Lecture Notes in Computer Science 12106

Anne Canteaut · Yuval Ishai (Eds.)

Advances in Cryptology – EUROCRYPT 2020

39th Annual International Conference on the Theory
and Applications of Cryptographic Techniques
Zagreb, Croatia, May 10–14, 2020
Proceedings, Part II

 Springer

Editors
Anne Canteaut (ID)
Équipe-projet COSMIQ
Inria
Paris, France

Yuval Ishai
Computer Science Department
Technion
Haifa, Israel

ISSN 0302-9743   ISSN 1611-3349   (electronic)
Lecture Notes in Computer Science
ISBN 978-3-030-45723-5   ISBN 978-3-030-45724-2   (eBook)
https://doi.org/10.1007/978-3-030-45724-2

LNCS Sublibrary: SL4 – Security and Cryptology

This Springer imprint is published by the registered company Springer Nature Switzerland AG
The registered company address is: Gewerbestrasse 11, 6330 Cham, Switzerland

Preface

Eurocrypt 2020, the 39th Annual International Conference on the Theory and Applications of Cryptographic Techniques, was held in Zagreb, Croatia, during May 10–14, 2020.[1] The conference was sponsored by the International Association for Cryptologic Research (IACR). Lejla Batina (Radboud University, The Netherlands) and Stjepan Picek (Delft University of Technology, The Netherlands) were responsible for the local organization. They were supported by a local organizing team consisting of Marin Golub and Domagoj Jakobovic (University of Zagreb, Croatia). Peter Schwabe acted as the affiliated events chair and Simona Samardjiska helped with the promotion and local organization. We are deeply indebted to all of them for their support and smooth collaboration.

The conference program followed the now established parallel-track system where the works of the authors were presented in two concurrently running tracks. The invited talks and the talks presenting the best paper/best young researcher spanned over both tracks.

We received a total of 375 submissions. Each submission was anonymized for the reviewing process and was assigned to at least three of the 57 Program Committee (PC) members. PC members were allowed to submit at most two papers. The reviewing process included a rebuttal round for all submissions. After extensive deliberations the PC accepted 81 papers. The revised versions of these papers are included in these three volume proceedings, organized topically within their respective track.

The PC decided to give the Best Paper Award to the paper "Optimal Broadcast Encryption from Pairings and LWE" by Shweta Agrawal and Shota Yamada and the Best Young Researcher Award to the paper "Private Information Retrieval with Sublinear Online Time" by Henry Corrigan-Gibbs and Dmitry Kogan. Both papers, together with "Candidate iO from Homomorphic Encryption Schemes" by Zvika Brakerski, Nico Döttling, Sanjam Garg, and Giulio Malavolta, received invitations for the *Journal of Cryptology*.

The program also included invited talks by Alon Rosen, titled "Fine-Grained Cryptography: A New Frontier?", and by Alice Silverberg, titled "Mathematics and Cryptography: A Marriage of Convenience?".

We would like to thank all the authors who submitted papers. We know that the PC's decisions can be very disappointing, especially rejections of very good papers which did not find a slot in the sparse number of accepted papers. We sincerely hope that these works eventually get the attention they deserve.

We are also indebted to the members of the PC and all external reviewers for their voluntary work. The PC work is quite a workload. It has been an honor to work with

---

[1] This preface was written before the conference took place, under the assumption that it will take place as planned in spite of travel restrictions related to the coronavirus.

everyone. The PC's work was simplified by Shai Halevi's submission software and his support, including running the service on IACR servers.

Finally, we thank everyone else – speakers, session chairs, and rump-session chairs – for their contribution to the program of Eurocrypt 2020. We would also like to thank the many sponsors for their generous support, including the Cryptography Research Fund that supported student speakers.

May 2020   Anne Canteaut
                                                                        Yuval Ishai

Eurocrypt 2020

The 39th Annual International Conference on the Theory and Applications of Cryptographic Techniques

Sponsored by *the International Association for Cryptologic Research (IACR)*

May 10–14, 2020
Zagreb, Croatia

General Co-chairs

Lejla Batina	Radboud University, The Netherlands
Stjepan Picek	Delft University of Technology, The Netherlands

Program Co-chairs

Anne Canteaut	Inria, France
Yuval Ishai	Technion, Israel

Program Committee

Divesh Aggarwal	National University of Singapore, Singapore
Benny Applebaum	Tel Aviv University, Israel
Fabrice Benhamouda	Algorand Foundation, USA
Elette Boyle	IDC Herzliya, Israel
Zvika Brakerski	Weizmann Institute of Science, Israel
Anne Broadbent	University of Ottawa, Canada
Nishanth Chandran	MSR India, India
Yilei Chen	Visa Research, USA
Aloni Cohen	Boston University, USA
Ran Cohen	Boston University and Northeastern University, USA
Geoffroy Couteau	CNRS, IRIF, Université de Paris, France
Joan Daemen	Radboud University, The Netherlands
Luca De Feo	IBM Research Zurich, Switzerland
Léo Ducas	CWI Amsterdam, The Netherlands
Maria Eichlseder	Graz University of Technology, Austria
Thomas Eisenbarth	University of Lübeck and WPI, Germany
Thomas Fuhr	ANSSI, France
Romain Gay	Cornell Tech, USA
Benedikt Gierlichs	KU Leuven, Belgium
Rishab Goyal	UT Austin, USA

Vipul Goyal — Carnegie Mellon University, USA
Tim Güneysu — Ruhr-Universität Bochum and DFKI, Germany
Jian Guo — Nanyang Technological University, Singapore
Mohammad Hajiabadi — UC Berkeley, USA
Carmit Hazay — Bar-Ilan University, Israel
Susan Hohenberger — Johns Hopkins University, USA
Pavel Hubáček — Charles University Prague, Czech Republic
Abhishek Jain — Johns Hopkins University, USA
Marc Joye — Zama, France
Bhavana Kanukurthi — IISc Bangalore, India
Nathan Keller — Bar-Ilan University, Israel
Susumu Kiyoshima — NTT Research, USA
Eyal Kushilevitz — Technion, Israel
Gregor Leander — Ruhr-Universität Bochum, Germany
Tancrède Lepoint — Google, USA
Tal Malkin — Columbia University, USA
Alexander May — Ruhr-Universität Bochum, Germany
Bart Mennink — Radboud University, The Netherlands
Kazuhiko Minematsu — NEC Corporation, Japan
María Naya-Plasencia — Inria, France
Ryo Nishimaki — NTT Secure Platform Laboratories, Japan
Cécile Pierrot — Inria and Université de Lorraine, France
Sondre Rønjom — University of Bergen, Norway
Ron Rothblum — Technion, Israel
Alessandra Scafuro — North Carolina State University, USA
Peter Schwabe — Radboud University, The Netherlands
Adam Smith — Boston University, USA
François-Xavier Standaert — KU Leuven, Belgium
Yosuke Todo — NTT Secure Platform Laboratories, Japan
Gilles Van Assche — STMicroelectronics, Belgium
Prashant Nalini Vasudevan — UC Berkeley, USA
Muthuramakrishnan Venkitasubramaniam — University of Rochester, USA
Frederik Vercauteren — KU Leuven, Belgium
Damien Vergnaud — Sorbonne Université and Institut Universitaire de France, France
Eylon Yogev — Technion, Israel
Yu Yu — Shanghai Jiao Tong University, China
Gilles Zémor — Université de Bordeaux, France

External Reviewers

Aysajan Abidin
Ittai Abraham
Thomas Agrikola
Navid Alamati
Nils Albartus
Martin Albrecht
Ghada Almashaqbeh
Joël Alwen
Miguel Ambrona
Ghous Amjad
Nicolas Aragon
Gilad Asharov
Tomer Ashur
Thomas Attema
Nuttapong Attrapadung
Daniel Augot
Florian Bache
Christian Badertscher
Saikrishna
   Badrinarayanan
Shi Bai
Josep Balasch
Foteini Baldimtsi
Marshall Ball
Zhenzhen Bao
James Bartusek
Lejla Batina
Enkhtaivan Batnyam
Carsten Baum
Gabrielle Beck
Christof Beierle
Amos Beimel
Sebastian Berndt
Dan J. Bernstein
Francesco Berti
Ward Beullens
Rishabh Bhadauria
Obbattu Sai Lakshmi
   Bhavana
Jean-Francois Biasse
Begül Bilgin
Nina Bindel
Nir Bitansky

Olivier Blazy
Naresh Boddu
Koen de Boer
Alexandra Boldyreva
Xavier Bonnetain
Carl Bootland
Jonathan Bootle
Adam Bouland
Christina Boura
Tatiana Bradley
Marek Broll
Olivier Bronchain
Ileana Buhan
Mark Bun
Sergiu Bursuc
Benedikt Bünz
Federico Canale
Sébastien Canard
Ran Canetti
Xavier Caruso
Ignacio Cascudo
David Cash
Gaëtan Cassiers
Guilhem Castagnos
Wouter Castryck
Hervé Chabanne
André Chailloux
Avik Chakraborti
Hubert Chan
Melissa Chase
Cong Chen
Hao Chen
Jie Chen
Ming-Shing Chen
Albert Cheu
Jérémy Chotard
Arka Rai Choudhuri
Kai-Min Chung
Michele Ciampi
Benoit Cogliati
Sandro Coretti-Drayton
Jean-Sébastien Coron
Adriana Suarez Corona

Alain Couvreur
Jan-Pieter D'Anvers
Bernardo David
Thomas Decru
Claire Delaplace
Patrick Derbez
Apoorvaa Deshpande
Siemen Dhooghe
Denis Diemert
Itai Dinur
Christoph Dobraunig
Yevgeniy Dodis
Jack Doerner
Jelle Don
Nico Döttling
Benjamin Dowling
John Schank
Markus Duermuth
Orr Dunkelman
Fréderic Dupuis
Iwan Duursma
Sébastien Duval
Stefan Dziembowski
Aner Moshe Ben Efraim
Naomi Ephraim
Thomas Espitau
Andre Esser
Brett Hemenway Falk
Antonio Faonio
Serge Fehr
Patrick Felke
Rex Fernando
Dario Fiore
Ben Fisch
Marc Fischlin
Nils Fleischhacker
Cody Freitag
Benjamin Fuller
Ariel Gabizon
Philippe Gaborit
Steven Galbraith
Chaya Ganesh
Juan Garay

Rachit Garg
Pierrick Gaudry
Nicholas Genise
Essam Ghadafi
Satrajit Ghosh
Kristian Gjøsteen
Aarushi Goel
Junqing Gong
Alonso Gonzalez
Lorenzo Grassi
Jens Groth
Aurore Guillevic
Berk Gulmezoglu
Aldo Gunsing
Chun Guo
Qian Guo
Siyao Guo
Shai Halevi
Shuai Han
Abida Haque
Phil Hebborn
Brett Hemenway
Shoichi Hirose
Dennis Hofheinz
Justin Holmgren
Akinori Hosoyamada
Senyang Huang
Paul Huynh
Kathrin Hövelmanns
Andreas Hülsing
Ilia Iliashenko
Laurent Imbert
Takanori Isobe
Tetsu Iwata
Håkon Jacobsen
Tibor Jager
Aayush Jain
Samuel Jaques
Jéremy Jean
Yanxue Jia
Zhengzhong Jin
Thomas Johansson
Kimmo Järvinen
Saqib Kakvi
Daniel Kales
Seny Kamara

Gabe Kaptchuk
Martti Karvonen
Shuichi Katsumata
Raza Ali Kazmi
Florian Kerschbaum
Dakshita Khurana
Jean Kieffer
Ryo Kikuchi
Eike Kiltz
Sam Kim
Elena Kirshanova
Fuyuki Kitagawa
Dima Kogan
Lisa Kohl
Markulf Kohlweiss
Ilan Komargodski
Yashvanth Kondi
Venkata Koppula
Lucas Kowalczyk
Karel Kral
Ralf Kuesters
Ashutosh Kumar
Ranjit Kumaresan
Srijita Kundu
Peter Kutasp
Thijs Laarhoven
Gijs Van Laer
Russell Lai
Virginie Lallemand
Baptiste Lambin
Julien Lavauzelle
Phi Hung Le
Eysa Lee
Hyung Tae Lee
Jooyoung Lee
Antonin Leroux
Gaëtan Leurent
Xin Li
Xiao Liang
Chengyu Lin
Huijia (Rachel) Lin
Wei-Kai Lin
Eik List
Guozhen Liu
Jiahui Liu
Qipeng Liu

Shengli Liu
Tianren Liu
Pierre Loidreau
Alex Lombardi
Patrick Longa
Sébastien Lord
Julian Loss
George Lu
Atul Luykx
Vadim Lyubashevsky
Fermi Ma
Varun Madathil
Roel Maes
Bernardo Magri
Saeed Mahloujifar
Christian Majenz
Eleftheria Makri
Giulio Malavolta
Mary Maller
Alex Malozemoff
Nathan Manohar
Daniel Masny
Simon Masson
Takahiro Matsuda
Noam Mazor
Audra McMillan
Lauren De Meyer
Peihan Miao
Gabrielle De Micheli
Ian Miers
Brice Minaud
Pratyush Mishra
Ahmad Moghimi
Esfandiar Mohammadi
Victor Mollimard
Amir Moradi
Tal Moran
Andrew Morgan
Mathilde de la Morinerie
Nicky Mouha
Tamer Mour
Pratyay Mukherjee
Marta Mularczyk
Koksal Mus
Pierrick Méaux
Jörn Müller-Quade

Yusuke Naito
Mridul Nandi
Samuel Neves
Ngoc Khanh Nguyen
Anca Nitulescu
Ariel Nof
Sai Lakshmi Bhavana
    Obbattu
Maciej Obremski
Tobias Oder
Frédérique Oggier
Miyako Ohkubo
Mateus de Oliveira
    Oliveira
Tron Omland
Maximilian Orlt
Michele Orrù
Emmanuela Orsini
Morten Øygarden
Ferruh Ozbudak
Carles Padro
Aurel Page
Jiaxin Pan
Omer Paneth
Lorenz Panny
Anat Paskin-Cherniavsky
Alain Passelègue
Sikhar Patranabis
Michaël Peeters
Chris Peikert
Alice Pellet-Mary
Olivier Pereira
Léo Perrin
Edoardo Persichetti
Thomas Peters
George Petrides
Thi Minh Phuong Pham
Duong-Hieu Phan
Krzysztof Pietrzak
Oxana Poburinnaya
Supartha Podder
Bertram Poettering
Antigoni Polychroniadou
Claudius Pott
Bart Preneel
Robert Primas

Luowen Qian
Willy Quach
Ahmadreza Rahimi
Somindu Ramannai
Matthieu Rambaud
Hugues Randriam
Shahram Rasoolzadeh
Divya Ravi
Mariana P. Raykova
Christian Rechberger
Ling Ren
Joost Renes
Leonid Reyzin
Joao Ribeiro
Silas Richelson
Peter Rindal
Francisco
    Rodríguez-Henríquez
Schuyler Rosefield
Mélissa Rossi
Mike Rosulek
Dragos Rotaru
Lior Rotem
Arnab Roy
Paul Rösler
Reihaneh Safavi-Naini
Amin Sakzad
Simona Samardjiska
Antonio Sanso
Yu Sasaki
Pascal Sasdrich
Or Sattath
John Schanck
Sarah Scheffler
Tobias Schneider
Markus Schofnegger
Peter Scholl
Jan Schoone
André Schrottenloher
Sven Schäge
Adam Sealfon
Jean-Pierre Seifert
Gregor Seiler
Sruthi Sekar
Okan Seker
Karn Seth

Yannick Seurin
Ido Shahaf
Ronen Shaltiel
Barak Shani
Sina Shiehian
Omri Shmueli
Jad Silbak
Thierry Simon
Luisa Sinischalchi
Veronika Slivova
Benjamin Smith
Yifan Song
Pratik Soni
Jessica Sorrell
Nicholas Spooner
Akshayaram Srinivasan
Damien Stehlé
Ron Steinfeld
Noah
    Stephens-Davidowitz
Martin Strand
Shifeng Sun
Ridwan Syed
Katsuyuki Takashima
Titouan Tanguy
Stefano Tessaro
Enrico Thomae
Jean-Pierre Tillich
Benjamin Timon
Junichi Tomida
Deniz Toz
Rotem Tsabary
Daniel Tschudi
Yiannis Tselekounis
Yi Tu
Dominique Unruh
Bogdan Ursu
Vinod Vaikuntanathan
Kerem Varici
Philip Vejre
Marloes Venema
Daniele Venturi
Fernando Virdia
Vanessa Vitse
Damian Vizár
Chrysoula Vlachou

Mikhail Volkhov
Satyanarayana Vusirikala
Hendrik Waldner
Alexandre Wallet
Michael Walter
Haoyang Wang
Meiqin Wang
Weijia Wang
Xiao Wang
Yohei Watanabe
Hoeteck Wee
Mor Weiss
Weiqiang Wen
Benjamin Wesolowski
Jan Wichelmann
Daniel Wichs

Friedrich Wiemer
Christopher Williamson
Jonas Wloka
Wessel van Woerden
Lennert Wouters
David J. Wu
Shai Wyborski
Brecht Wyseur
Keita Xagawa
Xiang Xie
Chaoping Xing
Sophia Yakoubov
Shota Yamada
Takashi Yamakawa
Avishay Yanai
Kang Yang

Kevin Yeo
Arkady Yerukhimovich
Øyvind Ytrehus
Aaram Yun
Mohammad Zaheri
Mark Zhandry
Jiayu Zhang
Liangfeng Zhang
Ren Zhang
Zhenfei Zhang
Zhongxiang Zheng
Hong-Sheng Zhou
Vassilis Zikas
Giorgos Zirdelis
Vincent Zucca

Contents – Part II

Foundations

Isogeny-Based Cryptography

Lattice-Based Cryptography

Symmetric Cryptography II

Secure Computation II

Generic Models

Separate Your Domains: NIST PQC KEMs, Oracle Cloning and Read-Only Indifferentiability

Mihir Bellare[1]([✉]), Hannah Davis[1]([✉]), and Felix Günther[2]([✉])

[1] Department of Computer Science and Engineering,
University of California San Diego, San Diego, USA
{mihir,h3davis}@eng.ucsd.edu
[2] Department of Computer Science, ETH Zürich, Zürich, Switzerland
mail@felixguenther.info
https://cseweb.ucsd.edu/~mihir/, https://cseweb.ucsd.edu/~mihir/,
https://www.felixguenther.info

Abstract. It is convenient and common for schemes in the random oracle model to assume access to multiple random oracles (ROs), leaving to implementations the task—we call it oracle cloning—of constructing them from a single RO. The first part of the paper is a case study of oracle cloning in KEM submissions to the NIST Post-Quantum Cryptography standardization process. We give key-recovery attacks on some submissions arising from mistakes in oracle cloning, and find other submissions using oracle cloning methods whose validity is unclear. Motivated by this, the second part of the paper gives a theoretical treatment of oracle cloning. We give a definition of what is an "oracle cloning method" and what it means for such a method to "work," in a framework we call read-only indifferentiability, a simple variant of classical indifferentiability that yields security not only for usage in single-stage games but also in multi-stage ones. We formalize domain separation, and specify and study many oracle cloning methods, including common domain-separating ones, giving some general results to justify (prove read-only indifferentiability of) certain classes of methods. We are not only able to validate the oracle cloning methods used in many of the unbroken NIST PQC KEMs, but also able to specify and validate oracle cloning methods that may be useful beyond that.

1 Introduction

Theoretical works giving, and proving secure, schemes in the random oracle (RO) model [11], often, for convenience, assume access to *multiple, independent* ROs. Implementations, however, like to implement them all via a *single* hash function like SHA256 that is assumed to be a RO.

The transition from one RO to many is, in principle, easy. One can use a method suggested by BR [11] and usually called "domain separation." For example to build three random oracles H_1, H_2, H_3 from a single one, H, define

$$H_1(x) = H(\langle 1 \rangle \| x), H_2(x) = H(\langle 2 \rangle \| x) \text{ and } H_3(x) = H(\langle 3 \rangle \| x) , \qquad (1)$$

© International Association for Cryptologic Research 2020
A. Canteaut and Y. Ishai (Eds.): EUROCRYPT 2020, LNCS 12106, pp. 3–32, 2020.
https://doi.org/10.1007/978-3-030-45724-2_1

where $\langle i \rangle$ is the representation of integer i as a bit-string of some fixed length, say one byte. One might ask if there is justifying theory: a proof that the above "works," and a definition of what "works" means. A likely response is that it is obvious it works, and theory would be pedantic.

If it were merely a question of the specific domain-separation method of Eq. (1), we'd be inclined to agree. But we have found some good reasons to revisit the question and look into theoretical foundations. They arise from the NIST Post-Quantum Cryptography (PQC) standardization process [35].

We analyzed the KEM submissions. We found attacks, breaking some of them, that arise from incorrect ways of turning one random oracle into many, indicating that the process is error-prone. We found other KEMs where methods other than Eq. (1) were used and whether or not they work is unclear. In some submissions, instantiations for multiple ROs were left unspecified. In others, they differed between the specification and reference implementation.

Domain separation as per Eq. (1) is a *method*, not a *goal*. We identify and name the underlying goal, calling it *oracle cloning*—given one RO, build many, independent ones. (More generally, given m ROs, build $n > m$ ROs.) We give a definition of what is an "oracle cloning method" and what it means for such a method to "work," in a framework we call read-only indifferentiability, a simple variant of classical indifferentiability [29]. We specify and study many oracle cloning methods, giving some general results to justify (prove read-only indifferentiability of) certain classes of them. The intent is not only to validate as many NIST PQC KEMs as possible (which we do) but to specify and validate methods that will be useful beyond that.

Below we begin by discussing the NIST PQC KEMs and our findings on them, and then turn to our theoretical treatment and results.

NIST PQC KEMs. In late 2016, NIST put out a call for post-quantum cryptographic algorithms [35]. In the first round they received 28 submissions targeting IND-CCA-secure KEMs, of which 17 remain in the second round [37].

Recall that in a KEM (Key Encapsulation Mechanism) KE, the encapsulation algorithm KE.E takes the public key pk (but no message) to return a symmetric key K and a ciphertext C^* encapsulating it, $(C^*, K) \leftarrow\!\!\!_\$\, \mathsf{KE.E}(pk)$. Given an IND-CCA KEM, one can easily build an IND-CCA PKE scheme by hybrid encryption [18], explaining the focus of standardization on the KEMs.

Most of the KEM submissions (23 in the first round, 15 in the second round) are constructed from a weak (OW-CPA, IND-CPA, ...) PKE scheme using either a method from Hofheinz, Hövelmanns and Kiltz (HHK) [24] or a related method from [21,27,40]. This results in a KEM KE_4, the subscript to indicate that it uses up to four ROs that we'll denote H_1, H_2, H_3, H_4. Results of [21,24,27,40] imply that KE_4 is provably IND-CCA, *assuming the ROs H_1, H_2, H_3, H_4 are independent*.

Next, the step of interest for us, the oracle cloning: they build the multiple random oracles via a single RO H, replacing H_i with an oracle $\mathbf{F}[H](i, \cdot)$, where we refer to the construction $\mathbf{F}$ as a "cloning functor," and $\mathbf{F}[H]$ means that $\mathbf{F}$ gets oracle access to H. This turns KE_4 into a KEM KE_1 that uses only a *single*

RO H, allowing an implementation to instantiate the latter with a single NIST-recommended primitive like SHA3-512 or SHAKE256 [36]. (In some cases, KE_1 uses a number of ROs that is more than one but less than the number used by KE_4, which is still oracle cloning, but we'll ignore this for now.)

Often the oracle cloning method (cloning functor) is not specified in the submission document; we obtained it from the reference implementation. Our concern is the security of this method and the security of the final, single-RO-using KEM KE_1. (As above we assume the starting KE_4 is secure if its four ROs are independent.)

ORACLE CLONING IN SUBMISSIONS. We surveyed the relevant (first- and second-round) NIST PQC KEM submissions, looking in particular at the reference code, to determine what choices of cloning functor $\mathbf{F}$ was made, and how it impacted security of KE_1. Based on our findings, we classify the submissions into groups as follows.

First is a group of *successfully attacked* submissions. We discover and specify attacks, enabled through erroneous RO cloning, on three (first-round) submissions: BIG QUAKE [8], DAGS [7] and Round2 [22]. (Throughout the paper, first-round submissions are in gray, second-round submissions in **bold**.) Our attacks on BIG QUAKE and Round2 recover the symmetric key K from the ciphertext C^* and public key. Our attack on DAGS succeeds in partial key recovery, recovering 192 bits of the symmetric key. These attacks are very fast, taking at most about the same time as taken by the (secret-key equipped, prescribed) decryption algorithm to recover the key. None of our attacks needs access to a decryption oracle, meaning we violate much more than IND-CCA.

Next is submissions with *questionable oracle cloning*. We put just one in this group, namely **NewHope** [2]. Here we do not have proof of security in the ROM for the final instantiated scheme KE_1. We do show that the cloning methods used here do not achieve our formal notion of rd-indiff security, but this does not result in an attack on KE_1, so we do not have a practical attack either. We recommend changes in the cloning methods that permit proofs.

Next is a group of ten submissions that use *ad-hoc oracle cloning* methods—as opposed, say, to conventional domain separation as per Eq. (1)—but for which our results (to be discussed below) are able to prove security of the final single-RO scheme. In this group are **BIKE** [3], KCL [44], LAC [28], Lizard [16], LOCKER [4], Odd Manhattan [38], **ROLLO-II** [30], **Round5** [6], **SABER** [19] and Titanium [43]. Still, the security of these oracle cloning methods remains brittle and prone to vulnerabilities under slight changes.

A final group of twelve submissions *did well*, employing something like Eq. (1). In particular our results can prove these methods secure. In this group are **Classic McEliece** [13], **CRYSTALS-Kyber** [5], EMBLEM [41], **FrodoKEM** [34], **HQC** [32], LIMA [42], NTRU-HRSS-KEM [25], **NTRU Prime** [14], **NTS-KEM** [1], RQC [31], **SIKE** [26] and **ThreeBears** [23].

This classification omits 14 KEM schemes that do not fit the above framework. (For example they do not target IND-CCA KEMs, do not use HHK-style transforms, or do not use multiple random oracles.)

LESSONS AND RESPONSE. We see that oracle cloning is error-prone, and that it is sometimes done in ad-hoc ways whose validity is not clear. We suggest that oracle cloning not be left to implementations. Rather, scheme designers should give proof-validated oracle cloning methods for their schemes. To enable this, we initiate a theoretical treatment of oracle cloning. We formalize oracle cloning methods, define what it means for one to be secure, and specify a library of proven-secure methods from which designers can draw. We are able to justify the oracle cloning methods of many of the unbroken NIST PQC KEMs. The framework of read-only indifferentiability we introduce and use for this purpose may be of independent interest.

The NIST PQC KEMs we break are first-round candidates, not second-round ones, and in some cases other attacks on the same candidates exist, so one may say the breaks are no longer interesting. We suggest reasons they are. Their value is illustrative, showing not only that errors in oracle cloning occur in practice, but that they can be devastating for security. In particular, the extensive and long review process for the first-round NIST PQC submissions seems to have missed these simple attacks, perhaps due to lack of recognition of the importance of good oracle cloning.

INDIFFERENTIABILITY BACKGROUND. Let SS, ES be sets of functions. (We will call them the starting and ending function spaces, respectively.) A functor $\mathbf{F} \colon \mathsf{SS} \to \mathsf{ES}$ is a deterministic algorithm that, given as oracle a function $s \in \mathsf{SS}$, defines a function $\mathbf{F}[s] \in \mathsf{ES}$. Indifferentiability of $\mathbf{F}$ is a way of defining what it means for $\mathbf{F}[s]$ to emulate e when s, e are randomly chosen from SS, ES, respectively. It permits a "composition theorem" saying that if $\mathbf{F}$ is indifferentiable then use of e in a scheme can be securely replaced by use of $\mathbf{F}[s]$.

Maurer, Renner and Holenstein (MRH) [29] gave the first definition of indifferentiability and corresponding composition theorem. However, Ristenpart, Shacham and Shrimpton (RSS) [39] pointed out a limitation, namely that it only applies to single-stage games. MRH-indiff fails to guarantee security in multi-stage games, a setting that includes many goals of interest including security under related-key attack, deterministic public-key encryption and encryption of key-dependent messages. Variants of MRH-indiff [17,20,33,39] tried to address this, with limited success.

RD-INDIFF. Indifferentiability is the natural way to treat oracle cloning. A cloning of one function into n functions ($n = 4$ above) can be captured as a functor (we call it a cloning functor) $\mathbf{F}$ that takes the single RO s and for each $i \in [1..n]$ defines a function $\mathbf{F}[s](i, \cdot)$ that is meant to emulate a RO. We will specify many oracle cloning methods in this way.

We define in Sect. 4 a variant of indifferentiability we call read-only indifferentiability (rd-indiff). The simulator—unlike for reset-indiff [39]—has access to a game-maintained state st, but—unlike MRH-indiff [29]—that state is read-only, meaning the simulator cannot alter it across invocations. Rd-indiff is a stronger requirement than MRH-indiff (if $\mathbf{F}$ is rd-indiff then it is MRH-indiff) but a weaker one than reset-indiff (if $\mathbf{F}$ is reset-indiff then it is rd-indiff). Despite the latter, rd-indiff, like reset-indiff, admits a composition theorem showing that an rd-indiff $\mathbf{F}$ may securely substitute a RO even in multi-stage games. (The proof of RSS [39] for reset-indiff extends to show this.) We do not use reset-indiff because some of our cloning functors do not meet it, but they do meet rd-indiff, and the composition benefit is preserved.

GENERAL RESULTS. In Sect. 4, we define *translating* functors. These are simply ones whose oracle queries are non-adaptive. (In more detail, a translating functor determines from its input W a list of queries, makes them to its oracle and, from the responses and W, determines its output.) We then define a condition on a translating functor $\mathbf{F}$ that we call *invertibility* and show that if $\mathbf{F}$ is an invertible translating functor then it is rd-indiff. This is done in two parts, Theorems 1 and 2, that differ in the degree of invertibility assumed. The first, assuming the greater degree of invertibility, allows a simpler proof with a simulator that does not need the read-only state allowed in rd-indiff. The second, assuming the lesser degree of invertibility, depends on a simulator that makes crucial use of the read-only state. It sets the latter to a key for a PRF that is then used to answer queries that fall outside the set of ones that can be trivially answered under the invertibility condition. This use of a computational primitive (a PRF) in the indifferentiability context may be novel and may seem odd, but it works.

We apply this framework to analyze particular, practical cloning functors, showing that these are translating and invertible, and then deducing their rd-indiff security. But the above-mentioned results are stronger and more general than we need for the application to oracle cloning. The intent is to enable further, future applications.

ANALYSIS OF ORACLE CLONING METHODS. We formalize oracle cloning as the task of designing a functor (we call it a cloning functor) $\mathbf{F}$ that takes as oracle a function $s \in \mathsf{SS}$ in the starting space and returns a two-input function $e = \mathbf{F}[s] \in \mathsf{ES}$, where $e(i, \cdot)$ represents the i-th RO for $i \in [1..n]$. Section 5 presents the cloning functors corresponding to some popular and practical oracle cloning methods (in particular ones used in the NIST PQC KEMs), and shows that they are translating and invertible. Our above-mentioned results allow us to then deduce they are rd-indiff, which means they are safe to use in most applications, even ones involving multi-stage games. This gives formal justification for some common oracle cloning methods. We now discuss some specific cloning functors that we treat in this way.

The prefix (cloning) functor $\mathbf{F}_{\mathrm{pf}(\mathbf{p})}$ is parameterized by a fixed, public vector $\mathbf{p}$ such that no entry of $\mathbf{p}$ is a prefix of any other entry of $\mathbf{p}$. Receiving function s as an oracle, it defines function $e = \mathbf{F}_{\mathrm{pf}(\mathbf{p})}[s]$ by $e(i, X) = s(\mathbf{p}[i] \| X)$, where $\mathbf{p}[i]$ is the ith element of vector $\mathbf{p}$. When $\mathbf{p}[i]$ is a fixed-length bitstring representing the integer i, this formalizes Eq. (1).

Some NIST PQC submissions use a method we call output splitting. The simplest case is that we want $e(i, \cdot), \ldots, e(n, \cdot)$ to all have the same output length L. We then define $e(i, X)$ as bits $(i-1)L + 1$ through iL of the given function s applied to X. That is, receiving function s as an oracle, the splitting (cloning) functor $\mathbf{F}_{\mathrm{spl}}$ returns function $e = \mathbf{F}_{\mathrm{spl}}[s]$ defined by $e(i, X) = s(X)[(i-1)L+1..iL]$.

An interesting case, present in some NIST PQC submissions, is trivial cloning: just set $e(i, X) = s(X)$ for all X. We formalize this as the identity (cloning) functor $\mathbf{F}_{\mathrm{id}}$ defined by $\mathbf{F}_{\mathrm{id}}[s](i, X) = s(X)$. Clearly, this is not always secure. It can be secure, however, for usages that restrict queries in some way. One such restriction, used in several NIST PQC KEMs, is length differentiation: $e(i, \cdot)$ is queried only on inputs of some length l_i, where $l_1, \ldots, l_n$ are chosen to be distinct. We are able to treat this in our framework using the concept of working domains that we discuss next, but we warn that this method is brittle and prone to misuse.

WORKING DOMAINS. One could capture trivial cloning with length differentiation as a restriction on the domains of the ending functions, but this seems artificial and dangerous because the implementations do not enforce any such restriction; the functions there are defined on their full domains and it is, apparently, left up to applications to use the functions in a way that does not get them into trouble. The approach we take is to leave the functions defined on their full domains, but define and ask for security over a subdomain, which we called the working domain. A choice of working domain $\mathcal{W}$ accordingly parameterizes our definition of rd-indiff for a functor, and also the definition of invertibility of a translating functor. Our result says that the identity functor is rd-indiff for certain choices of working domains that include the length differentiation one.

Making the working domain explicit will, hopefully, force the application designer to think about, and specify, what it is, increasing the possibility of staying out of trouble. Working domains also provide flexibility and versatility under which different applications can make different choices of the domain.

Working domains not being present in prior indifferentiability formalizations, the comparisons, above, of rd-indiff with these prior formalizations assume the working domain is the full domain of the ending functions. Working domains alter the comparison picture; a cloning functor which is rd-indiff on a working domain may not be even MRH-indiff on its full domain.

APPLICATION TO KEMs. The framework above is broad, staying in the land of ROs and not speaking of the usage of these ROs in any particular cryptographic primitive or scheme. As such, it can be applied to analyze RO instantiation in many primitives and schemes. In the full version of this paper [10], we exemplify its application in the realm of KEMs as the target of the NIST PQC designs.

This may seem redundant, since an indifferentiability composition theorem says exactly that once indifferentiability of a functor has been shown, "all" uses of it are secure. However, prior indifferentiability frameworks do not consider working domains, so the known composition theorems apply only when the working domain is the full one. (Thus the reset-indiff composition theorem of [39] extends to rd-indiff so that we have security for applications whose security definitions are underlain by either single or multi-stage games, but only for full working domains.)

To give a composition theorem that is conscious of working domains, we must first ask what they are, or mean, in the application. We give a definition of the *working domain of a KEM* KE. This is the set of all points that the scheme algorithms query to the ending functions in usage, captured by a certain game we give. (Queries of the adversary may fall outside the working domain.) Then we give a working-domain-conscious composition theorem for KEMs that says the following. Say we are given an IND-CCA KEM KE whose oracles are drawn from a function space KE.FS. Let $\mathbf{F}$: SS $\to$ KE.FS be a functor, and let $\overline{\mathsf{KE}}$ be the KEM obtained by implementing the oracles of the KE via $\mathbf{F}$. (So the oracles of this second KEM are drawn from the function space $\overline{\mathsf{KE}}.\mathsf{FS} = \mathsf{SS}$.) Let $\mathcal{W}$ be the working domain of KE, and assume $\mathbf{F}$ is rd-indiff over $\mathcal{W}$. Then $\overline{\mathsf{KE}}$ is also IND-CCA. Combining this with our rd-indiff results on particular cloning functors justifies not only conventional domain separation as an instantiation technique for KEMs, but also more broadly the instantiations in some NIST PQC submissions that do not use domain separation, yet whose cloning functors are rd-diff over the working domain of their KEMs. The most important example is the identity cloning functor used with length differentiation.

A key definitional element of our treatment that allows the above is, following [9], to embellish the *syntax* of a scheme (here a KEM KE) by having it name a function space KE.FS from which it wants its oracles drawn. Thus, the scheme specification must say how many ROs it wants, and of what domains and ranges. In contrast, in the formal version of the ROM in [11], there is a single, scheme-independent RO that has some fixed domain and range, for example mapping $\{0,1\}^*$ to $\{0,1\}$. This leaves a gap, between the object a scheme wants and what the model provides, that can lead to error. We suggest that, to reduce such errors, schemes specified in standards include a specification of their function space.

2 Oracle Cloning in NIST PQC Candidates

NOTATION. A KEM scheme KE specifies an encapsulation KE.E that, on input a public encryption key pk returns a session key K, and a ciphertext C^* encapsulating it, written $(C^*, K) \leftarrow\!\!\!{}_{\$}\, \mathsf{KE.E}(pk)$. A PKE scheme PKE specifies an encryption algorithm PKE.E that, on input pk, message $M \in \{0,1\}^{\mathsf{PKE.ml}}$ and randomness R, deterministically returns ciphertext $C \leftarrow \mathsf{PKE.E}(pk, M; R)$. For neither primitive will we, in this section, be concerned with the key generation or decapsulation/decryption algorithm. We might write $\mathsf{KE}[X_1, X_2, \ldots]$ to indicate that the scheme has oracle access to functions $X_1, X_2, \ldots$, and correspondingly then write $\mathsf{KE.E}[X_1, X_2, \ldots]$, and similarly for PKE.

2.1 Design Process

The literature [21,24,27,40] provides many transforms that take a public-key encryption scheme PKE, assumed to meet some weaker-than-IND-CCA notion of security we denote $\mathsf{S_{pke}}$ (for example, OW-CPA, OW-PCA or IND-CPA), and, with the aid of some number of random oracles, turn PKE into a KEM that is guaranteed (proven) to be IND-CCA *assuming the ROs are independent*. We'll refer to such transforms as *sound*. Many (most) KEMs submitted to the NIST

Post-Quantum Cryptography standardization process were accordingly designed as follows:

(1) First, they specify a S_{pke}-secure public-key encryption scheme PKE.

(2) Second, they pick a sound transform $\mathbf{T}$ and obtain KEM $KE_4[H_1, H_2, H_3, H_4]$ $= \mathbf{T}[PKE, H_2, H_3, H_4]$. (The notation is from [24]. The transforms use up to three random oracles that we are denoting H_2, H_3, H_4, reserving H_1 for possible use by the PKE scheme.) We refer to KE_4 (the subscript refers to its using 4 oracles) as the *base* KEM, and, as we will see, it differs across the transforms.

(3) Finally—the under-the-radar step that is our concern—the ROs $H_1, \ldots, H_4$ are constructed from cryptographic hash functions to yield what we call the *final* KEM KE_1. In more detail, the submissions make various choices of cryptographic hash functions $F_1, \ldots, F_m$ that we call the *base functions*, and, for $i = 1, 2, 3, 4$, specify constructions $\mathbf{C}_i$ that, with oracle access to the base functions, define the H_i, which we write as $H_i \leftarrow \mathbf{C}_i[F_1, \ldots, F_m]$. We call this process oracle cloning, and we call H_i the *final functions*. (Common values of m are $1, 2$.) The actual, submitted KEM KE_1 (the subscript because m is usually 1) uses the final functions, so that its encapsulation algorithm can be written as:

$KE_1.E[F_1, \ldots, F_m](pk)$
For $i = 1, 2, 3, 4$ do $H_i \leftarrow \mathbf{C}_i[F_1, \ldots, F_m]$
$(C^*, K) \leftarrow_\$ KE_4.E[H_1, H_2, H_3, H_4](pk)$
Return (C^*, K)

The question now is whether the final KE_1 is secure. We will show that, for some submissions, it is not. This is true for the choices of base functions $F_1, \ldots, F_m$ made in the submission, but also if these are assumed to be ROs. It is true despite the soundness of the transform, meaning insecurity arises from poor oracle cloning, meaning choices of the constructions $\mathbf{C}_i$. We will then consider submissions for which we have not found an attack. In the latter analysis, we are willing to assume (as the submissions implicitly do) that $F_1, \ldots, F_m$ are ROs, and we then ask whether the final functions are "close" to independent ROs.

2.2   The Base KEM

We need first to specify the base KE_4 (the result of the sound transform, from step (2) above). The NIST PQC submissions typically cite one of HHK [24], Dent [21], SXY [40] or JZCWM [27] for the sound transform they use, but our examinations show that the submissions have embellished, combined or modified the original transforms. The changes do *not* (to best of our knowledge) violate soundness (meaning the used transforms still yield an IND-CCA KE_4 if H_2, H_3, H_4 are independent ROs and PKE is S_{pke}-secure) but they make a succinct exposition challenging. We address this with a framework to unify the designs via a single, but parameterized, transform, capturing the submission transforms by different parameter choices.

Figure 1 (top) shows the encapsulation algorithm $KE_4.E$ of the KEM that our parameterized transform associates to PKE and H_1, H_2, H_3, H_4. The parameters are the variables X, Y, Z (they will be functions of other quantities in the algorithms), a boolean D, and an integer k^*. When choices of these are made, one

---

Algorithm $KE_4.E[H_1, H_2, H_3, H_4](pk)$:

1 $M \leftarrow_\$ \{0,1\}^{PKE.ml}$; $R \leftarrow \varepsilon$
2 If $(D = true)$ then $R \| K' \leftarrow H_2(X)$ $/\!/ \ |K'| = k^*$
3 $C \leftarrow PKE.E[H_1](pk, M; R)$
4 $C^* \leftarrow C \| Y$
5 $K \leftarrow H_4(Z)$; Return (C^*, K)

	D	k*	X	Y	Z	Used in
T_1	true	0	M	ε	M	LIMA, Odd Manhattan
T_2	true	0	$pk\|M$	ε	$pk\|M$	**ThreeBears**
T_3	true	0	M	ε	$M\|C$	**BIKE-1-CCA** **BIKE-3-CCA**, LAC
T_4	true	0	$M\|pk$	ε	$M\|C$	**SIKE**
T_5	true	0	M	$H_3(X)$	$M\|C$	**HQC**, **RQC**, Titanium
T_6	true	>0	$M\|H_3(pk)$	ε	$K'\|C$	**SABER**
T_7	true	>0	$H_3(pk)\|H_3(M)$	ε	$K'\|H_3(C)$	**CRYSTALS-Kyber**
T_8	true	0	M	$H_3(X)$	M	DAGS, NTRU-HRSS-KEM
T_9	true	0	M	$H_3(X)$	$M\|C\|Y$	ROLLO-II, EMBLEM, Lizard, LOCKER, BIG QUAKE
T_{10}	true	>0	$H_4(M)\|H_4(pk)$	$H_3(X)$	$K'\|H_4(C\|Y)$	**NewHope**
T_{11}	true	>0	$M\|pk$	$H_3(X)$	$K'\|C\|Y$	FrodoKEM, Round2 **Round5**
T_{12}	true	>0	$pk\|M$	$H_3(X)$	$K'\|C$	KCL
T_{13}	true	>0	$H_3(pk)\|M$	ε	$C\|K'$	**FrodoKEM**
T_{14}	false	0	$\bot$	$H_3(M)$	$M\|C\|Y$	**Classic McEliece**
T_{15}	true	0	M	ε	$R\|M$	**NTS-KEM**
T_{16}	false	0	$\bot$	$M\|pk$	$M\|C\|Y$	**Streamlined NTRU Prime**
T_{17}	true	0	M	$M\|pk$	$M\|C\|Y$	**NTRU LPRime**

Fig. 1. Top: Encapsulation algorithm of the base KEM scheme produced by our parameterized transform. **Bottom:** Choices of parameters X, Y, Z, D, k^* resulting in specific transforms used by the NIST PQC submissions. Second-round submissions are in **bold**, first-round submissions in gray. Submissions using different transforms in the two rounds appear twice.

gets a fully-specified transform and corresponding base KEM KE_4. Each row in the table in the same Figure shows one such choice of parameters, resulting in 15 fully-specified transforms. The final column shows the submissions that use the transform.

The encapsulation algorithm at the top of Fig. 1 takes input a public key pk and has oracle access to functions H_1, H_2, H_3, H_4. At line 1, it picks a random seed M of length the message length of the given PKE scheme. Boolean D being true (as it is with just one exception) means PKE.E is randomized. In that case, line 2 applies H_2 to X (the latter, determined as per the table, depends on M and possibly also on pk) and parses the output to get coins R for PKE.E and possibly (if the parameter $k^* \neq 0$) an additional string K'. At line 3, a ciphertext C is produced by encrypting the seed M using PKE.E with public key pk and coins R. In some schemes, a second portion of the ciphertext, Y, often called the "confirmation", is derived from X or M, using H_3, as shown in the table, and line 4 then defines C^*. Finally, H_4 is used as a key derivation function to extract a symmetric key K from the parameter Z, which varies widely among transforms.

In total, 26 of the 39 NIST PQC submissions which target KEMs in either the first or second round use transforms which fall into our framework. The remaining schemes do not use more than one random oracle, construct KEMs without transforming PKE schemes, or target security definitions other than IND-CCA.

2.3   Submissions We Break

We present attacks on BIG QUAKE [8], DAGS [7], and Round2 [22]. These attacks succeed in full or partial recovery of the encapsulated KEM key from a ciphertext, and are extremely fast. We have implemented the attacks to verify them.

Although none of these schemes progressed to Round 2 of the competition without significant modification, to the best of our knowledge, none of the attacks we described were pointed out during the review process. Given the attacks' superficiality, this is surprising and suggests to us that more attention should be paid to oracle cloning methods and their vulnerabilities during review.

RANDOMNESS-BASED DECRYPTION. The PKE schemes used by BIG QUAKE and Round2 have the property that given a ciphertext $C \leftarrow$ PKE.E$(pk, M; R)$ and also given the coins R, it is easy to recover M, even without knowledge of the secret key. We formalize this property, saying PKE allows randomness-based decryption, if there is an (efficient) algorithm PKE.DecR such that PKE.DecR$(pk, $ PKE.E$(pk, M; R), R) = M$ for any public key pk, coins R and message m. This will be used in our attacks.

ATTACK ON BIG QUAKE. The base KEM $KE_1[H_1, H_2, H_3, H_4]$ is given by the transform $\mathbf{T}_9$ in the table of Fig. 1. The final KEM $KE_2[F]$ uses a single function F to instantiate the random oracles, which it does as follows. It sets $H_3 = H_4 = F$ and $H_2 = W[F] \circ F$ for a certain function W (the rejection sampling algorithm) whose details will not matter for us. The notation $W[F]$

meaning that W has oracle access to F. The following attack (explanations after the pseudocode) recovers the encapsulated KEM key K from ciphertext $C^* \leftarrow_\$ \mathsf{KE}_1.\mathsf{E}[F](pk)$—

Adversary $\mathcal{A}[F](pk, C^*)$ // Input public key and ciphertext, oracle for F

1. $C \| Y \leftarrow C^*$ // Parse C^* to get PKE ciphertext C and $Y = H_3(M)$
2. $R \leftarrow W[F](Y)$ // Apply function $W[F]$ to Y to recover coins R
3. $M \leftarrow \mathsf{PKE.DecR}(pk, C, R)$ // Use randomness-based decryption for PKE
4. $K \leftarrow F(M)$; Return K

As per $\mathbf{T}_9$ we have $Y = H_3(M) = F(M)$. The coins for $\mathsf{PKE.E}$ are $R = H_2(M) = (W[F] \circ F)(M) = W[F](F(M)) = W[F](Y)$. Since Y is in the ciphertext, the coins R can be recovered as shown at line 2. The PKE scheme allows randomness-based decryption, so at line 3 we can recover the message M underlying C using algorithm $\mathsf{PKE.DecR}$. But $K = H_4(M) = F(M)$, so K can now be recovered as well. In conclusion, the specific cloning method chosen by BIG QUAKE leads to complete recovery of the encapsulated key from the ciphertext.

ATTACK ON Round2. The base KEM $\mathsf{KE}_1[H_2, H_3, H_4]$ is given by the transform $\mathbf{T}_{11}$ in the table of Fig. 1. The final KEM $\mathsf{KE}_2[F]$ uses a single base function F to instantiate the final functions, which it does as follows. It sets $H_4 = F$. The specification and reference implementation differ in how H_2, H_3 are defined: In the former, $H_2(x) = F(F(x)) \| F(x)$ and $H_3(x) = F(F(F(x)))$, while in the latter, $H_2(x) = F(F(F(x))) \| F(x)$ and $H_3(x) = F(F(X))$. These differences arise from differences in the way the output of a certain function $W[F]$ is parsed.

Our attack is on the reference-implementation version of the scheme. We need to also know that the scheme sets k^* so that $R \| K' \leftarrow H_2(X)$ with $H_2(X) = F(F(F(X))) \| F(X)$ results in $R = F(F(F(X)))$. But $Y = H_3(X) = F(F(X))$, so $R = F(Y)$ can be recovered from the ciphertext. Again exploiting the fact that the PKE scheme allows randomness-based decryption, we obtain the following attack that recovers the encapsulated KEM key K from ciphertext $C^* \leftarrow_\$ \mathsf{KE}_1.\mathsf{E}[F](pk)$—

Adversary $\mathcal{A}[F](pk, C^*)$ // Input public key and ciphertext, oracle for F

1. $C \| Y \leftarrow C^*$; $R \leftarrow F(Y)$
2. $M \leftarrow \mathsf{PKE.DecR}(pk, C, R)$; $K \leftarrow F(M)$; Return K

This attack exploits the difference between the way H_2, H_3 are defined across the specification and implementation, which may be a bug in the implementation with regard to the parsing of $W[F](x)$. However, the attack also exploits dependencies between H_2 and H_3, which ought not to exist when instantiating what are required to be distinct random oracles.

Round2 was incorporated into the second-round submission **Round5**, which specifies a different base function and cloning functor (the latter of which uses the secure method we call "output splitting") to instantiate oracles H_2 and H_3. This attack therefore does not apply to **Round5**.

ATTACK ON DAGS. If x is a byte string we let $x[i]$ be its i-th byte, and if x is a bit string we let x_i be its i-th bit. We say that a function V is an extendable output function if it takes input a string x and an integer ℓ to return an ℓ-byte output, and $\ell_1 \le \ell_2$ implies that $V(x, \ell_1)$ is a prefix of $V(x, \ell_2)$. If $v = v_1 v_2 v_3 v_4 v_5 v_6 v_7 v_8$ is a byte then let $Z(v) = 00 v_3 v_4 v_5 v_6 v_7 v_8$ be obtained by zeroing out the first two bits. If y is a string of ℓ bytes then let $Z'(y) = Z(y[1]) \| \cdots \| Z(y[\ell])$. Now let $V'(x, \ell) = Z'(V(x, \ell))$.

The base KEM $\mathsf{KE}_1[H_1, H_2, H_3, H_4]$ is given by the transform $\mathbf{T}_8$ in the table of Fig. 1. The final KEM $\mathsf{KE}_2[V]$ uses an extendable output function V to instantiate the random oracles, which it does as follows. It sets $H_2(x) = V'(x, 512)$ and $H_3(x) = V'(x, 32)$. It sets $H_4(x) = V(x, 64)$.

As per $\mathbf{T}_8$ we have $K = H_4(M)$ and $Y = H_3(M)$. Let L be the first 32 bytes of the 64-byte K. Then $Y = Z'(L)$. So Y reveals $32 \cdot 6 = 192$ bits of K. Since Y is in the ciphertext, this results in a partial encapsulated-key recovery attack. The attack reduces the effective length of K from $64 \cdot 8 = 512$ bits to $512 - 192 = 320$ bits, meaning 37.5% of the encapsulated key is recovered. Also $R = H_2(M)$, so Y, as part of the ciphertext, reveals 32 bytes of R, which does not seem desirable, even though it is not clear how to exploit it for an attack.

2.4 Submissions with Unclear Security

For the scheme NewHope [2], we can give neither an attack nor a proof of security. However, we can show that the final functions H_2, H_3, H_4 produced by the cloning functor $\mathbf{F}_{\texttt{NewHope}}$ with oracle access to a single extendable-output function V are differentiable from independent random oracles. The cloning functor $\mathbf{F}_{\texttt{NewHope}}$ sets $H_1(x) = V(x, 128)$ and $H_4 = V(x, 32)$. It computes H_2 and H_3 from V using the output splitting cloning functor. Concretely, KE_2 parses $V(x, 96)$ as $H_2(x) \| H_3(x)$, where H_2 has output length 64 bytes and H_3 has output length 32 bytes. Because V is an extendable-output function, $H_4(x)$ will be a prefix of $H_2(x)$ for any string x.

We do not know how to exploit this correlation to attack the IND-CCA security of the final KEM scheme $\mathsf{KE}_2[V]$, and we conjecture that, due to the structure of $\mathbf{T}_{10}$, no efficient attack exists. We can, however, attack the rd-indiff security of functor $\mathbf{F}_{\texttt{NewHope}}$, showing that that the security proof for the base KEM $\mathsf{KE}_1[H_2, H_3, H_4]$ does not naturally transfer to $\mathsf{KE}_2[V]$. Therefore, in order to generically extend the provable security results for KE_1 to KE_2, it seems advisable to instead apply appropriate oracle cloning methods.

2.5 Submissions with Provable Security but Ambiguous Specification

In their reference implementations, these submissions use cloning functors which we can and do validate via our framework, providing provable security in the random oracle model for the final KEM schemes. However, the submission documents do not clearly specify a secure cloning functor, meaning that variant implementations or adaptations may unknowingly introduce weaknesses. The schemes

BIKE [3], KCL [44], LAC [28], Lizard [16], LOCKER [4], Odd Manhattan [38], **ROLLO-II** [30], **Round5** [6], **SABER** [19] and Titanium [43] fall into this group.

LENGTH DIFFERENTIATION. Many of these schemes use the "identity" functor in their reference implementations, meaning that they set the final functions $H_1 = H_2 = H_3 = H_4 = F$ for a single base function F. If the scheme $\mathsf{KE}_1[H_1, H_2, H_3, H_4]$ never queries two different oracles on inputs of a single length, the domains of $H_1, \ldots, H_4$ are implicitly separated. Reference implementations typically enforce this separation by fixing the input length of every call to F. Our formalism calls this query restriction "length differentiation" and proves its security as an oracle cloning method. We also generalize it to all methods which prevent the scheme from querying any two distinct random oracles on a single input.

In the following, we discuss two schemes from the group, **ROLLO-II** and Lizard, where ambiguity about cloning methods between the specification and reference implementation jeopardizes the security of applications using these schemes. It will be important that, like BIG QUAKE and RoundTwo, the PKE schemes defined by **ROLLO-II** and Lizard allow randomness-based decryption.

The scheme **ROLLO-II** [30] defines its base KEM $\mathsf{KE}_1[H_1, H_2, H_3, H_4]$ using the $\mathbf{T}_9$ transform from Fig. 1. The submission document states that H_1, H_2, H_3, and H_4 are "typically" instantiated with a single fixed-length hash function F, but does not describe the cloning functors used to do so. If the identity functor is used, so that $H_1 = H_2 = H_3 = H_4 = F$, (or more generally, any functor that sets $H_2 = H_3$), an attack is possible. In the transform $\mathbf{T}_9$, both H_2 and H_3 are queried on the same input M. Then $Y = H_3(M) = F(M) = H_2(M) = R$ leaks the PKE's random coins, so the following attack will allow total key recovery via the randomness-based decryption.

Adversary $\mathcal{A}[F](pk, C^*)$ // Input public key and ciphertext, oracle for F

1. $C\|Y \leftarrow C^*$; $M \leftarrow \mathsf{PKE.DecR}(pk, C, Y)$ // ($Y = R$ is the coins)
2. $K \leftarrow F(M\|C\|Y)$; Return K

In the reference implementation of **ROLLO-II**, however, H_2 is instantiated using a second, independent function V instead of F, which prevents the above attack. Although the random oracles H_1, H_3 and H_4 are instantiated using the identity functor, they are never queried on the same input thanks to length differentiation. As a result, the reference implementation of **ROLLO-II** is provably secure, though alternate implementations could be both compliant with the submission document and completely insecure. The relevant portions of both the specification and the reference implementation were originally found in the corresponding first-round submission (LOCKER).

Lizard [16] also follows transform $\mathbf{T}_9$ to produce its base KEM $\mathsf{KE}_1[H_2, H_3, H_4]$. Its submission document suggests instantiation with a single function F as follows: it sets $H_3 = H_4 = F$, and it sets $H_2 = W \circ F$ for some postprocessing function W whose details are irrelevant here. Since, in $\mathbf{T}_9$, $Y = H_3(M) = F(M)$ and $R = H_2(M) = W \circ F(M) = W(Y)$, the randomness R will again be leaked through Y in the ciphertext, permitting a key-recovery attack using randomness-based decryption much like the others we have described. This attack is prevented in the reference implementation of Lizard, which instantiates H_3 and H_4 using an independent function G. The domains of H_3 and H_4 are separated by length differentiation. This allows us to prove the security of the final KEM $\mathsf{KE}_2[G, F]$, as defined by the reference implementation.

However, the length differentiation of H_3 and H_4 breaks down in the chosen-ciphertext-secure PKE variant specification of Lizard, which transforms KE_1. The PKE scheme, given a plaintext M, computes $R = H_2(M)$ and $Y = H_3(M)$ according to $\mathbf{T}_9$, but it computes $K = H_4(M)$, then includes the value $B = K \oplus M$ as part of the ciphertext C^*. Both the identity functor and the functor used by the KEM reference implementation set $H_3 = H_4$, so the following attack will extract the plaintext from any ciphertext–

Adversary $\mathcal{A}(pk, C^*)$ // Input public key and ciphertext
1. $C\|B\|Y \leftarrow C^*$ // Parse C^* to get Y and $B = M \oplus K$
2. $M \leftarrow Y \oplus B$; Return M // $Y = H_3(M) = H_4(M) = K$ is the mask.

The reference implementation of the public-key encryption schemes prevents the attack by cloning H_3 and H_4 from G via a third cloning functor, this one using the output splitting method. Yet, the inconsistency in the choice of cloning functors between the specification and both implementations underlines that ad-hoc cloning functors may easily "get lost" in modifications or adaptations of a scheme.

2.6 Submissions with Clear Provable Security

Here we place schemes which explicitly discuss their methods for domain separation and follow good practice in their implementations: Classic McEliece [13], CRYSTALS-Kyber [5], EMBLEM [41], FrodoKEM [34], HQC [32], LIMA [42], NTRU-HRSS-KEM [25], NTRU Prime [14], NTS-KEM [1], RQC [31], SIKE [26] and ThreeBears [23]. These schemes are careful to account for dependencies between random oracles that are considered to be independent in their security models. When choosing to clone multiple random oracles from a single primitive, the schemes in this group use padding bytes, deploy hash functions designed to accommodate domain separation, or restrictions on the length of the inputs which are codified in the specification. These explicit domain separation techniques can be cast in the formalism we develop in this work.

HQC and RQC are unique among the PQC KEM schemes in that their specifications warn that the identity functor admits key-recovery attacks. As protection, they recommend that H_2 and H_3 be instantiated with unrelated primitives.

SIGNATURES. Although the main focus of this paper is on domain separation in KEMs, we wish to note that these issues are not unique to KEMs. At least one digital signature scheme in the second round of the NIST PQC competition, MQDSS [15], models multiple hash functions as independent random oracles in its security proof, then clones them from the same primitive without explicit domain separation. We have not analyzed the NIST PQC digital signature schemes' security to see whether more subtle domain separation is present, or whether oracle collisions admit the same vulnerabilities to signature forgery as they do to session key recovery. This does, however, highlight that the problem of random oracle cloning is pervasive among more types of cryptographic schemes.

3 Preliminaries

BASIC NOTATION. By $[i..j]$ we abbreviate the set $\{i, \ldots, j\}$, for integers $i \leq j$. If $\mathbf{x}$ is a vector then $|\mathbf{x}|$ is its length (the number of its coordinates), $\mathbf{x}[i]$ is its i-th coordinate and $[\mathbf{x}] = \{\mathbf{x}[i] : i \in [1..|\mathbf{x}|]\}$ is the set of its coordinates. The empty vector is denoted (). If S is a set, then S^* is the set of vectors over S, meaning the set of vectors of any (finite) length with coordinates in S. Strings are identified with vectors over $\{0, 1\}$, so that if $x \in \{0, 1\}^*$ is a string then $|x|$ is its length, $x[i]$ is its i-th bit, and $x[i..j]$ is the substring from its i-th to its j-th bit (including), for $i \leq j$. The empty string is ε. If x, y are strings then we write $x \preceq y$ to indicate that x is a prefix of y. If S is a finite set then $|S|$ is its size (cardinality). A set $S \subseteq \{0, 1\}^*$ is *length closed* if $\{0, 1\}^{|x|} \subseteq S$ for all $x \in S$.

We let $y \leftarrow A[O_1, \ldots](x_1, \ldots; r)$ denote executing algorithm A on inputs $x_1, \ldots$ and coins r, with access to oracles $O_1, \ldots$, and letting y be the result. We let $y \leftarrow_\$ A[O_1, \ldots](x_1, \ldots)$ be the resulting of picking r at random and letting $y \leftarrow A[O_1, \ldots](x_1, \ldots; r)$. We let $\mathrm{OUT}(A[O_1, \ldots](x_1, \ldots))$ denote the set of all possible outputs of algorithm A when invoked with inputs $x_1, \ldots$ and access to oracles $O_1, \ldots$. Algorithms are randomized unless otherwise indicated. Running time is worst case. An adversary is an algorithm.

We use the code-based game-playing framework of [12]. A game G (see Fig. 2 for an example) starts with an INIT procedure, followed by a non-negative number of additional procedures, and ends with a FIN procedure. Procedures are also called oracles. Execution of adversary $\mathcal{A}$ with game G consists of running $\mathcal{A}$ with oracle access to the game procedures, with the restrictions that $\mathcal{A}$'s first call must be to INIT, its last call must be to FIN, and it can call these two procedures at most once. The output of the execution is the output of FIN. We write $\Pr[\mathrm{G}(\mathcal{A})]$ to denote the probability that the execution of game G with adversary $\mathcal{A}$ results in the output being the boolean true. Note that our adversaries have no output. The role of what in other treatments is the adversary output is, for us, played by the query to FIN. We adopt the convention that the running time of an adversary is the worst-case time to execute the game with the adversary, so the time taken by game procedures (oracles) to respond to queries is included.

FUNCTIONS. As usual $g \colon \mathcal{D} \to \mathcal{R}$ indicates that g is a function taking inputs in the domain set $\mathcal{D}$ and returning outputs in the range set $\mathcal{R}$. We may denote these sets by $\mathrm{Dom}(g)$ and $\mathrm{Rng}(g)$, respectively.

We say that $g \colon \mathrm{Dom}(g) \to \mathrm{Rng}(g)$ has output length ℓ if $\mathrm{Rng}(g) = \{0, 1\}^\ell$. We say that g is a single output-length (sol) function if there is some ℓ such that g has output length ℓ and also the set $\mathcal{D}$ is length closed. We let $\mathrm{SOL}(\mathcal{D}, \ell)$ denote the set of all sol functions $g\colon \mathcal{D} \to \{0,1\}^\ell$.

We say g is an extendable output length (xol) function if the following are true: (1) $\mathrm{Rng}(g) = \{0,1\}^*$ (2) there is a length-closed set $\mathrm{Dom}_*(g)$ such that $\mathrm{Dom}(g) = \mathrm{Dom}_*(g) \times \mathbb{N}$ (3) $|g(x,\ell)| = \ell$ for all $(x, \ell) \in \mathrm{Dom}(g)$, and (4) $g(x,\ell) \preceq g(x, \ell')$ whenever $\ell \leq \ell'$. We let $\mathrm{XOL}(\mathcal{D})$ denote the set of all xol functions $g\colon \mathcal{D} \to \{0,1\}^*$.

4   Read-Only Indifferentiability of Translating Functors

We define read-only indifferentiability (rd-indff) of functors. Then we define a class of functors called translating, and give general results about their rd-indiff security. Later we will apply this to analyze the security of cloning functors, but the treatment in this section is broader and, looking ahead to possible future applications, more general than we need for ours.

4.1   Functors and Read-Only Indifferentiability

A random oracle, formally, is a function drawn at random from a certain space of functions. A construction (functor) is a mapping from one such space to another. We start with definitions for these.

FUNCTION SPACES AND FUNCTORS. A function space FS is simply a set of functions, with the requirement that all functions in the set have the same domain $\mathsf{Dom}(\mathsf{FS})$ and the same range $\mathsf{Rng}(\mathsf{FS})$. Examples are $\mathrm{SOL}(\mathcal{D}, \ell)$ and $\mathrm{XOL}(\mathcal{D})$. Now $f \leftarrow_\$ \mathsf{FS}$ means we pick a function uniformly at random from the set FS.

Sometimes (but not always) we want an extra condition called input independence. It asks that the values of f on different inputs are identically and independently distributed when $f \leftarrow_\$ \mathsf{FS}$. More formally, let $\mathcal{D}$ be a set and let Out be a function that associates to any $W \in \mathcal{D}$ a set $\mathrm{Out}(W)$. Let $\mathrm{Out}(\mathcal{D})$ be the union of the sets $\mathrm{Out}(W)$ as W ranges over $\mathcal{D}$. Let $\mathrm{FUNC}(\mathcal{D}, \mathrm{Out})$ be the set of all functions $f\colon \mathcal{D} \to \mathrm{Out}(\mathcal{D})$ such that $f(W) \in \mathrm{Out}(W)$ for all $W \in \mathcal{D}$. We say that FS provides input independence if there exists such a Out such that $\mathsf{FS} = \mathrm{FUNC}(\mathsf{Dom}(\mathsf{FS}), \mathrm{Out})$. Put another way, there is a bijection between FS and the set S that is the cross product of the sets $\mathrm{Out}(W)$ as W ranges over $\mathsf{Dom}(\mathsf{FS})$. (Members of S are $|\mathsf{Dom}(\mathsf{FS})|$-vectors.) As an example the function space $\mathrm{SOL}(\mathcal{D}, \ell)$ satisfies input independence, but $\mathrm{XOL}(\mathcal{D})$ does *not* satisfy input independence.

Let SS be a function space that we call the starting space. Let ES be another function space that we call the ending space. We imagine that we are given a function $s \in \mathsf{SS}$ and want to construct a function $e \in \mathsf{ES}$. We refer to the object doing this as a functor. Formally a *functor* is a deterministic algorithm $\mathbf{F}$ that, given as oracle a function $s \in \mathsf{SS}$, returns a function $\mathbf{F}[s] \in \mathsf{ES}$. We write $\mathbf{F}\colon \mathsf{SS} \to \mathsf{ES}$ to emphasize the starting and ending spaces of functor $\mathbf{F}$.

RD-INDIFF. We want the ending function to "emulate" a random function from ES. Indifferentiability is a way of defining what this means. The original definition

Game $\mathbf{G}_{\mathbf{F},\mathsf{SS},\mathsf{ES},\mathcal{W},\mathsf{S}}^{\text{rd-indiff}}$	PRIV(W):
	5 If $W \in \mathcal{W}$ then return $e_b(W)$
INIT:	6 Else return $\perp$
1 $s \leftarrow_\$ \mathsf{SS}$	
2 $e_1 \leftarrow \mathbf{F}[s]$; $e_0 \leftarrow_\$ \mathsf{ES}$	PUB(U):
3 $b \leftarrow_\$ \{0,1\}$	7 if ($b = 1$) then return $s(U)$
4 $st \leftarrow_\$ \mathsf{S}.\text{Setup}()$	8 else return $\mathsf{S}.\text{Ev}[e_0](st, U)$
	FIN(b'):
	9 return ($b = b'$)

Fig. 2. Game defining read-only indifferentiability.

of MRH [29] has been followed by many variants [17,20,33,39]. Here we give ours, called read-only indifferentiability, which implies composition not just for single-stage games, but even for multi-stage ones [20,33,39].

Let ES and SS be function spaces, and let $\mathbf{F}: \mathsf{SS} \to \mathsf{ES}$ be a functor. Our variant of indifferentiability mandates a particular, strong simulator, which can read, but not write, its (game-maintained) state, so that this state is a static quantity. Formally a *read-only simulator* S for $\mathbf{F}$ specifies a *setup algorithm* S.Setup which outputs the state, and a deterministic *evaluation algorithm* S.Ev that, given as oracle a function $e \in \mathsf{ES}$, and given a string $st \in \text{OUT}(\mathsf{S}.\text{Setup})$ (the read-only state), defines a function $\mathsf{S}.\text{Ev}[e](st, \cdot): \text{Dom}(\mathsf{SS}) \to \text{Rng}(\mathsf{SS})$.

The intent is that $\mathsf{S}.\text{Ev}[e](st, \cdot)$ play the role of a starting function $s \in \mathsf{SS}$ satisfying $\mathbf{F}[s] = e$. To formalize this, consider the read-only indifferentiability game $\mathbf{G}_{\mathbf{F},\mathsf{SS},\mathsf{ES},\mathcal{W},\mathsf{S}}^{\text{rd-indiff}}$ of Fig. 2, where $\mathcal{W} \subseteq \text{Dom}(\mathsf{ES})$ is called the working domain. The adversary $\mathcal{A}$ playing this game is called a distinguisher. Its advantage is defined as

$$\mathbf{Adv}_{\mathbf{F},\mathsf{SS},\mathsf{ES},\mathcal{W},\mathsf{S}}^{\text{rd-indiff}}(\mathcal{A}) = 2 \cdot \Pr\left[\mathbf{G}_{\mathbf{F},\mathsf{SS},\mathsf{ES},\mathcal{W},\mathsf{S}}^{\text{rd-indiff}}(\mathcal{A})\right] - 1.$$

To explain, in the game, b is a challenge bit that the distinguisher is trying to determine. Function e_b is a random member of the ending space ES if $b = 0$ and is $\mathbf{F}[s](\cdot)$ if $b = 1$. The query W to oracle PRIV is required to be in $\text{Dom}(\mathsf{ES})$. The oracle returns the value of e_b on W, but only if W is in the working domain, otherwise returning $\perp$. The query U to oracle PUB is required to be in $\text{Dom}(\mathsf{SS})$. The oracle returns the value of s on U in the $b = 1$ case, but when $b = 0$, the simulator evaluation algorithm S.Ev must answer the query with access to an oracle for e_0. The distinguisher ends by calling FIN with its guess $b' \in \{0, 1\}$ of b and the game returns true if $b' = b$ (the distinguisher's guess is correct) and false otherwise.

The working domain $\mathcal{W} \subseteq \text{Dom}(\mathsf{ES})$, a parameter of the definition, is included as a way to allow the notion of read-only indifferentiability to provide results for oracle cloning methods like length differentiation whose security depends on domain restrictions.

The S.Ev algorithm is given direct access to e_0, rather than access to PRIV as in other definitions, to bypass the working domain restriction, meaning it may query e_0 at points in Dom(ES) that are outside the working domain.

All invocations of S.Ev$[e_0]$ are given the same (static, game-maintained) state st as input, but S.Ev$[e_0]$ cannot modify this state, which is why it is called read-only. Note INIT does not return st, meaning the state is not given to the distinguisher.

DISCUSSION. To compare rd-indiff to other indiff notions, we set $W = $ Dom(ES), because prior notions do not include working domains. Now, rd-indiff differs from prior indiff notions because it requires that the simulator state be just the immutable string chosen at the start of the game. In this regard, rd-indiff falls somewhere between the original MRH-indiff [29] and reset indiff [39] in the sense that our simulator is more restricted than in the first and less than in the second. A construction (functor) that is reset-indiff is thus rd-indiff, but not necessarily vice-versa, and a construct that is rd-indiff is MRH-indiff, but not necessarily vice-versa. Put another way, the class of rd-indff functors is larger than the class of reset-indiff ones, but smaller than the class of MRH-indiff ones. Now, RSS's proof [39] that reset-indiff implies security for multi-stage games extends to rd-indiff, so we get this for a potentially larger class of functors. This larger class includes some of the cloning functors we have described, which are not necessarily reset-indiff.

4.2   Translating Functors

TRANSLATING FUNCTORS. We focus on a class of functors that we call translating. This class includes natural and existing oracle cloning methods, in particular all the effective methods used by NIST KEMs, and we will be able to prove general results for translating functors that can be applied to the cloning methods.

A translating functor $\mathbf{T}$: SS $\to$ ES is a functor that, with oracle access to s and on input $W \in$ Dom(ES), non-adaptively calls s on a fixed number of inputs, and computes its output $\mathbf{T}[s](W)$ from the responses and W. Its operation can be split into three phases which do not share state: (1) a pre-processing phase which chooses the inputs to s based on W alone (2) the calls to s to obtain responses (3) a post-processing phase which uses W and the responses collected in phase 2 to compute the final output value $\mathbf{T}[s](W)$.

Proceeding to the definitions, let SS, ES be function spaces. A (SS, ES)-*query translator* is a function (deterministic algorithm) QT: Dom(ES) $\to$ Dom(SS)*, meaning it takes a point W in the domain of the ending space and returns a vector of points in the domain of the starting space. This models the pre-processing. A (SS, ES)-*answer translator* is a function (deterministic algorithm) AT: Dom(ES) $\times$ Rng(SS)* $\to$ Rng(ES), meaning it takes the original W, and a vector of points in the range of the starting space, to return a point in the range of the ending space. This models the post-processing. To the pair (QT, AT), we associate the functor $\mathbf{TF}_{\text{QT,AT}}$: SS $\to$ ES, defined as follows:

Algorithm $\mathbf{TF}_{\mathsf{QT},\mathsf{AT}}[s](W)$ // Input $W \in \mathrm{Dom}(\mathsf{ES})$ and oracle $s \in \mathsf{SS}$

$U \leftarrow \mathsf{QT}(W)$
For $j = 1, \ldots, |U|$ do $V[j] \leftarrow s(U[j])$ // $U[j] \in \mathrm{Dom}(\mathsf{SS})$
$Y \leftarrow \mathsf{AT}(W, V)$; Return Y

The above-mentioned calls of phase (2) are done in the second line of the code above, so that this implements a translating functor as we described. Formally we say that a functor $\mathbf{F}\colon \mathsf{SS} \to \mathsf{ES}$ is *translating* if there exists a $(\mathsf{SS}, \mathsf{ES})$-query translator QT and a $(\mathsf{SS}, \mathsf{ES})$-answer translator AT such that $\mathbf{F} = \mathbf{TF}_{\mathsf{QT},\mathsf{AT}}$.

INVERSES. So far, query and answer translators may have just seemed an unduly complex way to say that a translating oracle construction is one that makes non-adaptive oracle queries. The purpose of making the query and answer translators explicit is to define *invertibility*, which determines rd-indiff security.

Let SS and ES be function spaces. Let QTI be a function (deterministic algorithm) that takes an input $U \in \mathrm{Dom}(\mathsf{SS})$ and returns a vector W over $\mathrm{Dom}(\mathsf{ES})$. We allow QTI to return the empty vector (), which is taken as an indication of failure to invert. Define the *support* of QTI, denoted $\mathbf{sup}(\mathsf{QTI})$, to be the set of all $U \in \mathrm{Dom}(\mathsf{SS})$ such that $\mathsf{QTI}(U) \neq ()$. Say that QTI has *full support* if $\mathbf{sup}(\mathsf{QTI}) = \mathrm{Dom}(\mathsf{SS})$, meaning there is no $U \in \mathrm{Dom}(\mathsf{SS})$ such that $\mathsf{QTI}(U) = ()$. Let ATI be a function (deterministic algorithm) that takes $U \in \mathrm{Dom}(\mathsf{SS})$ and a vector Y over $\mathrm{Rng}(\mathsf{ES})$ to return an output in $\mathrm{Rng}(\mathsf{SS})$. Given a function $e \in \mathsf{ES}$, we define the function $\mathrm{P}[e]_{\mathsf{QTI},\mathsf{ATI}}\colon \mathrm{Dom}(\mathsf{SS}) \to \mathrm{Rng}(\mathsf{SS})$ by

---

Function $\mathrm{P}[e]_{\mathsf{QTI},\mathsf{ATI}}(U)$ // $U \in \mathrm{Dom}(\mathsf{SS})$

$W \leftarrow \mathsf{QTI}(U)$; $Y \leftarrow e(W)$; $V \leftarrow \mathsf{ATI}(U, Y)$; Return V

Above, e is applied to a vector component-wise, meaning $e(W)$ is defined as the vector $(e(W[1]), \ldots, e(W[|W|]))$.

We require that the function $\mathrm{P}[e]_{\mathsf{QTI},\mathsf{ATI}}$ belong to the starting space SS. Now let QT be a $(\mathsf{SS}, \mathsf{ES})$-query translator and AT a $(\mathsf{SS}, \mathsf{ES})$-answer translator. Let $\mathcal{W} \subseteq \mathrm{Dom}(\mathsf{ES})$ be a working domain. We say that $\mathsf{QTI}, \mathsf{ATI}$ *are inverses of* QT, AT *over* $\mathcal{W}$ if two conditions are true. The first is that for all $e \in \mathsf{ES}$ and all $W \in \mathcal{W}$ we have

$$\mathbf{TF}_{\mathsf{QT},\mathsf{AT}}[\mathrm{P}[e]_{\mathsf{QTI},\mathsf{ATI}}](W) = e(W) . \tag{2}$$

This equation needs some parsing. Fix a function $e \in \mathsf{ES}$ in the ending space. Then $s = \mathrm{P}[e]_{\mathsf{QTI},\mathsf{ATI}}$ is in SS. Recall that the functor $\mathbf{F} = \mathbf{TF}_{\mathsf{QT},\mathsf{AT}}$ takes a function s in the starting space as an oracle and defines a function $e' = \mathbf{F}[s]$ in the ending space. Equation (2) is asking that e' is identical to the original function e, on the working domain $\mathcal{W}$. The second condition (for invertibility) is that if $U \in \{\mathsf{QT}(W)[i] : W \in \mathcal{W}\}$—that is, U is an entry of the vector U returned by QT on some input W—then $\mathsf{QTI}(U) \neq ()$. Note that if QTI has full support then this condition is already true, but otherwise it is an additional requirement.

$$\begin{array}{|l|}
\hline
\textbf{Game } \mathbf{G}^{\mathrm{ti}}_{\mathsf{SS,ES,QTI,ATI}} \\
\hline
\text{INIT:} \\
\quad 1 \;\; b \leftarrow\!\!\$ \{0,1\} \;;\; e \leftarrow\!\!\$ \mathsf{ES} \\
\quad 2 \;\; s_1 \leftarrow\!\!\$ \mathsf{SS} \;;\; s_0 \leftarrow \mathrm{P}[e]_{\mathsf{QTI,ATI}} \\
\text{PUB}(U): \;\;\; /\!\!/ \; U \in \mathrm{Dom}(\mathsf{SS}) \\
\quad 3 \;\; \text{If } \mathbf{QTI}(U) = () \text{ then return } \bot \\
\quad 4 \;\; \text{return } s_b(U) \\
\text{FIN}(b'): \\
\quad 5 \;\; \text{return } (b = b') \\
\hline
\end{array}$$

Fig. 3. Game defining translation indistinguishability.

Algorithm S.Setup:	Algorithm S.Ev$[e](st, U)$:
1 Return ε	1 $\mathbf{W} \leftarrow \mathbf{QTI}(U)$; $\mathbf{Y} \leftarrow e(\mathbf{W})$; $V \leftarrow \mathbf{ATI}(U, \mathbf{Y})$
	2 Return V

Algorithm S.Setup:	Algorithm S.Ev$[e](st, U)$:
1 $st \leftarrow\!\!\$ \{0,1\}^{\mathsf{G.kl}}$	1 $\mathbf{W} \leftarrow \mathbf{QTI}(U)$
2 Return st	2 If $\mathbf{W} = ()$ then return $\mathbf{G}_{st}[e](U)$
	3 $\mathbf{Y} \leftarrow e(\mathbf{W})$; $V \leftarrow \mathbf{ATI}(U, \mathbf{Y})$
	4 Return V

Fig. 4. Simulators for Theorem 1 (top) and Theorem 2 (bottom).

We say that $(\mathsf{QT}, \mathsf{AT})$ is invertible over $\mathcal{W}$ if there exist $\mathsf{QTI}, \mathsf{ATI}$ such that $\mathsf{QTI}, \mathsf{ATI}$ are inverses of QT, AT over $\mathcal{W}$, and we say that a translating functor $\mathbf{TF}_{\mathsf{QT,AT}}$ is invertible over $\mathcal{W}$ if $(\mathsf{QT}, \mathsf{AT})$ is invertible over $\mathcal{W}$.

In the rd-indiff context, function $\mathrm{P}[e]_{\mathsf{QTI,ATI}}$ will be used by the simulator. Roughly, we try to set $\mathsf{S.Ev}[e](st, U) = \mathrm{P}[e]_{\mathsf{QTI,ATI}}(U)$. But we will only be able to successfully do this for $U \in \mathbf{sup}(\mathsf{QTI})$. The state st is used by S.Ev to provide replies when $U \notin \mathbf{sup}(\mathsf{QTI})$.

Equation (2) is a correctness condition. There is also a security metric. Consider the *translation indistinguishability* game $\mathbf{G}^{\mathrm{ti}}_{\mathsf{SS,ES,QTI,ATI}}$ of Fig. 3. Define the ti-advantage of adversary $\mathcal{B}$ via

$$\mathbf{Adv}^{\mathrm{ti}}_{\mathsf{SS,ES,QTI,ATI}}(\mathcal{B}) = 2 \cdot \Pr\left[\mathbf{G}^{\mathrm{ti}}_{\mathsf{SS,ES,QTI,ATI}}(\mathcal{B})\right] - 1.$$

In reading the game, recall that () is the empty vector, whose return by QTI represents an inversion error. TI-security is thus asking that if e is randomly chosen from the ending space, then the output of $\mathrm{P}[e]_{\mathsf{QTI,ATI}}$ on an input U is distributed like the output on U of a random function in the starting space, *but only as long as* $\mathsf{QTI}(U)$ *was non-empty*. We will see that the latter restriction creates some challenges in simulation whose resolution exploits using read-only state. We say that $(\mathsf{QTI}, \mathsf{ATI})$ provides perfect translation indistinguishability if $\mathbf{Adv}^{\mathrm{ti}}_{\mathsf{SS},\mathsf{ES},\mathsf{QTI},\mathsf{ATI}}(\mathcal{B}) = 0$ for all $\mathcal{B}$, regardless of the running time of $\mathcal{B}$.

Additionally we of course ask that the functions $\mathsf{QT}, \mathsf{AT}, \mathsf{QTI}, \mathsf{ATI}$ all be efficiently computable. In an asymptotic setting, this means they are polynomial time. In our concrete setting, they show up in the running-time of the simulator or constructed adversaries. (The latter, as per our conventions, being the time for the execution of the adversary with the overlying game.)

4.3 Rd-Indiff of Translating Functors

We now move on to showing that invertibility of a pair $(\mathsf{QT}, \mathsf{AT})$ implies rd-indifferentiability of the translating functor $\mathbf{TF}_{\mathsf{QT},\mathsf{AT}}$. We start with the case that QTI has full support.

Theorem 1. *Let SS and ES be function spaces. Let $\mathcal{W}$ be a subset of $\mathrm{Dom}(\mathsf{ES})$. Let QT, AT be $(\mathsf{SS}, \mathsf{ES})$ query and answer translators, respectively. Let $\mathsf{QTI}, \mathsf{ATI}$ be inverses of QT, AT over $\mathcal{W}$. Assume QTI has full support. Define read-only simulator S as per the top panel of Fig. 4. Let $\mathbf{F} = \mathbf{TF}_{\mathsf{QT},\mathsf{AT}}$. Let $\mathcal{A}$ be any distinguisher. Then we construct a ti-adversary $\mathcal{B}$ such that*

$$\mathbf{Adv}^{\mathrm{rd\text{-}indiff}}_{\mathbf{F},\mathsf{SS},\mathsf{ES},\mathcal{W},\mathsf{S}}(\mathcal{A}) \leq \mathbf{Adv}^{\mathrm{ti}}_{\mathsf{SS},\mathsf{ES},\mathsf{QTI},\mathsf{ATI}}(\mathcal{B}) \ .$$

Let ℓ be the maximum output length of QT. If $\mathcal{A}$ makes $q_{\mathrm{PRIV}}, q_{\mathrm{PUB}}$ queries to its PRIV, PUB oracles, respectively, then $\mathcal{B}$ makes $\ell \cdot q_{\mathrm{PRIV}} + q_{\mathrm{PUB}}$ queries to its PUB oracle. The running time of $\mathcal{B}$ is about that of $\mathcal{A}$.

Proof (Theorem 1). Consider the games of Fig. 5. In the left panel, line 1 is included only in G_0 and line 2 only in G_1, and this is the only way the games differ. Game G_0 is the real game, meaning the case $b = 1$ in game $\mathbf{G}^{\mathrm{rd\text{-}indiff}}_{\mathbf{F},\mathsf{SS},\mathsf{ES},\mathcal{W},\mathsf{S}}$. In game G_2, oracle PRIV is switched to a random function e_0. From the description of the simulator in Fig. 4 we see that

$$\mathsf{S}.\mathrm{Ev}[e_0](\varepsilon, U) = \mathsf{P}[e_0]_{\mathsf{QTI},\mathsf{ATI}}(U)$$

for all $U \in \mathrm{Dom}(\mathsf{SS})$ and all $e_0 \in \mathsf{ES}$, so that oracle PUB in game G_2 is responding according to the simulator based on e_0. So game G_2 is the case $b = 0$ in game $\mathbf{G}^{\mathrm{rd\text{-}indiff}}_{\mathbf{F},\mathsf{SS},\mathsf{ES},\mathcal{W},\mathsf{S}}$. Thus

$$\begin{aligned} \mathbf{Adv}^{\mathrm{rd\text{-}indiff}}_{\mathbf{F},\mathsf{SS},\mathsf{ES},\mathcal{W},\mathsf{S}}(\mathcal{A}) &= \Pr[G_0(\mathcal{A})] - \Pr[G_2(\mathcal{A})] \\ &= (\Pr[G_0(\mathcal{A})] - \Pr[G_1(\mathcal{A})]) + (\Pr[G_1(\mathcal{A})] - \Pr[G_2(\mathcal{A})]) \ . \end{aligned}$$

We define translation-indistinguishability adversary $\mathcal{B}$ in Fig. 5 so that

$$\Pr[G_0(\mathcal{A})] - \Pr[G_1(\mathcal{A})] \leq \mathbf{Adv}^{\mathrm{ti}}_{\mathsf{SS},\mathsf{ES},\mathsf{QTI},\mathsf{ATI}}(\mathcal{B}) \ .$$

Adversary $\mathcal{B}$ is playing game $\mathbf{G}^{\mathrm{ti}}_{\mathsf{SS},\mathsf{ES},\mathsf{QTI},\mathsf{ATI}}$. Using its PUB oracle, it presents the interface of G_0 and G_1 to $\mathcal{A}$. In order to simulate the PRIV oracle, $\mathcal{B}$ runs

Games G_0, G_1	Game G_2
INIT:	INIT:
1 $s \leftarrow_\$ SS$ // Game G_0	1 $e_0 \leftarrow_\$ ES$
2 $e_0 \leftarrow_\$ ES$; $s \leftarrow P[e_0]_{QTI,ATI}$ // Game G_1	2 $s \leftarrow P[e_0]_{QTI,ATI}$
PRIV(W):	PRIV(W):
3 If $W \in \mathcal{W}$ then return $\mathbf{F}[s](W)$	3 If $W \in \mathcal{W}$ then return $e_0(W)$
4 Else return $\bot$	4 Else return $\bot$
PUB(U):	PUB(U):
5 return $s(U)$	5 return $s(U)$
FIN(b'):	FIN(b'):
6 return $(b' = 1)$	6 return $(b' = 1)$

Adversary $\mathcal{B}$:	
1 INIT()	PRIV$'$(W):
2 $\mathcal{A}[\text{INIT}', \text{PUB}', \text{PRIV}', \text{FIN}']()$	5 if $W \notin \mathcal{W}$ then return $\bot$
	6 $U \leftarrow QT(W)$
INIT$'$:	7 For $j = 1, \ldots, |U|$ do $V[j] \leftarrow \text{PUB}(U[j])$
3 Return	8 return $AT(W, V)$
PUB$'$(U):	FIN$'$(b'):
4 return PUB(U)	9 FIN(b')

Fig. 5. Top: Games for proof of Theorem 1. Bottom: Adversary for proof of Theorem 1.

$\mathbf{TF}_{QT,AT}[\text{PUB}]$. This is consistent with G_0 and G_1. If $b = 1$ in $\mathbf{G}^{ti}_{SS,ES,QTI,ATI}$, then $\mathcal{B}$ perfectly simulates G_0 for $\mathcal{A}$. If $b = 1$, then $\mathcal{B}$ correctly simulates G_1 for $\mathcal{A}$. To complete the proof we claim that

$$\Pr[G_1(\mathcal{A})] = \Pr[G_2(\mathcal{A})] \,.$$

This is true by the correctness condition. The latter says that if $s \leftarrow P[e_0]_{QTI,ATI}$ then $\mathbf{F}[s]$ is just e_0 itself. So e_1 in game G_1 is the same as e_0 in game G_2, making their PRIV oracles identical. And their PUB oracles are identical by definition. $\square$

The simulator in Theorem 1 is stateless, so when $\mathcal{W}$ is chosen to be Dom(ES) the theorem is establishing reset indifferentiability [39] of $\mathbf{F}$.

For translating functors where QTI does not have full support, we need an auxiliary primitive that we call a (SS, ES)-oracle aided PRF. Given an oracle for a function $e \in ES$, an (SS, ES)-oracle aided PRF G defines a function $G[e]: \{0,1\}^{G.kl} \times \text{Dom(SS)} \to \text{Rng(SS)}$. The first input is a key. For $\mathcal{C}$ an adversary, let $\mathbf{Adv}^{prf}_{G,SS,ES}(\mathcal{C}) = 2\Pr[\mathbf{G}^{prf}_{G,SS,ES}(\mathcal{C})] - 1$, where the game is in Fig. 6. The simulator uses its read-only state to store a key st for G, then using $G(st, \cdot)$ to answer queries outside the support $\mathbf{sup}(QTI)$.

$$
\boxed{
\begin{array}{ll}
\mathbf{G}^{\mathrm{prf}}_{\mathsf{G,SS,ES}} & \mathrm{RO}(W): \\
& \quad 6 \ \text{Return } e(W) \\
\mathrm{INIT}(): & \\
\quad 1 \ b \leftarrow\!\!\$ \ \{0,1\} & \mathrm{FNO}(U): \\
\quad 2 \ e \leftarrow\!\!\$ \ \mathsf{ES} & \quad 7 \ V \leftarrow s_b(U) \\
\quad 3 \ st \leftarrow\!\!\$ \ \{0,1\}^{\mathsf{G.kl}} & \quad 8 \ \text{Return } V \\
\quad 4 \ s_1 \leftarrow \mathsf{G}[e](st, \cdot) & \mathrm{FIN}(b'): \\
\quad 5 \ s_0 \leftarrow\!\!\$ \ \mathsf{SS} & \quad 9 \ \text{Return } (b' = b)
\end{array}
}
$$

Fig. 6. Game to define PRF security of $(\mathsf{SS}, \mathsf{ES})$-oracle aided PRF G.

We introduce this primitive because it allows multiple instantiations. The simplest is that it is a PRF, which happens when it does not use its oracle. In that case the simulator is using a computational primitive (a PRF) in the indifferentiability context, which seems novel. Another instantiation prefixes st to the input and then invokes e to return the output. This works for certain choices of ES, but not always. Note G is used only by the simulator and plays no role in the functor.

The proof of the following is in [10].

Theorem 2. *Let* SS *and* ES *be function spaces, and assume they provide input independence. Let* $\mathcal{W}$ *be a subset of* $\mathrm{Dom}(\mathsf{ES})$. *Let* QT, AT *be* $(\mathsf{SS}, \mathsf{ES})$ *query and answer translators, respectively. Let* $\mathsf{QTI}, \mathsf{ATI}$ *be inverses of* QT, AT *over* $\mathcal{W}$. *Define read-only simulator* S *as per the bottom panel of Fig. 4. Let* $\mathbf{F} = \mathbf{TF}_{\mathsf{QT,AT}}$. *Let* $\mathcal{A}$ *be any distinguisher. Then we construct a ti-adversary* $\mathcal{B}$ *and a prf-adversary* $\mathcal{C}$ *such that*

$$
\mathbf{Adv}^{\mathrm{rd\text{-}indiff}}_{\mathbf{F},\mathsf{SS,ES},\mathcal{W},\mathsf{S}}(\mathcal{A}) \leq \mathbf{Adv}^{\mathrm{ti}}_{\mathsf{SS,ES,QTI,ATI}}(\mathcal{B}) + \mathbf{Adv}^{\mathrm{prf}}_{\mathsf{G,SS}}(\mathcal{C}) .
$$

Let ℓ *be the maximum output length of* QT *and* ℓ' *the maximum output length of* QTI. *If* $\mathcal{A}$ *makes* $q_{\mathrm{PRIV}}, q_{\mathrm{PUB}}$ *queries to its* PRIV, PUB *oracles, respectively, then* $\mathcal{B}$ *makes* $\ell \cdot q_{\mathrm{PRIV}} + q_{\mathrm{PUB}}$ *queries to its* PUB *oracle and* $\mathcal{C}$ *makes at most* $\ell \cdot \ell' \cdot q_{\mathrm{PRIV}} + q_{\mathrm{PUB}}$ *queries to its* RO *oracle and at most* $q_{\mathrm{PUB}} + \ell \cdot q_{\mathrm{PRIV}}$ *queries to its* FNO *oracle. The running times of* $\mathcal{B}, \mathcal{C}$ *are about that of* $\mathcal{A}$.

5 Analysis of Cloning Functors

Section 4 defined the rd-indiff metric of security for functors and give a framework to prove rd-indiff of translating functors. We now apply this to derive security results about particular, practical cloning functors.

ARITY-n FUNCTION SPACES. The cloning functors apply to function spaces where a function specifies sub-functions, corresponding to the different random oracles we are trying to build. Formally, a function space FS is said to have arity n if its members are two-argument functions f whose first argument is an integer $i \in$

$[1..n]$. For $i \in [1..n]$ we let $f_i = f(i, \cdot)$ and $\mathsf{FS}_i = \{f_i : f \in \mathsf{FS}\}$, and refer to the latter as the i-th subspace of FS. We let $\mathsf{Dom}_i(\mathsf{FS})$ be the set of all X such that $(i, X) \in \mathsf{Dom}(\mathsf{FS})$.

We say that FS has sol subspaces if FS_i is a set of sol functions with domain $\mathsf{Dom}_i(\mathsf{FS})$, for all $i \in [1..n]$. More precisely, there must be integers $\mathsf{OL}_1(\mathsf{FS}), \ldots,$ $\mathsf{OL}_n(\mathsf{FS})$ such that $\mathsf{FS}_i = \mathsf{SOL}(\mathsf{Dom}_i(\mathsf{FS}), \mathsf{OL}_i(\mathsf{FS}))$ for all $i \in [1..n]$. In this case, we let $\mathsf{Rng}_i(\mathsf{FS}) = \{0, 1\}^{\mathsf{OL}_i(\mathsf{FS})}$. This is the most common case for practical uses of ROs.

To explain, access to n random oracles is modeled as access to a two-argument function f drawn at random from FS, written $f \twoheadleftarrow \mathsf{FS}$. If FS has sol subspaces, then for each i, the function f_i is a sol function, with a certain domain and output length depending only on i. All such functions are included. This ensures input independence as we defined it earlier. Thus if $f \twoheadleftarrow \mathsf{FS}$, then for each i and any distinct inputs to f_i, the outputs are independently distributed. Also functions $f_1, \ldots, f_n$ are independently distributed when $f \twoheadleftarrow \mathsf{FS}$. Put another way, we can identify FS with $\mathsf{FS}_1 \times \cdots \times \mathsf{FS}_n$.

DOMAIN-SEPARATING FUNCTORS. We can now formalize the domain separation method by seeing it as defining a certain type of (translating) functor.

Let the ending space ES be an arity n function space. Let $\mathbf{F} \colon \mathsf{SS} \to \mathsf{ES}$ be a translating functor and QT, AT be its query and answer translations, respectively. Assume QT returns a vector of length 1 and that $\mathsf{AT}((i, X), \mathbf{V})$ simply returns $\mathbf{V}[1]$. We say that $\mathbf{F}$ is *domain separating* if the following is true: $\mathsf{QT}(i_1, X_1) \neq \mathsf{QT}(i_2, X_2)$ for any $(i_1, X_1), (i_2, X_2) \in \mathsf{Dom}(\mathsf{ES})$ that satisfy $i_1 \neq i_2$.

To explain, recall that the ending function is obtained as $e \leftarrow \mathbf{F}[s]$, and defines e_i for $i \in [1..n]$. Function e_i takes input X, lets $(u) \leftarrow \mathsf{QT}(i, X)$ and returns $s(u)$. The domain separation requirement is that if $(u_i) \leftarrow \mathsf{QT}(i, X_i)$ and $(u_j) \leftarrow \mathsf{QT}(j, X_j)$, then $i \neq j$ implies $u_i \neq u_j$, regardless of X_i, X_j. Thus if $i \neq j$ then the inputs to which s is applied are always different. The domain of s has been "separated" into disjoint subsets, one for each i.

PRACTICAL CLONING FUNCTORS. We show that many popular methods for oracle cloning in practice, including ones used in NIST KEM submissions, can be cast as translating functors.

In the following, the starting space $\mathsf{SS} = \mathsf{SOL}(\{0, 1\}^*, \mathsf{OL}(\mathsf{SS}))$ is assumed to be a sol function space with domain $\{0, 1\}^*$ and an output length denoted $\mathsf{OL}(\mathsf{SS})$. The ending space ES is an arity n function spaces that has sol subspaces.

PREFIXING. Here we formalize the canonical method of domain separation. Prefixing is used in the following NIST PQC submissions: **ClassicMcEliece**, **FrodoKEM**, LIMA, **NTRU Prime**, SIKE, QC-MDPC, **ThreeBears**.

Let $\mathbf{p}$ be a vector of strings. We require that it be *prefix-free*, by which we mean that $i \neq j$ implies that $\mathbf{p}[i]$ is not a prefix of $\mathbf{p}[j]$. Entries of this vector will be used as prefixes to enforce domain separation. One example is that the entries of $\mathbf{p}$ are distinct strings all of the same length. Another is that a $\mathbf{p}[i] = \mathsf{E}(i)$ for some prefix-free code E like a Huffman code.

Assume $OL_i(ES) = OL(SS)$ for all $i \in [1..n]$, meaning all ending functions have the same output length as the starting function. The functor $\mathbf{F}_{pf(\mathbf{p})}$: $SS \to ES$ corresponding to $\mathbf{p}$ is defined by $\mathbf{F}_{pf(\mathbf{p})}[s](i, X) = s(\mathbf{p}[i]\|X)$. To explain, recall that the ending function is obtained as $e \leftarrow \mathbf{F}_{pf(\mathbf{p})}[s]$, and defines e_i for $i \in [1..n]$. Function e_i takes input X, prefixes $\mathbf{p}[i]$ to X to get a string X', applies the starting function s to X' to get Y, and returns Y as the value of $e_i(X)$.

We claim that $\mathbf{F}_{pf(\mathbf{p})}$ is a translating functor that is also a domain-separating functor as per the definitions above. To see this, define query translator $QT_{pf(\mathbf{p})}$ by $QT_{pf(\mathbf{p})}(i, X) = (\mathbf{p}[i]\|X)$, the 1-vector whose sole entry is $\mathbf{p}[i]\|X$. The answer translator $AT_{pf(\mathbf{p})}$, on input (i, X), $\mathbf{V}$, returns $\mathbf{V}[1]$, meaning it ignores i, X and returns the sole entry in its 1-vector $\mathbf{V}$.

We proceed to the inverses, which are defined as follows:

Algorithm $QTI_{pf(\mathbf{p})}(U)$	Algorithm $ATI_{pf(\mathbf{p})}(U, \mathbf{Y})$
$\mathbf{W} \leftarrow ()$	If $\mathbf{Y} \neq ()$ then $V \leftarrow \mathbf{Y}[1]$
For $i = 1, \ldots, n$ do	Else $V \leftarrow 0^{OL(SS)}$
If $\mathbf{p}[i] \preceq U$ then $\mathbf{p}[i]\|X \leftarrow U$; $\mathbf{W}[1] \leftarrow (i, X)$	Return V
Return $\mathbf{W}$	

The working domain is the full one: $\mathcal{W} = \text{Dom}(ES)$. We now verify Eq. (2). Let QT, QTI, AT, ATI be $QT_{pf(\mathbf{p})}, QTI_{pf(\mathbf{p})}, AT_{pf(\mathbf{p})}, ATI_{pf(\mathbf{p})}$, respectively. Then for all $W = (i, X) \in \text{Dom}(ES)$, we have:

$$\mathbf{TF}_{QT,AT}[P[e]_{QTI,ATI}](W) = P[e]_{QTI,ATI}(\mathbf{p}[i]\|X)$$
$$= ATI(\mathbf{p}[i]\|X, (e(i, X)))$$
$$= e(i, X).$$

We observe that $(QTI_{pf(\mathbf{p})}, ATI_{pf(\mathbf{p})})$ provides perfect translation indistinguishability. Since $QTI_{pf(\mathbf{p})}$ does not have full support, we can't use Theorem 1, but we can conclude rd-indiff via Theorem 2.

IDENTITY. Many NIST PQC submissions simply let $e_i(X) = s(X)$, meaning the ending functions are identical to the starting one. This is captured by the identity functor $\mathbf{F}_{id}$: $SS \to ES$, defined by $\mathbf{F}_{id}[s](i, X) = s(X)$. This again assumes $OL_i(ES) = OL(SS)$ for all $i \in [1..n]$, meaning all ending functions have the same output length as the starting function. This functor is translating, via $QT_{id}(i, X) = X$ and $AT_{id}((i, X), \mathbf{V}) = \mathbf{V}[1]$. It is however *not*, at least in general, domain separating.

Clearly, this functor is not, in general, rd-indiff. To make secure use of it nonetheless, applications can restrict the inputs to the ending functions to enforce a virtual domain separation, meaning, for $i \neq j$, the schemes never query e_i and e_j on the same input. One way to do this is length differentiation. Here, for $i \in [1..n]$, the inputs to which e_i is applied all have the same length l_i, and $l_1, \ldots, l_n$ are distinct. Length differentiation is used in the following NIST PQC submissions: **BIKE**, EMBLEM, **HQC**, **RQC**, LAC, LOCKER, **NTS-KEM**, **SABER**, Round2,

Round5, Titanium. There are, of course, many other similar ways to enforce the virtual domain separation.

There are two ways one might capture this with regard to security. One is to restrict the domain Dom(ES) of the ending space. For example, for length differentiation, we would require that there exist distinct $l_1, \ldots, l_n$ such that for all $(i, X) \in \mathrm{Dom}(\mathsf{ES})$ we have $|X| = l_i$. For such an ending space, the identity functor would provide security. The approach we take is different. We don't restrict the domain of the ending space, but instead define security with respect to a subdomain, which we called the working space, where the restriction is captured. This, we believe, is better suited for practice, for a few reasons. One is that a single implementation of the ending functions can be used securely in different applications that each have their own working domain. Another is that implementations of the ending functions do not appear to enforce any restrictions, leaving it up to applications to figure out how to securely use the functions. In this context, highlighting the working domain may help application designers think about what is the working domain in their application and make this explicit, which can reduce error.

But we warn that the identity functor approach is more prone to misuse and in the end more dangerous and brittle than some others.

As per the above, inverses can only be given for certain working domains. Let us say that $\mathcal{W} \subseteq \mathrm{Dom}(\mathsf{ES})$ separates domains if for all $(i_1, X_1), (i_2, X_2) \in \mathcal{W}$ satisfying $i_1 \neq i_2$, we have $X_1 \neq X_2$. Put another way, for any $(i, X) \in \mathcal{W}$ there is at most one j such that $X \in \mathrm{Dom}_j(\mathsf{ES})$. We assume an efficient inverter for $\mathcal{W}$. This is a deterministic algorithm $\mathrm{In}_{\mathcal{W}}$ that on input $X \in \{0,1\}^*$ returns the unique i such that $(i, X) \in \mathcal{W}$ if such an i exists, and otherwise returns $\bot$. (The uniqueness is by the assumption that $\mathcal{W}$ separates domains.)

As an example, for length differentiation, we pick some *distinct* integers $l_1, \ldots, l_n$ such that $\{0,1\}^{l_i} \subseteq \mathrm{Dom}_i(\mathsf{ES})$ for all $i \in [1..n]$. We then let $\mathcal{W} = \{(i, X) \in \mathrm{Dom}(\mathsf{ES}) : |X| = l_i\}$. This separates domains. Now we can define $\mathrm{In}_{\mathcal{W}}(X)$ to return the unique i such that $|X| = l_i$ if $|X| \in \{l_1, \ldots, l_n\}$, otherwise returning $\bot$.

The inverses are then defined using $\mathrm{In}_{\mathcal{W}}$, as follows, where $U \in \mathrm{Dom}(\mathsf{SS}) = \{0,1\}^*$:

Algorithm $\mathsf{QTI}_{\mathrm{id}}(U)$	Algorithm $\mathsf{ATI}_{\mathrm{id}}(U, \boldsymbol{Y})$
$\boldsymbol{W} \leftarrow ()$; $i \leftarrow \mathrm{In}_{\mathcal{W}}(U)$	If $\boldsymbol{Y} \neq ()$ then $V \leftarrow \boldsymbol{Y}[1]$
If $i \neq \bot$ then $\boldsymbol{W}[1] \leftarrow (i, U)$	Else $V \leftarrow 0^{\mathsf{OL}(\mathsf{SS})}$
Return $\boldsymbol{W}$	Return V

The correctness condition of Eq. (2) over $\mathcal{W}$ is met, and since $\mathrm{In}_{\mathcal{W}}(X)$ never returns $\bot$ for $X \in \mathcal{W}$, the second condition of invertibility is also met. $(\mathsf{QTI}_{\mathrm{id}}, \mathsf{ATI}_{\mathrm{id}})$ provides perfect translation indistinguishability. Since $\mathsf{QTI}_{\mathrm{id}}$ does not have full support, we can't use Theorem 1, but we can conclude rd-indiff via Theorem 2.

Adversary $\mathcal{A}^{\text{INIT,PUB,PRIV,FIN}}$

INIT()

$y \leftarrow \text{PUB}(0)$; $d \leftarrow\!\!\text{\$} \{1,2\}$; $y_d \leftarrow \text{PRIV}(d,0)$

If $(y_d[1..256]) = y[1..256]$ then FIN(1) else FIN(0)

Fig. 7. Adversary against the rd-indiff security of $\mathbf{F}_{\text{NewHope}}$.

OUTPUT-SPLITTING. We formalize another method that we call output splitting. It is used in the following NIST PQC submissions: FrodoKEM, NTRU-HRSS-KEM, Odd Manhattan,QC-MDPC, Round2, **Round5**.

Let $\ell_i = \text{OL}_1(\text{ES}) + \cdots + \text{OL}_i(\text{ES})$ for $i \in [1..n]$. Let $\ell = \text{OL}(\text{SS})$ be the output length of the sol functions $s \in \text{SS}$, and assume $\ell = \ell_n$. The output-splitting functor $\mathbf{F}_{\text{spl}}\colon \text{SS} \to \text{ES}$ is defined by $\mathbf{F}_{\text{spl}}[s](i,X) = s(X)[\ell_{i-1}+1..\ell_i]$. That is, if $e \leftarrow \mathbf{F}_{\text{spl}}[s]$, then $e_i(X)$ lets $Z \leftarrow s(X)$ and then returns bits $\ell_{i-1}+1$ through ℓ_i of Z. This functor is translating, via $\text{QT}_{\text{spl}}(i,X) = X$ and $\text{AT}_{\text{spl}}((i,X),\mathbf{V}) = \mathbf{V}[1][\ell_{i-1}+1..\ell_i]$. It is however *not* domain separating.

The inverses are defined as follows, where $U \in \text{Dom}(\text{SS}) = \{0,1\}^*$:

Algorithm $\text{QTI}_{\text{spl}}(U)$	Algorithm $\text{ATI}_{\text{spl}}(U,\mathbf{Y})$
For $i = 1,\ldots,n$ do $\mathbf{W}[i] \leftarrow (i,U)$	$V \leftarrow \mathbf{Y}[1]\|\cdots\|\mathbf{Y}[n]$
Return $\mathbf{W}$	Return V

The correctness condition of Eq. (2) over $\mathcal{W} = \text{ES}$ is met, and $(\text{QTI}_{\text{spl}}, \text{ATI}_{\text{spl}})$ provides perfect translation indistinguishability. Since QTI_{spl} has full support, we can conclude rd-indiff via Theorem 1.

RD-INDIFF OF **NewHope**. We next demonstrate how read-only indifferentiability can highlight subpar methods of oracle cloning, using the example of **NewHope** [2]. The base KEM KE_1 defined in the specification of **NewHope** relies on just two random oracles, G and H_4. (The base scheme defined by transform $\mathbf{T}_{10}$, which uses 3 random oracles H_2, H_3, and H_4, is equivalent to KE_1 and can be obtained by applying the output-splitting cloning functor to instantiate H_2 and H_3 with G. **NewHope**'s security proof explicitly claims this equivalence [2].)

The final KEM KE_2 instantiates these two functions through SHAKE256 without explicit domain separation, setting $H_4(X) = \text{SHAKE256}(X,32)$ and $G(X) = \text{SHAKE256}(X,96)$. For consistency with our results, which focus on sol function spaces, we model SHAKE256 as a random member of a sol function space SS with some very large output length L, and assume that the adversary does not request more than L bits of output from SHAKE256 in a single call. We let ES be the arity-2 sol function space defining sub-functions G and H_4. In this setting, the cloning functor $\mathbf{F}_{\text{NewHope}} : \text{SS} \to \text{ES}$ used by **NewHope** is defined by $\mathbf{F}_{\text{NewHope}}[s](1,X) = s(X)[1..256]$ and $\mathbf{F}_{\text{NewHope}}[s](2,X) = s(X)[1..768]$. We will show that this functor cannot achieve rd-indiff for the given oracle spaces and the working domain $\mathcal{W} = \{0,1\}^*$. In Fig. 7, we give an adversary $\mathcal{A}$ which has high advantage in the rd-indiff game $\mathbf{G}^{\text{rd-indiff}}_{\mathbf{F}_{\text{NewHope}},\text{SS,ES},\mathcal{W},\mathsf{S}}$ for any indifferentiability simulator S. When $b = 1$ in game $\mathbf{G}^{\text{rd-indiff}}_{\mathbf{F}_{\text{NewHope}},\text{SS},\text{ES},\mathcal{W},\text{S}}$, we have that

$$y_d[1..256] = \mathbf{F}_{\text{NewHope}}[s](d,0)[1..256] = s(0)[1..256] = y[1..256],$$

so adversary $\mathcal{A}$ will always call FIN on the bit 1 and win. When $b = 0$ in game $\mathbf{G}^{\text{rd-indiff}}_{\mathbf{F}_{\text{NewHope}},\text{SS},\text{ES},\mathcal{W},\text{S}}$, the two strings $y_1 = e_0(1, X)$ and $y_2 = e_0(2, X)$ will have different 256-bit prefixes, except with probability $\epsilon = 2^{-256}$. Therefore, when $\mathcal{A}$ queries PUB(0), the simulator's response y can share the prefix of most one of the two strings y_1 and y_2. Its response must be independent of d, which is not chosen until after the query to PUB, so $\Pr[y[1..256] = y_d[1..256]] \leq 1/2 + \epsilon$, regardless of the behavior of S. Hence, $\mathcal{A}$ breaks the indifferentiability of $\mathbf{Q}^{\text{NewHope}}$ with probability roughly $1/2$, rendering NewHope's random oracle functor differentiable.

The implication of this result is that NewHope's implementation differs noticeably from the model in which its security claims are set, even when SHAKE256 is assumed to be a random oracle. This admits the possibility of hash function collisions and other sources of vulnerability that are not eliminated by the security proof. To claim provable security for NewHope's implementation, further justification is required to argue that these potential collisions are rare or unexploitable. We do not claim that an attack on read-only indifferentiability implies an attack on the IND-CCA security of NewHope, but it does highlight a gap that needs to be addressed. Read-only indifferentiability constitutes a useful tool for detecting such gaps and measuring the strength of various oracle cloning methods.

Acknowledgments. The authors were supported in part by NSF grant CNS-1717640 and a gift from Microsoft. Günther was additionally supported by Research Fellowship grant GU 1859/1-1 of the German Research Foundation (DFG).

References

1. Albrecht, M., Cid, C., Paterson, K.G., Tjhai, C.J., Tomlinson, M.: NTS-KEM. NIST PQC Round 2 Submission (2019)
2. Alkim, E., et al.: NewHope: algorithm specifications and supporting documentation. NIST PQC Round 2 Submission (2019)
3. Aragon, N., et al.: BIKE: bit flipping key encapsulation. NIST PQC Round 2 Submission (2019)
4. Aragon, N., et al.: LOCKER: low rank parity check codes encryption. NIST PQC Round 1 Submission (2017)
5. Avanzi, R., et al.: CRYSTALS-Kyber: algorithm specifications and supporting documentation. NIST PQC Round 2 Submission (2019)
6. Baan, H., et al.: Round5: KEM and PKE based on (ring) learning with rounding. NIST PQC Round 2 Submission (2019)
7. Banegas, G., et al.: DAGS: key encapsulation from dyadic GS codes. NIST PQC Round 1 Submission (2017)
8. Bardet, M., et al.: BIG QUAKE: binary goppa quasi-cyclic key encapsulation. NIST PQC Round 1 Submission (2017)
9. Bellare, M., Bernstein, D.J., Tessaro, S.: Hash-function based PRFs: AMAC and its multi-user security. In: Fischlin, M., Coron, J.-S. (eds.) EUROCRYPT 2016, Part I. LNCS, vol. 9665, pp. 566–595. Springer, Heidelberg (2016). https://doi.org/10.1007/978-3-662-49890-3_22

10. Bellare, M., Davis, H., Günther, F.: Separate your domains: NIST PQC KEMs, oracle cloning and read-only indifferentiability. Cryptology ePrint Archive (2020)
11. Bellare, M., Rogaway, P.: Random oracles are practical: a paradigm for designing efficient protocols. In: Denning, D.E., Pyle, R., Ganesan, R., Sandhu, R.S., Ashby, V. (eds.) ACM CCS 1993, pp. 62–73. ACM Press, November 1993
12. Bellare, M., Rogaway, P.: The security of triple encryption and a framework for code-based game-playing proofs. In: Vaudenay, S. (ed.) EUROCRYPT 2006. LNCS, vol. 4004, pp. 409–426. Springer, Heidelberg (2006). https://doi.org/10.1007/11761679_25
13. Bernstein, D.J., et al.: Classic McEliece: conservative code-based cryptography. NIST PQC Round 2 Submission (2019)
14. Bernstein, D.J., Chuengsatiansup, C., Lange, T., van Vredendaal, C.: NTRU Prime. NIST PQC Round 2 Submission (2019)
15. Chen, M.-S., Hülsing, A., Rijneveld, J., Samardjiska, S., Schwabe, P.: MQDSS specifications. NIST PQC Round 2 Submission (2019)
16. Cheon, J.H., et al.: Lizard public key encryption. NIST PQC Round 1 Submission (2017)
17. Coron, J.-S., Dodis, Y., Malinaud, C., Puniya, P.: Merkle-Damgård revisited: how to construct a hash function. In: Shoup, V. (ed.) CRYPTO 2005. LNCS, vol. 3621, pp. 430–448. Springer, Heidelberg (2005). https://doi.org/10.1007/11535218_26
18. Cramer, R., Shoup, V.: Design and analysis of practical public-key encryption schemes secure against adaptive chosen ciphertext attack. SIAM J. Comput. 33(1), 167–226 (2003)
19. D'Anvers, J.-P., Karmakar, A., Roy, S.S., Vercauteren, F.: SABER: Mod-LWR based KEM. NIST PQC Round 2 Submission (2019)
20. Demay, G., Gaži, P., Hirt, M., Maurer, U.: Resource-restricted indifferentiability. In: Johansson, T., Nguyen, P.Q. (eds.) EUROCRYPT 2013. LNCS, vol. 7881, pp. 664–683. Springer, Heidelberg (2013). https://doi.org/10.1007/978-3-642-38348-9_39
21. Dent, A.W.: A designer's guide to KEMs. In: Paterson, K.G. (ed.) Cryptography and Coding 2003. LNCS, vol. 2898, pp. 133–151. Springer, Heidelberg (2003). https://doi.org/10.1007/978-3-540-40974-8_12
22. Garcia-Morchon, O., Zhang, Z.: Round2: KEM and PKE based on GLWR. NIST PQC Round 1 Submission (2017)
23. Hamburg, M.: Post-quantum cryptography proposal: ThreeBears. NIST PQC Round 2 Submission (2019)
24. Hofheinz, D., Hövelmanns, K., Kiltz, E.: A modular analysis of the Fujisaki-Okamoto transformation. In: Kalai, Y., Reyzin, L. (eds.) TCC 2017, Part I. LNCS, vol. 10677, pp. 341–371. Springer, Cham (2017). https://doi.org/10.1007/978-3-319-70500-2_12
25. Hülsing, A., Rijneveld, J., Schanck, J.M., Schwabe, P.: NTRU-HRSS-KEM: algorithm specifications and supporting documentations. NIST PQC Round 1 Submission (2017)
26. Jao, D., et al.: Supersingular isogeny key encapsulation. NIST PQC Round 2 Submission (2019)
27. Jiang, H., Zhang, Z., Chen, L., Wang, H., Ma, Z.: IND-CCA-secure key encapsulation mechanism in the quantum random oracle model, revisited. In: Shacham, H., Boldyreva, A. (eds.) CRYPTO 2018, Part III. LNCS, vol. 10993, pp. 96–125. Springer, Cham (2018). https://doi.org/10.1007/978-3-319-96878-0_4
28. Lu, X., Liu, Y., Jia, D., Xue, H., He, J., Zhang, Z.: LAC: Lattice-based cryptosystems. NIST PQC Round 2 Submission (2019)

29. Maurer, U., Renner, R., Holenstein, C.: Indifferentiability, impossibility results on reductions, and applications to the random oracle methodology. In: Naor, M. (ed.) TCC 2004. LNCS, vol. 2951, pp. 21–39. Springer, Heidelberg (2004). https://doi.org/10.1007/978-3-540-24638-1_2

30. Melchor, C.A., et al.: ROLLO: rank-ouroboros, LAKE, & LOCKER. NIST PQC Round 2 Submission (2018)

31. Melchor, C.A., et al.: Rank quasi-cyclic (RQC). NIST PQC Round 2 Submission (2019)

32. Melchor, C.A., et al.: Hamming quasi-cyclic (HQC). NIST PQC Round 2 Submission (2019)

33. Mittelbach, A.: Salvaging indifferentiability in a multi-stage setting. In: Nguyen, P.Q., Oswald, E. (eds.) EUROCRYPT 2014. LNCS, vol. 8441, pp. 603–621. Springer, Heidelberg (2014). https://doi.org/10.1007/978-3-642-55220-5_33

34. Naehrig, M., et al.: FrodoKEM: learning with errors key encapsulation. NIST PQC Round 2 Submission (2019)

35. NIST. Post-Quantum Cryptography Standardization Process. https://csrc.nist.gov/projects/post-quantum-cryptography

36. NIST. Federal Information Processing Standard 202, SHA-3 Standard: Permutation-Based Hash and Extendable-Output Functions, August 2015

37. NIST. PQC Standardization Process: Second Round Candidate Announcement, January 2019. https://csrc.nist.gov/news/2019/pqc-standardization-process-2nd-round-candidates

38. Plantard, T.: Odd Manhattan's algorithm specifications and supporting documentation. NIST PQC Round 1 Submission (2017)

39. Ristenpart, T., Shacham, H., Shrimpton, T.: Careful with composition: limitations of the indifferentiability framework. In: Paterson, K.G. (ed.) EUROCRYPT 2011. LNCS, vol. 6632, pp. 487–506. Springer, Heidelberg (2011). https://doi.org/10.1007/978-3-642-20465-4_27

40. Saito, T., Xagawa, K., Yamakawa, T.: Tightly-secure key-encapsulation mechanism in the quantum random oracle model. In: Nielsen, J.B., Rijmen, V. (eds.) EUROCRYPT 2018, Part III. LNCS, vol. 10822, pp. 520–551. Springer, Cham (2018). https://doi.org/10.1007/978-3-319-78372-7_17

41. Seo, M., Park, J.H., Lee, D.H., Kim, S., Lee, S.-J.: Proposal for NIST post-quantum cryptography standard: EMBLEM and R.EMBLEM. NIST PQC Round 1 Submission (2017)

42. Smart, N.P., et al.: LIMA: a PQC encryption scheme. NIST PQC Round 1 Submission (2017)

43. Steinfeld, R., Sakzad, A., Zhao, R.K.: Titanium: proposal for a NIST post-quantum public-key encryption and KEM standard. NIST PQC Round 1 Submission (2017)

44. Zhao, Y., Jin, Z., Gong, B., Sui, G.: A modular and systematic approach to key establishment and public-key encryption based on LWE and its variants. NIST PQC Round 1 Submission (2017)

On the Memory-Tightness of Hashed ElGamal

Ashrujit Ghoshal$^{(\boxtimes)}$ and Stefano Tessaro$^{(\boxtimes)}$

Paul G. Allen School of Computer Science & Engineering,
University of Washington, Seattle, USA
{ashrujit,tessaro}@cs.washington.edu

Abstract. We study the memory-tightness of security reductions in public-key cryptography, focusing in particular on Hashed ElGamal. We prove that any *straightline* (i.e., without rewinding) black-box reduction needs memory which grows linearly with the number of queries of the adversary it has access to, as long as this reduction treats the underlying group generically. This makes progress towards proving a conjecture by Auerbach *et al.* (CRYPTO 2017), and is also the first lower bound on memory-tightness for a concrete cryptographic scheme (as opposed to generalized reductions across security notions). Our proof relies on compression arguments in the generic group model.

Keywords: Public-key cryptography · Memory-tightness · Lower bounds · Generic group model · Foundations · Compression arguments

1 Introduction

Security proofs rely on *reductions*, i.e., they show how to transform an adversary $\mathcal{A}$ breaking a scheme into an adversary $\mathcal{B}$ solving some underlying assumed-to-be-hard problem. Generally, the reduction ought to be *tight* – the resources used by $\mathcal{B}$, as well as the attained advantage, should be as close as possible to those of $\mathcal{A}$. Indeed, the more resources $\mathcal{B}$ needs, or the smaller its advantage, the weaker the reduction becomes.

Auerbach *et al.* [2] were the first to explicitly point out that *memory* resources have been ignored in reductions, and that this leads to a loss of quality in security results. Indeed, it is conceivable that $\mathcal{A}$'s memory is naturally bounded (say, at most 2^{64} bits), and the underlying problem is very sensitive to memory. For example, the best-known algorithm for discrete logarithms in a 4096-bit prime field runs in time (roughly) 2^{156} using memory 2^{80}. With less memory, the best algorithm is the generic one, requiring time $\Theta(\sqrt{p}) \approx 2^{2048}$. Therefore, if $\mathcal{B}$ also uses memory at most 2^{64}, we can infer a larger lower bound on the necessary time complexity for $\mathcal{A}$ to break the scheme, compared to the case where $\mathcal{B}$ uses 2^{100} bits instead.

WHAT CAN BE MEMORY-TIGHT? One should therefore target reductions that are *memory-tight*, i.e., the memory usage of $\mathcal{B}$ is similar to that of $\mathcal{A}$.[1] The work

---

[1] Generally, $\mathcal{B} = \mathcal{R}^{\mathcal{A}}$ for a black-box reduction $\mathcal{R}$, and one imposes the slightly stronger requirement that $\mathcal{R}$ uses small memory, independent of that of $\mathcal{A}$.

© International Association for Cryptologic Research 2020
A. Canteaut and Y. Ishai (Eds.): EUROCRYPT 2020, LNCS 12106, pp. 33–62, 2020.
https://doi.org/10.1007/978-3-030-45724-2_2

of Auerbach *et al.* [2], and its follow-up by Wang *et al.* [13], pioneered the study of memory-tight reductions. In particular, and most relevant to this work, they show *negative* results (i.e., that certain reductions cannot be memory tight) using *streaming lower bounds*.

Still, these lower bounds are tailored at general notions (e.g., single- to multi-challenge reductions), and lower bounds follow from a natural connection with classical frequency problems on streams. This paper tackles the more ambitious question of proving impossibility of memory-tight reductions for concrete *schemes*, especially those based on algebraic structures. This was left as an open problem by prior works.

HASHED ELGAMAL. Motivated by a concrete open question posed in [2], we consider here the CCA-security of Hashed ElGamal. In its KEM variant, the scheme is based on a cyclic group $G = \langle g \rangle$ – the secret key sk is a random element from $\mathbb{Z}_{|G|}$, whereas the public key is $pk = g^{sk}$. Then, encapsulation produces a ciphertext-key pair

$$C \leftarrow g^r, \quad K \leftarrow H(pk^r).$$

for $r \leftarrow \mathbb{Z}_{|G|}$ and a hash function $H : G \rightarrow \{0,1\}^\ell$. Decapsulation occurs by computing $K \leftarrow H(C^{sk})$.

The CCA-security of Hashed ElGamal in the random-oracle model was proved by Abdalla, Bellare, and Rogaway [1] based on the *Strong Diffie-Hellman* (SDH) assumption (also often called GapDH), and we briefly review the proof.[2] First, recall that in the SDH assumption, the attacker is asked to compute g^{uv} from g^u and g^v, given additionally access to a *decision* oracle O_v which on input $h, y \in G$, tells us whether $h^v = y$.

The reduction sets the Hashed ElGamal public-key to $pk = g^v$ (setting implicitly $sk = v$), the challenge ciphertext to be $C^* = g^u$, and the corresponding key K^* to be a random string. Then, it simulates both the random oracle and the decapsulation oracle to the adversary $\mathcal{A}$ (which is run on inputs pk, C^* and K^*), until a random-oracle query for g^{uv} is made (this can be detected using the O_v oracle). The challenge is to simulate both oracles consistently: As the reduction cannot compute discrete logarithms, it uses the oracle O_v to detect whether a random-oracle query X and a decapsulation query C_i satisfy $O_v(C_i, X) = \text{true}$, and, if this is the case, answers them with the same value.

This reduction requires memory to store all prior decapsulation and random-oracle queries. Unlike other reductions, the problem here is not to store the random-oracle output values (which could be compressed using a PRF), but the actual *inputs* to these queries, which are under adversarial control. This motivates the conjecture that a reduction using little memory does not exist, but the main challenge is of course to prove this is indeed the case.

---

[2] Abdalla et al. [1] do not phrase their paper in terms of the KEM/DEM paradigm [6,12], which was introduced concurrently – instead, they prove that an intermediate assumption, called Oracle Diffie-Hellman (ODH), follows from SDH in the ROM. However, the ODH assumption is structurally equivalent to the CCA security of Hashed ElGamal KEM for one challenge ciphertext.

OUR RESULT, IN SUMMARY. We provide a *memory* lower bound for reductions that are *generic* with respect to the underlying group G. Specifically, we show the existence of an (inefficient) adversary $\mathcal{A}$ in *the generic group model (GGM)* which breaks the CCA security of Hashed ElGamal via $O(k)$ random oracle/decapsulation queries, but such that no reduction using less than $k \cdot \lambda$ bits of memory can break the SDH assumption *even* with access to $\mathcal{A}$, where λ is the bit-size of the underlying group elements.

Our lower bound is strong in that it shows we do not even have a trade-off between advantage and memory, i.e., if the memory is smaller than $k \cdot \lambda$, then the advantage is very small, as long as the reduction makes a polynomial number of queries to O_v and to the generic group oracle. It is however also important to discuss two limitations of our lower bound. The first one is that the reduction – which receives g, g^v in the SDH game – uses $\mathsf{pk} = g^v$ as the public key to the Hashed ElGamal adversary. The second one is that the reduction is straightline, i.e., it does not perform any rewinding.

We believe that our impossibility result would extend even when the reduction is not straightline. However, allowing for rewinding appears to be out of reach of our techniques. Nonetheless, we *do* conjecture a lower bound on the memory of $\Omega(k \log k)$ bits, and discuss the reasoning behind our conjecture in detail in the full version.

We stress that our result applies to reductions in the GGM, but treats the adversary as a black box. This captures reductions which are black-box in their usage of the group and the adversary. (In particular, the reduction cannot see generic group queries made by the adversary, as in a GGM security proofs.) Looking at the GGM reduces the scope of our result. However, it is uncommon for reductions to depend on the specifics of the group, although our result can be bypassed for specific groups, e.g., if the group has a pairing.

CONCURRENT RELATED WORK. Concurrently to our work, Bhattacharyya [4] provides memory-tight reductions of KEM-CCA security for variants of Hashed ElGamal. At first glance, the results seem to contradict ours. However, they are entirely complementary – for example, a first result shows a memory tight reduction for the KEM-CCA security of the "Cramer-Shoup" variant of Hashed ElGamal – this variant differs from the (classical) Hashed ElGamal we consider here and is less efficient. The second result shows a memory-tight reduction for the version considered in this paper, but assumes that the underlying group has a pairing. This is a good example showing our result can be bypassed for specific groups i.e. groups with pairings, but we also note that typical instantiations of the scheme are on elliptic curves for which no pairing exists.

1.1   Our Techniques

We give a high-level overview of our techniques here. We believe some of these to be novel and of broader interest in providing other impossibility results.

THE SHUFFLING GAME. Our adversary against Hashed ElGamal[3] $\mathcal{A}$ first attempts to detect whether the reduction is using a sufficient amount of memory. The adversary $\mathcal{A}$ is given as input the public key g^v, as well as g^u, as well as a string $C^* \in \{0,1\}^\ell$, which is either a real encapsulation or a random string. It first samples k values $i_1, \ldots, i_k$ from $\mathbb{Z}_p$. It then:

(1) Asks for decapsulation queries for $C_j \leftarrow g^{i_j}$, obtaining values K_j, for $j \in [k]$
(2) Picks a random permutation $\pi : [k] \to [k]$.
(3) Asks for RO queries for $H_j \leftarrow \mathsf{H}(V_j)$ for $j \in [k]$, where $V_j \leftarrow g^{v \cdot i_{\pi(j)}}$.

After this, the adversary checks whether $K_j = H_{\pi(j)}$ for all $j \in [k]$, and if so, it continues its execution, breaking the ODH assumption (inefficiently). If not, it just outputs a random guess.

The intuition here is that no reduction using substantially less than $k \cdot \log p$ bits succeeds in passing the above test – in particular, because the inputs C_j and V_j are (pseudo-)random, and thus incompressible. If the test does not pass, the adversary $\mathcal{A}$ is rendered useless, and thus not helpful to break SDH.

Remark 1. The adversary here is described in a way that requires secret randomness, not known to the reduction, and it is easier to think of $\mathcal{A}$ in this way. We will address in the body how to generically make the adversary deterministic.

Remark 2. We stress that this adversary requires memory – it needs to remember the answers $C_1, \ldots, C_k$. However, recall that we adopt a black-box approach to memory-tightness, where our requirement is that the reduction itself uses little memory, regardless of the memory used by the adversary. We also argue this is somewhat necessary – it is not clear how to design a reduction which adapts its memory usage to the adversary, even if given this information in a non-black-box manner. Also, we conjecture different (and much harder to analyze) memory-less adversaries exist enabling a separation. An example is multi-round variant, where each round omits **(2)**, and **(3)** only asks a single query $\mathsf{H}(V_j)$ for a random $j \leftarrow_\$ [k]$, and checks consistency. Intuitively, the chance of passing each round is roughly $k \log p / s$, but we do not know how to make this formal.

INTRODUCING THE GGM. Our intuition is however *false* for an arbitrary group. For instance, if the discrete logarithm (DL) problem is easy in the group, then the reduction can simply simulate the random oracle via a PRF, as suggested in [2]. Ideally, we could prove that if the DL problem is hard in G, then any PPT reduction given access to $\mathcal{A}$ and with less than $k \cdot \log p$ bits of memory fails to break SDH.[4] Unfortunately, it will be hard to capture a single hardness property of G sufficient for our proof to go through. Instead, we will model the group via the *generic group model* (GGM) [9,11]: We model a group of prime

---

[3] The paper will in fact use the cleaner formalization of the ODH assumption, so we stick to Hashed ElGamal only in the introduction.

[4] This statement is somewhat confusing, so note that in general, the existence of a reduction is *not* a contradiction with the hardness of DL, as the reduction is meant to break SDH only given access to an adversary breaking the scheme, and this does not imply the ability to break SDH *without* access to the adversary.

order p defined via a random injection $\sigma : \mathbb{Z}_p \to \mathcal{L}$. An algorithm in the model typically has access to $\sigma(1)$ (in lieu of g) and an evaluation oracle which on input $\mathbf{a}, \mathbf{b} \in \mathcal{L}$ returns $\sigma(\sigma^{-1}(\mathbf{a}) + \sigma^{-1}(\mathbf{b}))$. (We will keep writing g^i instead of $\sigma(i)$ in the introduction, for better legibility.)

THE PERMUTATION GAME. In order to fool $\mathcal{A}$, the reduction can learn information about π via the O_v oracle. For example, it can try to input $C_j = g^{i_j}$ and $V_{j'} = g^{v i_{\pi(j')}}$ (both obtained from $\mathcal{A}$'s queries), and $\mathsf{O}_\mathsf{v}(C_j, V_{j'}) = \mathsf{true}$ if and only if $\pi(j') = j$. More generally, the reduction can compute, for any $\vec{a} = (a_1, \ldots, a_k)$ and $\vec{b} = (b_1, \ldots, b_k)$,

$$C^* = g^{\sum_{j=1}^{k} a_j i_j} = \prod_{j=1}^{k} C_j^{a_j} \ , \quad V^* = g^{\sum_{j=1}^{k} b_j v \cdot i_{\pi(j)}} = \prod_{j=1}^{k} V_j^{b_j},$$

and the query $\mathsf{O}_\mathsf{v}(C^*, V^*)$ returns true iff $b_j = a_{\pi(j)}$ for all $j \in [k]$, which we write as $\vec{b} = \pi(\vec{a})$. We abstract this specific strategy in terms of an information-theoretic game – which we refer to as the *permutation game* – which gives the adversary access to an oracle O which takes as inputs pairs of vectors $(\vec{a}, \vec{b})$ from $\mathbb{Z}_p^k$, and returns true iff $\vec{b} = \pi(\vec{a})$ for a secret permutation π. The goal of the adversary is to recover π.

Clearly, a strategy can win with $O(k^2)$ oracle queries $(\vec{e}_i, \vec{e}_j)$ for all i, j, where $\vec{e}_i \in \mathbb{Z}_p^k$ is the unit vector with a 1 in the i-th coordinate, and 0 elsewhere. This strategy requires in particular querying, in its first component, vectors which have rank k. Our first result will prove that this is necessary – namely, assume that an adversary makes a sequence of q queries $(\vec{x}_1, \vec{y}_1), \ldots, (\vec{x}_q, \vec{y}_q)$ such that the rank of $\vec{x}_1, \ldots, \vec{x}_p$ is at most ℓ, then the probability to win the permutation game is of the order $O(q^\ell / k!)$. We will prove this via a compression argument.

Note that roughly, this bound tells us that to win with probability ϵ and q queries to the oracle, the attacker needs

$$\ell = \Omega \left(\frac{k \log k - \log(1/\epsilon)}{\log(q)} \right).$$

A REDUCTION TO THE PERMUTATION GAME. We will think of the execution of the reduction against our adversary as consisting of two stages – we refer to them as $\mathcal{R}_1$ and $\mathcal{R}_2$. The former learns the decapsulation queries $g^{i_1}, \ldots, g^{i_k}$, whereas the latter learns the RO queries $g^{i_{\pi(1)} v}, \ldots, g^{i_{\pi(k)} v}$, and (without loss of generality) attempts to guess the permutation π. We will lower bound the size of the state ϕ that $\mathcal{R}_1$ passes on to $\mathcal{R}_2$. Both stages can issue O_v and Eval queries.

Note that non-trivial O_v queries (i.e., those revealing some information about the permutation), are (except with very small probability) issued by $\mathcal{R}_2$, since no information about π is ever revealed to $\mathcal{R}_1$. As one of our two key steps, we will provide a reduction from the execution of $\mathcal{R}_1, \mathcal{R}_2$ against $\mathcal{A}$ in the GGM to the permutation game – i.e., we build an adversary $\mathcal{D}$ for the latter game simulating the interaction between $\mathcal{R}_1, \mathcal{R}_2$ and $\mathcal{A}$, and such that $\mathcal{R}_1, \mathcal{R}_2$ "fooling" $\mathcal{A}$ results in $\mathcal{D}$ guessing the permutation.

MEMORY VS. RANK. The main question, however, is to understand the complexity of $\mathcal{D}$ in the permutation game, and in particular, the *rank* ℓ of the first component of its queries – as we have seen above, this affects its chance of winning the game.

To do this, we will take a slight detour, and specifically consider a set $\mathcal{Z} \subseteq \mathcal{L}$ of labels (i.e., outputs of σ) that the reduction $\mathcal{R}_2$ comes up with (as inputs to either of Eval or O_v) on its own (in the original execution), i.e., no earlier Eval query of $\mathcal{R}_2$ returned them, and that have been previously learnt by $\mathcal{R}_1$ as an output of its Eval queries. (The actual definition of $\mathcal{Z}$ is more subtle, and this is due to the ability of the adversary to come up with labels *without* knowing the corresponding pre-image.)

Then, we will show two statements about $\mathcal{Z}$:

(i) On the one hand, we show that the rank ℓ of the oracle queries of the adversary $\mathcal{D}$ is upper bound by $|\mathcal{Z}|$ in its own simulation of the execution of $\mathcal{R}_1, \mathcal{R}_2$ with $\mathcal{A}$.

(ii) On the other hand, via a compression argument, we prove that the size of $\mathcal{Z}$ is related to the length of ϕ, and this will give us our final upper bound.

This latter statement is by itself not very surprising – one can look at the execution of $\mathcal{R}_2$, and clearly every label in $\mathcal{Z}$ that appears "magically" in the execution must be the result of storing them into the state ϕ. What makes this different from more standard compression arguments is the handling of the generic group model oracle (which admits non-trivial operations). In particular, our compression argument will compress the underlying map σ, and we will need to be able to figure out the pre-images of these labels in $\mathcal{Z}$. We give a very detailed technical overview in the body explaining the main ideas.

MEMORY-TIGHT AGM REDUCTION. The Algebraic Group Model (AGM) was introduced in [8]. AGM reductions make strong extractability assumptions, and the question of their memory-tightness is an interesting one. In the full version we construct a reduction to the discrete logarithm problem that runs an adversary against the KEM-CCA security of Hashed ElGamal in the AGM such that the reduction is memory-tight but not tight with respect to advantage. We note that the model of our reduction is different than a (full-fledged) GGM reduction which is not black-box, in that it can observe the GGM queries made by the adversary. Our result does not imply any impossibility for these. In turn, AGM reductions are weaker, but our results do not imply anything about them, either.

2 Preliminaries

In this section, we review the formal definition of the generic group model. We also state ODH and SDH as introduced in [1] in the generic group model.

NOTATION. Let $\mathbb{N} = \{0, 1, 2, \cdots\}$ and, for $k \in \mathbb{N}$, let $[k] = \{1, 2, \cdots, k\}$. We denote by $\mathsf{InjFunc}(S_1, S_2)$ the set of all injective function from S_1 to S_2.

We also let $*$ denote a wildcard element. For example $\exists t : (t, *) \in T$ is true if the set T contains an ordered pair whose first element is t (the type of the wildcard element shall be clear from the context). Let $\mathcal{S}_k$ denote the set of all permutations on $[k]$. We use $f : \mathsf{D} \to \mathsf{R} \cup \{\bot\}$ to denote a partial function, where $f(x) = \bot$ indicates the value of $f(x)$ is undefined. Define in particular $D(f) = \{d \in \mathsf{D} : f(d) \neq \bot\}$ and $R(f) = \{r \in \mathsf{R} : \exists d \in \mathsf{D} : \sigma(d) = r\}$. Moreover, we let $\overline{D(f)} = \mathsf{D} \setminus D(f)$ and $\overline{R(f)} = \mathsf{R} \setminus R(f)$.

We shall use pseudocode descriptions of games inspired by the code-based framework of [3]. The output of a game is denoted using the symbol $\Rightarrow$. In all games we assume the flag bad is set to false initially. In pseudocode, we denote random sampling using $\leftarrow\!\!\$ $, assignment using $\leftarrow$ and equality check using $=$. In games that output boolean values, we use the term "winning" the game to mean that the output of the game is true.

We also introduce some linear-algebra notation. Let S be a set vectors with equal number of coordinates. We denote the rank and the linear span of the vectors by $\mathsf{rank}(S)$ and $\mathsf{span}(S)$ respectively. Let $\vec{x}, \vec{y}$ be vectors of dimension k. We denote $\vec{z}$ of dimension $2k$ which is the concatenation of $\vec{x}, \vec{y}$ as $\vec{z} = (\vec{x}, \vec{y})$. We denote the element at index i of a vector $\vec{x}$ as $\vec{x}[i]$.

2.1   Generic Group Model

The *generic group model* [11] captures algorithms that do not use any special property of the encoding of the group elements, other than assuming every element of the group has a unique representation, and that the basic group operations are allowed. This model is useful in proving lower bounds for some problems, but we use it here to capture reductions that are not specific to the underlying group.

More formally, let the order of the group be a large prime p. Let $\mathbb{Z}_p = \{0, 1, 2, \cdots, p-1\}$. Let $\mathcal{L} \subset \{0,1\}^*$ be a set of size p, called the set of *labels*. Let σ be a random injective mapping from $\mathbb{Z}_p$ to $\mathcal{L}$. The idea is that now every group element in $\mathbb{Z}_p$ is represented by a label in $\mathcal{L}$. An algorithm in this model takes as input $\sigma(1), \sigma(x_1), \sigma(x_2), \cdots, \sigma(x_n)$ for some $x_1, \cdots, x_n \in \mathbb{Z}_p$ (and possibly other inputs which are not group elements). The algorithm also has access to an oracle named Eval which takes as input two labels $\mathbf{a}, \mathbf{b} \in \mathcal{L}$ and returns $\mathbf{c} = \sigma(\sigma^{-1}(\mathbf{a}) + \sigma^{-1}(\mathbf{b}))$. Note that for any d, given $\sigma(x_i)$, $\sigma(d \cdot x_i)$ can be computed using $O(\log d)$ queries to Eval. We denote this operation as $\mathsf{Exp}(\sigma(x_i), d)$. We assume that all labels queried by algorithms in the generic group model are valid i.e. all labels queried by algorithms in the generic group model are in $\mathcal{L}$.[5]

ORACLE DIFFIE-HELLMAN ASSUMPTION (ODH). We first formalize the Oracle Diffie-Hellman Assumption (ODH) [1], which we are going to use in lieu of the CCA security of Hashed ElGamal. Suppose, a group has generator g and order p. The domain of hash function H is all finite strings and range is $\{0,1\}^{\mathsf{hLen}}$. The assumption roughly states for $u, v \leftarrow\!\!\$ \mathbb{Z}_p, W \leftarrow\!\!\$ \{0,1\}^{\mathsf{hLen}}$, the distributions $(g^u, g^v, \mathsf{H}(g^{uv}))$ and (g^u, g^v, W) are indistinguishable to an adversary who has access to the oracle H_v where $\mathsf{H}_v(g^x)$ returns $\mathsf{H}(g^{xv})$ with the restriction that it is not queried on g^u.

---

[5] We stress that we assume a strong version of the model where the adversary *knows* $\mathcal{L}$.

Game $\mathbb{G}^{\text{ODH-REAL-GG}}_{\mathcal{L},p,\text{hLen}}(\mathcal{A})$:	Game $\mathbb{G}^{\text{ODH-RAND-GG}}_{\mathcal{L},p,\text{hLen}}(\mathcal{A})$:
1: $\sigma \leftarrow_\$ \text{InjFunc}(\mathbb{Z}_p \rightarrow \mathcal{L})$	1: $\sigma \leftarrow_\$ \text{InjFunc}(\mathbb{Z}_p \rightarrow \mathcal{L})$
2: $u \leftarrow_\$ \mathbb{Z}_p; U \leftarrow \sigma(u)$	2: $u \leftarrow_\$ \mathbb{Z}_p; U \leftarrow \sigma(u)$
3: $v \leftarrow_\$ \mathbb{Z}_p; V \leftarrow \sigma(v)$	3: $v \leftarrow_\$ \mathbb{Z}_p; V \leftarrow \sigma(v)$
4: $\text{H} \leftarrow_\$ \Omega_{\text{hLen}}$	4: $\text{H} \leftarrow_\$ \Omega_{\text{hLen}}$
5: $W \leftarrow \text{H}(\sigma(uv))$	5: $W \leftarrow \{0,1\}^{\text{hLen}}$
6: $b \leftarrow \mathcal{A}^{\text{H}_v(\cdot),\text{H}(\cdot),\text{Eval}(\cdot,\cdot)}(U,V,W,\sigma(1))$	6: $b \leftarrow \mathcal{A}^{\text{H}_v(\cdot),\text{H}(\cdot),\text{Eval}(\cdot,\cdot)}(U,V,W,\sigma(1))$
7: **return** b	7: **return** b

Oracle Eval(a, b) :	Oracle H_v(a) :
1: **return** $\sigma(\sigma^{-1}(\mathbf{a}) + \sigma^{-1}(\mathbf{b}))$	1: **if** $\mathbf{a} = U$ **thenreturn** $\perp$
	2: **else return** $\text{H}(\sigma(\sigma^{-1}(\mathbf{a}) \cdot v))$

Game $\mathbb{G}^{\text{SDH-GG}}_{\mathcal{L},p,\text{hLen}}(\mathcal{A})$:	Oracle O_v(a, b) :
1: $\sigma \leftarrow_\$ \text{InjFunc}(\mathbb{Z}_p \rightarrow \mathcal{L})$	1: **return** $(\sigma^{-1}(\mathbf{a}) \cdot v = \sigma^{-1}(\mathbf{b}))$
2: $u \leftarrow_\$ \mathbb{Z}_p; U \leftarrow \sigma(u)$	
3: $v \leftarrow_\$ \mathbb{Z}_p; V \leftarrow \sigma(v)$	
4: $z \leftarrow \mathcal{A}^{\text{Eval}(\cdot,\cdot),\text{O}_v(\cdot,\cdot)}(U,V,\sigma(1))$	
5: **return** $(z = \sigma(uv))$	

Fig. 1. Games for ODH and SDH assumptions

We give a formalization of this assumption in the random-oracle and generic group models. For a fixed $\text{hLen} \in \mathbb{N}$, let Ω_{hLen} be the set of hash functions mapping $\{0,1\}^*$ to $\{0,1\}^{\text{hLen}}$. In Fig. 1, we formally define the Games $\mathbb{G}^{\text{ODH-REAL-GG}}_{\mathcal{L},p,\text{hLen}}$, $\mathbb{G}^{\text{ODH-RAND-GG}}_{\mathcal{L},p,\text{hLen}}$. The advantage of violating ODH is defined as

$$\text{Adv}^{\text{ODH-GG}}_{\mathcal{L},p,\text{hLen}}(\mathcal{A}) = \left| \Pr\left[\mathbb{G}^{\text{ODH-REAL-GG}}_{\mathcal{L},p,\text{hLen}}(\mathcal{A}) \Rightarrow 1\right] - \Pr\left[\mathbb{G}^{\text{ODH-RAND-GG}}_{\mathcal{L},p,\text{hLen}}(\mathcal{A}) \Rightarrow 1\right] \right|.$$

STRONG DIFFIE-HELLMAN ASSUMPTION (SDH). This is a stronger version of the classical CDH assumption. This assumption roughly states that CDH is hard even in the presence of a DDH-oracle O_v where $\text{O}_v(g^x, g^y)$ is true if and only if $x \cdot v = y$.

We formally define the game $\mathbb{G}^{\text{SDH-GG}}$ in the generic group model in Fig. 1. The advantage of violating SDH is defined as

$$\text{Adv}^{\text{SDH-GG}}_{\mathcal{L},p,\text{hLen}}(\mathcal{A}) = \left| \Pr\left[\mathbb{G}^{\text{SDH-GG}}_{\mathcal{L},p,\text{hLen}}(\mathcal{A}) \Rightarrow \text{true}\right] \right|.$$

Note in particular that one *can* upper bound this advantage unconditionally. We shall drop the $\mathcal{L}$ from the subscript of advantages and games henceforth since the set of labels $\mathcal{L}$ remains the same throughout our paper.

BLACK BOX REDUCTIONS IN THE GGM. We consider black-box reductions in the generic group model. We will limit ourselves to an informal description, but this can easily be formalized within existing formal frameworks for reductions (see e.g. [10]). We let the reduction $\mathcal{R}$ access an adversary $\mathcal{A}$, and denote by $\mathcal{R}^{\mathcal{A}}$ the resulting algorithm – understood here is that $\mathcal{R}$ supplies inputs, answers queries, etc. In addition, we let $\mathcal{R}$ and $\mathcal{A}$ access the Eval oracle available in the GGM. We stress that the GGM oracle is not under the reduction's control here – typically, the reduction itself will break a (hard) problem in the GGM with help of $\mathcal{A}$. We will allow (for simplicity) $\mathcal{A}$ to be run depending on some secret private coins[6] not accessible by $\mathcal{R}$. Reductions can run $\mathcal{A}$ several times (with fresh private coins). We call a reduction *straigthline* if it only runs $\mathcal{A}$ *once*.

In our case, the reduction $\mathcal{R}$ will be playing $\mathbb{G}_{p,\text{hLen}}^{\text{SDH-GG}}$. It receives as inputs $\sigma(1)$, $U = \sigma(u)$, $V = \sigma(v)$, and has access to the Eval, O_v oracles, as well as an adversary $\mathcal{A}$ for $\mathbb{G}_{p,\text{hLen}}^{\text{ODH-REAL-GG}}$ or $\mathbb{G}_{p,\text{hLen}}^{\text{ODH-RAND-GG}}$. The reduction needs therefore to supply inputs $(\sigma(1), U', V', W)$ to $\mathcal{A}$, and to answer its queries to the oracles H_v, as well as queries to H. We will call such a reduction *restricted* if it is straightline and $V' = V$.

2.2   Compression Lemma

In our lower bound proof we use the compression lemma that was formalized in [7] which roughly means that it is impossible to compress every element in a set with cardinality c to a string less than $\log c$ bits long, even relative to a random string. We state the compression lemma here as a proposition.

Proposition 1. *Suppose, there is a (not necessarily efficient) procedure* Encode : $\mathcal{X} \times \mathcal{R} \to \mathcal{Y}$ *and a (not necessarily efficient) decoding procedure* Decode : $\mathcal{Y} \times \mathcal{R} \to \mathcal{X}$ *such that*

$$\Pr_{x \in \mathcal{X}, r \in \mathcal{R}} [\text{Decode}(\text{Encode}(x, r), r) = x] \geqslant \epsilon \,,$$

then $\log |\mathcal{Y}| \geqslant \log |\mathcal{X}| - \log(1/\epsilon)$.

2.3   Polynomials

Let $\mathsf{p}(X_1, \cdots, X_n)$ be a n variate polynomial. We denote by $\mathsf{p}(x_1, \cdots, x_n)$ the evaluation of p at the point $(x_1, \cdots, x_n)$ throughout the paper. The polynomial ring in variables $X_1, \cdots, X_n$ over the field $\mathbb{Z}_p$ is denoted by $\mathbb{Z}_p[X_1, \cdots, X_n]$.

2.4   Key Encapsulation Mechanism (KEM)

A key-encapsulation mechanism (KEM) consists of three probabilistic polynomial time (PPT) algorithms Gen, Encap, Decap. The key generation algorithm Gen is probabilistic and outputs a key-pair $(\mathsf{pk}, \mathsf{sk})$. The encapsulation algorithm Encap is a probabilistic algorithm that takes pk as input and outputs a ciphertext c and a key K where $K \in \mathcal{K}$ for some non-empty set $\mathcal{K}$. The decapsulation algorithm Decap is a deterministic algorithm that takes as input the secret key sk and a ciphertext c outputs a key $K \in \mathcal{K}$ if (sk, c) is a valid secret key-ciphertext pair and $\perp$ otherwise. For correctness, it is required that for all pairs

---

[6] If we want to allow the reduction to control random bits, we model them explicitly as an additional input.

(pk, sk) output by Gen, if (K, c) is output by Encap(pk) then K is the output of Decap(sk, c).

SINGLE CHALLENGE KEM-CCA SECURITY. The single challenge CCA security of a KEM is defined by a pair of games called $\mathbb{G}^{\text{KEM-CCA-REAL}}$, $\mathbb{G}^{\text{KEM-CCA-RAND}}$. In both games a (pk, sk) pair is generated by Gen, and (c, K) is output by the encapsulation algorithm Encap on input pk. The adversary is provided with (pk, c, K) in $\mathbb{G}^{\text{KEM-CCA-REAL}}$ and with (pk, c, K') in $\mathbb{G}^{\text{KEM-CCA-RAND}}$ where K' is a randomly sampled element of $\mathcal{K}$. The adversary has access to the decapsulation oracle with sk as the secret key and it can make decapsulation queries on any ciphertext except the ciphertext c and has to output a bit. We define the advantage of violating single challenge KEM-CCA security is defined as the absolute value of the difference of probabilities of the adversary outputting 1 in the two games. A KEM is single challenge CCA-secure if for all non-uniform PPT adversaries the advantage of violating single challenge KEM-CCA security is negligible.

SINGLE CHALLENGE KEM-CCA OF HASHED ELGAMAL. We describe the KEM for Hashed ElGamal in a group with order p and generator g and a hash function H. The function Gen samples v at random from $\mathbb{Z}_p$, and returns (g^v, v) as the (pk, sk) pair. The function Encap on input v, samples u at random from $\mathbb{Z}_p$ and returns g^u as the ciphertext and $\mathsf{H}(g^{uv})$ as the key K. The function Decap on input c, returns $\mathsf{H}(c^v)$. Note that Decap in KEM of Hashed ElGamal is identical to the H_v function as defined in the ODH assumption. It follows that the single challenge KEM-CCA security of Hashed ElGamal is equivalent to the ODH assumption. In particular, in the generic group model when H is modeled as a random oracle, the single challenge KEM-CCA security of Hashed ElGamal is equivalent to the ODH assumption in the random oracle and generic group model.

3   Memory Lower Bound on the ODH-SDH Reduction

3.1   Result and Proof Outline

In this section, we prove a memory lower bound for restricted black-box reductions from ODH to SDH. We stress that the restricted reduction has access only to the H, H_v queries of the adversary. As discussed above, the ODH assumption is equivalent to the single-challenge KEM-CCA security of Hashed ElGamal, this proves a memory lower-bound for (restricted) black-box reductions of single challenge KEM-CCA security of Hashed ElGamal to the SDH assumption.

Theorem 1 (Main Theorem). *In the generic group model, with group order p, there exists an ODH adversary $\mathcal{A}$ that makes k H queries and k H_v queries (where k is a polynomial in $\log p$), a function $\epsilon_1(p, \mathsf{hLen})$ which is negligible in $\log p$, hLen, and a function $\epsilon_2(p)$ which is negligible in $\log p$, such that,*

1. $\mathsf{Adv}_{p,\mathsf{hLen}}^{\text{ODH-GG}}(\mathcal{A}) = 1 - \epsilon_1(p, \mathsf{hLen})$.

2. *For all restricted black-box reductions $\mathcal{R}$, with s bits of memory and making a total of q (assuming $q \geqslant k$) queries to O_v, Eval,*

$$\mathsf{Adv}^{\mathsf{SDH\text{-}GG}}_{p,\mathsf{hLen}}(\mathcal{R}^{\mathcal{A}}) \leqslant 2 \cdot 2^{\frac{s}{2}} \left(\frac{48q^3}{p} \right)^{\frac{k}{8c}} \left(1 + \frac{6q}{p} \right)^q + \frac{4q^2 \log p + 13q^2 + 5q}{p} + \epsilon_2(p) \,,$$

where $c = 4\lceil \frac{\log q}{\log k} \rceil$.

This result implies that if $\mathsf{Adv}^{\mathsf{SDH\text{-}GG}}_{p,\mathsf{hLen}}(\mathcal{R}^{\mathcal{A}})$ is non-negligible for a reduction $\mathcal{R}$ making q queries where q is a polynomial in $\log p$, then $s = \Omega(k \log p)$ i.e. the memory required by any restricted black-box reduction grows with the number of queries by $\mathcal{A}$. Hence, there does not exist any efficient restricted black-box reduction from ODH to SDH that is memory-tight.

In the full version, we discuss how rewinding can slightly improve the memory complexity to (roughly) $O(k \log k)$, with heavy computational cost (essentially, one rewinding per oracle query of the adversary). We conjecture this to be optimal, but a proof seems to evade current techniques.

DE-RANDOMIZATION. Before we turn to the proof – which also connects several technical lemmas presented across the next sections, let us discuss some aspects of the results. As explained above, our model allows for the adversary $\mathcal{A}$ to be run with randomness unknown to $\mathcal{R}$. This aspect *may* be controversial, but we note that there is a generic way for $\mathcal{A}$ to be made deterministic. Recall that $\mathcal{A}$ must be inefficient for the separation to even hold true. For example, $\mathcal{A}$ can use the injection σ from the generic group model to generate its random coin – say, using $\sigma^{-1}(\mathbf{a}_i)$ as coins a priori fixed labels $\mathbf{a}_1, \mathbf{a}_2, \ldots$. It is a standard – albeit tedious and omitted – argument to show that unless the reduction ends up querying the pre-images (which happens with negligible probability only), the $\sigma^{-1}(\mathbf{a}_i)$'s are good random coins.

STRENGTHENING BEYOND SDH. We would like to note that our result can be strengthened without much effort to a reduction between ODH and a more general version of SDH. Informally, we can extend our result to every problem which is hard in the generic group model in presence of an O_v oracle. For example, this could be a problem where given g, g^u, and g^v, the attacker needs to output $g^{f(u,v)}$, where f is (a fixed) two-variate polynomial with degree at least 2. We do not include the proof for the strengthened version for simplicity. However, it appears much harder to extend our result to different types of oracles than O_v, as our proof is tailored at this oracle.

Proof. Here, we give the overall structure, the key lemmas, and how they are combined – quantitatively – to obtain the final result.

First off, Lemma 1 establishes that there exists an adversary $\mathcal{A}$ such that $\mathsf{Adv}^{\mathsf{ODH\text{-}GG}}_{p,\mathsf{hLen}}(\mathcal{A})$ is close to 1, which we will fix (i.e., when we refer to $\mathcal{A}$, we refer to the one guaranteed to exist by the lemma). The proof of Lemma 1 is in Sect. 4.1 and the proof of Lemma 2 is in Sect. 4.2.

Lemma 1. *There exists an adversary $\mathcal{A}$ and a function $\epsilon_1(p, \mathsf{hLen})$ such that is negligible in $\log p, \mathsf{hLen}$, and*

$$\mathsf{Adv}_{p,\mathsf{hLen}}^{\mathsf{ODH\text{-}GG}}(\mathcal{A}) = 1 - \epsilon_1(p, \mathsf{hLen}).$$

After that, we introduce a game, called $\mathbb{G}_1$ and described in Fig. 3 in Sect. 4.2. Very informally, this is a game played by a two-stage adversary $\mathcal{R}_1, \mathcal{R}_2$ which can pass a state to each other of size s bits and have access to the $\mathsf{Eval}, \mathsf{O_v}$ oracles. The game captures the essence of the reduction $\mathcal{R}$ the adversary $\mathcal{A}$ of having a sufficient amount of memory. This is made formal in Lemma 2, where we show that the probability of the reduction $\mathcal{R}$ winning the $\mathsf{SDH\text{-}GG}$ game while running $\mathcal{A}$ is bounded by the probability of winning $\mathbb{G}_1$.

Lemma 2. *For every restricted black box reduction $\mathcal{R}$ to $\mathsf{SDH\text{-}GG}$ that runs $\mathcal{A}$, there exist adversaries $\mathcal{R}_1, \mathcal{R}_2$ playing $\mathbb{G}_1$, such that the number of queries made by $\mathcal{R}_1, \mathcal{R}_2$ to $\mathsf{Eval}, \mathsf{O_v}$ is same as the number of queries made by $\mathcal{R}$ to $\mathsf{Eval}, \mathsf{O_v}$, the state passed from $\mathcal{R}_1$ to $\mathcal{R}_2$ is upper bounded by the memory used by $\mathcal{R}$ and,*

$$\mathsf{Adv}_{p,\mathsf{hLen}}^{\mathsf{SDH\text{-}GG}}(\mathcal{R}^{\mathcal{A}}) \leqslant \Pr\left[\mathbb{G}_1 \Rightarrow \mathsf{true}\right] + \frac{4k^2(\log p)^2}{p} + \frac{4qk\log p + q^2}{p}.$$

We introduce Games $\mathbb{G}_2, \mathbb{G}_3$ in Fig. 4 in Sect. 4.2. These games are identical to $\mathbb{G}_1$ except for the condition to output true. The condition to output true in these games are disjoint and the disjunction of the two conditions is equivalent to the condition to output true in $\mathbb{G}_1$. A little more specifically, both games depend on a parameter l, which can be set arbitrarily, and in $\mathbb{G}_3$ and $\mathbb{G}_2$ the winning condition of $\mathbb{G}_1$ is strengthened by additional ensuring that a certain set defined during the execution of the game is smaller or larger than l, respectively. Therefore, tautologically,

$$\Pr\left[\mathbb{G}_1 \Rightarrow \mathsf{true}\right] = \Pr\left[\mathbb{G}_2 \Rightarrow \mathsf{true}\right] + \Pr\left[\mathbb{G}_3 \Rightarrow \mathsf{true}\right]. \tag{1}$$

We now prove the following two lemmas below, in Sects. 4.3 and 4.4,

Lemma 3. *For the game $\mathbb{G}_2$,*

$$\Pr\left[\mathbb{G}_2 \Rightarrow \mathsf{true}\right] \leqslant \frac{q^l}{k!} + \frac{2q(2k + 3q + 2)}{p} + \frac{5q}{p} + \frac{k^2 + k + 2}{p}.$$

Lemma 4. *If the size of the state ϕ output by $\mathcal{R}_1$ is s bits and $(\mathcal{R}_1, \mathcal{R}_2)$ make q queries in total in $\mathbb{G}_3$, then*

$$\Pr\left[\mathbb{G}_3 \Rightarrow \mathsf{true}\right] \leqslant 2 \cdot 2^{\frac{s}{2}} \left(\frac{8q^2(2k + 2 + 3q)}{p}\right)^{\frac{l}{2}} \left(1 + \frac{6q}{p}\right)^{\frac{2q-l}{2}} + \frac{k^2 + k + 2}{p}.$$

Combining (1) and the result of Lemmas 3 and 4 we get,

$$\Pr\left[\mathbb{G}_1 \Rightarrow \mathsf{true}\right] \leqslant 2 \cdot 2^{\frac{s}{2}} \left(\frac{8q^2(2k + 2 + 3q)}{p}\right)^{\frac{l}{2}} \left(1 + \frac{6q}{p}\right)^{\frac{2q-l}{2}} +$$

$$\frac{2(k^2 + k + 2)}{p} + \frac{q^l}{k!} + \frac{2q(2k + 3q + 2)}{p} + \frac{5q}{p}. \tag{2}$$

Since $\left(1 + \frac{6q}{p}\right)^{\frac{2q-l}{2}} \leqslant \left(1 + \frac{6q}{p}\right)^q$, combining Lemma 2, (2) we get,

$$\mathsf{Adv}^{\mathsf{SDH\text{-}GG}}_{p,\mathsf{hLen}}(\mathcal{R}^\mathcal{A}) \leqslant 2 \cdot 2^{\frac{s}{2}} \left(\frac{8q^2(2k+2+3q)}{p}\right)^{\frac{l}{2}} \left(1 + \frac{6q}{p}\right)^q + \frac{2(k^2+k+2)}{p} +$$

$$\frac{2q(2k+3q+2)}{p} + \frac{5q}{p} + \frac{4k^2(\log p)^2}{p} + \frac{4qk\log p + q^2}{p} + \frac{q^l}{k!}.$$

We let,

$$\epsilon_2(p) = \frac{q^l}{k!} + \frac{2(k^2+k+2)}{p} + \frac{4k^2(\log p)^2}{p}.$$

Setting $c = \lceil \frac{\log q}{\log k} \rceil$ and $l = \frac{k}{4c}$, $\frac{q^l}{k!} \leqslant \frac{k^{k/4}}{k!}$. By Sterling's approximation $k! \geqslant k^{k+1/2}e^{-k}$. Therefore,

$$\frac{k^{k/4}}{k!} = \frac{k^{k/4}}{k^{k/4}} \frac{e^k}{k^{k/4}} \frac{1}{k^{k/2+1/2}}.$$

For $k > e^4$ (we can set $k > e^4$), $\frac{q^l}{k!} \leqslant \frac{1}{k^{k/2+1/2}}$ i.e. $\frac{q^l}{k!}$ is negligible in $\log p$ for k polynomial in $\log p$. Also, $\frac{2(k^2+k+2)}{p} + \frac{4k^2(\log p)^2}{p}$ is negligible in $\log p$ (since k is a polynomial in $\log p$). So, $\epsilon_2(p)$ is negligible in $\log p$. We have that,

$$\mathsf{Adv}^{\mathsf{SDH\text{-}GG}}_{p,\mathsf{hLen}}(\mathcal{R}^\mathcal{A}) \leqslant 2 \cdot 2^{\frac{s}{2}} \left(\frac{8q^2(2k+2+3q)}{p}\right)^{\frac{k}{8c}} \left(1 + \frac{6q}{p}\right)^q +$$

$$\frac{2q(2k+3q+2)}{p} + \frac{5q}{p} + \frac{4qk\log p + q^2}{p} + \epsilon_2(p).$$

where $c = 4\lceil \frac{\log q}{\log k} \rceil$. Assuming $q \geqslant k$ (and thus $q > e^4 > 2$), we get,

$$\mathsf{Adv}^{\mathsf{SDH\text{-}GG}}_{p,\mathsf{hLen}}(\mathcal{R}^\mathcal{A}) \leqslant 2 \cdot 2^{\frac{s}{2}} \left(\frac{48q^3}{p}\right)^{\frac{k}{8c}} \left(1 + \frac{6q}{p}\right)^q + \frac{4q^2\log p + 13q^2 + 5q}{p} + \epsilon_2(p).$$

$\square$

4   Proof of Theorem

4.1   Adversary $\mathcal{A}$ Against ODH

In this section, we construct the ODH adversary $\mathcal{A}$ needed for the proof.

Lemma 1. *There exists an adversary $\mathcal{A}$ and a function $\epsilon_1(p, \mathsf{hLen})$ such that is negligible in $\log p, \mathsf{hLen}$, and*

$$\mathsf{Adv}^{\mathsf{ODH\text{-}GG}}_{p,\mathsf{hLen}}(\mathcal{A}) = 1 - \epsilon_1(p, \mathsf{hLen}).$$

Adversary $\mathcal{A}^{\mathsf{H_v}(\cdot),\mathsf{H}(\cdot),\mathsf{Eval}(\cdot,\cdot)}(U,V,W,\sigma(1))$:

1 : $i_1,\cdots,i_k \leftarrow\!\!\$\ \mathbb{Z}_p$
2 : **foreach** $j \in [k]$ **do**
3 : $Q_1[j] \leftarrow \mathsf{Exp}(\sigma(1),i_j); Q_2[j] \leftarrow \mathsf{Exp}(V,i_j)$
4 : $\mathsf{honest} \leftarrow 1$
5 : **foreach** $j \in [k]$ **do**
6 : $\mathsf{ans}_1[j] \leftarrow \mathsf{H_v}(Q_1[j])$
7 : $\pi \leftarrow\!\!\$\ \mathcal{S}_k$
8 : **foreach** $j \in [k]$ **do**
9 : $\mathsf{ans}_2[\pi(j)] \leftarrow \mathsf{H}(Q_2[\pi(j)])$
10 : **if** $\exists j,l \in [k], j \neq l : (\mathsf{ans}_1[j] = \mathsf{ans}_1[l] \vee \mathsf{ans}_2[j] = \mathsf{ans}_2[l])$ **then** $\mathsf{honest} \leftarrow 0$
11 : **if** $\exists j \in [k] : \mathsf{ans}_1[j] \neq \mathsf{ans}_2[j]$ **then** $\mathsf{honest} \leftarrow 0$
12 : **if** $\mathsf{honest} = 1$ **then**
13 : $\mathsf{temp} \leftarrow \sigma(1); v \leftarrow 1$
14 :   **while** $(\mathsf{temp} \neq V)$
15 : $\mathsf{temp} \leftarrow \mathsf{Eval}(\mathsf{temp}, \sigma(1)); v \leftarrow v + 1$
16 : $\mathsf{inp} \leftarrow \mathsf{Exp}(U, v); W' \leftarrow \mathsf{H}(\mathsf{inp}); b \leftarrow (W' = W)$
17 : **else** $b \leftarrow\!\!\$\ \{0, 1\}$
18 : **return** b

Fig. 2. The adversary $\mathcal{A}$

The adversary $\mathcal{A}$ is formally defined in Fig. 2. The proof of Lemma 1 itself is deferred to the full version. Adversary $\mathcal{A}$ samples $i_1, \cdots, i_k$ from $\mathbb{Z}_p$, and computes $\sigma(i_j), \sigma(i_j \cdot v)$ for all j in $[k]$. It then makes $\mathsf{H_v}$ queries on $\sigma(i_j)$'s for all j in $[k]$. Adversary $\mathcal{A}$ then samples a permutation π on $[k] \rightarrow [k]$, and then makes H queries on $\sigma(i_{\pi(j)} \cdot v)$'s for all j in $[k]$. If answers of all the H queries are distinct and the answers of all the $\mathsf{H_v}$ queries are distinct and for all j in $[k]$, $\mathsf{H_v}(\sigma(i_j)) = \mathsf{H}(\sigma(i_j \cdot v))$, $\mathcal{A}$ computes the discrete logarithm of V outputs the correct answer. Otherwise it returns a bit uniformly at random. Note that $\mathcal{A}$ is inefficient, but only if it is satisfied from the responses it gets from the reduction using it.

4.2 The Shuffling Games

THE GAME $\mathbb{G}_1$. We first introduce the two-stage game $\mathbb{G}_1$ played by a pair of adversaries $\mathcal{R}_1$ and $\mathcal{R}_2$. (With some foresight, these are going to be two stages of the reduction.) It is formally described in Fig. 3. Game $\mathbb{G}_1$ involves sampling $\sigma, i_1, \cdots, i_k, v$ from $\mathbb{Z}_p$, then running $\mathcal{R}_1$, followed by sampling permutation π from $\mathcal{S}_k$ and then running $\mathcal{R}_2$. The first stage $\mathcal{R}_1$ has inputs $\sigma(i_1), \cdots, \sigma(i_k)$ and it outputs a state ϕ of s bits along with k strings in $\{0,1\}^{\mathsf{hLen}}$. The second stage $\mathcal{R}_2$ has inputs $\phi, \sigma(i_{\pi(1)} \cdot v), \cdots, \sigma(i_{\pi(k)} \cdot v)$ and it outputs k strings in $\{0,1\}^{\mathsf{hLen}}$. Both the stages $\mathcal{R}_1, \mathcal{R}_2$ have access to oracles $\mathsf{Eval}, \mathsf{O_v}$. Game $\mathbb{G}_1$ outputs true if all the k strings output by $\mathcal{R}_1$ are distinct, and if all the k strings output by $\mathcal{R}_2$ are distinct, and if for all $j \in [k]$, the jth string output by $\mathcal{R}_2$ is identical to the $\pi(j)^{\mathsf{th}}$ string output by $\mathcal{R}_1$. Additionally, $\mathbb{G}_1$ involves some bookkeeping. The $\mathsf{Eval}, \mathsf{O_v}$ oracles in $\mathbb{G}_1$ take an extra parameter named from as input which indicates whether the query was from $\mathcal{R}_1$ or $\mathcal{R}_2$.

Game $\mathbb{G}_1$:

1: $\sigma \leftarrow\!\!\text{\$ } \mathsf{InjFunc}(\mathbb{Z}_p, \mathcal{L}); i_1, \cdots, i_k, v \leftarrow\!\!\text{\$ } \mathbb{Z}_p$

2: $\mathcal{X} \leftarrow \{\sigma(1), \sigma(v), \sigma(i_1), \cdots, \sigma(i_k)\}; \mathcal{Y}_1 \leftarrow \{\sigma(1), \sigma(v), \sigma(i_1), \cdots, \sigma(i_k)\}$

3: $\phi, s_1, \cdots, s_k \leftarrow \mathcal{R}_1^{\mathsf{Eval}(\cdot,\cdot,1), \mathsf{O}_v(\cdot,\cdot,1)}(\sigma(1), \sigma(v), \sigma(i_1), \cdots, \sigma(i_k))$

4: $\pi \leftarrow\!\!\text{\$ } S_k; \mathcal{Y}_2 \leftarrow \{\sigma(1), \sigma(v), \sigma(i_1 \cdot v), \cdots, \sigma(i_k \cdot v)\}; \mathcal{Z} \leftarrow \varnothing$

5: $s'_1, s'_2, \cdots, s'_k \leftarrow \mathcal{R}_2^{\mathsf{Eval}(\cdot,\cdot,2), \mathsf{O}_v(\cdot,\cdot,2)}(\phi, \sigma(1), \sigma(v), \sigma(i_{\pi(1)} \cdot v), \cdots, \sigma(i_{\pi(k)} \cdot v))$

6: $\mathsf{win} \leftarrow (\forall j \in [k] : s_{\pi(j)} = s'_j) \wedge (\forall j, l \in [k] : j \neq l \implies s_j \neq s_l \wedge s'_j \neq s'_l)$

7: **return** win

Oracle $\mathsf{Eval}(\mathbf{a}, \mathbf{b}, \mathrm{from})$:

1: $\mathbf{c} \leftarrow \sigma(\sigma^{-1}(\mathbf{a}) + \sigma^{-1}(\mathbf{b}))$

2: **if** $\mathrm{from} = 1$ **then**

3:     **if** $\mathbf{c} \notin \mathcal{Y}_1$ **then** $\mathcal{X} \xleftarrow{\cup} \{\mathbf{c}\}$

4:     $\mathcal{Y}_1 \xleftarrow{\cup} \{\mathbf{a}, \mathbf{b}, \mathbf{c}\}$

5: **if** $\mathrm{from} = 2$ **then**

6:     **if** $\mathbf{a} \in \mathcal{X} \backslash \mathcal{Y}_2$ **then** $\mathcal{Z} \xleftarrow{\cup} \{\mathbf{a}\}$

7:     **if** $\mathbf{b} \in \mathcal{X} \backslash \mathcal{Y}_2$ **then** $\mathcal{Z} \xleftarrow{\cup} \{\mathbf{b}\}$

8:     $\mathcal{Y}_2 \xleftarrow{\cup} \{\mathbf{a}, \mathbf{b}, \mathbf{c}\}$

9: **return** $\mathbf{c}$

Oracle $\mathsf{O}_v(\mathbf{a}, \mathbf{b}, \mathrm{from})$:

1: **if** $\mathrm{from} = 1$ **then** $\mathcal{Y}_1 \xleftarrow{\cup} \{\mathbf{a}, \mathbf{b}\}$

2: **if** $\mathrm{from} = 2$ **then**

3:     **if** $\mathbf{a} \in \mathcal{X} \backslash \mathcal{Y}_2$ **then** $\mathcal{Z} \xleftarrow{\cup} \{\mathbf{a}\}$

4:     **if** $\mathbf{b} \in \mathcal{X} \backslash \mathcal{Y}_2$ **then** $\mathcal{Z} \xleftarrow{\cup} \{\mathbf{b}\}$

5:     $\mathcal{Y}_2 \xleftarrow{\cup} \{\mathbf{a}, \mathbf{b}\}$

6: **return** $(v \cdot \sigma^{-1}(\mathbf{a}) = \sigma^{-1}(\mathbf{b}))$

Fig. 3. Game $\mathbb{G}_1$. We use the phrase $\mathcal{R}_1, \mathcal{R}_2$ win $\mathbb{G}_1$ to mean $\mathbb{G}_1 \Rightarrow \mathsf{true}$. We shall use this convention for all games in the paper that output boolean values.

We introduce the phrase "seen by" before describing the bookkeeping. A label has been "seen by" $\mathcal{R}_1$ if it was an input to $\mathcal{R}_1$, queried by $\mathcal{R}_1$ or an answer to a previously made $\mathsf{Eval}(., ., 1)$ query. A label has been "seen by" $\mathcal{R}_2$ if it was an input to $\mathcal{R}_2$, queried by $\mathcal{R}_2$ or an answer to a previously made $\mathsf{Eval}(., ., 2)$ query. We describe the sets $\mathcal{X}, \mathcal{Y}_1, \mathcal{Y}_2, \mathcal{Z}$ which are used for bookkeeping in $\mathbb{G}_1$.

- The labels in $\mathcal{X}$ are answers to $\mathsf{Eval}(., ., 1)$ queries such that it has not yet been "seen by" $\mathcal{R}_1$ before the query.
- $\mathcal{Y}_1$ contains all the labels that are input to $\mathcal{R}_1$, queried by $\mathcal{R}_1$ or answers to $\mathsf{Eval}(., ., 1)$ queries i.e. it is the set of labels "seen by" $\mathcal{R}_1$.
- $\mathcal{Y}_2$ contains all the labels that are input to $\mathcal{R}_2$, queried by $\mathcal{R}_1$ or answers to $\mathsf{Eval}(., ., 2)$ queries i.e. it is the set of labels "seen by" $\mathcal{R}_2$.
- All labels in $\mathcal{Z}$ are queried by $\mathcal{R}_2$ and have not been "seen by" $\mathcal{R}_2$ before the query and are in $\mathcal{X}$

The following lemma tells us that we can (somewhat straightforwardly) take a reduction as in the theorem statement, and transform it into an equivalent pair $\mathcal{R}_1, \mathcal{R}_2$ of adversaries for $\mathbb{G}_1$. The point here is that the reduction is very unlikely to succeed in breaking the SDH assumption without doing an effort equivalent to winning $\mathbb{G}_1$ to get $\mathcal{A}$'s help – otherwise, it is left with breaking SDH directly in the generic group model, which is hard. The proof is deferred to the full version.

Game $\boxed{\mathbb{G}_2}$, $\boxed{\mathbb{G}_3}$:

1 : $\quad \sigma \leftarrow\!\!\$\ \mathsf{InjFunc}(\mathbb{Z}_p, \mathcal{L}); i_1, \cdots, i_k, v \leftarrow\!\!\$\ \mathbb{Z}_p$

2 : $\quad \mathcal{X} \leftarrow \{\sigma(1), \sigma(v), \sigma(i_1), \cdots, \sigma(i_k)\}; \mathcal{Y}_1 \leftarrow \{\sigma(1), \sigma(v), \sigma(i_1), \cdots, \sigma(i_k)\}$

3 : $\quad \phi, s_1, \cdots, s_k \leftarrow \mathcal{R}_1^{\mathsf{Eval}(\cdot,\cdot,1), \mathsf{O_v}(\cdot,\cdot,1)}(\sigma(1), \sigma(v), \sigma(i_1), \cdots, \sigma(i_k))$

4 : $\quad \pi \leftarrow\!\!\$\ \mathcal{S}_k; \mathcal{Y}_2 \leftarrow \{\sigma(1), \sigma(v), \sigma(i_1 \cdot v), \cdots, \sigma(i_k \cdot v)\}; \mathcal{Z} \leftarrow \varnothing$

5 : $\quad s'_1, s'_2, \cdots, s'_k \leftarrow \mathcal{R}_2^{\mathsf{Eval}(\cdot,\cdot,2), \mathsf{O_v}(\cdot,\cdot,2)}(\phi, \sigma(1), \sigma(v), \sigma(i_{\pi(1)} \cdot v), \cdots, \sigma(i_{\pi(k)} \cdot v))$

6 : $\quad \mathsf{win} \leftarrow (\forall j \in [k] : s_{\pi(j)} = s'_j) \wedge (\forall j, l \in [k] : j \neq l \implies s_j \neq s_l \wedge s'_j \neq s'_l)$

7 : $\quad \boxed{\textbf{return } (\mathsf{win} \wedge |\mathcal{Z}| < l)} \quad \boxed{\textbf{return } (\mathsf{win} \wedge |\mathcal{Z}| \geqslant l)}$

Fig. 4. Games $\mathbb{G}_2, \mathbb{G}_3$. The $\mathsf{Eval}, \mathsf{O_v}$ oracles in $\mathbb{G}_2, \mathbb{G}_3$ are identical to those in $\mathbb{G}_1$ and hence we do not rewrite it here. The newly introduced changes compared to $\mathbb{G}_1$ are highlighted. The statement within the thinner box is present only in $\mathbb{G}_3$ and the statement within the thicker box is present only in $\mathbb{G}_2$.

Lemma 2. *For every restricted black box reduction $\mathcal{R}$ to SDH-GG that runs $\mathcal{A}$, there exist adversaries $\mathcal{R}_1, \mathcal{R}_2$ playing $\mathbb{G}_1$, such that the number of queries made by $\mathcal{R}_1, \mathcal{R}_2$ to $\mathsf{Eval}, \mathsf{O_v}$ is same as the number of queries made by $\mathcal{R}$ to $\mathsf{Eval}, \mathsf{O_v}$, the state passed from $\mathcal{R}_1$ to $\mathcal{R}_2$ is upper bounded by the memory used by $\mathcal{R}$ and,*

$$\mathsf{Adv}_{p,\mathsf{hLen}}^{\mathsf{SDH\text{-}GG}}(\mathcal{R}^{\mathcal{A}}) \leqslant \Pr\left[\mathbb{G}_1 \Rightarrow \mathsf{true}\right] + \frac{4k^2 (\log p)^2}{p} + \frac{4qk \log p + q^2}{p}.$$

THE GAMES $\mathbb{G}_2$ AND $\mathbb{G}_3$. In Fig. 4 we define $\mathbb{G}_2, \mathbb{G}_3$ which have an added check on the cardinality of $\mathcal{Z}$ to output true. Everything else remains unchanged (in particular $\mathsf{Eval}, \mathsf{O_v}$ are unchanged from $\mathbb{G}_1$ and we do not specify them again here). The statement within the thinner box is present only in $\mathbb{G}_3$ and statement within the thicker box is present only in $\mathbb{G}_2$. The changes from $\mathbb{G}_1$ have been highlighted. We shall follow these conventions of using boxes and highlighting throughout the paper.

The games $\mathbb{G}_2, \mathbb{G}_3$ are identical to $\mathbb{G}_1$ except for the condition to output true. Since this disjunction of the conditions to output true in $\mathbb{G}_2, \mathbb{G}_3$ is equivalent to the condition to output true in $\mathbb{G}_1$, and the conditions to output true in $\mathbb{G}_2, \mathbb{G}_3$ are disjoint, we have,

$$\Pr\left[\mathbb{G}_1 \Rightarrow \mathsf{true}\right] = \Pr\left[\mathbb{G}_2 \Rightarrow \mathsf{true}\right] + \Pr\left[\mathbb{G}_3 \Rightarrow \mathsf{true}\right].$$

4.3 Proof of Lemma 3

Recall we are going to prove the following lemma.

Lemma 3. *For the game $\mathbb{G}_2$,*

$$\Pr\left[\mathbb{G}_2 \Rightarrow \mathsf{true}\right] \leqslant \frac{q^l}{k!} + \frac{2q(2k + 3q + 2)}{p} + \frac{5q}{p} + \frac{k^2 + k + 2}{p}.$$

Game $\mathbb{PG}(\mathcal{A})$:	Oracle $O(\vec{x}, \vec{y})$: // $\vec{x} \in \mathbb{Z}_p^k, \vec{y} \in \mathbb{Z}_p^k$
1 : $\pi \leftarrow\!\!\$\; S_k$	1 : **return** $(\forall i \in [k] : \vec{x}[\pi(i)] = \vec{y}[i])$
2 : $\pi' \leftarrow \mathcal{A}^{O(\cdot,\cdot)}$	
3 : **return** $(\pi = \pi')$	

Fig. 5. The permutation game $\mathbb{PG}$ being played by adversary $\mathcal{A}$ is denoted by $\mathbb{PG}(\mathcal{A})$

We introduce a new game – called the *permutation game* and denoted $\mathbb{PG}$ – in order to upper bound $\Pr[\mathbb{G}_2 \Rightarrow \text{true}]$. In the rest of this proof, we are going to first define the game, and upper bound the winning probability of an adversary. Then, we are going to reduce an adversary for $\mathbb{G}_2$ to one for $\mathbb{PG}$.

THE PERMUTATION GAME. In Game $\mathbb{PG}$, an adversary has to guess a randomly sampled permutation π over $[k]$. The adversary has access to an oracle that takes as input two vectors of length k and returns true if the elements of the first vector, when permuted using π, results in the second vector and false otherwise. Figure 5 formally describes the game $\mathbb{PG}$.

In the following, we say an adversary playing $\mathbb{PG}$ is a (q, l)-query adversary if it makes at most q queries to O, and the rank of the vectors that were the first argument to the O queries returning true is at most l.

The following lemma – which we prove via a compression argument – yields an upper bound on the probability of winning the game for a (q, l)-query adversary.

Lemma 5. *For a (q, l)-query adversary $\mathcal{A}$ playing $\mathbb{PG}$ the following is true.*

$$\Pr[\mathbb{PG}(\mathcal{A}) \Rightarrow \text{true}] \leqslant \frac{q^l}{k!}.$$

Proof. We construct an encoding of π by running adversary $\mathcal{A}$. In order to run $\mathcal{A}$, all the O queries need to be correctly answered. This can be naively done by storing the sequence number of queries whose answers are true. In fact, of all such queries, we need to just store the sequence number of just those whose first argument is not in the linear span of vectors which were the first argument of previous such queries i.e. we store the sequence number of only those O queries returning true whose first argument form a basis of the first argument of all O queries returning true. This approach works because for every vector $\vec{x}$, there is only a unique vector $\vec{y}$ such that $O(\vec{x}, \vec{y}) = 1$. The random tape of the adversary can be derived using the common randomness of Encode, Decode and hence the adversary produces identical queries and output. For simplicity, we do not specify this explicitly in the algorithms and treat $\mathcal{A}$ as deterministic. The formal description of the algorithms Encode, Decode are in Fig. 6.

Observe that S is a basis of vectors $\vec{x}$ such that $O(\vec{x}, \vec{y}) = \text{true}$. Note that for an $O(\vec{x}, \vec{y})$ query returning true, if $\vec{x} \in S$ then the sequence number of the query is stored in enc. Therefore, $(\vec{x}, \vec{y}) \in S'$ in Decode. Again, for an $O(\vec{x}, \vec{y})$ query returning true, if $\vec{x} \notin S$ then the sequence number of the query is not stored in enc and therefore $(\vec{x}, \vec{y}) \notin S'$. So, for an $O(\vec{x}, \vec{y})$ query returning true,

Procedure Encode(π) :	**Oracle** $O(\vec{x}, \vec{y})$:
1 : $c \leftarrow 0$	1 : $c \leftarrow c + 1$
2 : $S \leftarrow \varnothing$	2 : **if** $(\exists i \in [k] : \vec{x}[\pi(i)] \neq \vec{y}[i])$ **then**
3 : enc $\leftarrow \varnothing$	3 : **return false**
4 : $\pi' \leftarrow \mathcal{A}^{O(\cdot,\cdot)}$	4 : **else**
5 : **return** enc	5 : **if** $\vec{x} \notin \text{span}(S)$ **then**
	6 : $S \leftarrow S \cup \{\vec{x}\}$
	7 : enc $\leftarrow$ enc $\cup \{c\}$
	8 : **return true**
Procedure Decode(enc) :	**Oracle** $O(\vec{x}, \vec{y})$:
1 : $c \leftarrow 0$	1 : $c \leftarrow c + 1$
2 : $S' \leftarrow \varnothing$	2 : **if** $c \in$ enc **then**
3 : $\pi' \leftarrow \mathcal{A}^{O(\cdot,\cdot)}$	3 : $S' \leftarrow S' \cup \{(\vec{x}, \vec{y})\}$
4 : **return** π'	4 : **return true**
	5 : **return** $((\vec{x}, \vec{y}) \in \text{span}(S'))$

Fig. 6. Encoding and decoding π using $\mathcal{A}$

$(\vec{x}, \vec{y}) \in S'$ iff $\vec{x} \in S$. Since, for all $(\vec{x}, \vec{y})$ such that $O(\vec{x}, \vec{y}) = \text{true}$ we have that for all $i \in [k]$, $\vec{y}[i] = \vec{x}[\pi^{-1}(i)]$, it follows that S' forms a basis of vectors $(\vec{x}, \vec{y})$ such that $O(\vec{x}, \vec{y}) = \text{true}$.

In Decode(enc), the simulation of $O(\vec{x}, \vec{y})$ is perfect because

- If c is in enc, then $\vec{x} \in S$ in Encode. From the definition of S in Encode, it follows that $O(\vec{x}, \vec{y})$ should return true.
- Otherwise we check if $(\vec{x}, \vec{y}) \in \text{span}(S')$ and return true if the check succeeds, false otherwise. This is correct since in S' is a basis of vectors $(\vec{x}, \vec{y})$ such that $O(\vec{x}, \vec{y}) = \text{true}$.

The encoding is a set of $|S|$ query sequence numbers. Since there are at most q queries, the encoding space is at most $\binom{q}{|S|}$. Using $\mathcal{X}$ to be the set S_k, $\mathcal{Y}$ to be the set of all possible encodings, $\mathcal{R}$ to be the set of random tapes of $\mathcal{A}$, it follows from Proposition 1 that,

$$\Pr\left[\text{Decoding is sucessful}\right] \leqslant \frac{\binom{q}{|S|}}{k!}.$$

Since the simulation of $O(\vec{x}, \vec{y})$ is perfect in Decode, decoding is successful if $\mathbb{PG}(\mathcal{A}) \Rightarrow \text{true}$. Therefore,

$$\Pr\left[\mathbb{PG}(\mathcal{A}) \Rightarrow \text{true}\right] \leqslant \frac{\binom{q}{|S|}}{k!} \leqslant \frac{q^{|S|}}{k!}.$$

Since $\mathcal{A}$ is a (q, l)-query adversary, $|S| \leqslant l$. Thus, we have,

$$\Pr\left[\mathbb{PG}(\mathcal{A}) \Rightarrow \text{true}\right] \leqslant \frac{q^l}{k!} \tag{3}$$

$\square$

Procedure PopulateSetsEval$(\mathbf{a}, \mathbf{b}, \mathbf{c}, \text{from})$:	**Procedure** PopulateSetsO$_\mathsf{v}(\mathbf{a}, \mathbf{b}, \text{from})$:
1 : **if** from = 1 **then**	1 : **if** from = 1 **then** $\mathcal{Y}_1 \xleftarrow{\cup} \{\mathbf{a}, \mathbf{b}\}$
2 : **if** $\mathbf{c} \notin \mathcal{Y}_1$ **then** $\mathcal{X} \xleftarrow{\cup} \{\mathbf{c}\}$	2 : **if** from = 2 **then**
3 : $\mathcal{Y}_1 \xleftarrow{\cup} \{\mathbf{a}, \mathbf{b}, \mathbf{c}\}$	3 : **if** $\mathbf{a} \in \mathcal{X} \backslash \mathcal{Y}_2$ **then** $\mathcal{Z} \xleftarrow{\cup} \{\mathbf{a}\}$
4 : **if** from = 2 **then**	4 : **if** $\mathbf{b} \in \mathcal{X} \backslash \mathcal{Y}_2$ **then** $\mathcal{Z} \xleftarrow{\cup} \{\mathbf{b}\}$
5 : **if** $\mathbf{a} \in \mathcal{X} \backslash \mathcal{Y}_2$ **then** $\mathcal{Z} \xleftarrow{\cup} \{\mathbf{a}\}$	5 : $\mathcal{Y}_2 \xleftarrow{\cup} \{\mathbf{a}, \mathbf{b}\}$
6 : **if** $\mathbf{b} \in \mathcal{X} \backslash \mathcal{Y}_2$ **then** $\mathcal{Z} \xleftarrow{\cup} \{\mathbf{b}\}$	
7 : $\mathcal{Y}_2 \xleftarrow{\cup} \{\mathbf{a}, \mathbf{b}, \mathbf{c}\}$	

Fig. 7. Subroutines PopulateSetsEval, PopulateSetsO$_\mathsf{v}$

REDUCTION TO $\mathbb{PG}$. We next show that the $\Pr[\mathbb{G}_2 \Rightarrow \text{true}]$ is upper bounded in terms of the probability of a (q, l)-query adversary winning the game $\mathbb{PG}$.

Lemma 6. *There exists a (q, l)-query adversary $\mathcal{D}$ against the permutation game $\mathbb{PG}$ such that*

$$\Pr[\mathbb{G}_2 \Rightarrow \text{true}] \leqslant \Pr[\mathbb{PG}(\mathcal{D}) \Rightarrow \text{true}] + \frac{2q(2k + 3q + 2)}{p} + \frac{5q}{p} + \frac{k^2 + k + 2}{p}.$$

Proof. We transform $\mathcal{R}_1, \mathcal{R}_2$ playing $\mathbb{G}_2$ to an adversary $\mathcal{D}$ playing the game $\mathbb{PG}$ through a sequence of intermediate games and use the upper bound on the probability of winning the game $\mathbb{PG}$ established previously to prove an upper bound on $\Pr[\mathbb{G}_2 \Rightarrow \text{true}]$. In order to make the pseudocode for subsequent games compact we define the two subroutines PopulateSetsEval, PopulateSetsO$_\mathsf{v}$ and invoke them from Eval, O$_\mathsf{v}$. The subroutines PopulateSetsEval, PopulateSetsO$_\mathsf{v}$ are formally described in Fig. 7.

THE GAME $\mathbb{G}_4$. We next describe game $\mathbb{G}_4$ where we introduce some additional bookkeeping. In $\mathbb{G}_4$, every valid label that is an input to $\mathcal{R}_1, \mathcal{R}_2$ or queried by $\mathcal{R}_1, \mathcal{R}_2$ or an answer to a query of $\mathcal{R}_1, \mathcal{R}_2$, is mapped to a polynomial in $\mathbb{Z}_p[I_1, \cdots, I_k, V, T_1, \cdots, T_{2q}]$ where q is the total number of Eval, O$_\mathsf{v}$ queries made by $\mathcal{R}_1, \mathcal{R}_2$. The polynomial associated with label $\mathbf{a}$ is denoted by $\mathsf{p_a}$. Similarly, we define Λ to be a mapping from polynomials to labels. For all labels $\mathbf{a} \in \mathcal{L}$, $\Lambda(\mathsf{p_a}) = \mathbf{a}$. The mapping from labels to polynomials is done such that for every label $\mathbf{a}$ mapped to $\mathsf{p_a}$,

$$\sigma^{-1}(\mathbf{a}) = \mathsf{p_a}(i_1, \cdots, i_k, v, t_1, \cdots, t_{2q}).$$

For compactness, let us denote $(i_1, \cdots, i_k, v, t_1, \cdots, t_{2q})$ by $\vec{i}$. Before running $\mathcal{R}_1$, $\mathsf{p}_{\sigma(1)}, \mathsf{p}_{\sigma(v)}, \mathsf{p}_{\sigma(i_1)}, \cdots, \mathsf{p}_{\sigma(i_k)}, \mathsf{p}_{\sigma(i_1 \cdot v)}, \cdots, \mathsf{p}_{\sigma(i_k \cdot v)}$ are assigned polynomials $1, V, I_1, \cdots, I_k, I_1 V, \cdots, I_k V$ respectively and for all other labels $\mathbf{a} \in \mathcal{L}$, $\mathsf{p_a} = \perp$. The function Λ is defined accordingly. For labels $\mathbf{a}$ queried by $\mathcal{R}_1, \mathcal{R}_2$ that have not been previously mapped to any polynomial (i.e. $\mathsf{p_a} = \perp$), $\mathsf{p_a}$ is assigned T_{new} (new starting from 1 and being incremented for every such label queried), the

---

Game $\mathbb{G}_4$:

1 : $\quad \sigma \leftarrow_\$ \mathsf{InjFunc}(\mathbb{Z}_p, \mathcal{L});\, \mathbf{foreach}\ \mathsf{a} \in \mathcal{L}\ \mathbf{do}\ \mathsf{p_a} \leftarrow \bot$

2 : $\quad \mathbf{foreach}\ \mathsf{p'} \in \mathbb{Z}_p[I_1, \cdots, I_k, V, T_1, \cdots, T_{2q}]\ \mathbf{do}\ \Lambda(\mathsf{p'}) \leftarrow \bot$

3 : $\quad i_1, \cdots, i_k, v \leftarrow_\$ \mathbb{Z}_p;\, \mathsf{p}_{\sigma(1)} \leftarrow 1;\, \Lambda(1) \leftarrow \sigma(1)$

4 : $\quad \mathbf{if}\ \mathsf{p}_{\sigma(v)} = \bot\ \mathbf{then}\ \mathsf{p}_{\sigma(v)} \leftarrow V$

5 : $\quad \Lambda(V) \leftarrow \sigma(v)$

6 : $\quad \mathbf{foreach}\ j \in [k]\ \mathbf{do}$

7 : $\quad\quad \mathbf{if}\ \mathsf{p}_{\sigma(i_j)} = \bot\ \mathbf{then}\ \mathsf{p}_{\sigma(i_j)} \leftarrow I_j$

8 : $\quad\quad \Lambda(I_j) \leftarrow \sigma(i_j)$

9 : $\quad\quad \mathbf{if}\ \mathsf{p}_{\sigma(v \cdot i_j)} = \bot\ \mathbf{then}\ \mathsf{p}_{\sigma(v \cdot i_j)} \leftarrow VI_j$

10 : $\quad\quad \Lambda(VI_j) \leftarrow \sigma(v \cdot i_j)$

11 : $\quad \mathsf{new} \leftarrow 0;\, \mathcal{X} \leftarrow \{\sigma(1), \sigma(v), \sigma(i_1), \cdots, \sigma(i_k)\};\, \mathcal{Y}_1 \leftarrow \{\sigma(1), \sigma(v), \sigma(i_1), \cdots, \sigma(i_k)\}$

12 : $\quad \phi, s_1, \cdots, s_k \leftarrow \mathcal{R}_1^{\mathsf{Eval}(\cdot, \cdot, 1), \mathsf{O_v}(\cdot, \cdot, 1)}(\sigma(1), \sigma(v), \sigma(i_1), \cdots, \sigma(i_k))$

13 : $\quad \pi \leftarrow_\$ \mathcal{S}_k;\, \mathcal{Y}_2 \leftarrow \{\sigma(1), \sigma(v), \sigma(i_1 \cdot v), \cdots, \sigma(i_k \cdot v)\};\, \mathcal{Z} \leftarrow \varnothing$

14 : $\quad s_1', s_2', \cdots, s_k' \leftarrow \mathcal{R}_2^{\mathsf{Eval}(\cdot, \cdot, 2), \mathsf{O_v}(\cdot, \cdot, 2)}(\phi, \sigma(1), \sigma(v), \sigma(i_{\pi(1)} \cdot v), \cdots, \sigma(i_{\pi(k)} \cdot v))$

15 : $\quad \mathsf{win} \leftarrow (\forall j \in [k] : s_{\pi(j)} = s_j') \wedge (\forall j, l \in [k] : j \neq l \implies s_j \neq s_l \wedge s_j' \neq s_l')$

16 : $\quad \mathbf{return}\ (\mathsf{win} \wedge |\mathcal{Z}| < l)$

Oracle $\mathsf{Eval}(\mathbf{a}, \mathbf{b}, \mathsf{from})$:

1 : $\quad \mathbf{if}\ \mathsf{p_a} = \bot\ \mathbf{then}$

2 : $\quad\quad \mathsf{AssignPoly}(\mathbf{a})$

3 : $\quad \mathbf{if}\ \mathsf{p_b} = \bot\ \mathbf{then}$

4 : $\quad\quad \mathsf{AssignPoly}(\mathbf{b})$

5 : $\quad \mathsf{p'} \leftarrow \mathsf{p_a} + \mathsf{p_b}$

6 : $\quad \mathbf{if}\ \Lambda(\mathsf{p'}) = \bot\ \mathbf{then}$

7 : $\quad\quad \mathbf{if}\ \exists c' \in \mathcal{L} : \mathsf{p}_{c'}(\vec{i}) = \mathsf{p'}(\vec{i})\ \mathbf{then}$

8 : $\quad\quad\quad \Lambda(\mathsf{p'}) \leftarrow c'$

9 : $\quad\quad \mathbf{else}$

10 : $\quad\quad\quad \Lambda(\mathsf{p'}) \leftarrow \sigma(\sigma^{-1}(\mathbf{a}) + \sigma^{-1}(\mathbf{b}));$

11 : $\quad\quad\quad \mathsf{p}_{\Lambda(\mathsf{p'})} \leftarrow \mathsf{p'}$

12 : $\quad \mathsf{PopulateSetsEval}(\mathbf{a}, \mathbf{b}, \Lambda(\mathsf{p'}), \mathsf{from})$

13 : $\quad \mathbf{return}\ \Lambda(\mathsf{p'})$

Oracle $\mathsf{O_v}(\mathbf{a}, \mathbf{b}, \mathsf{from})$:

1 : $\quad \mathbf{if}\ \mathsf{p_a} = \bot\ \mathbf{then}$

2 : $\quad\quad \mathsf{AssignPoly}(\mathbf{a})$

3 : $\quad \mathbf{if}\ \mathsf{p_b} = \bot\ \mathbf{then}$

4 : $\quad\quad \mathsf{AssignPoly}(\mathbf{b})$

5 : $\quad \mathsf{ans} \leftarrow (V\mathsf{p_a} = \mathsf{p_b})$

6 : $\quad \mathbf{if}\ (v\mathsf{p_a}(\vec{i}) = \mathsf{p_b}(\vec{i})) \neq \mathsf{ans}\ \mathbf{then}$

7 : $\quad\quad \mathsf{ans} \leftarrow (v\mathsf{p_a}(\vec{i}) = \mathsf{p_b}(\vec{i}))$

8 : $\quad\quad \mathsf{PopulateSetsO_v}(\mathbf{a}, \mathbf{b}, \mathsf{from})$

9 : $\quad \mathbf{return}\ \mathsf{ans}$

Procedure $\mathsf{AssignPoly}(\mathsf{l})$:

1 : $\quad \mathsf{new} \leftarrow \mathsf{new} + 1;\, t_{\mathsf{new}} \leftarrow \sigma^{-1}(\mathsf{l});\, \mathsf{p_l} \leftarrow T_{\mathsf{new}};\, \Lambda(T_{\mathsf{new}}) \leftarrow \mathsf{l}$

Fig. 8. $\mathbb{G}_4$ introduces additional bookkeeping. The newly introduced changes compared to $\mathbb{G}_2$ are highlighted.

variable t_{new} is assigned the pre-image of the label and $\Lambda(T_{\mathsf{new}})$ is assigned $\mathbf{a}$. Since there are q queries (each with two inputs), there can be at most $2q$ labels that had not previously been mapped to any polynomial. Hence, the polynomials have variables $I_1, \cdots, I_k, V, T_1, \cdots, T_{2q}$.

For an $\mathsf{Eval}(\mathbf{a}, \mathbf{b}, .)$ query where $\mathbf{c} = \sigma(\sigma^{-1}(\mathbf{a}) + \sigma^{-1}(\mathbf{b}))$, let $\mathsf{p'} = \mathsf{p_a} + \mathsf{p_b}$. From the definition of p, we have that $\mathsf{p'}(\vec{i}) = \sigma^{-1}(\mathbf{a}) + \sigma^{-1}(\mathbf{b})$. If $\Lambda(\mathsf{p'}) \neq \bot$, then by definition of $\varLambda$, we have $\varLambda(\mathsf{p'}) = \mathbf{c}$. If $\varLambda(\mathsf{p'}) = \perp$, then exactly one of the following two must be true.

1. The label $\mathbf{c}$ has been mapped to a polynomial which is different from $\mathsf{p'}$. In this case $\mathsf{p_c}(\vec{i}) = \mathsf{p'}(\vec{i})$ and $\varLambda(\mathsf{p'})$ is assigned $\mathbf{c}$.
2. The label $\mathbf{c}$ has not been mapped to any polynomial. In this case, $\mathsf{p_c}$ is assigned $\mathsf{p'}$ and $\varLambda(\mathsf{p'})$ is assigned $\mathbf{c}$.

The label $\varLambda(\mathsf{p'})$ is returned as the answer of the Eval query. Note that the output of Eval is $\mathbf{c} = \sigma(\sigma^{-1}(\mathbf{a}) + \sigma^{-1}(\mathbf{b}))$ in all cases, i.e. it is the same as the output of Eval in $\mathbb{G}_2$.

For an $\mathsf{O_v}(\mathbf{a}, \mathbf{b}, .)$ query, we first assign the boolean value $V\mathsf{p_a} = \mathsf{p_b}$ to ans. Note that if ans is true, then $v \cdot \sigma^{-1}(\mathbf{a}) = \sigma^{-1}(\mathbf{b})$. However, we might have that $v \cdot \sigma^{-1}(\mathbf{a}) = \sigma^{-1}(\mathbf{b})$ and $V\mathsf{p_a} \neq \mathsf{p_b}$. When this happens, the boolean value $v(\mathsf{p_a}(\vec{i}) = \mathsf{p_b}(\vec{i}))$ is assigned to ans. Oracle $\mathsf{O_v}$ returns ans. From the definition of p, it follows that the value returned by $\mathsf{O_v}$ in $\mathbb{G}_4$ is $(v \cdot \sigma^{-1}(\mathbf{a}) = \sigma^{-1}(\mathbf{b}))$ i.e. it is the same as the output of $\mathsf{O_v}$ in $\mathbb{G}_2$.

Figure 8 formally describes $\mathbb{G}_4$. The changes in $\mathbb{G}_4$ compared to $\mathbb{G}_2$ have been highlighted. We have already pointed out that the outputs of $\mathsf{O_v}$, Eval in $\mathbb{G}_4$ are identical to those in $\mathbb{G}_2$. Since the other changes involve only additional bookkeeping, the outputs of $\mathbb{G}_2, \mathbb{G}_4$ are identical. Therefore

$$\Pr[\mathbb{G}_4 \Rightarrow \mathsf{true}] = \Pr[\mathbb{G}_2 \Rightarrow \mathsf{true}]. \tag{4}$$

THE GAME $\mathbb{G}_{11}$. We introduce a new game named $\mathbb{G}_{11}$ in Fig. 9. Initially, for all polynomials p, $\varLambda(\mathsf{p}) = \perp$. In this game $\varLambda(1), \varLambda(V)$, $\varLambda(I_j)$'s, and $\varLambda(VI_j)$'s are assigned distinct labels sampled from $\mathcal{L}$. Adversary $\mathcal{R}_1$ is run with input labels $\varLambda(1), \varLambda(V), \varLambda(I_1), \cdots, \varLambda(I_k)$ and $\mathcal{R}_2$ has input labels $\varLambda(1), \varLambda(V), \varLambda(I_{\pi(1)} \cdot V), \cdots, \varLambda(I_{\pi(k)} \cdot V)$. The bookkeeping is identical to that in $\mathbb{G}_4$. Observe from the pseudocode that the mapping $\varLambda$ is injective in this game and hence $\varLambda^{-1}$ is well defined.

For every Eval or $\mathsf{O_v}$ query, if for the input label l, $\varLambda^{-1}(\mathsf{l})$ is $\perp$, then l is assigned to $\varLambda(T_{\mathsf{new}})$. For every such input label, new is incremented. For an Eval$(\mathbf{a}, \mathbf{b}, .)$ query, if $\varLambda(\varLambda^{-1}(\mathbf{a}) + \varLambda^{-1}(\mathbf{b}))$ is not defined, then it is assigned a random label in $\overline{R(\varLambda)}$. The label $\varLambda(\varLambda^{-1}(\mathbf{a}) + \varLambda^{-1}(\mathbf{b}))$ is returned as answer. For $\mathsf{O_v}(\mathbf{a}, \mathbf{b}, .)$, query true is returned iff $V\varLambda^{-1}(\mathbf{a})$ and $\varLambda^{-1}(\mathbf{b})$ are the same polynomials.

We next upper bound $\Pr[\mathbb{G}_4 \Rightarrow \mathsf{true}]$ in terms of $\Pr[\mathbb{G}_{11} \Rightarrow \mathsf{true}]$ in Lemma 7.

Lemma 7. *For the games $\mathbb{G}_4, \mathbb{G}_{11}$, we have,*

$$\Pr[\mathbb{G}_4 \Rightarrow \mathsf{true}] \leqslant \Pr[\mathbb{G}_{11} \Rightarrow \mathsf{true}] + \frac{2q(2k + 3q + 2)}{p} + \frac{5q}{p} + \frac{k^2 + k + 2}{p}.$$

The proof of Lemma 7 has been deferred to the full version.

THE ADVERSARY $\mathcal{D}$. Next, we construct the adversary $\mathcal{D}$ that plays $\mathbb{PG}$ by simulating $\mathbb{G}_{11}$ to $\mathcal{R}_1, \mathcal{R}_2$, where the permutation π is the secret permutation

---

Game $\mathbb{G}_{11}$:

1 :   **foreach** $p \in \mathbb{Z}_p[I_1, \cdots, I_k, V, T_1, \cdots, T_{2q}]$ **do** $\Lambda(p) \leftarrow \bot; \Lambda(1) \leftarrow\!\!{\scriptstyle\$}\, \mathcal{L}$

2 : $\Lambda(V) \leftarrow\!\!{\scriptstyle\$}\, \overline{R(\Lambda)}$

3 :   **foreach** $j \in [k]$ **do**

4 : $\Lambda(I_j) \leftarrow\!\!{\scriptstyle\$}\, \overline{R(\Lambda)}; \Lambda(VI_j) \leftarrow\!\!{\scriptstyle\$}\, \overline{R(\Lambda)}$

5 : $\text{new} \leftarrow 0; \mathcal{X} \leftarrow \Lambda(1), \Lambda(V), \Lambda(I_1), \cdots, \Lambda(I_k)\}; \mathcal{Y}_1 \leftarrow \{\Lambda(1), \Lambda(V), \Lambda(I_1), \cdots, \Lambda(I_k)\}$

6 : $\phi, s_1, \cdots, s_k \leftarrow \mathcal{R}_1^{\mathsf{Eval}(\cdot,\cdot,1),\mathsf{O_v}(\cdot,\cdot,1)}(\Lambda(1), \Lambda(V), \Lambda(I_1), \cdots, \Lambda(I_k))$

7 : $\pi \leftarrow\!\!{\scriptstyle\$}\, \mathcal{S}_k; \mathcal{Y}_2 \leftarrow \{\Lambda(1), \Lambda(V), \Lambda(VI_1), \cdots, \Lambda(VI_k)\}; \mathcal{Z} \leftarrow \varnothing$

8 : $s'_1, s'_2, \cdots, s'_k \leftarrow \mathcal{R}_2^{\mathsf{Eval}(\cdot,\cdot,2),\mathsf{O_v}(\cdot,\cdot,2)}(\phi, \Lambda(1), \Lambda(V), \Lambda(I_{\pi(1)} \cdot V), \cdots, \Lambda(I_{\pi(k)} \cdot V))$

9 : $\text{win} \leftarrow (\forall j \in [k] : s_{\pi(j)} = s'_j) \wedge (\forall j, l \in [k] : j \neq l \implies s_j \neq s_l \wedge s'_j \neq s'_l)$

10 : **return** $(\text{win} \wedge |\mathcal{Z}| < l)$

Oracle $\mathsf{Eval}(a, b, from)$:	**Oracle $\mathsf{O_v}(a, b, from)$:**
1 : **if** $\Lambda^{-1}(a) = \bot$ **then**	1 : **if** $\Lambda^{-1}(a) = \bot$ **then**
2 : $\text{new} \leftarrow \text{new} + 1; \Lambda(T_{\text{new}}) \leftarrow a$	2 : $\text{new} \leftarrow \text{new} + 1; \Lambda(T_{\text{new}}) \leftarrow a$
3 : **if** $\Lambda^{-1}(b) = \bot$ **then**	3 : **if** $\Lambda^{-1}(b) = \bot$ **then**
4 : $\text{new} \leftarrow \text{new} + 1; \Lambda(T_{\text{new}}) \leftarrow b$	4 : $\text{new} \leftarrow \text{new} + 1; \Lambda(T_{\text{new}}) \leftarrow b$
5 : $p \leftarrow \Lambda^{-1}(a) + \Lambda^{-1}(b)$	5 : $\mathsf{PopulateSetsO_v}(a, b, from)$
6 : **if** $\Lambda(p) = \bot$ **then**	6 : **return** $(V\Lambda^{-1}(a) = \Lambda^{-1}(b))$
7 : $\Lambda(p) \leftarrow\!\!{\scriptstyle\$}\, \overline{R(\Lambda)}$	
8 : $\mathsf{PopulateSetsEval}(a, b, \Lambda(p), from)$	
9 : **return** $\Lambda(p)$	

Fig. 9. Game $\mathbb{G}_{11}$

Procedure PolyMultCheck(p_a, p_b) :

1 : **if** $\exists j : (\text{coefficient}(p_a, T_j) \neq 0 \vee \text{coefficient}(p_a, VI_j) \neq 0)$ **thenreturn** false

2 : **if** $\exists j : (\text{coefficient}(p_b, T_j) \neq 0 \vee \text{coefficient}(p_b, I_j) \neq 0)$ **thenreturn** false

3 : **if** $\text{coefficient}(p_b, V) \neq \text{coefficient}(p_a, 1)$ **thenreturn** false

4 : **foreach** $j \in [k]$ **do** $\vec{x}[j] \leftarrow \text{coefficient}(p_a, I_j); \vec{y}[j] \leftarrow \text{coefficient}(p_b, VI_j)$

5 : **if** $O(\vec{x}, \vec{y}) = \text{true}$ **then**

6 :   **if** $\vec{x} \notin \text{span}(S)$ **then** $S \overset{\cup}{\leftarrow} \{\vec{x}\}; \mathcal{Z}' \overset{\cup}{\leftarrow} \{a\}$

7 :   **if** $|S| = l$ **then** ABORT

8 :   **return** true

9 : **else return** false

Fig. 10. Subroutine PolyMultCheck for simulating $\mathsf{O_v}$. In particular, $\text{coefficient}(p, M)$ returns the coefficient of the monomial M in the polynomial p. The sets S and $\mathcal{Z}'$ have no effect on the behavior, and are only used in the analysis of $\mathcal{D}$. The symbol ABORT indicates that $\mathcal{D}$ aborts and outputs $\bot$.

from $\mathbb{PG}$. As we will discuss below, the core of the adversary $\mathcal{D}$ will boil down to properly simulating the $\mathsf{O_v}$ oracle using the O oracle from $\mathbb{PG}$ *and* simulating the labels $\sigma(i_{\pi(j)})$ (and the associated polynomials) correctly without knowing π. After a correct simulation, $\mathcal{D}$ will simply extract the permutation π.

Adversary $\mathcal{D}$:

1: **foreach** $p \in \mathbb{Z}_p[I_1, \cdots, I_k, V, K_1, \cdots, K_k, T_1, \cdots, T_{2q}]$ **do** $\Lambda(p) \leftarrow \perp$

2: $\Lambda(1) \leftarrow_\$ \mathcal{L}; \Lambda(V) \leftarrow_\$ \overline{R(\Lambda)}$

3: **foreach** $j \in [k]$ **do**

4: $\quad \Lambda(I_j) \leftarrow_\$ \overline{R(\Lambda)}; \Lambda(K_j) \leftarrow_\$ \overline{R(\Lambda)}$

5: new $\leftarrow 0; \mathcal{X} \leftarrow \{\Lambda(1), \Lambda(V), \Lambda(I_1), \cdots, \Lambda(I_k)\}; \mathcal{Y}_1 \leftarrow \{\Lambda(1), \Lambda(V), \Lambda(I_1), \cdots, \Lambda(I_k)\}$

6: $\phi, s_1, \cdots, s_k \leftarrow \mathcal{R}_1^{\mathsf{Eval}(\cdot,\cdot,1),\mathsf{O}_v(\cdot,\cdot,1)}(\Lambda(1), \Lambda(V), \Lambda(I_1), \cdots, \Lambda(I_k))$

7: $\mathcal{Y}_2 \leftarrow \{\Lambda(1), \Lambda(V), \Lambda(K_1), \cdots, \Lambda(K_k)\}; \mathcal{Z} \leftarrow \varnothing; \mathcal{Z}' \leftarrow \varnothing; S \leftarrow \varnothing$

8: $s'_1, s'_2, \cdots, s'_k \leftarrow \mathcal{R}_2^{\mathsf{Eval}(\cdot,\cdot,2),\mathsf{O}_v(\cdot,\cdot,2)}(\phi, \Lambda(1), \Lambda(V), \Lambda(K_1), \cdots, \Lambda(K_k))$

9: win$' \leftarrow (\{s_1, \cdots, s_l\} = \{s'_1, \cdots, s'_l\}) \wedge (\forall j, l \in [k] : j \neq l \implies s_j \neq s_l \wedge s'_j \neq s'_l)$

10: **if** win$'$ = true **then**

11: $\quad$ **foreach** $i, j \in [k]$ **do if** $s_i = s'_j$ **then** $\pi(i) = j$

12: $\quad$ **return** π

13: **else return** $\perp$

Oracle $\mathsf{Eval}(\mathbf{a}, \mathbf{b}, \text{from})$:

1: **if** $\Lambda^{-1}(\mathbf{a}) = \perp$ **then**

2: $\quad$ new $\leftarrow$ new $+ 1; \Lambda(T_{\text{new}}) \leftarrow \mathbf{a}$

3: **if** $\Lambda^{-1}(\mathbf{b}) = \perp$ **then**

4: $\quad$ new $\leftarrow$ new $+ 1; \Lambda(T_{\text{new}}) \leftarrow \mathbf{b}$

5: $\mathbf{p} \leftarrow \mathbf{p_a} + \mathbf{p_b}$

6: **if** $\Lambda(\mathbf{p}) = \perp$ **then** $\Lambda(\mathbf{p}) \leftarrow_\$ \overline{R(\Lambda)}$

7: PopulateSetsEval$(\mathbf{a}, \mathbf{b}, \Lambda(\mathbf{p}), \text{from})$

8: **return** $\Lambda(\mathbf{p})$

Oracle $\mathsf{O}_v(\mathbf{a}, \mathbf{b}, \text{from})$:

1: **if** $\Lambda^{-1}(\mathbf{a}) = \perp$ **then**

2: $\quad$ new $\leftarrow$ new $+ 1; \Lambda(T_{\text{new}}) \leftarrow \mathbf{a}$

3: **if** $\Lambda^{-1}(\mathbf{b}) = \perp$ **then**

4: $\quad$ new $\leftarrow$ new $+ 1; \Lambda(T_{\text{new}}) \leftarrow \mathbf{b}$

5: PopulateSetsO$_v(\mathbf{a}, \mathbf{b}, \text{from})$

6: PolyMultCheck$(\mathbf{p_a}, \mathbf{p_b})$

Procedure PopulateSetsEval$(\mathbf{a}, \mathbf{b}, \mathbf{c}, \text{from})$:

1: **if** from = 1 **then**

2: $\quad$ **if** $\mathbf{c} \notin \mathcal{Y}_1$ **then** $\mathcal{X} \xleftarrow{\cup} \{\mathbf{c}\}$

3: $\quad \mathcal{Y}_1 \xleftarrow{\cup} \{\mathbf{a}, \mathbf{b}, \mathbf{c}\}$

4: **if** from = 2 **then**

5: $\quad$ **if** $\mathbf{a} \in \mathcal{X} \backslash \mathcal{Y}_2$ **then** $\mathcal{Z} \xleftarrow{\cup} \{\mathbf{a}\}$

6: $\quad$ **if** $\mathbf{b} \in \mathcal{X} \backslash \mathcal{Y}_2$ **then** $\mathcal{Z} \xleftarrow{\cup} \{\mathbf{b}\}$

7: $\quad \mathcal{Y}_2 \xleftarrow{\cup} \{\mathbf{a}, \mathbf{b}, \mathbf{c}\}$

Procedure PopulateSetsO$_v(\mathbf{a}, \mathbf{b}, \text{from})$:

1: **if** from = 1 **then** $\mathcal{Y}_1 \xleftarrow{\cup} \{\mathbf{a}, \mathbf{b}\}$

2: **if** from = 2 **then**

3: $\quad$ **if** $\mathbf{a} \in \mathcal{X} \backslash \mathcal{Y}_2$ **then** $\mathcal{Z} \xleftarrow{\cup} \{\mathbf{a}\}$

4: $\quad$ **if** $\mathbf{b} \in \mathcal{X} \backslash \mathcal{Y}_2$ **then** $\mathcal{Z} \xleftarrow{\cup} \{\mathbf{b}\}$

5: $\quad \mathcal{Y}_2 \xleftarrow{\cup} \{\mathbf{a}, \mathbf{b}\}$

Fig. 11. Adversary $\mathcal{D}$ which plays the permutation game $\mathbb{PG}$. The changes in $\mathcal{D}$ compared to $\mathbb{G}_{11}$ have been highlighted.

To see how this can be done, let us first have a closer look at $\mathbb{G}_{11}$. Let us introduce the shorthand $K_j = VI_{\pi(j)}$ for $j \in [k]$. With this notation, every polynomial input to or output from Eval is a linear combination of the monomials $1, I_1, \ldots, I_k, V, K_1, \ldots, K_k, T_1, T_2, \ldots$. Now, it is convenient to slightly rethink the check of whether $V\mathbf{p_a} = \mathbf{p_b}$ within O_v with this notation. First off, we observe that if either of the polynomial contains a monomial of the form T_i, the check fails. In fact, it is immediately clear that the check can only possibly succeed is if p_a is a linear combination of 1 and the I_j's and p_b is a linear combination of V and the K_j's. Now, assume that

$$p_a(I_1, \ldots, I_k) = a_0 + \sum_{j=1}^{k} \vec{x}[j] \cdot I_j,$$

$$p_b(V, K_1, \ldots K_k) = b_0 \cdot V + \sum_{j=1}^{k} \vec{y}[j] \cdot K_j.$$

Then, $V \cdot p_a = p_b$ if and only if $a_0 = b_0$ and $\vec{y}[j] = \vec{x}[\pi(j)]$ for all $j \in [k]$. If we are now in Game $\mathbb{PG}$, and π is the chosen permutation, then this is equivalent to $O(\vec{x}, \vec{y}) = \text{true}$ and $a_0 = b_0$.

This leads naturally to the adversary $\mathcal{D}$, which we formally describe in Fig. 11. The adversary will simply sample labels $\mathbf{f}_1, \ldots, \mathbf{f}_k$ for $\sigma(v \cdot i_{\pi(1)}), \ldots, \sigma(v \cdot i_{\pi(k)})$, and associate with them polynomials in the variables $K_1, \ldots, K_j$. Other than that, it simulates the game $\mathbb{G}_{11}$, with the exception that the check $V \cdot p_a = p_b$ is not implemented using the above approach – summarized in Fig. 10. Note that $\mathcal{D}$ aborts when $|S| = l$ and makes at most q queries to O. Thus $\mathcal{D}$ is a-query adversary against $\mathbb{PG}$. If $\mathcal{D}$ does not abort, then its simulation of $\mathbb{G}_{11}$ is perfect. If $\mathbb{G}_{11} \Rightarrow \text{true}$ and $\mathcal{D}$ does not abort, then win' shall be true and $\mathcal{D}$ will output the correct π.

The rest of the proof will now require proving that whenever $\mathbb{G}_{11}$ outputs true our adversary $\mathcal{D}$ will never abort due to the check $|S| = l$. Since $\mathbb{G}_{11} \Rightarrow \text{true}$ only if $|\mathcal{Z}| < l$, the following lemma implies that $\mathcal{D}$ does not abort if $\mathbb{G}_{11} \Rightarrow \text{true}$.

Lemma 8. *Let* $(\vec{x}_1, \vec{y}_1), \cdots, (\vec{x}_u, \vec{y}_u)$ *be the queries made by* $\mathcal{D}$ *to* O *which return* true. *Then,*

$$\text{rank}(\vec{x}_1, \cdots, \vec{x}_u) \leqslant |\mathcal{Z}|.$$

The proof of Lemma 8 has been deferred to the full version.

We have established that if $\mathbb{G}_{11}$ outputs true, then $\mathcal{D}$ will not abort and hence $\mathcal{D}$ simulates $\mathbb{G}_{11}$ to $\mathcal{R}_1, \mathcal{R}_2$ perfectly. If win = true in $\mathbb{G}_{11}$, the checks by $\mathcal{D}$ succeed and $\mathcal{D}$ outputs the correct permutation and wins $\mathbb{PG}$. Therefore, $\mathcal{D}$ is a (q, l)-query adversary such that $\mathbb{PG}(\mathcal{D}) \Rightarrow \text{true}$ if $\mathbb{G}_{11} \Rightarrow \text{true}$. Hence,

$$\Pr[\mathbb{G}_{11} \Rightarrow \text{true}] \leqslant \Pr[\mathbb{PG}(\mathcal{D}) \Rightarrow \text{true}]. \tag{5}$$

Combining Lemma 7 and (4), (5) we get,

$$\Pr[\mathbb{G}_2 \Rightarrow \text{true}] \leqslant \Pr[\mathbb{PG}(\mathcal{D}) \Rightarrow \text{true}] + \frac{2q(2k + 3q + 2)}{p} + \frac{5q}{p} + \frac{k^2 + k + 2}{p}. \tag{6}$$

$\square$

Combining (3) and (6), we get,

$$\Pr[\mathbb{G}_2 \Rightarrow \text{true}] \leqslant \frac{q^l}{k!} + \frac{2q(2k + 3q + 2)}{p} + \frac{5q}{p} + \frac{k^2 + k + 2}{p}.$$

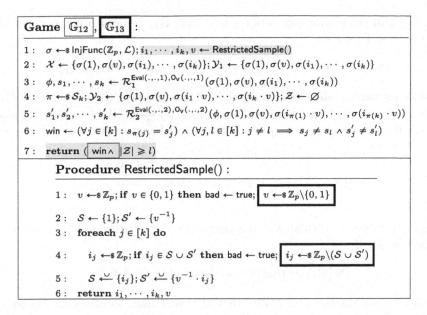

Fig. 12. Games $\mathbb{G}_{12}, \mathbb{G}_{13}$. The Eval, O_v oracles in $\mathbb{G}_{12}, \mathbb{G}_{13}$ are identical to those in $\mathbb{G}_3$ and hence we do not rewrite it here. The statement within the thinner box is present only in $\mathbb{G}_{12}$ and the statement within the thicker box is present only in $\mathbb{G}_{13}$. The newly introduced changes compared to $\mathbb{G}_3$ are highlighted.

4.4 Memory Lower Bound When $|\mathcal{Z}| \geqslant l$ (Proof of Lemma 4)

Recall that we need to prove the following lemma, which we do by using a compression argument.

Lemma 4. *If the size of the state ϕ output by $\mathcal{R}_1$ is s bits and $(\mathcal{R}_1, \mathcal{R}_2)$ make q queries in total in $\mathbb{G}_3$, then*

$$\Pr\left[\mathbb{G}_3 \Rightarrow \mathsf{true}\right] \leqslant 2 \cdot 2^{\frac{s}{2}} \left(\frac{8q^2(2k+2+3q)}{p}\right)^{\frac{l}{2}} \left(1 + \frac{6q}{p}\right)^{\frac{2q-l}{2}} + \frac{k^2+k+2}{p} .$$

Proof. Our proof does initial game hopping, with easy transitions. It first introduces a new game, $\mathbb{G}_{12}$ (Fig. 12) whose minor difference from game $\mathbb{G}_3$ is that it samples $i_1, \cdots, i_k, v$ using RestrictedSample which was previously used in game $\mathbb{G}_{11}$. It adds a bad flag while sampling $i_1, \cdots, i_k, v$ which is set to true if v is in $\{0, 1\}$ or if $|1, v, i_1, \cdots, i_k, i_1 \cdot v, \cdots, i_k \cdot v| < 2k + 2$. The bad event does not affect the output of $\mathbb{G}_{12}$ in any way. Observe that even though the sampling of $i_1, \cdots, i_k, v$ is written in a different manner in $\mathbb{G}_{12}$, it is identical to that in $\mathbb{G}_3$. In all other respects these two games are identical.

$$\Pr\left[\mathbb{G}_3 \Rightarrow \mathsf{true}\right] = \Pr\left[\mathbb{G}_{12} \Rightarrow \mathsf{true}\right]. \tag{7}$$

Games $\mathbb{G}_{12}, \mathbb{G}_{13}$ differ in the procedure RestrictedSample and the condition to return true. Note that the conditions of bad being set to true is identical in

$\mathbb{G}_{12}, \mathbb{G}_{13}$ and given that bad is not set to true, $\mathbb{G}_{13}$ returns true whenever $\mathbb{G}_{12}$ returns true. Therefore,

$$\Pr\left[\mathbb{G}_{12} \Rightarrow \text{true}\right] \leqslant \Pr\left[\mathbb{G}_{13} \Rightarrow \text{true}\right] + \Pr\left[\text{bad} = \text{true in } \mathbb{G}_{13}\right] .$$

It is not hard to show (details in the full version) that the probability of bad being set to true in RestrictedSample is at most $\frac{k^2+k+2}{p}$. Since in $\mathbb{G}_{13}$ bad is set only in RestrictedSample, the probability of bad being set to true is the same. Hence, we get,

$$\Pr\left[\mathbb{G}_{12} \Rightarrow \text{true}\right] \leqslant \Pr\left[\mathbb{G}_{13} \Rightarrow \text{true}\right] + \frac{k^2 + k + 2}{p} . \tag{8}$$

THE COMPRESSION ARGUMENT. We assume $\Pr\left[\mathbb{G}_{13} \Rightarrow \text{true}\right] = 2\epsilon$. We say a σ is "good" in $\mathbb{G}_{13}$ if

$$\Pr\left[\mathbb{G}_{13} \Rightarrow \text{true} \mid \sigma \text{ was sampled in } \mathbb{G}_{13}\right] \geqslant \epsilon.$$

It follows from Markov's inequality that at least ϵ fraction of σ's are "good".

The following lemma captures the essence of our compression argument.

Lemma 9. *If the state output by $\mathcal{R}_1$ has size s bits, all the "good" σ's can be encoded in an encoding space of size at most*

$$2^s p! \left(1 + \frac{6q}{p}\right)^{(2q-l)} \left(\frac{p}{8q^2(2k+2+3q)}\right)^{-l} ,$$

and decoded correctly with probability ϵ.

We next give some intuition regarding how we achieve compression and defer the formal proof of Lemma 9 to the full version.

INTUITION REGARDING COMPRESSION. Observe in $\mathbb{G}_{13}$, the labels in $\mathcal{Z}$ were queried by $\mathcal{R}_2$ (these labels were not seen by $\mathcal{R}_2$ before they were queried) and were answers to $\mathcal{R}_1$ and were not seen by $\mathcal{R}_1$ before the query. The core idea is that for all $\mathbf{a} \in \mathcal{L} \setminus \mathcal{Z}$, we store exactly one of $\mathbf{a}$ or its pre-image in the encoding and for all labels in $\mathcal{Z}$, we store neither the label nor its pre-image. Since $\mathcal{R}_2$ queries all the labels in $\mathcal{Z}$, these labels can be found by running $\mathcal{R}_2$ while decoding. Since all the labels in $\mathcal{Z}$ are answers to queries of $\mathcal{R}_1$ and were not seen by $\mathcal{R}_1$ before the query, their pre-images can be figured out while running $\mathcal{R}_1$.

HIGH LEVEL OUTLINES OF Encode, Decode. In Encode, we simulate the steps of $\mathbb{G}_{13}$ to $\mathcal{R}_1, \mathcal{R}_2$, including bookkeeping and then run $\mathcal{R}_1$ again assuming the particular σ we are compressing is sampled in $\mathbb{G}_{13}$. In Decode, we run $\mathcal{R}_2$ and then $\mathcal{R}_1$ to recover σ. We treat the values $i_1, \cdots, i_k, v, \pi$ as part of the common randomness provided to Encode, Decode (we assume they are sampled from the same distribution they are sampled from in $\mathbb{G}_{13}$). The random tapes of $\mathcal{R}_1, \mathcal{R}_2$

can also be derived from the common randomness of Encode, Decode. For simplicity, we do not specify this explicitly in the algorithms and treat $\mathcal{R}_1, \mathcal{R}_2$ as deterministic.

RUNNING $\mathcal{R}_2$. First off, we assume that $\mathcal{R}_1$ queries labels that it has "seen" before and $\mathcal{R}_2$ queries labels that $\mathcal{R}_1$ has "seen" or it has "seen" before. We shall relax this assumption later. Ideally, we would want to just store only ϕ, the inputs labels to $\mathcal{R}_2$ and the labels that are answers to $\mathcal{R}_2$'s queries. We append the input labels of $\mathcal{R}_2$ and labels that are answers to its Eval queries that it has not "seen" before to a list named Labels. However, it is easy to see that this information is not enough to answer O_v queries during decoding, as answering O_v queries inherently requires knowledge about pre-images of $\mathcal{R}_2$. This naturally leads to the idea of maintaining a mapping of all the labels "seen by" $\mathcal{R}_2$ to their pre-images.

THE MAPPING T OF LABELS TO PRE-IMAGE EXPRESSIONS. The pre-images of input labels and the labels that were results of sequence of Eval queries on its input labels by $\mathcal{R}_2$, are known. However, $\mathcal{R}_2$ might query labels which were neither an input to it nor an answer to one of its Eval queries. Such a label is in $\mathcal{Z}$ since we have assumed that all labels queried by $\mathcal{R}_2$ were "seen by" $\mathcal{R}_1$ or "seen by" $\mathcal{R}_2$ before. We represent the pre-images of labels in $\mathcal{Z}$ using a placeholder variable X_n where n is incremented for every such label. Note that the pre-image of every label seen by $\mathcal{R}_2$ can be expressed as a linear polynomial in the X_n's (these linear polynomials are referred to as pre-image expressions from hereon). Therefore we maintain a mapping of all labels "seen by" and their pre-image expressions in a list of tuples named T. Our approach is inspired by a similar technique used by Corrigan-Gibbs and Kogan in [5]. Like in [5], we *stress* that the mapping T is not a part of the encoding.

For Eval queries, we can check if there is a tuple in T whose pre-image expression is the sum of the pre-image expressions of the input labels. If that is the case, we return the label of such a tuple. Otherwise, we append the answer label to Labels. For O_v queries, we can return true if the pre-image expression of the first input label multiplied by v gives the pre-image expression of the second input label. Otherwise we return false.

SURPRISES. There is a caveat, however. There might arise a situation that the label which is the answer to the Eval query is present in T but its pre-image expression is not the sum of the pre-image expressions of the input labels. We call such a situation a "surprise" and we call the answer label in that case a "surprise label". For O_v queries, there might be a surprise when the answer of the O_v query is true but the pre-image expression of the first input label multiplied by v is different pre-image expression of the second input label. In this case we call the second input label the surprise label. We assign a sequence number to each query made by $\mathcal{R}_2$, starting from 1 and an index to each tuple in T, with the indices being assigned to tuples in the order they were appended to T. To detect the query where the surprise happens, we maintain a set named Srps_1 that contains tuples of query sequence numbers and indices of the surprise label in T. This set Srps_1 is a part of the encoding. Note that whenever there is a surprise, it means that two different pre-image expressions evaluate to the same value. Since these two pre-image expressions are linear polynomials, at least one variable can be eliminated from T by equating the two pre-image expressions.

RUNNING $\mathcal{R}_1$. Now that we have enough information in the encoding to run $\mathcal{R}_2$, we consider the information we need to add to the encoding to run $\mathcal{R}_1$ after $\mathcal{R}_2$ is run. First, we need to provide $\mathcal{R}_1$ its input labels. Our initial attempt would be to append the input labels of $\mathcal{R}_1$ (except $\sigma(1), \sigma(v)$, which are already present) to Labels. However, some of these input labels to $\mathcal{R}_1$ might have already been "seen by" $\mathcal{R}_2$. Since all labels "seen by" $\mathcal{R}_2$ are in T, we need a way to figure out which of $\sigma(i_j)$'s are in T. Note that such a label was either queried by $\mathcal{R}_2$ or an answer to a query of $\mathcal{R}_2$ (cannot have been an input to $\mathcal{R}_2$ given the restrictions on $i_1, \cdots, i_k, v$). Suppose q was the sequence number of the query in which $\sigma(i_j)$ was queried or an answer. The tuple (q, b, j) is added to the set Inputs where b can take values $\{1, 2, 3\}$ depending on whether $\sigma(i_j)$ was the first input label, the second input label or the answer label respectively. This set Inputs is a part of the encoding. The rest of the labels $\sigma(i_j)$, which do not appear in T, are added to T with their pre-images and the labels are appended to Labels. Note that for all queries of $\mathcal{R}_1$, it follows from our assumption that the input labels will be in T. For every surprise, we add a tuple of sequence number and an index in T to the set Srps_2.

RELAXING THE ASSUMPTION. When we allow $\mathcal{R}_2$ to query labels it has not seen before or $\mathcal{R}_1$ has not seen, there are two issues. First, we need to add a tuple for the label in T (since T, by definition contains a tuple for all labels queried by $\mathcal{R}_2$). We solve this issue by adding the tuple made of the label and its pre-image. We have no hope of recovering the pre-image later, hence, we append the pre-image to a list named Vals. This list needs to be a part of the encoding since the pre-image of the label needs to be figured out to be added to T during decoding. For queries of $\mathcal{R}_1$, if the input label is not present in T, we do the same thing. The second issue that comes up when we relax the assumption is that we need to distinguish whether an input label was in $\mathcal{Z}$ or not. We solve this issue by maintaining a set of tuples named Free. For all labels in $\mathcal{Z}$ that are not an input label to $\mathcal{R}_1$, we add the tuple consisting of the sequence number of the query of $\mathcal{R}_2$ and b to Free where b set to 1 indicates it was the first input label and b set to 2 indicates it was the second input label.

THE FINAL STEPS. The labels the are absent in T are appended to a list named RLabels. If $|\mathcal{Z}| < l$, a fixed encoding D (the output of Encode for some fixed σ when $|\mathcal{Z}| \geqslant l$) is returned. Otherwise the encoding of σ consisting of Labels, RLabels, Vals, Inputs, Srps_1, Srps_2, Free, ϕ is returned.

WRAPPING UP. The set of all "good" σ's has size at least $\epsilon p!$ (where we have used that the total number of injective functions from $\mathbb{Z}_p \to \mathcal{L}$ is $p!$). Using $\mathcal{X}$ to be the set of the "good" σ's, $\mathcal{Y}$ to be the set of encodings, $\mathcal{R}$ to be the set of cartesian product of the domains of $i_1, \cdots, i_k, v, \pi$, the set of all random tapes of $\mathcal{R}_1$ the set of all random tapes of $\mathcal{R}_2$ and $\mathcal{L}$, it follows from Lemma 9 and

Proposition 1 that

$$\log\left(\Pr\left[\text{Decoding is correct}\right]\right) \leqslant s + (2q - l)\log\left(1 + \frac{6q}{p}\right)$$
$$- l\log\left(\frac{p}{8q^2(2k + 2 + 3q)}\right) - \log\epsilon .$$

We have from Lemma 9 that $\Pr\left[\text{Decoding is correct}\right] \leqslant \epsilon$. Therefore,

$$2\log\epsilon \leqslant s + (2q - l)\log\left(1 + \frac{6q}{p}\right) - l\log\left(\frac{p}{8q^2(2k + 2 + 3q)}\right).$$

Since $\Pr\left[\mathbb{G}_{13}\right] = 2\epsilon$, using (7) and (8) we have,

$$\Pr\left[\mathbb{G}_3 \Rightarrow \text{true}\right] \leqslant 2 \cdot 2^{\frac{s}{2}}\left(\frac{8q^2(2k + 2 + 3q)}{p}\right)^{\frac{l}{2}}\left(1 + \frac{6q}{p}\right)^{\frac{2q-l}{2}} + \frac{k^2 + k + 2}{p}.$$

$\square$

5 Conclusions

Despite a clear restriction of our result to straightline reductions, we believe the main contribution of this work is the introduction of novel techniques for proving lower bounds on the memory of reductions that will find wider applicability. In particular, we clearly departed from the framework of prior works [2,13] tailored at the usage of lower bounds for streaming algorithms, and provided the first lower bound for "algebraic" proofs in the public-key domain. The idea of a problem-specific proof of memory could be helpful elsewhere.

Of course, there are several open problems. It seems very hard to study the role of rewinding for such reductions. In particular, the natural approach is to resort to techniques from communication complexity (and their incarnation as streaming lower bounds), as they are amenable to the multi-pass case. The simple combinatorial nature of these lower bounds however is at odds with the heavily structured oracles we encounter in the generic group model. Another problem we failed to solve is to give an adversary $\mathcal{A}$ in our proof which uses little memory – we discuss a candidate in the body, but analyzing it seems to give us difficulties similar to those of rewinding.

This latter point makes a clear distinction, not discussed by prior works, between the *way* in which we prove memory-tightness (via reductions using small memory), and its most general interpretation, as defined in [2], which would allow the reduction to adapt its memory usage to that of $\mathcal{A}$.

Acknowledgements. We thank the anonymous reviewers of EUROCRYPT 2020 for helpful comments. This work was partially supported by NSF grants CNS-1553758 (CAREER), CNS-1719146, and by a Sloan Research Fellowship.

References

1. Abdalla, M., Bellare, M., Rogaway, P.: The Oracle Diffie-Hellman assumptions and an analysis of DHIES. In: Naccache, D. (ed.) CT-RSA 2001. LNCS, vol. 2020, pp. 143–158. Springer, Heidelberg (2001). https://doi.org/10.1007/3-540-45353-9_12
2. Auerbach, B., Cash, D., Fersch, M., Kiltz, E.: Memory-tight reductions. In: Katz, J., Shacham, H. (eds.) CRYPTO 2017. LNCS, vol. 10401, pp. 101–132. Springer, Cham (2017). https://doi.org/10.1007/978-3-319-63688-7_4
3. Bellare, M., Rogaway, P.: The security of triple encryption and a framework for code-based game-playing proofs. In: Vaudenay, S. (ed.) EUROCRYPT 2006. LNCS, vol. 4004, pp. 409–426. Springer, Heidelberg (2006). https://doi.org/10.1007/11761679_25
4. Bhattacharyya, R.: Memory-tight reductions for practical key encapsulation mechanisms. In: PKC (2020)
5. Corrigan-Gibbs, H., Kogan, D.: The discrete-logarithm problem with preprocessing. In: Nielsen, J.B., Rijmen, V. (eds.) EUROCRYPT 2018, Part II. LNCS, vol. 10821, pp. 415–447. Springer, Cham (2018). https://doi.org/10.1007/978-3-319-78375-8_14
6. Cramer, R., Shoup, V.: Design and analysis of practical public-key encryption schemes secure against adaptive chosen ciphertext attack. SIAM J. Comput. **33**(1), 167–226 (2003)
7. De, A., Trevisan, L., Tulsiani, M.: Time space tradeoffs for attacks against one-way functions and PRGs. In: Rabin, T. (ed.) CRYPTO 2010. LNCS, vol. 6223, pp. 649–665. Springer, Heidelberg (2010). https://doi.org/10.1007/978-3-642-14623-7_35
8. Fuchsbauer, G., Kiltz, E., Loss, J.: The algebraic group model and its applications. In: Shacham, H., Boldyreva, A. (eds.) CRYPTO 2018, Part II. LNCS, vol. 10992, pp. 33–62. Springer, Cham (2018). https://doi.org/10.1007/978-3-319-96881-0_2
9. Maurer, U.: Abstract models of computation in cryptography. In: Smart, N.P. (ed.) Cryptography and Coding 2005. LNCS, vol. 3796, pp. 1–12. Springer, Heidelberg (2005). https://doi.org/10.1007/11586821_1
10. Reingold, O., Trevisan, L., Vadhan, S.: Notions of reducibility between cryptographic primitives. In: Naor, M. (ed.) TCC 2004. LNCS, vol. 2951, pp. 1–20. Springer, Heidelberg (2004). https://doi.org/10.1007/978-3-540-24638-1_1
11. Shoup, V.: Lower bounds for discrete logarithms and related problems. In: Fumy, W. (ed.) EUROCRYPT 1997. LNCS, vol. 1233, pp. 256–266. Springer, Heidelberg (1997). https://doi.org/10.1007/3-540-69053-0_18
12. Shoup, V.: A proposal for an ISO standard for public key encryption. Cryptology ePrint Archive, Report 2001/112 (2001). http://eprint.iacr.org/2001/112
13. Wang, Y., Matsuda, T., Hanaoka, G., Tanaka, K.: Memory lower bounds of reductions revisited. In: Nielsen, J.B., Rijmen, V. (eds.) EUROCRYPT 2018, Part I. LNCS, vol. 10820, pp. 61–90. Springer, Cham (2018). https://doi.org/10.1007/978-3-319-78381-9_3

Blind Schnorr Signatures and Signed ElGamal Encryption in the Algebraic Group Model

Georg Fuchsbauer[1(✉)], Antoine Plouviez[2,3(✉)], and Yannick Seurin[4]

[1] TU Wien, Vienna, Austria
georg.fuchsbauer@tuwien.ac.at
[2] Inria, Paris, France
[3] ENS, CNRS, PSL, Paris, France
antoine.plouviez@ens.fr
[4] ANSSI, Paris, France
yannick.seurin@m4x.org

Abstract. The Schnorr blind signing protocol allows blind issuing of Schnorr signatures, one of the most widely used signatures. Despite its practical relevance, its security analysis is unsatisfactory. The only known security proof is informal and in the combination of the generic group model (GGM) and the random oracle model (ROM) assuming that the "ROS problem" is hard. The situation is similar for (Schnorr-)signed ElGamal encryption, a simple CCA2-secure variant of ElGamal.

We analyze the security of these schemes in the algebraic group model (AGM), an idealized model closer to the standard model than the GGM. We first prove tight security of Schnorr signatures from the discrete logarithm assumption (DL) in the AGM+ROM. We then give a rigorous proof for blind Schnorr signatures in the AGM+ROM assuming hardness of the one-more discrete logarithm problem and ROS.

As ROS can be solved in sub-exponential time using Wagner's algorithm, we propose a simple modification of the signing protocol, which leaves the signatures unchanged. It is therefore compatible with systems that already use Schnorr signatures, such as blockchain protocols. We show that the security of our modified scheme relies on the hardness of a problem related to ROS that appears much harder. Finally, we give tight reductions, again in the AGM+ROM, of the CCA2 security of signed ElGamal encryption to DDH and signed hashed ElGamal key encapsulation to DL.

Keywords: Schnorr signatures · Blind signatures · Algebraic group model · ElGamal encryption · Blockchain protocols

1 Introduction

SCHNORR SIGNATURES. The Schnorr signature scheme [Sch90, Sch91] is one of the oldest and simplest signature schemes based on prime-order groups. Its adoption was hindered for years by a patent which expired in February 2008, but it

© International Association for Cryptologic Research 2020
A. Canteaut and Y. Ishai (Eds.): EUROCRYPT 2020, LNCS 12106, pp. 63–95, 2020.
https://doi.org/10.1007/978-3-030-45724-2_3

is by now widely deployed: EdDSA [BDL+12], a specific instantiation based on twisted Edward curves, is used for example in OpenSSL, OpenSSH, GnuPG and more. Schnorr signatures are also expected to be implemented in Bitcoin [Wui18], enabling multi-signatures supporting public key aggregation, which will result in considerable scalability and privacy enhancements [BDN18, MPSW19].

The security of the Schnorr signature scheme has been analyzed in the random oracle model (ROM) [BR93], an idealized model which replaces cryptographic hash functions by truly random functions. Pointcheval and Stern [PS96b, PS00] proved Schnorr signatures secure in the ROM under the discrete logarithm assumption (DL). The proof, based on the so-called Forking Lemma, proceeds by rewinding the adversary, which results in a loose reduction (the success probability of the DL solver is a factor q_h smaller than that of the adversary, where q_h is the number of the adversary's random oracle queries). Using the "meta reduction" technique, a series of works showed that this security loss is unavoidable when the used reductions are either algebraic [PV05, GBL08, Seu12] or generic [FJS19]. Although the security of Schnorr signatures is well understood (in the ROM), the same cannot be said for two related schemes, namely blind Schnorr signatures and Schnorr-signed ElGamal encryption.

BLIND SCHNORR SIGNATURES. A blind signature scheme allows a user to obtain a signature from a signer on a message m in such a way that (i) the signer is unable to recognize the signature later (*blindness*, which in particular implies that m remains hidden from the signer) and (ii) the user can compute one single signature per interaction with the signer (*one-more unforgeability*). Blind signature schemes were introduced by Chaum [Cha82] and are a fundamental building block for applications that guarantee user anonymity, e.g. e-cash [Cha82, CFN90, OO92, CHL05, FPV09], e-voting [FOO93], direct anonymous attestation [BCC04], and anonymous credentials [Bra94, CL01, BCC+09, BL13a, Fuc11].

Constructions of blind signature schemes range from very practical schemes based on specific assumptions and usually provably secure in the ROM [PS96a, PS00, Abe01, Bol03, FHS15, HKL19] to theoretical schemes provably secure in the standard model from generic assumptions [GRS+11, BFPV13, GG14].

The blind Schnorr signature scheme derives quite naturally from the Schnorr signature scheme [CP93]. It is one of the most efficient blind signature schemes and increasingly used in practice. Anticipating the implementation of Schnorr signatures in Bitcoin, developers are already actively exploring the use of blind Schnorr signatures for *blind* coin swaps, trustless tumbler services, and more [Nic19].

While the hardness of computing discrete logarithms in the underlying group $\mathbb{G}$ is obviously necessary for the scheme to be unforgeable, Schnorr [Sch01] showed that another problem that he named ROS, which only depends on the order p of the group $\mathbb{G}$, must also be hard for the scheme to be secure. Informally, the ROS_ℓ problem, parameterized by an integer ℓ, asks to find $\ell + 1$ vectors $\vec{\rho}_i = (\rho_{i,j})_{j \in [\ell]}$ such that the system of $\ell + 1$ linear equations in unknowns $c_1, \ldots, c_\ell$ over $\mathbb{Z}_p$

$$\sum_{j=1}^{\ell} \rho_{i,j} c_j = \mathsf{H}_{\mathrm{ros}}(\vec{\rho}_i), \quad i \in [\ell + 1]$$

has a solution, where $H_{ros} \colon (\mathbb{Z}_p)^\ell \to \mathbb{Z}_p$ is a random oracle. Schnorr showed that an attacker able to solve the ROS_ℓ problem can produce $\ell + 1$ valid signatures while interacting (concurrently) only ℓ times with the signer. Slightly later, Wagner [Wag02] showed that the ROS_ℓ problem can be reduced to the $(\ell + 1)$-sum problem, which can solved with time and space complexity $O\big((\ell+1)2^{\lambda/(1+\lfloor \lg(\ell+1) \rfloor)}\big)$, where λ is the bit size of p. For example, for $\lambda = 256$, this attack yields 16 valid signatures after $\ell = 15$ interactions with the signer in time and space close to 2^{55}. For $\ell + 1 = 2^{\sqrt{\lambda}}$, the attack has sub-exponential time and space complexity $O(2^{2\sqrt{\lambda}})$, although the number of signing sessions becomes arguably impractical. Asymptotically, this attack can be thwarted by increasing the group order, but this would make the scheme quite inefficient.

From a provable-security point of view, a number of results [FS10, Pas11, BL13b] indicate that blind Schnorr signatures cannot be proven one-more unforgeable under standard assumptions, not even in the ROM. The only positive result by Schnorr and Jakobsson [SJ99] and Schnorr [Sch01] states that blind Schnorr signatures are secure in the combination of the generic group model and the ROM assuming hardness of the ROS problem.

The recent analysis by Hauck, Kiltz, and Loss [HKL19] of blind signatures derived from linear identification schemes does not apply to Schnorr. The reason is that the underlying linear function family $F \colon \mathbb{Z}_p \to \mathbb{G}, x \mapsto xG$ lacks the property of having a pseudo torsion-free element from the kernel (see [HKL19, Def. 3.1]). In particular, F is one-to-one, whereas Hauck et al. reduce blind signature unforgeability to collision resistance of the underlying function family.

THE ALGEBRAIC GROUP MODEL. The *generic group model* (GGM) [Nec94, Sho97] is an idealized model for the security analysis of cryptosystems defined over cyclic groups. Instead of receiving concrete group elements, the adversary only gets "handles" for them and has access to an oracle that performs the group operation (denoted additively) on handles. This implies that if the adversary is given a list of (handles of) group elements $(X_1, \ldots, X_n)$ and later returns (a handle of) a group element Z, then by inspecting its oracle calls one can derive a "representation" $\vec{z} = (z_1, \ldots, z_n)$ such that $Z = \sum_{i=1}^{n} z_i X_i$.

Fuchsbauer, Kiltz, and Loss [FKL18] introduced the *algebraic group model* (AGM), a model that lies between the standard model and the GGM. On the one hand, the adversary has direct access to group elements; on the other hand, it is assumed to only produce new group elements by applying the group operation to received group elements. In particular, with every group element Z that it outputs, the adversary also gives a representation $\vec{z}$ of Z in terms of the group elements it has received so far. While the GGM allows for proving information-theoretic guarantees, security results in the AGM are proved via reductions to computationally hard problems, like in the standard model.

Our starting point is the observation that in the combination[1] AGM+ROM Schnorr signatures have a *tight* security proof under the DL assumption. This is because we can give a reduction which works *straight-line*, i.e., unlike the forking-

---

[1] This combination was already considered when the AGM was first defined [FKL18].

lemma-based reduction [PS96b, PS00], which must rewind the adversary, it runs the adversary only once.[2] Motivated by this, we then turn to blind Schnorr signatures, whose security in the ROM remains elusive, and study their security in the AGM+ROM.

OUR RESULTS ON BLIND SCHNORR SIGNATURES. Our first contribution is a rigorous analysis of the security of blind Schnorr signatures in the AGM+ROM. Concretely, we show that any algebraic adversary successfully producing $\ell + 1$ forgeries after at most ℓ interactions with the signer must either solve the one-more discrete logarithm (OMDL) problem or the ROS_ℓ problem. Although this is not overly surprising in view of the previous results in the GGM [SJ99, Sch01], this gives a more satisfying characterization of the security of this protocol. Moreover, all previous proofs [SJ99, Sch01] were rather informal; in particular, the reduction solving ROS was not explicitly described. In contrast, we provide precise definitions (in particular for the ROS problem, whose exact specification is central for a security proof) and work out the details of the reductions to both OMDL and ROS, which yields the first rigorous proof.

Nevertheless, the serious threat by Wagner's attack for standard-size group orders remains. In order to remedy this situation, we propose a simple modification of the scheme which only alters the signing protocol (key generation and signature verification remain the same) and thwarts (in a well-defined way) any attempt at breaking the scheme by solving the ROS problem. The idea is that the signer and the user engage in two parallel signing sessions, of which the signer only finishes one (chosen at random) in the last round. Running this tweak takes thus around twice the time of the original protocol. We show that an algebraic adversary successfully mounting an $(\ell + 1)$-forgery attack against this scheme must either solve the OMDL problem or a *modified* ROS problem, which appears much harder than the standard ROS problem for large values of ℓ, which is precisely when the standard ROS problem becomes tractable.

Our results are especially relevant to applications that impose the signature scheme and for which one then has to design a blind signing protocol. This is the case for blockchain-based systems where modifying the signature scheme used for authorizing transactions is a heavy process that can take years (if possible at all). We see a major motivation for studying blind Schnorr signatures in its real-world relevance for protocols that use Schnorr signatures or will in the near future, such as Bitcoin. For these applications, Wagner's attack represents a significant risk, which can be thwarted by using our modified signing protocol.

CHOSEN-CIPHERTEXT-SECURE ELGAMAL ENCRYPTION. Recall the ElGamal public-key encryption (PKE) scheme [ElG85]: given a cyclic group $(\mathbb{G}, +)$ of prime order p and a generator G, a secret/public key pair is of the form $(y, yG) \in \mathbb{Z}_p \times \mathbb{G}$. A message $M \in \mathbb{G}$ is encrypted as $(X := xG, M + xY)$

---

[2] A similar result [ABM15] shows that Schnorr signatures, when viewed as non-interactive proofs of knowledge of the discrete logarithm of the public key, are simulation-sound extractable, via a straight-line extractor. Our proof is much simpler and gives a concrete security statement.

for a random $x \leftarrow_\$ \mathbb{Z}_p$. This scheme is IND-CPA-secure under the decisional Diffie-Hellman (DDH) assumption [TY98], that is, no adversary can distinguish encryptions of two messages. Since the scheme is homomorphic, it cannot achieve IND-CCA2 security, where the adversary can query decryptions of any ciphertext (except of the one it must distinguish). However, ElGamal has been shown to be IND-CCA1-secure (where no decryption queries can be made after receiving the challenge ciphertext) in the AGM under a "q-type" variant of DDH [FKL18].[3]

A natural way to make ElGamal encryption IND-CCA2-secure is to add a proof of knowledge of the randomness x used to encrypt. (Intuitively, this would make the scheme *plaintext-aware* [BR95].) The reduction of IND-CCA2 security can then extract x to answer decryption queries. Since x together with the first part X of the ciphertext form a Schnorr key pair, a natural idea is to use a Schnorr signature [Jak98, TY98], resulting in (Schnorr-)signed ElGamal encryption. This scheme has a number of attractive properties: ciphertext validity can be checked without knowledge of the decryption key, and one can work homomorphically with the "core" ElGamal ciphertext (a property sometimes called "submission-security" [Wik08]), which is very useful in e-voting.

Since Schnorr signatures are extractable in the ROM, one would expect that signed ElGamal can be proved IND-CCA2 under, say, the DDH assumption (in the ROM). However, turning this intuition into a formal proof has remained elusive. The main obstacle is that Schnorr signatures are not *straight-line* extractable in the ROM [BNW17]. As explained by Shoup and Gennaro [SG02], the adversary could order its random-oracle and decryption queries in a way that makes the reduction take exponential time to simulate the decryption oracle.

Schnorr and Jakobsson [SJ00] showed IND-CCA2 security in the GGM+ROM, while Tsiounis and Yung [TY98] gave a proof under a non-standard "knowledge assumption", which amounts to assuming that Schnorr signatures are straight-line extractable. On the other hand, impossibility results tend to indicate that IND-CCA2 security cannot be proved in the ROM [ST13, BFW16].

OUR RESULTS ON SIGNED ELGAMAL ENCRYPTION. Our second line of contributions is twofold. First, we prove (via a tight reduction) that in the AGM+ROM, Schnorr-signed ElGamal encryption is IND-CCA2-secure under the DDH assumption. While intuitively this should follow naturally from the straight-line extractability of Schnorr proofs of knowledge for algebraic adversaries, the formal proof is technically quite delicate: since messages are group elements, the "basis" of group-element inputs in terms of which the adversary

---

[3] [FKL18] showed IND-CCA1 security for the corresponding key-encapsulation mechanism, which returns a key $K = xY$ and an encapsulation $X = xG$. The ElGamal PKE scheme is obtained by combining it with the one-time-secure DEM $M \mapsto M + K$. Generic results on hybrid schemes [HHK10] imply IND-CCA1 security of the PKE.

provides representations contains not only the three group elements of the challenge ciphertext but also grows as the adversary queries the decryption oracle.[4]

We finally consider the "hashed" variant of ElGamal (also known as DHIES) [ABR01], in which a key is derived as $k = H(xY)$. In the ROM, the corresponding key-encapsulation mechanism (KEM) is IND-CCA2-secure under the strong Diffie-Hellman assumption (i.e., CDH is hard even when given a DDH oracle) [CS03]. We propose to combine the two approaches: concretely, we consider the hashed ElGamal KEM together with a Schnorr signature proving knowledge of the randomness used for encapsulating the key and give a *tight* reduction of the IND-CCA2 security of this scheme to the DL problem in the AGM+ROM.

2   Preliminaries

GENERAL NOTATION. We denote the (closed) integer interval from a to b by $[a, b]$ and let $[b] := [1, b]$. A function $\mu \colon \mathbb{N} \to [0, 1]$ is *negligible* (denoted $\mu = \mathsf{negl}$) if $\forall c \in \mathbb{N} \; \exists \lambda_c \in \mathbb{N} \; \forall \lambda \geq \lambda_c : \mu(\lambda) \leq \lambda^{-c}$. A function ν is *overwhelming* if $1 - \nu = \mathsf{negl}$. The logarithm in base 2 is denoted $\lg$ and $x \equiv_p y$ denotes $x \equiv y \pmod{p}$. For a non-empty finite set S, sampling an element x from S uniformly at random is denoted $x \leftarrow_\$ S$. All algorithms are probabilistic unless stated otherwise. By $y \leftarrow \mathcal{A}(x_1, \ldots, x_n)$ we denote running algorithm $\mathcal{A}$ on inputs $(x_1, \ldots, x_n)$ and uniformly random coins and assigning the output to y. If $\mathcal{A}$ has oracle access to some algorithm ORACLE, we write $y \leftarrow \mathcal{A}^{\mathrm{ORACLE}}(x_1, \ldots, x_n)$. A list $\vec{z} = (z_1, \ldots, z_n)$, also denoted $(z_i)_{i \in [n]}$, is a finite sequence. The length of a list $\vec{z}$ is denoted $|\vec{z}|$. The empty list is denoted $(\,)$.

A *security game* GAME_{par} (see e.g. in Fig. 1) indexed by a set of parameters *par* consists of a main and oracle procedures. The main procedure has input the security parameter λ and runs an adversary $\mathcal{A}$, which interacts with the game by calling the provided oracles. When the adversary stops, the game computes its output b, which we write $b \leftarrow \mathrm{GAME}_{par}^{\mathcal{A}}(\lambda)$. For truth values we identify **false** with 0 and **true** with 1. Games are either computational or decisional. The *advantage* of $\mathcal{A}$ in GAME_{par} is defined as $\mathsf{Adv}_{par,\mathcal{A}}^{\mathrm{game}}(\lambda) := \Pr[1 \leftarrow \mathrm{GAME}_{par}^{\mathcal{A}}(\lambda)]$ if the game is computational and as $\mathsf{Adv}_{par,\mathcal{A}}^{\mathrm{game}}(\lambda) := 2 \cdot \Pr[1 \leftarrow \mathrm{GAME}_{par}^{\mathcal{A}}(\lambda)] - 1$ if it is decisional, where the probability is taken over the random coins of the game and the adversary. We say that GAME_{par} is *hard* if $\mathsf{Adv}_{par,\mathcal{A}}^{\mathrm{game}}(\lambda) = \mathsf{negl}(\lambda)$ for any probabilistic polynomial-time (p.p.t.) adversary $\mathcal{A}$.

ALGEBRAIC ALGORITHMS. A *group description* is a tuple $\Gamma = (p, \mathbb{G}, G)$ where p is an odd prime, $\mathbb{G}$ is an abelian group of order p, and G is a generator of $\mathbb{G}$. We will use additive notation for the group law throughout this paper, and denote group elements (including the generator G) with italic uppercase letters. We assume the existence of a p.p.t. algorithm GrGen which, on input the security

---

[4] Bernhard et al. [BFW16] hastily concluded that, in the AGM+ROM, IND-CCA2-security of signed ElGamal followed from straight-line extractability of Schnorr signatures showed in [ABM15]. Our detailed proof shows that this was a bit optimistic.

parameter 1^λ in unary, outputs a group description $\Gamma = (p, \mathbb{G}, G)$ where p is of bit-length λ. Given an element $X \in \mathbb{G}$, we let $\log_G(X)$ denote the discrete logarithm of X in base G, i.e., the unique $x \in \mathbb{Z}_p$ such that $X = xG$. We write $\log X$ when G is clear from context.

An *algebraic security game* (w.r.t. GrGen) is a game $\text{GAME}_{\text{GrGen}}$ that (among other things) runs $\Gamma \leftarrow \text{GrGen}(1^\lambda)$ and runs the adversary on input $\Gamma = (p, \mathbb{G}, G)$. An algorithm $\mathcal{A}_{\text{alg}}$ executed in an algebraic game $\text{GAME}_{\text{GrGen}}$ is *algebraic* if for all group elements Z that it outputs, it also provides a representation of Z relative to all previously received group elements: if $\mathcal{A}_{\text{alg}}$ has so far received $\vec{X} = (X_0, \ldots, X_n) \in \mathbb{G}^{n+1}$ (where by convention we let $X_0 = G$), then $\mathcal{A}_{\text{alg}}$ must output Z together with $\vec{z} = (z_0, \ldots, z_n) \in (\mathbb{Z}_p)^{n+1}$ such that $Z = \sum_{i=0}^n z_i X_i$. We let $Z_{[\vec{z}]}$ denote such an augmented output. When writing $\vec{z}$ explicitly, we simply write $Z_{[z_0, \ldots, z_n]}$ (rather than $Z_{[(z_0, \ldots, z_n)]}$) to lighten the notation.

Game $\text{DL}^{\mathcal{A}}_{\text{GrGen}}(\lambda)$	Game $\text{OMDL}^{\mathcal{A}}_{\text{GrGen}}(\lambda)$	Oracle $\text{CHAL}()$
$(p, \mathbb{G}, G) \leftarrow \text{GrGen}(1^\lambda)$	$(p, \mathbb{G}, G) \leftarrow \text{GrGen}(1^\lambda)$	$x \leftarrow_\$ \mathbb{Z}_p\,;\; X := xG$
$x \leftarrow_\$ \mathbb{Z}_p\,;\; X := xG$	$\vec{x} := (\,)\,;\; q := 0$	$\vec{x} := \vec{x} \,\|\, (x)$
$y \leftarrow \mathcal{A}(p, \mathbb{G}, G, X)$	$\vec{y} \leftarrow \mathcal{A}^{\text{CHAL}, \text{DLOG}}(p, \mathbb{G}, G)$	**return** X
return $(y = x)$	**return** $(\vec{y} = \vec{x} \,\wedge\, q < |\vec{x}|)$	
		Oracle $\text{DLOG}(X)$
		$q := q + 1\,;\; x := \log_G(X)$
		return x

Fig. 1. The DL and OMDL problems.

ALGEBRAIC ALGORITHMS IN THE RANDOM ORACLE MODEL. The original paper [FKL18] considered the algebraic group model augmented by a random oracle and proved tight security of BLS signatures [BLS04] in this model. The random oracle in that work is of type $\text{H} \colon \{0,1\}^* \to \mathbb{G}$, and as the outputs are group elements, the adversary's group element representations could depend on them.

In this work the RO is typically of type $\text{H} \colon \mathbb{G} \times \{0,1\}^* \to \mathbb{Z}_p$. Thus, an algebraic adversary querying H on some input (Z, m) must also provide a representation $\vec{z}$ for the group-element input Z. In a game that implements the random oracle by lazy sampling, to ease readability, we will define an auxiliary oracle $\widetilde{\text{H}}$, which is used by the game itself (and thus does not take representations of group elements as input) and implements the same function as H.

THE ONE-MORE DISCRETE LOGARITHM PROBLEM. We recall the discrete logarithm (DL) problem in Fig. 1. The one-more discrete logarithm (OMDL) problem, also defined in Fig. 1, is an extension of the DL problem and consists in finding the discrete logarithm of q group elements by making strictly less than

q calls to an oracle solving the discrete logarithm problem. It was introduced in [BNPS03] and used for example to prove the security of the Schnorr identification protocol against active and concurrent attacks [BP02].

3   Schnorr Signatures

3.1   Definitions

A signature scheme SIG consists of the following algorithms:

- $par \leftarrow$ SIG.Setup(1^λ): the setup algorithm takes as input the security parameter λ in unary and outputs public parameters par;
- $(sk, pk) \leftarrow$ SIG.KeyGen(par): the key generation algorithm takes parameters par and outputs a secret key sk and a public key pk;
- $\sigma \leftarrow$ SIG.Sign(sk, m): the signing algorithm takes as input a secret key sk and a message $m \in \{0, 1\}^*$ and outputs a signature σ;
- $b \leftarrow$ SIG.Ver(pk, m, σ): the (deterministic) verification algorithm takes pk, a message m, and a signature σ; it returns 1 if σ is valid and 0 otherwise.

Game EUF-CMA$_{\mathsf{SIG}}^{\mathcal{A}}(\lambda)$	Oracle SIGN(m)
$par \leftarrow$ SIG.Setup(1^λ)	$\sigma \leftarrow$ SIG.Sign(sk, m)
$(sk, pk) \leftarrow$ SIG.KeyGen(par) ; $\mathsf{Q} := ()$	$\mathsf{Q} := \mathsf{Q} \,\|\, (m)$
$(m^*, \sigma^*) \leftarrow \mathcal{A}^{\mathrm{SIGN}}(pk)$	**return** σ
return $\big(m^* \notin \mathsf{Q} \wedge$ SIG.Ver(pk, m^*, σ^*)$\big)$	

Fig. 2. The EUF-CMA security game for a signature scheme SIG.

Correctness requires that for any λ and any message m, when running $par \leftarrow$ SIG.Setup(1^λ), $(sk, pk) \leftarrow$ SIG.KeyGen(par), $\sigma \leftarrow$ SIG.Sign(sk, m), and $b \leftarrow$ SIG.Ver(pk, m, σ), one has $b = 1$ with probability 1. The standard security notion for a signature scheme is *existential unforgeability under chosen-message attack* (EUF-CMA), formalized via game EUF-CMA, which we recall in Fig. 2. The Schnorr signature scheme [Sch91] is specified in Fig. 3.

3.2   Security of Schnorr Signatures in the AGM

As a warm-up and to introduce some of the techniques used later, we reduce security of Schnorr signatures to hardness of DL in the AGM+ROM.

Sch.Setup(1^λ)	Sch.KeyGen(*par*)
$(p, \mathbb{G}, G) \leftarrow \mathsf{GrGen}(1^\lambda)$	$(p, \mathbb{G}, G, \mathsf{H}) := par;\; x \leftarrow_\$ \mathbb{Z}_p;\; X := xG$
Select $\mathsf{H}: \{0,1\}^* \to \mathbb{Z}_p$	$sk := (par, x);\; pk := (par, X)$
return $par := (p, \mathbb{G}, G, \mathsf{H})$	**return** (sk, pk)
Sch.Sign(sk, m)	Sch.Ver(pk, m, σ)
$(p, \mathbb{G}, G, \mathsf{H}, x) := sk;\; r \leftarrow_\$ \mathbb{Z}_p;\; R := rG$	$(p, \mathbb{G}, G, \mathsf{H}, X) := pk;\; (R, s) := \sigma$
$c := \mathsf{H}(R, m);\; s := r + cx \bmod p$	$c := \mathsf{H}(R, m)$
return $\sigma := (R, s)$	**return** $(sG = R + cX)$

Fig. 3. The Schnorr signature scheme Sch[GrGen] based on a group generator GrGen.

Theorem 1. *Let* GrGen *be a group generator. Let* $\mathcal{A}_{\mathrm{alg}}$ *be an algebraic adversary against the EUF-CMA security of the Schnorr signature scheme* Sch[GrGen] *running in time at most* τ *and making at most* q_s *signature queries and* q_h *queries to the random oracle. Then there exists an algorithm* $\mathcal{B}$ *solving the DL problem w.r.t.* GrGen, *running in time at most* $\tau + O(q_\mathrm{s} + q_\mathrm{h})$, *such that*

$$\mathsf{Adv}^{\mathrm{euf\text{-}cma}}_{\mathsf{Sch[GrGen]}, \mathcal{A}_{\mathrm{alg}}}(\lambda) \leq \mathsf{Adv}^{\mathrm{dl}}_{\mathsf{GrGen}, \mathcal{B}}(\lambda) + \frac{q_\mathrm{s}(q_\mathrm{s} + q_\mathrm{h}) + 1}{2^{\lambda-1}}.$$

We start with some intuition for the proof. In the random oracle model, Schnorr signatures can be simulated without knowledge of the secret key by choosing random c and s, setting $R := sG - cX$ and then programming the random oracle so that $\mathsf{H}(R, m) = c$. On the other hand, an adversary that returns a signature forgery $(m^*, (R^*, s^*))$ can be used to compute the discrete logarithm of the public key X. In the ROM this can be proved by rewinding the adversary and using the Forking Lemma [PS96b, PS00], which entails a security loss.

In the AGM+ROM, extraction is straight-line and the security proof thus tight: A valid forgery satisfies $R^* = s^*G - c^*X$, with $c^* := \mathsf{H}(R^*, m^*)$. On the other hand, since the adversary is algebraic, when it made its first query $\mathsf{H}(R^*, m^*)$, it provided a representation of R^* in basis (G, X), that is (γ^*, ξ^*) with $R^* = \gamma^*G + \xi^*X$. Together, these equations yield

$$(\xi^* + c^*)X = (s^* - \gamma^*)G.$$

Since c^* was chosen at random *after* the adversary chose ξ^*, the probability that $\xi^* + c^* \neq_p 0$ is overwhelming, in which case we can compute the discrete logarithm of X from the above equation.

Proof of Theorem 1. Let $\mathcal{A}_{\mathrm{alg}}$ be an algebraic adversary in EUF-CMA$_{\mathsf{Sch[GrGen]}}$ and making at most q_s signature queries and q_h RO queries. We proceed by a sequence of games specified in Fig. 4.

Game$_0$. The first game is EUF-CMA (Fig. 2) for the Schnorr signature scheme (Fig. 3) with a random oracle H. The game maintains a list Q of queried messages and T of values sampled for H. To prepare the change to Game$_1$, we have written the finalization of the game in an equivalent way: it first checks that $m^* \notin Q$ and then runs Sch.Ver($pk, m^*, (R^*, s^*)$), which we have written explicitly. Since the adversary is algebraic, it must provide a representation (γ^*, ξ^*) for its forgery $(m^*, (R^*_{[\gamma^*, \xi^*]}, s^*))$ such that $R^* = \gamma^* G + \xi^* X$, and similarly for each RO query $H(R_{[\gamma, \xi]}, m)$. By definition,

$$\mathsf{Adv}^{\mathrm{game}_0}_{\mathcal{A}_{\mathrm{alg}}}(\lambda) = \mathsf{Adv}^{\mathrm{euf\text{-}cma}}_{\mathrm{Sch[GrGen]},\mathcal{A}_{\mathrm{alg}}}(\lambda). \tag{1}$$

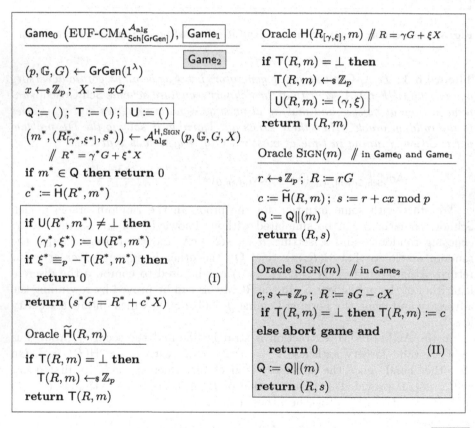

Fig. 4. Games in the proof of Theorem 1. Game$_0$ is defined by ignoring all boxes; boxes are included in Game$_1$ and Game$_2$; Gray boxes are only included in Game$_2$.

Game$_1$. We introduce an auxiliary table U that for each query $H(R_{[\gamma, \xi]}, m)$ stores the representation (γ, ξ) of R. Second, when the adversary returns its forgery $(m^*, (R^*_{[\gamma^*, \xi^*]}, s^*))$ and previously made a query $H(R^*_{[\gamma', \xi']}, m^*)$ for some (γ', ξ'), then we consider this previous representation of R^*, that is, we set

$(\gamma^*, \xi^*) := (\gamma', \xi')$. The only actual difference to Game_0 is that Game_1 returns 0 in case $\xi^* \equiv_p -\mathsf{T}(R^*, m^*)$ (line (I)).

We show that this happens with probability $1/p \leq 1/2^{\lambda-1}$. First note that line (I) is only executed if $m^* \notin \mathsf{Q}$, as otherwise the game would already have returned 0. Hence $\mathsf{T}(R^*, m^*)$ can only have been defined either (1) during a call to H or (2), if it is still undefined when $\mathcal{A}_{\mathrm{alg}}$ stops, by the game when defining c^*. In both cases the probability of returning 0 in line (I) is $1/p$:

(1) If $\mathsf{T}(R^*, m^*)$ was defined during a H query of the form $\mathsf{H}(R^*_{[\gamma', \xi']}, m^*)$ then $\mathsf{T}(R^*, m^*)$ is drawn uniformly at random and independently from ξ'. Since then $\mathsf{U}(R^*, m^*) \neq \bot$, the game sets $\xi^* := \xi'$ and hence $\xi^* \equiv_p -\mathsf{T}(R^*, m^*)$ holds with probability exactly $1/p$. (2) If $\mathsf{T}(R^*, m^*)$ is only defined after the adversary output ξ^* then again we have $\xi^* \equiv_p -\mathsf{T}(R^*, m^*)$ with probability $1/p$. Hence,

$$\mathsf{Adv}_{\mathcal{A}_{\mathrm{alg}}}^{\mathsf{game}_1}(\lambda) \geq \mathsf{Adv}_{\mathcal{A}_{\mathrm{alg}}}^{\mathsf{game}_0}(\lambda) - \frac{1}{2^{\lambda-1}}. \tag{2}$$

Game_2. In the final game we use the standard strategy of simulating the SIGN oracle without the secret key x by programming the random oracle. Game_1 and Game_2 are identical unless Game_2 returns 0 in line (II). For each signature query, R is uniformly random, and the size of table T is at most $q_{\mathrm{s}} + q_{\mathrm{h}}$, hence the game aborts in line (II) with probability at most $(q_{\mathrm{s}} + q_{\mathrm{h}})/p \leq (q_{\mathrm{s}} + q_{\mathrm{h}})/2^{\lambda-1}$. By summing over the at most q_{s} signature queries, we have

$$\mathsf{Adv}_{\mathcal{A}_{\mathrm{alg}}}^{\mathsf{game}_2}(\lambda) \geq \mathsf{Adv}_{\mathcal{A}_{\mathrm{alg}}}^{\mathsf{game}_1}(\lambda) - \frac{q_{\mathrm{s}}(q_{\mathrm{s}} + q_{\mathrm{h}})}{2^{\lambda-1}}. \tag{3}$$

REDUCTION TO DL. We now construct an adversary $\mathcal{B}$ solving DL with the same probability as $\mathcal{A}_{\mathrm{alg}}$ wins Game_2. On input $(p, \mathbb{G}, G)$ and X, the adversary runs $\mathcal{A}_{\mathrm{alg}}$ on input $(p, \mathbb{G}, G, X)$ and simulates Game_2, which can be done without knowledge of $\log_G(X)$. Assume that the adversary wins Game_2 by returning (m^*, R^*, s^*) and let $c^* := \mathsf{T}(R^*, m^*)$ and (γ^*, ξ^*) be defined as in the game. Thus, $\xi^* \neq -c^* \bmod p$ and $R^* = \gamma^* G + \xi^* X$; moreover, validity of the forgery implies that $s^* G = R^* + c^* X$. Hence, $(s^* - \gamma^*)G = (\xi^* + c^*)X$ and $\mathcal{B}$ can compute $\log X = (s^* - \gamma^*)(\xi^* + c^*)^{-1} \bmod p$. Combining this with Eqs. (1)–(3), we have

$$\mathsf{Adv}_{\mathsf{GrGen}, \mathcal{B}}^{\mathrm{dl}}(\lambda) = \mathsf{Adv}_{\mathcal{A}_{\mathrm{alg}}}^{\mathsf{game}_2}(\lambda) \geq \mathsf{Adv}_{\mathsf{Sch}[\mathsf{GrGen}], \mathcal{A}_{\mathrm{alg}}}^{\mathrm{euf\text{-}cma}}(\lambda) - \frac{q_{\mathrm{s}}(q_{\mathrm{s}} + q_{\mathrm{h}}) + 1}{2^{\lambda-1}}.$$

Assuming that scalar multiplications in $\mathbb{G}$ and assignments in tables T and U take unit time, the running time of $\mathcal{B}$ is $\tau + O(q_{\mathrm{s}} + q_{\mathrm{h}})$. □

4 Blind Schnorr Signatures

4.1 Definitions

We start with defining the syntax and security of blind signature schemes and focus on schemes with a 2-round (i.e., 4 messages) signing protocol for concreteness.

<u>SYNTAX.</u> A blind signature scheme BS consists of the following algorithms:

- $par \leftarrow$ BS.Setup(1^λ) and $(sk, pk) \leftarrow$ BS.KeyGen(par) and $b \leftarrow$ BS.Ver(pk, m, σ) are defined as for regular signature schemes (Sect. 3.1).
- $(b, \sigma) \leftarrow \langle$BS.Sign$(sk),$ BS.User$(pk, m)\rangle$: an interactive protocol is run between the signer with private input a secret key sk and the user with private input a public key pk and a message m; the signer outputs $b = 1$ if the interaction completes successfully and $b = 0$ otherwise, while the user outputs a signature σ if it terminates correctly, and $\perp$ otherwise. For a 2-round protocol the interaction can be realized by the following algorithms:

$$(msg_{U,0}, state_{U,0}) \leftarrow \text{BS.User}_0(pk, m)$$
$$(msg_{S,1}, state_S) \leftarrow \text{BS.Sign}_1(sk, msg_{U,0})$$
$$(msg_{U,1}, state_{U,1}) \leftarrow \text{BS.User}_1(state_{U,0}, msg_{S,1})$$
$$(msg_{S,2}, b) \leftarrow \text{BS.Sign}_2(state_S, msg_{U,1})$$
$$\sigma \leftarrow \text{BS.User}_2(state_{U,1}, msg_{S,2})$$

(Typically, BS.User$_0$ just initiates the session, and thus $msg_{U,0} = ()$ and $state_{U,0} = (pk, m)$.)

Correctness requires that for any λ and m, when running $par \leftarrow$ BS.Setup(1^λ), $(sk, pk) \leftarrow$ BS.KeyGen(par), $(b, \sigma) \leftarrow \langle$BS.Sign$(sk),$ BS.User$(pk, m)\rangle$, and $b' \leftarrow$ BS.Ver(pk, m, σ), we have $b = 1 = b'$ with probability 1.

Game $\text{UNF}_{\text{BS}}^{\mathcal{A}}(\lambda)$	Oracle $\text{SIGN}_1(msg)$
$par \leftarrow$ BS.Setup(1^λ)	$k_1 := k_1 + 1$ // session id
$(sk, pk) \leftarrow$ BS.KeyGen(par)	$(msg', state_{k_1}) \leftarrow$ BS.Sign$_1(sk, msg)$
$k_1 := 0$; $k_2 := 0$; $\mathcal{S} := \emptyset$	$\mathcal{S} := \mathcal{S} \cup \{k_1\}$ // open sessions
$(m_i^*, \sigma_i^*)_{i \in [n]} \leftarrow \mathcal{A}^{\text{SIGN}_1, \text{SIGN}_2}(pk)$	$\textbf{return } (k_1, msg')$
$\textbf{return } \big(k_2 < n$	
$\quad \wedge \ \forall i \neq j \in [n] : (m_i^*, \sigma_i^*) \neq (m_j^*, \sigma_j^*)$	Oracle $\text{SIGN}_2(j, msg)$
$\quad \wedge \ \forall i \in [n] : \text{BS.Ver}(pk, m_i^*, \sigma_i^*) = 1\big)$	$\textbf{if } j \notin \mathcal{S} \textbf{ then return } \perp$
	$(msg', b) \leftarrow$ BS.Sign$_2(state_j, msg)$
	$\textbf{if } b = 1 \textbf{ then } \mathcal{S} := \mathcal{S} \setminus \{j\}$; $k_2 := k_2 + 1$
	$\textbf{return } msg'$

Fig. 5. The (strong) unforgeability game for a blind signature scheme BS with a 2-round signing protocol.

<u>UNFORGEABILITY.</u> The standard security notion for blind signatures demands that no user, after interacting arbitrary many times with a signer and k of these interactions were considered successful by the signer, can produce more than k

signatures. Moreover, the adversary can schedule and interleave its sessions with the signer in any arbitrary way.

In game $\mathrm{UNF}_{\mathrm{BS}}^{\mathcal{A}}$ defined in Fig. 5 the adversary has access to two oracles SIGN_1 and SIGN_2 corresponding to the two phases of the interactive protocol. The game maintains two counters k_1 and k_2 (initially set to 0), where k_1 is used as session identifier, and a set $\mathcal{S}$ of "open" sessions. Oracle SIGN_1 takes the user's first message (which for blind Schnorr signatures is empty), increments k_1, adds k_1 to $\mathcal{S}$ and runs the first round on the signer's side, storing its state as $state_{k_1}$. Oracle SIGN_2 takes as input a session identifier j and a user message; if $j \in \mathcal{S}$, it runs the second round on the signer's side; if successful, it removes j from $\mathcal{S}$ and increments k_2, which thus represents the number of successful interactions.

BS satisfies unforgeability if $\mathrm{Adv}_{\mathrm{BS},\mathcal{A}}^{\mathrm{unf}}(\lambda)$ is negligible for all p.p.t. adversaries $\mathcal{A}$. Note that we consider "strong" unforgeability, which only requires that all pairs (m_i^*, σ_i^*) returned by the adversary (rather than all messages m_i^*) are distinct.

BLINDNESS. Blindness requires that a signer cannot link a message/signature pair to a particular execution of the signing protocol. Formally, the adversary chooses two messages m_0 and m_1 and the experiment runs the signing protocol acting as the user with the adversary, first obtaining a signature σ_b on m_b and then σ_{1-b} on m_{1-b} for a random bit b. If both signatures are valid, the adversary is given (σ_0, σ_1) and must determine the value of b. A formal definition can be found in the full version [FPS19].

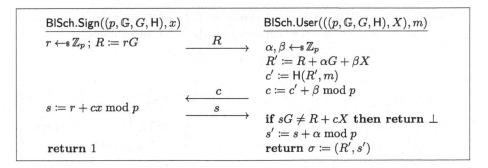

Fig. 6. The signing protocol of the blind Schnorr signature scheme.

BLIND SCHNORR SIGNATURES. A blind signature scheme BlSch is obtained from the scheme Sch in Fig. 3 by replacing Sch.Sign with the interactive protocol specified in Fig. 6 (the first message $msg_{U,0}$ from the user to the signer is empty and is not depicted). Correctness follows since a signature (R', s') obtained by the user after interacting with the signer satisfies Sch.Ver:

$$s'G = sG + \alpha G = (r + cx)G + \alpha G = R + \alpha G + \beta X + (-\beta + c)X$$
$$= R' + c'X = R' + \mathsf{H}(R', m)\, X.$$

Moreover, Schnorr signatures achieve perfect blindness [CP93].

4.2 The ROS Problem

The security of blind Schnorr signatures is related to the ROS (Random inhomogeneities in an Overdetermined, Solvable system of linear equations) problem, which was introduced by Schnorr [Sch01]. Consider the game $\mathsf{ROS}_{\mathsf{GrGen},\ell,\Omega}$ in Fig. 7, parameterized by a group generator GrGen,[5] an integer $\ell \geq 1$, and a set Ω (we omit GrGen and Ω from the notation when they are clear from context). The adversary $\mathcal{A}$ receives a prime p and has access to a random oracle $\mathsf{H}_{\mathrm{ros}}$ taking as input $(\vec{\rho}, \mathsf{aux})$ where $\vec{\rho} \in (\mathbb{Z}_p)^\ell$ and $\mathsf{aux} \in \Omega$. Its goal is to find $\ell + 1$ distinct pairs $(\vec{\rho}_i, \mathsf{aux}_i)_{i \in [\ell+1]}$ together with a solution $(c_j)_{j \in [\ell]}$ to the linear system $\sum_{j=1}^\ell \rho_{i,j} c_j \equiv_p \mathsf{H}_{\mathrm{ros}}(\vec{\rho}_i, \mathsf{aux}_i)$, $i \in [\ell + 1]$.[6]

The lemma below, which refines Schnorr's observation [Sch01], shows how an algorithm $\mathcal{A}$ solving the ROS_ℓ problem can be used to break the one-more unforgeability of blind Schnorr signatures. The proof is deferred to the full version [FPS19] due to space constraints.

Lemma 1. *Let GrGen be a group generator. Let $\mathcal{A}$ be an algorithm for game $\mathsf{ROS}_{\mathsf{GrGen},\ell,\Omega}$, where $\Omega = (\mathbb{Z}_p)^2 \times \{0,1\}^*$, running in time at most τ and making at most q_{h} random oracle queries. Then there exists an (algebraic) adversary $\mathcal{B}$ running in time at most $\tau + O(\ell + q_{\mathsf{h}})$, making at most ℓ queries to SIGN_1 and SIGN_2 and q_{h} random oracle queries, such that*

$$\mathsf{Adv}^{\mathsf{unf}}_{\mathsf{BlSch}[\mathsf{GrGen}],\mathcal{B}}(\lambda) \geq \mathsf{Adv}^{\mathsf{ros}}_{\mathsf{GrGen},\ell,\Omega,\mathcal{A}}(\lambda) - \frac{q_{\mathsf{h}}^2 + (\ell+1)^2}{2^{\lambda-1}}.$$

The hardness of ROS critically depends on ℓ. In particular, for small values of ℓ, ROS is statistically hard, as captured by the following lemma.

Game $\mathsf{ROS}^{\mathcal{A}}_{\mathsf{GrGen},\ell,\Omega}(\lambda)$	Oracle $\mathsf{H}_{\mathrm{ros}}(\vec{\rho}, \mathsf{aux})$
$(p, \mathbb{G}, G) \leftarrow \mathsf{GrGen}(1^\lambda)$; $\mathsf{T}_{\mathrm{ros}} := ()$	**if** $\mathsf{T}_{\mathrm{ros}}(\vec{\rho}, \mathsf{aux}) = \bot$ **then**
$\big((\vec{\rho}_i, \mathsf{aux}_i)_{i \in [\ell+1]}, (c_j)_{j \in [\ell]}\big) \leftarrow \mathcal{A}^{\mathsf{H}_{\mathrm{ros}}}(p)$	$\quad \mathsf{T}_{\mathrm{ros}}(\vec{\rho}, \mathsf{aux}) \leftarrow_{\$} \mathbb{Z}_p$
$/\!\!/ \ \vec{\rho}_i = (\rho_{i,1}, \ldots, \rho_{i,\ell})$	**return** $\mathsf{T}_{\mathrm{ros}}(\vec{\rho}, \mathsf{aux})$
return $\big(\forall i \neq i' \in [\ell+1] : (\vec{\rho}_i, \mathsf{aux}_i) \neq (\vec{\rho}_{i'}, \mathsf{aux}_{i'})$	
$\quad \wedge \ \forall i \in [\ell+1] : \sum_{j=1}^\ell \rho_{i,j} c_j \equiv_p \mathsf{H}_{\mathrm{ros}}(\vec{\rho}_i, \mathsf{aux}_i)\big)$	

Fig. 7. The ROS game, where $\mathsf{H}_{\mathrm{ros}} \colon (\mathbb{Z}_p)^\ell \times \Omega \to \mathbb{Z}_p$ is a random oracle.

---

[5] The group generator GrGen is only used to generate a prime p of length λ; the group $\mathbb{G}$ is not used in the game.

[6] The original definition of the problem by Schnorr [Sch01] sets $\Omega := \emptyset$. Our more general definition does not seem to significantly modify the hardness of the problem while allowing to prove Theorem 2.

Lemma 2. *Let* GrGen *be a group generator,* $\ell \geq 1$, *and* Ω *be some arbitrary set. Then for any adversary* $\mathcal{A}$ *making at most* q_h *queries to* H_{ros},

$$\mathsf{Adv}^{ros}_{\mathsf{GrGen},\ell,\Omega,\mathcal{A}}(\lambda) \leq \frac{\binom{q_h}{\ell+1} + 1}{2^{\lambda-1}}.$$

Proof. Consider a modified game $\mathsf{ROS}^*_{\mathsf{GrGen},\ell,\Omega}$ that is identical to ROS, except that it returns 0 when the adversary outputs $((\vec{\rho}_i, aux_i)_{i \in [\ell+1]}, (c_j)_{j \in [\ell]})$ such that for some $i \in [\ell + 1]$ it has not made the query $H_{ros}(\vec{\rho}_i, aux_i)$. Games ROS and ROS* are identical unless in game ROS the adversary wins and has not made the query $H_{ros}(\vec{\rho}_i, aux_i)$ for some i, which happens with probability at most $1/p \leq 1/2^{\lambda-1}$. Hence,

$$\mathsf{Adv}^{ros}_{\mathsf{GrGen},\ell,\Omega,\mathcal{A}}(\lambda) \leq \mathsf{Adv}^{ros^*}_{\mathsf{GrGen},\ell,\Omega,\mathcal{A}}(\lambda) + \frac{1}{2^{\lambda-1}}.$$

In order to win the modified game ROS*, $\mathcal{A}$ must in particular make $\ell+1$ distinct random oracle queries $(\vec{\rho}_i, aux_i)_{i \in [\ell+1]}$ such that the system

$$\sum_{j=1}^{\ell} \rho_{i,j} c_j \equiv_p H_{ros}(\vec{\rho}_i, aux_i), \quad i \in [\ell + 1] \tag{4}$$

with unknowns $c_1, \ldots, c_\ell$ has a solution. Consider any subset of $\ell + 1$ queries $(\vec{\rho}_i, aux_i)_{i \in [\ell+1]}$ made by the adversary to the random oracle and let M denote the $(\ell + 1) \times \ell$ matrix whose i-th row is $\vec{\rho}_i$ and let $t \leq \ell$ denote its rank. Then, Eq. (4) has a solution if and only if the row vector $\vec{h} := (H_{ros}(\vec{\rho}_i, aux_i))^T_{i \in [\ell+1]}$ is in the span of the columns of M. Since $\vec{h}$ is uniformly random, this happens with probability $p^t/p^{\ell+1} \leq 1/p \leq 1/2^{\lambda-1}$. By the union bound,

$$\mathsf{Adv}^{ros^*}_{\mathsf{GrGen},\ell,\Omega,\mathcal{A}}(\lambda) \leq \frac{\binom{q_h}{\ell+1}}{2^{\lambda-1}},$$

which concludes the proof. □

On the other hand, the ROS_ℓ problem can be reduced the $(\ell+1)$-sum problem, for which Wagner's generalized birthday algorithm [Wag02, MS12, NS15] can be used. More specifically, consider the $(\ell + 1) \times \ell$ matrix

$$(\rho_{i,j}) = \begin{bmatrix} 1 & 0 & \cdots & 0 \\ 0 & 1 & \cdots & 0 \\ & & \ddots & \\ 0 & \cdots & 0 & 1 \\ 1 & \cdots & & 1 \end{bmatrix}$$

and let $\vec{\rho}_i$ denote its i-th line, $i \in [\ell + 1]$. Let $q := 2^{\lambda/(1+\lfloor \lg(\ell+1) \rfloor)}$. The solving algorithm builds lists $L_i = (H_{ros}(\vec{\rho}_i, aux_{i,k}))_{k \in [q]}$ for $i \in [\ell]$ and $L_{\ell+1} = (-H_{ros}(\vec{\rho}_{\ell+1}, aux_{\ell+1,k}))_{k \in [q]}$ for arbitrary values $aux_{i,k}$ and uses Wagner's algorithm to find an element e_i in each list L_i such that $\sum_{i=1}^{\ell+1} e_i \equiv_p 0$. Then, it is easily seen that $((\vec{\rho}_i, aux_i)_{i \in [\ell+1]}, (e_j)_{j \in [\ell]})$, where aux_i is such that $e_i = H_{ros}(\vec{\rho}_i, aux_i)$, is a solution to the ROS problem. This algorithm makes $q_h = (\ell + 1)2^{\lambda/(1+\lfloor \lg(\ell+1) \rfloor)}$ random oracle queries, runs in time an space $O((\ell + 1)2^{\lambda/(1+\lfloor \lg(\ell+1) \rfloor)})$, and succeeds with constant probability.

4.3   Security of Blind Schnorr Signatures

We now formally prove that blind Schnorr signatures are unforgeable assuming the hardness of the one-more discrete logarithm problem and the ROS problem.

Theorem 2. *Let* GrGen *be a group generator. Let* $\mathcal{A}_{\mathrm{alg}}$ *be an algebraic adversary against the UNF security of the blind Schnorr signature scheme* BlSch[GrGen] *running in time at most* τ *and making at most* q_{s} *queries to* SIGN$_1$ *and* q_{h} *queries to the random oracle. Then there exist an algorithm* $\mathcal{B}_{\mathrm{ros}}$ *for the* ROS$_{q_{\mathrm{s}}}$ *problem making at most* $q_{\mathrm{h}} + q_{\mathrm{s}} + 1$ *random oracle queries and an algorithm* $\mathcal{B}_{\mathrm{omdl}}$ *for the OMDL problem w.r.t.* GrGen *making at most* q_{s} *queries to its oracle* DLOG*, both running in time at most* $\tau + O(q_{\mathrm{s}} + q_{\mathrm{h}})$*, such that*

$$\mathrm{Adv}_{\mathsf{BlSch[GrGen]},\mathcal{A}_{\mathrm{alg}}}^{\mathrm{unf}}(\lambda) \leq \mathrm{Adv}_{\mathsf{GrGen},\mathcal{B}_{\mathrm{omdl}}}^{\mathrm{omdl}}(\lambda) + \mathrm{Adv}_{\ell,\mathcal{B}_{\mathrm{ros}}}^{\mathrm{ros}}(\lambda).$$

We start with explaining the proof idea. Consider an adversary in the unforgeability game, let X be the public key and $R_1, \ldots, R_\ell$ be the elements returned by the oracle SIGN$_1$ and let (R_i^*, s_i^*) be the adversary's forgeries on messages m_i^*. As $\mathcal{A}_{\mathrm{alg}}$ is algebraic, it must also output a representation $(\gamma_i, \xi_i, \vec{\rho}_i)$ for R_i^* w.r.t. the group elements received from the game: $R_i^* = \gamma_i G + \xi_i X + \sum_{j=1}^\ell \rho_{i,j} R_j$. Validity of the forgeries implies another representation, namely $R_i^* = s_i^* G - c_i^* X$ with $c_i^* = \mathsf{H}(R_i^*, m_i^*)$. Together, these yield

$$(c_i^* + \xi_i^*)X + \sum_{j=1}^\ell \rho_{i,j} R_j = (s_i^* - \gamma_i^*)G, \tag{5}$$

which intuitively can be used to compute $\log X$.

However, the reduction also needs to simulate SIGN$_2$ queries, for which, contrary to the proof for standard Schnorr signatures (Theorem 1), it cannot rely on programming the random oracle. In fact, the reduction can only win OMDL, which is an *easier* game than DL. In particular, the reduction obtains $X, R_1, \ldots, R_q$ from its challenger and must compute their logarithms. It can make q logarithm queries, which it uses to simulate the SIGN$_2$ oracle: on input (j, c_j), it simply returns $s_j \leftarrow \mathrm{DLOG}(R_j + c_j X)$.

But this means that in Eq. (5) the reduction does not know the logarithms of the R_j's; all it knows is $R_j = s_j G - c_j X$, which, when plugged into Eq. (5) yields

$$\underbrace{\left(c_i^* + \xi_i^* - \sum_{j=1}^\ell \rho_{i,j}^* c_j\right)}_{=:\chi_i} X = \left(s_i^* - \gamma_i^* - \sum_{j=1}^\ell \rho_{i,j}^* s_j\right)G.$$

Thus, if for some i, $\chi_i \neq 0$, the reduction can compute $x = \log X$, and derive $r_j = \log R_j = s_j - c_j x$. Together, $x, r_1, \ldots, r_q$ constitute an OMDL solution.

On the other hand, we can show that if $\chi_i = 0$ for *all* i, then the adversary has actually found a solution to the ROS problem (Fig. 7): A reduction to ROS would answer the adversary's queries $\mathsf{H}(R_{[\gamma,\xi,\vec{\rho}]}, m)$ by $\mathsf{H}_{\mathrm{ros}}(\vec{\rho}, (\gamma, \xi, m)) - \xi$; then $\chi_i = 0$ implies (recall that $c_i^* = \mathsf{H}(R_i^*, m_i^*)$)

$$0 = \chi_i = \mathsf{H}(R_i^*, m_i^*) + \xi_i^* - \sum_{j=1}^\ell \rho_{i,j}^* c_j = \mathsf{H}_{\mathrm{ros}}(\vec{\rho}_i^*, (\gamma_i^*, \xi_i^*, m_i^*)) - \sum_{j=1}^\ell \rho_{i,j}^* c_j,$$

meaning $\left((\vec{\rho}_i^*, (\gamma_i^*, \xi_i^*, m_i^*))_i, (c_j)_j\right)$ is a solution to ROS.

To simplify the proof we first show the following lemma.

Lemma 3. *Let* GrGen *be a group generator and let* $\mathcal{A}$ *be an adversary against the UNF security of the blind Schnorr signature scheme* BlSch[GrGen] *running in time at most* τ *and making at most* q_s *queries to* SIGN$_1$ *and* q_h *queries to the random oracle. Then there exists an adversary* $\mathcal{B}$ *that makes exactly* q_s *queries to* SIGN$_1$ *and* q_s *queries to* SIGN$_2$ *that do not return* $\bot$*, and returns* $q_s + 1$ *forgeries, running in time at most* $\tau + O(q_s)$*, such that*

$$\mathsf{Adv}^{\mathsf{unf}}_{\mathsf{BlSch[GrGen]},\mathcal{A}}(\lambda) = \mathsf{Adv}^{\mathsf{unf}}_{\mathsf{BlSch[GrGen]},\mathcal{B}}(\lambda).$$

Proof. We construct the following adversary that plays game UNF (Fig. 5). On input pk, adversary $\mathcal{B}$ runs $\mathcal{A}(pk)$ and relays all oracle queries and responses between its challenger and $\mathcal{A}$. Let q be the number of $\mathcal{A}$'s SIGN$_1$ queries, let $R_1, \ldots, R_q$ be the answers, and let $\mathcal{C}$ be the completed sessions, that is, the set of values j such that $\mathcal{A}$ queried SIGN$_2$ on some input $(j, *)$ and SIGN$_2$ did not reply $\bot$. Let $(m_i^*, (R_i^*, s_i^*))_{i \in [n]}$ be $\mathcal{A}$'s output, for which we must have $k = |\mathcal{C}| < n$ when $\mathcal{A}$ wins.

$\mathcal{B}$ then makes $q_s - q$ queries to SIGN$_1$ to receive $R_{q+1}, \ldots, R_{q_s}$. Next, $\mathcal{B}$ completes all $q_s - k$ open signing sessions for distinct messages by following the protocol in Fig. 6: for every $j \in \mathcal{S} := [1, \ldots, q_s] \setminus \mathcal{C}$, adversary $\mathcal{B}$ picks a fresh message $m_j \notin \{m_i^*\}_{i \in [n]} \cup \{m_i\}_{i \in \mathcal{S} \setminus [j]}$ and $\alpha_j, \beta_j \leftarrow_\$ \mathbb{Z}_p$, computes $R'_j := R_j + \alpha_j G + \beta_j X$, queries $\mathsf{H}(R', m_j)$ to get c'_j, computes $c_j := c'_j + \beta_j \bmod p$ and queries (j, c_j) to SIGN$_2$. Upon receiving s_j, $\mathcal{B}$ computes $s'_j := s_j + \alpha_j \bmod p$, which yields a signature (R'_j, s'_j) on message m_j.

Finally, $\mathcal{B}$ concatenates $\mathcal{A}$'s output with $q_s + 1 - n \leq q_s - k$ signatures: let $\mathcal{S} = \{j_1, \ldots, j_{q_s-k}\}$; then $\mathcal{B}$ returns $(m_i^*, (R_i^*, s_i^*))_{i \in [n]} \| (m_{j_i}, (R'_{j_i}, s'_{j_i}))_{i \in [q_s+1-n]}$. When $\mathcal{A}$ wins the game, all tuples $(m_i^*, (R_i^*, s_i^*))$ are different; as all remaining messages also differ, all tuples output by $\mathcal{B}$ are distinct. By correctness of the scheme, $\mathcal{B}$'s signatures are valid. Thus whenever $\mathcal{A}$ wins, then so does $\mathcal{B}$. $\square$

Proof of Theorem 2. Let $\mathcal{A}_{\mathrm{alg}}$ be an algebraic adversary making at most q_s queries to SIGN$_1$ and q_h random oracle queries. By the above lemma, we can assume that $\mathcal{A}_{\mathrm{alg}}$ makes exactly $\ell := q_s$ queries to SIGN$_1$, closes all sessions, and returns $\ell + 1$ valid signatures. We proceed with a sequence of games defined in Fig. 8.

Game$_0$. The first game is the UNF game (Fig. 5) for scheme BlSch[GrGen] played with $\mathcal{A}_{\mathrm{alg}}$ in the random oracle model. We have written the finalization of the game in a different but equivalent way. In particular, instead of checking that $(m_i^*, (R_i^*, s_i^*)) \neq (m_{i'}^*, (R_{i'}^*, s_{i'}^*))$ for all $i \neq i' \in [\ell + 1]$, we simply check that $(m_i^*, R_i^*) \neq (m_{i'}^*, R_{i'}^*)$. This is equivalent since for any pair (m, R), there is a single $s \in \mathbb{Z}_p$ such that (R, s) is a valid signature for m. Hence, if the adversary returns $(m_i^*, (R_i^*, s_i^*))$ and $(m_{i'}^*, (R_{i'}^*, s_{i'}^*))$ with $(m_i^*, R_i^*) = (m_{i'}^*, R_{i'}^*)$ and $s_i^* \neq s_{i'}^*$, at least one of the two forgeries is invalid. Thus,

$$\mathsf{Adv}^{\mathsf{game}_0}_{\mathcal{A}_{\mathrm{alg}}}(\lambda) = \mathsf{Adv}^{\mathsf{unf}}_{\mathsf{BlSch[GrGen]},\mathcal{A}_{\mathrm{alg}}}(\lambda). \tag{6}$$

Fig. 8. Games used in the proof of Theorem 2. Game_0 ignores all boxes. The light-gray comments in Game_1 and oracle H show how reduction $\mathcal{B}_{\mathrm{ros}}$ solves ROS; the comments in the SIGN oracles show how $\mathcal{B}_{\mathrm{omdl}}$ embeds its challenges and simulates Game_1.

Game_1. In Game_1, we make the following changes (which are analogous to those in the proof of Theorem 1). First, we introduce an auxiliary table U that for each query $\mathsf{H}(R_{[\gamma,\xi,\vec{\rho}]}, m)$ stores the representation $(\gamma, \xi, \vec{\rho})$ of R. Second, when the adversary returns its forgeries $(m_i^*, (R_{i\,[\gamma_i,\xi_i,\vec{\rho}_i]}^*, s_i^*))_{i \in [\ell+1]}$, then for each $i \in [\ell+1]$ for which $\mathsf{T}(R_i^*, m_i^*)$ is undefined, we emulate a call to $\mathsf{H}(R_{i\,[\gamma_i,\xi_i,\vec{\rho}_i]}^*, m_i^*)$. Again, this does not change the output of the game, since in Game_0, the value $\mathsf{T}(R_i^*, m_i^*)$ would be randomly assigned when the game calls $\widetilde{\mathsf{H}}$ to check the signature. Finally, for each $i \in [\ell+1]$, we retrieve $(\gamma_i^*, \xi_i^*, \vec{\rho}_i^*) := \mathsf{U}(R_i^*, m_i^*)$ (which is necessarily defined at this point) and return 0 if $\sum_{i=1}^{\ell} \rho_{i,j}^* c_j \equiv_p c_i^* + \xi_i^*$ for all $i \in [\ell+1]$, where c_j is the (unique) value submitted to SIGN$_2$ together with j and not answered by $\bot$.

Game_0 and Game_1 are identical unless Game_1 returns 0 in line (I). We reduce indistinguishability of the games to ROS by constructing an algorithm $\mathcal{B}_{\mathrm{ros}}$ solving the ROS_ℓ problem whenever Game_1 stops in line (I). Algorithm $\mathcal{B}_{\mathrm{ros}}$, which has access to oracle $\mathsf{H}_{\mathrm{ros}}$, runs $\mathcal{A}_{\mathrm{alg}}$ and simulates Game_1 in a straightforward way, except for using its $\mathsf{H}_{\mathrm{ros}}$ oracle to define the entries of T.

In particular, consider a query $\mathsf{H}(R_{[\gamma,\xi,\vec{\rho}]}, m)$ by $\mathcal{A}_{\mathrm{alg}}$ such that $\mathsf{T}(R, m) = \bot$. Then $\mathcal{B}_{\mathrm{ros}}$ pads the vector $\vec{\rho}$ with 0's to make it of length ℓ (at this point, not all $R_1, \ldots, R_\ell$ are necessarily defined, so $\vec{\rho}$ might not be of length ℓ), and assigns $\mathsf{T}(R, m) := \mathsf{H}_{\mathrm{ros}}(\vec{\rho}, (\gamma, \xi, m)) - \xi$ (cf. comments in Fig. 8). Similarly, when $\mathcal{A}_{\mathrm{alg}}$ returns its forgeries $(m_i^*, (R_{i\,[\gamma_i, \xi_i, \vec{\rho}_i]}^*, s_i^*))_{i \in [\ell+1]}$, then for each $i \in [\ell+1]$ with $\mathsf{T}(R_i^*, m_i^*) = \bot$, reduction $\mathcal{B}_{\mathrm{ros}}$ assigns $\mathsf{T}(R_i^*, m_i^*) := \mathsf{H}_{\mathrm{ros}}(\vec{\rho}_i, (\gamma_i, \xi_i, m_i^*)) - \xi_i$. Since $\mathsf{H}_{\mathrm{ros}}$ returns uniformly random elements in $\mathbb{Z}_p$, the simulation is perfect.

If Game_1 aborts in line (I), $\mathcal{B}_{\mathrm{ros}}$ returns $((\vec{\rho}_i^*, (\gamma_i^*, \xi_i^*, m_i^*))_{i \in [\ell+1]}, (c_j)_{j \in [\ell]})$, where $(\gamma_i^*, \xi_i^*, \vec{\rho}_i^*) := \mathsf{U}(R_i^*, m_i^*)$. We show that this is a valid ROS solution.

First, for all $i \neq i' \in [\ell+1]$: $(\vec{\rho}_i^*, (\gamma_i^*, \xi_i^*, m_i^*)) \neq (\vec{\rho}_{i'}^*, (\gamma_{i'}^*, \xi_{i'}^*, m_{i'}^*))$. Indeed, otherwise we would have $(m_i^*, R_i^*) = (m_{i'}^*, R_{i'}^*)$ and the game would have returned 0 earlier. Second, since the game returns 0 in line (I), we have $\sum_{j=1}^{\ell} \rho_{i,j}^* c_j \equiv_p c_i^* + \xi_i^*$ for all $i \in [\ell+1]$. Hence, to show that the ROS solution is valid, it is sufficient to show that for all $i \in [\ell+1]$, $c_i^* = \mathsf{H}_{\mathrm{ros}}(\vec{\rho}_i^*, (\gamma_i^*, \xi_i^*, m_i^*)) - \xi_i^*$. This is clearly the case if $\mathsf{T}(R_i^*, m_i^*) = \bot$ when the adversary returns its forgeries. Indeed, in that case $(\gamma_i^*, \xi_i^*, \vec{\rho}_i^*) = (\gamma_i, \xi_i, \vec{\rho}_i)$ and

$$c_i^* = \mathsf{T}(R_i^*, m_i^*) = \mathsf{H}_{\mathrm{ros}}(\vec{\rho}_i, (\gamma_i, \xi_i, m_i^*)) - \xi_i = \mathsf{H}_{\mathrm{ros}}(\vec{\rho}_i^*, (\gamma_i^*, \xi_i^*, m_i^*)) - \xi_i^*.$$

Otherwise, $\mathsf{T}(R_i^*, m_i^*)$ was necessarily assigned during a call to H, and this call was of the form $\mathsf{H}(R_{i\,[\gamma_i^*, \xi_i^*, \vec{\rho}_i^*]}^*, m_i^*)$, which implies that $c_i^* = \mathsf{T}(R_i^*, m^*) = \mathsf{H}_{\mathrm{ros}}(\vec{\rho}_i^*, (\gamma_i^*, \xi_i^*, m_i^*)) - \xi_i^*$. Hence,

$$\mathsf{Adv}_{\mathcal{A}_{\mathrm{alg}}}^{\mathsf{game}_1}(\lambda) \geq \mathsf{Adv}_{\mathcal{A}_{\mathrm{alg}}}^{\mathsf{game}_0}(\lambda) - \mathsf{Adv}_{\ell, \mathcal{B}_{\mathrm{ros}}}^{\mathrm{ros}}(\lambda). \tag{7}$$

Moreover, it is easy to see that $\mathcal{B}_{\mathrm{ros}}$ makes at most $q_{\mathrm{h}} + \ell + 1$ queries to $\mathsf{H}_{\mathrm{ros}}$ and runs in time at most $\tau + O(\ell + q_{\mathrm{h}})$, assuming scalar multiplications in $\mathbb{G}$ and table assignments take unit time.

REDUCTION TO OMDL. In our last step, we construct an algorithm $\mathcal{B}_{\mathrm{omdl}}$ solving OMDL whenever $\mathcal{A}_{\mathrm{alg}}$ wins Game_1. Algorithm $\mathcal{B}_{\mathrm{omdl}}$, which has access to two oracles CHAL and DLOG (see Fig. 1) takes as input a group description $(p, \mathbb{G}, G)$, makes a first query $X \leftarrow \mathrm{CHAL}()$, and runs $\mathcal{A}_{\mathrm{alg}}$ on input $(p, \mathbb{G}, G, X)$, simulating Game_1 as follows (cf. comments in Fig. 8). Each time $\mathcal{A}_{\mathrm{alg}}$ makes a $\mathrm{SIGN}_1()$ query, $\mathcal{B}_{\mathrm{omdl}}$ queries its CHAL oracle to obtain R_j. It simulates $\mathrm{SIGN}_2(j, c)$ without knowledge of x and r_j by querying $s_j \leftarrow \mathrm{DLOG}(R_j + cX)$.

Assume that Game_1 returns 1, which implies that all forgeries (R_i^*, s_i^*) returned by $\mathcal{A}_{\mathrm{alg}}$ are valid. We show how $\mathcal{B}_{\mathrm{omdl}}$ solves OMDL. First, note that $\mathcal{B}_{\mathrm{omdl}}$ made exactly ℓ calls to its oracle DLOG in total (since it makes exactly one call for each (valid) SIGN_2 query made by $\mathcal{A}_{\mathrm{alg}}$).

Since Game_1 did not return 0 in line (I), there exists $i \in [\ell+1]$ such that

$$\sum_{j=1}^{\ell} \rho_{i,j}^* c_j \not\equiv_p c_i^* + \xi_i^*. \tag{8}$$

For all i, the adversary returned a representation $(\gamma_i^*, \xi_i^*, \vec{\rho}_i^*)$ of R_i^*, thus

$$R_i^* = \gamma_i^* G + \xi_i^* X + \sum_{j=1}^{\ell} \rho_{i,j}^* R_j. \tag{9}$$

On the other hand, validity of the i-th forgery yields another representation: $R_i^* = s_i^* G + c_i^* X$. Combining these two, we get

$$(c_i^* + \xi_i^*) X + \sum_{j=1}^{\ell} \rho_{i,j}^* R_j = (s_i^* - \gamma_i^*) G. \tag{10}$$

Finally, for each $j \in [\ell]$, s_j was computed with a call $s_j \leftarrow \text{DLog}(R_j + c_j X)$, hence

$$R_j = s_j G - c_j X. \tag{11}$$

Injecting Eq. (11) in Eq. (10), we obtain

$$\left(c_i^* + \xi_i^* - \sum_{j=1}^{\ell} \rho_{i,j}^* c_j \right) X = \left(s_i^* - \gamma_i^* - \sum_{j=1}^{\ell} \rho_{i,j}^* s_j \right) G. \tag{12}$$

Since by Eq. (8) the coefficient in front of X is non-zero, this allows $\mathcal{B}_{\text{omdl}}$ to compute $x := \log X$. Furthermore, from Eq. (11) we have $r_j := \log R_j = s_j - c_j x$ for all $j \in [\ell]$. By returning $(x, r_1, \ldots, r_\ell)$, $\mathcal{B}_{\text{omdl}}$ solves the OMDL problem whenever $\mathcal{A}_{\text{alg}}$ wins Game_1, which implies

$$\text{Adv}_{\text{GrGen}, \mathcal{B}_{\text{omdl}}}^{\text{omdl}}(\lambda) = \text{Adv}_{\mathcal{A}_{\text{alg}}}^{\text{game}_1}(\lambda). \tag{13}$$

The theorem now follows from Eqs. (6), (7) and (13). $\square$

CBlSch.Sign$((p, \mathbb{G}, G, \mathsf{H}), x)$		CBlSch.User$(((p, \mathbb{G}, G, \mathsf{H}), X), m)$
$r_0, r_1 \leftarrow_\$ \mathbb{Z}_p$		
$R_0 := r_0 G ; R_1 := r_1 G$	$\xrightarrow{\quad R_0, R_1 \quad}$	$\alpha_0, \beta_0, \alpha_1, \beta_1 \leftarrow_\$ \mathbb{Z}_p$
		$R_0' := R_0 + \alpha_0 G + \beta_0 X$
		$R_1' := R_1 + \alpha_1 G + \beta_1 X$
		$c_0' := \mathsf{H}(R_0', m)$
		$c_1' := \mathsf{H}(R_1', m)$
		$c_0 := c_0' + \beta_0 \bmod p$
	$\xleftarrow{\quad c_0, c_1 \quad}$	$c_1 := c_1' + \beta_1 \bmod p$
$b \leftarrow_\$ \{0, 1\}$		
$s := r_b + c_b x \bmod p$	$\xrightarrow{\quad b, s \quad}$	if $sG \neq R_b + c_b X$ then return $\bot$
		$s' := s + \alpha_b \bmod p$
return 1		**return** $\sigma := (R_b', s')$

Fig. 9. The clause blind Schnorr signing protocol.

5   The Clause Blind Schnorr Signature Scheme

We present a variation of the blind Schnorr signature scheme that only modifies the signing protocol. The scheme thus does not change the signatures themselves, meaning that it can be very smoothly integrated in existing applications.

The signature issuing protocol is changed so that it prevents the adversary from attacking the scheme by solving the ROS problem using Wagner's algorithm [Wag02,MS12]. The reason is that, as we show in Theorem 3, the attacker must now solve a *modified* ROS problem, which we define in Fig. 10.

We start with explaining the modified signing protocol, formally defined in Fig. 9. In the first round the signer and the user execute two parallel runs of the blind signing protocol from Fig. 6, of which the signer only finishes one at random in the last round, that is, it finishes $(\text{Run}_1 \vee \text{Run}_2)$: the clause from which the scheme takes its name.

This minor modification has major consequences. In the attack against the standard blind signature scheme (see Sect. 4.2), the adversary opens ℓ signing sessions, receiving $R_1, \ldots, R_\ell$, then searches a solution $\vec{c}$ to the ROS problem and closes the signing sessions by sending $c_1, \ldots, c_\ell$. Our modified signing protocol prevents this attack, as now for every opened session the adversary must *guess* which of the two challenges the signer will reply to. Only if all its guesses are correct is the attack successful. As the attack only works for large values of ℓ, this probability vanishes exponentially.

Game $\text{MROS}_{\mathsf{GrGen},\ell,\Omega}^{\mathcal{A}}(\lambda)$

$(p, \mathbb{G}, G) \leftarrow \mathsf{GrGen}(1^\lambda)$

$\mathsf{T}_{\text{ros}} := (\,)$

$(\vec{\rho}_{i,0}, \vec{\rho}_{i,1}, \text{aux}_i)_{i \in [\ell+1]} \leftarrow \mathcal{A}^{\mathsf{H}_{\text{ros}}, \text{SELECT}}(p)$

$/\!/ \ \vec{\rho}_{i,b} = (\rho_{i,b,1}, \ldots, \rho_{i,b,\ell})$

$\textbf{return } \big(\forall i \neq i' : (\vec{\rho}_{i,0}, \vec{\rho}_{i,1}, \text{aux}_i) \neq (\vec{\rho}_{i',0}, \vec{\rho}_{i',1}, \text{aux}_{i'})$

$\wedge \ \forall i \in [\ell+1] : \sum_{j=1}^{\ell} \rho_{i,b_j,j} c_j \equiv_p \mathsf{H}_{\text{ros}}(\vec{\rho}_{i,0}, \vec{\rho}_{i,0}, \text{aux}_i)$

$\wedge \ \forall i \in [\ell+1] \forall j \in [\ell] : \rho_{i,1-b_j,j} = 0 \big)$

Oracle $\mathsf{H}_{\text{ros}}(\vec{\rho}_0, \vec{\rho}_1, \text{aux})$

$\textbf{if } \mathsf{T}_{\text{ros}}(\vec{\rho}_0, \vec{\rho}_1, \text{aux}) = \bot \textbf{ then}$

$\quad \mathsf{T}_{\text{ros}}(\vec{\rho}_0, \vec{\rho}_1, \text{aux}) \leftarrow_{\$} \mathbb{Z}_p$

$\textbf{return } \mathsf{T}_{\text{ros}}(\vec{\rho}_0, \vec{\rho}_1, \text{aux})$

Oracle $\text{SELECT}(j, c_0', c_1')$

$/\!/ \text{ must be queried } \forall j \in [\ell]$

$b_j \leftarrow_{\$} \{0, 1\} \, ; \ c_j := c_{b_j}'$

$\textbf{return } b_j$

Fig. 10. The modified ROS problem.

In Theorem 3 we make this intuition formal; that is, we define a modified ROS game, which we show any successful attacker (which does not solve OMDL) must solve.

We have used two parallel executions of the basic protocol for the sake of simplicity, but the idea can be straightforwardly generalized to $t > 2$ parallel runs, of which the signer closes only one at random in the last round, that is, it closes $(\text{Run}_1 \vee \ldots \vee \text{Run}_t)$. This decreases the probability that the user correctly guesses which challenges will be answered by the signer in ℓ concurrent sessions.

THE MODIFIED ROS PROBLEM. Consider Fig. 10. The difference to the original ROS problem (Fig. 7) is that the queries to the H_{ros} oracle consist of *two* vectors $\vec{\rho}_0, \vec{\rho}_1$ and additional *aux* information. Analogously, the adversary's task is to return $\ell + 1$ tuples $(\vec{\rho}_{i,0}, \vec{\rho}_{i,1}, aux_i)$, except that the ROS solution $c_1^*, \ldots, c_\ell^*$ is selected as follows: for every index $j \in [\ell]$ the adversary must query an additional oracle $\text{SELECT}(j, c_{j,0}, c_{j,1})$, which flips a random bit b_j and sets the j-th coordinate of the solution to $c_j^* := c_{j,b_j}$.

Up to now, nothing really changed, as an adversary could always choose $\vec{\rho}_{i,0} = \vec{\rho}_{i,1}$ and $c_{j,0} = c_{j,1}$ for all indices, and solve the standard ROS problem. What complicates the task for the adversary considerably is the additional winning condition, which demands that in *all* tuples returned by the adversary, the ρ values that correspond to the complement of the selected bit must be zero, that is, for all $i \in [\ell+1]$ and all $j \in [\ell]$: $\rho_{i,1-b_j,j} = 0$. The adversary thus must commit to the solution coordinate c_j^* before it learns b_j, which then restricts the format of its ρ values.

We conjecture that the best attack against this modified ROS problem is to guess the ℓ bits b_j and to solve the standard ROS problem based on this guess using Wagner's algorithm. Hence, the complexity of the attack is increased by a factor 2^ℓ and requires time

$$O\left(2^\ell \cdot (\ell + 1) 2^{\lambda/(1+\lfloor \lg(\ell+1) \rfloor)}\right).$$

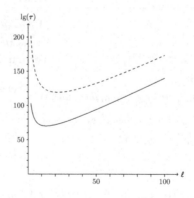

Fig. 11. Estimated complexity τ of conjectured best attack against the modified ROS problem as a function of parameter ℓ for $\lambda = 256$ (solid line) and $\lambda = 512$ (dashed line).

This estimated complexity is plotted for $\lambda \in \{256, 512\}$ in Fig. 11. This should be compared to the standard Wagner attack with $\ell + 1 = 2^{\sqrt{\lambda}}$ running in time 2^{32} and 2^{45}, respectively, for the same values of the security parameter.

We now prove that the Schnorr signature scheme from Fig. 3, with the signing algorithm replaced by the protocol in Fig. 9 is secure under the OMDL assumption for the underlying group and hardness of the modified ROS problem.

Theorem 3. *Let* GrGen *be a group generator. Let* $\mathcal{A}_{\mathrm{alg}}$ *be an algebraic adversary against the UNF security of the clause blind Schnorr signature scheme* CBlSch[GrGen] *running in time at most* τ *and making at most* q_{s} *queries to* SIGN₁ *and* q_{h} *queries to the random oracle. Then there exist an algorithm* $\mathcal{B}_{\mathrm{mros}}$ *for the* $MROS_{q_{\mathrm{s}}}$ *problem making at most* $q_{\mathrm{h}}+q_{\mathrm{s}}+1$ *random oracle queries and an algorithm* $\mathcal{B}_{\mathrm{omdl}}$ *for the OMDL problem w.r.t.* GrGen *making at most* q_{s} *queries to its oracle* DLOG, *both running in time at most* $\tau + O(q_{\mathrm{s}} + q_{\mathrm{h}})$, *such that*

$$\mathsf{Adv}^{\mathrm{unf}}_{\mathsf{BlSch[GrGen]},\mathcal{A}_{\mathrm{alg}}}(\lambda) \leq \mathsf{Adv}^{\mathrm{omdl}}_{\mathsf{GrGen},\mathcal{B}_{\mathrm{omdl}}}(\lambda) + \mathsf{Adv}^{\mathrm{mros}}_{\ell,\mathcal{B}_{\mathrm{mros}}}(\lambda).$$

The theorem follows by adapting the proof of Theorem 2; we therefore discuss the changes and refer to Fig. 12, which compactly presents all the details.

The proof again proceeds by one game hop, where an adversary behaving differently in the two games is used to break the modified ROS problem; the only change to the proof of Theorem 2 is that when simulating SIGN₂, the reduction $\mathcal{B}_{\mathrm{mros}}$ calls SELECT($j, c_{j,0}, c_{j,1}$) to obtain bit b instead of choosing it itself. By definition, Game₁ aborts in line (I) if and only if $\mathcal{B}_{\mathrm{mros}}$ has found a solution for MROS.

The difference in the reduction to OMDL of the modified game is that the adversary can fail to solve MROS in two ways: (1) its values $((\rho_{i,b_j,j})_{i,j}, (c_j)_j)$ are not a ROS solution; in this case the reduction can solve OMDL as in the proof of Theorem 2; (2) these values *are* a ROS solution, but for some i, j, we have $\rho_{i,1-b_j,j} \neq 0$. We show that in this case the OMDL reduction can compute the discrete logarithm of one of the values $R_{j,1-b_j}$.

More in detail, the main difference to Theorem 2 is that the representation of the values R_i^* in the adversary's forgery depend on both the $R_{j,0}$ and the $R_{j,1}$ values; we can thus write them as

$$R_i^* = \gamma_i^* G + \xi_i^* X + \sum_{j=1}^{\ell} \rho_{i,b_j,j}^* R_{j,b_j} + \sum_{j=1}^{\ell} \rho_{i,1-b_j,j}^* R_{j,1-b_j}$$

(this corresponds to Eq. (9) in the proof of Theorem 2). Validity of the forgery implies $R_i^* = s_i^* G - c_i^* X$, which together with the above yields

$$(c_i^* + \xi_i^*)X + \sum_{j=1}^{\ell} \rho_{i,b_j,j}^* R_{j,b_j} = (s_i^* - \gamma_i^*)G - \sum_{j=1}^{\ell} \rho_{i,1-b_j,j}^* R_{j,1-b_j}$$

(cf. Eq. (10)). By definition of s_j, we have $R_{j,b_j} = s_j G - c_j X$ for all $j \in [\ell]$; the above equation becomes thus

$$\left(c_i^* + \xi_i^* - \sum_{j=1}^{\ell} \rho_{i,b_j,j}^* c_j\right) X \tag{14}$$
$$= \left(s_i^* - \gamma_i^* - \sum_{j=1}^{\ell} \rho_{i,b_j,j}^* s_j\right) G - \sum_{j=1}^{\ell} \rho_{i,1-b_j,j}^* R_{j,1-b_j}$$

$\text{Game}_0 \left(\text{UNF}_{\text{CBlSch[GrGen]}}^{\mathcal{A}_{\text{alg}}}(\lambda)\right),\; \boxed{\text{Game}_1}$

$(p, \mathbb{G}, G) \leftarrow \text{GrGen}(1^\lambda)$

$x \leftarrow_{\$} \mathbb{Z}_p\,;\; X := xG$

$k_1 := 0\,;\; k_2 := 0\,;\; \mathcal{S} := \emptyset\,;\; \mathsf{T} := (\,)\,;\; \boxed{\mathsf{U} := (\,)}$

$(m_i^*, (R_i^*{}_{[\gamma_i, \xi_i, \vec\rho_{i,0}, \vec\rho_{i,1}]}, s_i^*))_{i \in [\ell+1]}$

$\qquad\qquad \leftarrow \mathcal{A}_{\text{alg}}^{\mathsf{H}, \text{Sign}_1, \text{Sign}_2}(p, \mathbb{G}, G, X)$

$/\!/\; R_i^* = \gamma_i G + \xi_i X + \sum \rho_{i,0,j} R_{j,0} + \sum \rho_{i,1,j} R_{j,1}$

if $k_2 > \ell$ **then return** 0

if $\exists i \neq i' \in [\ell+1] : (m_i^*, R_i^*) = (m_{i'}^*, R_{i'}^*)$

$\quad$ **then return** 0

---

for $i = 1 \ldots \ell + 1$ **do**

$\quad$ **if** $\mathsf{T}(R_i^*, m_i^*) = \perp$ **then**

$\qquad \mathsf{T}(R_i^*, m_i^*) \leftarrow_{\$} \mathbb{Z}_p$

$\qquad /\!/\; \mathsf{T}(R_i^*, m_i^*) := \mathsf{H}_{\text{ros}}(\vec\rho_{i,0}, \vec\rho_{i,1}, (\gamma_i, \xi_i, m_i^*)) - \xi_i$

$\qquad \mathsf{U}(R_i^*, m_i^*) := (\gamma_i, \xi_i, \vec\rho_{i,0}, \vec\rho_{i,1})$

---

for $i = 1 \ldots \ell + 1$ **do**

$\quad c_i^* := \widetilde{\mathsf{H}}(R_i^*, m_i^*)$ $\;/\!/$ does not modify T in Game_1

$(\gamma_i^*, \xi_i^*, \vec\rho_{i,0}^*, \vec\rho_{i,1}^*) := \mathsf{U}(R_i^*, m_i^*)$

if $\forall i \in [\ell+1] : \sum_{j=1}^{\ell} \rho_{i,b_j,j}^* c_j \equiv_p c_i^* + \xi_i^*$

$\quad \wedge\; \forall i \in [\ell+1], \forall j \in [\ell] : \rho_{i,1-b_j,j}^* = 0$

$\quad$ **then return** 0 $\hspace{3cm}$ (I)

$/\!/\; ((\vec\rho_{i,0}^*, \vec\rho_{i,1}^*, (\gamma_i^*, \xi_i^*, m_i^*))_{i\in[\ell+1]}$ solves MROS

return $(\forall i \in [\ell+1] : s_i^* G = R_i^* + c_i^* X)$

$/\!/ \begin{cases} \varphi_i := s_i^* - \gamma_i^* - \sum_{j=1}^{\ell} \rho_{i,b_j,j}^* s_j \\ \textbf{if } \chi_i := c_i^* + \xi_i^* - \sum_{j=1}^{\ell} \rho_{i,b_j,j}^* c_j \not\equiv_p 0 \\ \quad x := \chi_i^{-1} \varphi_i \bmod p \\ \quad \textbf{for } j \in [\ell] : r_{j,1-b_j} \leftarrow \text{DLog}(R_{j,1-b_j}) \\ \textbf{else if } \psi := \rho_{i,1-b_j,j}^* \neq 0 \text{ for some } i, \hat\jmath \\ \quad \textbf{for } j \neq \hat\jmath : r_{j,1-b_j} \leftarrow \text{DLog}(R_{j,1-b_j}) \\ \quad r_{\hat\jmath, 1-b_j} := \psi^{-1}(\varphi_i - \sum_{j \neq \hat\jmath} \rho_{i,1-b_j,j}^* r_{j,1-b_j}) \\ \quad x \leftarrow \text{DLog}(X) \\ \quad \textbf{for } j \in [\ell] : r_{j,b_j} := s_j - c_j x \\ (x, r_{1,0}, \ldots, r_{\ell,0}, r_{1,1}, \ldots, r_{\ell,1}) \text{ solves OMDL} \end{cases}$

Oracle $\widetilde{\mathsf{H}}(R, m)$

if $\mathsf{T}(R, m) = \perp$ **then**

$\quad \mathsf{T}(R, m) \leftarrow_{\$} \mathbb{Z}_p$

return $\mathsf{T}(R, m)$

Oracle $\mathsf{H}(R_{[\gamma, \xi, \vec\rho_0, \vec\rho_1]}, m)$

$/\!/\; R = \gamma G + \xi X + \sum \rho_{0,j} R_{j,0}$

$/\!/\qquad\qquad + \sum \rho_{1,j} R_{j,1}$

if $\mathsf{T}(R, m) = \perp$ **then**

$\quad \mathsf{T}(R, m) \leftarrow_{\$} \mathbb{Z}_p$

$\quad /\!/\; \mathsf{T}(R, m) :=$

$\quad /\!/\; \mathsf{H}_{\text{ros}}(\vec\rho_0, \vec\rho_1, (\gamma, \xi, m)) - \xi$

$\quad \boxed{\mathsf{U}(R, m) := (\gamma, \xi, \vec\rho_0, \vec\rho_1)}$

return $\mathsf{T}(R, m)$

Oracle $\text{Sign}_1()$

$k_1 := k_1 + 1$

$r_{k_1,0}, r_{k_1,1} \leftarrow_{\$} \mathbb{Z}_p$

$R_{k_1,0} := r_{k_1,0} G$ $\;/\!/\; R_{k_1,0} \leftarrow \text{Chal}()$

$R_{k_1,1} := r_{k_1,1} G$ $\;/\!/\; R_{k_1,1} \leftarrow \text{Chal}()$

$\mathcal{S} := \mathcal{S} \cup \{k_1\}$

return $(k_1, R_{k_1,0}, R_{k_1,1})$

Oracle $\text{Sign}_2(j, c_{j,0}, c_{j,1})$

if $j \notin \mathcal{S}$ **then return** $\perp$

$b_j \leftarrow_{\$} \{0, 1\}$

$/\!/\; b_j \leftarrow \text{Select}(j, c_{j,0}, c_{j,1})$

$c_j := c_{j,b_j}$

$s_j := r_{j,b_j} + c_j x$

$/\!/\; s_j \leftarrow \text{DLog}(R_{j,b_j} + c_j X)$

$\mathcal{S} := \mathcal{S} \setminus \{j\}$

$k_2 := k_2 + 1$

return (b_j, s_j)

Fig. 12. Games used in the proof of Theorem 3. The comments in light gray show how $\mathcal{B}_{\text{mros}}$ solves MROS; the dark comments show how $\mathcal{B}_{\text{omdl}}$ solves OMDL.

(which corresponds to Eq. (12) in Theorem 2). In Theorem 2, not solving ROS implied that for some i, the coefficient of X in the above equation was non-zero, which allowed computation of $\log X$.

However, if the adversary sets all these coefficients to 0, it could still fail to solve MROS if $\rho^*_{i^*, 1-b_{j^*}, j^*} \neq 0$ for some i^*, j^* (this is case (2) defined above). In this case Game_1 does not abort and the OMDL reduction $\mathcal{B}_{\mathrm{omdl}}$ must succeed. Since in this case the left-hand side of Eq. (14) is then 0, $\mathcal{B}_{\mathrm{omdl}}$ can, after querying $\mathrm{DLOG}(R_{j,1-b_j})$ for all $j \neq j^*$, compute $\mathrm{DLOG}(R_{j^*, 1-b_{j^*}})$, which breaks OMDL.

We finally note that the above case distinction was merely didactic, as the same OMDL reduction can handle both cases simultaneously, which means that our reduction does not introduce any additional security loss. In particular, the reduction obtains X and all values $(R_{j,0}, R_{j,1})$ from its OMDL challenger, then handles case (2) as described, and case (1) by querying $R_{1,1-b_1}, \ldots, R_{\ell, 1-b_\ell}$ to its DLOG oracle. In both cases it made 2ℓ queries to DLOG and computed the discrete logarithms of all $2\ell + 1$ challenges.

Figure 12 presents the unforgeability game and Game_1, which aborts if the adversary solved MROS. The gray and dark gray comments also precisely define how a reduction $\mathcal{B}_{\mathrm{mros}}$ solves MROS whenever Game_1 aborts in line (I), and how a reduction $\mathcal{B}_{\mathrm{omdl}}$ solves OMDL whenever $\mathcal{A}_{\mathrm{alg}}$ wins Game_1.

BLINDNESS OF THE CLAUSE BLIND SCHNORR SIGNATURE SCHEME. Blindness of the "clause" variant in Fig. 9 follows via a hybrid argument from blindness of the standard scheme (Fig. 6). In the game defining blindness the adversary impersonates a signer and selects two messages m_0 and m_1. The game flips a bit b, runs the signing protocol with the adversary for m_b and then for m_{1-b}. If both sessions terminate, the adversary is given the resulting signatures and must determine b.

In the blindness game for scheme CBISch, the challenger runs *two* instances of the issuing protocol from BISch for m_b of which the signer finishes one, as determined by its message (β_b, s_b) in the third round (β_b corresponds to b in Fig. 9), and then *two* instances for m_{1-b}.

If $b = 0$, the challenger thus asks the adversary for signatures on m_0, m_0, m_1 and then m_1. We define a hybrid game where the order of the messages is $m_1, m_0, \underline{m_0}, m_1$; this game thus lies between the blindness games for $b = 0$ and $b = 1$, where the messages are m_1, m_1, m_0, m_0. The original games differ from the hybrid game by exactly one message pair; intuitively, they are thus indistinguishable by blindness of BISch.

A technical detail is that the above argument only works when $\beta_0 = \beta_1$, as otherwise both reductions (between each original game and the hybrid game) abort one session and do not get any signatures from its challenger. The reductions thus guess the values β_0 and β_1 (and return a random bit if the guess turns out wrong). The hybrid game then replaces the β_0-th message of the first two and the β_1-th of the last two (as opposed to the ones underlined as above). Following this argument, in the full version [FPS19] we prove the following:

Theorem 4. *Let $\mathcal{A}$ be a p.p.t. adversary against blindness of the scheme* CBISch. *Then there exist two p.p.t. algorithms $\mathcal{B}_1$ and $\mathcal{B}_2$ against blindness of*

BlSch *such that*

$$\mathsf{Adv}^{\text{blind}}_{\text{CBlSch},\mathcal{A}}(\lambda) \leq 4 \cdot \left(\mathsf{Adv}^{\text{blind}}_{\text{BlSch},\mathcal{B}_1}(\lambda) + \mathsf{Adv}^{\text{blind}}_{\text{BlSch},\mathcal{B}_2}(\lambda) \right).$$

Since the (standard) blind Schnorr signature scheme is perfectly blind [CP93], by the above, our variant also satisfies perfect blindness.

6 Schnorr-Signed ElGamal Encryption

A public key for the ElGamal public-key encryption (PKE) scheme is a group element $Y \in \mathbb{G}$. Messages are group elements $M \in \mathbb{G}$ and to encrypt M under Y, one samples a random $x \in \mathbb{Z}_p$ and derives an ephemeral key $K := xY$ to blind the message: $C := xY + M$. Given in addition the value $X := xG$, the receiver that holds $y = \log Y$ can derive $K := yX$ and recover $M := C - K$.

Game $\mathsf{DDH}^{\mathcal{A}}_{\mathsf{GrGen}}(\lambda)$

$(p, \mathbb{G}, G) \leftarrow \mathsf{GrGen}(1^{\lambda})$; $b \leftarrow_{\$} \{0,1\}$; $x, y, z \leftarrow_{\$} \mathbb{Z}_p$

$X := xG$; $Y := yG$; $Z_0 := xyG$; $Z_1 := zG$

$b' \leftarrow \mathcal{A}(p, \mathbb{G}, G, X, Y, Z_b)$

return $(b = b')$

Fig. 13. The DDH problem.

SEG.Setup(λ)

$(p, \mathbb{G}, G) \leftarrow \mathsf{GrGen}(1^{\lambda})$

Select $\mathsf{H}: \{0,1\}^{*} \rightarrow \mathbb{Z}_p$

return $par := (p, \mathbb{G}, G, \mathsf{H})$

SEG.KeyGen(par)

$(p, \mathbb{G}, G, \mathsf{H}) := par$; $y \leftarrow_{\$} \mathbb{Z}_p$; $Y := yG$

$sk := (par, y)$; $pk := (par, Y)$

return (sk, pk)

SEG.Enc(pk, M)

$(p, \mathbb{G}, G, \mathsf{H}, Y) := pk$; $x, r \leftarrow_{\$} \mathbb{Z}_p$

$X := xG$; $R := rG$; $C := xY + M$

$s := r + \mathsf{H}(X, C, R) \cdot x \bmod p$

return (X, C, R, s)

SEG.Dec($sk, (X, C, R, s)$)

$(p, \mathbb{G}, G, \mathsf{H}, y) := sk$

if $sG \neq R + \mathsf{H}(X, C, R) \cdot X$ **then**

   return $\perp$

return $M := C - yX$

Fig. 14. The Schnorr-Signed ElGamal PKE scheme SEG[GrGen].

Under the decisional Diffie-Hellman (DDH) assumption (see Fig. 13), ciphertexts of different messages are computationally indistinguishable: replacing K

by a random value K' makes the ciphertext C perfectly hide the message. In the AGM, ElGamal, viewed as a key-encapsulation mechanism (KEM) was shown to satisfy CCA1-security (where the adversary can only make decryption queries before seeing the challenge key) under a parametrized variant of DDH [FKL18].

The idea of *Schnorr-signed* ElGamal is to accompany the ciphertext by a proof of knowledge of the randomness $x = \log X$ used to encrypt, in particular, a Schnorr signature on the pair (X, C) under the public key X. The scheme is detailed in Fig. 14. (Note that we changed the argument order in the hash function call compared to Sect. 3 so that it is the same as in ciphertexts.)

The strongest security notion for PKE is indistinguishability of ciphertexts under adaptive chosen-ciphertext attack (IND-CCA2), where the adversary can query decryptions of ciphertexts of its choice even after receiving the challenge. The (decisional) game IND-CCA2 is defined in Fig. 15.

When ephemeral keys are hashed (that is, defined as $k := \mathsf{H}'(xY)$) and the scheme is viewed as a KEM, then CCA2-security can be reduced to the *strong* Diffie-Hellman (SDH) assumption[7] [ABR01,CS03] in the ROM. In the full version [FPS19] we show that when key hashing is applied to the Schnorr-signed ElGamal scheme from Fig. 14, then in the AGM+ROM we can directly reduce CCA2-security of the corresponding KEM to the DL assumption (Fig. 1); in particular, we do so using a *tight* security proof (note that SDH is equivalent to DL in the AGM [FKL18] but the reduction from DL to SDH is non-tight). Here we prove that the Schnorr-signed ElGamal PKE is IND-CCA2-secure in the AGM+ROM under the DDH assumption.

Game IND-CCA2$^{\mathcal{A}}_{\mathsf{PKE}}(\lambda)$	Oracle $\mathrm{ENC}(m_0, m_1)$ // one time
$par \leftarrow \mathsf{PKE.Setup}(\lambda)$	$c^* \leftarrow \mathsf{PKE.Enc}(pk, m_b)$; **return** c^*
$(pk, sk) \leftarrow \mathsf{PKE.KeyGen}(par)$	
$b \leftarrow_\$ \{0, 1\}$	Oracle $\mathrm{DEC}(c)$
$b' \leftarrow \mathcal{A}^{\mathrm{ENC}, \mathrm{DEC}}(pk)$	**if** $c = c^*$ **then return** $\bot$
return $(b = b')$	**return** $\mathsf{PKE.Dec}(sk, c)$

Fig. 15. The IND-CCA2 security game for a PKE scheme PKE.

Theorem 5. *Let* GrGen *be a group generator. Let* $\mathcal{A}_{\mathrm{alg}}$ *be an algebraic adversary against the IND-CCA2 security of the Schnorr-signed ElGamal PKE scheme* SEG[GrGen] *making at most* q_d *decryption queries and* q_h *queries to the random oracle. Then there exist two algorithms* $\mathcal{B}_1$ *and* $\mathcal{B}_2$ *solving respectively the DL problem and the DDH problem w.r.t.* GrGen, *such that*

---

[7] SDH states that given $X = xG$ and Y it is infeasible to compute xY even when given access to an oracle which on input (Y', Z') returns 1 if $Z' = xY'$ and 0 otherwise.

$$\mathsf{Adv}^{\mathsf{ind\text{-}cca2}}_{\mathsf{SEG[GrGen]},\mathcal{A}_{\mathsf{alg}}}(\lambda) \le 2 \cdot \mathsf{Adv}^{\mathsf{ddh}}_{\mathsf{GrGen},\mathcal{B}_2}(\lambda) + \mathsf{Adv}^{\mathsf{dl}}_{\mathsf{GrGen},\mathcal{B}_1}(\lambda) + \frac{q_{\mathsf{d}} + \frac{1}{2^{\lambda-1}}(q_{\mathsf{d}} + q_{\mathsf{h}})}{2^{\lambda-1}}.$$

We start with the proof idea. The full proof can be found in the full version [FPS19]. Let Y be the public key, let P_0 and P_1 denote the challenge plaintexts, and let $(X^* = x^*G, C^* = x^*Y + P_b, R^*, s^*)$ be the challenge ciphertext. Under the DDH assumption, given Y and X^*, the value x^*Y looks random. We can thus replace x^*Y by a random group element Z^*, which perfectly hides P_b and leads to a game where the adversary gains no information about the challenge bit b.

It remains to show how the reduction can simulate the game without knowledge of $\log X^*$ (needed to sign the challenge ciphertext) and $\log Y$ (needed to answer decryption queries). The Schnorr signature under X^* contained in the challenge ciphertext can be simulated by programming the random oracle H as for Theorem 1.

Decryption queries leverage the fact that the Schnorr signature contained in a queried ciphertext (X, C, R, s) proves knowledge of x with $X = xG$. Thus, intuitively, the reduction should be able to answer a query by extracting x and returning $M = C - xY$. However, this extraction is a lot trickier than in the proof of Theorem 1: During the game the adversary obtains group elements Y, X^*, C^*, and R^*, as well as the answers $M_1, \ldots, M_{q_{\mathsf{d}}}$ to its queries to DEC. The adversary's representations of group elements can thus depend on all these elements. In particular, since DEC on input $(X, C, \ldots)$ computes $M := C - yX$, by successive calls to DEC, the adversary can obtain arbitrary powers of y.

In our proof we first show that from a representation given by the adversary, we can always (efficiently) derive a representation in basis

$$(G, X^*, Y = yG, \ldots, y^{q_{\mathsf{d}}+1}G, x^*yG, \ldots, x^*y^{q_{\mathsf{d}}+1}G).$$

Now consider a decryption query (X, C, R, s), each group element represented as

$$X = \gamma_x G + \xi_x X^* + \sum_{i=1}^{q_{\mathsf{d}}+1} v_x^{(i)} y^i G + \sum_{i=1}^{q_{\mathsf{d}}+1} \zeta_x^{(i)} x^* y^i G, \qquad R = \gamma_r G + \ldots \quad (15)$$

We show that each query falls into one of three categories:

(1) The choice of $c = \mathsf{H}(X, C, R)$ was unlucky, which only happens with negligible probability
(2) The representation of X is independent of Y, that is, $X = \gamma_x G + \xi_x X^*$. Then xY (and hence the answer $M = C - xY$ to the query) can be computed as $xY := \gamma_x Y + \xi_x Z^*$ (where $Z^* := x^*Y$ is known by the reduction).
(3) Otherwise we show that the adversary has computed $\log Y$ If the DEC query was valid then $sG = R + cX$, which, by plugging in the representations (15) yields

$$0 = (\gamma_r + c\gamma_x - s)G + (\xi_r + c\xi_x)X^* + \sum_{i=1}^{q_{\mathsf{d}}+1} \big(\underbrace{(v_r^{(i)} + x^*\zeta_r^{(i)}) + c\overbrace{(v_x^{(i)} + x^*\zeta_x^{(i)})}^{=:\beta^{(i)}}}_{=:\alpha^{(i)}} \big) y^i G$$

If $\beta^{(i)} \equiv_p 0$ for all i, we are in case (2). If $\beta^{(j)} \not\equiv_p 0$ for some j and $\alpha^{(i)} \equiv_p 0$ for all i, then $c \equiv_p -(v_r^{(j)} + x^* \zeta_r^{(j)}) \cdot (\beta^{(j)})^{-1}$ was an unlucky choice (made *after* the adversary chose its representations from (15)) (case (1)). Otherwise $\alpha^{(j)} \equiv_p 0$ for some j and

$$0 = \gamma_r + c\gamma_x - s + (\xi_r + c\xi_x)x^* + \sum_{i=1}^{q_d+1} \alpha^{(i)} y^i$$

can be solved for y. (Note that the reduction to DL chooses x^* itself.)

Acknowledgements. The first author is supported by the Vienna Science and Technology Fund (WWTF) through project VRG18-002. Parts of this work were done while he was visiting the Simons Institute for the Theory of Computing. This is work is funded in part by the *MSR–Inria Joint Centre*.

References

[Abe01] Abe, M.: A secure three-move blind signature scheme for polynomially many signatures. In: Pfitzmann, B. (ed.) EUROCRYPT 2001. LNCS, vol. 2045, pp. 136–151. Springer, Heidelberg (2001). https://doi.org/10.1007/3-540-44987-6_9

[ABM15] Abdalla, M., Benhamouda, F., MacKenzie, P.: Security of the J-PAKE password-authenticated key exchange protocol. In: 2015 IEEE Symposium on Security and Privacy, pp. 571–587 (2015)

[ABR01] Abdalla, M., Bellare, M., Rogaway, P.: The oracle Diffie-Hellman assumptions and an analysis of DHIES. In: Naccache, D. (ed.) CT-RSA 2001. LNCS, vol. 2020, pp. 143–158. Springer, Heidelberg (2001). https://doi.org/10.1007/3-540-45353-9_12

[BCC04] Brickell, E.F., Camenisch, J., Chen, L.: Direct anonymous attestation. In: ACM CCS 2004, pp. 132–145 (2004)

[BCC+09] Belenkiy, M., Camenisch, J., Chase, M., Kohlweiss, M., Lysyanskaya, A., Shacham, H.: Randomizable proofs and delegatable anonymous credentials. In: Halevi, S. (ed.) CRYPTO 2009. LNCS, vol. 5677, pp. 108–125. Springer, Heidelberg (2009). https://doi.org/10.1007/978-3-642-03356-8_7

[BDL+12] Bernstein, D.J., Duif, N., Lange, T., Schwabe, P., Yang, B.-Y.: High-speed high-security signatures. J. Cryptogr. Eng. $\mathbf{2}$(2), 77–89 (2012). https://doi.org/10.1007/s13389-012-0027-1

[BDN18] Boneh, D., Drijvers, M., Neven, G.: Compact multi-signatures for smaller blockchains. In: Peyrin, T., Galbraith, S. (eds.) ASIACRYPT 2018, Part II. LNCS, vol. 11273, pp. 435–464. Springer, Cham (2018). https://doi.org/10.1007/978-3-030-03329-3_15

[BFPV13] Blazy, O., Fuchsbauer, G., Pointcheval, D., Vergnaud, D.: Short blind signatures. J. Comput. Secur. $\mathbf{21}$(5), 627–661 (2013)

[BFW16] Bernhard, D., Fischlin, M., Warinschi, B.: On the hardness of proving CCA-security of signed ElGamal. In: Cheng, C.-M., Chung, K.-M., Persiano, G., Yang, B.-Y. (eds.) PKC 2016, Part I. LNCS, vol. 9614, pp. 47–69. Springer, Heidelberg (2016). https://doi.org/10.1007/978-3-662-49384-7_3

[BL13a] Baldimtsi, F., Lysyanskaya, A.: Anonymous credentials light. In: ACM CCS 2013, pp. 1087–1098 (2013)

[BL13b]   Baldimtsi, F., Lysyanskaya, A.: On the security of one-witness blind signature schemes. In: Sako, K., Sarkar, P. (eds.) ASIACRYPT 2013, Part II. LNCS, vol. 8270, pp. 82–99. Springer, Heidelberg (2013). https://doi.org/10.1007/978-3-642-42045-0_5

[BLS04]   Boneh, D., Lynn, B., Shacham, H.: Short signatures from the Weil pairing. J. Cryptol. **17**(4), 297–319 (2004). https://doi.org/10.1007/s00145-004-0314-9

[BNPS03] Bellare, M., Namprempre, C., Pointcheval, D., Semanko, M.: The one-more-RSA-inversion problems and the security of Chaum's blind signature scheme. J. Cryptol. **16**(3), 185–215 (2003). https://doi.org/10.1007/s00145-002-0120-1

[BNW17]   Bernhard, D., Nguyen, N.K., Warinschi, B.: Adaptive proofs have straight-line extractors (in the random oracle model). In: Gollmann, D., Miyaji, A., Kikuchi, H. (eds.) ACNS 2017. LNCS, vol. 10355, pp. 336–353. Springer, Cham (2017). https://doi.org/10.1007/978-3-319-61204-1_17

[Bol03]   Boldyreva, A.: Threshold signatures, multisignatures and blind signatures based on the gap-Diffie-Hellman-group signature scheme. In: Desmedt, Y.G. (ed.) PKC 2003. LNCS, vol. 2567, pp. 31–46. Springer, Heidelberg (2003). https://doi.org/10.1007/3-540-36288-6_3

[BP02]   Bellare, M., Palacio, A.: GQ and Schnorr identification schemes: proofs of security against impersonation under active and concurrent attacks. In: Yung, M. (ed.) CRYPTO 2002. LNCS, vol. 2442, pp. 162–177. Springer, Heidelberg (2002). https://doi.org/10.1007/3-540-45708-9_11

[BR93]   Bellare, M., Rogaway, P.: Random oracles are practical: a paradigm for designing efficient protocols. In: ACM CCS 1993, pp. 62–73 (1993)

[BR95]   Bellare, M., Rogaway, P.: Optimal asymmetric encryption. In: De Santis, A. (ed.) EUROCRYPT 1994. LNCS, vol. 950, pp. 92–111. Springer, Heidelberg (1995). https://doi.org/10.1007/BFb0053428

[Bra94]   Brands, S.: Untraceable off-line cash in wallet with observers: extended abstract. In: Stinson, D.R. (ed.) CRYPTO 1993. LNCS, vol. 773, pp. 302–318. Springer, Heidelberg (1994). https://doi.org/10.1007/3-540-48329-2_26

[CFN90]   Chaum, D., Fiat, A., Naor, M.: Untraceable electronic cash. In: Goldwasser, S. (ed.) CRYPTO 1988. LNCS, vol. 403, pp. 319–327. Springer, New York (1990). https://doi.org/10.1007/0-387-34799-2_25

[Cha82]   Chaum, D.: Blind signatures for untraceable payments. In: Chaum, D., Rivest, R.L., Sherman, A.T. (eds.) Advances in Cryptology, pp. 199–203. Springer, Boston (1983). https://doi.org/10.1007/978-1-4757-0602-4_18

[CHL05]   Camenisch, J., Hohenberger, S., Lysyanskaya, A.: Compact e-cash. In: Cramer, R. (ed.) EUROCRYPT 2005. LNCS, vol. 3494, pp. 302–321. Springer, Heidelberg (2005). https://doi.org/10.1007/11426639_18

[CL01]   Camenisch, J., Lysyanskaya, A.: An efficient system for non-transferable anonymous credentials with optional anonymity revocation. In: Pfitzmann, B. (ed.) EUROCRYPT 2001. LNCS, vol. 2045, pp. 93–118. Springer, Heidelberg (2001). https://doi.org/10.1007/3-540-44987-6_7

[CP93]   Chaum, D., Pedersen, T.P.: Wallet databases with observers. In: Brickell, E.F. (ed.) CRYPTO 1992. LNCS, vol. 740, pp. 89–105. Springer, Heidelberg (1993). https://doi.org/10.1007/3-540-48071-4_7

[CS03]   Cramer, R., Shoup, V.: Design and analysis of practical public-key encryption schemes secure against adaptive chosen ciphertext attack. SIAM J. Comput. **33**(1), 167–226 (2003)

[ElG85] ElGamal, T.: A public key cryptosystem and a signature scheme based on discrete logarithms. IEEE Trans. Inf. Theory **31**(4), 469–472 (1985)

[FHS15] Fuchsbauer, G., Hanser, C., Slamanig, D.: Practical round-optimal blind signatures in the standard model. In: Gennaro, R., Robshaw, M. (eds.) CRYPTO 2015, Part II. LNCS, vol. 9216, pp. 233–253. Springer, Heidelberg (2015). https://doi.org/10.1007/978-3-662-48000-7_12

[FJS19] Fleischhacker, N., Jager, T., Schröder, D.: On tight security proofs for Schnorr signatures. J. Cryptol. **32**(2), 566–599 (2019). https://doi.org/10.1007/s00145-019-09311-5

[FKL18] Fuchsbauer, G., Kiltz, E., Loss, J.: The algebraic group model and its applications. In: Shacham, H., Boldyreva, A. (eds.) CRYPTO 2018, Part II. LNCS, vol. 10992, pp. 33–62. Springer, Cham (2018). https://doi.org/10.1007/978-3-319-96881-0_2

[FOO93] Fujioka, A., Okamoto, T., Ohta, K.: A practical secret voting scheme for large scale elections. In: Seberry, J., Zheng, Y. (eds.) AUSCRYPT 1992. LNCS, vol. 718, pp. 244–251. Springer, Heidelberg (1993). https://doi.org/10.1007/3-540-57220-1_66

[FPS19] Fuchsbauer, G., Plouviez, A., Seurin, Y.: Blind Schnorr signatures and signed ElGamal encryption in the algebraic group model. Cryptology ePrint Archive, Report 2019/877 (2019). https://eprint.iacr.org/2019/877

[FPV09] Fuchsbauer, G., Pointcheval, D., Vergnaud, D.: Transferable constant-size fair e-cash. In: Garay, J.A., Miyaji, A., Otsuka, A. (eds.) CANS 2009. LNCS, vol. 5888, pp. 226–247. Springer, Heidelberg (2009). https://doi.org/10.1007/978-3-642-10433-6_15

[FS10] Fischlin, M., Schröder, D.: On the impossibility of three-move blind signature schemes. In: Gilbert, H. (ed.) EUROCRYPT 2010. LNCS, vol. 6110, pp. 197–215. Springer, Heidelberg (2010). https://doi.org/10.1007/978-3-642-13190-5_10

[Fuc11] Fuchsbauer, G.: Commuting signatures and verifiable encryption. In: Paterson, K.G. (ed.) EUROCRYPT 2011. LNCS, vol. 6632, pp. 224–245. Springer, Heidelberg (2011). https://doi.org/10.1007/978-3-642-20465-4_14

[GBL08] Garg, S., Bhaskar, R., Lokam, S.V.: Improved bounds on security reductions for discrete log based signatures. In: Wagner, D. (ed.) CRYPTO 2008. LNCS, vol. 5157, pp. 93–107. Springer, Heidelberg (2008). https://doi.org/10.1007/978-3-540-85174-5_6

[GG14] Garg, S., Gupta, D.: Efficient round optimal blind signatures. In: Nguyen, P.Q., Oswald, E. (eds.) EUROCRYPT 2014. LNCS, vol. 8441, pp. 477–495. Springer, Heidelberg (2014). https://doi.org/10.1007/978-3-642-55220-5_27

[GRS+11] Garg, S., Rao, V., Sahai, A., Schröder, D., Unruh, D.: Round optimal blind signatures. In: Rogaway, P. (ed.) CRYPTO 2011. LNCS, vol. 6841, pp. 630–648. Springer, Heidelberg (2011). https://doi.org/10.1007/978-3-642-22792-9_36

[HHK10] Herranz, J., Hofheinz, D., Kiltz, E.: Some (in)sufficient conditions for secure hybrid encryption. Inf. Comput. **208**(11), 1243–1257 (2010)

[HKL19] Hauck, E., Kiltz, E., Loss, J.: A modular treatment of blind signatures from identification schemes. In: Ishai, Y., Rijmen, V. (eds.) EUROCRYPT 2019, Part III. LNCS, vol. 11478, pp. 345–375. Springer, Cham (2019). https://doi.org/10.1007/978-3-030-17659-4_12

[Jak98]   Jakobsson, M.: A practical mix. In: Nyberg, K. (ed.) EUROCRYPT 1998. LNCS, vol. 1403, pp. 448–461. Springer, Heidelberg (1998). https://doi.org/10.1007/BFb0054145

[MPSW19] Maxwell, G., Poelstra, A., Seurin, Y., Wuille, P.: Simple Schnorr multi-signatures with applications to Bitcoin. Des. Codes Crypt. **87**(9), 2139–2164 (2019). https://doi.org/10.1007/s10623-019-00608-x

[MS12]   Minder, L., Sinclair, A.: The extended k-tree algorithm. J. Cryptol. **25**(2), 349–382 (2012). https://doi.org/10.1007/s00145-011-9097-y

[Nec94]   Nechaev, V.I.: Complexity of a determinate algorithm for the discrete logarithm. Math. Notes **55**(2), 165–172 (1994). https://doi.org/10.1007/BF02113297

[Nic19]   Nick, J.: Blind signatures in scriptless scripts. Presentation given at *Building on Bitcoin* 2019 (2019). Slides and video. https://jonasnick.github.io/blog/2018/07/31/blind-signatures-in-scriptless-scripts/

[NS15]   Nikolić, I., Sasaki, Y.: Refinements of the *k*-tree algorithm for the generalized birthday problem. In: Iwata, T., Cheon, J.H. (eds.) ASIACRYPT 2015, Part II. LNCS, vol. 9453, pp. 683–703. Springer, Heidelberg (2015). https://doi.org/10.1007/978-3-662-48800-3_28

[OO92]   Okamoto, T., Ohta, K.: Universal electronic cash. In: Feigenbaum, J. (ed.) CRYPTO 1991. LNCS, vol. 576, pp. 324–337. Springer, Heidelberg (1992). https://doi.org/10.1007/3-540-46766-1_27

[Pas11]   Pass, R.: Limits of provable security from standard assumptions. In: 43rd ACM STOC, pp. 109–118 (2011)

[PS96a]   Pointcheval, D., Stern, J.: Provably secure blind signature schemes. In: Kim, K., Matsumoto, T. (eds.) ASIACRYPT 1996. LNCS, vol. 1163, pp. 252–265. Springer, Heidelberg (1996). https://doi.org/10.1007/BFb0034852

[PS96b]   Pointcheval, D., Stern, J.: Security proofs for signature schemes. In: Maurer, U. (ed.) EUROCRYPT 1996. LNCS, vol. 1070, pp. 387–398. Springer, Heidelberg (1996). https://doi.org/10.1007/3-540-68339-9_33

[PS00]   Pointcheval, D., Stern, J.: Security arguments for digital signatures and blind signatures. J. Cryptol. **13**(3), 361–396 (2000). https://doi.org/10.1007/s001450010003

[PV05]   Paillier, P., Vergnaud, D.: Discrete-log-based signatures may not be equivalent to discrete log. In: Roy, B. (ed.) ASIACRYPT 2005. LNCS, vol. 3788, pp. 1–20. Springer, Heidelberg (2005). https://doi.org/10.1007/11593447_1

[Sch90]   Schnorr, C.P.: Efficient identification and signatures for smart cards. In: Brassard, G. (ed.) CRYPTO 1989. LNCS, vol. 435, pp. 239–252. Springer, New York (1990). https://doi.org/10.1007/0-387-34805-0_22

[Sch91]   Schnorr, C.P.: Efficient signature generation by smart cards. J. Cryptol. **4**(3), 161–174 (1991). https://doi.org/10.1007/BF00196725

[Sch01]   Schnorr, C.P.: Security of blind discrete log signatures against interactive attacks. In: Qing, S., Okamoto, T., Zhou, J. (eds.) ICICS 2001. LNCS, vol. 2229, pp. 1–12. Springer, Heidelberg (2001). https://doi.org/10.1007/3-540-45600-7_1

[Seu12]   Seurin, Y.: On the exact security of Schnorr-type signatures in the random oracle model. In: Pointcheval, D., Johansson, T. (eds.) EUROCRYPT 2012. LNCS, vol. 7237, pp. 554–571. Springer, Heidelberg (2012). https://doi.org/10.1007/978-3-642-29011-4_33

[SG02] Shoup, V., Gennaro, R.: Securing threshold cryptosystems against chosen ciphertext attack. J. Cryptol. **15**(2), 75–96 (2002). https://doi.org/10.1007/s00145-001-0020-9

[Sho97] Shoup, V.: Lower bounds for discrete logarithms and related problems. In: Fumy, W. (ed.) EUROCRYPT 1997. LNCS, vol. 1233, pp. 256–266. Springer, Heidelberg (1997). https://doi.org/10.1007/3-540-69053-0_18

[SJ99] Schnorr, C.-P., Jakobsson, M.: Security of discrete log cryptosystems in the random oracle and the generic model (1999). https://core.ac.uk/download/pdf/14504220.pdf

[SJ00] Schnorr, C.P., Jakobsson, M.: Security of signed ElGamal encryption. In: Okamoto, T. (ed.) ASIACRYPT 2000. LNCS, vol. 1976, pp. 73–89. Springer, Heidelberg (2000). https://doi.org/10.1007/3-540-44448-3_7

[ST13] Seurin, Y., Treger, J.: A robust and plaintext-aware variant of signed ElGamal encryption. In: Dawson, E. (ed.) CT-RSA 2013. LNCS, vol. 7779, pp. 68–83. Springer, Heidelberg (2013). https://doi.org/10.1007/978-3-642-36095-4_5

[TY98] Tsiounis, Y., Yung, M.: On the security of ElGamal based encryption. In: Imai, H., Zheng, Y. (eds.) PKC 1998. LNCS, vol. 1431, pp. 117–134. Springer, Heidelberg (1998). https://doi.org/10.1007/BFb0054019

[Wag02] Wagner, D.: A generalized birthday problem. In: Yung, M. (ed.) CRYPTO 2002. LNCS, vol. 2442, pp. 288–304. Springer, Heidelberg (2002). https://doi.org/10.1007/3-540-45708-9_19

[Wik08] Wikström, D.: Simplified submission of inputs to protocols. In: Ostrovsky, R., De Prisco, R., Visconti, I. (eds.) SCN 2008. LNCS, vol. 5229, pp. 293–308. Springer, Heidelberg (2008). https://doi.org/10.1007/978-3-540-85855-3_20

[Wui18] Wuille, P.: Schnorr signatures for secp256k1. Bitcoin Improvement Proposal (2018). https://github.com/sipa/bips/blob/bip-schnorr/bip-schnorr.mediawiki

On Instantiating the Algebraic Group Model from Falsifiable Assumptions

Thomas Agrikola[1]($^{\boxtimes}$), Dennis Hofheinz[2]($^{\boxtimes}$), and Julia Kastner[2]

[1] Karlsruhe Institute of Technology, Karlsruhe, Germany
thomas.agrikola@kit.edu
[2] ETH Zürich, Zürich, Switzerland
{hofheinz,julia.kastner}@inf.ethz.ch

Abstract. We provide a standard-model implementation (of a relaxation) of the algebraic group model (AGM, [Fuchsbauer, Kiltz, Loss, CRYPTO 2018]). Specifically, we show that every algorithm that uses our group is algebraic, and hence "must know" a representation of its output group elements in terms of its input group elements. Here, "must know" means that a suitable extractor can extract such a representation efficiently. We stress that our implementation relies only on falsifiable assumptions in the standard model, and in particular does not use any knowledge assumptions.

As a consequence, our group allows to transport a number of results obtained in the AGM into the standard model, under falsifiable assumptions. For instance, we show that in our group, several Diffie-Hellman-like assumptions (including computational Diffie-Hellman) are equivalent to the discrete logarithm assumption. Furthermore, we show that our group allows to prove the Schnorr signature scheme tightly secure in the random oracle model.

Our construction relies on indistinguishability obfuscation, and hence should not be considered as a practical group itself. However, our results show that the AGM is a realistic computational model (since it can be instantiated in the standard model), and that results obtained in the AGM are also possible with standard-model groups.

Keywords: Indistinguishability obfuscation · Algebraic group model · Schnorr signatures

1 Introduction

The generic group model. In order to analyze the plausibility and relative strength of computational assumptions in cyclic groups, Shoup [38] and Maurer [31] have

Work done while all authors were at Karlsruhe Institute of Technology.

T. Agrikola and J. Kastner—Supported by ERC Project PREP-CRYPTO 724307.

D. Hofheinz—Supported by ERC Project PREP-CRYPTO 724307, and by DFG project GZ HO 4534/4-2.

A. Canteaut and Y. Ishai (Eds.): EUROCRYPT 2020, LNCS 12106, pp. 96–126, 2020.
https://doi.org/10.1007/978-3-030-45724-2_4

proposed the *generic group model* (GGM). In the GGM, any adversary can only interact with the modeled group through an oracle. In particular, all computations in that group must be explicitly expressed in terms of the group operation. To prevent an adversary from locally performing computations, that adversary gets to see only truly random strings (in [38]) or independent handles (in [31]) as representations of group elements.[1]

The discrete logarithm and even many Diffie-Hellman-style problems are hard generically (i.e., when restricting group operations in the above way) [32,38]. Hence, the only way to break such a generically hard assumption in a concrete group is to use the underlying group representation in a nontrivial way. In that sense, the GGM can be very useful as a sanity check for the validity of a given assumption, or even the security of a given cryptographic scheme. However, generic groups cannot be implemented: there exist cryptographic schemes that are secure in the GGM, but insecure when instantiated with *any* concrete group [15].

The algebraic group model. The algebraic group model (AGM, [21]) is a relaxation of the GGM that tries to avoid impossibilities as in [15] while preserving the GGM's usefulness. Specifically, the AGM only considers *algebraic* (rather than generic) adversaries. An algebraic adversary $\mathcal{A}$ can make arbitrary use of the representation of group elements, but must supply an explicit decomposition for any of its output group elements in terms of input group elements. In other words, $\mathcal{A}$ must also output an explanation of how any group element in its output was computed from its input using the group operation.

Now [21] show that many GGM proofs only use this type of algebraicity of an adversary, and carry over to the AGM. At the same time, GGM impossibilities like [15] do not apply to the AGM, since algebraic adversaries are able to work with the actual group (and not only with random or abstract representations of group elements).

The AGM and knowledge assumptions. The AGM is closely related to the notions of knowledge assumptions and extractability. To illustrate, assume that for any (possibly non-algebraic) adversary $\mathcal{A}$, we can find an extractor $\mathcal{E}$ that manages to extract from $\mathcal{A}$ a decomposition of $\mathcal{A}$'s output in terms of $\mathcal{A}$'s input. Then, composing $\mathcal{E}$ and $\mathcal{A}$ yields an algebraic adversary $\mathcal{A}_{\mathrm{alg}}$. In this situation, we can then say that without loss of generality, any adversary can be assumed to be algebraic.[2] Conversely, any algebraic adversary by definition yields the results of such an extraction in its output.

This observation also provides a blueprint to *instantiating* the AGM: simply prove that any adversary $\mathcal{A}$ can be replaced by an algebraic adversary $\mathcal{A}_{\mathrm{alg}}$, possibly using an extraction process as above. If this extraction requires $\mathcal{A}$'s code

---

[1] Other black-box abstractions of groups with similar ramifications exist [6,34].

[2] This observation about algebraic adversaries has already been made in [9,35]. Also, similar but more specific knowledge assumptions have been used to prove concrete cryptographic constructions secure, e.g., [4,14,16,25].

and randomness but no other trapdoor, we obtain an AGM instantiation based on a knowledge assumption such as the knowledge of exponent assumption [14]. Indeed, this was recently done by [30] under a very strong generalized version of the knowledge of exponent assumption. Unfortunately, such knowledge assumptions are not falsifiable in the sense of Naor [33]. It is thus not entirely clear how to assess the plausibility of such a universal and strong knowledge assumption. Naturally, the question arises whether an AGM implementation inherently requires such strong and non-falsifiable assumptions. Or, more generally:

Can we achieve knowledge-type properties
from falsifiable assumptions?

Note that in the AGM, the discrete logarithm assumption implies the existence of extractable one-way functions (EOWFs) with unbounded auxiliary input. The existence of such EOWFs, however, conflicts with the existence of indistinguishability obfuscation, [5]. Due to this barrier, we can only hope for an instantiation of some suitably relaxed variant of the AGM from falsifiable assumptions.

Our strategy: private extraction. There is also another way to instantiate the AGM: show that it is possible to extract a decomposition of $\mathcal{A}$'s outputs *from these outputs* and a suitable (secret) extraction trapdoor. In other words, our idea is to avoid non-falsifiable knowledge assumptions by assuming that extraction requires a special trapdoor that can be generated alongside the public parameters of the group. This entails a number of technical difficulties (see below), but allows us to rely entirely on falsifiable assumptions.

Specifically, our main result is an *algebraic wrapper* that transforms a given cyclic group into a new one which allows for an extraction of representations. More specifically, an element of the new group carries an encrypted representation of this group element relative to a fixed basis (i.e., set of group elements). Upon group operations, this representation is updated, and a special trapdoor (generated alongside the public parameters) allows to extract it.

Our results. Our strategy allows us to retrieve several AGM results (from [21,22]) in the standard model, in the sense that the group can be concretely implemented from falsifiable assumptions.[3] In particular, we show that in our group,

- the discrete logarithm assumption, the computational Diffie-Hellman assumption, the square Diffie-Hellman assumption, and the linear-combination Diffie-Hellman assumption (see [21]) are all equivalent,

---

[3] Note that by "standard model", we mean that the group itself is formulated without idealizations and can be concretely implemented. While our construction itself does not rely on the ROM, we still can transfer some ROM proofs in the AGM to ROM proofs using our concrete group instantiation. We stress that a standard model instantiation of the (full-fledged) AGM from very strong *non-falsifiable* assumptions is already known due to [30].

- the security of the Schnorr signature scheme [37] can be *tightly* reduced to the discrete logarithm assumption escaping impossibility results due to [19].[4]

While, on a technical level, the AGM proofs from [21,22] need to be adapted, the general AGM proof strategies (that rely on extraction) can be replicated.

Limitations. We note that not all known AGM proofs can be transported to the standard model. For instance, [21] also prove the Boneh-Lynn-Shacham [7] signature scheme tightly secure in the AGM. Their reduction relies on the fact that the view of a signature forger is statistically independent of how simulated signatures are prepared by the reduction. However, with our algebraic wrapper, group elements (and thus BLS signatures) always carry an encrypted representation of how they were generated. In this case, our private extraction strategy also reveals additional (statistical, computationally hidden) information to an adversary. This additional information is problematic in the AGM-based BLS proof of [21]. We believe it is an interesting open problem to obtain a tight security proof for the BLS scheme with our group.[5]

Furthermore, as we will detail below, the amount of information we can extract from a group element is limited by the size of that group element. In particular, in settings in which no a-priori bound on the size of a desired algebraic representation is known, our techniques do not apply. This can be problematic, e.g., for constructions that depend on q-type assumptions.

Our assumptions. We stress that our algebraic wrapper relies on a strong (but falsifiable) computational assumption: the existence of subexponentially strong indistinguishability obfuscation (subexp-iO).[6] Additionally, we assume a re-randomizable encryption scheme. Together with subexp-iO, this implies a number of other strong primitives that we use: a variant of probabilistic iO (see [11]), fully homomorphic encryption (see [11]), and dual-mode non-interactive zero-knowledge (see [27]).

Interpretation. Due to their inefficiency, we view algebraic wrappers not as a tool to obtain practical cryptographic primitives. Rather, we believe that algebraic wrappers show that the AGM is a useful and realistic abstraction and not merely an idealized model which heuristically captures known adversaries: we show that AGM proofs *can* be replicated in the standard model, and even without resorting to knowledge assumptions.

---

[4] Tight security reductions provide a tight relation between the security of cryptographic schemes and the hardness of computational problems. Apart from their theoretical importance, tight reductions are also beneficial for practice, since they allow smaller keylength recommendations.

[5] We note that impossibility results for tight reductions of schemes like BLS (e.g., [12]) do not apply in our case, as the representation of our group elements is not unique.

[6] We note that iO and knowledge assumptions contradict each other [5]. However, we stress that the notion of *private* extractability we obtain does *not* contradict iO.

On implementing idealized models. Replacing idealized (heuristic) models with concrete standard-model implementations is a widely studied intriguing problem. A well-known example for this is the line of work on programmable hash functions. A programmable hash function due to [26] is a cryptographic primitive which can be used to replace random oracles in several cryptographic schemes. Following their introduction, a line of work [20, 28, 29] leveraged multi-linear maps or indistinguishability obfuscation to transport proofs from the random oracle model to the standard model. Our results can be interpreted as following this endeavor by leveraging indistinguishability obfuscation to replace the AGM with a standard model implementation (from falsifiable assumptions). From this angle, our algebraic wrapper relates to the AGM as programmable hash functions relate to the ROM.

1.1 Technical Overview

Algebraic wrappers. In the following, we speak of *group schemes* ([3], also called encoding schemes in [23]) as a generalization of groups with potentially non-unique encodings of group elements. This implies that a dedicated algorithm is required to determine if two given group elements are equal.[7] Our algebraic wrapping process takes a group $\mathbb{G}$ (which we call "base group") as input, and outputs a new group scheme $\mathbb{H}$ which allows for an efficient extraction process. Concretely, every $\mathbb{H}$-element $\widehat{h}$ can be viewed as a $\mathbb{G}$-element $h \in \mathbb{G}$, plus auxiliary information *aux*.

Intuitively, *aux* carries (encrypted) information that allows to express h as a linear combination of fixed base elements $b_1, \ldots, b_n \in \mathbb{G}$. The corresponding decryption key (generated alongside the group parameters) allows to extract this information, and essentially yields the information any algebraic adversary (in the sense of the AGM) would have to provide for any output group element. However, we are facing a number of technical problems:

(a) The group operation algorithm should update *aux* (in the sense that the linear combinations encrypted in the input elements should be added).
(b) Validity of *aux* should be ensured (so that no adversary can produce an $\mathbb{H}$-element from which no valid linear combination can be extracted from *aux*).
(c) It should be possible to switch the basis elements $b_1, \ldots, b_n$ to an application-dependent basis. (For instance, to prove a signature scheme like Schnorr's [37] secure, one would desire to set the basis vectors to elements from an externally given computational challenge.)
(d) To preserve tightness of reductions from the AGM (which is necessary in some of our applications), it should be possible to re-randomize group element encodings statistically.

---

[7] That is, formally, the group is defined as the quotient set of all well-formed bitstrings modulo the equivalence relation induced by the equality test.

Our solution largely follows the group scheme from [3]. In particular, (a) will be solved by encrypting the coefficients $z_1, \ldots, z_n$ with $h = \sum_i b_i^{z_i}$ using a homomorphic encryption scheme in aux. Hence, such coefficient vectors can be added homomorphically during the group operation. For (b), we will add a suitable non-interactive zero-knowledge proof of consistency in aux.[8] For (c), we adapt a "switching" lemma from [3]. In [3], that lemma allows to switch between two different representations of the same group element, but under a fixed basis. In our case, we show that similar techniques allow to also switch the group elements that form this basis. This switching property already implies a notion of computational re-randomizability. Finally, for (d), we introduce a re-randomization lemma using techniques from (c) in conjunction with a novel notion for probabilistic iO.

At this point, one main conceptual difference to the line of work [1,3,17] is that the basis elements $b_1, \ldots, b_n$ appear as part of the functionality of the new group scheme $\mathbb{H}$, not only in a proof. In particular, our construction must be able to deal with arbitrary b_i that are not necessarily randomly chosen. This issue is dealt with by additional linear randomization of the base group elements.

Another main conceptual difference to [1,3,17] is the notion of statistical re-randomizability of group elements. The group schemes from [1,3,17] do not satisfy this property. This will be resolved by developing a stronger notion of *statistically correct* probabilistic iO which may be of independent interest.

We note, however, that our techniques are inherently limited in the following sense: our extraction can only extract as much information as contained in (the auxiliary information of) group elements. Technically speaking, we cannot treat settings in which the size of the basis $b_1, \ldots, b_n$ is not known in advance (e.g., in case of constructions based on q-type assumptions).

Applications. The applications we consider have already been considered for the AGM in [21,22]. Hence, in this description, we focus on the technical differences that our extraction approach entails for these proofs.

First, recall that in the AGM by [21], an adversary outputs an algebraic representation of each output group element to the basis of its input group elements. Therefore, this basis depends also on the respective security game. On the other hand, in security proofs with our algebraic wrapper, a reduction needs to select such a basis in advance. The appropriate selection of such a basis is one of the main challenges when transferring proofs from the AGM to our setting. Namely, even though the basis as well as the representation of each group element is hidden, the choice of representations will still be information-theoretically known to the adversary. Therefore, security games that are identically distributed in the AGM might only be computationally indistinguishable in the wrapper, depending on the choice of a basis.

When transferring proofs from the AGM to our new group scheme, we thus use a technique we call *symmetrization* to extend the basis in such a way that

---

[8] Note that this approach is related to [8] in the sense that we restrict the homomorphic operations an adversary can perform on encodings by requiring a consistency proof.

security games are identically distributed in the relevant situations. In a nutshell, symmetrization achieves a uniform way to express challenge elements across most games of a security proof, and yields statistical security guarantees.

Another challenge is the implementation of tight security reductions in the wrapper. In some security reductions, the basis of the group and the algebraic representations of oracle responses need to be switched in order to be able to extract a useful algebraic representation. However, as we only achieve computationally indistinguishable group element representations, switching the representations of q oracle responses would lead to a q-fold computational loss, compromising the tightness of the reduction.

We show that it is possible to circumvent this loss by constructing oracle responses via the group operation from so-called *origin elements*, reducing the number of elements whose representation gets switched to a constant. In a nutshell, we derive many coordinated oracle answers from just few group elements (the "origin elements"), such that switching these origin elements affects (and changes) all oracle answers.

1.2   Related Work

This work builds upon the line of work [1,3,17] who build group schemes from iO. [3] lays the conceptual foundations for the construction of group schemes with non-unique encodings from iO and uses this framework to equip groups with multilinear maps. [17] extends this approach by allowing partial evaluations of the multilinear map yielding a graded encoding scheme. In contrast to [1,3,17] does not extend the functionality of an underlying group, but builds a group scheme with reduced functionality (group elements lack a unique representation). The resulting group scheme allows to mimic commonly used proof techniques from the generic group model. This is demonstrated by proving the validity of an adaptive variant of the Uber assumption family [10] in the constructed group scheme. Our results can hence be viewed as an extension of [1].

[30] make a first step towards instantiating the AGM. The authors identify an equivalence between the AGM and a very strong generalized version of the knowledge of exponent assumption [14], thus giving rise to the first instantiation of the AGM.

Roadmap

In Sect. 2, we recall some preliminaries and develop the mentioned variant of probabilistic iO. In Sect. 3, we present our notion of algebraic wrappers and give an iO-based instantiation. Section 4 contains results transported from the AGM to our wrapper setting, along with a description of how AGM proof techniques can be adapted. In the full version of this paper [2], we provide (besides further standard definitions and more motivation) an analysis of the Schnorr-signed ElGamal encryption scheme with our algebraic wrapper.

2   Preliminaries

Notation

Throughout this paper λ denotes the security parameter. For a natural number $n \in \mathbb{N}$, $[n]$ denotes the set $\{1, \ldots, n\}$. A function $\mathsf{negl}\colon \mathbb{N} \to \mathbb{R}$ is negligible in λ if for every constant $c \in \mathbb{N}$, there exists a bound $n_c \in \mathbb{R}$, such that for all $n \geq n_c$, $|\mathsf{negl}(n)| \leq n^{-c}$. Given a finite set S, the notation $x \leftarrow S$ means a uniformly random assignment of an element of S to the variable x. Given an algorithm A, the notation $y \leftarrow A(x)$ means evaluation of A on input of x with fresh random coins and assignment to the variable y. The notation $\mathcal{A}^{\mathcal{O}}$ indicates that the algorithm $\mathcal{A}$ is given oracle access to $\mathcal{O}$. Given a random variable B, $\mathsf{supp}(B)$ denotes the support of B.

Let $\mathbb{G}$ be a finite cyclic group with generator g and order p. For $x \in \mathbb{Z}_p$, the notation $[x]_{\mathbb{G}}$ denotes the group element g^x. Note that using this notation does not imply knowledge of x. Let $\mathbb{K}$ be a field and V be a vector space over $\mathbb{K}$ of finite dimension n. For $i \in [n]$, $\mathbf{e_i}$ denotes the vector which carries 1 in its i-th entry and 0 in all other entries.

In game based proofs, out_i denotes the output of game G_i.

2.1   Subset Membership Problem

Let $\mathcal{L} = (\mathcal{L}_\lambda)_{\lambda \in \mathbb{N}}$ be a family of families of languages $L \subseteq X_\lambda$ in a universe $X_\lambda = X$. Further, let R be an efficiently computable witness relation, such that $x \in L$ if and only if there exists a witness $w \in \{0,1\}^{\mathsf{poly}(|x|)}$ with $R(x, w) = 1$ (for a fixed polynomial poly). We assume that we are able to efficiently and uniformly sample elements from L together with a corresponding witness, and that we are able to efficiently and uniformly sample elements from $X \setminus L$.

Definition 1 (Subset membership problem, [13]). *A subset membership problem $L \subseteq X$ is hard, if for any PPT adversary $\mathcal{A}$, the advantage*

$$\mathrm{Adv}^{\mathrm{smp}}_{L,\mathcal{A}}(\lambda) := \Pr[x \leftarrow L \colon \mathcal{A}(1^\lambda, x) = 1] - \Pr[x \leftarrow X \setminus L \colon \mathcal{A}(1^\lambda, x) = 1]$$

is negligible in λ.

We additionally require that for every L and every $x \in L$, there exists exactly one witness $r \in \{0,1\}^*$ with $R(x, w) = 1$. Note that given a cyclic group $\mathbb{G}$ of prime order p in which DDH is assumed to hold, the Diffie-Hellman language $L_{[(1,x)]_{\mathbb{G}}} := \{[(y, xy)]_{\mathbb{G}} \mid y \in \mathbb{Z}_p\}$ (for randomly chosen generators $[1]_{\mathbb{G}}, [x]_{\mathbb{G}}$) satisfies this definition. Another instantiation of Definition 1 is the language containing all commitments to a fixed value using a perfectly binding commitment scheme with unique opening.

2.2   Dual-mode NIWI

A dual-mode NIWI proof system is a variant of NIWI proofs [18] offering two computationally indistinguishable modes to setup the common reference string (CRS). A binding mode CRS provides perfect soundness guarantees whereas a hiding mode CRS provides perfect witness indistinguishability guarantees.

Definition 2 (Dual-mode NIWI proof system (syntax), [3,24]). *A dual mode non-interactive witness-indistinguishable (NIWI) proof system for a relation $\mathcal{R}$ is a tuple of PPT algorithms* $\Pi = (\mathsf{Setup}, \mathsf{HSetup}, \mathsf{Prove}, \mathsf{Verify}, \mathsf{Ext})$.

$\mathsf{Setup}(1^\lambda)$. *On input of* 1^λ, Setup *outputs a perfectly binding common reference string* crs *and a corresponding extraction trapdoor* $\mathsf{td}_{\mathsf{ext}}$.

$\mathsf{HSetup}(1^\lambda)$. *On input of* 1^λ, HSetup *outputs a perfectly hiding common reference string* crs.

$\mathsf{Prove}(\mathsf{crs}, x, w)$. *On input of the CRS* crs, *a statement* x *and a corresponding witness* w, Prove *produces a proof* π.

$\mathsf{Verify}(\mathsf{crs}, x, \pi)$. *On of the CRS* crs, *a statement* x *and a proof* π, Verify *outputs* 1 *if the proof is valid and* 0 *otherwise.*

$\mathsf{Ext}(\mathsf{td}_{\mathsf{ext}}, x, \pi)$. *On input the extraction trapdoor* $\mathsf{td}_{\mathsf{ext}}$, *a statement* x *and a proof* π, Ext *outputs a witness* w.

We require Π *to satisfy the CRS indistinguishability, perfect completeness, perfect soundness, perfect extractability and perfect witness-indistinguishability.*

For a more detailed definition, we refer the reader to the full version [2]. There are several instantiations of dual-mode NIWI proof systems satisfying the above definition (or statistical variants), [24,27,36].

2.3   Probabilistic Indistinguishability Obfuscation

Let $\mathcal{C} = (\mathcal{C}_\lambda)_{\lambda \in \mathbb{N}}$ be a family of sets $\mathcal{C}_\lambda$ of probabilistic circuits. A *circuit sampler* for $\mathcal{C}$ is defined as a family of (efficiently samplable) distributions $S = (S_\lambda)_{\lambda \in \mathbb{N}}$, where S_λ is a distribution over triplets (C_0, C_1, z) with $C_0, C_1 \in \mathcal{C}_\lambda$ such that C_0 and C_1 take inputs of the same length and $z \in \{0,1\}^{poly(\lambda)}$.

Definition 3 (X-ind sampler, [11]). *Let $X(\lambda)$ be a function upper bounded by 2^λ. The class $\mathcal{S}^{X\text{-ind}}$ of X-ind samplers for a circuit family $\mathcal{C}$ contains all circuit samplers $S = (S_\lambda)_{\lambda \in \mathbb{N}}$ for $\mathcal{C}$ such that for all $\lambda \in \mathbb{N}$, there exists a set $\mathcal{X}_\lambda \subseteq \{0,1\}^*$ with $|\mathcal{X}| \leq X(\lambda)$, such that*

X-differing inputs. With overwhelming probability over the choice of $(C_0, C_1, z) \leftarrow S_\lambda$, for every $x \notin \mathcal{X}_\lambda$, for all $r \in \{0,1\}^{m(\lambda)}$, $C_0(x;r) = C_1(x;r)$.

X-indistinguishability. For all (non-uniform) adversaries $\mathcal{A}$, the advantage

$$X(\lambda) \cdot \left(\Pr[\mathsf{Exp}_{S,\mathcal{A}}^{\mathsf{sel-ind}}(\lambda) = 1] - \frac{1}{2} \right)$$

is negligible, where $\text{Exp}_{S,A}^{\text{sel-ind}}(\lambda)$ *requires* A *to statically choose an input, samples circuits* C_0, C_1 *(and auxiliary information* z*) afterwards, evaluates the circuit* C_b *(for randomly chosen* b*) on the adversarially chosen input (let the output be* y*) and outputs 1 if* A *on input of* (C_0, C_1, z, y) *guesses* b *correctly.*

Definition 4 (Probabilistic indistinguishability obfuscation for a class of samplers S **(syntax), [11]).** *A probabilistic indistinguishability obfuscator (pIO) for a class of samplers* S *is a uniform PPT algorithm* pIO*, such that correctness and security with respect to* S *hold.*

For a more detailed definition, we refer the reader to the full version [2].

[11] present the to date only known construction of pIO for X-ind samplers over the family of all polynomial sized probabilistic circuits.

2.4 Re-randomizable and Fully Homomorphic Encryption

We define an IND-CPA secure PKE scheme as a tuple of PPT algorithms PKE = (KGen, Enc, Dec) in the usual sense. Furthermore, without loss of generality, we assume that sk is the random tape used for key generation. Therefore, making the random tape of KGen explicit, we write $(pk, sk) = \text{KGen}(1^\lambda; sk)$.

A re-randomizable PKE scheme additionally provides an algorithm Rerand which re-randomizes a given ciphertext perfectly.

Finally, a fully homomorphic PKE scheme additionally provides an algorithm Eval which given the public key pk, an circuit C (expecting a inputs from the message space) and a ciphertexts $C_1, \ldots, C_a$, produces a ciphertext encrypting $C(\text{Dec}(sk, C_1), \ldots, \text{Dec}(sk, C_a))$.

Due to [11], probabilistic indistinguishability obfuscation in conjunction with (slightly super-polynomially secure) perfectly correct and perfectly re-randomizable public-key encryption yields a perfectly correct and perfectly re-randomizable fully homomorphic encryption scheme.

We refer the reader to the full version [2] for more detailed definitions.

2.5 Statistically Correct Input Expanding pIO

Looking ahead, instead of computationally correct pIO, we require a notion of statistically correct pIO, i.e. statistical closeness between evaluations of the original (probabilistic) circuit and the obfuscated (deterministic) circuit. Clearly, in general, this is impossible since the obfuscated circuit is deterministic and hence has no source of entropy other than its input. However, as long as a portion of the circuit's input is guaranteed to be outside the view of the adversary (and has sufficiently high min-entropy), the output of the obfuscated circuit and the actual probabilistic circuit can be statistically close. Therefore, we compile probabilistic circuits such that they receive an auxiliary input aux but simply ignore this input in their computation. Even though the obfuscated circuit is deterministic, the auxiliary input can be used as a source of actual entropy.

First try. We recall that the pIO construction from [11] obfuscates a probabilistic circuit C by using IO to obfuscate the deterministic circuit $\overline{C}(x) := C(x; F_K(x))$. A natural idea to achieve statistical correctness is to modify this construction such that the auxiliary input *aux* is directly XORed on the random tape which is derived using F, i.e. to obfuscate the circuit $\overline{C}(x, aux; F_K(x) \oplus aux)$. For uniform auxiliary input *aux*, statistical correctness follows immediately. However, security breaks down. Consider two circuits C_1 and C_2 such that C_1 outputs the first bit on its random tape and C_2 outputs the second bit on its random tape. Since C_1 and C_2 produce identical output distributions, it is desirable that a probabilistic indistinguishability obfuscator conceals which of the two circuits was obfuscated. However, this construction admits a successful attack. An adversary can evaluate the obfuscated circuit Λ on inputs (x, aux) and $(x, aux \oplus 1)$. If both evaluations yield identical outputs, C_2 was obfuscated, otherwise C_1 was obfuscated.

Using an extracting PRF. Our construction of statistically correct pIO applies an extracting puncturable PRF on the entire input (including the auxiliary input) of the circuit to derive the random tape for the probabilistic circuit. An extracting PRF guarantees that PRF outputs are uniformly distributed (even given the PRF key) as long as the input has high min-entropy. This is achieved using a universal hash function and the leftover hash lemma. For more details, we refer the reader to the full version [2].

Let $\{C_\lambda\}_{\lambda \in \mathbb{N}}$ be a family of sets C_λ of probabilistic circuits of polynomial size $p(\lambda)$ expecting inputs from $\{0,1\}^{n'(\lambda)}$ and randomness from $\{0,1\}^{r(\lambda)}$. Let $\mathcal{E}_\ell$ denote a compiler which on input of a probabilistic circuit $C \in C_\lambda$ appends $\ell(\lambda)$ input gates (without any additional edges) to the original circuit. The expanded circuit $\widehat{C}$ is of size $p'(\lambda) = p(\lambda) + \ell(\lambda)$, expects inputs from $\{0,1\}^{n'(\lambda)+\ell(\lambda)}$ and randomness from $\{0,1\}^{r(\lambda)}$. We refer to these additional input bits as auxiliary input $aux \in \{0,1\}^{\ell(\lambda)}$.

Our input expanding pIO scheme satisfies similar correctness and security properties as defined in [11] but additionally guarantees statistical correctness.

Definition 5 (ℓ-expanding pIO for the class of samplers $\mathcal{S}$). *An ℓ-expanding probabilistic indistinguishability obfuscator for the class of samplers $\mathcal{S}$ over $C = (C_\lambda)_{\lambda \in \mathbb{N}}$ is a uniform PPT algorithm $\mathsf{piO}_\ell^\star$, satisfying the following properties.*

Input expanding correctness. *For all PPT adversaries $\mathcal{A}$, all circuits $C \in \mathcal{C}$,*

$$\left| \Pr[\mathcal{A}^{\mathcal{O}_C(\cdot,\cdot)}(1^\lambda, C) = 1] - \Pr[\Lambda \leftarrow \mathsf{piO}_\ell^\star(1^{p(\lambda)}, C) : \mathcal{A}^{\mathcal{O}_\Lambda(\cdot,\cdot)}(1^\lambda, C) = 1] \right|$$

is negligible, where the oracles must not be called twice on the same input (x, aux).

$$\frac{\mathcal{O}_C(x, aux)}{r \leftarrow \{0,1\}^m} \qquad \frac{\mathcal{O}_\Lambda(x, aux)}{\textbf{return } \Lambda(x, aux)}$$
$$\textbf{return } C(x; r)$$

Security with respect to $\mathcal{S}$. *For all circuit samplers $S \in \mathcal{S}$, for all PPT adversaries $\mathcal{A}$, the advantage*

$$\mathrm{Adv}^{\mathrm{pio\text{-}ind}(\star)}_{\mathrm{piO}^\star_\ell, S, \mathcal{A}}(\lambda) :=$$

$$\left| \Pr\left[(C_0, C_1, z) \leftarrow S(1^\lambda) : \mathcal{A}(1^\lambda, C_0, C_1, z, \mathrm{piO}^\star_\ell(1^{p(\lambda)}, C_0)) = 1 \right] \right.$$

$$\left. - \Pr\left[(C_0, C_1, z) \leftarrow S(1^\lambda) : \mathcal{A}(1^\lambda, C_0, C_1, z, \mathrm{piO}^\star_\ell(1^{p(\lambda)}, C_1)) = 1 \right] \right|$$

is negligible in λ.

Support respecting. *For all circuits $C \in \mathcal{C}_\lambda$, all inputs $x \in \{0,1\}^{n'(\lambda)}$, all $aux \in \{0,1\}^{\ell(\lambda)}$, all $\Lambda \in \mathrm{supp}(\mathrm{piO}^\star_\ell(1^{p(\lambda)}, C))$, $\Lambda(x, aux) \in \mathrm{supp}(C(x))$.*

Statistical correctness with error $2^{-e(\lambda)}$. *For all $C \in \mathcal{C}_\lambda$ and all joint distributions (X_1, X_2) over $\{0,1\}^{n'(\lambda)} \times \{0,1\}^{\ell(\lambda)}$ with average min-entropy $\ell(\lambda) \geq \widetilde{\mathrm{H}}_\infty(X_2 \mid X_1) > m(\lambda) + 2e(\lambda) + 2$, the statistical distance between*

$$\left\{ \Lambda \leftarrow \mathrm{piO}^\star_\ell(1^{p(\lambda)}, C) : (\Lambda, \Lambda(X_1, X_2)) \right\}$$

$$and \left\{ \Lambda \leftarrow \mathrm{piO}^\star_\ell(1^{p(\lambda)}, C) : (\Lambda, C(X_1; U_{m(\lambda)})) \right\}$$

is at most $2^{-e(\lambda)}$.

We note that setting $\ell := 0$ recovers the original definition of pIO for X-ind samplers due to [11]. Looking ahead, our application does not require input expanding correctness.

Let S be a circuit sampler and let $\widehat{S}$ denote the circuit sampler which calls S and outputs ℓ-expanded circuits. Unfortunately, if S is an X-ind sampler does not imply that $\widehat{S}$ also satisfies the requirements to be an X-ind sampler. On a high level this is because $\widehat{X}(\lambda) := X(\lambda) \cdot 2^{\ell(\lambda)}$ is necessary for $\widehat{S}$ to satisfy the X-differing inputs property. Then, however, X-indistinguishability of S does not suffice to prove $\widehat{X}$-indistinguishability of $\widehat{S}$. Thus, we introduce the notion of ℓ-expanding X-ind samplers.

Definition 6 (ℓ-expanding X-ind sampler). *Let S be a circuit sampler. With $\widehat{S}$ we denote the circuit sampler which on input of $1^{p(\lambda)+\ell(\lambda)}$ samples $(C_0, C_1, z) \leftarrow S(1^{p(\lambda)})$ and outputs the circuits $\widehat{C}_0 := \mathcal{E}_\ell(C_0), \widehat{C}_1 := \mathcal{E}_\ell(C_1)$ and auxiliary information $\widehat{z} := (C_0, C_1, z)$. The class $\mathcal{S}^{X\text{-}(\star)\text{-ind}}_\ell$ of ℓ-expanding X-ind samplers for a circuit family $\mathcal{C}$ contains all circuit samplers $S = (S_\lambda)_{\lambda \in \mathbb{N}}$ for $\mathcal{C}$ such that the circuit sampler $\widehat{S}$ is an X-ind sampler according to Definition 3, i.e. $\widehat{S} \in \mathcal{S}^{X\text{-ind}}$.*

On a high level, we instantiate the construction of pIO for X-ind samplers due to [11] with a suitably extracting puncturable pseudorandom function (pPRF). By suitably extracting we mean that the PRF output is guaranteed to be statistically close to uniform randomness as long as the average min-entropy of the input of the PRF is sufficiently high. Such a pPRF can be constructed by composing a pPRF with a universal hash function.

Theorem 1. *Let e be an efficiently computable function. Let F be a sub-exponentially secure special extracting PRF family with distinguishing advantage $2^{-\lambda^e}$ (for some constant ϵ) and error $2^{-e(\lambda)}$ mapping $n(\lambda) = n'(\lambda) + \ell(\lambda)$ bits to $m(\lambda)$ bits which is extracting if the input average min-entropy is greater than $m(\lambda) + 2e(\lambda) + 2$. Then, there exists a statistically correct input expanding pIO $\mathsf{piO}_\ell^\star$ for the class of samplers $\mathcal{S}_\ell^{X\text{-}(\star)\text{-ind}}$.*

For additional explanations and a formal proof, we refer the reader to the full version [2].

3   How to Simulate Extraction – Algebraic Wrappers

In order to instantiate the AGM, we need to first find a way to conceptualize what it means to be a group in a cryptographic sense. This is captured by the notion of a *group scheme* or *encoding scheme*, [23]. In a nutshell, a group scheme provides an interface of algorithms abstracting the handling of a cryptographic group. As we want to prove hardness of certain problems based on hardness assumptions in an already existing base group, we incorporate this existing group into our group scheme.

More specifically, we introduce the concept of an *algebraic wrapper*, i.e. a group scheme that allows to extract a representation which – similar to the AGM – can be used in a security reduction. A similar approach has already been taken by [30]. [30] define their group scheme as a linear subspace of $\mathbb{G} \times \mathbb{G}$ for an existing group $\mathbb{G}$ in such a way that the Generalized Knowledge of Exponent Assumption (GKEA) can be used to extract a representation (membership can for instance be tested via a symmetric pairing). Hence, that group scheme can also be viewed as an extension, or a *wrapper*, for the underlying base group. However, [30] relies on GKEA in the base group which more or less directly yields an equivalence between algebraic groups and GKEA. The existence of algebraic groups, however, implies the existence of extractable one-way functions with unbounded auxiliary input (since the AGM allows an additional unstructured input from $\{0,1\}^*$) which in turn conflicts with the existence of indistinguishability obfuscation, [5]. Due to this contradiction and the difficulty to assess the plausibility of knowledge-type assumptions, we strive for a weaker model which can purely be based on falsifiable assumptions.

Extraction trapdoors. In [30], extraction is possible as long as the code and the randomness which where used to produce a group element are known. Since we strive to avoid knowledge-type assumptions, we need to find a different mechanism of what enables extraction. We observe that in order to reproduce proof strategies from the algebraic group model, extraction is only necessary during security reductions. Since the reduction to some assumption in the base group is in control of the group parameters of the wrapper, the reduction may use corresponding trapdoor information which we define to enable extraction. We call this notion *private extractability*.

3.1   Group Schemes

A group scheme or encoding scheme [23] abstracts the properties of mathematical groups used in cryptography. Group schemes have recently been studied in [1,3,17,30]. In contrast to traditional groups, group elements are not bound to be represented by a unique bitstring (henceforth referred to as encoding). This allows to encode auxiliary information inside group elements.

Formally, a group scheme $\mathbb{H}$ consists of the algorithms $(\mathsf{GGen}_{\mathbb{H}}, \mathsf{Sam}_{\mathbb{H}}, \mathsf{Val}_{\mathbb{H}}, \mathsf{Add}_{\mathbb{H}}, \mathsf{Eq}_{\mathbb{H}}, \mathsf{GetID}_{\mathbb{H}})$. A group generation algorithm $\mathsf{GGen}_{\mathbb{H}}$, which given 1^{λ}, samples group parameters $\mathsf{pp}_{\mathbb{H}}$. A sampling algorithm $\mathsf{Sam}_{\mathbb{H}}$, given the group parameters and an additional parameter determining the exponent of the desired group element, produces an encoding corresponding to that exponent. A validation algorithm $\mathsf{Val}_{\mathbb{H}}$, given the group parameters and a bitstring, decides whether the given bitstring is a valid encoding. The algorithm $\mathsf{Add}_{\mathbb{H}}$ implements the group operation, i.e. expects the group parameters and two encodings as input and produces an encoding of the resulting group element. Since group elements do not necessarily possess unique encodings, the equality testing algorithm $\mathsf{Eq}_{\mathbb{H}}$ enables to test whether two given encodings correspond to the same group element (with respect to the given group parameters). Note that $\mathsf{Eq}_{\mathbb{H}}(\mathsf{pp}_{\mathbb{H}}, \cdot)$ defines an equivalence relation on the set of valid bitstrings. Finally, again compensating for the non-unique encodings, a group scheme describes a "get-identifier" algorithm which given the group parameters and an encoding of a group element, produces a bitstring which is unique for all encodings of the same group element.[9] Note that $\mathsf{Eq}_{\mathbb{H}}(\mathsf{pp}_{\mathbb{H}}, a, b)$ can be implemented using $\mathsf{GetID}_{\mathbb{H}}$ by simply comparing $\mathsf{GetID}_{\mathbb{H}}(\mathsf{pp}_{\mathbb{H}}, a)$ and $\mathsf{GetID}_{\mathbb{H}}(\mathsf{pp}_{\mathbb{H}}, b)$ as bitstrings. The "get-identifier" algorithm compensates for the potential non-uniqueness of encodings and allows to extract, for instance, symmetric keys from group elements.

For a group scheme it is required that the quotient set

$$\{a \in \{0,1\}^{*} \mid \mathsf{Val}_{\mathbb{H}}(\mathsf{pp}_{\mathbb{H}}, a) = 1\}/\mathsf{Eq}_{\mathbb{H}}(\mathsf{pp}_{\mathbb{H}}, \cdot)$$

equipped with the operation defined via $\mathsf{Add}_{\mathbb{H}}(\mathsf{pp}_{\mathbb{H}}, \cdot, \cdot)$ defines a mathematical group (with overwhelming probability over the choice of $\mathsf{pp}_{\mathbb{H}} \leftarrow \mathsf{GGen}_{\mathbb{H}}(1^{\lambda})$). We say that an a is (an encoding of) a group element (relative to $\mathsf{pp}_{\mathbb{H}}$), written as $a \in \mathbb{H}$, if and only if $\mathsf{Val}_{\mathbb{H}}(\mathsf{pp}_{\mathbb{H}}, a) = 1$.

A group scheme requires that encodings corresponding to the same group element are computationally indistinguishable as formalized by the "Switching Lemma(s)" in [1,3,17].

Due to the non-uniqueness of encodings, we henceforth use the notation $\hat{h}$ to denote an encoding of a group element.

3.2   An Algebraic Wrapper

Given a cyclic group, an algebraic wrapper is a group scheme which equips a given group $\mathbb{G}$ with a notion of extractability while preserving its group

---

[9] Previous work refers to this algorithm as "extraction algorithm". However, in order not to overload the word "extraction", we rename this algorithm in this work.

structure and complexity theoretic hardness guarantees. In particular, we achieve a property which we refer to as "private extractability" with respect to a given set of group elements in the base group. More precisely, the group generation algorithm expects group parameters $\mathsf{pp}_\mathbb{G}$ of the base group together with a set of group elements $[\mathbf{b}]_\mathbb{G} \in \mathbb{G}^n$ in that base group, henceforth referred to as *basis*, and produces group parameters $\mathsf{pp}_\mathbb{H}$ of the wrapper group together with a corresponding trapdoor $\tau_\mathbb{H}$. This trapdoor enables to extract a representation with respect to the basis $[\mathbf{b}]_\mathbb{G}$ from every encoding. Looking ahead, this property will allow to implement proof strategies of the algebraic group model, [21].

More precisely, encodings can be seen to always carry computationally hidden representation vectors with respect to the basis $[\mathbf{b}]_\mathbb{G}$. The private extraction recovers this representation vector. Given the trapdoor, we require that it is possible to "privately" sample encodings which carry a specific dictated representation vector. We require that publicly sampled encodings and privately sampled encodings are computationally indistinguishable. We refer to this property as "switching". In order to preserve tightness of security reductions when implementing AGM proofs with our algebraic wrapper, we require a statistical re-randomization property. Furthermore, we require that representation vectors compose additively (in $\mathbb{Z}_p^n$) with the group operation and do not change when encodings are re-randomized.

Let $\mathcal{B}_{\mathsf{pp}_\mathbb{G}}^n := \{([1]_\mathbb{G}, [x_2]_\mathbb{G}, \ldots, [x_n]_\mathbb{G})^\intercal \in \mathbb{G}^n \mid x_2, \ldots, x_n \in \mathbb{Z}_p^\times\}$ be the set of what we call "legitimate basis vectors". Note that we require the first group element to be the generator of the group. This is necessary to allow public sampling.

Definition 7 (Algebraic wrapper for $\mathbb{G}$). *An algebraic wrapper $\mathbb{H}$ for $\mathbb{G}$ is a tuple of PPT algorithms* $(\mathsf{GGen}_\mathbb{H}, \mathsf{Sam}_\mathbb{H}, \mathsf{Val}_\mathbb{H}, \mathsf{Add}_\mathbb{H}, \mathsf{Eq}_\mathbb{H}, \mathsf{GetID}_\mathbb{H}, \mathsf{Rerand}_\mathbb{H}, \mathsf{PrivSam}_\mathbb{H}, \mathsf{PrivExt}_\mathbb{H}, \mathsf{Unwrap}_\mathbb{H})$ *such that* $(\mathsf{GGen}_\mathbb{H}, \mathsf{Sam}_\mathbb{H}, \mathsf{Val}_\mathbb{H}, \mathsf{Add}_\mathbb{H}, \mathsf{Eq}_\mathbb{H}, \mathsf{GetID}_\mathbb{H})$ *constitutes a group scheme and the following properties are satisfied.*

$\mathbb{G}$-wrapping. *The algorithm $\mathsf{Unwrap}_\mathbb{H}(\mathsf{pp}_\mathbb{H}, \cdot)$ is deterministic and for all $\mathsf{pp}_\mathbb{G} \in \mathsf{supp}(\mathsf{GGen}_\mathbb{G}(1^\lambda))$, all $[\mathbf{b}]_\mathbb{G} \in \mathcal{B}_{\mathsf{pp}_\mathbb{G}}^n$, all $(\mathsf{pp}_\mathbb{H}, \tau_\mathbb{H}) \in \mathsf{supp}(\mathsf{GGen}_\mathbb{H}(\mathsf{pp}_\mathbb{G}, [\mathbf{b}]_\mathbb{G}))$, $\mathsf{Unwrap}_\mathbb{H}(\mathsf{pp}_\mathbb{H}, \cdot)$ defines a group isomorphism from $\mathbb{H}$ to $\mathbb{G}$.*

Extractability. *The algorithm $\mathsf{PrivExt}_\mathbb{H}$ is deterministic. Furthermore, for all $\mathsf{pp}_\mathbb{G} \in \mathsf{supp}(\mathsf{GGen}_\mathbb{G}(1^\lambda))$, all $[\mathbf{b}]_\mathbb{G} \in \mathcal{B}_{\mathsf{pp}_\mathbb{G}}^n$, all $(\mathsf{pp}_\mathbb{H}, \tau_\mathbb{H}) \in \mathsf{supp}(\mathsf{GGen}_\mathbb{H}(\mathsf{pp}_\mathbb{G}, [\mathbf{b}]_\mathbb{G}))$, all $\widehat{h} \in \mathbb{H}$, we require that $\mathsf{PrivExt}_\mathbb{H}$ always extracts a representation of $[x]_\mathbb{G}$ with respect to $[\mathbf{b}]_\mathbb{G}$, i.e. for $\mathbf{z} := \mathsf{PrivExt}_\mathbb{H}(\tau_\mathbb{H}, \widehat{h})$, $[\mathbf{z}^\intercal \cdot \mathbf{b}]_\mathbb{G} = \mathsf{Unwrap}_\mathbb{H}(\mathsf{pp}_\mathbb{H}, \widehat{h})$.*

Correctness of extraction. *For all $\mathsf{pp}_\mathbb{G} \in \mathsf{supp}(\mathsf{GGen}_\mathbb{G}(1^\lambda))$, all $[\mathbf{b}]_\mathbb{G} \in \mathcal{B}_{\mathsf{pp}_\mathbb{G}}^n$, all $(\mathsf{pp}_\mathbb{H}, \tau_\mathbb{H}) \in \mathsf{supp}(\mathsf{GGen}_\mathbb{H}(\mathsf{pp}_\mathbb{G}, [\mathbf{b}]_\mathbb{G}))$, all $\widehat{h_0}, \widehat{h_1} \in \mathbb{H}$, we require that private extraction respects the group operation in the sense that for all $\widehat{h_2} \in \mathsf{supp}(\mathsf{Add}_\mathbb{H}(\mathsf{pp}_\mathbb{H}, \widehat{h_0}, \widehat{h_1}))$, $\mathbf{z}^{(i)} := \mathsf{PrivExt}_\mathbb{H}(\tau_\mathbb{H}, \widehat{h_i})$ satisfy $\mathbf{z}^{(2)} = \mathbf{z}^{(0)} + \mathbf{z}^{(1)}$. Furthermore, for all $\mathsf{pp}_\mathbb{G} \in \mathsf{supp}(\mathsf{GGen}_\mathbb{G}(1^\lambda))$, all $[\mathbf{b}]_\mathbb{G} \in \mathcal{B}_{\mathsf{pp}_\mathbb{G}}^n$, all $(\mathsf{pp}_\mathbb{H}, \tau_\mathbb{H}) \in \mathsf{supp}(\mathsf{GGen}_\mathbb{H}(\mathsf{pp}_\mathbb{G}, [\mathbf{b}]_\mathbb{G}))$, all $\widehat{h} \in \mathbb{H}$, we require that re-randomization does not interfere with private extraction in the sense that for all $\widehat{h'} \in \mathsf{supp}(\mathsf{Rerand}_\mathbb{H}(\mathsf{pp}_\mathbb{H}, \widehat{h}))$, $\mathsf{PrivExt}_\mathbb{H}(\tau_\mathbb{H}, \widehat{h}) = \mathsf{PrivExt}_\mathbb{H}(\tau_\mathbb{H}, \widehat{h'})$.*

Correctness of sampling. *For all* $\mathsf{pp}_{\mathbb{G}} \in \mathsf{supp}(\mathsf{GGen}_{\mathbb{G}}(1^\lambda))$, *all* $[\mathbf{b}]_{\mathbb{G}} \in \mathcal{B}^n_{\mathsf{pp}_{\mathbb{G}}}$, *all*
$(\mathsf{pp}_{\mathbb{H}}, \tau_{\mathbb{H}}) \in \mathsf{supp}(\mathsf{GGen}_{\mathbb{H}}(\mathsf{pp}_{\mathbb{G}}, [\mathbf{b}]_{\mathbb{G}}))$, *we require that*
- *for all* $\mathbf{v} \in \mathbb{Z}^n_p$, $\Pr[\mathsf{PrivExt}_{\mathbb{H}}(\tau_{\mathbb{H}}, \mathsf{PrivSam}_{\mathbb{H}}(\tau_{\mathbb{H}}, \mathbf{v})) = \mathbf{v}] = 1$, *and*
- *for all* $x \in \mathbb{Z}_p$, $\Pr[\mathsf{PrivExt}_{\mathbb{H}}(\tau_{\mathbb{H}}, \mathsf{Sam}_{\mathbb{H}}(\mathsf{pp}_{\mathbb{H}}, x \cdot \mathbf{e_1})) = x \cdot \mathbf{e_1}] = 1$.

k**-Switching.** *We say a PPT adversary* $\mathcal{A}$ *is a legitimate k-switching adversary if on input of base group parameters* $\mathsf{pp}_{\mathbb{G}}$, $\mathcal{A}$ *outputs two bases* $([\mathbf{b}]^{(j)}_{\mathbb{G}})_{j \in \{0,1\}}$ *and two lists comprising k representation vectors* $(\mathbf{v}^{(j),(i)})_{i \in [k], j \in \{0,1\}}$ *(and an internal state st) such that* $[\mathbf{b}]^{(0)}_{\mathbb{G}}, [\mathbf{b}]^{(1)}_{\mathbb{G}} \in \mathcal{B}^n_{\mathsf{pp}_{\mathbb{G}}}$ *and* $\mathbf{v}^{(0),(i)}, \mathbf{v}^{(1),(i)} \in \mathbb{Z}^n_p$ *for some* $n \in \mathbb{N}$ *and all* $i \in [k]$ *and* $[(\mathbf{v}^{(0),(i)})^{\mathsf{T}} \cdot \mathbf{b}^{(0)}]_{\mathbb{G}} = [(\mathbf{v}^{(1),(i)})^{\mathsf{T}} \cdot \mathbf{b}^{(1)}]_{\mathbb{G}}$ *for all* $i \in [k]$.

For all legitimate k-switching PPT adversaries $\mathcal{A}$,

$$\mathsf{Adv}^{k\text{-switching}}_{\mathbb{H},\mathcal{A}}(\lambda) := \left| \Pr[\mathsf{Exp}^{k\text{-switching}}_{\mathbb{H},\mathcal{A},0}(\lambda) = 1] - \Pr[\mathsf{Exp}^{k\text{-switching}}_{\mathbb{H},\mathcal{A},1}(\lambda) = 1] \right|$$

is negligible, where $\mathsf{Exp}^{k\text{-switching}}_{\mathbb{H},\mathcal{A},b}(\lambda)$ *(for $b \in \{0,1\}$) is defined in Fig. 1.*

Statistically re-randomizable. *We say an unbounded adversary* $\mathcal{A}$ *is a legitimate re-randomization adversary if on input of base group parameters* $\mathsf{pp}_{\mathbb{G}}$, $\mathcal{A}$ *outputs* $[\mathbf{b}]_{\mathbb{G}}$ *and a state st such that* $[\mathbf{b}]_{\mathbb{G}} \in \mathcal{B}^n_{\mathsf{pp}_{\mathbb{G}}}$ *and, in a second phase, $\mathcal{A}$ on input of* $(\mathsf{pp}_{\mathbb{H}}, \tau_{\mathbb{H}}, st)$ *outputs two valid encodings* $\widehat{h_0}, \widehat{h_1}$ *(and a state st) such that* $\mathsf{PrivExt}_{\mathbb{H}}(\tau_{\mathbb{H}}, \widehat{h_0}) = \mathsf{PrivExt}_{\mathbb{H}}(\tau_{\mathbb{H}}, \widehat{h_1})$.

For all unbounded legitimate re-randomization adversaries $\mathcal{A}$,

$$\mathsf{Adv}^{\mathsf{rerand}}_{\mathbb{H},\mathcal{A}}(\lambda) := \left| \Pr[\mathsf{Exp}^{\mathsf{rerand}}_{\mathbb{H},\mathcal{A},0}(\lambda) = 1] - \Pr[\mathsf{Exp}^{\mathsf{rerand}}_{\mathbb{H},\mathcal{A},1}(\lambda) = 1] \right| \le \frac{1}{2^\lambda},$$

where $\mathsf{Exp}^{\mathsf{rerand}}_{\mathbb{H},\mathcal{A},b}(\lambda)$ *(for $b \in \{0,1\}$) is defined in Fig. 1.*

$\underline{\mathsf{Exp}^{\mathsf{rerand}}_{\mathbb{H},\mathcal{A},b}(\lambda)}$

$\mathsf{pp}_{\mathbb{G}} \leftarrow \mathsf{GGen}_{\mathbb{G}}(1^\lambda)$
$([\mathbf{b}]_{\mathbb{G}}, st) \leftarrow \mathcal{A}(1^\lambda, \mathsf{pp}_{\mathbb{G}})$
$(\mathsf{pp}_{\mathbb{H}}, \tau_{\mathbb{H}}) \leftarrow \mathsf{GGen}_{\mathbb{H}}(\mathsf{pp}_{\mathbb{G}}, [\mathbf{b}]_{\mathbb{G}})$
$(\widehat{h_0}, \widehat{h_1}, st) \leftarrow \mathcal{A}(\mathsf{pp}_{\mathbb{H}}, \tau_{\mathbb{H}}, st)$
$\widehat{h} \leftarrow \mathsf{Rerand}_{\mathbb{H}}(\mathsf{pp}_{\mathbb{H}}, \widehat{h_b})$
$\mathbf{return}\ \mathcal{A}(\widehat{h}, st)$

$\underline{\mathsf{Exp}^{k\text{-switching}}_{\mathbb{H},\mathcal{A},b}(\lambda)}$

$\mathsf{pp}_{\mathbb{G}} \leftarrow \mathsf{GGen}_{\mathbb{G}}(1^\lambda)$
$(([\mathbf{b}]^{(j)}_{\mathbb{G}})_{j \in \{0,1\}},$
$\quad (\mathbf{v}^{(j),(i)})_{i \in [k], j \in \{0,1\}}, st) \leftarrow \mathcal{A}(1^\lambda, \mathsf{pp}_{\mathbb{G}})$
$(\mathsf{pp}_{\mathbb{H}}, \tau_{\mathbb{H}}) \leftarrow \mathsf{GGen}_{\mathbb{H}}(\mathsf{pp}_{\mathbb{G}}, [\mathbf{b}]^{(b)}_{\mathbb{G}})$
$\widehat{h^*_i} \leftarrow \mathsf{PrivSam}_{\mathbb{H}}(\tau_{\mathbb{H}}, \mathbf{v}^{(b),(i)})$
$\mathbf{return}\ \mathcal{A}(\mathsf{pp}_{\mathbb{H}}, (\widehat{h^*_i})_{i \in [k]}, st)$

Fig. 1. The re-randomization and k-switching games.

For simplicity we require that encodings are always in $\{0,1\}^{p_{\mathsf{enc}}(\lambda)}$ for a fixed polynomial $p_{\mathsf{enc}}(\lambda)$.

The k-switching property allows to simultaneously switch the representation vectors of multiple group element encodings. It is necessary to switch all encodings simultaneously since private sampling can only be simulated knowing the trapdoor $\tau_{\mathbb{H}}$ which is not the case in $\mathsf{Exp}^{k\text{-switching}}_{\mathbb{H},\mathcal{A},b}(\lambda)$.

3.3 Construction

Our construction follows the ideas from [1,3,17]. Let $\mathsf{GGen}_\mathbb{G}$ be a group generator for a cyclic group $\mathbb{G}$. Let $\mathcal{TD}$ be a family of hard subset membership problems. Let $\mathsf{FHE} = (\mathsf{KGen}, \mathsf{Enc}, \mathsf{Dec}, \mathsf{Eval}, \mathsf{Rerand})$ be a perfectly correct and perfectly re-randomizable fully homomorphic public-key encryption scheme. Let $\mathsf{pp}_\mathbb{G}$ be group parameters for $\mathbb{G}$ and $[\mathbf{\Omega}]_\mathbb{G} \in \mathbb{G}^n$ for some $n \in \mathbb{N}$. Let $\mathsf{TD} \subseteq X$ be a subset membership problem from $\mathcal{TD}$ and $y \leftarrow X \setminus \mathsf{TD}$ and pk be a public key for FHE. For ease of notation, we define $\mathsf{pars} := (\mathsf{pp}_\mathbb{G}, \mathsf{TD}, y, pk, [\mathbf{\Omega}]_\mathbb{G})$. Let $\varPi := (\mathsf{Setup}, \mathsf{Prove}, \mathsf{Verify}, \mathsf{HSetup}, \mathsf{Ext})$ be a perfectly complete, perfectly sound and perfectly witness-indistinguishable dual-mode NIZK proof system for the language

$$\mathcal{L} := \big\{ y := (\mathsf{pars}, [x]_\mathbb{G}, C) \mid \exists w \colon (y, w) \in \mathcal{R} := \mathcal{R}_1 \vee \mathcal{R}_2 \vee \mathcal{R}_3 \big\}.$$

The relations $\mathcal{R}_1, \mathcal{R}_2, \mathcal{R}_3$ are defined as follows.

$$\mathcal{R}_1 = \left\{ \left((\mathsf{pars}, [x]_\mathbb{G}, C), (sk, \mathbf{v}) \right) \;\middle|\; \begin{array}{l} \mathsf{KGen}(1^\lambda; sk) = (pk, sk) \\ \wedge \quad \mathsf{Dec}(sk, C) = \mathbf{v} \\ \wedge \quad [\mathbf{\Omega}^\mathsf{T} \cdot \mathbf{v}]_\mathbb{G} = [x]_\mathbb{G} \end{array} \right\}$$

$$\mathcal{R}_2 = \left\{ \left((\mathsf{pars}, [x]_\mathbb{G}, C), (r, \mathbf{v}) \right) \;\middle|\; \begin{array}{l} \mathsf{Enc}(pk, \mathbf{v}; r) = C \\ \wedge \quad [\mathbf{\Omega}^\mathsf{T} \cdot \mathbf{v}]_\mathbb{G} = [x]_\mathbb{G} \end{array} \right\}$$

$$\mathcal{R}_3 = \left\{ \left((\mathsf{pars}, [x]_\mathbb{G}, C), (w_y) \right) \;\middle|\; (y, w_y) \in R_{\mathsf{TD}} \right\}$$

With $m'(\lambda)$ we denote a polynomial upper bound on the number of random bits $\mathsf{FHE}.\mathsf{Rerand}(1^\lambda, \cdot, \cdot)$ expects and with $m''(\lambda)$ we denote a polynomial upper bound on the number of random bits $\varPi.\mathsf{Prove}(1^\lambda, \cdot, \cdot, \cdot)$ expects. Let $\ell(\lambda) := m'(\lambda) + m''(\lambda) + 2(\lambda + 1) + 3$. Let piO be a pIO scheme for the class of samplers $\mathcal{S}^{X\text{-ind}}$ and let $\mathsf{piO}_\ell^\star$ be an ℓ-expanding pIO scheme for the class of samplers $\mathcal{S}_\ell^{X\text{-}(\star)\text{-ind}}$. Further, let $p_{\mathsf{add}}(\lambda)$ denote a polynomial upper bound on the size of addition circuits and $p_{\mathsf{rerand}}(\lambda)$ denote a polynomial upper bound on the size of re-randomization circuits which are used during the proof, see the full version [2] for details.

Our algebraic wrapper $\mathbb{H}$ is composed of the PPT algorithms ($\mathsf{GGen}_\mathbb{H}$, $\mathsf{Sam}_\mathbb{H}, \mathsf{Val}_\mathbb{H}, \mathsf{Add}_\mathbb{H}, \mathsf{Eq}_\mathbb{H}, \mathsf{Rerand}_\mathbb{H}, \mathsf{PrivExt}_\mathbb{H}, \mathsf{PrivSam}_\mathbb{H}, \mathsf{GetID}_\mathbb{H}, \mathsf{Unwrap}_\mathbb{H}$) which are defined in Figs. 2a and 2b. We note that the algorithm $\mathsf{Val}_\mathbb{H}$ which is evaluated inside C_{Add} and C_{rerand} only requires a certain part of the public parameters as input. In particular, $\mathsf{Val}_\mathbb{H}$ does not depend on Λ_{Add} and $\Lambda_{\mathsf{rerand}}$.

During "honest" use of our algebraic wrapper, encodings carry proofs produced for relation $\mathcal{R}_1$ or relation $\mathcal{R}_2$. Relation $\mathcal{R}_2$ enables sampling without knowledge of any trapdoors. Re-randomized encodings always carry proofs for relation $\mathcal{R}_1$. Relation $\mathcal{R}_3$ is a trapdoor branch enabling simulation. Note that during "honest" use of the algebraic wrapper $y \notin \mathsf{TD}$ and, hence, due to perfect soundness of $\varPi$, there exists no proof for relation $\mathcal{R}_3$.

$\underline{\mathsf{GGen}_\mathbb{H}(\mathsf{pp}_\mathbb{G}, [\mathbf{b}]_\mathbb{G} = [(b_1, \ldots, b_n)^\top]_\mathbb{G})}$

$\alpha_1 := 1, \alpha_2, \ldots, \alpha_n \leftarrow \mathbb{Z}_p^\times$

$[\boldsymbol{\Omega}]_\mathbb{G} := ([b_1]_\mathbb{G}^{\alpha_1}, \ldots, [b_n]_\mathbb{G}^{\alpha_n})^\top$

$(pk, sk) \leftarrow \mathsf{FHE.KGen}(1^\lambda)$

$\mathsf{crs} \leftarrow \Pi.\mathsf{Setup}(1^\lambda), \mathsf{TD} \leftarrow \mathcal{TD}, y \leftarrow \overline{\mathcal{TD}}$

$\Lambda_{\mathsf{Add}} \leftarrow \mathsf{piO}(1^{P_{\mathsf{add}}(\lambda)}, C_{\mathsf{Add}})$

$\Lambda_{\mathsf{rerand}} \leftarrow \mathsf{piO}_\ell^\star(1^{P_{\mathsf{rerand}}(\lambda)}, C_{\mathsf{rerand}})$

$\mathsf{pars} := (\mathsf{pp}_\mathbb{G}, \mathsf{TD}, y, pk, [\boldsymbol{\Omega}]_\mathbb{G})$

$\mathsf{pp}_\mathbb{H} := (\mathsf{crs}, \mathsf{pars}, \Lambda_{\mathsf{Add}}, \Lambda_{\mathsf{rerand}})$

$\tau_\mathbb{H} := (\mathsf{pp}_\mathbb{H}, sk, \alpha_1, \ldots, \alpha_n, [\mathbf{b}]_\mathbb{G})$

$\mathbf{return}\ (\mathsf{pp}_\mathbb{H}, \tau_\mathbb{H})$

$\underline{\mathsf{Sam}_\mathbb{H}(\mathsf{pp}_\mathbb{H}, \mathbf{v} \in \mathbb{Z}_p^n)}$

$C = \mathsf{Enc}(pk, \mathbf{v}; r)$

$[x]_\mathbb{G} := [\boldsymbol{\Omega}^\top \cdot \mathbf{v}]_\mathbb{G}$

$\pi = \mathsf{Prove}(\mathsf{crs}, (\mathsf{pars}, [x]_\mathbb{G}, C), (r, \mathbf{v}))$

$\mathbf{return}\ \widehat{h} := ([x]_\mathbb{G}, C, \pi)_\mathbb{H}$

$\underline{\mathsf{Val}_\mathbb{H}(\mathsf{pp}_\mathbb{H}, \widehat{h})}$

$\mathrm{parse}\ \widehat{x} =: ([x]_\mathbb{G}, C, \pi)_\mathbb{H}$

$\mathbf{return}\ \Pi.\mathsf{Verify}(\mathsf{crs}, (\mathsf{pars}, [x]_\mathbb{G}, C), \pi)$

$\underline{\mathsf{Unwrap}_\mathbb{H}(\mathsf{pp}_\mathbb{H}, \widehat{h})}$

$\mathbf{if}\ \neg \mathsf{Val}_\mathbb{H}((\mathsf{crs}, \mathsf{pars}), \widehat{h})\ \mathbf{then}$

  $\mathbf{return}\ \bot$

$\mathrm{parse}\ \widehat{h} =: ([x]_\mathbb{G}, C, \pi)_\mathbb{H}$

$\mathbf{return}\ [x]_\mathbb{G}$

$\underline{\mathsf{Eq}_\mathbb{H}(\mathsf{pp}_\mathbb{H}, \widehat{h_1}, \widehat{h_2})}$

$\mathbf{if}\ \exists j \in [2]: \neg \mathsf{Val}_\mathbb{H}((\mathsf{crs}, \mathsf{pars}), \widehat{h_j})\ \mathbf{then}$

  $\mathbf{return}\ \bot$

$\mathrm{parse}\ \widehat{h_i} =: ([x_i]_\mathbb{G}, C_i, \pi_i)_\mathbb{H}$

$\mathbf{return}\ [x_1]_\mathbb{G} = [x_2]_\mathbb{G}$

$\underline{\mathsf{GetID}_\mathbb{H}(\mathsf{pp}_\mathbb{H}, \widehat{h})}$

$\mathbf{if}\ \neg \mathsf{Val}_\mathbb{H}((\mathsf{crs}, \mathsf{pars}), \widehat{h})\ \mathbf{then}$

  $\mathbf{return}\ \bot$

$\mathrm{parse}\ \widehat{h} =: ([x]_\mathbb{G}, C, \pi)_\mathbb{H}$

$\mathbf{return}\ [x]_\mathbb{G}$

$\underline{\mathsf{Add}_\mathbb{H}(\mathsf{pp}_\mathbb{H}, \widehat{h_1}, \widehat{h_2})}$

$\mathbf{return}\ \Lambda_{\mathsf{Add}}(\widehat{h_1}, \widehat{h_2})$

$\underline{C_{\mathsf{Add}}[\mathsf{pars}, \mathsf{crs}, sk](\widehat{h_1}, \widehat{h_2}; r)}$

$\mathbf{if}\ \exists j \in [2]: \neg \mathsf{Val}_\mathbb{H}((\mathsf{crs}, \mathsf{pars}), \widehat{h_j})\ \mathbf{then}$

  $\mathbf{return}\ \bot$

$\mathrm{parse}\ \widehat{h_i} =: ([x_i]_\mathbb{G}, C_i, \pi_i)_\mathbb{H}$

$[x_{\mathsf{out}}]_\mathbb{G} := [x_1]_\mathbb{G} \cdot [x_2]_\mathbb{G}$

$C_{\mathsf{out}} \leftarrow \mathsf{FHE.Eval}(pk, C^{(+)}[\mathbb{Z}_p^n], C_1, C_2)$

$/\!/\ C^{(+)}[\mathbb{Z}_p^n]\ \text{computes addition in}\ \mathbb{Z}_p^n$

$\mathbf{v}_i \leftarrow \mathsf{Dec}(sk, C_i)$

$\mathbf{v}_{\mathsf{out}} := \mathbf{v}_1 + \mathbf{v}_2$

$\pi_{\mathsf{out}} \leftarrow \mathsf{Prove}(\mathsf{crs},$

  $(\mathsf{pars}, [x_{\mathsf{out}}]_\mathbb{G}, C_{\mathsf{out}}), (sk, \mathbf{v}_{\mathsf{out}}))$

$\mathbf{return}\ \widehat{h_{\mathsf{out}}} := ([x_{\mathsf{out}}]_\mathbb{G}, C_{\mathsf{out}}, \pi_{\mathsf{out}})$

(a) Definition of the algorithms $\mathsf{GGen}_\mathbb{H}, \mathsf{Sam}_\mathbb{H}, \mathsf{Val}_\mathbb{H}, \mathsf{Eq}_\mathbb{H}, \mathsf{GetID}_\mathbb{H}, \mathsf{Add}_\mathbb{H}, \mathsf{Unwrap}_\mathbb{H}$ and the circuit C_{Add}.

$\underline{\mathsf{PrivSam}_\mathbb{H}(\tau_\mathbb{H}, \mathbf{v} \in \mathbb{Z}_p^n)}$

$\mathbf{v}^* := (v_1 \cdot \alpha_1^{-1}, \ldots, v_n \cdot \alpha_n^{-1})^\top$

$[x]_\mathbb{G} := [\mathbf{b}^\top \cdot \mathbf{v}]_\mathbb{G} = [\boldsymbol{\Omega}^\top \cdot \mathbf{v}^*]_\mathbb{G}$

$C = \mathsf{Enc}(pk, \mathbf{v}^*; r)$

$\pi = \mathsf{Prove}(\mathsf{crs}, (\mathsf{pars}, [x]_\mathbb{G}, C), (sk, \mathbf{v}^*))$

$\mathbf{return}\ ([x]_\mathbb{G}, C, \pi)_\mathbb{H}$

$\underline{\mathsf{PrivExt}_\mathbb{H}(\tau_\mathbb{H}, \widehat{h})}$

$\mathbf{if}\ \neg \mathsf{Val}_\mathbb{H}(\mathsf{pp}_\mathbb{H}, \widehat{h})\ \mathbf{then}$

  $\mathbf{return}\ \bot$

$\mathrm{parse}\ \widehat{h} =: ([x]_\mathbb{G}, C, \pi)_\mathbb{H}$

$(v_1, \ldots, v_n)^\top =: \mathbf{v} = \mathsf{Dec}(sk, C)$

$\mathbf{return}\ (v_1 \cdot \alpha_1, \ldots, v_n \cdot \alpha_n)^\top$

$\underline{\mathsf{Rerand}_\mathbb{H}(\mathsf{pp}_\mathbb{H}, \widehat{h})}$

$u \leftarrow \{0,1\}^{\ell(\lambda)}$

$\mathbf{return}\ \Lambda_{\mathsf{rerand}}(\widehat{h}, u)$

$\underline{C_{\mathsf{rerand}}[\mathsf{pars}, \mathsf{crs}, sk](\widehat{h}; r_1, r_2)}$

$\mathbf{if}\ \neg \mathsf{Val}_\mathbb{H}((\mathsf{crs}, \mathsf{pars}), \widehat{h})\ \mathbf{then}$

  $\mathbf{return}\ \bot$

$\mathrm{parse}\ \widehat{h} =: ([x]_\mathbb{G}, C, \pi)_\mathbb{H}$

$\mathbf{v} := \mathsf{Dec}(sk, C)$

$C_{\mathsf{out}} := \mathsf{FHE.Rerand}(pk, C; r_1)$

$\pi_{\mathsf{out}} \leftarrow \mathsf{Prove}(\mathsf{crs},$

  $(\mathsf{pars}, [x]_\mathbb{G}, C_{\mathsf{out}}), (sk, \mathbf{v}); r_2)$

$\mathbf{return}\ \widehat{h_{\mathsf{out}}} := ([x]_\mathbb{G}, C_{\mathsf{out}}, \pi_{\mathsf{out}})_\mathbb{H}$

(b) Definition of the algorithms $\mathsf{PrivSam}_\mathbb{H}, \mathsf{PrivExt}_\mathbb{H}, \mathsf{Rerand}_\mathbb{H}$ and the circuit C_{rerand}.

Fig. 2. Algorithms of our algebraic wrapper construction.

Differences to [1,3,17]. [3,17] introduce similar constructions of a group scheme featuring a multilinear map and of a graded encoding scheme, respectively. More precisely, [3,17] equip a base group with encodings carrying auxiliary information which can be used (in an obfuscated circuit) to "multiply in the exponent". We observe that these constructions already *wrap* a given base group in the sense that "unwrapping" encodings yields a group isomorphism to the base group.

Our construction builds upon these group schemes. In order to enable extractability with respect to a dynamically chosen basis[10], our group parameters must be generated depending on that basis.

This modification, however, comes at the cost of the multilinear map functionality. This is because any implementation of a multilinear map requires knowledge of discrete logarithms of each group element encoding to a fixed generator. This is undesirable for our purposes, since we want to be able to use sets of group elements as basis which we do not know discrete logarithms of (for instance group elements provided by a reduction). Thus, we have to give up the multiplication functionality.

Furthermore, looking ahead, we crucially require that the basis can be altered via computational game hops during proofs. We solve this problem by linearly perturbing the given basis $[\mathbf{b}]_{\mathbb{G}}$ (except for its first entry to enable meaningful public sampling). We refer to this perturbed basis as $[\mathbf{\Omega}]_{\mathbb{G}}$. Our group element encodings are defined to carry representation vectors with respect to $[\mathbf{\Omega}]_{\mathbb{G}}$. By construction of C_{Add}, these representation vectors are treated homomorphically by the group operation.

To preserve tightness of security reductions, we additionally introduce a statistical re-randomization mechanism.

As opposed to [1,3,17] uses a quite different approach. In [1], the group scheme is constructed from scratch, meaning there is no necessity for an underlying group. The consequences are twofold. On one hand, very strong decisional assumptions can be proven to hold in the resulting group scheme. On the other hand, however, the group scheme from [1] lacks a $\mathsf{GetID}_{\mathbb{H}}$ algorithm limiting its applicability.

Theorem 2. *Let (i)* $\mathsf{GGen}_{\mathbb{G}}$ *be a group generator for a cyclic group* $\mathbb{G}$, *(ii)* $\mathcal{TD}$ *be a family of hard subset membership problems, (iii)* $\mathsf{FHE} = (\mathsf{KGen}, \mathsf{Enc}, \mathsf{Dec}, \mathsf{Eval}, \mathsf{Rerand})$ *be a perfectly correct and perfectly re-randomizable fully homomorphic public-key encryption scheme, (iv)* $\Pi := (\mathsf{Setup}, \mathsf{Prove}, \mathsf{Verify}, \mathsf{HSetup}, \mathsf{Ext})$ *be a perfectly complete, perfectly sound and perfectly witness-indistinguishable dual-mode NIZK proof system for the language* $\mathcal{L}$, *(v)* piO *be a pIO scheme for the class of samplers* $\mathcal{S}^{X\text{-ind}}$ *and (vi)* $\mathsf{piO}_{\ell}^{\star}$ *be an* ℓ-*expanding pIO scheme for the class of samplers* $\mathcal{S}_{\ell}^{X\text{-}(\star)\text{-ind}}$. *Then,* $\mathbb{H}$ *defined in Figs. 2a and 2b is an algebraic wrapper.*

Here we provide a formal proof of the statistical re-randomization property and a high-level idea for the remaining properties. For a formal analysis of the remaining properties, we refer the reader to the full version [2].

---

[10] With basis we mean a set of group elements in the base group.

Proof (sketch). Since piO is support respecting, the algorithms defined in Fig. 2a equip the base group $\mathbb{G}$ with non-unique encodings but respect its group structure. Thus, the tuple $(\mathsf{GGen}_{\mathbb{H}}, \mathsf{Sam}_{\mathbb{H}}, \mathsf{Val}_{\mathbb{H}}, \mathsf{Eq}_{\mathbb{H}}, \mathsf{Add}_{\mathbb{H}}, \mathsf{GetID}_{\mathbb{H}})$ forms a group scheme such that $\mathsf{Unwrap}_{\mathbb{H}}(\mathsf{pp}_{\mathbb{H}}, \cdot)$ defines a group isomorphism from $\mathbb{H}$ to $\mathbb{G}$. Therefore, $\mathbb{H}$ satisfies $\mathbb{G}$-wrapping. Extractability follows (more or less) directly by the soundness of the consistency proof and correctness of FHE. Correctness of extraction follows by construction and the correctness of FHE and the fact that piO and $\mathsf{piO}_\ell^\star$ are support respecting. Correctness of sampling follows directly by correctness of FHE.

Since our construction builds upon techniques developed in [3], we also employ similar strategies to remove information about the secret decryption key from the public group parameters $\mathsf{pp}_{\mathbb{H}}$. To prove k-switching, we next use the IND-CPA security of FHE to remove all information about the basis from the group element encodings. Finally, the only remaining information about the basis used to setup the group parameters resides in $[\mathbf{\Omega}]_{\mathbb{G}}$ which thus looks uniformly random to even an unbounded adversary.

A crucial technical difference to previous work [1,3,17] is the ability to statistically re-randomize encodings. The key ingredient enabling this is our statistically correct pIO scheme due to Theorem 1.

Lemma 1. *The group scheme $\mathbb{H}$ defined in Figs. 2a and 2b satisfies statistical re-randomizability.*

Proof (of Lemma 1). The circuit C_{rerand} takes inputs from $\{0,1\}^{\mathcal{P}\mathsf{enc}(\lambda)}$ and expects a randomness from $\{0,1\}^{m'(\lambda)} \times \{0,1\}^{m''(\lambda)}$. We recall that $\mathsf{piO}_\ell^\star$ is an ℓ-expanding pIO scheme for $\ell(\lambda) = m'(\lambda) + m''(\lambda) + 2(\lambda+1) + 3$. Since for every distribution X_1 over $\{0,1\}^{\mathcal{P}\mathsf{enc}(\lambda)}$, $\widetilde{\mathrm{H}}_\infty(U_{\ell(\lambda)} \mid X_1) = \ell(\lambda) > m'(\lambda) + m''(\lambda) + 2(\lambda+1) + 2$, the statistical distance between

$$\left\{ \varLambda_{\mathsf{rerand}} \leftarrow \mathsf{piO}_\ell^\star(C_{\mathsf{rerand}}): (\varLambda_{\mathsf{rerand}}, \varLambda_{\mathsf{rerand}}(X_1, X_2)) \right\}$$

and $\left\{ \varLambda_{\mathsf{rerand}} \leftarrow \mathsf{piO}_\ell^\star(C_{\mathsf{rerand}}): (\varLambda_{\mathsf{rerand}}, C_{\mathsf{rerand}}(X_1; U_{m'(\lambda)+m''(\lambda)})) \right\}$

is at most $2^{-(\lambda+1)}$.

Let $\widehat{h_0} =: ([x_0]_{\mathbb{G}}, C_0, \pi_0)_{\mathbb{H}}, \widehat{h_1} =: ([x_1]_{\mathbb{G}}, C_1, \pi_1)_{\mathbb{H}} \in \mathbb{H}$ be the encodings chosen by the adversary $\mathcal{A}$. Since $\mathcal{A}$ is a legitimate re-randomization adversary, $\mathsf{PrivExt}_{\mathbb{H}}(\tau_{\mathbb{H}}, \widehat{h_0}) = \mathsf{PrivExt}_{\mathbb{H}}(\tau_{\mathbb{H}}, \widehat{h_1})$. Due to perfect correctness of FHE and since $\alpha_1, \ldots, \alpha_n \in \mathbb{Z}_p^\times$ are invertible, $\mathsf{Dec}(sk, C_0) = \mathsf{Dec}(sk, C_1)$. Due to perfect re-randomizability of FHE, the ciphertexts produced by $C_{\mathsf{rerand}}(\widehat{h_0})$ and $C_{\mathsf{rerand}}(\widehat{h_1})$ are identically distributed. Furthermore, since $C_{\mathsf{rerand}}(\widehat{h_b})$ produces the consistency proof using the witness $(sk, \mathsf{Dec}(sk, C_b))$, the distributions produced by $C_{\mathsf{rerand}}(\widehat{h_0})$ and $C_{\mathsf{rerand}}(\widehat{h_1})$ are identical. Therefore, $\mathsf{Adv}_{\mathbb{H}, \mathcal{A}}^{\mathsf{rerand}}(\lambda) \leq 2 \cdot 2^{-(\lambda+1)} = 2^{-\lambda}$.

Note that since $\mathbb{G}$ has unique encodings, $\mathcal{A}$ is unable to extract auxiliary information from the encodings of $\mathsf{Unwrap}_{\mathbb{H}}(\mathsf{pp}_{\mathbb{H}}, \widehat{h})$. This is crucial since such auxiliary information may be used to distinguish whether $\widehat{h_0}$ or $\widehat{h_1}$ was used to derive $\widehat{h}$. $\qquad\square$

4 How to Use Algebraic Wrappers – Implementing Proofs from the AGM

In the following, we demonstrate how proof techniques from the algebraic group model can be implemented with our algebraic wrapper. Mainly, we want to use the extracted representation provided by the algebraic wrapper in a similar way as in AGM proofs. We adapt the proofs of Diffie-Hellman assumptions from [21] in Sect. 4.1 as well as the proof for the EUF-CMA security of Schnorr signatures from [22] in Sect. 4.2. Before we demonstrate how to use the algebraic wrapper, we sketch two modifications which will be necessary when we replace the AGM with the algebraic wrapper.

The symmetrization technique. Information-theoretically, the basis[11] the algebraic wrapper enables extraction for, as well as the representation vectors inside group element encodings are known to the adversary. However, several security reductions in [21] employ case distinctions where different reduction algorithms embed their challenge in different group elements. For instance, in the CDH game, the discrete logarithm challenge Z can be embedded either in $[x]_{\mathbb{H}}$ or $[y]_{\mathbb{H}}$, leading to two different security reductions. Due to the ideal properties of the AGM, both reductions simulate identically distributed games.

However, transferring this strategy directly using algebraic wrappers fails, since the two reductions are information-theoretically distinguishable depending on the choice of basis. An unbounded adversary who knows which game he is playing could therefore influence the representation of his output in such a way that it always becomes impossible for the reduction to use the representation to compute the discrete logarithm. We call such a situation a *bad case*. It is necessary that the different reduction subroutines have mutually exclusive bad cases, so that extraction is always possible in at least one game type. Thus, we need find a way that even these representations (and the basis used to generate $\mathsf{pp}_{\mathbb{H}}$) are identically distributed.

We therefore introduce a proof technique which we call *symmetrization*. We extend the basis and group element representations in such a way that the games played by different reduction subroutines are identically distributed (as they would be in the AGM). This is done by choosing additional base elements to which the reduction knows the discrete logarithm (or partial logarithms), so that these additional base elements do not add any unknowns when solving for the discrete logarithm. With this technique, we achieve that the games defined by the different reduction algorithms are identically distributed but entail different mutually-exclusive bad cases. For the CDH reduction, this means that both challenge elements $[x]_{\mathbb{H}}$ and $[y]_{\mathbb{H}}$ are contained in the basis, so that it is not known to the adversary which one is the reduction's discrete logarithm challenge. This allows to adopt the proofs from AGM.

---

[11] With *basis* we mean the set of group elements in the base group to which we can extract.

The origin element trick. Applying the algebraic wrapper to AGM proofs where an oracle (e.g. a random oracle or a signing oracle) is present, entails the need to change the representation vectors of all oracle responses. One possibility to realize this is to apply Q-switching, where Q denotes a polynomial upper bound on the number of oracle queries. However, as the switching property only provides computational guarantees, this naive approach results in a non-tight reduction. Since we are interested in preserving the tightness of AGM proofs when applying the algebraic wrapper, we use so-called *origin elements* from which we construct the oracle responses using the group operation. This enables to use n-switching for a constant number n of origin elements instead of Q-switching for Q oracle responses.

Limitations of our techniques. While our algebraic wrapper provides an extraction property that is useful for many proofs in the AGM, it also has its limitations. Mainly, the base elements to which the PrivExt algorithm can extract need to be fixed at the time of group parameter generation. Therefore, we cannot mimic reductions to assumptions with a variable amount of challenge elements, where extraction needs to be possible with respect to all these challenge elements. For instance, q-type assumptions which are used in [21] to prove CCA1-security of ElGamal and the knowledge-soundness of Groth's ZK-SNARK.

Furthermore, there are security proofs in the AGM that rely on the representation used by the reduction being information-theoretically hidden from the adversary. An example for this is the tight reduction for the BLS scheme from [21]. As the reduction can forge a signature for any message, it relies on the representations provided by the adversary being different from what the reduction could have computed on its own. In the AGM, it is highly unlikely that the adversary computes the forged signature in the exact same way as the reduction simulates the signing oracle, because the reduction does not provide the adversary with an algebraic representation. However, since we need to be able to extract privately from group element encodings, the group elements output by the reduction information theoretically contain algebraic representations. Therefore, information-theoretically, an adversary sees how the reduction simulates hash responses and signatures, and thus could provide signatures with a representation that is useless to the reduction.

This problem is circumvented in the Schnorr proof in Sect. 4.2 due to the representation provided by the adversary already being fixed by the time it receives a challenge through the Random Oracle. We leave it as an open problem to transfer the BLS proof to the algebraic wrapper.

Another limitation is that due to the reduction being private, we cannot use the extraction in reductions between problems in the same group. That is, our wrapper does not allow for "multi-step" reductions as in the AGM.

4.1 Diffie-Hellman Assumptions

We show how to adapt the security reductions for Diffie-Hellman problems from [21] to our algebraic wrapper (see Fig. 3 for the definitions). The main proof idea, namely to use the representation of the adversary's output to compute the discrete logarithm, stays the same; however, due to the nature of our wrapper, we need to apply the symmetrization technique to achieve the same distributions as in the AGM.

cdh	sqdh	lcdh
$x, y \leftarrow \mathbb{Z}_p$	$x \leftarrow \mathbb{Z}_p$	$x, y \leftarrow \mathbb{Z}_p$
$s \leftarrow \mathcal{A}([1]_{\mathbb{G}}, [x]_{\mathbb{G}}, [y]_{\mathbb{G}})$	$s \leftarrow \mathcal{A}([1]_{\mathbb{G}}, [x]_{\mathbb{G}})$	$u, v, w, s \leftarrow \mathcal{A}([1]_{\mathbb{G}}, [x]_{\mathbb{G}}, [y]_{\mathbb{G}})$
return $s = [xy]_{\mathbb{G}}$	**return** $s = \left[x^2\right]_{\mathbb{G}}$	**return** $s = \left[u \cdot x^2 + v \cdot xy + w \cdot y^2\right]_{\mathbb{G}}$

Fig. 3. The different types of Diffie-Hellman games shown in [21]

Theorem 3. *Let $\mathbb{G}$ be a group where the discrete logarithm is hard. Then, the computational Diffie-Hellman assumption holds in an algebraic wrapper $\mathbb{H}$ for $\mathbb{G}$ of dimension ≥ 3.*

We sketch the proof here and refer the reader to the full version [2] for the full proof.

G_0

$\mathsf{pp}_{\mathbb{G}} \leftarrow \mathsf{GGen}_{\mathbb{G}}(1^\lambda)$
$\beta_2, \beta_3 \leftarrow \mathbb{Z}_p$
$(\mathsf{pp}_{\mathbb{H}}, \tau_{\mathbb{H}}) \leftarrow \mathsf{GGen}_{\mathbb{H}}(\mathsf{pp}_{\mathbb{G}}, ([1]_{\mathbb{G}}, [\beta_2]_{\mathbb{G}}, [\beta_3]_{\mathbb{G}})^\mathsf{T})$
$x, y \leftarrow \mathbb{Z}_p$
$\widehat{1} = \mathsf{Rerand}_{\mathbb{H}}(\mathsf{pp}_{\mathbb{H}}, \mathsf{Sam}_{\mathbb{H}}(\mathsf{pp}_{\mathbb{H}}, 1))$
$\widehat{x} = \mathsf{Rerand}_{\mathbb{H}}(\mathsf{pp}_{\mathbb{H}}, \mathsf{Sam}_{\mathbb{H}}(\mathsf{pp}_{\mathbb{H}}, x))$
$\widehat{y} = \mathsf{Rerand}_{\mathbb{H}}(\mathsf{pp}_{\mathbb{H}}, \mathsf{Sam}_{\mathbb{H}}(\mathsf{pp}_{\mathbb{H}}, y))$
$s \leftarrow \mathcal{A}(\mathsf{pp}_{\mathbb{H}}, \widehat{1}, \widehat{x}, \widehat{y})$
return $\mathsf{Eq}_{\mathbb{H}}(\widehat{x}^y, s)$

G_1

$\mathsf{pp}_{\mathbb{G}} \leftarrow \mathsf{GGen}_{\mathbb{G}}(1^\lambda)$
$X \leftarrow \mathbb{G}$
$z \leftarrow \mathbb{Z}_p$
$(\mathsf{pp}_{\mathbb{H}}, \tau_{\mathbb{H}}) \leftarrow \mathsf{GGen}_{\mathbb{H}}(\mathsf{pp}_{\mathbb{G}}, ([1]_{\mathbb{G}}, \boxed{[x]_{\mathbb{G}}}, \boxed{[y]_{\mathbb{G}}})^\mathsf{T})$
$\widehat{1} = \mathsf{Rerand}_{\mathbb{H}}(\mathsf{pp}_{\mathbb{H}}, \mathsf{Sam}_{\mathbb{H}}(\mathsf{pp}_{\mathbb{H}}, 1))$
$\widehat{x} = \mathsf{Rerand}_{\mathbb{H}}(\mathsf{pp}_{\mathbb{H}}, \mathsf{PrivSam}_{\mathbb{H}}(\tau_{\mathbb{H}}, (0, \boxed{1}, 0)^\mathsf{T}))$
$\widehat{y} = \mathsf{Rerand}_{\mathbb{H}}(\mathsf{pp}_{\mathbb{H}}, \mathsf{PrivSam}_{\mathbb{H}}(\tau_{\mathbb{H}}, (0, 0, \boxed{1})^\mathsf{T}))$
$s \leftarrow \mathcal{A}(\mathsf{pp}_{\mathbb{H}}, \widehat{1}, \widehat{x}, \widehat{y})$
return $\mathsf{Eq}_{\mathbb{H}}([xy]_{\mathbb{G}}, s)$

Fig. 4. The CDH games used in the security proof. G_0 corresponds to the honest CDH-game. Games of type G_1 allow the reduction to embed its discrete logarithm challenge and extract a useful representation.

Proof (sketch). We use an algebraic wrapper with basis $[1]_{\mathbb{G}}, [x]_{\mathbb{G}}, [y]_{\mathbb{G}}$. Initially, we perform game hops starting from the CDH game (where every encoding carries representation vectors in the first component), see G_0 in Fig. 4 and reach a game, where the encodings produced as CDH challenge carry representation vectors of $\mathbf{e_1}, \mathbf{e_2}$ and $\mathbf{e_3}$, respectively, see G_1 in Fig. 4. These game hops are justified by 2-switching and rerand.

The reduction flips a coin whether to embed the DLOG challenge Z as $[x]_{\mathbb{G}}$ or $[y]_{\mathbb{G}}$, i.e. it applies the symmetrization technique. In both cases, the view of the CDH adversary is identical. When the CDH adversary outputs a solution, the reduction is able to compute the discrete logarithm of the embedded DLOG challenge from the representation vector extracted from the solution.   □

We additionally show the following in the full version [2].

Theorem 4. *Let $\mathbb{G}$ be a group where the discrete logarithm is hard. Then, the square Diffie-Hellman assumption holds in an algebraic wrapper $\mathbb{H}$ of dimension ≥ 2 for $\mathbb{G}$.*

Theorem 5. *Let $\mathbb{G}$ be a group where DLOG is hard and $\mathbb{H}$ be an algebraic wrapper of dimension ≥ 3 for $\mathbb{G}$. Then, the linear-combination Diffie-Hellman problem is hard in $\mathbb{H}$.*

4.2   Schnorr Signatures

We apply the algebraic wrapper to mimic the proof of tight EUF-CMA security of Schnorr Signatures from [22].

Theorem 6. *Let $\mathsf{GGen}_{\mathbb{G}}$ be a group generator for a cyclic group $\mathbb{G}$ such that DLOG is hard relative to $\mathsf{GGen}_{\mathbb{G}}$ and let $\mathbb{H}$ be an algebraic wrapper of dimension ≥ 2 for $\mathbb{G}$. Then, the Schnorr signature scheme in $\mathbb{H}$ (Fig. 5) is tightly EUF-CMA secure in the random oracle model.*

More precisely, for all PPT adversaries $\mathcal{A}$, there exists a PPT adversary $\mathcal{B}$ and a legitimate switching adversary $\mathcal{A}''$ both running in time $T(\mathcal{B}) \approx T(\mathcal{A}) + (q_s + q_h) \cdot \mathsf{poly}(\lambda)$ and $T(\mathcal{A}'') \approx T(\mathcal{A}) + (q_s + q_h) \cdot \mathsf{poly}(\lambda)$ such that

$$\mathrm{Adv}_{\Sigma_{\mathrm{schnorr}}, \mathcal{A}}^{\mathrm{euf\text{-}cma}}(\lambda) \leq \mathrm{Adv}_{\mathcal{B}, \mathbb{G}}^{DLOG}(\lambda) + \mathrm{Adv}_{\mathcal{A}'', \mathbb{H}}^{\text{1-switching}}(\lambda) + \frac{O(q_s(q_s + q_h))}{2^{\lambda}},$$

where q_h is a polynomial upper bound on the number of random oracle queries, q_s is a polynomial upper bound on the number of signing queries and poly is a polynomial independent of q_s and q_h.

$\mathsf{KGen}(\mathsf{pp}_{\mathbb{H}})$	$\mathsf{Sign}(sk, m)$
$x \leftarrow \mathbb{Z}_p$	$r \leftarrow \mathbb{Z}_p$
$\widehat{1} := \mathsf{Rerand}_{\mathbb{H}}(\mathsf{pp}_{\mathbb{H}}, \mathsf{Sam}_{\mathbb{H}}(\mathsf{pp}_{\mathbb{H}}, 1))$	$\widehat{R} \leftarrow \mathsf{Rerand}_{\mathbb{H}}(\mathsf{pp}_{\mathbb{H}}, \mathsf{Sam}_{\mathbb{H}}(\mathsf{pp}_{\mathbb{H}}, r))$
$\widehat{X} := \mathsf{Rerand}_{\mathbb{H}}(\mathsf{pp}_{\mathbb{H}}, \mathsf{Sam}_{\mathbb{H}}(\mathsf{pp}_{\mathbb{H}}, x))$	$c := H(\widehat{R}, m)$
$pk := (\mathsf{pp}_{\mathbb{H}}, \widehat{1}, \widehat{X})$	$s := r + c \cdot x \mod p$
$sk := (pk, x)$	$\mathbf{return}\ \sigma := (\widehat{R}, s)$
$\mathbf{return}\ (pk, sk)$	

$\mathsf{Ver}(pk = (\mathsf{pp}_{\mathbb{H}}, \widehat{1}, \widehat{X}), m, \sigma = (\widehat{R}, s))$

$c := H(\widehat{R}, m)$

$\mathbf{return}\ \mathsf{Eq}_{\mathbb{H}}(\mathsf{pp}_{\mathbb{H}}, \mathsf{Sam}_{\mathbb{H}}(\mathsf{pp}_{\mathbb{H}}, s), \widehat{R} \cdot \widehat{X}^c)$

Fig. 5. The Schnorr signature scheme $\Sigma_{\mathrm{schnorr}}$. Note that to compensate for the non-uniqueness of group element encodings, the (random oracle) hash value of a group element encoding is computed for the unique identifier produced by $\mathsf{GetID}_{\mathbb{H}}(\mathsf{pp}_{\mathbb{H}}, \cdot)$.

$\mathrm{Exp}^{\mathsf{euf\text{-}cma}}_{\Sigma_{\mathrm{schnorr}}, \mathcal{A}}(\lambda)$	$H(\widehat{R}, m)$
$\mathsf{pp}_{\mathbb{G}} \leftarrow \mathsf{GGen}_{\mathbb{G}}(1^\lambda)$	$\mathbf{if}\ T[(\mathsf{GetID}_{\mathbb{H}}(\mathsf{pp}_{\mathbb{H}}, \widehat{R}), m)] = \bot\ \mathbf{then}$
$(\mathsf{pp}_{\mathbb{H}}, \tau_{\mathbb{H}}) \leftarrow \mathsf{GGen}_{\mathbb{H}}(\mathsf{pp}_{\mathbb{G}}, ([1]_{\mathbb{G}}, [\beta_2]_{\mathbb{G}})^\mathsf{T})$	$\quad T[(\mathsf{GetID}_{\mathbb{H}}(\mathsf{pp}_{\mathbb{H}}, \widehat{R}), m)] \leftarrow \mathbb{Z}_p$
$x \leftarrow \mathbb{Z}_p$	$\quad \mathbf{return}\ T[(\mathsf{GetID}_{\mathbb{H}}(\mathsf{pp}_{\mathbb{H}}, \widehat{R}), m)]$
$\xi_1 \leftarrow \mathsf{Rerand}_{\mathbb{H}}(\mathsf{pp}_{\mathbb{H}}, \mathsf{Sam}_{\mathbb{H}}(\mathsf{pp}_{\mathbb{H}}, 1))$	
$\xi_2 \leftarrow \mathsf{Rerand}_{\mathbb{H}}(\mathsf{pp}_{\mathbb{H}}, \mathsf{Sam}_{\mathbb{H}}(\mathsf{pp}_{\mathbb{H}}, x))$	$\mathsf{Sign}(m)$
$pk := (\mathsf{pp}_{\mathbb{H}}, \xi_1, \xi_2)$	$r \leftarrow \mathbb{Z}_p$
$Q := \varnothing, T := []$	$\widehat{R} \leftarrow \mathsf{Rerand}_{\mathbb{H}}(\mathsf{pp}_{\mathbb{H}}, \mathsf{Sam}_{\mathbb{H}}(\mathsf{pp}_{\mathbb{H}}, r))$
$(m^*, \widehat{R^*}, s^*) \leftarrow \mathcal{A}^{H, \mathsf{Sign}}(1^\lambda, pk)$	$c := H(\widehat{R}, m)$
$\mathbf{if}\ m^* \in Q\ \mathbf{then\ return}\ 0$	$s := r + cx$
$c^* = H(\widehat{R^*}, m^*)$	$Q := Q \cup \{m\}$
$\mathbf{return}\ \mathsf{Eq}_{\mathbb{H}}(\mathsf{pp}_{\mathbb{H}}, \mathsf{Sam}_{\mathbb{H}}(\mathsf{pp}_{\mathbb{H}}, s^*), \widehat{R^*} \cdot \xi_2^{c^*})$	$\mathbf{return}\ (\widehat{R}, s)$

Fig. 6. The EUF-CMA game for Schnorr signatures. Note that β_2 can be chosen arbitrarily.

Proof. We use the origin element trick to avoid using q_s-switching (see Definition 7) which would compromise tightness of the reduction. Figure 6 shows the EUF-CMA game with Schnorr signatures instantiated with the algebraic wrapper. We note that for groups with non-unique encodings, the hash function hashes the unique identifier returned by $\mathsf{GetID}_{\mathbb{H}}$, hence, encodings corresponding to the same group element are mapped to the same hash value. The reduction uses a table T to keep track of previously made hash queries and their responses, as well as a set Q to keep track of the messages the adversary has requested signatures for.

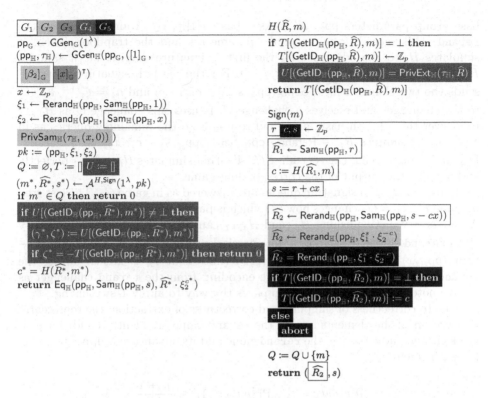

Fig. 7. Games G_1, G_2, G_3. Boxed content happens in the corresponding games and following games if no replacement is defined. The randomness for signatures is drawn using an x-component in G_1. G_1 is identically distributed to $\text{Exp}^{\text{euf-cma}}_{\Sigma_{\text{schnorr}},\mathcal{A}}(\lambda)$. In G_2, the second origin element is sampled through private sampling and the random part of the signatures is generated through origin elements. G_2 is statistically close to G_1 due to re-randomizability. In G_3, we switch the basis and representation of ξ_2; this hop is justified by 1-switching.

Game hop from $\text{Exp}^{\text{euf-cma}}_{\Sigma_{\text{schnorr}},\mathcal{A}}(\lambda) \rightsquigarrow G_1$**.** Since $r = s - cx \bmod p$ and hence $\text{GetID}_\mathbb{H}(\text{pp}_\mathbb{H}, \widehat{R_1}) = \text{GetID}_\mathbb{H}(\text{pp}_\mathbb{H}, \widehat{R_2})$, these two games are identically distributed.

Game hop $G_1 \rightsquigarrow G_2$**.** In G_2 (see Fig. 7), we construct $\widehat{R_2}$ from origin elements through the group operation instead of sampling. This game hop is justified by the re-randomizability of the algebraic wrapper. A reduction to this property works as a series of $q_s + 1$ hybrids where H_0 is G_1, where q_s denotes a polynomial upper bound on the number of signing queries. In H_i, the first i signature queries are answered as in G_2 and the $i + 1$-th to q_s-th signature queries are answered as in G_1. In the last hybrid, the public key is also changed to private sampling. If there is an (unbounded) adversary that distinguishes H_i and H_{i+1}, the reduction $\mathcal{A}'$ uses this adversary to attack the re-randomizability as follows. On input of base group parameters $\mathsf{pp}_\mathbb{G}$, $\mathcal{A}'$ picks a basis $([1]_\mathbb{G}, [\beta_2]_\mathbb{G})$ and gives it to the **rerand** challenger. It receives public parameters and the trapdoor. Then, it simulates H_i to the adversary for the first i signature queries, i.e. it samples $\widehat{R_{2,j}} \leftarrow \mathsf{Rerand}_\mathbb{H}(\mathsf{pp}_\mathbb{H}, \xi_1^{s_j} \cdot \xi_2^{-c_j})$ for $j < i$. For the $i + 1$-th signature query, $\mathcal{A}'$ sends the two elements $\widehat{h_0} = \mathsf{Sam}_\mathbb{H}(\mathsf{pp}_\mathbb{H}, s_{i+1} - c_{i+1} \cdot x)$ and $\widehat{h_1} = \xi_1^{s_{i+1}} \cdot \xi_2^{-c_{i+1}}$ to the challenger and receives a challenge $\widehat{C}$. It uses this challenge $\widehat{C}$ as $\widehat{R_{2,i+1}}$ to answer the $i + 1$-th hash query and responds to the remaining queries as in H_{i+1}, i.e. it samples $\widehat{R_j} \leftarrow \mathsf{Rerand}_\mathbb{H}(\mathsf{pp}_\mathbb{H}, \mathsf{Sam}_\mathbb{H}(\mathsf{pp}_\mathbb{H}, s_j - c_j \cdot x))$ for $j > i + 1$. Depending on the challenge encoding $\widehat{C}$, $\mathcal{A}'$ either simulates H_i or H_{i+1} perfectly and outputs the output of the corresponding game.

In hybrid H_{q_s}, all signature queries are answered as in game G_2. The last step to game $H_{q_s+1} = G_2$ changes how ξ_2 (which is part of the public key) is sampled. An adversary distinguishing H_{q_s} and H_{q_s+1} can be used to build an adversary $\mathcal{A}'$ in **rerand** similarly as above. More precisely, $\mathcal{A}'$ outputs the encodings $\widehat{h_0} \leftarrow \mathsf{Sam}_\mathbb{H}(\mathsf{pp}_\mathbb{H}, x)$ and $\widehat{h_1} \leftarrow \mathsf{PrivSam}_\mathbb{H}(\tau_\mathbb{H}, x)$ (note that $\tau_\mathbb{H}$ is known during the **rerand** game) and uses the challenge encoding from the **rerand** challenger as ξ_2. We note that this last game hop paves the way to apply 1-switching.

Due to correctness of sampling and correctness of extraction, the representation vectors of the elements used in the **rerand** game are identical and hence $\mathcal{A}'$ is a legitimate adversary in the **rerand** game and its advantage is upper bounded by $\frac{1}{2^\lambda}$. Therefore,

$$|\Pr\left[out_1 = 1\right] - \Pr\left[out_2 = 1\right]| \leq \frac{q_s + 1}{2^\lambda}.$$

Game hop $G_2 \rightsquigarrow G_3$. In game G_3 (see Fig. 7) we switch the basis and the representation of the origin element ξ_2. This game hop is justified by 1-switching. Let $\mathcal{A}$ be an adversary distinguishing G_2 and G_3. We construct an adversary $\mathcal{A}''$ on 1-switching as follows. Initially, $\mathcal{A}''$ on input of $\mathsf{pp}_\mathbb{G}$, outputs $[\mathbf{b}]_\mathbb{G}^{(G_2)} = [(1, \beta_2)^\intercal]_\mathbb{G}$ and $[\mathbf{b}]_\mathbb{G}^{(G_3)} = [(1, x)^\intercal]_\mathbb{G}$ and the representation vectors $\mathbf{v}^{(\mathbf{G_2})} := (x, 0)^\intercal$ and $\mathbf{v}^{(\mathbf{G_3})} := (0, 1)^\intercal$. In return, $\mathcal{A}''$ receives public parameters $\mathsf{pp}_\mathbb{H}$ and an encoding $\widehat{C}$ and samples $\xi_2 \leftarrow \mathsf{Rerand}_\mathbb{H}(\mathsf{pp}_\mathbb{H}, \widehat{C})$. The trapdoor $\tau_\mathbb{H}$ is not necessary to simulate G_3 and G_4 (except for sampling ξ_2). Hence, $\mathcal{A}''$ perfectly simulates G_3 or G_4 for $\mathcal{A}$ depending on the challenge provided by the 1-switching challenger. Thus, $|\Pr[out_3 = 1] - \Pr[out_2 = 1]| \leq \mathsf{Adv}_{\mathbb{H}, \mathcal{A}''}^{\text{1-switching}}(\lambda)$. Note that $\mathcal{A}''$ is a legitimate switching adversary since $[(1, \beta_2)]_\mathbb{G} \cdot (x, 0)^\intercal = [x]_\mathbb{G} = [(1, x)]_\mathbb{G} \cdot (0, 1)^\intercal$ and hence $\mathsf{Adv}_{\mathbb{H}, \mathcal{A}''}^{\text{1-switching}}(\lambda)$ is negligible.

Game hop $G_3 \rightsquigarrow G_4$. In G_4 (see Fig. 7), we introduce a list U to keep track of the representations of group elements used in Random Oracle queries. The games G_3 and G_4 differ in the fact that G_4 extracts the representation vectors contained in the encoding of a group element when this group element message tuple is queried for the first time and stores this representation in a list. Furthermore, G_4 introduces an abort condition which is triggered if the representation of $\widehat{R^*}$ originally used to query the random oracle on $(\widehat{R^*}, m^*)$ already contained the response in the second component ζ^*. This corresponds to the game hop from G_0 to G_1 in [22]. The game only aborts if the hash $T[(\mathsf{GetID}_{\mathbb{H}}(\mathsf{pp}_{\mathbb{H}}, \widehat{R^*}), m^*)]$ is the same as the second component ζ^* of the representation extracted from $\widehat{R^*}$. Since the hash $T[(\mathsf{GetID}_{\mathbb{H}}(\mathsf{pp}_{\mathbb{H}}, \widehat{R^*}), m^*)]$ is chosen uniformly at random *after* the representation (γ^*, ζ^*) is fixed, the probability that an unbounded adversary can find such an $(\widehat{R^*}, m^*)$ is upper bounded by $\frac{q_h}{p} \leq \frac{q_h}{2^\lambda}$, where q_h denotes a polynomial upper bound on the number of random oracle queries. Hence, $|\Pr[out_4 = 1] - \Pr[out_3 = 1]| \leq \frac{q_h}{2^\lambda}$.

Game hop $G_4 \rightsquigarrow G_5$. In game G_5 (see Fig. 7), we change how signature queries are answered such that it is not necessary anymore to know the discrete logarithm of the public key. This game hop corresponds to the hop from G_1 to G_2 in [22]. On one hand, since $\mathsf{GetID}_{\mathbb{H}}(\mathsf{pp}_{\mathbb{H}}, \widehat{R_1}) = \mathsf{GetID}_{\mathbb{H}}(\mathsf{pp}_{\mathbb{H}}, \widehat{R_2})$, replacing $\widehat{R_1}$ with $\widehat{R_2}$ does not change the distribution. On the other hand, as we are only able to answer a signing query if we can program the random oracle at $(\widehat{R_2}, m)$ (for randomly chosen $\widehat{R_2}$), the signing oracle has to abort in case the hash was already queried before. Since $\widehat{R_2}$ is a independently sampled uniformly random group element, this happens only with probability $\frac{1}{p} \leq \frac{1}{2^\lambda}$. Hence, by a union bound, this abort occurs at most with probability $\frac{q_s(q_s+q_h)}{2^\lambda}$ cases, where q_s denotes a polynomial upper bound on the number of signing queries and q_h denotes a polynomial upper bound on the number of random oracle queries. Conditioned on the event that no abort occurs, G_4 and G_5 are distributed identically. Hence, by the Difference Lemma due to Shoup [39], we have $|\Pr[out_5 = 1] - \Pr[out_4 = 1]| \leq \frac{q_s(q_s+q_h)}{2^\lambda}$. As in [22], on extraction of the initial representation (γ^*, ζ^*) of $\widehat{R^*}$ from a valid signature $(\widehat{R^*}, s^*)$ output by the adversary, the reduction can use that $\widehat{R^*} = [\gamma^*]_{\mathbb{H}} \cdot [\zeta^* \cdot z]_{\mathbb{H}} = [s^* - c^* \cdot z]_{\mathbb{H}}$. Therefore,

$$ z = \frac{s^* - \gamma^*}{\zeta^* - c^*}. $$

Due to the added check in G_4, an adversary can only win G_4 or G_5 when $\zeta^* - c^* \neq 0$ which concludes the proof. $\qquad\square$

Acknowledgments. We would like to thank the anonymous reviewers of EC20 for many helpful comments and for pointing out an error in previous versions of Lemma 1 and the proof of the switching property.

References

1. Agrikola, T., Hofheinz, D.: Interactively secure groups from obfuscation. In: Abdalla, M., Dahab, R. (eds.) PKC 2018, Part II. LNCS, vol. 10770, pp. 341–370. Springer, Cham (2018). https://doi.org/10.1007/978-3-319-76581-5_12
2. Agrikola, T., Hofheinz, D., Kastner, J.: On instantiating the algebraic group model from falsifiable assumptions. Cryptology ePrint Archive, Report 2020/070 (2020). https://eprint.iacr.org/2020/070

3. Albrecht, M.R., Farshim, P., Hofheinz, D., Larraia, E., Paterson, K.G.: Multilinear maps from obfuscation. In: Kushilevitz, E., Malkin, T. (eds.) TCC 2016-A, Part I. LNCS, vol. 9562, pp. 446–473. Springer, Heidelberg (2016). https://doi.org/10. 1007/978-3-662-49096-9_19
4. Bellare, M., Palacio, A.: The knowledge-of-exponent assumptions and 3-round zero-knowledge protocols. In: Franklin, M. (ed.) CRYPTO 2004. LNCS, vol. 3152, pp. 273–289. Springer, Heidelberg (2004). https://doi.org/10.1007/978-3-540-28628-8_17
5. Bitansky, N., Canetti, R., Paneth, O., Rosen, A.: On the existence of extractable one-way functions. In: Shmoys, D.B. (ed.) 46th ACM STOC, pp. 505–514. ACM Press, May/June 2014
6. Boneh, D., Lipton, R.J.: Algorithms for black-box fields and their application to cryptography. In: Koblitz, N. (ed.) CRYPTO 1996. LNCS, vol. 1109, pp. 283–297. Springer, Heidelberg (1996). https://doi.org/10.1007/3-540-68697-5_22
7. Boneh, D., Lynn, B., Shacham, H.: Short signatures from the Weil pairing. J. Cryptol. 17(4), 297–319 (2004). https://doi.org/10.1007/s00145-004-0314-9
8. Boneh, D., Segev, G., Waters, B.: Targeted malleability: homomorphic encryption for restricted computations. In: Goldwasser, S. (ed.) ITCS 2012, pp. 350–366. ACM, January 2012
9. Boneh, D., Venkatesan, R.: Breaking RSA may not be equivalent to factoring. In: Nyberg, K. (ed.) EUROCRYPT 1998. LNCS, vol. 1403, pp. 59–71. Springer, Heidelberg (1998). https://doi.org/10.1007/BFb0054117
10. Boyen, X.: The uber-assumption family. In: Galbraith, S.D., Paterson, K.G. (eds.) Pairing 2008. LNCS, vol. 5209, pp. 39–56. Springer, Heidelberg (2008). https:// doi.org/10.1007/978-3-540-85538-5_3
11. Canetti, R., Lin, H., Tessaro, S., Vaikuntanathan, V.: Obfuscation of probabilistic circuits and applications. In: Dodis, Y., Nielsen, J.B. (eds.) TCC 2015, Part II. LNCS, vol. 9015, pp. 468–497. Springer, Heidelberg (2015). https://doi.org/10. 1007/978-3-662-46497-7_19
12. Coron, J.-S.: On the exact security of full domain hash. In: Bellare, M. (ed.) CRYPTO 2000. LNCS, vol. 1880, pp. 229–235. Springer, Heidelberg (2000). https://doi.org/10.1007/3-540-44598-6_14
13. Cramer, R., Shoup, V.: Universal hash proofs and a paradigm for adaptive chosen ciphertext secure public-key encryption. In: Knudsen, L.R. (ed.) EUROCRYPT 2002. LNCS, vol. 2332, pp. 45–64. Springer, Heidelberg (2002). https://doi.org/10. 1007/3-540-46035-7_4
14. Damgård, I.: Towards practical public key systems secure against chosen ciphertext attacks. In: Feigenbaum, J. (ed.) CRYPTO 1991. LNCS, vol. 576, pp. 445–456. Springer, Heidelberg (1992). https://doi.org/10.1007/3-540-46766-1_36
15. Dent, A.W.: Adapting the weaknesses of the random oracle model to the generic group model. In: Zheng, Y. (ed.) ASIACRYPT 2002. LNCS, vol. 2501, pp. 100–109. Springer, Heidelberg (2002). https://doi.org/10.1007/3-540-36178-2_6
16. Dent, A.W.: The cramer-shoup encryption scheme is plaintext aware in the standard model. In: Vaudenay, S. (ed.) EUROCRYPT 2006. LNCS, vol. 4004, pp. 289–307. Springer, Heidelberg (2006). https://doi.org/10.1007/11761679_18
17. Farshim, P., Hesse, J., Hofheinz, D., Larraia, E.: Graded encoding schemes from obfuscation. In: Abdalla, M., Dahab, R. (eds.) PKC 2018, Part II. LNCS, vol. 10770, pp. 371–400. Springer, Cham (2018). https://doi.org/10.1007/978-3-319-76581-5_13
18. Feige, U., Shamir, A.: Witness indistinguishable and witness hiding protocols. In: 22nd ACM STOC, pp. 416–426. ACM Press, May 1990

19. Fleischhacker, N., Jager, T., Schröder, D.: On tight security proofs for Schnorr signatures. J. Cryptol. **32**(2), 566–599 (2019). https://doi.org/10.1007/s00145-019-09311-5
20. Freire, E.S.V., Hofheinz, D., Paterson, K.G., Striecks, C.: Programmable hash functions in the multilinear setting. In: Canetti, R., Garay, J.A. (eds.) CRYPTO 2013, Part I. LNCS, vol. 8042, pp. 513–530. Springer, Heidelberg (2013). https://doi.org/10.1007/978-3-642-40041-4_28
21. Fuchsbauer, G., Kiltz, E., Loss, J.: The algebraic group model and its applications. In: Shacham, H., Boldyreva, A. (eds.) CRYPTO 2018, Part II. LNCS, vol. 10992, pp. 33–62. Springer, Cham (2018). https://doi.org/10.1007/978-3-319-96881-0_2
22. Fuchsbauer, G., Plouviez, A., Seurin, Y.: Blind Schnorr signatures in the algebraic group model. Cryptology ePrint Archive, Report 2019/877 (2019). http://eprint.iacr.org/2019/877
23. Garg, S., Gentry, C., Halevi, S.: Candidate multilinear maps from ideal lattices. In: Johansson, T., Nguyen, P.Q. (eds.) EUROCRYPT 2013. LNCS, vol. 7881, pp. 1–17. Springer, Heidelberg (2013). https://doi.org/10.1007/978-3-642-38348-9_1
24. Groth, J., Sahai, A.: Efficient non-interactive proof systems for bilinear groups. In: Smart, N. (ed.) EUROCRYPT 2008. LNCS, vol. 4965, pp. 415–432. Springer, Heidelberg (2008). https://doi.org/10.1007/978-3-540-78967-3_24
25. Hada, S., Tanaka, T.: On the existence of 3-round zero-knowledge protocols. In: Krawczyk, H. (ed.) CRYPTO 1998. LNCS, vol. 1462, pp. 408–423. Springer, Heidelberg (1998). https://doi.org/10.1007/BFb0055744
26. Hofheinz, D., Kiltz, E.: Programmable hash functions and their applications. J. Cryptol. **25**(3), 484–527 (2012). https://doi.org/10.1007/s00145-011-9102-5
27. Hofheinz, D., Ursu, B.: Dual-mode NIZKs from obfuscation. In: Galbraith, S.D., Moriai, S. (eds.) ASIACRYPT 2019. LNCS, vol. 11921, pp. 311–341. Springer, Cham (2019). https://doi.org/10.1007/978-3-030-34578-5_12. https://eprint.iacr.org/2019/475
28. Hohenberger, S., Sahai, A., Waters, B.: Full domain hash from (leveled) multilinear maps and identity-based aggregate signatures. In: Canetti, R., Garay, J.A. (eds.) CRYPTO 2013, Part I. LNCS, vol. 8042, pp. 494–512. Springer, Heidelberg (2013). https://doi.org/10.1007/978-3-642-40041-4_27
29. Hohenberger, S., Sahai, A., Waters, B.: Replacing a random oracle: full domain hash from indistinguishability obfuscation. In: Nguyen, P.Q., Oswald, E. (eds.) EUROCRYPT 2014. LNCS, vol. 8441, pp. 201–220. Springer, Heidelberg (2014). https://doi.org/10.1007/978-3-642-55220-5_12
30. Kastner, J., Pan, J.: Towards instantiating the algebraic group model. Cryptology ePrint Archive, Report 2019/1018 (2019). https://eprint.iacr.org/2019/1018
31. Maurer, U.: Abstract models of computation in cryptography. In: Smart, N.P. (ed.) Cryptography and Coding 2005. LNCS, vol. 3796, pp. 1–12. Springer, Heidelberg (2005). https://doi.org/10.1007/11586821_1
32. Maurer, U., Wolf, S.: Lower bounds on generic algorithms in groups. In: Nyberg, K. (ed.) EUROCRYPT 1998. LNCS, vol. 1403, pp. 72–84. Springer, Heidelberg (1998). https://doi.org/10.1007/BFb0054118
33. Naor, M.: On cryptographic assumptions and challenges. In: Boneh, D. (ed.) CRYPTO 2003. LNCS, vol. 2729, pp. 96–109. Springer, Heidelberg (2003). https://doi.org/10.1007/978-3-540-45146-4_6
34. Nechaev, V.I.: Complexity of a determinate algorithm for the discrete logarithm. Math. Notes **55**(2), 165–172 (1994). https://doi.org/10.1007/BF02113297

35. Paillier, P., Vergnaud, D.: Discrete-log-based signatures may not be equivalent to discrete log. In: Roy, B. (ed.) ASIACRYPT 2005. LNCS, vol. 3788, pp. 1–20. Springer, Heidelberg (2005). https://doi.org/10.1007/11593447_1

36. Peikert, C., Shiehian, S.: Noninteractive zero knowledge for NP from (plain) learning with errors. In: Boldyreva, A., Micciancio, D. (eds.) CRYPTO 2019, Part I. LNCS, vol. 11692, pp. 89–114. Springer, Cham (2019). https://doi.org/10.1007/978-3-030-26948-7_4

37. Schnorr, C.P.: Efficient signature generation by smart cards. J. Cryptol. 4(3), 161–174 (1991). https://doi.org/10.1007/BF00196725

38. Shoup, V.: Lower bounds for discrete logarithms and related problems. In: Fumy, W. (ed.) EUROCRYPT 1997. LNCS, vol. 1233, pp. 256–266. Springer, Heidelberg (1997). https://doi.org/10.1007/3-540-69053-0_18

39. Shoup, V.: Sequences of games: a tool for taming complexity in security proofs. Cryptology ePrint Archive, Report 2004/332 (2004). http://eprint.iacr.org/2004/332

Secure Computation I

Resource-Restricted Cryptography: Revisiting MPC Bounds in the Proof-of-Work Era

Juan Garay[1], Aggelos Kiayias[2]([✉]), Rafail M. Ostrovsky[3],
Giorgos Panagiotakos[4]([✉]), and Vassilis Zikas[2]

[1] Department of Computer Science and Engineering,
Texas A&M University, College Station, USA
`garay@cse.tamu.edu`
[2] School of Informatics, University of Edinburgh & IOHK, Edinburgh, UK
`{akiayias,vzikas}@inf.ed.ac.uk`
[3] Department of Computer Science and Department of Mathematics,
UCLA, Los Angeles, USA
`rafail@cs.ucla.edu`
[4] School of Informatics, University of Edinburgh, Edinburgh, UK
`giorgos.pan@inf.ed.ac.uk`

Abstract. Traditional bounds on synchronous Byzantine agreement (BA) and secure multi-party computation (MPC) establish that in absence of a private correlated-randomness setup, such as a PKI, protocols can tolerate up to $t < n/3$ of the parties being malicious. The introduction of "Nakamoto style" consensus, based on Proof-of-Work (PoW) blockchains, put forth a somewhat different flavor of BA, showing that even a majority of corrupted parties can be tolerated as long as the majority of the computation resources remain at honest hands. This assumption on honest majority of some resource was also extended to other resources such as stake, space, etc., upon which blockchains achieving Nakamoto-style consensus were built that violated the $t < n/3$ bound in terms of number of party corruptions. The above state of affairs begs the question of whether the seeming mismatch is due to different goals and models, or whether the resource-restricting paradigm can be generically used to circumvent the $n/3$ lower bound.

In this work we study this question and formally demonstrate how the above paradigm changes the rules of the game in cryptographic definitions. First, we abstract the core properties that the resource-restricting paradigm offers by means of a functionality *wrapper*, in the UC framework, which when applied to a standard point-to-point network restricts the ability (of the adversary) to send new messages. We show that such a wrapped network can be implemented using the resource-restricting paradigm—concretely, using PoWs and honest majority of computing power—and that the traditional $t < n/3$ impossibility results fail when the parties have access to such a network. Our construction is in the *fresh* Common Reference String (CRS) model—i.e., it assumes a CRS which becomes available to the parties at the same time as to the adversary.

© International Association for Cryptologic Research 2020
A. Canteaut and Y. Ishai (Eds.): EUROCRYPT 2020, LNCS 12106, pp. 129–158, 2020.
https://doi.org/10.1007/978-3-030-45724-2_5

We then present constructions for BA and MPC, which given access to such a network tolerate $t < n/2$ corruptions without assuming a private correlated randomness setup. We also show how to remove the freshness assumption from the CRS by leveraging the power of a random oracle. Our MPC protocol achieves the standard notion of MPC security, where parties might have dedicated roles, as is for example the case in Oblivious Transfer protocols. This is in contrast to existing solutions basing MPC on PoWs, which associate roles to pseudonyms but do not link these pseudonyms with the actual parties.

1   Introduction

Byzantine agreement (BA), introduced by Lamport, Shostak, and Pease [31], is a fundamental primitive in distributed computing and is at the core of many secure multi-party computation (MPC) protocols. The problem comes in two main flavors, *Consensus* and *Broadcast*—although a number of relaxations have also been proposed. Consensus considers a set of n parties $\mathcal{P} = \{P_1, \ldots, P_n\}$ each of whom has an input x_i, and who wish to agree on an output y (Consistency) such that if $x_i = x$ for all honest parties then $y = x$ (Validity), despite the potentially malicious behavior of up to t of them. In the Broadcast version, on the other hand, only a single party, often called the *sender* has an input x_s, and the goal is to agree on an output y (Consistency) which, when the sender is honest equals x (Validity).

The traditional setting in which the problem was introduced and investigated considers synchronous communication and protocol execution. In a nutshell, this means that the protocol advances in rounds such that: (1) parties have a consistent view of the current round—i.e., no party advances to round $\rho + 1$ before all other parties are finished with their round ρ instructions; and (2) all messages sent in round ρ are delivered to their respective recipients by the beginning of round $\rho + 1$. Furthermore, the underlying communication network is a complete point-to-point authenticated channels network, where every pair (P_i, P_j) of parties is connected by a channel, such that when P_j receives a message on this channel it knows it was indeed sent by P_i (or the adversary, in case P_i is corrupted). We refer to the above setting as the *(standard) LSP setting*.

In this model, Lamport *et al.* [21,31] proved that there exists no Consensus or Broadcast protocol which can tolerate $t \geq n/3$ Byzantine parties, i.e., parties controlled by a (central) active and malicious adversary. The original formulation considered perfect security (i.e., information-theoretic security with zero error probability) and no correlated randomness shared among the parties.[1] This impossibility result was later extended by Borcherding [7] to computational security—i.e., it was proved to hold even under strong computational assumptions, such as one-way

---

[1] Lamport *et al.* also considered the case of "signed messages." The information-theoretic setting was referred to as the "oral messages" setting.

permutations.[2] Furthermore, it applies even when the point-to-point channels used by the parties are secure, i.e., both authenticated and private, and even if we assume an arbitrary public correlated randomness setup and/or a random oracle (RO).[3] (A *public* correlated randomness setup can be viewed as a functionality which samples a string and distributes it to all parties, e.g, a *common reference string* (CRS). This is in contrast to a *private* correlated randomness setup which might keep part of the sampled string private and distribute different parts of it to different parties, e.g., a PKI.) For ease of reference we state the above as a corollary:

Corollary 1 (Strong $t \geq n/3$ impossibility [7]). *In the synchronous point-to-point channels setting, there exists no Broadcast protocol tolerating $t \geq n/3$ corrupted parties. The statement holds both in the authenticated and in the secure channels settings, both for unconditional adversaries and assuming (even enhanced) trapdoor permutations, and even assuming an arbitrary public correlated randomness setup and/or a random oracle.*

Finally, Cohen et al. [16], show that this line of impossibility results can be extended to the case of symmetric functionalities, i.e., functionalities where all parties receive the same output.

The effect of BA lower bounds on MPC. MPC allows a set of parties to compute an arbitrary function of their (potentially private) inputs in a secure way even in the presence of an adversary. Ben-Or, Goldwasser and Wigderson [5] presented a protocol which computes any function with perfect security in the synchronous setting while tolerating $t < n/3$ malicious parties assuming the parties have access to a complete network of instant delivery point-to-point *secure*—i.e., authenticated and private—channels (we shall refer to this model as the *BGW communication model*). The lower bound holds even if a Broadcast channel—i.e., an ideal primitive guaranteeing the input/output properties of Broadcast—is available to the parties. Rabin and Ben-Or [34] proved that if we allow for a negligible error probability and assume broadcast, then there exists a general MPC protocol tolerating up to $t < n/2$ of the parties being corrupted, even if the adversary is computationally unbounded.

Observe, however, that just allowing negligible error probability is not sufficient for circumventing the $t < n/3$ barrier. Indeed, it is straightforward to verify that fully secure MPC as considered in [26,34]—with fairness and guaranteed output delivery—against malicious/Byzantine adversaries implies Broadcast: Just consider the function which takes input only from a designated party, the sender, and outputs it to everyone.[4] In fact, using the above observation

---

[2] The original result by Borcherding just treats the case of assumptions sufficient for the existence of existentially unforgeable signatures, but it can easily be extended to arbitrary cryptographic hardness assumptions.

[3] As usual, the implicit assumption here is that no party of adversary can query the RO more times than its running time.

[4] There are some delicate matters to handle when capturing Broadcast as MPC, which will become relevant for our results, but for clarity we defer discussing them for when they are needed.

and Corollary 1 directly implies that $t < n/3$ is tight even assuming a computational adversary, secure point-to-point channels, an arbitrary public correlated randomness setup, e.g., a CRS, and/or a random oracle.

The public-key infrastructure (PKI) model. With the exception of perfect security[5], the above landscape changes if we assume a *private correlated randomness setup*, such as a PKI. Indeed, in this case Dolev and Strong [19] proved that assuming a PKI and intractability assumptions implying existentially unforgeable digital signatures (e.g., one way functions) Broadcast tolerating arbitrarily many (i.e., $t < n$) malicious corruptions is possible. We refer to this protocol as *Dolev-Strong Broadcast.* In fact, as shown later by Pfitzmann and Waidner [33], by assuming more complicated correlations—often referred to as a setup for *information-theoretic (pseudo-)signatures*—it is also possible to obtain an unconditionally (i.e., information-theoretically) secure protocol for Broadcast tolerating. Clearly, by plugging the above constructions in [34], we obtain a computationally or even i.t. secure MPC protocol tolerating any dishonest minority in the private correlated randomness setting. Recall that this task was impossible for honest majorities in the public correlated randomness setting.

The blockchain revolution. The introduction and systematic study of blockchains in the *permissionless* setting, such as the Bitcoin blockchain, demonstrated how Consensus and Broadcast can be reached even in settings where a majority of the participants might be adversarial (as long as the majority of the computing power remains honest) and even without a private correlated randomness setup. And although it was proven that such constructions work under the different assumption of honest-majority computing power, a confusion still remained driven mainly by the fact that the investigation of the type of consensus achieved by Bitcoin ("Nakamoto consensus") considered more involved models that closer capture its execution parameters (e.g., "partial synchrony" [20]), and that the Bitcoin backbone protocol [23,32] was shown to achieve *eventual* consensus, a property closer to the traditional state-machine replication problem from distributed computing [35][6]. In fact, similar approaches were also used for alternative blockchains that relied on assumptions about restricting other resource, such as for example a majority of honest stake ("proof of stake"—PoS) [6,25,30], a majority of honest space [3,6,15,18,30], etc., which were however also analyzed in more complex network settings; see also Remark 1.

The resource-restricting paradigm. We will use this general term to refer to all the above approaches. Thus, an intriguing question remained:

> *Does Corollary* 1 *still apply to the standard LSP model (of instant delivery authenticated channels and full synchrony) under the resource-restricting paradigm?*

---

[5] Since perfect security allows no error probability, a setup does not help.

[6] Although it was also shown in [23] how to achieve the standard version of Consensus, as defined above, but in a way radically different from the existing protocols.

In this work we first answer this question in the negative by abstracting the essence of the above resource-restricting paradigm as an access restriction on the underlying communication network. Intuitively, the assumption of restricting (the adversary's access to) the relative resource can be captured by disallowing any party—and in particular any adversarial party—to send unboundedly many more new messages than any other party. To avoid ambiguity and allow using the related assumption in higher level constructions, we choose to work on Canetti's Universal Composition framework [10]. In particular, we describe the assumption induced by restricting the resources available to the adversary by means of a functionality *wrapper*, which wraps a communication network and restricts the ability of parties (or the adversary) to send new messages through this network.

We then demonstrate how our wrapper, when applied to the standard instant-delivery synchronous network, makes it impossible for the adversary to launch the attack from [7]. In particular, the classical impossibilities (or even their extension stated in Corollary 1) in the same model as the one they were proven, and with the required properties from the target primitive, do not apply to protocols in this new restricted network. We note in passing that the idea of restricting the resources available to the adversary compared to those available to the parties in order to limit the adversary's attacking power was also previously explored in [8, 24].

In order to prove that our network restriction is an appropriate abstraction of the mechanisms implied by the resource-restricting paradigm, we focus on the case of proofs of work (PoW) and prove how to implement the wrapped LSP-style network from a public correlated randomness setup (in particular, any high min-entropy CRS) and an access-restricted random oracle. Concretely, along the lines of the composable analyses of Bitcoin [4], we capture the assumption of honest majority of hashing power by means of a wrapped RO, which allows each party (honest or corrupted) at most q queries per communication round (cf. [23]) for any given q (polynomial in the security parameter).[7] An important consideration of our transformation is the need for a *freshness* property on the assumed CRS. Specifically, our protocol for realizing the wrapped network assumes that the adversary gets access to the CRS at the same time as honest parties do (and crucially relies on this fact). Intuitively, the reason is that our protocol will rely on PoW-style hash puzzles in order to restrict the ability of the adversary to create many new valid messages. Clearly, if the adversary has access to the initial CRS—which will play the role of the genesis block—way before the honest parties do, then he can start potentially precomputing valid messages thus making the implementation of communication restriction infeasible.

We note that such freshness of the CRS might be considered a non-standard assumption and seems relevant only in combination with the resource-restricting paradigm. Nonetheless, in Sect. 6, we discuss how this freshness can be replaced using PoWs on challenges exchanged between parties, along the lines of [1]. The absence of freshness yields a somewhat relaxed wrapper which offers analogous

---

[7] The wrapper actually puts a restriction to adversarial parties as honest parties can be restricted by their protocol (cf. [4]).

restrictions as our original wrapper, but guarantees only limited transferability of the messages sent, and is not as strict towards the adversary as our original one (i.e., adversarial messages can be transferred more times than honest ones). Still, as we argue, this relaxed wrapper is sufficient for obtaining all the positive results in this work.

The above sheds light on the seemingly confusing landscape, but leaves open the question of how powerful the new assumption of the resource-restricting wrapper (and hence the resource-restricting paradigm in general) is. In particular, although the above demonstrates that the resource-restricting paradigm allows to circumvent the limitation of Corollary 1, it still leaves open the question:

Does the resource-restricting methodology allow for fully secure MPC in the public correlated randomness model, and if so, under what assumptions on the 'number of corrupted parties?

We investigate the question of whether we can obtain honest majority MPC in this setting, and answer it in the affirmative. (Recall that without the resource-restricting methodology and associated assumptions this is impossible since MPC implied Broadcast.) Note that a consensus impossibility due to Fitzi [22] proved that the $t < n/2$ bound is actually necessary for Consensus in the standard LSP communication model. And the lower bound holds even if we assume a broadcast primitive. In fact, by a simple inspection of the results one can observe that the underlying proof uses only honest strategies (for different selections of corruption sets) and therefore applies even under the resource-restricting paradigm— where, as above, this paradigm is captured by wrapping the network with our communication-restricting wrapper.

Towards the feasibility goal, we provide a protocol which allows us to establish a PKI assuming only our resource-restricted (wrapped) LSP network and one-way functions (or any other assumption which allows for existentially unforgeable signatures). More specifically, we show that our PKI establishment mechanism implements the key registration functionality $\mathcal{F}_{\text{REG}}$ from [11]. Our protocol is inspired by the protocol of Andrychowicz and Dziembowski [1]. Their protocol, however, achieved a non-standard notion of MPC in which inputs are associated to public-keys/pseudonyms. In particular, in the standard MPC setting, computing a function $f(x_1, \ldots, x_n)$ among parties $P_1, \ldots, P_n$ means having each P_i contribute input x_i and output $f(x_1, \ldots, x_n)$—this is reflected both in the original definitions of MPC [26,36] and in the UC SFE functionality $\mathcal{F}_{\text{SFE}}$ [10] and the corresponding standalone evaluation experiment from [9]. Instead, in the MPC evaluation from [1], every party P_i is represented by a pseudonym j_i, which is not necessarily equal to i and where the mapping between i and j_i is unknown to the honest participants.[8] Then the party contributing the ℓth input to the computation of f is P_i such that $j_i = \ell$. This evaluation paradigm was termed *pseudonymous MPC* in [29].

---

[8] In fact, $(j_1, \ldots, j_n)$ is a permutation of $(1, \ldots, n)$.

It is not hard to see, however, that the above evaluation paradigm makes the corresponding solution inapplicable to classical scenarios where MPC would be applied, where parties have distinguished roles. Examples include decentralized auctions—where the auctioneer should not bid—and asymmetric functionalities such as oblivious transfer. We note in passing that the above relaxation of traditional MPC guarantees seems inherent in the permissionless peer-to-peer setting setting of [1,29]. Instead, our protocol adapts the techniques from [1] in a white-box manner to leverage the authenticity of our underlying communication network—recall that our protocol is in the (wrapped) BGW communication setting—in order to ensure that the registered public keys are publicly linked to their respective owners. This allows us to evaluate the standard MPC functionality.

Getting from an implementation of $\mathcal{F}_{\mathrm{REG}}$ where the keys are linked to their owners to standard MPC is then fairly straightforward by using the modularity of the UC framework. As proved in [11], $\mathcal{F}_{\mathrm{REG}}$ can be used to realize the certified signature functionality (aka *certification functionality*) $\mathcal{F}_{\mathrm{CERT}}$ which, in turn, can be used to realize a Broadcast functionality against even adaptive adversaries [27]. By plugging this functionality into the honest-majority protocol (compiler) by Cramer *et al.* [17]—an adaptation of the protocol from [34] to tolerate adaptive corruptions—we obtain an MPC protocol which is adaptively secure.

Organization of the paper. In Sect. 2 we discuss our model. In Sect. 3 we introduce our wrapper-based abstraction of the resource-restricting paradigm and demonstrate how the impossibility from Corollary 1 fails when parties can use it. Section 4 presents our implementation of this wrapper from PoWs and a fresh CRS, and Sect. 5 discusses how to use it to obtain certified digital signatures and MPC. Finally in Sect. 6 we discuss how to remove the freshness assumption by leveraging PoWs.

2   Model

To allow for a modular treatment and ensure universal composition of our results, we will work in Canetti's UC model [9]. We assume some familiarity of the reader with UC but we will restrict the properties we use to those that are satisfied by any composable security framework. In fact, technically speaking, our underlying framework is the UC with global setups (GUC) [12], as we aim to accurately capture a global notion of time (see below). Nonetheless, the low level technicalities of the GUC framework do not affect our arguments and the reader can treat our proofs as standard UC proofs.

Parties, functionalities, and the adversary and environment are (instances of) interactive Turing machines (ITMs) running in probabilistic polynomial time (PPT). We prove our statements for a static active adversary; however, the static restriction is only for simplicity as our proofs can be directly extended to handle adaptive corruptions. In (G)UC, security is defined via the standard simulation paradigm: In a nutshell, a protocol π realizes a functionality $\mathcal{F}$ (in UC, this is described as emulation of the dummy/ideal $\mathcal{F}$-hybrid protocol ϕ) if for any adversary attacking π there exists a simulator attacking ϕ making the executions of the two protocols indistinguishable in the eyes of any external environment. Note that π might (and in our cases will, as discussed below) have access to its own hybrid functionalities.

Synchrony. We adopt the global clock version of the synchronous UC model by Katz *et al.* [28] as described in [4]. Concretely, we assume that parties have access to a global clock functionality which allows them to advance rounds at the same pace. For generality, we will allow the clock to have a dynamic party set, as in [4].

Global Functionality $\mathcal{G}_{\text{CLOCK}}$

The functionality manages the set $\mathcal{P}$ of registered identities, i.e, parties $P = (\text{pid}, \text{sid})$. It also manages the set F of registered functionalities (together with their session identifier). Initially, $\mathcal{P} = \emptyset$ and $F = \emptyset$. For each session sid the clock maintains a variable τ_{sid}. For each identity $P = (\text{pid}, \text{sid}) \in \mathcal{P}$ it manages variable d_P. For each pair $(\mathcal{F}, \text{sid}) \in F$ it manages variable $d_{(\mathcal{F}, \text{sid})}$ (all integer variables are initially set to 0).

Synchronization:
- Upon receiving (CLOCK-UPDATE, sid_C) from some party $P \in \mathcal{P}$ set $d_P := 1$; execute *Round-Update* and forward (CLOCK-UPDATE, sid_C, P) to $\mathcal{A}$.
- Upon receiving (CLOCK-UPDATE, sid_C) from some functionality $\mathcal{F} \in F$ in a session sid such that $(\mathcal{F}, \text{sid}) \in F$, set $d_{(\mathcal{F}, \text{sid})} = 1$, execute *Round-Update* and return (CLOCK-UPDATE, sid_C, $\mathcal{F}$) to $\mathcal{A}$.
- Upon receiving (CLOCK-READ, sid_C) from any participant (including the environment, the adversary, or any ideal—shared or local—functionality) return (CLOCK-READ, sid_C, τ_{sid}) to the requestor.

Procedure Round-Update: For each session sid do: If $d_{(\mathcal{F}, \text{sid})} = 1$ for all $\mathcal{F} \in F$ and $d_P = 1$ for all honest $P = (\cdot, \text{sid})$ in $\mathcal{P}$, then set $\tau_{\text{sid}} = \tau_{\text{sid}} + 1$ and reset $d_{\mathcal{F}} = 0$ and $d_P = 0$ for all parties $P = (\cdot, \text{sid}) \in \mathcal{P}$.

Communication network. We capture point-to-point authenticated communication, modeling the LSP channels in UC, by means of a multi-party multi-use version of the authenticated channel functionality with instant delivery along the lines of [4]. (The original network from [4] had bounded delay; hence here we need to set this bound to 1.) Note that in this network once an honest party P_i inserts a message to be sent to P_j, the message is buffered, and it is delivered after at most Δ attempts from the receiver (here $\Delta = 1$). Syntactically, we allow the simulator to query the network and learn if a buffered message was received by the respective receiver. This step—despite being redundant in most cases as the simulator should be able to defer this fact by observing the activations forwarded to him—is not only an intuitive addition, as it captures that the adversary is aware of delivery of message, but will also simplify the protocol description and simulation. For completeness, we include the authenticated network functionality below.

Note that the BGW-style secure point-to-point network functionality can be trivially derived by the authenticated one by replacing in the message $(\text{SENT}, \text{sid}, m, P_i, P_j, mid)$ which the adversary receives upon some m being inserted to the network, the value of m by $\bot$ (of by $|m|$ if this is implemented by standard encryption).

Functionality $\mathcal{F}_{\text{AUTH}}$

The functionality is parameterized by a set of possible senders and receivers, denoted by $\mathcal{P}$, a list M, and integer variables of the form D_z, where $z \in \{0,1\}^*$, that are dynamically created. For every party $P \in \mathcal{P}$ it maintains a fetch counter f_P. Initially, $M := \emptyset$ and $f_P := 0$, for every $P \in \mathcal{P}$.

— Upon receiving $(\text{SEND}, \text{sid}, m, P_j)$ from $P_i \in \mathcal{P}$, set $D_{mid} := 1$ and $M = M \| (m, P_i, P_j, mid)$, where mid is a unique message-ID, and send $(\text{SENT}, \text{sid}, m, P_i, P_j, mid)$ to $\mathcal{A}$.

— Upon receiving $(\text{FETCH}, \text{sid})$ from some honest party $P_j \in \mathcal{P}$, increment f_P by 1, set $M' = \emptyset$, and do the following:
  1. For all tuples $(m, P_i, P_j, mid) \in M$, set $D_{mid} := D_{mid} - 1$,
  2. for all tuples $(m, P_i, P_j, mid) \in M$, where $D_{mid} \leq 0$, delete (m, P_i, P_j, mid) from M, and add (m, P_i) to M'.
  3. Send $(\text{SENT}, \text{sid}, M')$ to P_j.

— Upon receiving $(\text{FETCH-REQUESTS}, \text{sid}, P)$ from $\mathcal{A}$, output $(\text{FETCH-REQUESTS}, \text{sid}, f_P)$.

The random oracle functionality. As is typical in the proof-of-work literature, we will abstract puzzle-friendly hash functions by means of a random oracle functionality.

Functionality $\mathcal{F}_{\text{RO}}$

The functionality is parameterized by a security parameter λ and a set of parties $\mathcal{P}$. It maintains a (dynamically updatable) map H that is initially empty.

— Upon receiving $(\text{EVAL}, \text{sid}, x)$ from some party $P \in \mathcal{P}$ (or from $\mathcal{A}$ on behalf of a corrupted P), do the following:
  1. If $H[x] = \bot$, sample a value y uniformly at random from $\{0,1\}^\lambda$, and set $H[x] := y$.
  2. Return $(\text{EVAL}, \text{sid}, x, H[x])$ to the requestor.

Furthermore, following [4], we will use the wrapper to capture the assumption that no party gets more than q queries to the RO per round. This wrapper in combination with the honest majority of parties captures the assumption that the adversary does not control a majority of the systems hashing power.

Wrapper Functionality $\mathcal{W}_{\text{RO}}^q(\mathcal{F})$

The wrapper functionality is parameterized by a set of parties $\mathcal{P}$, and an upper bound q which restricts the $\mathcal{F}$-evaluations of each corrupted party per round. (To keep track of rounds the functionality registers with the global clock $\mathcal{G}_{\text{CLOCK}}$.) The functionality manages the variable τ and the current set of corrupted miners $\mathcal{P}$. For each party $P \in \mathcal{P}$ it manages variables q_P. Initially, $\tau = 0$.

General:
- The wrapper stops the interaction with the adversary as soon as the adversary tries to exceed its budget of q queries per corrupted party.

Relaying inputs to the random oracle:
- Upon receiving (EVAL, sid, x) from $\mathcal{A}$ on behalf of a corrupted party $P \in \mathcal{P}'$, then first execute *Round Reset*. Then, set $q_P := q_P + 1$ and only if $q_P \leq q$ forward the request to $\mathcal{F}_{\text{RO}}$ and return to $\mathcal{A}$ whatever $\mathcal{F}_{\text{RO}}$ returns.
- Any other request from any participant or the adversary is simply relayed to the underlying functionality without any further action and the output is given to the destination specified by the hybrid functionality.

Standard UC Corruption Handling:
- Upon receiving (CORRUPT, sid, P) from the adversary, set $\mathcal{P}' := \mathcal{P}' \cup P$. If P has already issued $t > 0$ random oracle queries in this round, set $q_P := t$. Otherwise set $q_P := 0$.

Procedure Round-Reset:
Send (CLOCK-READ, sid_C) to $\mathcal{G}_{\text{CLOCK}}$ and receive (CLOCK-READ, sid_C, τ') from $\mathcal{G}_{\text{CLOCK}}$. If $|\tau' - \tau| > 0$ (i.e., a new round started), then set $q_P := 0$ for each participant $P \in \mathcal{P}$ and set $\tau := \tau'$.

Correlated randomness setup. Finally, we make use of the CRS functionality [13], which models a public correlated randomness setup.

Functionality $\mathcal{F}_{\text{CRS}}^{\mathcal{D}}$

When activated for the first time on input (RETRIEVE, sid), choose a value $d \leftarrow \mathcal{D}$, and send (RETRIEVE, d) back to the activating party. In each other activation return the value d to the activating party.

---

3   Inapplicability of Strong BA Impossibility

In this section we present our abstraction of the resource-restricting paradigm as a communication-restricting wrapper for the underlying communication network, and show that the strong BA impossibility (Corollary 1) does not apply to this wrapped network. In particular, as we discussed, in [7] it was argued that assuming $3t \geq n$, no private correlated randomness setup, the existence of signatures, and authenticated point-to-point channels, no protocol solves the broadcast problem. In this section, we show that if parties have access to a simple channel that is restricted in such a way that spam or sybil attacks are infeasible, the impossibility proof of [7] does not go through.

3.1   Modeling a Communication-Restricted Network

Our filtering wrapper restricts the per-round accesses of each party to the functionality, in a probabilistic manner. In more detail, for parameters p, q, each party has a quota of q SEND requests per round, each of them succeeding with probability p. Note that after a message has been sent through the filter, the sender, as well as the receiver, can re-send the same message for free. This feature captures the fact that if a message has passed the filtering mechanism once, it should be freely allowed to circulate in the network. We explicitly differentiate this action in our interface, by introducing the RESEND request; parties have to use RESEND to forward for free messages they have already received.

Wrapper Functionality $\mathcal{W}_{\text{FLT}}^{p,q}(\mathcal{F})$

The wrapper functionality is parameterized by $p \in [0, 1]$ and $q \in \mathbb{N}$, which restrict the probability of success and number of $\mathcal{F}$-evaluations of each party per round, respectively, and a set of parties $\mathcal{P}$. It registers with the global clock $\mathcal{G}_{\text{CLOCK}}$. It manages the round integer variable τ, the current set of corrupted parties $\tilde{\mathcal{P}}$, and a list $\mathcal{T}$. For each party $P \in \mathcal{P}$, it manages the integer variable t_P. Initially $\tau := 0$, $\mathcal{T} := \emptyset$, and $t_P := 0$, for each $P \in \mathcal{P}$.

Filtering:
- Upon receiving (SEND, sid, m, P_j) from party $P_i \in \mathcal{P}$, execute *Round-Reset*, and do the following:
    - Set $t_{P_i} := t_{P_i} + 1$. If $t_{P_i} \leq q$, with probability p, do:
        1. Add (m, P_i) to $\mathcal{T}$ and output (SUCCESS, sid) to P_i.
        2. On response (CONTINUE, sid, m) from P_i, forward (SEND, sid, m, P_j) to $\mathcal{F}$.
      In any other case, send (FAIL, sid) to P_i.
- Upon receiving (RESEND, sid, m, P_j) from honest party $P_i \in \mathcal{P} \setminus \tilde{\mathcal{P}}$, if $(m, P_i) \in \mathcal{T}$ then forward (SEND, sid, m, P_j) to $\mathcal{F}$.
- Upon receiving (RESEND, sid, m, P_J) from $\mathcal{A}$ on behalf of corrupted $P_i \in \tilde{\mathcal{P}}$, if $(m, P) \in \mathcal{T}$ for some $P \in \mathcal{P}$, then forward (SEND, sid, m, P_j) to $\mathcal{F}$.
- Upon $\mathcal{F}$ sending (SENT, sid, m, P_i) to P_j, add (m, P_j) to $\mathcal{T}$ and forward the message to P_j.

Standard UC Corruption Handling:

- Upon receiving (CORRUPT, sid, P) from the adversary, set $\tilde{\mathcal{P}} \leftarrow \tilde{\mathcal{P}} \cup \mathcal{P}$.

General:

- Any other request from (resp. towards) any participant or the adversary, is simply relayed to the underlying functionality (resp . any participant of the adversary) without any further action.

Procedure Round-Reset:
- Send (CLOCK-READ, sid_C) to $\mathcal{G}_{\text{CLOCK}}$ and receive (CLOCK-READ, sid_C, τ') from $\mathcal{G}_{\text{CLOCK}}$.
- If $|\tau' - \tau| > 0$, then set $t_P := 0$ for each $P \in \mathcal{P}$ and set $\tau := \tau'$.

3.2   The Impossibility Theorem, Revisited

Next, we show that if parties have access to $\mathcal{W}_{\text{FLT}}^{p,q}(\mathcal{F}_{\text{AUTH}})$, for some noticeable p and $q \geq 1$, the BA attack from the impossibility proof of [7] does not go through. The proof relies on the fact that the adversary can simulate the behavior of multiple honest parties. In a nutshell, we describe a protocol where parties send messages through $\mathcal{W}_{\text{FLT}}^{p,q}(\mathcal{F}_{\text{AUTH}})$, and due to the restricted number of SEND attempts the adversary has at his disposal, it is impossible for him to simulate multiple parties running this protocol.

Lemma 1. *Let $n = 3, t = 1$, p be a noticeable function, and $q \geq 1$. There exists a polynomial time protocol in the $(\mathcal{G}_{\text{CLOCK}}, \mathcal{F}_{\text{AUTH}}, \mathcal{W}_{\text{FLT}}^{p,q}(\mathcal{F}_{\text{AUTH}}), \mathcal{F}_{\text{SIG}})$-hybrid model that invalidates the $t \geq n/3$ BA attack from the impossibility theorem of [7].*

Proof. The impossibility proof considers the class of full information protocols, where if some party receives a message at some round r, it signs the message with its own signing key, and sends it to all other parties. We are going to show a subclass of protocols that use $\mathcal{W}_{\text{FLT}}^{p,q}(\mathcal{F}_{\text{AUTH}})$ and are not captured by the proof.

We first briefly recall the proof in [7] for the case $n = 3$ and $t = 1$. The proof is based on constructing three scenarios $\sigma_1, \sigma_2, \sigma_3$, where broadcast cannot possibly be achieved. Let the sender be P_1. We proceed to describe $\sigma_1, \sigma_2, \sigma_3$. In σ_1, P_1 has input 0 and P_2 is corrupted. In σ_2, P_1 has input 1 and P_3 is corrupted. In σ_3, P_1 is corrupted.

By Validity, it follows that in σ_1 P_3 should output 0, and in σ_2 P_2 should output 1, no matter the behavior of the adversary. Moreover, due to the Agreement (Consistency) property, the output of P_2 and P_3 in σ_3 must be the same. The proof then proceeds to describe a way of making the view of P_3 (resp. P_2) indistinguishable in scenarios σ_1 (resp. σ_2) and σ_3, and thus reaching a contradiction since they are going to decide on different values in σ_3.

The main idea is for P_2 in σ_1 to behave as if P_1 had input 1, by creating a set of fake keys and changing the signatures of P_1 to the ones with the fake keys and different input where possible. Since there is no PKI, P_3 cannot tell whether: (i) P_1 is corrupted and sends messages signed with different keys to P_2, or (ii) P_2 is corrupted. Symmetrically, P_3 in σ_2 simulates P_1 with input 0. Finally, P_1 in σ_3 simulates *both behaviors*, i.e., P_1 running the protocol honestly with input 1 in its communication with P_2, and P_1 with input 0 in its communication with P_3. This is exactly where the impossibility proof does not go through anymore.

For the moment, assume that we are in the setting where $p = 1 - \mathsf{negl}(\lambda)$ and $q = 1$. Let Π be a full information protocol, where in the first round the sender P_1 uses $\mathcal{W}_{\mathrm{FLT}}^{1-\mathsf{negl}(\lambda),1}(\mathcal{F}_{\mathrm{AUTH}})$ to transmit its message to the other two parties. Further, assume that this message is different for the cases where the sender input is 0 and 1, with probability α. It follows that P_1 has to send two *different* messages to parties P_2 and P_3 at the first round of σ_3, with probability α. However, this is not possible anymore, as the network functionality only allows for one new message to be send by P_1 at each round, with overwhelming probability. Hence, with probability α the impossibility proof cannot go through anymore.

For the case where p is noticeable and $q \geq 1$, we can design a similar protocol that cannot be captured by the proof. The protocol begins with a first "super round" of size $\frac{\lambda}{pq}$ regular rounds, where each party should successfully send its first message m at least $\frac{3\lambda}{4}$ times using $\mathcal{W}_{\mathrm{FLT}}^{p,q}(\mathcal{F}_{\mathrm{AUTH}})$ for it to be considered valid. Since the functionality allows sending the same message twice for free, the sequence of $\frac{3\lambda}{4}$ messages is encoded as follows: $(m, 1), \ldots, (m, \frac{3\lambda}{4})$.

Next, we analyze the probability that $\mathcal{A}$ can use the strategy described in the impossibility proof in [7]. Note that each party can query $\mathcal{W}_{\mathrm{FLT}}^{p,q}(\mathcal{F}_{\mathrm{AUTH}})$ up to λ/p times during the super round. We will show that: (i) honest parties will be able to send $\frac{3\lambda}{4}$ messages with overwhelming probability, and (ii) that the adversary in σ_3 will not be able to send the $2 \cdot \frac{3\lambda}{4}$ messages it has to. Let random variable X_i be 1 if the i-th query to $\mathcal{W}_{\mathrm{FLT}}^{p,q}(\mathcal{F}_{\mathrm{AUTH}})$ of some party P succeeds, and 0 otherwise. Also, let $X = \sum_{i=1}^{\lambda/p} X_i$. It holds that $\mathbb{E}[X] = p \cdot \lambda/p = \lambda$. By an application of the Chernoff bound, for $\delta = \frac{1}{4}$, it holds that

$$\Pr[X \leq (1 - \delta)\mathbb{E}[X]] = \Pr[X \leq \frac{3\lambda}{4}] \leq e^{-\Omega(\lambda)}.$$

Hence, with overwhelming probability each party will be able to send at least $\frac{3\lambda}{4}$ messages in the first $\frac{\lambda}{pq}$ rounds. On the other hand, we have that

$$\Pr[X \geq (1 + \delta)\mathbb{E}[X]] = \Pr[X \geq \frac{5\lambda}{4}] \leq e^{-\Omega(\lambda)}.$$

Hence, no party will be able to send more than $\frac{5\lambda}{4}$ messages in the first super round. This concludes the proof, since the adversary, in order to correctly follow the strategy described before, must send in total $\frac{6\lambda}{4}(> \frac{5\lambda}{4})$ messages in the first super round. Thus, with overwhelming probability it is going to fail to do so. Finally, note that the length of the super round is polynomial, since $1/p$ is bounded by some polynomial. Thus, the theorem follows.   □

The proof of Corollary 1 works along the same lines as the proof of [7]; since only public correlated randomness is assumed, nothing prevents the adversary from simulating an honest party. Finally, we note that the same techniques used above can also be used to refute an appropriate adaptation of Corollary 1, where parties have access to $\mathcal{W}_{\text{FLT}}^{p,q}(\mathcal{F}_{\text{AUTH}})$.

4   Implementing a Communication-Restricted Network

In this section we describe our implementation of $\mathcal{W}_{\text{FLT}}^{p,q}(\mathcal{F}_{\text{AUTH}})$ that is based on the resource-restricted RO functionality $\mathcal{W}_{\text{RO}}^{q}(\mathcal{F}_{\text{RO}})$ and a standard authenticated network. As discussed in the introduction, we also make use of an enhanced version of the $\mathcal{F}_{\text{CRS}}$ functionality, where it is guaranteed that the adversary learns the shared string after the honest parties. We capture this restriction in a straightforward way: A wrapper $\mathcal{W}_{\text{FRESH}}(\mathcal{F}_{\text{CRS}}^{\mathcal{D}})$ which does not allow the adversary to learn the CRS before the round honest parties are spawned. W.l.o.g., in the rest of the paper we are going to assume that all parties are spawned at round 1.

Our protocol makes uses of the proof-of-work construction of [2]. Every time a party wants to send a new message, it tries to find a hash of the message and some nonce, that is smaller than some target value D, and if successful it forwards this message through $\mathcal{F}_{\text{AUTH}}$ to the designated recipient. Moreover, if it has received such a message and nonce, it can perform a RESEND by forwarding this message through $\mathcal{F}_{\text{AUTH}}$. To be sure that the adversary does not precompute small hashes before the start of the protocol, and thus violates the SEND quota described in the wrapper, parties make use of the string provided by $\mathcal{W}_{\text{FRESH}}^{\mathcal{D}}(\mathcal{F}_{\text{CRS}})$, where $\mathcal{D}$ will be a distribution with sufficient high min-entropy. They use this string as a prefix to any hash they compute, thus effectively disallowing the adversary to use any of the small hashes it may have precomputed.

Protocol Wrapped-Channel$^{D,q}(P)$

Initialization:
- We assume that P is in the party set of $\mathcal{W}_{\text{RO}}^{q}(\mathcal{F}_{\text{RO}})$, $\mathcal{F}_{\text{AUTH}}$, and $\mathcal{W}_{\text{FRESH}}(\mathcal{F}_{\text{CRS}}^{\mathcal{D}})$, and is registered with $\mathcal{G}_{\text{CLOCK}}$. The protocol maintains a list of valid message/nonce/hash tuples $\mathcal{T}$, initially empty, and a counter t initially set to 0. When P is first activated, it gets the CRS from $\mathcal{W}_{\text{FRESH}}(\mathcal{F}_{\text{CRS}}^{\mathcal{D}})$, and uses it as a prefix of all messages it sends to $\mathcal{W}_{\text{RO}}^{q}(\mathcal{F}_{\text{RO}})$. For simplicity, we avoid explicitly including this term bellow.

Message Exchange:
- Upon receiving (SEND, sid, m, P'), execute *Round-Reset*, set $t := t + 1$, and if $t > q$ output (FAIL, sid) to P. Otherwise, do the following:
  1. Send (EVAL, sid, (m, r)) to $\mathcal{W}_{\text{RO}}^{q}(\mathcal{F}_{\text{RO}})$, where $r \leftarrow \{0, 1\}^{\lambda}$.
  2. On response (EVAL, sid, (m, r), v), if $(v > D)$, output (FAIL, sid) to P.
  3. Otherwise, if no entry of the form (m, r', v') exists in $\mathcal{T}$, store (m, r, v) in $\mathcal{T}$. Then, send (SUCCESS, sid) to P. On response (CONTINUE, sid), pick r', v' such that (m, r', v') is an entry in $\mathcal{T}$, and send (SEND, sid, (m, r', v'), P') to $\mathcal{F}_{\text{AUTH}}$.
- Upon receiving (RESEND, sid, m, P'), if r, v exist such that (m, r, v) is an entry in $\mathcal{T}$, send (SEND, sid, (m, r, v), P') to $\mathcal{F}_{\text{AUTH}}$. Otherwise, output (FAIL, sid) to P.

- Upon receiving (FETCH, sid), forward the message to $\mathcal{F}_{\text{AUTH}}$.
- Upon receiving (SENT, sid, $(m, r, v), P'$) from $\mathcal{F}_{\text{AUTH}}$, send (EVAL, sid, (m, r)) to $\mathcal{W}_{\text{RO}}^q(\mathcal{F}_{\text{RO}})$. On response (EVAL, sid, $(m, r), v'$), if $(v \leq D)$ and $(v' = v)$, remove any entry of the form (m, r', v') from $\mathcal{T}$ and instead add (m, r, v), and output (SENT, sid, m, P').
- Upon receiving (FETCH-REQUESTS, sid), forward the message to $\mathcal{F}_{\text{AUTH}}$, and output its response.

Clock Update:
Upon receiving (CLOCK-UPDATE, sid_C), send (CLOCK-UPDATE, sid_C) to $\mathcal{G}_{\text{CLOCK}}$.

Procedure Round-Reset:
Send (CLOCK-READ, sid_C) to $\mathcal{G}_{\text{CLOCK}}$ and receive (CLOCK-READ, sid_C, τ') from $\mathcal{G}_{\text{CLOCK}}$. If $|\tau' - \tau| > 0$, then set $t := 0$ and $\tau := \tau'$.

Next, we prove that $\texttt{Wrapped-Channel}^{D,q}$ UC realizes the $\mathcal{W}_{\text{FLT}}^{p,q}(\mathcal{F}_{\text{AUTH}})$ functionality, for appropriate values of p. The main idea of the proof is that the simulator is going to simulate new messages sent through the ideal functionality in the eyes of $\mathcal{A}$, by appropriately programming the random oracle. All other actions can be easily simulated.

Lemma 2. *Let* $p := \frac{D}{2^\kappa}$, *and* $\mathcal{D}$ *be a distribution with min-entropy at least* $\omega(\log(\lambda))$. *Protocol* $\texttt{Wrapped-Channel}^{D,q}$ *UC-realizes functionality* $\mathcal{W}_{\text{FLT}}^{p,q}(\mathcal{F}_{\text{AUTH}})$ *in the* $(\mathcal{G}_{\text{CLOCK}}, \mathcal{W}_{\text{RO}}^q(\mathcal{F}_{\text{RO}}), \mathcal{F}_{\text{AUTH}}, \mathcal{W}_{\text{FRESH}}(\mathcal{F}_{\text{CRS}}^D))$-*hybrid model.*

Proof. We consider the following simulator that is parameterized by some real-world adversary $\mathcal{A}$:

Simulator $\mathcal{S}_1$

The simulator manages a set of parties P. It sets up an empty network buffer M, an empty random oracle table H, and a table of received messages $\mathcal{T}$. The simulator also manages integer variables of the form D_z, where $z \in \{0, 1\}^*$, that are dynamically created, and f_P, for $P \in \mathcal{P}$. Initially, M is empty, and $f_P := 0$, for $P \in \mathcal{P}$.

Simulating the CRS:
- Sample a value from $\mathcal{D}$ once, and only output it after the round the protocol starts.

Simulating the Random Oracle:
- As in the protocol above, we always include the CRS value as a prefix of all messages to $\mathcal{W}_{\text{RO}}^q(\mathcal{F}_{\text{RO}})$. Again, for clarity we avoid explicitly including this term bellow.
- Upon receiving (EVAL, sid, u) for $\mathcal{W}_{\text{RO}}^q(\mathcal{F}_{\text{RO}})$ from $\mathcal{A}$ on behalf of corrupted $P \in \mathcal{P}$, do the following:
  1. If $H[u]$ is already defined, output (EVAL, sid, $u, H[u]$),

2. If u is of the form (m, r), send (SEND, sid, m, P) to $\mathcal{W}_{\text{FLT}}^{p,q}(\mathcal{F}_{\text{AUTH}})$ on behalf of P. On response (FAIL, sid), set $H[u]$ to a uniform value in $\{0,1\}^\lambda$ larger than D. On response (SUCCESS, sid), set $H[u]$ to a uniform value in $\{0,1\}^\lambda$ smaller or equal to D. Output (EVAL, sid, $v, H[u]$).

3. Otherwise, set $H[u]$ to a uniform value in $\{0,1\}^\lambda$ and output (EVAL, sid, $u, H[u]$).

Simulating the Network:

– Upon receiving (SEND, sid, u, P') for $\mathcal{F}_{\text{AUTH}}$ from $\mathcal{A}$ on behalf of corrupted $P \in \mathcal{P}$, do the following:

1. If u is of the form (m, r, v), $H[(m, r)]$ is defined, $H[(m, r)] = v$, and $v \leq D$, add (u, P) to $\mathcal{T}$, and send (RESEND, sid, m, P') to $\mathcal{W}_{\text{FLT}}^{p,q}(\mathcal{F}_{\text{AUTH}})$ on behalf of P. On response (SENT, sid, m, P, P', mid), set $D_{mid} = 1$ and $\boldsymbol{M} = \boldsymbol{M}\|(u, P, P', mid)$, and send (SENT, sid, u, P, P', mid) to $\mathcal{A}$.

2. Otherwise, send (SENT, sid, u, P, P', mid) to $\mathcal{A}$, where mid is a unique message-ID.

– Upon receiving (FETCH-REQUESTS, sid, P) for $\mathcal{F}_{\text{AUTH}}$ from $\mathcal{A}$, execute *Network-Update* and output (FETCH-REQUESTS, sid, P, f_P).

Interaction with $\mathcal{W}_{\text{FLT}}^{p,q}(\mathcal{F}_{\text{AUTH}})$:

– Upon receiving (SENT, sid, m, P, P', mid) from $\mathcal{W}_{\text{FLT}}^{p,q}(\mathcal{F}_{\text{AUTH}})$, execute *Network-Update*, and do the following :

1. If $(\nexists(r', v') : ((m, r', v'), P) \in \mathcal{T})$, pick an r uniformly at random from $\{0,1\}^\lambda$ and set $H[(m, r)] := v$, where v is a uniform value in $\{0,1\}^\lambda$ smaller or equal to D. Then, add $((m, r, v), P)$ to $\mathcal{T}$.

2. Otherwise, pick r, v such that $((m, r, v), P)$ is an entry in $\mathcal{T}$.

Add $((m, r, v), P, P', mid)$ to $\boldsymbol{M}$, set $D_{mid} = 1$, and output (SENT, sid, $(m, r, v), P, P', mid$) to $\mathcal{A}$.

Procedure Network-Update: For each $P \in \mathcal{P}$, send (FETCH-REQUESTS, sid, P) to $\mathcal{W}_{\text{FLT}}^{p,q}(\mathcal{F}_{\text{AUTH}})$. On response (FETCH-REQUESTS, sid, P, f'_P), if $f'_P > f_P$, set $f_P := f'_P$ and do the following

1. For all tuples $((m, r, v), P', P, mid) \in \boldsymbol{M}$, set $D_{mid} := D_{mid} - 1$.

2. For all tuples $((m, r, v), P', P, mid) \in \boldsymbol{M}$, where $D_{mid} \leq 0$, delete $((m, r, v), P', P, mid)$ from $\boldsymbol{M}$, delete any entry of the form $((m, r', v'), P_j)$ from $\mathcal{T}$, and add $((m, r, v), P_j)$ to $\mathcal{T}$.

We will argue that for every PPT adversary $\mathcal{A}$ in the real world, no PPT environment $\mathcal{Z}$ can distinguish between the real execution against $\mathcal{A}$ and the ideal execution against $\mathcal{S}_1$.

First, let E_1 denote the event where honest parties in the real world, and on input SEND, repeat a query to the random oracle. Each time an honest party issues a new RO query, a random string of size λ bits is sampled. The probability that the same string is sampled twice in a polynomial execution is negligible in λ. Moreover, E_1 implies this event. Hence, the probability of E_1 happening in a polynomially bounded execution is at most $\text{negl}(\lambda)$. Note, that if E_1 does not occur, the distribution of SEND commands invoked by honest parties that succeed is identical in the real and the ideal world.

Next, we turn our attention to adversarial attempts to send a new message. Let E_2 be the event where $\mathcal{A}$ sends a message of the form (m, r, v) to $\mathcal{F}_{\text{AUTH}}$, such that it hasn't queried (m, r) on the random oracle and $H[(m, r)] = v$. The probability of this event happening, amounts to trying to guess a random value sampled uniformly over an exponential size domain, and is $\mathsf{negl}(\lambda)$. Moreover, if E_2 does not occur, the adversary can only compute new "valid" messages by querying the RO. Define now E_3 to be the event where the adversary makes a query to the RO containing the CRS value, before round 1. By the fact that the CRS value is sampled by a high min-entropy distribution, and that $\mathcal{A}$ is PPT, it is implied that $\Pr[E_3] \leq \mathsf{negl}(\lambda)$. Hence, if E_2 and E_3 do not occur, the distribution of adversarially created messages is identical in both worlds.

Now if E_1, E_2, E_3 do no occur, the view of the adversary and the environment in both worlds is identical, as all requests are perfectly simulated. By an application of the union bound, it is easy to see that $\neg(E_1 \vee E_2 \vee E_3)$ occurs with only negligible probability. Hence, the real and the ideal execution are statistically indistinguishable in the eyes of $\mathcal{Z}$, and the theorem follows.   □

Regarding the round and communication complexity of our protocol, we note the following: It takes on expectation $1/p$ SEND requests to send a message, i.e., $1/pq$ rounds, and the communication cost is only one message. Regarding implementing $\mathcal{W}_{\text{FLT}}^{p,q}(\mathcal{F}_{\text{AUTH}})$ using virtual resources, we point to Remark 1.

Corollary 2. *Let $n = 3, t = 1$, p be a noticeable function, $q \geq 1$, and any distribution $\mathcal{D}$ with min-entropy at least $\omega(\log(\lambda))$. Then, there exist a polynomial time protocol in the $(\mathcal{G}_{\text{CLOCK}}, \mathcal{W}_{\text{RO}}^q(\mathcal{F}_{\text{RO}}), \mathcal{F}_{\text{AUTH}}, \mathcal{W}_{\text{FRESH}}(\mathcal{F}_{\text{CRS}}^{\mathcal{D}}), \mathcal{F}_{\text{SIG}})$-hybrid model, that invalidates the proof of the impossibility theorem of [7].*

Remark 1. The resource-restricted crypto paradigm can be also applied to virtual resources. For PoS, the implicit PKI associated with PoS blockchains seems sufficient for a simple implementation of our resource-restricted wrapper using a verifiable random function (VRF). However, this PoS-implicit PKI typically assigns keys to coins instead of parties. Thus, a transformation, e.g. through our wrapper (see Sect. 5), would be needed that shifts from the honest majority assumption on coins to parties. This validates the generality of our abstraction; however, with PoS in the permissioned setting, there might be more direct ways of getting standard MPC by leveraging the implicit coin-PKI.

5   Implementing a Registration Functionality

In this section, we show how to implement a key registration functionality (cf. [11]) in the resource-restricted setting, and in the presence of an honest majority of parties.

5.1   The Registration Functionality

The registration functionality allows any party to submit a key, which all other parties can later retrieve. Our specific formulation $\mathcal{F}_{\text{REG}}^r$, is parameterized by an integer r that specifies the round after which key retrieval becomes available.[9] Note, that $\mathcal{F}_{\text{REG}}$ does not guarantee that the keys submitted belong to the corresponding parties, i.e., a corrupted party can submit a key it saw another party submit.

Following the paradigm of [4] to deal with synchrony, $\mathcal{F}_{\text{REG}}$ also has a MAINTAIN command, which is parameterized by an implementation dependent function predict-time. We use this mechanism, to capture the behavior of the real world protocol with respect to $\mathcal{G}_{\text{CLOCK}}$, and appropriately delay $\mathcal{F}_{\text{REG}}$ from sending its clock update until all honest parties get enough activations. In more detail, predict-time takes as input a timed honest input sequence of tuples $\boldsymbol{I}_H^T = (\ldots, (x_i, id_i, \tau_i), \ldots)$, where x_i is the i-th input provided to $\mathcal{F}_{\text{REG}}$ by honest party id_i at round τ_i. We say that a protocol Π has a *predictable synchronization pattern*, if there exists a function predict-time such that for any possible execution of Π, with timed honest input sequence $\boldsymbol{I}_H^T$, predict-time$(\boldsymbol{I}_H^T) = \tau + 1$ if all honest parties have received enough activations to proceed to round $\tau + 1$.

Functionality $\mathcal{F}_{\text{REG}}^r$

The functionality is parameterized by a set of parties $\mathcal{P}$, and an integer r. It maintains integer variables τ, d_u, and a owner/key set $\mathcal{T}$. Initially, $\mathcal{T}$ is empty and τ is equal to 0.

Upon receiving any input I from any party or the adversary, send (CLOCK-READ, sid_C) to $\mathcal{G}_{\text{CLOCK}}$. On response (CLOCK-READ, sid_C, t'), if $|\tau' - \tau| > 0$, set $\tau := \tau'$, $d_u := 0$. Then, if I was received from an honest party $P \in \mathcal{P} \setminus \tilde{\mathcal{P}}$, set $\boldsymbol{\mathcal{I}}_H^T := \boldsymbol{\mathcal{I}}_H^T \| (I, P_i, \tau)$. Depending on the input I and the ID of the sender, execute the respective code:

- On input $I = (\text{SUBMIT}, \text{sid}, v)$ from honest party P, if there is no v' such that $(P, v') \in \mathcal{T}$, add (P, v) to $\mathcal{T}$ and send (SUBMIT, sid, v) to $\mathcal{A}$.
- On input $I = (\text{SUBMIT}, \text{sid}, v)$ from corrupted party P, if $\tau \leq r$ and there is a v' such that $(P, v') \in \mathcal{T}$, delete it and add (P, v) instead. Then, send (SUBMIT, sid, v) to $\mathcal{A}$.
- On input $I = (\text{RETRIEVE}, \text{sid})$ from party P, if $\tau > r$, output (RETRIEVE, sid, $\mathcal{T}$) to P.
- Upon receiving (MAINTAIN, sid) from honest party P, if predict-time$(\boldsymbol{I}_H^T) > \tau$, and $d_u = 0$, set $d_u := 1$ and send (CLOCK-UPDATE, sid_C) to $\mathcal{G}_{\text{CLOCK}}$. Otherwise, send (I, ID) to $\mathcal{A}$.

5.2   The Identity-Assignment Protocol

To implement the above functionality we follow an adaptation of the protocol from [1], with the difference that instead of relating keys to pseudonyms, parties are able to create a PKI relating keys to identities. First, we deal with a technical issue.

---

[9] We sometimes omit r when it is clear from the context.

Our protocol contains commands that perform a sequence of operations. It is possible that during the execution of this operation, the party will lose the activation. Following the formulation of [4], we perform some of the commands in an interruptible manner. That is, a command I is I-*interruptible* executed, if in case activation is lost, an anchor is stored so that in the next invocation of this command it continues from the place it stopped in the previous activation. For more details on how implement this mechanism, we refer to [4].

Next, we give an informal description of the protocol, which makes use of $\mathcal{W}_{\text{FLT}}(\mathcal{F}_{\text{AUTH}})$, $\mathcal{F}_{\text{AUTH}}$, $\mathcal{G}_{\text{CLOCK}}$, and the signature functionality $\mathcal{F}_{\text{SIG}}$ of [11], adapted for many signers and being responsive, i.e., the one who is issuing a command is not losing its activation, as for example is done in the context of the key evolving signature functionality $\mathcal{F}_{\text{KES}}$ of [3].

The protocol is structured in 2 different phases. In the first phase, lasting up to round $r + n + 1$, parties use $\mathcal{W}_{\text{FLT}}(\mathcal{F}_{\text{AUTH}})$ to partially agree on a "graded" PKI. In more detail, for the first r rounds (procedure *PoWGeneration*) they attempt to send through $\mathcal{W}_{\text{FLT}}(\mathcal{F}_{\text{AUTH}})$ messages containing a verification key pk and an increasing counter c. A key is going to be taken in account, only if a sufficient number of messages related to this key and with different counter values are sent. This way keys are linked to resource accesses. And since resource accesses are restricted, so is going to be the number of generated keys. Unlike [1], to establish that keys are linked to identities, at round r parties sign the submitted key $\hat{pk}$ and their identity with their verification key pk, and multicast it to all other parties.

For the remaining $n+1$ rounds (procedure *KeyAgreement*), parties depending on when they received the messages related to some key, assign it a grade from 0 for the earliest, to n for the latest. To ensure that these grades differ by at most one for the same key, they immediately send the relevant messages they received to all other parties. This allows them to establish a form of a graded PKI, denoted by $\mathcal{K}$ in the protocol, where parties are proportionally represented, and which is going to be later used for broadcast. Finally, key/identity pairs received that have been signed with a key in $\mathcal{K}$ of grade 0 are added to a separate set $\mathcal{M}$. This set is going to be used in the second phase, which we describe next, to correctly relate keys to identities.

Starting at round $r + n + 2$, parties use an adaptation of the "Dolev-Strong" protocol to reliably broadcast $\mathcal{M}$ (procedure *Broadcast*). The way the protocol works, is by accepting messages as correctly broadcast only if a progressively bigger number of keys of sufficient grade in $\mathcal{K}$ have signed it. At the last round of the protocol, round $r + 2n + 2$, it is ensured that if an honest party accepts a message, then so do all other honest parties. Finally, by using a simple majority rule on the key/identity pairs contained in the broadcast sets $\mathcal{M}$, parties are able to agree on a key/identity set, denoted by $\mathcal{N}$ in the protocol, where each party is related to exactly one key and honest parties are correctly represented. $\mathcal{N}$ is output whenever a RETRIEVE command is issued. Next, we give a formal description of protocol **Graded-Agreement**.

Protocol Graded-Agreement(P)

Initialization:
- We assume that P is registered to $\mathcal{G}_{\text{CLOCK}}$ and is in the party sets of $\mathcal{W}_{\text{FLT}}^{q}(\mathcal{F}_{\text{RO}})$, $\mathcal{F}_{\text{AUTH}}$ and $\mathcal{F}_{\text{SIG}}$. The protocol maintains a list $\mathcal{K}$ of key/grade pairs, a list $\mathcal{M}$ of key/owner tuples, a list $\mathcal{N}$ of key/owner pairs, and a list $\mathcal{T}$ of message/key pairs, all initially empty, keys $pk, \hat{pk}$, initially set to $\bot$, and integer variables $\tau := 0, r := \frac{4n^2\lambda}{\min(1,pq)}, c := 1$.

Upon receiving any input I from any party or the adversary, send (CLOCK-READ, sid_C) to $\mathcal{G}_{\text{CLOCK}}$. On response (CLOCK-READ, sid_C, t'), if $|\tau' - \tau| > 0$, set $\tau := \tau'$ and $d_r, d_u := 0$, and do the following:
- On input $I = (\text{MAINTAIN}, \text{sid})$, if $d_r = 0$ execute in a (MAINTAIN, sid)-interruptible manner the following:
  1. If $1 \leq \tau \leq r$, execute *PowGeneration*.
  2. Else if $r < \tau \leq r + n + 1$, execute *KeyAgreement*.
  3. Else, if $r + n + 1 < \tau \leq r + 2n + 2$, execute *Broadcast*.
  4. Finally, if $d_u = 1$, send (CLOCK-UPDATE, sid_C) to $\mathcal{G}_{\text{CLOCK}}$. Set $d_r := 1$.
- On input $I = (\text{SUBMIT}, \text{sid}, v)$, if $\hat{pk} = \bot$, set $\hat{pk} := v$.
- On input $I = (\text{RETRIEVE}, \text{sid})$, if $\tau > r + 2n$, output $\mathcal{N}$.
- On input $I = (\text{CLOCK-UPDATE}, \text{sid}_C)$, if $d_r = 1$ and $d_u = 0$, send (CLOCK-UPDATE, sid_C) to $\mathcal{G}_{\text{CLOCK}}$. Set $d_u := 1$.

Procedure PoWGeneration:
If $pk = \bot$, then send (KEYGEN, sid) to $\mathcal{F}_{\text{SIG}}$, and on response (VERIFICATION KEY, sid, v), set $pk := v$. If $\hat{pk} = \bot$, give the activation to $\mathcal{Z}$, and in the next activation repeat this step. Otherwise, do the following:
1. Repeat q times: Send (SEND, sid, $(pk, c), P$) to $\mathcal{W}_{\text{FLT}}^{p,q}(\mathcal{F}_{\text{AUTH}})$. On response (SUCCESS, sid), increase c by 1, and for each $P' \in \mathcal{P}$ send (RESEND, sid, $(pk, c-1), P'$) through $\mathcal{W}_{\text{FLT}}^{p,q}(\mathcal{F}_{\text{AUTH}})$.
2. If $\tau = r$, send (SIGN, sid, $pk, (\hat{pk}, P)$) to $\mathcal{F}_{\text{SIG}}$. On response, (SIGNED, sid, $pk, (\hat{pk}, P'), \sigma$), for each $P' \in \mathcal{P}$ send (SEND, sid, $(pk, \hat{pk}, \sigma), P'$) to $\mathcal{F}_{\text{AUTH}}$.

Procedure KeyAgreement:
1. Send (FETCH, sid) to $\mathcal{W}_{\text{FLT}}^{p,q}(\mathcal{F}_{\text{AUTH}})$.
2. On response, (SENT, sid, M) from $\mathcal{W}_{\text{FLT}}^{p,q}(\mathcal{F}_{\text{AUTH}})$, for every subset of messages in M of the form $M' = \{(\text{SENT}, \text{sid}, (pk', i), P'_i)\}_{i \in [\lceil (1-\delta)pqr \rceil]}$, for δ equal to $1/4t$, if no entry of the form $(pk', \cdot)$ exists in $\mathcal{K}$, add $(pk', \tau - (r+1))$ to $\mathcal{K}$ and forward the messages in M' to all other parties through $\mathcal{W}_{\text{FLT}}^{p,q}(\mathcal{F}_{\text{AUTH}})$.
3. If $\tau = r + 1$, send (FETCH, sid) to $\mathcal{F}_{\text{AUTH}}$. On response (SENT, sid, M') from $\mathcal{F}_{\text{AUTH}}$, for every message in M of the form (SENT, sid, $(pk', \hat{pk}', \sigma), P'$), if there exists a entry of the form $(pk', \cdot)$ in $\mathcal{K}$, send (VERIFY, sid, $pk', (\hat{pk}', P'), \sigma$) to $\mathcal{F}_{\text{SIG}}$. On response (VERIFIED, sid, $pk', (\hat{pk}', P'), \sigma, f$), if $f = 1$, add $(\hat{pk}', P')$ to $\mathcal{M}$.

Procedure Broadcast:

1. If $\tau = r + n + 2$, send (SIGN, sid, pk, $(\mathcal{M}, pk)$) to $\mathcal{F}_{\text{SIG}}$. On response, (SIGNED, sid, pk, $(\mathcal{M}, pk)$, σ), send (SEND, sid, $((\mathcal{M}, pk), (pk, \sigma))$, P') to every party $P' \in \mathcal{P}$ through $\mathcal{F}_{\text{AUTH}}$.
2. If $r + n + 2 < \tau \leq r + 2n + 2$, send (FETCH, sid) to $\mathcal{F}_{\text{AUTH}}$. On response, (SENT, sid, M) from $\mathcal{F}_{\text{AUTH}}$, do the following:
   (a) For every message in M of the form
       (SENT, sid, $((m, pk_1), (pk_1, \sigma_1), \ldots, (pk_k, \sigma_k))$, P'), for $k = \tau - (r + n + 2)$,
       send (VERIFY, sid, pk_i, (m, pk_1), σ_i) to $\mathcal{F}_{\text{SIG}}$, for $i \in [k]$. If for all responses of
       the form (VERIFIED, sid, pk_i, (m, pk_1), σ_i, f_i), for $i \in [k]$, it holds that $f_i = 1$,
       $pk_1, \ldots, pk_k$ are all different, and $(pk_i, g_i) \in \mathcal{K}$ for $g_i \leq k$, add (m, pk_1) to T.
   (b) For every new entry (m, pk_1) in T, send (SIGN, sid, pk, (m, pk_1)) to $\mathcal{F}_{\text{SIG}}$. On
       response, (SIGNED, sid, pk, (m, pk_1), σ), add (pk, σ) to the relevant message
       received, and forward it to all other parties through $\mathcal{F}_{\text{AUTH}}$.
3. If $\tau = r + 2n + 2$, do the following:
   (a) For every pk_i, where $\exists m \neq m' : (m, pk_i), (m', pk_i) \in T$, delete all entries of
       the form $(\cdot, pk_i)$ from T.
   (b) For every $P' \in \mathcal{P}$, if there exists a unique key $\hat{pk}'$, where at least $n/2$ entries
       of T contain an entry of the form $(\hat{pk}', P')$ and do not contain any other
       entry of the form $(\cdot, P')$, add $(\hat{pk}', P')$ to $\mathcal{N}$.

We are going to show that protocol **Graded-Agreement** implements functionality $\mathcal{F}_{\text{REG}}$. First, note that there exists a function **predict-time** for our protocol that successfully predicts when honest parties are done for the round; honest parties lose their activation in a predictable manner when they get MAINTAIN as input. Moreover, a simulator can easily simulate the real world execution in the eyes of $\mathcal{Z}$, since it has all the information it needs to simulate honest parties' behavior and functionalities $\mathcal{W}_{\text{FLT}}(\mathcal{F}_{\text{AUTH}})$, $\mathcal{F}_{\text{AUTH}}$, and $\mathcal{F}_{\text{SIG}}$. Finally, due to the properties of the protocol, also proved in [1], all parties are going to agree on the same key/identity set $\mathcal{N}$, and thus provide the same responses on a RETRIEVE command from $\mathcal{Z}$. We proceed to state our theorem.

Theorem 1. *Let $n > 2t$, p be a noticeable function, $q \in \mathbb{N}^+$. The protocol* **Graded-Agreement** *UC-realizes functionality $\mathcal{F}_{\text{REG}}^{\frac{4n^2\lambda}{\min(1, pq)} + 2n + 3}$ in the $(\mathcal{G}_{\text{CLOCK}}, \mathcal{F}_{\text{AUTH}}, \mathcal{W}_{\text{FLT}}^{p,q}(\mathcal{F}_{\text{AUTH}}), \mathcal{F}_{\text{SIG}})$-hybrid model.*

Proof. Let $r = \frac{4n^2\lambda}{\min(1, pq)}$ and w.l.o.g., let $p \cdot q \leq 1$. We start by making some observations about the protocol.

Claim. The set $\mathcal{K}$ of each honest party, at the end of round $r + 1$, will contain the keys of all other honest parties, with overwhelming probability in λ.

Proof. We first show that the claim holds for a single honest party. Let random variable X_i be equal to 1, if the i-th invocation of SEND to $\mathcal{W}_{\text{FLT}}^{p,q}(\mathcal{F}_{\text{AUTH}})$ by some honest party P is successful, and 0 otherwise. It holds that $\Pr[X_i = 1] = p$, and that $X_1, \ldots, X_{r \cdot q}$ is a set of independent random variables; each party invokes

SEND exactly $r \cdot q$ times up to round r. Let $X = \sum_{i=1}^{rq} X_i$. By an application of the Chernoff bound, it holds that:

$$\Pr[X \leq (1 - \frac{1}{4t})pqr] = \Pr[X \leq (1 - \frac{1}{4t})\mathbb{E}[X]] \leq e^{-\Omega(\lambda)}$$

Since X is an integer, with overwhelming probability each honest party will send at least $\lceil(1 - \frac{1}{4t})pqr\rceil$ messages to each other party. Hence, its key will be included in $\mathcal{K}$. By an application of the union bound the claim follows.   ⊣

In addition to the previous claim, we also note two things: (i) The grade of each such key will be 0, and (ii) due to the correctness of the signature scheme, all honest parties will add the associated key $\hat{pk}$ and the correct owner of key pk in $\mathcal{M}$. These two facts will be useful later, when we will argue that all honest keys make it to the final list of keys $\mathcal{N}$, along with their correct owner.

Next, we show that the total number of keys generated will be at most n.

Claim. The set $\mathcal{K}$ of each honest party contains at most n elements, with overwhelming probability.

Proof. As before let $Z = \sum_{i=1}^{qt(r+n)} Z_i$, denote the successful attempts of the adversary to send a message through $\mathcal{W}_{\text{FLT}}(\mathcal{F}_{\text{AUTH}})$. Note that, starting from round 1, she has $r + n$ rounds in her disposal to send messages. After some computations we can show that:

$$(1 + \frac{1}{4t})\mathbb{E}[Z] = (1 + \frac{1}{4t})pqt(r+n) \leq (1 - \frac{1}{4t})pqr(t+1)$$

By the Chernoff bound, it holds that:

$$\Pr[Z \geq (1 - \frac{1}{4t})pqr(t+1)] \leq \Pr[Z \geq (1 + \frac{1}{4t})\mathbb{E}[Z]] \leq e^{-\Omega(\lambda)}$$

Note now, that $\lceil(1 - \frac{1}{4t})pqr\rceil$ different messages are required for a new key to be added to $\mathcal{K}$. It follows, that the adversary will add at most t keys of its choice to $\mathcal{K}$. Moreover, by the design of the protocol, honest parties will add at most $n - t$ keys to $\mathcal{K}$. Thus, the set $\mathcal{K}$ of any honest party will contain at most n keys with overwhelming probability.   ⊣

Next, note that if an honest party adds a key to $\mathcal{K}$ with grade $g < n$, due to the fact that the relevant messages for this key are multicast to all other parties in the network together with an additional valid signature, all honest parties will add the same key in $\mathcal{K}$ with grade at most $g + 1$.

Using all facts proved above, we can now proceed and show that during the Broadcast phase of the protocol, all honest parties will reliably broadcast set $\mathcal{M}$. Moreover, the adversary will not be able to confuse them about her broadcast input, if any. We start by arguing about the values broadcast by honest parties.

Claim. At the end of round $r + 2n + 2$, the set $\mathcal{N}$ of each honest party will contain the keys of all honest parties, along with their correct identity, with overwhelming probability.

Proof. Let P be some honest party, $(pk, \hat{pk})$ be her public keys, $\mathcal{K}', \mathcal{M}'$ be her key sets, and $m = (\mathcal{M}', pk)$. By our previous claim, all honest parties will have added $(pk, 0)$ to their key set $\mathcal{K}$. Moreover, they will all receive the message $(\hat{pk}, P)$ signed w.r.t. pk at round $r + 1$ by party P, and thus include $(\hat{pk}, P)$ in $\mathcal{M}$. Note, that no honest party will include another entry related to P, as P will not send any other such message. Moreover, all parties will receive $(m, (pk, \sigma))$, where σ is a valid signature for m. Hence, they will all add m to $\mathcal{T}$. Again, due to unforgeability, they will not add any other entry related to pk in $\mathcal{T}$. Hence, since $\mathcal{T}$ has at most n elements (one for each key) and $2n > t$, $(\hat{pk}, P)$ will be the only entry that appears exactly once with respect to P in at least $n/2$ sets of $\mathcal{T}$. Thus, all honest parties will add (pk, P) in $\mathcal{N}$, and the claim follows. $\dashv$

Next, we argue that the key sets $\mathcal{N}$ of all honest parties will be the same.

Claim. At the end of round $r + 2n + 2$, all honest parties will have the same set $\mathcal{N}$, with at most one entry per party, with overwhelming probability.

Proof. First, we argue that all honest parties have same set $\mathcal{T}$ at the end of round $r + 2n + 2$. For the sake of contradiction assume that the opposite was true. This would imply that some honest party P has added $(m, pk) \in \mathcal{T}$ at some round r', while some other party P' has not. We take two cases. If $r' < r + 2n + 2$, then P will forward the message relevant to entry (m, pk) together with its own signature to all other parties. Since its key has grade 0, all other honest parties will add (m, pk) to $\mathcal{T}$ in the next round. On the other hand, if $r' = r + 2n + 2$, it holds that (m, pk) is signed by n keys in the set $\mathcal{K}$ of P, and by our previous claims at least one of these keys was of an honest party. Thus, this party must have accepted this message earlier, and by our previous argument all other honest parties will also receive and add this message to $\mathcal{T}$. This is a contradiction. Hence, honest parties agree on their entries in $\mathcal{T}$.

Now, since all parties agree on $\mathcal{T}$, and $\mathcal{N}$ is a deterministic function of $\mathcal{T}$, it is implied that they will also agree on $\mathcal{N}$. Moreover, by construction each party P is associated with at most one key in $\mathcal{N}$. The claim follows. $\dashv$

Our last two claims imply that all parties agree on $\mathcal{N}$, all honest parties will be represented, and at most one key will be assigned to each identity.

Having established these properties of the protocol, we next give a sketch of the simulator, which we denote by $\mathcal{S}_2$. The first thing the simulator must deal with is clock updates. In the ideal world, clock updates sent by $\mathcal{Z}$ to honest parties, are directly forwarded to $\mathcal{G}_{\text{CLOCK}}$, which in turn notifies $\mathcal{S}_2$. This is not the case in the real world. Parties send updates to $\mathcal{G}_{\text{CLOCK}}$ only after a sufficient number of MAINTAIN and CLOCK-UPDATE inputs have been provided by $\mathcal{Z}$. The way we simulate this behavior, is by having $\mathcal{S}_2$ deduce exactly when honest parties will send their updates in the real world, by keeping track of when $\mathcal{F}_{\text{REG}}$ will send its clock update in the ideal world, as well as the activations it gets after a MAINTAIN command has been issued to $\mathcal{F}_{\text{REG}}$ or a CLOCK-UPDATE command has been issued to $\mathcal{G}_{\text{CLOCK}}$. Note, that a new round starts only after either of the two commands has been issued, and thus $\mathcal{S}_2$ has been activated.

Since $\mathcal{S}_2$ can tell when parties are done for each round, it can also simulate the interaction of $\mathcal{A}$ with $\mathcal{W}_{\text{FLT}}(\mathcal{F}_{\text{AUTH}})$, $\mathcal{F}_{\text{AUTH}}$ and $\mathcal{F}_{\text{SIG}}$. It does that by simulating the behavior of honest parties. All information needed to do this are public, or in the case of the honest parties' signatures can be faked by the simulator itself. Note, that care has been taken so that $\mathcal{S}_2$ never throughout the protocol has to sign anything with the keys submitted to $\mathcal{F}_{\text{REG}}$ for honest parties; it only signs with the keys generated by the parties themselves. This is the reason that each party uses two different keys, pk and $\hat{pk}$.

Finally, at round $r + 2n + 2$ the simulator submits to $\mathcal{F}_{\text{REG}}$ the keys that corrupted parties choose based on key set $\mathcal{N}$; with overwhelming probability this set is the same for all honest parties. Thus, the response of $\mathcal{F}_{\text{REG}}$ to any RETRIEVE query after this round is $\mathcal{N}$. It follows that the view of $\mathcal{Z}$ in the two executions is going to be indistinguishable, and the theorem follows.   □

As discussed in the introduction, getting from an implementation of $\mathcal{F}_{\text{REG}}$ where the keys are linked to their owners to standard MPC is fairly straightforward by using the modularity of the UC framework. As proved in [11], $\mathcal{F}_{\text{REG}}$ can be used to realize the certified signature functionality (aka *certification functionality*) $\mathcal{F}_{\text{CERT}}$ which, in turn, can be used to realize a Broadcast functionality against even adaptive adversaries [27] if we additionally assume the existence of secure channels; for details about implementing the secure channel functionality $\mathcal{F}_{\text{SC}}$ from $\mathcal{F}_{\text{AUTH}}$ we point to [14]. By plugging the Broadcast functionality into the honest-majority protocol (compiler) by Cramer *et al.* [17]—an adaptation of the protocol from [34] to tolerate adaptive corruptions—we obtain an MPC protocol which is adaptively secure.

Corollary 3. *Let $n > 2t$, p be a noticeable function, and $q \in \mathbb{N}^+$. Then, there exists a protocol that UC-realizes functionality $\mathcal{F}_{\text{MPC}}$ in the $(\mathcal{G}_{\text{CLOCK}}, \mathcal{F}_{\text{SC}}, \mathcal{W}_{\text{FLT}}^{p,q}(\mathcal{F}_{\text{AUTH}}), \mathcal{F}_{\text{SIG}})$-hybrid model.*

6   Removing the Freshness Assumption

So far, we have assumed that all parties, including the adversary, get access to the CRS at the same time, i.e., when the protocol starts. In this section, we give a high level overview of how our analysis can be adapted to the case where we remove the fresh CRS and instead assume the existence of a random oracle. The protocol we devise is based on techniques developed initially in [1].

The main function of the CRS in the implementation of $\mathcal{W}_{\text{FLT}}(\mathcal{F}_{\text{AUTH}})$, is to ensure that all parties agree on which hash evaluations are "fresh", i.e., performed after the CRS became known. Consequently, sent messages are fully transferable, in the sense that they can be forwarded an arbitrary number of times and still be valid. Without a CRS we have to sacrifice full transferability and instead settle with a limited version of the property (cf. [33]).

Next, we describe the filtering functionality we implement in this setting, denoted $\mathcal{W}_{\text{FLT-LIM}}(\mathcal{F}_{\text{AUTH}})$. The functionality has the same syntax as $\mathcal{W}_{\text{FLT}}(\mathcal{F}_{\text{AUTH}})$, with one difference: each message sent is accompanied by a grade g, which signifies the number of times that this message can be forwarded by different parties and is also related to when the message was initially sent. For example, if party P_1 receives a message with grade 2, the message can be forwarded to party P_2 with grade 1, and party P_2 can forward to party P_3 with grade 0. Party P_3 cannot forward the message any further, while party P_2 can still forward the message to any other party it wants to. Moreover, the initial grade assigned to a message sent using the SEND command is equal to the round that this command was issued minus 1, i.e., messages with higher grades can be computed at later rounds, for honest parties. The adversary has a small advantage: the initial grade of messages he sends is equal to the current round. Finally, we enforce the participation of honest parties the same way we do for the $\mathcal{F}_{REG}$ functionality in Sect. 5. Next, we formally describe $\mathcal{W}_{FLT\text{-}LIM}$.

Wrapper Functionality $\mathcal{W}_{FLT\text{-}LIM}^{p,q}(\mathcal{F})$

The wrapper functionality is parameterized $p \in [0, 1]$ and $q \in \mathbb{N}$, which restrict the probability of success and number of $\mathcal{F}$-evaluations of each party per round, respectively, and a set of parties $\mathcal{P}$. It manages the round integer variable τ, a boolean flag d_u, the current set of corrupted parties $\tilde{\mathcal{P}}$, and a list $\mathcal{T}$. For each party $P \in \mathcal{P}$, it manages the integer variable t_P.
Initially $\tau, d_u := 0$, $\mathcal{T} := \emptyset$, and $t_P := 0$, for each $P \in \mathcal{P}$.

Upon receiving any input I from any party or the adversary, send (CLOCK-READ, sid_C) to $\mathcal{G}_{CLOCK}$. On response (CLOCK-READ, sid_C, t'), if $|\tau' - \tau| > 0$, set $\tau := \tau'$, $d_u := 0$ and $t_P := 0$ for each $P \in \mathcal{P}$. Then, if I was received from an honest party $P \in \mathcal{P} \setminus \tilde{\mathcal{P}}$, set $\boldsymbol{\mathcal{I}}_H^T := \boldsymbol{\mathcal{I}}_H^T || (I, P_i, \tau)$. Depending on the input I and the ID of the sender, execute the respective code.

Filtering:

- Upon receiving (SEND, sid, m, P_j) from party $P_i \in \mathcal{P}$, do the following:
  - Set $t_{P_i} := t_{P_i} + 1$. If $t_{P_i} \leq q$, with probability p, do:
    1. If P_i is honest, let local variable $g := \tau - 1$. Otherwise, let $g := \tau$.
    2. Add (m, P_i, g) to $\mathcal{T}$, and output (SUCCESS, sid) to P_i,
    3. On response (CONTINUE, sid, m) from P_i, forward (SEND, $\mathsf{sid}, (m, g), P_j$) to $\mathcal{F}$.

    In any other case, send (FAIL, sid) to P_i.
- Upon receiving (RESEND, sid, m, g, P_j) from honest party $P_i \in \mathcal{P} \setminus \tilde{\mathcal{P}}$, if $(m, P_i, g) \in \mathcal{T}$ and $g > 0$, then forward (SEND, $\mathsf{sid}, (m, g), P_j$) to $\mathcal{F}$.
- Upon receiving (RESEND, sid, m, g, P_j) from $\mathcal{A}$ on behalf of corrupted $P_i \in \tilde{\mathcal{P}}$, if for some $g' \geq g$ and some $P \in \mathcal{P}$, $(m, P, g') \in \mathcal{T}$, and $g > 0$, forward (SEND, $\mathsf{sid}, (m, g), P_j$) to $\mathcal{F}$.
- Upon $\mathcal{F}$ sending (SENT, $\mathsf{sid}, (m, g), P_i$) to P_j, add $(m, P_j, g - 1)$ to $\mathcal{T}$ and forward the message to P_j.

Ensure Honest Participation:

- Upon receiving (MAINTAIN, sid) from honest party P, if predict-time($\boldsymbol{I}_H^T$) > τ and $d_u = 0$, set $d_u := 1$ and send (CLOCK-UPDATE, sid_C) to $\mathcal{G}_{CLOCK}$. Otherwise, send (I,ID) to $\mathcal{A}$.

Standard UC Corruption Handling:

- Upon receiving (CORRUPT, sid, P) from the adversary, set $\tilde{\mathcal{P}} \leftarrow \tilde{\mathcal{P}} \cup \mathcal{P}$.

General:

- Any other request from (resp. towards) any participant or the adversary, is simply relayed to the underlying functionality (resp . any participant of the adversary) without any further action.

The way we implement this functionality is by introducing a repeated challenge-exchange procedure to protocol Wrapped-Channel: at each round parties sample a random string, which they then hash together with the challenges sent by other parties at the previous round to compute a new challenge, that they multicast to the network. The new challenge computed at each round is used as a prefix to the queries they are making to the restricted RO functionality. If a query is successful, they send the query value along with a pre-image of the challenge, in order for other parties to be sure that the challenge *they* multicast earlier was used in the computation, and thus ensure freshness. The receiving party can forward the message by also including a pre-image of its own challenge, thus ensuring all honest parties will accept it as valid. Obviously, in the first round of the protocol parties cannot send any message as they haven't yet exchanged any random challenges, in the second round the messages cannot be transferred, in the third they can be transferred once, and so on. We formally describe the new protocol and state our lemma next. The relevant security proof proceeds as that of Lemma 2, except that we have to show the the that the adversary cannot precomputes hashes that are related to some challenge at a round earlier than the one that this challenge was generated. Due to lack of space we omit it.

Protocol Wrapped-Channel-Lim$^{D,q}(P)$

Initialization:
- We assume that P is in the party set of $\mathcal{W}_{\text{RO}}^q(\mathcal{F}_{\text{RO}})$, $\mathcal{F}_{\text{AUTH}}$, $\mathcal{F}_{\text{RO}}$. The protocol maintains a list of valid message/nonce/hash tuples $\mathcal{T}$, initially empty, a counter t initially set to 0, flags d_n, d_u, d_r all set to 0, a set M_{buf}, and sequences of sets M_j and integers c_j, for $j \in \mathbb{N}$.

Upon receiving any input I from any party or the adversary, send (CLOCK-READ, sid$_C$) to $\mathcal{G}_{\text{CLOCK}}$. On response (CLOCK-READ, sid$_C$, t'), if $|\tau' - \tau| > 0$, set $\tau := \tau'$ and $t, d_r, d_u, d_n := 0$, and do the following:

Message Exchange:
- Upon receiving (SEND, sid, m, P'), set $t := t + 1$, and if $t > q$ output (FAIL, sid) to P. Otherwise, do the following:

1. If $d_n = 0$, execute *MaintainNetwork*.
2. Send (EVAL, sid, (c_τ, m, r)) to $\mathcal{W}^q_{RO}(\mathcal{F}_{RO})$, where $r \leftarrow \{0, 1\}^\lambda$.
3. On response (EVAL, sid, $(c_\tau, m, r), v$), if $(v > D)$, output (FAIL, sid) to P.
4. Otherwise, if no entry of the form $(\tau - 1, M', m, r', v')$ exists in T, store $(\tau - 1, (M_\tau), m, r, v)$ in T. Then, send (SUCCESS, sid) to P. On response (CONTINUE, sid), pick M', r', v' such that $(\tau - 1, M', m, r', v')$ is an entry in T, and send (SEND, sid, $(\tau - 1, M', m, r', v'), P'$) to $\mathcal{F}_{AUTH}$.

- Upon receiving (RESEND, sid, m, g, P'), if $g > 0$ and M, r, v exists such that $(g, M, m, r, v) \in T$, send (SEND, sid, $(g, M, m, r, v), P'$) to $\mathcal{F}_{AUTH}$.
- Upon receiving (FETCH, sid), if $d_n = 0$, then execute *MaintainNetwork*. Set $M' = \emptyset$, and for each message of the form (SENT, sid, $(g, M, m, r, v), P'$) in M_{buf}, do the following:
  1. Let $M = (M_i, M_{i-1}, \ldots, M_{g+1})$. For $j \in \{g + 1, \ldots, i\}$, sent (EVAL, sid, M_j). On response (EVAL, sid, M_j, v), initialize variable $H[M_j] := v$.
  2. If $c_g \notin M_{g+1}$ or $H[M_j] \notin M(j + 1)$, for $j \in \{g + 1, \ldots, i - 1\}$, do nothing. *(Ensure freshness.)*
  3. Send (EVAL, sid, $(H[M_i], m, r)$) to $\mathcal{W}^q_{RO}(\mathcal{F}_{RO})$.
  4. On response (EVAL, sid, $(H[M_i], m, r), v'$), if $(v \le D)$ and $(v' = v)$, remove any entries of the form $(g - 1, M'', m, r'', v'')$ from T and add $(g - 1, M \cup M_g, m, r, v)$ instead. Set $M' := M' \cup ((g - 1, m), P')$.

  Finally, empty M_{buf} and output (SENT, sid, M').
- Upon receiving (FETCH-REQUESTS, sid), forward the message to $\mathcal{F}_{AUTH}$, and output its response.
- Upon receiving (MAINTAIN, sid), if $d_r = 0$, execute in a (MAINTAIN, sid)-interruptible manner the following:
  1. If $d_n = 0$, then execute *MaintainNetwork*.
  2. Send (SEND, sid, $(challenge, c_\tau), P_i$), to all $P_i \in \mathcal{P}$.
  3. Set $d_r := 1$. If $d_u = 1$, send (CLOCK-UPDATE, sid$_C$) to $\mathcal{G}_{CLOCK}$.
- Upon receiving (CLOCK-UPDATE, sid$_C$), if $d_r = 1$ and $d_u = 0$, send (CLOCK-UPDATE, sid$_C$) to $\mathcal{G}_{CLOCK}$. Set $d_u := 1$.

Procedure MaintainNetwork:
1. Send (FETCH, sid) to $\mathcal{F}_{AUTH}$.
2. On response (SENT, sid, M), do the following:
   (a) Sample $r_\tau \leftarrow \{0, 1\}^\lambda$, and let $M_\tau := \{r_\tau\}$.
   (b) For any tuple of the form $((challenge, c), P') \in M$, for $P' \in \mathcal{P}$, set $M_\tau := M_\tau \cup \{c\}$, and remove this message from M.
   (c) Set $M_{buf} := M$.
3. Send (EVAL, sid, M_τ) to $\mathcal{F}_{RO}$. On response (EVAL, sid, M_τ, v), set $c_\tau := v$.
4. Set $d_n := 1$.

Lemma 3. *Let $p := \frac{D}{2^\lambda}$. The protocol* Wrapped-Channel-Lim^{D,q} *UC-realizes functionality* $\mathcal{W}^{p,q}_{FLT-LIM}(\mathcal{F}_{AUTH})$ *in the* $(\mathcal{G}_{CLOCK}, \mathcal{W}^q_{RO}(\mathcal{F}_{RO}), \mathcal{F}_{AUTH}, \mathcal{F}_{RO})$-*hybrid model.*

Next, we observe that $\mathcal{W}_{FLT-LIM}(\mathcal{F}_{AUTH})$ is sufficient to implement $\mathcal{F}_{REG}$. The protocol is similar to protocol Graded-Agreement, with two differences: (i) parties start sending messages through $\mathcal{W}_{\text{FLT-LIM}}(\mathcal{F}_{\text{AUTH}})$ after $n + 2$ rounds have passed, and (ii) during the *KeyAgreement* phase of the protocol, parties take in account messages with grade bigger than n at the first round, $n - 1$ at the second, $\ldots$, 0 at the last one. The rest of the protocol is exactly the same. Note, that parties can always forward the messages received during the *KeyAgreement* phase, since the grade of the relevant messages is bigger than 0. The analysis of [1] is built on the same idea.

As a result, we are able to implement $\mathcal{F}_{\text{REG}}$, and subsequently $\mathcal{F}_{\text{MPC}}$, without having to assume a "fresh" CRS. With the techniques described above, the following theorem can be proven.

Theorem 2. *Let $n > 2t$ and $q \in \mathbb{N}^+$. Then, there exists a protocol that UC-realizes functionality $\mathcal{F}_{\text{MPC}}$ in the $(\mathcal{G}_{\text{CLOCK}}, \mathcal{F}_{\text{SC}}, \mathcal{W}_{\text{RO}}^q(\mathcal{F}_{\text{RO}}), \mathcal{F}_{\text{SIG}}, \mathcal{F}_{\text{RO}})$-hybrid model.*

Acknowledgements. Juan Garay, Rafail Ostrovsky and Vassilis Zikas were supported in part by the Office of the Director of National Intelligence (ODNI), Intelligence Advanced Research Projects Activity (IARPA), via 2019-1902070008. This work was performed in part while Juan Garay was consulting for Stealth Software Technologies, Inc., and supported in part by DARPA/SPAWAR N66001-15-C-4065. Aggelos Kiayias was supported in part by EU Project No.780477, PRIVILEDGE. Rafail Ostrovsky was also supported in part by NSF-BSF Grant 1619348, DARPA/SPAWAR N66001-15-C-4065, US-Israel BSF grant 2012366, JP Morgan Faculty Award, Google Faculty Research Award, OKAWA Foundation Research Award, IBM Faculty Research Award, Xerox Faculty Research Award, B. John Garrick Foundation Award, Teradata Research Award, and Lockheed-Martin Corporation Research Award. This work was done in part while Vassilis Zikas was visiting the Simons Institute for the Theory of Computing, UC Berkeley, and UCLA. The views and conclusions contained herein are those of the authors and should not be interpreted as necessarily representing the official views or policies, either expressed or implied, of the Department of Defense, DARPA, ODNI, IARPA, or the U.S. Government. The U.S. Government is authorized to reproduce and distribute reprints for governmental purposes notwithstanding any copyright annotation therein.

References

1. Andrychowicz, M., Dziembowski, S.: PoW-based distributed cryptography with no trusted setup. In: Gennaro, R., Robshaw, M. (eds.) CRYPTO 2015, Part II. LNCS, vol. 9216, pp. 379–399. Springer, Heidelberg (2015). https://doi.org/10.1007/978-3-662-48000-7_19
2. Back, A.: Hashcash (1997). http://www.cypherspace.org/hashcash
3. Badertscher, C., Gazi, P., Kiayias, A., Russell, A., Zikas, V.: Ouroboros genesis: composable proof-of-stake blockchains with dynamic availability. In: Proceedings of the 2018 ACM SIGSAC Conference on Computer and Communications Security, CCS 2018, Toronto, ON, Canada, 15–19 October 2018, pp. 913–930 (2018)
4. Badertscher, C., Maurer, U., Tschudi, D., Zikas, V.: Bitcoin as a transaction ledger: a composable treatment. In: Katz, J., Shacham, H. (eds.) CRYPTO 2017, Part I. LNCS, vol. 10401, pp. 324–356. Springer, Cham (2017). https://doi.org/10.1007/978-3-319-63688-7_11

5. Ben-Or, M., Goldwasser, S., Wigderson, A.: Completeness theorems for non-cryptographic fault-tolerant distributed computation (extended abstract). In: Simon, J. (ed.) Proceedings of the 20th Annual ACM Symposium on Theory of Computing, Chicago, Illinois, USA, 2–4 May 1988, pp. 1–10. ACM (1988)

6. Bentov, I., Pass, R., Shi, E.: Snow white: provably secure proofs of stake. Cryptology ePrint Archive, Report 2016/919 (2016). http://eprint.iacr.org/2016/919

7. Borcherding, M.: Levels of authentication in distributed agreement. In: Babaoğlu, Ö., Marzullo, K. (eds.) WDAG 1996. LNCS, vol. 1151, pp. 40–55. Springer, Heidelberg (1996). https://doi.org/10.1007/3-540-61769-8_4

8. Cachin, C., Maurer, U.M.: Unconditional security against memory-bounded adversaries. In: Kaliski Jr., B.S. (ed.) CRYPTO 1997. LNCS, vol. 1294, pp. 292–306. Springer, Heidelberg (1997). https://doi.org/10.1007/BFb0052243

9. Canetti, R.: Security and composition of multiparty cryptographic protocols. J. Cryptol. 13(1), 143–202 (2000)

10. Canetti, R.: Universally composable security: a new paradigm for cryptographic protocols. In: 42nd Annual Symposium on Foundations of Computer Science, pp. 136–145. IEEE Computer Society Press, October 2001

11. Canetti, R.: Universally composable signature, certification, and authentication. In: 17th IEEE Computer Security Foundations Workshop (CSFW-17 2004), Pacific Grove, CA, USA, 28–30 June 2004, p. 219 (2004)

12. Canetti, R., Dodis, Y., Pass, R., Walfish, S.: Universally composable security with global setup. In: Vadhan, S.P. (ed.) TCC 2007. LNCS, vol. 4392, pp. 61–85. Springer, Heidelberg (2007). https://doi.org/10.1007/978-3-540-70936-7_4

13. Canetti, R., Fischlin, M.: Universally composable commitments. In: Kilian, J. (ed.) CRYPTO 2001. LNCS, vol. 2139, pp. 19–40. Springer, Heidelberg (2001). https://doi.org/10.1007/3-540-44647-8_2

14. Canetti, R., Krawczyk, H.: Universally composable notions of key exchange and secure channels. In: Knudsen, L.R. (ed.) EUROCRYPT 2002. LNCS, vol. 2332, pp. 337–351. Springer, Heidelberg (2002). https://doi.org/10.1007/3-540-46035-7_22

15. Chen, J., Micali, S.: Algorand. arXiv preprint arXiv:1607.01341 (2016)

16. Cohen, R., Haitner, I., Omri, E., Rotem, L.: Characterization of secure multiparty computation without broadcast. In: Kushilevitz, E., Malkin, T. (eds.) TCC 2016, Part I. LNCS, vol. 9562, pp. 596–616. Springer, Heidelberg (2016). https://doi.org/10.1007/978-3-662-49096-9_25

17. Cramer, R., Damgård, I., Dziembowski, S., Hirt, M., Rabin, T.: Efficient multiparty computations secure against an adaptive adversary. In: Stern, J. (ed.) EUROCRYPT 1999. LNCS, vol. 1592, pp. 311–326. Springer, Heidelberg (1999). https://doi.org/10.1007/3-540-48910-X_22

18. David, B., Gaži, P., Kiayias, A., Russell, A.: Ouroboros Praos: an adaptively-secure, semi-synchronous proof-of-stake blockchain. In: Nielsen, J.B., Rijmen, V. (eds.) EUROCRYPT 2018, Part II. LNCS, vol. 10821, pp. 66–98. Springer, Cham (2018). https://doi.org/10.1007/978-3-319-78375-8_3

19. Dolev, D., Strong, H.R.: Authenticated algorithms for Byzantine agreement. SIAM J. Comput. 12(4), 656–666 (1983)

20. Dwork, C., Lynch, N., Stockmeyer, L.: Consensus in the presence of partial synchrony. J. ACM (JACM) 35(2), 288–323 (1988)

21. Fischer, M.J., Lynch, N.A., Merritt, M.: Easy impossibility proofs for distributed consensus problems. In: Malcolm, M.A., Strong, H.R. (eds.) 4th ACM Symposium Annual on Principles of Distributed Computing, pp. 59–70. Association for Computing Machinery, August 1985

22. Fitzi, M.: Generalized communication and security models in Byzantine agreement. Ph.D. thesis, ETH Zurich (2002)
23. Garay, J.A., Kiayias, A., Leonardos, N.: The bitcoin backbone protocol: analysis and applications. In: Oswald, E., Fischlin, M. (eds.) EUROCRYPT 2015, Part II. LNCS, vol. 9057, pp. 281–310. Springer, Heidelberg (2015). https://doi.org/10.1007/978-3-662-46803-6_10
24. Garay, J.A., MacKenzie, P.D., Prabhakaran, M., Yang, K.: Resource fairness and composability of cryptographic protocols. J. Cryptol. **24**(4), 615–658 (2011)
25. Gilad, Y., Hemo, R., Micali, S., Vlachos, G., Zeldovich, N.: Algorand: scaling Byzantine agreements for cryptocurrencies. Cryptology ePrint Archive, Report 2017/454 (2017). http://eprint.iacr.org/2017/454
26. Goldreich, O., Micali, S., Wigderson, A.: How to play any mental game or a completeness theorem for protocols with honest majority. In: Aho, A. (ed.) 19th Annual ACM Symposium on Theory of Computing, pp. 218–229. ACM Press, New York (1987)
27. Hirt, M., Zikas, V.: Adaptively secure broadcast. In: Gilbert, H. (ed.) EUROCRYPT 2010. LNCS, vol. 6110, pp. 466–485. Springer, Heidelberg (2010). https://doi.org/10.1007/978-3-642-13190-5_24
28. Katz, J., Maurer, U., Tackmann, B., Zikas, V.: Universally composable synchronous computation. In: Sahai, A. (ed.) TCC 2013. LNCS, vol. 7785, pp. 477–498. Springer, Heidelberg (2013). https://doi.org/10.1007/978-3-642-36594-2_27
29. Katz, J., Miller, A., Shi, E.: Pseudonymous broadcast and secure computation from cryptographic puzzles. Cryptology ePrint Archive, Report 2014/857 (2014). http://eprint.iacr.org/2014/857
30. Kiayias, A., Russell, A., David, B., Oliynykov, R.: Ouroboros: a provably secure proof-of-stake blockchain protocol. In: Katz, J., Shacham, H. (eds.) CRYPTO 2017, Part I. LNCS, vol. 10401, pp. 357–388. Springer, Cham (2017). https://doi.org/10.1007/978-3-319-63688-7_12
31. Lamport, L., Shostak, R.E., Pease, M.C.: The Byzantine generals problem. ACM Trans. Program. Lang. Syst. **4**(3), 382–401 (1982)
32. Pass, R., Seeman, L., Shelat, A.: Analysis of the blockchain protocol in asynchronous networks. In: Coron, J., Nielsen, J.B. (eds.) EUROCRYPT 2017, Part II. LNCS, vol. 10211, pp. 643–673. Springer, Cham (2017). https://doi.org/10.1007/978-3-319-56614-6_22
33. Pfitzmann, B., Waidner, M.: Unconditional Byzantine agreement for any number of faulty processors. In: Finkel, A., Jantzen, M. (eds.) STACS 1992. LNCS, vol. 577, pp. 339–350. Springer, Heidelberg (1992). https://doi.org/10.1007/3-540-55210-3_195
34. Rabin, T., Ben-Or, M.: Verifiable secret sharing and multiparty protocols with honest majority (extended abstract). In: 21st Annual ACM Symposium on Theory of Computing, pp. 73–85. ACM Press, May 1989
35. Schneider, F.B.: Implementing fault-tolerant services using the state machine approach: a tutorial. ACM Comput. Surv. **22**(4), 299–319 (1990)
36. Yao, A.C.-C.: Protocols for secure computations (extended abstract). In: 23rd Annual Symposium on Foundations of Computer Science, pp. 160–164. IEEE Computer Society Press, November 1982

Efficient Constructions
for Almost-Everywhere
Secure Computation

Siddhartha Jayanti[✉], Srinivasan Raghuraman, and Nikhil Vyas[✉]

Massachusetts Institute of Technology (CSAIL MIT), Cambridge, USA
{jayanti,srirag,nikhilv}@mit.edu

Abstract. We study the problem of *almost-everywhere reliable message transmission*; a key component in designing efficient and secure Multiparty Computation (MPC) protocols for sparsely connected networks. The goal is to design low-degree networks which allow a large fraction of honest nodes to communicate reliably even when a small constant fraction of nodes experience byzantine corruption and deviate arbitrarily from the assigned protocol.

In this paper, we achieve a log-degree network with a polylogarithmic work complexity protocol, thereby improving over the state-of-the-art result of Chandran *et al.* (ICALP 2010) who required a polylogarithmic-degree network and had a linear work complexity. In addition, we also achieve:

- A work efficient version of Dwork et al.'s (STOC 1986) butterfly network.
- An improvement upon the state of the art protocol of Ben-or and Ron (Information Processing Letters 1996) in the randomized corruption model—both in work-efficiency and in resilience.

1 Introduction

Many real world applications involve computing functions on large data sets that are distributed across machines in a global network. For instance, hospitals across the world have confidential patient data that can be used to create accurate disease models and improve treatment plans. Data held by any particular agent may need to be kept private. The ubiquitous need for such distributed private computations has motivated research on efficient multiparty computation (MPC) [2,9,14,22]. MPC protocols enable a set of parties to compute a joint function on their inputs while keeping them private [6]. MPC protocols for various important tasks, such as elections, were discovered in the twentieth century, but most of these protocols have not seen practical application as they were designed for densely connected networks. For MPC to see widespread use, it is important for

Siddhartha Jayanti was supported by an NDSEG Fellowship from the United States Department of Defense, and Nikhil Vyas was supported by NSF CCF-1909429.

A. Canteaut and Y. Ishai (Eds.): EUROCRYPT 2020, LNCS 12106, pp. 159–183, 2020.
https://doi.org/10.1007/978-3-030-45724-2_6

protocols to rely only on the sparse connectivity that is available in modern large scale networks while simultaneously meeting the efficiency needs of practice. In this paper, we focus on designing sparse networks, and secure communication protocols for these networks that are resilient to large fractions of the machines being hacked, and thereby deviating arbitrarily from the assigned protocols.

All secure distributed protocols rely on the ability of machines to communicate. In particular, if A and B are two nodes in a network, A must be able to send a message to B in a way that satisfies the following two properties: (1) *reliable transmission*: B receives the message that A intended to send, and (2) *authentication*: B must be able to confirm that A was indeed the sender of the received message [1]. The first—reliable transmission—is the focus of our paper. Reliable transmission becomes trivial if we assume every pair of nodes has a dedicated *secure link* to pass messages over. However, it is impractical to create pairwise secure links in modern large scale networks—a network on even just a thousand nodes would need half a million secure links!

In a seminal work, Dwork *et al.* [12] considered the question of designing sparse networks that are tolerant to nodes experiencing *byzantine* failures—nodes that fail can deviate arbitrarily from the protocol. The problem is to design a network G of degree d on n nodes in which *honest nodes* can continue to communicate and execute protocols, even after t nodes are *corrupted*, i.e., experience byzantine failures. The challenge is to make the degree d as small as possible (ideally constant), even while allowing up to $t = \varepsilon n$ corruptions for some constant ε. Since we allow many more corruptions, t, than the degree of the graph, d, any set of $\Omega(t/d)$ honest nodes can be isolated from the other nodes if all of their neighbors are corrupted. Thereby, it is impossible for all the honest nodes to communicate with each other in this failure model. So, Dwork *et al.* allow x honest nodes to become *doomed*, and only require that a set of $n - t - x$ honest nodes be able to pairwise communicate with each other after t corruptions occur. This set of honest nodes are called *privileged nodes*, and the class of primitives that work on these privileged nodes in the presence of byzantine failures are called *almost-everywhere (AE)* primitives. Our paper's main result, is the design of a new sparse graph and a corresponding communication protocol that improve the state of the art in AE reliable message transmission.

Our protocol for AE reliable message transmission immediately implies an improved protocol for AE Secure Multi-party Computation (MPC) in the following way. The problem of byzantine agreement [18,20] is one where nodes start with an initial value but wish to agree, at the end of execution of some protocol, on some value, despite malicious or byzantine behavior of some subset of nodes. Prior to [12], this problem was considered assuming all pairs of nodes had a secure link for communication [10,18,20]. Dwork *et al.* introduced the notion of *almost-everywhere agreement* where only privileged nodes need to reach agreement. We note that *AE reliable message transmission*, which would guarantee that a large subset of the network can transmit messages to each other reliably, implies a protocol for *AE agreement*, and an AE agreement protocol implies a protocol for *AE secure MPC* that is unconditionally or information-theoretically secure as formulated in the work of Garay and Ostrovsky [13].

1.1   Previous Work

AE reliable transmission protocols are generally compared by the following three properties:

1. *degree*: the degree, d, of graph of secure links needed for the protocol.
2. *resilience*: a protocol is $(f(n), g(t))$-resilient if it can sustain up to $t = f(n)$ corruptions while dooming at most $x = g(t)$ nodes when t nodes are corrupted.
3. *work complexity*: the total amount of work (both local and message passing) required for a single communication from node u to node v in the network.

The ideal solution would give a protocol on a constant degree graph that is $(\varepsilon n, O(t))$-resilient for a small constant $\varepsilon \in (0, 1)$, and have low work complexity. This ideal remains an open problem. In the remainder of this section, we discuss the three previous results which are mutually incomparable, and thereby, jointly form the state-of-the-art for the AE reliable transmission problem. We remark that ε continues to be used in resilience guarantees throughout the paper, and it simply represents some constant in $(0, 1)$ when it appears.

Dwork *et al.*'s seminal work introduced the AE reliable transmission problem, and gave the first solution to the problem [12]. Their famous *Butterfly network* is a constant degree graph and their protocol is $(\varepsilon n / \log n, O(t))$-resilient, and has linear work complexity. While the Butterfly network is a simple network and Dwork *et al.*'s protocol, the possibility of increasing the resilience of the network to be resistant to a linear number of corruptions spurred further research into the AE reliable transmission.

Upfal showed the remarkable result that both optimal graph degree and optimal resilience were simultaneously possible [21]. He produced a constant degree graph and a protocol that is $(\varepsilon n, O(t))$-resilient on that graph. While these advantages make Upfal's work of great information theoretic importance, his protocol is practically intractable, since it requires nodes to do an exponential amount of computation. In particular, when a node u is sending a message to a node v, Upfal's algorithm requires v to loop through all possible subsets of corrupted nodes before it can correctly decipher the message it has received (even when u and v are both privileged). Thus, the work complexity of Upfal's algorithm is the exponential $O\left(\binom{n}{t}\right)$.

The third work at the frontier of the field was Chandran *et al.*'s protocol. This work tries to combine the work efficiency of Dwork *et al.*'s protocol with the resiliency of Upfal's work. Chandran *et al.* succeed in getting a linear work protocol, and in fact achieve the very strong property of $(\varepsilon n, O(t / \log n))$-resilience. However, the significant weakness of their work is the complexity and degree of their graph. Unlike the other two works, their protocol is designed for a graph of polylogarithmic-degree.

In summary, the state-of-the-art on the AE reliable transmission problem consisted of three incomparable results: Dwork *et al.*'s linear work protocol with low resiliency on a constant degree graph, Upfal's exponential work protocol with high resiliency on a constant degree graph, and Chandran *et al.*'s linear work protocol with high resiliency on a polylogarithmic degree graph.

1.2 Our Contributions

The primary contribution of our paper is an AE reliable transmission protocol on a graph of logarithmic degree that is $(\varepsilon n, O(t/\log n))$-resilient while requiring only polylogarithmic work per communication. The significance of our result lies in the low degree of the graph and the work-efficiency of the protocol. Our result is a strict improvement over Chandran *et al.*'s result, as our graph's degree is smaller—only logarithmic, compared to polylogarithmic—and our protocol's work complexity is polylogarithmic as opposed to linear, while our protocol's resiliency is the same as their protocol's. Also, our protocol is the first AE reliable transmission protocol to achieve sublinear work complexity. In particular, the small work complexity of our message-passing protocol enables us to simulate any protocol on a (dense) complete graph with only polylogarithmic multiplicative overhead on our nearly-sparse logarithmic degree graph, while all previous protocols required at least linear multiplicative overhead. The primary result of our paper is stated as Theorem 1 below.

Theorem 1 (Main Theorem: Efficient Worst-case Corruptions). *For sufficiently large n, there exists an n-node network $G_{wc} = (V, E)$, a protocol $\Pi_{wc,eff}$ for message transmission on it, and constants α and β, such that:*

1. *The network G_{wc} is of degree $O(\log n)$.*
2. *The Work complexity of $\Pi_{wc,eff}$ is $O(\text{polylog}(n))$.*
3. *$\Pi_{wc,eff}$ is $(\alpha n, \beta t/\log n)$-resilient.*

Remark 1. The protocoled-network $(G_{wc}, \Pi_{wc,eff})$ of Theorem 1 is efficiently constructible in the following sense. In the paper, we give an efficient probabilistic construction that takes the number of nodes n and outputs a protocoled-network satisfying the conditions of the theorem with all but exponentially small probability. However, we do not know how to efficiently verify that the obtained construction indeed satisfies the conditions of the theorem.

We compare our work to previous works in Table 1.

Table 1. In general, total work can be further broken down into message passing work and internal computations of the nodes. For Upfal's protocol the message passing work is linear, and internal computations take exponential work. For the rest of the protocols, message passing work and internal computation work are identical.

Result	Degree	Corruptions	Doomed	Total Work
Dwork et al. [12]	$O(1)$	$\varepsilon n/\log n$	$O(t)$	$O(n)$
Upfal [21]	$O(1)$	εn	$O(t)$	$O\left(\binom{n}{t}\right)$
Chandran et al. [7]	$\text{polylog}(n)$	εn	$O(t/\log n)$	$O(n)$
This paper	$O(\log n)$	εn	$O(t/\log n)$	$\text{polylog}(n)$

A secondary contribution of our work is an improvement over the state of the art in AE reliable transmission when the adversary corrupts nodes at *random*. Ben-or and Ron [3] introduced the *random corruption model* in which nodes are corrupted independently and at random and the protocol only needs to be resilient with some large probability, called the *probability of resiliency*. So, algorithms in this model are evaluated by *four* parameters: degree, resiliency, work complexity, and probability of resiliency. (If the probability of resiliency becomes equal to one, then the protocol is resilient in the standard model.) Ben-or and Ron exhibited a constant degree network that is $(\varepsilon n, O(t))$-resilient with high probability, and thereby almost resolved the random corruption model [3]. En route to our main construction, we produce a different constant degree network that has the same $(\varepsilon n, O(t))$-resilience, just with even higher probability than Ben-or and Ron's construction. Interestingly, the *improvement in probability* that we attain for the random corruption model drives our ability to get such a *low degree* graph in the standard model of corruption.

1.3 Our Techniques

In this section, we describe the main ideas in the paper and how they fit together to build our main result.

At a high level, our AE transmission protocol is constructed in two parts: the first part yields a network and protocol that have the $(\varepsilon n, O(t/\log n))$-resilience and logarithmic-degree; this immediately yields an improvement over Chandran *et al.*'s protocol, which has the same resiliency but polylogarithmic degree. Our construction in the first part, uses the protocol of Dwork *et al.* on the Butterfly Network as a black box.

In the second part, we improve this communication protocol significantly—reducing the linear work to only polylogarithmic work, while maintaining the resiliency parameters. Modularly replacing the Dwork *et al.* protocol with the new efficient protocol immediately yields our main theorem: a logarithmic degree graph and a polylogarithmic work protocol with $(\varepsilon n, O(t/\log n))$-resilience.

Better Resilience. We achieve a highly resilient graph with low degree in two steps. In the first step, we combine the ideas of Dwork *et al.* and Upfal to construct a constant degree graph that is resilient to a linear number of corruptions with high probability in the random corruption model. Upfal constructed an exponential work protocol Π_{Upfal} on a constant degree expander graph G_{Upfal}. We notice that while Upfal's protocol is too slow to be run on a full sized graph of n nodes, it can be run on *committees* of sub-logarithmic size, and thereby split the n nodes into disjoint committees of size $O(\log \log n)$ each. In order for nodes in one committees to communicate with nodes in other committees, we view the individual committees as super-nodes, and connect these super-nodes through the butterfly network, G_{But}, of Dwork *et al.* An important theorem we prove at the end of this step shows that this construction (which we fully specify in Sect. 3) along with a carefully constructed protocol gives high resilience in the random corruption model with high probability.

Theorem 2 (Random Corruptions). *For sufficiently large n, there exists an n-node network $G_{rand} = (V, E)$, a protocol Π_{rand} for message transmission on it, and constants α_3 and β_3, such that:*

1. *The network G_{rand} is of constant degree.*
2. *If a subset of nodes $T \subset V$ is randomly corrupt, where $|T| \leq \alpha_3 n$, with probability $1 - (t/n)^{\alpha_2 t/(4 \log(n))}$, there exists a set of nodes $S \subset V$ where $|S| \geq n - \beta_3 |T|$ such that every pair of nodes in S can communicate reliably with each other by invoking Π_{rand}.*

In the second step, we strengthen the graph from the first step by adding multiple (perturbed) copies of the edges to it and modify the protocol to get a graph that is resilient to linearly many worst-case corruptions. In particular, let $G^i_{rand} = (V, E_i)$ be graphs of the type constructed in the first step where the vertex labels are permuted randomly and independently for each $1 \leq i \leq f(n)$ for some $f(n) = O(\log n)$. Our graph in the second step is the union of all of these graphs, i.e., $G_{wc} = \left(V, \bigcup_{i=1}^{f(n)} E_i\right)$. Since $O(\log n)$ different edge sets are combined to form this graph, the degree of the graph goes up to $O(\log n)$. However, the graph now has very high probability of being resilient to linearly many *worst-case* corruptions. Intuitively, this resilience is built from the fact that the protocol from the first step can be executed independently on each set of edges E_i, and it suffices if a majority of these protocols succeed. Since there is some probability of success, i.e. that the random graph G_{wc} is indeed resilient to linearly many worst-case corruptions, the probabilistic method yields Theorem 3 (stated below) which strictly improves over the construction of Chandran *et al.*

Theorem 3. *For sufficiently large n, there exists an n-node network $G_{wc} = (V, E)$, a protocol Π_{wc} for message transmission on it, and constants α_4 and β_4, such that:*

1. *The network G_{wc} is of degree $O(\log n)$.*
2. *Π_{wc} is $(\alpha_4 n, \beta_4 t/ \log n)$-resilient.*

Better Efficiency. Our protocols for network resiliency used the G_{But} and Dwork *et al.*'s protocol designed for the graph as primitives. In this part of the paper we design a communication protocol on the Butterfly Network that is more work-efficient than Dwork *et al.*'s protocol. A communication from node u to node v in Dwork *et al.*'s protocol floods many paths between u and v in G_{But} with the message and makes v take the majority of the messages it receives to decipher the true message reliably. In this step of our work, we show that if paths are chosen correctly, it suffices to use only polylogarithmically many paths per pair of nodes. Once again, our result goes through the probabilistic method to show that such paths exist.

Theorem 4. *For the $n = m2^m$-node network $G_{But} = (V, E)$ there is a protocol Π^*_{Eff} for message transmission on it such that the following holds:*

1. *The network G_{But} has degree 11.*
2. *The total work of the protocol Π^*_{Eff} is $O(\text{polylog}(n))$.*
3. *There is a constant $\varepsilon \in (0, 1)$ such that Π^*_{Eff} is $(\varepsilon n / \log n, O(t \log t))$-resilient.*

Getting Efficient and Resilient Networks. Modularly substituting the more efficient protocol on the Butterfly graph from the second part for Dwork *et al.*'s protocol in the highly resilient network from the first part yields the main result of our paper:

Reminder of Theorem 1. *For sufficiently large n, there exists an n-node network $G_{wc} = (V, E)$, a protocol $\Pi_{wc,eff}$ for message transmission on it, and constants α and β, such that:*

1. *The network G_{wc} is of degree $O(\log n)$.*
2. *The Work complexity of $\Pi_{wc,eff}$ is $O(\text{polylog}(n))$.*
3. *$\Pi_{wc,eff}$ is $(\alpha n, \beta t / \log n)$-resilient.*

1.4 Related Work

There have been a plethora of works asking for various different measures of quality of an agreement or MPC protocol. A sequence of works seek to improve the round complexity of protocols for byzantine consensus [4,5]. Another goal is to optimize the communication complexity of byzantine agreement protocols [11,15–17]. Another model of corruptions is that of edge corruptions [8]. As observed in the work of Chandran *et al.*, an almost-everywhere secure computation protocol for node corruptions can be readily transformed into a corresponding almost-everywhere protocol also tolerating edge corruptions, for a reduced fraction of edge corruptions (by a factor of d, the degree of the network). We note that all our results hence also extend to the edge corruption model, both worst-case and random.

1.5 Organization

We discuss preliminary notation and definitions in Sect. 2. Next, we describe our network for the randomized corruption model in Sect. 3. We describe our solution in the face of worst-case corruptions in Sect. 4. Our polylogarithmic efficiency protocol on the Butterfly Network is specified in Sect. 5, and our main result which combines resiliency in the face of worst-case corruptions with work efficiency is described in Sect. 5.

2 Preliminaries

2.1 Notation

For $n \in \mathbb{N}$, let $[n] = \{1, 2, \dots, n\}$. We assume that all logarithms are taken to the base 2.

2.2 Approximation and Concentration Inequalities

Chernoff bound. Let X be a random variable with $\mathbb{E}[X] = \mu$. For $0 \leq \delta \leq 1$,

$$\Pr[X \geq (1+\delta)\mu] \leq e^{-\frac{\delta^2 \mu}{3}} \tag{1}$$

Stirling's approximation. For any $n, t \in \mathbb{N}$ with $t \leq n$,

$$\binom{n}{t} \leq \left(\frac{en}{t}\right)^t$$

2.3 Expanders

Definition 1. *A graph $G = (V, E)$ is an expander if there exists a constant $\theta < 1$ such that for every subset $U \subset V$ of vertices of size $|U| \leq \frac{|V|}{2}$, the set of vertices outside U that have at least one neighbor in U is at least $\theta|U|$.*

Constructions of expanders of constant degree are known [19].

2.4 Network Parameters

Given a graph $G = (V, E)$, a *message transmission protocol* or simply *protocol* Π on the graph, is a specification for how messages are routed between every pair of nodes. In particular, $\Pi(u, v)$ is the protocol for node $u \in V$ to *transmit* to node $v \in V$. A protocol is comprised of discrete synchronous *rounds*. In each round, we allow each node $w \in V$ to perform local computations and pass a different one bit message to each of its neighbors in G.

We call a pair $N = (G, \Pi)$ a *protocoled-network* (or simply a *network*) if Π is a protocol for graph G. We define the following properties of the network, where u and v are two different nodes in G:

1. **Work complexity**, or, **Total work:** The total work of $\Pi(u, v)$ is the number computations, $W(u, v)$, performed across all processors in the network in a transmission from u to v. The *total work* of Π is $W = \max_{u,v \in V} W(u, v)$.
2. **Graph degree:** The degree of u is the number of neighbors, $d(u)$, that u has in G. The *degree* of G is $d = \max_{u \in V} d(u)$.
3. **Resilience:** We say a network (G, Π) is *resilient* to a set of nodes T, of size $t = |T|$, being *corrupted* while dooming only x nodes if there is a subset $S \subseteq V$ of $n - t - x$ *privileged* nodes that can reliably transmit messages between each other, after the nodes in T experience byzantine failure. Nodes in set S are called *privileged*, nodes in $X = V - (S \cup T)$ are called *doomed*, and nodes in $X \cup T$ are called *unprivileged*. We say a network is $(f(n), g(t))$-resilient if it can sustain an arbitrary set of up to $t \leq f(n)$ corruptions while dooming at most $x = g(t)$ nodes. When corruptions are randomized (see Sect. 2.7), we say that a network is $(f(n), g(t))$-resilient with probability p, if it can sustain a random subset of up to $t \leq f(n)$ corruptions, and at most $x = g(t)$ nodes get doomed with probability at least p. Informally speaking, a network is highly resilient if $f(n)$ is large while $g(t)$ is not too large, and thus the set of privileged nodes is large.

Our goal is to design a highly resilient low degree network of low work complexity.

2.5   Notion of Almost-Everywhere Security

The notion of almost-everywhere secure primitives was introduced by Dwork *et al.* [12]. In this setting, we consider a sparse communication network on the nodes. We assume a synchronous network and that the communication is divided into rounds. In every round, each node can send (possibly different) messages on its incident edges; these messages are delivered before the next round. Suppose a certain subset of the nodes may be adversarially corrupt, in particular adaptive, rushing and computationally unbounded. This implies that a protocol for any task on this network must "give up" a certain number of honest nodes on account of their poor connectivity to other honest nodes. We set up the following notation. Consider a network of n nodes connected by a communication network $G = (V, E)$ of degree d. On executing a protocol Π on this network in the presence of a subset $T \subset V$ of adversarial or *corrupt* nodes, let $X \subset V$ be the set of honest nodes that are given up, or *doomed*, and let $P \subset V$ be the set of honest nodes for whom the protocol requirements of correctness and security hold, or *privileged* nodes. The nodes that are not privileged are *unprivileged* nodes. Let $|T| = t$, $|X| = x$ and $|S| = s$. We have $t + x + s = n$.

2.6   Almost-Everywhere Reliable Message Transmission

We present some prior networks for almost-everywhere reliable message transmission that will be useful in our constructions.

Dwork, Peleg, Pippenger, Upfal [12]. Dwork *et al.* define the *butterfly* protocol-network.

Definition 2. *The butterfly network* (G_{But}, Π_{But}) *is as follows.*

> **Graph:** $G_{But} = (V_{But}, E_{But})$ *where* $V_{But} = \{(i, j)\}$ *where* $0 \leq i \leq m - 1$ *and* $j \in \{0, 1\}^m$ *is a set of* $n = m2^m$ *nodes, and* $E_{But} = \{(i, j), (i', j')\}$ *is the set of edges where* $i' = (i + 1) \mod m$ *and* j *and* j' *only possibly differ in the* i^{th} *bit.*
> **Protocol:** *Let* u *and* v *be distinct vertices in* V_{But}. *There exists as set of paths* $P_{u,v}$ *from* u *to* v *such that* $|P_{u,v}| = 2^m = \Theta(n / \log n)$. *The message transmission protocol* Π *from* u *to* v *in* G_{But} *is as follows:* u *sends the message along all paths* $P_{u,v}$, v *receives all the messages and takes majority.*

Theorem 5 ([12]).   *For the* $n = m2^m$-*node network* $G_{But} = (V, E)$ *and the protocol* Π_{But} *for message transmission on it, there exists constants* α_1 *and* β_1, *such that:*

1. *The network* G_{But} *is of constant degree, namely 11.*
2. *The work complexity is* $\tilde{O}(n)$.
3. *If a subset of nodes* $T \subset V$ *is corrupt, where* $|T| \leq \alpha_1 n / \log n$, *there exists a set of nodes* $S \subset V$ *where* $|S| \geq n - \beta_1 |T| \log |T|$[1] *such that for every pair of nodes* (u, v) *in* S, $(2/3)^{rd}$ *of the paths in* $P_{u,v}$ *have no corrupted nodes in them which implies that all pairs of nodes in* S *can communicate reliably with each other by invoking* Π_{But}.

---

[1] [12] also achieved an improved theorem with $|S| \geq n - \beta_1 |T|$ but we use this version as G_{But} is a simpler graph.

Upfal [21]

Theorem 6. *For sufficiently large n, there exists an n-node network $G_{Upfal} = (V, E)$, a protocol Π_{Upfal} for message transmission on it, and constants α_2 and β_2, such that:*

1. *The network G_{Upfal} is of constant degree[2].*
2. *The work complexity is Π_{Upfal} is $O(2^n)$.*
3. *Π_{Upfal} is $(\alpha_2 n, \beta_2 t)$-resilient.*

2.7   Corruption Models

We consider two models where a subset T of size t in the n node network can be corrupted.

Worst-case Model. The worst-case model is the strongest of our adversary models. In this model, the subset of T corrupt nodes can be chosen adversarially after the network topology and protocol for communication have been fixed.

Random Model. The randomized adversary model assumes that the t corrupted nodes are chosen uniformly at random from the set of n nodes. We call this model of picking a random subset of size t the Hamming Random Model or corruption. Alternately, a randomized adversary may make each node corrupt with probability t/n; we call this the Shannon model. Basic Chernoff bounds show that the Shannon and Hamming models are equivalent up to a constant factor difference in t with all but exponentially small probability. Thus, we freely switch between the two models in our exposition. While this model of corruption is primarily good for simulating phishing and password guessing attacks, our probabilistic approaches show that it can be the starting point for state of the art protocols against random and worst-case adversaries.

3   Constant-Degree Networks in the Random Model

In this section we will build a network that is resistant to linearly many random corruptions with an improved success probability as compared to Ben-or and Ron's work [3].

We turn our attention to the protocol of Chandran *et al.* [7]. Their protocol builds on the following observation. Consider the protocols of Dwork *et al.* [12] and Upfal [21] where if node A wishes to communicate with node B, A floods all paths from A to B (possibly of a bounded length) with the message. In Dwork *et al.* [12], the parameters are set to ensure that a majority of such paths contain no corrupt nodes (for most pairs of nodes A, B) while Upfal [21] employs an

---

[2] G_{Upfal} is an n node Ramanjuan graph, and we know such graphs with large enough constant degree.

exhaustive search to determine which paths may have contained corrupt nodes. These protocols face the disadvantage that paths that pass through even one corrupt node are lost. The work of Chandran *et al.* [7] introduced the idea of local correction through the use of Bracha committees. If we were able to create committees that had the ability to locally correct the message transmission, we can potentially tolerate a lot more corruptions than in Dwork *et al.* [12] and perform the final decoding more efficiently than in Upfal [21]. Chandran *et al.* [7] however considers many overlapping committees in order to ensure that even if a constant fraction of the nodes are corrupt, a sub-constant fraction of the committees are corrupt, where a committee is considered corrupt if a certain fraction of its nodes is corrupt. This calls for a larger degree. We show in this section that in our model of random corruptions, it suffices to construct fewer committees to achieve the same goal. Going forward, we refer to the networks (protocol, resp.) of Upfal [21] by G_{Upfal} (Π_{Upfal} resp.) respectively.

Let the set of nodes that wish to communicate be $V = [n]$ for $n \in \mathbb{N}$. We arbitrarily divide the nodes of V into n/s committees of size $s = (2/\alpha_2) \log \log n$ where α_2 is from Theorem 6. Within each committee, we instantiate G_{Upfal}, which is an expander of constant degree $d = O(1)$. We then connect the n/s committees using the network G_{But} from Theorem 5, where in order to connect two committees, we connect them by means of a perfect matching between the two sets of s nodes.

Definition 3.

Graph: *Our graph that is resistant to random errors is $G_{rand} = (V, E)$, where $V = [n]$. The edge set is as follows. Arbitrarily partition the nodes of V into n/s committees of size $s = (2/\alpha_2) \log \log n$. We let C_v denote the committee containing node v, where $C_u = C_v$ if u and v are in the same committee. Within each committee, we instantiate G_{Upfal}, which is an expander of constant degree $d = O(1)$. We then connect the n/s committees using the network G_{But}, where in order to connect two committees, we connect them by means of a perfect matching between the two sets of s nodes.*

Protocol: *We now describe the communication protocol Π_{rand} over this network. To this end, we first describe two building block protocols Π_{edge} and Π_{maj}.*

- *Π_{edge} is the protocol that is invoked when we wish to send a message from one committee, C to another C' that are connected in the G_{But} network (connected by means of a perfect matching). We will assume that each node in C is initialized with some message. In the protocol Π_{edge}, each node in C sends its message to the node it is matched to in C'.*

- *Π_{maj} is a majority protocol invoked within a committee C. We will assume that each node i in C is initialized with some message m_i. The goal of the Π_{maj} protocol is for each node in C to compute the majority function $m = \text{maj}\{m_i\}_i$. The protocol proceeds as follows: every node in C invokes Π_{Upfal} to send its message to every other node in C. Each node then simply computes (locally) the majority of the messages it received.*

Now, if a node A wishes to send a message m to node B:

(a) *If A and B are in the same committee C, then A simply sends the message to B by invoking Π_{Upfal} within the committee C.*

(b) *If A and B are in different committees, C_A and C_B respectively, then:*

   i. *A invokes Π_{Upfal} to send m to every other node in its committee C_A.*

   ii. *The committee C_A then invokes Π_{But} to send a message to the committee C_B. In the invocation of Π_{But}, whenever two committees C and C' connected by G_{But} wish to communicate with each other, they invoke Π_{edge} and then C' invokes Π_{maj}.*

   iii. *Finally, every node other than B in committee C_B invokes Π_{Upfal} to send the message they received to B. B computes (locally) the majority of the messages it received.*

Degree. The network constructed is of constant degree, namely $D = d + 11$.

We now wish to argue that in the presence of a set $T \subset V$ of randomly corrupt nodes with $|T| \leq \alpha_3 n$, there exists a set $S \subset V$ with $|S| \geq n - \beta_3 |T|$ such that every pair of nodes in S can communicate reliably with each other, for appropriately chosen universal constants α_3, β_3 to be determined later. The proof proceeds as follows. Under these choices of α_3, β_3, we first show that most committees must in fact contain less than an α_2-fraction of corrupt nodes. In such committees, Π_{Upfal} works successfully for all but an $\epsilon = O(\alpha_2)$-fraction of nodes in that committee by Theorem 6. Call such committees as *good* committees. From Theorem 6, in good committees there exists a set of *privileged* nodes of size at least $s - O(\alpha_2 s)$ that can communicate reliably with each other.

We now consider nodes A, B that wish to communicate with each other, and are *privileged* nodes in *good* committees. Hence, all but an ϵ-fraction of the nodes in C_A (the committee containing A) receive A's message correctly on executing Π_{Upfal}. On any execution of Π_{edge} between C_A and another committee C', all but at most an ϵ-fraction of the nodes in C' receive the correct value. Now, if C' is *good*, in the execution of the Π_{maj} protocol in C', all but at most a $\epsilon + \alpha_2 = O(\alpha_2)$-fraction of the nodes begin with the correct value and Π_{Upfal} works successfully for all but an ϵ-fraction of nodes. This ensures that as long as $\epsilon + \alpha_2 < 1/2$, all but at most an ϵ-fraction of the nodes compute the majority of the incoming messages correctly. Inductively, this would show that at the end of the emulation of the Π_{But} protocol, all but an ϵ-fraction of the nodes in the committee containing B receive A's message correctly and since C_B is a good committee and $\epsilon + \alpha_2 < 1/2$, B receives A's message correctly as B is *privileged*.

We now formalize this argument. We call a committee *good* if the fraction of corrupt nodes in it is at most α_2 and *bad* otherwise. Let $T \subset V$ be a set of randomly corrupt nodes with $|T| = t = \alpha_3 n$ where $\alpha_3 \leq \min\{\alpha_1, (\alpha_2/e)^2\}$ where the constant α_2 is from Theorem 6.

Lemma 1. *The probability that a committee is* good *is at least* $1 - (t/n)^{\log \log n}$.

Proof. The probability that a committee is bad is

$$\Pr[\text{A committee is bad}] \leq \binom{s}{\alpha_2 s}\left(\frac{t}{n}\right)^{\alpha_2 s}$$

$$\leq \left(\frac{es}{\alpha_2 s}\right)^{\alpha_2 s}\left(\frac{t}{n}\right)^{\alpha_2 s}$$

$$\leq \left(\frac{et}{\alpha_2 n}\right)^{\alpha_2 s}$$

Taking $\alpha_3 \leq (\alpha_2/e)^2$ which implies $\frac{e\alpha_3}{\alpha_2} \leq \sqrt{\alpha_3}$, i.e., $\frac{et}{\alpha_2 n} \leq \sqrt{\frac{t}{n}}$, we get

$$\Pr[\text{A committee is bad}] \leq \left(\frac{t}{n}\right)^{\frac{\alpha_2 s}{2}}$$

$$\leq \left(\frac{t}{n}\right)^{\log \log(n)}$$

as $s = (2/\alpha_2) \log \log(n)$.

Lemma 2. *The number of* bad *committees is at most* $\frac{t/s}{\log(n)}$ *with probability at least* $1 - (t/n)^{\alpha_2 t/(4\log(n))}$.

Proof. Let $\zeta = (t/n)^{\log \log n}$. Note that

$$1/\sqrt{\zeta} = (t/n)^{-\log \log n/2}$$

$$= (1/\alpha_3)^{\log \log n/2}$$

$$= (1/\alpha_3)(1/\alpha_3)^{\log \log n/2-1}$$

$$\geq (1/\alpha_3) \cdot (8)^{\log \log n/2-1}$$

$$= (1/\alpha_3) \cdot 2^{1.5 \log \log n-3}$$

$$\gg (1/\alpha_3) \cdot 2^{\log \log n+\log_2(e)}$$

$$= (1/\alpha_3) \cdot e \log(n) = en \log(n)/t \tag{2}$$

The probability that the number of bad committees is more than $\frac{t/s}{\log(n)}$ is

$$\leq \binom{n/s}{t/(s\log(n))}\zeta^{t/(s\log(n))}$$

$$\leq \left(\frac{en/s}{t/(s\log(n))}\right)^{t/(s\log(n))}\zeta^{t/(s\log(n))}$$

$$= \left(\zeta \cdot \frac{en \log(n)}{t} \right)^{t/(s \log(n))}$$

$$\leq \left(\sqrt{\zeta} \right)^{t/(s \log(n))} \qquad \text{from (2)}$$

$$= \left(\frac{t}{n} \right)^{\frac{\log \log(n) t}{2s \log(n)}}$$

$$= \left(\frac{t}{n} \right)^{\frac{\alpha_2 t}{4 \log(n)}}$$

$$= (t/n)^{\alpha_2 t/(4 \log(n))}$$

We have that if C is a *good* committee with $t' \leq \alpha_2 s$ corrupt nodes, from Theorem 6, there exists a set S_C (privileged nodes) of at least $s - \beta_2 t'$ nodes in C that can communicate reliably with each other. We say that a committee holds value v if all the privileged nodes in the committee hold value v.

Lemma 3. *If C and C' are* good *committees connected by an edge in G_{But} and if C holds value v, after invoking Π_{edge} and Π_{maj}, C' holds value v.*

Proof. Since C holds value v, at least $s - \beta_2 \alpha_2 s$ nodes in C' receive the value v after invoking Π_{edge}. Since C' is *good* at most $\alpha_2 s$ nodes in C' are corrupt. Hence, at least $s - (\beta_2 + 1)\alpha_2 s$ nodes in C' begin with the value v while invoking Π_{maj} in C'. Consider a node Z in the set $S_{C'}$ of privileged nodes in C'. As C' is good, we have $|S_{C'}| \geq s - \beta_2 \alpha_2 s$. Nodes in $S_{C'}$ receive messages reliably from each other. Out of the messages received by Z from nodes in $S_{C'}$ during the execution of Π_{maj}, at most $(\beta_2 + 1)\alpha_2 s$ may be unequal to v. The messages received by Z from the $\beta_2 \alpha_2 s$ non-privileged nodes may not be equal to v. Still each node in $S_{C'}$ will receive at least $s - (2\beta_2 + 1)\alpha_2 s$ copies of v. Hence, if $(2\beta_2 + 1)\alpha_2 < 1/2$, the claim follows. We note from [21] that it is possible to take $\alpha_2 = 1/72$ and $\beta_2 = 6$ which satisfies $(2\beta_2 + 1)\alpha_2 < 1/2$.

Considering the *bad* committees as corrupt nodes in G_{But}, there are at most $\frac{t/s}{\log n}$ of them with overwhelming probability by Lemma 2. From Theorem 5, there exists a set of committees P (privileged committees) that can communicate with each other reliably.

Lemma 4. *Let A and B be two nodes in privileged (good) committees $C_A \in P$ and $C_B \in P$ respectively. If $A \in S_{C_A}$ and $B \in S_{C_B}$, then the above protocol guarantees reliable message transmission from A to B.*

Proof. Note that if $C_A = C_B$, we are done by Theorem 6 as A and B are privileged. We consider the case $C_A \neq C_B$. Since $A \in S_{C_A}$, all nodes in S_{C_A} receive A's message, m, correctly and C_A holds m. Since $C_A, C_B \in P$, after the invocation of Π_{But}, C_B holds m. Since $B \in S_{C_B}$, it receives m from each node in $S_{C'}$. Hence B will receive at least $s - \beta_2 \alpha_2 s$ copies of v. If $\beta_2 \alpha_2 < 1/2$, the claim follows. We note from [21] that it is possible to take $\alpha_2 = 1/72$ and $\beta_2 = 6$ which satisfies $\beta_2 \alpha_2 < 1/2$.

Lemma 5. *With probability* $1 - (t/n)^{\alpha_2 t/(4 \log(n))}$, *there exists a set of nodes* $S \subset V$ *where* $|S| \geq n - \beta_3 |T|$ *such that every pair of nodes in S can communicate reliably with each other.*

Proof. The set S consists of nodes that are privileged nodes in privileged committees. We have that the total number of committees is $N_C = n/s$. Let t_C denote the number of bad committees. Note that with probability at least $1 - (t/n)^{\alpha_2 t/(4 \log(n))}$, $t_C \leq \frac{t/s}{\log n}$. Furthermore, since $t = \alpha_3 n \leq \alpha_1 n$ (by the choice of $\alpha_3 \leq \min\{\alpha_1, (\alpha_2/e)^2\}$), $t_C \leq \frac{t/s}{\log n} \leq \alpha_1 \cdot \frac{n/s}{\log n} \leq \alpha_1 \cdot \frac{N_C}{\log N_C}$. This implies that Theorem 5 is now applicable. From Theorem 5, the number of unprivileged committees is bounded by $O(t_C \log t_C) = O(t/s)$. Thus, the number of nodes in unprivileged committees is bounded by $s \cdot O(t/s) = O(t)$. Finally, we consider the unprivileged nodes in privileged committees. Let t_i denote the number of corrupt nodes in committee C_i for $i \in [n/s]$. The number of unprivileged nodes in privileged committees is upper bounded by

$$\sum_i O(t_i) = O\left(\sum_i t_i\right) = O(t)$$

from Theorem 6. Thus, $|S| \geq n - \beta_3 t$ for some constant β_3.

We summarize the result from this section in the theorem below.

Reminder of Theorem 2. *For sufficiently large n, there exists an n-node network* $G_{rand} = (V, E)$, *a protocol* Π_{rand} *for message transmission on it, and constants* α_3 *and* β_3, *such that:*

1. *The network* G_{rand} *is of constant degree.*
2. *If a subset of nodes* $T \subset V$ *is randomly corrupt, where* $|T| \leq \alpha_3 n$, *with probability* $1 - (t/n)^{\alpha_2 t/(4 \log(n))}$, *there exists a set of nodes* $S \subset V$ *where* $|S| \geq n - \beta_3 |T|$ *such that every pair of nodes in S can communicate reliably with each other by invoking* Π_{rand}.

Note that at $t = \Theta(n)$ we get that the protocol works with probability $1 - 2^{-\Omega\left(\frac{n}{\log(n)}\right)}$ which improves upon [3] which achieved $1 - 2^{-\Omega\left(\frac{n}{\log^2(n)}\right)}$.

We end this section with the following remark. Let $|T| = t$. Note that in [7], the number of nodes that can communicate with each other reliably is $n - t - O(t/\log n)$, that is, we give up at most $O(t/\log n) = o(t)$ nodes. We remark that this is not achievable in networks of constant degree even in the random model. In an adversarial corruption setting, one can corrupt the neighbors of $O(t/d)$ nodes, and hence if $d = O(1)$, any protocol must give up $O(t)$ nodes. This is true even in the random corruption model: a node has corrupt neighbors with some constant probability if $t = O(n)$ and hence any protocol must give up $O(t)$ nodes. Similarly, in networks of $\log \log n$ degree, any protocol must give up $O(t/(\log n)^{\Theta(1)})$ nodes.

4   Logarithmic Degree Networks in the Worst-Case Model

In the worst-case model, the current best networks are those constructed by Chandran, Garay and Ostrovsky [7]. They construct a graph with degree $d = \log^q n$ for some fixed constant $q > 1$, that is resilient to $t = O(n)$ adversarial corruptions. We show using a probabilistic argument the existence of a network of degree $O(\log n)$ that is resilient to $t = O(n)$ adversarial corruptions. Furthermore, the probabilistic construction works with all but negligibly small probability.

Our construction is also rather simple, and uses our network that is resilient to random errors as a black box. This style of our argument provides further motivation for studying the random corruption model, even if the ultimate goal is to be resilient to adversarial corruptions.

Definition 4.

Graph: *Our graph that is resistant to worst-case errors is $G_{wc} = (V, E)$, where $V = [n]$. The edge set is as follows. Let $\{G^i_{rand}\}_i = \{(V^R_i, E_i)\}_i$ be our network, G_{rand}, resilient to random corruptions on a randomly permutation V^R_i of the vertex set V, for $1 \leq i \leq z \triangleq k \cdot \log n$ for $k = 40/\alpha_2$, where α_2 is the constant from Theorem 6. Define $E \triangleq \bigcup_{i=1}^z E_i$.*

Protocol: *We now describe the communication protocol Π_{wc} over this network. Let Π^i_{rand} be the reliable transmission protocol associated with the network G^i_{rand} as described in Definition 3, for each $1 \leq i \leq z$. Now, if a node A wishes to send a message m to node B:*

(a) A will invoke the protocol Π^i_{rand} to transmit the message m to B over the network G^i_{rand}.

(b) B receives z messages, corresponding to the z executions of Π^i_{rand} for $1 \leq i \leq z$. B takes the majority of all these messages.

Degree. The network constructed is of degree $O(\log n)$, since the network is constructed using $z = O(\log n)$ copies of the constant degree network G_{rand} from Definition 3.

We proceed to prove resiliency of the protocol. We will first consider an arbitrary fixed adversary $T \subset V$, estimate the probability of resilience against it and finally perform a union bound over all adversaries. Consider an arbitrary fixed adversary. We will say that the ith layer is bad for this fixed adversary if the conditions in Theorem 2 do not hold for G^i_{rand}. Correspondingly we call a layer good for this adversary if the conditions in Theorem 2 hold. In Lemma 6, we prove that with high probability only at most $(1/5)$th of the layers are bad.

Consider a good layer i, for some $1 \leq i \leq z$. We define D_i to be set of doomed nodes in protocol Π^i_{rand}. By Theorem 2, $|D_i| \leq \beta_3 |T|$. For an arbitrary fixed adversary, we will show that the set D_i behaves as a small random set as a result of permuting the vertex set V to obtain V^R_i over which G^i_{rand} is constructed. For any honest node $v \in V$, let L^D_v denote the set of all good layers i such that $v \in D_i$, that is, v is doomed in layer i. We will finally show that, with high probability, for most nodes v, $|L^D_v|$ is small.

To wrap up the proof, we designate a node $v \in V$ as doomed for Π_{wc} with respect to this fixed adversary if $|L_v^D| > (1/10)z$. Consider a pair of privileged nodes (nodes that are honest and not designated as doomed for Π_{wc}) $A, B \in V$. Since, with high probability, at most $(1/5)$th of the layers are bad and, by definition, A, B are doomed in at most $(1/10)$th of the good layers, A, B are both privileged in at least $(3/5)$th of the good layers with respect to this adversary. Hence a majority of the messages sent by A in Π_{wc} reach B correctly and B's majority is computed correctly. By our earlier claim, with high probability, the number of doomed nodes is small, that is, most nodes are privileged and can hence communicate reliably in the presence of this fixed adversary with high probability. Performing a union bound over all possible adversaries, we get our final result.

We now formalize this argument. Let $T \subset V$ be an arbitrary set of corrupt nodes with $|T| = t = \alpha_4 n$ where $\alpha_4 \leq \min\{\alpha_3, 1/10, \frac{1}{11^{4/3}e^{3/2}\beta_3^{4/3}} \approx \frac{.01}{\beta_3^{4/3}}\}$ where the constant α_3 is from Theorem 2.

Lemma 6. *For a fixed adversary, with probability at least* $1 - n^{\frac{32}{\alpha_2}} \cdot \left(\frac{n}{t}\right)^{-2t}$, *at most* $\delta = \frac{1}{5}$ *fraction of the layers are bad.*

Proof. Note that the ith layer is constructing by randomly and independently permuting the vertex set V to obtain V_i^R over which G_{rand}^i is constructed. This is equivalent to constructing G_{rand}^i over V and thinking of the adversary as being a random subset of V of size $|T|$. This enables to apply Theorem 2. By Theorem 2, for a fixed adversary, the ith layer is bad independently with probability $\leq (t/n)^{\alpha_2 t/(4 \log n)}$. So the probability that δz out of the z layers are bad is

$$\Pr[\delta z \text{ out of the } z \text{ layers are bad}] \leq \binom{z}{\delta z}\left(\left(\frac{t}{n}\right)^{\alpha_2 t/(4 \log n)}\right)^{\delta z}$$

$$\leq \left(\frac{ez}{\delta z}\right)^{\delta z}\left(\left(\frac{t}{n}\right)^{\alpha_2 t/(4 \log n)}\right)^{\delta k \log n}$$

$$= \left(\frac{e}{\delta}\right)^{\delta k \log n}\left(\left(\frac{t}{n}\right)^{\alpha_2 t/4}\right)^{\frac{8}{\alpha_2}}$$

$$= (5e)^{(8/\alpha_2)\cdot \log n}\left(\frac{t}{n}\right)^{2t}$$

$$= (5e)^{(8/\alpha_2)\cdot \log n}\left(\frac{n}{t}\right)^{-2t}$$

$$= n^{(8/\alpha_2)\cdot \log(5e)}\left(\frac{n}{t}\right)^{-2t}$$

$$\leq n^{32/\alpha_2} \cdot \left(\frac{n}{t}\right)^{-2t}$$

Lemma 7. *For a fixed adversary and a fixed layer i, the probability that $D_i = S \subset V \setminus T$ only depends on $|S|$.*

Proof. Consider a fixed adversary and a fixed layer i. Let π_i be a permutation of V and let $\pi_i(V) = V_i^R$. Also, let $\pi_i(T) = T_i^R$. Let $D_i^R \subset V_i^R \setminus T_i^R$ be the doomed nodes in V_i^R with respect to this adversary. Note that D_i^R is fixed by the choice of T_i^R, or equivalently, by the choice of $\pi_i(T)$. Let $D_i \subset V \setminus T$ be the set of doomed nodes in V. Note that $\pi_i(D_i) = D_i^R$. By symmetry, for any two subsets $S_1, S_2 \subset V \setminus T$ with $|S_1| = |S_2| = |D_i^R|$, the number of permutations π such that:

- $\pi(T) = T_i^R$ and $\pi(S_1) = D_i^R$
- $\pi(T) = T_i^R$ and $\pi(S_2) = D_i^R$

is the same, and is equal to the number of permutations of the remaining $|V| - |T| - |D_i^R|$ nodes. Hence, the probability that $D_i = S \subset V \setminus T$ only depends on $|S|$. $\qquad\blacksquare$

For a fixed adversary and a fixed honest node $v \in V \setminus T$, let L_v^D denote the set of all good layers i such that $v \in D_i$, that is, v is doomed in layer i.

Lemma 8. *For a fixed adversary, with probability $1 - \left(\frac{11e\beta_3 t}{n}\right)^{8t}$, the number of honest nodes v such that $|L_v^D| \geq z/10$ is at most $\beta_4 t / \log n$. ($\beta_4 = 2\alpha_2$)*

Proof. Let layer i be good. This implies that $|D_i| \leq \beta_3 t$ by Theorem 2. Without loss of generality we can assume that $|D_i| = \beta_3 t$ as more doomed nodes is worse for us. Let v be an arbitrary honest node. By Lemma 7,

$$\Pr[v \in D_i] = \frac{\beta_3 t}{n - t}$$

as all subsets of honest nodes of size $\beta_3 t$ are equally likely and the number of honest nodes is $n - t$.

As all layers are sampled independently, we have

$$\Pr[|L_v^D| \geq z/10] \leq \binom{z}{z/10} \left(\frac{\beta_3 t}{n - t}\right)^{z/10}$$

$$\leq \left(\frac{ez}{z/10}\right)^{z/10} \left(\frac{\beta_3 t}{n - t}\right)^{z/10}$$

$$\leq \left(\frac{10e\beta_3 t}{n - t}\right)^{z/10}$$

$$\leq \left(\frac{11e\beta_3 t}{n}\right)^{z/10}$$

where the last inequality follows from $t \leq n/10$.

Let u, v be two honest nodes. We have that $\Pr[v \in D_i] = \frac{\beta_3 t}{n-t}$, while $\Pr[u \in D_i | v \in D_i] = \frac{\beta_3 t - 1}{n-t-1} < \frac{\beta_3 t}{n-t}$. Hence the events $u \in D_i$ and $v \in D_i$ are anti-correlated. This implies that $|L_v^D| \geq z/10$ and $|L_u^D| \geq z/10$ are also anti-correlated. As we want to upper bound the number of nodes A which satisfy $|L_A^D| \geq z/10$, we can assume that the events $|L_v^D| \geq z/10$ and $|L_u^D| \geq z/10$ are independent.

The probability that for more than $\beta_4 t / \log n$ honest nodes $|L_v^D| \geq z/10$ with $\beta_4 = \alpha_2/2$ is

$$
\begin{aligned}
\Pr \left[\text{For over } t / \log n \text{ honest nodes, } |L_v^D| \geq z/10 \right] &\leq \left(\left(\frac{11 e \beta_3 t}{n} \right)^{z/10} \right)^{\beta_4 t / \log n} \\
&= \left(\frac{11 e \beta_3 t}{n} \right)^{k \beta_4 t / 10} \\
&= \left(\frac{11 e \beta_3 t}{n} \right)^{4 \beta_4 t / \alpha_2} \\
&= \left(\frac{11 e \beta_3 t}{n} \right)^{8t}
\end{aligned}
$$

Reminder of Theorem 3. *For sufficiently large n, there exists an n-node network $G_{wc} = (V, E)$, a protocol Π_{wc} for message transmission on it, and constants α_4 and β_4, such that:*

1. *The network G_{wc} is of degree $O(\log n)$.*
2. *Π_{wc} is $(\alpha_4 n, \beta_4 t / \log n)$-resilient.*

Proof. For a fixed adversary A, let E_1^A be the event that less than $z/5$ of the layers are bad. Then by Lemma 6, $\Pr[E_1^A] \geq 1 - n^{\frac{32}{\alpha_2}} \cdot \left(\frac{n}{t}\right)^{-2t}$. Let E_1 be the event that E_1^A holds for all adversaries A with t corruptions. By a union bound over all such adversaries,

$$
\begin{aligned}
\Pr[E_1] &\geq 1 - \binom{n}{t} \cdot n^{\frac{32}{\alpha_2}} \cdot \left(\frac{n}{t}\right)^{-2t} \\
&\geq 1 - \left(\frac{en}{t}\right)^t \cdot \left(\frac{n}{t}\right)^{-2t} \cdot n^{\frac{32}{\alpha_2}} \\
&= 1 - \left(\frac{et}{n}\right)^t \cdot n^{\frac{32}{\alpha_2}} \\
&\geq 1 - \left(\frac{t}{n}\right)^{.5t} \cdot n^{\frac{32}{\alpha_2}} \qquad \text{As } t = n/10 \text{ which implies } e \leq \sqrt{\frac{n}{t}} \\
&\geq 1 - 1/n^{\omega(1)} \qquad [\text{For } t = \omega(1)]^3
\end{aligned}
$$

Let E_2^A be the event that the number of honest nodes v such that $|L_v^D| \geq z/10$ is at most $\beta_4 t / \log n$. Then by Lemma 8 for a fixed adversary $\Pr[E_2^A] \geq 1 - \left(\frac{11e\beta_3 t}{n} \right)^{8t}$. Let E_2 be the event that E_2^A holds for all adversaries A with t corruptions. By a union bound over all such adversaries,[3]

$$
\begin{aligned}
\Pr[E_2] &\geq 1 - \binom{n}{t} \left(\frac{11e\beta_3 t}{n} \right)^{8t} \\
&\geq 1 - \left(\frac{en}{t} \right)^t \cdot \left(\frac{11e\beta_3 t}{n} \right)^{8t} \\
&\geq 1 - \left(\frac{11^8 \cdot e^9 \cdot \beta_3^8 \cdot t^7}{n^7} \right)^t \\
&\geq 1 - \left(\frac{t}{n} \right)^t \qquad \text{As } t \leq \frac{n}{11^{4/3} e^{3/2} \beta_3^{4/3}} \\
&\geq 1 - 1/n^{\omega(1)} \qquad \text{[For } t = \omega(1)\text{]}
\end{aligned}
$$

Hence by union bound $\Pr[E_1 \wedge E_2] \geq 1 - 1/n^{\omega(1)} - 1/n^{\omega(1)} = 1 - 1/n^{\omega(1)}$.

E_1 implies that for any adversary $\leq 1/5$ fraction of the layers are bad. E_2 implies that for any adversary there exists a set of honest nodes $S, |S| \geq n - t - \beta_4 t \log n$ such that for all $v \in S$ $L_v^D \leq z/10$. Hence for any two nodes $A, B \in S$ they are both privileged in at least $1 - 1/5 - 1/10 - 1/10 > 1/2$ fraction of the layers. Hence the message from A to B will be correctly delivered on $> 1/2$ fraction of the layers hence B will find the correct message after taking majority. The set S behaves as the privileged set for the network G_{wc}, Π_{wc}.

5   Low-Work Protocols in the Worst-Case Model

It is our goal to design low degree graphs with efficient communication protocols for AE reliable message transmission. Our final networks are constructed by composing several simpler graph structures. An important graph that our work builds on is Dwork et al.'s *butterfly* network [12]. The diameter of a graph is a fundamental lower bound on the amount of work required for message transmission. Any graph with constant degree will necessarily have work complexity $\Omega(\log n)$. Thus, the logarithmic diameter of the butterfly network is optimal up to constant factors. Since the diameter is a fundamental lower bound on the work complexity of point to point transmissions in a network, we think of a polynomial work complexity in the diameter—polylogarithmic work complexity—as a reasonable definition for *work-efficient* in this context. Dwork et al.'s protocol which requires $\Omega(n)$ work complexity for a single point to point message transmission is thereby work-inefficient. Another weakness of Dwork et al.'s protocol,

---

[3] The case of $t = O(1)$ is trivial and can be handled by Theorem 5.

is that it floods the network, and thus nearly every node in the network is necessarily involved in every point to point message transmission. It would aid both efficiency and parallelizability of higher level protocols to significantly limit the number of nodes used for a point to point transmission.

We make simple modifications to Dwork *et al.*'s ideas to achieve a work-efficient protocol that requires only polylogarithmically many nodes to be active in any point to point communication in this section. Our main observation is that a u to v transmission over the Butterfly network need not flood all $\Theta(n/\log n)$ paths in the network to ensure reliable transmission. In fact, we show that picking a set of just $\Theta(\log n)$ paths between every pair of vertices, and sending the message only over those paths suffices. This reduces both the number of nodes used per point to point transmission and total work to $O(\log^2 n)$.

Definition 5. *The* efficient Butterfly *protocoled-network* $N_{Eff} = (G_{But}, \Pi_{Eff})$ *is as follows:*

> **Graph***: We use the Butterfly graph* $G_{But} = (V, E)$ *as defined in Definition 2 such that* $|V| = n = m2^m$. *For every pair* u, v *of distinct vertices in* V, *there exists a set of paths* $P_{u,v}$ *as defined in Definition 2 between* u *and* v. *Let* $Q_{u,v}$ *be a random subset of* $P_{u,v}$ *of size* $\Theta(\log n)$. *The subset* $Q_{u,v}$ *is sampled before the protocol and is fixed, in particular it is known to all the nodes as well as the adversary.*
>
> **Protocol***: The message transmission protocol* Π_{Eff} *from* u *to* v *in* G_{Eff} *is as follows:* u *sends the message along all paths in* $Q_{u,v}$, v *receives all the messages and takes majority.*

Lemma 9. *For the* $n = m2^m$*-node network* $G_{But} = (V, E)$ *and the protocol* Π_{Eff} *for message transmission on it the following statements hold:*

1. *The network* G_{But} *has degree 11.*
2. *The total work is* $O(\text{polylog}(n))$.
3. *There is a constant* $\varepsilon \in (0,1)$ *such that* Π_{Eff} *is* $(\varepsilon n/\log n, O(t\log t))$-*resilient with probability* $1 - o(1)$.

Proof. It is clear that the degree of the network is 11 and that the work complexity in the protocol are $O(\text{polylog}(n))$ as we send $\Theta(\log n)$ messages on paths of length $\Theta(\log n)$.

We now prove the resilience guarantee. Consider any fixed subset $T \subset V$ with $t = |T| \leq \alpha_1 n/\log n$, where α_1 is that of Theorem 5. By Theorem 5, we know that there is a set V' of size $n - \beta_1 t \log t$ that can communicate reliably with each other by invoking Π_{But}. For any pair of vertices $u, v \in V'$, we let $P_{u,v}$ be the set of paths used in message transmissions from u to v by protocol Π_{But}. By Theorem 5 property (3) we know that at least a 2/3 fraction of the paths in each $P_{u,v}$ contain no corrupt node. We will assume that exactly 2/3 fraction of the paths in each $P_{u,v}$ contain no corrupt node as that is only worse for us. If a message is sent through a path with no corrupt nodes, the correct message reaches v. Let $Q_{u,v}$ be a random sample of $h = 144 \log_e(n) \approx 100 \log n$ paths from $P_{u,v}$. The protocol Π_{Eff} sends a message from u to v as follows:

1. u sends the message along all the paths $Q_{u,v}$,
2. v receives all h messages that were sent along the paths in $Q_{u,v}$ and takes the majority.

We now argue when this majority will be the correct message with high probability. Fix two nodes $u, v \in V'$ and fix an adversary (the subset of corrupted nodes). We look at the paths $Q_{u,v}$ in a communication from u to v. The expected number of paths, μ, in $Q_{u,v}$ with a corrupted node is $\mu = h/3$. So, we define $\delta = \frac{1/2}{1/3} - 1$ and by the Chernoff bound from Eq. 1, the probability that a majority of the paths $Q_{u,v}$ contain a corrupt node is:

$$\Pr[\text{majority of paths } Q_{u,v} \text{ are incorrect}] \le e^{-\delta^2 \mu/3}$$

$$\le e^{-(1/2)^2 \cdot (h/9)}$$

$$\left[\text{As } \delta = \frac{1/2}{1/3} - 1 \text{ and } \mu = h/3 \right]$$

$$= e^{-h/36}$$

$$= e^{-4 \log_e(n)}$$

$$= 1/n^4$$

We call a pair of vertices $\{u, v\}$ a *doomed-pair* if a majority of paths between them contain a corrupt node. For a fixed adversary, the probability that there are more than g doomed-pairs is bounded above by

$$\binom{n^2}{g} \left(\frac{1}{n^4} \right)^g \le \left(\frac{en^2}{g} \right)^g \left(\frac{1}{n^4} \right)^g < \left(\frac{e}{n^2} \right)^g$$

since the probability of pair corruptions is independent conditioned on the adversary. To show that the construction works for an adversarially chosen set of corruptions, we take a union bound over all adversaries. The probability that there is an adversary with t corruptions for which the number of doomed-pairs is at least g is bounded above by:

$$\binom{n}{t} \left(\frac{e}{n^2} \right)^g$$

Setting $g = t$ we get $\binom{n}{t} \left(\frac{e}{n^2} \right)^g \le \left(\frac{en}{t} \right)^t \left(\frac{e}{n^2} \right)^t \le \left(\frac{e^2}{n} \right)^t = o(1)$. Hence the number of doomed-pairs $u, v \in V'$ is $\le t$ w.p. $1 - o(1)$. Let S be the set of vertices $v \in V'$ which are not in any doomed-pair. The set S is privileged for N_{eff} as for any $A, B \in S$ the majority of paths $Q_{A,B}$ have no corrupt nodes and hence B decodes the correct message by taking majority. As w.p. $1 - o(1)$ the number of doomed-pairs is $\le t$ which implies that number of nodes in any doomed-pair is $\le 2t$. Hence $|S| \ge |V'| - 2t$ w.p. $1 - o(1)$. By Theorem 5, $|V'| \ge n - \beta_1 t \log t$ hence $|S| \ge n - (\beta_1 + 2)t \log t$ w.p. $1 - o(1)$ which implies that the number of doomed nodes is $O(t \log t)$.

Lemma 9 shows that the network $N_{Eff} = (G_{But}, \Pi_{Eff})$ satisfies resilience only with high probability—not deterministically. We now show, via the probabilistic method, that the resilience guarantee can be made deterministic; yet we state it explicitly, because this is the protocol that we use to enable our main theorem.

Reminder of Theorem 4. *For the* $n = m2^m$-*node network* $G_{But} = (V, E)$ *there is a protocol* Π^*_{Eff} *for message transmission on it such that the following holds:*

1. *The network* G_{But} *has degree 11.*
2. *The total work of the protocol is* $O(\text{polylog}(n))$.
3. *There is a constant* $\varepsilon \in (0, 1)$ *such that* Π^*_{Eff} *is* $(\varepsilon n/\log n, O(t \log t))$-*resilient.*

Proof. Since Lemma 9 holds with probability greater than 0, and the randomness is just over the protocol Π_{Eff}, there is some specific protocol Π^*_{Eff} in the support of Π_{Eff} that has properties (1–3). $\square$

5.1 Resilient and Efficient Networks

We now show how to modularly substitute-in our work-efficient protocol on the Butterfly network, in order to get work-efficient versions of Theorems 2 and 3. The high level idea is simple. The protocol Π_{rand} uses Π_{But} as a blackbox, and the protocol Π_{wc} uses a Π_{rand} as a blackbox. Substituting the efficient protocol Π^*_{Eff} in for Π_{But} into Π_{rand} creates an efficient version of Π_{rand}, which we call $\Pi_{rand,eff}$ below; and substituting $\Pi_{rand,eff}$ into Π_{wc} creates an efficient version of Π_{wc}, which we call $\Pi_{wc,eff}$ below. We describe the details of these subsitutions in the following theorems.

We substitute Π^*_{Eff} in for Π_{But} in Π_{rand} to strengthen Theorem 2 to the following:

Theorem 7. *For sufficiently large* n, *there exists an* n-*node network* $G_{rand} = (V, E)$, *a protocol* $\Pi_{rand,eff}$ *for message transmission on it, and constants* α_3 *and* β_3, *such that:*

1. *The network* $G_{rand,eff}$ *is of constant degree.*
2. *The Work complexity of* $G\Pi_{rand,eff}$ *is* $O(\text{polylog}(n))$.
3. *If a subset of nodes* $T \subset V$ *is randomly corrupt, where* $|T| \leq \alpha_3 n$, *with probability* $1 - (t/n)^{\alpha_2 t/(4\log(n))}$, *there exists a set of nodes* $S \subset V$ *where* $|S| \geq n - \beta_3|T|$ *such that every pair of nodes in* S *can communicate reliably with each other by invoking* $\Pi_{rand,eff}$.

Proof. In Theorem 2 we note that work done inside a single committee was exponential in the size of the committee as we instantiate G_{Upfal} (from Theorem 6) inside every committee. But as the size of the committee is $s = O(\log \log(n))$ this is only $O(\text{polylog}(n))$. Thinking of committees as super-nodes we had instantiated G_{But} over super-nodes. The total number of super-nodes used in a single message transmission was $\Omega(n/s)$ as we have n/s super-nodes. By using Π_{eff}

instead of Π_{But} we can bring this down to polylog$(n/s) \leq$ polylog(n), Sending a single message from a super-node to its neighbor requires running G_{Upfal} inside the committee which takes $O(\text{polylog}(n))$ work. Thus the total work is $O(\text{polylog}(n) \cdot \text{polylog}(n)) = O(\text{polylog}(n))$.

Finally, we substitute $\Pi^*_{rand,eff}$ in for Π_{rand} in Π_{wc} to strengthen Theorem 3 to our main theorem:

Reminder of Theorem 1. *For sufficiently large n, there exists an n-node network $G_{wc} = (V, E)$, a protocol $\Pi_{wc,eff}$ for message transmission on it, and constants α and β, such that:*

1. *The network G_{wc} is of degree $O(\log n)$.*
2. *The Work complexity of $\Pi_{wc,eff}$ is $O(\text{polylog}(n))$.*
3. *$\Pi_{wc,eff}$ is $(\alpha n, \beta t/\log n)$-resilient.*

Proof. The protocol Π_{wc} uses Π_{rand} as a blackbox $O(\log n)$ times, one for each layer. We substitute Π_{rand} with $\Pi_{rand,eff}$. This brings down the work complexity to $O(\log n \cdot \text{polylog} n) = \text{polylog} n$.

References

1. Barak, B., Canetti, R., Lindell, Y., Pass, R., Rabin, T.: Secure computation without authentication. In: Shoup, V. (ed.) CRYPTO 2005. LNCS, vol. 3621, pp. 361–377. Springer, Heidelberg (2005). https://doi.org/10.1007/11535218_22
2. Ben-Or, M., Goldwasser, S., Wigderson, A.: Completeness theorems for non-cryptographic fault-tolerant distributed computation (extended abstract). In: Proceedings of the 20th Annual ACM Symposium on Theory of Computing, Chicago, Illinois, USA, 2–4 May 1988, pp. 1–10 (1988)
3. Ben-Or, M., Ron, D.: Agreement in the presence of faults, on networks of bounded degree. Inf. Process. Lett. **57**(6), 329–334 (1996)
4. Berman, P., Garay, J.A.: Asymptotically optimal distributed consensus. In: Ausiello, G., Dezani-Ciancaglini, M., Della Rocca, S.R. (eds.) ICALP 1989. LNCS, vol. 372, pp. 80–94. Springer, Heidelberg (1989). https://doi.org/10.1007/BFb0035753
5. Berman, P., Garay, J.A.: Fast consensus in networks of bounded degree. In: van Leeuwen, J., Santoro, N. (eds.) WDAG 1990. LNCS, vol. 486, pp. 321–333. Springer, Heidelberg (1991). https://doi.org/10.1007/3-540-54099-7_22
6. Canetti, R.: Security and composition of cryptographic protocols: a tutorial (part I). SIGACT News **37**(3), 67–92 (2006)
7. Chandran, N., Garay, J., Ostrovsky, R.: Improved fault tolerance and secure computation on sparse networks. In: Abramsky, S., Gavoille, C., Kirchner, C., Meyer auf der Heide, F., Spirakis, P.G. (eds.) ICALP 2010, Part II. LNCS, vol. 6199, pp. 249–260. Springer, Heidelberg (2010). https://doi.org/10.1007/978-3-642-14162-1_21
8. Chandran, N., Garay, J., Ostrovsky, R.: Edge fault tolerance on sparse networks. In: Czumaj, A., Mehlhorn, K., Pitts, A., Wattenhofer, R. (eds.) ICALP 2012, Part II. LNCS, vol. 7392, pp. 452–463. Springer, Heidelberg (2012). https://doi.org/10.1007/978-3-642-31585-5_41

9. Chaum, D., Crépeau, C., Damgård, I.: Multiparty unconditionally secure protocols (extended abstract). In: Proceedings of the 20th Annual ACM Symposium on Theory of Computing, Chicago, Illinois, USA, 2–4 May 1988, pp. 11–19 (1988)
10. Dolev, D., Fischer, M.J., Fowler, R.J., Lynch, N.A., Strong, H.R.: An efficient algorithm for byzantine agreement without authentication. Inf. Control **52**(3), 257–274 (1982)
11. Dolev, D., Reischuk, R.: Bounds on information exchange for Byzantine agreement. In: ACM SIGACT-SIGOPS Symposium on Principles of Distributed Computing, Ottawa, Canada, 18–20 August 1982, pp. 132–140 (1982)
12. Dwork, C., Peleg, D., Pippenger, N., Upfal, E.: Fault tolerance in networks of bounded degree (preliminary version). In: Proceedings of the 18th Annual ACM Symposium on Theory of Computing, Berkeley, California, USA, 28–30 May 1986, pp. 370–379 (1986)
13. Garay, J.A., Ostrovsky, R.: Almost-everywhere secure computation. In: Smart, N. (ed.) EUROCRYPT 2008. LNCS, vol. 4965, pp. 307–323. Springer, Heidelberg (2008). https://doi.org/10.1007/978-3-540-78967-3_18
14. Goldreich, O., Micali, S., Wigderson, A.: How to play any mental game or a completeness theorem for protocols with honest majority. In: 1987 Proceedings of the 19th Annual ACM Symposium on Theory of Computing, New York, New York, USA, pp. 218–229 (1987)
15. King, V., Saia, J.: From almost everywhere to everywhere: Byzantine agreement with $\tilde{O}(n^{3/2})$ bits. In: Keidar, I. (ed.) DISC 2009. LNCS, vol. 5805, pp. 464–478. Springer, Heidelberg (2009). https://doi.org/10.1007/978-3-642-04355-0_47
16. King, V., Saia, J., Sanwalani, V., Vee, E.: Scalable leader election. In: Proceedings of the Seventeenth Annual ACM-SIAM Symposium on Discrete Algorithms, SODA 2006, Miami, Florida, USA, 22–26 January 2006, pp. 990–999 (2006)
17. King, V., Saia, J., Sanwalani, V., Vee, E.: Towards secure and scalable computation in peer-to-peer networks. In: Proceedings of the 47th Annual IEEE Symposium on Foundations of Computer Science (FOCS 2006), Berkeley, California, USA, 21–24 October 2006, pp. 87–98 (2006)
18. Lamport, L., Shostak, R.E., Pease, M.C.: The Byzantine generals problem. ACM Trans. Program. Lang. Syst. **4**(3), 382–401 (1982)
19. Lubotzky, A., Phillips, R., Sarnak, P.: Explicit expanders and the Ramanujan conjectures. In: Proceedings of the 18th Annual ACM Symposium on Theory of Computing, Berkeley, California, USA, 28–30 May 1986, pp. 240–246 (1986)
20. Pease, M.C., Shostak, R.E., Lamport, L.: Reaching agreement in the presence of faults. J. ACM **27**(2), 228–234 (1980)
21. Upfal, E.: Tolerating linear number of faults in networks of bounded degree. In: Proceedings of the Eleventh Annual ACM Symposium on Principles of Distributed Computing, Vancouver, British Columbia, Canada, 10–12 August 1992, pp. 83–89 (1992)
22. Yao, A.C.: Protocols for secure computations (extended abstract). In: 23rd Annual Symposium on Foundations of Computer Science, Chicago, Illinois, USA, 3–5 November 1982, pp. 160–164 (1982)

The Price of Active Security
in Cryptographic Protocols

Carmit Hazay[1]([⊠]), Muthuramakrishnan Venkitasubramaniam[2]([⊠]),
and Mor Weiss[3]

[1] Bar-Ilan University, Ramat Gan, Israel
carmit.hazay@biu.ac.il
[2] University of Rochester, Rochester, USA
vmuthu@gmail.com
[3] IDC Herzliya, Herzliya, Israel

Abstract. We construct the first actively-secure Multi-Party Computation (MPC) protocols with an *arbitrary* number of parties in the dishonest majority setting, for an *arbitrary* field $\mathbb{F}$ with *constant communication overhead* over the "passive-GMW" protocol (Goldreich, Micali and Wigderson, STOC '87). Our protocols rely on passive implementations of Oblivious Transfer (OT) in the boolean setting and Oblivious Linear function Evaluation (OLE) in the arithmetic setting. Previously, such protocols were only known over sufficiently large fields (Genkin et al. STOC '14) or a constant number of parties (Ishai et al. CRYPTO '08).

Conceptually, our protocols are obtained via a new compiler from a passively-secure protocol for a distributed multiplication functionality $\mathcal{F}_{\mathrm{MULT}}$, to an actively-secure protocol for general functionalities. Roughly, $\mathcal{F}_{\mathrm{MULT}}$ is parameterized by a linear-secret sharing scheme $\mathcal{S}$, where it takes $\mathcal{S}$-shares of two secrets and returns $\mathcal{S}$-shares of their product.

We show that our compilation is concretely efficient for sufficiently large fields, resulting in an overhead of 2 when securely computing natural circuits. Our compiler has two additional benefits: (1) it can rely on *any* passive implementation of $\mathcal{F}_{\mathrm{MULT}}$, which, besides the standard implementation based on OT (for boolean) and OLE (for arithmetic) allows us to rely on implementations based on threshold cryptosystems (Cramer et al. Eurocrypt '01); and (2) it can rely on weaker-than-passive (i.e., imperfect/leaky) implementations, which in some parameter regimes yield actively-secure protocols with overhead less than 2.

Instantiating this compiler with an "honest-majority" implementations of $\mathcal{F}_{\mathrm{MULT}}$, we obtain the first honest-majority protocol with optimal corruption threshold for boolean circuits with constant communication overhead over the best passive protocol (Damgård and Nielsen, CRYPTO '07).

1 Introduction

The problem of Secure Multi-party Computation (MPC) considers a set of parties with private inputs that wish to jointly compute a function of their inputs while simultaneously preserving *correctness* of the outputs, and guaranteeing

© International Association for Cryptologic Research 2020
A. Canteaut and Y. Ishai (Eds.): EUROCRYPT 2020, LNCS 12106, pp. 184–215, 2020.
https://doi.org/10.1007/978-3-030-45724-2_7

privacy of the inputs, i.e., nothing but the output is revealed. These properties are required to hold in the presence of an adversary that controls a subset of the parties, and attacks the protocol in an attempt to breach its security, e.g., learn more than it should about the honest parties' inputs.

Secure computation was first defined and explored in the mid 80s [5,7,19,50], and has been the focus of intensive study ever since. In the first two decades, research focused mainly on theoretical foundations, establishing the boundaries of feasibility and complexity. More recently, the focus has shifted to making MPC efficient and reducing its overhead over insecure implementations, both in terms of asymptotic and concrete efficiency (See [14,20,27,32,33,37,48,49], and references therein.)

A basic classification in MPC considers protocols in which security is guaranteed with: (1) an *honest majority*, namely when the adversary corrupts a minority of the participants; or (2) a *dishonest majority*, where the adversary can corrupt arbitrarily many parties. The second category, which captures two-party protocols as a special case, has the advantage that any single party need not trust anyone but itself. Designing protocols from the second category is significantly more challenging, and they can only guarantee computational security, i.e., against computationally-bounded adversaries. On the other hand, the first category admits conceptually simpler solutions with statistical (or even perfect) security, namely against computationally-unbounded adversaries.

An orthogonal classification of MPC protocols is based on the adversarial behavior: (1) *passive* adversaries that follow the protocol's instructions but try to learn more than the prescribed information; and (2) *active* adversaries that may arbitrarily deviate from the protocol. A common paradigm in MPC is to design first a passively-secure protocol, and then compile it into an actively-secure one.

Hence, an important efficiency metric for MPC protocols is the *overhead* of actively-secure protocols over (the best) passively-secure ones. A primary goal in MPC today is to reduce this overhead, and specifically to design actively-secure protocols with *constant overhead* over *state-of-the-art passively-secure* protocols. That is, to design protocols whose communication and computation overheads grow only by a constant factor compared to the underlying passive protocols.

This work focuses on one of the most challenging MPC settings: *active security with an arbitrary number of parties*. Ideally, we would like the price of achieving active security to be minimal compared to the passively-secure counterparts.

The past decade has seen tremendous progress in the design of concretely-efficient actively-secure protocols for arbitrary functions, specified as boolean or arithmetic circuits, in either the two-party [21,26,29,35,37,38,40–44,46–48,51], or the multi-party setting with an arbitrary number of parties [12,14,27,32,34, 39,49]. See Sect. 1.2 below for more details.

Despite this impressive progress there still remains important gaps between what is achievable with passive and active security. Indeed, no protocols for boolean computations with an arbitrary number of parties and constant communication overhead (even asymptotically) are known, both in the honest and the dishonest majority settings. For arithmetic computations with an arbitrary number of parties and over sufficiently large fields, the best concrete overhead (of 12x [17]) still seems large. In the honest majority setting an overhead of 2 has been achieved only for large fields [9].

Given this state of affairs, in this work we set out to answer the following fundamental open problem:

Can actively-secure protocols over an arbitrary field match the complexity of passively-secure protocols, in the dishonest and honest majority settings, with an arbitrary number of parties?

We resolve this open problem in terms of communication complexity in the affirmative, designing an asymptotically-efficient *actively-secure* protocol for *boolean* circuits (as well as arithmetic circuits over any field) in both the *honest majority* and *dishonest majority* settings, with *constant communication overhead* over the (best known) passively-secure counterparts.

We note that constant-overhead protocols are known based on general zero-knowledge proofs [19], but these solutions rely on "heavy" tools and are *practically inefficient*. Instead, we focus on designing protocols that make *black-box* use of simpler (and lightweight) primitives such as One-Way Functions (OWFs), and parallel Oblivious-Transfer (OT) or parallel Oblivious Linear function Evaluation (OLE) in the boolean and arithmetic settings (resp.). Relying on OTs/OLEs is, in a sense, necessary since these are special cases of secure computation in their respective settings. Moreover, since our protocols make black-box use of these primitives, they will benefit from future improvements in the costs of OT/OLE implementations, which have been steadily decreasing.

Moreover, to frame a clean theoretical question, we focus on designing modular protocols in which the (relatively) computationally-expensive "cryptographic" component is separated from the rest of the protocol, and abstracted as an ideal functionality. Specifically, the "cryptographic" abstraction we consider in this work is a (constant-round) parallel protocol for computing distributed multiplication. Relying on a general multiplication functionality instead of OT/OLE allows us to simultaneously capture many settings of interest (boolean/arithmetic computations, two/multi-party, honest/dishonest majority) in a unified way. More specifically, we abstract distributed multiplication as an $\mathcal{F}_{\text{MULT}}$ functionality that is parameterized by a secret sharing scheme $\mathcal{S}$ over some field $\mathbb{F}$, takes $\mathcal{S}$-shares of two secrets, and produces $\mathcal{S}$-shares of their product. It is easy to see that one can use a general reduction from OT (resp. OLE) to a random instance $\mathcal{F}_{\text{RMULT}}$ of $\mathcal{F}_{\text{MULT}}$ (which generates additive shares of random multiplication triples in the sense of Beaver's triples [3]) for boolean (resp. arithmetic) computations. In the multi-party setting, one can also realize $\mathcal{F}_{\text{MULT}}$ using more general protocols based on threshold additively-homomorphic encryption schemes [10].

Given the previous discussion, we can rephrase our motivating question:

Can actively-secure protocols over an arbitrary field match the complexity of passively-secure implementations of $\mathcal{F}_{\mathrm{MULT}}$, in the dishonest and honest majority settings, with an arbitrary number of parties?

1.1   Our Results – A New Framework

In this work we answer the open problem stated above with respect to communication complexity on the affirmative, introducing the first actively-secure protocol with constant communication overhead over passive GMW [19], for any number of parties and over any field, in the $\mathcal{F}_{\mathrm{MULT}}$-hybrid model.

We obtain our result via a new compiler which transforms a passively-secure protocol for $\mathcal{F}_{\mathrm{MULT}}$ into an actively-secure protocol for arbitrary functionalities, while inheriting the setting of the $\mathcal{F}_{\mathrm{MULT}}$ protocol (i.e., boolean/arithmetic, two/multi-party, and honest/dishonest majority). Specifically, the compiler is described in the $\mathcal{F}_{\mathrm{MULT}}$-hybrid model, and using different instantiations of $\mathcal{F}_{\mathrm{MULT}}$ we obtain actively-secure protocols with constant communication overhead in the boolean and arithmetic, two-party and multi-party, and honest and dishonest majority settings. Moreover, the overhead of our protocols is 2 for large fields and "typical" circuits (i.e., that have sufficiently many parallel multiplication gates; for our asymptotic result, it suffices for this width to be $\Omega(s)$, where s is a statistical security parameter).

Working in the $\mathcal{F}_{\mathrm{MULT}}$-hybrid model allows us to preserve a clear separation between the "passive" (alternatively, cryptographic) components of our protocol, namely the implementation of $\mathcal{F}_{\mathrm{MULT}}$, which relies on cryptographic assumptions; and the "correctness-enforcing" (alternatively, non-cryptographic) components which involve tools from the literature of honest-majority protocols, employing consistency tests to enforce honest behavior. Besides scalability (and reduced communication complexity), we believe our approach is simple and modular.

Our compiler improves over the state-of-the-art in several settings; see Table 1 for a summary, and Sect. 6 for a detailed discussion.

Table 1. Asymptotic communication overheads of our results in both the dishonest and honest majority settings for boolean and arithmetic computations. The "best passive" column refers to the passively-secure protocol over which the overhead is computed. The "theorem number" column specifies the theorem which implies the corresponding result.

Corruption Threshold	Number of Parties	Field Size	Hybrid Model	Asymptotic Overhead	Best Passive	Theorem Number
$t < n$	Arbitrary	$O(1)$	OT	Constant	[19]	Theorem 3
$t < n$	Arbitrary	Arbitrary	OLE	Constant*	[19]	Theorem 5
$t < n/2$**	Arbitrary	Arbitrary	—	Constant	[5]	Theorem 6

*Concretely, this constant is 2 for moderately wide circuits.
**We note that though in the honest majority setting guaranteed output delivery is achievable, our protocol only guarantees security with abort.

New protocols in the dishonest majority setting. Our compiler exhibits the most substantial improvements in the dishonest majority setting, yielding the *first* constant-overhead actively-secure protocol with a dishonest majority over an arbitrary number of parties for boolean circuits. The concrete constants of our compiler are yet unknown since they depend on the concrete efficiency of Algebraic Geometric (AG) secret sharing schemes over constant-size fields [8]. The result is summarized in the following informal theorem; see Theorem 3 for the formal statement.

Theorem 1 (Informal). *Any m-party function f over a constant-size field (resp., arbitrary size field) can be securely realized by an $O(d)$-round protocol in the OT-hybrid (resp., OLE-hybrid) model against an active adversary corrupting an arbitrary number of parties with total communication $O(m^2 |C|) + \mathsf{poly}(\kappa, d, m)$ field elements, where C is a depth-d circuit for f, and κ is a computational security parameter.*

For arithmetic computations, we can concretely analyze the constants introduced by our compiler, and show that they can be as small as 2 for moderately wide circuits and sufficiently large fields. This improves over [17] in two aspects. First, their work requires at least 12 invocations of an active implementation of $\mathcal{F}_{\mathrm{MULT}}$, while ours requires only two invocation of a passive implementation. This allows us to instantiate our compiler with passive implementations of $\mathcal{F}_{\mathrm{MULT}}$ based on threshold additively homomorphic encryption schemes [6,10]. Second, their result is only useful for computations over sufficiently large fields (where the statistical error $O(|C| / |\mathbb{F}|)$ is small), whereas our result applies to fields of arbitrary size.

Building on the recent result of Hazay et al. [25], we can extend our compiler to rely on a weaker-than-passive (e.g., imperfect or leaky) implementation of $\mathcal{F}_{\mathrm{MULT}}$. Consequently $\mathcal{F}_{\mathrm{MULT}}$ can be instantiated with lattice-based protocols with "aggressive" (weaker) parameters, yielding actively-secure compiled protocols whose communication cost almost matches that of the best passive protocols, namely, essentially achieving active security at the cost of passive!

Additionally, we achieve an interesting corollary in the constant-round regime for boolean computations. By viewing distributed garbling [4] as an arithmetic functionality over $\mathbb{GF}(2^\kappa)$, we can instantiate our compiler for arithmetic circuits to achieve constant-overhead over that passive variant of [4] instantiated with $\mathcal{F}_{\mathrm{MULT}}$ over $\mathbb{GF}(2^\kappa)$. See the full version [28] for details.

We believe our protocols can also be made to tolerate adaptive corruptions by instantiating the underlying cryptographic primitives (namely, $\mathcal{F}_{\mathrm{MULT}}$ and $\mathcal{F}_{\mathrm{COM}}$) with their adaptively-secure counterparts, and leave this to future work.

New protocols in the honest majority setting. In the honest majority regime for $t < n/2$, our compiler gives an actively-secure protocol for boolean circuits with constant overhead over a variant of passive-BGW [5] that is instantiated using AG secret sharing schemes. This result improves over the recent protocol by Chida et al. [9], which only achieves constant overhead for large fields (introducing an extra statistical security parameter s for small fields with an overhead of $s/\log_2(|\mathbb{F}|)$), and over Ishai et al. [31] who achieve constant-overhead for arbitrary fields, but only for few parties. We note that [11] achieves constant-rate secure protocols, but only for suboptimal corruption thresholds. For boolean computation with an arbitrary number of parties and optimal threshold, the best protocols are due to Genkin et al. [18] and achieve a $\mathsf{poly}\log(|C|,s)$ overhead, where $|C|$ is the circuit size.

1.2   Related Work

We give a brief overview of recent efficient protocols, summarized in Table 2.

The state-of-the-art: Boolean multi-party setting. For boolean circuits, secure protocol against a dishonest majority with an (asymptotic) constant overhead over passively-secure protocols, was achieved for constant number of parties by Ishai, Prabhakaran and Sahai [32] (referred to as the "IPS-compiler"). Their protocol operates in the OT-hybrid model, achieving constant overhead over passive-GMW. It also achieves constant rate, namely the communication complexity of evaluating a circuit C is $O(|C|) + \mathsf{poly}(\log|C|, d, m, \kappa)$, where d, m, κ are the depth of C, the number of parties, and a security parameter, respectively. For an arbitrary number of parties, the protocol of Genkin et al. [18] obtains $\mathsf{poly}\log(|C|, s)$ overhead over passive-GMW, where s is a statistical security parameter. This result is obtained by converting a boolean circuit C into a functionally-equivalent randomized circuit C' that is immune against so called "additive attacks", and evaluating C' using the semi-honest protocol of [19]. (This technique was originally introduced by [17], but was essentially only useful over large fields, see discussion below.)

The state-of-the-art: arithmetic multi-party setting. In the arithmetic setting in which the computation is performed over an arbitrary field $\mathbb{F}$, Genkin et al. [17] designed MPC protocols in the OLE-hybrid model, with a statistical error of $O(|C|/\mathbb{F})$, and constant communication overhead compared to an algebraic variant of passive-GMW [19], for sufficiently large fields $\mathbb{F}$. As described above, their result is obtained by converting a circuit C over some field $\mathbb{F}$ into its additively-secure variant C', and evaluating C' using passive-GMW and actively secure implementation of OLE. In practice, the constant in the communication overhead of their protocol is 12, and moreover their protocol is only useful for circuits over large fields (for which $O(|C|/\mathbb{F})$ is sufficiently small). For arbitrary fields, the work of Döttling et al. [15] give an actively secure protocol where the overhead is 22 invocations of an actively secure implementation of $\mathcal{F}_{\mathrm{MULT}}$ per multiplication gate of the circuit. A practical implementation for arbitrary number of parties was given in [34] based on "tailor-made" zero-knowledge proofs to achieve active security.

We note that in the *honest majority* setting, the recent work by Chida et al. [9] presents a new actively-secure protocol for arithmetic circuits that obtains overhead 2 over passive protocols for sufficiently large fields. Similar to our protocol, their protocol is in the $\mathcal{F}_{\mathrm{MULT}}$-hybrid model, where $\mathcal{F}_{\mathrm{MULT}}$ can be instantiated with any passively-secure protocol that further guarantees a notion of "security up to additive attacks" in the presence of active adversaries. It is unclear whether their paradigm extends to the dishonest majority setting, since their model of additive attacks is weaker than the standard one formulated in [17], where in all natural candidates an active attack translates into an additive attack in the latter (stronger) attack model, and is therefore not protected against by the framework of [9].

In an orthogonal vein, we note that Applebaum et al. [2] designed the first (variant of) passively-secure OLE based on LPN-style assumptions, implying secure arithmetic computation with asymptotic constant computational overhead over an insecure evaluation of the circuit.

The state-of-the-art: two-party setting. In the boolean setting, the protocols of [32] and [26] achieve (asymptotic) constant communication overhead over the passive protocols of [19] and [50], respectively. The latter has the added benefit of matching the number of OT calls in [50], which (unlike [19]) is sublinear in the circuit size. Practical implementations of [32] have been studied in [36], who identified bottlenecks in obtaining concretely-efficient protocols based on the IPS protocol due to the implementation of the so-called "watchlist channels". In the arithmetic setting, a recent work by Hazay et al. [25] instantiated the framework of [32] with a concretely-efficient honest majority protocol, obtaining small multiplicative overheads (between 2–8) compared to the passive protocol of [19].

Table 2. Asymptotic and concrete communication overheads of state-of-the-art 2PC and MPC protocols in the dishonest majority setting. The overhead is measured as the number of calls to the underlying (passively or actively secure) OT or OLE functionality, compared to the number of calls made by the passive-GMW to the corresponding (passively secure) functionality (OT or OLE). The concrete overhead column is specified only when the overhead is constant, and holds over sufficiently large fields. s denotes a statistical security parameter, and C is the circuit being evaluated.

Construction	Number of Parties	Hybrid Model	Asymptotic Overhead	Concrete Overhead
[32]	Constant	OT (passive)	Constant*	Unexplored
[41]	Two	OT** (active)	$O(s/\log s)$	—
[17]	Arbitrary	OLE (active)	Constant	12***
[15]	Two	OLE (active)	Constant	22[†]
[49]	Arbitrary	OT** (active)	$O(s/\log|C|)$	—
This work	Arbitrary	$\mathcal{F}_{\text{MULT}}$ (passive)	Constant	2

*In terms of asymptotic complexity, we note that [32] also achieves constant rate.
**Security is proven in the random oracle model.
***Based on personal communication with the authors.
[†]This constant holds for a particular instantiation of OLE based on noisy encoding.

2   Our Techniques

We first recall the so-called "IPS framework" of Ishai, Prabhakaran and Sahai [32], that constructs actively-secure m-party protocols for a function f using the following two weaker ingredients as a black-box: (1) an actively-secure honest-majority protocol (the "outer protocol") for f with m clients and n servers, tolerating active corruption of a minority $t < n/2$ of the servers and an arbitrary number of clients; and (2) a passively secure m-party protocol (the "inner protocol") for a "simpler" functionality, tolerating an arbitrary number of corruptions.

Using appropriate instantiations of the outer and inner protocols, this framework yields a constant-overhead (in fact, constant-rate) actively-secure protocol for boolean functionalities in the dishonest majority setting with a constant number of parties m. However, it does not obtain constant overhead for a super-constant m, as we now explain.

To watch or not to watch? The high-level idea of the IPS compiler it to have the m parties "virtually" execute the outer protocol by emulating its n servers. Specifically, the parties first obtain (through some joint computation) secret shares of the initial server states, then use the inner protocol on the shared states to generate (secret shares) of the outputs of the "next message" functions of each server. Since the outer protocol is only secure when a majority of the servers are honest, the parties must insure that most servers were correctly emulated, for which it suffices to verify that the parties behave honestly in sufficiently many of the inner protocol executions. The IPS compiler introduces a novel "watchlist" mechanism in which parties "watch" each other to enforce such honest behaviour. More precisely, every party P_i picks a random subset of t servers for which it learns the entire internal state throughout the computation. Consequently, P_i can check that all parties honest emulated the t servers, and abort if some party misbehaves. The identity of servers watched by honest parties remains hidden from the adversary, thus even a single honest party forces the adversary to honestly emulate most (specifically, a majority) of the servers. In terms of parameters, obtaining a $2^{-\Omega(s)}$ soundness error for a statistical security parameter s requires $t, n = \Omega(s)$. Since each corrupted party can choose an arbitrary subset of t watched servers, and there could be $m - 1$ corrupted parties, privacy is only preserved when $(m-1)t < n/2$. Since achieving constant-overhead requires $n = O(s)$, this is only possible for $m = O(1)$.

Compute first, check later. To solve this problem, our first idea is to have a *single* random subset of t servers which are *simultaneously* watched by *all* parties. Of course, now that the identity of the watched servers is known to all parties, it cannot be revealed before the computation has been completed. Instead, the subset is chosen using joint coin-tossing after the circuit has been evaluated, but before the output is reconstructed from the output shares. Correctness is preserved similarly to the original IPS compiler, but checking honest behavior after-the-fact might violate privacy. Indeed, unlike the IPS compiler we can no longer "catch" the adversary as soon as it deviates from the protocol, which raises two privacy concerns. First, by actively deviating from the protocol, the adversary can potentially violate the inner protocol privacy, and learn intermediate values during the circuit evaluation. Second, the adversary can potentially violate the privacy of the outer protocol, by "corrupting" a majority of the servers in the outer protocol (i.e., by not emulating them correctly). We note that even if the inner protocol has the stronger guarantee of remaining *private* even against *active* adversaries, this does not resolve the second issue because as long as the inner protocol is *not actively-secure*, active corruptions in it might violate correctness, which corresponds to corrupting servers in the outer protocol. Thus, an active adversary might still violate privacy in the outer protocol by violating correctness in the inner protocol (thus, in effect, corrupting possibly a majority of the servers).

Our approach. Due to these issues, we take a step back, and (instead of extending the IPS framework) focus on designing a new compiler that amplifies the security of a passively-secure inner protocol via a tailor-made outer protocol. Since we use different instantiates of the inner protocol, we model it more generally, assuming the parties have oracle access to an ideal multiplication functionality $\mathcal{F}_{\text{MULT}}$ that works over some agreed-upon secret sharing scheme $\mathcal{S}$. We note that in our compiler, we will not refer to "servers" (or an "outer" protocol), but rather think of these as "copies" of the circuit.

The combined protocol. To highlight the main components of our framework, we describe a basic MPC variant that will loosely rely on the passive BGW [5] protocol. Though this does not yield our asymptotic results, it will serve as a good starting point, which we build on to obtain our final framework (as described towards the end of the section).

At the onset of the computation each party P_i secret shares its input x_i using Shamir's secret sharing scheme with privacy parameter t, to obtain the shares $(X^1, \ldots, X^n)$ (as in the passive-BGW protocol). Then, P_i generates additive shares (x_j^l) of each Shamir share X^l, and sends $(x_j^l)_{l \in [n]}$ to P_j. The protocol will evaluates the circuit gate-by-gate as in passive-BGW, where addition gates are locally computed. We will preserve the invariant that when parties evaluate a gate G, they collectively hold additive shares of Shamir shares of the values of its input wires. That is, if G's inputs are values a, b which in the passive-BGW protocol have Shamir shares $(A^1, \ldots, A^n)$, $(B^1, \ldots, B^n)$ (respectively), then for every $l \in [n]$, party P_i holds values a_i^l, b_i^l such that $\sum_i a_i^l = A^l$ and $\sum_i b_i^l = B^l$.

In passive-BGW, multiplications are performed by having each party locally multiply its Shamir shares A^l, B^l, followed by all parties jointly running a degree-reduction sub-protocol on these products. However, in our modified protocol parties can no longer locally compute the products $A^l \cdot B^l$, because no party knows A^l, B^l (parties only know additive shares of these values). To solve this issue, we use an ideal distributed-multiplication functionality $\mathcal{F}_{\text{MULT}}$ which takes as input additive shares of two values x, y, and outputs a (fresh) additive sharing of their product $x \cdot y$. (We discuss $\mathcal{F}_{\text{MULT}}$ instantiations below.) This allows parties to learn additive shares of each product $A^l \cdot B^l$.

Once (additive shares of) the products $A^l \cdot B^l$ have been computed, degree reduction should be performed. In the classical passive-BGW protocol, degree reduction requires expensive communication, which is improved by protocols such as [13]. We use a new approach that significantly reduces the communication complexity, leveraging the fact that degree-reduction is a linear operation over the Shamir shares.

Local degree-reduction. Each party *locally* performs degree reduction over its additive shares of the Shamir shares. Across all parties, the additive shares obtained as a result of this procedure constitute a valid Shamir sharing of the "right" value, due to the linearity properties of Shamir's secret sharing scheme. Intuitively, the second secret-sharing layer allows parties to locally perform degree reduction, because it gives each party a *global "view"* of the protocol execution, as an additive share of the global view of the protocol execution.

Enforcing correctness. Once the computation is completed in all copies, we ensure it was performed correctly by incorporating a "correctness-enforcing" mechanism into the protocol. Specifically, before opening the output shares obtained at the outputs of all copies, we first run some correctness tests which will check that (with high probability) all parties honestly executed the computation. The output shares are revealed (and the output is reconstructed from these shares) only if all correctness tests pass.

To explain our correctness tests, we first analyze possible malicious strategies of corrupted parties. Roughly, a corrupted party can deviate from the protocol in one of four ways. First, it can incorrectly share its input (i.e., the "sharing" isn't of the right degree t). Second, it can incorrectly perform the degree-reduction procedure, by generating a fresh sharing that either isn't of the right degree (i.e., t), or doesn't share the right value (i.e., the value shared before degree reduction). Third, when evaluating a multiplication gate (i.e., computing the product of Shamir shares as described above), it can use different values than the ones provided by $\mathcal{F}_{\mathrm{MULT}}$. Fourth, it can incorrectly perform the local linear computations.

To handle such deviations from the protocol, we introduce three tests. The first is a *degree* test, which checks that the secrets sharings used by all parties, either to share their inputs or as input to multiplication gates, have the right degree. The second is an *equality* test, which checks that the secret sharings before and after degree reduction share the same value. The degree and equality tests jointly guarantee that with overwhelming probability, the input sharings are valid, and the degree reduction procedure was executed correctly (in most copies). Similar degree and equality tests were used in [1,25] to check similar conditions. The last test is a *consistency* test, which verifies that (with high probability) parties correctly performed the local computations in (most) copies of the circuit. This checks that the values used by the parties when evaluating a multiplication gate are consistent with the values they obtained from $\mathcal{F}_{\mathrm{MULT}}$, that the local linear operations were performed correctly, and will also guarantee the soundness of the degree and equality tests. For this test, a random subset of copies is chosen, each party reveals its local view of the computation in those copies, and all parties check that the views are consistent with each other. Similar tests were used in the context of MPC-in-the-head [30,32].

We note that this high-level overview omits important details (see Sect. 4). For example, the order in which parties commit and reveal the correctness tests' values is crucial to preserving privacy even when the computations in most copies are incorrect. Using this combination of correctness tests, and proving the security of this approach is novel to our work, and requires subtle analysis.

Achieving constant communication overhead. Our basic MPC protocol does not achieve constant communication overhead since it increases the communication complexity of the underlying BGW protocol [5] by $O(s)$, where s is a security parameter. We reduce this overhead to constant by replacing [5] with the protocol of Franklin and Yung [16] that uses packed secret sharing.

Loosely speaking, packed secret sharing extends Shamir's secret sharing, allowing a block of $\mathcal{B}$ secrets to be shared within a single set of shares. To exploit the advantages of packed secret sharing, we will assume the circuit is arranged in layers that contain only one type (addition/multiplication) of gates, where each phase of the protocol evaluates the gates in one layer.

Using packed secret sharing introduces two main differences from the basic protocol. First, before evaluating a specific layer the parties need to rearrange (repack) the shared secrets corresponding to the input wire values of that layer, to align the packing in blocks with the order of gates within the layer. Then, the layer can be evaluated similarly to the basic protocol (where additions are computed locally, and multiplications involve a call to $\mathcal{F}_{\text{MULT}}$, followed by a local degree-reduction step). The second difference from the basic protocol is that to insure correctness we must now check that the parties correctly rearranged the shared secrets between layers. This is checked through an additional "permutation test" [1,11]. See Sect. 5 for further details.

This protocol reduces the amortized per-gate communication overhead to constant, because in effect the packed secret sharing allows us to evaluate many gates in one "shot". In particular, the wider the circuit to be evaluated, the larger the gains from employing packed secret sharing.

Instantiating the multiplication functionality $\mathcal{F}_{\text{MULT}}$. We instantiate $\mathcal{F}_{\text{MULT}}$ through a reduction to a simpler functionality $\mathcal{F}_{\text{RMULT}}$ which generates (unauthenticated) random triples. All prior protocols that relied on this abstraction (apart from [32]), used actively-secure multiplication protocols to instantiate $\mathcal{F}_{\text{MULT}}$. Interestingly, we can greatly weaken the security of the multiplication protocol, requiring only a passively-secure instantiation, together with a coin tossing protocol to ensure correctly-sampled randomness. Moreover, our protocol can benefit from a preprocessing stage in an offline/online setting, where the triples are generated in the offline phase, and used in the online phase. The consistency test (described for our basic MPC protocol) will ensure, at the cost of a small overhead, that the triples were correctly generated with respect to the tossed coins. We note that unlike prior works, our security analysis can tolerate a small number of ill-formed triples without violating secrecy.

Related techniques. Conceptually, our consistency test can be viewed as a combination of the cut-and-choose approach [37] and the watchlist mechanism of [32]. Indeed, on the one hand we maintain multiple copies of the computed circuit, yet unlike the cut-and-choose technique the checked copies are not discarded, but rather used in the remainder of the computation to reconstruct the outputs. On the other hand, the purpose of our consistency test is similar to the watchlist channels, which add privacy and correctness to passively-secure protocols. The main difference between our tests and the watchlists of [32] is that in IPS these channels are used to *constantly* enforce correct behaviour *throughout* the protocol execution (and consequently also cause a high overhead), whereas we perform a single consistency test *after the protocol execution has (essentially) ended*, right before the output is reconstructed. These correctness enforcement mechanisms are known to have limitations to achieving scalable MPC. Specifically, the asymptotic limit of cut-and-choose is $O(s/\log|C|)$ [49], whereas the watchlists mechanism requires $O(s \cdot n)$ virtual servers for the outer protocol [36]. In both cases, the communication grows with some statistical parameter, and is hence neither constant-overhead nor scalable.

3   Preliminaries

In this section we provide necessary preliminaries. Further preliminaries are deferred to the full version [28].

Basic notations. We denote a security parameter by κ. We say that a function $\mu : \mathbb{N} \to \mathbb{N}$ is *negligible* if for every positive polynomial $p(\cdot)$ and all sufficiently large κ's it holds that $\mu(\kappa) < \frac{1}{p(\kappa)}$. We use the abbreviation PPT to denote probabilistic polynomial-time and denote by $[n]$ the set of elements $\{1, \ldots, n\}$ for some $n \in \mathbb{N}$. We assume functions to be represented by an arithmetic circuit C (with addition and multiplication gates of fan-in 2), and denote the size of C by $|C|$. By default we define the size of the circuit to include the total number of gates including input gates. For a random variable X, we use $\mathsf{Supp}(X)$ to denote the set of values which X takes with positive probability.

3.1   Layered Arithmetic Circuits

An arithmetic circuit defined over a finite field $\mathbb{F}$ is a directed acyclic graph, where nodes (or *gates*) are labelled either as input gates, output gates or computation gates. Input gates have no incoming edges (or *wires*), while output gates have a single incoming wire and no outgoing wires. Computation gates are labelled with a field operations (either addition or multiplication),[1] and have exactly two incoming wires, which we denote as the left and right wire. A circuit with i input gates and o output gates over a field $\mathbb{F}$ represents a function

---

[1] Subtraction gates can be handled analogously to addition gates, and we ignore them here for simplicity.

Functionality $\mathcal{F}_{\text{MULT}}$

Functionality $\mathcal{F}_{\text{MULT}}$ communicates with parties $P_1, \ldots, P_m$ and adversary $\mathcal{S}$ corrupting a subset $I \subset [m]$ of parties. It is parameterized by a secret sharing scheme $\mathcal{S} = (\text{Share}, \text{Recon})$ (see Section 3.3 below).

1. Upon receiving the input (sid, a_j, b_j) from P_j record $(\text{sid}, (a_j, b_j))$.
2. If a tuple is recorded from all parties continue as follows:
   (a) Compute $c = \text{Recon}(a_1, \ldots, a_m) \cdot \text{Recon}(b_1, \ldots, b_m)$.
   (b) Receive corrupted parties' shares $\{c_j\}_{j \in I}$.
   (c) Sample a secret sharing $(c'_1, \ldots, c'_m)$ uniformly at random from $\text{Supp}(\text{Share}(c))$ subject to the constraint that $c'_j = c_j$ for every $j \in I$. For every $j \notin I$, set $c_j = c'_j$.
   (d) Forward c_j to party P_j.

Fig. 1. The multiplication functionality.

$f : \mathbb{F}^i \to \mathbb{F}^o$ whose value on input $x = (x_1, \ldots, x_i)$ can be computed by assigning a value to each wire of the circuit. Note that this abstraction captures boolean circuits as well, by setting $\mathbb{F} = \text{GF}(2)$. In this work, we will exploit an additional structure of the circuit. Specifically, the gates of an arithmetic circuit can be partitioned into ordered layers $\mathcal{L}_1, \ldots, \mathcal{L}_d$, such that i) a layer only consists of gates of the same type (i.e., addition, multiplication, input or output gates belonging to the same party), and ii) the incoming wires of all gates of layer i originate from gates in layers 0 to $i - 1$.

3.2 Multiplication Functionalities

A core building block in our protocols is a multiplication functionality $\mathcal{F}_{\text{MULT}}$ shown in Fig. 1, that takes additive shares of two secrets over some field $\mathbb{F}$ and produces additive shares of their product. In fact, we will reduce $\mathcal{F}_{\text{MULT}}$ to a random instance $\mathcal{F}_{\text{RMULT}}$, shown in Fig. 2, where all shares are chosen uniformly at random from $\mathbb{F}$. The reduction, due to Beaver [3], is as follows. Denote by $[a]$ the additive sharing of some value $a \in \mathbb{F}$, namely, the tuple $(a_1, \ldots, a_m)$. Then, given a random triple $[a], [b], [c]$ obtained as the output of $\mathcal{F}_{\text{RMULT}}$, and inputs $[x], [y]$ for $\mathcal{F}_{\text{MULT}}$, we can compute $[xy]$ by first reconstructing $e = [x + a]$ and $d = [y + b]$. Next, the parties compute a (trivial) secret sharing $[ed]$ of ed by having P_1 set its share to ed, and the rest of the parties set their shares to 0. Finally, the parties compute the following equation (each party locally computes the equation on its own shares)

$$[xy] = [c] + e[y] + d[x] - [ed] = [ab] + (x + a)[y] + (y + b)[x] - (x + a)(y + b).$$

Functionality $\mathcal{F}_{\text{RMULT}}$

Functionality $\mathcal{F}_{\text{RMULT}}$ communicates with parties $P_1, \ldots, P_m$ and adversary $\mathcal{S}$ corrupting the subset of parties in $I \subset [m]$. It is parameterized by a secret sharing scheme $\mathcal{S} = (\text{Share}, \text{Recon})$ (see Section 3.3 below).

1. Receive corrupted parties' shares $\{a_j, b_j, c_j\}_{j \in I}$.
2. Sample secret shares $(a'_1, \ldots, a'_m)$ and $(b'_1, \ldots, b'_m)$ uniformly at random from $\text{Supp}(\text{Share}(\cdot))$ subject to the constraint that $a'_j = a_j$ and $b'_j = b_j$ for every $j \in I$. For every $j \notin I$, set $a_j = a'_j$ and $b_j = b'_j$.
3. Compute $c = \text{Recon}(a_1, \ldots, a_m) \cdot \text{Recon}(b_1, \ldots, b_m)$.
4. Sample a secret sharing $(c'_1, \ldots, c'_m)$ uniformly at random from $\text{Supp}(\text{Share}(c))$ subject to the constraint that $c'_j = c_j$ for every $j \in I$. For every $j \notin I$, set $c_j = c'_j$.
5. Forward a_j, b_j, c_j to party P_j.

Fig. 2. The random multiplication functionality.

3.3 Secret-Sharing

A secret-sharing scheme allows a dealer to distribute a secret among n parties, where each party receives a share (or piece) of the secret during a *sharing phase*. In its simplest form, the goal of (threshold) secret-sharing is to allow only subsets of players of size at least $t + 1$ to reconstruct the secret. More formally a $t + 1$-out-of-n secret sharing scheme comes with a sharing algorithm that on input a secret s outputs n shares $s_1, \ldots, s_n$ and a reconstruction algorithm that takes as input $((s_i)_{i \in S}, S)$ where $|S| > t$ and outputs either a secret s' or $\bot$. In this work, we will use Shamir's secret sharing scheme [45] with secrets in $\mathbb{F} = \mathbb{GF}(2^\kappa)$. We present the sharing and reconstruction algorithms below:

Sharing algorithm: For any input $s \in \mathbb{F}$, pick a random polynomial $p(\cdot)$ of degree t in the polynomial-field $\mathbb{F}[x]$ with the condition that $p(0) = s$ and output $p(1), \ldots, p(n)$.

Reconstruction algorithm: For any input $(s'_i)_{i \in S}$ where none of the s'_i are $\bot$ and $|S| > t$, compute a polynomial $g(x)$ such that $g(i) = s'_i$ for every $i \in S$. This is possible using Lagrange interpolation where g is given by

$$g(x) = \sum_{i \in S} s'_i \prod_{j \in S/\{i\}} \frac{x - j}{i - j}.$$

Finally the reconstruction algorithm outputs $g(0)$.

Packed secret-sharing. The concept of packed secret-sharing was introduced by Franking and Yung in [16] in order to reduce the communication complexity of secure multi-party protocols, and is an extension of standard secret-sharing.

In particular, the authors considered Shamir's secret sharing with the difference that the number of secrets $s_1, \ldots, s_\ell$ is now ℓ instead of a single secret, where the secrets are represented as the evaluations of a polynomial $p(\cdot)$ at ℓ distinct points. To ensure privacy in case of t colluding corrupted parties, $p(\cdot)$ must have degree at least $t + \ell$. Packed secret sharing inherits the linearity property of Shamir's secret sharing, with the added benefit that it supports batch (block-wise) multiplications. This was used to design secure computation protocols with an honest majority and constant amortized overhead [11]. For this reason, we use this tool in our honest majority MPC protocol embedded within our dishonest majority protocol from Sect. 4, leveraging its advantages to improve the overhead of the former protocol.

3.4 Error Correcting Codes

A crucial ingredient in our construction is the use of Reed-Solomon codes as a packed secret sharing scheme [16] (as defined in Sect. 3.3). In what follows, we provide our coding notations and related definitions.

Coding notation. For a code $C \subseteq \Sigma^n$ and vector $v \in \Sigma^n$, we denote by $d(v, C)$ the minimal distance of v from C, namely the number of positions in which v differs from the closest codeword in C, and by $\Delta(v, C)$ the set of positions in which v differs from such a closest codeword (in case of a tie, take the lexicographically first closest codeword). For any $k \leq d(v, C)$, we say that v is k-close to C, and for every $k > d(v, C)$, we say that v is k-far from C. We further denote by $d(V, C)$ the minimal distance between a vector set V and a code C, namely $d(V, C) = \min_{v \in V}\{d(v, C)\}$.

Definition 1 (Reed-Solomon code). *For positive integers n, k, finite field $\mathbb{F}$, and a vector $\eta = (\eta_1, \ldots, \eta_n) \in \mathbb{F}^n$ of distinct field elements, the code $\mathsf{RS}_{\mathbb{F},n,k,\eta}$ is the $[n, k, n - k + 1]$-linear code[2] over $\mathbb{F}$ that consists of all n-tuples $(p(\eta_1), \ldots, p(\eta_n))$ where p is a polynomial of degree $< k$ over $\mathbb{F}$.*

Definition 2 (Encoded message). *Let $L = \mathsf{RS}_{\mathbb{F},n,k,\eta}$ be an RS code and $\zeta = (\zeta_1, \ldots, \zeta_w)$ be a sequence of distinct elements of $\mathbb{F}$ for $w \leq k$. For $u \in L$ we define the message $\mathsf{Decode}_\zeta(u)$ to be $(p_u(\zeta_1), \ldots, p_u(\zeta_w))$, where p_u is the polynomial (of degree $< k$) corresponding to u. For $U \in L^m$ with rows $u^1, \ldots, u^m \in L$, we let $\mathsf{Decode}_\zeta(U)$ be the length mw vector $x = (x_{11}, \ldots, x_{1w}, \ldots, x_{m1}, \ldots, x_{mw})$ such that $(x_{i1}, \ldots, x_{iw}) = \mathsf{Decode}_\zeta(u^i)$ for $i \in [m]$. We say that u L-encodes x (or simply encodes x) if $x = \mathsf{Decode}_\zeta(u)$.*

Moreover, we recall that $\mathsf{Decode}_\zeta(\cdot)$ is a linear operation, i.e. for any $a, b \in \mathbb{F}^n$ (even if a, b are not in L), $\mathsf{Decode}_\zeta(a + b) = \mathsf{Decode}_\zeta(a) + \mathsf{Decode}_\zeta(b)$.

It will be convenient to view m-tuples of codewords in L as codewords in an interleaved code L^m. We formally define this notion below.

---

[2] We denote by $[n, k, d]$-linear code a linear code of length n, rank k and minimum distance d, where the minimum distance of the code is the minimal weight of a codeword in the code.

Definition 3 (Interleaved code). *Let $L \subset \mathbb{F}^n$ be an $[n, k, d]$ linear code over $\mathbb{F}$. We let L^m denote the $[n, mk, d]$ (interleaved) code over $\mathbb{F}^m$ whose codewords are all $m \times n$ matrices U such that every row U_i of U satisfies $U_i \in L$. For $U \in L^m$ and $j \in [n]$, we denote by $U[j]$ the j'th symbol (column) of U.*

4   Basic MPC Protocol

In this section we describe a simple variant of our MPC protocol, which we build on in Sect. 5 to achieve constant overhead.

Our starting point is a passively-secure variant of the BGW protocol [5], which we amplify to the actively-secure dishonest-majority setting. Amplifying the security of this protocol requires facing three challenges: (1) high overhead due to the degree-reduction sub-protocol; (2) security holds only with a dishonest minority; and (3) security holds only against passive corruptions.

Our strategy towards addressing the first issue is to have parties *locally* perform the degree-reduction procedure which the degree-reduction sub-protocol implements, thus (almost) eliminating the interaction it requires. This is achieved by using a second layer of secret-sharing.

Concretely, our MPC protocol with m parties relies on two layers of secret sharing schemes: (1) first layer sharing: Reed-Solomon codes (which can be thought of as Shamir's secret sharing), denoted by L-encoding, where $L = \mathrm{RS}_{\mathbb{F},n,k,\eta}$ (cf. Sect. 3.4); and (2) second layer sharing: additive secret sharing.[3] Throughout the execution, the parties hold additive shares of the L-encodings of the wires of the evaluated circuit C. We note that using this two-layer secret sharing decouples the number of parties m from the length of the encoding n, since (unlike passive-BGW) parties no longer hold the symbols of the L-encodings. In fact, it will be useful to have $m \neq n$. Intuitively, this can be though of as having the parties emulate n copies of C, where the wires of the l'th copy carry the l'th symbol in the L-encodings of the wire values of C, and these symbols are additively shared among the parties. The execution maintains the invariant that when evaluating the gates in layer $\mathcal{L}$, the parties hold for each copy l additive shares of the l'th symbols in the L-encodings of the outputs of previous layers.

Our protocol is described in the $\mathcal{F}_{\mathrm{RMULT}}$-hybrid model (cf. Sect. 3.2) which generates m additive shares of random triples, and is used to execute multiplications. In more detail, the parties evaluate the n copies of C layer by layer, locally performing additions, substractions and multiplications by a constant (this is possible due to the linear nature of our secret sharing schemes), whereas multiplication gates require communication.

Roughly, a multiplication gate G in the l'th copy of C is evaluated as follows. The parties hold additive shares of the l'th symbols A^l, B^l at the inputs of G,

---

[3] We note that the second layer sharing is added "on top" of the secret sharing used in BGW, and differs from the resharing performed in BGW (in which Shamir shares are reshared using *Shamir*'s scheme). This additional layer of additive sharing allows us to exploit the linearity of BGW's degree reduction procedure to perform degree reduction *locally*.

and use $\mathcal{F}_{\text{RMULT}}$ (and a reduction from $\mathcal{F}_{\text{MULT}}$ to $\mathcal{F}_{\text{RMULT}}$, described in Sect. 3.2) to obtain additive shares of the product $A^l B^l$. Across all copies, these products form an $\tilde{L}$-encoding of the output wire of G, where $\tilde{L} = \text{RS}_{\mathbb{F},n,2k,\eta}$. To obtain a fresh L-encoding of the output wire, each party interprets its additive shares of the $\tilde{L}$-encoding (across all copies) as an encoding in $\text{RS}_{\mathbb{F},n,n,\eta}$, decodes it, and then generates a fresh L-encoding of this decoded value. The additive shares obtained through this procedure reconstruct to the correct value because degree reduction is a linear operation.

Employing a second secret-sharing layer solves the second challenge (that passive-BGW is only private in the honest majority setting) since a subset of parties learn only a strict subset of additive shares. The third challenge (passive-BGW is only secure against passive corruptions) is handled by incorporating correctness-enforcing tests into the protocol, as described in Sect. 2.

Our detailed protocol is given in Figs. 3, 4 and 5. We next state the following theorem; its proof appears in the full version [28].

Theorem 1. *Protocol Φ described in Figs. 3, 4 and 5 securely realizes $\mathcal{F}$ in the $(\mathcal{F}_{\text{COM}}, \mathcal{F}_{\text{RMULT}}, \mathcal{F}_{\text{COIN}})$-hybrid model, tolerating $m-1$ active (static) corruptions, with statistical security error*

$$(1 - e/n)^{\delta} + \frac{n - k + 2}{|\mathbb{F}|} + 2^{-\Omega(e)}$$

where $k > \delta + 4e, n > 2k + 4e$ and $e \leq (n - k + 1)/3$.

Proof sketch. The simulation follows by having the simulator Sim execute the protocol with the adversary, emulating the ideal functionalities for it, and emulating the honest parties on dummy 0-inputs. Before executing the output decommitment step, Sim performs several checks regarding the actions of the corrupted parties. Specifically, the simulator determines the set E of copies for which, if they were chosen during the consistency test, the test would fail. It also identifies the set E' of copies in which the $\mathcal{F}_{\text{RMULT}}$ values the corrupted parties committed to are inconsistent with the ones Sim provided to them. Then, it verifies that $|E| \leq e, |E|' \leq 3e$, and that there exist $\hat{U}, \hat{X}_i, i \in [m]$, and $\hat{z}$ which are valid encodings in the appropriate (interleaved) codes that agree with $\sum_{i \in [m]} U_i, X_i, i \in [m]$, and $\sum_{i \in [m]} z_i$ (respectively) except for the copies in E. It also verifies that there exists a $\hat{V}$ in the interleaved code over $\tilde{L}$ that agrees with $\sum_{i \in [m]} V_i$ except for the copies in $E \cup E'$. We note that Sim can perform these checks because it emulated the internal ideal functionalities for the adversary, whereas the honest parties in the protocol cannot perform these checks. If all checks pass then Sim can extract effective inputs for the corrupted parties, and use them to obtain the output from the trusted party. Finally, Sim "corrects" the output shares of the honest parties to share the correct outputs.

Next, we highlight some of the challenges we face when proving indistinguishability of the simulated and real views. Recall that unlike [32] we run a single consistency test, right before output reconstruction. Thus, we essentially

Protocol Φ.

- **Inputs.** P_i's input is x_i for all $i \in [m]$. The parties share a description of an arithmetic circuit C with fan-in 2 which contains h multiplication gates and implements functionality $\mathcal{F}$.

- **Initialization.**
  The parties invoke the $\mathcal{F}_{\mathrm{RMULT}}$ functionality hn times. Each invocation yields additive shares $(r_1^1, \ldots, r_m^1)$, $(r_1^2, \ldots, r_m^2)$ and $(r_1^3, \ldots, r_m^3)$, with party P_i holding (r_i^1, r_i^2, r_i^3), such that $r^j = \sum_{i=1}^m r_i^j$ for $j \in \{1, 2, 3\}$, and $r^3 = r^1 \cdot r^2$. Each party P_i generates a random L-encoding $\gamma_i = (\gamma_i^1, \ldots, \gamma_i^n)$ of a random value, a random L encoding $\nu_i = (\nu_i^1, \ldots, \nu_i^n)$ of 0, and a random $\tilde{L}$ encoding $\tilde{\gamma}_i = (\tilde{\gamma}_i^1, \ldots, \tilde{\gamma}_i^n)$ of 0. P_i samples a tuple $(\psi_i^1, \ldots, \psi_i^m)$ such that $\psi_i^j \in \mathbb{F}^n$ and $\sum_{j=1}^m \psi_i^j$ is the all-**0** vector. P_i sends ψ_i^j to party P_j. These "blinding" encodings are used in the degree and equality tests of Figure 4.
  Then, for every copy $l \in [n]$, P_i commits using $\mathcal{F}_{\mathrm{COM}}$ to:
  - The triples obtained from the $(l-1) \cdot h + 1, \ldots, hl$'th invocations of the $\mathcal{F}_{\mathrm{RMULT}}$ oracle.

  - $\gamma_i^l, \nu_i^l, \tilde{\gamma}_i^l$ and $\psi_i^{j,l}$ (i.e., the l'th element of ψ_i^j) for every j.

- **Input sharing.** Each party P_i generates a random L-encoding $\boldsymbol{X}_i = (X_i^1, \ldots, X_i^n)$ of its input x_i (where X_i^l will be used in the evaluation of the l'th copy of C), and commits to $X_i^1, \ldots, X_i^n$ using $\mathcal{F}_{\mathrm{COM}}$. For every $1 \leq l \leq n$, P_i generates an additive sharing $(x_{i,1}^l, \ldots, x_{i,m}^l)$ of X_i^l, and sends $(x_{i,j}^l)_{l \in [n]}$ to P_j. Each party P_i uses the shares $x_{j,i}^l$ ($j \in [n]$) as its inputs to the l'th copy.

- **Emulating the computation.** For every copy $l \in [n]$ of C, every layer $\mathcal{L} \in [d]$ in C, and every gate $G \in [w]$ in layer $\mathcal{L}$ (where w is the width of C), do:
  1. **Additions/subtractions.** If G is an addition or subtraction gate, each P_i performs the gate operation by applying it locally on the additive shares maintained as the inputs of that gate in the l'th copy.

  2. **Multiplications.** To compute a multiplication gate, the parties invoke the following multiplication protocol, where each party uses as inputs its l'th-copy shares of the inputs of G.
     - For every i, let a_i^l, b_i^l denote the shares of the inputs of G which P_i holds in the l'th copy of C. Then the parties compute additive shares $(\tilde{c}_1^l, \ldots, \tilde{c}_m^l)$ of $(\sum_{i=1}^m a_i^l)(\sum_{i=1}^m b_i^l)$, where P_i receives $\tilde{c}_i^l$, via the reduction from $\mathcal{F}_{\mathrm{MULT}}$ to $\mathcal{F}_{\mathrm{RMULT}}$ (described in Section 3.2), using the first unused triple obtained from $\mathcal{F}_{\mathrm{RMULT}}$ in the (next unused portion of the) randomness generation phase above.

     - Then, P_i locally performs degree reduction on its shares $\tilde{c}_i^1, \ldots, \tilde{c}_i^n$ as follows: it interprets $(\tilde{c}_i^1, \ldots, \tilde{c}_i^n)$ as an encoding in $\mathrm{RS}_{\mathbb{F},n,n,\eta}$, and applies the decoding procedure to obtain a value o_i. It then generates a fresh L-encoding $(c_i^1, \ldots, c_i^n)$ of o_i, which it uses as the additive shares of the output of G across the n copies. (We note that $\tilde{c}_i^1, \ldots, \tilde{c}_i^n$ are additive shares of a purported $\tilde{L}$-encoding where $\tilde{L} = \mathrm{RS}_{\mathbb{F},n,2\cdot k,\eta}$, but as a length-$n$ encoding it is always consistent with *some* valid encoding in $\mathrm{RS}_{\mathbb{F},n,n,\eta}$.)

- **Output commitments.** For the output wire z, let $\boldsymbol{w}_i$ be the additive shares held by party P_i for the output. Then, P_i computes $\boldsymbol{z}_i = \boldsymbol{w}_i + \nu_i$ where ν_i is the L-encoding of 0 committed to during the initialization step. Then, P_i commits using $\mathcal{F}_{\mathrm{COM}}$ to its shares $\boldsymbol{z}_i = (z_i^1, \ldots, z_i^n)$.

Fig. 3. Actively secure MPC Φ – Part 1 (circuit emulation).

Correctness tests. The following tests are performed to verify that the parties correctly evaluated the n copies of C (including the degree reduction step executed after each multiplication gate).

- **Commit to degree test.** *This test checks that the input encodings and the shares produced by all parties at the end of every degree reduction step are valid L-encodings. This is done by checking that a random linear combination of the sum of all these shares is a valid encoding in* $L = \mathsf{RS}_{\mathbb{F},n,k,\eta}$.
  More precisely, the parties first obtain from $\mathcal{F}_{\mathrm{COIN}}$ random vectors $\boldsymbol{r} \in \mathbb{F}^h$, $\boldsymbol{r}' \in \mathbb{F}^m$, and $r'' \in \mathbb{F}$ (recall that h is the number of multiplication gates in C, and m is the number of inputs — one from each party). Next, each party P_i constructs the matrix $U_i \in \mathbb{F}^{h \times n}$ that contains the L-encodings obtained after the degree reduction step of all multiplication gates (arranged in some arbitrary order, agreed upon by all parties). Then, P_i locally computes

  $$q_i = \boldsymbol{r}^T U_i + r_i' \boldsymbol{X}_i + r'' \boldsymbol{\nu}_i + \boldsymbol{\gamma}_i,$$

  where $\boldsymbol{X}^i$ is the L-encoding of P_i's input x_i committed at the input sharing step, $\boldsymbol{\nu}_i$ is the L-encoding of 0 committed to by P_i at the initialization step and $\boldsymbol{\gamma}_i$ is the blinding L-encoding committed to at the initialization step. P_i then commits to each element of q_i, and each column of U_i, using $\mathcal{F}_{\mathrm{COM}}$.

- **Commit to equality test.** *This test checks that the degree reduction step was performed correctly. This is done by checking that a random linear combination of the sum of differences of shares before and after the degree reduction step (performed as part of evaluating a multiplication gate) is a valid encoding of 0 in* $\tilde{L} = \mathsf{RS}_{\mathbb{F},n,2k,\eta}$.
  Specifically, the parties obtain from $\mathcal{F}_{\mathrm{COIN}}$ a random vector $\boldsymbol{\alpha} = (\alpha_1, \dots, \alpha_h) \in \mathbb{F}^h$ and random element $\beta \in \mathbb{F}$. P_i sets V_i to contain the additive shares which P_i obtains from the $\mathcal{F}_{\mathrm{MULT}}$ to $\mathcal{F}_{\mathrm{RMULT}}$ reduction computed during the evaluation of multiplication gates. Next, P_i locally computes:
  $$\tilde{q}_i = \boldsymbol{\alpha}^T (V_i - U_i) + \beta \boldsymbol{\nu}_i + \tilde{\boldsymbol{\gamma}}_i + \boldsymbol{b}_i$$
  where $b_i^l = \sum_{j=1}^m \psi_j^{i,l}$, $\tilde{\boldsymbol{\gamma}}_i$ is the $\tilde{L}$-encoding of 0 from the initialization step. Finally, P_i commits to each element of $\tilde{q}_i$ using $\mathcal{F}_{\mathrm{COM}}$.

Fig. 4. Actively secure MPC Φ – Part 2 (correctness tests commitments).

have one "shot" to catch the adversary, causing the test to be more involved. Another challenge is that parties are only committed to small portions of the execution, whereas in [32] parties commit to *all their messages* via the watchlists channels. Consequently, Sim cannot verify correct behavior directly by checking the messages, and instead we need to show that the messages can be extracted from the partial information which parties commit to. Fortunately, we show that correctness can be defined based on the $\mathcal{F}_{\mathrm{RMULT}}$ inputs, and the transcript of the reduction from $\mathcal{F}_{\mathrm{MULT}}$ to $\mathcal{F}_{\mathrm{RMULT}}$. Finally, correctness is guaranteed by the combination of local and global checks in our protocol. Specifically, the consistency

- **Consistency test.** *This test checks that the parties correctly executed the local computations in each copy.*

  $P_1, \ldots, P_m$ obtain from $\mathcal{F}_{\text{COIN}}$ a random subset $\Gamma \subset [n]$ of size δ. For every $l \in \Gamma$, each P_i opens its entire view of the execution of the l'th copy of C. Specifically, P_i decommits X_i^l, and the randomness (including all components of the commitments generated in the initialization step) it used in the execution of the l'th copy. It also opens the commitments to the degree and equality tests, and the additive shares of the final outputs of the l'th copy. Then, P_i checks (as described next) that all local computations in the copies in Γ were performed correctly, aborting if an inconsistency is detected.

  To check the l'th copy, P_i first checks that for every $j \in [m]$, $\sum_{j' \in [m]} \psi_j^{j',l} = 0$. Then, it obtains the l'th column of U_j and z_j from the decommitments of P_j, and uses the decommitments to $\mathcal{F}_{\text{RMULT}}$ values to determine the multiplication triples used by all parties for the l'th copy. Using these triples, P_i determines the inputs and outputs each party used in each multiplication gate of the l'th copy. Having determined the outputs of multiplication gates, P_j can reconstruct the l'th column of V_j. Moreover, since the final output is a linear combination of outputs of multiplication gates and parties' inputs, $\sum_j \boldsymbol{w}_j^l$ can be obtained by computing this linear combination over the corresponding rows in $\sum_j U_j$'s and the $\boldsymbol{X}_j$'s.

  Since addition gates are evaluated locally, correct execution of addition gates can be verified by checking that the inputs to all multiplication gates were computed correctly. Recall that an input to a multiplication gate is a linear combination of outputs of previous multiplication gates and parties' inputs. Thus, correctness can be checked by verifying that the sum of additive shares used as inputs to multiplication gates by all parties (as inferred from the $\mathcal{F}_{\text{RMULT}}$ triples, and the transcript), and the linear combination of the corresponding rows in $\sum_j U_j$ and the $\boldsymbol{X}_j$'s, are equal. Parties also verify that the reduction from $\mathcal{F}_{\text{MULT}}$ to $\mathcal{F}_{\text{RMULT}}$ was computed correctly in the l'th copy, and that $z_i^l = w_i^l + \nu_i^l$ for every i.

- **Degree test check.** The parties decommit the degree test commitments for all remaining copies $l \notin \Gamma$, namely each P_i opens the commitment to the value q_i computed in Figure 4. (Note that the parties do not decommit the remaining columns of U_i.) Each party computes the vector $q = (q_1 + \ldots + q_m)$ and aborts if q is not a valid L-encoding.

- **Equality test check.** The parties decommit their equality test commitments for all copies $l \notin \Gamma$, namely each P_i opens the commitment to the value $\tilde{q}_i$ computed in Figure 4. Each party computes $\tilde{q} = (\tilde{q}_1 + \ldots + \tilde{q}_m)$, and aborts if either $\tilde{q} \notin \tilde{L}$ or $\tilde{q}$ does not decode to the value 0.

- **Output decommitments.** If the consistency, degree and equality tests pass correctly, then every party P_i decommits its output commitments for all copies $l \notin \Gamma$. The parties then locally reconstruct $\boldsymbol{z} = \sum_i \boldsymbol{z}_i$, and if it is an L-encoding, decode the output of C from the encoding.

Fig. 5. Actively secure MPC Φ – Part 3 (correctness tests).

test verifies *local* correctness of the computation within each copy, by inspecting a subset of copies; and the degree and equality tests verify that some *global* relation holds over all copies (i.e., all additive shares).

In the proof, we show that if all the protocol tests pass then except with negligible probability, all the conditions checked by the simulator before the output reconstruction phase hold, and moreover the output is consistent with the outputs of the honest parties, and the effective outputs that Sim extracts for the corrupted parties. Thus, it suffices to prove indistinguishability of the simulated distribution and a hybrid distribution which is obtained from the real execution by performing Sim's checks, and aborting if they are violated. The difference between the hybrid and simulated distributions is that the honest parties use their real inputs in the former, and 0-inputs in the latter. We prove indistinguishability by a case analysis based on which tests pass. Intuitively, the views revealed during the consistency tests are identically distributed due to the secrecy of Shamir's secret sharing scheme (alternatively, Reed-Solomon codes). The degree test values are indistinguishable because the honest parties' values are valid L-encodings, which are uniformly random due to the masking by the γ_i's. The equality test values are indistinguishable because the sum of honest parties' values are valid $\tilde{L}$-encodings of $\mathbf{0}$, which are uniformly random subject to this constraint due to the masking by the $\tilde{\gamma}_i$'s. Since the equality test values are masked by additive shares of $\mathbf{0}$, the values themselves are identically distributed. Finally, conditioned on all tests passing, the output shares are uniformly random L-encodings whose sum encodes the correct output, due to the masking by the ν_i's.

Communication complexity of protocol Φ. Assuming the existence of a PRG, parties can commit to their $\mathcal{F}_{\text{RMULT}}$ triples by committing (during the initialization step) to a PRG seed for each copy (the other initialization-phase commitments are generated as in Fig. 3). Consequently, the total communication, assuming rate-1 commitments, is:

$$\underbrace{n \cdot m \cdot (\kappa + (3+m) \cdot \log_2 |\mathbb{F}|)}_{\text{rnd/blind com.}} + \underbrace{m \cdot n \cdot \log_2 |\mathbb{F}|}_{\text{input commitments}} + \underbrace{m^2 \cdot n \cdot \log_2 |\mathbb{F}|}_{\text{input sharing}}$$

$$+ \underbrace{n \cdot h \cdot \text{CC}_{\text{MULT}}}_{\text{multiplication}} + \underbrace{|\Gamma| \cdot m \cdot (\kappa + (4+m) \cdot \log_2 |\mathbb{F}|)}_{\text{consistency test}}$$

$$+ \underbrace{2 \cdot m \cdot n \cdot \log_2 |\mathbb{F}|}_{\text{degree test com. and dec.}} + \underbrace{2 \cdot m \cdot n \cdot \log_2 |\mathbb{F}|}_{\text{equality test com. and dec.}} + \underbrace{2 \cdot n \cdot m \cdot \log_2 |\mathbb{F}|}_{\text{output com. and dec.}}$$

where CC_{MULT} is the communication complexity of the m-party multiplication protocol (implementing $\mathcal{F}_{\text{RMULT}}$ and the $\mathcal{F}_{\text{MULT}}$ to $\mathcal{F}_{\text{RMULT}}$ reduction), and h is the number of multiplication gates in the circuit. (We note that the degree and equality test commitments revealed during the consistency test are counted as part of the degree and equality test terms, resp.) In order to get $2^{-\Omega(s)}$ soundness, we need to set $n = O(s)$. Assuming $s \leq \kappa$, the overall communication complexity can be bounded by $O(s \cdot h \cdot \text{CC}_{\text{MULT}}) + \text{poly}(m, \kappa, \log_2 |\mathbb{F}|)$. Since h represents the size of the circuit (i.e. number of multiplication gates), the best passive protocol in the $\mathcal{F}_{\text{MULT}}$-hybrid can be bounded by $O(h) \cdot \text{CC}_{\text{MULT}}$. Therefore, the communication overhead of our basic variant is $O(s)$.

4.1   Instantiating $\mathcal{F}_{\mathrm{RMULT}}$

Recall from Sect. 4.1 that $\mathcal{F}_{\mathrm{RMULT}}$ is the multiplication functionality that outputs three tuples of additive shares a, b, c such that the "inputs" a, b share random values a, b, and the "output" c shares the product $a \cdot b$. In this section we discuss how to realize this functionality, while identifying the minimal security properties required from it.

Our first observation is that we do not need an actively-secure implementation of the $\mathcal{F}_{\mathrm{RMULT}}$ functionality. In fact, it suffices to consider a protocol that is only "private" against active adversaries, in the sense that throughout the protocol execution, an actively corrupted party cannot violate the privacy of the honest parties' inputs. In particular, the underlying implementation does not have to retain correctness in this case, or provide a mechanism for extracting the adversary's inputs. Extraction in our protocol is achieved by requiring the adversary to commit to its input and randomness used for the $\mathcal{F}_{\mathrm{RMULT}}$-functionality. Correctness, on the other hand, is enforced through our consistency test that ensures correctness of the computations in most of the copies, by checking a random subset of δ copies.

When computing a boolean circuit, the pairwise products of the shares can be computed using Oblivious Transfer (OT) [3,41]. Based on the discussion above, it suffices to use a private OT protocol [24]. Indeed, consistency between the different OT executions will be verified during the consistency test of our protocol, as discussed above.[4] Intuitively, privacy is guaranteed because an OT sender has no output in the execution, and the security/privacy of OT ensures that even if the sender cheats it learns nothing about the receiver's input. Moreover, though an OT receiver can use inconsistent inputs in the OT executions with different honest parties, this can only violate correctness, and not privacy, since the output of each OT execution is an additive share of the cross product (e.g., $a_i \cdot b_j$), which reveals nothing about the other party's share. Similarly, when working over large fields, $\mathcal{F}_{\mathrm{RMULT}}$ can be realized using private OLE, where private OLE can be defined analogously to private OT, requiring that parties do not infer any additional information (except what can be inferred from their inputs and outputs).

Relaxing to passive implementation of the $\mathcal{F}_{\mathrm{RMULT}}$-functionality. We can further weaken the security requirement on the $\mathcal{F}_{\mathrm{RMULT}}$ implementation, by incorporating the reduction from defensible privacy to passive security. We first informally review the notion of *defensible privacy* which was introduced by Haitner in [22,23]; see [23] for the formal definitions. Let π be a two-party protocol between P_1 and P_2, and let trans $= (q_1, a_1, \ldots, q_\ell, a_\ell)$ be a transcript of an execution of π when P_1 is controlled by an adversary $\mathcal{A}$, where q_i denotes the i'th message from P_1, and a_i denotes the i'th message from P_2 (that is, a_i is the response to q_i). Informally, a *defence* of $\mathcal{A}$ relative to trans, which is

---

[4] More specifically, we use OT between pairs of parties to compute a 2-out-of-2 additive secret sharing of the product they should compute. Then. we perform the consistency check, and reconstruct the outputs of OTs only if this test passes.

provided after the protocol execution ends, is a pair (x, r) of input and random tape for P_1. We say that a defence (x, r) of $\mathcal{A}$ relative to trans is *good* if the transcript generated by running the honest P_1 with input x and random tape r against P_2's messages $a_1, \ldots, a_\ell$ results exactly in trans. Intuitively, a defense (x, r) is good relative to trans if, whenever P_i uses (x, r) in an honest execution of π, the messages sent by P_i are identical to the messages sent by the adversary in trans. Thus, in essence, a defense serves as a "proof" of honest behavior. Defensible privacy guarantees that when the adversary provides a good defence, then it learns nothing beyond what can be inferred from its input and prescribed output.[5]

The security of a passive protocol can be amplified to defensible privacy by adding a coin tossing phase (which, in our case, samples the inputs to $\mathcal{F}_{\text{RMULT}}$), and ensuring that these coins were indeed used in the passive execution. The latter can be checked as part of our consistency test, however to guarantee privacy we cannot postpone this check until the consistency test is performed at the end of the circuit emulation, since by that time the adversary could have already violated privacy by using badly-sampled randomness. Thus, we include in our protocol two consistency tests: the first is the consistency test described in Fig. 4, and the second checks consistency of $\mathcal{F}_{\text{RMULT}}$ inputs and the tossed coins, and is executed during the initialization phase. This second consistency test ensures that with overwhelming probability, all but (possibly) a small subset of random triples are correct (namely, the aggregated parties' shares correspond to $c = a \cdot b$), and consistent with the random coins. This will suffice for our security analysis, because the number of copies will be sufficiently large such that by cheating in a small number $(< k)$ of copies, the adversary learns nothing.

Relaxing further to weaker than passive. Following ideas from [25], our protocol can, in fact, tolerate an *imperfect* passive OLE, namely one that has a non-negligible statistical privacy or correctness error. This security feature can be turned into an efficiency advantage. For example, imperfect $\mathcal{F}_{\text{RMULT}}$ can be implemented more efficiently by aggressively setting the parameters in existing LWE-based OLE constructions, see the full version [28] for details.

5   Actively Secure MPC with Constant Communication Overhead

In this section we present our main result, namely, an MPC protocol for an arbitrary number of parties that achieves constant communication overhead over the passive GMW protocol.

---

[5] For instance, an OT protocol is defensibly private with respect to a corrupted sender if any adversary interacting with an honest receiver with input u, and providing a good defence at the end of the execution, does not learn u. Similarly, an OT protocol is defensibly private with respect to a corrupted receiver if for any input u, and any inputs (v_0, v_1) for the sender, any adversary interacting with the honest sender with input (v_0, v_1), that is able to provide a good defense for input u, does not learn v_{1-u}.

On a high-level, we will incorporate a variant of the protocol of Frankling and Yung [16] instead of [5] in our basic MPC protocol. Recall that the main overhead in the basic MPC protocol is caused by the $n = O(s)$ copies of the circuit used to perform the computation, where s is a statistical security parameter. Then, similar to [16] we improve the communication overhead, achieving *constant* overhead, by having all copies evaluate multiple gates in parallel using packed secret sharing. Our protocol will achieve constant-overhead for moderately wide circuits (See Sect. 6 for a more detailed discussion.)

In more detail, given a circuit C, and block-width parameter $\mathcal{B}$, the parties agree on a divisions of the circuit evaluation into layers, where at most $\mathcal{B}$ multiplication gates are evaluated in parallel in each layer, and arbitrary linear operations are performed between layers. During the evaluation of the protocol on a specific input, we can associate with each layer of gates G a vector (block) B_O^G of $\mathcal{B}$ values whose i'th position contains the output value assigned to the i'th gate in the layer (or 0 if the block has less than $\mathcal{B}$ gates). For each layer (except blocks of input gates), we will associate two additional blocks: a "left" block B_L^G and "right" block B_R^G whose i'th position contains the value of the left input wire and right input wire of the i'th gate, respectively. In other words, the value of the i'th gate of a multiplication block can be expressed as $(B_O^G)_i = (B_L^G)_i (B_R^G)_i$. In the protocol, the parties will collectively operate on an efficient (constant-rate) Reed-Solomon encoding (equivalently, packed secret shares) of each block. The protocol parameters include a description of the Reed-Solomon code $L = \mathsf{RS}_{\mathbb{F},n,k,\eta}$, and a vector of elements $\zeta = (\zeta_1, \ldots, \zeta_\mathcal{B}) \in \mathbb{F}^\mathcal{B}$ which is used for decoding.

Next, we describe our protocol, simulation and proof by specifying the main differences from the description of the basic protocol from Sect. 4.

- INITIALIZATION. Recall that each party generates $\gamma_i, \nu_i, \widetilde{\gamma}_i$ and $(\psi_i^1, \ldots, \psi_i^m)$. The parties generate the same vectors except that γ_i is a random L-encoding of a random block of values, and ν_i and $\widetilde{\gamma}_i$ are random L and $\tilde{L}$ encodings of the all 0's block. In addition, the parties generate a random L'-encoding $\gamma'^i = (\gamma'^i_1, \ldots, \gamma'^i_n)$ of a block of values that are random subject to the condition that they add up to 0, where $L' = \mathsf{RS}_{\mathbb{F},n,k+\mathcal{B},\eta}$.
- INPUT SHARING. The parties share a block rather than a single element. Namely, the parties embed their input value(s) into a block of length $\mathcal{B}$, and generates a packed secret sharing L-encoding for this block, distributing the outcome as in the basic protocol.
- EMULATING THE COMPUTATION. The computation proceed in layers of multiplication gates, where for each layer, we maintain the invariant that the parties hold additive shares of the inputs to the (at most) $\mathcal{B}$ multiplication gates in the layer. The difference from the basic protocol is that before evaluating a layer, the parties need to repack the inputs to the layer. (See discussion below on why repacking might be needed.)

  Concretely, to evaluate a layer, each party first rearranges the left wire values and right wire values of the multiplication gates in the layer into blocks B_L and B_R, and generates an L-encoding of each block. For every i, let a_i^l, b_i^l

denote P_i's shares of B_L, B_R (respectively) corresponding to the l'th copy. Then the parties compute (via the reduction from $\mathcal{F}_{\text{MULT}}$ to $\mathcal{F}_{\text{RMULT}}$) additive shares $(\tilde{c}_1^l, \ldots, \tilde{c}_m^l)$ of $(\sum_{i=1}^m a_i^l)(\sum_{i=1}^m b_i^l)$, where P_i receives $\tilde{c}_i^l$, just as in the basic MPC protocol. Then, each P_i locally performs the degree reduction procedure as in the basic MPC protocol, with the difference that P_i decodes $(\tilde{c}_i^1, \ldots, \tilde{c}_i^n)$ to obtain a *block* of values which it uses as the additive shares of the outputs of the multiplication gates in the layer.

Why repacking is needed. To see why rearranging the values within and between blocks might be necessary, consider a circuit that has a wire connecting the 3'rd value in the 2'nd block in layer 1 with the 5'th value in the 3'rd block in layer 2; or a wire connecting the 4'th value in the 1'st block in layer 1 with the 2'nd value in the 1'st block in layer 2.[6]

– CORRECTNESS TESTS. We will employ the equality test as before, modify the degree test to also check the repacked encodings, and add an additional *permutation test*, as described next.

– THE MODIFIED DEGREE TEST. As in the basic protocol, the degree test will compute a random linear combination of the tested encodings. These encodings include the blocks X_i encoding the parties' inputs (which were committed in the input sharing step), the block of 0s encoded in ν_i (which was committed in the initialization step), and the matrix U_i which contains L-encodings of the blocks of additive shares that were obtained from the degree reduction step following a multiplication step (U_i was committed to during the commit to degree test step). The difference from the degree test of the basic MPC protocol is that the linear combination will now also include an additional matrix U_i'' which contains the L-encodings of the repacked blocks of additive shares that were used as inputs to multiplication gates. (We note that these values are never committed to, but as explained in the proof of Corollary 2 below, can be extracted by the simulator from the transcript of the execution.) More formally, the parties will obtain from $\mathcal{F}_{\text{COIN}}$ random vectors r, r', r''', and a random value r'', and party P_i will compute

$$q_i = r^T U_i + r'''^T U_i'' + r_i' X_i + r'' \nu_i + \gamma_i.$$

Permutation test: This test verifies that the parties correctly permute (i.e., rearrange) the additive shares of wire values between layers. In particular, the test verifies that the encodings of the left and right input blocks of each computation layer correctly encode the values from the previous layers (and similarly for the output blocks). Note that the set of constraints that the blocks of values have to satisfy can be expressed as a set of linear equations in at most $m\mathcal{B}$ equations and $m\mathcal{B}$ variables (where w is the width, d is the depth of the computed circuit, and $m = dw/\mathcal{B}$), where variable $x_{i,j}$ represents the j'th value in the i'th block. (For example, if the circuit has a wire between

---

[6] Addition gates do not require repacking: they can be computed locally (because parties hold additive shares of the wire values), then repacked for the next multiplication layer.

the 3'rd value of the 2'nd block and the 5'th value in the 3'rd block, the corresponding constraint would be $x_{2,3} - x_{3,5} = 0$.) These linear equations can be represented in matrix form as $Ax = 0^{m\mathcal{B}}$, where $A \in \mathbb{F}^{m\mathcal{B} \times m\mathcal{B}}$ is a public matrix which only depends on the circuit being computed. The permutation test simply picks a random vector $r \in \mathbb{F}^{m\mathcal{B}}$ and checks that $(r^T A)x = 0$. To check these constraints, the parties obtain from $\mathcal{F}_{\text{COIN}}$ a random vector $r \in \mathbb{F}^{m\mathcal{B}}$ and compute

$$r^T A = (r'_{11}, \ldots, r'_{1\mathcal{B}}, \ldots, r'_{m1}, \ldots, r'_{m\mathcal{B}}).$$

Now, let $r_j(\cdot)$ be the unique polynomial of degree $< \mathcal{B}$ such that $r_j(\zeta_Q) = r'_{jQ}$ for every $Q \in [\mathcal{B}]$ and $j \in [m]$. Then party P_i locally computes $q'_i = (r_1(\zeta_i), \ldots, r_m(\zeta_i))^T U'_i + \gamma'_i$, where γ'_i is the blinding encoding from the initialization step (that encode in $\text{RS}_{\mathbb{F},n,k+\mathcal{B},\eta}$ random blocks of values that sum to 0), and U'_i is the matrix obtained by concatenating the rows of U_i and U''_i from the degree test. Notice that the rows of U'_i consist of the L-encodings which P_i obtained at the output of multiplication layers (after degree reduction), and the L-encodings it used as inputs to multiplication layers (after repacking). Finally, P_i commits to each element of q'_i using $\mathcal{F}_{\text{COM}}$.

– CONSISTENCY TEST CHECK. In the consistency test, we also check for all $l \in \Gamma$ that the permutation test values of copy l were computed correctly. Specifically, each party checks that for every $i \in [m]$, the l'th element of q'_i is consistent with the l'th element of γ'_i, the l'th column of U'_i, and r (the coins obtained from $\mathcal{F}_{\text{COIN}}$ for the permutation test).

– PERMUTATION TEST CHECK. The parties decommit their permutation test commitments for all copies $l \notin \Gamma$, namely each P_i opens the commitment to the value q'_i computed above. Each party computes $q' = (q'_1 + \ldots + q'_m)$, and aborts if $q' = (q'_1, \ldots, q'_n) \notin \text{RS}_{\mathbb{F},n,k+\mathcal{B},\eta}$ or $x_1 + \cdots + x_w \neq 0$ where $x = (x_1, \ldots, x_w) = \text{Decode}_\zeta(q')$.

The following Theorem follows from Theorem 1 and the discussion above; its proof appears in the full version [28].

Theorem 2. *The packed variant of protocol Φ of Figs. 3, 4 and 5 securely realizes $\mathcal{F}$ in the $(\mathcal{F}_{\text{COM}}, \mathcal{F}_{\text{RMULT}}, \mathcal{F}_{\text{COIN}})$-hybrid model, tolerating $m-1$ active (static) corruptions, with statistical security error*

$$(1 - e/n)^\delta + ((e + k + \mathcal{B})/n)^\delta + (n - k + 3)/|\mathbb{F}| + 2^{-\Omega(e)}$$

where $k > \delta + 4e + \mathcal{B}$, $n > 2k + 4e$, and $e < (n - k + 1)/3$.

Assuming that each layer of the circuit has at least $\mathcal{B}$ parallel multiplications, the communication complexity of this variant is given by $O(n \cdot \frac{h}{\mathcal{B}} \cdot \text{CC}_{\text{MULT}}) + \text{poly}(m, \kappa, \log_2 |\mathbb{F}|)$ since we amortize over $\mathcal{B}$ multiplications. By setting $n = O(s)$, the amortized communication overhead of this protocol becomes $O(1)$ per copy. Circuits of an arbitrary structure can be easily handled at a worst-case additional cost of $\text{poly}(s, d)$. The statistical error can be improved by repeating the tests. The analysis presented above works for fields of size larger than n, for smaller fields, we can rely on the analysis from [11].

6 Corollaries and Applications

In this section we consider several different instantiations of the $\mathcal{F}_{\mathrm{RMULT}}$ functionality, thus obtaining our main results in the different settings as instances of the generic protocol of Sect. 5.

6.1 Constant Overhead MPC for Constant-Size Fields

Dishonest majority. Our main result is obtained by replacing the Reed-Solomon codes in our protocol with Algebraic Geometric (AG) secret sharing over fields of constant size [8], instantiating the $\mathcal{F}_{\mathrm{RMULT}}$ functionality with pairwise calls to a passively-secure implementation of the $\mathcal{F}_{\mathrm{OT}}$ functionality, and instantiating commitments using a pseudorandom generator. Formally:

Theorem 3 (Theorem 1, restated). *Let κ, s denote computational and statistical security parameters (resp.), m denote the number of parties, and $\mathbb{F}$ be a constant-size field. Then there exists a protocol compiler that, given a pseudorandom generator G with seed length κ, s, a constant-round implementation of the $\mathcal{F}_{\mathrm{OT}}$ functionality with total communication complexity $\mathrm{CC}_{\mathrm{OT}}$, and a description of an m-party functionality expressed as a depth-d circuit C with constant fan-in, outputs a UC-secure $O(d)$-round m-party protocol realizing f with communication complexity $O(m^2 |C| \, \mathrm{CC}_{\mathrm{OT}}) + \mathrm{poly}(m, \kappa, d)$, where security holds against an active adversary corrupting an arbitrary number of parties.*

We note that the exact constants in the overhead of Theorem 3 depend on the concrete constants of the underlying AG code, which have not been studied before. The communication complexity of our protocol using a bit-OT protocol for the boolean setting asymptotically matches the communication complexity of the best known passively-secure protocol, namely [19] using a passively-secure OT protocol. The best known previous result for active security is due to Genkin et al. [18] who achieve $O(m^2 |C| \, \mathrm{poly} \log(s))$ communication complexity, i.e., a multiplicative factor of $\mathrm{poly} \log(s)$ over GMW.

Honest majority. To obtain our main result for the honest majority setting, we need to slightly modify our protocol in two ways. First, we will rely on the passive variant of a protocol of Damgård and Nielsen [13], instantiated with secret-sharing based on AG codes over constant-size finite fields, to instantiate the parallel $\mathcal{F}_{\mathrm{RMULT}}$ functionality (i.e., to generate the triples in the initialization phase). To achieve this, we replace the additive secret sharing used in our protocol with secret sharing based on AG codes for constant-size fields. We note that the passively-secure honest-majority m-party protocol of [13] can generate $T = \Omega(m)$ random triples with total communication complexity $O(mT)$. Second, we will consider $\mathcal{F}_{\mathrm{RMULT}}$ and $\mathcal{F}_{\mathrm{MULT}}$ whose underlying secret sharing scheme is based on the same AG secret sharing scheme. Specifically, parallel $\mathcal{F}_{\mathrm{RMULT}}$ distributes secret-shares of many triples a, b and c such that $a \cdot b = c$. Then the $\mathcal{F}_{\mathrm{MULT}}$ to $\mathcal{F}_{\mathrm{RMULT}}$ reduction works essentially as in the basic protocol, where the only difference is that the values e, d are reconstructed using the reconstruction procedure of the AG secret sharing scheme. Consequently, we obtain the following theorem.

Theorem 4. *Let κ, s denote computational and statistical security parameters (resp.), m denote the number of parties, and $\mathbb{F}$ be a constant-size field. Then there exists a protocol compiler that, given a pseudorandom generator G with seed length κ, s, and a description of an m-party functionality expressed as a depth-d circuit C with constant fan-in, outputs a UC-secure $O(d)$-round m-party protocol realizing f with $O(m|C|) + \mathsf{poly}(m, \kappa, d)$ bits total communication complexity, and security against a static adversary corrupting a minority of parties.*

We remark that this improves over the result of Chida et al. [9] that achieves $O(s)$ overhead for binary fields, and generalizes the result of Ishai et al. [31] that achieves the same result, but only for a constant number of parties. We remark that the latter protocol additionally achieve constant-rate, while our protocol only achieves constant-overhead.

6.2 Constant Overhead MPC over Fields of Arbitrary Size

Dishonest majority. To obtain our result for fields of arbitrary size, we realize the $\mathcal{F}_{\mathrm{RMULT}}$ functionality using a passively-secure OLE protocol. For fields of size $\leq s$ we rely on AG sharing, whereas for fields of size $\Omega(s)$ we use Reed-Solomon codes. Thus, we can re-derive a result of Genkin et al. [17] (Theorem 5.7 in the full version), who construct an actively-secure m-party protocol for arbitrary functionalities (represented by an arithmetic circuit C), in the dishonest majority setting, using $O(m^2 |C|)$ calls to an OLE oracle. More precisely, we have the following theorem:

Theorem 5. *Let κ, s denote computational and statistical security parameters (resp.), m denote the number of parties, and $\mathbb{F}$ be a field. Then there exists a protocol compiler that, given a pseudorandom generator G with seed length κ, s, a constant-round implementation of the $\mathcal{F}_{\mathrm{OLE}}$ functionality over $\mathbb{F}$ with total communication complexity $\mathrm{CC}_{\mathrm{OLE}}$, and a description of an m-party functionality expressed as a depth-d arithmetic circuit C over $\mathbb{F}$ with constant fan-in, outputs a UC-secure $O(d)$-round m-party protocol realizing f with communication complexity $O(m^2 |C| \, \mathrm{CC}_{\mathrm{OLE}}) + \mathsf{poly}(m, \kappa, d)$ field elements, with security against an active adversary corrupting an arbitrary number of parties.*

This result asymptotically matches the communication complexity of the best known passively-secure protocol [19] using a passively-secure OLE protocol. Furthermore, for sufficiently wide circuits, we can show that the overhead of our protocols is 2. We present the concrete parameters in the full version [28].

Honest majority. Just as in Sect. 6.1, we can obtain constant overhead over the best passively-secure protocol in the honest majority setting:

Theorem 6. *Let κ, s denote computational and statistical security parameters (resp.), m denote the number of parties, and $\mathbb{F}$ be a field. Then there exists a protocol compiler that, given a pseudorandom generator G with seed length κ, s, and a description of an m-party functionality expressed as a depth-d arithmetic circuit C over $\mathbb{F}$ with constant fan-in, outputs a UC-secure $O(d)$-round m-party protocol realizing f with total communication complexity $O(m|\mathsf{C}|) + \mathsf{poly}(m, \kappa, d)$ bits, where security holds against a static adversary corrupting a minority of parties.*

Applying the analysis of concrete parameters (see above and the full version [28]) we re-derive the result of Chida et al. [9] who show an overhead-2 actively-secure honest-majority protocol. Their result applies to arbitrary circuits over sufficiently large fields, whereas ours achieves overhead of 2 for sufficiently wide circuits.

Acknowledgments. The first author is supported by the BIU Center for Research in Applied Cryptography and Cyber Security in conjunction with the Israel National Cyber Bureau in the Prime Minister's Office, and by ISF grant 1316/18. The second author is supported by Google Faculty Research Grant, NSF Award CNS-1618884 and Intelligence Advanced Research Projects Activity (IARPA) via 2019-19-020700009. The views expressed are those of the author and do not reflect the official policy or position of Google, the Department of Defense, the National Science Foundation, or the U.S. Government. The third author is supported by ISF grants 1861/16 and 1399/17, and AFOSR Award FA9550-17-1-0069.

References

1. Ames, S., Hazay, C., Ishai, Y., Venkitasubramaniam, M.: Ligero: lightweight sublinear arguments without a trusted setup. In: CCS, pp. 2087–2104 (2017)
2. Applebaum, B., Damgård, I., Ishai, Y., Nielsen, M., Zichron, L.: Secure arithmetic computation with constant computational overhead. In: Katz, J., Shacham, H. (eds.) CRYPTO 2017. LNCS, vol. 10401, pp. 223–254. Springer, Cham (2017). https://doi.org/10.1007/978-3-319-63688-7_8
3. Beaver, D.: Efficient multiparty protocols using circuit randomization. In: Feigenbaum, J. (ed.) CRYPTO 1991. LNCS, vol. 576, pp. 420–432. Springer, Heidelberg (1992). https://doi.org/10.1007/3-540-46766-1_34
4. Beaver, D., Micali, S., Rogaway, P.: The round complexity of secure protocols (extended abstract). In: STOC, pp. 503–513 (1990)
5. Ben-Or, M., Goldwasser, S., Wigderson, A.: Completeness theorems for non-cryptographic fault-tolerant distributed computation (extended abstract). In: STOC, pp. 1–10 (1988)
6. Bendlin, R., Damgård, I., Orlandi, C., Zakarias, S.: Semi-homomorphic encryption and multiparty computation. In: Paterson, K.G. (ed.) EUROCRYPT 2011. LNCS, vol. 6632, pp. 169–188. Springer, Heidelberg (2011). https://doi.org/10.1007/978-3-642-20465-4_11
7. Chaum, D., Crépeau, C., Damgård, I.: Multiparty unconditionally secure protocols (abstract). In: Pomerance, C. (ed.) CRYPTO 1987. LNCS, vol. 293, p. 462. Springer, Heidelberg (1988). https://doi.org/10.1007/3-540-48184-2_43

8. Chen, H., Cramer, R.: Algebraic geometric secret sharing schemes and secure multi-party computations over small fields. In: Dwork, C. (ed.) CRYPTO 2006. LNCS, vol. 4117, pp. 521–536. Springer, Heidelberg (2006). https://doi.org/10.1007/11818175_31

9. Chida, K., et al.: Fast large-scale honest-majority MPC for malicious adversaries. In: Shacham, H., Boldyreva, A. (eds.) CRYPTO 2018. LNCS, vol. 10993, pp. 34–64. Springer, Cham (2018). https://doi.org/10.1007/978-3-319-96878-0_2

10. Cramer, R., Damgård, I., Nielsen, J.B.: Multiparty computation from threshold homomorphic encryption. In: Pfitzmann, B. (ed.) EUROCRYPT 2001. LNCS, vol. 2045, pp. 280–300. Springer, Heidelberg (2001). https://doi.org/10.1007/3-540-44987-6_18

11. Damgård, I., Ishai, Y.: Scalable secure multiparty computation. In: Dwork, C. (ed.) CRYPTO 2006. LNCS, vol. 4117, pp. 501–520. Springer, Heidelberg (2006). https://doi.org/10.1007/11818175_30

12. Damgård, I., Keller, M., Larraia, E., Pastro, V., Scholl, P., Smart, N.P.: Practical covertly secure MPC for dishonest majority – or: breaking the SPDZ limits. In: Crampton, J., Jajodia, S., Mayes, K. (eds.) ESORICS 2013. LNCS, vol. 8134, pp. 1–18. Springer, Heidelberg (2013). https://doi.org/10.1007/978-3-642-40203-6_1

13. Damgård, I., Nielsen, J.B.: Scalable and unconditionally secure multiparty computation. In: Menezes, A. (ed.) CRYPTO 2007. LNCS, vol. 4622, pp. 572–590. Springer, Heidelberg (2007). https://doi.org/10.1007/978-3-540-74143-5_32

14. Damgård, I., Pastro, V., Smart, N., Zakarias, S.: Multiparty computation from somewhat homomorphic encryption. In: Safavi-Naini, R., Canetti, R. (eds.) CRYPTO 2012. LNCS, vol. 7417, pp. 643–662. Springer, Heidelberg (2012). https://doi.org/10.1007/978-3-642-32009-5_38

15. Döttling, N., Ghosh, S., Nielsen, J.B., Nilges, T., Trifiletti, R.: TinyOLE: efficient actively secure two-party computation from oblivious linear function evaluation. In: CCS, pp. 2263–2276 (2017)

16. Franklin, M.K., Yung, M.: Communication complexity of secure computation (extended abstract). In: STOC, pp. 699–710 (1992)

17. Genkin, D., Ishai, Y., Prabhakaran, M., Sahai, A., Tromer, E.: Circuits resilient to additive attacks with applications to secure computation. In: STOC, pp. 495–504 (2014)

18. Genkin, D., Ishai, Y., Weiss, M.: Binary AMD circuits from secure multiparty computation. In: Hirt, M., Smith, A. (eds.) TCC-B 2016. LNCS, vol. 9985, pp. 336–366. Springer, Heidelberg (2016). https://doi.org/10.1007/978-3-662-53641-4_14

19. Goldreich, O., Micali, S., Wigderson, A.: How to play any mental game acompleteness theorem for protocols with honest majority. In: STOC, pp. 218–229 (1987)

20. Goyal, V., Liu, Y., Song, Y.: Communication-efficient unconditional MPC with guaranteed output delivery. In: Boldyreva, A., Micciancio, D. (eds.) CRYPTO 2019. LNCS, vol. 11693, pp. 85–114. Springer, Cham (2019). https://doi.org/10.1007/978-3-030-26951-7_4

21. Gueron, S., Lindell, Y., Nof, A., Pinkas, B.: Fast garbling of circuits under standard assumptions. In: CCS, pp. 567–578 (2015)

22. Haitner, I.: Semi-honest to malicious oblivious transfer—the black-box way. In: Canetti, R. (ed.) TCC 2008. LNCS, vol. 4948, pp. 412–426. Springer, Heidelberg (2008). https://doi.org/10.1007/978-3-540-78524-8_23

23. Haitner, I., Ishai, Y., Kushilevitz, E., Lindell, Y., Petrank, E.: Black-box constructions of protocols for secure computation. SIAM J. Comput. 40(2), 225–266 (2011)

24. Halevi, S., Kalai, Y.T.: Smooth projective hashing and two-message oblivious transfer. J. Cryptol. **25**(1), 158–193 (2012). https://doi.org/10.1007/s00145-010-9092-8

25. Hazay, C., Ishai, Y., Marcedone, A., Venkitasubramaniam, M.: Leviosa: Lightweight secure arithmetic computation. In: CCS, pp. 327–344 (2019)

26. Hazay, C., Ishai, Y., Venkitasubramaniam, M.: Actively secure garbled circuits with constant communication overhead in the plain model. In: Kalai, Y., Reyzin, L. (eds.) TCC 2017. LNCS, vol. 10678, pp. 3–39. Springer, Cham (2017). https://doi.org/10.1007/978-3-319-70503-3_1

27. Hazay, C., Scholl, P., Soria-Vazquez, E.: Low cost constant round MPC combining BMR and oblivious transfer. In: Takagi, T., Peyrin, T. (eds.) ASIACRYPT 2017. LNCS, vol. 10624, pp. 598–628. Springer, Cham (2017). https://doi.org/10.1007/978-3-319-70694-8_21

28. Hazay, C., Venkitasubramaniam, M., Weiss, M.: The price of active security in cryptographic protocols. IACR Cryptology ePrint Archive 2019, 1250 (2019). https://eprint.iacr.org/2019/1250

29. Huang, Y., Katz, J., Kolesnikov, V., Kumaresan, R., Malozemoff, A.J.: Amortizing garbled circuits. In: Garay, J.A., Gennaro, R. (eds.) CRYPTO 2014. LNCS, vol. 8617, pp. 458–475. Springer, Heidelberg (2014). https://doi.org/10.1007/978-3-662-44381-1_26

30. Ishai, Y., Kushilevitz, E., Ostrovsky, R., Sahai, A.: Zero-knowledge from secure multiparty computation. In: STOC, pp. 21–30 (2007)

31. Ishai, Y., Kushilevitz, E., Prabhakaran, M., Sahai, A., Yu, C.-H.: Secure protocol transformations. In: Robshaw, M., Katz, J. (eds.) CRYPTO 2016. LNCS, vol. 9815, pp. 430–458. Springer, Heidelberg (2016). https://doi.org/10.1007/978-3-662-53008-5_15

32. Ishai, Y., Prabhakaran, M., Sahai, A.: Founding cryptography on oblivious transfer – efficiently. In: Wagner, D. (ed.) CRYPTO 2008. LNCS, vol. 5157, pp. 572–591. Springer, Heidelberg (2008). https://doi.org/10.1007/978-3-540-85174-5_32

33. Ishai, Y., Prabhakaran, M., Sahai, A.: Secure arithmetic computation with no honest majority. In: Reingold, O. (ed.) TCC 2009. LNCS, vol. 5444, pp. 294–314. Springer, Heidelberg (2009). https://doi.org/10.1007/978-3-642-00457-5_18

34. Keller, M., Pastro, V., Rotaru, D.: Overdrive: making SPDZ great again. In: Nielsen, J.B., Rijmen, V. (eds.) EUROCRYPT 2018. LNCS, vol. 10822, pp. 158–189. Springer, Cham (2018). https://doi.org/10.1007/978-3-319-78372-7_6

35. Kolesnikov, V., Schneider, T.: Improved garbled circuit: free XOR gates and applications. In: Aceto, L., Damgård, I., Goldberg, L.A., Halldórsson, M.M., Ingólfsdóttir, A., Walukiewicz, I. (eds.) ICALP 2008. LNCS, vol. 5126, pp. 486–498. Springer, Heidelberg (2008). https://doi.org/10.1007/978-3-540-70583-3_40

36. Lindell, Y., Oxman, E., Pinkas, B.: The IPS compiler: optimizations, variants and concrete efficiency. In: Rogaway, P. (ed.) CRYPTO 2011. LNCS, vol. 6841, pp. 259–276. Springer, Heidelberg (2011). https://doi.org/10.1007/978-3-642-22792-9_15

37. Lindell, Y., Pinkas, B.: An efficient protocol for secure two-party computation in the presence of malicious adversaries. In: Naor, M. (ed.) EUROCRYPT 2007. LNCS, vol. 4515, pp. 52–78. Springer, Heidelberg (2007). https://doi.org/10.1007/978-3-540-72540-4_4

38. Lindell, Y., Pinkas, B.: Secure two-party computation via cut-and-choose oblivious transfer. J. Cryptol. **25**(4), 680–722 (2012). https://doi.org/10.1007/s00145-011-9107-0

39. Lindell, Y., Pinkas, B., Smart, N.P., Yanai, A.: Efficient constant round multi-party computation combining BMR and SPDZ. In: Gennaro, R., Robshaw, M. (eds.) CRYPTO 2015. LNCS, vol. 9216, pp. 319–338. Springer, Heidelberg (2015). https://doi.org/10.1007/978-3-662-48000-7_16

40. Lindell, Y., Riva, B.: Blazing fast 2PC in the offline/online setting with security for malicious adversaries. In: CCS, pp. 579–590 (2015)

41. Nielsen, J.B., Nordholt, P.S., Orlandi, C., Burra, S.S.: A new approach to practical active-secure two-party computation. In: Safavi-Naini, R., Canetti, R. (eds.) CRYPTO 2012. LNCS, vol. 7417, pp. 681–700. Springer, Heidelberg (2012). https://doi.org/10.1007/978-3-642-32009-5_40

42. Nielsen, J.B., Orlandi, C.: LEGO for two-party secure computation. In: Reingold, O. (ed.) TCC 2009. LNCS, vol. 5444, pp. 368–386. Springer, Heidelberg (2009). https://doi.org/10.1007/978-3-642-00457-5_22

43. Rindal, P., Rosulek, M.: Faster malicious 2-party secure computation with online/offline dual execution. In: 25th USENIX Security Symposium, USENIX Security 16, Austin, TX, USA, 10–12 August 2016, pp. 297–314 (2016)

44. Schoenmakers, B., Tuyls, P.: Practical two-party computation based on the conditional gate. In: Lee, P.J. (ed.) ASIACRYPT 2004. LNCS, vol. 3329, pp. 119–136. Springer, Heidelberg (2004). https://doi.org/10.1007/978-3-540-30539-2_10

45. Shamir, A.: How to share a secret. Commun. ACM **22**(11), 612–613 (1979)

46. Shelat, A., Shen, C.: Fast two-party secure computation with minimal assumptions. In: CCS, pp. 523–534 (2013)

47. Wang, X., Malozemoff, A.J., Katz, J.: Faster secure two-party computation in the single-execution setting. In: Coron, J.-S., Nielsen, J.B. (eds.) EUROCRYPT 2017. LNCS, vol. 10212, pp. 399–424. Springer, Cham (2017). https://doi.org/10.1007/978-3-319-56617-7_14

48. Wang, X., Ranellucci, S., Katz, J.: Authenticated garbling and efficient maliciously secure two-party computation. In: CCS, pp. 21–37 (2017)

49. Wang, X., Ranellucci, S., Katz, J.: Global-scale secure multiparty computation. In: CCS, pp. 39–56 (2017)

50. Yao, A.C.: How to generate and exchange secrets (extended abstract). In: FOCS, pp. 162–167 (1986)

51. Zahur, S., Rosulek, M., Evans, D.: Two halves make a whole - reducing data transfer in garbled circuits using half gates. In: Oswald, E., Fischlin, M. (eds.) EUROCRYPT 2015. LNCS, vol. 9057, pp. 220–250. Springer, Heidelberg (2015). https://doi.org/10.1007/978-3-662-46803-6_8

Succinct Non-interactive Secure Computation

Andrew Morgan[1(✉)], Rafael Pass[2(✉)], and Antigoni Polychroniadou[3]

[1] Cornell University, Ithaca, USA
asmorgan@cs.cornell.edu
[2] Cornell Tech, New York City, USA
rafael@cornell.edu
[3] J.P. Morgan AI Research, New York City, USA
antigonipoly@gmail.com

Abstract. We present the first *maliciously secure* protocol for *succinct non-interactive secure two-party computation* (SNISC): Each player sends just a single message whose length is (essentially) independent of the running time of the function to be computed. The protocol does not require any trusted setup, satisfies superpolynomial-time simulation-based security (SPS), and is based on (subexponential) security of the Learning With Errors (LWE) assumption. We do *not* rely on SNARKs or "knowledge of exponent"-type assumptions.

Since the protocol is non-interactive, the relaxation to SPS security is needed, as standard polynomial-time simulation is impossible; however, a slight variant of our main protocol yields a SNISC with polynomial-time simulation in the CRS model.

R. Pass—Supported in part by NSF Award SATC-1704788, NSF Award RI-1703846, and AFOSR Award FA9550-18-1-0267. This research is based upon work supported in part by the Office of the Director of National Intelligence (ODNI), Intelligence Advanced Research Projects Activity (IARPA), via 2019-19-020700006. The views and conclusions contained herein are those of the authors and should not be interpreted as necessarily representing the official policies, either expressed or implied, of ODNI, IARPA, or the U.S. Government. The U.S. Government is authorized to reproduce and distribute reprints for governmental purposes notwithstanding any copyright annotation therein.

A. Polychroniadou—This paper was prepared in part for information purposes by the Artificial Intelligence Research group of JPMorgan Chase & Co and its affiliates ("JP Morgan"), and is not a product of the Research Department of JP Morgan. JP Morgan makes no representation and warranty whatsoever and disclaims all liability, for the completeness, accuracy or reliability of the information contained herein. This document is not intended as investment research or investment advice, or a recommendation, offer or solicitation for the purchase or sale of any security, financial instrument, financial product or service, or to be used in any way for evaluating the merits of participating in any transaction, and shall not constitute a solicitation under any jurisdiction or to any person, if such solicitation under such jurisdiction or to such person would be unlawful. © 2020 JPMorgan Chase & Co. All rights reserved.

© International Association for Cryptologic Research 2020
A. Canteaut and Y. Ishai (Eds.): EUROCRYPT 2020, LNCS 12106, pp. 216–245, 2020.
https://doi.org/10.1007/978-3-030-45724-2_8

1   Introduction

Protocols for *secure two-party computation* (2PC) allow two parties to compute any function (f) of their private inputs (x and y) without revealing anything more than the output $f(x, y)$ of the function. Since their introduction by Yao [42] and Goldreich, Micali and Wigderson [22], they have become one of the most central tools in modern cryptography. In this work, our focus is on 2PC in a setting with a *non-interactivity* requirement: each player sends just a *single* message. The first player—typically referred to as the *receiver* (or R)—computes some message m_1 based on its input x and sends m_1 to the second player. The second player—referred to as the *sender* (S)—next computes a response m_2 (based on its input y and the message m_1 it received) and sends it back to the receiver. Upon receiving the response m_2, the receiver can finally compute and output $f(x, y)$. (Note that in such a non-interactive scenario, it is essential that only the receiver obtains the output—in other words, that the functionality is "one-sided"; otherwise, since the protocol only has two rounds, the sender will be able to compute the output given only m_1, meaning that it could obtain $f(x, y^*)$ on any number of inputs y^* of its choice.)

SNISC: Succinct Non-interactive Secure Computation. As far as we know, this notion of non-interactive 2PC was first formally studied in [30] under the name *non-interactive secure computation (NISC)*; however, informal versions of it became popular in connection with Gentry's breakthrough result on *fully homomorphic encryption* (FHE) [21]. One of the original applications of FHE was the *private outsourcing* of some computation to a remote party: for instance, consider a scenario where a client (the receiver) has some secret input x and wishes a powerful server (the sender) to compute some potentially time-consuming function f on x (and potentially another input y belonging to the server). Using FHE, the client/receiver simply lets m_1 be an FHE encryption of x; the server/sender can next use homomorphic evaluation to obtain an encryption m_2 of $f(x, y)$ to send back, which can be decrypted by the client/receiver. Indeed, an FHE scheme not only directly yields a NISC, but it also yields a *succinct NISC (SNISC)*—where both the communication complexity of the protocol and the running time of an honest receiver are "essentially" independent of the running time of f. More formally, we define a SNISC as a NISC where the communication complexity and receiver running time depend only on the length of the inputs and outputs, and *polylogarithmically* on the running time of the function f to be computed (where we assume that f is given as a Turing machine).

The problem with this folklore approach towards "private outsourcing" or succinct NISC is that using FHE alone only satisfies *semi-honest security*, as opposed to fully *malicious security*. For instance, a malicious sender could decide to compute any other function of its choice instead of the correct f! Of course, we could always extend the protocol using ZK-SNARKs (succinct non-interactive arguments of knowledge) [6,8,20,27,32] to prove correctness of the messages m_1 and m_2, but doing so comes at a cost. First, we now need to assume some trusted setup, such as a *common reference string* (CRS). Additionally, all known constructions of SNARKs are based on knowledge- or extractability-type assumptions, which in general are known to be problematic with respect to arbitrary auxiliary input [7,9].[1] Thus, the question as to whether succinct non-interactive secure computation with *malicious* security is possible in the plain model remains open:

> *Does there exist a succinct non-interactive secure computation protocol without any trusted setup (and without using extractability assumptions)?*

NISC protocols in models *with* trusted setup have been extensively studied. There exist known constructions of NISC in the OT-hybrid model [30], in the CRS model based on cut-and-choose [1,33], assuming tamper-proof stateful [26] and stateless [4,29] hardware tokens, and in the global random oracle model [15]. As far as we know, none of the above protocols are succinct.

The plain model, however, presents additional issues: Goldreich-Oren's [23] classic impossibility result for two-round zero-knowledge proofs immediately shows that even a non-succinct (let alone succinct) NISC with malicious security cannot satisfy the standard *polynomial-time* simulation-based notion of security.[2] Thus, to get *any* NISC, let alone a succinct one, we need to use some relaxed notion of simulatability for the definition of secure computation. *Superpolynomial-time simulation-based security* (SPS) [36,38] has emerged as the standard relaxation of simulation-based security: under SPS security, the attacker is restricted to be a non-uniform polynomial time algorithm, but the simulator (in the definition of secure computation) is allowed to run in (slightly) superpolynomial time (e.g., in quasi-polynomial time). Non-succinct NISC protocols with SPS simulation are known under various standard assumptions [3,36,41]. Most notably, the work of [3] constructs a maliciously secure (non-succinct) NISC with quasi-polynomial simulation in the plain model which can securely compute any functionality based on the subexponential security of various standard hardness assumptions; we return to this result in more detail later on. However, all previous works only construct NISC protocols that are non-succinct.

Towards achieving succinctness for NISC, a very recent work by Brakerski and Kalai [13] takes us a step on the way: they focus on a notion of "private delegation" where the receiver's/client's input x is publicly known (and thus does not need to be kept hidden) but the input y of the sender/server is considered private. The authors present a delegation protocol that achieves *witness indistinguishability (WI)* for the sender—as shown in [36], WI is a strict relaxation of

---

[1] Finally, even forgetting about the issues with extractability assumptions, formalizing this approach requires dealing with some subtle issues, which we will discuss later on. Works where this has been done (in the orthogonal setting of "laconic" function evaluation) include [16,39].

[2] Furthermore, if we restrict to black-box simulation, [19,31] proved that four rounds are necessary and sufficient for secure one-sided 2PC in the plain model.

SPS security.[3] While their protocol achieves the desired notion of succinctness, it still falls short of the goal of producing a succinct NISC protocol due to the fact that its only considers privacy for one of the players (namely, the sender); this significantly simplifies the problem. Additionally, their notion of privacy (witness indistinguishability) is also weaker than what we are aiming to achieve (i.e., simulation-based SPS security).

1.1 Our Results

In this work, we provide an affirmative answer to the above question, presenting the first SNISC for general functionalities. Our protocol is in the plain model (i.e., no trusted setup), and we do not rely on any extractability-based assumptions.

Theorem 1 (Informally stated). *Assuming subexponential security of the LWE assumption, there exists a maliciously SPS-secure SNISC for any efficient functionality. Furthermore, the simulator of the protocol runs in quasi-polynomial time.*

Our protocol relies on three primitives:

- A (leveled) FHE scheme [21] with quasi-polynomial security. For our purposes, we additionally require the FHE to satisfy *perfect correctness*. Such schemes can be based on the (quasi-polynomial security of the) LWE (Learning With Errors) assumption [40], as shown in [11,24].
- A (non-private) delegation scheme for polynomial time computations with quasi-polynomial security. For our purpose, we require a scheme that satisfies *perfect completeness* and allows the sender to adaptively choose the functionality (i.e., we need what is referred to as an "adaptive delegation scheme"). Such schemes can in fact be based on the above notion of quasi-polynomial FHE, and hence in turn on the quasi-polynomial security of the LWE assumption [12].
- A (non-succinct) SPS-secure NISC for general functionalities f with a quasi-polynomial simulator. Such a scheme exists based on the existence of a subexponentially-secure "weak oblivious transfer" protocol[4] [3][5]; this in turn can be based on the subexponential security of any one of the DDH [35], Quadratic Residuosity, or N^{th} Residuosity [28] assumptions, or (as shown in [10]) on subexponential security of the LWE assumption.

---

[3] In the context of interactive proofs, WI is equivalent to a relaxed form of SPS security where the simulator's running time is unbounded (as opposed to some "small" superpolynomial time).

[4] Roughly speaking, a weak oblivious transfer protocol is an OT protocol that satisfies SPS-security against a malicious receiver, but only indistinguishability-based ("game-based") security against a malicious sender.

[5] While [3] claim a construction of SPS NISC from just the existence of a weak OT protocol, their security proof additionally relies on the existence of an *onto* one-way function. As far as we know, onto one-way functions are not known based on the existence of Weak OT. Consequently, in the full version [34] we present a variant of their protocol that dispenses of this additional assumption.

More precisely, if the underlying NISC protocol has a $T(n) \cdot \text{poly}(n)$-time simulator, and if all the other primitives are secure against $T(n) \cdot \text{poly}(n)$ time attackers, the final protocol is secure and has a $T(n) \cdot \text{poly}(n)$-time simulator:

Theorem 2 (Informally stated). *Assuming the existence of a $T(n)$-time simulatable NISC protocol, a subexponentially sound adaptive delegation scheme for polynomial-time computations with perfect completeness, and a subexponentially secure leveled FHE scheme with perfect correctness, there exists $T(n) \cdot \boldsymbol{poly(n)}$-time simulatable SNISC for any efficient functionality.*

As a corollary, we can directly instantiate our protocol using a NISC with polynomial-time simulation in the CRS model based on a two-round universally composable OT protocol (in the CRS model), which [37] shows can be based on the polynomial security of LWE. Hence:

Corollary 1 (Informally stated). *Assuming the polynomial security of the LWE assumption, there exists a maliciously-secure SNISC (with a polynomial-time simulator) in the CRS model for any efficient functionality.*

We defer the proof of this corollary to the full version of our paper [34].

1.2 Technical Overview

At a high level, our approach begins with the semi-honestly secure approach of using FHE (which we detailed in the introduction) and attempts to compile it to become secure with respect to malicious attackers. Instead of using ZK-SNARKs (which rely on non-standard assumptions and trusted setup), we will instead use an adaptive delegation scheme and a non-succinct NISC. For our approach to work, we will strongly rely on *perfect correctness/completeness* properties of both the FHE and the delegation scheme; as far as we know, perfect correctness of these types of primitives has not previously been used to enable applications (where the goal itself isn't perfect correctness).[6] Despite this, though, recent constructions (or slight variants) of both FHE and delegation protocols fortunately do provide these guarantees.

Adaptive Delegation: A Starting Point. To explain the approach, we shall start from a (flawed) candidate which simply combines an FHE scheme and an adaptive delegation scheme. In an adaptive delegation scheme (as given in [12]), a verifier generates a public/secret key-pair $(\mathsf{pk}, \mathsf{sk})$ and sends pk to the prover. The prover next picks some statement $\tilde{x}$ and function g, computes the output $\tilde{y} = g(\tilde{x})$, and produces a "short" proof π of the validity of the statement that $\tilde{y} = g(\tilde{x})$. The prover finally sends $(\tilde{x}, g, \tilde{y}, \pi)$ to the verifier, who can use its secret key sk to check the validity of the proof. We will rely on an adaptive delegation scheme satisfying *perfect completeness*—that is, for all public keys in

---

[6] The only work we are aware that uses perfect correctness of a FHE is a very recent work [2] which uses perfectly correct FHE as a tool to get perfectly correct iO.

the range of the key generation algorithm, the prover can convince the verifier with probability 1.

The candidate SNISC leverages delegation to "outsource" the computation of the homomorphic evaluation to the sender: specifically, the receiver first generates a public/secret key-pair $(\mathsf{pk_{FHE}}, \mathsf{sk_{FHE}})$ for the FHE, encrypts its input x using the FHE (obtaining a ciphertext ct_x), generates a public/secret key pair $(\mathsf{pk_{Del}}, \mathsf{sk_{Del}})$ for the delegation scheme, and finally sends $(\mathsf{ct}_x, \mathsf{pk_{FHE}}, \mathsf{pk_{Del}})$ to the sender. The sender in turn encrypts its input y, obtaining a ciphertext ct_y; next, it lets g be the function for homomorphically evaluating f on two ciphertexts, computes $g(\mathsf{ct}_x, \mathsf{ct}_y)$ (i.e., homomorphically evaluates f on ct_x and ct_y) to obtain a ciphertext $\mathsf{ct_{out}}$, and computes a delegation proof π (with respect to $\mathsf{pk_{Del}}$) of the validity of the computation of g. Finally, the sender sends $(\mathsf{ct}_y, \mathsf{ct_{out}}, \pi)$ to the receiver, who verifies the proof and, if the proof is accepting, decrypts $\mathsf{ct_{out}}$ and outputs it.

Intuitively, this approach hides the input x of the receiver, but clearly fails to hide the input y of the sender, as the receiver can simply decrypt ct_y to obtain y. So, rather than providing ct_y and π in the clear (as even just the proof π could leak things about ct_y), we instead use the (non-succinct) NISC to run the verification procedure of the delegation scheme. That is, we can add to the protocol a NISC instance where the receiver inputs $\mathsf{sk_{Del}}$, the sender inputs $\mathsf{ct}_x, \mathsf{ct}_y, \mathsf{ct_{out}}, \pi$, and the functionality runs the verification algorithm for the delegation scheme, outputting either $\bot$ if verification fails or, otherwise, $\mathsf{ct_{out}}$ (which can be decrypted by the receiver).

Input Independence: Leveraging Perfect Correctness of FHE. The above approach intuitively hides the inputs of both players, and also ensures that the function is computed correctly. But there are many problems with it. For instance, while it guarantees that the sender does not learn the receiver's input x, it does *not* guarantee "input independence", or that the sender's input does not depend on the receiver's somehow: for instance, the sender can easily maul ct_x into, say, an encryption ct_y of $x + 1$ and use that as its input. On a more technical level, simulation-based security requires the simulator to be able to extract the inputs of malicious players, but it is not clear how this can be done here—in fact, a simulator *cannot* extract the sender's input y due to the above malleability attack.

To overcome this issue, we again leverage the non-succinct NISC to enable extractability: we add x and the randomness, r_x, needed to generate ct_x as an input from the receiver, and we add ct_x (i.e., the ciphertext obtained from the receiver), y, and the randomness needed to generate ct_y as input from the sender. The functionality additionally checks that the ciphertexts $\mathsf{ct}_x, \mathsf{ct}_y$ respectively are valid encryptions of the inputs x, y using the given randomness. (It is actually essential that the *sender* includes the ciphertext ct_x from the receiver as part of its input, as opposed to having the receiver input it, as otherwise we could not guarantee that the receiver is sending the same ciphertext to the sender as it is inputting to the NISC). If we have perfect correctness for the underlying FHE scheme with respect to the public-keys selected by the receiver, this approach guarantees that we can correctly extract the inputs of the players. The reason that we need perfect correctness is that the NISC only guarantees that the ciphertexts have been honestly generated using *some* randomness, but we have no guarantees that the randomness is honestly generated. Perfect correctness ensures that all randomness is "good" and will result in a "well-formed" ciphertext on which homomorphic computation, and subsequently decryption, will always lead to the correct output.

Dealing with a Malicious Receiver: Interactive Witness Encryption and Perfectly Correct Delegation. While the above protocol suffices to deal with a malicious sender (although, as we shall discuss later on, even this is not trivial due to the potential for "spooky interactions" [17]), it still does not allow us to deal with a malicious receiver. The problem is that the receiver could send invalid public keys, either for the FHE or for the delegation scheme. For instance, if the public key for the FHE is invalid, perfect correctness may no longer hold, and we may not be able to extract a correct input for the receiver. Likewise, if the public key for the delegation scheme is invalid, we will not be able to determine whether the verification algorithm of the delegation scheme will be accepting, and thus cannot carry out a simulation. Typically, dealing with a malicious receiver would require adding a zero-knowledge proof of well-formedness of its messages; however, given that the receiver is sending the first message, this seems problematic since, even with SPS-security, one-message ZK is impossible (with respect to non-uniform attackers [5,36]).

To explain our solution to this problem, let us first assume that we have access to a *witness encryption scheme* [18]. Recall that a witness encryption scheme enables encrypting a message m with a statement $\tilde{x}$ so that anyone having a witness w to $\tilde{x}$ can decrypt the message; if the statement is false, however, the encryption scheme conceals the message m. If we had access to such a witness encryption scheme, we could have the functionality in the NISC compute a witness encryption of ct_{out} with the statement being that the public keys have been correctly generated. This method ensures that the receiver does not get any meaningful output unless it actually generated the public keys correctly. Of course, it may still use "bad" randomness—we can only verify that the public keys are in the range of the key generating function. But, if the delegation scheme *also* satisfies a "perfect correctness" property (specifically, both correctness of the computation and *perfect completeness* of the generated proof), this enables us to simulate the verification of the delegation scheme (as once again, in this case, perfect correctness guarantees that there is no "bad" randomness).

We still have an issue: perfect correctness of the FHE will ensure that the decryption of the output is correct, but we also need to ensure that we can simulate the ciphertext output by the NISC. While this can be handled using an FHE satisfying an appropriate rerandomizability/simulatability property (also with respect to maliciously selected ciphertext), doing so introduces additional complications. Furthermore, while we motivated the above modification using witness encryption, currently known constructions of witness encryption rely on non-standard, and less understood, hardness assumptions; as such, we would like to altogether avoid using it as an underlying primitive.

So, to circumvent the use of witness encryption—while at the same time ensuring that the output of the NISC is simulatable—we realize that in our context, it in fact suffices to use a *two-round version of witness encryption*, where the receiver of the encryption chooses the statement and can first send a message corresponding to the statement. And such a non-interactive version of witness encryption can be readily implemented using a NISC! As we are already running an instance of a NISC, we can simply have the NISC also implement this interactive witness encryption. More precisely, we now additionally require the receiver to provide its witness—i.e., the randomness for the key generation algorithms—as an input to the NISC, while the sender additionally provides the public keys $\mathsf{pk}_{\mathsf{FHE}}$ and $\mathsf{pk}_{\mathsf{Del}}$ which it receives. The functionality will now only release the output $\mathsf{ct}_{\mathsf{out}}$ if it verifies that the keys input by the sender are correctly generated from the respective randomness input by the receiver. Better still, since the randomness used to generate the public/secret key-pair is now an input to the functionality, the functionality can *also* recover the secret key for the FHE, and next also decrypt $\mathsf{ct}_{\mathsf{out}}$ and simply output plain text corresponding to $\mathsf{ct}_{\mathsf{out}}$. This prevents the need for rerandomizing $\mathsf{ct}_{\mathsf{out}}$, since it is now internal to the NISC instance (and is no longer output). With all of the above modifications, we can now prove that the protocol satisfies SPS security.

The Final Protocol. For clarity, let us summarize the final protocol.

- The Receiver generates $(\mathsf{pk}_{\mathsf{FHE}}, \mathsf{sk}_{\mathsf{FHE}})$ and $(\mathsf{pk}_{\mathsf{Del}}, \mathsf{sk}_{\mathsf{Del}})$ using randomness r_{FHE} and r_{Del} (respectively) and generates an encryption ct_x of its input x using randomness r_x. It then sends $(\mathsf{pk}_{\mathsf{FHE}}, \mathsf{pk}_{\mathsf{Del}}, \mathsf{ct}_x)$ and the first message msg_1 of a NISC using the input $x' = (x, r_{\mathsf{FHE}}, r_{\mathsf{Del}}, r_x)$ (for a functionality to be specified shortly).
- The Sender, upon receiving $\mathsf{pk}_{\mathsf{FHE}}, \mathsf{pk}_{\mathsf{Del}}, \mathsf{msg}_1$ generates an encryption ct_y of its input y using randomness r_y, applies the homomorphic evaluation of f to ct_x and ct_y to obtain a ciphertext $\mathsf{ct}_{\mathsf{out}} = g(\mathsf{ct}_x, \mathsf{ct}_y)$, generates a proof π using the delegation scheme (w.r.t. $\mathsf{pk}_{\mathsf{Del}}$) of the correctness of the computation that $\mathsf{ct}_{\mathsf{out}} = g(\mathsf{ct}_x, \mathsf{ct}_y)$, and finally sends the second message msg_2 of the NISC using the input $y' = (y, \mathsf{pk}_{\mathsf{FHE}}, \mathsf{pk}_{\mathsf{Del}}, \mathsf{ct}_x, \mathsf{ct}_y, \mathsf{ct}_{\mathsf{out}}, \pi, r_y)$.
- Finally, the receiver, upon getting msg_2, computes the output z of the NISC protocol and outputs it.
- The functionality computed by the NISC on input $x' = (x, r_{\mathsf{FHE}}, r_{\mathsf{Del}}, r_x)$ and $y' = (y, \mathsf{pk}_{\mathsf{FHE}}, \mathsf{pk}_{\mathsf{Del}}, \mathsf{ct}_x, \mathsf{ct}_y, \mathsf{ct}_{\mathsf{out}}, \pi, r_y)$ does the following: it checks that:
  1. the public keys $\mathsf{pk}_{\mathsf{FHE}}, \mathsf{pk}_{\mathsf{Del}}$ were respectively generated using randomness $r_{\mathsf{FHE}}, r_{\mathsf{Del}}$;
  2. the ciphertexts $\mathsf{ct}_x, \mathsf{ct}_y$ are respectively encryptions of x, y using randomness r_x, r_y; and,
  3. π is a valid proof of $\mathsf{ct}_{\mathsf{out}} = g(\mathsf{ct}_x, \mathsf{ct}_y)$ w.r.t. $(\mathsf{pk}_{\mathsf{Del}}, \mathsf{sk}_{\mathsf{Del}})$ (as generated from r_{Del}).

If the checks pass, it decrypts $\mathsf{ct_{out}}$ (by first generating $\mathsf{sk_{FHE}}$ from r_{FHE}), obtaining the plaintext z, and finally outputs z. (If any of the checks fail, it instead outputs $\perp$.)

A summary of the message flow can be found in Fig. 1.

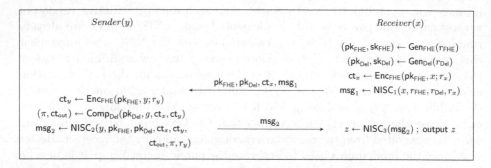

Fig. 1. The final SNISC protocol. $(\mathsf{NISC_1}, \mathsf{NISC_2}, \mathsf{NISC_3})$ denotes the underlying (non-succinct) NISC protocol and the functionality g denotes the homomorphic evaluation $g(c_1, c_2) = \mathsf{Eval_{FHE}}(\mathsf{pk_{FHE}}, f, c_1, c_2)$.

A Subtlety in the Security Proof. One subtle point that arises in the proof of security is that, to simulate a malicious sender, we need to simulate the ciphertext ct_x without knowledge of x. But the functionality of the underlying NISC takes as input the randomness used for both the key generation of $\mathsf{pk_{FHE}}$ and for encrypting ct_x, and thus the functionality implicitly knows how to decrypt ct_x. A similar issue has arisen in the related context of constructing delegation schemes from FHE and related primitives (see [17]), where it was shown that so-called "spooky interactions" can arise, where a malicious sender (even though it does not how to decrypt the ciphertext) can in fact use this dependence to make the receiver output values that correlate in undesirable ways with the input x (in particular, in ways that would not have been possible if using an "idealized" FHE). Fortunately, in our context, we are able to overcome this issue by using the perfect correctness of the FHE scheme and soundness of our underlying delegation scheme to perform a carefully designed hybrid argument.

A bit more precisely, the key point is that when simulating a malicious sender in communication with an *honest* receiver, the receiver's public key and ciphertext ct_x will always be correctly generated (as such, we do not have to perform the checks involving the receiver to simulate the underlying NISC's output); furthermore, by soundness of delegation and the perfect correctness of the FHE, the decryption of $\mathsf{ct_{out}}$ must equal $f(x, y)$ (with overwhelming probability) if π is accepting, so we can use this fact to show that decrypting $\mathsf{ct_{out}}$ is actually *also* unnecessary. As such, we do not need to use either r_{FHE} or r_x to emulate the experiment for a malicious sender, and we can create (and prove security in) a hybrid functionality for the underlying NISC which is independent of this randomness (and only depends on $\mathsf{pk_{FHE}}$).

2   Preliminaries

2.1   Fully Homomorphic Encryption

Definition 1 (based on [21]). *A **fully homomorphic encryption** (or FHE) scheme consists of a tuple of algorithms* (Gen, Enc, Eval, Dec), *where* Gen, Enc *are PPT and* Eval, Dec *are (deterministic) polynomial-time algorithms, such that:*

- $(\mathsf{pk}, \mathsf{sk}) \leftarrow \mathsf{Gen}(1^n; \rho)$: *takes the security parameter n as input and outputs a public key* pk *and secret key* sk.
- $\mathsf{ct} \leftarrow \mathsf{Enc}(\mathsf{pk}, m; \rho)$: *takes as input a public key* pk *and a message $m \in \{0, 1\}$, and outputs a ciphertext* ct. *(For multi-bit messages $\overrightarrow{m} \in \{0, 1\}^{p(n)}$, we let $\overrightarrow{\mathsf{ct}} \leftarrow \mathsf{Enc}(\mathsf{pk}, \overrightarrow{m})$ be such that $\mathsf{ct}_i = \mathsf{Enc}(\mathsf{pk}, m_i)$.)*
- $\mathsf{ct}' = \mathsf{Eval}(\mathsf{pk}, C, \overrightarrow{\mathsf{ct}})$: *takes as input a list of ciphertexts $\overrightarrow{\mathsf{ct}}$ and a circuit description C of some function to evaluate and outputs a ciphertext* ct'.
- $m' \leftarrow \mathsf{Dec}(\mathsf{sk}, \mathsf{ct})$: *takes as input a ciphertext* ct *and outputs a message* m'.

We furthermore require that the following properties are satisfied:

1. **Full homomorphism:** *There exist sets of boolean circuits $\{\mathcal{C}_n\}_{n \in \mathbb{N}}$, negligible function $\epsilon(n)$, and polynomial $p(\cdot)$ such that $\mathcal{C} = \bigcup_n \mathcal{C}_n$ includes the set of all arithmetic circuits over $GF(2)^7$, and, for any $n \in \mathbb{N}$, we have that, for all $C \in \mathcal{C}_n$ and $\overrightarrow{m} \in \{0, 1\}^{p(n)}$:*

$$Pr[z \neq C(\overrightarrow{m}) : (\mathsf{pk}, \mathsf{sk}) \leftarrow \mathsf{Gen}(1^n), \overrightarrow{\mathsf{ct}} \leftarrow \mathsf{Enc}(\mathsf{pk}, \overrightarrow{m}),$$

$$z \leftarrow \mathsf{Dec}(\mathsf{sk}, \mathsf{Eval}(C, \mathsf{pk}, \overrightarrow{\mathsf{ct}}))] < \epsilon(n),$$

   *Furthermore, if this probability is identically zero, we refer to the scheme as having **perfect correctness**.*
2. **Compactness:** *There exists a polynomial $q(\cdot)$ such that the output length of* Eval *given (any number of) inputs generated with security parameter n is at most $q(n)$.*

Definition 2 (based on [25]). *We say that an FHE* (Gen, Enc, Eval, Dec) *is **secure** if, for all non-uniform PPT D, there exists a negligible $\epsilon(\cdot)$ such that for any $n \in \mathbb{N}$:*

$$|Pr[D(1^n, \mathsf{pk}, \mathsf{Enc}(\mathsf{pk}, 0)) = 1] - Pr[D(1^n, \mathsf{pk}, \mathsf{Enc}(\mathsf{pk}, 1)) = 1]| < \epsilon(n)$$

*over $(\mathsf{pk}, \mathsf{sk}) \leftarrow \mathsf{Gen}(1^n)$. If this condition holds also with respect to subexponential size distinguishers D (i.e., algorithms implemented by circuits of size $poly(2^{n^\epsilon})$ for some $\epsilon > 0$), we refer to the scheme as being **subexponentially secure**.*

---

[7] GF(2) is the set of arithmetic circuits consisting only of $+$ and $\times$ gates over the field $\mathbb{F}_2$.

We have the following consequence for encryptions of poly(n)-bit messages $\overrightarrow{m_0}$ and $\overrightarrow{m_1}$:

Fact 1. *If an FHE scheme* (Gen, Enc, Eval, Dec) *is secure (resp., subexponentially secure), then, for any polynomial $p(\cdot)$ and for any non-uniform PPT (resp., subexponential-size) $(\mathcal{A}, D)$ where $\mathcal{A}$ outputs messages $\overrightarrow{m_0}, \overrightarrow{m_1} \in \{0,1\}^{p(n)}$ for polynomial $p(\cdot)$, there exists a negligible $\epsilon(\cdot)$ such that for any $n \in \mathbb{N}$:*

$$|Pr[D(1^n, \mathsf{pk}, \mathsf{Enc}(\mathsf{pk}, \overrightarrow{m_0})) = 1] - Pr[D(1^n, \mathsf{pk}, \mathsf{Enc}(\mathsf{pk}, \overrightarrow{m_1})) = 1]| < \epsilon(n)$$

where

$$(\mathsf{pk}, \mathsf{sk}) \leftarrow \mathsf{Gen}(1^n), (\overrightarrow{m_0}, \overrightarrow{m_1}) \leftarrow \mathcal{A}(1^n, \mathsf{pk})$$

We can construct an FHE scheme with all of the above properties based on the Learning With Errors (LWE) assumption:

Theorem 3 ([2,11,24]). *Based on computational (resp., subexponential) hardness of the Learning With Errors assumption, there exists a secure (resp., subexponentially secure) fully homomorphic encryption scheme satisfying perfect correctness.*

2.2 Adaptive Delegation Schemes

A delegation scheme allows for the effective "outsourcing" of computation from one party to another; that is, using delegation, the sender can compute both the correct result of some (possibly expensive) computation on a receiver's input and a (short) proof which can convince the receiver of the correctness of the computation without requiring the receiver to perform the computation themselves. We consider a notion of delegation with the additional property, formalized in [12], that the functionality $f(\cdot)$ whose computation is to be delegated can be decided *adaptively* after the keys pk, sk are computed (i.e., the key-generation algorithm Gen is independent from f). Formally:

Definition 3 (based on [12]). *An **adaptive delegation scheme** is given by a triple of algorithms* (Gen, Comp, Ver), *where* Comp *and* Ver *are (deterministic) polynomial-time algorithms and* Gen *is PPT, such that:*

- $(\mathsf{pk}, \mathsf{sk}) \leftarrow \mathsf{Gen}(1^n; \rho)$ *takes as input a security parameter n and probabilistically outputs a public key* pk *and secret key* sk.
- $(y, \pi, 1^T) \leftarrow \mathsf{Comp}(\mathsf{pk}, f, \overrightarrow{x})$ *takes as input a Turing machine description of the functionality f to be computed, as well as the inputs $\overrightarrow{x}$ to f, and produces a result y which the sender claims to be the result of the computation, a poly(n)-size proof π of its correctness, and the running time T of the computation in unary.*
- $\{\mathsf{Accept}, \mathsf{Reject}\} \leftarrow \mathsf{Ver}(\mathsf{sk}, f, \overrightarrow{x}, y, \pi, T)$ *takes as input the functionality f to be computed, inputs $\overrightarrow{x}$, result y, proof π, and running time T, and returns* Accept *or* Reject *depending on whether π is a valid proof of $f(\overrightarrow{x}) = y$.*

Furthermore, we require the following properties:

1. **Completeness:** *There exists a negligible function $\epsilon(\cdot)$ such that, for any $n \in \mathbb{N}$, any f computable by a Turing machine that runs in time at most 2^n, and any $\overrightarrow{x}$ in the domain of f:*

$$\Pr\left[(\mathsf{pk}, \mathsf{sk}) \leftarrow \mathsf{Gen}(1^n); (\pi, y, 1^T) = \mathsf{Comp}(\mathsf{pk}, f, \overrightarrow{x}) : \right.$$
$$\left. \mathsf{Ver}(\mathsf{sk}, f, \overrightarrow{x}, \pi, y, T) = \mathsf{Reject}\right] < \epsilon(n)$$

In addition, if the above probability is identically zero, we say that the adaptive delegation scheme satisfies **perfect completeness.**

2. **Correctness:** *For any $n \in \mathbb{N}$, any f computable by a Turing machine that runs in time at most 2^n, and any $\overrightarrow{x}$ in the domain of f:*

$$Pr\left[(\mathsf{pk}, \mathsf{sk}) \leftarrow \mathsf{Gen}(1^n) : \mathsf{Comp}(\mathsf{pk}, f, \overrightarrow{x}) = (f(\overrightarrow{x}), \cdot, \cdot)\right] = 1$$

3. **Soundness:** *For any non-uniform PPT adversary $\mathcal{A}$, there exists a negligible function $\epsilon(\cdot)$ such that, for any $n \in \mathbb{N}$:*

$$\Pr\left[(\mathsf{pk}, \mathsf{sk}) \leftarrow \mathsf{Gen}(1^n), (f, \overrightarrow{x}, y_1, y_2, \pi_1, \pi_2, 1^{T_1}, 1^{T_2}) \leftarrow \mathcal{A}(1^n, \mathsf{pk}) : \right.$$
$$T < 2^n \wedge \mathsf{Ver}(\mathsf{sk}, f, \overrightarrow{x}, y_1, \pi_1, T_1) = \mathsf{Accept}$$
$$\left. \wedge \mathsf{Ver}(\mathsf{sk}, f, \overrightarrow{x}, y_2, \pi_2, T_2) = \mathsf{Accept} \wedge y_1 \neq y_2\right] < \epsilon(n)$$

Furthermore, if this condition holds with respect to subexponential-size adversaries, we say that the scheme is **subexponentially sound.**

A construction of an adaptive delegation scheme with perfect completeness can be found in the work of Brakerski et al. [12], and is based on a secure private information retrieval (PIR) scheme, which in turn can be constructed based on a leveled FHE scheme (including the one presented in Theorem 3). Hence:

Theorem 4 ([2,11,12,24]). *Given computational (resp., subexponential) hardness of the Learning With Errors assumption, there exists a sound (resp., subexponentially sound) adaptive delegation scheme satisfying perfect completeness.*

2.3   Non-interactive Secure Computation

Definition 4 (based on [3,22,42]). *A* **non-interactive two-party computation protocol** *for computing some functionality $f(\cdot, \cdot)$ (we assume f to be computable by a polynomial-time Turing machine) is given by three PPT algorithms $(\mathsf{NISC}_1, \mathsf{NISC}_2, \mathsf{NISC}_3)$ defining an interaction between a sender S and a receiver R, where only R will receive the final output. The protocol will have common input 1^n (the security parameter); the receiver R will have input x, and the sender will have input y. The algorithms $(\mathsf{NISC}_1, \mathsf{NISC}_2, \mathsf{NISC}_3)$ are such that:*

- *$(\mathsf{msg}_1, \sigma) \leftarrow \mathsf{NISC}_1(1^n, x)$ generates R's message msg_1 and persistent state σ (which is not sent to S) given the security parameter n and R's input x.*

- $\mathsf{msg}_2 \leftarrow \mathsf{NISC}_2(\mathsf{msg}_1, y)$ *generates S's message msg_2 given S's input y and R's message msg_1.*
- $out \leftarrow \mathsf{NISC}_3(\sigma, \mathsf{msg}_2)$ *generates R's output out given the state σ and S's message msg_2.*

Furthermore, we require the following property:

- **Correctness.** *For any parameter $n \in \mathbb{N}$ and inputs x, y:*

$$Pr\left[(\mathsf{msg}_1, \sigma) \leftarrow \mathsf{NISC}_1(1^n, x) : \mathsf{NISC}_3(\sigma, \mathsf{NISC}_2(\mathsf{msg}_1, y)) \neq f(x, y)\right] \leq \epsilon(n)$$

Defining non-interactive *secure* computation will require us to add a security definition, which we formalize as follows:

Security. We adopt a standard notion of *simulation-based security*, with the relaxation that we allow superpolynomial-time simulation (as originally proposed in [36,38]). We define security by comparing two experiments conducted between the sender and receiver, either of whom may be corrupted and act arbitrarily (while the other is honest and follows the protocol). In the *real* experiment, the two parties will perform the actual protocol; in the *ideal* experiment, the two parties will instead send their inputs to a "trusted third party" who performs the computation and returns the result only to, in this case (because the protocol is one-sided), the receiver. Informally, we say that a protocol is secure if, for any adversary $\mathcal{A}$ against the *real* experiment, acting either as the sender or receiver, there is a simulated adversary $\mathcal{S}$ in the *ideal* experiment which produces a near-identical (i.e., computationally indistinguishable) result; intuitively, if this is the case, we can assert that the real adversary cannot "learn" anything more than they could by interacting with a trusted intermediary. Let us formalize this notion for the case of SNISC:

- Let the *real* experiment be defined as an interaction between a sender S with input y and a receiver R with input x, defined as follows:
  - R computes $(\mathsf{msg}_1, \sigma) \leftarrow \mathsf{NISC}_1(1^n, x)$, stores σ, and sends msg_1 to S.
  - S, on receiving msg_1, computes $\mathsf{msg}_2 \leftarrow \mathsf{NISC}_2(\mathsf{msg}_1, y)$ and sends msg_2 to R.
  - R, on receiving msg_2 computes $out \leftarrow \mathsf{NISC}_3(\sigma, \mathsf{msg}_2)$ and outputs out.
  In this interaction, one party $I \in \{S, R\}$ is defined as the *corrupted* party; we additionally define an *adversary*, or a polynomial-time machine $\mathcal{A}$, which receives the security parameter 1^n, an auxiliary input z, and the inputs of the corrupted party I, and sends messages (which it may determine arbitrarily) in place of I.
  Letting Π denote the protocol to be proven secure, we shall denote by $\mathsf{Out}_{\Pi, \mathcal{A}, I}(1^n, x, y, z)$ the random variable, taken over all randomness used by the honest party and the adversary, whose output is given by the outputs of the honest receiver (if $I = S$) and the adversary (which may output an arbitrary function of its view).
- Let the *ideal* experiment be defined as an interaction between a sender S, a receiver R, and a *trusted party* $\mathcal{T}_f$, defined as follows:

- R sends x to T_f, and S sends y to T_f.
- T_f, on receiving x and y, computes $out = f(x,y)$ and returns it to R.
- R, on receiving out, outputs it.

As with the real experiment, we say that one party $I \in \{S, R\}$ is corrupted in that, as before, their behavior is controlled by an adversary $\mathcal{A}$. We shall denote by $\mathsf{Out}^{T_f}_{\Pi_f, \mathcal{A}, I}(1^n, x, y, z)$ the random variable, once again taken over all randomness used by the honest party and the adversary, whose output is again given by the outputs of the honest receiver (if $I = S$) and the adversary.

Given the above, we can now formally define non-interactive secure computation:

Definition 5 (based on [3,22,36,38,42]). *Given a function $T(\cdot)$, a non-interactive two-party protocol $\Pi = (\mathsf{NISC}_1, \mathsf{NISC}_2, \mathsf{NISC}_3)$ between a sender S and a receiver R, and functionality $f(\cdot, \cdot)$ computable by a polynomial-time Turing machine, we say that Π* **securely computes** f **with** $T(\cdot)$**-time simulation**, *or that Π is a* **non-interactive secure computation (NISC) protocol (with** $T(\cdot)$**-time simulation)** *for computing f, if Π is a non-interactive two-party computation protocol for computing f and, for any polynomial-time adversary $\mathcal{A}$ corrupting party $I \in \{S, R\}$, there exists a $T(n) \cdot poly(n)$-time simulator S such that, for any $T(n) \cdot poly(n)$-time algorithm $D : \{0, 1\}^* \rightarrow \{0, 1\}$, there exists negligible $\epsilon(\cdot)$ such that for any $n \in \mathbb{N}$ and any inputs $x, y \in \{0, 1\}^n, z \in \{0, 1\}^*$, we have:*

$$\left| Pr\left[D(\mathsf{Out}_{\Pi, \mathcal{A}, I}(1^n, x, y, z)) = 1 \right] - Pr\left[D(\mathsf{Out}^{T_f}_{\Pi_f, S, I}(1^n, x, y, z)) = 1 \right] \right| < \epsilon(n)$$

where the experiments and distributions Out are as defined above.

Furthermore, if Π securely computes f with $T(\cdot)$-time simulation for $T(n) = n^{\log^c(n)}$ for some constant c, we say that Π **securely computes** f **with quasi-polynomial simulation**.

Succinctness. The defining feature of our construction will be a notion of *succinctness*; specifically, for functionality $f(\cdot, \cdot)$ with Turing machine description M and running time bounded by T_f, we show the existence of a NISC protocol $\Pi = (\mathsf{NISC}_1, \mathsf{NISC}_2, \mathsf{NISC}_3)$ for computing f whose message length (i.e., the combined output length of NISC_1 and NISC_2) and total receiver running time on input 1^n are relatively short and essentially independent of the running time of f. Formally:

Definition 6. *We say that a NISC protocol $\Pi = (\mathsf{NISC}_1, \mathsf{NISC}_2, \mathsf{NISC}_3)$ has* **communication complexity** $\rho(\cdot)$ *if, for any $n \in \mathbb{N}$, $x, y \in \{0, 1\}^n$, and $z \in \{0, 1\}^*$, the outputs of $\mathsf{NISC}_1(1^n, x)$ and $\mathsf{NISC}_2(1^n, y, z)$ contain at most $\rho(n)$ bits.*

We shall define a NISC protocol which, given functionality $f : \{0, 1\}^n \times \{0, 1\}^n \leftarrow \{0, 1\}^{\ell(n)}$ computable by a Turing machine M with running time $T_f(n)$, features communication complexity and receiver running time bounded above by $p(n, \log(T_f(n)), |M|, \ell(n))$ for an *a priori* fixed polynomial p.

There exist *non-succinct* non-interactive secure computation protocols in the standard model based on a notion of "weak oblivious transfer" [3], which in turn can be based on subexponential security of the Learning With Errors assumption [10]:

Theorem 5 ([3, 10]). *Assuming subexponential hardness of the Learning With Errors assumption, for any functionality $f(\cdot, \cdot)$ computable by a polynomial-time Turing machine there exists a (non-succinct) non-interactive secure computation protocol with quasi-polynomial simulation for computing f.*

We note that this theorem essentially follows from [3, 10]; however, [3] required as an additional assumption the existence of an *onto* one-way function. In the full version of our paper [34], we present a variant which demonstrates how to prove Theorem 5 without this added assumption.

3   Protocol

We state our main theorem:

Theorem 6. *Assuming subexponential hardness of the Learning With Errors assumption, there exists polynomial $p(\cdot, \cdot, \cdot, \cdot)$ such that, for any polynomials $T_f(\cdot)$ and $\ell(\cdot)$ and any Turing machine M with running time bounded by $T_f(\cdot)$ computing functionality $f(\cdot, \cdot) : \{0,1\}^n \times \{0,1\}^n \leftarrow \{0,1\}^{\ell(n)}$, there exists a non-interactive secure computation protocol for computing f with quasi-polynomial simulation which is additionally succinct in that both its communication complexity and the running time of the honest receiver are at most $p(n, log(T_f(n)), |M|, \ell(n))$.*

We propose the protocol Π given in Fig. 2 for secure non-interactive secure computation of a function $f(x, y)$ given a receiver input x and sender input y, where Π shall use the following primitives:

- Let $\pi = (\mathsf{NISC}_1, \mathsf{NISC}_2, \mathsf{NISC}_3)$ be a non-succinct NISC protocol with $T(n)$-time simulation for $T(n) = n^{\log^c(n)}$ (i.e., quasi-polynomial simulation), for which the functionality h will be determined in the first round of the protocol. (The existence of such a primitive is guaranteed by Theorem 5 under subexponential LWE.)
- Let $(\mathsf{Gen}_{\mathsf{FHE}}, \mathsf{Enc}_{\mathsf{FHE}}, \mathsf{Dec}_{\mathsf{FHE}}, \mathsf{Eval}_{\mathsf{FHE}})$ be a fully homomorphic encryption scheme satisfying perfect correctness, compactness, and subexponential security (in particular, with respect to $T(n) \cdot \mathsf{poly}(n)$-time adversaries). (The existence of such a primitive is guaranteed by Theorem 3 under subexponential LWE.)
- Let $(\mathsf{Gen}_{\mathsf{Del}}, \mathsf{Comp}_{\mathsf{Del}}, \mathsf{Ver}_{\mathsf{Del}})$ be an adaptive delegation scheme with perfect completeness, correctness, and subexponential soundness (in particular, with respect to $T(n) \cdot \mathsf{poly}(n)$-time adversaries). (The existence of such a primitive is guaranteed by Theorem 4 under subexponential LWE.)

Input: The receiver R and the sender S are given input $x, y \in \{0, 1\}^n$, respectively, and both parties have common input 1^n.

Output: R receives $f(x, y)$.

Round 1: R proceeds as follows:

1. Generate random coins $r_{\mathsf{FHE}} \leftarrow \{0, 1\}^*$ and compute $(\mathsf{pk}_{\mathsf{FHE}}, \mathsf{sk}_{\mathsf{FHE}}) = \mathsf{Gen}_{\mathsf{FHE}}(1^n; r_{\mathsf{FHE}})$.
2. Let T_g denote the running time of the functionality $g(c_1, c_2) = \mathsf{Eval}_{\mathsf{FHE}}(\mathsf{pk}_{\mathsf{FHE}}, f, c_1, c_2)$, and let $\lambda = \max(n, \log(T_g))$. Generate random coins $r_{\mathsf{Del}} \leftarrow \{0, 1\}^*$ and compute $(\mathsf{pk}_{\mathsf{Del}}, \mathsf{sk}_{\mathsf{Del}}) = \mathsf{Gen}_{\mathsf{Del}}(1^\lambda; r_{\mathsf{Del}})$.
3. Generate random coins $r_{\mathsf{Enc}(x)} \leftarrow \{0, 1\}^*$ and compute $\mathsf{ct}_x = \mathsf{Enc}_{\mathsf{FHE}}(\mathsf{pk}_{\mathsf{FHE}}, x; r_{\mathsf{Enc}(x)})$.
4. Generate message $\mathsf{msg}_1 \leftarrow \mathsf{NISC}_1(x, r_{\mathsf{FHE}}, r_{\mathsf{Del}}, r_{\mathsf{Enc}(x)})$ to compute the functionality h described in Figure 3.
5. Send $(\mathsf{pk}_{\mathsf{FHE}}, \mathsf{pk}_{\mathsf{Del}}, \mathsf{ct}_x, \mathsf{msg}_1)$ to S.

Round 2: S proceeds as follows:

1. Generate random coins $r_{\mathsf{Enc}(y)} \leftarrow \{0, 1\}^*$ and compute $\mathsf{ct}_y = \mathsf{Enc}_{\mathsf{FHE}}(\mathsf{pk}_{\mathsf{FHE}}, y; r_{\mathsf{Enc}(y)})$.
2. Compute $(\mathsf{ct}_{\mathsf{out}}, \pi_{\mathsf{Del}}, 1^T) = \mathsf{Comp}_{\mathsf{Del}}(\mathsf{pk}_{\mathsf{Del}}, g, \mathsf{ct}_x, \mathsf{ct}_y)$ for the functionality $g(c_1, c_2) = \mathsf{Eval}_{\mathsf{FHE}}(\mathsf{pk}_{\mathsf{FHE}}, f, c_1, c_2)$.
3. Generate message $\mathsf{msg}_2 \leftarrow \mathsf{NISC}_2(y, \mathsf{pk}_{\mathsf{FHE}}, \mathsf{pk}_{\mathsf{Del}}, \mathsf{ct}_x, \mathsf{ct}_y, \mathsf{ct}_{\mathsf{out}}, \pi_{\mathsf{Del}}, r_{\mathsf{Enc}(y)}, T)$ to compute the functionality h described in Figure 3.
4. Send msg_2 to R.

Output phase: R computes $\mathsf{out} = \mathsf{NISC}_3(\mathsf{msg}_2)$ and returns the result.

Fig. 2. Protocol Π for succinct non-interactive secure computation.

4   Proof

Overview. After first proving the succinctness and correctness of the protocol, we turn to proving its security. We do this in two steps. In the first step, we consider a "hybrid" model in which the underlying NISC protocol is replaced by an "ideal" third party $\mathcal{T}_h$. If the underlying protocol were universally composable [14], this step would be trivial; unfortunately, it is not, so we need to take care to formally reduce this transformation to the simulation-based security of the underlying protocol. Crucially, this will rely on the fact that we restrict our attention to two-round protocols.

Next, in the second step, we can create and prove the respective simulators for a corrupted sender and corrupted receiver in the $\mathcal{T}_h$-hybrid model. The corrupted receiver case follows in a fairly straightforward way, relying on the perfect correctness and completeness of the delegation and FHE schemes. The corrupted sender case, however, has some interesting subtleties in the reduction,

Input: The receiver R has input $(x, r_{\mathsf{FHE}}, r_{\mathsf{Del}}, r_{\mathsf{Enc}(x)})$, and the sender S has
input $(y, \mathsf{pk}_{\mathsf{FHE}}, \mathsf{pk}_{\mathsf{Del}}, \mathsf{ct}_x, \mathsf{ct}_y, \mathsf{ct}_{\mathsf{out}}, \pi_{\mathsf{Del}}, r_{\mathsf{Enc}(y)}, T)$
Output: Either a message out or the special symbol $\perp$.

Functionality:
1. Verify that all of the following checks hold. If any fail, return $\perp$.
   (a) $(\mathsf{pk}_{\mathsf{FHE}}, \cdot) = \mathsf{Gen}_{\mathsf{FHE}}(1^n; r_{\mathsf{FHE}})$
   (b) $(\mathsf{pk}_{\mathsf{Del}}, \cdot) = \mathsf{Gen}_{\mathsf{Del}}(1^\lambda; r_{\mathsf{Del}})$
   (c) $\mathsf{ct}_x = \mathsf{Enc}_{\mathsf{FHE}}(\mathsf{pk}_{\mathsf{FHE}}, x; r_{\mathsf{Enc}(x)})$
   (d) $\mathsf{ct}_y = \mathsf{Enc}_{\mathsf{FHE}}(\mathsf{pk}_{\mathsf{FHE}}, y; r_{\mathsf{Enc}(y)})$
2. Compute $(\cdot, \mathsf{sk}_{\mathsf{FHE}}) = \mathsf{Gen}_{\mathsf{FHE}}(1^n; r_{\mathsf{FHE}})$ and $(\cdot, \mathsf{sk}_{\mathsf{Del}}) = \mathsf{Gen}_{\mathsf{Del}}(1^\lambda; r_{\mathsf{Del}})$.
3. If $\mathsf{Ver}_{\mathsf{Del}}(\mathsf{sk}_{\mathsf{Del}}, g, \mathsf{ct}_x, \mathsf{ct}_y, \mathsf{ct}_{\mathsf{out}}, \pi_{\mathsf{Del}}, T) = \mathsf{Reject}$ for the functionality
   $g(c_1, c_2) = \mathsf{Eval}_{\mathsf{FHE}}(\mathsf{pk}_{\mathsf{FHE}}, f, c_1, c_2)$, then return $\perp$.
4. Compute $\mathsf{out} = \mathsf{Dec}_{\mathsf{FHE}}(\mathsf{sk}_{\mathsf{FHE}}, \mathsf{ct}_{\mathsf{out}})$ and return the result.

Fig. 3. Functionality h used for the underlying 2PC protocol π.

and in fact will require another hybrid with a slightly different third party $\mathcal{T}_{h'}$ to
complete; we discuss these subtleties in more detail when they arise during the
proof. We begin the formal proof by proving that the protocol Π is *succinct*:

Lemma 1. *There exists polynomial* $p(\cdot, \cdot, \cdot, \cdot)$ *such that, for any polynomials*
$T_f(\cdot)$ *and* $\ell(\cdot)$ *and any Turing machine* M *with running time bounded by* $T_f(\cdot)$
computing functionality $f(\cdot, \cdot) : \{0,1\}^n \times \{0,1\}^n \leftarrow \{0,1\}^{\ell(n)}$, *the respective*
non-interactive secure computation protocol Π *has communication complexity*
and honest receiver running time bounded above by $p(n, \log(T_f(n)), |M|, \ell(n))$.

Proof. We begin by analyzing the communication complexity, as succinctness of
the receiver's running time will follow immediately from this analysis. Aside from
messages msg_1 and msg_2 for the underlying NISC π, the only communication
consists of the public keys $\mathsf{pk}_{\mathsf{FHE}}$ and $\mathsf{pk}_{\mathsf{Del}}$ and the ciphertext ct_x. $\mathsf{pk}_{\mathsf{FHE}}$ has
length $\mathsf{poly}(n)$ since $\mathsf{Gen}_{\mathsf{FHE}}$ is a polynomial-time algorithm running on input
1^n, and the ciphertext ct_x (which consists of a ciphertext for each bit in $x \in$
$\{0,1\}^n$) also has length $\mathsf{poly}(n)$ since $\mathsf{Enc}_{\mathsf{FHE}}$ is polynomial-time and is run on
inputs of length $\mathsf{poly}(n)$. $\mathsf{pk}_{\mathsf{Del}}$ will have length $\mathsf{poly}(n, \log(T_f))$; specifically, its
length is given to be $\mathsf{poly}(\lambda) = \mathsf{poly}(n, \log(T_g))$, where T_g is the running time of
the functionality $g(c_1, c_2) = \mathsf{Eval}_{\mathsf{FHE}}(\mathsf{pk}_{\mathsf{FHE}}, f, c_1, c_2)$ with inputs generated from
common input 1^n. However, since $\mathsf{pk}_{\mathsf{FHE}}$ has $\mathsf{poly}(n)$ length, the input ciphertexts
both have $\mathsf{poly}(n)$ length by the efficiency of $\mathsf{Enc}_{\mathsf{FHE}}$, and f in this case is given as
a *circuit* description, which will have size $\mathsf{poly}(T_f(n))$, we have by the efficiency
of $\mathsf{Eval}_{\mathsf{FHE}}$ that $T_g = \mathsf{poly}(n, T_f(n))$, implying $\mathsf{poly}(\lambda) = \mathsf{poly}(n, \log(T_f(n)))$.

So it suffices now to bound the length of the NISC messages msg_1 and msg_2.
Specifically, even for a *non-succinct* NISC protocol π, the honest sender and
receiver must be efficient, and so the message length is still at most polynomial

in the input length and running time of the functionality h. We argue that these are $\mathsf{poly}(n, \log(T_f(n)), |M|, \ell(n))$ to complete the proof of the claim:

- The input length to π is given as the size of the inputs $(x, r_{\mathsf{FHE}}, r_{\mathsf{Del}}, r_{\mathsf{Enc}(x)})$ from the receiver and $(y, \mathsf{pk}_{\mathsf{FHE}}, \mathsf{pk}_{\mathsf{Del}}, \mathsf{ct}_x, \mathsf{ct}_y, \mathsf{ct}_{\mathsf{out}}, \pi_{\mathsf{Del}}, r_{\mathsf{Enc}(y)}, T)$ from the sender. x and y have length n by assumption. $\mathsf{pk}_{\mathsf{FHE}}, \mathsf{ct}_x$, and ct_y have length $\mathsf{poly}(n)$ as argued above, and $\mathsf{ct}_{\mathsf{out}}$ (which consists of a ciphertext output from $\mathsf{Eval}_{\mathsf{FHE}}$ for each bit of $f(x,y) \in \{0,1\}^{\ell(n)}$) has length $\mathsf{poly}(n, \ell(n))$ by the compactness of the FHE scheme. $\mathsf{pk}_{\mathsf{Del}}$ has length $\mathsf{poly}(n, \log(T_f(n)))$ as argued above, and π_{Del} also has length $\mathsf{poly}(\lambda) = \mathsf{poly}(n, \log(T_f(n)))$; T will have size $\lambda = \mathsf{poly}(n, \log(T_f(n)))$ as $T \leq 2^\lambda$ is required by the properties of the delegation scheme. Lastly, the randomness $r_{\mathsf{FHE}}, r_{\mathsf{Del}}, r_{\mathsf{Enc}(x)}, r_{\mathsf{Enc}(y)}$ cannot have length greater than the running times of the respective algorithms $\mathsf{Gen}_{\mathsf{FHE}}, \mathsf{Gen}_{\mathsf{Del}}, \mathsf{Enc}_{\mathsf{FHE}}$, all of which we have already noted are at most $\mathsf{poly}(n, \log(T_f(n)))$.
- To bound the running time of the functionality h, notice that it consists of the following:
  - $\mathsf{Gen}_{\mathsf{FHE}}$ (run twice), $\mathsf{Enc}_{\mathsf{FHE}}$ (run $2n$ times, once for each bit of x and y), $\mathsf{Eval}_{\mathsf{FHE}}$ (run $\ell(n)$ times, once for each bit of out), all of which are efficient algorithms run on inputs of at most length $\mathsf{poly}(n)$ (and hence have running time $\mathsf{poly}(n)$);
  - $\mathsf{Dec}_{\mathsf{FHE}}$ (run $\ell(n)$ times), which has inputs $\mathsf{sk}_{\mathsf{FHE}}$ with size $\mathsf{poly}(n)$ and $\mathsf{ct}_{\mathsf{out}}$ with size $\mathsf{poly}(n, \ell(n))$, and hence has running time $\mathsf{poly}(n, \ell(n))$;
  - $\mathsf{Gen}_{\mathsf{Del}}$ (run twice), which runs in time $\mathsf{poly}(\lambda) = \mathsf{poly}(n, \log(T_f(n)))$;
  - $\mathsf{Ver}_{\mathsf{Del}}$ (run once), which, given inputs $\mathsf{sk}_{\mathsf{Del}}, \pi_{\mathsf{Del}}$ of size $\mathsf{poly}(\lambda) = \mathsf{poly}(n, \log(T_f(n)))$, $\mathsf{ct}_x, \mathsf{ct}_y$ of size $\mathsf{poly}(n)$, $\mathsf{ct}_{\mathsf{out}}$ of size $\mathsf{poly}(n, \ell(n))$, g (the description of $g(c_1, c_2) = \mathsf{Eval}_{\mathsf{FHE}}(\mathsf{pk}_{\mathsf{FHE}}, f, c_1, c_2)$, where we here interpret f as the Turing machine M) of size $\mathsf{poly}(|M|)$, and $T \leq 2^\lambda$ of size at most $\lambda = \mathsf{poly}(n, \log(T_f(n)))$, has running time which is at most $\mathsf{poly}(n, \log(T_f(n)), |M|, \ell(n))$;

and a $\mathsf{poly}(n)$ number of comparisons between input values and function outputs which have already been established to have at most $\mathsf{poly}(n, \log(T_f(n)))$ length.

The above shows that the communication complexity of Π is succinct. Furthermore, as the honest receiver runs only $\mathsf{Gen}_{\mathsf{FHE}}, \mathsf{Gen}_{\mathsf{Del}}, \mathsf{Enc}_{\mathsf{FHE}}$, and the (efficient) receiver protocol for the underlying NISC on the aforementioned inputs, and as we have already established that all of these algorithms have running time $\mathsf{poly}(n, \log(T_f(n)), |M|, \ell(n))$, the receiver will inherit the same running time bound. $\qquad\square$

Towards proving security for Π, let $\mathsf{Out}_{\Pi, \mathcal{A}, I}(1^n, x, y, z)$ denote the random variable, taken over all randomness used by the honest party and the adversary, of the outputs of the honest receiver (if $I = S$) and the adversary in the execution of protocol Π given adversary $\mathcal{A}$ controlling corrupted party $I \in \{S, R\}$, receiver input x, sender input y, and adversary auxiliary input z. Let $\mathsf{Exec}_{\Pi, \mathcal{A}, I}(1^n, x, y, z)$ denote the respective experiment.

Let us also define the "ideal" execution by letting $\mathcal{T}_f$ denote the ideal functionality corresponding to the computation target $f(x, y)$ and letting Π_f be the "ideal" version of the protocol where R sends x to $\mathcal{T}_f$, S sends y to $\mathcal{T}_f$, and then R finally outputs the result out output by $\mathcal{T}_f$. We want to show the following theorem:

Theorem 7. *Assume, given functionality $f(\cdot, \cdot)$, the respective protocol Π described in Fig. 2 and the assumptions required in Theorem 6, and let $T(\cdot)$ be such that the underlying NISC π is secure with $T(\cdot)$-time simulation. For any efficient adversary $\mathcal{A}$ corrupting party $I \in \{S, R\}$, there exists a $T(n) \cdot \mathsf{poly}(n)$-time simulator $\mathcal{S}$ such that, for any non-uniform polynomial-time distinguisher D, there exists a negligible function $\epsilon(\cdot)$ such that, for all $n \in \mathbb{N}$, $x, y \in \{0, 1\}^n$, and auxiliary input z, D distinguishes the distributions $\mathsf{Out}_{\Pi, \mathcal{A}, I}(1^n, x, y, z)$ and $\mathsf{Out}_{\Pi_f, \mathcal{S}, I}^{\mathcal{T}_f}(1^n, x, y, z)$ with at most probability $\epsilon(n)$.*

Notice that correctness of Π holds trivially from the perfect correctness of the underlying FHE, the correctness and perfect completeness of the underlying adaptive delegation scheme, and the correctness of the underlying NISC protocol π; hence, Theorem 7, which proves security, and Lemma 1, which proves succinctness, will in conjunction directly imply Theorem 6 (where quasi-polynomial simulation results from our use of an underlying NISC protocol with quasi-polynomial simulation, as given in Theorem 5). The remainder of the section, then, is devoted to proving Theorem 7.

We begin by defining a "trusted third party" $\mathcal{T}_h$ which executes the ideal functionality for h—that is, given the corresponding sender and receiver inputs, $\mathcal{T}_h$ outputs the correct value of h computed on those inputs. Our first task is to show, then, that the "real" experiment's outputs $\mathsf{Out}_{\Pi, \mathcal{A}, I}(1^n, x, y, z)$ cannot be distinguished from those of a "hybrid" experiment, which we shall denote by $\mathsf{Out}_{\Pi_h, \mathcal{A}', I}^{\mathcal{T}_h}(1^n, x, y, z)$.

Formally, we let Π_h denote a protocol which is identical to Π with the exception that, in rounds 1 and 2, rather than generating msg_1 and msg_2, R and S instead send the respective inputs to $\mathcal{T}_h$, and, in the output phase, R receives and returns the output from $\mathcal{T}_h$ rather than unpacking msg_2. We then state the following lemma, the proof of which is deferred to the full version of our paper [34] as it is rather straightforward.

Lemma 2. *For any efficient adversary $\mathcal{A}$ corrupting party $I \in \{S, R\}$, there is a $T(n) \cdot \mathsf{poly}(n)$-time adversary $\mathcal{A}'$ such that, for any non-uniform polynomial-time distinguisher D, there exists a negligible function $\epsilon(\cdot)$ such that, for all $n \in \mathbb{N}$, $x, y \in \{0, 1\}^n$, and auxiliary input z, D distinguishes the distributions $\mathsf{Out}_{\Pi, \mathcal{A}, I}(1^n, x, y, z)$ and $\mathsf{Out}_{\Pi_h, \mathcal{A}', I}^{\mathcal{T}_h}(1^n, x, y, z)$ with at most probability $\epsilon(n)$.*

4.1   Comparing Hybrid and Ideal Executions

Next, we need to compare the hybrid execution $\mathsf{Exec}_{\Pi_h, \mathcal{A}', I}^{\mathcal{T}_h}(1^n, x, y, z)$ to the "ideal" execution $\mathsf{Exec}_{\Pi_f, \mathcal{S}, I}^{\mathcal{T}_f}(1^n, x, y, z)$ to finish the proof of Theorem 7.

Lemma 3. *For any $T(n) \cdot poly(n)$-time adversary $\mathcal{A}'$ corrupting some party $I \in \{S, R\}$, there exists a $T(n) \cdot poly(n)$-time simulator S such that, for any non-uniform polynomial-time distinguisher D, there exists a negligible function $\epsilon(\cdot)$ such that, for all $n \in \mathbb{N}$, $x, y \in \{0, 1\}^n$, and auxiliary input z, D distinguishes the distributions $\mathrm{Out}_{\Pi_h, \mathcal{A}', I}^{\mathcal{T}_h}(1^n, x, y, z)$ and $\mathrm{Out}_{\Pi_f, S, I}^{\mathcal{T}_f}(1^n, x, y, z)$ with at most probability $\epsilon(n)$.*

Proof. We again separate into two cases, based on whether $I = R$ (the receiver is corrupted) or $I = S$ (the sender is corrupted).

Corrupted Receiver. In this case, define a $T(n) \cdot poly(n)$-time simulator S_R which does as follows:

1. Run the corrupted receiver $\mathcal{A}'$. $\mathcal{A}'$, in the first round, will output a message $(x, r_{\mathsf{FHE}}, r_{\mathsf{Del}}, r_{\mathsf{Enc}})$ to be sent to $\mathcal{T}_h$. Send x to the ideal functionality $\mathcal{T}_f$.
2. Receive an output message out from the ideal functionality $\mathcal{T}_f$. If out is $\perp$, return $\perp$ to $\mathcal{A}'$ (as the output of $\mathcal{T}_h$).
3. Verify the following. If any checks fail, return $\perp$ to $\mathcal{A}'$.
   (a) $(\mathsf{pk}_{\mathsf{FHE}}, \cdot) = \mathsf{Gen}_{\mathsf{FHE}}(1^n; r_{\mathsf{FHE}})$
   (b) $(\mathsf{pk}_{\mathsf{Del}}, \cdot) = \mathsf{Gen}_{\mathsf{Del}}(1^\lambda; r_{\mathsf{Del}})$
   (c) $\mathsf{ct}_x = \mathsf{Enc}_{\mathsf{FHE}}(\mathsf{pk}_{\mathsf{FHE}}, x; r_{\mathsf{Enc}(x)})$
4. If all checks in the previous step pass, return out to $\mathcal{A}'$. Finally, output whatever $\mathcal{A}'$ outputs.

It suffices here to argue that the output which S_R returns to $\mathcal{A}'$ in the ideal experiment is identically distributed to the output which $\mathcal{T}_h$ would return to $\mathcal{A}'$ in the hybrid experiment, as this, combined with the observation that the only input $\mathcal{A}'$ receives (aside from the auxiliary input z) is the output from $\mathcal{T}_h$, allows us to conclude that $\mathcal{A}'$'s views in $\mathrm{Exec}_{\Pi_h, \mathcal{A}', R}^{\mathcal{T}_h}(1^n, x, y, z)$ and $\mathrm{Exec}_{\Pi_f, S_R, R}^{\mathcal{T}_f}(1^n, x, y, z)$ (and hence $\mathcal{A}'$'s outputs) are likewise identically distributed. We can argue this using the following claims:

Claim 1. *If S is honest, then, given the messages $(x, r_{\mathsf{FHE}}, r_{\mathsf{Del}}, r_{\mathsf{Enc}})$ and $(\mathsf{pk}_{\mathsf{FHE}}, \mathsf{pk}_{\mathsf{Del}}, \mathsf{ct}_x)$ from $\mathcal{A}'$, step (4) of S_R succeeds (i.e., does not return $\perp$) in Π_f if and only if all checks in step (1) of the functionality h described in Fig. 3 succeed in the respective instance of Π_h.*

Proof. The "if" direction is trivial since the checks in step (4) of S_R are a strict subset of the checks in step (1) of h.

The "only if" direction follows from the assumption that S is honest, and will hence compute $\mathsf{ct}_y = \mathsf{Enc}_{\mathsf{FHE}}(\mathsf{pk}_{\mathsf{FHE}}, y; r_{\mathsf{Enc}(y)})$ correctly using the correct inputs. $\square$

Claim 2. *If S is honest and all checks in step (1) of the functionality h described in Fig. 3 succeed in Π_h, then, with probability 1, step (3) of the functionality h will not return $\perp$.*

Proof. Since step (1) is successful, we know that $(\mathsf{pk}_{\mathsf{Del}}, \mathsf{sk}_{\mathsf{Del}}) = \mathsf{Gen}_{\mathsf{Del}}(1^\lambda, r_{\mathsf{Del}})$; moreover, since S is honest, we know that it must have computed $(\mathsf{ct}_{\mathsf{out}}, \pi_{\mathsf{Del}}, 1^T) = \mathsf{Comp}_{\mathsf{Del}}(\mathsf{pk}_{\mathsf{Del}}, g, \mathsf{ct}_x, \mathsf{ct}_y)$ correctly (and using the correct $\mathsf{pk}_{\mathsf{Del}}$ and ct_x, since the checks in step (1) passed). It follows by perfect completeness of the delegation scheme $(\mathsf{Gen}_{\mathsf{Del}}, \mathsf{Comp}_{\mathsf{Del}}, \mathsf{Ver}_{\mathsf{Del}})$ that

$$\mathsf{Ver}_{\mathsf{Del}}(\mathsf{sk}_{\mathsf{Del}}, g, \mathsf{ct}_x, \mathsf{ct}_y, \mathsf{ct}_{\mathsf{out}}, \pi_{\mathsf{Del}}, T) = \mathsf{Accept}$$

as desired. □

Claim 3. *If S is honest and, in Π_h, all checks in step (1) of the functionality h described in Fig. 3 succeed, and step (3) of the functionality h does not return $\bot$, then the value of* out *returned by step (4) of h will be equal to $f(x, y)$ with probability 1.*

Proof. Since S is honest and step (1) is successful, we know, as in the previous claim, that $(\mathsf{pk}_{\mathsf{Del}}, \mathsf{sk}_{\mathsf{Del}}) = \mathsf{Gen}_{\mathsf{Del}}(1^\lambda, r_{\mathsf{Del}})$ and furthermore $(\mathsf{ct}_{\mathsf{out}}, \pi_{\mathsf{Del}}, 1^T) = \mathsf{Comp}_{\mathsf{Del}}(\mathsf{pk}_{\mathsf{Del}}, g, \mathsf{ct}_x, \mathsf{ct}_y)$. It follows by correctness of the delegation scheme $(\mathsf{Gen}_{\mathsf{Del}}, \mathsf{Comp}_{\mathsf{Del}}, \mathsf{Ver}_{\mathsf{Del}})$ that

$$\mathsf{ct}_{\mathsf{out}} = g(\mathsf{ct}_x, \mathsf{ct}_y) = \mathsf{Eval}_{\mathsf{FHE}}(\mathsf{pk}_{\mathsf{FHE}}, f, \mathsf{ct}_x, \mathsf{ct}_y)$$

It suffices to show that this will decrypt to the correct output $\mathsf{out} = f(x, y)$. This holds due to perfect correctness of $(\mathsf{Gen}_{\mathsf{FHE}}, \mathsf{Enc}_{\mathsf{FHE}}, \mathsf{Dec}_{\mathsf{FHE}}, \mathsf{Eval}_{\mathsf{FHE}})$; specifically, since ct_x and ct_y are encryptions of x and y, respectively:

$$\mathsf{Dec}_{\mathsf{FHE}}(\mathsf{sk}_{\mathsf{FHE}}, \mathsf{ct}_{\mathsf{out}}) = \mathsf{Dec}_{\mathsf{FHE}}(\mathsf{sk}_{\mathsf{FHE}}, \mathsf{Eval}_{\mathsf{FHE}}(\mathsf{pk}_{\mathsf{FHE}}, f, \mathsf{ct}_x, \mathsf{ct}_y)) = f(x, y)$$

□

Chaining together Claims 1, 2, and 3 leads us to the conclusion that (by Claim 1), $\mathcal{S}_R$ returns $\bot$ in $\mathsf{Exec}_{\Pi_f, \mathcal{S}_R, R}^{\mathcal{T}_f}(1^n, x, y, z)$ if and only if $\mathcal{T}_h$ would return $\bot$ (from step (1)) in the respective execution of $\mathsf{Exec}_{\Pi_h, \mathcal{A}', R}^{\mathcal{T}_h}(1^n, x, y, z)$, and furthermore, if this event does not occur, then (by Claims 2 and 3 as well as the definition of $\mathcal{S}_R$) both $\mathcal{S}_R$ (in $\mathsf{Exec}_{\Pi_f, \mathcal{S}_R, R}^{\mathcal{T}_f}(1^n, x, y, z)$) and $\mathcal{T}_h$ (in the respective execution of $\mathsf{Exec}_{\Pi_h, \mathcal{A}', R}^{\mathcal{T}_h}(1^n, x, y, z)$) will return an output out that is precisely equal to $f(x, y)$, where x is the value sent by the adversary to $\mathcal{T}_h$ and y is the (honest) sender's input. This completes the argument for the case $I = R$.

Corrupted Sender. In the case $I = S$, define a $T(n) \cdot \mathsf{poly}(n)$-time simulator $\mathcal{S}_S$ which does as follows:

1. Generate $r_{\mathsf{FHE}}, r_{\mathsf{Del}}, r_{\mathsf{Enc}(x)} \leftarrow \{0, 1\}^*$, $(\mathsf{pk}_{\mathsf{FHE}}, \cdot) = \mathsf{Gen}_{\mathsf{FHE}}(1^n; r_{\mathsf{FHE}})$, $(\mathsf{pk}_{\mathsf{Del}}, \cdot)$ $= \mathsf{Gen}_{\mathsf{Del}}(1^\lambda; r_{\mathsf{Del}})$, $\mathsf{ct}_x = \mathsf{Enc}_{\mathsf{FHE}}(\mathsf{pk}_{\mathsf{FHE}}, 0; r_{\mathsf{Enc}(x)})$.
2. Run the corrupted sender $\mathcal{A}'$ using input $(\mathsf{pk}_{\mathsf{FHE}}, \mathsf{pk}_{\mathsf{Del}}, \mathsf{ct}_x)$. $\mathcal{A}'$ will generate a message $(y', \mathsf{pk}_{\mathsf{FHE}}', \mathsf{pk}_{\mathsf{Del}}', \mathsf{ct}_x', \mathsf{ct}_y', \mathsf{ct}_{\mathsf{out}}', \pi_{\mathsf{Del}}', r_{\mathsf{Enc}(y)}', T')$ to send to $\mathcal{T}_h$. Perform the following checks to verify this message, and return $\bot$ to $\mathcal{T}_f$ (causing it to output $\bot$) if any of them fail.

(a) $\mathsf{pk_{FHE}} = \mathsf{pk'_{FHE}}$, $\mathsf{pk_{Del}} = \mathsf{pk'_{Del}}$, $\mathsf{ct}_x = \mathsf{ct}'_x$.

(b) $\mathsf{ct}'_y = \mathsf{Enc_{FHE}}(\mathsf{pk_{FHE}}, y'; r'_{\mathsf{Enc}(y)})$

(c) $\mathsf{Ver_{Del}}(\mathsf{sk_{Del}}, g, \mathsf{ct}_x, \mathsf{ct}_y, \mathsf{ct}'_{\mathsf{out}}, \pi'_{\mathsf{Del}}, T') = \mathsf{Accept}$ for the functionality given by $g(c_1, c_2) = \mathsf{Eval_{FHE}}(\mathsf{pk_{FHE}}, f, c_1, c_2)$.

3. Otherwise (if the above checks pass), send y' to $\mathcal{T}_f$. Finally, output whatever $\mathcal{A}'$ outputs.

As this case has interesting subtleties, we lead the formal proof with a brief overview. Recall that, for this case, we need not only to verify that the adversary $\mathcal{A}'$'s views in the experiments $\mathsf{Exec}_{\Pi_h, \mathcal{A}', S}^{\mathcal{T}_h}(1^n, x, y, z)$ and $\mathsf{Exec}_{\Pi_f, S_S, S}^{\mathcal{T}_f}(1^n, x, y, z)$ (and hence $\mathcal{A}'$'s outputs) cannot be distinguished, but also that the honest receiver R's outputs cannot be distinguished between the two experiments.

The natural way to do this would be to begin by creating a hybrid protocol Π'_h where the receiver, instead of sending a ciphertext of their input x in the first round, sends the corresponding ciphertext of 0 (as the simulator does when running $\mathcal{A}'$ in Π_f). Ostensibly, this would allow us to show that the output distributions between Π_h and Π'_h are close by using the CPA-security of the underlying FHE protocol to assert that the ciphertexts, and hence the views of $\mathcal{A}'$, are indistinguishable between the two experiments. And while this does indeed directly imply that the *adversary's* outputs are close, we run into an issue the moment we consider the *receiver's* output; specifically, the receiver's output is the output from the ideal functionality $\mathcal{T}_h$, which among other things depends on *the secret key* $\mathsf{sk_{FHE}}$ *and the randomness* r_{FHE} *used to generate it*. In fact, this makes a reduction from Π'_h to the security of the FHE scheme impossible (using current techniques), since a hypothetical adversary simulating this functionality would only know $\mathsf{pk_{FHE}}$.

Instead we will have to consider an alternate functionality h' which only depends on the public key $\mathsf{pk_{FHE}}$ and does not use the randomness or secret key. Specifically, rather than decrypting the final result $\mathsf{ct_{out}}$, h' will instead simply return $f(x, y')$. We then show that the output distribution of $\Pi_{h'}$ is *statistically close* to that of Π_h. Specifically, they are identical except when the adversary $\mathcal{A}'$ can force the ideal functionality h' to verify a proof π_{Del} of an incorrect ciphertext $\mathsf{ct_{Out}}$—this implies that their statistical distance must be at most the (negligible) soundness error of delegation.[8] Now, given $\Pi_{h'}$, we can finally consider a protocol $\Pi'_{h'}$ where the receiver uses a ciphertext of 0; now that h' no longer depends on $\mathsf{sk_{FHE}}$, the reduction to the CPA-security will go through (for both the adversary's and receiver's outputs), and we can lastly compare $\mathsf{Exec}_{\Pi'_{h'}, \mathcal{A}', S}^{\mathcal{T}_h}(1^n, x, y, z)$ and $\mathsf{Exec}_{\Pi_f, S_S, S}^{\mathcal{T}_f}(1^n, x, y, z)$ to show that, actually, the output distributions are identically distributed.

---

[8] An attentive reader might wonder at this point why, in doing this, we are not simply backing ourselves into the same corner, since indeed $\mathcal{T}_h$ and even $\mathcal{T}_{h'}$ are very much dependent on the randomness r_{Del} and secret key $\mathsf{sk_{Del}}$. The intuitive answer is that, unlike with the reduction to FHE, we are able to "outsource" the dependence on $\mathsf{sk_{Del}}$ in $\mathcal{T}_{h'}$ to the security game for the soundness of delegation, allowing us to effectively *emulate* h' without said secret key in the adversary we construct.

We continue to the formal proof. Let h' be the functionality defined as h, but with four key differences:

- h', instead of taking input r_{FHE} from the receiver, takes input $\mathsf{pk}_{\mathsf{FHE}}$.
- In step (1), instead of verifying that $(\mathsf{pk}_{\mathsf{FHE}}, \cdot) = \mathsf{Gen}_{\mathsf{FHE}}(1^n, r_{\mathsf{FHE}})$, h' verifies that the sender's and receiver's inputs $\mathsf{pk}_{\mathsf{FHE}}$ match.
- In step (2), h' no longer computes $(\cdot, \mathsf{sk}_{\mathsf{FHE}}) = \mathsf{Gen}_{\mathsf{FHE}}(1^n; r_{\mathsf{FHE}})$.
- In step (4), h' returns $f(x, y)$ rather than $\mathsf{Dec}_{\mathsf{FHE}}(\mathsf{sk}_{\mathsf{FHE}}, \mathsf{ct}_{\mathsf{out}})$.

Let $\varPi_{h'}$ be defined identically to $\varPi_h$ except that both parties use the ideal functionality $\mathcal{T}_{h'}$ in place of $\mathcal{T}_h$ and the receiver inputs $\mathsf{pk}_{\mathsf{FHE}}$ to $\mathcal{T}_{h'}$ instead of r_{FHE} as specified above. We state the following claim:

Claim 4. *There exists negligible $\epsilon(\cdot)$ such that, for all $n \in \mathbb{N}$ and inputs x, y, z, the output distributions $\mathsf{Out}^{\mathcal{T}_h}_{\varPi_h, \mathcal{A}', S}(1^n, x, y, z)$ and $\mathsf{Out}^{\mathcal{T}_{h'}}_{\varPi_{h'}, \mathcal{A}', S}(1^n, x, y, z)$ are $\epsilon(n)$-statistically close.*

Proof. Intuitively, this will follow from the soundness of the delegation scheme $(\mathsf{Gen}_{\mathsf{Del}}, \mathsf{Comp}_{\mathsf{Del}}, \mathsf{Ver}_{\mathsf{Del}})$. First, observe that the adversary's views in experiments $\mathsf{Exec}^{\mathcal{T}_h}_{\varPi_h, \mathcal{A}', S}(1^n, x, y, z)$ and $\mathsf{Exec}^{\mathcal{T}_{h'}}_{\varPi_{h'}, \mathcal{A}', S}(1^n, x, y, z)$, and thus the adversary's outputs, are identically distributed; hence, it suffices to argue about the honest receiver's output, i.e., the output of $\mathcal{T}_h$ or $\mathcal{T}_{h'}$.

Second, since the receiver R is honest, the fact that h' verifies that the sender's and receiver's inputs $\mathsf{pk}_{\mathsf{FHE}}$ match is equivalent to the verification in h of the sender's $\mathsf{pk}_{\mathsf{FHE}}$ (that $(\mathsf{pk}_{\mathsf{FHE}}, \cdot) = \mathsf{Gen}_{\mathsf{FHE}}(1^n, r_{\mathsf{FHE}})$), since the receiver's input $\mathsf{pk}_{\mathsf{FHE}}$ will always be equal to $\mathsf{Gen}_{\mathsf{FHE}}(1^n, r_{\mathsf{FHE}})$. So the only change that can possibly affect the output of $\mathcal{T}_{h'}$ compared to $\mathcal{T}_h$ in the corrupted sender case is the fact that h' returns $f(x, y)$ rather than $\mathsf{Dec}_{\mathsf{FHE}}(\mathsf{sk}_{\mathsf{FHE}}, \mathsf{ct}_{\mathsf{out}})$.

Now, assume for the sake of contradiction that there is some polynomial $p(\cdot)$ such that, for infinitely many $n \in \mathbb{N}$, there exist x, y, z so that the ideal functionality's output is different between $\mathsf{Exec}^{\mathcal{T}_h}_{\varPi_h, \mathcal{A}', S}(1^n, x, y, z)$ and $\mathsf{Exec}^{\mathcal{T}_{h'}}_{\varPi_{h'}, \mathcal{A}', S}(1^n, x, y, z)$ with probability $1/p(n)$. We shall use this to construct a $T(n) \cdot \mathsf{poly}(n)$-time adversary $\mathcal{A}_{\mathsf{Del}}$ to break the soundness of the delegation scheme with probability $1/p(n)$. Specifically, let $\mathcal{A}_{\mathsf{Del}}$ do as follows on input $(1^n, \mathsf{pk}_{\mathsf{Del}})$:

1. Generate $r_{\mathsf{FHE}}, r_{\mathsf{Enc}(x)} \leftarrow \{0,1\}^*$ and $(\mathsf{pk}_{\mathsf{FHE}}, \cdot) = \mathsf{Gen}_{\mathsf{FHE}}(1^n; r_{\mathsf{FHE}}), \mathsf{ct}_x = \mathsf{Enc}_{\mathsf{FHE}}(\mathsf{pk}_{\mathsf{FHE}}, x; r_{\mathsf{Enc}(x)})$.
2. Run the corrupted sender $\mathcal{A}'$ on input y, auxiliary input z, and first-round message $(\mathsf{pk}_{\mathsf{FHE}}, \mathsf{pk}_{\mathsf{Del}}, \mathsf{ct}_x)$. $\mathcal{A}'$ will generate the message $(y', \mathsf{pk}'_{\mathsf{FHE}}, \mathsf{pk}'_{\mathsf{Del}}, \mathsf{ct}'_x, \mathsf{ct}'_y, \mathsf{ct}'_{\mathsf{out}}, \pi'_{\mathsf{Del}}, r'_{\mathsf{Enc}(y)}, T')$ to send to the ideal functionality $(\mathcal{T}_h$ or $\mathcal{T}_{h'})$.
3. Run $(\mathsf{ct}_{\mathsf{out}}, \pi_{\mathsf{Del}}, 1^T) \leftarrow \mathsf{Comp}_{\mathsf{Del}}(\mathsf{pk}_{\mathsf{Del}}, g, \mathsf{ct}_x, \mathsf{ct}'_y)$ for the functionality given by $g(c_1, c_2) = \mathsf{Eval}_{\mathsf{FHE}}(\mathsf{pk}_{\mathsf{FHE}}, f, c_1, c_2)$
4. Verify the following and abort if any are false.
   (a) $\mathsf{pk}_{\mathsf{FHE}} = \mathsf{pk}'_{\mathsf{FHE}}$, $\mathsf{pk}_{\mathsf{Del}} = \mathsf{pk}'_{\mathsf{Del}}$, $\mathsf{ct}_x = \mathsf{ct}'_x$
   (b) $\mathsf{ct}'_y = \mathsf{Enc}_{\mathsf{FHE}}(\mathsf{pk}_{\mathsf{FHE}}, y'; r'_{\mathsf{Enc}(y)})$

5. Otherwise, return $(g, \mathsf{ct}_x, \mathsf{ct}'_y, \mathsf{ct}_\mathsf{out}, \mathsf{ct}'_\mathsf{out}, \pi_\mathsf{Del}, \pi'_\mathsf{Del}, 1^T, 1^{T'})$.

We claim that $\mathcal{A}_\mathsf{Del}$ returns a tuple $(g, \mathsf{ct}_x, \mathsf{ct}'_y, \mathsf{ct}_\mathsf{out}, \mathsf{ct}'_\mathsf{out}, \pi_\mathsf{Del}, \pi'_\mathsf{Del}, 1^T, 1^{T'})$ such that $\mathsf{ct}_\mathsf{out} \neq \mathsf{ct}'_\mathsf{out}$ but $\mathsf{Ver}_\mathsf{Del}(\mathsf{sk}_\mathsf{Del}, g, \mathsf{ct}_x, \mathsf{ct}'_y, \mathsf{ct}_\mathsf{out}, \pi_\mathsf{Del}, T) = \mathsf{Ver}_\mathsf{Del}(\mathsf{sk}_\mathsf{Del}, g, \mathsf{ct}_x, \mathsf{ct}'_y, \mathsf{ct}'_\mathsf{out}, \pi'_\mathsf{Del}, T') = \mathsf{Accept}$—that is, $\mathcal{A}_\mathsf{Del}$ breaks soundness of the delegation scheme—precisely when h decrypts a ciphertext that is not equal to ct_out as returned by $\mathsf{Comp}_\mathsf{Del}(\mathsf{pk}_\mathsf{Del}, g, \mathsf{ct}_x, \mathsf{ct}_y)$ for the corresponding functionality and inputs; furthermore, we claim that this is the only case where h and h' may not be identically distributed.

To verify this, we start by observing that the input to $\mathcal{A}'$ in step (2) of $\mathcal{A}_\mathsf{Del}$ is identically distributed to the inputs in the experiments $\mathsf{Exec}_{\Pi_h, \mathcal{A}', S}^{\mathcal{T}_h}(1^n, x, y, z)$ and $\mathsf{Exec}_{\Pi_{h'}, \mathcal{A}', S}^{\mathcal{T}_{h'}}(1^n, x, y, z)$, since pk_Del is honestly generated and the receiver is honest. Furthermore, given the message from $\mathcal{A}'$ to the ideal functionality, as well as the fact that R is honest, we can assert that the checks in step (4) of $\mathcal{A}_\mathsf{Del}$ are equivalent to the checks in step (1) of h or h', since the receiver's inputs $\mathsf{pk}_\mathsf{FHE}, \mathsf{pk}_\mathsf{Del}, \mathsf{ct}_x$ are guaranteed to be honestly generated. So, comparing $\mathcal{T}_h$ and $\mathcal{T}_{h'}$ for a particular interaction, there are four possible outcomes, which we shall analyze:

1. Step (1) of h or h' fails, in which case both return $\perp$ (and $\mathcal{A}_\mathsf{Del}$ will abort).
2. Step (1) succeeds, but the verification in step (3) fails, in which case both will return $\perp$ (and $\mathcal{A}_\mathsf{Del}$ will produce output $(g, \mathsf{ct}_x, \mathsf{ct}'_y, \mathsf{ct}_\mathsf{out}, \mathsf{ct}'_\mathsf{out}, \pi_\mathsf{Del}, \pi'_\mathsf{Del}, 1^T, 1^{T'})$ which is *rejected* because $(\mathsf{ct}'_\mathsf{out}, \pi'_\mathsf{Del})$ fails to verify).
3. Steps (1) and (3) succeed, and $\mathsf{ct}'_\mathsf{out}$ given by the adversary is the same as the correct $(\mathsf{ct}_\mathsf{out}, \cdot, \cdot) = \mathsf{Comp}_\mathsf{Del}(\mathsf{pk}_\mathsf{Del}, g, \mathsf{ct}_x, \mathsf{ct}'_y)$, in which case the outputs of h and h' are identical and not $\perp$ by perfect correctness of Enc and Eval, as well as correctness of the delegation scheme.
   Specifically, considering the inputs to h, we know by correctness of delegation that, since $(\mathsf{ct}'_\mathsf{out}, \cdot, \cdot) = \mathsf{Comp}_\mathsf{Del}(\mathsf{pk}_\mathsf{Del}, g, \mathsf{ct}_x, \mathsf{ct}'_y)$, $\mathsf{ct}'_\mathsf{out} = g(\mathsf{ct}_x, \mathsf{ct}'_y) = \mathsf{Eval}_\mathsf{FHE}(\mathsf{pk}_\mathsf{FHE}, f, \mathsf{ct}_x, \mathsf{ct}'_y)$. Furthermore, by perfect correctness of the FHE scheme and the fact that ct_x and ct'_y are encryptions of x and y, respectively:

$$\mathsf{Dec}_\mathsf{FHE}(\mathsf{sk}_\mathsf{FHE}, \mathsf{ct}_\mathsf{out}) = \mathsf{Dec}_\mathsf{FHE}(\mathsf{sk}_\mathsf{FHE}, \mathsf{Eval}_\mathsf{FHE}(\mathsf{pk}_\mathsf{FHE}, f, \mathsf{ct}_x, \mathsf{ct}'_y)) = f(x, y')$$

   that is, the output of h will be identical to the output $f(x, y')$ of h'. In this case, $\mathcal{A}_\mathsf{Del}$ will produce output $(g, \mathsf{ct}_x, \mathsf{ct}'_y, \mathsf{ct}_\mathsf{out}, \mathsf{ct}'_\mathsf{out}, \pi_\mathsf{Del}, \pi'_\mathsf{Del}, 1^T, 1^{T'})$ which is *rejected* because $\mathsf{ct}'_\mathsf{out} = \mathsf{ct}_\mathsf{out}$.
4. Steps (1) and (3) succeed, and $\mathsf{ct}'_\mathsf{out}$ given by the adversary is *not* the same as the correct $(\mathsf{ct}_\mathsf{out}, \cdot, \cdot) = \mathsf{Comp}_\mathsf{Del}(\mathsf{pk}_\mathsf{Del}, g, \mathsf{ct}_x, \mathsf{ct}'_y)$, in which case the outputs of h and h' *may be different* (and $\mathcal{A}_\mathsf{Del}$ will produce output $(g, \mathsf{ct}_x, \mathsf{ct}'_y, \mathsf{ct}_\mathsf{out}, \mathsf{ct}'_\mathsf{out}, \pi_\mathsf{Del}, \pi'_\mathsf{Del}, 1^T, 1^{T'})$ which is *accepted* because $\mathsf{ct}'_\mathsf{out} \neq \mathsf{ct}_\mathsf{out}$ and $(\mathsf{ct}'_\mathsf{out}, \pi'_\mathsf{Del}, 1^{T'})$ verifies successfully).

The above implies that the probability over possible interactions that the outputs of h and h' are different—which, as we have argued above, is equal to the statistical distance between the distributions $\mathsf{Out}^{\mathcal{T}_h}_{\Pi_h,\mathcal{A}',S}(1^n,x,y,z)$ and $\mathsf{Out}^{\mathcal{T}_{h'}}_{\Pi_{h'},\mathcal{A}',S}(1^n,x,y,z)$—is no greater[9] than the probability with which $\mathcal{A}_{\mathsf{Del}}$'s output is accepted. In particular, by our assumption that, for infinitely many $n \in \mathbb{N}$, there were x,y,z such that this statistical distance was greater than $1/p(n)$, this implies that the probability that $\mathcal{A}_{\mathsf{Del}}$'s output is accepted (for the corresponding inputs) must be greater than $1/p(n)$ for infinitely many $n \in \mathbb{N}$. But this contradicts the soundness of delegation, so the claim is proven.   □

Now let $\Pi'_{h'}$ be identical to $\Pi_{h'}$, with the sole exception that the receiver's first-round message to the sender replaces the correctly generated $\mathsf{ct}_x = \mathsf{Enc}_{\mathsf{FHE}}(\mathsf{pk}_{\mathsf{FHE}},x;r_{\mathsf{Enc}(x)})$ with the simulated encryption $\mathsf{ct}_x = \mathsf{Enc}_{\mathsf{FHE}}(\mathsf{pk}_{\mathsf{FHE}},0;r_{\mathsf{Enc}(x)})$ of 0. We present the following claim comparing $\mathsf{Exec}^{\mathcal{T}_{h'}}_{\Pi_{h'},\mathcal{A}',S}(1^n,x,y,z)$ and $\mathsf{Exec}^{\mathcal{T}_{h'}}_{\Pi'_{h'},\mathcal{A}',S}(1^n,x,y,z)$:

Claim 5. *For any polynomial-time non-uniform distinguisher D, there exists negligible $\epsilon(\cdot)$ such that, for any $n \in \mathbb{N}$ and inputs x,y,z, the distributions $\mathsf{Out}^{\mathcal{T}_{h'}}_{\Pi_{h'},\mathcal{A}',S}(1^n,x,y,z)$ and $\mathsf{Out}^{\mathcal{T}_{h'}}_{\Pi'_{h'},\mathcal{A}',S}(1^n,x,y,z)$ cannot be distinguished by D with probability greater than $\epsilon(n)$.*

Proof. Intuitively, this follows from the CPA-security of the FHE scheme with respect to $T(n) \cdot \mathsf{poly}(n)$-time adversaries and the fact that both h' and the view of $\mathcal{A}'$ are independent of r_{FHE} and $\mathsf{sk}_{\mathsf{FHE}}$.

Formally, assume for contradiction that there exist some non-uniform polynomial-time distinguisher D and polynomial $p(\cdot)$ such that, for infinitely many $n \in \mathbb{N}$, there are inputs x,y,z such that D is able to distinguish the distributions $\mathsf{Out}^{\mathcal{T}_{h'}}_{\Pi_{h'},\mathcal{A}',S}(1^n,x,y,z)$ and $\mathsf{Out}^{\mathcal{T}_{h'}}_{\Pi'_{h'},\mathcal{A}',S}(1^n,x,y,z)$ with probability $1/p(n)$. We define a tuple of $T(n) \cdot \mathsf{poly}(n)$-time algorithms $(\mathcal{A}_{\mathsf{FHE}}, D')$ that can break the CPA-security of the FHE scheme $(\mathsf{Gen}_{\mathsf{FHE}}, \mathsf{Enc}_{\mathsf{FHE}}, \mathsf{Eval}_{\mathsf{FHE}}, \mathsf{Dec}_{\mathsf{FHE}})$ with probability $1/p(n)$ as follows:

- $\mathcal{A}_{\mathsf{FHE}}$, on input 1^n, outputs $(0,x)$.
- D', on input $(1^n, \mathsf{pk}_{\mathsf{FHE}}, \mathsf{ct}_x)$, where c is given as either $\mathsf{ct}^0_x = \mathsf{Enc}_{\mathsf{FHE}}(\mathsf{pk}_{\mathsf{FHE}},0)$ or $\mathsf{ct}^1_x = \mathsf{Enc}_{\mathsf{FHE}}(\mathsf{pk}_{\mathsf{FHE}},x)$, does the following:
  1. Generate $r_{\mathsf{Del}} \leftarrow \{0,1\}^*$ and $(\mathsf{pk}_{\mathsf{Del}}, \mathsf{sk}_{\mathsf{Del}}) = \mathsf{Gen}_{\mathsf{Del}}(1^\lambda;r_{\mathsf{Del}})$.
  2. Run the corrupted sender $\mathcal{A}'$ with sender input y, auxiliary input z, and first-round message $(\mathsf{pk}_{\mathsf{FHE}}, \mathsf{pk}_{\mathsf{Del}}, \mathsf{ct}_x)$. $\mathcal{A}'$ will generate a message $(y', \mathsf{pk}'_{\mathsf{FHE}}, \mathsf{pk}'_{\mathsf{Del}}, \mathsf{ct}'_x, \mathsf{ct}'_y, \mathsf{ct}'_{\mathsf{out}}, \pi'_{\mathsf{Del}}, r'_{\mathsf{Enc}(y)}, T')$ to send to $\mathcal{T}_{h'}$ and output $\mathsf{out}_{\mathcal{A}'}$. Store $\mathsf{out}_{\mathcal{A}'}$.
  3. Verify the following and set $\mathsf{out}_R = \bot$ if any are false. Otherwise, set $\mathsf{out}_R = f(x,y')$.
     (a) $\mathsf{pk}_{\mathsf{FHE}} = \mathsf{pk}'_{\mathsf{FHE}}$, $\mathsf{pk}_{\mathsf{Del}} = \mathsf{pk}'_{\mathsf{Del}}$, $\mathsf{ct}_x = \mathsf{ct}'_x$
     (b) $\mathsf{ct}'_y = \mathsf{Enc}_{\mathsf{FHE}}(\mathsf{pk}_{\mathsf{FHE}}, y'; r'_{\mathsf{Enc}(y)})$

---

[9] Note that equality is not guaranteed, as h could possibly accept a ciphertext $\mathsf{ct}'_{\mathsf{out}} \neq \mathsf{ct}_{\mathsf{out}}$ that still decrypts to $f(x,y)$.

(c) $\mathsf{Ver}_{\mathsf{Del}}(\mathsf{sk}_{\mathsf{Del}}, g, \mathsf{ct}_x, \mathsf{ct}'_y, \mathsf{ct}'_{\mathsf{out}}, \pi'_{\mathsf{Del}}, T') = \mathsf{Accept}$ for the functionality given by $g(c_1, c_2) = \widetilde{\mathsf{Eval}}_{\mathsf{FHE}}(\mathsf{pk}_{\mathsf{FHE}}, f, c_1, c_2)$

4. Return $D(1^n, (\mathsf{out}_{\mathcal{A}'}, \mathsf{out}_R))$.

First, notice that (given that the inputs $\mathsf{pk}_{\mathsf{FHE}}$ and $\mathsf{ct}_x = \mathsf{Enc}_{\mathsf{FHE}}(\mathsf{pk}_{\mathsf{FHE}}, m)$ for either $m = 0$ or $m = x$ are generated correctly) the inputs to $\mathcal{A}'$ in step (2) of D' are identically distributed to either the inputs in $\mathsf{Exec}^{\mathcal{T}_{h'}}_{\Pi'_{h'}, \mathcal{A}', S}(1^n, x, y, z)$ (if $m = x$) or the inputs in $\mathsf{Exec}^{\mathcal{T}_{h'}}_{\Pi'_{h'}, \mathcal{A}', S}(1^n, x, y, z)$ (if $m = 0$). Hence, the view of $\mathcal{A}'$ in D' is identically distributed to the corresponding view in the respective experiment, which implies that the output $\mathsf{out}_{\mathcal{A}'}$ must be as well, as must the message sent to $\mathcal{T}_{h'}$.

It remains to argue about the receiver's output out_R; recall that the honest receiver's output in either experiment is given by the output of the ideal functionality $\mathcal{T}_{h'}$. However, out_R as defined in step (3) of D' can easily be seen to be identically distributed to the output of h' in the respective experiment $\mathsf{Exec}^{\mathcal{T}_{h'}}_{\Pi'_{h'}, \mathcal{A}', S}(1^n, x, y, z)$ (if $m = x$) or $\mathsf{Exec}^{\mathcal{T}_{h'}}_{\Pi'_{h'}, \mathcal{A}', S}(1^n, x, y, z)$ (if $m = 0$). This holds because, since R is honest, R's inputs $(\mathsf{pk}_{\mathsf{FHE}}, \mathsf{pk}_{\mathsf{Del}}, \mathsf{ct}_x)$ are honestly generated and so the verifications in steps (3a) and (3b) are identical to the respective checks in step (1) of h. Furthermore, the verification in step (3c) of D' is identical to the verification in step (3) of h, so it follows that $\mathsf{out}_R = \perp$ exactly when h' in the respective experiment would return $\perp$, and that, otherwise, $\mathsf{out}_R = f(x, y')$, which by the definition of h' is identical to what h' would return if not $\perp$.

So we have argued that the distribution $(\mathsf{out}_{\mathcal{A}'}, \mathsf{out}_R)$ is identical to the distribution $\mathsf{Out}^{\mathcal{T}_{h'}}_{\Pi'_{h'}, \mathcal{A}', S}(1^n, x, y, z)$ when $m = x$ and to $\mathsf{Out}^{\mathcal{T}_{h'}}_{\Pi'_{h'}, \mathcal{A}', S}(1^n, x, y, z)$ when $m = 0$. But we have assumed that for infinitely many $n \in \mathbb{N}$ there exist x, y, z so that D can distinguish $\mathsf{Out}^{\mathcal{T}_{h'}}_{\Pi'_{h'}, \mathcal{A}', S}(1^n, x, y, z)$ and $\mathsf{Out}^{\mathcal{T}_{h'}}_{\Pi'_{h'}, \mathcal{A}', S}(1^n, x, y, z)$ with probability $1/p(n)$, i.e., that there is at least a $1/p(n)$ difference between the probability that $D(1^n, (\mathsf{out}_{\mathcal{A}'}, \mathsf{out}_R))$ returns 1 in the $m = x$ case and the respective probability in the $m = 0$ case. But, since D' returns precisely $D(1^n, (\mathsf{out}_{\mathcal{A}'}, \mathsf{out}_R))$, this gives us

$$|\Pr[D(1^n, \mathsf{pk}_{\mathsf{FHE}}, \mathsf{Enc}_{\mathsf{FHE}}(\mathsf{pk}_{\mathsf{FHE}}, 0)) = 1]$$
$$-\Pr[D(1^n, \mathsf{pk}_{\mathsf{FHE}}, \mathsf{Enc}_{\mathsf{FHE}}(\mathsf{pk}_{\mathsf{FHE}}, x)) = 1]| \geq 1/p(n)$$

which, since $\mathcal{A}_{\mathsf{FHE}}$ always returns $(0, x)$, means that $(\mathcal{A}_{\mathsf{FHE}}, D')$ is able to break the CPA-security of the underlying FHE scheme (w.r.t. $T(n) \cdot \mathsf{poly}(n)$-time adversaries) with probability $1/p(n)$ for infinitely many $n \in \mathbb{N}$, a contradiction. □

It remains to compare $\mathsf{Out}^{\mathcal{T}_{h'}}_{\Pi'_{h'}, \mathcal{A}', S}(1^n, x, y, z)$ and $\mathsf{Out}^{\mathcal{T}_f}_{\Pi_f, S_S, S}(1^n, x, y, z)$; we claim that in fact these distributions are already identical. First, observe that the input provided to $\mathcal{A}'$ in S_S is identically distributed to the input provided to $\mathcal{A}'$ in $\mathsf{Exec}^{\mathcal{T}_{h'}}_{\Pi'_{h'}, \mathcal{A}', S}(1^n, x, y, z)$; in both cases this consists of an honestly generated $\mathsf{pk}_{\mathsf{FHE}}, \mathsf{pk}_{\mathsf{Del}}, \mathsf{ct}_x$ such that ct_x is the respective encryption of 0. So it follows that the adversary's output, as well as the message sent by the adversary to the ideal functionality, must be identically distributed between the two experiments. Demonstrating that the receiver's outputs are identical—that is, that the output of h' in $\mathsf{Exec}^{\mathcal{T}_{h'}}_{\Pi'_{h'},\mathcal{A}',S}(1^n,x,y,z)$ is always equal to the output $f(x,y)$ in $\mathsf{Exec}^{\mathcal{T}_f}_{\Pi_f,\mathcal{S}_S,S}(1^n,x,y,z)$—will follow from the following claim, to which we have already alluded in the previous two reductions:

Claim 6. *If R is honest, then, given messages $(x,\mathsf{pk}_{\mathsf{FHE}},r_{\mathsf{Del}},r_{\mathsf{Enc}})$ sent to $\mathcal{T}_{h'}$, $(\mathsf{pk}_{\mathsf{FHE}},\mathsf{pk}_{\mathsf{Del}},\mathsf{ct}_x)$ sent to $\mathcal{A}'$, and $(y',\mathsf{pk}'_{\mathsf{FHE}},\mathsf{pk}'_{\mathsf{Del}},\mathsf{ct}'_x,\mathsf{ct}'_y,\mathsf{ct}'_{\mathsf{out}},\pi'_{\mathsf{Del}},r'_{\mathsf{Enc}(y)},T')$ sent by $\mathcal{A}'$ to $\mathcal{T}_{h'}$, the checks in step (2) of $\mathcal{S}_S$ succeed if and only if all checks in steps (1) and (3) of the functionality h' succeed.*

Proof. If R is honest, it must be the case that $(\mathsf{pk}_{\mathsf{Del}},\cdot) = \mathsf{Gen}_{\mathsf{Del}}(1^\lambda;r_{\mathsf{Del}})$ and $\mathsf{ct}_x = \mathsf{Enc}_{\mathsf{FHE}}(\mathsf{pk}_{\mathsf{FHE}},x;r_{\mathsf{Enc}(x)})$; hence step (2a) of $\mathcal{S}_S$ is equivalent to verifying $\mathsf{pk}'_{\mathsf{FHE}} = \mathsf{pk}_{\mathsf{FHE}}$, $(\mathsf{pk}'_{\mathsf{Del}},\cdot) = \mathsf{Gen}_{\mathsf{Del}}(1^\lambda;r_{\mathsf{Del}})$, and $\mathsf{ct}'_x = \mathsf{Enc}_{\mathsf{FHE}}(\mathsf{pk}'_{\mathsf{FHE}},x;r_{\mathsf{Enc}(x)})$, i.e., the first three checks of step (1) of h'. Step (2b) is trivially equivalent to the last check in step (1) of h' and step (2c) is trivially equivalent to the check in step (3) of h', completing the argument. $\square$

This implies that the receiver in $\mathsf{Exec}^{\mathcal{T}_{h'}}_{\Pi'_{h'},\mathcal{A}',S}(1^n,x,y,z)$ will return $\bot$ as the output from h' precisely when $\mathcal{S}_S$ will return $\bot$ to the ideal functionality (based on the checks in step (2)) and cause the receiver in $\mathsf{Exec}^{\mathcal{T}_f}_{\Pi_f,\mathcal{S}_S,S}(1^n,x,y,z)$ to return $\bot$. However, when $\mathcal{T}_f$ does not output $\bot$, it will always output $f(x,y')$ on the respective inputs x from the honest receiver and y' from $\mathcal{S}_S$; similarly, when $\mathcal{T}_{h'}$ does not return $\bot$, it will, by definition, *also* always output $f(x,y')$ on the respective input x from the honest receiver and y' from $\mathcal{A}'$. The above, then, is sufficient to conclude that the distributions $\mathsf{Out}^{\mathcal{T}_{h'}}_{\Pi'_{h'},\mathcal{A}',S}(1^n,x,y,z)$ and $\mathsf{Out}^{\mathcal{T}_f}_{\Pi_f,\mathcal{S}_S,S}(1^n,x,y,z)$ are identical.

We conclude the proof of the lemma with a standard hybrid argument; specifically, if there exists some non-uniform polynomial-time distinguisher D and polynomial $p(\cdot)$ such that, for infinitely many $n \in \mathbb{N}$, there are inputs x,y,z so that D can distinguish $\mathsf{Out}^{\mathcal{T}_h}_{\Pi_h,\mathcal{A}',S}(1^n,x,y,z)$ and $\mathsf{Out}^{\mathcal{T}_f}_{\Pi_f,S,S}(1^n,x,y,z)$ with probability $1/p(n)$, then D must likewise be able to distinguish one of the following pairs with probability $1/p'(n)$ for some polynomial $p'(\cdot)$:

– $\mathsf{Out}^{\mathcal{T}_h}_{\Pi_h,\mathcal{A}',S}(1^n,x,y,z)$ and $\mathsf{Out}^{\mathcal{T}_{h'}}_{\Pi_{h'},\mathcal{A}',S}(1^n,x,y,z)$
– $\mathsf{Out}^{\mathcal{T}_{h'}}_{\Pi_{h'},\mathcal{A}',S}(1^n,x,y,z)$ and $\mathsf{Out}^{\mathcal{T}_{h'}}_{\Pi'_{h'},\mathcal{A}',S}(1^n,x,y,z)$
– $\mathsf{Out}^{\mathcal{T}_{h'}}_{\Pi'_{h'},\mathcal{A}',S}(1^n,x,y,z)$ and $\mathsf{Out}^{\mathcal{T}_f}_{\Pi_f,S,S}(1^n,x,y,z)$

The first case would contradict Claim 4, the second case would contradict Claim 5, and the third case is impossible because we showed the distributions to be identical. Therefore, such a distinguisher D cannot exist. $\square$

By the same logic, a standard hybrid argument shows that Lemmas 2 and 3 imply Theorem 7: if there were some non-uniform polynomial-time distinguisher D and polynomial $p(\cdot)$ such that, for infinitely many $n \in \mathbb{N}$, there were inputs

x, y, z so that D could distinguish $\mathsf{Out}_{\Pi, \mathcal{A}, I}(1^n, x, y, z)$ and $\mathsf{Out}_{\Pi_f, \mathcal{S}, I}^{T_f}(1^n, x, y, z)$ with probability $1/p(n)$, then D would be able to distinguish either:

- $\mathsf{Out}_{\Pi, \mathcal{A}, I}(1^n, x, y, z)$ and $\mathsf{Out}_{\Pi_h, \mathcal{A}', I}^{T_h}(1^n, x, y, z)$, or
- $\mathsf{Out}_{\Pi_h, \mathcal{A}', I}^{T_h}(1^n, x, y, z)$ and $\mathsf{Out}_{\Pi_f, \mathcal{S}, I}^{T_f}(1^n, x, y, z)$

with probability $1/p'(n)$ for some polynomial $p'(\cdot)$. The first case would contradict Lemma 2 and the second Lemma 3; hence, Theorem 7 is proven.

References

1. Afshar, A., Mohassel, P., Pinkas, B., Riva, B.: Non-interactive secure computation based on cut-and-choose. In: Nguyen, P.Q., Oswald, E. (eds.) EUROCRYPT 2014. LNCS, vol. 8441, pp. 387–404. Springer, Heidelberg (2014). https://doi.org/10.1007/978-3-642-55220-5_22
2. Asharov, G., Ephraim, N., Komargodski, I., Pass, R.: On perfect correctness without derandomization. Cryptology ePrint Archive, Report 2019/1025 (2019). https://eprint.iacr.org/2019/1025
3. Badrinarayanan, S., Garg, S., Ishai, Y., Sahai, A., Wadia, A.: Two-message witness indistinguishability and secure computation in the plain model from new assumptions. In: Takagi, T., Peyrin, T. (eds.) ASIACRYPT 2017, Part III. LNCS, vol. 10626, pp. 275–303. Springer, Cham (2017). https://doi.org/10.1007/978-3-319-70700-6_10
4. Badrinarayanan, S., Jain, A., Ostrovsky, R., Visconti, I.: Non-interactive secure computation from one-way functions. In: Peyrin, T., Galbraith, S. (eds.) ASIACRYPT 2018, Part III. LNCS, vol. 11274, pp. 118–138. Springer, Cham (2018). https://doi.org/10.1007/978-3-030-03332-3_5
5. Barak, B., Pass, R.: On the possibility of one-message weak zero-knowledge. In: Naor, M. (ed.) TCC 2004. LNCS, vol. 2951, pp. 121–132. Springer, Heidelberg (2004). https://doi.org/10.1007/978-3-540-24638-1_7
6. Bitansky, N., Canetti, R., Chiesa, A., Tromer, E.: Recursive composition and bootstrapping for SNARKS and proof-carrying data. In: Boneh, D., Roughgarden, T., Feigenbaum, J. (eds.) 45th ACM STOC, pp. 111–120. ACM Press, June 2013. https://doi.org/10.1145/2488608.2488623
7. Bitansky, N., Canetti, R., Paneth, O., Rosen, A.: On the existence of extractable one-way functions. In: Shmoys, D.B. (ed.) 46th ACM STOC, pp. 505–514. ACM Press, May/June 2014. https://doi.org/10.1145/2591796.2591859
8. Bitansky, N., Chiesa, A., Ishai, Y., Paneth, O., Ostrovsky, R.: Succinct non-interactive arguments via linear interactive proofs. In: Sahai, A. (ed.) TCC 2013. LNCS, vol. 7785, pp. 315–333. Springer, Heidelberg (2013). https://doi.org/10.1007/978-3-642-36594-2_18
9. Boyle, E., Pass, R.: Limits of extractability assumptions with distributional auxiliary input. In: Iwata, T., Cheon, J.H. (eds.) ASIACRYPT 2015, Part II. LNCS, vol. 9453, pp. 236–261. Springer, Heidelberg (2015). https://doi.org/10.1007/978-3-662-48800-3_10
10. Brakerski, Z., Döttling, N.: Two-message statistically sender-private OT from LWE. In: Beimel, A., Dziembowski, S. (eds.) TCC 2018, Part II. LNCS, vol. 11240, pp. 370–390. Springer, Cham (2018). https://doi.org/10.1007/978-3-030-03810-6_14

11. Brakerski, Z., Gentry, C., Vaikuntanathan, V.: (Leveled) fully homomorphic encryption without bootstrapping. In: Goldwasser, S. (ed.) ITCS 2012, pp. 309–325. ACM, January 2012. https://doi.org/10.1145/2090236.2090262
12. Brakerski, Z., Holmgren, J., Kalai, Y.T.: Non-interactive delegation and batch NP verification from standard computational assumptions. In: Hatami, H., McKenzie, P., King, V. (eds.) 49th ACM STOC, pp. 474–482. ACM Press, June 2017. https://doi.org/10.1145/3055399.3055497
13. Brakerski, Z., Kalai, Y.T.: Monotone batch NP-delegation with applications to access control. Cryptology ePrint Archive, Report 2018/375 (2018). https://eprint.iacr.org/2018/375
14. Canetti, R.: Universally composable security: a new paradigm for cryptographic protocols. In: 42nd FOCS, pp. 136–145. IEEE Computer Society Press, October 2001. https://doi.org/10.1109/SFCS.2001.959888
15. Canetti, R., Jain, A., Scafuro, A.: Practical UC security with a global random oracle. In: Ahn, G.J., Yung, M., Li, N. (eds.) ACM CCS 2014, pp. 597–608. ACM Press, November 2014. https://doi.org/10.1145/2660267.2660374
16. Cho, C., Döttling, N., Garg, S., Gupta, D., Miao, P., Polychroniadou, A.: Laconic oblivious transfer and its applications. In: Katz, J., Shacham, H. (eds.) CRYPTO 2017, Part II. LNCS, vol. 10402, pp. 33–65. Springer, Cham (2017). https://doi.org/10.1007/978-3-319-63715-0_2
17. Dwork, C., Langberg, M., Naor, M., Nissim, K., Reingold, O.: Succinct proofs for NP and spooky interactions (2004)
18. Garg, S., Gentry, C., Sahai, A., Waters, B.: Witness encryption and its applications. In: Boneh, D., Roughgarden, T., Feigenbaum, J. (eds.) 45th ACM STOC, pp. 467–476. ACM Press, June 2013. https://doi.org/10.1145/2488608.2488667
19. Garg, S., Mukherjee, P., Pandey, O., Polychroniadou, A.: The exact round complexity of secure computation. In: Fischlin, M., Coron, J.-S. (eds.) EUROCRYPT 2016, Part II. LNCS, vol. 9666, pp. 448–476. Springer, Heidelberg (2016). https://doi.org/10.1007/978-3-662-49896-5_16
20. Gennaro, R., Gentry, C., Parno, B., Raykova, M.: Quadratic span programs and succinct NIZKs without PCPs. In: Johansson, T., Nguyen, P.Q. (eds.) EUROCRYPT 2013. LNCS, vol. 7881, pp. 626–645. Springer, Heidelberg (2013). https://doi.org/10.1007/978-3-642-38348-9_37
21. Gentry, C.: Fully homomorphic encryption using ideal lattices. In: Mitzenmacher, M. (ed.) 41st ACM STOC, pp. 169–178. ACM Press, May/June 2009. https://doi.org/10.1145/1536414.1536440
22. Goldreich, O., Micali, S., Wigderson, A.: How to play any mental game or a completeness theorem for protocols with honest majority. In: Aho, A. (ed.) 19th ACM STOC, pp. 218–229. ACM Press, May 1987. https://doi.org/10.1145/28395.28420
23. Goldreich, O., Oren, Y.: Definitions and properties of zero-knowledge proof systems. J. Cryptol. 7(1), 1–32 (1994). https://doi.org/10.1007/BF00195207
24. Goldwasser, S., Kalai, Y.T., Popa, R.A., Vaikuntanathan, V., Zeldovich, N.: Reusable garbled circuits and succinct functional encryption. In: Boneh, D., Roughgarden, T., Feigenbaum, J. (eds.) 45th ACM STOC, pp. 555–564. ACM Press, June 2013. https://doi.org/10.1145/2488608.2488678
25. Goldwasser, S., Micali, S.: Probabilistic encryption. J. Comput. Syst. Sci. 28(2), 270–299 (1984)
26. Goyal, V., Ishai, Y., Sahai, A., Venkatesan, R., Wadia, A.: Founding cryptography on tamper-proof hardware tokens. In: Micciancio, D. (ed.) TCC 2010. LNCS, vol. 5978, pp. 308–326. Springer, Heidelberg (2010). https://doi.org/10.1007/978-3-642-11799-2_19

27. Groth, J.: Short pairing-based non-interactive zero-knowledge arguments. In: Abe, M. (ed.) ASIACRYPT 2010. LNCS, vol. 6477, pp. 321–340. Springer, Heidelberg (2010). https://doi.org/10.1007/978-3-642-17373-8_19

28. Halevi, S., Kalai, Y.T.: Smooth projective hashing and two-message oblivious transfer. J. Cryptol. **25**(1), 158–193 (2012)

29. Hazay, C., Polychroniadou, A., Venkitasubramaniam, M.: Composable security in the tamper-proof hardware model under minimal complexity. In: Hirt, M., Smith, A. (eds.) TCC 2016, Part I. LNCS, vol. 9985, pp. 367–399. Springer, Heidelberg (2016). https://doi.org/10.1007/978-3-662-53641-4_15

30. Ishai, Y., Kushilevitz, E., Ostrovsky, R., Prabhakaran, M., Sahai, A.: Efficient non-interactive secure computation. In: Paterson, K.G. (ed.) EUROCRYPT 2011. LNCS, vol. 6632, pp. 406–425. Springer, Heidelberg (2011). https://doi.org/10.1007/978-3-642-20465-4_23

31. Katz, J., Ostrovsky, R.: Round-optimal secure two-party computation. In: Franklin, M. (ed.) CRYPTO 2004. LNCS, vol. 3152, pp. 335–354. Springer, Heidelberg (2004). https://doi.org/10.1007/978-3-540-28628-8_21

32. Micali, S.: CS proofs (extended abstracts). In: 35th FOCS, pp. 436–453. IEEE Computer Society Press, November 1994. https://doi.org/10.1109/SFCS.1994.365746

33. Mohassel, P., Rosulek, M.: Non-interactive secure 2PC in the offline/online and batch settings. In: Coron, J.-S., Nielsen, J.B. (eds.) EUROCRYPT 2017, Part III. LNCS, vol. 10212, pp. 425–455. Springer, Cham (2017). https://doi.org/10.1007/978-3-319-56617-7_15

34. Morgan, A., Pass, R., Polychroniadou, A.: Succinct non-interactive secure computation (full version). Cryptology ePrint Archive, Report 2019/1341 (2019). https://eprint.iacr.org/2019/1341

35. Naor, M., Pinkas, B.: Efficient oblivious transfer protocols. In: SODA, pp. 448–457 (2001)

36. Pass, R.: Simulation in quasi-polynomial time, and its application to protocol composition. In: Biham, E. (ed.) EUROCRYPT 2003. LNCS, vol. 2656, pp. 160–176. Springer, Heidelberg (2003). https://doi.org/10.1007/3-540-39200-9_10

37. Peikert, C., Vaikuntanathan, V., Waters, B.: A framework for efficient and composable oblivious transfer. In: Wagner, D. (ed.) CRYPTO 2008. LNCS, vol. 5157, pp. 554–571. Springer, Heidelberg (2008). https://doi.org/10.1007/978-3-540-85174-5_31

38. Prabhakaran, M., Sahai, A.: New notions of security: achieving universal composability without trusted setup. In: Babai, L. (ed.) 36th ACM STOC, pp. 242–251. ACM Press, June 2004. https://doi.org/10.1145/1007352.1007394

39. Quach, W., Wee, H., Wichs, D.: Laconic function evaluation and applications. In: Thorup, M. (ed.) 59th FOCS, pp. 859–870. IEEE Computer Society Press, October 2018. https://doi.org/10.1109/FOCS.2018.00086

40. Regev, O.: On lattices, learning with errors, random linear codes, and cryptography. In: Gabow, H.N., Fagin, R. (eds.) 37th ACM STOC, pp. 84–93. ACM Press, May 2005. https://doi.org/10.1145/1060590.1060603

41. Schröder, D., Unruh, D.: Round optimal blind signatures. Cryptology ePrint Archive, Report 2011/264 (2011). https://eprint.iacr.org/2011/264

42. Yao, A.C.: Protocols for secure computations (extended abstract). In: FOCS, pp. 160–164 (1982)

Quantum I

Finding Hash Collisions with Quantum Computers by Using Differential Trails with Smaller Probability than Birthday Bound

Akinori Hosoyamada[1,2]($\boxtimes$) and Yu Sasaki[1]($\boxtimes$)

[1] NTT Secure Platform Laboratories, Tokyo, Japan
{akinori.hosoyamada.bh,yu.sasaki.sk}@hco.ntt.co.jp
[2] Nagoya University, Nagoya, Japan
hosoyamada.akinori@nagoya-u.jp

Abstract. In this paper we spot light on dedicated quantum collision attacks on concrete hash functions, which has not received much attention so far. In the classical setting, the generic complexity to find collisions of an n-bit hash function is $O(2^{n/2})$, thus classical collision attacks based on differential cryptanalysis such as rebound attacks build differential trails with probability higher than $2^{-n/2}$. By the same analogy, generic quantum algorithms such as the BHT algorithm find collisions with complexity $O(2^{n/3})$. With quantum algorithms, a pair of messages satisfying a differential trail with probability p can be generated with complexity $p^{-1/2}$. Hence, in the quantum setting, some differential trails with probability up to $2^{-2n/3}$ that cannot be exploited in the classical setting may be exploited to mount a collision attack in the quantum setting. In particular, the number of attacked rounds may increase. In this paper, we attack two international hash function standards: AES-MMO and Whirlpool. For AES-MMO, we present a 7-round differential trail with probability 2^{-80} and use it to find collisions with a quantum version of the rebound attack, while only 6 rounds can be attacked in the classical setting. For Whirlpool, we mount a collision attack based on a 6-round differential trail from a classical rebound distinguisher with a complexity higher than the birthday bound. This improves the best classical attack on 5 rounds by 1. We also show that those trails are optimal in our approach. Our results have two important implications. First, there seems to exist a common belief that classically secure hash functions will remain secure against quantum adversaries. Indeed, several second-round candidates in the NIST post-quantum competition use existing hash functions, say SHA-3, as quantum secure ones. Our results disprove this common belief. Second, our observation suggests that differential trail search should not stop with probability $2^{-n/2}$ but should consider up to $2^{-2n/3}$. Hence it deserves to revisit the previous differential trail search activities.

Keywords: Symmetric key cryptography · Hash function · Cryptanalysis · Collision · Quantum attack · AES-MMO · Whirlpool · Rebound attack

© International Association for Cryptologic Research 2020
A. Canteaut and Y. Ishai (Eds.): EUROCRYPT 2020, LNCS 12106, pp. 249–279, 2020.
https://doi.org/10.1007/978-3-030-45724-2_9

1   Introduction

Recently, post-quantum security has received a lot of attention from the cryptographic community. The security of public-key cryptographic schemes is often reduced to some mathematically difficult problem, which can be affected by quantum machines directly. In contrast, symmetric-key cryptographic schemes may not have such a security reduction and post-quantum security of symmetric-key cryptographic schemes has not been discussed until recently. In 2010, Kuwakado and Morii [28] pointed out that the 3-round Feistel network would be distinguished only with polynomially many queries by using Simon's algorithm [40] in the quantum setting. After their discovery, a lot of researchers have tried to apply Simon's algorithm to symmetric-key schemes to obtain a drastic reduction of the complexity in the quantum setting, e.g. key-recovery attacks against the Even-Mansour construction [29] and universal forgery attacks on various message authentication codes (MACs) [24].

Simon's algorithm allows to find a "hidden period" by only polynomially many queries. From its nature, all the previous applications of Simon's algorithm are keyed primitives. Namely, a key or a key-dependent secret value takes a role of the hidden period. Then, queries need to be made in a quantum manner, which is called "superposition queries." (An exception is a recently published paper that utilizes Simon's algorithm without superposition queries [6], but this is the only exception.) Superposition queries can still be practical if one considers the situation that keyed primitives are implemented in a keyless manner, white-box implementation for example. Meanwhile, there seems to exist consensus that to make superposition queries is more difficult than to make classical queries.

In contrast, the analysis of the keyless primitives does not require any online queries because all computations can be done offline. In this work, we are targeting hash functions, and thus do not make any superposition queries to keyed oracles.

To find collisions of hash functions in the quantum setting is indeed important. Recently many public-key schemes have been proven to be post-quantum secure in the quantum random oracle model (QROM) [5], which is an analogue of the random oracle model in the classical setting. These schemes include many second-round candidates in the NIST post-quantum public-key standardization process [36]. A quantum random oracle is an ideal model of concrete hash functions that allows superposed quantum queries for adversaries, and the QROM implicitly assumes that there exists a concrete hash function that behaves like a random oracle against adversaries that make quantum superposed queries. In particular, if a hash function is used to instantiate a quantum random oracle, there should not exist any dedicated quantum collision attack on the hash function that is faster than the generic quantum collision attack. When the best collision attack on a hash function is the generic one in the classical setting, it is often believed to be also the case in the quantum setting. Thus, to find dedicated quantum collision attacks on classically collision-resistant hash functions will give significant impacts in the real world.

In the classical setting, the generic attack complexity to find collisions against an n-bit hash function is $O(2^{n/2})$ by the birthday paradox. Therefore any dedicated attack that finds collisions with less than $O(2^{n/2})$ complexity is regarded as a meaningful attack. In the quantum setting, the generic attack complexity depends on the model (or assumptions) of the actual quantum machines. Irrespective of the model, the lower bound of the query complexity is proven to be $\Omega(2^{n/3})$ [45] and there is an attack matching this bound if $O(2^{n/3})$ qubits are available (BHT) [11]. By the same analogy, any dedicated attack with less than $O(2^{n/3})$ quantum complexity should be regarded as a meaningful attack.

However, in the quantum setting, dedicated attacks need to be compared with the generic attack complexity very carefully because the generic attack complexity depends on the model of the quantum computations. For example, BHT cannot be better than the classical computations by considering the fact that each qubit can behave as either processor or memory [4]. (By running $2^{n/3}$ processors in parallel, collisions can be found in time $O(2^{n/6})$ even with classical machines.) However, if a quantum computer of polynomial size with exponentially large quantum random access memory (qRAM) is available, BHT is the best collision attack. It is hard to predict which model is more likely to be realized in the future than others, and it would be useful to discuss advantages of attacks in various models with various generic attack complexities.

While there are various generic attacks, we observe that there does not exist any dedicated quantum attack against hash functions. This is a strange tendency especially considering the fact that there are many attempts to speed up dedicated cryptanalysis against block ciphers e.g. differential and linear cryptanalysis [25], impossible differential cryptanalysis [44], meet-in-the-middle attacks [8,20], slide attacks [7], and so on. In this paper, we explore dedicated collision attacks against hash functions to find collisions faster than generic quantum attacks.

Here we briefly review dedicated collision attacks in the classical setting. Some of famous collision attacks are ones presented by Wang et al. against SHA-1 [41] and MD5 [42]. In short, they first derive the differential trail, and then efficiently find message pairs which satisfy the first part of the differential trail by using a "message modification" technique. The generated message pairs are simply propagated to the last round to probabilistically satisfy the differential trail of the remaining part. When the cost of message modification is 1, the latter part of the differential trail can be up to $2^{-n/2}$ (if the differential probability is smaller than $2^{-n/2}$, the attack becomes worse than the birthday attack). Another important direction is the rebound attack by Mendel et al. [31,32] which is particularly useful against hash functions based on the substitution-permutation network (SPN). In short, it divides the computation into three parts (outbound, inbound, and another outbound), and derives a differential trail such that the probability of the differential propagation in the outbound parts is high. Then, pairs of messages to satisfy the inbound part are found with average cost 1 and those are propagated to outbound parts. Hence, the probability of the outbound differential trail can be up to $2^{-n/2}$ to be faster than the birthday attack.

1.1   Our Contribution

This paper gives an observation that dedicated quantum collision attacks based on differential cryptanalysis may break hash functions that are secure in the classical setting, and shows that we can actually mount quantum versions of rebound attacks that find collisions of 7-round AES-MMO and 6-round Whirlpool, on which there has not been found any dedicated collision attack that is faster than the generic collision attack in the classical setting.

An observation on quantum differential cryptanalysis. In the classical setting, if we mount an attack that uses a differential trail with differential probability p, the attack requires at least $1/p$ operations. Thus, the trail cannot be used to find hash collisions if $p < 2^{-n/2}$. On the other hand, in the quantum setting, Kaplan et al. [25] showed that we can find a message pair that satisfies the differential in time around $\sqrt{1/p}$. Thus, if we have a differential trail with probability p, we can mount a collision attack in time around $\sqrt{1/p}$. Such an attack is faster than the generic attack (BHT) if $\sqrt{1/p} < 2^{n/3}$, or equivalently $p > 2^{-2n/3}$ (in the quantum setting where a small quantum computer with exponentially large qRAM is available). In particular, if we find a differential trail for a hash function with probability $2^{-n/2} > p > 2^{-2n/3}$, we can make a dedicated quantum collision attack that is faster than the quantum generic attack.

Observations without qRAM. So far we have discussed the setting where qRAM is available and the best generic attack is BHT. The generic attack changes in other settings where qRAM of exponential size is not available. In this paper we consider two settings in which qRAM is not available, and observe that we can still use differential trails with smaller differential probabilities than $2^{-n/2}$ to find collisions: In the first setting, the efficiency of quantum algorithms is measured by the tradeoff between time T and space S (the maximum of the size of quantum computer and classical memory) and parallelizations are taken into account. Since qubits for computation and qubits for quantum memory may be realized in physically the same way, if a quantum algorithm requires lots of qubits for quantum memory, it is plausible to compare the algorithm to other algorithms that use the same amount of qubits for parallelization [18]. In the second setting, a small quantum computer of polynomial size and exponentially large classical memory are available (and we do not consider parallelizations).

In the first setting of time-space tradeoff, the generic collision finding algorithm is the parallel rho method [37] that gives the tradeoff $T = 2^{n/2}/S$ even in the quantum setting, as observed by Bernstein [4]. Thus, in this setting, we have to compare the efficiency of dedicated quantum attacks to the parallel rho method. As briefly introduced before, rebound attacks consist of *inbound phase* and *outbound phase*. Intuitively, if we use a differential trail of probability p_{out} for the outbound phase, the time complexity for the outbound phase becomes about $\sqrt{1/p_{out}}$ with the Grover search. The inbound phase can be done in a constant time if large memory (and qRAM) is available, but here we aim to construct space-efficient attacks since now we are in the setting without qRAM where quantum memory is usually quite expensive. Suppose that we can construct a quantum circuit of size S_0 that performs the inbound phase in time T_{in}. Then the rebound attack runs in time $T = T_{in} \cdot \sqrt{1/p_{out}}$ on a quantum computer of size around S_0. We observe that this attack is more efficient than the generic attack (the parallel rho method) if $p_{out} > T_{in}^2 S_0^2 2^{-n}$ holds. In addition, if a quantum computer of size $S(\geq S_0)$ is available, by parallelizing the Grover search for the outbound phase we obtain the tradeoff $T = T_{in} \cdot \sqrt{1/p_{out}}\sqrt{S_0/S}$, which is better than the generic tradeoff $T = 2^{n/2}/S$ as long as $S < 2^n \cdot p_{out}/(T_{in}^2 \cdot S_0)$.

In the second setting that a small computer of polynomial size and exponentially large classical memory is available, the best collision-finding algorithm is the one by Chailloux et al. [13] that runs in time $\tilde{O}(2^{2n/5})$ with a quantum computer of size $\tilde{O}(1)$ and classical memory of size $O(2^{n/5})$. We observe that our rebound attack is faster than this algorithm if $p_{out} > T_{in}^2 2^{-4n/5}$ holds.

Rebound attacks on 7-round AES-MMO and 6-round Whirlpool

Rebound attacks on 7-round AES-MMO. AES-MMO is an AES-based compression function that is widely considered for practical use. AES-MMO is standardized by Zigbee [1] and used to be standardized by IETF [12]. In addition, due to its efficiency with a support by AES-NI, many multi-party computation protocols are implemented by using AES-MMO, e.g. [19,27]. Here, the Matyas-Meyer-Oseas (MMO) construction [26, Section 9.4] makes a compression function $h^E : \{0,1\}^n \times \{0,1\}^n \to \{0,1\}$ from an n-bit block cipher $E_k(m)$ as $h^E(\text{iv}, m) := E_{\text{iv}}(m) \oplus m$. The compression function can be used to construct hash functions by using the Merkle-Damgård construction [15,33].

In the classical setting, the best collision attacks on AES-MMO are for 6 rounds [16,30]. Here, the goal of collision attacks on the compression function is to find messages $m, m' \in \{0,1\}^n$ such that $h^E(\text{iv}, m) = h^E(\text{iv}, m')$ (E is AES-128), given iv $\in \{0,1\}^n$ *arbitrarily*. If we can mount such a collision attack on h^E, we can extend it to the entire hash function.

In this paper, we give a new 7-round differential trail of AES with the differential probability $p_{out} = 2^{-80}(> 2^{-128 \cdot 2/3})$ and show that it can be used to mount rebound attacks in the quantum settings: In the setting that a small computer with qRAM is available, we can mount a rebound attack that is slightly faster than the generic attack (BHT) by using large classical and quantum memory.[1] In the setting that the efficiency of quantum algorithms is measured by the tradeoff between time and space, we can also mount a rebound attack and its time-tradeoff is better than the generic one. However, in the setting that a small

---

[1] Our attack in this setting is just a demonstration that differential trails with such a small probability can actually be used to mount rebound attacks that are comparable to the generic attack. We assume that 1 memory access is faster than 1 execution of the entire function, which allows a memory size (2^{48}) to be larger than the time complexity $(2^{42.5})$ counted by the unit time (see also Table 1). Since some readers may disagree this counting and the advantage of our attack over BHT is small, we do not claim that 7-round AES-MMO is broken by our attack in this setting.

Table 1. Comparison of dedicated attacks against AES hashing modes and Whirlpool

AES-MMO and AES-MP

Attack	Rounds	Time	Space	Setting	Model	Ref.
collision	5	2^{56}	2^4	classic		[32]
collision	6	2^{56}	2^{32}	classic		[16,30]
collision	7	$2^{42.5}$	(2^{48})	quantum	qRAM	Ours
collision	7	$2^{59.5}/\sqrt{S/2^3}$	$2^3 \leq S < 2^6$	quantum	time-space	Ours
preimage	7	2^{120}	2^8	classic		[38]

Whirlpool

Attack	Rounds	Time	Space	Setting	Model	Ref.
collision	4	2^{120}	2^{16}	classic		[32]
collision	5	2^{120}	2^{64}	classic		[16,30]
collision	6	$2^{228}/\sqrt{S/2^8}$	$2^8 \leq S < 2^{48}$	quantum	time-space	Ours
semi-free-start coll	5	2^{120}	2^{16}	classic		[32]
semi-free-start coll	7	2^{184}	2^8	classic		[30]
free-start collision	8	2^{120}	2^8	classic		[39]
preimage	5	2^{504}	2^8	classic		[38]
preimage	5	$2^{481.5}$	2^{64}	classic		[43]
preimage	6	2^{481}	2^{256}	classic		[39]
distinguisher	9	2^{368}	2^{64}	classic		[23]
distinguisher	10	2^{188}	2^8	classic		[30]

Semi-free-start collisions, free-start collisions, and differential distinguishers are attacks on the compression function and cannot be applied to real Whirlpool with fixed IV.

quantum computer of polynomial size and exponentially large classical memory is available, our rebound attack is lower than the best attack by Chailloux et al. See Table 1 for details on attack complexities and comparisons. As well as the best classical attack, in which the Super-Sbox technique [16,30] is used to perform inbound phases.

Our attacks are also valid for AES-MP, where the Miyaguchi-Preneel (MP) construction [26, Section 9.4] makes a compression function $h^E : \{0,1\}^n \times \{0,1\}^n \to \{0,1\}^n$ from a block cipher $E_k(m)$ as $h^E(\mathrm{iv}, m) = E_{\mathrm{iv}}(m) \oplus m \oplus \mathrm{iv}$.

A Rebound Attack on 6-round Whirlpool. Whirlpool is a hash function of 512-bit output designed by Barreto and Rijmen [3], which is recommended by the NESSIE project and adopted by ISO/IEC 10118-3 standard [22]. Whirlpool is a block cipher based hash function that uses a 10-round AES-like cipher as the underlying block cipher. Both of the block and key lengths of the block cipher are 512 bits. Unlike AES, it performs MixColumns in the last round.

In this paper, we show that a technique for the classical distinguishing attack [23], which covers three full active rounds for the inbound phase can be used to find collisions of 6-round Whirlpool in the quantum setting. The attack on 6-round Whirlpool is only valid in the setting that the efficiency of quantum algorithms is measured by the tradeoff between time and space, and the attack is worse than generic attacks in other quantum settings. See Table 1 for details.

Optimality. We also show that our 7-round differential trail for AES and 6-round differential trail for Whirlpool are optimal from the view point of rebound attacks to find collisions. We show the optimality by using MILP.

Future work. An important future work is to search for more differential trails of which differential probabilities are too small in the classical setting but large enough in the quantum settings. The number of attacked rounds of other concrete hash functions may be improved in the quantum settings.

1.2 Paper Outline

Section 2 gives preliminaries on AES-like block ciphers and quantum computations. Section 3 reviews generic quantum collision attacks in various settings. Section 4 reviews the framework of classical rebound attacks. Section 5 gives our main observation on quantum computation and differential trails with smaller differential probabilities than the birthday bound. Sections 6 and 7 show our rebound attacks in the quantum settings on 7-round AES-MMO and 6-round Whirlpool, respectively. Section 8 shows optimality of our differential trails given in Sects. 6 and 7. Section 9 concludes the paper.

2 Preliminaries

2.1 AES-like Ciphers

An AES-like cipher is a $(c \cdot r^2)$-bit block cipher based on Substitution-Permutation Network (SPN) such that its internal states consist of $r \times r$ c-bit cells (each cell is regarded as an element in $GF(2^c)$) and each round transformation consists of the four operations SubBytes (SB), ShiftRows (SR), Mix-Columns (MC), and AddRoundKey (AK). SubBytes is the non-linear operation that applies a c-bit S-box to each cell. ShiftRows is the linear operation that rotates the i-th row by i cells to the left. MixColumns is the linear operation that multiplies an $r \times r$ matrix over $GF(2^c)$ to each column vector. AddRound-Key is the operation that adds a round key to the state. Given an input message to encrypt, an AES-like cipher first adds a pre-whitening key to message, and then applies the round transformation iteratively.

In this paper, when we consider attacks on compression functions based on AES-like ciphers, the keys of the ciphers are fixed to constants (initialization vectors). Thus, we call the operation of adding a round key AddConstant instead of AddRoundKey.

AES. The original AES is a 128-bit block cipher designed by Daemen and Rijmen [14]. The parameters r and c are set as $r = 4$ and $c = 8$. The key length k can be chosen from 128, 192, or 256, and the number of rounds r is specified depending on k as $r = 6 + (k/32)$. AES uses $4 \times r$ S-box applications in its key schedules. Thus one encryption with AES requires $20 \times r$ S-box applications in total. In particular, one encryption with AES-128 requires 200 S-box applications in total. An important feature of the original AES is that MixColumns is skipped in the last round. In our attacks in later sections, whether or not MixColumns in the last round is skipped impacts to the number of attacked rounds.

Whirlpool. Whirlpool is a hash function designed by Barreto and Rijmen [3]. It is constructed from an AES-like 512-bit block cipher E^2 with Merkle-Damgård and Miyaguchi-Preneel constructions [26, Section 9.4]. The parameters r and c of the underlying block cipher E are set as $r = 8$ and $c = 8$. The key length k and the number of rounds r are specified as $k = 512$ and $r = 10$, respectively. The key schedule of E is the same as the round transformations for internal states except that fixed constants are added instead of round keys. Thus, one encryption with E requires $(64 + 64) \times r = 1280$ S-box applications. Unlike AES, E does not skip MixColumns in the last round.

2.2 Quantum Computation

We use the standard quantum circuit model [35] and adopt the basic gate set $\{H, CNOT, T\}$ (Clifford+T gates). Here, H is the single qubit Hadamard gate $H : |b\rangle \mapsto \frac{1}{\sqrt{2}}(|0\rangle + (-1)^b |1\rangle)$, $CNOT$ is the two-qubit CNOT gate $CNOT : |a\rangle |b\rangle \mapsto |a\rangle |b \oplus a\rangle$, and T is the $\pi/8$ gate defined as $T : |0\rangle \mapsto |0\rangle$ and $T : |1\rangle \mapsto e^{i\pi/4} |1\rangle$. We denote the identity operator on n-qubit states by I_n. The quantum oracle of a function $f : \{0,1\}^m \to \{0,1\}^n$ is modeled as the unitary operator U_f defined by $U_f : |x\rangle |y\rangle \mapsto |x\rangle |y \oplus f(x)\rangle$. We also use an alternative model for the quantum oracle of f, which is the unitary operator defined as $\tilde{U}_f : |x\rangle |y\rangle \mapsto (-1)^{y \cdot f(x)} |x\rangle |y\rangle$. When f is a Boolean function, $\tilde{U}_f = (I_n \otimes H)U_f(I_n \otimes H)$ holds. Thus $\tilde{U}_f$ can be simulated with one application of U_f, and vice versa.

When we estimate time complexity of an attack on a primitive, we assume unit of time to be the time required to run the primitive once (e.g., the time required for one encryption if the primitive is a block cipher). The actual time to run a quantum attack will depend on hardware architectures of quantum computers, but we just consider the simple computational model that each pair of qubits in a quantum computer can interact with one another. Based on this model, we evaluate the time of dedicated attacks on a primitive to discuss if it is more efficient than the generic attacks in this model. In addition, when we estimate space complexity of a quantum attack on a primitive, we regard the number of qubits to implement the target primitive as the unit of space size.

---

[2] In the specification of Whirlpool [3] Shift "Columns" and Mix "Rows" operations are used instead of ShiftRows and MixColumns, but they are mathematically equivalent up to transposition of internal states.

Grover's algorithm. Consider the following *database search problem.*

Problem 1. Let $F : \{0,1\}^n \to \{0,1\}$ be a Boolean function. Suppose that F is given as a black-box. Then, find x such that $F(x) = 1$.

Let $a := |f^{-1}(1)|/2^n$, which is the probability that we obtain x such that $F(x) = 1$ when we randomly choose $x \in \{0,1\}^n$. Suppose that $a > 0$. In the classical setting, we have to make $1/a$ queries to find x such that $F(x) = 1$. On the other hand, in the quantum setting, when F is given as a quantum black-box oracle and $a > 0$, Grover's algorithm finds x by making $\Theta(\sqrt{1/a})$ quantum queries to F [9,10,17]. That is, Grover's algorithm achieves a quadratic speed up compared to classical algorithms. Below we review Grover's algorithm and its variants.

Let S_F and S_0 be the unitary operators that act on n-qubit states defined as $S_F |x\rangle = (-1)^{F(x)} |x\rangle$ for $x \in \{0,1\}^n$, and $S_0 |x\rangle = |x\rangle$ if $x \neq 0^n$ and $S_0 |0^n\rangle = -|0^n\rangle$, respectively. (Note that S_F can be simulated by using the operator $\tilde{U}_F$ since $(S_F |x\rangle) \otimes |1\rangle = \tilde{U}_F(|x\rangle \otimes |1\rangle)$ holds.) Let $V_F := -H^{\otimes n} S_0 H^{\otimes n} S_F$. Then the following proposition holds.

Proposition 1 (Grover's algorithm [10,17]). *Let θ be the parameter such that $0 \leq \theta \leq \pi/2$ and $\sin^2 \theta = a$. Set $m := \lfloor \pi/4\theta \rfloor$. When we compute $V_F^m H^{\otimes n} |0^n\rangle$ and measure the resulting state, we will obtain $x \in \{0,1\}^n$ such that $F(x) = 1$ with a probability at least $\max\{1 - p, p\}$.*[3]

Grover's algorithm with certainty. Grover's algorithm can be modified so that it will return the solution with certainty by slightly changing the last application of V_F and doing some rotations [10]. In this case we will obtain the superposition $\sum_{x \in f^{-1}(1)} \frac{1}{\sqrt{|f^{-1}(1)|}} |x\rangle$ before the final measurement. In particular, if there exists only a single x_0 such that $f(x_0) = 1$, we will obtain the state $|x_0\rangle$.[4]

Parallelization. Suppose that P *classical* processors can be used for parallelization to solve Problem 1. Then, by dividing $\{0,1\}^n$ into P subspaces $X_1, \ldots, X_P$ such that $|X_i| = 2^n/P$ for each i and using the i-th classical processor to search in X_i, we can solve Problem 1 in time $1/(a \cdot P)$ (provided $a > 0$). On the other hand, when Q quantum processors (small quantum computers) can be used for parallelization, by using the i-th quantum processor to run Grover search on X_i, we can solve Problem 1 in time $O(\sqrt{1/(a \cdot P)})$.

---

[3] Here we are assuming that the probability a is known in advance. However, even if we do not know the probability a in advance, we can find x such that $F(x) = 1$ with $O(\sqrt{1/a})$ quantum queries by introducing some intermediate measurements.

[4] To be more precise, in the real world, we will still have some small errors since we can only approximate unitary operators by using Clifford + T gates. However, since we can efficiently make such approximation errors sufficiently small, we ignore these errors.

3   Generic Quantum Collision-Finding Algorithms

This section reviews generic quantum collision-finding algorithms and their complexities in various settings. Here we consider finding collisions of a random function with range $\{0,1\}^n$ and sufficiently large domain (e.g., $\{0,1\}^n$).

The BHT algorithm (the setting with qRAM). The first important generic quantum collision-finding algorithm is the BHT algorithm (BHT) developed by Brassard, Høyer, and Tapp [11]. It finds a collision in time $\tilde{O}(2^{n/3})$ by making $O(2^{n/3})$ quantum queries when exponentially large quantum random access memory (qRAM) is available.

Here, qRAM is a quantum analogue of random access memory (RAM), which allows us to efficiently access stored data in quantum superpositions. Suppose that there is a list of classical data $L = (x_0, \ldots, x_{2^m-1})$, where $x_i \in \{0,1\}^n$ for each i. Then, the qRAM for L is modeled as an unitary operator $U_{\mathsf{qRAM}}(L)$ defined by

$$U_{\mathsf{qRAM}}(L) : |i\rangle \otimes |y\rangle \mapsto |i\rangle \otimes |y \oplus x_i\rangle \tag{1}$$

for $i \in \{0,1\}^m$ and $y \in \{0,1\}^n$. When we say that qRAM is available, we assume that a quantum gate that realizes the unitary operation (1) (for a list L of classical data) is available in addition to basic quantum gates.

BHT consists of two steps. Suppose that our current goal is to find a collision of a random function $f : \{0,1\}^n \to \{0,1\}^n$. The first step performs a classical precomputation that chooses a subset $X \subset \{0,1\}^n$ of size $|X| = 2^{n/3}$ and computes the value $f(x)$ for all $x \in X$ (which requires queries and time in $O(2^{n/3})$). The $2^{n/3}$ pairs $L = \{(x, f(x))\}_{x \in X}$ are stored into qRAM so that they can be accessed in quantum superpositions. Then, the second step performs the Grover search to find $x' \in \{0,1\}^n \setminus X$ such that $(x, f(x)) \in L$ and $f(x) = f(x')$ for some $x \in X$, which runs in time $O(\sqrt{2^n/|L|}) = O(2^{n/3})$ on average. If we find such an $x' \in \{0,1\}^n \setminus X$ (and $x \in X$), it implies that we find a collision for f since $f(x') = f(x)$.

Consider the model that a small quantum computer of polynomial size and a qRAM that allows us to access exponentially many classical data in quantum superposition are available. Here we do not consider any parallelized computations. In this model, the best collision-finding algorithm is BHT since we can implement it with qRAM (of size $O(2^{n/3})$) and its time complexity matches the tight quantum query complexity $\Theta(2^{n/3})$.

Tradeoffs between time and space. BHT achieves time complexity $\tilde{O}(2^{n/3})$, however, it also uses a large qRAM of size $\tilde{O}(2^{n/3})$. The model that each adversary can use a small quantum computer with qRAM is simple and theoretically worth studying since it generalizes the classical attack model that each adversary can use a single processor and large memory, but it is not clear whether such qRAM will be available in some future. Even if qRAM of size $O(2^{n/3})$ is not available, we can simulate it with a quantum circuit of size $O(2^{n/3})$. However, such a usage of exponentially large number of qubits causes discussions on parallelizations: When we evaluate the efficiency of a quantum algorithm that uses exponentially many qubits to realize quantum memory, it is plausible to compare the algorithm to other quantum algorithms that may use the same amount of qubits for parallel computations.

As observed by Bernstein [4], from the view point of time-space complexity, BHT is worse than the classical parallel rho method by Oorschot and Wiener [37]: Roughly speaking, when P classical processors are available, the parallel rho method finds a collision in time $O(2^{n/2}/P)$. Thus, if a quantum computer of size $2^{n/3}$ is available but qRAM is not available, by just running the parallel rho method on the quantum computer, we can find a collision in time $2^{n/6}$, which is much faster than BHT.[5]

In the classical setting, there exists a memory-less collision finding algorithm that finds a collision in time $O(2^{n/2})$, which matches the classical tight bound for query complexity. On the other hand, in the quantum setting, there has not been known any memory-less quantum collision finding algorithm such that its *time* complexity matches the optimal query complexity $2^{n/3}$.

Let S denote the size of computational resources required for a quantum algorithm (i.e., S is the maximum size of quantum computers and classical memory) and T denote its time complexity. Then the tradeoff $T \cdot S = 2^{n/2}$ given by the parallel rho method is the best one even in the quantum setting.

Small quantum computer with large classical memory. Next, suppose that only a small quantum computer of polynomial size is available but we can use a exponentially large classical memory. In this situation, Chailloux et al. [13] showed that we can find a collision in time $\tilde{O}(2^{2n/5})$ with a quantum computer of size $\tilde{O}(1)$ and $\tilde{O}(2^{n/5})$ classical memory. The product of T and S becomes around $2^{3n/5}$, which is larger than $2^{n/2}$, but it is quite usual to consider a classical memory of size $\tilde{O}(2^{n/5})$, which is usually available. The algorithm by Chailloux et al. shows that we can obtain another better tradeoff between time and space if we treat the sizes of quantum hardware and classical hardware separately.

Remark 1. To be precise, it is not clear what the term "quantum computer of polynomial size" means in practical settings since the security parameter n is usually fixed to a constant in concrete primitives. For convenience, by "quantum computer of polynomial size" we arbitrarily denote a quantum computer of size at most n^2. (Note that we regard the space (the number of qubits) required to implement the target primitive as the unit of space.)

4 Previous Works in the Classical Setting

In this section, we briefly review the previous work of collision attacks against AES-like hash functions. Note that whether or not the MixColumns operation

---

[5] Here we are considering the model that is called *free communication model* by Banegas and Bernstein [2].

in the last round is omitted impacts on the number of attacked rounds with respect to the collision attack, which is different from the number of attacked rounds for differential distinguishers.

4.1 Framework of Collision Attacks

Our target constructions are the MMO and Miyaguchi-Preneel modes that compute the output as $E_k(p) \oplus p$ or $E_k(p) \oplus p \oplus k$ respectively, where E_k is AES or an AES-like cipher and p is a plaintext input to the cipher. Moreover, we assume that the key input k is fixed to an initial value iv. Namely, for a 1-block message m, the hash value is computed as $E_{\mathrm{iv}}(m) \oplus m$ or $E_{\mathrm{iv}}(m) \oplus m \oplus \mathrm{iv}$, respectively.

Given the above target, the attackers' strategy is to inject a non-zero difference Δ on the plaintext input m and to process m and $m \oplus \Delta$ with fixed iv with zero difference. If the ciphertext difference matches the plaintext difference, i.e. $E_{\mathrm{iv}}(m) \oplus E_{\mathrm{iv}}(m \oplus \Delta) = \Delta$, two hash values collide because the differences are canceled through the feed-forward operation.

AES-like ciphers with r rows and r columns (with MixColumns in the last round) is known to allow the 4-round differential propagation with the following number of active S-boxes per round: $1 \longrightarrow r \longrightarrow r^2 \longrightarrow r \longrightarrow 1$, where the second, third, and fourth rounds have r active bytes in a column, fully active, and have r active bytes in a diagonal, respectively. If the active-byte positions at the beginning and the end, as well as the actual difference, are identical, collisions are obtained.

For AES (with $r = 4$, without MixColumns in the last round), one more rounds can be attacked by the following pattern of the number of active S-boxes: $1 \longrightarrow 4 \longrightarrow 16 \longrightarrow 4 \longrightarrow 1 \longrightarrow 1$.

The most interesting part of hash function analysis is to find the minimum complexity to find a pair of values that satisfies such differential propagation patterns. Owing to the nature of the keyless primitives, the attacker can first choose pairs such that the most difficult part (unlikely to be satisfied by randomly chosen pairs) is satisfied, and then the remaining propagation is satisfied probabilistically. This strategy, in particular for AES-like ciphers, was explored by Mendel et al. [32] as the "rebound attack" framework. Very intuitively, the differential propagation is designed to be dense in the middle and sparse at the beginning and the end. The attacker first efficiently collects paired values satisfying the middle part. This procedure is called "inbound phase" and the paired values are called "starting points." Then, starting points are simply propagated to the beginning and the end to check if the sparse propagation is probabilistically satisfied or not. This procedure is called "outbound phase."

Mendel et al. showed that a pair of values satisfying the 2-round transformation $r \longrightarrow r^2 \longrightarrow r$ can be generated with complexity 1 on average. Hence, 4-round collisions can be generated only by satisfying the differential transformation $r \longrightarrow 1$ twice and 1-byte cancellation for the feed-forward operation.

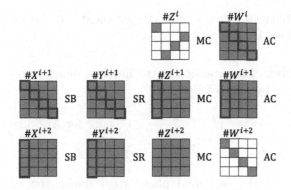

Fig. 1. Inbound phase of Super-Sbox cryptanalysis.

4.2 Super-Sbox Cryptanalysis

There are many previous works that improve or extend the rebound attack. An important improvement is the Super-Sbox cryptanalysis presented by Gilbert and Peyrin [16] and independently observed by Lamberger et al. [30], which generates a pair of values satisfying the 3-round transformation $r \longrightarrow r^2 \longrightarrow r^2 \longrightarrow r$ with complexity 1 on average.

Inbound Phase. The involved states are depicted in Fig. 1 for the case of $r = 4$. The procedure is iterated for all the choices of the difference at state $\#Z^i$. Hence for each iteration, the difference at $\#Z^i$ is fixed. Because MixColumns is a linear operation, the corresponding difference at state $\#X^{i+1}$ is uniquely computed. From the opposite side, the number of possible differences at state $\#W^{i+2}$ is 2^{rc} and those are handled in parallel. The attacker computes the corresponding 2^{rc} differences at state $\#Y^{i+2}$ and stores them in a list L.

The attacker then searches for the paired values that connect $\#X^{i+1}$ and $\#Y^{i+2}$. The core observation is that this part can be computed independently for each group of r bytes, which is known to the Super-Sbox. One of the r-byte groups is highlighted by thick squares in Fig. 1. For each of 2^{rc} input values to a Super-Sbox at $\#X^{i+1}$, the corresponding difference (along with paired values) at $\#Y^{i+2}$ is computed. Each difference in L will be hit once on average because L contains 2^{rc} differences. The same analysis is applied for r Super-Sboxes. Then, each of the 2^{rc} difference in L can be produced once on average from all the Super-Sboxes.

Complexity of the Inbound Phase. L requires a memory of size 2^{rc}. Each Super-Sbox is computed for 2^{rc} distinct inputs. Considering that the size of each Super-Sbox is $1/r$ of the entire state, computations of r Super-Sboxes are regarded as a single computation for the entire construction. After the analysis, the attacker obtains 2^{rc} starting points, hence the average complexity to obtain a starting point is 1. The inbound phase can be iterated up to 2^{rc} times by choosing 2^{rc} differences at State $\#Z^i$. Hence the degrees of freedom to satisfy the outbound phase is up to 2^{2rc}.

Outbound Phase. The extension of the inbound phase increases the number of attacked rounds by one as follows.

$$1 \xleftarrow{2^{-(r-1)c}} r - r^2 - r^2 - r \xrightarrow{2^{-(r-1)c}} 1 \qquad \text{for AES-like ciphers,}$$

$$1 \xleftarrow{2^{-24}} 4 - 16 - 16 - 4 \xrightarrow{2^{-24}} 1 \xrightarrow{1} 1 \qquad \text{for AES.}$$

The probability for the outbound phase stays unchanged from the original rebound attack, which is $2^{-2(r-1)c}$ to satisfy the transformation $r \longrightarrow 1$ twice and 2^{-c} for the cancellation at the feed-forward operation. Hence, collisions of 5-round Whirlpool are generated with complexity $2^{120}(= 2^{2(8-1)8} \times 2^8)$ and collisions of 6-round AES-MMO are generated with complexity $2^{56}(= 2^{2(4-1)8} \times 2^8)$.

4.3   Covering Three Full Active Rounds on 8×8 State

Jean et al. presented another extension of the rebound attack, which covers one more fully active state for the inbound phase [23], namely

$$r \longleftarrow 1 \xleftarrow{2^{-(r-1)c}} r - r^2 - r^2 - r^2 - r \xrightarrow{2^{-(r-1)c}} 1 \longrightarrow r \longrightarrow \mathcal{L}(r),$$

where $\mathcal{L}(r)$ is a linear subspace of dimension 2^{rc}. However the drawback of this analysis is that the amortized cost to find a starting point is $2^{r^2 c/2}$, which reaches the complexity of the birthday paradox. This is significantly more expensive than the amortized cost 1 for the original rebound attack and the Super-Sbox analysis. Owing to its complexity, the technique cannot be used for finding collisions, while it is still sufficient to mount a differential distinguisher up to 9 rounds. Here we briefly explain the procedure to satisfy the inbound phase with complexity $2^{r^2 c/2}$ and omit the explanation of the outbound phase and advantages of the distinguisher because our goal is to find collisions.

The involved states are depicted in Fig. 2 for the case of $r = 8$. The analysis of the inbound phase starts with a fixed pair of difference at state $\#Z^i$ and $\#W^{i+3}$. Similarly to the Super-Sbox cryptanalysis, the corresponding differences at $\#X^{i+1}$ and $\#Y^{i+3}$ are linearly computed. The attacker then computes r Super-Sboxes that cover from $\#X^{i+1}$ to $\#Y^{i+2}$. The results for the i-th Super-Sbox are stored in a list L_j^f, where $0 \leq j < r$. To be precise, each L_j^f contains 2^{rc} pairs of r-byte values ($2r$-byte values) at $\#Y^{i+2}$. Similarly, the attacker computes r inverse Super-Sboxes from $\#Y^{i+3}$ to $\#Y^{i+2}$, and the results are stored in a list L_j^b, where $0 \leq j < r$.

The attacker then finds a match of those $2r$ lists. The attacker exhaustively tries $r^2/2$-byte values at $\#Y^{i+2}$ that can be fixed by choosing the entries of $L_0^f, L_1^f, \ldots, L_{r/2-1}^f$ (a half of the Super-Sboxes). As shown in Fig. 2, this will fix a pair of values for $r^2/2$ bytes at $\#Y^{i+2}$, i.e. r^2-byte values are fixed for

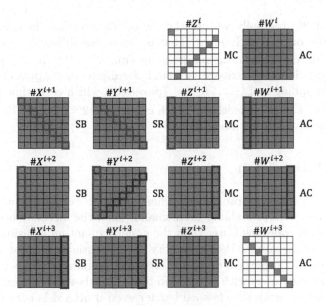

Fig. 2. Inbound phase for covering three rounds with fully active states.

the left-half of $\#Y^{i+2}$. The attacker then checks if those fixed values can be produced from L_j^b. For each L_j^b, r-byte values have already been fixed, and those play a role of the rc-bit filter. Considering that the degrees of freedom in each L_j^b is 2^{rc}, the attacker can expect one match on average for each L_j^b, and the state $\#Y^{i+2}$ is now fully fixed. The attacker finally checks if the paired values at $\#Y^{i+2}$ for the remaining $r^2/2$-byte value (right-half of $\#Y^{i+2}$) can be produced from $L_{r/2}^f, L_{r/2+1}^f, \ldots, L_{r-1}^f$. The number of the constraints is 2^{r^2c} while the total degrees of freedom in $r/2$ Super-Sboxes is $2^{r^2c/2}$. Therefore, a match will be found with probability $2^{-r^2c/2}$, and by exhaustively testing $2^{r^2c/2}$ choices of $L_0^f, L_1^f, \ldots, L_{r/2-1}^f$ at the beginning, a solution can be found.

The procedure of the inbound phase can be summarized as follows.

1. For exhaustive combinations of the values of $L_0^f, \ldots, L_{r/2-1}^f$, do as follows.
2. Find an entry of L_j^b for each $0 \le j < r$.
3. Check if the fixed state can be produced by $L_{r/2}^f, \ldots, L_{r-1}^f$.

The attacker can find a starting point after $2^{r^2c/2}$ iterations of the first step. Note that the computation of each L_j^f and L_j^b only requires 2^{rc} computations and memory. The bottleneck is to find a match in the middle, which requires $2^{r^2c/2}$ computations, while the required memory is negligible in the context of finding a match.

A memoryless variant. The technique for the inbound phase introduced above can easily converted into a memoryless variant by increasing the running time by a factor of 2^{rc} (actually we use the memoryless variant in a later section rather than the original technique). That is, given the differences at state $\#Z^i$ and $\#W^{i+3}$, we can find a starting point in time $2^{r^2c/2+rc}$ by using negligible memory by just doing the exhaustive search for inputs or outputs of the Super-Sboxes corresponding to $L_0^f, \ldots, L_{r/2-1}^f$ (parallelly, which costs time $2^{r^2c/2}$) and L_j^b for each $0 \le j < r$ (sequentially, which costs time 2^{rc}). See Section A in this paper's full version [21] for more details.

5 New Observation

This section gives a new observation: when quantum computers are available, differential trails with probability even smaller than the birthday bound can be used to find hash collisions faster than the generic quantum collision attacks.

Section 5.1 observes that the probability of differential trails that can be used in classical rebound attacks is up to the birthday bound. Section 5.2 shows that small quantum computers with qRAM can break the classical barrier. Section 5.3 shows that we can break the classical barrier even if qRAM is not available.

5.1 Birthday Bound Barrier for Classical Differential Probabilities

Recall that rebound attacks consist of inbound phase and outbound phase (see Sect. 4). Roughly speaking, for an input difference Δ_{in} and output difference Δ_{out} for some intermediate rounds of E (Δ_{in} and Δ_{out} correspond to the differences at state $\#Z^i$ and $\#W^{i+2}$ in Fig. 1, respectively), firstly the inbound phase searches for an input pair (M, M') and an output pair $(\tilde{M}, \tilde{M}')$ that satisfy the differential propagation $\Delta_{in} \longrightarrow \Delta_{out}$ (i.e., starting points). Then the outbound phase checks whether the pairs (M, M') and $(\tilde{M}, \tilde{M}')$ satisfy differential transformations for the remaining rounds (which implies that we find a collision of the target compression function).

Let p_{out} be the probability that the pairs (M, M') and $(\tilde{M}, \tilde{M}')$ satisfy differential transformations for the outbound phase (including the cancellation for the feed-forward operation). Then, since the inbound phase can usually be done in a constant time by doing some precomputations and using some classical memory, the whole time complexity of the attack becomes $T = 1/p_{out}$.

If $p_{out} > 2^{-n/2}$, $T < 2^{n/2}$ holds and the rebound attack is faster than the classical generic collision finding algorithm. However, the attack is worse than the generic attack if $2^{-n/2} > p_{out}$. Thus, a differential trail for the outbound phase can be used only if $p_{out} > 2^{-n/2}$ holds. In other words, $2^{-n/2}$ is the barrier for differential probabilities to be used in classical rebound attacks.

5.2 Breaking the Barrier with Quantum Computers and qRAM

Below we explain how the attack complexity and the limitation for differential probability p_{out} changes in the quantum setting. To simplify explanations, here we consider the theoretically simple setting that a small quantum computer of polynomial size and exponentially large qRAM is available.

In the quantum setting, to implement rebound attacks on quantum computers, we use the Grover search on a Boolean function $F(\Delta_{in}, \Delta_{out})$ defined as $F(\Delta_{in}, \Delta_{out}) = 1$ if and only if both of the following conditions hold.

1. In the inbound phase, there exists an input pair (M, M') and output pair $(\tilde{M}, \tilde{M}')$ that satisfies the differential trail $\Delta_{in} \longrightarrow \Delta_{out}$ (i.e., starting points), and

2. The pairs (M, M') and $(\tilde{M}, \tilde{M}')$ satisfy the differential transformation in the outbound phase.

(Here, without loss of generality we assume that $M < M'$. We ignore the possibility that two or more starting points exist in the inbound phase, to simplify explanations.) For each input $(\Delta_{in}, \Delta_{out})$, we have to perform the inbound and outbound phases to compute the value $F(\Delta_{in}, \Delta_{out})$. Once we find a pair $(\Delta_{in}, \Delta_{out})$ such that $F(\Delta_{in}, \Delta_{out}) = 1$, we can easily find a collision by performing the inbound and outbound phases again.

Small quantum computer with qRAM. Recall that, the generic collision finding attack in this setting (a small quantum computer of polynomial size and exponentially large qRAM is available) is BHT that finds a collision in time $O(2^{n/3})$. (See Sect. 3. We do not consider any parallelized computations in this setting.) Therefore, dedicated attacks that can find collisions in time less than $O(2^{n/3})$ with a small quantum computer of polynomial size and qRAM are regarded to be valid. To mount rebound attacks, we perform some classical precomputations and store the results into qRAM so that we can perform the inbound phase in a constant time. Then the time complexity for the Grover search becomes $\sqrt{1/p_{out}}$. Let T_{pre} denote the time required for the classical precomputation.

Recall that BHT performs $2^{n/3}$ classical precomputations and then does $2^{n/3}$ iterations in the Grover search. Suppose that the time for our classical precomputation T_{pre} satisfies $T_{pre} \leq 2^{n/3}$, for simplicity. Then, our rebound attack is more efficient than the generic attack (BHT) if $\sqrt{1/p_{out}} < 2^{n/3}$, or equivalently $p_{out} > 2^{-2n/3}$ holds. Thus, roughly speaking, even if a compression function is secure in the classical setting, if there exists a differential trail for the outbound phase with $2^{-n/2} > p_{out} > 2^{-2n/3}$, there exists a collision attack for the function that is more efficient than the generic attack in this setting. In other words, we can break the birthday bound barrier $2^{-n/2}$ for the differential probability with quantum computers and qRAM.

5.3 Breaking the Barrier Without qRAM

Here we show that the barrier of the birthday bound can be broken even if qRAM is not available.

If we perform heavy precomputations for the inbound phase, it may use huge quantum memory. When qRAM is not available, quantum memory is usually very expensive and sometimes only a small number of qubits can be used to store data. To reduce the amount of quantum memory required, when we implement rebound attacks on quantum computers without qRAM, we do not perform heavy precomputations and increase the time to perform the inbound phase if necessary. Let T_{in} denote the time to perform the inbound phase.

Tradeoffs between time and space. Consider the setting that efficiency of a quantum algorithm is measured by the tradeoff between time T and space S (S is the maximum of the size of quantum computer and the size of classical memory), and parallelized computations are taken into account. In this setting, the generic collision finding algorithm is the parallel rho method (see Sect. 3), which gives the tradeoff $T \cdot S = 2^{n/2}$, or equivalently $T = 2^{n/2}/S$.

Suppose that the inbound phase of a rebound attack can be done in time T_{in} by using a quantum circuit of size S_0, where S_0 may be exponentially large. Then the rebound attack runs in time $T = T_{in} \cdot \sqrt{1/p_{out}}$. When we measure the efficiency of a quantum algorithm by tradeoff between time and space, this rebound attack is more efficient than the generic attack (that uses a quantum computer and classical memory of size at most S_0) if $T = T_{in} \cdot \sqrt{1/p_{out}} < 2^{n/2}/S_0$, or equivalently $p_{out} > T_{in}^2 S_0^2 2^{-n}$ holds.

In other words, even if a compression function is secure in the classical setting, if we can construct a quantum algorithm that performs the inbound phase in time T_{in} by using a quantum circuit of size S_0 and there exists a differential trail for the outbound phase with probability p_{out} such that $2^{-n/2} > p_{out} > T_{in}^2 S_0^2 2^{-n}$, there exists a collision attack for the function that is more efficient than the generic attack in this setting.

Parallelization of the rebound attack. If a quantum computer of size $S(\geq S_0)$ is available, we can use it to parallelize the Grover search in the rebound attack, which leads to the time-memory tradeoff $T = T_{in} \cdot \sqrt{1/p_{out}} \cdot \sqrt{S_0/S}$. Since the time-memory tradeoff for the generic attack in this setting is $T = 2^{n/2}/S$, our rebound attack works if a quantum computer of size $S \geq S_0$ is available and it is more efficient than the generic attack as long as $T_{in} \cdot \sqrt{1/p_{out}} \cdot \sqrt{S_0/S} < 2^{n/2}/S$, or equivalently $S < 2^n \cdot p_{out}/(T_{in}^2 \cdot S_0)$.

Small quantum computer with large classical memory. Consider the setting that a small quantum computer of polynomial size and exponentially large classical memory are available (here we do not consider parallelization). In this setting, the generic collision finding algorithm is the one by Chailloux et al. that finds a collision in time $\tilde{O}(2^{2n/5})$ (see Sect. 3).

Suppose that the outbound phase can be done in time T_{in} by using a quantum circuit of size S_0, where S_0 is relatively small (polynomial in n). When we are in the situation that a quantum computer of polynomial size and large classical memory is available, this rebound attack is more efficient than the generic attack (the algorithm by Chailloux et al.) if $T = T_{in} \cdot \sqrt{1/p_{out}} < 2^{2n/5}$, or equivalently $p_{out} > T_{in}^2 2^{-4n/5}$ holds.

In other words, even if a compression function is secure in the classical setting, if we can construct a quantum algorithm that performs the inbound phase in time T_{in} with a quantum circuit of polynomial size and there exists a differential trail for the outbound phase with probability p_{out} such that $2^{-n/2} > p_{out} > T_{in}^2 2^{-4n/5}$, there exists a collision attack for the compression function that is more efficient than the generic attack in this setting.

6   Finding Collisions for 7-Round AES-MMO

This section gives a new differential trail for 7-round AES and shows how to use the trail to mount rebound attacks on 7-round AES-MMO in the quantum settings.

6.1   New Differential Trail for 7-Round AES

Here we give a new differential trail with the differential probability $p_{out} = 2^{-80}$ for 7-round AES that can be used to find collisions for 7-round AES-MMO: With some effort, we can come up with a differential trail shown in Fig. 3. Here, each 4×4 square in Fig. 3 shows the active byte pattern at the beginning of each round except for the square on the right hand side. The square on the right hand side shows the active byte pattern at the end of the last round. (See Fig. 4 in Section B.1 in this paper's full version [21] for more details on the differential transformations.) This trail gives $p_{out} = 2^{-80}$ since the probability for the 8-byte cancellation for the feed-forward operation is 2^{-64}.

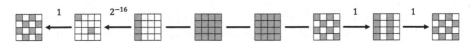

Fig. 3. A new differential trail for 7-round AES. The numbers over arrows are the probabilities for differential transformations.

The cancellation probability 2^{-64} is too small to be used in classical rebound attacks since it reaches the classical birthday bound barrier, but it can be used when quantum computers are available. We use this trail to mount rebound attacks on 7-round AES-MMO in the quantum settings.

In a later section (Sect. 8) we show that there exists no trail with $p_{out} > 2^{-80}$ for 7-round AES and there exist another trail with $p_{out} = 2^{-80}$.

6.2   Demonstration: An Attack with qRAM

Here we consider to use the above differential trail with probability 2^{-80} to implement a rebound attack on a small quantum computer with qRAM. Note that here we do not consider any parallelized computations. Our attack is based on the framework in Sect. 5.2, but here we give more detailed discussions to analyze attack complexities precisely. The attack in this section is just a demonstration that we can use very small differential probability (less than $2^{-n/2}$) to mount attacks that are comparable to the generic collision-finding algorithm. In particular, we do not intend to claim that 7-round AES-MMO is "broken" by our attack.

Detailed settings and remarks. Since the S-box can be implemented by using random access memory, we regard that 1 random access to a classical memory or qRAM is equivalent to 1 application of the S-box, which is further equivalent to $1/140$ encryption with 7-round AES (recall that 7-round AES requires 140 S-box applications). We assume that the cost for sequential accesses to classical data is negligible.

Let $\Delta_{in}, \Delta_{out} \in \{0,1\}^{128}$ be the input and output differences for the inbound phase (i.e., the difference just after the SubBytes of the 3rd round ($\#Y^3$ in Fig. 4 in Section B.1 of this paper's full version [21]) and at the beginning of the 6-th round ($\#X^6$ in Fig. 4 in Section B.1 of this paper's full version [21]), respectively). Note that 4 cells (2^{32} bits) and 8 cells (2^{64} bits) are active in Δ_{in} and Δ_{out}, respectively. Since now the differential probability is 2^{-80}, we have to make 2^{80} starting points. As well as classical rebound attacks, we expect that one starting point exists for each pair $(\Delta_{in}, \Delta_{out})$ on average. Thus we check 2^{16} values for Δ_{in} and 2^{64} values for Δ_{out}. Then we can expect that there exists 1 starting point that leads to a collision of 7-round AES-MMO among the 2^{80} pairs of $(\Delta_{in}, \Delta_{out})$.

Recall that an initialization vector iv $\in \{0,1\}^{128}$ is given before we start attacks on 7-round AES-MMO. We precompute and store all the round constants that are derived from iv and added in the AddConstant phase in each round. Since the cost to compute the round constants is negligible and we need the constants only for *sequential* applications of AddConstant in our attack (in particular, we do not need random accesses to the round constants in quantum super positions), we ignore the cost to precompute and store the round constants.

Precomputation for the inbound phase. We label the 4 Super-Sboxes involved in the inbound phase as $\mathsf{SSB}^{(1)}, \ldots, \mathsf{SSB}^{(4)}$. We perform the following precomputations and store the results in qRAM so that the inbound phase can be done efficiently.

1. For $1 \le i \le 4$, do the following Steps 2–9.
2. Let L_i and L'_i be empty lists.
3. Compute $\mathsf{SSB}^{(i)}(x)$ for each $x \in \{0,1\}^{32}$ and store the pair $(x, \mathsf{SSB}^{(i)}(x))$ into L'_i.

4. For each $x \in \{0, 1\}^{32}$, do Steps 5–9.
5. Compute $y := \mathsf{SSB}^{(i)}(x)$ by accessing to the stored list L'_i.
6. For each value of Δ_{in} (from 2^{16} values), do the following Steps 7–9:
7. Compute the corresponding input difference $\delta^{(i)}_{in}$ for $\mathsf{SSB}^{(i)}$.
8. If $x \leq x \oplus \delta^{(i)}_{in}$, do Step 9:
9. Compute $y' := \mathsf{SSB}^{(i)}(x \oplus \delta^{(i)}_{in})$ and $\delta^{(i)}_{out} := y \oplus y'$ by accessing to the stored list L'_i, and add $((\delta^{(i)}_{in}, \delta^{(i)}_{out}), \{x, x \oplus \delta^{(i)}_{in}\}, \{y, y'\})$ into the list L_i (each element of L_i is indexed by $(\delta^{(i)}_{in}, \delta^{(i)}_{out})$).

Analysis for the precomputation for the inbound phase. Here we give an analysis for the time T_{pre} required to perform the precomputation. First, we estimate the cost of Steps 2–9 for each i: Step 3 requires $8 \cdot 2^{32} = 2^{35}$ S-box applications. Each iteration of Step 5 requires 1 random memory access. Each iteration of Step 9 requires around 1 random memory access (here we regard the combination of reading data from L'_i and writing data into L_i as a single random memory access). Since there exists around $2^{32} \cdot 2^{16}/2 = 2^{47}$ pairs of (x, Δ_{in}) such that $x \leq x \oplus \delta^{(i)}_{in}$, Step 9 is performed 2^{47} times in total for each i. In addition, Step 5 is performed 2^{32} times in total. Therefore, Steps 5–9 require $2^{32} + 2^{47} \approx 2^{47}$ random memory accesses in total. This is equivalent to 2^{47} S-box applications. Thus the cost for Steps 2–8 is around $(2^{35} + 2^{47}) \approx 2^{47}$ S-box applications for each i.

Since a single S-box application is equivalent to $1/140$ single encryption by 7-round AES and we have to treat 4 Super-Sboxes, the total cost for these precomputations is equal to the cost of $4 \times 2^{47}/140 < 2^{42}$ encryptions.[6] Therefore we have $T_{pre} < 2^{42}$.

Precomputations for the outbound phase. We also perform some additional precomputations so that the outbound phase will run efficiently. We compute input-output tables of the Super-Sboxes for the 2nd and 3rd rounds, and 6th and 7th rounds, in advance. We also precompute the entire table of the 4-parallel S-box applications $(x, y, z, w) \mapsto (\mathsf{SB}(x), \mathsf{SB}(y), \mathsf{SB}(z), \mathsf{SB}(w))$ so that the computation for the 1st round in the outbound phase can be done efficiently. These computations require time $2^{32} \times c$ for a small constant c, which is negligible compared to T_{pre}.

Application of the Grover search. Recall that, when we mount rebound attacks in the quantum setting, we define a function $F(\Delta_{in}, \Delta_{out})$ so that $F(\Delta_{in}, \Delta_{out}) = 1$ if and only if there exists a starting point corresponding to $(\Delta_{in}, \Delta_{out})$ that satisfies the differential transformations for the outbound phase, and we apply the Grover search on F. Here Δ_{in} and Δ_{out} are chosen from 2^{16} and 2^{64} values, respectively.

---

[6] Because the entire truth table of the Super-Sbox is computed and stored in qRAM in the precomputation phase, we assume that the time for a single qRAM access is equivalent to a single S-box evaluation.

Given a pair $(\Delta_{in}, \Delta_{out})$, if there exists one input-output pair (x, x') and (y, y') that satisfies the differential trail $\delta_{in}^{(i)} \longrightarrow \delta_{out}^{(i)}$ for $\mathsf{SSB}^{(i)}$ for each $1 \leq i \leq 4$, there exist $(2 \cdot 2 \cdot 2 \cdot 2)/2 = 8$ choices for starting points for each $(\Delta_{in}, \Delta_{out})$. To simplify the explanations, temporarily we assume that there exist exactly 8 starting points for each $(\Delta_{in}, \Delta_{out})$ under the condition that at least one starting point exists for $(\Delta_{in}, \Delta_{out})$. We slightly modify the definition of F so that it will take additional 3-bit input α as inputs that specify which starting point we choose among 8 choices. Since here we check 2^{16} values for Δ_{in} and 2^{64} values for Δ_{out}, the size of the domain of $F(\Delta_{in}, \Delta_{out}; \alpha)$ becomes $2^{16} \cdot 2^{64} \cdot 2^3 = 2^{83}$.

We implement the function $F(\Delta_{in}, \Delta_{out}; \alpha)$ on quantum computers as follows:

1. (Inbound phase.) Given an input $(\Delta_{in}, \Delta_{out})$ (in addition to the 3-bit additional input α), we obtain the corresponding starting point (pairs of messages (M, M') and $(\tilde{M}, \tilde{M}')$ that satisfies the differential trail $\Delta_{in} \longrightarrow \Delta_{out}$) by accessing the precomputed lists $L_1, \ldots, L_4$ stored in qRAM.
2. (Outbound phase.) Propagate (M, M') and $(\tilde{M}, \tilde{M}')$ to the beginning and the end of the cipher to check whether the differential transformations are satisfied, and compute the value of $F(\Delta_{in}, \Delta_{in}; \alpha)$.
3. Uncompute Steps 1 and 2.

Analysis for the Grover search. Step 1 (inbound phase) of F requires 4 qRAM accesses. Step 2 (outbound phase) of F can be done with $2 \times ((4+4)+4) = 24$ random access to the precomputed tables (recall that we precomputed the tables of the Super-Sboxes and the 4-parallel S-box applications). Then the computational cost for F is around $2 \times (4 + 24) = 56$ qRAM accesses, which is equivalent to $56/140 = 2/5$ 7-round AES encryptions. Since we can expect there exists exactly 1 input $(\Delta_{in}, \Delta_{out}; \alpha)$ such that $F(\Delta_{in}, \Delta_{out}; \alpha) = 1$, the Grover search requires about $\frac{\pi}{4}\sqrt{2^{83}} = \frac{\pi}{4}2^{41.5}$ evaluations of F, of which cost is around $\frac{\pi}{4} \cdot \frac{2}{5} \cdot 2^{41.5} \leq 2^{40}$ encryptions.

Even if there exist more than 8 starting points for some $(\Delta_{in}, \Delta_{out})$, we can still find collisions in time 2^{41} by slightly modifying the definition of F. See Section B.2 in this paper's full version [21] for details on how to find collisions in such a general setting.

Summary. Our rebound attack requires $T_{pre} < 2^{42}(< 2^{128/3})$ classical precomputations and $2^{41}(< 2^{128/3})$ costs for the Grover search. On the other hand, the generic collision finding attack in the current setting (BHT) performs $2^{128/3}$ classical precomputations and requires time $2^{128/3}$ for the Grover search on quantum computers. Therefore, our rebound attack is slightly faster than the generic collision finding attack in this setting and it runs in time around $2^{42.5}$. It uses large memory of size 2^{48}.

6.3 Attack Without qRAM: A Time-Space Tradeoff

Here we show a rebound attack that is more efficient than the current generic attack in the setting that efficiency of a quantum algorithm is measured by tradeoff between time T and space S (S is the maximum of the size of quantum computer and classical memory), and parallelized computations are taken into account. We again use the differential trail of $p_{out} = 2^{-80}$ for the outbound phase. Recall that the generic collision finding algorithm in this setting is the parallel rho method (see Sect. 3), which gives the tradeoff $T \cdot S = 2^{n/2}$, or equivalently $T = 2^{n/2}/S$. Recall that we regard the size (the number of qubits) required to implement the attack target (here, 7-round AES) as the unit of space size.

Again, let $\Delta_{in}, \Delta_{out} \in \{0,1\}^{128}$ be the input and output differences for the inbound phase. Unlike Sect. 6.2, here we check 2^{32} values for Δ_{in} and 2^{48} values for Δ_{out}. (Again we expect that there exists 1 starting point that leads to a collision of 7-round AES-MMO among the 2^{80} pairs of $(\Delta_{in}, \Delta_{out})$.) As in Sect. 6.2, we precompute and store all the round constants that are derived from iv and added in the AddConstant phase in each round, and ignore the costs related to those constants.

We again assume that there exist exactly 8 starting points for each $(\Delta_{in}, \Delta_{out})$ under the condition that at least one starting point exists for $(\Delta_{in}, \Delta_{out})$, temporarily, to simplify explanations. We define the function $F(\Delta_{in}, \Delta_{out}; \alpha)$ in the same way as we did in Sect. 6.2, but here we implement the function F on quantum computers without heavy precomputation. To reduce the amount of quantum memory required, instead of doing heavy precomputation, we just use the Grover search to find a starting point for each $(\Delta_{in}, \Delta_{out}; \alpha)$ to perform the inbound phase in F. Explanations on how to deal with pairs $(\Delta_{in}, \Delta_{out})$ with more than 8 starting points will be given later.

Implementation of F with the Grover search. Here we carefully explain how to implement F on quantum computers, or equivalently, how to implement the unitary operator U_F that is defined by $U_F : |\Delta_{in}, \Delta_{out}; \alpha\rangle |y\rangle \mapsto |\Delta_{in}, \Delta_{out}; \alpha\rangle |y \oplus F(\Delta_{in}, \Delta_{out}; \alpha)\rangle$. First, to solve the equation $\mathsf{SSB}^{(i)}(x_i) \oplus \mathsf{SSB}^{(i)}(x_i \oplus \delta_{in}^{(i)}) = \delta_{out}^{(i)}$ for x_i in the inbound phase in F, we define additional functions $G^{(i)}$ for $1 \leq i \leq 4$.

For $1 \leq i \leq 3$, let us define a Boolean function $G^{(i)}(\delta_{in}^{(i)}, \delta_{out}^{(i)}, \alpha_i; x_i)$ (here $\delta_{in}^{(i)}, \delta_{out}^{(i)}, x_i \in \{0,1\}^{32}$ and $\alpha_i \in \{0,1\}$) by $G^{(i)}(\delta_{in}^{(i)}, \delta_{out}^{(i)}, \alpha_i; x_i) = 1$ if and only if: $x_i < x_i \oplus \delta_{in}^{(i)}$ (if $\alpha_i = 0$) or $x_i > x_i \oplus \delta_{in}^{(i)}$ (if $\alpha_i = 1$) and $\mathsf{SSB}^{(i)}(x_i) \oplus \mathsf{SSB}^{(i)}(x_i \oplus \delta_{in}^{(i)}) = \delta_{out}^{(i)}$ holds. In addition, we define a Boolean function $G^{(4)}(\delta_{in}^{(4)}, \delta_{out}^{(4)}; x_4)$ by $G^{(4)}(\delta_{in}^{(4)}, \delta_{out}^{(4)}; x_4) = 1$ if and only if $x_i < x_i \oplus \delta_{in}^{(i)}$ and $\mathsf{SSB}^{(4)}(x_4) \oplus \mathsf{SSB}^{(4)}(x_4 \oplus \delta_{in}^{(4)}) = \delta_{out}^{(4)}$ holds.

Note that the following unitary operator U_F is defined regardless of whether or not we assume there exists exactly 8 starting points for each $(\Delta_{in}, \Delta_{out})$ under the condition that there exists at least one starting point for $(\Delta_{in}, \Delta_{out})$.

Implementation of U_F.

1. Suppose that $|\Delta_{in}, \Delta_{out}; \alpha\rangle |y\rangle$ is given as an input ($\alpha = \alpha_1 \| \alpha_2 \| \alpha_3$ and $\alpha_i \in \{0,1\}$).

2. Compute the corresponding differences $\delta_{in}^{(i)} \longrightarrow \delta_{out}^{(i)}$ for $\mathsf{SSB}^{(i)}$ for $1 \leq i \leq 4$ from $(\Delta_{in}, \Delta_{out})$.
3. Do Step 4 for $1 \leq i \leq 3$.
4. Run the Grover search with certainty on the function $G^{(i)}(\delta_{in}^{(i)}, \delta_{out}^{(i)}, \alpha_i; \cdot)$: $\{0,1\}^{32} \to \{0,1\}$. Let x_i be the output and set $x_i' := x_i \oplus \delta_{in}^{(i)}$.
5. Run the Grover search with certainty on the function $G^{(4)}(\delta_{in}^{(4)}, \delta_{out}^{(4)}, \cdot)$: $\{0,1\}^{32} \to \{0,1\}$. Let x_4 be the output and set $x_4' := x_4 \oplus \delta_{in}^{(4)}$.
6. Set $M := x_1 \| \cdots \| x_4$ and $M' := x_1' \| \cdots \| x_4'$ (now (M, M') is chosen as a candidate for the starting point for $(\Delta_{in}, \Delta_{out}; \alpha)$).
7. Check if the (M, M') is in fact a starting point for $(\Delta_{in}, \Delta_{out})$ (i.e., it satisfies the differential $\Delta_{in} \longrightarrow \Delta_{out}$). If so, set a 1-bit flag flag_1 as $\mathsf{flag}_1 := 1$. If not, set the flag as $\mathsf{flag}_1 := 0$.
8. Do the outbound phase with the starting point (M, M') to check whether (M, M') leads to a collision. If so, set a 1-bit flag flag_2 as $\mathsf{flag}_2 := 1$. If not, set the flag as $\mathsf{flag}_2 := 0$.
9. Return 1 as the value for $F(\Delta_{in}, \Delta_{out}; \alpha)$ (i.e., add the value 1 into the $|y\rangle$ register) if $\mathsf{flag}_1 = \mathsf{flag}_2 = 1$. Return 0 (i.e., do nothing for the $|y\rangle$ register) otherwise.
10. Uncompute Steps 2–8.

Properties and the cost estimation for U_F are summarized in the following lemma.

Lemma 1. $U_F |\Delta_{in}, \Delta_{out}; \alpha\rangle |y\rangle = |\Delta_{in}, \Delta_{out}; \alpha\rangle |y \oplus F(\Delta_{in}, \Delta_{out}; \alpha)\rangle$ *holds for all y if there does not exist any starting point for $(\Delta_{in}, \Delta_{out})$ that leads to a collision of 7-round AES-MMO. If $(\Delta_{in}, \Delta_{out}; \alpha)$ is a tuple such that there exists exactly 8 starting points for $(\Delta_{in}, \Delta_{out})$ and $(\Delta_{in}, \Delta_{out}; \alpha)$ leads to a collision of 7-round AES-MMO, $U_F |\Delta_{in}, \Delta_{out}; \alpha\rangle |y\rangle = |\Delta_{in}, \Delta_{out}; \alpha\rangle |y \oplus F(\Delta_{in}, \Delta_{out}; \alpha)\rangle$ holds for all y. We can implement U_F on a quantum circuit in such a way that it runs in time around $2^{16.5}$ encryptions with 7-round AES, by using ancillary quantum register of size around 2^3.*

See Section B.3 in this paper's full version [21] for a proof of Lemma 1.

Our rebound attack in the current setting. Finally we describe our rebound attack and give its complexity analysis in the current setting that efficiency of a quantum algorithm is measured by the tradeoff between time T and space S. Recall that 4 cells (2^{32} bits) and 8 cells (2^{64} bits) are active in Δ_{in} and Δ_{out}, respectively. In addition, recall that we consider to check 2^{32} values and 2^{48} values for Δ_{in} and Δ_{out}, respectively, when we perform the Grover search on F. In particular, 2^{48} values for Δ_{out} are randomly chosen among 2^{64} possible values.

Description of the rebound attack.

1. Iterate the following Steps 2 and 3 until a collision of 7-round AES-MMO is found (change the choice of 2^{48} values for Δ_{out} completely (among possible 2^{64} values), for each iteration):

2. Apply the Grover search on F and let $(\Delta_{in}, \Delta_{out}; \alpha)$ be the output.
3. Apply the inbound and outbound phases again for the obtained tuple $(\Delta_{in}, \Delta_{out}; \alpha)$ and check if it leads to a collision of 7-round AES-MMO.

Analysis. First, assume that there exist exactly 8 starting points for each $(\Delta_{in}, \Delta_{out})$. Then, there exists exactly one tuple $(\Delta_{in}, \Delta_{out}; \alpha)$ such that $F(\Delta_{in}, \Delta_{out}; \alpha) = 1$ holds, and thus we can find a collision with only one iteration of Steps 2 and 3, from Lemma 1.

Since the domain size of F is 2^{83}, it follows that Step 2 runs in time around $\frac{\pi}{4} \cdot 2^{41.5} \cdot 2^{16.5} \approx 2^{58}$ encryptions with 7-round AES by using ancillary quantum register of size around 2^3 from Lemma 1. The time required for Step 3 is negligible compared to Step 2, and Step 3 can be done by using almost the same number of qubits as used in Step 2. Thus each iteration of Steps 2 and 3 runs in time around 2^{58} encryptions with AES, and uses a quantum circuit of size around 2^3.

Even if we consider the general case in which there exist more than 8 starting points for some $(\Delta_{in}, \Delta_{out})$, we can show that only 3 iterations of Steps 2 and 3 find a collision with a high probability. (See Section B.4 in this paper's full version [21] for a detailed proof.) Therefore our attack runs in time around $3 \cdot 2^{58} \approx 2^{59.5}$ encryptions with AES-MMO, by using a quantum circuit of size 2^3. When a quantum computer of size S $(S \geq 2^3)$ is available, by parallelizing the Grover search for F we can mount the attack in time $T = 2^{59.5}/\sqrt{S/2^3}$.

Summary. When the efficiency of a quantum algorithm is measured by the tradeoff between time T and space S, the generic attack gives time-space tradeoff $T = 2^{64}/S$. On the other hand, when a quantum computer of size S is available, our rebound attack runs in time around $T = 2^{59.5}/\sqrt{S/2^3} \approx 2^{61}/\sqrt{S}$. Therefore our attack works for $S \geq 2^3$ and it is more efficient than the generic attack as long as $S < 2^6$.

6.4   Small Quantum Computer with Large Classical Memory

When a small (polynomial size) quantum computer and large (exponential size) classical memory is available, the generic collision finding attack is the one by Chailloux et al., which runs in time around $2^{2n/5} = 2^{51.2}$ encryptions with 7-round AES when we apply the algorithm on 7-round AES-MMO. Since our rebound attack in Sect. 6.3 requires time $2^{59.5}$ (if it is not parallelized), it is slower than the generic attack in this setting. We do not know whether we can mount a quantum attack that is better than the generic attack in this setting.

7   Finding Collisions for 6-Round Whirlpool

This section shows a quantum rebound attack that finds collisions for 6-round Whirlpool. Basically this section considers the setting that the efficiency of quantum algorithms are measured by the tradeoff of time and space. (Our attack is worse than the generic attack in other settings.)

Recall that there exists a 5-round differential propagation

$$1 \xleftarrow{2^{-(r-1)c}} r - r^2 - r^2 - r \xrightarrow{2^{-(r-1)c}} 1$$

for Whirlpool, which can be used to mount a classical rebound attack with Super-Sboxes (see Sect. 4.2). Here we use the 6-round differential propagation

$$1 \xleftarrow{2^{-(r-1)c}} r - r^2 - r^2 - r^2 - r \xrightarrow{2^{-(r-1)c}} 1$$

with the technique that covers three active rounds on 8×8 state introduced in Sect. 4.3, instead of usual Super-Sboxes (See Fig. 5 in Section C.1 in this paper's full version [21]). We use the memoryless variant rather than the original technique, which runs in time $2^{r^2c/2+rc}$. The technique can be used for classical *distinguishing attacks* but cannot be used for classical *collision attacks* since its time complexity reaches the birthday bound $2^{r^2c/2} = 2^{n/2}$. However, the power of quantum computation enables us to use the technique. The optimality of the 6-round differential trail is shown in Sect. 8.

When we implement the rebound attack with the above 6-round differential propagation and the memoryless variant of the technique from Sect. 4.3 in the *classical* setting, the attack time complexity becomes $2^{(r-1)c} \cdot 2^{(r-1)c} \cdot 2^c \cdot 2^{r^2c/2+rc} = 2^{(r^2+6r-2)c/2} = 2^{440}$ (here $r = 8$ and $c = 8$). This attack is essentially a combination of an exhaustive search on differences in the two internal states (the difference just after the SubBytes application in the 2nd round ($\#Y^2$ in Fig. 5 in Section C.1 of this paper's full version [21]) and the difference at the beginning of the 6th round ($\#X^6$ in Fig. 5 in Section C.1 of this paper's full version [21])) with the exhaustive search for the inbound phase (the memoryless variant introduced in Sect. 4.3). Since we can obtain the quadratic speed up for exhaustive searches with Grover's algorithm in the quantum setting, roughly speaking, we can implement the attack so that it runs in time around 2^{220} on a small size quantum computer. Roughly speaking, if S quantum computers are available, we will obtain a time-space tradeoff $T = 2^{220}/\sqrt{S}$, which is better than the generic time-space tradeoff $T = 2^{n/2}/S = 2^{256}/S$ for $S \leq 2^{72}$. Note that this rough cost analysis gives just an underestimation since it ignores additional costs such as uncomputations and ancilla qubits to implement Boolean functions for the Grover search. The precise tradeoff will be somewhat worse than $T = 2^{220}/\sqrt{S}$ in practice, but $T \leq 2^{232}/\sqrt{S}$ holds. (See Section C.2 in this paper's full version [21] for detailed discussions on precise analysis.) We assume that our attack follows the worst-case tradeoff $T = 2^{232}/\sqrt{S}$.

Summary. Our rebound attack on 6-round Whirlpool runs in time $T = 2^{228}$ on a quantum computer of size $S_0 = 2^8$. When a large quantum computer of size S ($S \geq 2^8$) is available and we use them to parallelize the Grover search, our rebound attack runs in time $T = 2^{232}/\sqrt{S}$. It is better than the generic attack in the setting where the efficiency of a quantum algorithm is measured by the tradeoff between time T and space S as long as $2^8 \leq S < 2^{48}$, but it is worse than the generic attack in other settings. (See Section C.3 in this paper's full version [21] for detailed discussions in other settings.)

8   Optimality of Differential Trails

MILP Model. We checked the optimality of the differential trail by using the Mixed Integer Linear Programming (MILP) based tool. The MILP model to derive the minimum number of active S-boxes for AES was described by Mouha et al. [34]. We modify the model by Mouha et al. to minimize the complexity of the collision attack. The model by Mouha et al. describes valid differential propagation patterns according to the AES diffusion. The model can simply be converted to the collision search by adding the constraints such that the active byte patterns of the first round input and the last round output are identical.

The objective function of the model by Mouha et al. is to minimize the number of active S-boxes, while we need a different objective function to minimize the complexity of the collision attack in the rebound attack framework. Regarding AES-MMO, we assume the usage of the Super-Sbox analysis, which generates a pair of values satisfying MixColumns in three consecutive rounds by cost 1 per starting point. For each model, we fix a position of the inbound phase. Namely we fix the round index r in which MixColumns in rounds $r, r+1$, and $r+2$ are satisfied with cost 1. Because the last round does not have MixColumns, we only have 4 choices in the case of the 7-round attack: $r \in \{1, 2, 3, 4\}$ by starting the round counting from 1. For example, the 7-round trail introduced in Sect. 6.1 is the case with $r = 3$. The probability of the outbound phase is affected by two factors.

1. the number of difference cancellation in MixColumns
2. the number of difference cancellation in the feed-forward

The latter can be simply counted by counting the number of active S-boxes in the first round. Let $x0, x1, \ldots, x15$ be 16 binary variables to denote whether the ith byte of the initial state is active or not. Then, the number of canceling bytes in the feed-forward is $x_0 + x_1 + \cdots + x_{15}$. The impact of the former is evaluated by counting the number of inactive bytes in active columns in MixColumns. Suppose that xi_0, xi_1, xi_2, xi_3 are 4 binary variables to denote whether each of 4 input bytes to a MixColumns is active or not. Similarly yi_0, yi_1, yi_2, yi_3 denote the same for output bytes. Also let d be a binary variable to denote whether the column is active or not. Note that the model proposed by Mouha et al. satisfies this configuration. We introduce an integer variable $b, 0 \le b \le 3$ for each column to count the number of inactive bytes in active columns. Then, proper relationships can be modeled in the following equality.

$$\begin{cases} -xi_0 - xi_1 - xi_2 - xi_3 + 4d = b & \text{for backward outbound,} \\ -yi_0 - yi_1 - yi_2 - yi_3 + 4d = b & \text{for forward outbound.} \end{cases}$$

For the rounds located before the Super-Sbox (the first round to round $r-1$) we compute in backwards, hence we use the first equation. For the rounds located after the Super-Sbox (round $r+3$ to the last round) we compute in forwards, hence we use the second equation. When the column is inactive, all of x_i, y_i and d are 0, thus b becomes 0. When column is active, b is set to 4 minus the sum of the number active bytes, which is the number of bytes with difference cancellation. In the end, the objective function can be to minimize the sum of x_0 to x_{15} for the feed-forward and b for all the columns.

Regarding the Whirlpool, the only difference from the AES-MMO is the number of rounds covered by the inbound phase (and the last round transformation). The extension is straightforward and thus we omit the details.

Search Results. The resulted system of linear inequalities can be solved easily by using a standard laptop in a few seconds. The result shows that the minimum number of difference cancellation to derive 7-round collisions is 10, i.e. probability 2^{-80}. Hence the trail introduced in Sect. 6.1 is one of the best.

As noted before, we generated different models depending on the starting round of the Super-Sbox. An interesting result is that besides $r = 3$ (the trail introduced in Sect. 6.1), $r = 2$ also achieves the trail with probability 2^{-80}. (No such trail for $r = 1$ and $r = 4$.) To the completeness, we show the detected trail in Fig. 6 in Section D in this paper's full version [21].

We also verified the optimality for Whirlpool and difficulty of attacking 1 more round with the approaches considered in this paper.

9   Concluding Remarks

This paper observed that there is a possibility that differential trails of which differential probabilities are smaller than the birthday bound can be used to mount collision attacks in the quantum settings and classically secure hash functions may be broken in the quantum settings. In fact we showed the quantum versions of rebound attacks on 7-round AES-MMO and 6-round Whirlpool, on which there has not been found any dedicated collision attack that is faster than the generic one in the classical setting.

An important future work is to find differential trails (that are suitable to mount collision-finding attacks) such that the differential probabilities are too small to be used for collision finding attacks in the classical setting but large enough to be used in the quantum settings. Our observation suggests that differential trail search should not stop with probability $2^{-n/2}$ but should consider up to $2^{-2n/3}$ or more. By revisiting previous differential trail search activities, we will be able to construct more and more dedicated quantum collision-finding attacks.

References

1. ZigBee Alliance: ZigBee -2007 Specification (2007). https://zigbee.org/. Document 053474r17
2. Banegas, G., Bernstein, D.J.: Low-communication parallel quantum multi-target preimage search. In: Adams, C., Camenisch, J. (eds.) SAC 2017. LNCS, vol. 10719, pp. 325–335. Springer, Cham (2018). https://doi.org/10.1007/978-3-319-72565-9_16

3. Barreto, P.S., Rijmen, V.: The WHIRLPOOL Hashing Function. Submitted to NESSIE (2000). Accessed 24 May 2003
4. Bernstein, D.J.: Cost analysis of hash collisions: will quantum computers make SHARCS obsolete? In: SHARCS (2009)
5. Boneh, D., Dagdelen, Ö., Fischlin, M., Lehmann, A., Schaffner, C., Zhandry, M.: Random oracles in a quantum world. In: Lee, D.H., Wang, X. (eds.) ASIACRYPT 2011. LNCS, vol. 7073, pp. 41–69. Springer, Heidelberg (2011). https://doi.org/10.1007/978-3-642-25385-0_3
6. Bonnetain, X., Hosoyamada, A., Naya-Plasencia, M., Sasaki, Y., Schrottenloher, A.: Quantum attacks without superposition queries: the offline Simon's algorithm. In: Galbraith, S.D., Moriai, S. (eds.) ASIACRYPT 2019, Part I. LNCS, vol. 11921, pp. 552–583. Springer, Cham (2019). https://doi.org/10.1007/978-3-030-34578-5_20
7. Bonnetain, X., Naya-Plasencia, M., Schrottenloher, A.: On quantum slide attacks. In: Paterson, K.G., Stebila, D. (eds.) SAC 2019. LNCS, vol. 11959, pp. 492–519. Springer, Cham (2020). https://doi.org/10.1007/978-3-030-38471-5_20
8. Bonnetain, X., Naya-Plasencia, M., Schrottenloher, A.: Quantum security analysis of AES. IACR Trans. Symmetric Cryptol. **2019**(2), 55–93 (2019)
9. Boyer, M., Brassard, G., Høyer, P., Tapp, A.: Tight bounds on quantum searching. Fortschritte der Physik: Progress of Physics **46**(4–5), 493–505 (1998)
10. Brassard, G., Hoyer, P., Mosca, M., Tapp, A.: Quantum amplitude amplification and estimation. Contemp. Math. **305**, 53–74 (2002)
11. Brassard, G., Høyer, P., Tapp, A.: Quantum cryptanalysis of hash and claw-free functions. In: Lucchesi, C.L., Moura, A.V. (eds.) LATIN 1998. LNCS, vol. 1380, pp. 163–169. Springer, Heidelberg (1998). https://doi.org/10.1007/BFb0054319
12. Campagna, M., Zaverucha, G., Corp, C.: A Cryptographic Suite for Embedded Systems (SuiteE). Internet-Draft, October 2012
13. Chailloux, A., Naya-Plasencia, M., Schrottenloher, A.: An efficient quantum collision search algorithm and implications on symmetric cryptography. In: Takagi, T., Peyrin, T. (eds.) ASIACRYPT 2017, Part II. LNCS, vol. 10625, pp. 211–240. Springer, Cham (2017). https://doi.org/10.1007/978-3-319-70697-9_8
14. Daemen, J., Rijmen, V.: The Design of Rijndeal: AES – The Advanced Encryption Standard (AES). Springer, Heidelberg (2002). https://doi.org/10.1007/978-3-662-04722-4
15. Damgård, I.B.: A design principle for hash functions. In: Brassard, G. (ed.) CRYPTO 1989. LNCS, vol. 435, pp. 416–427. Springer, New York (1990). https://doi.org/10.1007/0-387-34805-0_39
16. Gilbert, H., Peyrin, T.: Super-Sbox cryptanalysis: improved attacks for AES-like permutations. In: Hong, S., Iwata, T. (eds.) FSE 2010. LNCS, vol. 6147, pp. 365–383. Springer, Heidelberg (2010). https://doi.org/10.1007/978-3-642-13858-4_21
17. Grover, L.K.: A fast quantum mechanical algorithm for database search. In: ACM STOC 1996, pp. 212–219. ACM (1996)
18. Grover, L.K., Rudolph, T.: How significant are the known collision and element distinctness quantum algorithms? Quantum Inf. Comput. **4**(3), 201–206 (2004)
19. Guo, C., Katz, J., Wang, X., Yu, Y.: Efficient and secure multiparty computation from fixed-key block ciphers. IACR Cryptology ePrint Archive 2019/74 (2019)
20. Hosoyamada, A., Sasaki, Y.: Quantum Demiric-Selçuk meet-in-the-middle attacks: applications to 6-round generic Feistel constructions. In: Catalano, D., De Prisco, R. (eds.) SCN 2018. LNCS, vol. 11035, pp. 386–403. Springer, Cham (2018). https://doi.org/10.1007/978-3-319-98113-0_21

21. Hosoyamada, A., Sasaki, Y.: Finding hash collisions with quantum computers by using differential trails with smaller probability than birthday bound. IACR Cryptology ePrint Archive 2020/213 (2020)
22. ISO: IT Security techniques - Hash-functions - Part 3: Dedicated hash-functions, ISO/IEC 10118–3:2018 (2018)
23. Jean, J., Naya-Plasencia, M., Peyrin, T.: Improved rebound attack on the finalist Grøstl. In: Canteaut, A. (ed.) FSE 2012. LNCS, vol. 7549, pp. 110–126. Springer, Heidelberg (2012). https://doi.org/10.1007/978-3-642-34047-5_7
24. Kaplan, M., Leurent, G., Leverrier, A., Naya-Plasencia, M.: Breaking symmetric cryptosystems using quantum period finding. In: Robshaw, M., Katz, J. (eds.) CRYPTO 2016, Part II. LNCS, vol. 9815, pp. 207–237. Springer, Heidelberg (2016). https://doi.org/10.1007/978-3-662-53008-5_8
25. Kaplan, M., Leurent, G., Leverrier, A., Naya-Plasencia, M.: Quantum differential and linear cryptanalysis. IACR Trans. Symmetric Cryptol. 2016(1), 71–94 (2016)
26. Katz, J., Menezes, A.J., Van Oorschot, P.C., Vanstone, S.A.: Handbook of Applied Cryptography. CRC Press, Boca Raton (1996)
27. Keller, M., Orsini, E., Scholl, P.: MASCOT: faster malicious arithmetic secure computation with oblivious transfer. In: ACM SIGSAC 2016, pp. 830–842 (2016)
28. Kuwakado, H., Morii, M.: Quantum distinguisher between the 3-round Feistel cipher and the random permutation. In: ISIT 2010, pp. 2682–2685. IEEE (2010)
29. Kuwakado, H., Morii, M.: Security on the quantum-type Even-Mansour cipher. In: ISITA 2012, pp. 312–316. IEEE (2012)
30. Lamberger, M., Mendel, F., Rechberger, C., Rijmen, V., Schläffer, M.: Rebound distinguishers: results on the full Whirlpool compression function. In: Matsui, M. (ed.) ASIACRYPT 2009. LNCS, vol. 5912, pp. 126–143. Springer, Heidelberg (2009). https://doi.org/10.1007/978-3-642-10366-7_8
31. Lamberger, M., Mendel, F., Schläffer, M., Rechberger, C., Rijmen, V.: The rebound attack and subspace distinguishers: application to Whirlpool. J. Cryptol. 28(2), 257–296 (2015). https://doi.org/10.1007/s00145-013-9166-5
32. Mendel, F., Rechberger, C., Schläffer, M., Thomsen, S.S.: The rebound attack: cryptanalysis of reduced Whirlpool and Grøstl. In: Dunkelman, O. (ed.) FSE 2009. LNCS, vol. 5665, pp. 260–276. Springer, Heidelberg (2009). https://doi.org/10.1007/978-3-642-03317-9_16
33. Merkle, R.C.: A certified digital signature. In: Brassard, G. (ed.) CRYPTO 1989. LNCS, vol. 435, pp. 218–238. Springer, New York (1990). https://doi.org/10.1007/0-387-34805-0_21
34. Mouha, N., Wang, Q., Gu, D., Preneel, B.: Differential and linear cryptanalysis using mixed-integer linear programming. In: Wu, C.-K., Yung, M., Lin, D. (eds.) Inscrypt 2011. LNCS, vol. 7537, pp. 57–76. Springer, Heidelberg (2012). https://doi.org/10.1007/978-3-642-34704-7_5
35. Nielsen, M.A., Chuang, I.L.: Quantum Computation and Quantum Information: 10th Anniversary Edition. Cambridge University Press, Cambridge (2010)
36. NIST: Post-quantum cryptography standardization, 26 September 2019. See https://csrc.nist.gov/Projects/post-quantum-cryptography/Post-Quantum-Cryptography-Standardization
37. van Oorschot, P.C., Wiener, M.J.: Parallel collision search with application to hash functions and discrete logarithms. In: ACM CCS 1994, pp. 210–218. ACM (1994)
38. Sasaki, Y.: Meet-in-the-middle preimage attacks on AES hashing modes and an application to Whirlpool. In: Joux, A. (ed.) FSE 2011. LNCS, vol. 6733, pp. 378–396. Springer, Heidelberg (2011). https://doi.org/10.1007/978-3-642-21702-9_22

39. Sasaki, Y., Wang, L., Wu, S., Wu, W.: Investigating fundamental security require-
    ments on Whirlpool: improved preimage and collision attacks. In: Wang, X., Sako,
    K. (eds.) ASIACRYPT 2012. LNCS, vol. 7658, pp. 562–579. Springer, Heidelberg
    (2012). https://doi.org/10.1007/978-3-642-34961-4_34
40. Simon, D.R.: On the power of quantum computation. SIAM J. Comput. **26**(5),
    1474–1483 (1997)
41. Wang, X., Yin, Y.L., Yu, H.: Finding collisions in the full SHA-1. In: Shoup, V.
    (ed.) CRYPTO 2005. LNCS, vol. 3621, pp. 17–36. Springer, Heidelberg (2005).
    https://doi.org/10.1007/11535218_2
42. Wang, X., Yu, H.: How to break MD5 and other hash functions. In: Cramer, R.
    (ed.) EUROCRYPT 2005. LNCS, vol. 3494, pp. 19–35. Springer, Heidelberg (2005).
    https://doi.org/10.1007/11426639_2
43. Wu, S., Feng, D., Wu, W., Guo, J., Dong, L., Zou, J.: (Pseudo) preimage attack
    on round-reduced Grøstl hash function and others. In: Canteaut, A. (ed.) FSE
    2012. LNCS, vol. 7549, pp. 127–145. Springer, Heidelberg (2012). https://doi.org/
    10.1007/978-3-642-34047-5_8
44. Xie, H., Yang, L.: Quantum impossible differential and truncated differential crypt-
    analysis. CoRR abs/1712.06997 (2017)
45. Zhandry, M.: A note on the quantum collision and set equality problems. Quantum
    Inf. Comput. **15**(7–8), 557–567 (2015)

Implementing Grover Oracles
for Quantum Key Search
on AES and LowMC

Samuel Jaques[1]($\boxtimes$), Michael Naehrig[2]($\boxtimes$), Martin Roetteler[3],
and Fernando Virdia[4]

[1] Department of Materials, University of Oxford, Oxford, UK
samuel.jaques@materials.ox.ac.uk
[2] Microsoft Research, Redmond, WA, USA
mnaehrig@microsoft.com
[3] Microsoft Quantum, Redmond, WA, USA
[4] Information Security Group, Royal Holloway, University of London, Egham, UK

Abstract. Grover's search algorithm gives a quantum attack against block ciphers by searching for a key that matches a small number of plaintext-ciphertext pairs. This attack uses $O(\sqrt{N})$ calls to the cipher to search a key space of size N. Previous work in the specific case of AES derived the full gate cost by analyzing quantum circuits for the cipher, but focused on minimizing the number of qubits.

In contrast, we study the cost of quantum key search attacks under a depth restriction and introduce techniques that reduce the oracle depth, even if it requires more qubits. As cases in point, we design quantum circuits for the block ciphers AES and LowMC. Our circuits give a lower overall attack cost in both the gate count and depth-times-width cost models. In NIST's post-quantum cryptography standardization process, security categories are defined based on the concrete cost of quantum key search against AES. We present new, lower cost estimates for each category, so our work has immediate implications for the security assessment of post-quantum cryptography.

As part of this work, we release Q# implementations of the full Grover oracle for AES-128, -192, -256 and for the three LowMC instantiations used in Picnic, including unit tests and code to reproduce our quantum resource estimates. To the best of our knowledge, these are the first two such full implementations and automatic resource estimations.

Keywords: Quantum cryptanalysis · Grover's algorithm · AES · LowMC · Post-quantum cryptography · Q# implementation

S. Jaques—Partially supported by the University of Oxford Clarendon fund.
S. Jaques and F. Virdia—This work was done while Fernando and Sam were interns at Microsoft Research.
F. Virdia—Partially supported by the EPSRC and the UK government as part of the Centre for Doctoral Training in Cyber Security at Royal Holloway, University of London (EP/P009301/1).

A. Canteaut and Y. Ishai (Eds.): EUROCRYPT 2020, LNCS 12106, pp. 280–310, 2020.
https://doi.org/10.1007/978-3-030-45724-2_10

1   Introduction

The prospect of a large-scale, cryptographically relevant quantum computer has prompted increased scrutiny of the post-quantum security of cryptographic primitives. Shor's algorithm for factoring and computing discrete logarithms introduced in [45] and [46] will completely break public-key schemes such as RSA, ECDSA and ECDH. But symmetric schemes like block ciphers and hash functions are widely considered post-quantum secure. The only caveat thus far is a security reduction due to key search or pre-image attacks with Grover's algorithm [22]. As Grover's algorithm only provides at most a square root speedup, the rule of thumb is to simply double the cipher's key size to make it post-quantum secure. Such conventional wisdom reflects the asymptotic behavior and only gives a rough idea of the security penalties that quantum computers inflict on symmetric primitives. In particular, the cost of evaluating the Grover oracle is often ignored.

In their call for proposals to the standardization of post-quantum cryptography [37], the National Institute of Standards and Technology (NIST) proposes security categories for post-quantum public-key schemes such as key encapsulation and digital signatures. Categories are defined by the cost of quantum algorithms for exhaustive key search on the block cipher AES and collision search for the hash function SHA-3, and measure the attack cost in the number of quantum gates. Because the gate count of Grover's algorithm increases with parallelization, they impose a total upper bound on the depth of a quantum circuit, called MAXDEPTH, and account for this in the gate counts. An algorithm meets the requirements of a specific security category if the best known attack uses more resources (gates) than are needed to solve the reference problem. Hence, a concrete and meaningful definition of these security categories depends on precise resource estimates of the Grover oracle for key search on AES. Security categories 1, 3 and 5 correspond to key recovery against AES-128, AES-192 and AES-256, respectively. The NIST proposal derives gate cost estimates from the concrete, gate-level descriptions of the AES oracle by Grassl *et al.* [21]. Grassl *et al.* aim to minimize the circuit width, i.e. the number of qubits needed.

Prior Work. Since the publication of [21], other works have studied quantum circuits for AES, the AES Grover oracle and its use in Grover's algorithm. Almazrooie *et al.* [3] improve the quantum circuit for AES-128. As in [21], the focus is on minimizing the number of qubits. The improvements are a slight reduction in the total number of Toffoli gates and the number of qubits by using a wider binary field inversion circuit that saves one multiplication. Kim *et al.* [29] discuss time-space trade-offs for key search on block ciphers in general and use AES as an example. They discuss NIST's MAXDEPTH parameter and hence study parallelization strategies for Grover's algorithm to address the depth constraint. They take the Toffoli gate depth as the relevant metric for the MAXDEPTH bound arguing that it is a conservative approximation.

Recently, independent and concurrent to parts of this work, Langenberg *et al.* [31] developed quantum circuits for AES that demonstrate significant improvements over those presented in [21] and [3]. The main source of optimization is a different S-box design derived from work by Boyar and Peralta in [10] and [11], which greatly reduces the number of Toffoli gates in the S-box as well as its Toffoli depth. Another improvement is that fewer auxiliary qubits are required for the AES key expansion. Again, this work aligns with the objectives in [21] to keep the number of qubits small.

Bonnetain *et al.* [9] study the post-quantum security of AES within a new framework for classical and quantum structured search. The work cites [21] for deducing concrete gate counts for reduced-round attacks.

Our Contributions. We present implementations of the full Grover oracle for key search on AES and LowMC in Q# [49], including full implementations of the block ciphers themselves. In contrast to previous work [3,21] and [31], having a concrete implementation allows us to get more precise, flexible and automatic estimates of the resources required to compute these operations. It also allows us to unit test our circuits, to make sure that the implementations are correct.

The source code is publicly available[1] under a free license. We hope that it can serve as a useful starting point for cryptanalytic work to assess the post-quantum security of other schemes.

We review the literature on the parallelization of Grover's algorithm [13,23, 29,55] to explore the cost of attacking AES and LowMC in the presence of a bound on the total depth, such as MAXDEPTH proposed by NIST. We conclude that using parallelization by dividing the search space is advantageous. We also give a rigorous justification for the number of plaintext-ciphertext blocks needed in Grover's oracle in the context of parallelization. Smaller values than those proposed by Grassl *et al.* [21] are sufficient, as is also pointed out in [31].

Our quantum circuit optimization approach differs from those in the previous literature [3,21] and [31] in that our implementations do not aim for the lowest possible number of qubits. Instead, we designed them to minimize the gate-count and depth-times-width cost metrics for quantum circuits under a depth constraint. The gate-count metric is relevant for defining the NIST security categories and the depth-times-width cost metric is a more realistic measure of quantum resources when quantum error correction is deployed. Favoring lower depth at the cost of a slightly larger width in the oracle circuit leads to costs that are smaller in both metrics than for the circuits presented in [3,21] and [31]. Grover's algorithm does not parallelize well, meaning that minimizing depth rather than width is crucial to make the most out of the available depth.

To the best of our knowledge, our work results in the most shallow quantum circuit of AES so far, and the first ever for LowMC. We chose to also implement LowMC as an example of a quantum circuit for another block cipher. It is used in the Picnic signature scheme [14,56], a round-2 candidate in the NIST standardization process. Thus, our implementation can contribute to more precise cost estimates for attacks on Picnic and its post-quantum security assessment.

We present our results for quantum key search on AES in the context of the NIST post-quantum cryptography standardization process and derive new and

---

[1] https://github.com/microsoft/grover-blocks.

lower cost estimates for the definition of the NIST security strength categories. We see a consistent gate cost reduction between 11 and 13 bits, making it easier for submitters to claim a certain quantum security category.

2   Finding a Block Cipher Key with Grover's Algorithm

Given plaintext-ciphertext pairs created by encrypting a small number of messages under a block cipher, Grover's quantum search algorithm [22] can be used to find the secret key [54]. This section provides some preliminaries on Grover's algorithm, how it can be applied to the key search problem and how it parallelizes under depth constraints.

2.1   Grover's Algorithm

Grover's algorithm [22] searches through a space of N elements; for simplicity, we restrict to $N = 2^k$ right away and label elements by their indices in $\{0,1\}^k$. The algorithm works with a superposition $|\psi\rangle = 2^{-k/2} \sum_{x \in \{0,1\}^k} |x\rangle$ of all indices, held in a register of k qubits. It makes use of an operator U_f for evaluating a Boolean function $f : \{0,1\}^k \to \{0,1\}$ that marks solutions to the search problem, i.e. $f(x) = 1$ if and only if the element corresponding to x is a solution. When applying the Grover oracle U_f to a state $|x\rangle |y\rangle$ for a single qubit $|y\rangle$, it acts as $|x\rangle |y\rangle \mapsto |x\rangle |y \oplus f(x)\rangle$ in the computational basis. When $|y\rangle$ is in the state $|\varphi\rangle = (|0\rangle - |1\rangle)/\sqrt{2}$, then this action can be written as $|x\rangle |\varphi\rangle \mapsto (-1)^{f(x)} |x\rangle |\varphi\rangle$. This means that the oracle applies a phase shift to exactly the solution indices.

The algorithm first prepares the state $|\psi\rangle |\varphi\rangle$ with $|\psi\rangle$ and $|\varphi\rangle$ as above. It then repeatedly applies the so-called Grover iteration $G = (2|\psi\rangle\langle\psi| - I)U_f$, an operator that consists of the oracle U_f followed by the operator $2|\psi\rangle\langle\psi| - I$, which can be viewed as an inversion about the mean amplitude. Each iteration can be visualized as a rotation of the state vector in the plane spanned by two orthogonal vectors: the superposition of all indices corresponding to solutions and non-solutions, respectively. The operator G rotates the vector by a constant angle towards the superposition of solution indices. Let $1 \leq M \leq N$ be the number of solutions and let $0 < \theta \leq \pi/2$ such that $\sin^2(\theta) = M/N$. Note that if $M \ll N$, then $\sin(\theta)$ is very small and $\theta \approx \sin(\theta) = \sqrt{M/N}$.

When measuring the first k qubits after $j > 0$ iterations of G, the success probability $p(j)$ for obtaining one of the solutions is $p(j) = \sin^2((2j + 1)\theta)$ [13], which is close to 1 for $j \approx \frac{\pi}{4\theta}$. Hence, after $\left\lfloor \frac{\pi}{4}\sqrt{\frac{N}{M}} \right\rfloor$ iterations, measurement yields a solution with overwhelming probability of at least $1 - \frac{M}{N}$.

Grover's algorithm is optimal in the sense that any quantum search algorithm needs at least $\Omega(\sqrt{N})$ oracle queries to solve the problem [13]. In [55], Zalka shows that for any number of oracle queries, Grover's algorithm gives the largest probability to find a solution.

2.2 Key Search for a Block Cipher

Let C be a block cipher with block length n and key length k; for a key $K \in \{0,1\}^k$ denote by $C_K(m) \in \{0,1\}^n$ the encryption of message block $m \in \{0,1\}^n$ under the key K. Given r plaintext-ciphertext pairs (m_i, c_i) with $c_i = C_K(m_i)$, we aim to apply Grover's algorithm to find the unknown key K [54]. The Boolean function f for the Grover oracle takes a key K as input, and is defined as $f(K) = 1$ if $C_K(m_i) = c_i$ for all $1 \le i \le r$, and $f(K) = 0$ otherwise.

Possibly, there exist other keys than K that encrypt the known plaintexts to the same ciphertexts. We call such keys *spurious keys*. If their number is known to be, say $M - 1$, the M-solution version of Grover's algorithm has the same probability of measuring each spurious key as measuring the correct K.

Spurious Keys. We assume that under a fixed key K, the map $\{0,1\}^n \to \{0,1\}^n, m \mapsto C_K(m)$ is a pseudo-random permutation; and under a fixed message block m, the map $\{0,1\}^k \to \{0,1\}^n, K \mapsto C_K(m)$ is a pseudo-random function. Now let K be the correct key, i.e. the one used for the encryption. It follows that for a single message block of length n, $\Pr_{K \ne K'}(C_K(m) = C_{K'}(m)) = 2^{-n}$.

This probability becomes smaller when the equality condition is extended to multiple blocks. Given r distinct messages $m_1, \ldots, m_r \in \{0,1\}^n$, we have

$$\Pr_{K \ne K'}\left((C_K(m_1), \ldots, C_K(m_r)) = (C_{K'}(m_1), \ldots, C_{K'}(m_r))\right) = \prod_{i=0}^{r-1} \frac{1}{2^n - i}, \quad (1)$$

which is $\approx 2^{-rn}$ for $r^2 \ll 2^n$. Since the number of keys different from K is $2^k - 1$, we expect the number of spurious keys for an r-block message to be $\approx (2^k - 1)2^{-rn}$. Choosing r such that this quantity is very small ensures with high probability that there is a unique key and we can parameterize Grover's algorithm for a single solution.

Remark 1. Grassl *et al.* [21, §3.1] work with a similar argument. They take the probability over pairs (K', K'') of keys with $K' \ne K''$. Since there are $2^{2k} - 2^k$ such pairs, they conclude that about $(2^{2k} - 2^k)2^{-rn}$ satisfy the above condition that the ciphertexts coincide on all r blocks. But this also counts pairs of keys for which the ciphertexts match each other, but do not match the images under the correct K. Thus, using the number of pairs overestimates the number of spurious keys and hence the number r of message blocks needed to ensure a unique key.

Based on the above heuristic assumptions, one can determine the probability for a specific number of spurious keys. Let X be the random variable whose value is the number of spurious keys for a given set of r message blocks and a given key K. Then, X is distributed according to a binomial distribution: $\Pr(X = t) = \binom{2^k-1}{t} p^t (1 - p)^{2^k - 1 - t}$, where $p = 2^{-rn}$. We use the Poisson limit theorem to conclude that this is approximately a Poisson distribution with

$$\Pr(X = t) \approx e^{-\frac{2^k - 1}{2^{rn}}} \frac{(2^k - 1)^t (2^{-rn})^t}{t!} \approx e^{-2^{k-rn}} \frac{2^{t(k-rn)}}{t!}. \quad (2)$$

The probability that K is the unique key consistent with the r plaintext-ciphertext pairs is $\Pr(X = 0) \approx e^{-2^{k-rn}}$. Thus we can choose r such that rn is slightly larger than k; $rn = k + 10$ gives $\Pr(X = 0) \approx 0.999$. In a block cipher where $k = b \cdot n$ is a multiple of n, taking $r = b + 1$ will give the unique key K with probability at least $1 - 2^{-n}$, which is negligibly close to 1 for typical block sizes. If $rn < k$, then K is almost certainly not unique. Even $rn = k - 3$ gives less than a 1% chance of a unique key. Hence, r must be at least $\lceil k/n \rceil$.

The case $k = rn$, when the total message length is equal to the key length, remains interesting if one aims to minimize the number of qubits. The probability for a unique K is $\Pr(X = 0) \approx 1/e \approx 0.3679$, and the probability of exactly one spurious key is the same. Kim *et al.* [29, Equation (7)] describe the success probability after a certain number of Grover iterations when the number of spurious keys is unknown. The optimal number of iterations gives a maximum success probability of 0.556, making it likely that the first attempt will not find the correct key and one must repeat the algorithm.

Depth Constraints for Cryptanalysis. In this work, we assume that any quantum adversary is bounded by a constraint on its total depth for running a quantum circuit. In its call for proposals to the post-quantum cryptography standardization effort [37], NIST introduces the parameter MAXDEPTH as such a bound and suggests that reasonable values are between 2^{40} and 2^{96}. Whenever an algorithm's overall depth exceeds this bound, parallelization becomes necessary. We do assume that MAXDEPTH constitutes a hard upper bound on the total depth of a quantum attack, including possible repetitions of a Grover instance.

In general, an attacker can be assumed to have a finite amount of resources, in particular a finite time for an attack. This is equivalent to postulating an upper bound on the total depth of a quantum circuit as suggested by NIST. Unlike in the classical case, the required parallelization increases the gate cost for Grover's algorithm, which makes it important to study attacks with bounded depth.

We consider it reasonable to expect that the overall attack strategy is guaranteed to return a solution with high probability close to 1 within the given depth bound. E.g., a success probability of 1/2 for a Grover instance to find the correct key requires multiple runs to increase the overall probability closer to 1. These runs, either sequentially or in parallel, need to be taken into account for determining the overall cost and must respect the depth limit. While this setting is our main focus, it can be adequate to allow and cost a quantum algorithm with a success probability noticeably smaller than 1. Where not given in this paper, the corresponding analysis can be derived in a straightforward manner.

2.3 Parallelization

There are different ways to parallelize Grover's algorithm. Kim *et al.* [29] describe two, which they denote as *inner* and *outer* parallelization. Outer parallelization runs multiple instances of the full algorithm in parallel. Only one instance must succeed, allowing us to reduce the necessary success probability, and hence number of iterations, for all. Inner parallelization divides the search space into disjoint subsets and assigns each subset to a parallel machine. Each machine's search space is smaller, so the number of necessary iterations shrinks.

Zalka [55] concludes that in both cases, one only obtains a factor $\sqrt{S}$ gain in the number of Grover iterations when working with S parallel Grover oracles, and that this is asymptotically optimal. Compared to many classical algorithms, this is an inefficient parallelization, since we must increase the width by a factor of S to reduce the depth by a factor of $\sqrt{S}$. Both methods avoid any communication, quantum or classical, during the Grover iterations. They require communication at the beginning, to distribute the plaintext-ciphertext pairs to each machine and to delegate the search space for inner parallelization, and communication at the end to collect the measured keys and decide which one, if any, is the true key. The next section discusses why our setting favours inner parallelization.

Advantages of Inner Parallelization. Consider S parallel machines that we run for j iterations, using the notation of Sect. 2.1, and a unique key. For a single machine, the success probability is $p(j) = \sin^2((2j+1)\theta)$. Using outer parallelization, the probability that at least one machine recovers the correct key is $p_S(j) = 1 - (1 - p(j))^S$. We hope to gain a factor $\sqrt{S}$ in the number of iterations, so instead of iterating $\lfloor \frac{\pi}{4\theta} \rfloor$ times, we run each machine for $j_S = \lfloor \frac{\pi}{4\theta\sqrt{S}} \rfloor$ iterations.

Considering some small values of S, we get $S = 1 : p_1(j_1) \approx 1$, $S = 2 : p_2(j_2) \approx 0.961$ and $S = 3 : p_3(j_3) \approx 0.945$. As S gets larger, we use a series expansion to find that

$$p_S(j_S) \approx 1 - \left(1 - \frac{\pi^2}{4S} + O\left(\frac{1}{S^2}\right)\right)^S \xrightarrow{S \to \infty} 1 - e^{-\frac{\pi^2}{4}} \approx 0.915. \tag{3}$$

This means that by simply increasing S, it is not possible to gain a factor $\sqrt{S}$ in the number of iterations if one aims for a success probability close to 1. In contrast, with inner parallelization, the correct key lies in the search space of exactly one machine. With j_S iterations, this machine has near certainty of measuring the correct key, while other machines are guaranteed not to measure the correct key. Overall, we have near-certainty of finding the correct key. Inner parallelization thus achieves a higher success probability with the same number S of parallel instances and the same number of iterations.

Another advantage of inner parallelization is that dividing the search space separates any spurious keys into different subsets and reduces the search problem to finding a unique key. This allows us to reduce the number r of message blocks in the Grover oracle and was already observed by Kim et al. [29] in the context of measure-and-repeat methods. In fact, the correct key lies in exactly one subset of the search space. If the spurious keys fall into different subsets, the respective machines measure spurious keys, which can be discarded classically after measurement with access to the appropriate number of plaintext-ciphertext pairs. The only relevant question is whether there is a spurious key in the correct key's subset of size $2^k/S$. The probability for this is $\text{SKP}(k, n, r, S) = \sum_{t=1}^{\infty} \Pr(X = t) \approx 1 - e^{-\frac{2^{k-rn}}{S}}$, using Eq. (2) with 2^k replaced by $2^k/S$. If $k = rn$, this probability is roughly $1/S$ when S gets larger. In general, high parallelization makes spurious keys irrelevant, and the Grover oracle can simply use the smallest r such that $\text{SKP}(k, n, r, S)$ is less than a desired bound.

3 Quantum Circuit Design

Quantum computation is usually described in the quantum circuit model. This section describes our interpretation of quantum circuits, methods and criteria for quantum circuit design, and cost models to estimate quantum resources.

3.1 Assumptions About the Fault-Tolerant Gate Set and Architecture

The quantum circuits we are concerned with in this paper operate on qubits. They are composed of so-called Clifford+T gates, which form a commonly used universal fault-tolerant gate set exposed by several families of quantum error-correcting codes. The primitive gates consist of single-qubit Clifford gates, controlled-NOT (CNOT) gates, T gates, and measurements. We make the standard assumption of *full parallelism*, meaning that a quantum circuit can apply any number of gates simultaneously so long as these gates act on disjoint sets of qubits [8,23].

All quantum circuits for AES and LowMC described in this paper were designed, tested, and costed in the Q# programming language [49], which supports all assumptions discussed here. We adopt the computational model presented in [25]. The Q# compiler allows us to compute circuit depth automatically by moving gates around through a circuit if the qubits it acts on were previously idle. In particular, this means that the depth of two circuits applied in series may be less than the sum of the individual depths of each circuit. The Q# language allows the circuit to *allocate* auxiliary qubits as needed, which adds new qubits initialized to $|0\rangle$. If an auxiliary qubit is returned to the state $|0\rangle$ after it has been operated on, the circuit can *release* it. Such a qubit is no longer entangled with the state used for computation and the circuit can now maintain or measure it.

Grover's algorithm is a far-future quantum algorithm, making it difficult to decide on the right cost for each gate. Previous work assumed that T gates constitute the main cost [3,21,31]. They are exceptionally expensive for a surface code [19]; however, for a future error-correcting code, T gates may be transversal and cheap while a different gate may be expensive. Thus, we present costs for both counting T gates only, and costing all gates equally. For most of the circuits, these concerns do not change the optimal design.

We ignore all concerns of layout and communication costs for the Grover oracle circuit. Though making this assumption is unrealistic for a surface code, where qubits can only interact with neighboring ones, other codes may not have these issues. A single oracle circuit uses relatively few logical qubits ($<2^{20}$), so these costs are unlikely to dominate. This allows us to compare our work with previous proposals, which also ignore these costs. This also implies that uncontrolled swaps are free, since the classical controller can simply track such swaps and rearrange where it applies subsequent gates.

While previous work on quantum circuits for AES such as [3,21] and [31] mainly uses Toffoli gates, we use AND gates instead. A quantum AND gate has the same functionality as a Toffoli gate, except the target qubit is assumed to be in the state $|0\rangle$, rather than an arbitrary state. We use a combination[2] of Selinger's [44] and Jones' [28] circuits to express the AND gate in terms of Clifford and T gates. This circuit uses $4\,T$ gates and 11 Clifford gates in T-depth 1 and total depth 8. It uses one auxiliary qubit which it immediately releases, while its adjoint circuit is slightly smaller.

3.2 Automated Resource Estimation and Unit Tests

One incentive for producing full implementations of the Grover oracle and its components is to obtain precise resource estimates automatically and directly from the circuit descriptions. Another incentive is to test the circuits for correctness and to compare results on classical inputs against existing classical software implementations that are known (or believed) to be correct. Yet quantum circuits are in general not testable, since they rely on hardware yet to be constructed. To partially address this issue, the Q# compiler can classically simulate a subset of quantum circuits, enabling partial test coverage. We thus designed our circuits such that this tool can fully classically simulate them, by using X, CNOT, CCNOT, SWAP, and AND gates only, together with measurements (denoted throughout as M "gates"). This approach limits the design space since we cannot use true quantum methods within the oracle. Yet, it is worthwhile to implement components that are testable and can be fully simulated to increase confidence in the validity of resource estimates deduced from such implementations.

As part of the development process, we first implemented AES (resp. LowMC) in Python3, and tested the resulting code against the AES implementation in PyCryptodome 3.8.2 [39] (resp. the C++ reference implementation in [33]). Then, we proceeded to write our Q# implementations (running on the Dotnet Core version 2.1.507, using the Microsoft Quantum Development Kit version 0.7.1905.3109), and tested these against our Python3 implementations, by making use of the IQ# interface (see [35,36]. For the Q# simulator to run, we are required to use the Microsoft QDK standard library's Toffoli gate for evaluating both Toffoli and AND gates, which results in deeper than necessary circuits. We also have to explicitly SWAP values across wires, which costs 3 CNOT gates, rather than simply keeping track of the necessary free rewiring. Hence, to mitigate these effects, our functions admit a Boolean flag indicating whether the code is being run as part of a unit test by the simulator, or as part

---

[2] We thank Mathias Soeken for providing the implementation of the AND gate circuit.

of a cost estimate. In the latter case, Toffoli and AND gate designs are automatically replaced by shallower ones, and SWAP instructions are disregarded as free (after manually checking that this does not allow for incompatible circuit optimizations). All numbers reporting the total width of a circuit include the initial number of qubits plus the maximal number of temporarily allocated auxiliary qubits within the Q# function. For numbers describing the total depth, all gates such as Clifford gates, CNOT and T gates as well as measurements are assigned a depth of 1.

The AND and Toffoli gate designs we chose use measurements, hence CNOT, 1-qubit Clifford, measurement and depth counts are probabilistic. The Q# simulator does not currently support PRNG seeding for de-randomizing the measurements,[3] which means that estimating differently sized circuits with the same or similar depth (or re-estimating the same circuit multiple times) may result in slightly different numbers. We also note that the compiler is currently unable to optimize a given circuit by, e.g., searching through small circuit variations that may result in functionally the same operation at a smaller cost (say by allowing better use of the circuit area).

3.3 Reversible Circuits for Linear Maps

Linear maps $f\colon \mathbb{F}_2^n \to \mathbb{F}_2^m$ for varying dimensions n and m are essential building blocks of AES and LowMC. In general, such a map f, expressed as multiplication by a constant matrix $M_f \in \mathbb{F}_2^{m \times n}$, can be implemented as a reversible circuit on n input wires and m additional output wires (initialized to $|0\rangle$), by using an adequate sequence of CNOT gates: if the (i, j)-th coefficient of M_f is 1, we set a CNOT gate targeting the i-th output wire, controlled on the j-th input wire.

Yet, if a linear map $g\colon \mathbb{F}_2^n \to \mathbb{F}_2^n$ is invertible, one can reversibly compute it in-place on the input wires via a PLU decomposition of M_g, $M_g = P \cdot L \cdot U$ [51, Lecture 21]. The lower- and upper-triangular components L and U of the decomposition can be implemented as described above by using the appropriate CNOT gates, while the final permutation P does not require any quantum gates and instead, is realized by appropriately keeping track of the necessary rewiring. While rewiring is not easily supported in Q#, the same effect can be obtained by defining a custom REWIRE operation that computes an in-place swap of any two wires when testing an implementation, and that can be disabled when costing it. We note that such decompositions are not generally unique, but it is not clear whether sparser decompositions can be consistently obtained with any particular technique. For our implementations, we adopt the PLU decomposition algorithm from [51, Algorithm 21.1], as implemented in SageMath 8.1 [48].

3.4 Cost Metrics for Quantum Circuits

For a meaningful cost analysis, we assume that an adversary has fixed constraints on its total available resources, and a specific cost metric they wish to minimize. Most importantly, we assume a total depth limit $D_{\max}$ as explained in Sect. 2.2.

---

[3] https://github.com/microsoft/qsharp-runtime/issues/30, visited 2019-08-24.

In this paper, we use the two cost metrics that are considered by Jaques and Schanck in [25]. The first is the total number of gates, the *G-cost*. It assumes non-volatile ("passive") quantum memory, and therefore models circuits that incur some cost with every gate, but no cost is incurred in time units during which a qubit is not operated on.

The second cost metric is the product of circuit depth and width, the *DW-cost*. This is a more realistic cost model when quantum error correction is necessary. It assumes a volatile ("active") quantum memory, which incurs some cost to correct errors on every qubit in each time step, i.e. each layer of the total circuit depth. In this cost model, a released auxiliary qubit would not require error correction, and the cost to correct it could be omitted. But we assume an efficient strategy for qubit allocation that avoids long idle periods for released qubits and thus choose to ignore this subtlety. Instead, we simply cost the maximum width at any point in the oracle, times its total depth. For both cost metrics, we can choose to count only T-gates towards gate count and depth, or count all gates equally.

The Cost of Grover's Algorithm. As in Sect. 2.1, let the search space have size $N = 2^k$. Suppose we use an oracle G such that a single Grover iteration costs G_G gates, has depth G_D, and uses G_W qubits. Let $S = 2^s$ be the number of parallel machines that are used with the inner parallelization method by dividing the search space in S disjoint parts (see Sect. 2.3). In order to achieve a certain success probability p, the required number of iterations can be deduced from $p \leq \sin^2((2j+1)\theta)$ which yields $j_p = \lceil (\arcsin(\sqrt{p})/\theta - 1)/2 \rceil \approx \arcsin(\sqrt{p})/2 \cdot \sqrt{N/S}$. Let $c_p = \arcsin(\sqrt{p})/2$, then the total depth of a j_p-fold Grover iteration is

$$D = j_p \mathsf{G}_D \approx c_p \sqrt{N/S} \cdot \mathsf{G}_D = c_p 2^{\frac{k-s}{2}} \mathsf{G}_D \text{ cycles.} \tag{4}$$

Note that for $p \approx 1$ we have $c_p \approx c_1 = \frac{\pi}{4}$. Each machine uses $j_p \mathsf{G}_G \approx c_p \sqrt{N/S} \cdot \mathsf{G}_G = c_p 2^{\frac{k-s}{2}} \mathsf{G}_G$ gates, i.e. the total G-cost over all S machines is

$$G = S \cdot j_p \mathsf{G}_G \approx c_p \sqrt{N \cdot S} \cdot \mathsf{G}_G = c_p 2^{\frac{k+s}{2}} \mathsf{G}_G \text{ gates.} \tag{5}$$

Finally, the total width is $W = S \cdot \mathsf{G}_W = 2^s \mathsf{G}_W$ qubits, which leads to a DW-cost

$$DW \approx c_p \sqrt{N \cdot S} \cdot \mathsf{G}_D \mathsf{G}_W = c_p 2^{\frac{k+s}{2}} \mathsf{G}_D \mathsf{G}_W \text{ qubit-cycles.} \tag{6}$$

These cost expressions show that minimizing the number $S = 2^s$ of parallel machines minimizes both G-cost and DW-cost. Thus, under fixed limits on depth, width, and the number of gates, an adversary's best course of action is to use the entire depth budget and parallelize as little as possible. Under this premise, the depth limit fully determines the optimal attack strategy for a given Grover oracle. Limits on width or the number of gates simply become binary feasibility criteria and are either too tight and the adversary cannot finish the attack, or one of the limits is loose. If one resource limit is loose, we may be able to modify the oracle to use this resource to reduce depth, lowering the overall cost.

Optimizing the Oracle Under a Depth Limit. Grover's full algorithm parallelizes so badly that it is generally preferable to parallelize *within* the oracle circuit. Reducing its depth allows more iterations within the depth limit, thus reducing the necessary parallelization.

Let $D_{\max}$ be a fixed depth limit. Given the depth G_D of the oracle, we are able to run $j_{\max} = \lfloor D_{\max}/G_D \rfloor$ Grover iterations of the oracle G. For a target success probability p, we obtain the number S of parallel instances to achieve this probability in the instance whose key space partition contains the key from $p \leq \sin^2((2j_{\max}+1)\sqrt{S/N})$ as

$$S = \left\lceil \frac{N \cdot \arcsin^2(\sqrt{p})}{(2 \cdot \lfloor D_{\max}/G_D \rfloor + 1)^2} \right\rceil \approx c_p^2 2^k \frac{G_D^2}{D_{\max}^2}. \tag{7}$$

Using this in Eq. (5) gives a total gate count of

$$G = c_p^2 2^k \frac{G_D G_G}{D_{\max}} \text{ gates.} \tag{8}$$

It follows that for two oracle circuits G and F, the total G-cost is lower for G if and only if $G_D G_G < F_D F_G$. That is, we wish to minimize the product $G_D G_G$. Similarly, the total DW-cost under the depth constraint is

$$DW = c_p^2 2^k \frac{G_D^2 G_W}{D_{\max}} \text{ qubit-cycles.} \tag{9}$$

Here, we wish to minimize $G_D^2 G_W$ of the oracle circuit to minimize total DW-cost.

4   A Quantum Circuit for AES

The Advanced Encryption Standard (AES) [15,16] is a block cipher standardized by NIST in 2001. Using the notation from [15], AES is composed of an S-box, a Round function (with subroutines ByteSub, ShiftRow, MixColumn, AddRound-Key; with the last round slightly differing from the others), and a KeyExpansion function (with subroutines SubByte, RotByte). Three different instances of AES have been standardized, for key lengths of 128, 192 and 256 bits. Grassl *et al.* [21] describe their quantum circuit implementation of the S-box and other components, resulting in a full description of all three instances of AES (but no testable code has been released). Grassl *et al.* take care to reduce the number of auxiliary qubits required, i.e. reducing the circuit *width* as much as possible. The recent improvements by Langenberg *et al.* [31] build on the work by Grassl *et al.* with similar objectives.

In this section, we describe our implementation of AES in the quantum programming language Q# [49]. Some of the components are taken from the description in [21], while others are implemented independently, or ported from other sources. We take the circuit description from [21] as the basis for our work and compare to the results in [31]. In general, we aim at reducing the *depth* of the AES circuit, while limitations on width are less important. Width restrictions are not explicitly considered by the NIST call for proposals [37, § 4.A.5].

The internal state of AES contains 128 bits, arranged in four 32-bit (or 4-byte) words. In the rest of this section, when referring to a 'word', we intend a 4-byte word. In all tables below, we denote by #CNOT, the number of CNOT gates, by #1qCliff the number of 1-qubit Clifford gates, by #T the number of T gates, by #M the number of measurement operations and by width the number of qubits.

S-box, ByteSub and SubByte. The AES S-box is a transformation that inverts the input as an element of $\mathbb{F}_{256}$, and maps 0 to 0. The S-box is the only source of T gates in a quantum circuit of AES. On classical hardware, it can be implemented easily using a lookup-table. Yet, on a quantum computer, this is not efficient (see [5,32] and [20]). Alternatively, the inversion can be computed either by using some variant of Euclid's algorithm (taking care of the special case of 0), or by applying Lagrange's theorem and raising the input to the $(|\mathbb{F}_{256}^{\times}| - 1)^{th}$ power (i.e. the 254th power), which incidentally also takes care of the 0 input. Grassl *et al.* [21] suggest an Itoh-Tsujii inversion algorithm [24], following [4], and compute all required multiplications over $\mathbb{F}_2[x]/(x^8 + x^4 + x^3 + x + 1)$. This idea had already been extensively explored in the vast[4] literature on hardware design for AES, and requires a different construction of $\mathbb{F}_{256}$ to be most effective. Following this lead, we port the S-box circuit by Boyar and Peralta from [11] to Q#. The specified linear program combining AND and XOR operations can be easily expressed as a sequence of equivalent CNOT and AND operations (we use cheaper T-depth-1 AND gates [28,44] instead of T-depth-1 CCNOT gates [44]). Cost estimates for the AESS-box are in Table 1. We compare to our own Q# implementation of the S-box circuits from [21] and [31]. ByteSub is a state-wide parallel application of the S-box, requiring new output auxiliary qubits to store the result, while SubByte is a similar word-wide application of the S-box.

Table 1. Comparison of our reconstruction of the original [21] S-box circuit with the one from [10] as used in [31] and the one in this work based on [11]. In our implementation of [10] from [31], we replace CCNOT gates with AND gates to allow a fairer comparison.

Operation	#CNOT	#1qCliff	#T	#M	T-depth	Full depth	Width
[21] S-box	8683	1028	3584	0	217	1692	44
[10] S-box	818	264	164	41	35	497	41
[11] S-box	654	184	136	34	6	101	137

---

[4] E.g. see [10,12,27,38,40–43,52,53].

Remark 2. Langenberg *et al.* [31] independently introduced a new AES quantum circuit design using the S-box circuit proposed in [10]. They also present a ProjectQ [47] implementation of the S-box, albeit without unit tests. We ported their source code to Q#, tested and costed it. For a fairer comparison, we replaced their CCNOT gates with the AND gate design that our circuits use. Cost estimates can be found in Table 1. Overall, the [11] S-box leads to a more cost effective circuit for our purposes in both the *G*-cost and *DW*-cost metrics, and hence we did not proceed further in our analysis of costs using the [10] design. Note that the results obtained here differ from the ones presented in [31, §3.2]. This is due to the difference in counting gates and depth. While [31] counts Toffoli gates, the Q# resource estimator costs at a lower level of T gates and also counts all gates needed to implement a Toffoli gate.

ShiftRow and RotByte. ShiftRow is a permutation on the full 128-bit AES state, happening across its four words [15, §4.2.2]. As a permutation of qubits, it can be entirely encoded as rewiring. As in [21], we consider rewiring as free and do not include it in our cost estimates. Similarly, RotByte is a circular left shift of a word by 8 bits, and can be implemented by appropriate rewiring as well.

MixColumn. The operation MixColumn interprets each word in the state as a polynomial in $\mathbb{F}_{256}[x]/(x^4+1)$. Each word is multiplied by a fixed polynomial $c(x)$ [15, § 4.2.3]. Since the latter is coprime to x^4+1, this operation can be seen as an invertible linear transformation, and hence can be implemented in place by a PLU decomposition of a matrix in $\mathbb{F}_2^{32\times32}$. To simplify this tedious operation, we use SageMath [48] code that performs the PLU decomposition, and outputs equivalent Q# code. Note that [21] describes the same technique, while achieving a significantly smaller design than the one we obtain (ref. Table 2), but we were not able to reproduce these results. However, highly optimized, shallower circuits have been proposed in the hardware design literature such as [7,18,26,30,50]. Hence, we chose to use one of those and experiment with a recent design by Maximov [34]. Both circuits are costed independently in Table 2. Maximov's circuit has a much lower depth, but it only reduces the total depth, does not reduce the T-depth (which is already 0) and comes at the cost of an increased width. Our experiments show that without a depth restriction, it seems advantageous to use the in-place version to minimize both *G*-cost and *DW*-cost metrics, while for a depth restricted setting, Maximov's circuit seems better due to the square in the depth term in Eq. (9).

Table 2. Comparison of an in-place implementation of MixColumn (via PLU decomposition) versus the recent shallow out-of-place design in [34].

Operation	#CNOT	#1qCliff	#T	#M	T-depth	Full depth	Width
In-place MixColumn	1108	0	0	0	0	111	128
[34] MixColumn	1248	0	0	0	0	22	318

AddRoundKey. AddRoundKey performs a bitwise XOR of a round key to the internal AES state and can be realized with a parallel application of 128 CNOT gates, controlled on the round key qubits and targeted on the state qubits. Grassl *et al.* [21] and Langenberg *et al.* [31] use the same approach.

KeyExpansion. Key expansion is one of the two sources of T gates in the design of AES, and hence might have a strong impact on the overall efficiency of the circuit. A simple implementation of KeyExpansion would allocate enough auxiliary qubits to store the full expanded key, including all round keys. This is easy to implement with relatively low depth, but uses more qubits than necessary. The authors of [21] amortize this width cost by caching only those key bytes that require S-box evaluations. Instead, we minimize width by not requiring auxiliary qubits at all. At the same time, we reduce the depth in comparison with the naive key expansion using auxiliary qubits for all key bits as described above.

Let $|k\rangle_0$ denote the AES key consisting of $N_k \in \{4, 6, 8\}$ key words and $|k\rangle_i$ the i-th set of N_k consecutive round key words. The first such block $|k\rangle_1$ can be computed in-place as shown in the appropriately sized circuit in Fig. 1. This circuit produces the i-th set of N_k key words from the $(i-1)$-th set. Note that for AES-128, these sets correspond to the actual round keys as the key size is

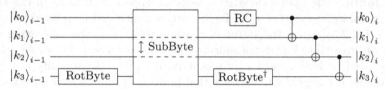

(a) AES-128 in-place key expansion step producing the i-th round key.

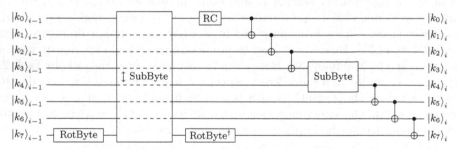

(b) AES-256 in-place key expansion step producing the i-th set of 8 round key words.

Fig. 1. In-place AES key expansion for AES-128 and AES-256, deriving the ith set of N_k round key works from the $(i-1)^{th}$. AES-192 is identical to AES-128, but with 6 key words. Each $|k_j\rangle_i$ represents the jth word of $|k\rangle_i$. SubByte takes the input state on the top wire, and returns the output on the bottom wire, while $\updownarrow$ SubByte takes inputs on the bottom wire, and returns outputs on the top. Dashed lines indicate wires that are not used in the $\updownarrow$ SubByte operation. RC is the round constant addition, implemented by applying X gates as appropriate.

equal to the block size, for AES-192 and AES-256, each round key set generates more words than needed in a single round key. The full operation mapping $|k\rangle_{i-1} \mapsto |k\rangle_i$ is denoted by KE. As for the two larger key sizes, each round only needs parts of these sets of round key words, we specify KE_j^l to denote the part of the operation KE that produces the words $j \dots l$ of the new set, disregarding other words. KE_j^l can be used as part of the round strategy described below to only compute as many words of the round key as necessary, resulting in an overall narrower and shallower circuit.

Remark 3. In addition to improving the S-box circuit over [21], Langenberg *et al.* [31, §4] demonstrate significant savings by reducing the number of qubits and the depth of key expansion. This is achieved by an improved scheduling of key expansion during AES encryption, namely by computing round key words only at the time they are required and un-computing them early. While their method is based on the one in [21] using auxiliary qubits for the round keys, our approach works completely in place and reduces width and depth at the same time.

Round, FinalRound and Full AES. To encrypt a message block using AES-128 (resp. -192, -256), we initially XOR the input message with the first 4 words of the key, and then execute 10 (resp. 12, 14) rounds consisting of ByteSub, ShiftRow, MixColumn (except in the final round) and AddRoundKey. The quantum circuits for AES we propose follow the same blueprint with the exception that key expansion is interleaved with the algorithm in such a way that the operations KE_j^l only produce the key words that are immediately required.

The resulting circuits are shown in Fig. 2. For formatting reasons, we omit the repeating round pattern and AES-256, and only represent a subset of the full set of qubits used. In AES-128, each round is identical until round 9. In AES-192 rounds 5, 8 and 11 use the same KE call and order as round 2; rounds 6 and 9 do as round 3; rounds 7 and 10 do as round 4. In AES-256, rounds 4, 6, 8, 10, 12 (resp. 5, 7, 9, 11, 13) use the same KE call and order as round 2 (resp. 3). Cost estimates for the resulting AES encryption circuits are in Table 3. In contrast to [21] and [31], we aim to reduce circuit depth, hence un-computing of rounds is delayed until the output ciphertext is produced. For easier testability and modularity, the Round circuit is divided into two parts: a ForwardRound operator that computes the output state but does not clean auxiliary qubits, and its adjoint. For unit-testing Round in isolation, we compose ForwardRound with its adjoint operator. For testing AES, we first run all ForwardRound instances without auxiliary qubit cleaning, resulting in a similar ForwardAES operator, copy out the ciphertext, and then undo the ForwardAES operation.

Table 3 presents results for the AES circuit for both versions of MixColumn, the in-place implementation using a PLU decomposition as well as Maximov's out-of-place, but lower depth circuit. We use both because each has advantages for different applications. The full depth corresponds to G_D as in Sect. 3.4 and Sect. 2.3, while width corresponds to G_W. While for AES-128 and AES-192, $G_D G_W$ is smaller for the in-place implementation, $G_D^2 G_W$ is smaller for Maximov's circuit. Hence, Sect. 2.3 indicates Maximov's circuit gives a lower DW-cost under a depth restriction. If there is no depth restriction, the in-place design has a lower DW-cost.

Table 3. Circuit cost estimates for the AES operator, using the [11] S-box and for Mix-Column design ("MC") either in-place ("IP") or Maximov's [34] ("M"). The apparently inconsistent T-depth is discussed under T-**depth**.

Operation	MC	#CNOT	#1qCliff	#T	#M	T-depth	Full depth	Width
AES-128	IP	291150	83116	54400	13600	120	2827	1785
AES-192	IP	328612	93160	60928	15232	120	2987	2105
AES-256	IP	402878	114778	75072	18768	126	3353	2425
AES-128	M	293730	83236	54400	13600	120	2094	2937
AES-192	M	331752	93280	60928	15232	120	1879	3513
AES-256	M	406288	114318	75072	18768	126	1955	4089

T-**depth.** Every round of AES (as implemented in Fig. 2) computes at least one layer of S-boxes as part of ByteSub, which must later be uncomputed. We would thus expect the T-depth of n rounds of AES to be $2n$ times the T-depth of the S-box. Instead, Table 3 shows smaller depths. We find this effect when using either the AND circuit or the unit-testable CCNOT implementation. To test if this is a bug, we used a placeholder S-box circuit which has an arbitrary T-depth d and which the compiler cannot parallelize. This "dummy" AES design had the expected T-depth of $2n \cdot d$. Thus we believe the Q# compiler found non-trivial parallelization between components of the S-box and the surrounding circuit. This provides a strong case for full explicit implementations of quantum cryptanalytic algorithms in Q# or other languages that allow automatic resource estimates and optimizations; in our case the T-depth of AES-256 is 25% less than naively expected. Unfortunately, Q# cannot yet generate full circuit diagrams, so we do not know exactly where the parallelization takes place[5].

5   A Quantum Circuit for LowMC

LowMC [1,2] is a family of block ciphers aiming for low multiplicative complexity circuits. Originally designed to reduce the high cost of binary multiplication in the MPC and FHE scenarios, it has been adopted as a fundamental component by the Picnic signature scheme (see [14] and [56]) proposed for standardization as part of the NIST process for standardizing post-quantum cryptography.

To achieve low multiplicative complexity, LowMC uses an S-box layer of AND-depth 1, which contains a user-defined number of parallel 3-bit S-box computations. In general, any instantiation of LowMC comprises a specific number of rounds. Each round calls an S-box layer, an affine transformation, and a

---

[5] https://github.com/microsoft/qsharp-runtime/issues/31, visited 2019-09-03.

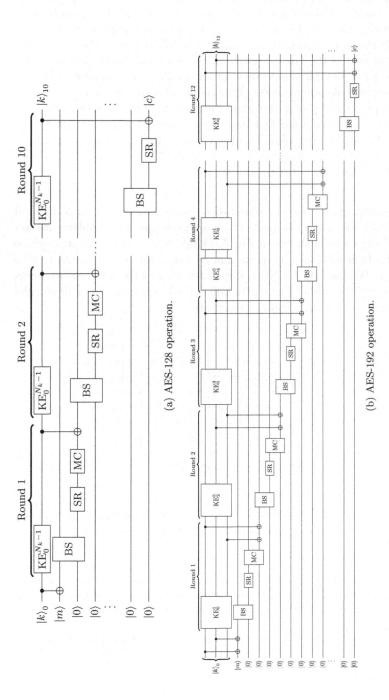

(a) AES-128 operation.

(b) AES-192 operation.

Fig. 2. Circuit sketches for the AES-128 and AES-192 operation. Each wire under the $|k\rangle_0$ label represents 4 words of the key for AES-128 and 2 words for AES-192. Each subsequent wire (initially labeled $|m\rangle$ and $|0\rangle$) represents 4 words. CNOT gates between word-sized wires should be read as multiple parallel CNOT gates applied bitwise (e.g. at the beginning of AES-192 the intention is of XORing 128 bits from $|k\rangle_0$ onto the state). BS stands for ByteSub, SR for ShiftRow and MC for MixColumn. For AES-128, the circuit shows an in-place implementation of MixColumn, while for AES-192, it uses an out-of-place version like Maximov's MixColumn linear program [34].

round key addition. Key-scheduling can either be precomputed or computed on the fly. In this work, we study the original LowMC design. This results in a sub-optimal circuit, which can clearly be improved by porting the more recent version from [17] instead. Even for the original LowMC, our work shows that the overhead from the cost of the Grover oracle is very small, in particular under the T-depth metric. Since LowMC could be standardized as a component of Picnic, we deem it appropriate to point out the differences in Grover oracle cost between different block ciphers and that generalization from AES requires caution.

In this section we describe our Q# implementation of the LowMC instances used as part of Picnic. In particular, Picnic proposes three parameter sets, with (key size, block size, rounds) $\in \{(128, 128, 20), (192, 192, 30), (256, 256, 38)\}$, all with 10 parallel S-boxes per substitution layer.

S-box and S-boxLayer. The LowMC S-box can be naturally implemented using Toffoli (CCNOT) gates. In particular, a simple in-place implementation with depth 5 (T-depth 3) is shown in Fig. 3, alongside a T-depth 1 out-of-place circuit, both of which were produced manually. Costs for both circuits can be found in Table 4. We use the CCNOT implementation with no measurements from [44]. For LowMC inside of Picnic, the full S-boxLayer consists of 10 parallel S-boxes run on the 30 low order bits of the state.

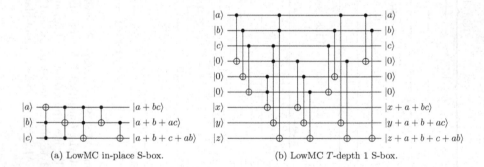

(a) LowMC in-place S-box.   (b) LowMC T-depth 1 S-box.

Fig. 3. Alternative quantum circuit designs for the LowMC S-box. The in-place design requires auxiliary qubits as part of the concrete CCNOT implementation.

Table 4. Cost estimates for a single LowMC S-box circuit, following the two designs proposed in Fig. 3. We note that the circuit size may seem different at first sight due to Fig. 3 not displaying the concrete CCNOT implementation.

Operation	#CNOT	#1qCliff	#T	#M	T-depth	Full depth	Width
In-place S-box	50	6	21	0	3	23	7
Shallow S-box	60	6	21	0	1	11	13

LinearLayer, ConstantAddition and AffineLayer. AffineLayer is an affine transformation applied to the state at every round. It consists of a matrix multiplication (LinearLayer) and the addition of a constant vector (ConstantAddition). Both matrix and vector are different for every round and are predefined constants that are populated pseudo-randomly. ConstantAddition is implemented by applying X gates for entries of the vector equal to 1. In Picnic, for every round and every parameter set, all LinearLayer matrices are invertible (due to LowMC's specification requirements), and hence we use a PLU decomposition for matrix multiplication (Sect. 3.3). Cost estimates for the first round affine transformation in LowMC as used in Picnic are in Table 5.

Table 5. Costs for in-place circuits implementing the first round (R1) AffineLayer transformation for the three instantiations of LowMC used in Picnic.

Operation	#CNOT	#1qCliff	#T	#M	T-depth	Full depth	Width
AffineLayer L1 R1	8093	60	0	0	0	2365	128
AffineLayer L3 R1	18080	90	0	0	0	5301	192
AffineLayer L5 R1	32714	137	0	0	0	8603	256

KeyExpansion and KeyAddition. To generate the round keys rk_i, in each round i the LowMC key k is multiplied by a different key derivation pseudo-random matrix KM_i. For Picnic, each KM_i is invertible, so we compute rk_i from rk_{i-1} as $rk_i = KM_i \cdot KM_{i-1}^{-1} \cdot rk_{i-1}$. We compute this in-place using a PLU decomposition of $KM_i \cdot KM_{i-1}^{-1}$. This saves matrix multiplications and qubits compared to computing rk_i directly. We call this operation KeyExpansion. KeyAddition is equivalent to AddRoundKey in AES, and is implemented the same way. Cost estimates for the first round key expansion in LowMC as used in Picnic can be found in Table 6.

Table 6. Costs for in-place circuits implementing the first round (R1) KeyExpansion operation for the three instantiations of LowMC used in Picnic.

Operation	#CNOT	#1qCliff	#T	#M	T-depth	Full depth	Width
KeyExpansion L1 R1	8104	0	0	0	0	2438	128
KeyExpansion L3 R1	18242	0	0	0	0	4896	192
KeyExpansion L5 R1	32525	0	0	0	0	9358	256

Round and LowMC. The LowMC round sequentially applies S-boxLayer, AffineLayer and KeyAddition to the state. Our implementation also runs KeyExpansion before AffineLayer. For a full LowMC encryption, we first add the LowMC key k to the message to produce the initial state, then run the specified number of rounds on it. Costs of the resulting encryption circuit are in Table 7.

Table 7. Costs for the full encryption circuit for LowMC as used in Picnic.

Operation	#CNOT	#1qCliff	#T	#M	T-depth	Full depth	Width
LowMC L1	689944	4932	8400	0	40	98699	991
LowMC L3	2271870	9398	12600	0	60	319317	1483
LowMC L5	5070324	14274	15960	0	76	693471	1915

6   Grover Oracles and Key Search Resource Estimates

Equipped with Q# implementations of the AES and LowMC encryption circuits, this section describes the implementation of full Grover oracles for both block ciphers. Eventually, based on the cost estimates obtained automatically from these Q# Grover oracles, we provide quantum resource estimates for full key search attacks via Grover's algorithm. Beyond comparing to previous work, our emphasis is on evaluating algorithms that respect a total depth limit, for which we consider NIST's values for MAXDEPTH from [37]. This means we *must* parallelize. We use inner parallelization via splitting up the search space, see Sect. 2.3.

6.1   Grover Oracles

As discussed in Sect. 2.2 and Sect. 2.3, we must determine the parameter r, the number of known plaintext-ciphertext pairs that are required for a successful key-recovery attack. The Grover oracle encrypts r plaintext blocks under the same candidate key and computes a Boolean value that encodes whether all r resulting ciphertext blocks match the given classical results. A circuit for the block cipher allows us to build an oracle for any r by simply fanning out the key qubits to the r instances and running the r block cipher circuits in parallel. Then a comparison operation with the classical ciphertexts conditionally flips the result qubit and the r encryptions are un-computed. Figure 4 shows the construction for AES and $r = 2$, using the ForwardAES operation from Sect. 4.

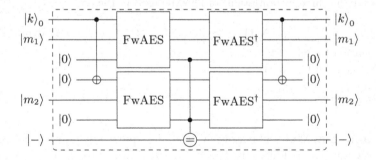

Fig. 4. Grover oracle construction from AES using two message-ciphertext pairs. FwAES represents the ForwardAES operator described in Sect. 4. The middle operator "=" compares the output of AES with the provided ciphertexts and flips the target qubit if they are equal.

The Required Number of Plaintext-Ciphertext Blocks. The explicit computation of the probabilities in Eq. (1) shows that using $r = 2$ (resp. 2, 3) for AES-128 (resp. -192, -256) guarantees a unique key with overwhelming probability. The probabilities that there are no spurious keys are $1 - \epsilon$, where $\epsilon < 2^{-128}$, 2^{-64}, and 2^{-128}, respectively. Grassl *et al.* [21, § 3.1] used $r = 3$, $r = 4$ and $r = 5$, respectively. Hence, these values are too large and the Grover oracle can work correctly with fewer full AES evaluations.

If one is content with a success probability lower than 1, it suffices to use $r = \lceil k/n \rceil$ blocks of plaintext-ciphertext pairs. In this case, it is enough to use $r = 1$, 2, and 3 for AES-128, -192, -256, respectively. Langenberg *et al.* [31] also propose these values. As an example, if we use $r = 1$ for AES-128, the probability of not having spurious keys is $1/e \approx 0.368$, which could be a high enough chance for a successful attack in certain scenarios, e.g., when there is a strict limit on the width of the attack circuit. Furthermore, when a large number of parallel machines are used in an instance of the attack, as discussed in Sect. 2.3, even the value $r = 1$ can be enough in order to guarantee with high probability that the relevant subset of the key space contains the correct key as a unique solution.

The LowMC parameter sets we consider here all have $k = n$. Therefore, $r = 2$ plaintext-ciphertext pairs are enough for all three sets ($k \in \{128, 192, 256\}$). Then, the probability that the key is unique is $1 - \epsilon$, where $\epsilon < 2^{-k}$, i.e. this probability is negligibly close to 1. With high parallelization, $r = 1$ is sufficient for a success probability very close to 1.

Grover Oracle Cost for AES. Table 8 shows the resources needed for the full AES Grover oracle for the relevant values of $r \in \{1, 2, 3\}$. Even without parallelization, more than 2 pairs are never required for AES-128 and AES-192. The same holds for 4 or more pairs for AES-256.

Table 8. Costs for the AES Grover oracle operator for $r = 1$, 2 and 3 plaintext-ciphertext pairs. "MC" is the MixColumn design, either in-place ("IP") or Maximov's [34] ("M").

Operation	MC	r	#CNOT	#1qCliff	#T	#M	T-depth	Full depth	Width
AES-128	IP	1	292313	84428	54908	13727	121	2816	1665
AES-192	IP	1	329697	94316	61436	15359	120	2978	1985
AES-256	IP	1	404139	116286	75580	18895	126	3353	2305
AES-128	IP	2	585051	169184	109820	27455	121	2815	3329
AES-192	IP	2	659727	188520	122876	30719	120	2981	3969
AES-256	IP	2	808071	231124	151164	37791	126	3356	4609
AES-256	IP	3	1212905	347766	226748	56687	126	3347	6913
AES-128	M	1	294863	84488	54908	13727	121	2086	2817
AES-192	M	1	332665	94092	61436	15359	120	1879	3393
AES-256	M	1	407667	116062	75580	18895	126	1951	3969
AES-128	M	2	589643	168288	109820	27455	121	2096	5633
AES-192	M	2	665899	188544	122876	30719	120	1890	6785
AES-256	M	2	815645	231712	151164	37791	126	1952	7937
AES-256	M	3	1223087	346290	226748	56687	126	1956	11905

Grover Oracle Cost for LowMC. The resources for our implementation of the full LowMC Grover oracle for the relevant values of $r \in \{1, 2\}$ are shown in Table 9. No setting needs more than $r = 2$ plaintext-ciphertext pairs.

Table 9. Cost estimates for the LowMC Grover oracle operator for $r = 1$ and 2 plaintext-ciphertext pairs. LowMC parameter sets are as used in Picnic.

Operation	r	#CNOT	#1qCliff	#T	#M	T-depth	Full depth	Width
LowMC L1	1	690961	5917	8908	191	41	98709	1585
LowMC L3	1	2273397	10881	13364	286	61	319323	2377
LowMC L5	1	5072343	16209	16980	372	77	693477	3049
LowMC L1	2	1382143	11774	17820	362	41	98707	3169
LowMC L3	2	4547191	21783	26732	576	61	319329	4753
LowMC L5	2	10145281	32567	33964	783	77	693483	6097

6.2 Cost Estimates for Block Cipher Key Search

Using the cost estimates for the AES and LowMC Grover oracles from Sect. 6.1, this section provides cost estimates for full key search attacks on both block ciphers. For the sake of a direct comparison to the previous results in [21] and [31], we first ignore any limit on the depth and present the same setting as in these works. Then, we provide cost estimates with imposed depth limits and the consequential parallelization requirements.

Comparison to Previous Work. Table 10 shows cost estimates for a full run of Grover's algorithm when using $\lfloor \frac{\pi}{4} 2^{k/2} \rfloor$ iterations of the AES Grover operator without parallelization. We only take into account the costs imposed by the oracle operator U_f (in the notation of Sect. 2.1) and ignore the costs of the operator $2 |\psi\rangle\langle\psi| - I$. If the number of plaintext-ciphertext pairs ensures a unique key, this number of operations maximizes the success probability p_{succ} to be negligibly close to 1. For smaller values of r such as those proposed in [31], the success probability is given by the probability that the key is unique.

The G-cost is the total number of gates, which is the sum of the first three columns in the table, corresponding to the numbers of 1-qubit Clifford and CNOT gates, T gates and measurements. Table 10 shows that the G-cost is always better in our work when comparing values for the same AES instance and the same value for r. The same holds for the DW-cost as we increase the width by factors less than 4 and simultaneously reduce the depth by more than that.

Table 11 shows cost estimates for LowMC in the same setting. Despite LowMC's lower multiplicative complexity and a relatively lower number of T gates, the large number of CNOT gates leads to overall higher G-cost and DW-cost than AES, as we count all gates.

Cost Estimates Under a Depth Limit. Tables 13a and b show cost estimates for running Grover's algorithm against AES and LowMC under a given depth limit. This restriction is proposed in the NIST call for proposals for standardization of post-quantum cryptography [37]. We use the notation and example values for `MAXDEPTH` from the call. Imposing a depth limit forces the parallelization of Grover's algorithm, which we assume uses inner parallelization, see Sect. 2.3.

The values in the table follow Sect. 3.4. Given cost estimates G_G, G_D and G_W for the oracle circuit, we determine the maximal number of Grover iterations that can be carried out within the `MAXDEPTH` limit. Then the required number S of parallel instances is computed via Eq. (7) and the G-cost and DW-cost follow from Eqs. (8) and (9). The number r of plaintext-ciphertext pairs is the minimal value such that the probability SKP for having spurious keys in the subset of the key space that holds the target key is less than 2^{-20}.

Table 10. Comparison of cost estimates for Grover's algorithm with $\left\lfloor \frac{\pi}{4} 2^{k/2} \right\rfloor$ AES oracle iterations for attacks with high success probability, disregarding `MAXDEPTH`. CNOT and 1-qubit Clifford gate counts are added to allow easier comparison to the previous work from [21,31], who report both kinds of gates under "Clifford". [31] uses the S-box design from [10]. "IP MC" (resp. "M's MC") means the oracle uses an in-place (resp. Maximov's [34]) MixColumn design. The circuit sizes for AES-128 (resp. -192, -256) in the second block have been extrapolated from Grassl *et al.* by multiplying gate counts and circuit width by 1/3 (resp. 1/2, 2/5), while keeping depth values intact. p_s reports the approximate success probability.

Scheme	r	#Clifford	#T	#M	T-depth	Full depth	Width	G-cost	DW-cost	p_s
					Grassl *et al.* [21]					
AES-128	3	$1.55 \cdot 2^{86}$	$1.19 \cdot 2^{86}$	0	$1.06 \cdot 2^{80}$	$1.16 \cdot 2^{81}$	2953	$1.37 \cdot 2^{87}$	$1.67 \cdot 2^{92}$	1
AES-192	4	$1.17 \cdot 2^{119}$	$1.81 \cdot 2^{118}$	0	$1.21 \cdot 2^{112}$	$1.33 \cdot 2^{113}$	4449	$1.04 \cdot 2^{120}$	$1.44 \cdot 2^{125}$	1
AES-256	5	$1.83 \cdot 2^{151}$	$1.41 \cdot 2^{151}$	0	$1.44 \cdot 2^{144}$	$1.57 \cdot 2^{145}$	6681	$1.62 \cdot 2^{152}$	$1.28 \cdot 2^{158}$	1
				Extrapolation of Grassl *et al.* [21] to lower r						
AES-128	1	$1.03 \cdot 2^{85}$	$1.59 \cdot 2^{84}$	0	$1.06 \cdot 2^{80}$	$1.16 \cdot 2^{81}$	984	$1.83 \cdot 2^{85}$	$1.11 \cdot 2^{91}$	$1/e$
AES-192	2	$1.17 \cdot 2^{118}$	$1.81 \cdot 2^{117}$	0	$1.21 \cdot 2^{112}$	$1.33 \cdot 2^{113}$	2224	$1.04 \cdot 2^{119}$	$1.44 \cdot 2^{124}$	1
AES-256	2	$1.46 \cdot 2^{150}$	$1.13 \cdot 2^{150}$	0	$1.44 \cdot 2^{144}$	$1.57 \cdot 2^{145}$	2672	$1.30 \cdot 2^{151}$	$1.02 \cdot 2^{157}$	$1/e$
					Langenberg *et al.* [31]					
AES-128	1	$1.46 \cdot 2^{82}$	$1.47 \cdot 2^{81}$	0	$1.44 \cdot 2^{77}$	$1.39 \cdot 2^{79}$	865	$1.10 \cdot 2^{83}$	$1.17 \cdot 2^{89}$	$1/e$
AES-192	2	$1.71 \cdot 2^{115}$	$1.68 \cdot 2^{114}$	0	$1.26 \cdot 2^{109}$	$1.23 \cdot 2^{111}$	1793	$1.27 \cdot 2^{116}$	$1.08 \cdot 2^{122}$	1
AES-256	2	$1.03 \cdot 2^{148}$	$1.02 \cdot 2^{147}$	0	$1.66 \cdot 2^{141}$	$1.61 \cdot 2^{143}$	2465	$1.54 \cdot 2^{148}$	$1.94 \cdot 2^{154}$	$1/e$
				This work (with "in-place" MixColumn)						
AES-128	1	$1.13 \cdot 2^{82}$	$1.32 \cdot 2^{79}$	$1.32 \cdot 2^{77}$	$1.48 \cdot 2^{70}$	$1.08 \cdot 2^{75}$	1665	$1.33 \cdot 2^{82}$	$1.76 \cdot 2^{85}$	$1/e$
AES-128	2	$1.13 \cdot 2^{83}$	$1.32 \cdot 2^{80}$	$1.32 \cdot 2^{78}$	$1.48 \cdot 2^{70}$	$1.08 \cdot 2^{75}$	3329	$1.34 \cdot 2^{83}$	$1.75 \cdot 2^{86}$	1
AES-192	2	$1.27 \cdot 2^{115}$	$1.47 \cdot 2^{112}$	$1.47 \cdot 2^{110}$	$1.47 \cdot 2^{102}$	$1.14 \cdot 2^{107}$	3969	$1.50 \cdot 2^{115}$	$1.11 \cdot 2^{119}$	1
AES-256	2	$1.56 \cdot 2^{147}$	$1.81 \cdot 2^{144}$	$1.81 \cdot 2^{142}$	$1.55 \cdot 2^{134}$	$1.29 \cdot 2^{139}$	4609	$1.84 \cdot 2^{147}$	$1.45 \cdot 2^{151}$	$1/e$
AES-256	3	$1.17 \cdot 2^{148}$	$1.36 \cdot 2^{145}$	$1.36 \cdot 2^{143}$	$1.55 \cdot 2^{134}$	$1.28 \cdot 2^{139}$	6913	$1.38 \cdot 2^{148}$	$1.08 \cdot 2^{152}$	1
			This work (with "in-place" MixColumn), using Grassl *et al.* [21] values for r							
AES-128	3	$1.69 \cdot 2^{83}$	$1.97 \cdot 2^{80}$	$1.97 \cdot 2^{78}$	$1.48 \cdot 2^{70}$	$1.09 \cdot 2^{75}$	4993	$1.00 \cdot 2^{84}$	$1.32 \cdot 2^{87}$	1
AES-192	4	$1.27 \cdot 2^{116}$	$1.47 \cdot 2^{113}$	$1.47 \cdot 2^{111}$	$1.47 \cdot 2^{102}$	$1.15 \cdot 2^{107}$	7937	$1.50 \cdot 2^{116}$	$1.11 \cdot 2^{120}$	1
AES-256	5	$1.95 \cdot 2^{148}$	$1.13 \cdot 2^{146}$	$1.13 \cdot 2^{144}$	$1.55 \cdot 2^{134}$	$1.28 \cdot 2^{139}$	11521	$1.15 \cdot 2^{149}$	$1.81 \cdot 2^{152}$	1

Table 11. Cost estimates for Grover's algorithm with $\left\lfloor \frac{\pi}{4} 2^{k/2} \right\rfloor$ LowMC oracle iterations for attacks with high success probability, without a depth restriction.

Scheme	r	# CNOT	#1qCliff	#T	#M	T-depth	Full depth	Width	G-cost	DW-cost	p_s
LowMC L1	1	$1.04 \cdot 2^{83}$	$1.13 \cdot 2^{76}$	$1.71 \cdot 2^{76}$	$1.17 \cdot 2^{71}$	$1.01 \cdot 2^{69}$	$1.18 \cdot 2^{80}$	1585	$1.06 \cdot 2^{83}$	$1.83 \cdot 2^{90}$	$1/e$
LowMC L3	1	$1.70 \cdot 2^{116}$	$1.04 \cdot 2^{109}$	$1.28 \cdot 2^{109}$	$1.75 \cdot 2^{103}$	$1.50 \cdot 2^{101}$	$1.91 \cdot 2^{113}$	2377	$1.72 \cdot 2^{116}$	$1.11 \cdot 2^{125}$	$1/e$
LowMC L5	1	$1.90 \cdot 2^{149}$	$1.55 \cdot 2^{141}$	$1.63 \cdot 2^{141}$	$1.14 \cdot 2^{136}$	$1.89 \cdot 2^{133}$	$1.04 \cdot 2^{147}$	3049	$1.91 \cdot 2^{149}$	$1.55 \cdot 2^{158}$	$1/e$
LowMC L1	2	$1.04 \cdot 2^{84}$	$1.13 \cdot 2^{77}$	$1.71 \cdot 2^{77}$	$1.11 \cdot 2^{72}$	$1.01 \cdot 2^{69}$	$1.18 \cdot 2^{80}$	3169	$1.06 \cdot 2^{84}$	$1.83 \cdot 2^{91}$	1
LowMC L3	2	$1.70 \cdot 2^{117}$	$1.04 \cdot 2^{110}$	$1.28 \cdot 2^{110}$	$1.77 \cdot 2^{104}$	$1.50 \cdot 2^{101}$	$1.91 \cdot 2^{113}$	4753	$1.72 \cdot 2^{117}$	$1.11 \cdot 2^{126}$	1
LowMC L5	2	$1.90 \cdot 2^{150}$	$1.56 \cdot 2^{142}$	$1.63 \cdot 2^{142}$	$1.20 \cdot 2^{137}$	$1.89 \cdot 2^{133}$	$1.04 \cdot 2^{147}$	6097	$1.91 \cdot 2^{150}$	$1.55 \cdot 2^{159}$	1

The impact of imposing a depth limit on the key search algorithm can directly be seen by comparing, for example Table 13a with Table 10 in the case of AES. Key search against AES-128 without depth limit has a G-cost of $1.34 \cdot 2^{83}$ gates and a DW-cost of $1.75 \cdot 2^{86}$ qubit-cycles. Now, setting MAXDEPTH $= 2^{40}$ increases both the G-cost and the DW-cost by a factor of roughly 2^{34} to $1.07 \cdot 2^{117}$ gates and $1.76 \cdot 2^{120}$ qubit-cycles. For MAXDEPTH $= 2^{64}$, the increase is by a factor of roughly 2^{10}. We note that for MAXDEPTH $= 2^{96}$, key search on AES-128 does not require any parallelization.

Implications for Post-quantum Security Categories. The security strength categories 1, 3 and 5 in the NIST call for proposals [37] are defined by the resources needed for key search on AES-128, AES-192 and AES-256, respectively. For a cryptographic scheme to satisfy the security requirement at a given level, the best known attack must take at least as many resources as key search against the corresponding AES instance.

As guidance, NIST provides a table with gate cost estimates via a formula depending on the depth bound MAXDEPTH. This formula is deduced as follows: assume that non-parallel Grover search requires a depth of $D = x \cdot$ MAXDEPTH for some $x \geq 1$ and the circuit has G gates. Then, about x^2 machines are needed that each run for a fraction $1/x$ of the time and use roughly G/x gates in order for the quantum attack to fit within the depth budget given by MAXDEPTH while attaining the same attack success probability. Hence, the total gate count for a parallelized Grover search is roughly $(G/x) \cdot x^2 = G \cdot D/$MAXDEPTH. The cost formula reported in the NIST table (also provided in Table 12 for reference) is deduced by using the values for G-cost and depth D from Grassl et al. [21].

The above formula does not take into account that parallelization often allows us to reduce the number of required plaintext-ciphertext pairs, resulting in a G-cost reduction for search in each parallel Grover instance by a factor larger than x. Note also that [37, Footnote 5] mentions that using the formula for very small values of x (very large values of MAXDEPTH such that $D/$MAXDEPTH < 1, where no parallelization is required) underestimates the quantum security of AES. This is the case for AES-128 with MAXDEPTH $= 2^{96}$.

In Table 12, we compare NIST's numbers with our gate counts for parallel Grover search. Our results for each specific setting incorporate the reduction of plaintext-ciphertext pairs through parallelization, provide the correct cost if parallelization is not necessary and use improved circuit designs. The table shows that for most situations, AES is less quantum secure than the NIST estimates predict. For each category, we provide a very rough approximation formula that could be used to replace NIST's formula. We observe a consistent reduction in G-cost for quantum key search by 11–13 bits.

Since NIST clearly defines its security categories 1, 3 and 5 based on the computational resources required for key search on AES, the explicit gate counts should be lowered to account for the best known attack. This would mean that it is now easier for submitters to claim equivalent security, with the exception of category 1 with MAXDEPTH $= 2^{96}$. A possible consequence of our work is that some of the NIST submissions might profit from slightly tweaking certain parameter sets to allow more efficient implementations, while at the same time satisfying the (now weaker) requirements for their intended security category.

Remark 4. The G-cost results in Table 13b show that key recovery against the LowMC instances we implemented requires at least as many gates as key recovery against AES with the same key size. If NIST replaces its explicit gate cost estimates for AES with the ones in this work, these LowMC instances meet the post-quantum security requirements as defined in the NIST call [37]. On the other hand, the same results show that they do not meet the explicit gate count requirements for the original NIST security categories. For example, LowMC L1 can be broken with an attack having G-cost $1.25 \cdot 2^{123}$ when MAXDEPTH $= 2^{40}$, while the original bound in category 1 requires a scheme to not be broken by an attack using less than 2^{130} gates. In all settings considered here, a LowMC key can be found with a slightly smaller G-cost than NIST's original estimates for AES, again with the exception when no parallelization is needed. The margin is relatively small. We cannot finalize conclusions about the relative security of LowMC and AES until quantum circuits for LowMC are optimized as much as the ones for AES.

Table 12. Comparison of our cost estimate results with NIST's approximations based on Grassl *et al.* [21]. The *approximation* column displays NIST's formula from [37] and a rough approximation to replace the NIST formula based on our results. Under MAXDEPTH $= 2^{96}$, AES-128 is a special case as the attack does not require any parallelization and the approximation underestimates its cost.

NIST security		G-cost for MAXDEPTH ($\log_2$)			
Category	Source	2^{40}	2^{64}	2^{96}	Approximation
1 AES-128	[37]	130.0	106.0	74.0	2^{170}/MAXDEPTH
	This work	117.1	93.1	*83.4	$\approx 2^{157}$/MAXDEPTH
3 AES-192	[37]	193.0	169.0	137.0	2^{233}/MAXDEPTH
	This work	181.1	157.1	126.1	$\approx 2^{221}$/MAXDEPTH
5 AES-256	[37]	258.0	234.0	202.0	2^{298}/MAXDEPTH
	This work	245.5	221.5	190.5	$\approx 2^{285}$/MAXDEPTH

Table 13. Cost estimates for parallel Grover key search against block ciphers under a depth limit MAXDEPTH with *inner* parallelization (see Sect. 2.3). MD is MAXDEPTH, r is the number of plaintext-ciphertext pairs used in the Grover oracle, S is the number of subsets into which the key space is divided, SKP is the probability that spurious keys are present in the subset holding the target key, W is the qubit width of the full circuit and D the full depth. Each of the S candidate keys measured from the Grover search are classically checked against plaintext-ciphertext pairs. AES-128, -192, and -256 need 2, 2, and 3 such pairs, respectively, while LowMC needs 2 pairs for all sizes.

Scheme	MD	r	S	$\log_2(\mathrm{SKP})$	D	W	G-cost	DW-cost
AES-128	2^{40}	1	$1.28 \cdot 2^{69}$	-69.36	$1.00 \cdot 2^{40}$	$1.76 \cdot 2^{80}$	$1.07 \cdot 2^{117}$	$1.76 \cdot 2^{120}$
AES-192	2^{40}	1	$1.04 \cdot 2^{133}$	-69.05	$1.00 \cdot 2^{40}$	$1.72 \cdot 2^{144}$	$1.09 \cdot 2^{181}$	$1.72 \cdot 2^{184}$
AES-256	2^{40}	1	$1.12 \cdot 2^{197}$	-69.16	$1.00 \cdot 2^{40}$	$1.08 \cdot 2^{209}$	$1.39 \cdot 2^{245}$	$1.08 \cdot 2^{249}$
AES-128	2^{64}	1	$1.28 \cdot 2^{21}$	-21.36	$1.00 \cdot 2^{64}$	$1.76 \cdot 2^{32}$	$1.07 \cdot 2^{93}$	$1.76 \cdot 2^{96}$
AES-192	2^{64}	1	$1.04 \cdot 2^{85}$	-21.05	$1.00 \cdot 2^{64}$	$1.72 \cdot 2^{96}$	$1.09 \cdot 2^{157}$	$1.72 \cdot 2^{160}$
AES-256	2^{64}	1	$1.12 \cdot 2^{149}$	-21.16	$1.00 \cdot 2^{64}$	$1.08 \cdot 2^{161}$	$1.39 \cdot 2^{221}$	$1.08 \cdot 2^{225}$
AES-128*	2^{96}	2	$1.00 \cdot 2^{0}$	$-\infty$	$1.08 \cdot 2^{75}$	$1.63 \cdot 2^{11}$	$1.34 \cdot 2^{83}$	$1.75 \cdot 2^{86}$
AES-192	2^{96}	2	$1.05 \cdot 2^{21}$	$-\infty$	$1.00 \cdot 2^{96}$	$1.74 \cdot 2^{33}$	$1.09 \cdot 2^{126}$	$1.74 \cdot 2^{129}$
AES-256	2^{96}	2	$1.12 \cdot 2^{85}$	-85.16	$1.00 \cdot 2^{96}$	$1.09 \cdot 2^{98}$	$1.39 \cdot 2^{190}$	$1.09 \cdot 2^{194}$

(a) Grover oracle for AES

Scheme	MD	r	S	$\log_2(\mathrm{SKP})$	D	W	G-cost	DW-cost
LowMC L1	2^{40}	1	$1.40 \cdot 2^{80}$	-80.48	$1.00 \cdot 2^{40}$	$1.08 \cdot 2^{91}$	$1.25 \cdot 2^{123}$	$1.08 \cdot 2^{131}$
LowMC L3	2^{40}	1	$1.83 \cdot 2^{147}$	-147.87	$1.00 \cdot 2^{40}$	$1.06 \cdot 2^{159}$	$1.65 \cdot 2^{190}$	$1.06 \cdot 2^{199}$
LowMC L5	2^{40}	1	$1.08 \cdot 2^{214}$	-214.11	$1.00 \cdot 2^{40}$	$1.61 \cdot 2^{225}$	$1.99 \cdot 2^{256}$	$1.61 \cdot 2^{265}$
LowMC L1	2^{64}	1	$1.40 \cdot 2^{32}$	-32.48	$1.00 \cdot 2^{64}$	$1.08 \cdot 2^{43}$	$1.25 \cdot 2^{99}$	$1.08 \cdot 2^{107}$
LowMC L3	2^{64}	1	$1.83 \cdot 2^{99}$	-99.87	$1.00 \cdot 2^{64}$	$1.06 \cdot 2^{111}$	$1.65 \cdot 2^{166}$	$1.06 \cdot 2^{175}$
LowMC L5	2^{64}	1	$1.08 \cdot 2^{166}$	-166.11	$1.00 \cdot 2^{64}$	$1.61 \cdot 2^{177}$	$1.99 \cdot 2^{232}$	$1.61 \cdot 2^{241}$
LowMC L1	2^{96}	2	$1.00 \cdot 2^{0}$	$-\infty$	$1.18 \cdot 2^{80}$	$1.55 \cdot 2^{11}$	$1.06 \cdot 2^{84}$	$1.83 \cdot 2^{91}$
LowMC L3	2^{96}	1	$1.83 \cdot 2^{35}$	-35.87	$1.00 \cdot 2^{96}$	$1.06 \cdot 2^{47}$	$1.65 \cdot 2^{134}$	$1.06 \cdot 2^{143}$
LowMC L5	2^{96}	1	$1.08 \cdot 2^{102}$	-102.11	$1.00 \cdot 2^{96}$	$1.61 \cdot 2^{113}$	$1.99 \cdot 2^{200}$	$1.61 \cdot 2^{209}$

(b) Grover oracle for LowMC

7 Future Work

This work's main focus is on exploring the setting proposed by NIST where quantum attacks are limited by a total bound on the depth of quantum circuits. Previous works [3,21,31] aim to minimize cost under a tradeoff between circuit depth and a limit on the total number of qubits needed, say a hypothetical bound MAXDEPTH. Depth limits are not discussed when choosing a Grover strategy. Since it is somewhat unclear what exact characteristics and features a future scalable quantum hardware might have, quantum circuit and Grover strategy optimization with the goal of minimizing different cost metrics under different constraints than MAXDEPTH could be an interesting avenue for future research.

We have studied key search problems for a single target. In classical cryptanalysis, multi-target attacks have to be taken into account for assessing the security of cryptographic systems. We leave the exploration of estimating the cost of quantum multi-target attacks, for example using the algorithm by Banegas and Bernstein [6] under MAXDEPTH (or alternative regimes), as future work.

Further, implementing quantum circuits for cryptanalysis in Q# or another quantum programming language for concrete cost estimation is worthwhile to increase confidence in the security of proposed post-quantum schemes. For example, quantum lattice sieving and enumeration appear to be prime candidates.

Acknowledgements. We thank Chris Granade and Bettina Heim for their help with the Q# language and compiler, Mathias Soeken and Thomas Häner for general discussions on optimizing quantum circuits and Q#, Mathias Soeken for providing the AND gate circuit we use, and Daniel Kales and Greg Zaverucha for their input on Picnic and LowMC.

References

1. Albrecht, M.R., Rechberger, C., Schneider, T., Tiessen, T., Zohner, M.: Ciphers for MPC and FHE. In: Oswald, E., Fischlin, M. (eds.) EUROCRYPT 2015. LNCS, vol. 9056, pp. 430–454. Springer, Heidelberg (2015). https://doi.org/10.1007/978-3-662-46800-5_17

2. Albrecht, M.R., Rechberger, C., Schneider, T., Tiessen, T., Zohner, M.: Ciphers for MPC and FHE. Cryptology ePrint Archive, Report 2016/687 (2016)

3. Almazrooie, M., Samsudin, A., Abdullah, R., Mutter, K.N.: Quantum reversible circuit of AES-128. Quantum Inf. Process. **17**(5), 1–30 (2018). https://doi.org/10.1007/s11128-018-1864-3

4. Amento, B., Steinwandt, R., Roetteler, M.: Efficient quantum circuits for binary elliptic curve arithmetic: reducing T-gate complexity. arXiv:1209.6348 (2012)

5. Babbush, R., et al.: Encoding electronic spectra in quantum circuits with linear T complexity. Phys. Rev. X **8**(4), 041015 (2018)

6. Banegas, G., Bernstein, D.J.: Low-communication parallel quantum multi-target preimage search. In: Adams, C., Camenisch, J. (eds.) SAC 2017. LNCS, vol. 10719, pp. 325–335. Springer, Cham (2018). https://doi.org/10.1007/978-3-319-72565-9_16

7. Banik, S., Funabiki, Y., Isobe, T.: More results on shortest linear programs. Cryptology ePrint Archive, Report 2019/856 (2019)

8. Beals, R., et al.: Efficient distributed quantum computing. Proc. Roy. Soc. A Math. Phys. Eng. Sci. **469**, 20120686 (2013)

9. Bonnetain, X., Naya-Plasencia, M., Schrottenloher, A.: Quantum security analysis of AES. IACR Trans. Symmetric Cryptol. **2019**(2), 55–93 (2019)

10. Boyar, J., Peralta, R.: A new combinational logic minimization technique with applications to cryptology. In: Festa, P. (ed.) SEA 2010. LNCS, vol. 6049, pp. 178–189. Springer, Heidelberg (2010). https://doi.org/10.1007/978-3-642-13193-6_16

11. Boyar, J., Peralta, R.: A small depth-16 circuit for the AES S-Box. In: Gritzalis, D., Furnell, S., Theoharidou, M. (eds.) SEC 2012. IAICT, vol. 376, pp. 287–298. Springer, Heidelberg (2012). https://doi.org/10.1007/978-3-642-30436-1_24
12. Boyar, J., Find, M.G., Peralta, R.: Small low-depth circuits for cryptographic applications. Crypt. Commun. 11(1), 109–127 (2018). https://doi.org/10.1007/s12095-018-0296-3
13. Boyer, M., Brassard, G., Høyer, P., Tapp, A.: Tight bounds on quantum searching. Fortschr. Phys. 46(4–5), 493–505 (1998)
14. Chase, M., et al.: Post-quantum zero-knowledge and signatures from symmetric-key primitives. In: ACM CCS 2017. ACM (2017)
15. Daemen, J., Rijmen, V.: AES proposal: Rijndael (1999)
16. Daemen, J., Rijmen, V.: Specification for the advanced encryption standard (AES). Federal Information Processing Standards Publication 197 (2001)
17. Dinur, I., Kales, D., Promitzer, A., Ramacher, S., Rechberger, C.: Linear equivalence of block ciphers with partial non-linear layers: application to LowMC. In: Ishai, Y., Rijmen, V. (eds.) EUROCRYPT 2019. LNCS, vol. 11476, pp. 343–372. Springer, Cham (2019). https://doi.org/10.1007/978-3-030-17653-2_12
18. Ekdahl, P., Johansson, T., Maximov, A., Yang, J.: A new SNOW stream cipher called SNOW-V. Cryptology ePrint Archive, Report 2018/1143 (2018)
19. Fowler, A.G., Mariantoni, M., Martinis, J.M., Cleland, A.N.: Surface codes: towards practical large-scale quantum computation. Phys. Rev. A 86, 032324 (2012)
20. Gidney, C.: Windowed quantum arithmetic. arXiv preprint arXiv:1905.07682 (2019)
21. Grassl, M., Langenberg, B., Roetteler, M., Steinwandt, R.: Applying Grover's algorithm to AES: quantum resource estimates. In: Takagi, T. (ed.) PQCrypto 2016. LNCS, vol. 9606, pp. 29–43. Springer, Cham (2016). https://doi.org/10.1007/978-3-319-29360-8_3
22. Grover, L.K.: A fast quantum mechanical algorithm for database search. In: STOC 1996. ACM (1996)
23. Grover, L.K., Rudolph, T.: How significant are the known collision and element distinctness quantum algorithms? QIC 4(3), 201–206 (2004)
24. Itoh, T., Tsujii, S.: A fast algorithm for computing multiplicative inverses in $GF(2^m)$ using normal bases. Inf. Comput. 78(3), 171–177 (1988)
25. Jaques, S., Schanck, J.M.: Quantum cryptanalysis in the RAM model: claw-finding attacks on SIKE. In: Boldyreva, A., Micciancio, D. (eds.) CRYPTO 2019. LNCS, vol. 11692, pp. 32–61. Springer, Cham (2019). https://doi.org/10.1007/978-3-030-26948-7_2
26. Jean, J., Moradi, A., Peyrin, T., Sasdrich, P.: Bit-sliding: a generic technique for bit-serial implementations of SPN-based primitives. In: Fischer, W., Homma, N. (eds.) CHES 2017. LNCS, vol. 10529, pp. 687–707. Springer, Cham (2017). https://doi.org/10.1007/978-3-319-66787-4_33
27. Jeon, Y.-S., Kim, Y.-J., Lee, D.-H.: A compact memory-free architecture for the AES algorithm using resource sharing methods. JCSC 19, 1109–1130 (2010)
28. Jones, C.: Low-overhead constructions for the fault-tolerant Toffoli gate. Phys. Rev. A 87(2), 022328 (2013)
29. Kim, P., Han, D., Jeong, K.C.: Time-space complexity of quantum search algorithms in symmetric cryptanalysis: applying to AES and SHA-2. Quantum Inf. Process. 17(12), 1–39 (2018). https://doi.org/10.1007/s11128-018-2107-3
30. Kranz, T., Leander, G., Stoffelen, K., Wiemer, F.: Shorter linear straight-line programs for MDS matrices. IACR Trans. Symm. Cryptol. 2017(4), 188–211 (2017)

31. Langenberg, B., Pham, H., Steinwandt, R.: Reducing the cost of implementing AES as a quantum circuit. Cryptology ePrint Archive, Report 2019/854 (2019)
32. Low, G.H., Kliuchnikov, V., Schaeffer, L.: Trading T-gates for dirty qubits in state preparation and unitary synthesis. arXiv preprint arXiv:1812.00954 (2018)
33. LowMC: LowMC/lowmc at e847fb160ad8ca1f373efd91a55b6d67f7deb425 (2019). https://github.com/LowMC/lowmc/tree/e847fb160ad8ca1f373efd91a55b6d67f7deb425
34. Maximov, A.: AES MixColumn with 92 XOR gates. Cryptology ePrint Archive, Report 2019/833 (2019)
35. Microsoft: Getting started with Python and Q# — Microsoft Docs (2019). https://docs.microsoft.com/en-us/quantum/install-guide/python
36. Microsoft: microsoft/iqsharp: Microsoft's IQ# server (2019). https://github.com/microsoft/iqsharp
37. NIST: Submission requirements and evaluation criteria for the Post-Quantum Cryptography standardization process (2016)
38. Nogami, Y., Nekado, K., Toyota, T., Hongo, N., Morikawa, Y.: Mixed bases for efficient inversion in $\mathbb{F}((2^2)^2)2$ and conversion matrices of SubBytes of AES. In: Mangard, S., Standaert, F.-X. (eds.) CHES 2010. LNCS, vol. 6225, pp. 234–247. Springer, Heidelberg (2010). https://doi.org/10.1007/978-3-642-15031-9_16
39. PyCryptodome: Welcome to PyCryptodome's documentation - PyCryptodome 3.8.2 documentation (2019). https://pycryptodome.readthedocs.io/en/stable/index.html
40. Reyhani-Masoleh, A., Taha, M., Ashmawy, D.: New area record for the AES combined S-box/inverse S-box. In: ARITH. IEEE (2018)
41. Reyhani-Masoleh, A., Taha, M., Ashmawy, D.: Smashing the implementation records of AES S-box. TCHES **2018**, 298–336 (2018)
42. Rijmen, V.: Efficient implementation of the Rijndael S-box. Katholieke Universiteit Leuven, Dept. ESAT, Belgium (2000)
43. Satoh, A., Morioka, S., Takano, K., Munetoh, S.: A compact rijndael hardware architecture with S-Box optimization. In: Boyd, C. (ed.) ASIACRYPT 2001. LNCS, vol. 2248, pp. 239–254. Springer, Heidelberg (2001). https://doi.org/10.1007/3-540-45682-1_15
44. Selinger, P.: Quantum circuits of T-depth one. Phys. Rev. A **87**, 042302 (2013)
45. Shor, P.W.: Algorithms for quantum computation: discrete logarithms and factoring. In: FOCS 1994, pp. 124–134. IEEE Computer Society (1994)
46. Shor, P.W.: Polynomial-time algorithms for prime factorization and discrete logarithms on a quantum computer. SIAM J. Comput. **26**(5), 1484–1509 (1997)
47. Steiger, D.S., Häner, T., Troyer, M.: ProjectQ: an open source software framework for quantum computing. Quantum **2**(49), 10–22331 (2018)
48. Stein, W., et al.: Sage Mathematics Software Version 8.1 (2017)
49. Svore, K.M., et al.: Q#: enabling scalable quantum computing and development with a high-level DSL. In: RWDSL@CGO 2018 (2018)
50. Tan, Q.Q., Peyrin, T.: Improved heuristics for short linear programs. Cryptology ePrint Archive, Report 2019/847 (2019)
51. Trefethen, L., Bau, D.: Numerical Linear Algebra. Other Titles in Applied Mathematics. SIAM, Philadelphia (1997)
52. Ueno, R., Homma, N., Sugawara, Y., Nogami, Y., Aoki, T.: Highly efficient $GF(2^8)$ inversion circuit based on redundant GF arithmetic and its application to AES design. In: Güneysu, T., Handschuh, H. (eds.) CHES 2015. LNCS, vol. 9293, pp. 63–80. Springer, Heidelberg (2015). https://doi.org/10.1007/978-3-662-48324-4_4

53. Wei, Z., Sun, S., Hu, L., Wei, M., Boyar, J., Peralta, R.: Scrutinizing the tower field implementation of the $\mathbb{F}_{2^8}$ inverter - with applications to AES, Camellia, and SM4. Cryptology ePrint Archive, Report 2019/738 (2019)
54. Yamamura, A., Ishizuka, H.: Quantum cryptanalysis of block ciphers (algebraic systems, formal languages and computations), vol. 1166, pp. 235–243 (2000). https://repository.kulib.kyoto-u.ac.jp/dspace/bitstream/2433/64334/1/1166-29.pdf
55. Zalka, C.: Grover's quantum searching algorithm is optimal. Phys. Rev. A **60**(4), 2746 (1999)
56. Zaverucha, G., et al.: Picnic. Technical report, NIST (2017)

Optimal Merging in Quantum k-xor and k-sum Algorithms

María Naya-Plasencia[✉] and André Schrottenloher[✉]

Inria, Paris, France
{maria.naya_plasencia,andre.schrottenloher}@inria.fr

Abstract. The k-xor or Generalized Birthday Problem aims at finding, given k lists of bit-strings, a k-tuple among them XORing to 0. If the lists are unbounded, the best classical (exponential) time complexity has withstood since Wagner's CRYPTO 2002 paper. If the lists are bounded (of the same size) and such that there is a single solution, the *dissection algorithms* of Dinur *et al.* (CRYPTO 2012) improve the memory usage over a simple meet-in-the-middle.

In this paper, we study quantum algorithms for the k-xor problem. With unbounded lists and quantum access, we improve previous work by Grassi *et al.* (ASIACRYPT 2018) for almost all k. Next, we extend our study to lists of any size and with classical access only.

We define a set of "merging trees" which represent the best known strategies for quantum and classical merging in k-xor algorithms, and prove that our method is optimal among these. Our complexities are confirmed by a Mixed Integer Linear Program that computes the best strategy for a given k-xor problem. All our algorithms apply also when considering modular additions instead of bitwise xors.

This framework enables us to give new improved quantum k-xor algorithms for all k and list sizes. Applications include the subset-sum problem, LPN with limited memory and the multiple-encryption problem.

Keywords: Generalized Birthday Problem · Quantum cryptanalysis · List-merging algorithms · k-list problems · Approximate k-list problem · Multiple encryption · MILP · LPN · Subset-sum

1 Introduction

As constant progress is being made in the direction of quantum computing devices with practical applications, the inherent threat to cryptography has led to massive amounts of research in designing secure post-quantum primitives. To design these cryptosystems and justify their parameters, one must rely on generic levels of quantum security. Therefore a precise study of the *query* and *time* complexities of quantum algorithms for relevant problems is needed. Furthermore,

The original version of this chapter was revised: The title has been corrected as "Optimal Merging in Quantum k-xor and k-sum Algorithms". The correction to this chapter is available at https://doi.org/10.1007/978-3-030-45724-2_29

improved quantum algorithms may increase the vulnerabilities of some cryptosystems. In this work, we study, from a quantum point of view, an ubiquitous generic problem with many variants and applications: the Generalized Birthday Problem, or k-xor problem.

Generalized Birthday Problem. The birthday problem, or collision problem, may be formulated as the following: given a random oracle $H : \{0,1\}^n \rightarrow \{0,1\}^n$, find a collision pair, *i.e.* $x, y \in \{0,1\}^n$ such that $H(x) = H(y)$. It is well-known that $\Omega(2^{n/2})$ classical queries are necessary and sufficient. In a seminal paper, Wagner [32] generalized a method credited to Camion and Patarin [15] to solve a variant of this problem for k-tuples:

> Given some lists $L_1, \ldots, L_k$ of n-bit strings, find a k-tuple $x_1, \ldots, x_k$ of $L_1 \times \ldots \times L_k$ such that $x_1 \oplus x_2 \oplus \ldots \oplus x_k = 0$.

Although Wagner studied the case of unbounded lists, many cryptographic applications are concerned with lists of limited size. For example, if the lists (of uniformly random n-bit strings) have size $2^{\lfloor n/k \rfloor}$, we expect a single solution with constant probability. The best classical algorithms for this case are given in [18], and apply *e.g.* to the multiple-encryption or subset-sums problems. Alternatively, if the lists have size $2^{\lfloor n/(k-1) \rfloor}$ we may want to find all the expected $2^{\lfloor n/(k-1) \rfloor}$ solutions.

Extension to Other Operations. We choose to focus on the bitwise XOR operation $\oplus$ for simplicity. In all algorithms studied throughout this paper, it can be replaced by modular additions. We provide more details in the full version of the paper [28].

Classical Complexity of k-xor. Intuitively, increasing k can only make the problem easier on average, since new degrees of freedom are available. The optimal query complexity of k-xor is $\widetilde{\Omega}(2^{n/k})$ queries: with them it is possible to build $\mathcal{O}(2^n)$ k-tuples, and retrieve a XOR to zero with constant probability. The main contribution of Wagner in [32] is to give an algorithm which, although far from optimal in queries, reaches an efficient time complexity for any k. Its time complexity is $\widetilde{\mathcal{O}}\left(2^{n/(\lfloor \log_2(k) \rfloor + 1)}\right)$, using k lists of size $2^{n/(\lfloor \log_2(k) \rfloor + 1)}$.

Quantum Complexity. The optimal quantum query complexity of k-xor is known to be $\Omega\left(2^{n/(k+1)}\right)$ [5]. In [20] some quantum algorithms for solving the k-xor problem with quantum oracle access are given. For a general k, a time complexity of $\widetilde{\mathcal{O}}\left(2^{n/(\lfloor \log_2(k) \rfloor + 2)}\right)$ is obtained in the MNRS quantum walk framework [26]. As for Wagner's algorithm, the exponent decreases only at powers of 2. However, the authors also observed an exponential separation between the quantum collision and 3-xor time complexities. While collision search requires provably $\Omega(2^{n/3})$ quantum queries, they present a 3-xor algorithm running in time $\mathcal{O}\left(2^{3n/10}\right)$. A natural question is whether this extends to all k.

Furthermore, this previous work for general k covers only the case of unbounded lists. As highlighted above, in many applications we would like to consider a general k *and* lists of bounded size, as in [18,27].

This paper. In this work, we first answer the open questions stated in [20], which were far from intuitive or trivial as explained in Sect. 3. We introduce for this the "merging trees", that describe in a systematic way merging strategies to solve the quantum k-xor problem. This enables us to reach better exponential time complexities than [20], with exponents that decrease strictly at each new value of k. With $poly(n)$ qubits and without qRAM, we give quantum speedups for half of the values of k. We prove that our results are optimal among all merging trees.

While [20] studied the problem with quantum oracle access, we extend our framework to classically given lists *and* lists of limited size, up to the case where k lists of size only $2^{n/k}$ are given as input, improving the best algorithms for most values of k. We give the first quantum k-list algorithms applicable for all bicomposite problems as defined in [18]. We obtain also the first quantum time-memory product below $2^{n/2}$ for a generic k-list problem with lists of size $2^{n/k}$.

We provide several applications of these algorithms, improving the best known quantum algorithms for subset sums, the BKW algorithm, multiple-encryption and the approximate k-list problem.

Outline. In Sect. 2, we recall some preliminaries of quantum computing, state the different problems that we will solve and recall previous results. Section 3 summarizes our main algorithmic results. Sections 4 and 5 concern the case of unbounded lists. In Sect. 4, we present Wagner's algorithm and show how to generalize its idea with the concept of *merging trees*, which can be adapted to the quantum setting. These strategies cover all the previously known quantum algorithms for k-xor and the new ones in this paper. Our results were first obtained experimentally with the help of Mixed Integer Linear Programming, as the complexity of a merging tree appears naturally as the solution to a simple linear optimization problem. This is why our definition focuses on *variables* and *constraints*. In Sect. 5, we give the optimal merging trees for quantum k-xor and prove their optimality among all strategies of our framework. We also compare our new results with the ones from [20]. Next, in Sect. 6, we extend to limited input domains, *i.e.* smaller lists. Finally, in Sect. 7, we give some applications, using our new k-list algorithms as black boxes: subset-sums, LPN, the approximate k-list and multiple-encryption problems. We conclude the paper with some open questions.

2   Preliminaries

In this section we introduce the problems under study, cover some basic required notions of quantum computing and summarize the state-of-the-art of algorithms for these k-xor problems.

2.1   Variants of the k-xor Problem

All algorithms in this paper have exponential time complexities in n, written $\widetilde{\mathcal{O}}\left(2^{\alpha_k n}\right)$ for some α_k depending *only* on k. We consider k as a constant and neglect the multiplicative factors in k and n.

The k-xor problem has two main variants: the input data can be accessed via *input lists* or via an *oracle*. Classically, this does not make any (more than constant in k) difference. Quantumly, it implicitly determines whether we authorize *quantum access* or only classical access to the data.

Problem 1 (k-xor with lists). Given $L_1, \ldots L_k$ lists of uniformly random n-bit strings, find $x_1, \ldots, x_k \in L_1 \times \ldots \times L_k$ such that $x_1 \oplus \ldots \oplus x_k = 0$ in minimal time.

Problem 1 is the original problem solved by Wagner in [32], in which the sizes of the lists is arbitrary, and not a concern. In that case, there exists an optimal list size, which is exponential in n (otherwise we wouldn't expect a solution) and the same for all lists (otherwise we could increase the size of the non-maximal lists and simply drop the additional elements). The *oracle* version of this problem is as follows.

Problem 2 (k-xor with an oracle). Given oracle access to a random n-bit to n-bit function H, find $x_1, \ldots, x_k \in L_1 \times \ldots \times L_k$ such that $H(x_1) \oplus \ldots \oplus H(x_k) = 0$.

Alternatively, one can define Problem 2 with k different random functions, or Problem 1 with a single input list. These formulations are equivalent up to a constant factor in k and both will be used in the rest of this paper.

Problem 2 is the one studied in [20], when quantum oracle access to H is allowed. In that case, instead of querying H for a fixed input x, we are allowed superposition queries to a quantum oracle O_H. This models a situation in which the production of the lists is entirely controlled by the adversary, and can be easily implemented on a quantum computer.

Finally, we will allow a limitation of the domain of H, or alternatively, of the sizes of the lists L_i. The limit case happens when there is on average a single k-tuple with a XOR to zero. We name these problems "unique k-xor".

Problem 3 (Unique k-xor with an oracle). Given query access to a random $\lceil n/k \rceil$-bit to n-bit function H, expecting that there exists a single k-tuple $x_1, \ldots, x_k$ such that $H(x_1) \oplus H(x_2) \oplus \ldots \oplus H(x_k) = 0$, find it.

Although we choose to focus on these limit cases, our framework will encompass all intermediate cases where the domain size of H (or the size of L_i) is restricted to 2^d with $\lceil \frac{n}{k} \rceil \leq d \leq n$.

Problem 4 (Unique k-xor with lists). Given classical data as k lists $L_1, \ldots, L_k$ of uniformly random n-bit strings, of size $2^{n/k}$, find a k-tuple $x_1, \ldots, x_k \in L_1 \times \ldots \times L_k$ such that $x_1 \oplus \ldots \oplus x_k = 0$, if it exists.

2.2   Quantum Computing Model and Preliminaries

We use the quantum circuit model. However, as we are only interested in exponential time complexities, we allow ourselves a level of abstraction which should make our algorithms and complexities understandable even for a non-expert audience. For the interested reader, a thorough introduction to quantum computing can be found in [29].

The quantum circuit model is a universal way of describing a quantum computation. We compute with a set of qubits, which are two-dimensional quantum systems. Their state is described by a vector in a Hilbert space $\mathcal{H}$, of the form $\alpha\,|0\rangle + \beta\,|1\rangle$, where $|0\rangle, |1\rangle$ is the canonical basis of $\mathcal{H}$ (named the computational basis), α, β are complex numbers and $|\alpha|^2 + |\beta|^2 = 1$. A quantum circuit starts with a system of (possibly many) qubits in the state $|0\rangle$; then a sequence of unitary operators (formed of operators known as *quantum gates*), possibly interleaved with oracle calls, is applied. At the end of the computation, the qubits are measured.

A widely known example of quantum algorithm is Grover's algorithm [21]. From a uniform superposition over a search space X, it creates the superposition over the subset $G = \{x \in X, f(x) = 1\}$ for some function f, assuming that a superposition oracle for f is given: $O_f(|x\rangle\,|b\rangle) = |x\rangle\,|b \oplus f(x)\rangle$. As this procedure consists in iterating $\sqrt{|X|2^{-t}}$ times the same unitary, we speak of "iterations". Grover search is known to be optimal when the test f is a black-box oracle [6].

Lemma 1 (Grover Search, from [21]). *Let X be a search space, whose elements are represented on $\lceil \log_2(|X|) \rceil$ qubits, such that the uniform superposition $\frac{1}{\sqrt{|X|}} \sum_{x \in X} |x\rangle$ is computable in $\widetilde{\mathcal{O}}(1)$ time. Assume that we can implement a superposition oracle O_f for f in $\widetilde{\mathcal{O}}(1)$ time. Let $G = \{x \in X, f(x) = 1\}$. Then there exists a quantum algorithm using $\lceil \log_2(|X|) \rceil$ qubits, running in time $\widetilde{O}(\sqrt{|X|/|G|})$ that returns some $x \in G$. In particular, if $|G| = 1$, the running time is $\widetilde{O}(\sqrt{|X|})$.*

Amplitude Amplification. A generalization of Grover search given in [12] enables to run a search with a structured search space: if there are 2^t partial solutions amongst the search space X, and if the superposition of elements of X can be constructed with a quantum algorithm $\mathcal{A}$ of complexity $|\mathcal{A}|$, we can recover the superposition of all preimages of 1 with total time $\widetilde{\mathcal{O}}\left(\sqrt{|X|2^{-t}}(|\mathcal{A}| + |O_f|)\right)$.

In the rest of this paper, we use Grover search as a subroutine. We perform sequences of Grover searches, and also, nested instances, using Amplitude Amplification. We do the complexity estimates as if Grover's algorithm ran in exact time $\sqrt{|X|/|G|}$ and with success probability 1. More justification is provided in the full version of the paper [28].

Benchmarking. We focus on the single-processor model, and count the asymptotic *quantum time* complexity (the number of gates in the circuit), *quantum space* complexity (the number of qubits in the circuit) and, when necessary, classical time and space. This is contrary to works which focus primarily on quantum *query complexity* (*e.g.* [23]), or detailed quantum gate counts. When an oracle is given, we consider oracle calls in time $\mathcal{O}(1)$ and suppose a constant quantum space overhead. Asymptotically, we consider that one quantum gate is equivalent to one classical gate. In practice, there should be a massive (but constant) factor in-between.

qRAM Models. Classical random-access memory authorizes a constant-time access to memory cell whose indices are known only at runtime. However, during a quantum computation, the index register of such a query, since it depends on previous computations, is likely to be in superposition. This is why many quantum algorithms require quantum RAM.

A qRAM authorizes *superposition* access to its contents, using so-called "qRAM gates", an add-on to a traditional universal gate set. Assume that the quantum circuit holds qubit registers $x_0 \ldots x_{2^n-1}$. Then on input:

$$\left(\bigotimes_{j \in \{0,1\}^n} |x_j\rangle \right) \otimes |i\rangle |0\rangle \quad \text{we compute} \quad \left(\bigotimes_{j \in \{0,1\}^n} |x_j\rangle \right) \otimes |i\rangle |x_i\rangle$$

in a single time step, realizing *superposition access* to the qubit registers. Using qRAM gates, it is possible to obtain quantum data structures with fast lookups (for example the combination of a skip list and a hash table in [2] or the radix trees of [7]). The access time is generally logarithmic and often neglected as a global multiplicative factor.

In this paper, we will extensively refer to three settings.

- "Low-qubits": the quantum computation uses only $\mathcal{O}(n)$ qubits and there are no qRAM gates. The quantum computer can still make use of a classical memory of exponential size, by performing classically controlled operations. This model was already considered in [20] and [16].
- QACM (quantum-accessible classical memory): there are qRAM gates, but the data accessed must be classical. This is the model required by the collision-finding algorithm of [13] or the QBKW algorithm of [19]. Some authors [25] consider it more relevant than the QAQM model.
- QAQM (quantum-accessible quantum memory): the quantum computation can use as many qubits as needed. The data accessed in superposition can be quantum. This model is obviously the most powerful. The unique collision-finding algorithm of [2] and the quantum algorithms for subset-sum of [7,22] require QAQM, as do all cryptographic applications of the MNRS quantum walk framework [26].

2.3   Overview of Previous Related Work

Classical Algorithms for the k-xor Problem. In Sect. 4, we will describe in detail Wagner's algorithm [32], that provides the current best classical exponential time complexity of $\widetilde{\mathcal{O}}\left(2^{n/(\lfloor \log_2(k) \rfloor + 1)}\right)$ for any k (there are logarithmic improvements for non-powers of 2). Many subsequent works have improved the memory consumption and given new trade-offs [8,30].

Minder and Sinclair [27] study the success probability and limit the sizes of the lists at the first level of Wagner's k-tree. This corresponds to taking an oracle

$H : \{0,1\}^{dn} \to \{0,1\}^n$ with $d < 1$. The authors use MILP to derive the optimal list sizes depending on the domain restriction. Their optimal algorithms roughly run in two steps: in the first levels of the binary tree, all pairs of elements are produced, increasing the list sizes; after that, classical merging is used. They also perform a precise estimation of the success probability of Wagner's algorithm.

In [18], the authors study a family of *bicomposite* problems with a single solution, which include hard knapsacks, multiple-encryption, and k-xor with a single solution. They generalize the technique of Schroeppel and Shamir [31] to improve the memory complexity of these problems. Their method consists in guessing some intermediate values, then producing efficiently lists of partial guesses, before matching them. A bigger meet-in-the-middle instance is broken down into smaller ones.

Later on, more generalized frameworks have appeared, like [3] in the context of the Short Integer Solution problem, or [17], in which Dinur gives a memory improvement for some values of k and better time-memory tradeoffs in general, by combining parallel collision search, which is used in [30], with dissection [18,31]. Although we have considered various potential improvements, our best algorithms for k-xor combine merging (as done by Wagner in [32]) and guessing intermediate values (as done in [18]), which is why we focus only on these techniques.

Quantum Algorithms for $k = 2$. The first algorithm to find quantum collisions was found by Brassard, Høyer and Tapp in 1998 [13,14]. With a two-to-one function $H : \{0,1\}^n \to \{0,1\}^n$, it runs in time $\widetilde{\mathcal{O}}\left(2^{n/3}\right)$, using as much quantum queries. The bound $\Omega\left(2^{n/3}\right)$ was later proven to be optimal [1] and extended to random functions [33]. This corresponds to the 2-xor problem with no bound on the list size. This algorithm also requires a QACM of size $2^{n/3}$.

When all 2^n outputs of H are distinct, except two of them, Ambainis' celebrated algorithm [2], based on a quantum walk, finds the pair in time $\widetilde{\mathcal{O}}\left(2^{2n/3}\right)$ using $2^{2n/3}$ QAQM. This corresponds to the 2-xor problem with a single solution. In the QACM model, there is, to date, no quantum algorithm with better time than the classical meet-in-the-middle.

Chailloux *et al.* [16] showed that the unbounded 2-xor problem could be solved in quantum time $\mathcal{O}\left(2^{2n/5}\right)$ in the low-qubits setting. The uses a classical memory of size $2^{n/5}$. Indeed, a superposition query to a QACM of size $2^{n/5}$ can be emulated by $2^{n/5}$ sequential quantum computations. The cost of these queries is mitigated by the fact that the algorithm makes only $2^{n/5}$ of them.

Quantum Algorithms for Bigger k. Given a random function $H : \{0,1\}^n \to \{0,1\}^n$, the classical (information-theoretic) query lower bound of the k-xor problem is $\Omega(2^{n/k})$. The quantum query lower bound is $\Omega(2^{n/(k+1)})$ [5].

Unbounded Domain Size. Grassi *et al.* [20] proposed quantum algorithms for solving the k-xor problem with a quantum oracle for a random function $H :$

$\{0,1\}^n \to \{0,1\}^n$, hence in the case of unbounded lists, as in [32]. They proposed a quantum analogue of Wagner's algorithm based on a quantum walk, running in the QAQM model, in time $\widetilde{\mathcal{O}}\left(2^{n\frac{1}{2+\lfloor \log_2 k \rfloor}}\right)$ and obtained some quantum time speedups in the low-qubits model. They also obtained a 3-xor QACM algorithm of quantum time complexity $\widetilde{\mathcal{O}}\left(2^{0.3n}\right)$, with an exponential improvement over quantum collision search. In this paper, we subsume and improve all these results. Notably, our new algorithms in this case require QACM only.

Restricted Domain and Unique k-xor. To the best of our knowledge, the k-xor problem with limited domain size, including Problem 3, has never been studied for a general k from a quantum algorithmic perspective. For $k = 4$, a quantum walk algorithm (originally designed for solving subset sums) is given in [7]. It solves Problem 3 in time $\widetilde{\mathcal{O}}\left(2^{0.3n}\right)$, using $\widetilde{\mathcal{O}}\left(2^{0.2n}\right)$ QAQM. This represents an exponential quantum time and memory improvement with respect to $k = 2$. However, for other values of k, *e.g.* $k = 5$, we must revert to a simple meet-in-the-middle strategy using Ambainis' algorithm.

Moreover, while Ambainis' algorithm gives a general meet-in-the-middle result, the 4-list algorithm of [7] is not a general 4-dissection algorithm; it does not apply to 4-encryption (we will explain this in Sect. 7).

3   Summary of Our Main Results

In this section we summarize the optimal time complexities, *in our merging tree framework*, for solving Problems 1, 2, 3 and 4, with XORs and modular additions. The details will be given in the following sections.

The origin of this work was realizing that for some values of k, we were able to obtain merging algorithms that were more efficient than the ones from [20]. This could be done by decomposing the original k-xor problem on n bits in smaller problems, with smaller values of k' and a smaller number of bits, and merging them together. At the beginning, we did not find an intuitive way to predict the best merging strategies for a given k. We decided to implement a Mixed Integer Linear program[1] that gave us the best possible algorithms for $k \leq 20$. From these results, we were able to understand the optimal methods and extrapolate the results given below

New quantum algorithms for LPN, subset-sums, multiple-encryption and the parity check problem. Whenever a classical algorithm makes use of a black-box k-xor procedure, we can replace this inner machinery with a quantum merging algorithm and optimize the strategy using MILP. We have identified various cryptographic applications of our framework. However, we defer the details to Sect. 7 and concentrate here only on the black-box k-xor problems.

---

[1] Our code is available at https://project.inria.fr/quasymodo/files/2019/05/merging_kxor_eprint.tar.gz.

3.1   Quantum Algorithms for Problem 2

In the QACM setting, we prove Theorem 1 and, answering one of the open questions of [20], show that the time complexity exponent of our method decreases strictly for each k (see Fig. 1 for a comparison).

Theorem 1. *Let $k \geq 2$ be an integer and $\kappa = \lfloor \log_2(k) \rfloor$. The best quantum merging tree finds a k-xor on n bits in quantum time and memory $\widetilde{O}(2^{\alpha_k n})$ where $\alpha_k = \frac{2^\kappa}{(1+\kappa)2^\kappa + k}$. For $c \leq 1$, the same method finds 2^{nc} k-xor with a quantum (time and memory) complexity exponent of $n \max(\alpha_k + 2\alpha_k c, c)$.*

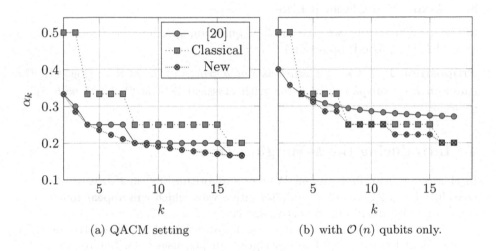

(a) QACM setting   (b) with $\mathcal{O}(n)$ qubits only.

Fig. 1. Comparison of time complexity exponents between the classical case, the algorithms of [20] and our new results. The complexities are $\widetilde{O}(2^{\alpha_k n})$.

In the low-qubits setting, we find the following. Except in the cases $k = 3$ and $k = 5$, quantum optimal merging trees give an exponential time speedup for half of the values of k, where the merging is mostly done classically. This also answers a question in [20] (see Fig. 1 for a comparison).

Theorem 2. *Let $k > 2, k \neq 3, 5$ be an integer and $\kappa = \lfloor \log_2(k) \rfloor$. The best quantum merging tree finds a k-xor on n bits in quantum time and classical memory $\widetilde{O}(2^{\alpha_k n})$ where:*

$$\alpha_k = \begin{cases} \frac{1}{\kappa+1} & \text{if } k < 2^\kappa + 2^{\kappa-1} \\ \frac{2}{2\kappa+3} & \text{if } k \geq 2^\kappa + 2^{\kappa-1} \end{cases}$$

The same method finds 2^{nc} k-xor with a (quantum time and classical memory) complexity exponent of $n \max(\alpha_k + \alpha_k c, c)$.

3.2   Quantum Algorithms for Unique k-xor

For Problems 4 and 3, we give algorithms in the QAQM model starting from $k = 3$. We improve over the previously known techniques for all k that are not multiples of 4. Our time complexity is given by Theorem 3.

Theorem 3. *Let $k > 2$ be an integer. The best merging tree finds, given k lists of uniformly distributed n-bit strings, of size $2^{n/k}$ each, a k-xor on n bits (if it exists) in quantum time $\widetilde{\mathcal{O}}\left(2^{\beta_k n}\right)$ where $\beta_k = \frac{1}{k}\frac{k+\lceil k/5 \rceil}{4}$. In particular, it converges towards a minimum 0.3, which is reached by multiples of 5. For $k \geq 5$ the memory (QAQM) used is $2^{\gamma_k n}$ with $\gamma_k \leq 0.2$.*

3.3 k-xor with Classical Lists

In the QAQM setting, we give the first quantum speedups for Problem 1 for a general k. We prove Proposition 1.

Proposition 1. *Let $k > 2$ which is not a power of 2, let $\kappa = \lfloor \log_2 k \rfloor$. The quantum time complexity of k-xor with classical lists is $\widetilde{\mathcal{O}}\left(2^{\alpha_k n}\right)$ with $\alpha_k \leq \frac{1}{2+\lfloor \log_2 k \rfloor}$.*

4   Introducing the k-Merging Trees

In this section, we first present Wagner's algorithm [32] in two ways: first, as introduced in [32], second, as an alternative way, which will appear much more compliant with quantum exhaustive search.

Wagner's algorithm is a recursive generalization of an idea introduced by Camion and Patarin [15]. The description in [32] uses lists, but to emphasize the translation to a quantum algorithm, *we will start by considering Problem 2 instead*, with a random function $H : \{0,1\}^n \to \{0,1\}^n$.

We will next introduce and define the context of k-merging trees. They provide a unified framework for merging quantumly (and classically) and enable automatic search of optimal merging strategies. We will show how to use these trees in the quantum case, and how to optimize them.

4.1   Wagner's Binary Tree in a Breadth-First Order

We now fix the constant k. Wagner notices that given two sorted lists L_1 and L_2 of random n-bit elements, it is easy to "merge" L_1 and L_2 according to some prefix of length u. Let L_u be the lists of pairs $x_1 \in L_1, x_2 \in L_2$ such that $x_1 \oplus x_2$ has its first u bits to zero. We say that such x_1 and x_2 *partially collide* on u bits. Then L_u can be produced in time $\max\left(|L_u|, \min(|L_1|, |L_2|)\right)$.

For example, if L_1 and L_2 contain 2^u elements and we want the merged list of partial collisions on the first u bits, then this list will have a size of around 2^u and can be obtained in time 2^u.

If k is given, and if H is a random oracle, Wagner's algorithm is a *strategy of successive merges* building a sequence of lists of *partial ℓ-xor* on u bits, for increasing values of $u < n$ and $\ell < k$, culminating into a single k-xor.

Example: 4-*xor.* The strategy for 4-xor is depicted on Fig. 2. We start from 4 lists of $2^{n/3}$ random elements each. At the second level of the tree, we build two lists of $2^{n/3}$ partial $\frac{n}{3}$-bit collisions (2-xors on $u = n/3$ bits), by merging the two pairs of lists in time $2^{n/3}$. At the root, we merge the two lists of collisions. There are $2^{2n/3}$ 4-tuples to form, with $2n/3$ remaining bits to put to zero.

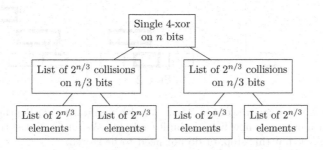

Fig. 2. Structure of Wagner's 4-xor-tree

General k. If k is a power of 2, we write $k = 2^{\kappa}$. In the remaining of this paper, when k is an integer, we write $\kappa = \lfloor \log_2(k) \rfloor$ for ease of notation. In the context of Wagner's algorithm, if k is not a power of 2, we first take $k - 2^{\kappa}$ arbitrary elements $z_1, \ldots, z_{k-2^{\kappa}}$ and then find a 2^{κ}-xor on their sum. So assume without loss of generality that $k = 2^{\kappa}$. All the lists in the tree will have size $2^{\frac{n}{\kappa+1}}$.

- At the lowest level of the tree (level 0), we build k lists of $2^{\frac{n}{\kappa+1}}$ single elements, making random queries to H.
- At level 1, we merge the lists by pairs, obtaining $2^{\kappa-1}$ lists, each one containing $2^{\frac{n}{\kappa+1}}$ collisions on $\frac{n}{\kappa+1}$ bits.
- At level i ($0 \leq i \leq \kappa - 1$), we have $2^{\kappa-i}$ lists of 2^i-tuples which XOR to zero on $\frac{in}{\kappa+1}$ bits: each level puts $\frac{n}{\kappa+1}$ new bits to zero. Notice that all these bit-positions are arbitrary and fixed, for example prefixes of increasing size.
- At the final level, we merge two lists of $2^{\kappa-1}$-tuples which XOR to zero on $\frac{(\kappa-1)n}{\kappa+1}$ bits, both lists having size $2^{\frac{n}{\kappa+1}}$. We expect on average one 2^{κ}-tuple to entirely XOR to zero.

4.2   Building a k-tree in a Depth-First Order

To build a node of the tree, it suffices to have built its children; not necessarily all nodes of bigger depth. Wagner [32] already remarks that this allows to reduce the memory requirement of his algorithm from 2^{κ} lists to κ.

On Fig. 3, we highlight the difference between these two strategies, by considering the 4-xor tree of Fig. 2. In a breadth-first manner, we go from one level to the other by building all the nodes (the new nodes are put in bold). Four lists need to be stored (the whole lower level). In a depth-first manner, only two lists need to be stored.

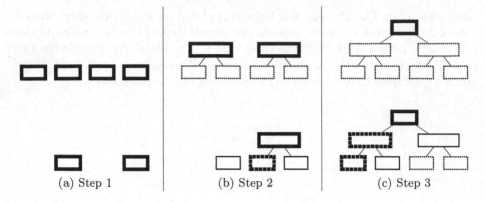

(a) Step 1   (b) Step 2   (c) Step 3

Fig. 3. Building the 4-xor tree of Fig. 2 in a breadth-first (above) or depth-first manner (below). At each new step, new lists are built (in bold). We put in dotted the lists which are either discarded at this step, or do not need to be stored.

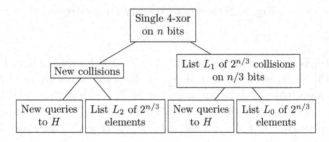

Fig. 4. Depth-first order in which to build the lists.

Example: 4-xor. We illustrate this depth-first tree traversal with the 4-xor example of before. Lists are numbered as in Fig. 4.

1. We build and store the list L_0 of $2^{n/3}$ elements.
2. We build the list L_1 of pairs x, x_0 such that $x_0 \in L_0$, x is a new queried element, and $x \oplus x_0$ is 0 on $n/3$ bits. To build a list of $2^{n/3}$ elements, we need time $2^{n/3}$, as each new x has on average one partial collision ($n/3$-bit condition) with some x_0 in L_0 ($2^{n/3}$ elements).
3. We discard L_0. We build and store the list L_2 of $2^{n/3}$ elements.
4. We find a 4-xor on n bits as follows: we make new queries x. Given an element x, we expect a partial $n/3$-bit collision with some $x_2 \in L_2$ (if there is none, abort). Given $x \oplus x_2$, we expect a partial $2n/3$-bit collision with some $(x' \oplus x_0) \in L_1$ (if there is none, abort). Then value $x \oplus x_2 \oplus (x' \oplus x_0)$ has $2n/3$ bits to zero. It remains to nullify $n/3$ remaining bits, which is why we repeat this operation for $2^{n/3}$ values of x.

Ensuring a Success Probability of 1. Minder and Sinclair [27] provided a study of the probability of failure in Wagner's algorithm. By building the tree in a depth-first manner, we can easily ensure an exponentially high success probability, that will hold in the quantum setting as well as in the classical. The idea is to always ensure that, given a candidate, a list will yield at least one partially colliding element on the bits that we wish to put to zero. This makes our analysis simpler, but we must pay a logarithmic overhead. The details can be found in the full version of the paper.

4.3 Limitations of the Extension to Quantum k-trees

In the breadth-first variant of Wagner's algorithm, it does not seem easy to use Grover's algorithm as a subroutine, as the initial lists are all fixed (although this is proposed in [17]). Since the time complexity depends on the size of the output list, the necessity to write this list in memory forbids a quantum improvement.

This fundamental problem is the main limitation on the quantum k-xor algorithms of [20]. In their quantum walk approach, they mimic Wagner's algorithm. Given a set of queries to H, one reproduces the k-tree and moves from one set to another in the MNRS quantum walk framework [26]. The inherent limitation of this procedure is that it reproduces the classical steps, and cannot yield a better time when k is not a power of 2. In their low-qubits approach, they use trees of depth 1: the leaf nodes are produced using some (classical or quantum) precomputation, and then, they do a Grover search for the final element.

However, in the depth-first variant, each new step corresponds to *some new exhaustive search*. New elements x are queried and *matched* (not merged) against the currently stored lists. Hence, classical search can easily be replaced with quantum search. We apply this idea in the next section.

4.4 Examples of Quantum Merging

In the *depth-first* tree traversal for 4-xor of Fig. 4, we now allow quantum computations. Each new node in the tree will be potentially built using *quantum* queries to H and lookups to the previously computed nodes. We reuse the numbering of lists of Fig. 4.

1. We build and store classically the list L_0 of $2^{n/3}$ elements.
2. We build the list L_1 of pairs x, x_0 such that $x_0 \in L_0$, x is a new queried element, and $x \oplus x_0$ is 0 on $n/3$ bits. Since the list is of size $2^{n/3}$, and it needs to be written down, we still need time $2^{n/3}$.
3. We discard the list L_0. We build and store the list L_2 of $2^{n/3}$ elements.
4. To find the final 4-xor, we are testing $2^{n/3}$ values of x, after which we expect that the partial collision with a candidate in L_2 and a candidate in L_1 also nullifies the last $n/3$ bits. This step can be done using Grover search, in time $2^{n/6}$.

At this point, it becomes clear that the tree of Fig. 2 must be re-optimized, so that all steps, including the last Grover search, take the same time. This new strategy is specific to the quantum setting. We obtain a time complexity of $\widetilde{\mathcal{O}}\left(2^{n/4}\right)$, which is that of [20] for 4-xor. We don't use a quantum walk anymore, but the procedure still requires $\widetilde{\mathcal{O}}\left(2^{n/4}\right)$ QACM to hold the intermediate lists L_2 and L_1 during the final Grover search.

Moreover, the example of 3-xor shows that there exists *inherently quantum* merging strategies. In Algorithm 1, which also improves over [20], the corresponding "3-xor-tree" is of depth one. Classically, it does not yield a speedup over the collision exponent $\frac{1}{2}$.

Algorithm 1. Quantum 3-xor Algorithm with QACM

1: Store a list L_0 of $2^{2n/7}$ elements;
2: Using Grover subroutines, build a list L_1 of $2^{n/7}$ elements with a $\frac{2n}{7}$-bit zero prefix;
3: Use Grover's algorithm to find an element x such that $f(x) = 1$, where f is defined as:
   - Find $x_0 \in L_0$ which collides with x on the first $\frac{2n}{7}$ bits, in time $\widetilde{\mathcal{O}}\left(1\right)$, with probability of success 1,
   - Find $x_1 \in L_1$ such that $x_0 \oplus x_1 \oplus x$ is zero on $\frac{3n}{7}$ bits,
   - If $x_0 \oplus x_1 \oplus x = 0$, return 1, else 0.
   This requires $\sqrt{2^{4n/7}}$ iterations, as $x_0 \oplus x_1 \oplus x$ has always $\frac{3n}{7}$ bits to zero; there remains $\frac{4n}{7}$ bits to nullify.

4.5 Definition of Merging Trees

In order to emphasize that our trees are constructed in a depth-first manner, and to make their definition more suitable, we start from now on to represent them as *unbalanced* trees where each node introduces a new exhaustive search, as on Fig. 5.

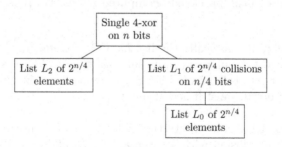

Fig. 5. Tree of Fig. 4 as an unbalanced quantum merging tree.

Since all the complexities throughout this paper are exponential in the output bit-size n and we focus on the exponent, we write them in $\log_2$ as $\alpha_k n$ for some α_k which depends only on k. We notice that n is a common factor in all complexities, so it can actually by removed. Next, we define our unbalanced *merging trees*. A tree represents a possible strategy for computing a k-xor; due to our specific writing, its number of nodes is k. Each node corresponds to computing a new list, starting from the leaves, computing the root last.

Definition 1. *A k-merging tree is defined recursively as follows:*

- *If $k = 1$, it has no children: this corresponds to "simple queries" to H.*
- *If $k > 1$, it can have up to $k - 1$ children $T_0, \ldots, T_{\ell-1}$, which are k_i-merging trees respectively, with the constraint $k_0 + \ldots + k_{\ell-1} = k - 1$.*

In other words, a k-sum to zero can be obtained by summing some k_i-sums, such that the k_i sum to k (here a $+1$ comes from the exhaustive search at the root of the tree).

Next, we label each node of the tree with some variables, which represents the characteristics of the list computed:

- The number ℓ of nodes of the subtree
- The number u of bits to zero (relatively to n)
- The size s of this list: s represents a size of 2^{sn}
- The (time) cost c of producing this list: c represents a time complexity of 2^{cn}

We obtain the general shape of a tree represented on Fig. 6.

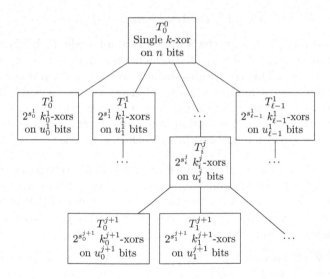

Fig. 6. k-merging tree

The Merging Strategy. We now consider a k-node T and the ℓ subtrees (of children) $T_0, \ldots, T_{\ell-1}$ attached to it. We suppose that they are ordered by their number of nodes (hence the lists will contain k_0-xors, k_1-xors, $\ldots, k_{\ell-1}$-xors, with $k_0 + \ldots + k_{\ell-1} + 1 = k$). The *merging strategy* is inherent to the definition of merging trees, and independent of the computation model. It generalizes the depth-first examples of Sect. 4.

Each element of T is built using exhaustive search, with $T_0, \ldots, T_{\ell-1}$ as intermediate data. We impose that the zero-prefixes of $T_0, \ldots, T_{\ell-1}$ are contained in one another. Let $u_0, u_1, \ldots u_{\ell-1}$ be the sizes of these prefixes and $s_0, s_1, \ldots, s_{\ell-1}$ the sizes of the lists. Given x in the search space of T, the test proceeds in ℓ steps. First, we make sure that x has zero-prefix u_0. Then we can match it with the first child T_0. Since this child contains 2^{s_0} elements, we can expect to find $x_0 \in T_0$ such that $x \oplus x_0$ has $u_0 + s_0$ bits to zero. Now we search T_1 for some x_1 which increases the number of zeroes in $x \oplus x_0 \oplus x_1$. We would like T_1 to have a zero-prefix of size $u_1 = u_0 + s_0$. Then $x \oplus x_0 \oplus x_1$ will have $u_1 + s_1 = u_0 + s_0 + s_1$ zero, and so on.

We see that for this depth-first merging strategy to work, we need a constraint relating the sizes of the lists and of the prefix of each node. It must hold at any non-leaf node in the tree.

Constraint 1 (A pyramid of zeroes). *Let $T_0, \ldots, T_{\ell-1}$ be the ℓ subtrees attached to a given k-node T, ordered by their number of nodes. Let $u_0, u_1, \ldots, u_{\ell-1}$ be their prefix sizes and $s_0, s_1, \ldots, s_{\ell-1}$ be their sizes. We have:*

$$\forall 1 \leq i \leq \ell - 1, u_i = u_{i-1} + s_{i-1}.$$

In other words, given x in the search space for node T, having u_0 zeroes, we expect only one candidate $x_0 \in T_0$ such that $x_0 \oplus x_1$ has u_1 zeroes, one candidate in T_1, *etc.* This constraint also ensures a success probability of 1 by the argument of Sect. 4.2. Since the list of node T_i is responsible for putting $u_{i+1} - u_i$ bits to zero exactly, we ensure that it takes all the values in this range. Notice that at this point, our definition of merging trees encompasses the binary tree of Wagner's algorithm, created in a depth-first manner.

Computation of the cost of a Tree. Since the goal of our strategy is to obtain the best time complexity for merging, we enforce *computational* constraints, which relate the *cost* of a k-node T with his size and zero-prefix and that of its children. These constraints depend on the computation model used; whether we authorize classical or quantum computation, QACM or not.

Constraint 2 (Cost of a leaf node). *A leaf node T with size s and zero prefix u has a cost c such that classically $c = u + s$ and quantumly $c = s + \frac{u}{2}$.*

Classically, finding a single x with a prefix of u bits requires 2^u queries to H. Quantumly, it requires $2^{u/2}$ superposition queries with Grover's algorithm.

Constraint 3 (Cost of a non-leaf node). *A k-node T with size s and zero prefix u, with children $T_0, \ldots, T_{\ell-1}$ having sizes $s_0, \ldots, s_{\ell-1}$ and prefix sizes $u_0, \ldots, u_{\ell-1}$ has a cost c such that:*

- *Classically $c = s + u + u_0 - u_{\ell-1} - s_{\ell-1}$*
- *Quantumly, with QACM: $c = s + \frac{1}{2}(u + u_0 - u_{\ell-1} - s_{\ell-1})$*
- *Quantumly, low-qubits: $c = s + \frac{1}{2}(u - u_{\ell-1} - s_{\ell-1}) + \max\left(\frac{u_0}{2}, s_0, \ldots, s_{\ell-1}\right)$*

In the classical setting, there are 2^s elements in the node to build and u zeroes to obtain. We must start from an element with u_0 zeroes, which requires already 2^{u_0} queries. Next, we traverse all intermediate lists, which give us a k-xor on $u_{\ell-1} + s_{\ell-1}$ zeroes. There remains $u - u_{\ell-1} - s_{\ell-1}$ zeroes to obtain, so we have to repeat this $2^{u-u_{\ell-1}-s_{\ell-1}}$ times. Quantumly, if we have quantum random access to the previously computed children, we use Grover's algorithm. We take the square root of the classical complexity for finding one element and multiply it by 2^s, the total number of elements in the node. If we don't have quantum random access, we can emulate a QACM by a sequential lookup of classically stored data. This was done in [16] in the case of quantum collision search (2-xor) and further used in [20] for low-qubit k-xor algorithms. Checking whether $x \in T_i$ can be done in time $n2^{s_i}$ using a sequence of comparisons. Finding a partially colliding element on some target takes the same time. Since each child list is queried this way, for each iteration of Grover search, the time complexity becomes:

$$2^{s+\frac{1}{2}(u-u_{\ell-1}-s_{\ell-1})}\left(2^{\frac{u_0}{2}} + 2^{s_0} + \ldots + 2^{s_\ell}\right).$$

We approximate the right sum by $2^{\max\left(\frac{u_0}{2}, s_0, \ldots, s_\ell\right)}$. This remains valid up to a constant factor in k. In the quantum setting, we will also authorize to fall back on classical computations if there is no better choice.

Finally, the size and number of zeroes of the final list (the root node) are parameters of the problem.

Constraint 4 (Final number of solutions). *The root T of the tree has zero-prefix $u = 1$ (since it requires n zeroes). Its size s is 0 if we want a single tuple, or γ if we want $2^{\gamma n}$ of them for some constant γ.*

Example. We can take as example Algorithm 1, which builds a 3-xor using two intermediate lists. We have a merging tree T, where the root has children T_0 and T_1. At T_0, we build a list of $2^{2n/7}$ elements: $u_0 = 0$, $s_0 = \frac{2}{7}$. At T_1 we build a list of $2^{n/7}$ elements with a $\frac{2n}{7}$-bit zero prefix: $u_1 = \frac{2}{7}$, $s_1 = \frac{1}{7}$. At the root we have $s = 0$ and $u = 1$. The costs of all nodes are $c_0 = c_1 = c = \frac{2}{7}$. We can verify that $u_1 = u_0 + s_0$ and $c = s + \frac{1}{2}(u + u_0 - u_1 - s_1) = 0 + \frac{1}{2}(1 - 1/7 - 2/7) = \frac{2}{7}$.

4.6   Optimization of Merging Trees

The description of merging trees that we have given above has two purposes: first, to provide a unified framework for merging quantumly and classically; second, to enable automatic search of optimal merging strategies. Given a tree structure, minimizing the total time complexity (the maximum of c_i for all T_i) is a linear problem, that we can solve with Mixed Integer Linear Programming (MILP). Given k, we can try different possible tree structures and find an optimal one.

Linear Program. We minimize the total time complexity of the merging tree. By definition of c_i, this is the sum of all 2^{nc_i} for all nodes T_i, starting from the leaf nodes (which are traversed first) up to the root (which is produced last). We approximate it to $2^{n \max_i(c_i)}$, up to a constant factor in k. Hence we minimize $c = \max_i(c_i)$ under the constraints outlined above.

Adaptations. The constraints of Sect. 4.5 are the only ones required to solve efficiently Problem 2. We will amend the framework in Sect. 6 to solve efficiently Problems 1, 4 and 3.

5   Optimal Merging Trees

In this section, we present our main results regarding Problem 2. We first describe the shape of the optimal trees, and next, the complexities in the QACM and in the low-qubit setting. Our results are compared with the ones from [20] on Fig. 1 and Table 3 in the full version of the paper [28].

5.1   Description of the Optimal Trees

By testing the different possible merging trees, and optimizing each tree with a MILP solver, we obtained optimal merging-tree strategies for solving the k-xor problem in the quantum setting, improving on [20] for many values of k. Furthermore, the quantum walk of [20] uses QAQM, while our method relies only on QACM. For non-powers of 2, we reach new and strictly better complexity exponents for all k. In the low-qubits case, we obtain non-trivial improvements for $k = 5, 6, 7$ and a new quantum speedup for half the values of k.

Optimal Trees. First of all, we define a family of trees $\mathcal{T}_k$ which will represent some optimal strategies for k-xor. The root of $\mathcal{T}_k$ (a k-xor) has $\lceil \log_2(k) \rceil$ children. The first child contains $\lfloor \frac{k}{2} \rfloor$-xors on some bits, the second contains $\lfloor \frac{1}{2}(k - \lfloor \frac{k}{2} \rfloor) \rfloor$-xors. In general, child i contains k_i-xors, and child $i+1$ contains $k_{i+1} = \lfloor \frac{1}{2}(k - \sum_{j=1}^{i} k_j) \rfloor$. The children subtrees are all $\mathcal{T}_{k_i}$.

If the $\mathcal{T}_k$ trees are solved with the classical constraints, we recover the complexities of Wagner's algorithm. Quantumly, we can make use of the additional nodes when k is not a power of 2. Indeed, Grover's algorithm allows to create elements with some zero-prefix quadratically faster. This is the source of the 3-xor quantum speedup (see Algorithm 1), and it can be generalized. We point out that $\mathcal{T}_k$ provides the optimal complexity both in the QACM and low-qubits setting (for $k > 5$) however it is not the only merging tree with such optimization.

QACM Setting. In the QACM case, each node that has a non-empty zero prefix is produced using Grover search. We note $\kappa = \lfloor \log_2(k) \rfloor$ and $\alpha_k = \frac{2^\kappa}{(1+\kappa)2^\kappa + k}$. In the optimization of $\mathcal{T}_k$, all the nodes have exactly the same cost (so all the lists are generated in the same quantum time). For all nodes of the tree, the optimal values of s_i and u_i are multiples of $\frac{1}{(1+\kappa)2^\kappa+k}$. The whole description of the optimal tree is easily derived from the constraints, but we do not have a clear description of it for a given k. We give the tree and constraints in the example of 11-xor in the full version of the paper [28].

Low-qubits Setting. In the low-qubits case, for $k \neq 2, 3, 5$, the best strategy is always to use classical searches, except at some leaves of the tree, where some elements with zero-prefixes are produced using Grover search. This gives one intermediate level of complexity between two successive powers of 2. For collision search, we obtain the algorithm of [16] with $\alpha_2 = \frac{2}{5}$. For $k = 3$, we obtain the algorithm of [20] with $\alpha_3 = \frac{5}{14}$, showing that it remains optimal in our extended framework (contrary to 3-xor with QACM, see Algorithm 1). The case $k = 5$ is the last using Grover search at the root of the tree, with a surprisingly non-trivial $\alpha_5 = \frac{14}{45}$. We describe it in full detail in the full version of the paper [28].

Memory. The memory used by our algorithms, for an equal time, is always equal or better than the one from [20], in both settings. Notice that the low-qubits variants use classical memory only (it can be seen as a quantum-classical tradeoff), its $\mathcal{O}(n)$ qubits being dedicated to computing. For a time $\widetilde{\mathcal{O}}(2^{\alpha_k n})$, the QACM variant requires $\widetilde{\mathcal{O}}(2^{\alpha_k n})$ QACM (it is needed to store the leaf lists).

5.2 Optimality in the QACM Setting

The MILP experiments helped us find the time complexity exponents α_k for $k \leq 20$, and acquire an intuition of the optimal algorithms for any k. We can prove this optimality in the QACM setting among all merging trees.

Theorem 1. *Let $k \geq 2$ be an integer and $\kappa = \lfloor \log_2(k) \rfloor$. The best quantum merging tree finds a k-xor on n bits in quantum time (and memory) $\widetilde{\mathcal{O}}(2^{\alpha_k n})$ where $\alpha_k = \frac{2^\kappa}{(1+\kappa)2^\kappa+k}$. The same method finds 2^{nc} k-xor with a quantum (time and memory) complexity exponent of $n \max(\alpha_k + 2\alpha_k c, c)$.*

Furthermore, for every k, the optimum is realized by $\mathcal{T}_k$.

One can verify that α_k gives the expected exponent for powers of 2, where it is equal to $\frac{1}{\kappa+2}$.

The idea of the proof is an induction on k. It is possible to prove that, if the last child of the root node is a list of partial k_ℓ-xors, then the optimal exponent α_k satisfies: $\frac{1}{\alpha_k} \leq 1 + \frac{1}{2\alpha_{k-k_\ell}} + \frac{1}{2\alpha_{k_\ell}}$.

This is where the structure $\mathcal{T}_k$ appears naturally. Since α_k is a decreasing function of k, to minimize the sum on the right, we need k_ℓ equal to $\lfloor k/2 \rfloor$. By plugging in this value and using the recurrence hypothesis, we obtain immediately the formula for α_k, and show that it is attained by $\mathcal{T}_k$. The full proof is given in the full version of the paper [28].

5.3   Theoretical Result in the Low-Qubits Setting

In the low-qubits setting, we can explain why Theorem 2 gives the optimal complexities.

Theorem 2. *Let $k > 2, k \neq 3, 5$ be an integer and $\kappa = \lfloor \log_2(k) \rfloor$. The best quantum merging tree finds a k-xor on n bits in quantum time and classical memory $\widetilde{\mathcal{O}}(2^{\alpha_k n})$ where:*

$$\alpha_k = \begin{cases} \frac{1}{\kappa+1} & \text{if } k < 2^\kappa + 2^{\kappa-1} \\ \frac{2}{2\kappa+3} & \text{if } k \geq 2^\kappa + 2^{\kappa-1} \end{cases}$$

The same method finds 2^{nc} k-xors with a (quantum time and classical memory) complexity exponent of $\max(\alpha_k n + \alpha_k c, c)$.

Furthermore, for every $k \neq 3, 5$, the optimum is realized by $\mathcal{T}_k$.

Informally, when k is bigger than 6, the merging operation at the root of the tree is performed using classical search. Grover search cannot be used anymore, as each iteration requires to pay the full length of the children (to emulate the qRAM lookups). In that case, we single out the first child T_0. We can rewrite the k-tree as a single merge between T_0, which is a k_0-tree, and a $k - k_0$-tree. The costs of producing these trees should be balanced, hence we should have $k_0 = \lfloor k/2 \rfloor$ as before, and we obtain the tree $\mathcal{T}_k$. Now we can remark that if $k < 2^\kappa + 2^{\kappa-1}$, then $\lfloor k/2 \rfloor < 2^{\kappa-1} + 2^{\kappa-2}$; and conversely, if $k \geq 2^\kappa + 2^{\kappa-1}$, then $\lfloor k/2 \rfloor \geq 2^{\kappa-1} + 2^{\kappa-2}$. In other words, we fall back very easily on the recurrence hypothesis.

6   Extended Merging Trees and Quantum Dissections

In this section, we extend merging trees to a much broader setting. We limit the input domain size, solving Problems 3 and 4 with time complexities better than the previous algorithms for most of the values of k. All new algorithms in this section run in the QAQM model.

First we will show how to adapt the merging trees of Sect. 4 to this new situation. We will present some examples of algorithms and our general results. Recall that in our formulation of Problems 4 and 3, the *input domain* of the oracle H is restricted to n/k bits and the codomain is n bits; alternatively, the input lists are of size $2^{n/k}$.

6.1   Generalized Merging Trees for Problems 1, 3 and 4

Our observation is that the *dissection* technique of [18, Section 3] finds a very simple analogue in terms of merging trees.

We remark that a merging tree as defined in Sect. 4 has many unused degrees of freedom. Indeed, suppose that we are building a tree T with children $T_0, \ldots T_{\ell-1}$. Each T_i has a zero-prefix of u_i bits. We deliberately used the term "zero-prefix", but we can actually take any value for these bits. During a search for a new element of T, we still look for successive collisions, but the values required depend on the prefixes of each child. All the prefixes are ours to choose, except for the root, since we still want the final k-tuple to XOR to zero.

This allows to *repeat* the node T up to $2^{u_0} \times 2^{u_1} \times \ldots \times 2^{u_{\ell-1}}$ times, and to overcome a limitation in the domain size. We write a merging tree as before, but expect only a small probability of success for the search at the root; so we interleave this tree with repetitions. The root search can be performed many more times, by changing the children.

The final time complexity depends on the complexity of the children, and the number of times that they are repeated. Indeed, suppose that the children $T_0, \ldots, T_{\ell-1}$ are built in time $t_0, \ldots, t_{\ell-1}$ (all of this in $\log_2$ and multiples of n). Suppose also that the root search requires time t. With a total number of repetitions r before we find a solution, the children will respectively be repeated $r_0, \ldots, r_{\ell-1}$ times (up to the choices they have in their prefixes) with $r_0 + \ldots + r_{\ell-1} = r$. We can write the time complexity as:

$$r_0(t_0 + r_1(t_1 + \ldots) \ldots + t)$$

by taking an arbitrary order for the children and writing the algorithm as ℓ nested loops:

0. The first loop iterates r_0 times on child T_0

1. Inside the first loop, after building T_0, the second loop iterates r_1 times on child T_1

. . .

$\ell - 1$ Inside all $\ell - 1$ previous loops, after building $T_0, \ldots, T_{\ell-2}$, the ℓ-th loop iterates on child $T_{\ell-1}$. Inside this loop:

- We build the child T_ℓ
- We perform the exhaustive search of the root T, using the children $T_0, \ldots, T_{\ell-1}$

In particular, this method subsumes the algorithms of [18, Section 3] in a classical setting. It also generalizes the idea of guessing intermediate values (which are the prefixes of the children T_i) and running an exhaustive search of these, and extends [18, Section 3] to all intermediate domain sizes.

The quantum correspondence works in a very simple way: these ℓ nested loops become ℓ nested Grover searches. We search among choices for T_i, *i.e.* choices for the fixed prefix. The setup (producing the superposition over the whole search space) remains easy. The test of a choice performs the nested computations: creating the list T_i itself and running the other searches.

Example: Quantum and Classical 4-dissection. We take the example of Problem 3. We suppose quantum access to a random function $H : \{0,1\}^{n/4} \to \{0,1\}^n$. Classically, the best algorithm is Algorithm 2, from [31], in time $2^{n/2}$ and memory $2^{n/4}$. Quantumly, the best algorithm is in [7], in time $2^{0.3n}$ using $2^{0.2n}$ QAQM. Our method is Algorithm 3. It runs in quantum time $2^{0.3125n}$, smaller than a simple meet-in-the-middle, and QAQM $2^{0.25n}$. It is worse than [7] for Problems 4 and 3, but we will see in Sect. 7 that it can be used to attack the 4-encryption problem, contrary to [7].

Algorithm 2. Classical 4-dissection

1: Query H and store all the elements $H(x)$ in a list L_0
2: **for** each $u \in \{0,1\}^{0.25n}$ **do**
3:     Create the list L_1 of pairs x, y with $x \oplus y = u|*$. This takes time $2^{0.25n}$, L_1 contains $2^{0.25n}$ elements (indeed, for each element $x \in L_0$ we expect a partial collision on $0.25n$ bits with some other element $y \in L_0$).
4:     **for** each $z \in L_0$ **do**
5:         Find $t \in L_0$ such that $t \oplus z = u|*$.
6:         Find $x \oplus y \in L_1$ such that $x \oplus y \oplus z \oplus t$ gives a $0.5n$-bit zero prefix.
7:         If $x \oplus y \oplus z \oplus t$ is all-zero and all are distinct, then return this result.
8:     **end for**
9: **end for**
10: Return the 4-tuple that XORs to zero.

Algorithm 3. Optimal merging tree algorithm for Problems 4 and 3 with $k = 4$

1: Query H and store all the elements $H(x)$ in a list L_0
2: **for** each $u \in \{0,1\}^{0.25n}$ **do**
3:     **for** $2^{0.125n}$ repetitions **do**
4:         Build a list L_1 of $2^{0.125n}$ partial collisions $x \oplus y = u|*$, in time $2^{0.125n}$, using exhaustive search with L_0 as intermediate (if we take any element, we expect a partial collision on $0.25n$ bits with some other in L_0)
5:         **for** each $z \in L_0$ **do**
6:             Find $t \in L_0$ such that $z \oplus t = u|*$
7:             Find $x \oplus y \in L_1$ that collides with $z \oplus t$ on $0.25n$ more bits
8:             If $x \oplus y \oplus z \oplus t = 0$ and all are distinct, then return this result
9:         **end for**
10:     **end for**
11: **end for**
12: Return the 4-tuple that XORs to zero.

The classical time complexity of Algorithm 3 would be:

$$\underbrace{2^{0.25n}}_{\text{choice of } u} \left(2^{0.125n} \left(\underbrace{2^{0.125n}}_{\substack{\text{Intermediate} \\ \text{list } L_1}} + \underbrace{2^{0.25n}}_{\substack{\text{Exhaustive} \\ \text{search}}} \right) \right) = 2^{0.625n}$$

which is not optimal. However, as a quantum algorithm with nested Grover searches, it optimizes differently, since exhaustive search factors are replaced by their square roots:

$$2^{0.125n/2} \times 2^{0.125n/2} \left(2^{0.125n} + 2^{0.25n/2} \right) = 2^{0.3125n}.$$

6.2 Quantum Algorithms for Unique k-xor

In what follows, we solve together Problems 4 and 3 in the QAQM model, with the same time complexities. The reason why there is little difference between these problems is that, as long as quantum random-access is allowed (QACM or QAQM), it allows to simulate quantum oracle queries. It suffices to store the input data in QACM and replace an oracle query by a query to the whole memory. For $k \geq 4$, the cost of storing the whole domain of size $2^{n/k}$ is not dominant. For $k = 3$, there is a difference in the memory complexity. For completeness, the two procedures for $k = 3$ are given in the full version of the paper [28].

From our observations, we derive the optimal merging-tree time complexity for Problems 4 and 3. When k is a multiple of 5, we can just apply our 5-xor algorithm with an increased domain size, and obtain an exponent 0.3. For other values of k, a good combination of Grover searches allows to approach it.

Theorem 3. *Let $k > 2$ be an integer. The best merging tree finds, given k lists of uniformly distributed n-bit strings, of size $2^{n/k}$ each, a k-xor on n bits if it exists in quantum time $\widetilde{\mathcal{O}}\left(2^{\beta_k n}\right)$ where $\beta_k = \frac{1}{k}\frac{k+\lceil k/5 \rceil}{4}$. In particular, it converges towards a minimum 0.3, which is reached by multiples of 5. For $k \geq 5$ the memory (QAQM) used is $2^{\gamma_k n}$ with $\gamma_k \leq 0.2$.*

Memory Usage. One of the advantages of the Dissection technique is its memory consumption. On Fig. 7, we compare the time complexities of the classical Dissection [18, Section 3] and of our quantum algorithm, for increasing k, when the memory available is limited to $2^{n/k}$. We remark that our technique often reaches a square root speedup upon [18, Section 3].

Without QAQM. Problem 4 becomes more difficult if QAQM is replaced by QACM. Indeed, assume that we are making a loop on a prefix of u bits, under which we build and store a list L of elements with u-prefix (before moving to other computations). It is crucial for our technique to be able to loop over this prefix with Grover search, in $2^{u/2}$ iterations. However, the list L written in each iteration is now in superposition as well, since it depends on u: it cannot be stored in classical memory. The solution would be to iterate classically on the prefix, in 2^u iterations. But then, we seem to loose the advantage over classical computations.

An algorithm for Problem 4 without QAQM can be obtained for $k = 3$ (and any multiple of 3) as follows: we store classically one of the lists and we do a Grover search on the product of the two others. The time complexity is always $\widetilde{\mathcal{O}}\left(2^{n/3}\right)$. We leave as an open problem to find QACM algorithms for unique k-xor (for any $k \geq 3$) with a factor less than $1/3$ in the complexity exponent, or even to find algorithms in the low-qubits model.

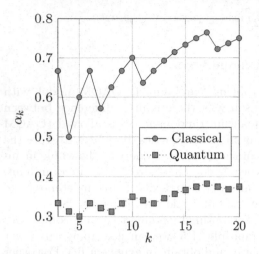

k	Classical α_k	Quantum α_k
3	2/3	1/3
4	1/2	5/16
5	3/5	3/10
6	2/3	1/3
7	4/7	9/28
8	5/8	5/16
9	2/3	1/3
10	7/10	7/20
11	7/11	15/44
12	2/3	1/3
13	9/13	9/26

Fig. 7. Smallest classical (using [18, Section 3]) and quantum time (using our algorithms) for merging k lists of size $2^{n/k}$ for a single solution, with a memory limit of $2^{n/k}$ (RAM or QAQM). The complexities are $\widetilde{O}\left(2^{\alpha_k n}\right)$.

7   Applications

In this section, we elaborate on various applications of our new algorithms. The common point of all the problems below is their k-list or *bicomposite* structure.

7.1   Improved Quantum Time – Memory Tradeoff for Subset-sums

Using the extended merging trees for Problem 3, we reach a better quantum time – memory product with respect to the current literature for low-density knapsacks, as was the case in [18] for classical algorithms.

Let $a_1, \ldots, a_n, t$ be randomly chosen integers on ℓ bits. We are looking for a subset of indices $I \subset \{1, \ldots, n\}$ such that $\sum_{i \in I} a_i \equiv t \mod 2^{\ell}$. The hardness of this problem is related to the density n/ℓ. When $\ell = poly(n)$, and we expect a single solution with high probability, the best classical algorithm [4], runs in time and memory $\widetilde{O}\left(2^{0.291n}\right)$. The current best quantum algorithm [22] takes time $\widetilde{O}\left(2^{0.226n}\right)$, using as much QAQM.

A subset-sum problem can easily be translated to a k-sum problem with a single solution. Indeed, it suffices to separate the set $\{1, \ldots, n\}$ into k disjoint parts $J_1 \cup \ldots \cup J_k$ and to start from the lists $L_1, \ldots, L_k$, with list L_j containing all the sums $\sum_{i \in I} a_i$ for $I \subset J_j$.

Both the quantum time and memory (QAQM) complexities of the k-xor (or k-sum) problem with a single solution vary with k. Optimizing the time-memory product (more details are given in the full version of the paper), we find that $k = 12$ seems the most interesting, with a time $\widetilde{O}\left(2^{n/3}\right)$ and a memory $2^{n/12}$. The product is $\widetilde{O}\left(2^{5n/12}\right) = \widetilde{O}\left(2^{0.412n}\right)$, which is less than the previous $0.452n$.

7.2 New Quantum Algorithms for LPN and LWE

We consider the LPN problem in dimension n with constant error rate $0 \leq p < 1/2$. Given a certain number of samples of the form $(a, a \cdot s + e)$ where $a \in \{0,1\}^n$ is chosen uniformly at random and $e \in \{0,1\}$ is a Bernoulli noise: $e \sim Ber_p$ i.e. $P(e = 1) = p$. The LWE problem is the generalization from $\mathbb{F}_2$ to $\mathbb{F}_q$ for some prime q.

In [9], Blum, Kalai and Wasserman introduced an algorithm solving LPN in time $\mathcal{O}\left(2^{n/\log n}\right)$, using $2^{n/\log n}$ samples. Their idea is to combine samples: given $(a_1, a_1 \cdot s + e_1)$ and $(a_2, a_2 \cdot s + e_2)$ one can compute $(a_1 \oplus a_2, (a_1 \oplus a_2) \cdot s + e_1 + e_2)$. When summing k Bernoulli errors of correlation $\epsilon = 1 - 2p$, one obtains a Bernoulli error of correlation ϵ^k by the Piling-Up Lemma. Hence, the goal is to produce sufficiently many sums of a_i with almost all bits to zero, with sufficiently few a_i summed, so that one can obtain a bit of s from the samples gathered. The same principle applies to LWE, although we focus on LPN for simplicity.

In its original version, the BKW algorithm uses $2^{n/\log n}$ samples and memory. It starts from the list of samples and repeatedly finds partial collisions, cancelling $n/\log n$ bits in the a_i, until it produces a list of $2^{n/\log n}$ samples with a single nonzero bit. In [19], the authors find that there are many advantages of combining $c > 2$ samples at a time, that is, using a c-list algorithm in place of a simple 2-list merge operation. First of all, this reduces the memory used, which is crucial for practical implementations of the BKW algorithm. Second, this reduces the number of samples: we start from a smaller list. Finally, they give the first quantum version of the BKW algorithm.

The c-sum-BKW algorithm is build upon the c-Sum-Problem as defined in [19, Definition 3.1]: *given a list L of N uniformly random b-bit strings, given $t \in \{0,1\}^n$ find at least N distinct c-tuples of elements of L that xor to t.*

They prove that, given an algorithm solving this problem in time $T_{c,N}$ and memory $M_{c,N}$ with overwhelming probability, for $b = \log c \frac{n(1+\epsilon)}{\log n}$ and $N \geq 2^{\frac{b+c\log c+1}{c-1}}$, then their adapted BKW algorithm solves LPN in dimension n in time $T_{c,N}^{1+o(1)}$ and memory $M_{c,N}^{1+o(1)}$.

The authors study the solving of this c-sum problem via the Dissection method [18] and obtain new time-memory trade-offs. They also study a quantum version of this algorithm, hereby using a naive Grover search in the QACM model: we store L in QACM and perform a Grover search on all $c-1$ tuples of L, for those who xor to an element of L. The memory used is N. As the parameters are tailored for N solutions in total, the quantum time complexity is $N^{c/2-1}$ for a single solution and $N^{c/2}$ for all of them. They leave as an open question (end of Sect. 1) whether a quantum k-list algorithm could be used in replacement.

New Trade-Offs. We are in a situation in which the input list is of size N_c and there are N_c solutions to recover. It is as if we were solving a c-xor problem on b bits with c lists of size $N_c = 2^{b/(c-1)}$ each, and wanted all the $2^{b/(c-1)}$ expected solutions. Furthermore, we limit the memory (QAQM) used to N_c. We simply solve the problem $\widetilde{\mathcal{O}}\left(2^{b/(c-1)}\right)$ times, as in the naive Grover case (Table 1).

Table 1. Improvements on the quantum-BKW algorithm of [19] (see Table 1 in [19])

c	Previous (naive + Grover)		This paper		
	Memory	Time	Memory	Time	Time exponent
3	N_c	$N_c^{3/2}$	N_c	$N_c^{5/3}$	$5/3 = 1.667$
4	N_c	N_c^2	N_c	$N_c^{13/7}$	$13/7 = 1.857$
5	N_c	$N_c^{5/2}$	N_c	N_c^2	2
6	N_c	N_c^3	N_c	$N_c^{5/2}$	$5/2 = 2.5$
7	N_c	$N_c^{7/2}$	N_c	$N_c^{11/4}$	$11/4 = 2.75$
8	N_c	N_c^4	N_c	N_c^3	3

7.3 New Quantum Algorithms for the Multiple-Encryption Problem

The multiple-encryption problem is an example of a *bicomposite* problem extensively studied in [18]. Consider a block cipher E_k with message space and key space of size n both. We consider the encryption by $E_{k_1} \circ \ldots \circ E_{k_r}$ with a sequence of independent keys $k_1, \ldots, k_r$. Given r plaintext-ciphertext pairs (enough to discriminate the good sequence with high probability), we want to retrieve $k_1, \ldots, k_r$. Classically, the best time complexity to date is essentially $2^{\lceil r/2 \rceil n}$ and the question is to obtain better time-memory trade-offs, as it is the case in [18]. We do not know of any r-list algorithm that wouldn't be applicable to r-encryption as well.

In [24], Kaplan proves that 2-encryption is (quantumly) equivalent to element distinctness[2]. However, already for $r = 4$, we remark that the 4-xor algorithm of [7] cannot be used to attack 4-encryption. Indeed, in the quantum optimization of [7], the size of the "intermediate value" that is guessed is not a multiple of n bits. This has no consequence on Problem 3, but if we try to translate the algorithm to attack multiple-encryption, we cannot solve efficiently the smaller meet-in-the middle problems. It would require to produce efficiently (in time $2^{0.8n}$), from $2^{0.8n}$ choices of k_1 and k_2, the list of $2^{0.8n}$ pairs k_1, k_2 such that $E_{k_1} \circ E_{k_2}(P)$ has some fixed $0.8n$-bit prefix.

We remark that all our r-xor algorithms (on nr bits) can be naturally converted to r-encryption: the size of the prefixes guessed is always a multiple of n, so we remain in a similar situation as [18], while this was not the case for quantum-walk based methods. For example, Algorithm 3 provides the best quantum time for 4-encryption that we know of, in quantum time $2^{1.25n}$ and QAQM 2^n to obtain the $4n$-bit key. Theorem 3 gives the best quantum time complexities for r-encryption for $r \geq 4$ and also shows an exponential decrease in the quantum time complexity with respect to 2-encryption.

---

[2] Kaplan [24] also gives an algorithm for 4-encryption, but we could not verify its time complexity.

7.4 Approximate k-list Problem

In [10], Both and May introduce and study the *approximate k-list problem*. It is a generalization of k-xor in which the final n-bit value only needs to have a Hamming weight lower than αn for some fraction $0 \le \alpha \le \frac{n}{2}$ (so the k-xor is the special case $\alpha = 0$). Its main application is solving the parity check problem: given an irreducible polynomial $P(X) \in \mathbb{F}_2[X]$ of degree n, find a multiple $Q(X)$ of $P(X)$ of a certain weight and degree. This is used in fast correlation attacks on stream ciphers. For this application, we can consider quantum oracle access (the lists actually contain polynomials of the form $X^a \mod P(X)$ for many choices of a).

The match-and-filter algorithm of [10, Section 3] consists in running a k-xor algorithm with a restricted number of bits to put to zero, and to tailor the length of the final list so that it will contain one element of low Hamming weight with certainty. With a quantum k-merging tree, we can always improve on this classical method in the QACM model. Let α_k be the k-xor optimal QACM time exponent as defined in Theorem 1. We cut the tree at its root: in time $\widetilde{\mathcal{O}}\left(2^{\alpha_k un}\right)$, we can obtain a tuple of lists $L_1, \ldots L_t$ such that, given an n-bit element x, we can find $x_1 \in L_1, \ldots, x_t \in L_t$ such that $x \oplus x_1 \ldots \oplus x_t$ has $(1 - 2\alpha_k)un$ bits to zero. Indeed, the Grover search at the root of the tree has also cost $\widetilde{\mathcal{O}}\left(2^{\alpha_k un}\right)$ since everything is balanced, so it eliminates $2\alpha_k un$ bits.

Hence, if we want to be able to eliminate un bits for some fraction $0 \le u \le 1$, we build all these lists in time $\widetilde{\mathcal{O}}\left(2^{\frac{\alpha_k}{(1-2\alpha_k)}un}\right)$.

Now we do a modified Grover search at the root: given any n-bit element x, the structure puts un bits to zero. There remains $(1 - u)n$ (random) bits. We want the Hamming weight of the result to be less than a target $c_w n$. The proportion of $(1 - u)n$-bit strings of Hamming weight less than $c_w n$ is approximately:

$$\binom{(1 - u)n}{c_w n} \Big/ 2^{(1-u)n} \simeq 2^{(1-u)n(\mathrm{H}(c_w/(1-u))-1))} \text{ if } c \le (1 - u) \text{ and } 1 \text{ otherwise,}$$

where H is the binary entropy function. Hence the number of Grover iterations in this last step is: $2^{\frac{1}{2}(1-u)n(1-\mathrm{H}_e(c_w/(1-u))))}$ where $\mathrm{H}_e(x) = 0$ if $x \ge 1$. It suffices to look for $0 \le u \le 1$ which optimizes the sum of the time complexities of the two steps:

$$2^{\frac{\alpha_k}{(1-2\alpha_k)}un} + 2^{\frac{1}{2}(1-u)n(1-\mathrm{H}_e(c_w/(1-u))))}.$$

We obtain the results of Table 2 by numerical optimization.

8 Conclusion

Better Quantum k-xor Algorithms. In this paper, we proposed new algorithms improving the complexities from [20] for most values of k in both the QACM and low-qubits settings. We gave quantum algorithms for the k-xor problem with limited input size. This enabled us to gave algorithms for k-encryption running exponentially faster than double-encryption and to reach the best quantum time – memory product known for solving the subset-sum problem. All our algorithms can be used by replacing xors by sums modulo 2^n.

Table 2. Quantum speedup of the approximate k-list problem of [10], in the QACM model.

c_w	$\log T/n$ (classical)	$\log T/n$ (quantum)	c_w	$\log T/n$ (classical)	$\log T/n$ (quantum)	c_w	$\log T/n$ (classical)	$\log T/n$ (quantum)
	$k = 2$			$k = 3$			$k = 4$	
0	0.5000	0.3333	0	0.5000	0.2857	0	0.3333	0.2500
0.1	0.2920	0.1876	0.1	0.2769	0.1641	0.1	0.2040	0.1460
0.2	0.1692	0.1046	0.2	0.1590	0.0935	0.2	0.1238	0.0846
0.3	0.0814	0.0481	0.3	0.0778	0.0440	0.3	0.0630	0.0407
0.4	0.0232	0.0129	0.4	0.0221	0.0122	0.4	0.0195	0.0116
	$k = 8$			$k = 32$			$k = 1024$	
0	0.2500	0.2000	0	0.1667	0.1429	0	0.1667	0.1429
0.1	0.1576	0.1200	0.1	0.1091	0.0889	0.1	0.1091	0.0889
0.2	0.0984	0.0714	0.2	0.0704	0.0548	0.2	0.0704	0.0548
0.3	0.0518	0.0355	0.3	0.0387	0.0284	0.3	0.0387	0.0284
0.4	0.0170	0.0106	0.4	0.0914	0.0091	0.4	0.0914	0.0091

Optimal Strategies from MILP. We defined the framework of *merging trees*, which allows to write strategies for solving k-list problems (classically and quantumly) in an abstract and systematic way. Our optimization results were obtained using Mixed Integer Linear Programming. We used this experimental evidence to move on to actual proofs and systematic descriptions of our optimums.

Future Work. The merging trees we defined might be extended with more advanced techniques, inspired by the classical literature on k-list problems. We tried some of these techniques and could not find a quantum advantage so far. There are also many cryptographic applications for quantum k-list algorithms (*e.g.* lattice algorithms or decoding random linear codes [11]) that we did not cover yet.

Open Questions. We have proven some optimality results *among all merging trees*, which is a set of strategies that we carefully defined, but we do not know whether an extended framework could be suitable to improve the quantum algorithms. In particular, the time complexity of our merging tree algorithms for r-encryption encounters a limit $2^{0.3n}$. Whether an extended framework could allow to break this bound remains unknown to us. It would also be interesting to obtain better algorithms for Problem 4 (unique k-xor) without QAQM, or even in the low-qubits model.

Acknowledgments. The authors would like to thank Xavier Bonnetain, André Chailloux, Lorenzo Grassi, Marc Kaplan and Yu Sasaki for helpful discussions and comments. This project has received funding from the European Research Council (ERC) under the European Union's Horizon 2020 research and innovation programme (grant agreement no. 714294 - acronym QUASYModo).

References

1. Aaronson, S., Shi, Y.: Quantum lower bounds for the collision and the element distinctness problems. J. ACM **51**(4), 595–605 (2004)
2. Ambainis, A.: Quantum walk algorithm for element distinctness. SIAM J. Comput. **37**(1), 210–239 (2007)
3. Bai, S., Galbraith, S.D., Li, L., Sheffield, D.: Improved combinatorial algorithms for the inhomogeneous short integer solution problem. J. Cryptol. **32**(1), 35–83 (2019). https://doi.org/10.1007/s00145-018-9304-1
4. Becker, A., Coron, J., Joux, A.: Improved generic algorithms for hard knapsacks. In: Paterson, K.G. (ed.) EUROCRYPT 2011. LNCS, vol. 6632, pp. 364–385. Springer, Heidelberg (2011). https://doi.org/10.1007/978-3-642-20465-4_21
5. Belovs, A., Spalek, R.: Adversary lower bound for the k-sum problem. In: Innovations in Theoretical Computer Science, ITCS 2013, pp. 323–328. ACM (2013)
6. Bennett, C.H., Bernstein, E., Brassard, G., Vazirani, U.V.: Strengths and weaknesses of quantum computing. SIAM J. Comput. **26**(5), 1510–1523 (1997). https://doi.org/10.1137/S0097539796300933
7. Bernstein, D.J., Jeffery, S., Lange, T., Meurer, A.: Quantum algorithms for the subset-sum problem. In: Gaborit, P. (ed.) PQCrypto 2013. LNCS, vol. 7932, pp. 16–33. Springer, Heidelberg (2013). https://doi.org/10.1007/978-3-642-38616-9_2
8. Bernstein, D.J., Lange, T., Niederhagen, R., Peters, C., Schwabe, P.: FSBday. In: Roy, B., Sendrier, N. (eds.) INDOCRYPT 2009. LNCS, vol. 5922, pp. 18–38. Springer, Heidelberg (2009). https://doi.org/10.1007/978-3-642-10628-6_2
9. Blum, A., Kalai, A., Wasserman, H.: Noise-tolerant learning, the parity problem, and the statistical query model. J. ACM **50**(4), 506–519 (2003)
10. Both, L., May, A.: The approximate k-list problem. IACR Trans. Symmetric Cryptol. **2017**(1), 380–397 (2017). https://doi.org/10.13154/tosc.v2017.i1.380-397
11. Both, L., May, A.: Decoding linear codes with high error rate and its impact for LPN security. In: Lange, T., Steinwandt, R. (eds.) PQCrypto 2018. LNCS, vol. 10786, pp. 25–46. Springer, Cham (2018). https://doi.org/10.1007/978-3-319-79063-3_2
12. Brassard, G., Hoyer, P., Mosca, M., Tapp, A.: Quantum amplitude amplification and estimation. Contemp. Math. **305**, 53–74 (2002)
13. Brassard, G., Høyer, P., Tapp, A.: Quantum cryptanalysis of hash and claw-free functions. In: Lucchesi, C.L., Moura, A.V. (eds.) LATIN 1998. LNCS, vol. 1380, pp. 163–169. Springer, Heidelberg (1998). https://doi.org/10.1007/BFb0054319
14. Brassard, G., Høyer, P., Tapp, A.: Quantum algorithm for the collision problem. In: Encyclopedia of Algorithms, pp. 1662–1664 (2016)
15. Camion, P., Patarin, J.: The knapsack hash function proposed at Crypto'89 can be broken. In: Davies, D.W. (ed.) EUROCRYPT 1991. LNCS, vol. 547, pp. 39–53. Springer, Heidelberg (1991). https://doi.org/10.1007/3-540-46416-6_3

16. Chailloux, A., Naya-Plasencia, M., Schrottenloher, A.: An efficient quantum collision search algorithm and implications on symmetric cryptography. In: Takagi, T., Peyrin, T. (eds.) ASIACRYPT 2017. LNCS, vol. 10625, pp. 211–240. Springer, Cham (2017). https://doi.org/10.1007/978-3-319-70697-9_8
17. Dinur, I.: An algorithmic framework for the generalized birthday problem. Cryptology ePrint Archive, Report 2018/575 (2018). https://eprint.iacr.org/2018/575
18. Dinur, I., Dunkelman, O., Keller, N., Shamir, A.: Efficient dissection of composite problems, with applications to cryptanalysis, knapsacks, and combinatorial search problems. In: Safavi-Naini, R., Canetti, R. (eds.) CRYPTO 2012. LNCS, vol. 7417, pp. 719–740. Springer, Heidelberg (2012). https://doi.org/10.1007/978-3-642-32009-5_42
19. Esser, A., Heuer, F., Kübler, R., May, A., Sohler, C.: Dissection-BKW. In: Shacham, H., Boldyreva, A. (eds.) CRYPTO 2018. LNCS, vol. 10992, pp. 638–666. Springer, Cham (2018). https://doi.org/10.1007/978-3-319-96881-0_22
20. Grassi, L., Naya-Plasencia, M., Schrottenloher, A.: Quantum algorithms for the k-xor problem. In: Peyrin, T., Galbraith, S. (eds.) ASIACRYPT 2018. LNCS, vol. 11272, pp. 527–559. Springer, Cham (2018). https://doi.org/10.1007/978-3-030-03326-2_18
21. Grover, L.K.: A fast quantum mechanical algorithm for database search. In: Proceedings of the Twenty-Eighth Annual ACM Symposium on the Theory of Computing 1996, pp. 212–219. ACM (1996). http://doi.acm.org/10.1145/237814.237866
22. Helm, A., May, A.: Subset sum quantumly in 1.17^n. In: TQC. LIPIcs, vol. 111, pp. 5:1–5:15. Schloss Dagstuhl - Leibniz-Zentrum fuer Informatik (2018)
23. Hosoyamada, A., Sasaki, Y., Xagawa, K.: Quantum multicollision-finding algorithm. In: Takagi, T., Peyrin, T. (eds.) ASIACRYPT 2017. LNCS, vol. 10625, pp. 179–210. Springer, Cham (2017). https://doi.org/10.1007/978-3-319-70697-9_7
24. Kaplan, M.: Quantum attacks against iterated block ciphers. CoRR abs/1410.1434 (2014). http://arxiv.org/abs/1410.1434
25. Kuperberg, G.: Another subexponential-time quantum algorithm for the dihedral hidden subgroup problem. In: TQC. LIPIcs, vol. 22, pp. 20–34. Schloss Dagstuhl - Leibniz-Zentrum fuer Informatik (2013)
26. Magniez, F., Nayak, A., Roland, J., Santha, M.: Search via quantum walk. SIAM J. Comput. **40**(1), 142–164 (2011)
27. Minder, L., Sinclair, A.: The extended k-tree algorithm. J. Cryptol. **25**(2), 349–382 (2012)
28. Naya-Plasencia, M., Schrottenloher, A.: Optimal merging in quantum k-xor and k-sum algorithms. IACR Cryptology ePrint Archive 2019, 501 (2019)
29. Nielsen, M.A., Chuang, I.: Quantum computation and quantum information (2002)
30. Nikolić, I., Sasaki, Y.: Refinements of the k-tree algorithm for the generalized birthday problem. In: Iwata, T., Cheon, J.H. (eds.) ASIACRYPT 2015. LNCS, vol. 9453, pp. 683–703. Springer, Heidelberg (2015). https://doi.org/10.1007/978-3-662-48800-3_28
31. Schroeppel, R., Shamir, A.: A $T = O(2^{n/2})$, $S = O(2^{n/4})$ algorithm for certain NP-complete problems. SIAM J. Comput. **10**(3), 456–464 (1981)
32. Wagner, D.: A generalized birthday problem. In: Yung, M. (ed.) CRYPTO 2002. LNCS, vol. 2442, pp. 288–304. Springer, Heidelberg (2002). https://doi.org/10.1007/3-540-45708-9_19
33. Zhandry, M.: A note on the quantum collision and set equality problems. Quantum Inf. Comput. 15(7–8), 557–567 (2015). http://dl.acm.org/citation.cfm?id=2871411.2871413

On the Quantum Complexity of the Continuous Hidden Subgroup Problem

Koen de Boer[1](✉), Léo Ducas[1], and Serge Fehr[1,2](✉)

[1] Cryptology Group, Centrum Wiskunde & Informatica (CWI),
Amsterdam, The Netherlands
{K.de.Boer,serge.fehr}@cwi.nl
[2] Mathematical Institute, Leiden University, Leiden, The Netherlands

Abstract. The Hidden Subgroup Problem (HSP) aims at capturing all problems that are susceptible to be solvable in quantum polynomial time following the blueprints of Shor's celebrated algorithm. Successful solutions to this problems over various commutative groups allow to efficiently perform number-theoretic tasks such as factoring or finding discrete logarithms.

The latest successful generalization (Eisenträger et al. STOC 2014) considers the problem of finding a full-rank lattice as the hidden subgroup of the continuous vector space $\mathbb{R}^m$, even for large dimensions m. It unlocked new cryptanalytic algorithms (Biasse-Song SODA 2016, Cramer et al. EUROCRYPT 2016 and 2017), in particular to find mildly short vectors in ideal lattices.

The cryptanalytic relevance of such a problem raises the question of a more refined and quantitative complexity analysis. In the light of the increasing physical difficulty of maintaining a large entanglement of qubits, the degree of concern may be different whether the above algorithm requires only linearly many qubits or a much larger polynomial amount of qubits.

This is the question we start addressing with this work. We propose a detailed analysis of (a variation of) the aforementioned HSP algorithm, and conclude on its complexity as a function of all the relevant parameters. Our modular analysis is tailored to support the optimization of future specialization to cases of cryptanalytic interests. We suggest a few ideas in this direction.

Keywords: Quantum algorithm · Hidden subgroup · Period finding · Fourier transform · Cryptanalysis

1 Introduction

The Hidden Subgroup Problem. Among all quantum algorithms, Shor's algorithm [32] for factoring and finding discrete logarithms stands out as

All three authors were supported by the European Union H2020 Research and Innovation Program Grant 780701 (PROMETHEUS). Additionally, K.d.B. was supported by the ERC Advanced Grant 740972 (ALGSTRONGCRYPTO) and L.D. was supported by the Veni Innovational Research Grant from NWO under project number 639.021.645.

© International Association for Cryptologic Research 2020
A. Canteaut and Y. Ishai (Eds.): EUROCRYPT 2020, LNCS 12106, pp. 341–370, 2020.
https://doi.org/10.1007/978-3-030-45724-2_12

demonstrating the largest complexity gap between classical and quantum computing. It is also singular by its cryptanalytic implications, and, due to progress toward the realization of large quantum computers, this celebrated algorithm is now motivating the standardization of quantum-resistant schemes [23], in preparation of a global update of widely deployed encryption and authentication protocols.

The core idea of quantum period finding from [32] is not limited to factoring and discrete logarithm, and the Hidden Subgroup Problem formalized in [22] serves as a convenient interface between the quantum-algorithmic techniques for period finding, and applications to solve other computational problems, in particular problems arising from number theory. We will here discuss only the case of commutative groups. The cases of non-abelian groups such as dihedral groups are very interesting as well and have fascinating connections with lattice problems [29]; however, no polynomial time algorithm is known for those cases, and the best known algorithm has sub-exponential complexity [19], using very different techniques.

The simplest version of the Hidden Subgroup Problem consists of finding a hidden subgroup H in a *finite* abelian group G, when given access to a strictly H-periodic function $f : G \to R$. Here, in the language of representation theory, the off-the-shelf period-finding quantum algorithm finds a uniformly random character $\chi \in \hat{G}$ that acts trivially on H. Shor's original algorithm [32] for integer factoring finds a hidden subgroup H in the ambient group $\mathbb{Z}$. The infiniteness of $\mathbb{Z}$ induces some "cut-off" error; nevertheless, the distribution of the algorithm's output is still concentrated around the multiples of the inverse period.

A generalization to the real line $H = \mathbb{R}$ was given by Hallgren [16] and allows to solve Pell's equation. The case of real vector space of constant dimension $H = \mathbb{R}^c$ has also been studied in [15,31], and permits the computation of unit groups of number fields of finite degree.

The *Continuous* Hidden Subgroup Problem in Large Dimension. The latest generalization of the HSP algorithm, given by Eisenträger, Hallgren, Kitaev and Song in an extended abstract [11], targets the ambient group $G = \mathbb{R}^m$ (for a non-constant dimension m) with a hidden discrete subgroup $H = \Lambda$, i.e. a *lattice*. Next to the ambient group $\mathbb{R}^m$ being *continuous*, an additional special feature is that the Λ-periodic function f is assumed to produce a "quantum output". More formally, $f : \mathbb{R}^m \to \mathcal{S}$, $x \mapsto |f(x)\rangle$, where $\mathcal{S}$ is the state space of a quantum system, and the HSP algorithm is given access to a unitary that maps $|x\rangle|0\rangle$ to $|x\rangle|f(x)\rangle$. A crucial observation here is that $|f(x)\rangle$ and $|f(y)\rangle$ are *not* necessarily orthogonal (or even distinct) for distinct x and y modulo Λ. In other words, it is not assumed that f is *strictly* periodic, but merely that $|f(x)\rangle$ and $|f(y)\rangle$ are "somewhat orthogonal" for x and y that are "not too close" modulo Λ, and that f is Lipschitz continuous.

More specifically they consider a variation of the standard HSP algorithm in order to tackle the Continuous Hidden Subgroup Problem (CHSP). In order to deal with the continuous nature of the domain $\mathbb{R}^m$ of f, the given HSP algorithm acts on a bounded "grid" of points within $\mathbb{R}^m$. Additionally, the algorithm is modified in the following ways: (1) The initial state is not a uniform super-position (over the considered grid points in $\mathbb{R}^n$) but follows a trigonometric distribution, and (2) the quantum Fourier transform is done "remotely", i.e., rather than applying it to the actual register, the register is entangled with an ancilla and the quantum Fourier transform is then applied to the ancilla instead. According to [11], applying the quantum Fourier transform directly would make the resulting approximation errors difficult to analyze.

As an application, the work of [11] also gave a quantum polynomial time algorithm for computing the unit group of a number field in their article [11]. This was generalized by Biasse and Song [2] to the computation of S-unit groups, and therefore to the computation of class groups and to finding a generator of a principal ideals. This led to solving the short vector problem in certain ideal lattices for non-trivial approximation factors [7,8,27]. While the cryptanalytic consequences for ideal-lattice based cryptography seems limited so far [10], these results demonstrate a hardness gap between ideal lattices and general ones.

The algorithm of [11] has proved itself to be a key tool in quantum crypt-analysis, and, as such, the question of its precise range of application, and of its practical efficiency are therefore of cryptographic interest. Unfortunately, [11] offers only an informal treatment of the algorithm, both in terms of the analysis and in terms of the formulation of the result. Also, at the time of preparing this article, there was no full version publicly available.[1]

The extended abstract [11] explains convincingly that in the limit of choosing an unbounded and infinitely fine grid in $\mathbb{R}^m$ the algorithm does what it is supposed to do; however, the "rate of convergence" and thus the quantitative aspects of their result are not provided. Furthermore, it was not clear to us what "polynomial-time" formally meant when the input is an oracle, specified by various parameters. For example, in an application of the Continuous HSP algorithm it may be critical to know whether the running time grows polynomially in the Lipschitz constant of f (which is one of the 3 parameters of the Continuous HSP), or polynomially in its logarithm.

In an email from September 2018, Fang Song [33] partially answered early questions we had; technically his comments corresponds to a claim on the error term ϵ_{lip} in Part 2 Step 2 of our analysis of the Dual Lattice Sampling step (Sect. 5.2). We found that this claim could be related to Yudin-Jackson Theorem [37]. To make the analysis tighter, we found it preferable to generalize Yudin-Jackson Theorem to multi-dimensional ranges (see Appendix D of the full version [3]).

The urge to understand the security post-quantum cryptography motivates the elevation of the powerful result of [11] into an open and lively research topic.

Our Work. The goal of this paper is to provide a complete, modular, and quantitative analysis of (a slightly modified version of) the Continuous HSP

---

[1] The STOC 2014 submitted version [11] has been made publicly available online on November 2019 (after submissison of this paper) http://www.cse.psu.edu/~sjh26/units-stoc-submission.pdf. A full version is announced to be in preparation.

quantum algorithm given by [11]. More concretely, we provide an explicit bound on the number of qubits needed by the algorithm, clarifying the dependency on the parameters of the Continuous HSP instance and on the required precision and success probability. This shows explicitly in what parameters the algorithm is polynomial time and with what exponent.

The algorithm that we consider and analyze differs from the one considered [11] in the following points:

- First, we specify the initial state of the algorithm to have Gaussian amplitudes, while [11, Sec. 6.2] suggests to use a cropped trigonometric function; as far as we can see, our choice makes the analysis simpler and tighter thanks to the well known tail-cut and smoothness bounds of Banaszczyk [1] and Micciancio and Regev [20].
- Secondly, we do not make use of a "remote" Fourier transform but instead follow the blueprint of Shor's original algorithm in that respect; the claimed advantage of the "remote" Fourier transform is unclear to us.

These modifications simplify the algorithm and its analysis. Due to the lack of details given in [11], we can not state a complexity comparison, but we think this variation is at least as efficient as the original algorithm.

Our analysis is divided into four parts, each summarized by a formal statement given in Sects. 2.3 to 2.6, leading to the main theorem (Sect. 2.2). We insist on this modular presentation, so as to enable future work on optimization and specialization of this algorithm to instances of interests; specific suggestions follow.

In the first part (*Dual Lattice Sampling*), which is the technically more involved one, we show that the appropriately discretized and finitized, but otherwise (almost) standard HSP quantum algorithm produces sample points in $\mathbb{R}^m$ that lie close to the dual lattice Λ^* with high probability. More precisely, and more technically speaking, we show that the algorithm's output is a sample point close to $\ell^* \in \Lambda^*$ with probability close to $\langle c_{\ell^*} | c_{\ell^*} \rangle$, where the vectors $|c_{\ell^*}\rangle$ are the Fourier coefficients of the function f. This is in line with the general HSP approach, where for instance Shor's algorithm for period finding over $\mathbb{Z}$ produces a point that is close to a random multiple of the inverse period, except with bounded probability.

In this first part (Sect. 4 and Sect. 5), we bound the complexity of the core algorithm in terms of the error that we allow in the above context of a sampling algorithm, and depending on the Lipschitz constant of f. In particular, we show that the number of qubits grows as mQ, where Q, the "number of qubits per dimension", grows linearly in the logarithm of the Lipschitz constant of f, the logarithm of the inverse of the error probability and the logarithm of the inverse of the (absolute) precision, and quasi-linearly in m. The running time of the algorithm is then bounded[2] by $O(m^2 Q^2)$.

---

[2] This complexity estimate can be lowered to $O(mQ \log(kmQ))$ if we allow an error in the L_2-distance of $< 1/k^2$ [14], see Remark 1.

In the second part (*Full Dual Recovery*, Sect. 6), we then relate the parameters of the Continuous HSP instance to the number of sample points, and thus to how often the core algorithm needs to be repeated, necessary in order to have an approximation of the entire dual lattice Λ^*.

In the third part (*Primal Basis Reconstruction*, see Appendix B of the full version [3]), we study the numerical stability of reconstructing an approximate basis of the primal lattice Λ from a set of approximate generators of the dual lattice Λ^*. This is based on the Buchmann-Pohst algorithm [4] already mentioned in [11]. The claim of [11] involves intricate quantities related to sublattices of Λ, making the final complexity hard to derive; we provide a simpler statement with a detailed proof.

Finally, in the last part (see Appendix C of the full version [3]), we revisit the quantum poly-time algorithm for *Gaussian State Preparation* [13,18] used as a black-box in our first part, and provide its precise complexity.

These four parts leads to our formal and quantitative version of the informal CHSP Theorem of [11, Theorem 6.1], stated as Theorem 1 in Sect. 2.2.

Conclusion and Research Directions. Our conclusion is that, in its generic form, the Continuous Hidden Subgroup Problem is rather expensive to solve; not accounting for other parameters than the dimension m, it already requires $\tilde{O}(m^3)$ qubits and $\tilde{O}(m^7)$ quantum gates (or, $\tilde{O}(m^4)$ quantum gates if an approximate quantum Fourier transform is used). However, this inefficiency seems to be a consequence of its genericness. In particular, the core algorithm for Dual Lattice Sampling would only need $\tilde{O}(m^2)$ qubits, if it wasn't for accommodating for the terrible numerical stability of the Primal Basis Reconstruction step. Similarly, we expect the number of samples needed to generate the dual lattice to be significantly smaller for smoother oracle functions.

All in all, our modular analysis of the generic steps of the CHSP algorithm sets the stage for analyzing and optimizing its specializations, in particular to cryptanalytic applications [7,8]. We propose as few research directions towards this objective:

- Study the costs (qubits, quantum gates) and the parameters of the oracle functions from [2,11,34] for solving the Unit Group Problem, the Principal Ideal Problem (PIP), and for the computation of the class-group.
- Find stronger hypotheses satisfied by the above oracle functions (or by variant thereof) that improve this generic analysis of the CHSP algorithm; or resort to an ad-hoc analysis of the Full Dual Recovery step by directly studying the spectrum of these oracle functions.
- Explore the possibility of a trade-off between the (classical) Primal Basis Reconstruction step and the (quantum) Dual Lattice Sampling step, possibly up to small sub-exponential classical complexity. More specifically, does replacing LLL by BKZ with an medium block-size substantially improve the numerical stability of Buchmann-Pohst algorithm?
- Exploit prior knowledge of sublattices (potentially close to full-rank) of the hidden lattice to accelerate or skip the Full Dual Recovery and Primal Basis

Reconstruction steps. This is for example the case when solving PIP [2] while already knowing the unit group and the class group of a given number field. This would be applicable in the context of [7,8].

- Exploit known symmetries of the hidden sublattice to improve the Full Dual Recovery and Primal Basis Reconstruction steps. Such symmetries are for example induced by the Galois action on the log-unit lattice and the lattice of class relation, in particular in the case of the cyclotomic number fields. This would again be applicable in the context of [7,8].

2   Problem Statements and Results

2.1   Notation and Set-Up

Here and throughout the paper, $\mathcal{H}$ is a complex Hilbert space of dimension $N = 2^n$, and $\mathcal{S}$ is the unit sphere in $\mathcal{H}$; thus, a vector in $\mathcal{S}$ describes the state of a system of n qubits. For an arbitrary positive integer m, we consider a function

$$\boldsymbol{f} : \mathbb{R}^m \to \mathcal{S} \subset \mathcal{H}, \; x \mapsto |\boldsymbol{f}(x)\rangle$$

that is periodic with respect to a full rank lattice $\Lambda \subset \mathbb{R}^m$; hence, $\boldsymbol{f}$ may be understood as a function $\mathbb{R}^m/\Lambda \to \mathcal{S}$. The function $\boldsymbol{f}$ is assumed to be Lipschitz continuous with Lipschitz constant

$$\mathrm{Lip}(\boldsymbol{f}) = \inf\{L > 0 \mid \; \||\boldsymbol{f}(x)\rangle - |\boldsymbol{f}(y)\rangle\|_{\mathcal{H}} \le L\,\|x - y\|_{2,\mathbb{T}^m}\}.$$

Later, we will also require $\boldsymbol{f}$ to be "sufficiently non-constant". One should think of $\boldsymbol{f}$ as an oracle that maps a classical input x to a quantum state over n qubits, which is denoted $|\boldsymbol{f}(x)\rangle$.

We write Λ^* for the dual lattice of Λ. By $\lambda_1(\Lambda)$ we denote the length of a shortest non-zero vector of Λ, and correspondingly for $\lambda_1(\Lambda^*)$. Since Λ is typically clear from the context, we may just write λ_1 and λ_1^* instead of $\lambda_1(\Lambda)$ and $\lambda_1(\Lambda^*)$.

We denote by $\mathcal{B}_r(x) = \{y \in \mathbb{R}^m \mid \|y - x\| < r\}$ the open Euclidean ball with radius r around x, and by $B_r(x) = \mathcal{B}_r(x) \cap \mathbb{Z}^m$ its integer analogue. For the open ball around 0 we just denote $\mathcal{B}_r$, and for a set $X \subset \mathbb{R}^m$ we write $\mathcal{B}_r(X) = \bigcup_x \mathcal{B}_r(x)$ and $B_r(X) = \bigcup_x B_r(x)$ where the union is over all $x \in X$.

Definition 1 (Definition 1.1 from [11]). *A function $\boldsymbol{f} : \mathbb{R}^m \to \mathcal{S} \subset \mathcal{H}$ is said to be an (a, r, ϵ)-HSP oracle of the full-rank lattice $\Lambda \subset \mathbb{R}^m$ if*

- *$\boldsymbol{f}$ is Λ-periodic,*
- *$\boldsymbol{f}$ is a-Lipschitz: $\mathrm{Lip}(f) \le a$,*
- *For all $x, y \in \mathbb{R}^m$ such that $d_{\mathbb{R}^m/\Lambda}(x, y) \ge r$, it holds that $|\langle \boldsymbol{f}(x)|\boldsymbol{f}(y)\rangle| \le \epsilon$,*

where $d_{\mathbb{R}^m/\Lambda}(x, y) = \min_{v \in \Lambda} \|x - y - v\|$ denotes the distance induced by the Euclidean distance of $\mathbb{R}^n$ modulo Λ.

2.2   Main Theorem: Continuous Hidden Subgroup Problem

Theorem 1. *There exists a quantum algorithm that, given access to an (a, r, ϵ)-HSP oracle with period lattice Λ, $r < \lambda_1(\Lambda)/6$ and $\epsilon < 1/4$, computes, with constant success probability, an approximate basis $\tilde{B} = B + \Delta_B$ of this lattice Λ, satisfying $\|\Delta_B\| < \tau$.*

This algorithm makes k quantum oracle calls to the (a, r, ϵ)-HSP oracle, and uses $mQ+n$ qubits, $O(km^2Q^2)$ quantum gates and $poly(m, \log \frac{a}{\lambda_1^*}, \log \frac{a}{\tau})$ classical bit operations, where

$$Q = O(mk) + O\left(\log \frac{a}{\lambda_1^*}\right) + O\left(\log \frac{1}{\lambda_1^* \cdot \tau}\right), \tag{1}$$

$$k = O\left(m \cdot \log\left(\sqrt{m} \cdot a \cdot (\det \Lambda)^{1/m}\right)\right) \tag{2}$$

Remark 1. The quantum gate complexity in this theorem can be lowered to $O(kmQ \log(kmQ))$ if we *approximate* the quantum Fourier transform [14] over $\mathbb{Z}/q^m\mathbb{Z}$. For example, an approximation that is $1/k^2$-close in the induced matrix norm – which is sufficient for our purposes – can be computed using $O(mQ \log(kmQ))$ quantum gates (where $Q = \log q$). Repeating this approximate Fourier transform k times, one arrives at the complexity $O(kmQ \log(kmQ))$.

Remark 2. Note that the quantities inside logarithms are homogeneous. In particular, scaling the lattice Λ by a factor f, also scales τ, $1/a$ and $1/\lambda_1^*$ by the same factor f, leaving the complexity parameters Q and k unaffected.

Remark 3. The expert reader may expect the "distortion" parameter $\lambda_1 \cdot \lambda_1^*$ of the lattice Λ to have a bearing on the complexity of this algorithm. It is indeed implicitly the case: the assumption the HSP definition implies that $ar \geq 1 - \epsilon^2$, and therefore the theorem's hypothesis requires $a \geq \frac{45}{8\lambda_1}$.

Proof. This is obtained by instantiating Theorems 2 to 5. First, we obtain k samples close to the dual lattice by invoking k times Algorithm 1, whose correctness and complexity is given in Theorem 2. Samples whose Euclidean length exceed a certain threshold R are rejected. The approximate samples are collected into a matrix $\tilde{G}$.

The above step requires to prepare Gaussian states with parameter s over a grid of granularity q; this is obtained by k calls to Algorithm 1, whose cost and correctness is stated in Theorem 5. The cost of this subroutine is dominated by the cost of Algorithm 1.

According to Theorem 3, the approximated dual samples generate the dual lattice Λ^* with constant probability. Finally, one applies the Buchmann-Pohst algorithm [4,5] and matrix inversion to $\tilde{G}$, in order to recover an approximate basis of the primal lattice Λ. The loss of precision induced by this computation is given in Theorem 4. The parameters are instantiated as follows:

- the failure probability η of dual lattice sampling is set to $\eta = 1/k^2$,
- the parameter α driving the success of dual reconstruction is set to $\alpha = 1$,

- the relative error on dual lattice sample is set to

$$\delta = \frac{(\lambda_1^*)^2 \cdot \det(\Lambda^*)}{2^{O(mk)} \cdot \|\tilde{G}\|_\infty^{m+1}} \cdot \tau,$$

- the maximal entry size of the dual samples is $\|\tilde{G}\|_\infty \leq R$ where $R = \sqrt{m} \cdot a$,
- the discretization granularity is set to $q = 2^Q$,
- the Gaussian windowing parameter s is set to $s = O(\sqrt{m \log(\eta^{-1})})$.

We defer the detailed bookkeeping for deriving the parameters Q and k to Appendix A of the full version [3].   □

2.3 Dual Lattice Sampling Problem

Following our modular approach as outlined in the introduction, we first consider the following *Dual Lattice Sampling Problem* instead. Informally, the task is to sample points in $\mathbb{R}^m$ that are respectively close to points $\ell^* \in \Lambda^*$ that follow the distribution $\mathcal{D}_{ideal}(\ell^*) = \langle c_{\ell^*}|c_{\ell^*}\rangle$, where $|c_{\ell^*}\rangle$ are the vectorial Fourier coefficients of $\boldsymbol{f} : \mathbb{R}^m/\Lambda \to \mathcal{S}$ (see Sect. 3).

Problem 1 (Dual Lattice Sampling Problem). Given error parameter $\eta > 0$ and a relative distance parameter $\frac{1}{2} > \delta > 0$, and given oracle access to an HSP oracle $\boldsymbol{f}$ as above, sample according to a (finite) distribution $\mathcal{D}$ on $\mathbb{R}^m$ that satisfies, for any $S \subseteq \Lambda^*$,

$$p_S := \mathcal{D}\big(\mathcal{B}_{\delta\lambda_1^*}(S)\big) \geq \left(\sum_{\ell^* \in S} \langle c_{\ell^*}|c_{\ell^*}\rangle\right) - \eta. \tag{3}$$

In the problem statement above, $\mathcal{D}\big(\mathcal{B}_{\delta\lambda_1^*}(S)\big)$ denotes the cumulative weight of the set $\mathcal{B}_{\delta\lambda_1^*}(S)$ with respect to the distribution $\mathcal{D}$.

Theorem 2. *Algorithm 1 solves the Dual Lattice Sampling Problem with parameters η and δ; it uses m calls to the Gaussian superposition subroutine (see Theorem 5), one quantum oracle call to $\boldsymbol{f}$, $mQ + n$ qubits, and $O(m^2Q^2)$ quantum gates, where*

$$Q = O\left(m \log\left(m \log\frac{1}{\eta}\right)\right) + O\left(\log\left(\frac{\mathrm{Lip}(\boldsymbol{f})}{\eta \cdot \delta\lambda_1^*}\right)\right). \tag{4}$$

Remark 4. Note that this step only requires smoothness of the HSP oracle (via the Lipchitz constant), but does not rely on the "separability" assumption (third item of Definition 1). Indeed this third assumption will only play a role to ensure that those samples are actually non-trivial and usable.

2.4   Full Dual Lattice Recovery

Recovering the full lattice (or equivalently its dual) requires an extra assumption on the oracle function f, as captured by the third condition in the following definition, reformatted from Definition 1.1 of [11].

According to Eisenträger et al. [11], for (some undetermined) adequate parameters, Definition 1 ensures that the distribution on the dual lattice Λ^* is not concentrated on any proper sublattice, hence sufficiently many samples will generate the lattice fully. We formalize and quantify this proof strategy, and obtain the following quantitative conclusion. We note that the constraints on r and ϵ are milder that one could think, for example ϵ does not need to tend to 0 as a function of n or m.

Theorem 3. *Let $f : \mathbb{R}^m \to S$ be an (a, r, ϵ)-HSP oracle with $r \leq \lambda_1(\Lambda)/6$ and $\epsilon \in [0, 1/3)$, and let $\mathcal{D}_{\text{ideal}}$ be the distribution described above, given by $\mathcal{D}_{\text{ideal}}(\ell^*) = \langle c_{\ell^*} | c_{\ell^*} \rangle$ for $\ell^* \in \Lambda^*$. Furthermore, denote by S the random variable defined by the number of samples that need to be drawn from $\mathcal{D}_{\text{ideal}}$ such that the samples together generate Λ^* as a lattice. Then, for any $\alpha > 0$,*

$$\Pr\left[S > (2 + \alpha)\frac{t + m}{\frac{1}{2} - \frac{1}{4\pi^2} - \epsilon} \right] \leq \exp(-\alpha(t + m)/2)$$

where $t = m \log_2(\sqrt{m} \cdot a) + \log_2(\det(\Lambda))$.

The above Theorem is obtained by combining Lemmata 5 and 8 from Sect. 6, instantiating the parameter R to $R^2 = ma^2$. This choice is somewhat arbitrary and given for concreteness, however it does not have a critical quantitative impact.

2.5   Primal Basis Reconstruction

Theorem 4. *There exists a polynomial time algorithm, that, for any matrix $G \in \mathbb{R}^{k \times m}$ of k generators of a (dual) lattice Λ^*, and given an approximation $\tilde{G} = G + \Delta_G \in \mathbb{Q}^{k \times n}$, computes an approximation $\tilde{B} = B + \Delta_B$ of a basis B of the primal lattice Λ, such that*

$$\|\Delta_B\|_\infty \leq \frac{2^{O(mk)} \cdot \|\tilde{G}\|_\infty^{m+1}}{(\lambda_1^*)^3 \cdot \det(\Lambda^*)} \cdot \|\Delta_G\|_\infty,$$

under the assumption that $\|\Delta_G\|_\infty < \frac{\min(1, (\lambda_1^*)^2) \cdot \det(\Lambda^*)}{2^{O(km)} \cdot \|\tilde{G}\|_\infty^{m+1}}$.

Remark 5. More specifically, the algorithm from Theorem 4 essentially consists of the Buchmann-Pohst algorithm [4,5] and a matrix inversion. Its complexity is dominated by two calls to LLL on matrices of dimension $(m + k) \times k$ and entry bitsize $O(k^2 \log(\|\tilde{G}\|/\lambda_1^*))$ (see the discussion before [4, Cor. 4.1]). One can optimize the final running time by choosing the adequate variant of LLL [24,26] depending on the relative dimension and bitsizes of these inputs.

Our contribution on this step is merely a completed numerical analysis, with the help of a theorem from [6]. A claim with a similar purpose is given in [11], yet involves more intricate lattice quantities.

2.6   Gaussian State Preparation

The main algorithm of this paper requires the preparation of a multidimensional Gaussian initial state, which can be obtained by generating the one-dimensional Gaussian state on m parallel quantum registers. This task is known to be polynomial time [13,18], and we provide a quantitative analysis in Appendix C of the full version [3]. The precise running time of preparing this Gaussian state is summarized below.

Theorem 5. *For any positive integers q, p and for any $s > 1$, there exists a quantum algorithm that prepares the one-dimensional Gaussian state*

$$\frac{1}{\sqrt{\rho_{1/s}(\frac{1}{q}[q]_c)}} \sum_{x \in \frac{1}{q}[q]_c} \sqrt{\rho_{1/s}(x)}|x\rangle \tag{5}$$

up to trace distance $se^{-\pi s^2/8} + Q \cdot 2^{-p}$ using $O(Q + p)$ qubits and $O(Q \cdot p^{3/2} \cdot \text{polylog}(p))$ quantum gates, where $Q = \log(q)$ and $\frac{1}{q}[q]_c = [-\frac{1}{2}, \frac{1}{2}) \cap \frac{1}{q}\mathbb{Z}$.

The above theorem is obtained by instantiating Theorem 12 in Appendix C of the full version [3] with parameters $\mu = q/2$, $k = p$ and $\sigma = \sqrt{2}q/s$ and relabeling the basis states. Whenever above theorem is used as a subroutine in Theorem 2, choosing $p = \log(mQ/\eta^2)$ is sufficient, causing merely an extra error of η^2.

Remark 6. In Theorem 1, we chose η to be $1/k^2$, yielding $p = \log(mk^4Q)$. Therefore, one call to the one-dimensional Gaussian state preperation with the parameters of Theorem 1 takes $O(Q)$ qubits and $O(Q \log(kmQ))$ quantum gates. As Theorem 1 requires k subsequent preparations of the m-dimensional Gaussian state, the total costs of the Gaussian state preparation steps are $O(mQ)$ qubits and $\tilde{O}(kmQ)$ quantum gates. As this is negligible to the overall complexity of Theorem 1, we can ignore these costs.

3   Preliminaries

We start with a brief introduction to Fourier analysis over arbitrary locally compact Abelian groups. Our general treatment allows us to then apply the general principles to the different groups that play a role in this work. For the reader that is unfamiliar with such a general treatment, it is useful—and almost sufficient—to think of $\mathbb{R}$, of $\mathbb{T} = \mathbb{R}/\mathbb{Z}$, and a finite group. For more details and for the proofs we refer to [9].

3.1   Groups

Here and below we consider a *locally compact Abelian* group G. Such a group admits a *Haar measure* μ that is unique up to a normalization factor. The crucial property of such a Haar measure is that it is invariant under the group action.

Simple examples are $G = \mathbb{R}$ with μ the Lebesgue measure λ, or a finite group G with μ the counting measure $\#$.

The *dual group* $\hat{G}$, consisting of the continuous group homomorphisms χ from G into the multiplicative group of complex numbers of absolute value 1, is again a locally compact Abelian group. As we shall see soon, for a fixed choice of the normalization factor of the Haar measure μ for G, there is a natural choice for the normalization factor of the Haar measure $\hat{\mu}$ for $\hat{G}$.

Examples of locally compact Abelian groups that play an important role in this work are: the m-dimensional real vector space $\mathbb{R}^m$; the m-fold torus $\mathbb{T}^m := \mathbb{R}^m/\mathbb{Z}^m$ and more generally $\mathbb{R}^m/\Lambda$ for an arbitrary lattice Λ in $\mathbb{R}^m$; and the finite group $\mathbb{D}^m := \frac{1}{q}\mathbb{Z}^m/\mathbb{Z}^m \subset \mathbb{T}^m$ (which is isomorphic to $\mathbb{Z}^m/q\mathbb{Z}^m$) for a positive integer q. Figure 1 below shows the corresponding dual groups as well as the respective (dual) Haar measures as used in this paper.

G	μ	$\hat{G}$	$\hat{\mu}$
$\mathbb{R}^m$	λ	$\hat{\mathbb{R}}^m \simeq \mathbb{R}^m$	λ
$\mathbb{T}^m := \mathbb{R}^m/\mathbb{Z}^m$	λ	$\hat{\mathbb{T}}^m \simeq \mathbb{Z}^m$	$\#$
$\mathbb{D}^m := \frac{1}{q}\mathbb{Z}^m/\mathbb{Z}^m$	$\frac{1}{q^m}\#$	$\hat{\mathbb{D}}^m \simeq \mathbb{Z}^m/q\mathbb{Z}^m$	$\#$
$\mathbb{R}^m/\Lambda$	$\frac{1}{\det(\Lambda)}\lambda$	$(\widehat{\mathbb{R}^m/\Lambda}) \simeq \Lambda^*$	$\#$

Fig. 1. Some groups G and their respective dual groups $\hat{G}$, plus the considered (dual) Haar measures μ and $\hat{\mu}$. Here, λ denotes the Lebesgue and $\#$ the counting measure.

In some cases it will be useful to identify the quotient groups $\mathbb{T}^m = \mathbb{R}^m/\mathbb{Z}^m$ and $\mathbb{D}^m = \frac{1}{q}\mathbb{Z}^m/\mathbb{Z}^m$ with the respective representing sets

$$\mathbb{T}^m_{\text{rep}} := [-\tfrac{1}{2}, \tfrac{1}{2})^m \subset \mathbb{R}^m \quad \text{and} \quad \mathbb{D}^m_{\text{rep}} := \tfrac{1}{q}\mathbb{Z}^m \cap \mathbb{T}^m_{\text{rep}},$$

and similarly $\hat{\mathbb{D}}^m \simeq \mathbb{Z}^m/q\mathbb{Z}^m$ with

$$\hat{\mathbb{D}}^m_{\text{rep}} := [q]^m_c := \mathbb{Z}^m \cap [-\tfrac{q}{2}, \tfrac{q}{2})^m.$$

It will be useful to understand that if $H \subset G$ is a closed subgroup then G/H and H have dual groups that satisfy the following natural isomorphisms.

$$\widehat{G/H} \simeq H^\perp := \{\chi \in \hat{G} \mid \chi(h) = 1 \,\forall\, h \in H\} \subset \hat{G} \quad \text{and} \quad \hat{H} \simeq \hat{G}/H^\perp.$$

As we shall see soon, for any choice of the Haar measure μ_H for H there is a natural choice for the Haar measure $\mu_{G/H}$ for G/H, and vice versa.

3.2 Norms and Fourier Transforms

Let G be as above with a fixed choice for the Haar measure μ. For any $p \in [1, \infty]$, $L_p(G)$ denotes the vector space of measurable functions $f : G \to \mathbb{C}$ with finite norm $\|f\|_p$ (modulo the functions with vanishing norm), where

$$\|f\|_p^p := \int_{g \in G} |f(g)|^p d\mu \quad \text{for } p < \infty,$$

and

$$\|f\|_\infty := \operatorname*{ess\,sup}_{g \in G} |f(g)|,$$

the essential supremum of $|f|$. We write $\|f\|_{p,G}$ if we want to make G explicit. For any function $f \in L^1(G)$, the *Fourier transform* of f is the function

$$\mathcal{F}_G\{f\} : \hat{G} \to \mathbb{C}, \ \chi \mapsto \int_{g \in G} f(g)\bar{\chi}(g)d\mu,$$

also denoted by $\hat{f}$ when G is clear from the context. The Fourier transform of $f \in L^1(G)$ is continuous, but not necessarily in $L^1(\hat{G})$.

For example, for the group $\mathbb{D}^m := \frac{1}{q}\mathbb{Z}^m/\mathbb{Z}^m$ with the Haar measure as fixed in Fig. 1, the L_2-norm and the Fourier transform are respectively given by

$$\|f\|_2^2 = \frac{1}{q^m} \sum_{x \in \mathbb{D}^m} |f(x)|^2 \quad \text{and} \quad \mathcal{F}\{f\}(y) = \frac{1}{q^m} \sum_{x \in \mathbb{D}^m} f(x)e^{-2\pi i \langle x, y \rangle}.$$

We note that we use a different convention on the scaling than what is common in the context of the quantum Fourier transform.

Given the Haar measure μ for G, there exists a unique *dual* Haar measure $\hat{\mu}$ for $\hat{G}$ with the property that, for any $f \in L^1(G)$, if $\hat{f} = \mathcal{F}_G\{f\} \in L^1(\hat{G})$, then $f = \mathcal{F}_G^{-1}\{\hat{f}\}$, where

$$\mathcal{F}_G^{-1}\{\hat{f}\} : G \to \mathbb{C}, \ g \mapsto \int_{\chi \in \hat{G}} \hat{f}(\chi)\chi(g)d\hat{\mu}$$

is the *inverse Fourier transform*. From now on it is always understood that the Haar measure of the dual group is chosen to be the dual of the Haar measure of the primal group. With this choice, we also have the following well known fact [9, Thm. 3.4.8].

Theorem 6 (Plancherel's Identity). *For all $f \in L^1(G) \cap L^2(G)$,*

$$\|f\|_{2,G} = \|\mathcal{F}_G\{f\}\|_{2,\hat{G}}.$$

Finally, we recall the *convolution theorem*, which states that $\widehat{fg} = \hat{f} \star \hat{g} = \int_{x \in G} \hat{f}(x)\hat{g}(\cdot - x)d\mu(x)$ for all functions $f, g \in L^1(G)$ that have Fourier transforms $\hat{f}, \hat{g} \in L^1(G)$. This extends to functions $f \in L^1(G/H)$ and $g \in L^1(G)$, with f understood as an H-periodic function on G. Tailored to $G = \mathbb{R}^m$ and $H = \Lambda$, where $\mathbb{R}^m/\Lambda$ has dual group Λ^*, it then states that

$$\mathcal{F}_{\mathbb{R}^m}\{fg\}(y) = \mathcal{F}_{\mathbb{R}^m/\Lambda}\{f\} \star \mathcal{F}_{\mathbb{R}^m}\{g\}(y) = \sum_{\ell^* \in \Lambda^*} \mathcal{F}_{\mathbb{R}^m/\Lambda}\{f\}(\ell^*)\,\mathcal{F}_{\mathbb{R}^m}\{g\}(y - \ell^*)$$

for any $y \in \mathbb{R}^m$.

3.3   The Poisson Summation Formula

Poisson summation formula is well-known for the group $G = \mathbb{R}$, where it states that $\sum_{k \in \mathbb{Z}} \hat{f}(k) = \sum_{x \in \mathbb{Z}} f(x)$. In the case $G = \mathbb{Z}/N\mathbb{Z}$, it states that

$$\sum_{i=0}^{N/s} \hat{f}(is) = \sum_{j=1}^{s} f(j\tfrac{N}{s})$$

for any integer s that divides N. In order to formulate the Poisson summation formula for an arbitrary locally compact Abelian group G, we need to introduce the notion of *restriction* and *periodization* of functions.

Definition 2 (Restriction). *Let $H \subseteq G$ be a subset or a subgroup. For any continuous function $f : G \to \mathbb{C}$ we define $f\big|_H : H \to \mathbb{C}, h \mapsto f(h)$.*

Definition 3 (Periodization). *Let H be a closed subgroup of G with Haar measure μ_H. For any function $f \in L^1(G)$, we define*

$$f|^{G/H} : G/H \to \mathbb{C}, \; g + H \mapsto \int_{h \in H} f(g+h) d\mu_H.$$

For any closed subgroup of G with some fixed Haar measure μ and any choice of the Haar measure μ_H for H, there exists a Haar measure $\mu_{G/H}$ for G/H such that the *quotient integral formula*

$$\int_{G/H} \left(\int_H f(g+h) d\mu_H(h) \right) d\mu_{G/H}(g+H) = \int_G f(g) d\mu(g) \qquad (6)$$

holds for any continuous function $f : G \to \mathbb{C}$ with compact support (see [9, Section 1.5]).

   With this choice of Haar measure for G/H, and with the dual measures for the respective dual groups, we are ready to state the general form of the Poisson summation formula (obtained from [9, Section 3.6], see also Fig. 2).

Theorem 7 (Poisson Summation Formula). *For continuous $f \in L^1(G)$,*

$$\mathcal{F}_H\{f\big|_H\} = \mathcal{F}_G\{f\}\big|^{\hat{H}} \quad and \quad \mathcal{F}_{G/H}\{f|^{G/H}\} = \mathcal{F}_G\{f\}\big|_{\widehat{G/H}}.$$

$$
\begin{array}{ccccc}
L^1(H) & \xleftarrow{\quad |_H \quad} & L^1(G) & \xrightarrow{\quad |^{G/H} \quad} & L^1(G/H) \\[2pt]
\Big\downarrow{\scriptstyle \mathcal{F}_H} & & \Big\downarrow{\scriptstyle \mathcal{F}_G} & & \Big\downarrow{\scriptstyle \mathcal{F}_{G/H}} \\[2pt]
L^1(\hat{G}/\widehat{G/H}) & \xleftarrow{\quad |^{\hat{H}} \quad} & L^1(\hat{G}) & \xrightarrow{\quad |_{\widehat{G/H}} \quad} & L^1(\widehat{G/H})
\end{array}
$$

Fig. 2. Informal illustration of Theorem 7 by means of a diagram that commutes whenever the maps are well defined.

Applied to $G = \mathbb{R}^m$ and $H = \mathbb{Z}^m$, so that $G/H = \mathbb{T}^m$ and $\widehat{G/H} \simeq \mathbb{Z}^m$; and applied to $G = \mathbb{T}^m$ and $H = \mathbb{D}^m$ below, we obtain the following.

Corollary 1. *For continuous $h \in L^1(\mathbb{R}^m)$, we have $\mathcal{F}_{\mathbb{T}^m}\{h|^{\mathbb{T}^m}\} = \mathcal{F}_{\mathbb{R}^m}\{h\}|_{\mathbb{Z}^m}$.*

Corollary 2. *For continuous $t \in L^1(\mathbb{T}^m)$, we have $\mathcal{F}_{\mathbb{D}^m}\{t|_{\mathbb{D}^m}\} = \mathcal{F}_{\mathbb{T}^m}\{t\}|^{\hat{\mathbb{D}}^m}$.*

3.4   The Fourier Transform of Vector-Valued Functions

The Fourier transform as discussed above generalizes to vector-valued functions $\boldsymbol{f} : G \to \mathbb{C}^N$ simply by applying $\mathcal{F}$ to the N coordinate functions, resulting in a function $\mathcal{F}\{\boldsymbol{f}\} : \hat{G} \to \mathbb{C}^N$. By fixing an orthonormal basis, this extends to functions $\boldsymbol{f} : G \to \mathcal{H}$ for an arbitrary finite-dimensional complex Hilbert space, where, by linearity of the Fourier transform, $\mathcal{F}\{\boldsymbol{f}\} : \hat{G} \to \mathcal{H}$ is independent of the choice of the basis.

The norm $\|\cdot\|_{2,G}$ on functions $G \to \mathbb{C}$ generalizes to vector-valued functions $\boldsymbol{f} : G \to \mathcal{H}$, as well, by defining $\|\boldsymbol{f}\|_{2,G}$ to be the norm of the scalar function $x \mapsto \|\boldsymbol{f}(x)\|_{\mathcal{H}} = \sqrt{\langle \boldsymbol{f}(x)|\boldsymbol{f}(x)\rangle}$. The vectorial Fourier transforms and norms are compatible with each other, in the sense that Plancherel's identity (see Theorem 6) still holds; that is,

$$\|\boldsymbol{f}\|_{2,G} = \|\mathcal{F}_G\{\boldsymbol{f}\}\|_{2,\hat{G}}.$$

Also the Poisson summation formula (see Theorem 7) is still valid, as well as the convolution theorem whenever one of the functions in the product is scalar:

$$\mathcal{F}_G\{\boldsymbol{f}g\} = \mathcal{F}_G\{\boldsymbol{f}\} \star \mathcal{F}_G\{g\}.$$

An important example is the case $\boldsymbol{f} : \mathbb{R}^m/\Lambda \to \mathcal{H}$. Spelling out the above, we get

$$\mathcal{F}_{\mathbb{R}^m/\Lambda}\{\boldsymbol{f}\} : \Lambda^* \to \mathcal{H}, \ \ell^* \mapsto |c_{\ell^*}\rangle := \frac{1}{\det \Lambda} \int_{x \in \mathbb{R}^m/\Lambda} |\boldsymbol{f}(x)\rangle e^{-2\pi i\langle x,\ell^*\rangle} dx,$$

where the vectors $|c_{\ell^*}\rangle$ are also referred to as the *(vectorial) Fourier coefficients* of $\boldsymbol{f}$. The Parseval-Plancherel identity then becomes

$$\sum_{\ell^* \in \Lambda^*} \langle c_{\ell^*}|c_{\ell^*}\rangle = \|\boldsymbol{f}\|_{2,\mathbb{R}^m/\Lambda}^2 := \frac{1}{\det \Lambda} \int_{x \in \mathbb{R}^m/\Lambda} \langle \boldsymbol{f}(x)|\boldsymbol{f}(x)\rangle dx.$$

3.5   Trigonometric Approximation

As another application of the Poisson summation formula, we derive a relation between the Lipschitz constant of a function on $\mathbb{T}^m$ and the 'error of discretization' in the Fourier transform when restricting the function to $\mathbb{D}^m$.

Theorem 8. *For any Lipschitz function* $h : \mathbb{T}^m \to \mathcal{H}$ *with Lipschitz constant* $\mathrm{Lip}(h)$, *and any subset* $C \subseteq \hat{\mathbb{D}}^m$, *we have*

$$\left| \, \|1_C \cdot \mathcal{F}_{\mathbb{D}^m}\{h\}\|_{2,\hat{\mathbb{D}}^m} - \|1_C \cdot \mathcal{F}_{\mathbb{T}^m}\{h\}\|_{2,\mathbb{Z}^m} \, \right| \leq \frac{4\pi\sqrt{m}\,\mathrm{Lip}(h)}{q}$$

Here and below, we slightly abuse notation and use 1_C as indicator function acting on $\hat{\mathbb{D}}^m$ and on $\mathbb{Z}^m$, justified by identifying $\hat{\mathbb{D}}^m$ with $\hat{\mathbb{D}}^m_{\mathrm{rep}} = [q]^m_c \subset \mathbb{Z}^m$. Also, we write $\mathcal{F}_{\mathbb{D}^m}\{h\}$ instead of $\mathcal{F}_{\mathbb{D}^m}\{h|_{\mathbb{D}^m}\}$, taking it as understood that h is restricted to $\mathbb{D}^m$ when applying $\mathcal{F}_{\mathbb{D}^m}$.

Proof. Using a result of Yudin ([37, Example I after Theorem 2], see also[3] Appendix D of the full version [3]), there exists a trigonometric approximation t of h, i.e. a function $t : \mathbb{T}^m \to \mathbb{C}$ with $\hat{t}(x) := \mathcal{F}_{\mathbb{T}^m}\{t\}(x) = 0$ for all $x \notin [q]^m_c$ so that $\|h - t\|_\infty \leq \pi\sqrt{m}\,\mathrm{Lip}(h)/q$. Recalling that $\hat{\mathbb{D}}^m \simeq \mathbb{Z}^m/q\mathbb{Z}^m$, the fact that $\hat{t} : \mathbb{Z}^m \to \mathbb{C}$ vanishes outside of $[q]^m_c$ implies for all $x \in [q]^m_c$ that

$$\hat{t}(x) = \sum_{d \in q\mathbb{Z}^m} \hat{t}(x + d) = \hat{t}|^{\hat{\mathbb{D}}^m}(x + q\mathbb{Z}^m) = \mathcal{F}_{\mathbb{D}^m}\{t\}(x + q\mathbb{Z}^m),$$

where the last equality holds by Corollary 2 (and our convention of omitting the restriction to $\mathbb{D}^m$). In particular, we have $\|1_C \cdot \mathcal{F}_{\mathbb{D}^m}\{t\}\|_{2,\hat{\mathbb{D}}^m} = \|1_C \cdot \mathcal{F}_{\mathbb{T}^m}\{t\}\|_{2,\mathbb{Z}^m}$. Therefore, by the (reverse) triangle inequality and the linearity of the Fourier transform, one obtains

$$\left| \, \|1_C \cdot \mathcal{F}_{\mathbb{D}^m}\{h\}\|_{2,\hat{\mathbb{D}}^m} - \|1_C \cdot \mathcal{F}_{\mathbb{T}^m}\{h\}\|_{2,\mathbb{Z}^m} \, \right|$$
$$\leq \|1_C \cdot \mathcal{F}_{\mathbb{D}^m}\{h - t\}\|_{2,\hat{\mathbb{D}}^m} + \|1_C \cdot \mathcal{F}_{\mathbb{T}^m}\{h - t\}\|_{2,\mathbb{Z}^m}.$$

We now observe that

$$\|1_C \cdot \mathcal{F}_G\{h - t\}\|_{2,\hat{G}} \leq \|\mathcal{F}_G\{h - t\}\|_{2,\hat{G}} = \|h - t\|_{2,G} \leq \sqrt{\mu(G)}\,\|h - t\|_\infty$$

where $\mu(G) = \int_G d\mu$ denotes the total measure of G. We conclude by noting that $\mu(G) = 1$ for both groups at hand $G = \mathbb{D}^m$ and $G = \mathbb{T}^m$.   □

3.6 The Gaussian Function and Smoothing Errors

Let m be a fixed positive integer. For any parameter $\sigma > 0$, we consider the m-dimensional *Gaussian function*

$$\rho_\sigma : \mathbb{R}^m \to \mathbb{C}, \; x \mapsto e^{-\frac{\pi\|x\|^2}{\sigma^2}},$$

which is well known to satisfy the following basic properties.

---

[3] In Appendix D of the full version [3], we provide a slight generalization of Yudin's paper [37] to functions with vectorial output. In principle the bound of Theorem 8 can also derived without this generalization, but at the cost of an undesirable extra factor $\dim \mathcal{H} = 2^n$.

Lemma 1. *For all* $\sigma > 0$, $m \in \mathbb{N}$ *and* $x, y \in \mathbb{R}^m$, *we have* $\int_{z \in \mathbb{R}^m} \rho_\sigma(z) dz = \sigma^m$, $\mathcal{F}_{\mathbb{R}^m}\{\rho_\sigma\} = \sigma^m \rho_{1/\sigma}$, $\sqrt{\rho_\sigma(x)} = \rho_{\sqrt{2}\sigma}(x)$ *and* $\rho_\sigma(x)\rho_\sigma(y) = \rho_{\frac{\sigma}{\sqrt{2}}}(\frac{x+y}{2})\rho_{\frac{\sigma}{\sqrt{2}}}(\frac{x-y}{2})$.

Remark 7. From these properties it follows that the integral of the L_2-norm of $x \mapsto \sigma^{m/2} \cdot \sqrt{\rho_{1/\sigma}(x)}$ equals 1, i.e., $\left\| \sigma^{m/2} \cdot \sqrt{\rho_{1/\sigma}(x)} \right\|_{2,\mathbb{R}^m}^2 = 1$.

The following two results (and the variations we discuss below) will play an important role and will be used several times in this paper: *Banaszczyk's bound*, originating from [1], and the *smoothing error*[4], as introduced by Micciancio and Regev [20]. They allow us to control

$$\rho_\sigma(X) := \sum_{x \in X} \rho_\sigma(x),$$

for certain discrete subsets $X \subseteq \mathbb{R}^m$. For ease of notation, we let

$$\beta_z^{(m)} := \left(\frac{2\pi e z^2}{m} \right)^{m/2} e^{-\pi z^2},$$

which decays super-exponentially in z (for fixed m). The following formulation of Banaszczyk's lemma is obtained from [21, Equation (1.1)].

Lemma 2 (Banaszczyk's Bound). *Whenever* $r/\sigma \geq \sqrt{\frac{m}{2\pi}}$,

$$\rho_\sigma((\Lambda + t) \setminus \mathcal{B}_r) \leq \beta_{r/\sigma}^{(m)} \cdot \rho_\sigma(\Lambda),$$

where $\mathcal{B}_r = \mathcal{B}_r(0) = \{x \in \mathbb{R}^m \mid |x| < r\}$.

Imitating techniques from [20, Lemma 3.2], we have:

Lemma 3. *Let* $\sigma \geq \frac{\sqrt{m}}{\lambda_1(\Lambda^*)}$. *Then* $\rho_{1/\sigma}(\Lambda^* \setminus 0) \leq 2 \cdot \beta_{\sigma \lambda_1(\Lambda^*)}^{(m)}$.

As a direct corollary, we have the following result.

Corollary 3. *Let* $\sigma \geq 2\sqrt{m}$, *and let* $x \in \mathbb{R}^m$ *with* $\|x\|_\infty \leq 1/2$. *Then*

$$\rho_{1/\sigma}(\mathbb{Z}^m \setminus \{0\} + x) \leq 2\beta_{\sigma/2}^{(m)}.$$

Proof. We have $\rho_{1/\sigma}(\mathbb{Z}^m \setminus \{0\} + x) \leq \rho_{1/\sigma}((\mathbb{Z}^m + x) \setminus \mathcal{B}_{\frac{1}{2}}) \leq \beta_{\sigma/2}^{(m)} \rho_{1/\sigma}(\mathbb{Z}^m)$, where the second inequality follows from Lemma 2. Using Lemma 3 to argue that $\rho_{1/\sigma}(\mathbb{Z}^m) = 1 + \rho_{1/\sigma}(\mathbb{Z}^m \setminus 0) \leq 1 + 2\beta_\sigma^{(m)} \leq 2$ then proves the claim. $\square$

The following lemma, which combines [20, Lemma 4.1] and [20, Lemma 3.2], controls the fluctuation of the sum $\rho_s(\Lambda + t)$ for varying $t \in \mathbb{R}^m$.

---

[4] Although most literature on lattices analyze smoothing errors in terms of the *smoothing parameter* η_ϵ, we chose not to do so. Instead, this paper addresses smoothing errors in a reversed and more direct way, making the errors occurring in the later analysis more easy to describe.

Lemma 4 (Smoothing Error). *Let $\Lambda \in \mathbb{R}^m$ be a full rank lattice, and let $\sigma \geq \sqrt{m}/\lambda_1(\Lambda^*)$. Then, for any $t \in \mathbb{R}^m$,*

$$(1 - 2\beta^{(m)}_{\sigma\lambda_1(\Lambda^*)})\frac{\sigma^m}{\det \Lambda} \leq \rho_\sigma(\Lambda + t) \leq (1 + 2\beta^{(m)}_{\sigma\lambda_1(\Lambda^*)})\frac{\sigma^m}{\det \Lambda}. \tag{7}$$

Corollary 4. *For $\sigma \geq \frac{\sqrt{m}}{\lambda_1(\Lambda^*)}$ and for any $t \in \mathbb{R}^m$, we have $\rho_\sigma(\Lambda + t) \leq 2\frac{\sigma^m}{\det \Lambda}$.*

Proof. Using Lemma 4 and noticing $2\beta^{(m)}_{\sigma\lambda_1(\Lambda^*)} \leq 2\beta^{(m)}_{\sqrt{m}} \leq 1$ yields the result. □

3.7 Lipschitz Condition

Theorem 9 (Rademacher's theorem). *A Lipschitz function $f : \mathbb{R}^m/\Lambda \to \mathcal{H}$ has weak partial derivatives $\partial_{x_j} f : \mathbb{R}^m/\Lambda \to \mathcal{H}$ lying in $L_2(\mathbb{R}^m/\Lambda)$. In particular, $\sum_{j=1}^m \left\|\partial_{x_j} f\right\|^2_{2,\mathbb{R}^m/\Lambda} \leq \mathrm{Lip}(f)^2$.*

Proof. Combining the proof of [17, Theorem 4.1 and 4.9] and [35, Theorem 2] on measures of compact sets, we obtain this result.   □

Corollary 5. *Let $f : \mathbb{R}^m/\Lambda \to \mathcal{H}$ be a Lipschitz-continuous function, and denote by $|c_{\ell^*}\rangle$ the vectorial Fourier coefficients of f. Then,*

$$\sum_{\substack{\ell^* \in \Lambda^* \\ \|\ell^*\| \geq B}} \langle c_{\ell^*}|c_{\ell^*}\rangle \leq \frac{\mathrm{Lip}(f)^2}{4\pi^2 B^2}.$$

Proof. Since f is Lipschitz, we can apply Theorem 9. Furthermore, the identity $|f(x)\rangle = \sum_{\ell^* \in \Lambda^*} |c_{\ell^*}\rangle e^{2\pi i\langle x,\ell^*\rangle}$ implies $|\partial_{x_j} f(x)\rangle = 2\pi i \sum_{\ell^* \in \Lambda^*} \ell_j^* |c_{\ell^*}\rangle e^{2\pi i\langle x,\ell^*\rangle}$ almost everywhere ([36, Lemma V.2.11] or [30, Lemma 2.16]). Finally, given that $\sum_{j=1}^m \left\|\partial_{x_j} f\right\|^2_{2,\mathbb{R}^m/\Lambda} \leq \mathrm{Lip}(f)^2$, Plancherel's identity implies that

$$\mathrm{Lip}(f)^2 \geq \sum_{j=1}^m \left\|\partial_{x_j} f\right\|^2_{2,\mathbb{R}^m/\Lambda} = 4\pi^2 \sum_{\ell^* \in \Lambda^*} \|\ell^*\|_2^2 \langle c_{\ell^*}|c_{\ell^*}\rangle$$

$$\geq 4\pi^2 \sum_{\substack{\ell^* \in \Lambda^* \\ \|\ell^*\|_2 \geq B}} \|\ell^*\|_2^2 \langle c_{\ell^*}|c_{\ell^*}\rangle \geq 4B^2\pi^2 \sum_{\substack{\ell^* \in \Lambda^* \\ \|\ell^*\|_2 \geq B}} \langle c_{\ell^*}|c_{\ell^*}\rangle,$$

from which the claim follows.   □

4 Algorithm

4.1 The Algorithm

Given a Λ-periodic function $f : \mathbb{R}^m \to \mathcal{S}$ as discussed in Sect. 2, which maps a classical input x to a quantum state $|f(x)\rangle$, we consider the following quantum algorithm (see Fig. 3). The algorithm has oracle access to f, meaning that it has access to a unitary that maps $|x\rangle|0\rangle$ to $|x\rangle|\boldsymbol{f}(x)\rangle$. As a matter of fact, we may obviously assume the algorithm to have oracle access to a unitary that maps $|x\rangle|0\rangle$ to $|x\rangle|\boldsymbol{f}(Vx)\rangle$ for a parameter $V \in \mathbb{R}$ chosen by the algorithm. Per se, x may be arbitrary in $\mathbb{R}^m$; for any concrete algorithm it is of course necessary to restrict x to some finite subset of $\mathbb{R}^m$.

The algorithm we consider follows the blueprint of the standard hidden-subgroup algorithm. Notable differences are that we need to discretize (and finitize) the continuous domain $\mathbb{R}^m$ of the function, and the algorithm starts off with a superposition that is not uniform but follows a (discretized and finitized) Gaussian distribution. The reason for the latter choice is that Gaussian distributions decay very fast and behave nicely under the Fourier transform (as they are eigenfunctions of the Fourier transform).

The algorithm is given in Fig. 3 below. It uses two quantum registers, each one consisting of a certain number of qubits. Associated to the first register are orthonormal bases $\{|x\rangle_{\mathbb{D}^m}\}_{x\in\mathbb{D}^m}$ and $\{|y\rangle_{\hat{\mathbb{D}}^m}\}_{y\in\hat{\mathbb{D}}^m}$ where the basis vectors are labeled by $x \in \mathbb{D}^m$ and $y \in \hat{\mathbb{D}}^m$, respectively, which we identify with elements $x \in \mathbb{D}_{\mathrm{rep}}^m$ and $y \in \hat{\mathbb{D}}_{\mathrm{rep}}^m$ (see Sect. 3.1). The second register has state space $\mathcal{H}$. The algorithm is parameterized by $q \in \mathbb{N}$ (which determines $\mathbb{D}^m$), $s > 0$ and $V > 0$. Intuitively, the fraction $\frac{s}{V}$ is tightly related to the absolute precision of the output, whereas q is connected with the number of qubits needed.

Algorithm 1 : Quantum algorithm for the dual lattice sampling problem

---

1 **Prepare the Gaussian state** $|\psi_0\rangle := \sum_{x\in\mathbb{D}^m} \sqrt{\rho_{1/s}(x)} \cdot |x\rangle_{\mathbb{D}^m}|0\rangle$;

2 **Apply the $\boldsymbol{f}$-oracle,** yielding $\sum_{x\in\mathbb{D}^m} \sqrt{\rho_{1/s}(x)} \cdot |x\rangle_{\mathbb{D}^m}|\boldsymbol{f}(Vx)\rangle$;

3 **Apply the quantum Fourier transform on the first register,** yielding the unnormalized state $\sum_{x\in\mathbb{D}^m} \sum_{y\in\hat{\mathbb{D}}^m} \sqrt{\rho_{1/s}(x)} \cdot e^{-2\pi i\langle x,y\rangle} \cdot |y\rangle_{\hat{\mathbb{D}}^m}|\boldsymbol{f}(Vx)\rangle$;

4 **Measure the first register in the $\hat{\mathbb{D}}_{\mathrm{rep}}^m$-basis** yielding some $y \in \hat{\mathbb{D}}_{\mathrm{rep}}^m$, and output $\frac{y}{V}$;

Fig. 3. The continuous-hidden-subgroup quantum algorithm.

The description and Analysis of Step 1 is deferred to Appendix C of the full version [3]. It will be shown (as summarized in Theorem 5) that its cost is negligible compared to the main cost of Algorithm 1, while contributing an error of at most $o(\eta)$ in the trace distance.

4.2   The Figure of Merit

Recall that $N = \dim \mathcal{H} = 2^n$. Then the state after step (2) of Algorithm 1 equals, up to normalization,

$$|\psi\rangle := s^{m/2} \sum_{x \in \mathbb{D}^m} \sqrt{\rho_{1/s}(x)} \, |x\rangle_{\mathbb{D}^m} |\boldsymbol{f}(Vx)\rangle$$

which we can rewrite as

$$|\psi\rangle = \sum_{x \in \mathbb{D}^m} |x\rangle_{\mathbb{D}^m} |\boldsymbol{h}(x)\rangle$$

where

$$\boldsymbol{h}(x) := s^{m/2} \sqrt{\rho_{1/s}(x)} \cdot |\boldsymbol{f}(Vx)\rangle.$$

Applying the quantum Fourier transform in step (3) maps this to

$$|\hat{\psi}\rangle = q^{-m/2} \sum_{x \in \mathbb{D}^m} \sum_{y \in \hat{\mathbb{D}}^m} e^{-2\pi i \langle x, y \rangle} |y\rangle_{\hat{\mathbb{D}}^m} |\boldsymbol{h}(x)\rangle = q^{m/2} \sum_{y \in \hat{\mathbb{D}}^m} |y\rangle_{\hat{\mathbb{D}}^m} |\mathcal{F}_{\mathbb{D}^m} \{\boldsymbol{h}\}(y)\rangle,$$

where the factor $q^{m/2}$ comes from the fact that, by our convention, the Fourier transform $\mathcal{F}_{\mathbb{D}^m}$ is scaled with the factor q^{-m}, while the quantum Fourier transform comes with a scaling factor $q^{-m/2}$.

Up to normalization, the probability to observe outcome y in step (4) thus is

$$\langle \hat{\psi} | (|y\rangle\langle y| \otimes \mathbb{I}) | \hat{\psi} \rangle = q^m \, \|\mathcal{F}_{\mathbb{D}^m} \{\boldsymbol{h}\}(y)\|_{\mathcal{H}}^2 \, ,$$

and so, for any "target" subset $C \subset \hat{\mathbb{D}}^m$, the probability for the algorithm to produce an outcome $y \in C$ equals

$$\mathcal{D}(C) = \sum_{y \in C} \frac{\langle \hat{\psi} | (|y\rangle\langle y| \otimes \mathbb{I}) | \hat{\psi} \rangle}{\langle \psi_0 | \psi_0 \rangle} = \frac{\|1_C \cdot \mathcal{F}_{\mathbb{D}^m} \{\boldsymbol{h}\}\|_{2,\hat{\mathbb{D}}^m}^2}{\frac{s^m}{q^m} \sum_{x \in \mathbb{D}^m} \rho_{1/s}(x)}. \tag{8}$$

Intuitively, in the limit $q \to \infty$, the grid $\frac{1}{q}\mathbb{Z}^m$ becomes $\mathbb{R}^m$; thus, neglecting constant factors, the function $\mathcal{F}_{\mathbb{D}^m} \{\boldsymbol{h}\}$ is expected to converge to

$$\mathcal{F}_{\mathbb{R}^m} \{\rho_{\sqrt{2}/s} \boldsymbol{f}(V \cdot)\} = \rho_{s/\sqrt{2}} \star \mathcal{F}_{\mathbb{R}^m} \{\boldsymbol{f}(V \cdot)\}.$$

Furthermore, when V is large enough compared to s then, relative to the dual lattice $V\Lambda^*$, the Gaussian function behaves as a Dirac delta function. Thus, the above function is then supported by $V\Lambda^*$ and takes on the values $|c_{\ell^*}\rangle$. Hence, by taking square norms, we get the claimed $\langle c_{\ell^*} | c_{\ell^*} \rangle$.

Below, we prove that this intuition is indeed correct, and we work out the actual "rate of convergence".

5 Analysis

5.1 Proof Overview

In the overview here and in the formal analysis in the next section, we consider the case $V = 1$. This is without loss of generality; in order to deal with an arbitrary V we simply apply our analysis to the function $\boldsymbol{f}_V := \boldsymbol{f}(V\cdot)$, with the effect that in the error term, Λ^* becomes $V\Lambda^*$ and $\mathrm{Lip}(\boldsymbol{f}_V)$ becomes $V\,\mathrm{Lip}(\boldsymbol{f})$.

The error analysis (for $V = 1$) is divided into three parts. The first part consists of showing that the denominator from Eq. (8) satisfies

$$\frac{s^m}{q^m} \sum_{x \in \mathbb{D}^m} \rho_{1/s}(x) \approx 1.$$

In the second part, which is the most technical one, we show that for any $C \subset \hat{\mathbb{D}}^m$, also understood as a subset of $\hat{\mathbb{D}}^m_{\mathrm{rep}} = [q]^m_c \subset \mathbb{Z}^m$,

$$\|1_C \cdot \mathcal{F}_{\mathbb{D}^m}\{h\}\|^2_{2,\hat{\mathbb{D}}^m} \gtrsim \sum_{\substack{\ell^* \in \Lambda^* \\ B_{\delta\lambda_1^*}(\ell^*) \subseteq C}} \langle c_{\ell^*} | c_{\ell^*} \rangle. \tag{9}$$

We recall that $|c_{\ell^*}\rangle$ are the vectorial Fourier coefficients of $\boldsymbol{f}$ and $B_{\delta\lambda_1^*}(\ell^*) = \mathcal{B}_{\delta\lambda_1^*}(\ell^*) \cap \mathbb{Z}^m$. This approximation (9) is divided into the following five steps:

$$\|1_C\mathcal{F}_{\mathbb{D}^m}\{h\}\|^2_{2,\hat{\mathbb{D}}^m} \overset{(1)}{\approx} \left\|1_C\mathcal{F}_{\mathbb{D}^m}\left\{h\big|^{\mathbb{T}^m}\right\}\right\|^2_{2,\hat{\mathbb{D}}^m} \overset{(2)}{\approx} \left\|1_C\mathcal{F}_{\mathbb{T}^m}\{h\big|^{\mathbb{T}^m}\}\right\|^2_{2,\mathbb{Z}^m}$$

$$\overset{(3)}{=} \|1_C\mathcal{F}_{\mathbb{R}^m}\{h\}\|^2_{2,\mathbb{Z}^m} \overset{(4)}{\approx} \sum_{\ell^* \in \Lambda^*} \langle c_{\ell^*}|c_{\ell^*}\rangle \cdot \iota_C(\ell^*) \overset{(5)}{\geq} \sum_{\substack{\ell^* \in \Lambda^* \\ B_{\delta\lambda_1^*}(\ell^*) \subseteq C}} \langle c_{\ell^*}|c_{\ell^*}\rangle.$$

It thus follows that

$$\mathcal{D}(C) \gtrsim \sum_{\substack{\ell^* \in \Lambda^* \\ B_{\delta\lambda_1^*}(\ell^*) \subseteq C}} \langle c_{\ell^*}|c_{\ell^*}\rangle,$$

and therefore, applied to $C := B_{\delta\lambda_1^*}(S)$, that for any $S \subset \Lambda^*$ for which $B_{\delta\lambda_1^*}(S) \subset [q]^m_c$, requirement (3) is satisfied.

The third part of the analysis is to show that (3) is satisfied also for $S \subset \Lambda^*$ for which $B_{\delta\lambda_1^*}(S)$ is not fully contained in $[q]^m_c$. For such S, it is then sufficient to show that $\sum_{\ell^* \in S \setminus S_0} \langle c_{\ell^*}|c_{\ell^*}\rangle \approx 0$ then, where $S_0 = \{\ell^* \in S \mid B_{\delta\lambda_1^*}(\ell^*) \subseteq [q]^m_c\}$. We prove this by means of Corollary 5.

We emphasize that in the formal proof below, we explicitly follow this 3-part structure of the proof, with part 2 being divided into 5 steps as indicated above.

5.2 Formal Analysis

Part 1. By Lemma 4, we have (whenever $q/s \geq \sqrt{m}$),

$$\frac{s^m}{q^m} \sum_{x \in \mathbb{D}^m} \rho_{1/s}(x) \leq \frac{s^m}{q^m} \cdot \rho_{1/s}\left(\frac{1}{q}\mathbb{Z}^m\right) \leq 1 + 2\beta^{(m)}_{q/s}. \tag{10}$$

Therefore,

$$\frac{\|1_C \cdot \mathcal{F}_{\mathbb{D}^m}\{h\}\|_{2,\hat{\mathbb{D}}^m}^2}{\frac{s^m}{q^m}\sum_{x\in\mathbb{D}^m}\rho_{1/s}(x)} \geq \|1_C \cdot \mathcal{F}_{\mathbb{D}^m}\{h\}\|_{2,\hat{\mathbb{D}}^m}^2 - \varepsilon_{\mathrm{denom}} \tag{11}$$

with $\varepsilon_{\mathrm{denom}} = 2\beta_{q/s}^{(m)}$.

Part 2. Recall that $h = s^{m/2}\cdot f\cdot\rho_{\sqrt{2}/s}$ is a function $h:\mathbb{R}^m\to\mathcal{H}$. In the following, by slightly abusing notation, we also understand h as a function $h:\mathbb{T}^m\to\mathcal{H}$ by considering the restriction of h to $\mathbb{T}_{\mathrm{rep}}^m = [-\frac{1}{2},\frac{1}{2})^m$. Similarly, we understand h as a function $h:\mathbb{D}^m\to\mathcal{H}$ by considering its restriction to $\mathbb{D}_{\mathrm{rep}}^m = \mathbb{T}_{\mathrm{rep}}^m\cap\frac{1}{q}\mathbb{Z}^m$.

Step 1. Observe that

$$\left\|1_C\cdot\mathcal{F}_{\mathbb{D}^m}\{h\} - 1_C\cdot\mathcal{F}_{\mathbb{D}^m}\left\{h|^{\mathbb{T}^m}\right\}\right\|_{2,\hat{\mathbb{D}}^m} \leq \left\|\mathcal{F}_{\mathbb{D}^m}\left\{h - h|^{\mathbb{T}^m}\right\}\right\|_{2,\hat{\mathbb{D}}^m} = \left\|h|^{\mathbb{T}^m} - h\right\|_{2,\mathbb{D}^m}.$$

Writing out the definition of $h|^{\mathbb{T}^m}$ and h, we obtain (provided that $\frac{s}{2\sqrt{2}} \geq \sqrt{m}$)

$$\left\|h|^{\mathbb{T}^m} - h\right\|_{2,\mathbb{D}^m}^2 = \frac{1}{q^m}\sum_{x\in\mathbb{D}^m}\left\|\sum_{z\in\mathbb{Z}^m\setminus 0}h(x+z)\right\|_{\mathcal{H}}^2$$

$$\leq \frac{\|f\|_\infty^2\, s^m}{q^m}\sum_{x\in\mathbb{D}^m}\left(\sum_{z\in\mathbb{Z}^m\setminus 0}\rho_{\sqrt{2}/s}(x+z)\right)^2 \leq 4s^m(\beta_{\frac{s}{2\sqrt{2}}}^{(m)})^2,$$

as $\rho_{\sqrt{2}/s}(\mathbb{Z}^m\setminus\{0\}+x) \leq 2\beta_{\frac{s}{2\sqrt{2}}}^{(m)}$, from Corollary 3, combining with the fact that $\|f\|_\infty = 1$. Taking square roots and using the reverse triangle inequality yields

$$\left|\|1_C\cdot\mathcal{F}_{\mathbb{D}^m}\{h\}\|_{2,\hat{\mathbb{D}}^m} - \left\|1_C\cdot\mathcal{F}_{\mathbb{D}^m}\left\{h|^{\mathbb{T}^m}\right\}\right\|_{2,\hat{\mathbb{D}}^m}\right| \leq 2s^{m/2}\beta_{\frac{s}{2\sqrt{2}}}^{(m)} =: \varepsilon_{\mathrm{per}}$$

Step 2. Using Theorem 8 with $h|^{\mathbb{T}^m}$, one obtains

$$\left|\left\|1_C\cdot\mathcal{F}_{\mathbb{D}^m}\left\{h|^{\mathbb{T}^m}\right\}\right\|_{2,\hat{\mathbb{D}}^m} - \left\|1_C\cdot\mathcal{F}_{\mathbb{T}^m}\{h|^{\mathbb{T}^m}\}\right\|_{2,\mathbb{Z}^m}\right| \leq \varepsilon_{\mathrm{lip}},$$

where $\varepsilon_{\mathrm{lip}} = \frac{4\pi\sqrt{m}\,\mathrm{Lip}(h|^{\mathbb{T}^m})}{q}$. Recall that we use 1_C as indicator function acting on $\mathbb{Z}^m$ and on $\hat{\mathbb{D}}^m \simeq \mathbb{Z}^m/q\mathbb{Z}^m$ in the obvious way.

The Lipschitz constant of $h|^{\mathbb{T}^m}$ can be obtained by taking the maximum value of the absolute value of the derivative.

$$\frac{\partial}{\partial x_j}\left(h|^{\mathbb{T}^m}\right) = s^{m/2}\sum_{z\in\mathbb{Z}^m}\left(\frac{\partial}{\partial x_j}f(x+z)\cdot\rho_{\sqrt{2}/s}(x+z) + f(x+z)\frac{\partial}{\partial x_j}\rho_{\sqrt{2}/s}(x+z)\right)$$

The norm of $\nabla\left(\boldsymbol{h}|^{\mathbb{T}^m}\right)$ is therefore bounded by

$$s^{m/2}\left(\mathrm{Lip}(\boldsymbol{f})\rho_{\sqrt{2}/s}(x+\mathbb{Z}^m)+\pi s^2\,\|\boldsymbol{f}\|_\infty\sum_{z\in\mathbb{Z}^m}\|x+z\|\,\rho_{\sqrt{2}/s}(x+z)\right)$$

$$\leq s^{m/2}\left(2\,\mathrm{Lip}(\boldsymbol{f})+2\pi s^2\right)$$

where we used $\|\nabla\boldsymbol{f}\|=\sqrt{\sum_{j=1}^m\left\|\frac{\partial}{\partial x_j}\boldsymbol{f}\right\|_{\mathcal{H}}^2}\leq\mathrm{Lip}(\boldsymbol{f})$, $\|\boldsymbol{f}\|_\infty\leq 1$, $\nabla\rho_{\sqrt{2}/s}(x)=\pi s^2 x\cdot\rho_{\sqrt{2}/s}(x)$, $\rho_{\sqrt{2}/s}(x+\mathbb{Z}^m)\leq 2$ and $\sum_{z\in\mathbb{Z}^m}\|x+z\|\,\rho_{\sqrt{2}/s}(x+z)\leq 2$. The second last inequality follows from $\rho_{\sqrt{2}/s}(x+\mathbb{Z}^m)\leq 1+\rho_{\sqrt{2}/s}(\mathbb{Z}^m\backslash\{0\}+x)\leq 1+2\beta_{\frac{s}{2\sqrt{2}}}^{(m)}\leq 2$, see Corollary 3. The last inequality can be obtained by the fact that $\|x+z\|\,\rho_{\sqrt{2}/s}(x+z)\leq\rho_{\sqrt{2}/(s-1)}(x+z)$, and repeating the former argument.

Step 3. Apply Corollary 1 to conclude that

$$\left\|1_C\cdot\mathcal{F}_{\mathbb{T}^m}\{\boldsymbol{h}|^{\mathbb{T}^m}\}\right\|_{2,\mathbb{Z}^m}=\|1_C\cdot\mathcal{F}_{\mathbb{R}^m}\{\boldsymbol{h}\}\|_{2,\mathbb{Z}^m}\,,$$

where we continue to abuse notation here by identifying $\mathcal{F}_{\mathbb{R}^m}\{\boldsymbol{h}\}$ with its restriction to $\mathbb{Z}$.

Using $|a^2-b^2|=|a+b||a-b|\leq(|a-b|+2|a|)|a-b|$ and the fact that $\|1_C\cdot\mathcal{F}_{\mathbb{D}^m}\{\boldsymbol{h}\}\|_{2,\hat{\mathbb{D}}^m}\leq 2$ (which follows from Eq. (8) and Eq. (10)), we conclude that

$$\left|\|1_C\cdot\mathcal{F}_{\mathbb{D}^m}\{\boldsymbol{h}\}\|_{2,\hat{\mathbb{D}}^m}^2-\|1_C\cdot\mathcal{F}_{\mathbb{R}^m}\{\boldsymbol{h}\}\|_{2,\mathbb{Z}^m}^2\right|\leq 5(\varepsilon_{\mathrm{per}}+\varepsilon_{\mathrm{lip}}),$$

where we assume that $\varepsilon_{\mathrm{per}}+\varepsilon_{\mathrm{lip}}<1$.

Step 4. By applying the convolution theorem as outlined in Sect. 3.2, we see that

$$\mathcal{F}_{\mathbb{R}^m}\{\boldsymbol{h}\}[y]=\mathcal{F}_{\mathbb{R}^m/\Lambda}\{\boldsymbol{f}\}\star\mathcal{F}_{\mathbb{R}^m}\{s^{m/2}\rho_{s/\sqrt{2}}\}(y)=\left(\frac{2}{s}\right)^{m/2}\sum_{\ell^*\in\Lambda^*}|c_{\ell^*}\rangle\rho_{s/\sqrt{2}}(y-\ell^*)$$

where $|c_{\ell^*}\rangle$ are the vectorial Fourier coefficients of $\boldsymbol{f}$. Therefore,

$$\|\mathcal{F}_{\mathbb{R}^m}\{\boldsymbol{h}\}[y]\|_{\mathcal{H}}^2=\left(\frac{2}{s}\right)^m\sum_{k^*\in\Lambda^*}\sum_{\ell^*\in\Lambda^*}\langle c_{\ell^*}|c_{k^*}\rangle\rho_{s/\sqrt{2}}(y-\ell^*)\rho_{s/\sqrt{2}}(y-k^*)$$

$$=\left(\frac{2}{s}\right)^m\sum_{u^*\in\frac{1}{2}\Lambda^*}\sum_{v^*\in u^*+\Lambda^*}\langle c_{v^*+u^*}|c_{v^*-u^*}\rangle\rho_{s/2}(u^*)\rho_{s/2}(y-v^*),$$

where the latter is obtained by the variable substitution $u^*=\frac{\ell^*-k^*}{2}$, $v^*=\frac{\ell^*+k^*}{2}$, and using Lemma 1. Summing over $y\in C$, setting

$$\iota_C(\ell^*):=\left(\frac{2}{s}\right)^m\sum_{y\in C}\rho_{s/2}(y-\ell^*),$$

and splitting into $u^* = 0$ and $u^* \neq 0$, we obtain

$$\|1_C \mathcal{F}_{\mathbb{R}^m}\{h\}\|^2_{2,\mathbb{Z}^m} = \sum_{v^* \in \Lambda^*} \langle c_{v^*} | c_{v^*} \rangle \cdot \iota_C(v^*)$$

$$+ \sum_{u^* \in \frac{1}{2}\Lambda^* \setminus 0} \rho_{s/2}(u^*) \sum_{v^* \in u^* + \Lambda^*} \langle c_{v^*+u^*} | c_{v^*-u^*} \rangle \cdot \iota_C(v^*)$$

We now bound the second term. Assuming $s \geq \sqrt{m}$, we have that $\iota_C(v^*) \leq \left(\frac{2}{s}\right)^m \rho_{s/2}(\mathbb{Z}^m + t) \leq 2$ (see Corollary 4). Furthermore, by the Cauchy-Schwartz inequality,

$$\left| \sum_{v^* \in u^* + \Lambda^*} \langle c_{v^*+u^*} | c_{v^*-u^*} \rangle \right| \leq \sum_{v^* \in \Lambda^*} \sqrt{\langle c_{v^*+2u^*} | c_{v^*+2u^*} \rangle \langle c_{v^*} | c_{v^*} \rangle}$$

$$\leq \sum_{v^* \in \Lambda^*} (\langle c_{v^*+2u^*} | c_{v^*+2u^*} \rangle + \langle c_{v^*} | c_{v^*} \rangle) = 2\|f\|^2_{2,\mathbb{R}^m/\Lambda} = 2$$

Finally, using Lemma 3, we have

$$\sum_{u^* \in \frac{1}{2}\Lambda^* \setminus 0} \rho_{s/2}(u^*) = \rho_s\left(\Lambda^* \setminus 0\right) \leq 2 \cdot \beta^{(m)}_{\frac{\lambda_1^*}{s}}.$$

Putting all together, we obtain that

$$\left| \|1_C \mathcal{F}_{\mathbb{R}^m}\{h\}\|^2_{2,\mathbb{Z}^m} - \sum_{\ell^* \in \Lambda^*} \langle c_{\ell^*} | c_{\ell^*} \rangle \iota_C(\ell^*) \right| \leq \varepsilon_{\text{diag}},$$

where $\varepsilon_{\text{diag}} = 8 \cdot \beta^{(m)}_{\lambda_1^*/s}$.

Step 5. Recall the notation $B_{\delta\lambda_1^*}(\ell^*) = \{x \in \mathbb{Z}^m \mid |x - \ell^*| < \delta\lambda_1^*\}$. Whenever $\overline{B_{\delta\lambda_1^*}(\ell^*)} \subseteq C$, it obviously holds that

$$\iota_C(\ell^*) = \left(\frac{2}{s}\right)^m \sum_{y \in C} \rho_{s/2}(y - v^*) \geq \left(\frac{2}{s}\right)^m \sum_{y \in B_{\delta\lambda_1^*}(\ell^*)} \rho_{s/2}(y - \ell^*)$$

$$\geq \left(\frac{2}{s}\right)^m \rho_{s/2}(\mathbb{Z}^m)\left(1 - \beta^{(m)}_{2\delta\lambda_1^*/s}\right) \geq (1 - 2 \cdot \beta^{(m)}_{s/2})(1 - \beta^{(m)}_{2\delta\lambda_1^*/s}),$$

where the second inequality follows from Banaszczyk's bound (see Lemma 2) and the last from Lemma 4. It follows then that

$$\sum_{\ell^* \in \Lambda^*} \langle c_{\ell^*} | c_{\ell^*} \rangle \iota(\ell^*) \geq (1 - \varepsilon_{\text{smooth}}) \sum_{\substack{\ell^* \in \Lambda^* \\ B_{V\delta}(V\ell^*) \subseteq C}} \langle c_{\ell^*} | c_{\ell^*} \rangle.$$

where $\varepsilon_{\text{smooth}} = 2 \cdot \beta^{(m)}_{s/2} + \beta^{(m)}_{2\delta\lambda_1^*/s}$

Finalizing. By collecting all the error terms, we obtain that

$$\|1_C \cdot \mathcal{F}_{\mathbb{D}^m}\{h\}\|_{2,\hat{\mathbb{D}}^m}^2$$

$$\geq \sum_{\substack{\ell^* \in \Lambda^* \\ B_{\delta\lambda_1^*}(\ell^*) \subseteq C}} \langle c_{\ell^*}|c_{\ell^*}\rangle - \varepsilon_{\text{smooth}} - \varepsilon_{\text{diag}} - 5(\varepsilon_{\text{per}} + \varepsilon_{\text{lip}})$$

whenever s, δ and λ_1^* satisfy the following:

$$\frac{2\delta\lambda_1^*}{s} \geq \sqrt{m} \quad \text{and} \quad \frac{s}{2\sqrt{2}} \geq \sqrt{m}. \tag{12}$$

Part 3. Let $\mathcal{D}$ be the distribution defined by the output y of Algorithm 1 (recall that we assumed $V = 1$); note that $\mathcal{D}$ has support only on $[q]_c^m$. Throughout this part of the analysis, S denotes a subset of Λ^*.

By above analysis, we can conclude that whenever $B_{\delta\lambda_1^*}(S) \subseteq [q]_c^m$, we have (putting $C = B_{\delta\lambda_1^*}(S)$),

$$p_S := \mathcal{D}(B_{\delta\lambda_1^*}(S)) \geq \sum_{\ell^* \in S} \langle c_{\ell^*}|c_{\ell^*}\rangle - \eta',$$

where $\eta' = \varepsilon_{\text{smooth}} + \varepsilon_{\text{diag}} + \varepsilon_{\text{denom}} + 5(\varepsilon_{\text{per}} + \varepsilon_{\text{lip}})$.

For general $S \subseteq \Lambda^*$, write $S = S_0 \cup S_1$ as a disjoint union, where $S_0 = \{\ell^* \in S \mid B_{\delta\lambda_1^*}(\ell^*) \subseteq [q]_c^m\}$. Then it is evident that $S_1 \subseteq \Lambda^*\backslash[-\frac{q}{4},\frac{q}{4}]^m$. Then, putting $\varepsilon_{\text{tail}} = \frac{4m\,\text{Lip}(f)^2}{\pi^2 q^2} \geq \sum_{\ell^* \in \Lambda^*\backslash[-\frac{q}{4},\frac{q}{4}]^m} \langle c_{\ell^*}|c_{\ell^*}\rangle \geq \sum_{\ell^* \in S_1} \langle c_{\ell^*}|c_{\ell^*}\rangle$, (see Corollary 5), we have

$$\mathcal{D}(B_{\delta\lambda_1^*}(S)) \geq \mathcal{D}(B_{\delta\lambda_1^*}(S_0)) \geq \sum_{\ell^* \in S_0} \langle c_{\ell^*}|c_{\ell^*}\rangle - \eta' \geq \sum_{\ell^* \in S} \langle c_{\ell^*}|c_{\ell^*}\rangle - \varepsilon_{\text{tail}} - \eta',$$

$$= \sum_{\ell^* \in S} \langle c_{\ell^*}|c_{\ell^*}\rangle - \varepsilon_{\text{smooth}} - \varepsilon_{\text{diag}} - \varepsilon_{\text{denom}} - 5(\varepsilon_{\text{per}} + \varepsilon_{\text{lip}}) - \varepsilon_{\text{tail}} \tag{13}$$

5.3   Tuning Parameters

The left hand side of the table in Fig. 4 collects the different error terms obtained above, considering $V = 1$. The general case is obtained simply by applying the above analysis to the function $f_V := f(V\cdot)$. The hidden lattice of f_V is $\frac{1}{V}\Lambda$, which has $V\Lambda^*$ as its dual, and the Lipschitz constant of f_V is $V\,\text{Lip}(f)$. Thus, the requirements on the parameters (see Eq. (12)) change to

$$\frac{2\delta V\lambda_1^*}{s} \geq \sqrt{m} \quad \text{and} \quad \frac{s}{2\sqrt{2}} \geq \sqrt{m}, \tag{14}$$

and the different error terms become as listed in the table in Fig. 4.

Error	$V = 1$	V arbitrary
$\varepsilon_{\text{denom}}$	$2\beta^{(m)}_{q/s}$	$2\beta^{(m)}_{q/s}$
$\varepsilon_{\text{smooth}}$	$2\cdot\beta^{(m)}_{s/2} + \beta^{(m)}_{2\delta\lambda^*_1/s}$	$2\cdot\beta^{(m)}_{s/2} + \beta^{(m)}_{2\delta V\lambda^*_1/s}$
$\varepsilon_{\text{diag}}$	$8\beta^{(m)}_{\lambda^*_1/s}$	$8\beta^{(m)}_{V\lambda^*_1/s}$
ε_{per}	$2s^{m/2}\beta^{(m)}_{\frac{s}{2\sqrt2}}$	$2s^{m/2}\beta^{(m)}_{\frac{s}{2\sqrt2}}$
ε_{lip}	$\dfrac{4\pi\sqrt{m}s^{m/2}\big(2\,\text{Lip}(\boldsymbol{f})+2\pi s^2\big)}{q}$	$\dfrac{4\pi\sqrt{m}s^{m/2}\big(2V\,\text{Lip}(\boldsymbol{f})+2\pi s^2\big)}{q}$
$\varepsilon_{\text{tail}}$	$\dfrac{m\,\text{Lip}(\boldsymbol{f})^2}{\pi^2 q^2}$	$\dfrac{mV^2\,\text{Lip}(\boldsymbol{f})^2}{\pi^2 q^2}$

Fig. 4. Change of the errors when applying the analysis to f_V

Recall that $\beta^{(m)}_z := \big(\frac{2\pi ez^2}{m}\big)^{m/2}e^{-\pi z^2}$ and $N = 2^n$. We can now choose the parameters s, V and q of the algorithm appropriately to enforce all the error terms to be small. In detail, we can select:

- $s \in O(\sqrt{m\log(\eta^{-1})})$ so that $5\varepsilon_{\text{per}} \leq \eta/6$, and $2\beta^{(m)}_{s/2} \leq \eta/12$ in $\varepsilon_{\text{smooth}}$.
- $V \in O(\frac{\sqrt{m\log(\eta^{-1})}s}{\delta\lambda^*_1}) = O(\frac{m\log(\eta^{-1})}{\delta\lambda^*_1})$ so that $\varepsilon_{\text{smooth}}, \varepsilon_{\text{diag}} \leq \eta/6$.
- $Q = \log(q) \in O(m\log(s)+\log(V)+\log(\text{Lip}(f))+\log(\eta^{-1}))$ so that $5\varepsilon_{\text{lip}} \leq \eta/6$ and $\varepsilon_{\text{tail}} \leq \eta/6$.

With the above choice of parameters, $\varepsilon_{\text{smooth}} + \varepsilon_{\text{diag}} + \varepsilon_{\text{denom}} + 5(\varepsilon_{\text{per}} + \varepsilon_{\text{lip}}) + \varepsilon_{\text{tail}} \leq \eta$ in Eq. (13). Unrolling the expression of $Q = \log(q)$ and recalling that the quantum Fourier transform requires a quadratic number of gates [25, Ch. 5], we obtain the main theorem.

Theorem 10. *Algorithm 1 solves the Dual Lattice Sampling Problem with parameters η and δ; it uses m calls to the Gaussian superposition subroutine (see Theorem 5), one quantum oracle call to $\boldsymbol{f}$, $mQ + n$ qubits, and $O(m^2Q^2)$ quantum gates, where*

$$Q = O\left(m\log\left(m\log\frac{1}{\eta}\right)\right) + O\left(\log\left(\frac{\text{Lip}(\boldsymbol{f})}{\eta\cdot\delta\lambda^*_1}\right)\right). \tag{4}$$

6   From Sampling to Full Dual Lattice Recovery

We have so far focused on approximate sampling dual lattice points following weights $\langle c_{\ell^*}|c_{\ell^*}\rangle$ for $\ell^* \in \Lambda^*$, regardless of how useful this distribution may be. Indeed, until now, it could be that the function $\boldsymbol{f} : \mathbb{R}^m/\Lambda \to \mathcal{S}$ is constant, and therefore that the weight is concentrated on $0 \in \Lambda^*$. We would like now make sure we can reconstruct (approximately) Λ^* from such samples, i.e., that a sufficient number of sampled vectors from Λ^* will generate it. Informally, an equivalent condition is that the weight $\langle c_{\ell^*} | c_{\ell^*} \rangle$ is not concentrated on any proper sublattice $M^* \subsetneq \Lambda^*$. More formally, we give the following sufficient conditions.

Definition 4. *Let $L \subseteq \mathbb{R}^m$ be a full-rank lattice. A distribution $\mathcal{D}$ on L is called p-evenly distributed whenever $\Pr_{v \leftarrow \mathcal{D}}[v \in L'] \leq p$ for any proper sublattice $L' \subsetneq L$.*

Definition 5. *Let $L \subseteq \mathbb{R}^m$ be a full-rank lattice. A distribution $\mathcal{D}$ on L is called (R, q)-concentrated whenever $\Pr_{v \leftarrow \mathcal{D}}[\|v\| \geq R] \leq q$.*

Lemma 5. *Let $L \subseteq \mathbb{R}^m$ be a full-rank lattice with a p-evenly distributed and (R, q)-concentrated distribution $\mathcal{D}$. Denote by S the random variable defined by the number of samples that needs to be drawn from $\mathcal{D}$ such that the samples together generate L as a lattice. Then, for all $\alpha > 0$,*

$$\Pr\left[S > (2 + \alpha) \cdot \frac{(t + m)}{1 - p - q}\right] \leq \exp(-\alpha(t + m)/2)$$

where $t = m \log_2(R) - \log_2(\det(L))$.

Proof. First, we define the following sublattices of L, for any $v_1, \ldots, v_{j-1} \in L$.

$$L_{v_1, \ldots, v_{j-1}} = \begin{cases} \mathrm{span}_{\mathbb{R}}(v_1, \ldots, v_{j-1}) \cap L & \text{if } \dim(\mathrm{span}_{\mathbb{R}}(v_1, \ldots, v_{j-1})) < m \\ \langle v_1, \ldots, v_{j-1} \rangle & \text{otherwise.} \end{cases}$$

Consider a sequence of samples $(v_i)_{i>0}$ (from $\mathcal{D}$). We call v_j 'good' whenever $\|v_j\| \leq R$ and $v_j \notin L_{v_1, \ldots, v_{j-1}}$. We argue that we need at most $m + t$ good vectors to generate L.

Denote L' for the lattice generated by the $m + t$ good vectors. Then the first m good vectors ensure that L' is of rank m, whereas the last t good vectors will reduce the index of the L' lattice in L. Calculating determinants, using the fact that all good vectors are bounded by R, we have $\det(L') \leq R^m/2^t \leq \det(L)$. This yields $L' = L$.

Denote by X the random variable having the negative binomial distribution with success probability $p + q$ and number of 'failures' $m + t$. That is, X is the number of independent samples from a $(p + q)$-Bernoulli distribution until $m + t$ 'failures'[5] are obtained. We argue that the random variable S is dominated by the random variable X, i.e., $\Pr[S > x] \leq \Pr[X > x]$ for every $x \in \mathbb{N}$.

Again, consider a sequence of samples $(v_i)_{i>0}$ (from $\mathcal{D}$). The probability of v_j being a 'good' vector is at least $1 - p - q$, by the fact that $\mathcal{D}$ is (R, q)-concentrated and p-evenly distributed. Because at most $m + t$ 'good' vectors are needed to generate the whole lattice, S is indeed dominated by X. Therefore, for any $k \in \mathbb{N}$,

---

[5] In our case, the failures are the 'good' vectors. We nonetheless chose the word 'failure' because it is standard nomenclature for the negative binomial distribution.

$$\Pr\left[S > \frac{t+m+k}{1-p-q}\right] \leq \Pr\left[X > \frac{t+m+k}{1-p-q}\right] \leq \Pr\left[B < m+t\right] \qquad (15)$$

$$\leq \exp\left(-\frac{1}{2}\frac{k^2}{t+m+k}\right)$$

where B is binomially distributed with $\lfloor\frac{t+m+k}{1-p-q}\rfloor$ trials and success probability $1-p-q$. The first inequality follows from the fact that S is upper bounded by X. The second inequality comes from the close relationship between the negative binomial distribution and the binomial distribution [12, Ch. 8, Ex. 17]. The last inequality follows from Chernoff's bound. Putting $k = (1+\alpha)(t+m)$ into Eq. (15) yields the claim.   □

We conclude by relating the parameters (a, r, ϵ) of the HSP oracle (Definition 1) $f : \mathbb{R}^m/\Lambda \to \mathcal{S}$ and the assumption used in the above Lemma 5.

Lemma 6. *Let Λ be a lattice, and let $M \supsetneq \Lambda$ a proper super-lattice of Λ. Then there exists a $v \in M$ such that $d(v, \Lambda) \geq \lambda_1(\Lambda)/3$.*

Proof. Let $w \in M$ be the shortest non-zero vector in M and write $\|w\| = \alpha\lambda_1(\Lambda)$ for $\alpha < 1$. We show that $v = \lceil\frac{1}{3\alpha}\rceil \cdot w \in M$ suffices. If $\alpha \geq 1/3$ this is certainly true. For $\alpha < 1/3$ it is clear that $\|v\| \geq \lambda_1(\Lambda)/3$ and $\|v\| \leq \lambda_1(\Lambda)/3 + \|w\| \leq \frac{2}{3}\lambda_1(\Lambda)$. In particular, for any $\ell \in \Lambda \setminus \{0\}$, $\|v - \ell\| \geq \lambda_1(\Lambda) - \|v\| \geq \lambda_1(\Lambda)/3$. Therefore, $d(v, \Lambda) \geq \lambda_1(\Lambda)/3$.   □

Lemma 7. *Let Λ be a lattice and $M \supsetneq \Lambda$ a proper super-lattice of Λ. Then the number $N = \left|\{c \in M/\Lambda \mid d(c, \Lambda) < \frac{1}{6}\lambda_1(\Lambda)\}\right|$ of close cosets is at most $\frac{1}{2} \cdot |M/\Lambda|$.*

Proof. By Lemma 6 there exists a $v \in M$ such that $d(v, \Lambda) \geq \frac{1}{3}\lambda_1(\Lambda)$. Denoting $T = \{c \in M/\Lambda \mid d(c, \Lambda) < \frac{1}{6}\lambda_1(\Lambda)\}$, we can deduce that $T \cup (T + v)$ is a disjoint union in M/Λ. Indeed, elements $c \in T$ satisfy $d(c, \Lambda) \leq \frac{1}{6}\lambda_1(\Lambda)$, whereas $c' \in T + v$ satisfy $d(c', \Lambda) \geq d(v, \Lambda) - \frac{1}{6}\lambda_1(\Lambda) \geq \frac{1}{6}\lambda_1(\Lambda)$. Therefore $N = |T| \leq \frac{1}{2}|M/\Lambda|$.   □

Lemma 8. *Let $f : \mathbb{R}^m \to \mathcal{S}$ be an (a, r, ϵ)-HSP oracle of the full-rank lattice $\Lambda \subset \mathbb{R}^m$, with $r \leq \lambda_1(\Lambda)/6$. Let $\mathcal{D}_{\text{ideal}}$ be the distribution supported by Λ^*, with weight $\langle c_{\ell^*}|c_{\ell^*}\rangle$ at $\ell^* \in \Lambda^*$, where $|c_{\ell^*}\rangle$ are the vectorial Fourier coefficients of the function f. Then $\mathcal{D}_{\text{ideal}}$ is both $(\frac{1}{2} + \epsilon)$-evenly distributed and $(R, \frac{ma^2}{4\pi^2 R^2})$-concentrated for any $R > 0$.*

Proof. The distribution $\mathcal{D}_{\text{ideal}}$ being $(R, \frac{ma^2}{4\pi^2 R^2})$-concentrated for any $R > 0$ is a direct consequence of Corollary 5. For the $(\frac{1}{2} + \epsilon)$-evenly distributed part, we argue as follows. Let M^* be any strict sublattice of Λ^*, and let M be its dual, which is then a superlattice of Λ. Put $f|^{\mathbb{R}^m/M}(x) = \frac{1}{|M/\Lambda|}\sum_{v \in M/\Lambda} f(x + v)$, the periodization of f with respect to $\mathbb{R}^m/M$ (c.f. Definition 3). We have the following sequence of equalities, of which the first follows from the Poisson summation formula (see Theorem 7).

$$\sum_{v^* \in M^*} \langle c_{v^*} | c_{v^*} \rangle = \left\| f \right|^{\mathbb{R}^m/M} \right\|_{2, \mathbb{R}^m/M} = \frac{1}{\det M} \int_{x \in \mathbb{R}^m/M} \langle f |^{\mathbb{R}^m/M} | f |^{\mathbb{R}^m/M} \rangle dx,$$

$$= \frac{1}{|M/\Lambda|^2} \sum_{v,w \in M/\Lambda} \underbrace{\frac{1}{\det M} \int_{x \in \mathbb{R}^m/M} \langle f(x+v) | f(x+w) \rangle dx}_{I_{v,w}}$$

$$= \frac{1}{|M/\Lambda|^2} \sum_{\substack{v,w \in M/\Lambda \\ d_{\mathbb{R}^m/\Lambda}(v,w) < r}} I_{v,w} + \frac{1}{|M/\Lambda|^2} \sum_{\substack{v,w \in M/\Lambda \\ d_{\mathbb{R}^m/\Lambda}(v,w) \geq r}} I_{v,w}$$

By the definition of an (a, r, ϵ)-oracle, we have that $|I_{v,w}| \leq \epsilon$ whenever $d_{\mathbb{R}^m/\Lambda}(v, w) \geq r$. In the rest of the cases we have $|I_{v,w}| \leq 1$, because f maps to the unit sphere. Above expression is therefore bounded by $\frac{|M/\Lambda \cap \mathcal{B}_r|}{|M/\Lambda|} + \epsilon$, where $\mathcal{B}_r$ is the open unit ball with radius r. By Lemma 7, we have $\frac{|M/\Lambda \cap r\mathcal{B}|}{|M/\Lambda|} \leq \frac{1}{2}$ for $r \leq \lambda_1(\Lambda)/6$. Summarizing all results, we conclude that

$$\sum_{v^* \in M^*} \langle c_{v^*} | c_{v^*} \rangle \leq \frac{1}{2} + \epsilon.$$

Since M^* was chosen arbitrarily, we can conclude that $\mathcal{D}_{\text{ideal}}$ is $(\frac{1}{2} + \epsilon)$-evenly distributed.   □

Remark 8. A similar reasoning happens in [28, Lecture 12], though it specifically targets the discrete Gaussian distribution on lattices. Despite being not general enough for our purposes, it may well be helpful for optimizing a future specialization.

Acknowledgments. We would like to thank Stacey Jeffery, Oded Regev and Ronald de Wolf for helpful discussions on the topic of this article.

References

1. Banaszczyk, W.: New bounds in some transference theorems in the geometry of numbers. Mathematische Annalen **296**(4), 625–636 (1993). http://eudml.org/doc/165105
2. Biasse, J.F., Song, F.: Efficient quantum algorithms for computing class groups and solving the principal ideal problem in arbitrary degree number fields. In: Proceedings of the Twenty-Seventh Annual ACM-SIAM Symposium on Discrete Algorithms, pp. 893–902. Society for Industrial and Applied Mathematics (2016)
3. de Boer, K., Ducas, L., Fehr, S.: On the quantum complexity of the continuous hidden subgroup problem. Cryptology ePrint Archive, Report 2019/716 (2019). https://eprint.iacr.org/2019/716
4. Buchmann, J., Kessler, V.: Computing a reduced lattice basis from a generating system, August 1996
5. Buchmann, J., Pohst, M.: Computing a lattice basis from a system of generating vectors. In: Davenport, J.H. (ed.) EUROCAL 1987. LNCS, vol. 378, pp. 54–63. Springer, Heidelberg (1989). https://doi.org/10.1007/3-540-51517-8_89. http://dl.acm.org/citation.cfm?id=646658.700556

6. Chang, X., Stehlé, D., Villard, G.: Perturbation analysis of the QR factor R in the context of LLL lattice basis reduction. Math. Comput. **81**(279), 1487–1511 (2012). https://doi.org/10.1090/S0025-5718-2012-02545-2

7. Cramer, R., Ducas, L., Peikert, C., Regev, O.: Recovering short generators of principal ideals in cyclotomic rings. In: Fischlin, M., Coron, J.-S. (eds.) EUROCRYPT 2016. LNCS, vol. 9666, pp. 559–585. Springer, Heidelberg (2016). https://doi.org/10.1007/978-3-662-49896-5_20

8. Cramer, R., Ducas, L., Wesolowski, B.: Short stickelberger class relations and application to ideal-SVP. In: Coron, J.-S., Nielsen, J.B. (eds.) EUROCRYPT 2017. LNCS, vol. 10210, pp. 324–348. Springer, Cham (2017). https://doi.org/10.1007/978-3-319-56620-7_12

9. Deitmar, A., Echterhoff, S.: Principles of Harmonic Analysis, 2nd edn. Springer, Heidelberg (2016). https://doi.org/10.1007/978-0-387-85469-4

10. Ducas, L., Plançon, M., Wesolowski, B.: On the shortness of vectors to be found by the ideal-SVP quantum algorithm. In: Boldyreva, A., Micciancio, D. (eds.) CRYPTO 2019. LNCS, vol. 11692, pp. 322–351. Springer, Cham (2019). https://doi.org/10.1007/978-3-030-26948-7_12

11. Eisenträger, K., Hallgren, S., Kitaev, A., Song, F.: A quantum algorithm for computing the unit group of an arbitrary degree number field. In: Proceedings of the Forty-Sixth Annual ACM Symposium on Theory of Computing, pp. 293–302. ACM (2014)

12. Graham, R.L., Knuth, D.E., Patashnik, O.: Concrete Mathematics: A Foundation for Computer Science, 2nd edn. Addison-Wesley Longman Publishing Co., Inc., Boston (1994)

13. Grover, L., Rudolph, T.: Creating superpositions that correspond to efficiently integrable probability distributions. arXiv preprint quant-ph/0208112 (2002)

14. Hales, L., Hallgren, S.: An improved quantum Fourier transform algorithm and applications. In: Proceedings 41st Annual Symposium on Foundations of Computer Science, pp. 515–525, November 2000. https://doi.org/10.1109/SFCS.2000.892139

15. Hallgren, S.: Fast quantum algorithms for computing the unit group and class group of a number field. In: Proceedings of the Thirty-Seventh Annual ACM Symposium on Theory of Computing, pp. 468–474. ACM (2005)

16. Hallgren, S.: Polynomial-time quantum algorithms for Pell's equation and the principal ideal problem. J. ACM (JACM) **54**(1), 4 (2007)

17. Heinonen, J.: Lectures on Lipschitz analysis. http://www.math.jyu.fi/research/reports/rep100.pdf

18. Kitaev, A., Webb, W.A.: Wavefunction preparation and resampling using a quantum computer. arXiv preprint arXiv:0801.0342 (2008)

19. Kuperberg, G.: A subexponential-time quantum algorithm for the dihedral hidden subgroup problem. SIAM J. Comput. **35**(1), 170–188 (2005)

20. Micciancio, D., Regev, O.: Worst-case to average-case reductions based on Gaussian measures. SIAM J. Comput. **37**(1), 267–302 (2007). https://doi.org/10.1137/S0097539705447360

21. Miller, S.D., Stephens-Davidowitz, N.: Generalizations of Banaszczyk's transference theorems and tail bound. arXiv preprint arXiv:1802.05708 (2018)

22. Mosca, M., Ekert, A.: The hidden subgroup problem and eigenvalue estimation on a quantum computer. In: Williams, C.P. (ed.) QCQC 1998. LNCS, vol. 1509, pp. 174–188. Springer, Heidelberg (1999). https://doi.org/10.1007/3-540-49208-9_15

23. National Institute of Standards and Technology: Post-quantum cryptography standardization (2017). https://csrc.nist.gov/Projects/Post-Quantum-Cryptography/Post-Quantum-Cryptography-Standardization

24. Nguyen, P.Q., Stehlé, D.: An LLL algorithm with quadratic complexity. SIAM J. Comput. **39**(3), 874–903 (2009)
25. Nielsen, M.A., Chuang, I.L.: Quantum Computation and Quantum Information, 10th edn. Cambridge University Press, New York (2011)
26. Novocin, A., Stehlé, D., Villard, G.: An LLL-reduction algorithm with quasi-linear time complexity. In: Proceedings of the Forty-Third Annual ACM Symposium on Theory of Computing, pp. 403–412. ACM (2011)
27. Pellet-Mary, A., Hanrot, G., Stehlé, D.: Approx-SVP in ideal lattices with pre-processing. In: Ishai, Y., Rijmen, V. (eds.) EUROCRYPT 2019. LNCS, vol. 11477, pp. 685–716. Springer, Cham (2019). https://doi.org/10.1007/978-3-030-17656-3_24
28. Regev, O.: Lecture notes in 'lattices in computer science', November 2004
29. Regev, O.: Quantum computation and lattice problems. SIAM J. Comput. **33**(3), 738–760 (2004)
30. Reiter, M., Arthur, S.: Fourier transform & solobev spaces (lecture notes) (2008). https://www.mat.univie.ac.at/~stein/teaching/SoSem08/sobolev_fourier.pdf
31. Schmidt, A., Vollmer, U.: Polynomial time quantum algorithm for the computation of the unit group of a number field. In: Proceedings of the Thirty-Seventh Annual ACM Symposium on Theory of Computing, pp. 475–480. ACM (2005)
32. Shor, P.W.: Algorithms for quantum computation: discrete logarithms and factoring. In: Proceedings 35th Annual Symposium on Foundations of Computer Science, pp. 124–134. IEEE (1994)
33. Song, F.: Email, from September 2018
34. Song, F.: Quantum computing: a cryptographic perspective. Ph.D. thesis, The Pennsylvania State University (2013). https://etda.libraries.psu.edu/files/final_submissions/8820
35. Villani, A.: Another note on the inclusion $l^p(\mu) \subset l^q(\mu)$. Am. Math. Monthly **92**(7), 485–487 (1985). http://www.jstor.org/stable/2322503
36. Werner, D.: Funktionalanalysis. Springer, Heidelberg (2007)
37. Yudin, V.A.: The multidimensional Jackson theorem. Math. Notes Acad. Sci. USSR **20**(3), 801–804 (1976). https://doi.org/10.1007/BF01097255

Foundations

Formalizing Data Deletion in the Context of the Right to Be Forgotten

Sanjam Garg[1($\boxtimes$)], Shafi Goldwasser[2], and Prashant Nalini Vasudevan[1($\boxtimes$)]

[1] Department of Electrical Engineering and Computer Sciences,
University of California Berkeley, Berkeley, USA
{sanjamg,prashvas}@berkeley.edu
[2] Simons Institute for the Theory of Computing,
University of California Berkeley, Berkeley, USA
shafi@theory.csail.mit.edu

Abstract. The right of an individual to request the deletion of their personal data by an entity that might be storing it – referred to as *the right to be forgotten* – has been explicitly recognized, legislated, and exercised in several jurisdictions across the world, including the European Union, Argentina, and California. However, much of the discussion surrounding this right offers only an intuitive notion of what it means for it to be fulfilled – of what it means for such personal data to be deleted.

In this work, we provide a formal definitional framework for the right to be forgotten using tools and paradigms from cryptography. In particular, we provide a precise definition of what could be (or should be) expected from an entity that collects individuals' data when a request is made of it to delete some of this data. Our framework captures most, though not all, relevant aspects of typical systems involved in data processing. While it cannot be viewed as expressing the statements of current laws (especially since these are rather vague in this respect), our work offers technically precise definitions that represent possibilities for what the law could reasonably expect, and alternatives for what future versions of the law could explicitly require.

Finally, with the goal of demonstrating the applicability of our framework and definitions, we consider various natural and simple scenarios where the right to be forgotten comes up. For each of these scenarios, we highlight the pitfalls that arise even in genuine attempts at implementing systems offering deletion guarantees, and also describe technological solutions that provably satisfy our definitions. These solutions bring together techniques built by various communities.

S. Garg and P. N. Vasudevan—Supported in part from AFOSR Award FA9550-19-1-0200, AFOSR YIP Award, NSF CNS Award 1936826, DARPA and SPAWAR under contract N66001-15-C-4065, a Hellman Award and research grants by the Okawa Foundation, Visa Inc., and Center for Long-Term Cybersecurity (CLTC, UC Berkeley). The views expressed are those of the authors and do not reflect the official policy or position of the funding agencies.
S. Goldwasser—Supported in part by the C. Lester Hogan Chair in EECS, UC Berkeley, and Fintech@CSAIL.

© International Association for Cryptologic Research 2020
A. Canteaut and Y. Ishai (Eds.): EUROCRYPT 2020, LNCS 12106, pp. 373–402, 2020.
https://doi.org/10.1007/978-3-030-45724-2_13

1 Introduction

Everything we do in our lives leaves (or will soon leave) a digital trace, which can be analyzed. Recent advances in capturing and analyzing big data help us improve traffic congestion, accurately predict human behavior and needs in various situations, and much more. However, this mass collection of data can be used against people as well. Simple examples of this would be to charge individuals higher auto insurance premiums or decline mortgages and jobs based on an individual's profile as presented by the collected data. In the worst case, this wealth of information could be used by totalitarian governments to persecute their citizens years after the data was collected. In such ways, vast collection of personal data has the potential to present a serious infringement to personal liberty. Individuals could perpetually or periodically face stigmatization as a consequence of a specific past action, even one that has already been adequately penalized. This, in turn, threatens democracy as a whole, as it can force individuals to self-censor personal opinions and actions for fear of later retaliation.

One alternative for individuals wanting to keep personal information secret is to simply stay offline, or at least keep such information hidden from entities that are likely to collect it. Yet, this is not always desirable or possible. These individuals might want to share such information with others over an internet-based platform, or obtain a service based on their personal information, such as personalized movie recommendations based on previous movie watching history, or simply driving directions to their destination based on where they want to go. In such cases, it is reasonable to expect that an individual might later change their mind about having this data available to the service provider they sent it to. In order to provide useful functionality while keeping in mind the aforementioned perils of perennial persistence of data, an individual's ability to withdraw previously shared personal information is very important. For example, one might want to request deletion of all personal data contained in one's Facebook account.

However, in many cases, an individual's desire to request deletion of their private data may be in conflict with a data collector's[1] interests. In particular, the data collector may want to preserve the data because of financial incentives or simply because fulfilling these requests is expensive. It would seem that, in most cases, the data collector has nothing to gain from fulfilling such requests.

Thus, it seems imperative to have in place legal or regulatory means to grant individuals control over what information about them is possessed by different entities, how it is used, and, in particular, provide individuals the rights to request deletion of any (or all) of their personal data. And indeed, the legitimacy of this desire to request deletion of personal data is being increasingly widely discussed, codified in law, and put into practice (in various forms) in, for instance, the European Union (EU) [GDP16], Argentina [Car13], and California [CCP18]. The following are illustrative examples:

---

[1] Throughout this paper, we refer to any entity collecting individuals' data as a "data collector", and often refer such indivisuals whose data is collected as "users".

- The General Data Protection Regulation (GDPR) [GDP16], adopted in 2016, is a regulation in the EU aimed at protecting the data and privacy of individuals in the EU. Article 6 of the GDPR lists conditions under which an entity may lawfully process personal data. The first of these conditions is when "the data subject has given consent to the processing of his or her personal data for one or more specific purposes". And Article 7 states that, "The data subject shall have the right to withdraw his or her consent at any time". Further, Article 17 states that, "The data subject shall have the right to obtain from the controller the erasure of personal data concerning him or her without undue delay and the controller shall have the obligation to erase personal data without undue delay" under certain conditions listed there.
- The California Consumer Privacy Act (CCPA), passed in 2018, is a law with similar purposes protecting residents of California. Section 1798.105 of the CCPA states, "A consumer shall have the right to request that a business delete any personal information about the consumer which the business has collected from the consumer", and that "A business that receives a verifiable request from a consumer ... shall delete the consumer's personal information from its records."

Thus, if a data collector (that operates within the jurisdictions of these laws) wishes to process its consumers' data based on their consent, and wishes to do so lawfully, it would also need to have in place a mechanism to stop using any of its consumers' data. Only then can it guarantee the consumers' *right to be forgotten* as the above laws require. However, it is not straightforward to nail down precisely what this means and involves.

Defining Deletion: More that Meets the Eye. Our understanding of what it means to forget a user's data or honor a user deletion request is rather rudimentary, and consequently, the law does not precisely define what it means to delete something. Further, this lack of understanding is reflected in certain inconsistencies between the law and what would naturally seem desirable. For example, Article 7 of the GDPR, while describing the right of the data subject to withdraw consent for processing of personal data, also states, "the withdrawal of consent shall not affect the lawfulness of processing based on consent before its withdrawal." This seems to suggest that it is reasonable to preserve the result of processing performed on user data even if the data itself is requested to be deleted. However, processed versions of user data may encode all or most of the original data, perhaps even inadvertently. For instance, it is known that certain machine learning models end up memorizing the data they were trained on [SRS17, VBE18].

Thus, capturing the intuitive notion of what it means to truly delete something turns out be quite tricky. In our quest to do so, we ask the following question:

How does an honest data collector know whether it is in compliance with the right to be forgotten?

Here, by *honest* we mean a data collector that does in fact intend to guarantee its users' right to be forgotten in the intuitive sense – it wishes to truly forget all personal data it has about them. Our question is about how it can tell whether the algorithms and mechanisms it has in place to handle deletion requests are in fact working correctly.

Honest Data-Collectors. In this work, we focus on the simple case where the data-collector is assumed to be honest. In other words, we are only interested in the data-collectors that aim to faithfully honor all legitimate deletion requests. Thus, we have no adversaries in our setting. This deviates from many cryptographic applications where an adversary typically attempts to deviate from honest execution. Note that even in the case of semi-honest adversaries in multiparty computation, the adversary attempts to learn more than what it is supposed to learn while following protocol specification. In our case, we expect the data-collector to itself follow the prescribed procedures, including deleting any stored information that it is directed to delete.

With the above view, we do not attempt to develop methods by which a data collector could prove to a user that it did indeed delete the user's data. As a remark, we note here that this is in fact impossible in general, as a malicious data collector could always make additional secret copies of user data.[2] Finally, we note that even for this case of law-abiding data-collectors, the problem of defining what it means to delete data correctly is relevant. The goal of our definitions is to provide such data-collectors guidance in designing systems that handle data deletion, and a mechanism to check that any existing systems are designed correctly and are following the law (or some reasonable interpretation of it).

When is it Okay to Delete? Another challenge a data-collector faces in handling deletion requests is in establishing whether a particular deletion request should be honored. Indeed, in some cases a data collector may be legally required to preserve certain information to satisfy legal or archival needs, e.g. a data collector may be required to preserve some payment information that is evidence in a case in trial. This raises the very interesting question of how to determine whether a particular deletion request should indeed be honored, or even what factors should be taken into consideration while making this decision. However, this is not the focus of this work. Instead, we are only interested in cases where the data-collector does intend (or has already decided) to honor a received deletion request, after having somehow found it legitimate. In such cases, we aim to specify the requirements this places on the data-collector.

Our Contributions. In this work, we provide the first precise general notions of what is required of an honest data-collector trying to faithfully honor deletion requests. We say that a data-collector is *deletion-compliant* if it satisfies our requirements. Our notions are intended to capture the intuitive expectations

---

[2] Certifying deletion could be possible in specific settings though, such as under assumptions on the amount of storage available to the data collector [PT10, DKW11, KK14], or in the presence of quantum computers and data [CW19, BI19].

a user may have when issuing deletion requests. Furthermore, it seems to satisfy the requirements demanded, at least intuitively, by the GDPR and CCPA. However, we note that our definition should not be seen as being equivalent to the relevant parts of these laws – for one, the laws themselves are somewhat vague about what exactly they require in this respect, and also there are certain aspects of data-processing systems that are not captured by our framework (see Sect. 2.2 for a discussion). Instead, our work offers technically precise definitions for data deletion that represent possibilities for interpretations of what the law could reasonably expect, and alternatives for what future versions of the law could explicitly require.

Next, armed with these notions of deletion-compliance, we consider various natural scenarios where the right to be forgotten comes up. For each of these scenarios, we highlight the pitfalls that arise even in genuine attempts at writing laws or honest efforts in implementing systems with these considerations. Our definitions provide guidance towards avoiding these pitfalls by, for one, making them explicit as violations of the definitions. In particular, for each of the considered scenarios, we describe technological solutions that provably satisfy our definitions. These solutions bring together techniques built by various communities.

1.1 Our Notions

In this subsection, we explain our notions of deletion-compliance at a high level, building them up incrementally so as to give deeper insights. The formal definitions are in terms of building blocks from the UC framework [Can01], and details are provided in Sect. 2.1.

The Starting Challenge. We start with the observation that a deletion request almost always involves much more than the process of just erasing something from memory. In fact, this issue comes up even in the most seemingly benign deletion requests. For example, consider the very simple case where a user requests deletion of one of her files stored with a data-collector. In this setting, even if the server was to erase the file from its memory, it may be the case that not all information about it has been deleted. For example, if the files are stored contiguously in memory, it might be possible to recover the size of the file that was deleted. Furthermore, if the files of a user are kept on contiguous parts of the memory, it might be possible to pin-point the owner of the deleted file as well, or in most cases at least be able to tell that there was a file that was deleted.

Our Approach: Leave No Trace. In order to account for the aforementioned issues, we take the *leave-no-trace* approach to deletion in our definitions. In particular, a central idea of our definition is that execution of the deletion request should leave the data collector and the rest of the system in a state that is equivalent (or at least very similar) to one it would have been in if the data that is being deleted was never provided to the data-collector in the first place.

The requirement of leave-no-trace places several constraints on the data-collector. First, and obviously, the data that is requested to be deleted should no longer persist in the memory of the data-collector after the request is processed.

Second, as alluded to earlier, the data-collector must also remove the dependencies that other data could have on the data that is requested for deletion. Or at least, the data-collector should erase the other stored information which depends on this data. We note that we diverge from the GDPR in this sense, as it only requires deletion of data rather than what may have been derived from it via processing. Third, less obvious but clearly necessary demands are placed on the data-collector in terms of what it is allowed to do with the data it collects. In particular, the data-collector cannot reveal any data it collects to any external entity. This is because sharing of user data by the data-collector to external entities precludes it from honoring future deletion requests for the shared data. More specifically, on sharing user data with an external entity, the data-collector loses its the ability to ensure that the data can be deleted from everywhere where it is responsible for the data being present or known. That is, if this data were never shared with the data collector, then it would not have found its way to the external entity, and thus in order for the system to be returned to such a state after a deletion request, the collector should not reveal this data to the entity.

A more concrete consequence of the third requirement above is that the data-collector cannot share or sell user data to third parties. Looking ahead, in some settings this sharing or selling of user data is functionally beneficial and legally permitted as long as the collector takes care to inform the recipients of such data of any deletion requests. For instance, Article 17 of the GDPR says, "Where the controller has made the personal data public and is obliged ... to erase the personal data, the controller ... shall take reasonable steps, including technical measures, to inform controllers which are processing the personal data that the data subject has requested the erasure by such controllers of any links to, or copy or replication of, those personal data." We later see (in Sect. 2.3) how our definition can be modified to handle such cases and extended to cover data collectors that share data with external entities but make reasonable efforts to honor and forward deletion requests.

The Basic Structure of the Definition. In light of the above discussion, the basic form of the definition can be phrased as follows. Consider a user $\mathcal{Y}$ that shares certain data with a data-collector and later requests for the shared data to be deleted. We refer to this execution as a *real world* execution. In addition to this user, the data-collector might interact with other third parties. In this case, we are interested in the memory state of the data-collector post-deletion and the communication between the data-collector and the third parties. Next, we define the *ideal world* execution, which is same as the real world execution except that the user $\mathcal{Y}$ does not share anything with the data-collector and does not issue any deletion requests. Here again we are interested in the memory state of the data-collector and the communication between the data-collector and the third parties. More specifically, we require that the joint distribution of memory state of the data-collector and the communication between the data-collector and the third parties in the two worlds is identically distributed (or is at least very close). Further, this property needs to hold not just for a specific user, but hold for every user that *might* interact with the data-collector as part of its routine operation where it is interacting with any number of other users and processing their data and deletion requests as well. Note that the data-collector does not a priori know when and for what data it will receive deletion requests.

A More Formal Notion. Hereon, we refer to the data-collector as $\mathcal{X}$, and the deletion requester as $\mathcal{Y}$. In addition to these two entities, we model all other parties in the system using $\mathcal{Z}$, which we also refer to as the environment. Thus, in the real execution, the data-collector $\mathcal{X}$ interacts arbitrarily with the environment $\mathcal{Z}$. Furthermore, in addition to interactions with $\mathcal{Z}$, $\mathcal{X}$ at some point receives some data from $\mathcal{Y}$ which $\mathcal{Y}$ at a later point also requests to be deleted. In contrast, in the ideal execution, $\mathcal{Y}$ is replaced by a silent $\mathcal{Y}_0$ that does not communicate with $\mathcal{X}$ at all. In both of these executions, the environment $\mathcal{Z}$ represent both the rest of the users in the system under consideration, as well as an adversarial entity that possibly instructs $\mathcal{Y}$ on what to do and when. Finally, our definition requires that the state of $\mathcal{X}$ and the view of $\mathcal{Z}$ in the real execution and the ideal execution are similar. Thus, our definition requires that the deletion essentially has the same effect as if the deleted data was never sent to $\mathcal{X}$ to begin with. The two executions are illustrated in Fig. 1.

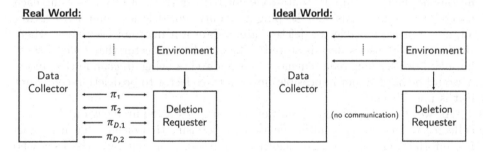

Fig. 1. The real and ideal world executions. In the real world, the deletion-requester talks to the data collector, but not in the ideal world. In the real world, π_1 and π_2 are interactions that contain data that is asked to be deleted by the deletion-requester through the interactions $\pi_{D,1}$ and $\pi_{D,2}$, respectively.

While $\mathcal{Y}$ above is represented as a single user sending some data and a corresponding deletion request, we can use the same framework for a more general modeling. In particular, $\mathcal{Y}$ can be used to model just the part of a user that contains the data to be deleted, or of multiple users, all of whom want some or all of their data to be deleted.

Dependencies in Data. While the above definition makes intuitive sense, certain user behaviors can introduce dependencies that make it impossible for the data-collector to track and thus delete properly. Consider a data-collector that assigns a pseudonym to each user, which is computed as the output of a pseudo-random permutation P (with the seed kept secret by the data-collector) on the user identity. Imagine a user who registers in the system with his real identity id and is assigned the pseudonym pd. Next, the user re-registers a fresh account using pd as his identity. Finally, the user requests deletion of the first account which used his real identity id. In this case, even after the data-collector deletes the requested account entirely, information about the real identity id is still preserved in its memory, i.e. $P^{-1}(pd) = id$. Thus, the actions of the user can make it impossible to keep track of and properly delete user data. In our definition, we resolve this problem by limiting the communication between $\mathcal{Y}$ and $\mathcal{Z}$. We do not allow $\mathcal{Y}$ to send any messages to the environment $\mathcal{Z}$, and require that $\mathcal{Y}$ ask for all (and only) the data it sent to be deleted. This implicitly means that the data that is requested to be deleted cannot influence other information that is stored with the data-collector, unless that is also explicitly deleted by the user.

Requirement that the Data-Collector Be Diligent. Our definitions of deletion compliance place explicit requirements on the data collector only when a deletion request is received. Nonetheless, these explicit requirements implicitly require the data-collector to organize (or keep track of the collected data) in a way that ensures that deletion requests can be properly handled. For example, our definitions implicitly require the data-collector to keep track of how it is using each user's data. In fact, this book-keeping is essential for deletion-compliance. After all, how can a data-collector delete a user's data if it does not even know where that particular user's data is stored? Thus, a data-collector that follows these implicit book-keeping requirements can be viewed as being *diligent*. Furthermore, it would be hard (if not impossible) for a data-collector to be deletion-compliant if it is not diligent.

As we discuss later, our definition also implies a requirement on the data-collector to have in place authentication mechanisms that ensure that it is sharing information only with the legitimate parties, and that only the user who submitted a piece of data can ask for it to be deleted.

Composition Properties. Finally, we also show, roughly, that under an assumption that different users operate independently of each other, a data collector that is deletion-compliant under our definition for a deletion request from a single user is also deletion-compliant for requests from (polynomially) many users (or polynomially many independent messages from a single user). This makes our definition easier to use in the analysis of certain data collectors, as demonstrated in our examples in Sect. 3.

1.2 Lessons from Our Definitions

Our formalization of the notion of data deletion enables us to design and analyze mechanisms that handle data obtained from others and process deletion requests, as demonstrated in Sect. 3. This process of designing systems that satisfy our definition has brought to light a number of properties such a mechanism needs to have in order to be deletion-compliant that may be seen as general principles in this respect.

To start with, satisfying our definition even while providing very simple functionalities requires a non-trivial authentication mechanism that uses randomness generated by the server. Otherwise many simple attacks can be staged that lead to observable differences based on whether some specific data was stored and deleted or never stored. The easier case to observe is when, as part of its functionality, the data collector provides a way for users to retrieve data stored with it. In this case, clearly if there is no good authentication mechanism, then one user can look at another user's data and be able to remember it even after the latter user has asked the collector to delete it. More broadly, our definition implicitly requires the data collector to provide certain privacy guarantees – that one user's data is not revealed to others.

But even if such an interface is not provided by the collector, one user may store data in another user's name, and then if the latter user ever asks for its data to be deleted, this stored data will also be deleted, and looking at the memory of the collector after the fact would indicate that such a request was indeed received. If whatever authentication mechanism the collector employs does not use any randomness from the collector's side, such an attack may be performed by any adversary that knows the initial state (say the user name and the password) of the user it targets.

Another requirement that our definition places on data collectors is that they handle metadata carefully. For instance, care has to be taken to use implementations of data structures that do not inadvertently preserve information about deleted data in their metadata. This follows from our definition as it talks about the state of the memory, and not just the contents of the data structure. Such requirements may be satisfied, for instance, by the use of "history-independent" implementations of data structures [Mic97,NT01], which have these properties.

Further, this kind of history-independence in other domains can also be used to provide other functionalities while satisfying our definition. For instance, recent work [CY15,GGVZ19,Sch20,BCC+19,BSZ20] has investigated the question of data deletion in machine learning models, and this can be used to construct a data collector that learns such a model based on data given to it, and can later delete some of this data not just from its database, but also from the model itself.

Finally, we observe that certain notions of privacy, such as differential privacy [DMNS06], can sometimes be used to satisfy deletion requirements without requiring any additional action from the data collector at all. Very roughly, a differentially private algorithm guarantees that the distribution of its output does not change by much if a small part of its input is changed. We show that if a data collector runs a differentially private algorithm on data that it is given, and is later asked to delete some of the data, it need not worry about updating the output of the algorithm that it may have stored (as long as not too much data is asked to be deleted). Following the guarantee of differential privacy, whether the deleted data was used or not in the input to this algorithm essentially does not matter.

1.3 Related Work

Cryptographic treatment of legal terms and concepts has been undertaken in the past. Prominent examples are the work of Cohen and Nissim [CN19] that formalizes and studies the notion of singling-out that is specified in the GDPR as a means to violate privacy in certain settings, and the work of Nissim et al. [NBW+17] that models the privacy requirements of FERPA using a game-based definition.

Recently, the notion of data deletion in machine learning models has been studied by various groups [CY15, GGVZ19, Sch20, BCC+19, BSZ20]. Closest to our work is the paper of Ginart et al. [GGVZ19], which gives a definition for what it means to retract some training data from a learned model, and shows efficient procedures to do so in certain settings like k-means clustering. We discuss the crucial differences between our definitions and theirs in terms of scope and modelling in Sect. 2.2.

There has been considerable past work on notions of privacy like differential privacy [DMNS06] that are related to our study, but very different in their considerations. Roughly, in differential privacy, the concern is to protect the privacy of each piece of data in a database – it asks that the output of an algorithm running on this database is roughly the same whether or not any particular piece of data is present. We, in our notion of deletion-compliance, ask for something quite different – unless any piece of data is requested to be deleted, the state of the data collector could depend arbitrarily on it; only *after* this deletion request is processed by the collector do the requirements of our definition come in. In this manner, while differential privacy could serve as a means to satisfy our definition, our setting and considerations in general are quite different from those there. For similar reasons, our definitions are able to require bounds on statistical distance without precluding all utility (and in some cases even perfect deletion-compliance is possible), whereas differential privacy has to work with a different notion of distance between distributions (see [Vad17, Section 1.6] for a discussion).

While ours is the first formal definition of data deletion in a general setting, there has been considerable work on studying this question in specific contexts, and in engineering systems that attempt to satisfy intuitive notions of data deletion, with some of it being specifically intended to support the right to be forgotten. We refer the reader to the comprehensive review article by Politou et al. [PAP18] for relevant references and discussion of such work.

2 Our Framework and Definitions

In this section we describe our framework for describing and analyzing data collectors, and our definitions for what it means for a data collector to be *deletion-compliance.* Our modeling uses building blocks that were developed for the Universal Composability (UC) framework of Canetti [Can01]. First, we present the formal description of this framework and our definitions. Explanations of the framework and definitions, and how we intend for them to be used are given in Sect. 2.1. In Sect. 2.2, we discuss the various choices made in our modelling and the implicit assumptions and restrictions involved. In Sect. 2.3, we present a weakening of our definition that covers data collectors that share data with external entities, and in Sect. 2.4 we demonstrate some composition properties that our definition has.

The Model of Execution. Looking ahead, our approach towards defining deletion-compliance of a data collector will be to execute it and have it interact with certain other parties, and at the end of the execution ask for certain properties of what it stores and its communication with these parties. Following [GMR89, Gol01, Can01], both the data collector and these other parties in our framework are modelled as *Interactive Turing Machines* (ITMs), which represent the program to be run within each party. Our definition of an ITM is very similar to the one in [CCL15], but adapted for our purposes.

Definition 1 (Interactive Turing Machine). *An Interactive Turing Machine (ITM) is a (possibly randomized) Turing Machine M with the following tapes: (i) a read-only identifier tape; (ii) a read-only input tape; (iii) a write-only output tape; (iv) a read-write work tape; (v) a single-read-only incoming tape; (vi) a single-write-only outgoing tape; (vii) a read-only randomness tape; and (viii) a read-only control tape.*

The state of an ITM M at any given point in its execution, denoted by $state_M$, consists of the content of its work tape at that point. Its view, denoted by $view_M$, consists of the contents of its input, output, incoming, outgoing, randomness, and control tapes at that point.

The execution of the system consists of several instances of such ITMs running and reading and writing on their own and each others' tapes, and sometimes instances of ITMs being created anew, according to the rules described in this subsection. We distinguish between ITMs (which represent static objects, or programs) and *instances of ITMs*, or ITIs, that represent instantiations of that ITM. Specifically, an ITI is an ITM along with an identifier that distinguishes it from other ITIs in the same system. This identifier is written on the ITI's identifier tape at the point when the ITI is created, and its semantics will be described in more detail later.

In addition to having the above access to its own tapes, each ITI, in certain cases, could also have access to read from or write on certain tapes of other ITI. The first such case is when an ITI M *controls* another ITI M'. M is said to control the ITIs whose identifiers are written on its control tape, and for each ITI M' on this tape, M can read M''s output tape and write on its input tape. This list is updated whenever, in the course of the execution of the system, a new ITI is created under the control of M.

The second case where ITIs have access to each others' tapes is when they are engaged in a *protocol*. A protocol is described by a set of ITMs that are allowed to write on each other's incoming tapes. Further, any "message" that any ITM writes on any other ITM's incoming tape is also written on its own outgoing tape. As with ITMs, a protocol is just a description of the ITMs involved in it and their prescribed actions and interactions; and an *instance* of a protocol, also referred to as a *session*, consists of ITIs interacting with each other (where indeed some of the ITIs may deviate from the prescribed behavior). Each such session has a unique session identifier (sId), and within each session each participating ITI is identified by a unique party identifier (pId). The identifier corresponding to an ITI participating in a session of a protocol with session identifier sId and party identifier pId is the unique tuple (sId, pId).

There will be small number of special ITIs in our system, as defined below, whose identifiers are assigned differently from the above. Unless otherwise specified, all ITMs in our system are probabilistic polynomial time (PPT) – an ITM M is PPT if there exists a constant $c > 0$ such that, at any point during its run, the overall number of steps taken by M is at most n^c, where n is the overall number of bits written on the *input tape* of M during its execution.

The Data Collector. We require the behavior of the data collector and its interactions with other parties to be specified by a tuple $(\mathcal{X}, \pi, \pi_D)$, where $\mathcal{X}$ specifies the algorithm run by the data collector, and π, π_D are protocols by means of which the data collector interacts with other entities. Here, π could be an arbitrary protocol (in the simplest case, a single message followed by local processing), and π_D is the corresponding *deletion* protocol – namely, a protocol to undo/reverse a previous execution of the protocol π.

For simplicity, in this work, we restrict to protocol π, π_D to the natural case of the two-party setting.[3] Specifically, each instance of the protocol π that is executed has specifications for a server-side ITM and a client-side ITM. The data collector will be represented in our system by a special ITI that we will also refer to as $\mathcal{X}$. When another ITI in the system, call it $\mathcal{W}$ for now, wishes to interact with $\mathcal{X}$, it does by initiating an instance (or session) of one of the protocols π or π_D. This initiation creates a pair of ITIs – the client and the server of this session – where $\mathcal{W}$ controls the client ITI and $\mathcal{X}$ the server ITI. $\mathcal{W}$ and $\mathcal{X}$ then interact by means of writing to and reading from the input and output tapes of these ITIs that they control. Further details are to be found below.

The only assumption we will place on the syntax of these protocols is the following interface between π and π_D. We require that at the end of any particular execution of π, a *deletion token* is defined that is a function solely of the sId of the execution and its transcript, and that π should specify how this token is computed. The intended interpretation is that a request to delete this instance of π consists of an instance of π_D where the client-side ITI is given this

---

[3] However, our model naturally generalizes to protocols with more parties.

deletion token as input. As we will see later, this assumption does not lose much generality in applications.

Recipe for Describing Deletion-Compliance. Analogous to how security is defined in the UC framework, we define *deletion-compliance* in three steps as follows. First, we define a *real execution* where certain other entities interact with the data collector ITI $\mathcal{X}$ by means of instances the protocols π and π_D. This is similar to the description of the "real world" in the UC framework. In this setting, we identify certain deletion requests (that is, executions of π_D) that are of special interest for us – namely, the requests that we will be requiring to be satisfied. Next, we define an *ideal execution*, where the instances of π that are asked to be deleted by these identified deletion requests are never executed in the first place. The "ideal execution" in our setting is different from the "ideal world" in the UC framework in the sense that we do not have an "ideal functionality". Finally, we say that $(\mathcal{X}, \pi, \pi_D)$ is *deletion-compliant* if the two execution process are essentially the same in certain respects. Below, we explain the model of the *real* execution, the *ideal* execution, and the notion of deletion-compliance.

Real Execution. The real execution involves the data collector ITI $\mathcal{X}$, and two other special ITIs: the *environment* $\mathcal{Z}$ and the *deletion requester* $\mathcal{Y}$. By intention, $\mathcal{Y}$ represents the part of the system whose deletion requests we focus on and will eventually ask to be respected by $\mathcal{X}$, and $\mathcal{Z}$ corresponds to the rest of the world – the (possibly adversarial) environment that interacts with $\mathcal{X}$. Both of these interact with $\mathcal{X}$ via instances of π and π_D, with $\mathcal{X}$ controlling the server-side of these instances and $\mathcal{Z}$ or $\mathcal{Y}$ the client-side.

The environment $\mathcal{Z}$, which is taken to be adversarial, is allowed to use arbitrary ITMs (ones that may deviate from the protocol) as the client-side ITIs of any instances of π or π_D it initiates. The deletion-requester $\mathcal{Y}$, on the other hand, is the party we are notionally providing the guarantees for, and is required to use honest ITIs of the ITMs prescribed by π and π_D in the instances it initiates, though, unless otherwise specified, it may provide them with any inputs as long as they are of the format required by the protocol.[4] In addition, we require that any instance of π_D run by $\mathcal{Y}$ is for an instance of π already initiated by $\mathcal{Y}$.[5] Finally, in our modeling, while $\mathcal{Z}$ can send arbitrary messages to $\mathcal{Y}$ (thereby influencing its executions), we do not allow any communication from $\mathcal{Y}$ back to $\mathcal{Z}$. This is crucial for ensuring that the $\mathcal{X}$ does not get any "to be deleted" information from other sources.

At any point, there is at most one ITI in the system that is *activated*, meaning that it is running and can reading from or writing to any tapes that it has access to. Each ITI, while it is activated, has access to a number of tapes that it can write to and read from. Over the course of the execution, various ITIs

---

[4] Note that it is essential that $\mathcal{Y}$ follow the honest protocol specifications to ensure that the deletion requests are successful.

[5] This corresponds to providing guarantees only for entities that do not (maliciously or otherwise) ask for others' data to be deleted.

are activated and deactivated following rules described below. When an ITI is activated, it picks up execution from the point in its "code" where it was last deactivated.

Now we provide a formal description of the real execution. We assume that all parties have a computational/statistical security parameter $\lambda \in \mathbb{N}$ that is written on their input tape as 1^λ the first time they are activated.[6] The execution consists of a sequence of *activations*, where in each activation a single participant (either $\mathcal{Z}, \mathcal{Y}, \mathcal{X}$ or some ITM) is activated, and runs until it writes on the incoming tape of another (at most *one* other) machine, or on its own output tape. Once this write happens, the writing participant is deactivated (its execution is paused), and another party is activated next—namely, the one on who incoming tape the message was written; or alternatively, if the message was written to the output tape then the party controlling the writing ITI is activated. If no message is written to the incoming tape (and its own output tape) of any party, then $\mathcal{Z}$ is activated. The real execution proceeds in two phases: (i) the alive phase, and (ii) the termination phase.

Alive Phase: This phase starts with an activation of the environment $\mathcal{Z}$, and $\mathcal{Z}$ is again activated if any other ITI halts without writing on a tape. The various ITIs run according to their code, and are allowed to act as follows:

- The environment $\mathcal{Z}$ when active is allowed to read the tapes it has access to, run, and perform any of the following actions:
  - Write an arbitrary message on the incoming tape of $\mathcal{Y}$.
  - Write on the input tape of any ITI that it controls (from protocol instances initiated in the past).
  - Initiate a new protocol instance of π or π_D with $\mathcal{X}$, whereupon the required ITIs are created and $\mathcal{Z}$ is given control of the client-side ITI of the instance and may write on its input tape. At the same time, $\mathcal{X}$ is given control of the corresponding server-side ITI that is created.
  - Pass on activation to $\mathcal{X}$ or $\mathcal{Y}$.
  - Declare the end of the Alive Phase, upon which the execution moves to the Terminate Phase. This also happens if $\mathcal{Z}$ halts.
- The deletion-requester $\mathcal{Y}$ on activation can read the tapes it has access to, run, and perform any of the following actions:
  - Write on the input tape of any ITI that it controls.
  - Initiate a new instance of π or π_D with $\mathcal{X}$, and write on the input tape of the created client-side ITI.
- The data collector $\mathcal{X}$ on activation can read the tapes it has access to, run, and write on the input tape of any ITI that it controls.
- Any other ITI that is activated is allowed to read any of the tapes that it has access to, and write to either the incoming tape of another ITI in the protocol instance it is a part of, or on its own output tape.

---

[6] We remark that this is done merely for convenience and is not essential for the model to make sense. In particular, in the perfect security case, no security parameter is needed.

Terminate Phase: In this phase, the various ITIs are allowed the same actions as in the Alive phase. The activation in this phase proceeds as follows:

1. First, each client-side ITI for π that was initiated by $\mathcal{Y}$ in the Alive phase is sequentially activated enough times until each one of them halts.
2. For any instance of π for which a client-side ITI was initiated by $\mathcal{Y}$ and which was executed to completion, an instance of π_D is initiated with input the deletion token for that instance of π (except if such an instance of π_D was already initiated).
3. Each client-side ITI for instances of π_D that were initiated by $\mathcal{Y}$ in the Alive phase or in the previous step is sequentially activated enough times until each one of them halts.

We denote by $\text{EXEC}_{\mathcal{Z},\mathcal{Y}}^{\mathcal{X},\pi,\pi_D}(\lambda)$ the tuple $(state_{\mathcal{X}}, view_{\mathcal{X}}, state_{\mathcal{Z}}, view_{\mathcal{Z}})$ resulting at the end of above-described real execution with security parameter λ.

Ideal Execution. Denote by $\mathcal{Y}_0$ the special $\mathcal{Y}$ that is completely silent – whenever it is activated, it simply halts. In particular, it does not initiate any ITIs and does not write on the incoming tape of any other machine. A real execution using such a $\mathcal{Y}_0$ as the deletion-requester is called an ideal execution. We denote by $\text{EXEC}_{\mathcal{Z},\mathcal{Y}_0}^{\mathcal{X},\pi,\pi_D}(\lambda)$ the tuple $(state_{\mathcal{X}}, view_{\mathcal{X}}, state_{\mathcal{Z}}, view_{\mathcal{Z}})$ resulting at the end of an ideal execution with data collector $\mathcal{X}$ and environment $\mathcal{Z}$, and with security parameter λ.

We are now ready to present our definition for the deletion-compliance of data collectors, which is as follows.

Definition 2 (Statistical Deletion-Compliance). *Given a data-collector $(\mathcal{X}, \pi, \pi_D)$, an environment $\mathcal{Z}$, and a deletion-requester $\mathcal{Y}$, let $(state_{\mathcal{X}}^{R,\lambda}, view_{\mathcal{X}}^{R,\lambda})$ denote the corresponding parts of the real execution $\text{EXEC}_{\mathcal{Z},\mathcal{Y}}^{\mathcal{X},\pi,\pi_D}(\lambda)$, and let $(state_{\mathcal{X}}^{I,\lambda}, view_{\mathcal{Z}}^{I,\lambda})$ represent those of the ideal execution $\text{EXEC}_{\mathcal{Z},\mathcal{Y}_0}^{\mathcal{X},\pi,\pi_D}(\lambda)$. We say that $(\mathcal{X}, \pi, \pi_D)$ is statistically deletion-compliant if, for any PPT environment $\mathcal{Z}$, any PPT deletion-requester $\mathcal{Y}$, and for all unbounded distinguishers D, there is a negligible function ε such that for all $\lambda \in \mathbb{N}$:*

$$\left| \Pr[D(state_{\mathcal{X}}^{R,\lambda}, view_{\mathcal{Z}}^{R,\lambda}) = 1] - \Pr[D(state_{\mathcal{X}}^{I,\lambda}, view_{\mathcal{Z}}^{I,\lambda}) = 1] \right| \leq \varepsilon(\lambda)$$

In other words, the statistical distance between these two distributions above is at most $\varepsilon(\lambda)$. If D above is required to be computationally bounded (allowed to run only in PPT time in λ), then we get the weaker notion of *computational deletion-compliance*. Analogously, if $\varepsilon(\lambda)$ is required to be 0, then we get the stronger notion of *perfect deletion-compliance*.

2.1 Explanation of the Definition

As indicated earlier, the central idea our definition is built around is that the processing of a deletion request should leave the data collector and the rest of the system in a state that is similar to one it would have been in if the data that was deleted was never given to the collector in the first place. This ensures that there is no trace left of deleted data, even in metadata maintained by some of the entities, etc.

The first question that arises here is which parts of the system to ask this of. It is clear that the deleted data should no longer persist in the memory of the data collector. A less obvious but clearly necessary demand is that the data collector also not reveal this data to any user other than the one it belongs to. Otherwise, unless whomever this data is revealed to provides certain guarantees for its later deletion, the data collector loses the ability to really delete this data from locations it reached due to actions of the data collector itself, which is clearly undesirable.[7]

Once so much is recognized, the basic form of the definition is clear from a cryptographic standpoint. We fix any user, let the user send the collector some data and then request for it to be deleted, and look at the state of the collector at this point together with its communication with the rest of the system so far. We also look at the same in a world where this user did not send this data at all. And we ask that these are distributed similarly. We then note that this property needs to hold not just when the collector is interacting solely with this user, but is doing so as part of its routine operation where it is interacting with any number of other users and processing their data and deletion requests as well.

The UC Framework. In order to make this definition formal, we first need to model all entities in a formal framework that allows us to clearly talk about the "state" or the essential memory of the entities, while also being expressive enough to capture all, or at least most, data collectors. We chose the UC framework for this purpose as it satisfies both of these properties and is also simple enough to describe clearly and succinctly. In this framework, the programs that run are represented by Interactive Turing Machines, and communication is modelled as one machine writing on another's tape. The state of an entity is then captured by the contents of the work tape of the machine representing it, and its view by whatever was written on its tapes by other machines. This framework does impose certain restrictions on the kind of executions that it captures, though, and this is discussed later, in Sect. 2.2.

Protocols and Interaction. Another choice of formality motivated by its usefulness in our definition is to have all communication with the data collector $\mathcal{X}$

---

[7] Of course, if the entity this data is revealed to does provide some guarantees for later deletion, then we may reasonably expect the data collector to provide deletion guarantees even while revealing data to this entity. In Sect. 2.3, we present a weaker definition of deletion-compliance that captures this.

be represented by instances of a protocol π. It should be noted that the term "protocol" here might belie the simplicity of π, which could just involve the sending of a piece of data by a user of the system to the data collector $\mathcal{X}$. This compartmentalisation of communication into instances of π is to let us (and the users) refer directly to specific instances later and request their deletion using instances of the deletion protocol π_D. As the reference to instances of π, we use a "deletion token" that is computable from the transcript of that instance – this is precise enough to enable us to refer to specific pieces of data that are asked to be deleted, and loose enough to capture many natural systems that might be implemented in reality for this purpose.

The Deletion-Requester $\mathcal{Y}$ and the Environment $\mathcal{Z}$. The role of the user in the above rudimentary description is played by the deletion-requester $\mathcal{Y}$ in our framework. In the "real" execution, $\mathcal{Y}$ interacts with the data collector $\mathcal{X}$ over some instances of π, and then asks for all information contained in these instances to be deleted. In the "ideal" execution, $\mathcal{Y}$ is replaced by a silent $\mathcal{Y}_0$ that does not communicate with $\mathcal{X}$ at all. And both of these happen in the presence of an environment $\mathcal{Z}$ that interacts arbitrarily with $\mathcal{X}$ (through instances of π and π_D) – this $\mathcal{Z}$ is supposed to represent both the rest of the users in the system that $\mathcal{X}$ interacts with, as well as an adversarial entity that, in a sense, attempts to catch $\mathcal{X}$ if it is not handling deletions properly. By asking that the state of $\mathcal{X}$ and the view of $\mathcal{Z}$ in both these executions be similar, we are asking that the deletion essentially have the same effect on the world as the data never being sent.

It is to be noted that while $\mathcal{Y}$ here is represented as a single entity, it does not necessarily represent just a single "user" of the system or an entire or single source of data. It could represent just a part of a user that contains the data to be deleted, or represent multiple users, all of whom want their data to be deleted. In other words, if a data collector $\mathcal{X}$ is deletion-compliant under our definition, and at some point in time has processed a certain set of deletion requests, then as long as the execution of the entire world at this point can be separated into $\mathcal{Z}$ and $\mathcal{Y}$ that follow our rules of execution, the deletion-compliance of $\mathcal{X}$ promises that all data that was sent to $\mathcal{X}$ from $\mathcal{Y}$ will disappear from the rest of the world.

Using the Definition. Our framework and definition may be used for two purposes: (i) to guide the design of data collectors $\mathcal{X}$ that are originally described within our framework (along with protocols π and π_D) and wish to handle deletion requests well, and (ii) to analyse the guarantees provided by existing systems that were not designed with our framework in mind and which handle data deletion requests.

In order to use Definition 2 to analyze the deletion-compliance of pre-existing systems, the first step is to rewrite the algorithm of the data collector to fit within our framework. This involves defining the protocols π and π_D representing the communication between "users" in the system and the data collector. This part of the process involves some subjectivity, and care has to be taken to not lose crucial but non-obvious parts of the data collector, such as metadata and memory allocation procedures, in this process. The examples of some simple systems presented in Sect. 3 illustrate this process) though they do not talk about modelling lower-level implementation details). Once the data collector and the protocols are described in our framework, the rest of the work in seeing whether they satisfy our definition of deletion-compliance is well-defined.

2.2   Discussion

A number of choices were made in the modelling and the definition above, the reasons for some of which are not immediately apparent. Below, we go through a few of these and discuss their place in our framework and definition.

Modelling Interactions. The first such choice is to include in the model the entire communication process between the data collector and its users rather than look just at what goes on internally in the data collector. For comparison, a natural and simpler definition of data deletion would be to consider a data collector that has a database, and maintains the result of some computation on this database. It then receives requests to delete specific rows in the database, and it is required to modify both the database and the processed information that it maintains so as to make it look like the deleted row was never present. The definition of data deletion in machine learning by Ginart et al. [GGVZ19], for instance, is of this form.

The first and primary reason for this choice is that the intended scope of our definitions is larger than just the part of the data collector that maintains the data. We intend to analyze the behavior of the data collector as a whole, including the memory used to implement the collector's algorithm and the mechanisms in place for interpreting and processing its interactions with external agents. For instance, as we discuss in Sect. 3, it turns out that any data collector that wishes to provide reasonable guarantees to users deleting their data needs to have in place a non-trivial authentication mechanism. This requirement follows easily from the requirements of our definition, but would not be apparent if only the part of the collector that directly manages the data is considered.

The second reason is that while the simpler kind of definition works well when the intention is to apply it to collectors that do indeed have such a static database that is given to them, it fails to capture crucial issues that arise in a more dynamic setting. Our inclusion of the interactions between parties in our definition enables us to take into account dependencies among the data in the system, which in turn enables us to keep our demands on the data collector more reasonable. Consider, for example, a user who sends its name to a data collector that responds with a hash of it under some secret hash function. And then the user asks the same collector to store a piece of data that is actually the same hash, but there is no indication given to the collector that this is the case. At some later time, the user asks the collector to delete its name. To a definition that only looks at the internal data storage of the collector, the natural expectation after this deletion request is processed would be that the collector's state should look as though it never learnt the user's name. However, this is an unreasonable demand – since the collector has no idea that the hash of the name was also given to it, it is not reasonable to expect that it also find the hash (which contains information about the name) and delete it. And indeed, under our definition, the collector is forgiven for not doing so unless the user explicitly asks for the hash also to be deleted. If our modelling had not kept track of the interactions between the collector and the user, we would not have been able to make this relaxation.

Restrictions on $\mathcal{Y}$. Another conspicuous choice is not allowing the deletion-requester $\mathcal{Y}$ in our framework to send messages to the environment $\mathcal{Z}$. This is, in fact, how we handle cases like the one just described where there are dependencies between the messages that the collector receives that are introduced on the users' side. By requiring that $\mathcal{Y}$ does not send messages to $\mathcal{Z}$ and that all interaction between $\mathcal{Y}$ and $\mathcal{X}$ are asked to be deleted over the course of the execution, we ensure that any data that depends on $\mathcal{X}$'s responses to $\mathcal{Y}$'s messages is also asked to be deleted. This admits the case above where both the name and the hash are requested to be deleted, and requires $\mathcal{X}$ to comply with such a request; but it excludes the case where only the name is asked to be deleted (as then the hash would have to be sent by $\mathcal{Z}$, which has no way of learning it), thus excusing $\mathcal{X}$ for not deleting it.

Also note that this restriction does not lose any generality outside of excluding the above kind of dependency. Take any world in which a user (or users) asks for some of its messages to be deleted, and where the above perverse dependency does not exist between these and messages not being asked to be deleted. Then, there is a pair of environment $\mathcal{Z}$ and deletion-requester $\mathcal{Y}$ that simulates that world exactly, and the deletion-compliance guarantees of $\mathcal{X}$ have the expected implications for such a deletion request. The same is true of the restriction that *all* of the messages sent by $\mathcal{Y}$ have to be requested to be deleted rather than just some of them – it does not actually lose generality. And also of the fact that $\mathcal{Y}$ is a single party that is asking for deletion rather than a collection – a set of users asking for deletion can be simulated by just one $\mathcal{Y}$ that does all their work.

The Ideal Deletion-Requester. An interesting variant of our definition would be one in which the $\mathcal{Y}$ is not replaced by a silent $\mathcal{Y}_0$ in the ideal world, but by another $\mathcal{Y}'$ that sends essentially the same kinds of messages to $\mathcal{X}$, but with different contents. Currently, our definition says that, after a deletion request, the collector does not even remember that it had some data that was deleted. This might be unnecessarily strong for certain applications, and this modification would relax the requirement to saying that it is fine for the collector to remember that it had some data that was deleted, just not what the data was. The modification is not trivial, though, as in general the number and kinds of messages that $\mathcal{Y}$ sends could depend on the contents of its messages and the responses from $\mathcal{X}$, which could change if the contents are changed. Nevertheless, under the assumption that $\mathcal{Y}$ behaves nicely in this sense, such an alternative definition could be stated and would be useful in simple applications.

Choices that Lose Generality. There are certain assumptions in our modelling that do break from reality. One of these is that all machines running in the system are sequential. Due to this, our definition does not address, for instance, the effects of race conditions in the data collector's implementation. This assumption, however, makes our definition much simpler and easier to work with, while still keeping it meaningful. We leave it as an open question to come up with a reasonable generalization of our definition (or an alternative to it) that accounts for parallel processing.

Another such assumption is that, due to the order of activations and the fact that activation is passed on in the execution by ITIs writing on tapes, we do not give $\mathcal{Z}$ the freedom to interlace its messages freely with those being sent by $\mathcal{Y}$ to $\mathcal{X}$. It could happen, for instance, that $\mathcal{X}$ is implemented poorly and simply fails to function if it does not receive all messages belonging to a particular protocol instance consecutively. This failure is not captured by our definition as is, but this is easily remedied by changing the activation rules in the execution to pass activation back to $\mathcal{Z}$ after each message from (an ITI controlled by) $\mathcal{Y}$ to $\mathcal{X}$ is sent and responded to. We do not do this for the sake of simplicity.

Finally, our modelling of the data collector's algorithm being the entire ITM corresponds to the implicit assumption of reality that the process running this algorithm is the only one running on the system. Or, at least, that the distinguisher between the real and ideal worlds does not get to see how memory for this process is allocated among all the available memory in the system, does not learn about scheduling in the system, etc. Side-channel attacks involving such information and definitions that provide protection against these would also be interesting for future study, though even more exacting than our definition.

2.3   Conditional Deletion-Compliance

As noted in earlier sections, any data collector that wishes to be deletion-compliant under Definition 2 cannot reveal the data that is given to it by a user to any other entity. There are several situations, however, where such an action is desirable and even safe for the purposes of deletion. And rules for how the collector should act when it is in fact revealing data in this way is even specified in some laws – Article 17 of the GDPR, for instance, says, "Where the controller has made the personal data public and is obliged ... to erase the personal data, the controller, taking account of available technology and the cost of implementation, shall take reasonable steps, including technical measures, to inform controllers which are processing the personal data that the data subject has requested the erasure by such controllers of any links to, or copy or replication of, those personal data."

Consider, for instance, a small company $\mathcal{X}$ that offers storage services using space it has rented from a larger company $\mathcal{W}$. $\mathcal{X}$ merely stores indexing information on its end and stores all of its consumers' data with $\mathcal{W}$, and when a user asks for its data to be deleted, it forwards (an appropriately modified version of) this request to the $\mathcal{W}$. Now, if $\mathcal{W}$ is deletion-compliant and deletes whatever data $\mathcal{X}$ asks it to, it could be possible for $\mathcal{X}$ to act in way that ensures that state of the entire system composed of $\mathcal{X}$ and $\mathcal{W}$ has no information about the deleted data. In other words, conditioned on some deletion-compliance properties of the environment (that includes $\mathcal{W}$ here), it is reasonable to expect deletion guarantees even from collectors that reveal some collected data. In this subsection, we present a definition of *conditional* deletion-compliance that captures this.

Specifically, we consider the case where the environment $\mathcal{Z}$ itself is deletion-compliant, though in a slightly different sense than Definition 2. In order to define this, we consider the deletion-compliance of a data collector $\mathcal{X}$ running its protocols (π, π_D) in the presence of other interaction going on in the system. So far, in our executions involving $(\mathcal{X}, \pi, \pi_D)$, we essentially required that $\mathcal{Y}$ and $\mathcal{Z}$ only interact with $\mathcal{X}$ by means of the protocols π and π_D. Now we relax this requirement and, in both phases of execution, allow an additional set of protocols $\Phi = \{\phi_1, \ldots\}$ that can be initiated by $\mathcal{X}$ to be run between $\mathcal{X}$ and $\mathcal{Z}$ (but not $\mathcal{Y}$) during the execution. We denote an execution involving $\mathcal{X}$, $\mathcal{Z}$ and $\mathcal{Y}$ under these rules by $\mathrm{EXEC}_{\mathcal{Z},\mathcal{Y},\Phi}^{\mathcal{X},\pi,\pi_D}$.

Finally, we also consider executions where, additionally, we also let $\mathcal{X}$ write on the incoming tape of $\mathcal{Y}$.[8] We call such an execution an *auxiliary* execution, and denote it by $\mathrm{AEXEC}_{\mathcal{Z},\mathcal{Y},\Phi}^{\mathcal{X},\pi,\pi_D}$. We define the following notion of auxiliary deletion-compliance that we will be the condition we will place on the environment in our eventual definition of conditional deletion-compliance.

Definition 3 (Auxiliary Deletion-Compliance). *Given a data-collector denoted by $(\mathcal{X}, \pi, \pi_D)$, an environment $\mathcal{Z}$, a deletion-requester $\mathcal{Y}$, and a set of protocols Φ, let $(state_{\mathcal{X}}^{R,\lambda}, view_{\mathcal{Z}}^{R,\lambda})$ denote the corresponding parts of the auxiliary execution $\mathrm{AEXEC}_{\mathcal{Z},\mathcal{Y},\Phi}^{\mathcal{X},\pi,\pi_D}(\lambda)$, and $(state_{\mathcal{X}}^{I,\lambda}, view_{\mathcal{Z}}^{I,\lambda})$ the corresponding parts of the ideal auxiliary execution $\mathrm{AEXEC}_{\mathcal{Z},\mathcal{Y}_0,\Phi}^{\mathcal{X},\pi,\pi_D}(\lambda)$. We say that $(\mathcal{X}, \pi, \pi_D)$ is statistically auxiliary-deletion-compliant in the presence of Φ if, for any PPT environment $\mathcal{Z}$, any PPT deletion-requester $\mathcal{Y}$, and for all unbounded distinguishers D, there is a negligible function ε such that for all $\lambda \in \mathbb{N}$:*

$$\left| \Pr[D(state_{\mathcal{X}}^{R,\lambda}, view_{\mathcal{Z}}^{R,\lambda}) = 1] - \Pr[D(state_{\mathcal{X}}^{I,\lambda}, view_{\mathcal{Z}}^{I,\lambda}) = 1] \right| \leq \varepsilon(\lambda)$$

Note that we do not ask $\mathcal{X}$ for any guarantees on being able to delete executions of the protocols in Φ. It may be seen that any data collector $(\mathcal{X}, \pi, \pi_D)$ that is deletion-compliant is also auxiliary deletion-compliant in the presence of any Φ, since it never runs any of the protocols in Φ.

We say that a data collector $\mathcal{X}$ is conditionally deletion-compliant if, whenever it is interacting with an environment that is auxiliary-deletion-compliant, it provides meaningful deletion guarantees.

---

[8] This weakens the definition of deletion-compliance, as it allows $\mathcal{X}$ to send to $\mathcal{Y}$ anything it wants, since the view or state of $\mathcal{Y}$ is not scrutinized by the requirements of deletion-compliance. And though as a definition of deletion-compliance this is not meaningful on its own, it is a property that, if the environment $\mathcal{Z}$ possesses it, seems necessary and sufficient to allow a data collector $\mathcal{X}$ to safely reveal data to $\mathcal{Z}$ that it may wish to delete later.

Definition 4 (Conditional Deletion-Compliance). *Given a data-collector* $(\mathcal{X}, \pi, \pi_D)$, *an environment* $\mathcal{Z}$, *a deletion-requester* $\mathcal{Y}$, *and a pair of protocols* $\Phi = (\phi, \phi_D)$, *let* $(state_{\mathcal{X}}^{R,\lambda}, state_{\mathcal{Z}}^{R,\lambda})$ *denote the corresponding parts of the real execution* $\mathrm{EXEC}_{\mathcal{Z},\mathcal{Y},\Phi}^{\mathcal{X},\pi,\pi_D}(\lambda)$, *and* $(state_{\mathcal{X}}^{I,\lambda}, state_{\mathcal{Z}}^{I,\lambda})$ *the corresponding parts of the ideal execution* $\mathrm{EXEC}_{\mathcal{Z},\mathcal{Y}_0,\Phi}^{\mathcal{X},\pi,\pi_D}(\lambda)$. *We say that* $(\mathcal{X}, \pi, \pi_D)$ *is conditionally statistically deletion-compliant in the presence of* Φ *if, for any PPT environment* $\mathcal{Z}$ *such that* $(\mathcal{Z}, \phi, \phi_D)$ *is statistically auxiliary-deletion-compliant in the presence of* (π, π_D), *any PPT deletion-requester* $\mathcal{Y}$, *and for all unbounded distinguishers* D, *there is a negligible function* ε *such that for all* $\lambda \in \mathbb{N}$:

$$\left| \Pr[D(state_{\mathcal{X}}^{R,\lambda}, state_{\mathcal{Z}}^{R,\lambda}) = 1] - \Pr[D(state_{\mathcal{X}}^{I,\lambda}, state_{\mathcal{Z}}^{I,\lambda}) = 1] \right| \leq \varepsilon(\lambda)$$

One implication of $\mathcal{X}$ being conditionally deletion-compliant is that if, in some execution, it is found that data that was requested of $\mathcal{X}$ to be deleted is still present in the system in some form, then this is not due to a failure on the part of $\mathcal{X}$, but was because the environment $\mathcal{Z}$ was not auxiliary-deletion-compliant and hence failed to handle deletions correctly. A setup like the one described at the beginning of this subsection is studied as an example of a conditionally deletion-compliant data collector in Sect. 3.1.

2.4   Properties of Our Definitions

In this section, we demonstrate a few properties of our definition of deletion-compliance that are meaningful to know on their own and will also make analyses of data collectors we design in later sections simpler. In order to describe them, we first define certain special classes of deletion-requesters. The first is one where we limit the number of protocol instances the deletion-requester $\mathcal{Y}$ is allowed to initiate.

Definition 5. *For* $k \in \mathbb{N}$, *a deletion-requester* $\mathcal{Y}$ *is said to be* k-representative *if, when interacting with a data collector* $\mathcal{X}$ *running* (π, π_D), *it initiates at most* k *instances of* π *with* $\mathcal{X}$.

The other is a class of deletion-requesters intended to represent the collected actions of several 1-representative deletion-requesters operating independently of each other. In other terms, the following represents, say, a collection of users that interact with a data collector by sending it a single message each, and further never interact with each other. This is a natural circumstance that arises in several situations of interest, such as when people respond to a survey or submit their medical records to a hospital, for example. Hence, even deletion-compliance guarantees that hold only in the presence of such deletion-requesters are already meaningful and interesting.

Definition 6. *A deletion-requester* $\mathcal{Y}$ *is said to be* oblivious *if, when interacting with a data collector* $\mathcal{X}$ *running* (π, π_D), *for any instance of* π *that it initiates, it never accesses the output tape of the corresponding client-side ITI except when running* π_D *to delete this instance, whereupon it merely computes the deletion token and provides it as input to* π_D.

Note that the deletion-requester $\mathcal{Y}$ not accessing the output tapes does not necessarily mean that the entities or users that it notionally represents similarly do not look at the responses they receive from the data collector – as long as each user in a collection of users does not communicate anything about such responses to another user, the collection may be faithfully represented by an oblivious $\mathcal{Y}$. Similarly, an oblivious $\mathcal{Y}$ could also represent a single user who sends multiple messages to the data collector, under the condition that the content of these messages, and whether and when the user sends them, does not depend on any information it receives from the data collector.

We also quantify the error that is incurred by a data collector in its deletion-compliance as follows. In our definition of deletion-compliance (Definition 2), we required this error to be negligible in the security parameter.

Definition 7 (Deletion-Compliance Error). *Let $k \in \mathbb{N}$. Given a data-collector $(\mathcal{X}, \pi, \pi_D)$, an environment $\mathcal{Z}$ and a deletion-requester $\mathcal{Y}$, denote by $(state_{\mathcal{X}}^{R,\lambda}, view_{\mathcal{Z}}^{R,\lambda})$ the corresponding parts of $\mathrm{EXEC}_{\mathcal{Z},\mathcal{Y}}^{\mathcal{X},\pi,\pi_D}(\lambda)$, and denote by $(state_{\mathcal{X}}^{I,\lambda}, view_{\mathcal{Z}}^{I,\lambda})$ the corresponding parts of $\mathrm{EXEC}_{\mathcal{Z},\mathcal{Y}_0}^{\mathcal{X},\pi,\pi_D}(\lambda)$. The (statistical) deletion-compliance error of $(\mathcal{X}, \pi, \pi_D)$ is a function $\varepsilon : \mathbb{N} \rightarrow [0,1]$ where for $\lambda \in \mathbb{N}$, the function value $\varepsilon(\lambda)$ is set to be the supremum, over all PPT environments $\mathcal{Z}$, all PPT deletion-requesters $\mathcal{Y}$, and all unbounded distinguishers D, of the following quantity when all parties are given λ as the security parameter:*

$$\left| \Pr[D(state_{\mathcal{X}}^{R,\lambda}, view_{\mathcal{Z}}^{R,\lambda}) = 1] - \Pr[D(state_{\mathcal{X}}^{I,\lambda}, view_{\mathcal{Z}}^{I,\lambda}) = 1] \right|$$

The oblivious deletion-compliance error is defined similarly, but only quantifying over all oblivious PPT deletion-requesters $\mathcal{Y}$. And the k-representative deletion-compliance error is defined similarly by quantifying over all k-representative PPT $\mathcal{Y}$'s.

We show that, for oblivious deletion-requesters, the deletion-compliance error of any data collector $(\mathcal{X}, \pi, \pi_D)$ grows at most linearly with the number of instances of π that are requested to be deleted. In other words, if k different users of $\mathcal{X}$ ask for their information to be deleted, and they all operate independently in the sense that none of them looks at the responses from $\mathcal{X}$ to any of the others, then the error that $\mathcal{X}$ incurs in processing all these requests is at most k times the error it incurs in processing one deletion request.

Apart from being interesting on its own, our reason for proving this theorem is that in the case of some data collectors that we construct in Sect. 3, it turns out to be much simpler to analyze the 1-representative deletion-compliance error than the error for a generic deletion-requester. The following theorem then lets us go from the 1-representative error to the error for oblivious deletion-requesters that make more deletion requests.

Theorem 1. *For $k \in \mathbb{N}$ and any data collector $(\mathcal{X}, \pi, \pi_D)$, the k-representative oblivious deletion-compliance error is no more than k times its 1-representative deletion-compliance error.*

We defer the proof of the above theorem to the full version. We also show that, given two data collectors that are each deletion-compliant, their combination is also deletion-compliant, assuming obliviousness of deletion-requesters. To be more precise, given a pair of data collectors $(\mathcal{X}_1, \pi_1, \pi_{1,D})$ and $(\mathcal{X}_2, \pi_2, \pi_{2,D})$, consider the "composite" data collector $((\mathcal{X}_1, \mathcal{X}_2), (\pi_1, \pi_2), (\pi_{1,D}, \pi_{2,D}))$ that works as follows:

- An instance of (π_1, π_2) is either an instance of π_1 or of π_2. Similarly, an instance of $(\pi_{1,D}, \pi_{2,D})$ is either an instance of $\pi_{1,D}$ or of $\pi_{2,D}$.
- The collector $(\mathcal{X}_1, \mathcal{X}_2)$ consists of a simulation of $\mathcal{X}_1$ and of $\mathcal{X}_2$, each running independently of the other.
- When processing an instance of π_1 or $\pi_{1,D}$, it forwards the messages to and from its simulation of $\mathcal{X}_1$, and similarly $\mathcal{X}_2$ for π_2 or $\pi_{2,D}$.
- The state of $(\mathcal{X}_1, \mathcal{X}_2)$ consists of the states of its simulations of $\mathcal{X}_1$ and $\mathcal{X}_2$.

Such an $\mathcal{X}$ would represent, for instance, two data collectors that operate separately but deal with the same set of users. We show that, if the constituting data collectors are deletion-compliant, then under the condition of the deletion-requester being oblivious, the composite data collector is also deletion-compliant.

Theorem 2. *If $(\mathcal{X}_1, \pi_1, \pi_{1,D})$ and $(\mathcal{X}_2, \pi_2, \pi_{2,D})$ are both statistically deletion-compliant, then the composite data collector $((\mathcal{X}_1, \mathcal{X}_2), (\pi_1, \pi_2), (\pi_{1,D}, \pi_{2,D}))$ is statistically deletion-compliant for oblivious deletion-requesters.*

We prove Theorem 2 in the full version. The above theorem extends to the composition of any k data collectors in this manner, where there is a loss of a factor of k in the oblivious deletion-compliance error (this will be evident from the proof below).

Proof of Theorem 2. The theorem follows by first showing that the composite collector is deletion-compliant for 1-representative data collectors, and then applying Theorem 1. Any 1-representative deletion-requester $\mathcal{Y}$ interacts either only with (the simulation of) $\mathcal{X}_1$ or with $\mathcal{X}_2$. And since both of these are deletion-compliant, the state of $(\mathcal{X}_1, \mathcal{X}_2)$ and the view of the environment are similarly distributed in both real and ideal executions. Thus, $((\mathcal{X}_1, \mathcal{X}_2), (\pi_1, \pi_2), (\pi_{1,D}, \pi_{2,D}))$ is 1-representative deletion-compliant. Applying Theorem 1 now gives us the theorem. □

3   Scenarios

In this section, we present examples of data collectors that satisfy our definitions of deletion-compliance with a view to illustrate both the modelling of collectors in our framework, and the aspects of the design of such collectors that are necessitated by the requirement of such deletion-compliance. In interest of space, we only present two of our data collectors here, and defer discussion of the ones based employing differential privacy and data deletion in machine learning to the full version.

3.1   Data Storage and History-Independence

Consider the following ostensibly simple version of data storage. A company wishes to provide the following functionality to its users. A user can ask the company to store a single piece of data, say their date-of-birth or a password. At a later point, the user can ask the company to retrieve this data, whence the company sends this stored data back to the user. And finally, the user can ask for this data to be deleted, at which point the company deletes any data the user has asked to be stored.

While a simple task, it is still not trivial to implement the deletion here correctly. The natural way to implement these functionalities is to use a dictionary data structure that stores key-value pairs and supports insertion, deletion and lookup operations. The collector could then store the data a user sends as the value and use a key that is somehow tied to the user, say the user's name or some other identifier. Unless care is taken, however, such data structures could prove insufficient – data that has been deleted could still leave a trace in the memory implementing the data structure. A pathological example is a dictionary that, to indicate that a certain key-value pair has been deleted, simply appends the string "deleted" to the value – note that such a dictionary can still provide valid insertion, deletion and lookup. While actual implementations of dictionaries do not explicitly maintain "deleted" data in this manner, no special care is usually taken to ensure that information about such data does not persist, for instance, in the metadata.

The simplest solution to this problem is to use an implementation of such a data structure that explicitly ensures that the above issue does not occur. History independent data structures, introduced by Micciancio [Mic97], are implementations of data structures that are such that their representation in memory at any point in time reveals only the "content" of the data structure at that point, and not the history of the operations (insertion, deletion, etc.) performed that resulted in this content. In particular, this implies that an insertion of some data into such a data structure followed by a deletion of the same data would essentially have the same effect on memory as not having done either in the first place.

More formally, these are described as follows by Naor and Teague [NT01]. Any abstract data structure supports a set of operations, each of which, without loss of generality, returns a result (which may be null). Two sequences of operations S_1 and S_2 are said to produce the same *content* if for any sequence T, the results returned by T with the prefix S_1 is the same as the results with the prefix S_2. An implementation of a data structure takes descriptions of operations and returns the corresponding results, storing what it needs to in its memory. Naor and Teague then define history independence as a property of how this memory is managed by the implementation.

Definition 8. *An implementation of a data structure is* history independent *if any two sequences of operations that produce the same content also induce the same distribution on the memory representation under the implementation.*

If data is stored by the data collector in a history independent data structure that supports deletion, then being deletion-compliant becomes a lot simpler, as the property of history independence helps satisfy much of the requirements. In our case, we will make us of a history-independent dictionary, a data structure defined as follows. History-independent dictionaries were studied and constructed by Naor and Teague [NT01].

Definition 9. *A* dictionary *is a data structure that stores key-value pairs, denoted by* (key, value), *and supports the following operations:*

- Insert(key, value): *stores the value* value *under the key* key. *If the key is already in use, does nothing.*
- Lookup(key): *returns the value previously stored under the key* key. *If there is no such key, returns* ⊥.
- Delete(key): *deletes the key-value pair stored under the key* key. *If there is no such key, does nothing.*

Our current approach, then, is to implement the data storage using a history-independent dictionary as follows. When a user sends a (key, value) pair to be stored, we insert it into the dictionary. When a user asks for the value stored under a key key, we look it up in the dictionary and return it. When a user asks to delete whatever is stored under the key key, we delete this from the dictionary. And the deletion, due to history-independence, would remove all traces of anything that was deleted.

There is, however, still an issue that arises from the fact that the channels in our model are not authenticated. Without authentication, any entity that knows a user's key could use it to learn from the data collector whether this user has any data stored with it. And later if the user asks for deletion, the data might be deleted from the memory of the collector, but the other entity has already learnt it, which it could not have done in an ideal execution. In order to deal with this, the data collector has to implement some form of authentication; and further, this authentication, as seen by the above example, has to use some randomness (or perhaps pseudorandomness) generated on the data collector's side. We implement the simplest form of authentication that suffices for this, and the resulting data collector $\mathcal{H}$ is described informally as follows.

. . . .

The data collector $\mathcal{H}$ maintains a history-independent dictionary Dict. Below, any information that is not required explicitly to be stored is erased as soon as each message is processed. It waits to receive a message from a user that is parsed as (instruction, auth, key, value), where either of auth or value could be ⊥, and processed as follows:

- If instruction = insert,
    - it samples a new random authentication string auth.
    - it runs Dict.Insert((key, auth), value) to add value to the dictionary under the key (key, auth).
    - it responds to the message with the string auth.

- If instruction = lookup,
  - it recovers the *value* stored under the key $(key, auth)$ by running the lookup algorithm Dict.Lookup$((key, auth))$, and responds with *value* (if the key is not in use, *value* will be $\perp$).
- If instruction = delete,
  - it deletes any entry under the key $(key, auth)$ by running the deletion algorithm Dict.Delete$((key, auth))$.

....

The formal description of the above data collector in our framework, along with the associated protocols π and π_D, is presented in the full version. We show that this collector is indeed statistically deletion-compliant.

Informal Theorem 1. *The data collector $\mathcal{H}$ presented above is statistically deletion-compliant.*

We present the formal version of the above theorem and its proof in the full version. The approach is to first observe that, due to the authentication mechanism, the probability that the environment $\mathcal{Z}$ will ever see any data that was stored by the deletion-requester $\mathcal{Y}$ is negligible in the security parameter. If this never happens, then the view of $\mathcal{Z}$ in the real and ideal executions (where $\mathcal{Y}$ does not store anything) is identical. And when the view is identical, the sequence of operations performed by $\mathcal{Z}$ in the two executions are also identical. Thus, since whatever $\mathcal{Y}$ asks to store it also asks to delete, the state of $\mathcal{X}$ at the end of the execution, due to its use of a history-independent dictionary, depends only on the operations of $\mathcal{Z}$, which are now the same in the real and ideal executions.

In summary, the lessons we learn from this process of constructing a deletion-compliant data collector for data storage are as follow:

1. Attention has to be paid to the implementation of the data structures used, which needs to satisfy some notion of independence from deleted data.
2. Authentication that involves some form of hardness or randomness from the data collector's side has to be employed even to support simple operations.

Outsourcing Data Storage. Next, we present a data collector that outsources its storage to an external system, maintaining only bookkeeping information in its own memory. As it actively reveals users' data to this external system, such a data collector cannot be deletion-compliant. However, we show that history-independence can be used to make it *conditionally* deletion-compliant. Again, it turns out to be crucial to ensure that an authentication mechanism is used, for reasons similar to that for the previously constructed data collector. This data collector $\mathcal{H}_2$ is informally described as follows, and is quite similar to $\mathcal{H}$.

....

The data collector $\mathcal{H}_2$ maintains a history-independent dictionary Dict, and interacts with another collector $\mathcal{W}$ that uses the same syntax for messages as the collector $\mathcal{H}$ from earlier in this section. It waits to receive a message that is parsed as (instruction, $auth, key, value$), where either of $auth$ or $value$ could be $\bot$, and processed as follows:

- If instruction = insert,
  - It samples a new authentication string $auth$ and a new "external key" $exkey$ at random.
  - It sends the message (insert, $exkey, value$) to $\mathcal{W}$ and waits to receive a response $exauth$.
  - It runs Dict.Insert$((key, auth), (exkey, exauth))$ to add $(exkey, exauth)$ to the dictionary under the key $(key, auth)$.
  - It responds to the initial message with the string $auth$.
- If instruction = lookup,
  - It recovers the $(exkey, exauth)$ stored under the key $(key, auth)$ by running Dict.Lookup$((key, auth))$. If the lookup fails, it responds with $\bot$.
  - It sends the message (lookup, $exkey, exauth$) to $\mathcal{W}$ and waits to receive a response $value$.
  - It responds to the initial message with $value$.
- If instruction = delete,
  - It recovers the $(exkey, exauth)$ stored under the key $(key, auth)$ by running Dict.Lookup$((key, auth))$. If the lookup fails, it halts.
  - If not, it sends the message (delete, $exkey, exauth$) to $\mathcal{W}$.
  - It deletes any entry under the key $(key, auth)$ by running the deletion algorithm Dict.Delete$((key, auth))$.

. . . .

The formal description of the above data collector in our framework, along with the associated protocols π and π_D, is presented in the full version. We show that this collector is conditionally deletion-compliant.

Informal Theorem 2. *The data collector $\mathcal{H}_2$ described above is conditionally statistically deletion-compliant.*

The formal version of this theorem and its proof is presented in the full version. The approach is again to first condition on $\mathcal{Z}$ not being able to guess any of the authentication strings given to $\mathcal{Y}$, an event that happens with overwhelming probability. After this, we show that the history-independence of the dictionary used by $\mathcal{X}$ can be used to effectively split $\mathcal{X}$ into two parts – one that handles protocols with $\mathcal{Y}$, and the other than handles protocols with $\mathcal{Z}$ – without affecting what essentially happens in the execution. At this point, we switch to looking at the execution as an auxiliary execution with $\mathcal{Z}$ as the data collector, the first part of $\mathcal{X}$ as the deletion-requester, and the second part as the environment, and apply the auxiliary deletion-compliance of $\mathcal{Z}$ to show that the states of $\mathcal{Z}$ and $\mathcal{X}$ are unchanged if $\mathcal{Y}$ is replaced with a silent $\mathcal{Y}_0$.

References

[BCC+19] Bourtoule, L., et al.: Machine unlearning. CoRR, abs/1912.03817 (2019)

[BI19] Broadbent, A., Islam, R.: Quantum encryption with certified deletion. arXiv preprint arXiv:1910.03551 (2019)

[BSZ20] Baumhauer, T., Schöttle, P., Zeppelzauer, M.: Machine unlearning: linear filtration for logit-based classifiers. CoRR, abs/2002.02730 (2020)

[Can01] Canetti, R.: Universally composable security: a new paradigm for cryptographic protocols. In: 42nd Annual Symposium on Foundations of Computer Science, pp. 136–145. IEEE Computer Society Press, October 2001

[Car13] Carter, E.L.: Argentina's right to be forgotten. Emory Int'l L. Rev. **27**, 23 (2013)

[CCL15] Canetti, R., Cohen, A., Lindell, Y.: A simpler variant of universally composable security for standard multiparty computation. In: Gennaro, R., Robshaw, M. (eds.) CRYPTO 2015, Part II. LNCS, vol. 9216, pp. 3–22. Springer, Heidelberg (2015). https://doi.org/10.1007/978-3-662-48000-7_1

[CCP18] California Consumer Privacy Act (CCPA) (2018). https://oag.ca.gov/privacy/ccpa

[CN19] Cohen, A., Nissim, K.: Towards formalizing the GDPR's notion of singling out. CoRR, abs/1904.06009 (2019)

[CW19] Coiteux-Roy, X., Wolf, S.: Proving erasure. In: IEEE International Symposium on Information Theory, ISIT 2019, Paris, France, 7–12 July 2019, pp. 832–836. IEEE (2019)

[CY15] Cao, Y., Yang, J.: Towards making systems forget with machine unlearning. In: 2015 IEEE Symposium on Security and Privacy, SP 2015, San Jose, CA, USA, 17–21 May 2015, pp. 463–480. IEEE Computer Society (2015)

[DKW11] Dziembowski, S., Kazana, T., Wichs, D.: One-time computable self-erasing functions. In: Ishai, Y. (ed.) TCC 2011. LNCS, vol. 6597, pp. 125–143. Springer, Heidelberg (2011). https://doi.org/10.1007/978-3-642-19571-6_9

[DMNS06] Dwork, C., McSherry, F., Nissim, K., Smith, A.D.: Calibrating noise to sensitivity in private data analysis. In: Halevi, S., Rabin, T. (eds.) TCC 2006. LNCS, vol. 3876, pp. 265–284. Springer, Heidelberg (2006). https://doi.org/10.1007/11681878_14

[GDP16] Regulation (EU) 2016/679 of the European parliament and of the council of 27 April 2016 on the protection of natural persons with regard to the processing of personal data and on the free movement of such data, and repealing directive 95/46 (general data protection regulation). Official J. Eur. Union (OJ) **59**(1–88), 294 (2016)

[GGVZ19] Ginart, A., Guan, M.Y., Valiant, G., Zou, J.: Making AI forget you: data deletion in machine learning. CoRR, abs/1907.05012 (2019)

[GMR89] Goldwasser, S., Micali, S., Rackoff, C.: The knowledge complexity of interactive proof systems. SIAM J. Comput. **18**(1), 186–208 (1989)

[Gol01] Goldreich, O.: Foundations of Cryptography: Basic Tools, vol. 1. Cambridge University Press, Cambridge (2001)

[KK14] Karvelas, N.P., Kiayias, A.: Efficient proofs of secure erasure. In: Abdalla, M., De Prisco, R. (eds.) SCN 2014. LNCS, vol. 8642, pp. 520–537. Springer, Cham (2014). https://doi.org/10.1007/978-3-319-10879-7_30

[Mic97] Micciancio, D.: Oblivious data structures: applications to cryptography. In: Leighton, F.T., Shor, P.W. (eds.) Proceedings of the Twenty-Ninth Annual ACM Symposium on the Theory of Computing, El Paso, Texas, USA, 4–6 May 1997, pp. 456–464. ACM (1997)

[NBW+17] Nissim, K., et al.: Bridging the gap between computer science and legal approaches to privacy. Harv. JL Tech. **31**, 687 (2017)

[NT01]   Naor, M., Teague, V.: Anti-presistence: history independent data struc-
         tures. In: Vitter, J.S., Spirakis, P.G., Yannakakis, M. (eds.) Proceedings
         on 33rd Annual ACM Symposium on Theory of Computing, Heraklion,
         Crete, Greece, 6–8 July 2001, pp. 492–501. ACM (2001)

[PAP18] Politou, E.A., Alepis, E., Patsakis, C.: Forgetting personal data and revok-
         ing consent under the GDPR: challenges and proposed solutions. J. Cyber-
         secur. 4(1), tyy001 (2018)

[PT10]   Perito, D., Tsudik, G.: Secure code update for embedded devices via
         proofs of secure erasure. In: Gritzalis, D., Preneel, B., Theoharidou, M.
         (eds.) ESORICS 2010. LNCS, vol. 6345, pp. 643–662. Springer, Heidelberg
         (2010). https://doi.org/10.1007/978-3-642-15497-3_39

[Sch20] Schelter, S.: "Amnesia" - machine learning models that can forget user
         data very fast. In: 10th Conference on Innovative Data Systems Research,
         CIDR 2020, Amsterdam, The Netherlands, 12–15 January 2020 (2020).
         Online Proceedings. www.cidrdb.org

[SRS17] Song, C., Ristenpart, T., Shmatikov, V.: Machine learning models that
         remember too much. In: Thuraisingham, B.M., Evans, D., Malkin, T., Xu,
         D. (eds.) Proceedings of the 2017 ACM SIGSAC Conference on Computer
         and Communications Security, CCS 2017, Dallas, TX, USA, 30 October–
         03 November 2017, pp. 587–601. ACM (2017)

[Vad17] Vadhan, S.P.: The complexity of differential privacy. In: Lindell, Y. (ed.)
         Tutorials on the Foundations of Cryptography. ISC, pp. 347–450. Springer,
         Cham (2017). https://doi.org/10.1007/978-3-319-57048-8_7

[VBE18] Veale, M., Binns, R., Edwards, L.: Algorithms that remember: model
         inversion attacks and data protection law. CoRR, abs/1807.04644 (2018)

OptORAMa: Optimal Oblivious RAM

Gilad Asharov[1]($\boxtimes$), Ilan Komargodski[2], Wei-Kai Lin[3], Kartik Nayak[4],
Enoch Peserico[5], and Elaine Shi[3]

[1] Bar-Ilan University, 52900 Ramat Gan, Israel
gilad.asharov@biu.ac.il
[2] NTT Research, Palo Alto, CA 94303, USA
ilan.komargodski@ntt-research.ac.il
[3] Cornell University, Ithaca, NY 14850, USA
w1572@cornell.edu, runting@gmail.com
[4] Duke University, Durham, NC 27708, USA
kartik@cs.duke.edu
[5] Università degli Studi di Padova, Padova, PD, Italy
enoch@dei.unipd.it

Abstract. Oblivious RAM (ORAM), first introduced in the ground-breaking work of Goldreich and Ostrovsky (STOC '87 and J. ACM '96) is a technique for provably obfuscating programs' access patterns, such that the access patterns leak no information about the programs' secret inputs. To compile a general program to an oblivious counterpart, it is well-known that $\Omega(\log N)$ amortized blowup is necessary, where N is the size of the logical memory. This was shown in Goldreich and Ostrovksy's original ORAM work for statistical security and in a somewhat restricted model (the so called *balls-and-bins* model), and recently by Larsen and Nielsen (CRYPTO '18) for computational security.

A long standing open question is whether there exists an *optimal* ORAM construction that matches the aforementioned logarithmic lower bounds (without making large memory word assumptions, and assuming a constant number of CPU registers). In this paper, we resolve this problem and present the first secure ORAM with $O(\log N)$ amortized blowup, assuming one-way functions. Our result is inspired by and non-trivially improves on the recent beautiful work of Patel et al. (FOCS '18) who gave a construction with $O(\log N \cdot \log \log N)$ amortized blowup, assuming one-way functions.

One of our building blocks of independent interest is a linear-time deterministic oblivious algorithm for tight compaction: Given an array of n elements where some elements are marked, we permute the elements in the array so that all marked elements end up in the front of the array. Our $O(n)$ algorithm improves the previously best known deterministic or randomized algorithms whose running time is $O(n \cdot \log n)$ or $O(n \cdot \log \log n)$, respectively.

Keywords: Oblivious RAM · Randomized algorithms · Tight compaction

© International Association for Cryptologic Research 2020
A. Canteaut and Y. Ishai (Eds.): EUROCRYPT 2020, LNCS 12106, pp. 403–432, 2020.
https://doi.org/10.1007/978-3-030-45724-2_14

1   Introduction

Oblivious RAM (ORAM), first proposed by Goldreich and Ostrovsky [22,23], is a technique to compile *any* program into a functionally equivalent one, but whose memory access patterns are independent of the program's secret inputs. The overhead of an ORAM is defined as the (multiplicative) blowup in runtime of the compiled program. Since Goldreich and Ostrovsky's seminal work, ORAM has received much attention due to its applications in cloud computing, secure processor design, multi-party computation, and theoretical cryptography (for example, [7,19–21,34–36,39,44,46,47,51–53]).

For more than three decades, the biggest open question in this line of work is regarding the *optimal* overhead of ORAM. Goldreich and Ostrovsky's original work [22,23] showed a construction with $O(\log^3 N)$ blowup in runtime, assuming the existence of one-way functions, where N denotes the memory size consumed by the original non-oblivious program. On the other hand, they proved that any ORAM scheme must incur at least $\Omega(\log N)$ overhead, but their lower bound is restricted to schemes that treat the contents of each memory word as "indivisible" (see Boyle and Naor [8]) and make no cryptographic assumptions. In a recent work, Larsen and Nielsen [30] showed that $\Omega(\log N)$ overhead is necessary for all *online* ORAM schemes,[1] even ones that use cryptographic assumptions and might perform non-trivial encodings on the contents of the memory. Since Goldreich and Ostrovsky's work, a long line of research has been dedicated to improving the asymptotic efficiency of ORAM [10,25,29,45,48,50]. Prior to our work, the best known scheme, allowing computational assumptions, is the elegant work by Patel et al. [40]: they showed the existence of an ORAM with $O(\log N \cdot \log \log N)$ overhead, assuming one-way functions. In comparison with Goldreich and Ostrovksy's original $O(\log^3 N)$ result, Patel's result seems tantalizingly close to matching the lower bound, but unfortunately we are still not there yet and the construction of an optimal ORAM continues to elude us even after more than 30 years.

1.1   Our Results: Optimal Oblivious RAM

We resolve this long-standing problem by showing a matching upper bound to Larsen and Nielsen's [30] lower bound: an ORAM scheme with $O(\log N)$ overhead and negligible security in λ, where N is the size of the memory and λ is the security parameter, assuming one-way functions. More concretely, we show:[2]

---

[1] An ORAM scheme is *online* if it supports accesses arriving in an online manner, one by one. Almost all known schemes have this property.

[2] Note that for the (sub-)exponential security regime, e.g., failure probability of $2^{-\lambda}$ or $2^{-\lambda^\epsilon}$ for some $\epsilon \in (0,1)$, perfectly secure ORAM schemes [12,16] asymptotically outperform known statistically or computationally secure constructions assuming that $N = \mathsf{poly}(\lambda)$.

Theorem 1.1. *Assume that there is a PRF family that is secure against any probabilistic polynomial-time adversary except with a negligible small probability in λ. Assume that $\lambda \leq N \leq T \leq \text{poly}(\lambda)$ for any fixed polynomial $\text{poly}(\cdot)$, where T is the number of accesses. Then, there is an ORAM scheme with $O(\log N)$ overhead and whose security failure probability is upper bounded by a suitable negligible function in λ.*

In the aforementioned results and throughout this paper, unless otherwise noted, we shall assume a standard word-RAM where each memory word has at least $w = \log N$ bits, i.e., large enough to store its own logical address. We assume that word-level addition and boolean operations can be done in unit cost. We assume that the CPU has constant number of private registers. For our ORAM construction, we additionally assume that a single evaluation of a pseudorandom function (PRF), resulting in at least word-size number of pseudo-random bits, can be done in unit cost.[3] Note that all earlier computationally secure ORAM schemes, starting with the work of Goldreich and Ostrovsky [22,23], make the same set of assumptions. Additionally, we remark that our result can be made statistically secure if one assumes a private random oracle to replace the PRF (the known logarithmic ORAM lower bound [22,23,30] still hold in this setting). Finally, we note that our construction suffers from huge constants due to the use of certain expander graphs; improving the concrete constant is left for future work.

In the full version [5], we provide a comparison with previous works, where we make the comparison more accurate and meaningful by explicitly stating the dependence on the error probability (which was assumed to be some negligible functions in previous works).

1.2 Our Results: Optimal Oblivious Tight Compaction

Closing the remaining $\log \log N$ gap for ORAM turns out to be highly challenging. Along the way, we actually construct an important building block, that is, a *deterministic*, linear-time, oblivious *tight compaction* algorithm. This result is an important contribution on its own, and has intimate connections to classical algorithms questions, as we explain below.

Tight compaction is the following task: given an input array of size n containing either real or dummy elements, output a permutation of the input array where all real elements appear in the front. Tight compaction can be considered as a restricted form of sorting, where each element in the input array receives a 1-bit key, indicating whether it is real or dummy. One naïve solution for tight compaction, therefore, is to rely on oblivious sorting to sort the input array [2,24]; unfortunately, due to recent lower bounds [17,33], we know that any oblivious sorting scheme must incur $\Omega(n \cdot \log n)$ time on a word-RAM, either assuming

---

[3] Alternatively, if we use number of IOs as an overhead metric, we only need to assume that the CPU can evaluate a PRF internally without writing to memory, but the evaluation need not be unit cost.

that the algorithm treats each element as "indivisible" [33] or assuming that the famous Li-Li network coding conjecture [32] is true [17].

A natural question, therefore, is whether we can do asymptotically better than just naïvely sorting the input. It turns out that this question is related to a line of work in the classical algorithms literature, that is, the design of switching networks and routing on such networks [2,4,6,18,42,43]. First, a line of combinatorial works showed the existence of linear-sized super-concentrators [41, 42,49], i.e., switching networks with n inputs and n outputs such that vertex-disjoint paths exist from any k elements in the inputs to any k positions in the outputs. One could leverage a linear-sized super-concentrator construction to *obliviously* route all the real elements in the input to the front of the output array deterministically and in linear time (by routing elements along the routes), but it is not clear yet how to find routes (i.e., a set of vertex-disjoint paths) from the real input positions to the front of the output array.

In an elegant work in 1996, Pippenger [43] showed a deterministic, linear-time algorithm for route-finding but unfortunately the algorithm is *not oblivious*. Shortly afterwards, Leighton et al. [31] showed a probabilistic algorithm that tightly compacts n elements in $O(n \cdot \log \log \lambda)$ time with $1 - \mathsf{negl}(\lambda)$ probability—their algorithm is *almost oblivious* except for leaking the number of reals and dummies. After Leighton et al. [31], this line of work remained somewhat stagnant for almost two decades. Only recently, did we see some new results: Mitchell and Zimmerman [38] as well as Lin et al. [33] showed how to achieve the same asymptotics as Leighton et al. [31] but now making the algorithm fully oblivious.

In this paper, we give an explicit construction of a deterministic, oblivious algorithm that tightly compacts any input array of n elements in linear time, as stated in the following theorem:

Theorem 1.2 (Linear-time oblivious tight compaction). *There is a deterministic, oblivious tight compaction algorithm that compacts n elements in $O(\lceil D/w \rceil \cdot n)$ time on a word-RAM where D is the bit-width for encoding each element and $w \geq \log n$ is the word size.*

Our algorithm is *not comparison-based* and *not stable* and this is inherent. Specifically, Lin et al. [33] recently showed that any stable, oblivious tight compaction algorithm (that treats elements as indivisible) must incur $\Omega(n \cdot \log n)$ runtime, where stability requires that the real elements in the output must appear in the same order as the input. Further, due to the well-known 0-1 principle [1,15], any comparison-based tight compaction algorithm must incur at least $\Omega(n \cdot \log n)$ runtime as well.[4]

Not only our ORAM construction relies on the above compaction algorithm in several key points, but it is a useful primitive independently. For example, we use our compaction algorithm to give a perfectly oblivious algorithm that

---

[4] Although the algorithm of Leighton et al. [31] appears to be comparison-based, it is in fact not since the algorithm must tally the number of reals/dummies and make use of this number.

randomly permutes arrays of n elements in (worst-case) $O(n \cdot \log n)$ time. All previously known such constructions have some probability of failure.

2   Technical Roadmap

We give a high-level overview of our results. In Sect. 2.1 we provide a high-level overview of our ORAM construction which uses an oblivious tight compaction algorithm. In Sect. 2.2 we give a high-level overview of the techniques underlying our tight compaction algorithm.

2.1   Oblivious RAM

In this section we present a high-level description of the main ideas and techniques underlying our ORAM construction. Full details are given later in the corresponding technical sections.

Hierarchical ORAM. The hierarchical ORAM framework, introduced by Goldreich and Ostrovsky [22, 23] and improved in subsequent works (e.g., [10, 25, 29]), works as follows. For a logical memory of N blocks, we construct a hierarchy of hash tables, henceforth denoted $T_1, \ldots, T_L$ where $L = \log N$. Each T_i stores 2^i memory blocks. We refer to table T_i as the i-th level. In addition, we store next to each table a flag indicating whether the table is *full* or *empty*. When receiving an access request to read/write some logical memory address addr, the ORAM proceeds as follows:

- **Read phase.** Access each non-empty levels $T_1, \ldots, T_L$ in order and perform Lookup for addr. If the item is found in some level T_i, then when accessing all non-empty levels $T_{i+1}, \ldots, T_L$ look for dummy.
- **Write back.** If this operation is read, then store the found data in the read phase and write back the data value to T_0. If this operation is write, then ignore the associated data found in the read phase and write the value provided in the access instruction in T_0.
- **Rebuild:** Find the first empty level ℓ. If no such level exists, set $\ell := L$. Merge all $\{T_j\}_{0 \le j \le \ell}$ into T_ℓ. Mark all levels $T_1, \ldots, T_{\ell-1}$ as empty and T_ℓ as full.

For each access, we perform $\log N$ lookups, one per hash table. Moreover, after t accesses, we rebuild the i-th table $\lceil t/2^i \rceil$ times. When implementing the hash table using the best known oblivious hash table (e.g., oblivious Cuckoo hashing [10, 25, 29]), building a level with 2^k items obliviously requires $O(2^k \cdot \log(2^k)) = O(2^k \cdot k)$ time. This building algorithm is based on oblivious sorting, and its time overhead is inherited from the time overhead of the oblivious sort procedure (specifically, the best known algorithm for obliviously sorting n elements takes $O(n \cdot \log n)$ time [2, 24]). Thus, summing over all levels (and ignoring the $\log N$ lookup operations across different levels for each access), t accesses require $\sum_{i=1}^{\log N} \lceil \frac{t}{2^i} \rceil \cdot O(2^i \cdot i) = O(t \cdot \log^2 N)$ time. On the other hand, lookup takes essentially constant time per level (ignoring searching in stashes which introduce an additive factor) and thus $O(\log N)$ per access. Thus, there is an asymmetry between build time and lookup time, and the main overhead is the build.

The work of Patel et al. [40]. Classically (e.g., [10, 22, 23, 25, 29]), oblivious hash tables were built to support (and be secure for) *every* input array. This required expensive oblivious sorting, causing the extra logarithmic factor. The key idea of Patel et al. [40] is to modify the hierarchical ORAM framework to realize ORAM from a weaker primitive: an oblivious hash table that works only for *randomly shuffled input* arrays. Patel et al. describe a novel oblivious hash table such that building a hash table containing n elements can be accomplished without oblivious sorting and consumes only $O(n \cdot \log \log \lambda)$ total time[5] and lookup consumes $O(\log \log n)$ total time. Patel et al. argue that their hash table construction retains security not necessarily for every input, but when the input array is randomly permuted, and moreover the input permutation must be unknown to the adversary.

To be able to leverage this relaxed hash table in hierarchical ORAM, a remaining question is the following: whenever a level is being rebuilt in the ORAM (i.e., a new hash table is being constructed), how do we make sure that the input array is randomly and secretly shuffled? A naïve answer is to employ an oblivious random permutation to permute the input, but known oblivious random permutation constructions require oblivious sorting which brings us back to our starting point. Patel et al. solve this problem and show that there is no need to completely shuffle the input array. Recall that when building some level T_ℓ, the input array consists of only unvisited elements in tables $T_0, \ldots, T_{\ell-1}$ (and T_ℓ too if ℓ is the largest level). Patel et al. argue that the unvisited elements in tables $T_0, \ldots, T_{\ell-1}$ are already randomly permuted *within each table* and the permutation is unknown to the adversary. Then, they presented a new algorithm, called *multi-array shuffle*, that combines these arrays to a shuffled array within $O(n \cdot \log \log \lambda)$ time, where $n = |T_0| + |T_1| + \ldots + |T_{\ell-1}|$.[6] The algorithm is somewhat involved, randomized, and has a negligible probability of failure.

The blueprint. Our construction builds upon and simplifies the construction of Patel et al. To get better asymptotic overhead, we improve their construction in two different aspects:

1. We show how to implement our variant of multi-array shuffle (called *intersperse*) in $O(n)$ time. Specifically, we show a new reduction from *intersperse* to tight compaction.
2. We develop a hash table that supports build in $O(n)$ time assuming that the input array is randomly shuffled. The lookup is $O(1)$, ignoring time spent on looking in stashes. Achieving this is rather non-trivial: first we use a "packing"

---

[5] λ denotes the security parameter. Since the size of the hash table n may be small, here we separate the security parameter from the hash table's size.

[6] The time overhead is a bit more complicated to state and the above expression is for the case where $|T_i| = 2|T_{i-1}|$ for every i (which is the case in a hierarchical ORAM construction).

style trick to construct oblivious Cuckoo hash tables for small sizes where $n \leq \mathsf{poly}\log\lambda$, achieving linear-time build and constant-time lookup. Relying on the advantage we gain for problems of small sizes, we then show how to solve problems of medium and large sizes, again relying on oblivious tight compaction as a building block. The bootstrapping step from medium to large is inspired by Patel et al. [40] at a very high level, but our concrete construction differs from Patel et al. [40] in many technical details.

We describe the core ideas behind these improvements next. In Sect. 2.1.1, we present our multi-array shuffle algorithm. In Sect. 2.1.2, we show how to construct a hash table for shuffled inputs achieving linear build time and constant lookup.

2.1.1   Interspersing Randomly Shuffled Arrays

Given two arrays, $\mathbf{I}_1$ and $\mathbf{I}_2$, of size n_1, n_2, respectively, where each array is randomly shuffled, our goal is to output a single array that contains all elements from $\mathbf{I}_1$ and $\mathbf{I}_2$ in a randomly shuffled order. Ignoring obliviousness, we could first initialize an output array of size $n = n_1 + n_2$, mark exactly n_1 random locations in the output array, and place the elements from $\mathbf{I}_1$ arbitrarily in these locations. The elements from $\mathbf{I}_2$ are placed in the unmarked locations.[7] The challenge is how to perform this placement obliviously, without revealing the mapping from the input array to the output array.

We observe that this routing problem is exactly the "reverse" problem of oblivious tight compaction, where one is given an input array of size n containing keys that are 1-bit and the goal is to sort the array such that all elements with key 0 appear before all elements with key 1. Intuitively, by running this algorithm "in reverse", we obtain a linear time algorithm for *obliviously* routing marked elements to an array with marked positions (that are not necessarily at the front). Since we believe that this procedure is useful in its own right, we formalize it independently and call it *oblivious distribution*. The full details appear in the full version [5].

2.1.2   An Optimal Hash Table for Shuffled Inputs

In this section, we first describe a warmup construction that can be used to build a hash table in $O(n \cdot \mathsf{poly}\log\log\lambda)$ time and supports lookups in $O(\mathsf{poly}\log\log\lambda)$ time. We will then get rid of the additional $\mathsf{poly}\log\log\lambda$ factor in both the build and lookup phases.

Warmup: oblivious hash table with **$\mathsf{poly}\log\log\lambda$** *slack.* Intuitively, to build a hash table, the idea is to randomly distribute the n elements in the input into $B := n/\mathsf{poly}\log\lambda$ bins of size $\mathsf{poly}\log\lambda$ in the clear. The distribution is done according to a pseudorandom function with some secret key K, where an

---

[7] Note that the number of such assignments is $\binom{n}{n_1, n_2}$. Assuming that each array is already permuted, the number of possible outputs is $\binom{n}{n_1, n_2} \cdot n_1! n_2! = n!$.

element with address addr is placed in the bin with index $\mathsf{PRF}_K(\mathsf{addr})$. Whenever we lookup for a real element $\mathsf{addr'}$, we access the bin $\mathsf{PRF}_K(\mathsf{addr'})$; in which case, we might either find the element there (if it was originally one of the n elements in the input) or we might not find it in the accessed bin (in the case where the element is not part of the input array). Whenever we perform a dummy lookup, we just access a random bin.

Since we assume that the n balls are secretly and randomly distributed to begin with, the build procedure does not reveal the mapping from original elements to bins. However, a problem arises in the lookup phase. Since the total number of elements in each bin is revealed, accessing in the lookup phase all real keys of the input array would produce an access pattern that is identical to that of the build process, whereas accessing n dummy elements results in a new, independent balls-into-bins process of n balls into B bins.

To this end, we first throw the n balls into the B bins as before, revealing loads $n_1, \ldots, n_B$. Then, we sample new *secret* loads $L_1, \ldots, L_B$ corresponding to an independent process of throwing $n' := n \cdot (1 - 1/\mathsf{poly}\log\lambda)$ balls into B bins. By a Chernoff bound, with overwhelming probability $L_i < n_i$ for every $i \in [B]$. We extract from each bin arbitrary $n_i - L_i$ balls obliviously and move them to an overflow pile (without revealing the L_i's). The overflow pile contains only $n/\mathsf{poly}\log\lambda$ elements so we use a standard Cuckoo hashing scheme such that it can be built in $O(m \cdot \log m) = O(n)$ time and supports lookups effectively in $O(1)$ time (ignoring the stash).[8] The crux of the security proof is showing that since the secret loads $L_1, \ldots, L_B$ are never revealed, they are large enough to mask the access pattern in the lookup phase so that it looks independent of the one leaked in the build phase.

We glossed over many technical details, the most important ones being how the bin sizes are truncated to the secret loads $L_1, \ldots, L_B$, and how each bin is being implemented. For the second question, since the bins are of $O(\mathsf{poly}\log\lambda)$ size, we support lookups using a perfectly secure ORAM constructions that can be built in $O(\mathsf{poly}\log\lambda \cdot \mathsf{poly}\log\log\lambda)$ and looked up in $O(\mathsf{poly}\log\log\lambda)$ time [12,16] (this is essentially where our $\mathsf{poly}\log\log$ factor comes from in this warmup). The first question is solved by employing our linear time tight compaction algorithm to extract the number of elements we want from each bin.

The full details of the construction appear in Sect. 5.

Remark 2.1 (Comparison of the warmup construction with Patel et al. [40]). *Our warmup construction borrows the idea of revealing loads and then sampling new secret loads from Patel et al. However, our concrete instantiation is different and this difference is crucial for the next step where we get an optimal hash table. Particularly, the construction of Patel et al. has $\log\log\lambda$ layers of hash tables of decreasing sizes, and one has to look for an element in each one of these hash tables, i.e., searching within $\log\log\lambda$ bins. In our solution, by tightening the analysis (that is, the Chernoff bound), we show that a single layer of hash tables suffices; thus, lookup accesses only a single bin. This allows us to focus on optimizing the implementation of a bin towards the optimal construction.*

---

[8] We refer to the full version [5] for background information on Cuckoo hashing.

Oblivious hash table with linear build time and constant lookup time. In the warmup construction, (ignoring the lookup time in the stash of the overflow pile[9]), the only super-linear operation that we have is the use of a perfectly secure ORAM, which we employ for bins of size $O(\mathsf{poly}\log\lambda)$. In this step, we replace this with a data structure with linear time build and constant time lookup: a Cuckoo hash table for lists of polylogarithmic size.

Recall that in a Cuckoo hash table each element receives two random bin choices (e.g., determined by a PRF) among a total of $c_{\mathsf{cuckoo}} \cdot n$ bins where $c_{\mathsf{cuckoo}} > 1$ is a suitable constant. During build-time, the goal is for all elements to choose one of the two assigned bins, such that every bin receives at most one element. At this moment it is not clear how to accomplish this build process, but suppose we can obliviously build such a Cuckoo hash table in linear time, then the problem would be solved. Specifically, once we have built such a Cuckoo hash table, lookup can be accomplished in constant time by examining both bin choices made by the element (ignoring the issue of the stash for now). Since the bin choices are (pseudo-)random, the lookup process retains security as long as each element is looked up at most once. At the end of the lookups, we can extract the unvisited elements through oblivious tight compaction in linear time—it is not hard to see that if the input array is randomly shuffled, the extracted unvisited elements appear in a random order too.

Therefore the crux is how to build the Cuckoo hash table for polylogarithmically-sized, randomly shuffled input arrays. Our observation is that classical oblivious Cuckoo hash table constructions can be split into three steps: (1) assigning two possible bin choices per element, (2) assigning either one of the bins or the stash for every element, and (3) routing the elements according to the Cuckoo assignment. We delicately handle each step separately:

1. For step (1) the $n = \mathsf{poly}\log\lambda$ elements in the input array can each evaluate the PRF on its associated key, and write down its two bin choices (this takes linear time).

2. Implementing step (2) in linear time is harder as this step is dominated by a sequence of oblivious sorts. To overcome this, we use the fact that the problem size n is of size $\mathsf{poly}\log\lambda$. As a result, the index of each item and its two bin choices can be expressed using $O(\log\log\lambda)$ bits which means that a single memory word (which is $\log\lambda$ bits long) can hold $O\left(\frac{\log\lambda}{\log\log\lambda}\right)$ many elements' metadata. We can now apply a "packed sorting" type of idea [3,11,14,28] where we use the RAM's word-level instructions to perform SIMD-style operations. Through this packing trick, we show that oblivious sorting and oblivious random permutation (of the elements' metadata) can be accomplished in $O(n)$ time!

---

[9] For the time being, the reader need not worry about how to perform lookup in the stash. Later, when we use our oblivious Cuckoo hashing scheme in the bigger hash table construction, we will merge the stashes of all Cuckoo hash tables into a single one and treat the merged stash specially.

3. Step (3) is classically implemented using oblivious bin distribution which again uses oblivious sorts. Here, we cannot use the packing trick since we operate on the elements themselves, so we use the fact that the input array is randomly shuffled and just route the elements in the clear.

There are many technical issues we glossed over, especially related to the fact that the Cuckoo hash tables are of size $c_{cuckoo} \cdot n$ bins, where $c_{cuckoo} > 1$. This requires us to pad the input array with dummies and later to use them to fill the empty slots in the Cuckoo assignment. Additionally, we also need to get rid of these dummies when extracting the set of unvisited element. All of these require several additional (packed) oblivious sorts or our oblivious tight compaction.

We refer the reader to Sect. 6 for the full details of the construction.

2.1.3   Additional Technicalities

The above description, of course, glossed over many technical details. To obtain our final ORAM construction, there are still a few concerns that have not been addressed. First, recall that we need to make sure that the unvisited elements in a hash table appear in a (pseudo-)random order such that we can make use of this residual randomness to re-initialize new hash tables faster. To guarantee this for the Cuckoo hash table that we employ for $\mathsf{poly}\log \lambda$-sized bins, we need that the underlying Cuckoo hash scheme we employ satisfy an additional property called the "indiscriminating bin assignment" property: specifically, we need that the two pseudo-random Cuckoo-bin choices for each element do not depend on the order in which they are added, their keys, or their positions in the input array. In our technical sections later, this property will allow us to do a coupling argument and prove that the residual unvisited elements in the Cuckoo hash table appear in random order.

Additionally, some technicalities remain in how we treat the smallest level of the ORAM and the stashes. The smallest level in the ORAM construction cannot use the hash table construction described earlier. This is because elements are added to the smallest level as soon as they are accessed and our hash table does not support such an insertion. We address this by using an oblivious dictionary built atop a perfectly secure ORAM for the smallest level of the ORAM. This incurs an additive $O(\mathsf{poly}\log\log \lambda)$ blowup. Finally, the stashes for each of the Cuckoo hash tables (at every level and every bin within the level) incur $O(\log \lambda)$ time. We leverage the techniques from Kushilevitz et al. [29] to merge all stashes into a common stash of size $O(\log^2 \lambda)$, which is added to the smallest level when it is rebuilt.

On deamortization. As the overhead of our ORAM is amortized over several accesses, it is natural to ask whether we can deamortize the construction to achieve the same overhead in the worst case, per access. Historically, Ostrovsky and Shoup [39] deamortized the hierarchical ORAM of Goldreich and Ostrovsky [23], and related techniques were later applied on other hierarchical ORAM schemes [10,26,29]. Unfortunately, the technique fails for our ORAM as we explain below (it fails for Patel et al. [40], as well, by the same reason).

Recall that in the hierarchical ORAM, the i-th level hash table stores 2^i keys and is rebuilt every 2^i accesses. The core idea of existing deamortization techniques is to spread the rebuilding work over the next sequence of 2^i ORAM accesses. That is, copy the 2^i keys (to be rebuilt) to another working space while performing lookup on the same level i to fulfill the next 2^i accesses. However, plugging such copy-while-accessing into our ORAM, an adversary can access a key in level i right after the same level is fully copied (as the copying had no way to foresee future accesses). Then, in the adversarial eyes, the copied keys are no longer randomly shuffled, which breaks the security of the hash table (which assumes that the inputs are shuffled). Indeed, in previous works, where hash tables were secure for *every* input, such deamortization works. Deamortizing our construction is left as an open problem.

2.2 Tight Compaction

Recall that tight compaction can be considered as a restricted form of sorting, where each element in the input array receives a 1-bit key, indicating whether it is real or dummy. The goal is to move all the real elements in the array to the front obliviously, and without leaking how many elements are reals. We show a deterministic algorithm for this task.

Reduction to loose compaction. Pippenger's self-routing super-concentrator construction [43] proposes a technique that reduces the task of tight compaction to that of loose compaction. Informally speaking, loose compaction receives as input a sparse array, containing a few real elements and many dummy elements. The output is a compressed output array, containing all real elements but the procedure does not necessarily remove all the dummy elements. More concretely, we care about a specific form of loose compactor (parametrized by n): consider a suitable bipartite expander graph that has n vertices on the left and $n/2$ vertices on the right where each node has constant degree. At most $1/128$ fraction of the vertices on the left will receive a real element, and we would like to route *all* real elements over vertex-disjoint paths to the right side such that every right vertex receives at most 1 element. The crux is to find a set of satisfying routes in linear time and obliviously. Once a set of feasible routes have been identified, it is easy to see that performing the actual routing can be done obliviously in linear time (and for obliviousness we need to route a dummy element over an edge that bears 0 load). During this process, we effectively compress the sparse input array (represented by vertices on the left) by $1/2$ without losing any element.

Using Pippenger's techniques [43] and with a little extra work, we can derive the following claim—at this point we simply state the claim while deferring algorithmic details to subsequent technical sections. Below D denotes the number of bits it takes to encode an element and w denotes the word size:

Claim: There exist appropriate constants $C, C' > 6$ such that the following holds: if we can solve the aforementioned loose compaction problem obliviously in time $T(n)$ for all $n \leq n_0$, then we can construct an oblivious algorithm that tightly compacts n elements in time $C \cdot T(n) + C' \cdot \lceil D/w \rceil \cdot n$ for all $n \leq n_0$.

As mentioned, the crux is to find satisfying routes for such a "loose compactor" bipartite graph obliviously and in linear time. Achieving this is non-trivial: for example, the recent work of Chan et al. [12] attempted to do this but their route-finding algorithm requires $O(n \log n)$ runtime—thus Chan et al. [12]'s work also implies a loose compaction algorithm that runs in time $O(n \log n + \lceil D/w \rceil \cdot n)$. To remove the extra $\log n$ factor, we introduce two new ideas, *packing*, and *decomposition*—in fact both ideas are remotely reminiscent of a line of works in the core algorithms literature on (non-comparison-based, non-oblivious) integer sorting on RAMs [3,14,28] but obviously we apply these techniques to a different context.

Packing: linear-time compaction for small instances. We observe that the offline route-finding phase operates only on metadata. Specifically, the route-finding phase receives the following as input: an array of n bits where the i-th bit indicates whether the i-th input position is real or dummy. If the problem size n is small, specifically, if $n \le w / \log w$ where w denotes the width of a memory word, we can pack the entire problem into a single memory word (since each element's index can be described in $\log n$ bits). In our technical sections we will show how to rely on word-level addition and boolean operations to solve such small problem instances in $O(n)$ time. At a high level, we follow the slow route-finding algorithm by Chan et al. [12], but now within a single memory word, we can effectively perform SIMD-style operations and we exploit this to speed up Chan et al. [12]'s algorithm by a logarithmic factor for small instances.

Relying on the above Claim that allows us to go from loose to tight, we now have an $O(n)$-time oblivious *tight* compaction algorithm for small instances where $n \le w / \log w$; specifically, if the loose compaction algorithm takes $C_0 \cdot n$ time, then the runtime of the tight compaction would be upper bounded by $C \cdot C_0 \cdot n + C' \cdot \lceil D/w \rceil \cdot n \le C \cdot C_0 \cdot C' \cdot \lceil D/w \rceil \cdot n$.

Decomposition: bootstrapping larger instances of compaction. With this logarithmic advantage we gain in small instances, our hope is to bootstrap larger instances by decomposing larger instances into smaller ones.

Our bootstrapping is done in two steps—as we calculate below, each time we bootstrap, the constant hidden inside the $O(n)$ runtime blows up by a constant factor; thus it is important that the bootstrapping is done for only $O(1)$ times.

1. *Medium instances: $n \le (w / \log w)^2$.* For medium instances, our idea is to divide the input array into $\sqrt{n}$ segments each of $B := \sqrt{n}$ size. As long as the input array has only $n/128$ or fewer real elements, then at most $\sqrt{n}/4$ segments can be dense, i.e., each containing more than $\sqrt{n}/4$ real elements (1/4 is loose but sufficient). We rely on tight compaction for small instances to move the dense segments in front of the sparse ones. For each of $3\sqrt{n}/4$ sparse segments, we next compress away 3/4 of the space using tight compaction for small instances. Clearly, the above procedure is a loose compaction and consumes at most $2 \cdot C \cdot C' \cdot C_0 \cdot \lceil D/w \rceil \cdot n + 6 \lceil D/w \rceil \cdot n \le 2.5 \cdot C \cdot C' \cdot C_0 \cdot \lceil D/w \rceil \cdot n$ runtime.

So far we have constructed a loose compaction algorithm for medium instances. Using the aforementioned Claim, we can in turn construct an algorithm that obliviously and *tightly* compacts a medium-sized instance of size $n \leq (w/\log w)^2$ in time at most $3C^2 \cdot C' \cdot C_0 \cdot \lceil D/w \rceil \cdot n$.

2. *Large instances: arbitrary n.* We can now bootstrap to arbitrary choices of n by dividing the problem into $m := n/(\frac{w}{\log w})^2$ segments where each segment contains at most $(\frac{w}{\log w})^2$ elements. Similar to the medium case, at most $1/4$ fraction of the segments can have real density exceeding $1/4$—which we call such segments *dense*. As before, we would like to move the dense segments in the front and the sparse ones to the end. Recall that Chan et al. [12]'s algorithm solves loose compaction for problems of arbitrary size m in time $C_1 \cdot (m \log m + \lceil D/w \rceil m)$ Thus due to the above claim we can solve tight compaction for problems of any size m in time $C \cdot C_1 \cdot (m \log m + \lceil D/w \rceil \cdot m) + C' \cdot \lceil D/w \rceil \cdot m$. Thus, in $O(\lceil D/w \rceil \cdot n)$ time we can move all the dense instances to the front and the sparse instances to the end. Finally, by invoking medium instances of tight compaction, we can compact within each segment in time that is linear in the size of the segment. This allows us to compress away $3/4$ of the space from the last $3/4$ segments which are guaranteed to be sparse. This gives us loose compaction for large instances in $O(\lceil D/w \rceil \cdot n)$ time—from here we can construct oblivious tight compaction for large instances using the above Claim.[10]

Remark 2.2. *In our formal technical sections later, we in fact directly use loose compaction for smaller problem sizes to bootstrap loose compaction for larger problem sizes (whereas in the above version we use* tight *compaction for smaller problems to bootstrap loose compaction for larger problems). The detailed algorithm is similar to the one described above: it requires slightly more complicated parameter calculation but results in better constants than the above more intuitive version.*

Organization. In Sect. 3 we highlight several building blocks that are necessary for our construction. In Sect. 4 we describe our oblivious tight compaction algorithm informally (due to lack of space). In Sect. 5 we provide our construction of hash table for shuffled input for long size inputs, and in Sect. 6 we provide our construction of hash table for small size input, i.e., how we organize the bins. Our ORAM construction is provided in Sect. 7.

3   Oblivious Building Blocks

Our ORAM construction uses many building blocks, some of which new to this work and some of which are known from the literature. The building blocks are

---

[10] We omit the concrete parameter calculation in the last couple of steps but from the calculations so far, it should be obvious by now that the there is at most a constant blowup in the constants hidden inside the big-O notation.

listed next. Due to lack of space, we just mention the building blocks and refer the reader to the full paper [5] for formal definitions.

Oblivious Sorting Algorithms: We state the classical sorting network of Ajtai et al. [2] and present a *new* oblivious sorting algorithm that is more efficient in settings where each memory word can hold multiple elements.

Oblivious Random Permutations: We show how to perform *efficient* oblivious random permutations in settings where each memory word can hold multiple elements.

Oblivious Bin Placement: We state the known results for oblivious bin placement of Chan et al. [10,13].

Oblivious Hashing: We present the formal functionality of a hash table that is used throughout our work. We also state the resulting parameters of a simple oblivious hash table that is achieved by compiling a non-oblivious hash table inside an existing ORAM construction. Due to its importance, we provide some high level of the functionality here.

In a nutshell, the functionality of hash function supports three commands: A "constructor" Build(I), receiving an array of n pairs of key/value (k_i, v_i). The array I is assumed to be randomly shuffled, and the instruction builds some internal structure for supporting fast (and oblivious) future accesses. Then, the construction supports several Lookup(k) instructions, where if $k \in I$ then the corresponding v should be returned, and otherwise $\bot$ is returned. Importantly, the Lookup should also support fictitious lookups, i.e., supports $k = \bot$. The construction should not leak whether $k \in I$, $k \notin I$ or $k = \bot$. Finally, the hash function also supports the "destructor" function Extract() – which returns a permuted array of size n consisting of all elements in I that were not accessed padded with dummies. The security definition requires that the joint distribution of access pattern, where the adversary can choose the sequence of instructions and the inputs to the instructions, is simulatable. The only restriction is that the adversary cannot ask for the same key more than once. We call this functionality "oblivious hash table for non-recurrent lookups", see full paper for formal definition.

Oblivious Cuckoo Hashing: We present and overview the state-of-the-art constructions of oblivious Cuckoo hash tables. We state their complexities and also make minor modifications that will be useful to us later.

Oblivious Dictionary: We present and analyze a simple construction of a dictionary that is achieved by compiling a non-oblivious dictionary (e.g., a red-black tree) inside an existing ORAM construction.

Oblivious Balls-into-Bins Sampling: We present an oblivious sampling of the approximated bin loads of throwing independently n balls into m bins, which uses the binomial sampling of Bringmann et al. [9].

Oblivious Tight Compaction: As was mentioned in the introduction, one of our main contributions is a deterministic linear time procedure (in the balls and bins model) for the following problem: given an input array containing n

balls, each of which marked with a 1-bit label that is either 0 or 1, output a permutation of the array such that all the 1 balls are moved to the front.

Intersperse: Given two arrays that are assumed to be randomly shuffled $\mathbf{I}_0, \mathbf{I}_1$ of sizes n_0, n_1, resp., we show a procedure $\mathsf{Intersperse}_{n_0+n_1}(\mathbf{I}_0\|\mathbf{I}_1, n_0, n_1)$ that returns a random permutation of $\mathbf{I}_0\|\mathbf{I}_1$. We generalize it also for interspersing k arrays $\mathsf{Intersperse}_{n_1,\ldots,n_k}^{(k)}(\mathbf{I}_1\|\ldots\|\mathbf{I}_k)$, each of which is randomly shuffled, and for interspersing real and dummy elements $\mathsf{IntersperseRD}$, assuming that the real elements are randomly shuffled but in which we have no guarantee of the relative positions of the real elements with respect to the dummy ones. In all of these variants, the goal is to return a random permutation of all elements in the input array, while the assumption on the input helps to reduces the running time.

Notation. Throughout the paper, we use the notation $\delta^{\mathcal{A}}$-*secure* PRF to mean that for every (non-uniform) probabilistic polynomial-time algorithm $\mathcal{A}$ has advantage at most $\delta^{\mathcal{A}}$ in distinguishing an output of the PRF from random. We additionally say that an algorithm is $(1 - \delta^{\mathcal{A}})$-*oblivious* if no (non-uniform) probabilistic polynomial-time algorithm $\mathcal{A}$ can distinguish its access pattern from a simulated one with probability better than $\delta^{\mathcal{A}}$. Formal definitions appear in the full paper.

4   Oblivious Tight Compaction in Linear Time

Our tight compaction algorithm works in two main steps. We first reduce the problem (in linear time) to a relaxed problem called *loose compaction*. Here, one is given an array $\mathbf{I}$ with n elements in which it is guaranteed that at most n/ℓ elements are real for some constant $\ell > 2$, and the goal is to return an array of size $n/2$ that contain all the real elements. Second, we implement loose compaction in linear time.

Reducing tight compaction to loose compaction. Given an input array $\mathbf{I}$ of n elements in which some are marked 0 and the rest are marked 1, we first count the number of total elements marked 0 in the input array, and let c be this number. The first observation is that all 0-elements in the input array that reside in locations $1, \ldots, c$, and all 1-elements in locations $c+1, \ldots, n$ are already placed correctly. Thus, we just need to handle the rest of the elements which we call the *misplaced* ones. The number of misplaced elements marked 0 equals to the number of misplaced elements marked 1, and all we have to do is to (obliviously) swap between each misplaced 0-element with a distinct misplaced 1-element.

The main idea here is to perform the swaps along the edges of a bipartite expander graph. Consider a bipartite expander graph where the left nodes are associated with the elements. The edges of the graph are the access pattern of our algorithm. We will swap two misplaced elements that have a different mark if they have a common neighbor on the right. To make sure this algorithm runs in linear time, the graph has to be d-regular for $d = O(1)$ and that the list of neighbors of every node can be computed using $O(1)$ basic operations. Such explicit expander graphs are known to exist (for example, Margulis [37]).

Using the expansion properties of the graph, we can upper bound the number of misplaced elements that were not swapped by this process: at most n/ℓ for some $\ell > 2$. Thus, we can invoke loose compaction where we consider the remaining misplaced element as real elements and the rest being dummy. This process reduced the problem from n elements to $n/2$ and we proceed in recursion to swap the misplaced elements on that first half of the array, until all 0-elements and 1-elements are swapped. (The reduction is of logarithmic depth and the problem size is shrunk by a factor two in each step so the complexity is linear overall.)

Loose compaction. The loose compaction algorithm LooseCompaction$_\ell$ receives as input an array $\mathbf{I}$ consisting of n balls, where at most n/ℓ are real and the rest are dummies for some $\ell > 2$. The goal is to return an array of size $n/2$ where all the real balls reside in the returned array. In this algorithm we again use a bipartite expander and combine it with ideas coming from the matching algorithm of Pippenger [43]. The main idea of the procedure is to first distribute the real balls to many bins, while ensuring that no bin consists of too many real balls. Then, as all bins have small load, we can merge several bins together and compact the array, as required.

The input/output of step 1, namely of the balanced distribution, is as follows. The input is an array $\mathbf{I}$ of size n that we interpret as n/B bins of size B each (simply by considering the array $\mathbf{I}[(i - 1) \cdot B + 1, \dots, iB]$ as the i-th bin, for $i = 1, \dots, n/B$). If a bin contains more than $B/4$ real balls, then we call it "dense", and otherwise we call it "sparse". Our goal is to distribute all *dense* bins in $\mathbf{I}$ into another array $\mathbf{I}'$ of size n which we think about as split into n/B bins of size B each. The procedure computes which target bins in $\mathbf{I}'$ we should distribute each one of the dense bins in $\mathbf{I}$, such that, the distribution would be balanced. In particular, the balanced distribution guarantees that no bin in $\mathbf{I}'$ receives more than $B/4$ real balls. Let us explain why this balanced distribution is enough.

After the balanced distribution, we can compact the arrays $\mathbf{I}, \mathbf{I}'$ into an array of size $n/2$ by "folding": Interpret $\mathbf{I} = (\mathbf{I}_0, \mathbf{I}_1), \mathbf{I}' = (\mathbf{I}'_0, \mathbf{I}'_1)$ where $|\mathbf{I}_0| = |\mathbf{I}_1| = |\mathbf{I}'_0| = |\mathbf{I}'_1|$ and each array consists of $n/(2B)$ bins of size B; Then, for every $i = 1, \dots, n/(2B)$, we merge all real balls in $(\mathbf{I}_{0,i}, \mathbf{I}_{1,i}, \mathbf{I}'_{0,i}, \mathbf{I}'_{1,i})$ into a bin of size B. As no bin consists of more than $B/4$ real balls, there is enough "room" in $\mathbf{I}_0$. We then output the concatenation of all these $n/(2B)$ bins, i.e., we return an array of size $n/2$.

Balanced distribution of the dense bins. The distribution of dense bins in $\mathbf{I}$ into $\mathbf{I}'$ relies (again) on a good expander graph. Fixing a proper constant ϵ, we consider a d_ϵ-regular graph $G_{\epsilon, n/B} = (L, R, E)$ with $|L| = |R| = n/B$, where L corresponds to $\mathbf{I}$, R corresponds to $\mathbf{I}'$ and we let $B = d_\epsilon/2$. Let $S \subset L$ be the set of dense bins in L. We look for a $(B, B/4)$-*matching for* S: We look for a set of edges $M \subseteq E$ such that (1) from every bin in S there are at least B out edges, and (2) for every bin in R there are at most $B/4$ incoming edges. Given such a matching M, every dense bin in $\mathbf{I}$ can be distributed to $\mathbf{I}'$ while guaranteeing that no bin in $\mathbf{I}'$ will have load greater than $B/4$, while the access pattern corresponds to edges in the graph which is public and known to the adversary.

Computing the matching. We first describe a non-oblivious algorithm for finding the matching; the algorithm is due to Pippenger [43]. Let $m = |L| = |R|$.[11] The algorithm proceeds in rounds, where initially all *dense* vertices in L are "unsatisfied", and in each round:

1. **Each unsatisfied *dense* vertex $u \in L$:** Send a request to each one of the neighbors of u.
2. **Each vertex $v \in R$:** If v receives more than $B/4$ requests in this round, it replies with "negative" to all the requests it received in this round. Otherwise, it replies "positive" to all requests it received.
3. **Each unsatisfied *dense* vertex $u \in L$:** If u received more than B positive replies then take these edges to the matching and change the status to "satisfied".

The output is the edges in the matching. In each round, there are $O(m)$ transmitted messages, where each message is a single bit. Using properties of the expander graphs, in each round the number of unsatisfied vertices decreases by a factor of 2. Thus, the algorithm proceeds in $O(\log m)$ rounds, and the total runtime of the algorithm is $O(m)$.[12] However, the algorithm is non-oblivious.

Oblivious slow matching (for any m). A simple way to make this algorithm oblivious (as observed by [12]) is by sending a message from every vertex in L to the relevant vertices in R in each round, that is, even a vertex is satisfied it still sends fictitious messages in the proceeding rounds. In particular, in each round the algorithm hides whether a vertex $v \in L$ is in the set of satisfied vertices ($v \notin L'$) or is still unsatisfied ($v \in L'$), and in fact, we run each iteration on the entire graph. This results in algorithm that takes overall $O(m \cdot \log m)$ time.

Oblivious fast matching (for small m). When m is really small, we use the packing trick. Concretely, when $m \leq \frac{w}{\log w}$, where w is the word size, all the information required for the algorithm can be packed into $O(1)$ words. Thus, when accessing information related to one node $u \in L$, we can access at the same time all the information regarding all other nodes in L. This enables us to hide which node is being visited (i.e., whether a node is in L' or not) and therefore the algorithm can now just visit the nodes in L' and does not have to make fictitious accesses on the entire graph. As a result, when m is small (as above) we are able to compute the matching in $O(m)$ word-level operations.

---

[11] Note that we are working here with a parameter m and not n, as m is the number of vertices in the graph G – e.g., the number of bins and not the number of balls.

[12] The set of unsatisfied vertices (in L) and its neighboring set (in R) are both stored in double-linked lists to visit and remove efficiently.

Combining slow match and fast match. We achieve loose compaction as follows:

- Given the array $\mathbf{I}$ of size n and word size $w = \Omega(\log n)$, we first break it into blocks of size $p^2 = (w/\log w)^2$, and our goal is to move all "dense" blocks to the beginning of the array. We find the matching obliviously using the "slow" matching algorithm, that takes $O(m \cdot \log m) = O\left(\frac{n}{p^2} \cdot \log \frac{n}{p^2}\right)$ time, which is linear. Then, compaction given the matching (by folding) takes $O(n)$. By running this compaction twice we get an output of size $n/4$, consisting of all dense blocks of size p^2.
- At this point, we want to run compaction on each one of the sparse blocks in $\mathbf{I}$ (where again, blocks are of size p^2) independently, and then take only the result of the compaction of each block for the remaining part of the output array.

  In order to run the compaction on each block of size p^2, we perform the same trick again. We break each instance into p sub-blocks of a *smaller* size p, and mark each sub-block as dense or sparse. As the number of sub-blocks we have in each instance is $p = w/\log w$, we can find the matching using the fast matching algorithm. Note that as previously, we did not handle the real balls in the sparse sub-blocks.
- Finally, we have to solve compaction of all sparse sub-blocks of the previous step. Each sparse sub-block is of size $p = w/\log w$, and thus can be solved in linear time using the fast matching algorithm.

The final output consists of the following: (i) The output of compaction of the dense block in $\mathbf{I}$ (to total size $n/4$), and (ii) a compaction of each one of the sparse blocks in $\mathbf{I}$ (sums up together to $n/4$). Note that each one of these sparse blocks (of size p^2), by itself, is divided to p sub-blocks (each of size p) and its compaction consists of (i) a compaction of its dense sub-blocks; and (ii) a compaction of each one of its sparse sub-blocks.

We refer to the full version [5] for the formal description and analysis.

5   BigHT: Oblivious Hashing for Non-Recurrent Lookups

The hash table construction we describe in this section suffers from poly log log λ extra multiplicative factor in Build and Lookup (which lead to similar overhead in the implied ORAM construction). Nevertheless, this hash table serves as a first step and we will get rid of the extra factor in Sect. 6. Hence, the parameter of expected bin load $\mu = \log^9 \lambda$ is seemingly loose in this section but is necessary later in Sect. 6 (to apply Cuckoo hash). Additionally, note that this hash table captures and simplifies many of the ideas in the oblivious hash table of Patel et al. [40] and can be used to get an ORAM with similar overhead to theirs.

Construction 5.1: Hash Table for Shuffled Inputs

Procedure BigHT.Build(I):

- **Input:** An array $\mathbf{I} = (a_1, \ldots, a_n)$ containing n elements, where each a_i is either dummy or a (key, value) pair denoted (k_i, v_i), where both the key k and the value v are D-bit strings where $D := O(1) \cdot w$.
- **Input assumption:** The elements in the array $\mathbf{I}$ are uniformly shuffled.
- **The algorithm:**
    1. Let $\mu := \log^9 \lambda$, $\epsilon := \frac{1}{\log^2 \lambda}$, $\delta := e^{-\log \lambda \cdot \log \log \lambda}$, and $B := \lceil n/\mu \rceil$.
    2. *Sample PRF key.* Sample a random PRF secret key sk.
    3. *Directly hash into major bins.* Throw the real $a_i = (k_i, v_i)$ into B bins using $\mathsf{PRF}_{\mathsf{sk}}(k_i)$. If $a_i = $ dummy, throw it to a uniformly random bin. Let $\mathsf{Bin}_1, \ldots, \mathsf{Bin}_B$ be the resulted bins.
    4. *Sample independent smaller loads.* Sample[a] the load of throwing n' balls into B bins with failure probability δ, where $n' = n \cdot (1 - \epsilon)$. Let $(L_1, \ldots, L_B)$ be the resulted loads. If there exists $i \in [B]$ such that $||\mathsf{Bin}_i| - \mu| > 0.5 \cdot \epsilon\mu$ or $\left|L_i - \frac{n'}{B}\right| > 0.5 \cdot \epsilon\mu$, then abort.
    5. *Create major bins.* Allocate new arrays $(\mathsf{Bin}'_1, \ldots, \mathsf{Bin}'_B)$, each of size μ. For every i, iterate in parallel on both Bin_i and Bin'_i, and copy the first L_i elements in Bin_i to Bin'_i. Fill the empty slots in Bin'_i with dummy. (L_i is not revealed during this process, by continuing to iterate over Bin_i after we cross the threshold L_i.)
    6. *Create overflow pile.* Obliviously merge all of the last $|\mathsf{Bin}_i| - L_i$ elements in each bin $\mathsf{Bin}_1, \ldots, \mathsf{Bin}_B$ into an overflow pile:
        - For each $i \in [B]$, replace the first L_i positions with dummy.
        - Concatenate all of the resulting bins and perform oblivious tight compaction on the resulting array such that the real balls appear in the front. Truncate the outcome to be of length ϵn.
    7. Prepare an oblivious hash table for elements in the overflow pile by calling the Build algorithm of the $(1 - O(\delta) - \delta^{\mathcal{A}}_{\mathsf{PRF}})$-oblivious Cuckoo hashing scheme (see Building blocks, Section 3) parameterized by δ (recall that $\delta = e^{-\Omega(\log \lambda \cdot \log \log \lambda)}$) and the stash size $\log(1/\delta)/\log n$. Let $\mathsf{OF} = (\mathsf{OF_T}, \mathsf{OF_S})$ denote the outcome data structure. Henceforth, we use $\mathsf{OF.Lookup}$ to denote a lookup operation to this oblivious Cuckoo hashing scheme.
    8. *Prepare data structure for efficient lookup.* For $i = 1, \ldots, B$, call naïveHT.Build(Bin'_i) on each major bin to construct an oblivious hash table, and let OBin_i denote the outcome for the i-th bin.
- **Output:** The algorithm stores in the memory a state that consists of ($\mathsf{OBin}_1, \ldots, \mathsf{OBin}_B, \mathsf{OF}, \mathsf{sk}$).

Procedure BigHT.Lookup(k):

- **Input:** The secret state ($\mathsf{OBin}_1, \ldots, \mathsf{OBin}_B, \mathsf{OF}, \mathsf{sk}$), and a key k to look for (that may be $\bot$, i.e., dummy).
- **The algorithm:**
    1. Call $v \leftarrow \mathsf{OF.Lookup}(k)$.

2. If $k = \bot$, choose a random bin $i \xleftarrow{\$} [B]$ and call $\mathsf{OBin}_i.\mathsf{Lookup}(\bot)$.

3. If $k \neq \bot$ and $v \neq \bot$ (i.e., v was found in OF), choose a random bin $i \xleftarrow{\$} [B]$ and call $\mathsf{OBin}_i.\mathsf{Lookup}(\bot)$.

4. If $k \neq \bot$ and $v = \bot$ (i.e., v was not found in OF), let $i := \mathsf{PRF}_{\mathsf{sk}}(k)$ and call $v \leftarrow \mathsf{OBin}_i.\mathsf{Lookup}(k)$.

– **Output:** The value v.

Procedure BigHT.Extract():

– **Input:** The secret state $(\mathsf{OBin}_1, \ldots, \mathsf{OBin}_B, \mathsf{OF}, \mathsf{sk})$.
– **The algorithm:**
  1. Let
     $$T = \mathsf{OBin}_1.\mathsf{Extract}() \| \mathsf{OBin}_2.\mathsf{Extract}() \| \ldots \| \mathsf{OBin}_B.\mathsf{Extract}() \| \mathsf{OF}.\mathsf{Extract}().$$
  2. Perform oblivious tight compaction on T, moving all the real balls to the front. Truncate the resulting array at length n. Let $\mathbf{X}$ be the outcome of this step.
  3. Call $\mathbf{X}' \leftarrow \mathsf{IntersperseRD}_n(\mathbf{X})$, to get a permutation of $\mathbf{X}$.
– **Output:** $\mathbf{X}'$.

---

[a] See the full paper for more information on how to perform this step obliviously.

We claim that our construction obliviously implements the hash table functionality for every sequence of instructions with non-recurrent lookups between two Build operations and as long as the input array to Build is randomly and secretly shuffled.

Theorem 5.2. *Assume a $\delta^{\mathcal{A}}_{\mathsf{PRF}}$-secure PRF. Then, Construction 5.1 $(1 - n^2 \cdot e^{-\Omega(\log \lambda \cdot \log \log \lambda)} - \delta^{\mathcal{A}}_{\mathsf{PRF}})$-obliviously implements the hash table functionality (see Sect. 3) for all $n \geq \log^{11} \lambda$, assuming that the input array (of size n) for Build is randomly shuffled. Moreover,*

– Build *and* Extract *each take* $O\left(n \cdot \mathsf{poly} \log \log \lambda + n \cdot \frac{\log n}{\log^2 \lambda}\right)$ *time; and*
– Lookup *takes* $O(\mathsf{poly} \log \log \lambda)$ *time in addition to linearly scanning a stash of size* $O(\log \lambda)$.

In particular, if $\log^{11} \lambda \leq n \leq \mathsf{poly}(\lambda)$, then hash table is $(1 - e^{-\Omega(\log \lambda \cdot \log \log \lambda)} - \delta^{\mathcal{A}}_{\mathsf{PRF}})$-obliviously and consumes $O(n \cdot \mathsf{poly} \log \log \lambda)$ time for the Build and Extract phases; and Lookup consumes $O(\mathsf{poly} \log \log \lambda)$ time in addition to linearly scanning a stash of size $O(\log \lambda)$.

The proof of security is given in the full version [5].

Remark 5.3. *As we mentioned, Construction 5.1 is only the first step towards the final oblivious hash table that we use in the final ORAM construction. We make significant optimizations in Sect. 6. We show how to improve upon the Build and Extract procedures from $O(n \cdot \mathsf{poly} \log \log \lambda)$ to $O(n)$ by replacing the naïveHT* *hash table with an optimized version (called SmallHT) that is more efficient for small lists. Additionally, while it may now seem that the $O(\log \lambda)$-stash overhead of Lookup is problematic, we will "merge" the stashes for different hash tables in our final ORAM construction and store them again in an oblivious hash table.*

6   SmallHT: Oblivious Hashing for Small Bins

In Sect. 5, we constructed an oblivious hashing scheme for randomly shuffled inputs where Build and Extract consumes $n \cdot \text{poly} \log \log \lambda$ time and Lookup consumes $\text{poly} \log \log \lambda$. The extra $\text{poly} \log \log \lambda$ factors arise from the oblivious hashing scheme (denoted naïveHT) which we use for each major bin of size $\approx \log^9 \lambda$. To get rid of the extra $\text{poly} \log \log \lambda$ factors, in this section, we will construct a new oblivious hashing scheme for $\text{poly} \log \lambda$-sized arrays which are randomly shuffled. In our new construction, Build and Extract takes linear time and Lookup takes constant time (ignoring the stash which we will treat separately later).

As mentioned in Sect. 2.1, the key idea is to rely on *packed* operations such that the metadata phase of Build (i.e., the cuckoo assignment problem) takes only linear time—this is possible because the problem size $n = \text{poly} \log \lambda$ is small. The more tricky step is how to route the actual balls into their destined location in the hash-table. We cannot rely on standard oblivious sorting to perform this routing since this would consume a logarithmic extra overhead. Instead, we devise a method to directly place the balls into the destined location in the hash-table in the clear—this is safe as long as the input array has been padded with dummies to the output length, and randomly shuffled; in this way only a random permutation is revealed. A technicality arises in realizing this idea: after figuring out the assigned destinations for real elements, we need to expand this assignment to include dummy elements too, and the dummy elements must be assigned at random to the locations unoccupied by the reals. At a high level, this is accomplished through a combination of packed oblivious random permutation and packed oblivious sorting over metadata.

We first describe two helpful procedures (mentioned in Sect. 2.1.2) in Sects. 6.1 and 6.2. Then, in Sect. 6.3, we give the full description of the Build, Lookup, and Extract procedures (Construction 6.5). Throughout this section, we assume for simplicity that $n = \log^9 \lambda$ (while in reality $n \in \log^9 \lambda \pm \log^7 \lambda$).

6.1   Step 1 – Add Dummies and Shuffle

We are given a randomly shuffled array **I** of length n that contains real and dummy elements. In Algorithm 6.1, we pad the input array with dummies to match the size of the hash-table to be built. Each dummy will receive a unique index label, and we rely on packed oblivious random permutation to permute the labeled dummies. Finally, we rely on Intersperse on the real balls to make sure that all elements, including reals and dummies, are randomly shuffled.

More formally, the output of Algorithm 6.1 is an array of size $n_{\text{cuckoo}} = c_{\text{cuckoo}} \cdot n + \log \lambda$, where c_{cuckoo} is the constant required for Cuckoo hashing, which contains all the real elements from **I** and the rest are dummies. Furthermore, each dummy receives a distinct random index from $\{1, \ldots, n_{\mathsf{cuckoo}} - n_R\}$, where n_R is the number of real elements in **I**. Assuming that the real elements in **I** are a-priori uniformly shuffled, then the output array is randomly shuffled.

Algorithm 6.1: Shuffle the Real and Dummy Elements

Input: An input array **I** of length n consisting of real and dummy elements.
Input Assumption: The real elements among **I** are randomly shuffled.
The algorithm:

1. Count the number of real elements in **I**. Let n_R be the output.
2. Write down a metadata array **MD** of length n_{cuckoo}, where the first n_R elements contain only a symbol **real**, and the remaining $n_{\mathsf{cuckoo}} - n_R$ elements are of the form $(\bot, 1), (\bot, 2), \ldots, (\bot, n_{\mathsf{cuckoo}} - n_R)$, i.e., each element is a $\bot$ symbol tagged with a dummy index.
3. Run packed oblivious random permutation (see Section 3)on **MD**, packing $O\left(\frac{w}{\log n}\right)$ elements into a single memory word. Run oblivious tight compaction on the resulting array, moving all the dummy elements to the end.
4. Run tight compaction on the input **I** to move all the real elements to the front.
5. Obliviously write down an array **I'** of length n_{cuckoo}, where the first n_R elements are the first n_R elements of **I** and the last $n_{\mathsf{cuckoo}} - n_R$ elements are the last $n_{\mathsf{cuckoo}} - n_R$ elements of **MD**, decompressed to the original length as every entry in the input **I**.
6. Run Intersperse on **I'** letting $n_1 := n_R$ and $n_2 := n_{\mathsf{cuckoo}} - n_R$. Let **X** denote the outcome (permuted) array.

Output: The array **X**.

Claim 6.2. *Algorithm 6.1 fails with probability at most $e^{-\Omega(\sqrt{n})}$ and completes in $O(n + \frac{n}{w} \cdot \log^3 n)$ time. Specifically, for $n = \log^9 \lambda$ and $w \geq \log^3 \log \lambda$, the algorithm completes in $O(n)$ time and fails with probability $e^{-\Omega(\log^{9/2} \lambda)}$.*

Proof. All steps except the oblivious random permutation in Step 3 incur $O(n)$ time and are perfectly correct by construction. Each element of **MD** can be expressed with $O(\log n)$ bits, so the packed oblivious random permutation incurs $O\left((n \cdot \log^3 n)/w\right)$ time and has failure probability at most $e^{-\Omega(\sqrt{n})}$. $\qquad\square$

6.2   Step 2 – Evaluate Assignment with Metadata Only

We obliviously emulate the Cuckoo hashing procedure, but doing it directly on the input array is too expensive (as it incurs oblivious sorting inside) so we do it directly on metadata (which is short since there are few elements), and use the packed version of oblivious sort (see Sect. 3). At the end of this step, every element in the input array should learn which bin (either in the main table or the stash) it is destined for. Recall that the Cuckoo hashing consists of a main table of $c_{cuckoo} \cdot n$ bins and a stash of $\log \lambda$ bins.

Algorithm 6.3: Evaluate Cuckoo Hash Assignment on Metadata

Input: An array $\mathbf{MD_X}$ of length $n_{cuckoo} = c_{cuckoo} \cdot n + \log \lambda$, where each element is either dummy or a pair $(\mathsf{choice}_{i,1}, \mathsf{choice}_{i,2})$, where $\mathsf{choice}_{i,b} \in [c_{cuckoo} \cdot n]$ for every $b \in \{1, 2\}$, and the number of real pairs is at most n.

Remark: All oblivious sorting in the algorithm below will be instantiated using packed oblivious sorting (including those called by $\overline{\text{cuckooAssign}}$ and oblivious bin placement).

The algorithm:

1. Run the indiscriminate oblivious Cuckoo assignment algorithm $\overline{\text{cuckooAssign}}$ with parameter $\delta = e^{-\log \lambda \log \log \lambda}$ (where $\overline{\text{cuckooAssign}}$ is formally described in the full paper) and let $\mathbf{Assign_X}$ be the result. For every i for which $\mathbf{MD_X}[i] = (\mathsf{choice}_{i,1}, \mathsf{choice}_{i,2})$, we have that $\mathbf{Assign_X}[i] \in \{\mathsf{choice}_{i,1}, \mathsf{choice}_{i,2}\} \cup S_{stash}$, i.e., either one of the two choices or the stash $S_{stash} = [n_{cuckoo}] \setminus [c_{cuckoo} \cdot n]$. For every i for which $\mathbf{MD_X}[i]$ is dummy we have that $\mathbf{Assign_X}[i] = \bot$.

2. Run oblivious bin placement on $\mathbf{Assign_X}$, and let $\mathbf{Occupied}$ be the output array (of length n_{cuckoo}). For every index j we have $\mathbf{Occupied}[j] = i$ if $\mathbf{Assign_X}[i] = j$ for some i. Otherwise, $\mathbf{Occupied}[j] = \bot$.

3. Label the i-th element in $\mathbf{Assign_X}$ with a tag $t = i$ for all i. Run oblivious sorting on $\mathbf{Assign_X}$ and let $\widetilde{\mathbf{Assign}}$ be the resulting array, such that all real elements appear in the front, and all dummies appear at the end, and ordered by their respective dummy-index (i.e. given in Algorithm 6.1, Step 2).

4. Label the i-th element in $\mathbf{Occupied}$ with a tag $t = i$ for all i. Run oblivious sorting on $\mathbf{Occupied}$ and let $\widetilde{\mathbf{Occupied}}$ be the resulting array, such that all occupied bins appear in the front and all empty bins appear at the end (where each empty bin contains an index (i.e., a tag t) of an empty bin in $\mathbf{Occupied}$).

5. Scan both arrays $\widetilde{\mathbf{Assign}}$ and $\widetilde{\mathbf{Occupied}}$ in parallel, updating the destined bin of each dummy element in $\widetilde{\mathbf{Assign}}$ with the respective tag in $\widetilde{\mathbf{Occupied}}$ (and each real element pretends to be updated).

6. Run oblivious sorting on the array $\widetilde{\mathbf{Assign}}$ (back to the original ordering in the array $\mathbf{Assign_X}$) according to the tag labeled in Step 3. Update the assignments of all dummy elements in $\mathbf{Assign_X}$ according to the output array of this step.

Output: The array $\mathbf{Assign_X}$.

Our input for this step is an array $\mathbf{MD_X}$ of length $n_{\mathsf{cuckoo}} := \mathsf{c_{cuckoo}} \cdot n + \log \lambda$ which consists of pairs of bin choices $(\mathsf{choice}_1, \mathsf{choice}_2)$, where each choice is an element from $[\mathsf{c_{cuckoo}} \cdot n] \cup \{\bot\}$. The real elements have choices in $[\mathsf{c_{cuckoo}} \cdot n]$ while the dummies have $\bot$. This array corresponds to the bin choices of the original elements in $\mathbf{X}$ (using a PRF) which is the original array $\mathbf{I}$ after adding enough dummies and randomly shuffling that array.

To compute the bin assignments we start with obliviously assigning the bin choices of the real elements in $\mathbf{MD_X}$. Next, we obliviously assign the remaining dummy elements to the remaining available locations. We do so by a sequence of oblivious sort algorithms. See Algorithm 6.3.

Claim 6.4. *For* $n \geq \log^9 \lambda$, *Algorithm 6.3 fails with probability at most* $e^{-\Omega(\log \lambda \cdot \log \log \lambda)}$ *and completes in* $O\left(n \cdot \left(1 + \frac{\log^3 n}{w}\right)\right)$ *time. Specifically, for* $n = \log^9 \lambda$ *and* $w \geq \log^3 \log \lambda$, *Algorithm 6.3 completes in* $O(n)$ *time.*

Proof. The input arrays is of size $n_{\mathsf{cuckoo}} = \mathsf{c_{cuckoo}} \cdot n + \log \lambda$ and the arrays $\mathbf{MD_X}$, $\mathbf{Assign_X}$, **Occupied**, $\widetilde{\mathbf{Occupied}}$, $\widetilde{\mathbf{Assign}}$ are all of length at most n_{cuckoo} and consist of elements that need $O(\log n_{\mathsf{cuckoo}})$ bits to describe. Thus, the cost of packed oblivious sort is $O((n_{\mathsf{cuckoo}}/w) \cdot \log^3 n_{\mathsf{cuckoo}}) \leq O((n \cdot \log^3 n)/w)$. The linear scans take time $O(n_{\mathsf{cuckoo}}) = O(n)$. The cost of the $\underline{\mathsf{cuckooAssign}}$ from Step 1 has failure probability $e^{-\Omega(\log \lambda \cdot \log \log \lambda)}$ and it takes time $O((n_{\mathsf{cuckoo}}/w) \cdot \log^3 n_{\mathsf{cuckoo}}) \leq O((n \cdot \log^3 n)/w)$. □

6.3 SmallHT Construction

The full description of the construction is given next. It invokes Algorithms 6.1 and 6.3.

Construction 6.5: SmallHT – Hash table for Small Bins

Procedure **SmallHT.Build(I)**:

- **Input:** An input array $\mathbf{I}$ of length n consisting of real and dummy elements. Each real element is of the form (k, v) where both the key k and the value v are D-bit strings where $D := O(1) \cdot w$.
- **Input Assumption:** The real elements among $\mathbf{I}$ are randomly shuffled.
- **The algorithm:**
    1. Run Algorithm 6.1 (prepare real and dummy elements) on input $\mathbf{I}$, and receive back an array $\mathbf{X}$.
    2. Choose a PRF key sk where PRF maps $\{0,1\}^D \to [\mathsf{c_{cuckoo}} \cdot n]$.
    3. Create a new metadata array $\mathbf{MD_X}$ of length n. Iterate over the the array $\mathbf{X}$ and for each real element $\mathbf{X}[i] = (k_i, v_i)$ compute two values $(\mathsf{choice}_{i,1}, \mathsf{choice}_{i,2}) \leftarrow \mathsf{PRF}_{\mathsf{sk}}(k_i)$, and write $(\mathsf{choice}_{i,1}, \mathsf{choice}_{i,2})$ in the i-th location of $\mathbf{MD_X}$. If $\mathbf{X}[i]$ is dummy, write $(\bot, \bot)$ in the i-th location of $\mathbf{MD_X}$.

4. Run Algorithm 6.3 on $\mathbf{MD_X}$ to compute the assignment for every element in $\mathbf{X}$. The output of this algorithm, denoted $\mathbf{Assign_X}$, is an array of length n, where in the i-th position we have the destination location of element $\mathbf{X}[i]$.

5. Route the elements of $\mathbf{X}$, in the clear, according to $\mathbf{Assign_X}$, into an array $\mathbf{Y}$ of size $c_{\text{cuckoo}} \cdot n$ and into a stash S.

– **Output:** The algorithm stores in the memory a secret state consists of the array $\mathbf{Y}$, the stash S and the secret key sk.

Procedure **SmallHT.Lookup(k)**:

– **Input:** A key k that might be dummy $\bot$. It receives a secret state that consists of an array $\mathbf{Y}$, a stash S, and a key sk.

– **The algorithm:**

1. If $k \neq \bot$:
   (a) Evaluate $(\text{choice}_1, \text{choice}_2) \leftarrow \text{PRF}_{\text{sk}}(k)$.
   (b) Visit $\mathbf{Y}_{\text{choice}_1}, \mathbf{Y}_{\text{choice}_2}$ and the stash S to look for the key k. If found, remove the element by overwriting $\bot$. Let v^* be the corresponding value (if not found, set $v^* := \bot$).

2. Otherwise:
   (a) Choose random $(\text{choice}_1, \text{choice}_2)$ independently at random from $[c_{\text{cuckoo}} \cdot n]$.
   (b) Visit $\mathbf{Y}_{\text{choice}_1}, \mathbf{Y}_{\text{choice}_2}$ and the stash S and look for the key k. Set $v^* := \bot$.

– **Output:** Return v^*.

Procedure **SmallHT.Extract()**.

– **Input:** The algorithm has no input; It receives the secret state that consists of an array $\mathbf{Y}$, a stash S, and a key sk.

– **The algorithm:**

1. Perform oblivious tight compaction on $\mathbf{Y} \| \mathbf{S}$, moving all the real elements to the front. Truncate the resulting array at length n. Let $\mathbf{X}$ be the outcome of this step.

2. Call $\mathbf{X}' \leftarrow \text{IntersperseRD}_n(\mathbf{X})$ to get a permuted array.

– **Output:** The array $\mathbf{X}'$.

We prove that our construction obliviously implements the oblivious hash table functionality for every sequence of instructions with non-recurrent lookups between two Build operations, assuming that the input array for Build is randomly shuffled.

Theorem 6.6. *Assume a $\delta^{\mathcal{A}}_{\text{PRF}}$-secure PRF. Suppose that $n = \log^9 \lambda$ and $w \geq \log^3 \log \lambda$. Then, Construction 6.5 $(1 - n \cdot e^{-\Omega(\log \lambda \cdot \log \log \lambda)} - \delta^{\mathcal{A}}_{\text{PRF}})$-obliviously implements the non-recurrent hash table functionality assuming that the input for Build (of size n) is randomly shuffled. Moreover, Build and Extract incur $O(n)$ time, Lookup has constant time in addition to linearly scanning a stash of size $O(\log \lambda)$.*

Proof. The proof of security is given in the full version [5]. We proceed with the efficiency analysis. The Build operation executes Algorithm 6.1 that consumes $O(n)$ time (by Claim 6.2), then performs additional $O(n)$ time, then executes Algorithm 6.3 that consumes $O(n)$ time (by Claim 6.4), and finally performs additional $O(n)$ time. Thus, the total time is $O(n)$. Lookup, by construction, incurs $O(1)$ time in addition to linearly scanning the stash S which is of size $O(\log \lambda)$. The time of Extract is $O(n)$ by construction. $\qquad\square$

6.4   CombHT: Combining BigHT with SmallHT

We use SmallHT in place of naïveHT for each of the major bins in the BigHT construction from Sect. 5. Since the load in the major bin in the hash table BigHT construction is indeed $n = \log^9 \lambda$, this modification is valid. Note that we still assume that the number of elements in the input to CombHT, is at least $\log^{11} \lambda$ (as in Theorem 5.2).

However, we make one additional modification that will be useful for us later in the construction of the ORAM scheme (Sect. 7). Recall that each instance of SmallHT has a stash S of size $O(\log \lambda)$ and so Lookup will require, not only searching an element in the (super-constant size) stash OF$_S$ of the overflow pile from BigHT, but also linearly scanning the super-constant size stash of the corresponding major bin. To this end, we merge the different stashes of the major bins and store the merged list in an oblivious Cuckoo hash (denoted as CombS later). (A similar idea has also been applied in several prior works [13, 25, 27, 29].) This results with a new hash table scheme we call CombHT. See the full version [5] for precise details.

7   Oblivious RAM

In this section, we utilize CombHT in the hierarchical framework of Goldreich and Ostrovsky [23] to construct our ORAM scheme. We denote by λ the security parameter. For simplicity, we assume that N, the size of the logical memory, is a power of 2. Additionally, we assume that w, the word size is $\Theta(\log N)$.

ORAM Initialization. Our structure consists of one dictionary D (see Sect. 3), and $O(\log N)$ levels numbered $\ell + 1, \dots, L$ respectively, where $\ell = \lceil 11 \log \log \lambda \rceil$, and $L = \lceil \log N \rceil$ is the maximal level.

- The dictionary D is an oblivious dictionary storing $2^{\ell+1}$ elements.
- Each level $i \in \{\ell + 1, \dots, L\}$ consists of an instance, called T_i, of the oblivious hash table CombHT from Sect. 6.4 that has capacity 2^i.

Additionally, each level is associated with an additional bit full$_i$, where 1 stands for *full* and 0 stands for *available*. Available means that this level is currently empty and does not contain any blocks, and thus one can rebuild into this level. Full means that this level currently contains blocks, and therefore an attempt to rebuild into this level will effectively cause a cascading merge. In addition, there is a global counter ctr that is initialized to 0.

Construction 7.1: Oblivious RAM Access(op, addr, data).

Input: op $\in \{\text{read}, \text{write}\}$, addr $\in [N]$ and data $\in \{0,1\}^w$.
Secret state: The dictionary D, levels $T_{\ell+1}, \ldots, T_L$, the bits full$_{\ell+1}, \ldots,$ full$_L$ and counter ctr.
The algorithm:

1. Initialize found := false, data* := $\perp$.
2. Perform fetched := D.Lookup(addr). If fetched $\neq \perp$, then set found := true.
3. For each $i \in \{\ell+1, \ldots, L\}$ in increasing order, do:
    (a) If found = false:
        i. Run fetched := T_i.Lookup(addr) with the following modifications:
            – Do not visit the stash of OF.
            – Do not visit the stash of CombS.
            (below, these stashes (OF$_S$, CombS$_S$) are merged into previous levels.)
        ii. If fetched $\neq \perp$, let found := true and data* := fetched.
    (b) Else, T_i.Lookup($\perp$).
4. If found = false, i.e., this is the first time addr is being accessed, set data* = 0.
5. Let $(k, v) := \{(\text{addr}, \text{data}^*)\}$ if this is a read operation; else let $(k, v) := \{(\text{addr},$ data$)\}$. Insert $(k, (\ell, \perp, v))$ into oblivious dictionary D using D.Insert($k, (\ell, \perp, v)$).
6. Increment ctr by 1. If ctr $\equiv 0 \mod 2^\ell$, perform the following.
    (a) Let j be the smallest level index such that full$_j = 0$ (i.e., available). If all levels are marked full, then $j := L$. In other words, j is the target level to be rebuilt.
    (b) Let $\mathbf{U} := D$.Extract()$\|T_{\ell+1}$.Extract()$\| \ldots \|T_{j-1}$.Extract() and set $j^* := j - 1$. If all levels are marked full, then additionally let $\mathbf{U} := \mathbf{U}\|T_L$.Extract() and set $j^* := L$. (Here, Extract() of CombHT does not extract the element from the stashes.)
    (c) Run Intersperse$_{2^{\ell+1}, 2^{\ell+1}, 2^{\ell+2}, \ldots, 2^{j^*}}^{(j^*-\ell)}(\mathbf{U})$ (see Section 3). Denote the output by $\tilde{\mathbf{U}}$. If $j = L$, then additionally do the following to shrink $\tilde{\mathbf{U}}$ to size $N = 2^L$:
        i. Run the tight compaction on $\tilde{\mathbf{U}}$ moving all real elements to the front. Truncate $\tilde{\mathbf{U}}$ to length N.
        ii. Run $\tilde{\mathbf{U}} \leftarrow$ IntersperseRD$_N(\tilde{\mathbf{U}})$ to get a permuted $\mathbf{U}$.
    (d) Rebuild the jth hash table with the 2^j elements from $\tilde{\mathbf{U}}$ via $T_j := $ CombHT.Build($\tilde{\mathbf{U}}$) and let OF$_S$, CombS$_S$ be the associated stashes (of size $O(\log \lambda)$ each). Mark full$_j := 1$.
        i. For each element (k, v) in the stash OF$_S$, run D.Insert(k, v).
        ii. For each element (k, v) in the stash CombS$_S$, run D.Insert(k, v).
    (e) For $i \in \{\ell+1, \ldots, j-1\}$, reset T_i to be empty structure and set full$_i := 0$.

Output: Return data*.

The next theorem is proven in the full version [5].

Theorem 7.2. *Let $N \in \mathbb{N}$ be the capacity of ORAM and $\lambda \in \mathbb{N}$ be a security parameter. Assume a $\delta_{\mathsf{PRF}}^{\mathcal{A}}$-secure PRF. For any number of queries $T = T(N, \lambda) \geq N$, Construction 7.1 $(1 - T \cdot N^2 \cdot e^{-\Omega(\log \lambda \cdot \log \log \lambda)} - \delta_{\mathsf{PRF}}^{\mathcal{A}})$-obliviously implements the ORAM functionality. Moreover, the construction has $O\left(\log N \cdot \left(1 + \frac{\log N}{\log^2 \lambda}\right) + \log^9 \log \lambda\right)$ amortized time overhead.*

Acknowledgments. We are grateful to Hubert Chan, Kai-Min Chung, Yue Guo, and Rafael Pass for helpful discussions. This work is supported in part by a Simons Foundation junior fellow award awarded to G.A., an AFOSR Award FA9550-18-1-0267, NSF grant CNS-1601879, a DARPA Brandeis award, a Packard Fellowship, a Sloan Fellowship, Google Faculty Research Awards, a VMware Research Award, and a Baidu Research Award. G.A. and I.K. were with Cornell Tech during most this research.

References

1. https://en.wikipedia.org/wiki/Sorting_network
2. Ajtai, M., Komlós, J., Szemerédi, E.: An $O(n \log n)$ sorting network. In: ACM STOC, pp. 1–9 (1983)
3. Andersson, A., Hagerup, T., Nilsson, S., Raman, R.: Sorting in linear time? In: ACM STOC, pp. 427–436 (1995)
4. Arora, S., Leighton, T., Maggs, B.: On-line algorithms for path selection in a nonblocking network. In: ACM STOC (1990)
5. Asharov, G., Komargodski, I., Lin, W.-K., Nayak, K., Peserico, E., Shi, E.: Optorama: optimal oblivious RAM. IACR Cryptology ePrint Archive 2018:892 (2018)
6. Batcher, K.E.: Sorting networks and their applications. In: American Federation of Information Processing Societies: AFIPS Conference Proceedings, vol. 32, pp. 307–314 (1968)
7. Bindschaedler, V., Naveed, M., Pan, X., Wang, X., Huang, Y.: Practicing oblivious access on cloud storage: the gap, the fallacy, and the new way forward. In: ACM CCS, pp. 837–849 (2015)
8. Boyle, E., Naor, M.: Is there an oblivious RAM lower bound? In: ACM ITCS, pp. 357–368 (2016)
9. Bringmann, K., Kuhn, F., Panagiotou, K., Peter, U., Thomas, H.: Internal DLA: efficient simulation of a physical growth model. In: Esparza, J., Fraigniaud, P., Husfeldt, T., Koutsoupias, E. (eds.) ICALP 2014, Part I. LNCS, vol. 8572, pp. 247–258. Springer, Heidelberg (2014). https://doi.org/10.1007/978-3-662-43948-7_21
10. Hubert Chan, T.-H., Guo, Y., Lin, W.-K., Shi, E.: Oblivious hashing revisited, and applications to asymptotically efficient ORAM and OPRAM. In: Takagi, T., Peyrin, T. (eds.) ASIACRYPT 2017, Part I. LNCS, vol. 10624, pp. 660–690. Springer, Cham (2017). https://doi.org/10.1007/978-3-319-70694-8_23
11. Hubert Chan, T.-H., Guo, Y., Lin, W.-K., Shi, E.: Cache-oblivious and data-oblivious sorting and applications. In: SODA, pp. 2201–2220 (2018)
12. Hubert Chan, T.-H., Nayak, K., Shi, E.: Perfectly secure oblivious parallel RAM. In: Beimel, A., Dziembowski, S. (eds.) TCC 2018, Part II. LNCS, vol. 11240, pp. 636–668. Springer, Cham (2018). https://doi.org/10.1007/978-3-030-03810-6_23

13. Hubert Chan, T.-H., Shi, E.: Circuit OPRAM: unifying statistically and computationally secure ORAMs and OPRAMs. In: Kalai, Y., Reyzin, L. (eds.) TCC 2017, Part II. LNCS, vol. 10678, pp. 72–107. Springer, Cham (2017). https://doi.org/10.1007/978-3-319-70503-3_3

14. Paul, J.C., Simon, W.: Decision trees and random access machines (1980)

15. Cormen, T.H., Leiserson, C.E., Rivest, R.L., Stein, C.: Introduction to Algorithms, 3rd edn, pp. 428–436. MIT Press, Cambridge (2009)

16. Damgård, I., Meldgaard, S., Nielsen, J.B.: Perfectly secure oblivious RAM without random oracles. In: Ishai, Y. (ed.) TCC 2011. LNCS, vol. 6597, pp. 144–163. Springer, Heidelberg (2011). https://doi.org/10.1007/978-3-642-19571-6_10

17. Farhadi, A., Hajiaghayi, M.T., Larsen, K.G., Shi, E.: Lower bounds for external memory integer sorting via network coding. In: ACM STOC (2019)

18. Feldman, P., Friedman, J., Pippenger, N.: Non-blocking networks. In: ACM STOC, pp. 247–254 (1986)

19. Fletcher, C.W., van Dijk, M., Devadas, S.: A secure processor architecture for encrypted computation on untrusted programs. In: Seventh ACM Workshop on Scalable Trusted Computing, pp. 3–8. ACM (2012)

20. Fletcher, C.W., Ren, L., Kwon, A., van Dijk, M., Devadas, S.: Freecursive ORAM: [nearly] free recursion and integrity verification for position-based oblivious RAM. In: ACM ASPLOS, pp. 103–116 (2015)

21. Gentry, C., Halevi, S., Jutla, C., Raykova, M.: Private database access with HE-over-ORAM architecture. In: Malkin, T., Kolesnikov, V., Lewko, A.B., Polychronakis, M. (eds.) ACNS 2015. LNCS, vol. 9092, pp. 172–191. Springer, Cham (2015). https://doi.org/10.1007/978-3-319-28166-7_9

22. Goldreich, O.: Towards a theory of software protection and simulation by oblivious RAMs. In: ACM STOC, pp. 182–194 (1987)

23. Goldreich, O., Ostrovsky, R.: Software protection and simulation on oblivious RAMs. J. ACM **43**(3), 431–473 (1996)

24. Goodrich, M.T.: Zig-zag sort: a simple deterministic data-oblivious sorting algorithm running in O(N Log N) time. In: ACM STOC, pp. 684–693 (2014)

25. Goodrich, M.T., Mitzenmacher, M.: Privacy-preserving access of outsourced data via oblivious RAM simulation. In: Aceto, L., Henzinger, M., Sgall, J. (eds.) ICALP 2011, Part II. LNCS, vol. 6756, pp. 576–587. Springer, Heidelberg (2011). https://doi.org/10.1007/978-3-642-22012-8_46

26. Goodrich, M.T., Mitzenmacher, M., Ohrimenko, O., Tamassia, R.: Oblivious RAM simulation with efficient worst-case access overhead. In: Proceedings of the 3rd ACM Workshop on Cloud Computing Security Workshop, CCSW 2011, pp. 95–100 (2011)

27. Goodrich, M.T., Mitzenmacher, M., Ohrimenko, O., Tamassia, R.: Privacy-preserving group data access via stateless oblivious RAM simulation. In: SODA, pp. 157–167 (2012)

28. Hagerup, T., Shen, H.: Improved nonconservative sequential and parallel integer sorting. Inf. Process. Lett. **36**(2), 57–63 (1990)

29. Kushilevitz, E., Lu, S., Ostrovsky, R.: On the (in)security of hash-based oblivious RAM and a new balancing scheme. In: SODA, pp. 143–156 (2012)

30. Larsen, K.G., Nielsen, J.B.: Yes, there is an oblivious RAM lower bound!. In: Shacham, H., Boldyreva, A. (eds.) CRYPTO 2018, Part II. LNCS, vol. 10992, pp. 523–542. Springer, Cham (2018). https://doi.org/10.1007/978-3-319-96881-0_18

31. Leighton, F.T., Ma, Y., Suel, T.: On probabilistic networks for selection, merging, and sorting. Theory Comput. Syst. **30**(6), 559–582 (1997)

32. Li, Z., Li, B.: Network coding: the case of multiple unicast sessions (2004)
33. Lin, W.-K., Shi, E., Xie, T.: Can we overcome the $n \log n$ barrier for oblivious sorting? In: SODA (2019)
34. Liu, C., Wang, X.S., Nayak, K., Huang, Y., Shi, E.: ObliVM: a programming framework for secure computation. In: IEEE S&P (2015)
35. Lu, S., Ostrovsky, R.: Distributed oblivious RAM for secure two-party computation. In: Sahai, A. (ed.) TCC 2013. LNCS, vol. 7785, pp. 377–396. Springer, Heidelberg (2013). https://doi.org/10.1007/978-3-642-36594-2_22
36. Maas, M., et al.: PHANTOM: practical oblivious computation in a secure processor. In: ACM CCS, pp. 311–324 (2013)
37. Margulis, G.A.: Explicit constructions of concentrators. Probl. Pereda. Inf. 9(4), 71–80 (1973)
38. Mitchell, J.C., Zimmerman, J.: Data-oblivious data structures. In: STACS, pp. 554–565 (2014)
39. Ostrovsky, R., Shoup, V.: Private information storage. In: ACM STOC, pp. 294–303 (1997)
40. Patel, S., Persiano, G., Raykova, M., Yeo, K.: Oblivious RAM with logarithmic overhead. In: IEEE FOCS, Panorama (2018)
41. Pinsker, M.S.: On the complexity of a concentrator. In: 7th International Teletraffic Conference (1973)
42. Pippenger, N.: Superconcentrators. SIAM J. Comput. 6(2), 298–304 (1977)
43. Pippenger, N.: Self-routing superconcentrators. J. Comput. Syst. Sci. 52(1), 53–60 (1996)
44. Ren, L., Yu, X., Fletcher, C.W., van Dijk, M., Devadas, S.: Design space exploration and optimization of path oblivious RAM in secure processors. In: ACM ISCA, pp. 571–582 (2013)
45. Shi, E., Hubert Chan, T.-H., Stefanov, E., Li, M.: Oblivious RAM with $O((\log N)^3)$ worst-case cost. In: Lee, D.H., Wang, X. (eds.) ASIACRYPT 2011. LNCS, vol. 7073, pp. 197–214. Springer, Heidelberg (2011). https://doi.org/10.1007/978-3-642-25385-0_11
46. Stefanov, E., Shi, E.: Oblivistore: high performance oblivious cloud storage. In: IEEE S&P, pp. 253–267 (2013)
47. Stefanov, E., Shi, E., Song, D.X.: Towards practical oblivious RAM. In: NDSS (2012)
48. Stefanov, E., et al.: Path ORAM: an extremely simple oblivious RAM protocol. In: ACM CCS, pp. 299–310 (2013)
49. Valiant, L.G.: Graph-theoretic properties in computational complexity. J. Comput. Syst. Sci. 13(3), 278–285 (1976)
50. Wang, X., Hubert Chan, T.-H., Shi, E.: Circuit ORAM: on tightness of the Goldreich-Ostrovsky lower bound. In: ACM CCS, pp. 850–861 (2015)
51. Wang, X.S., Huang, Y., Hubert Chan, T.-H., Shelat, A., Shi, E.: SCORAM: oblivious RAM for secure computation. In: ACM CCS, pp. 191–202 (2014)
52. Williams, P., Sion, R., Tomescu, A.: PrivateFS: a parallel oblivious file system. In: ACM CCS (2012)
53. Zahur, S., et al.: Revisiting square-root ORAM: efficient random access in multi-party computation. In: IEEE S&P, pp. 218–234 (2016)

On the Streaming Indistinguishability of a Random Permutation and a Random Function

Itai Dinur$^{(\boxtimes)}$

Department of Computer Science, Ben-Gurion University, Beersheba, Israel
dinuri@cs.bgu.ac.il

Abstract. An adversary with S bits of memory obtains a stream of Q elements that are uniformly drawn from the set $\{1, 2, \ldots, N\}$, either with or without replacement. This corresponds to sampling Q elements using either a random function or a random permutation. The adversary's goal is to distinguish between these two cases.

This problem was first considered by Jaeger and Tessaro (EURO-CRYPT 2019), which proved that the adversary's advantage is upper bounded by $\sqrt{Q \cdot S/N}$. Jaeger and Tessaro used this bound as a streaming switching lemma which allowed proving that known time-memory tradeoff attacks on several modes of operation (such as counter-mode) are optimal up to a factor of $O(\log N)$ if $Q \cdot S \approx N$. However, the bound's proof assumed an unproven combinatorial conjecture. Moreover, if $Q \cdot S \ll N$ there is a gap between the upper bound of $\sqrt{Q \cdot S/N}$ and the $Q \cdot S/N$ advantage obtained by known attacks.

In this paper, we prove a tight upper bound (up to poly-logarithmic factors) of $O(\log Q \cdot Q \cdot S/N)$ on the adversary's advantage in the streaming distinguishing problem. The proof does not require a conjecture and is based on a hybrid argument that gives rise to a reduction from the unique-disjointness communication complexity problem to streaming.

Keywords: Streaming algorithm · Time-memory tradeoff · Communication complexity · Provable security · Switching lemma · Mode of operation

1 Introduction

A classical result in cryptography asserts that an adversary attempting to distinguish a random permutation from a random function with an image size of N using Q queries has advantage that is upper bounded by about Q^2/N over a coin toss [3,13,14]. This bound serves as a switching lemma which has important implications in establishing the security of various cryptographic constructions. For example, the security of several modes of operation (such as counter-mode) is proved up to the birthday bound of $Q = \sqrt{N}$ by first idealizing the

© International Association for Cryptologic Research 2020
A. Canteaut and Y. Ishai (Eds.): EUROCRYPT 2020, LNCS 12106, pp. 433–460, 2020.
https://doi.org/10.1007/978-3-030-45724-2_15

underlying block cipher as a random permutation and then replacing it with a random function using the switching lemma.[1]

A limitation of the switching lemma is that it only bounds the advantage of the adversary as a function of the number of queries, whereas in practice, the adversary could have constraints on additional resources, notably on memory. At the same time, given $Q \approx \sqrt{N}$ unrestricted queries to the underlying primitive, it is possible to distinguish a random function from a random permutation with constant advantage using a negligible amount of $O(\log N)$ bits of memory by applying a "memory-less" cycle detection algorithm such as Floyd's algorithm [17] (or its variants, e.g., [6,21]).

Streaming Indistinguishability. Cycle detection algorithms are inapplicable when only given access to a stream of data produced by arbitrary queries to the underlying primitive which are not under the adversary's control. The streaming indistinguishability model was introduced in the context of symmetric-key cryptography by Jaeger and Tessaro at EUROCRYPT 2019 [15]. The authors considered an adversary (i.e. a randomized algorithm) with memory size of S bits and access to a stream of Q elements drawn from either a random permutation or from a random function with an image size of N. The main technical result of [15] is an adaptation of the switching lemma between a random permutation and random function to the streaming model. The streaming switching lemma asserts that the adversary's advantage is bounded by $\sqrt{Q \cdot S/N}$ as long as the queries to the underlying primitive are not repeated. The proof of the bound is based on tools from information theory and relies on a combinatorial conjecture regarding hypergraphs. We refer the reader to [15] for more details.

The main applications of the switching lemma described in [15] deal with cryptanalysis of modes of operations. Such modes are typically secure up to the birthday bound against adversaries with unbounded memory, yet [15] shows that they become more secure against memory-bounded adversaries. For example, in AES-based randomized counter-mode, message m_i is encrypted as $r_i, c_i = \text{AES}_K(r_i) \oplus m_i$, where r_i is a random 128-bit string. The best known distinguishing attack simply awaits a collision $r_i = r_j$ for $i \neq j$, in which case $c_i \oplus c_j = m_i \oplus m_j$. This attack stores the r_i's and requires memory of about $\sqrt{N} = 2^{64}$ to find a collision with high probability. Let us now assume that the memory is limited to storing only $S' \ll 2^{64}$ values (where $S' \approx S \cdot \log N$ bits, as storing an element requires $\log N$ bits). In this case, the probability of observing a collision with a stored element (i.e., the distinguishing advantage) is roughly $Q \cdot S'/N \approx Q \cdot S/N$ (ignoring a logarithmic factor in N). Hence, such a collision is likely to occur only after observing about $Q \approx N/S \gg 2^{64}$ elements.

Jaeger and Tessaro used their streaming switching lemma to show that the simple attack on randomized counter-mode describe above is optimal up to a factor of $O(\log N)$, if we require a constant advantage. The proof applies the

---

[1] For the sake of brevity, in this paper we use the term "switching lemma" to refer to a particular type of lemma that allows to switch between a random permutation and a random function.

streaming switching lemma to replace the random r_i's with random non-repeating ones and further replaces AES with a truly random permutation (assuming it is a PRP). Finally, it applies the streaming switching lemma again to replace the permutation with a random function, completely masking the messages. More details and additional applications are described in [15]. We further mention that attacks against counter-mode and other modes of operation have been shown to be meaningful in practice (refer to [4] for a recent example), giving an additional motivation to understand their limitations.

The streaming switching lemma of [15] is very useful, but has two limitations. First, it is based on an unproven combinatorial conjecture. Second, when $Q \cdot S \ll N$, there is a gap between the advantage upper bound $\sqrt{Q \cdot S/N}$ of the lemma and the $Q \cdot S/N$ advantage of the simple attack described above. In fact, it is easy to see that the bound $\sqrt{Q \cdot S/N}$ is not tight when $Q \cdot S \ll N$ and $S \approx Q$, as it evaluates to $Q/\sqrt{N}$. On the other hand, the true optimal advantage is Q^2/N, as obtained by the original switching lemma (since for $S \approx Q$, the adversary can store all the elements in the stream).

In order to demonstrate this gap, let us assume that for $N = 2^{128}$ the adversary has memory limited to storing $S = 2^{40}$ elements, and obtains a stream of $Q = 2^{64}$ elements. Jaeger and Tessaro's result upper bounds the adversary's advantage by about $\sqrt{2^{64+40-128}} = 2^{-12}$. On the other hand, the distinguishing advantage of the attack described above is $2^{64+40-128} = 2^{-24}$, which is significantly lower.

Our Results. In this paper, we overcome the two limitations of Jaeger and Tessaro's result. More specifically, we derive a streaming switching lemma which bounds the adversary's advantage by $O(\log Q \cdot Q \cdot S/N)$ via an alternative proof which it is not based on any conjecture. This matches the advantage of the simple distinguishing attack described above (up to poly-logarithmic factors in N), hence we resolve the streaming indistinguishability problem unconditionally.[2] Note that if we plug $S = Q$ into our bound, we obtain the original switching lemma (up to poly-logarithmic factors). Hence, our bound can also be viewed as a natural generalization of the original switching lemma to the case that the adversary cannot store all the Q elements of the stream (i.e. $S \ll Q$).

Finally, we extend the streaming switching lemma to show that the advantage of an adversary with S bits of memory that is allowed P passes over a stream of Q elements (drawn from a random permutation or a random function) is bounded by $O(\log Q \cdot Q \cdot S \cdot P/N)$. If we combine the multi-pass bound with the original switching lemma, we obtain the bound of about $\min\{\log Q \cdot Q \cdot S \cdot P/N, Q^2/N\}$, which is tight up to poly-logarithmic factors in N.

To understand the significance of our multi-pass bound, observe that for a fixed value of S, the P-pass streaming bound depends only on the total number of queries, $Q \cdot P$ (ignoring the small factor of $\log Q$). This essentially implies that repeating Q distinct queries P times does not give a P-pass algorithm

---

[2] We note, however, that Jaeger and Tessaro's result is superior to ours by a factor of up to $O(\sqrt{\log Q})$ when $S \cdot Q \approx N$.

an advantage over a single-pass algorithm that issues $Q \cdot P$ distinct queries. In contrast, in the non-streaming model repeating queries in an adaptive way has a big advantage, as cycle detection algorithms perform significantly better than the P-pass bound (obtaining constant advantage for $S = O(\log N)$ and $\sqrt{N}$ queries).

Our Techniques. The main novelty of the proof of our switching lemma is a hybrid argument that allows to devise a reduction from communication complexity to streaming. The hybrid argument is tailored to a common cryptographic setting where the goal is to distinguish between two pre-fixed distributions on streams. The cryptographic setting is different from the typical worst-case setting of streaming problems, where there is much more freedom in choosing the stream distributions in reductions from communication complexity, and hybrid arguments are not required. Although it is simple, this hybrid argument is somewhat non-trivial and allows us to apply strong bounds from communication complexity to the problem. This proof naturally extends to multi-pass adversaries. On the other hand, it seems challenging to extend the proof of [15] to multi-pass adversaries, where queries to the underlying primitive are repeated. This further demonstrates that our proof technique may be of independent interest.

Related Work. This work lies in the intersection between cryptography and streaming algorithms. The area of streaming algorithms is subject to active research in computer science, and has been largely influenced by the seminal work of Alon, Matias, and Szegedy on approximating frequency moments with limited space [1]. In the field of cryptography, several previous works investigated the security of cryptographic primitives against a space-bounded adversary whose input is given as a data stream composed of a sequence of elements that can be read only once (cf., [7,20]). More recently, Thiruvengadam and Tessaro initiated the study of the security of modes of operation against space-bounded adversaries [23]. Jaeger and Tessaro's work [15], as well as this paper, continue the line of research on streaming algorithms in cryptography.

Paper Organization. The rest of the paper is organized as follows. We give a technical overview of the proof in Sect. 2 and describe preliminaries in Sect. 3. In Sect. 4 we prove our main streaming switching lemma for single-pass algorithms, while our proof of the multi-pass variant is given in Sect. 5. Finally, we conclude the paper in Sect. 6.

2 Technical Overview

We consider an algorithm with S bits of memory that processes a stream of $Q \leq N$ elements from $[N] = \{1, 2, \ldots, N\}$, element by element. The goal of the algorithm is to decide whether the stream is drawn from a random permutation (i.e., the elements are drawn uniformly without replacement), or from a random function (i.e., the elements are drawn uniformly with replacement).

In [15] Jaeger and Tessaro approached the problem by considering the sequences of states maintained by the adversary for the two stream distributions, claiming that they remain statistically close.

In the rest of this section, we give an overview of our proof, which (unlike Jaeger and Tessaro's proof) does not directly analyze the states maintained by the adversary. For the sake of simplicity, in this overview we aim to show that the distinguishing advantage of any algorithm (compared to a random guess) is negligible as long as $Q \ll N/S$, but do not consider the concrete advantage.

2.1 Communication Complexity

A standard approach for obtaining bounds on streaming algorithms is via a reduction from communication complexity. Suppose that our goal is to distinguish between two distributions $\mathcal{D}_1$ and $\mathcal{D}_2$ on a stream $x_1, x_2, \ldots, x_Q \in [N]^Q$. We can reduce the problem from a 2-player communication game between $\mathcal{A}$ and $\mathcal{B}$ as follows. For some value of i, we partition the stream into two parts, $x_1, \ldots, x_i$ and $x_{i+1}, \ldots, x_Q$. We give the first part to $\mathcal{A}$ and the second part to $\mathcal{B}$. The goal of $\mathcal{A}$ and $\mathcal{B}$ is to decide whether the (concatenated) stream is drawn from $\mathcal{D}_1$ or from $\mathcal{D}_2$ with minimal one-way communication between $\mathcal{A}$ and $\mathcal{B}$.

In the reduction, $\mathcal{A}$ simulates a streaming algorithm on its input, sends its intermediate state to $\mathcal{B}$, which continues the simulation of the streaming algorithm and outputs its result. Thus, any streaming algorithm with memory S yields a one-way communication protocol with communication cost of S and the same distinguishing advantage. Therefore, an upper bound on the distinguishing advantage of $\mathcal{A}$ and $\mathcal{B}$ in any one-way communication protocol yields a bound on the distinguishing advantage of any streaming algorithm.

Obviously, in order to obtain a meaningful upper bound on the distinguishing advantage in the communication game, the communication problem induced from the streaming problem must be hard. In particular, a reduction from communication complexity to the streaming distinguishability game could be useful only if it has the property that for both stream distributions considered in the game, each player receives an input (partial stream) drawn from the same marginal distribution. Otherwise, a player could trivially distinguish between the two distributions locally with no communication (since $\mathcal{A}$ and $\mathcal{B}$ are unrestricted computationally).

Suppose that $\mathcal{D}_1$ is the distribution where $x_1, x_2, \ldots, x_Q$ are sampled using a random permutation, and $\mathcal{D}_2$ is the distribution where the elements are sampled using a random function. Unfortunately, for $Q > 2$ there is no way to partition the stream between $\mathcal{A}$ and $\mathcal{B}$ such that each player receives an input with the same marginal distribution in both cases.

In order to work around this difficulty, we define hybrid stream distributions between $\mathcal{D}_1$ and $\mathcal{D}_2$ with the aim of bounding the advantage between each pair of neighboring distributions using communication complexity, and applying a hybrid argument to bound the total advantage.

2.2   An Initial Approach

We start by informally outlining an initial approach that does not give the desired bound, but motivates the alternative approach that follows. We denote a stream drawn from a random permutation by $x_1, \ldots, x_Q$ and a stream drawn from a random function by $\hat{x}_1, \ldots, \hat{x}_Q$. We define $Q - 1$ intermediate stream distributions, which give rise to Q distinguishing games. The i'th game involves distinguishing between the stream distributions

$$x_1, \ldots, x_{Q-i}, \hat{x}_{Q-i+1}, \ldots, \hat{x}_Q \text{ and } x_1, \ldots, x_{Q-i-1}, \hat{x}_{Q-i}, \ldots, \hat{x}_Q,$$

which is equivalent to distinguishing between

$$x_1, \ldots, x_{Q-i} \text{ and } x_1, \ldots, x_{Q-i-1}, \hat{x}_{Q-i}.$$

Namely, the goal is to determine whether the last element already appears in the stream or not. In fact, even if the last element is chosen uniformly, it will not appear in the stream with probability $1 - (Q - i - 1)/N$. Hence, we can condition on the event that $\hat{x}_{Q-i}$ appears in the stream. As a result, the distinguishing advantage of any algorithm can be approximately bounded by $\alpha \cdot (Q - i - 1)/N$, where $\alpha = \alpha(i)$ is the advantage of the algorithm in distinguishing between $x_1, \ldots, x_{Q-i}$ and $x_1, \ldots, x_{Q-i-1}, \hat{x}_{Q-i}$, where $\hat{x}_{Q-i}$ is drawn uniformly from the first $Q - i - 1$ elements of the stream.

Unfortunately, this approach is insufficient to prove the bound we require via a hybrid argument (regardless of whether we use communication complexity of any other tool). In order to demonstrate this, consider the following distinguishing algorithm that uses only $O(\log N)$ bits of memory: we iteratively hash every element of $x_1, \ldots, x_{Q-i-1}$ to a single bit, maintaining the majority of the hashes. Then, we hash the final element and output 1 if and only if its hash is equal to the majority over the first $Q - i - 1$ hashes. Simple calculation shows that the advantage of the algorithm in distinguishing between the above streams is about $\alpha = 1/\sqrt{Q - i - 1}$. This implies that using this method cannot give a better upper bound than $1/\sqrt{Q - i - 1} \cdot (Q - i - 1)/N$ on the advantage of a streaming algorithm with memory $S = O(\log N)$ in distinguishing between neighboring stream distributions. If we sum over the advantages of the first $Q - 1$ games (the advantage is 0 in the last game), we obtain

$$\sum_{i=0}^{Q-2} \frac{1}{\sqrt{Q - i - 1}} \cdot \frac{Q - i - 1}{N} = \sum_{i=0}^{Q-2} \frac{\sqrt{Q - i - 1}}{N} = \Omega \left(\frac{Q^{3/2}}{N} \right),$$

which is already $\Omega(1)$ for $Q = N^{2/3}$. On the other hand, our goal is to show that if $S = O(\log N)$ and the distinguishing advantage is $\Omega(1)$, then $Q \approx N$.

2.3   The Improved Approach

The reason that the initial attempt above fails to prove the required bound is that distinguishing neighboring stream distributions is too easy, and the sum of the advantages over all Q games results in a loose bound. An alternative approach in attempt to overcome the loss is to try and avoid the straightforward sum of advantages by using more advanced techniques developed in the area of provable security for the purpose of obtaining tight bounds (e.g., the chi-squared method proposed in [10]). However, such techniques do not directly apply to the streaming model where the adversary no longer has access to answers of its previous queries. Moreover, it seems challenging to extend such techniques to the multi-pass setting in order to handle the dependencies between repeated queries to the underlying primitive. In this paper, we use a completely different approach by reconsidering our definition of intermediate hybrid distributions that lead from a stream produced by random permutation to a stream produced by a random function.

The Hybrid Distributions. We start by defining the first distinguishing game between $x_1, \ldots, x_Q$ (a stream drawn from a random permutation) and a second stream drawn from a carefully chosen hybrid distribution. Our goal is to make sure that the distinguishing advantage between two neighboring stream distributions is significantly lower compared to the basic approach. Furthermore, we would like to use communication complexity in order to analyze neighboring stream distributions, i.e., we require that the stream can be partitioned such that the marginal distributions of the inputs given to each player are identical.

We define our stream distributions using more convenient notation of $x_1, \ldots, x_{Q/2}, y_1, \ldots, y_{Q/2}$, where each of $x_1, \ldots, x_{Q/2}$ and $y_1, \ldots, y_{Q/2}$ is a stream drawn from a random permutation, such that the streams are either drawn from the same permutation (which corresponds to the original distribution), or drawn from independent permutations (which corresponds to the first intermediate hybrid). We then define the corresponding 2-player communication problem (which we call the *permutation-dependence* problem), where $\mathcal{A}$ and $\mathcal{B}$ obtain $x_1, \ldots, x_{Q/2}$ and $y_1, \ldots, y_{Q/2}$, respectively, and try to decide with minimal one-way communication whether their inputs are drawn from the same or from independent permutations.

To complete the distinguishability upper bound proof for the streaming game, we prove an upper bound on the distinguishing advantage of $\mathcal{A}$ and $\mathcal{B}$ in the permutation-dependence problem. The proof is by a reduction from the *set-disjointness* problem, which is a canonical 2-player problem in communication complexity [2, 16, 22], where the input of each player is a set and their goal is to determine whether their sets intersect, or are disjoint.[3]

The first hybrid breaks the dependency between the two halves of the stream. We can now continue recursively by dividing the halves into quarters, etc. This results in a binary tree of hybrids of hight $\log Q$, where a one-way communication game is played at every non-leaf node. The leaves are completely independent

---

[3] In fact, the reduction is from the *unique-disjointness* problem which is a variant of set-disjointness with the promise that if the sets of the players intersect, the intersection size is 1.

elements of $[N]$, whose concatenation is a stream sampled using a random function, as desired.[4]

Summing up the advantages over the hybrids in each level of the tree gives an upper bound of $O(Q \cdot S/N)$. The overall advantage is $O(\log Q \cdot Q \cdot S/N)$, as there are $\log Q$ levels in the tree.

3   Preliminaries

Unless stated explicitly, all parameters considered in this paper are positive integers. We define $[N] = \{1, 2, \ldots, N\}$ and $[N]^K = \underbrace{[N] \times [N] \times \ldots \times [N]}_{K}$. Given

bit strings x and y, we denote their concatenation by $x\|y$. For a positive integer K, we denote by $x^{(K)}$ the string $\underbrace{x\|x \ldots \|x}_{K}$, obtained by K repetitions of x. We

denote by $HW(x)$ the Hamming weight of x.

Given a bit string $a \in \{0,1\}^N$ such that $HW(a) = K$, we can treat it as an incidence vector of a set $\{x_1, x_2, \ldots, x_K\}$ such that $x_i \in [N]$ and $a[x_i] = 1$ for $i \in [K]$. We define $SEQ : \{0,1\}^N \to [N]^K$ as the sequence $SEQ(a) = x_1, x_2, \ldots, x_K$ (which includes the elements indicated by a in lexicographical order). Given incidence vectors $a \in \{0,1\}^N$ and $b \in \{0,1\}^N$, let $a \cap b$ denote the intersection of these sets, and $|a \cap b|$ the size of the intersection.

Given a distribution $\mathcal{X}$ on strings with finite support, we write $x \overset{\$}{\leftarrow} \mathcal{X}$ to denote a random variable x chosen from $\mathcal{X}$. We write $x \sim \mathcal{X}$ if x is a random variable that is distributed as $\mathcal{X}$.

For arbitrary distributions on strings $\mathcal{D}_1$ and $\mathcal{D}_2$, we denote by $\mathcal{D}_1\|\mathcal{D}_2$ the distribution on strings obtained by concatenating two strings sampled independently from $\mathcal{D}_1$ and $\mathcal{D}_2$.

Distinguishing Between Streams. We define our model for a randomized algorithm whose goal is to distinguish between streams. The model is similar to the one defined in [15], although we use slightly different notation.

For some parameters N, K, let $\mathcal{X}$ be some distribution over $[N]^K$. We denote by $O(\mathcal{X})$ an oracle that samples $x_1, x_2, \ldots, x_K$ from $\mathcal{X}$. The oracle receives up to K queries and answers query number i by x_i. Note that once the oracle outputs x_i, it is not output again. This implies that an algorithm $\mathcal{A}$ that interacts with $O(\mathcal{X})$ receives $x_1, x_2, \ldots, x_K$ as a stream, i.e., if $\mathcal{A}$ requires access to x_i after issuing query i, it has to store x_i in memory in some representation.

We denote by $\mathcal{A}^{O(\mathcal{X})}$ a randomized algorithm with oracle access to $O(\mathcal{X})$ and by $\mathcal{A}^{O(\mathcal{X})} \Rightarrow b$ the event that the algorithm outputs the bit $b \in \{0,1\}$.

---

[4] A hybrid argument on a binary tree is also used to prove the security of the classical pseudo-random function construction by Goldreich et al. [11]. However, the resemblance is superficial, as in [11] the construction itself is a binary tree, whereas in our case, we build it artificially only in the proof.

We say that an algorithm $\mathcal{A}$ is S-bounded, if the size of each state maintained by $\mathcal{A}$ during any execution is upper bounded by S bits.

Let $\mathcal{X}$ and $\mathcal{Y}$ be two distributions over $[N]^K$. The streaming distinguishing advantage of an algorithm $\mathcal{A}$ between $\mathcal{X}$ and $\mathcal{Y}$ is defined as

$$\text{Adv}^{\text{STR}}_{\mathcal{X},\mathcal{Y}}(\mathcal{A}) = \left| \Pr[\mathcal{A}^{O(\mathcal{X})} \Rightarrow 1] - \Pr[\mathcal{A}^{O(\mathcal{Y})} \Rightarrow 1] \right|.$$

We further define the optimal advantage for an S-bounded algorithm as

$$\text{Opt}^{\text{STR}}_{\mathcal{X},\mathcal{Y}}(S) = \max_{\mathcal{A}}\{\text{Adv}^{\text{STR}}_{\mathcal{X},\mathcal{Y}}(\mathcal{A}) \mid \mathcal{A} \text{ is } S - \text{bounded}\}.$$

Sampling with and Without Replacement. For a parameter $0 < K \leq N$, let $\mathcal{D}^K_N$ be the distribution over $[N]^K$ that is defined by a sampling procedure which uniformly draws K elements from $[N]$ without replacement.

For parameters $0 < K \leq N$ and $R > 0$, let $\mathcal{D}^{K \times R}_N$ be the distribution over $[N]^{K \cdot R}$ that is composed of R independent copies of $\mathcal{D}^K_N$. For example, $\mathcal{D}^{K \times 2}_N = \mathcal{D}^K_N \| \mathcal{D}^K_N$.

Note that sampling from $\mathcal{D}^{1 \times K}_N$ is equivalent to choosing K items from $[N]$ uniformly with replacement (i.e., from a random function), while sampling from $\mathcal{D}^K_N$ is equivalent to choosing K items from $[N]$ uniformly without replacement (i.e., from a random permutation).

The original switching lemma between a random permutation and a random function [3,13,14] asserts that any algorithm that issues Q queries to the underlying primitive has distinguishing advantage bounded by $Q^2/2N$. This bound obviously holds in the (more restricted) streaming model.

Theorem 1 (switching lemma [3,13,14]). *For any S and $Q \leq N$,*

$$\text{Opt}^{\text{STR}}_{\mathcal{D}^Q_N, \mathcal{D}^{1 \times Q}_N}(S) \leq \frac{Q^2}{2N}.$$

The Set-Disjointness and Unique-Disjointness Problems

The set-disjointness function $DISJ : \{0,1\}^N \times \{0,1\}^N \to \{0,1\}$ is defined as

$$DISJ(a,b) = \begin{cases} 0, & \text{there exists } i \in [N] \text{ for which } a[i] = b[i] = 1 \\ 1, & \text{otherwise.} \end{cases}$$

We can view a and b as subsets of $[N]$, encoded as incidence vectors, and then $DISJ(a,b) = 1$ if a and b are disjoint.

The *set-disjointness problem* (or *disjointness* in short) is a classical problem in communication complexity.[5] We consider its 2-player variant which is a game between $\mathcal{A}$ and $\mathcal{B}$ that run a protocol Π. In an instance of disjointness $\mathcal{A}$ receives $a \in \{0,1\}^N$, $\mathcal{B}$ receives $b \in \{0,1\}^N$ and their goal is to output $DISJ(a,b)$ with minimal communication in the worst case. Namely, the communication cost of

---

[5] For a (slightly outdated) survey on set-disjointness, refer to [8].

Π is defined as the maximal number of bits communicated among all possible protocol executions.

We consider a variant of the disjointness problem called *unique-disjointness*, which is identical to disjointness, but with the promise that in a 0-instance, there exists a *single* index $i \in [N]$ for which $a[i] = b[i] = 1$. We denote the corresponding function by $UDISJ$, where we define $UDISJ(a, b) = \perp$ if a, b do not satisfy the required promise. We will be interested in a public-coin randomized variant of unique-disjointness in which $\mathcal{A}, \mathcal{B}$ have access to a shared random string that is independent of their inputs.

We denote the output of the protocol Π on inputs a, b as $UDISJ_\Pi(a, b)$. Note that it is a random variable that depends on the shared randomness of $\mathcal{A}, \mathcal{B}$. Disjointness and its variants are worst case problems. This motivates the following notation for the error and advantage of the protocol.[6]

$$\mathrm{Err}_N^{\mathrm{UDISJ0}}(\Pi) = \max_{a,b}\{\Pr[UDISJ_\Pi(a,b) \neq 0 \mid UDISJ(a,b) = 0]\},$$

$$\mathrm{Err}_N^{\mathrm{UDISJ1}}(\Pi) = \max_{a,b}\{\Pr[UDISJ_\Pi(a,b) \neq 1 \mid UDISJ(a,b) = 1]\},$$

$$\mathrm{Err}_N^{\mathrm{UDISJ}}(\Pi) = \max\{\mathrm{Err}_N^{\mathrm{UDISJ0}}(\Pi), \mathrm{Err}_N^{\mathrm{UDISJ1}}(\Pi)\},$$

$$\mathrm{Adv}_N^{\mathrm{UDISJ}}(\Pi) = \left|1 - \mathrm{Err}_N^{\mathrm{UDISJ1}}(\Pi) - \mathrm{Err}_N^{\mathrm{UDISJ0}}(\Pi)\right|.$$

The following is a classical result in communication complexity.

Theorem 2 ([2, 16, 22, **adapted**]). *Any public-coin randomized protocol Π that solves unique-disjointness on all inputs $a, b \in \{0,1\}^N \times \{0,1\}^N$ such that $UDISJ(a, b) \in \{0, 1\}$ with error probability $\mathrm{Err}_N^{\mathrm{UDISJ}}(\Pi) \leq 1/3$, uses $\Omega(N)$ bits of communication in the worst case.*

Therefore, it is not possible to do much better than the trivial protocol in which $\mathcal{A}$ sends $\mathcal{B}$ its entire input a, and $\mathcal{B}$ outputs $UDISJ(a, b)$.

When analyzing the advantage γ of a protocol with communication cost of $o(N)$, we can repeat it with independent randomness and amplify its advantage using a majority vote to obtain an error probability of at most $1/3$. By applying a Chernoff bound and using Theorem 2, we can lower bound the communication cost required to achieve advantage of γ by $\Omega(\gamma^2 N)$. Unfortunately, this bound is insufficient for our purpose of obtaining a tight streaming switching lemma. On the other hand, relatively recent results [5, 12] prove a much stronger lower bound of $\Omega(\gamma N)$ on the communication cost by a more careful analysis. This stronger bound (summarized in the theorem below) will allow us to prove a tight streaming switching lemma. Nevertheless, we use the full power of the theorem only in the multi-pass version of the lemma in Sect. 5, whereas the main (single-pass) lemma only requires a weaker variant of the theorem for one-way communication protocols.

---

[6] Our notation for disjointness is consistent with the rest of the paper, yet it differs from standard notation used in communication complexity.

Theorem 3 (unique-disjointness bound). *There exists a constant $M \geq 1$ for which any public-coin randomized protocol Π for unique-disjointness that satisfies $\mathrm{Adv}_N^{\mathrm{UDISJ}}(\Pi) = \gamma$ must communicate at least $\frac{1}{M}\gamma N - M \log N$ bits in the worst case.*

The proof is heavily based on the proof of Theorem 2.2 in [5]. It is described in Appendix A for the sake of completeness, where we prove it with $M = 20$.

4 The Streaming Switching Lemma

Our main theorem is stated below. We refer to it as a "streaming switching lemma" (for the sake of compatibility with previous results).

Theorem 4 (streaming switching lemma). *There exists a constant $M_1 \geq 1$ such that any S-bounded randomized algorithm $\mathcal{A}$ for $S \geq \log N$ with access to a stream containing $\log N \leq Q \leq N/3$ elements drawn from $[N]$ via either a random permutation or a random function has a distinguishing advantage bounded by*

$$\mathrm{Adv}_{\mathcal{D}_N^Q, \mathcal{D}_N^{1 \times Q}}^{\mathrm{STR}}(\mathcal{A}) \leq \mathrm{Opt}_{\mathcal{D}_N^Q, \mathcal{D}_N^{1 \times Q}}^{\mathrm{STR}}(S) \leq \frac{M_1 \cdot \lceil \log Q \rceil \cdot Q}{N} \cdot (S + M_1 \cdot \log N).$$

Remark 1. The advantage is $O(\log Q \cdot Q \cdot S/N)$ given than $S = \Omega(\log N)$.

Remark 2. It follows from our proof that we can set $M_1 = 30$. However, a smaller value of M_1 can be derived by low-level optimizations.

Theorem 4 follows from the lemma below, which is proved in Sect. 4.1.

Lemma 1. *There exists a constant $M_1 \geq 1$ such that for any $K \leq N/3$ and $S \geq \log N$,*

$$\mathrm{Opt}_{\mathcal{D}_N^{2K}, \mathcal{D}_N^{K \times 2}}^{\mathrm{STR}}(S) \leq \frac{M_1 \cdot K}{N} \cdot (S + M_1 \cdot \log N).$$

Proof (of Theorem 4). Let M_1 be the constant implied by Lemma 1. We denote by $\Gamma = \Gamma(N, S) = \frac{M_1}{N} \cdot (S + M_1 \cdot \log N)$ the upper bound on $\mathrm{Opt}_{\mathcal{D}_N^{2K}, \mathcal{D}_N^{K \times 2}}^{\mathrm{STR}}(S)$ deduced in Lemma 1, divided by K. Note that $\Gamma(N, S)$ does not depend on K. Let k be a positive integer such that $K = 2^k < 2N/3$. We prove that for any S-bounded algorithm $\mathcal{A}$ with $S \geq \log N$,

$$\mathrm{Adv}_{\mathcal{D}_N^K, \mathcal{D}_N^{1 \times K}}^{\mathrm{STR}}(\mathcal{A}) \leq \frac{k \cdot K}{2} \cdot \Gamma. \tag{1}$$

The proof is by induction on k. The base case is for k such that $K \leq \log N$. It follows from the original switching lemma (Theorem 1), since

$$\mathrm{Adv}_{\mathcal{D}_N^K, \mathcal{D}_N^{1 \times K}}^{\mathrm{STR}}(\mathcal{A}) \leq \frac{K^2}{2N} \leq \frac{K \cdot S}{2N} \leq \frac{M_1 \cdot k \cdot K}{2N} \cdot (S + M_1 \cdot \log N).$$

Suppose that the hypothesis holds up to $k' = k$. We prove it for $k' = k+1$ (assuming $K \leq N/3$). We have

$$\mathrm{Adv}^{\mathrm{STR}}_{\mathcal{D}_N^{2K}, \mathcal{D}_N^{1 \times 2K}}(\mathcal{A}) =$$

$$\left| \Pr[\mathcal{A}^{O(\mathcal{D}_N^{2K})} \Rightarrow 1] - \Pr[\mathcal{A}^{O(\mathcal{D}_N^{1 \times 2K})} \Rightarrow 1] \right| =$$

$$\left| \left(\Pr[\mathcal{A}^{O(\mathcal{D}_N^{2K})} \Rightarrow 1] - \Pr[\mathcal{A}^{O(\mathcal{D}_N^{K \times 2})} \Rightarrow 1] \right) + \right.$$

$$\left. \left(\Pr[\mathcal{A}^{O(\mathcal{D}_N^{K \times 2})} \Rightarrow 1] - \Pr[\mathcal{A}^{O(\mathcal{D}_N^{1 \times 2K})} \Rightarrow 1] \right) \right| \leq$$

$$\left| \Pr[\mathcal{A}^{O(\mathcal{D}_N^{2K})} \Rightarrow 1] - \Pr[\mathcal{A}^{O(\mathcal{D}_N^{K \times 2})} \Rightarrow 1] \right| +$$

$$\left| \Pr[\mathcal{A}^{O(\mathcal{D}_N^{K \times 2})} \Rightarrow 1] - \Pr[\mathcal{A}^{O(\mathcal{D}_N^{1 \times 2K})} \Rightarrow 1] \right| \leq \qquad \text{(Lemma 1)}$$

$$K \cdot \Gamma +$$

$$\left| \left(\Pr[\mathcal{A}^{O(\mathcal{D}_N^{K \times 2})} \Rightarrow 1] - \Pr[\mathcal{A}^{O(\mathcal{D}_N^K \| \mathcal{D}_N^{1 \times K})} \Rightarrow 1] \right) + \right.$$

$$\left. \left(\Pr[\mathcal{A}^{O(\mathcal{D}_N^K \| \mathcal{D}_N^{1 \times K})} \Rightarrow 1] - \Pr[\mathcal{A}^{O(\mathcal{D}_N^{1 \times 2K})} \Rightarrow 1] \right) \right| \leq$$

$$K \cdot \Gamma +$$

$$\left| \Pr[\mathcal{A}^{O(\mathcal{D}_N^K \| \mathcal{D}_N^K)} \Rightarrow 1] - \Pr[\mathcal{A}^{O(\mathcal{D}_N^K \| \mathcal{D}_N^{1 \times K})} \Rightarrow 1] \right| +$$

$$\left| \Pr[\mathcal{A}^{O(\mathcal{D}_N^K \| \mathcal{D}_N^{1 \times K})} \Rightarrow 1] - \Pr[\mathcal{A}^{O(\mathcal{D}_N^{1 \times K} \| \mathcal{D}_N^{1 \times K})} \Rightarrow 1] \right| \leq \qquad \text{(hypothesis)}$$

$$K \cdot \Gamma + 2 \cdot \frac{k \cdot K}{2} \cdot \Gamma =$$

$$\frac{(k+1) \cdot 2K}{2} \cdot \Gamma.$$

This completes the proof of the induction.

Finally, let $\mathcal{A}$ be S-bounded as in the theorem. Let $q' = \lceil \log Q \rceil$ and $Q' = 2^{q'}$ (note that $Q \leq Q' \leq 2Q$). We have

$$\mathrm{Adv}^{\mathrm{STR}}_{\mathcal{D}_N^Q, \mathcal{D}_N^{1 \times Q}}(\mathcal{A}) \leq \mathrm{Adv}^{\mathrm{STR}}_{\mathcal{D}_N^{Q'}, \mathcal{D}_N^{1 \times Q'}}(\mathcal{A}) \leq \frac{q' \cdot Q'}{2} \cdot \Gamma \leq \lceil \log Q \rceil \cdot Q \cdot \Gamma,$$

where the second inequality follows from (1). This concludes the proof of Theorem 4. ∎

4.1   Reduction from Communication Complexity to Streaming

We now define the permutation-dependence problem and summarize the outcome of the reduction from this problem to streaming in Proposition 1. We then state a lower bound on the communication cost of the permutation-dependence problem in Proposition 2 (which is proved in Sect. 4.2), and use it to prove Lemma 1.

The Permutation-Dependence Problem. *Permutation-dependence* is a 2-player game between $\mathcal{A}$ and $\mathcal{B}$ that run a protocol Π. For an even parameter $K \leq N$, we choose the K elements

$$x_1, \ldots, x_{K/2}, y_1, \ldots, y_{K/2},$$

from either $\mathcal{D}_N^K$, or from $\mathcal{D}_N^{K/2 \times 2}$. We give $x_1, \ldots, x_{K/2}$ to $\mathcal{A}$ and $y_1, \ldots, y_{K/2}$ to $\mathcal{B}$. Note that regardless of the distribution from which the K elements are chosen, the input to each player is taken from the (marginal) distribution $\mathcal{D}_N^{K/2}$. However, the inputs are either dependent (chosen from $\mathcal{D}_N^K$) or independent (chosen from $\mathcal{D}_N^{K/2 \times 2}$) and the goal of the players is to distinguish between these cases.

After receiving their inputs x, y, players $\mathcal{A}, \mathcal{B}$ run a communication protocol Π and then one of the players outputs a bit which is the output of the protocol, denoted by $PDEP_{\Pi}(x, y)$. We say that Π has communication cost C if $\mathcal{A}, \mathcal{B}$ communicate at most C bits in all possible protocol executions. Similarly to the disjointness problem, we will be interested in public-coin randomized protocols for permutation-dependence.

Since it is a distributional communication complexity problem, we define the following notation for permutation-dependence:

$$\mathrm{Err}_{N,K}^{\mathrm{PDEP0}}(\Pi) = \Pr[PDEP_{\Pi}(x, y) \neq 0 \mid x, y \xleftarrow{\$} \mathcal{D}_N^{K/2 \times 2}],$$

$$\mathrm{Err}_{N,K}^{\mathrm{PDEP1}}(\Pi) = \Pr[PDEP_{\Pi}(x, y) \neq 1 \mid x, y \xleftarrow{\$} \mathcal{D}_N^K],$$

$$\mathrm{Adv}_{N,K}^{\mathrm{PDEP}}(\Pi) = \left| 1 - \mathrm{Err}_{N,K}^{\mathrm{PDEP1}}(\Pi) - \mathrm{Err}_{N,K}^{\mathrm{PDEP0}}(\Pi) \right|,$$

$$\mathrm{Opt}_{N,K}^{\mathrm{PDEP}}(C) = \max_{\Pi}\{ \mathrm{Adv}_{N,K}^{\mathrm{PDEP}}(\Pi) \mid \Pi \text{ has communication cost } C\}.$$

We further denote by $\mathrm{Opt}_{N,K}^{\mathrm{PDEP}\rightarrow}(C)$ the optimal advantage of a *one-way communication protocol* for permutation-dependence. Namely, we only consider protocols in which $\mathcal{A}$ sends a single message to $\mathcal{B}$, which outputs the answer. Clearly, $\mathrm{Opt}_{N,K}^{\mathrm{PDEP}\rightarrow}(C) \leq \mathrm{Opt}_{N,K}^{\mathrm{PDEP}}(C)$.

The Reduction from Permutation-Dependence to Streaming. The following proposition upper bounds the advantage of a (memory-bounded) streaming algorithm in distinguishing between $\mathcal{D}_N^K$ and $\mathcal{D}_N^{K/2 \times 2}$ by the advantage of an optimal one-way permutation-dependence protocol (with limited communication cost). It is a standard reduction from a 2-player one-way communication protocol to streaming (for example, refer to [18]).

Proposition 1. *For any S and even $K \leq N$,*

$$\mathrm{Opt}_{\mathcal{D}_N^K, \mathcal{D}_N^{K/2 \times 2}}^{\mathrm{STR}}(S) \leq \mathrm{Opt}_{N,K}^{\mathrm{PDEP}\rightarrow}(S).$$

Proof. Given black-box access to an S-bounded streaming algorithm $\mathcal{A}_1$, players $\mathcal{A}$ and $\mathcal{B}$ in the permutation-dependence protocol Π run $\mathcal{A}_1$ and answer its oracle queries using their inputs: $\mathcal{A}$ answers the first batch of $K/2$ queries (using $x_1, \ldots, x_{K/2}$) and then communicates the intermediate state of $\mathcal{A}_1$ to $\mathcal{B}$ which answers the second batch of $K/2$ queries (using $y_1, \ldots, y_{K/2}$). Finally, $\mathcal{B}$ outputs the same answer as $\mathcal{A}_1$.

Thus, $\mathcal{A}_1$ is given oracle access to O, where either $O = O(\mathcal{D}_N^K)$ or $O = O(\mathcal{D}_N^{K/2 \times 2})$, depending on the distribution of the inputs x, y of $\mathcal{A}, \mathcal{B}$. Clearly, Π is a one-way communication protocol. Moreover, since $\mathcal{A}_1$ is S-bounded and its state is communicated once, the communication cost of Π is bounded by S. Therefore,

$$\mathrm{Adv}^{\mathrm{STR}}_{\mathcal{D}_N^K, \mathcal{D}_N^{K/2 \times 2}}(\mathcal{A}_1) = \mathrm{Adv}^{\mathrm{PDEP}}_{N,K}(\Pi) \leq \mathrm{Opt}^{\mathrm{PDEP} \to}_{N,K}(S).$$

The proposition follows since the above inequality holds for any S-bounded algorithm $\mathcal{A}_1$.   ∎

Remark 3. In case $S > K/2$, a trivial reduction (where one party sends its input to the other) is more efficient than the one above. This gives

$$\mathrm{Opt}^{\mathrm{STR}}_{\mathcal{D}_N^K, \mathcal{D}_N^{K/2 \times 2}}(S) \leq \mathrm{Opt}^{\mathrm{PDEP} \to}_{N,K}(K/2).$$

Using this observation, it is possible to obtain a limited improvement to the streaming switching lemma (Theorem 4) in case $S = N^{\Omega(1)}$.

Proof of Lemma 1. In order to prove Lemma 1, we use the following proposition (proved in Sect. 4.2) which bounds the advantage of any protocol Π for permutation-dependence.

Proposition 2. *There exists a constant $M_1 \geq 1$ such that for any $K \leq N/3$ and $C \geq \log N$,*

$$\mathrm{Opt}^{\mathrm{PDEP}}_{N,2K}(C) \leq \frac{M_1 \cdot K}{N} \cdot (C + M_1 \cdot \log N).$$

Proof (of Lemma 1). Let M_1 be the constant implied by Proposition 2. Based on Proposition 1 and Proposition 2 we have

$$\mathrm{Opt}^{\mathrm{STR}}_{\mathcal{D}_N^{2K}, \mathcal{D}_N^{K \times 2}}(S) \leq \mathrm{Opt}^{\mathrm{PDEP} \to}_{N,2K}(S) \leq \mathrm{Opt}^{\mathrm{PDEP}}_{N,2K}(S) \leq \frac{M_1 \cdot K}{N} \cdot (S + M_1 \cdot \log N).$$

                                                                          ∎

Remark 4. Proposition 2 upper bounds $\mathrm{Opt}^{\mathrm{PDEP}}_{N,2K}(C)$, yet the proof of Lemma 1 only requires an upper bound on $\mathrm{Opt}^{\mathrm{PDEP} \to}_{N,2K}(S)$. This suggests that a (small) improvement to the bound of Lemma 1 (and hence to the bound of Theorem 4) may be possible.

4.2 Reduction from Unique-Disjointness to Permutation-Dependence

The proof of Proposition 2 is based on a reduction from the unique-disjointness problem to the permutation-dependence problem, summarized by the proposition below.

Proposition 3. *Let $K \leq N/3$ and $N' = \lfloor N/K \rfloor$. There exists a public-coin randomized local reduction, f_1, f_2, where $f_i : \{0,1\}^{N'} \to [N]^K$, such that for any $a, b \in \{0,1\}^{N'} \times \{0,1\}^{N'}$,*

$$f_1(a), f_2(b) \sim \begin{cases} \mathcal{D}_N^{K \times 2}, & \text{if } UDISJ(a,b) = 0 \\ \mathcal{D}_N^{2K}, & \text{if } UDISJ(a,b) = 1. \end{cases}$$

Here, a public-coin randomized local reduction means that f_1 only depends on a and on public randomness (but not on b), and similarly, f_2 does not depend on a. Hence, if a, b intersect at exactly 1 index, then the output of the reduction consists of two independent random permutation streams, each of K elements. On the other hand, if a, b are disjoint, then the output of the reduction consists of a single random permutation stream of $2K$ elements (that is split into two halves).

Proof. We describe the reduction f_1, f_2 as a procedure executed by two parties $\mathcal{A}, \mathcal{B}$ that do not communicate, but share a random string.

---

1. Given incidence vector inputs (bit arrays) $a, b \in \{0,1\}^{N'} \times \{0,1\}^{N'}$, let $S_A = a^{(K)} \| 0^{(N - N' \cdot K)}$, $S_B = b^{(K)} \| 0^{(N - N' \cdot K)}$. Namely, each party locally duplicates its array K times and appends zero entries such that $S_A \in \{0,1\}^N$ and $S_B \in \{0,1\}^N$.

2. Using their joint randomness, the parties sample a sequence of K indices $i_1, i_2, \ldots, i_K \xleftarrow{\$} \mathcal{D}_N^K$ (chosen from $[N]$ without replacement). The parties use the sampled indices to create new arrays: $\mathcal{A}$ defines an array $T_A \in \{0,1\}^K$, where $T_A[j] = S_A[i_j]$ for $j \in \{1, 2, \ldots, K\}$. Similarly, $\mathcal{B}$ defines $T_B \in \{0,1\}^K$, where $T_B[j] = S_B[i_j]$ for $j \in \{1, 2, \ldots, K\}$.

3. Each party locally extends its array from size K to size N such that its Hamming weight becomes K (the parties add disjoint 1 entries). More specifically, $\mathcal{A}$ computes

$$T_A^2 = T_A \| 1^{(K - HW(T_A))} \| 0^{(N - 2K + HW(T_A))},$$

and $\mathcal{B}$ computes

$$T_B^2 = T_B \| 0^{(K)} \| 1^{(K - HW(T_B))} \| 0^{(N - 3K + HW(T_B))}.$$

4. Each party applies (the same) uniform permutation $\sigma : \{0,1\}^N \to \{0,1\}^N$ to its array of size N (σ is specified in the joint randomness),

$$T_A^3[i] = T_A^2[\sigma(i)], \text{ and } T_B^3[i] = T_B^2[\sigma(i)],$$

for each $i \in [N]$.

5. Finally, $\mathcal{A}$ selects a uniform permutation $\sigma_1 : \{0,1\}^K \to \{0,1\}^K$ and uses it to output the elements indicated by its array T_A^3 (the 1 entries) in uniform order. $\mathcal{A}$ outputs

$$f_1(a)_i = SEQ(T_A^3)_{\sigma_1(i)}, \text{ for each } i \in [K].$$

$\mathcal{B}$ selects a uniform permutation $\sigma_2 : \{0,1\}^K \to \{0,1\}^K$ and outputs

$$f_2(b)_i = SEQ(T_B^3)_{\sigma_2(i)}, \text{ for each } i \in [K].$$

Analysis. Observe that $T_A^3 \in \{0,1\}^N$ satisfies $HW(T_A^3) = K$ and similarly $T_B^3 \in \{0,1\}^N$ satisfies $HW(T_B^3) = K$. Therefore, each party outputs a sequence of K elements.

Due to the randomization of σ (which randomizes the elements that are output by f_1, f_2) and of σ_1, σ_2 (which randomize the order of the elements output by f_1, f_2), we have the following property.

Property 1. Let $a, b \in \{0,1\}^{N'} \times \{0,1\}^{N'}$ and

$$x, y = x_1, \ldots, x_K, y_1, \ldots, y_K \in [N]^{2K}, \; x', y' = x_1', \ldots, x_K', y_1', \ldots, y_K' \in [N]^{2K},$$

where each K element sequence (x, y, x' and y') contains distinct elements and for some $0 \le t \le K$,

$$|\{x_1, \ldots, x_K\} \cap \{y_1, \ldots, y_K\}| = |\{x_1', \ldots, x_K'\} \cap \{y_1', \ldots, y_K'\}| = t.$$

Then,

$$\Pr[f_1(a), f_2(b) = x, y] = \Pr[f_1(a), f_2(b) = x', y'].$$

Hence, the distribution of $f_1(a), f_2(b)$ is completely determined by the distribution of the size of the intersection of the sequences $f_1(a)$ and $f_2(b)$ as sets. The intersection size is equal to $|T_A \cap T_B|$ (since $|T_A \cap T_B| = |T_A^3 \cap T_B^3|$), thus we analyze this variable below.

Observe that

$$|S_A \cap S_B| = K \cdot |a \cap b|.$$

Consider the case that $UDISJ(a, b) = 1$, or $|a \cap b| = 0$. We have $|S_A \cap S_B| = 0$ and therefore $|T_A \cap T_B| = 0$. Hence, $f_1(a)$ and $f_2(b)$ are disjoint as sets, and by Property 1, $f_1(a), f_2(b) \sim \mathcal{D}_N^{2K \times 1}$.

Otherwise, $UDISJ(a, b) = 0$, implying that $|a \cap b| = 1$ and therefore $|S_A \cap S_B| = K$. The number of options for selecting $i_1, i_2, \ldots, i_K$ in the second step such that they intersect the K common indices in S_A, S_B in exactly $0 \le t \le K$ places is $\binom{K}{t}\binom{N-K}{K-t}$. Since the total number of options for selecting $i_1, i_2, \ldots, i_K$ is $\binom{N}{K}$,

$$\Pr[|T_A \cap T_B| = t] = \frac{\binom{K}{t}\binom{N-K}{K-t}}{\binom{N}{K}}.$$

At the same time,

$$\Pr\left[\left|\{x_1,\ldots,x_K\} \cap \{y_1,\ldots,y_K\}\right| = t \mid x_1,\ldots,x_K, y_1,\ldots,y_K \xleftarrow{\$} \mathcal{D}_N^{K \times 2}\right] =$$

$$\frac{\binom{K}{t}\binom{N-K}{K-t}}{\binom{N}{K}} = \Pr[|T_A \cap T_B| = t].$$

Hence, by Property 1, $f_1(a), f_2(b) \sim \mathcal{D}_N^{K \times 2}$ as claimed.   ∎

Finally, Proposition 2 follows from Proposition 3 and Theorem 3.

Proof (of Proposition 2). We show that there exists a constant M_1 such that any permutation-dependence protocol Π' with communication cost $C \geq \log N$ satisfies $\mathrm{Adv}_{N,2K}^{\mathrm{PDEP}}(\Pi') \leq \frac{M_1 \cdot K}{N} \cdot (C + M_1 \cdot \log N)$. This proves Proposition 2.

Fix a permutation-dependence protocol Π' as above. We consider a protocol Π for unique-disjointness, where given an input $a, b \in \{0,1\}^{N'} \times \{0,1\}^{N'}$ (for $N' = \lfloor N/K \rfloor$), each party independently applies the reduction of Proposition 3 to its input using the public randomness. The parties then run the permutation-dependence protocol Π' on input $f_1(a), f_2(b)$ with communication cost (at most) C bits in the worst case and output the same value. In short,

$$UDISJ_\Pi(a,b) = PDEP_{\Pi'}(f_1(a), f_2(b)).$$

Proposition 3 implies that for every a, b such that $UDISJ(a,b) = 0$,

$$\Pr[UDISJ_\Pi(a,b) = 1 \mid UDISJ(a,b) = 0] =$$
$$\Pr[PDEP_{\Pi'}(f_1(a), f_2(b)) = 1 \mid UDISJ(a,b) = 0] = \mathrm{Err}_{N,2K}^{\mathrm{PDEP0}}(\Pi'),$$

and a similar equality holds for every a, b such that $UDISJ(a,b) = 1$. Hence

$$\mathrm{Err}_{N'}^{\mathrm{UDISJ0}}(\Pi) = \mathrm{Err}_{N,2K}^{\mathrm{PDEP0}}(\Pi'), \text{ and } \mathrm{Err}_{N'}^{\mathrm{UDISJ1}}(\Pi) = \mathrm{Err}_{N,2K}^{\mathrm{PDEP1}}(\Pi').$$

Denote

$$\alpha' = 1 - \mathrm{Err}_{N'}^{\mathrm{UDISJ1}}(\Pi), \quad \beta' = \mathrm{Err}_{N'}^{\mathrm{UDISJ0}}(\Pi),$$

and $\gamma' = \alpha' - \beta'$. We have

$$\mathrm{Adv}_{N'}^{\mathrm{UDISJ}}(\Pi) = \alpha' - \beta' = \gamma' =$$
$$1 - \mathrm{Err}_{N,2K}^{\mathrm{PDEP1}}(\Pi') - \mathrm{Err}_{N,2K}^{\mathrm{PDEP0}}(\Pi') = \mathrm{Adv}_{N,2K}^{\mathrm{PDEP}}(\Pi'),$$

where we assume that $\alpha' - \beta' \geq 0$ (otherwise, $\mathcal{A}, \mathcal{B}$ in Π simply negate the output of Π'). Hence, γ' is equal to the advantage of both the unique-disjointness and permutation-dependence protocols.

We apply Theorem 3 to Π, and since C upper bounds the communication cost of Π in the worst case, we conclude that $C \geq \frac{1}{M} \cdot N' \cdot \gamma' - M \log N'$. This gives

$$\gamma' \leq \frac{M}{N'} \cdot (C + M \cdot \log N') \leq \frac{M}{N'} \cdot (C + M \cdot \log N).$$

Define $M_1 = 3/2 \cdot M$. Note that since $K \leq N/3$, then

$$N' = \left\lfloor \frac{N}{K} \right\rfloor \geq \frac{N - K}{K} \geq \frac{2N}{3K},$$

hence $\frac{M}{N'} \leq \frac{M_1 \cdot K}{N}$. Therefore,

$$\gamma' \leq \frac{M_1 \cdot K}{N} \cdot (C + M_1 \cdot \log N),$$

as claimed.   ∎

5   The Multi-pass Streaming Switching Lemma

For a parameter $P \geq 1$, we consider a P-pass streaming algorithm which can access an input stream of Q elements P times at the same order. The P-pass algorithm attempts to distinguish between a stream chosen from a random permutation or from a random function. In our model, the algorithm interacts with an oracle that samples from one of the distributions defined below.

For $0 < K \leq N$, let $\mathcal{D}_N^{K \times R \otimes P}$ be the distribution over $[N]^{K \cdot R \cdot P}$ that is defined by a sampling procedure which first draws $x \xleftarrow{\$} \mathcal{D}_N^{K \times R}$ and then outputs $\underbrace{x \| x \| \dots \| x}_{P}$. In case $R = 1$, we simply write $\mathcal{D}_N^{K \otimes P}$.

Theorem 5 (multi-pass switching lemma). *There exists a constant $M_1 \geq 1$ such that any S-bounded randomized P-pass algorithm $\mathcal{A}$ for $S \geq \log N$ with access to a stream containing $\log N \leq Q \leq N/3$ elements drawn from $[N]$ via either a random permutation or a random function has a distinguishing advantage bounded by*

$$\mathrm{Adv}^{\mathrm{STR}}_{\mathcal{D}_N^{Q \otimes P}, \mathcal{D}_N^{1 \times Q \otimes P}}(\mathcal{A}) \leq \mathrm{Opt}^{\mathrm{STR}}_{\mathcal{D}_N^{Q \otimes P}, \mathcal{D}_N^{1 \times Q \otimes P}}(S) \leq \frac{M_1 \cdot \lceil \log Q \rceil \cdot Q}{N} \cdot (P \cdot S + M_1 \cdot \log N).$$

The proof of Theorem 5 is based on the lemma below, which is a generalization of Lemma 1.

Lemma 2. *There exists a constant $M_1 \geq 1$ such that for any $K \leq N/3$ and $S \geq \log N$,*

$$\mathrm{Opt}^{\mathrm{STR}}_{\mathcal{D}_N^{2K \otimes P}, \mathcal{D}_N^{K \times 2 \otimes P}}(S) \leq \frac{M_1 \cdot K}{N} \cdot (P \cdot S + M_1 \cdot \log N).$$

We omit the proof of Theorem 5, as it is essentially identical to the one of Theorem 4.

The proof of Lemma 2 uses the following proposition which generalizes Proposition 1.

Proposition 4. *For any S and even $K \leq N$,*

$$\mathrm{Opt}^{\mathrm{STR}}_{\mathcal{D}_N^{K \otimes P}, \mathcal{D}_N^{K/2 \times 2 \otimes P}}(S) \leq \mathrm{Opt}^{\mathrm{PDEP}}_{N, K}(P \cdot S).$$

Proof. The proof is via a reduction from the (multi-round) permutation-dependence problem to (multi-pass) streaming, which generalizes the proof of Proposition 1. The only difference is that in order to simulate the P-pass streaming algorithm, its state is communicated P times between the parties, hence the communication cost of the permutation-dependence protocol is bounded by $S \cdot P$. ∎

Proof (of Lemma 2). Let M_1 be the constant implied by Proposition 2. Based on Proposition 4 and Proposition 2 we have

$$\mathrm{Opt}^{\mathrm{STR}}_{\mathcal{D}_N^{2K} \otimes P, \mathcal{D}_N^{K \times 2 \otimes P}}(S) \leq \mathrm{Opt}^{\mathrm{PDEP}}_{N,2K}(P \cdot S) \leq \frac{M_1 \cdot K}{N} \cdot (P \cdot S + M_1 \cdot \log N).$$

∎

6   Conclusions and Future Work

In this paper we proved an upper bound on the streaming distinguishing advantage between a random permutation and a random function, which is tight up to poly-logarithmic factors. Our proof is based on a hybrid argument that gives rise to a reduction from the unique-disjointness communication complexity problem to streaming. In the future, it would be interesting to apply our techniques to additional streaming problems that are relevant to cryptography.

Acknowledgements. The author would like to thank Andrej Bogdanov for his helpful comment on a previous version of this work, which allowed to base the single-pass streaming switching lemma on a permutation-dependence problem with one-way communication (the previous version was based on a generalized variant of permutation-dependence with multi-round communication).

The author was supported by the Israeli Science Foundation through grant No. 573/16 and by the European Research Council under the ERC starting grant agreement No. 757731 (LightCrypt).

A   Concrete Parameters for Theorem 3

In this appendix we prove Theorem 3 for $M = 20$, as restated below.

Theorem 3 (restated with $M = 20$). *Any public-coin randomized protocol Π for unique-disjointness that satisfies $\mathrm{Adv}^{\mathrm{UDISJ}}_N(\Pi) = \gamma$ must communicate at least $\frac{1}{20}\gamma N - 20 \log N$ bits in the worst case.*

We first describe information theory preliminaries, which are heavily used in the proof (for more details refer to [9]). We then give an overview of the proof, which is based on the proof of Theorem 2.2 in [5, revision 1].

A.1   Information Theory

We begin with notations and definitions. Consider discrete random variables X, Y, Z. We denote the distribution of X by $p(X)$. We denote by $\mathcal{X}(x)$ the probability that a random variable drawn from the distribution $\mathcal{X}$ gets the value x.

The *entropy* of X is

$$\mathrm{H}(X) = \sum_x \Pr[X = x] \log(1/\Pr[X = x]).$$

The *conditional entropy* of X given Y is

$$\mathrm{H}(X|Y) = \sum_y \Pr[Y = x] H(X|Y = y) = \mathrm{H}[X, Y] - \mathrm{H}[Y].$$

The *mutual information* between X, Y is

$$I(X; Y) = H(X) - H(X|Y) = H(Y) - H(Y|X),$$

where $I(X; Y) = 0$ if and only if X and Y are independent. The *conditional mutual information* between X, Y given Z is

$$I(X; Y|Z) = H(X|Z) - H(X|Y, Z).$$

The *Kullback-Leibler divergence* (also known as the relative entropy) between two distributions $\mathcal{X}, \mathcal{Y}$ is

$$\mathrm{D}(\mathcal{X} \| \mathcal{Y}) = \sum_x \mathcal{X}(x) \log(\mathcal{X}(x)/\mathcal{Y}(x)).$$

Next, we describe the properties that we use.

The *chain rule of mutual information* asserts that

$$I(X; Y, Z) = I(X; Z) + I(X; Y|Z).$$

Since (conditional) mutual information is non-negative, this implies that

$$I(X; Y, Z) \geq I(X; Z).$$

We will use the following equalities:

$$I(X; Y) = \sum_x \Pr[X = x] \mathrm{D}(p(Y|X = x) \| p(Y)), \text{ and}$$

$$I(X; Y|Z) = \sum_z \Pr[Z = z] \mathrm{D}(p(X, Y|Z = z) \| p(X|Z = z), p(Y|Z = z)) =$$

$$\sum_{y,z} \Pr[Y = y, Z = x] \mathrm{D}(p(X|Y = y, Z = z) \| p(X|Z = z)).$$

Finally, *Pinsker's inequality* bounds the statistical distance between probability distributions as

$$\Delta(\mathcal{X}, \mathcal{Y}) \leq \sqrt{1/2 \cdot \mathrm{D}(\mathcal{X} \| \mathcal{Y})}.$$

A.2   Overview of the Proof

The main part of the proof (described in Sect. A.3) establishes a similar result to Theorem 3 for private-coin protocols. It is based on the proof of Theorem 2.2 by Braverman and Moitra [5, revision 1]. Then, in Sect. A.4, we complete the proof of the theorem by extending the result to public-coin protocols using the standard sparsification technique of [19].

We now give a short overview of the lower bound proof for private-coin protocols. It uses the *information complexity* approach, which has become a standard technique for proving communication complexity lower bounds (cf., [2]). In particular, we define a distribution on the inputs of the parties, which become random variables, denoted by (A, B). We analyze the amount of information that the concatenation of the messages in the protocol (namely, the protocol transcript, denoted as $\Pi(A, B)$) reveals to each player about the other player's input. This quantity is exactly $I(A; \Pi \mid B) + I(B; \Pi \mid A)$ (known as the internal information complexity of Π) and it immediately lower bounds $H(\Pi)$ and hence the communication cost of Π.

In order to lower bound $I(A; \Pi \mid B) + I(B; \Pi \mid A)$, we break down the inputs (A, B) into N mutually independent coordinates (A_j, B_j). This allows using a direct sum property which reduces the task of proving an $\Omega(\epsilon N)$ lower bound for the original problem (for $0 < \epsilon \leq 1$) to the task of proving an $\Omega(\epsilon)$ lower bound for a small "gadget". In particular, the disjointness function can be written as $DISJ(a, b) = \bigvee_{j \in [N]}(a_j \wedge b_j)$. Hence, in standard proofs that use this approach the gadget is the AND (or NAND) gate.

Unfortunately, it is shown in [5] that there is a protocol for AND that achieves an advantage of γ, but reveals only $O(\gamma^2)$ bits of information. This implies that the standard reduction to the AND gate only allows to prove a lower bound of $\Omega(\gamma^2 N)$ on the communication cost (which can also be obtained by straightforward majority amplification, as summarized in Sect. 3). We note that the protocol of [5] for AND can also be viewed as a one-way communication protocol in which $\mathcal{B}$ outputs the answer. Therefore, the standard reduction to the AND gate does not allow proving the required $\Omega(\gamma N)$ communication cost lower bound even for one-way protocols.

In order to prove a $\Omega(\gamma N)$ lower bound, Braverman and Moitra use a more complex gadget and the main part of the analysis involves proving that any protocol for this gadget that achieves advantage of γ must reveal $\Omega(\gamma)$ bits of information. The analysis essentially breaks the gadget down into 6 smaller AND gadgets which interact in a way that allows proving the required bound.

A.3   A Lower Bound for Private-Coin Protocols

We consider private-coin protocols for unique-disjointness.

Theorem 6. *Any private-coin protocol Π for unique-disjointness that satisfies* $\mathrm{Adv}_N^{\mathrm{UDISJ}}(\Pi) = \gamma$ *must communicate at least* $\frac{1}{19.5}\gamma N$ *bits in the worst case.*

Theorem 3 is a concrete variant of Theorem 2.2 in [5, revision 1] and its proof is very similar to that of [5]. However, we present the proof slightly differently and additionally calculate the constants involved. We note that the proof in [5] employed a so-called "smoothing" to the underlying disjointness protocol, yet this not necessary to prove the theorem and hence is omitted.[7]

Consider a private-coin protocol Π such that $\mathrm{Adv}_N^{\mathrm{UDISJ}}(\Pi) = \gamma$. We analyze the information complexity of Π with respect to the following distribution on inputs: we group the N bits into blocks of size exactly three, and for each pair of three bits we generate $a_j, b_j \in \{0,1\}^3$ (for $j \in [N/3]$) uniformly at random from the pairs of strings of length three bits where a_j and b_j have exactly one 1 and two 0's, and a_j and b_j are disjoint. Consequently, there are 6 possible a_j, b_j pairs. We define A, B as random variables for the inputs of the players and $A_j, B_j \in \{1, 2, 3\}$ as random variables for the location of the 1 bit in a_j, b_j, respectively.

We will be interested in lower bounding $\mathrm{H}(\Pi) = \mathrm{H}(\Pi(A, B))$ by proving a lower bound on the internal information complexity $\mathrm{I}(A; \Pi \mid B) + \mathrm{I}(B; \Pi \mid A)$ using the following fact.

Fact 1. $\frac{1}{2}\left[\sum_j \mathrm{I}(A_j; \Pi \mid A_{1\ldots j-1}, B_{j\ldots n}) + \mathrm{I}(B_j; \Pi \mid A_{1\ldots j}, B_{j+1\ldots n})\right] \le \mathrm{H}[\Pi]$.

Proof. By the chain rule for mutual information we obtain

$$\sum_j \mathrm{I}(A_j; \Pi \mid A_{1\ldots j-1}, B_{j\ldots n}) \le \sum_j \mathrm{I}(A_j; \Pi, B_{1\ldots j-1} \mid A_{1\ldots j-1}, B_{j\ldots n}) =$$

$$\sum_j \mathrm{I}(A_j; B_{1\ldots j-1} \mid A_{1\ldots j-1}, B_{j\ldots n}) + \sum_j \mathrm{I}(A_j; \Pi \mid A_{1\ldots j-1}, B) =$$

$$\sum_j \mathrm{I}(A_j; \Pi \mid A_{1\ldots j-1}, B) = \mathrm{I}(A; \Pi \mid B) \le \mathrm{H}(\Pi),$$

where $\mathrm{I}(A_j; B_{1\ldots j-1} \mid A_{1\ldots j-1}, B_{j\ldots n}) = 0$ by independence. Similarly,

$$\sum_j \mathrm{I}(B_j; \Pi \mid A_{1\ldots j}, B_{j+1\ldots n}) \le \mathrm{H}(\Pi).$$

Therefore,

$$\frac{1}{2}\left[\sum_j \mathrm{I}(A_j; \Pi \mid A_{1\ldots j-1}, B_{j\ldots n}) + \mathrm{I}(B_j; \Pi \mid A_{1\ldots j}, B_{j+1\ldots n})\right] \le \mathrm{H}(\Pi),$$

concluding the proof. ∎

We define $C_j = A_{1\ldots j-1}, B_{j+1\ldots n}$ and write

$$\mathrm{I}(A_j; \Pi \mid A_{1\ldots j-1}, B_{j\ldots n}) = \mathrm{I}(A_j; \Pi \mid C_j, B_j) =$$

$$\sum_{c,i} \sum_t \Pr[\Pi = t, C_j = c, B_j = i] \mathrm{D}(p(A_j \mid \Pi = t, C_j = c, B_j = i) \| p(A_j \mid C_j = c, B_j = i)),$$

and a similar equality holds for $\mathrm{I}(B_j; \Pi \mid A_{1\ldots j}, B_{j+1\ldots n})$.

---

[7] The fact that "smoothing" is not required is also mentioned in [24, Footnote 7].

Choosing C_j according to the distribution on the inputs, we obtain

$$\mathrm{I}(A_j; \Pi \mid C_j, B_j) + \mathrm{I}(B_j; \Pi \mid C_j, A_j) = \sum_t \mathrm{E}[\mathrm{adv}(t, C_j)], \qquad (2)$$

where the expectation is over C_j, and $\mathrm{adv}(t, C_j)$ is defined as

$$\mathrm{adv}(t, C_j) =$$
$$\sum_{i \in \{1,2,3\}} \Pr[\Pi = t, B_j = i \mid C_j] \mathrm{D}(p(A_j \mid \Pi = t, B_j = i, C_j) \| p(A_j \mid B_j = i, C_j)) +$$
$$\Pr[\Pi = t, A_j = i \mid C_j] \mathrm{D}(p(B_j \mid \Pi = t, A_j = i, C_j) \| p(B_j \mid A_j = i, C_j)).$$

Since B_j is independent of C_j and is uniform in $\{1, 2, 3\}$ (and the same property holds for A_j), then

$$\mathrm{adv}(t, C_j) =$$
$$\frac{1}{3} \sum_{i \in \{1,2,3\}} \Pr[\Pi = t \mid B_j = i, C_j] \mathrm{D}(p(A_j \mid \Pi = t, B_j = i, C_j) \| p(A_j \mid B_j = i, C_j)) + \qquad (3)$$
$$\Pr[\Pi = t \mid A_j = i, C_j] \mathrm{D}(p(B_j \mid \Pi = t, A_j = i, C_j) \| p(B_j \mid A_j = i, C_j)).$$

Our goal is to relate the expression $\sum_t \mathrm{E}[\mathrm{adv}(t, C_j)]$ to the advantage of the protocol, γ. For this purpose, we fix a transcript t where the output is one. We consider a fixed block j, and the matrix $N^t(C_j)$ that gives the probability of $\Pi = t$ for each pair of inputs for the parties $\mathcal{A}$ and $\mathcal{B}$, conditioned on the parts of their input C_j that we have already fixed (the probability here is taken over the randomness of the protocol and the remaining bits in the input of $\mathcal{A}$ and $\mathcal{B}$). To simplify notation we abbreviate $N^t(C_j)$ as N^t and write

$$N^t = \begin{bmatrix} N_{11}^t, & N_{12}^t, & N_{13}^t \\ N_{21}^t, & N_{22}^t, & N_{23}^t \\ N_{31}^t, & N_{32}^t, & N_{33}^t \end{bmatrix}.$$

Since Π is a private-coin protocol, $\mathcal{A}$ and $\mathcal{B}$ can privately sample their remaining bits conditioned on C_j. Therefore (similarly to [2, Lemma 6.7]), N^t is a rank one matrix that can be expressed as $N^t = [a_1, a_2, a_3][b_1, b_2, b_3]^T$. In particular, b_i is the probability over $B_{1...j-1}$ and the private randomness of $\mathcal{B}$ that $B = B_{1...j-1}, B_j = i; B_{j+1...n}$ is in the rectangle for $\Pi = t$.

Relating the terms in (3) to N^t, observe that for $i = 1$, $\Pr[\Pi = t \mid B_j = 1, C_j] = N_{21}^t + N_{31}^t = a_2 b_1 + a_3 b_1$. Moreover, using the convention that $0/0 = 0$, $p(A_j \mid \Pi = t, B_j = 1, C_j)$ is a Bernoulli distribution with parameter $a_2 b_1 / (a_2 b_1 + a_3 b_1)$ (which we denote by $\mathcal{B}_{a_2 b_1 / (a_2 b_1 + a_3 b_1)}$), while $p(A_j \mid B_j = 1, C_j)$ is a Bernoulli distribution with parameter $1/2$ (as $A_j \in \{2, 3\}$ is uniform). Consequently, we get the equality

$$\Pr[\Pi = t \mid B_j = 1, C_j] \mathrm{D}(p(A_j \mid \Pi = t, B_j = 1, C_j) \| p(A_j \mid B_j = 1, C_j)) =$$
$$(a_2 b_1 + a_3 b_1) \mathrm{D}(\mathcal{B}_{a_2 b_1 / (a_2 b_1 + a_3 b_1)} \| \mathcal{B}_{1/2}).$$

For any $x, y, z \in [0,1]$, define

$$IC(x,y,z) = (xy + xz)\mathrm{D}(\mathcal{B}_{xy/(xy+xz)} \| \mathcal{B}_{1/2}).$$

We generalize the above equality to all terms in (3), obtaining

$$\mathrm{adv}(t, C_j) = \frac{1}{3}(IC(b_1, a_2, a_3) + IC(a_1, b_2, b_3) + IC(b_2, a_1, a_3) + \\ IC(a_2, b_1, b_3) + IC(b_3, a_1, a_2) + IC(a_3, b_1, b_2)). \tag{4}$$

Let P be the ordered set of triplets $(i_1, i_2, i_3) \in \{1,2,3\}^3$ such that i_1, i_2, i_3 are all distinct. Note that P contains 6 triples. Since $IC(x,y,z) = IC(x,z,y)$, we can write (4) as

$$\mathrm{adv}(t, C_j) = \frac{1}{6} \sum_{(i_1, i_2, i_3) \in P} (IC(a_{i_1}, b_{i_2}, b_{i_3}) + IC(b_{i_2}, a_{i_1}, a_{i_3})). \tag{5}$$

Each expression $IC(a_{i_1}, b_{i_2}, b_{i_3}) + IC(b_{i_2}, a_{i_1}, a_{i_3})$ can be thought of the information revealed by the protocol for a small AND gadget. The sum of the 6 expressions in $\mathrm{adv}(t, C_j)$ can be thought of as a "covering" of the matrix $N^t(C_j)$ with 6 AND gadgets.

For the following fact, we use the proof of [24, Lemma 4] to obtain a slightly better constant than the one obtained in [5]. Let $\phi = (1 + \sqrt{5})/2 \approx 1.618$ be the golden ratio. Recall that $\phi^2 = \phi + 1$.

Fact 2 *For any* $x, y, z, u \in [0,1]$, $IC(x,y,z) + IC(y,x,u) \geq \frac{1}{2\phi}(xz + yu - xy - zu)$.

Proof. By Pinsker's inequality for Bernoulli distributions, we have

$$\mathrm{D}(\mathcal{B}_{xy/(zy+xz)} \| \mathcal{B}_{1/2}) \geq 2 \cdot \left(\frac{xy}{xy + xz} - \frac{1}{2}\right)^2 = \frac{1}{2}\left(\frac{z-y}{z+y}\right)^2$$

(if $xy + xz = 0$ the inequality follows from the definition $0/0 = 0$). Therefore,

$$IC(x,y,z) + IC(y,x,u) = \\ (xy + xz)\mathrm{D}(\mathcal{B}_{xy/(xy+xz)} \| \mathcal{B}_{1/2}) + (yx + yu)\mathrm{D}(\mathcal{B}_{yx/(yx+yu)} \| \mathcal{B}_{1/2}) \geq \\ \frac{1}{2}\left((xy + xz)\left(\frac{z-y}{z+y}\right)^2 + (yx + yu)\left(\frac{x-u}{x+u}\right)^2\right) = \\ \frac{1}{2}\left(\frac{x}{y+z} \cdot (z-y)^2 + \frac{y}{x+u} \cdot (x-u)^2\right).$$

Denote

$$R = \frac{x}{y+z} \cdot (z-y)^2 + \frac{y}{x+u} \cdot (x-u)^2,$$

$$L = xz + yu - xy - zu = (x-u)(z-y).$$

Thus, in order to complete the proof we show that $R \geq L/\phi$. If L is not positive, then $R \geq L$ (since R is non-negative) and we are done. It remains to consider the case that $x \geq u$ and $z \geq y$ (the remaining case, $x \leq u$ and $z \leq y$, is symmetric). If $z \leq (2\phi+1)y$ (implying that $y/(y+z) \geq 1/(2\phi+2)$) then since $x/(x+u) \geq 1/2$, the product of the two terms of R is at least $(x-u)^2(z-y)^2/(4\phi+4)$. Hence by the AM-GM inequality, $R \geq 2(x-u)(z-y)/\sqrt{4\phi+4} = L/\sqrt{\phi+1} = L/\phi$. If $z \geq (2\phi+1)y$ then $z+y \leq (z-y)(\phi+1)/\phi = \phi(z-y)$, hence the first term of R is at least $(x/\phi(z-y))(z-y)^2 = x(z-y)/\phi \geq L/\phi$.   ∎

We can now prove Theorem 6.

Proof (of Theorem 6). Combining (5) with Fact 2, we obtain

$$\mathrm{adv}(t, C_j) = \frac{1}{6} \sum_{(i_1,i_2,i_3)\in P} (IC(a_{i_1}, b_{i_2}, b_{i_3}) + IC(b_{i_2}, a_{i_1}, a_{i_3})) \geq$$

$$\frac{1}{12\phi} \sum_{(i_1,i_2,i_3)\in P} (a_{i_1}b_{i_3} + b_{i_2}a_{i_3} - a_{i_1}b_{i_2} - b_{i_3}a_{i_3}) =$$

$$\frac{1}{12\phi} \left(\sum_{i\neq i'} a_i b_{i'} - 2 \sum_{i\in\{1,2,3\}} a_i b_i \right) =$$

$$\frac{1}{12\phi} \left(\sum_{i\neq i'} (N_{ii'}^t(C_j)) - 2 \sum_{i\in\{1,2,3\}} N_{ii}^t(C_j) \right).$$

Therefore,

$$\sum_t \mathrm{E}[\mathrm{adv}(t, C_j)] \geq \frac{1}{12\phi} \sum_t \mathrm{E}\left[\sum_{i\neq i'} (N_{ii'}^t(C_j)) - 2 \sum_{i\in\{1,2,3\}} N_{ii}^t(C_j) \right] \geq \frac{1}{12\phi} \cdot 6\gamma = \gamma/(2\phi).$$

The second inequality follows since the advantage of Π is γ. In more detail, for some $\alpha \geq 0$, for each i, i' such that $i \neq i'$ we average the probability of outputting 1 over disjoint inputs and therefore we have $\sum_t \mathrm{E}[N_{ii'}^t(C_j)] \geq \alpha + \gamma$. On the other hand, for each $i \in \{1, 2, 3\}$ we average the probability of outputting 1 over inputs with intersection size of one and hence $\sum_t \mathrm{E}[N_{ii}^t(C_j)] \leq \alpha$.

Finally, combining with Fact 1 and (2),

$$\mathrm{H}[\Pi] \geq \frac{1}{2} \sum_j [\mathrm{I}(A_j; \Pi \mid C_j, B_j) + \mathrm{I}(B_j; \Pi \mid C_j, A_j)]] =$$

$$\frac{1}{2} \sum_j \sum_t \mathrm{E}[\mathrm{adv}(t, C_j)] \geq \frac{1}{4\phi} \sum_{j\in[N/3]} \gamma = \frac{1}{4\phi} \cdot \gamma N/3 \geq \gamma N/19.5,$$

concluding the proof.   ∎

A.4   The Proof of Theorem 3

We now use Theorem 6 to prove Theorem 3. The proof is based on the standard sparsification technique of [19].

Proof (of Theorem 3). We start with a public-coin protocol Π' for unique-disjointness with communication cost C' and advantage γ' and convert it into a private-coin protocol Π with communication cost at most $C = C' + 2.7 \log N + 17$ and advantage at least $\gamma \geq 0.99\gamma'$. By Theorem 6, we have $C \geq \gamma N/19.5$, or $C' + 2.7 \log N + 17 \geq \gamma' N/20$, implying that $C' \geq \gamma' N/20 - 2.7 \log N - 17 \geq \gamma' N/20 - 20 \log N$ and establishing Theorem 3 for $M = 20$.

Suppose Π' uses a string R as its randomness. For a parameter k, we pick k independent random strings $R_1, \ldots, R_k$, distributed as R. Fix an input (a, b) such that $UDISJ(a, b) = 0$ and denote $\alpha = \mathrm{Err}_N^{\mathrm{UDISJ0}}(\Pi')$. Among $R_1, \ldots, R_k$, the expected number of strings R_i for which $\Pi'(a, b)$ errs with randomness R_i is at most αk. Hence, by a Chernoff bound, the probability that the number of strings for which $\Pi'(a, b)$ errs is more than $(\alpha + \gamma'/256)k = (1 + \gamma'/(256\alpha))\alpha k$ is at most $e^{-(\gamma'/(256\alpha))^2 \cdot \alpha k/3} > e^{-(\gamma')^2 \cdot k \cdot 2^{-16}}$. Since $\gamma' \geq 1/N$ (otherwise, the theorem is trivial), this probability is upper bounded by $e^{-k \cdot 2^{-16} N^{-2}}$. A similar bound can be shown for an input (a, b) such that $UDISJ(a, b) = 1$ by considering $\beta = \mathrm{Err}_N^{\mathrm{UDISJ1}}(\Pi')$.

We call a sequence of strings $R_1, \ldots, R_k$ *good* if for any (legal) input (a, b) to unique-disjointness, the fraction of strings for which Π' errs deviates from the corresponding error probability of Π' ($\mathrm{Err}_N^{\mathrm{UDISJ0}}(\Pi')$ or $\mathrm{Err}_N^{\mathrm{UDISJ1}}(\Pi')$) by at most $\gamma'/256$. Otherwise, the sequence is called *bad*. Taking a union bound over the (at most) 2^{2N} possible inputs, the probability that the sequence $R_1, \ldots, R_k$ is bad is at most $2^{2N} \cdot e^{-k \cdot 2^{-16} N^{-2}}$. Setting $k = 2^{17} N^{2.7}$ ensures that this probability is less than 1, and therefore there exists a good sequence of $k = 2^{17} N^{2.7}$ random strings, which we fix.

In the private-coin protocol Π, $\mathcal{A}$ first samples a uniform index $i \in [k]$ and sends it to $\mathcal{B}$ with its first message. This requires $\log k = 17 + 2.7 \log N$ additional bits of communication. The parties then run Π' with randomness R_i. Since $R_1, \ldots, R_k$ is good, then the advantage of Π is at least $\gamma' - \gamma'/256 - \gamma'/256 \geq 0.99\gamma'$, as claimed. ∎

References

1. Alon, N., Matias, Y., Szegedy, M.: The space complexity of approximating the frequency moments. J. Comput. Syst. Sci. **58**(1), 137–147 (1999)
2. Bar-Yossef, Z., Jayram, T.S., Kumar, R., Sivakumar, D.: An information statistics approach to data stream and communication complexity. J. Comput. Syst. Sci. **68**(4), 702–732 (2004)
3. Bellare, M., Rogaway, P.: The security of triple encryption and a framework for code-based game-playing proofs. In: Vaudenay, S. (ed.) EUROCRYPT 2006. LNCS, vol. 4004, pp. 409–426. Springer, Heidelberg (2006). https://doi.org/10.1007/11761679_25

4. Bhargavan, K., Leurent, G.: On the practical (in-)security of 64-bit block ciphers: collision attacks on HTTP over TLS and OpenVPN. In: Weippl, E.R., Katzenbeisser, S., Kruegel, C., Myers, A.C., Halevi, S. (eds.) Proceedings of the 2016 ACM SIGSAC Conference on Computer and Communications Security, Vienna, Austria, 24–28 October 2016, pp. 456–467. ACM (2016)
5. Braverman, M., Moitra, A.: An information complexity approach to extended formulations. In: Boneh, D., Roughgarden, T., Feigenbaum, J. (eds.) Symposium on Theory of Computing Conference, STOC 2013, Palo Alto, CA, USA, 1–4 June 2013, pp. 161–170. ACM (2013)
6. Brent, R.P.: An improved Monte Carlo factorization algorithm. BIT Numer. Math. **20**(2), 176–184 (1980). https://doi.org/10.1007/BF01933190
7. Cachin, C., Maurer, U.: Unconditional security against memory-bounded adversaries. In: Kaliski, B.S. (ed.) CRYPTO 1997. LNCS, vol. 1294, pp. 292–306. Springer, Heidelberg (1997). https://doi.org/10.1007/BFb0052243
8. Chattopadhyay, A., Pitassi, T.: The story of set disjointness. SIGACT News **41**(3), 59–85 (2010)
9. Cover, T.M., Thomas, J.A.: Elements of Information Theory, 2nd edn. Wiley, Hoboken (2006)
10. Dai, W., Hoang, V.T., Tessaro, S.: Information-theoretic indistinguishability via the Chi-Squared method. In: Katz, J., Shacham, H. (eds.) CRYPTO 2017, Part III. LNCS, vol. 10403, pp. 497–523. Springer, Cham (2017). https://doi.org/10.1007/978-3-319-63697-9_17
11. Goldreich, O., Goldwasser, S., Micali, S.: How to construct random functions. J. ACM **33**(4), 792–807 (1986)
12. Göös, M., Watson, T.: Communication complexity of set-disjointness for all probabilities. Theory Comput. **12**(1), 1–23 (2016)
13. Hall, C., Wagner, D., Kelsey, J., Schneier, B.: Building PRFs from PRPs. In: Krawczyk, H. (ed.) CRYPTO 1998. LNCS, vol. 1462, pp. 370–389. Springer, Heidelberg (1998). https://doi.org/10.1007/BFb0055742
14. Impagliazzo, R., Rudich, S.: Limits on the provable consequences of one-way permutations. In: Johnson, D.S. (ed.) Proceedings of the 21st Annual ACM Symposium on Theory of Computing, 14–17 May 1989, Seattle, Washigton, USA, pp. 44–61. ACM (1989)
15. Jaeger, J., Tessaro, S.: Tight time-memory trade-offs for symmetric encryption. In: Ishai, Y., Rijmen, V. (eds.) EUROCRYPT 2019, Part I. LNCS, vol. 11476, pp. 467–497. Springer, Cham (2019). https://doi.org/10.1007/978-3-030-17653-2_16
16. Kalyanasundaram, B., Schnitger, G.: The probabilistic communication complexity of set intersection. SIAM J. Discrete Math. **5**(4), 545–557 (1992)
17. Knuth, D.E.: The Art of Computer Programming, Volume II: Seminumerical Algorithms. Addison-Wesley, Reading (1969)
18. Kushilevitz, E., Nisan, N.: Communication Complexity. Cambridge University Press, New York (1997)
19. Newman, I.: Private vs. common random bits in communication complexity. Inf. Process. Lett. **39**(2), 67–71 (1991)
20. Nisan, N.: Pseudorandom generators for space-bounded computation. Combinatorica **12**(4), 449–461 (1992)
21. Pollard, J.M.: A monte carlo method for factorization. BIT Numer. Math. **15**(3), 331–334 (1975). https://doi.org/10.1007/BF0193366
22. Razborov, A.A.: On the distributional complexity of disjointness. Theor. Comput. Sci. **106**(2), 385–390 (1992)

23. Tessaro, S., Thiruvengadam, A.: Provable time-memory trade-offs: symmetric cryptography against memory-bounded adversaries. In: Beimel, A., Dziembowski, S. (eds.) TCC 2018, Part I. LNCS, vol. 11239, pp. 3–32. Springer, Cham (2018). https://doi.org/10.1007/978-3-030-03807-6_1
24. Watson, T.: Communication complexity with small advantage. In: Servedio, R.A. (ed.) 33rd Computational Complexity Conference, CCC 2018, 22–24 June 2018, San Diego, CA, USA, volume 102 of LIPIcs, pp. 9:1–9:17. Schloss Dagstuhl - Leibniz-Zentrum fuer Informatik (2018)

Isogeny-Based Cryptography

He Gives C-Sieves on the CSIDH

Chris Peikert[(✉)]

University of Michigan, Ann Arbor, USA
cpeikert@alum.mit.edu

Abstract. Recently, Castryck, Lange, Martindale, Panny, and Renes proposed *CSIDH* (pronounced "sea-side") as a candidate post-quantum "commutative group action." It has attracted much attention and interest, in part because it enables noninteractive Diffie–Hellman-like key exchange with quite small communication. Subsequently, CSIDH has also been used as a foundation for digital signatures.

In 2003–04, Kuperberg and then Regev gave asymptotically subexponential quantum algorithms for "hidden shift" problems, which can be used to recover the CSIDH secret key from a public key. In late 2011, Kuperberg gave a follow-up quantum algorithm called the *collimation sieve* ("c-sieve" for short), which improves the prior ones, in particular by using exponentially less quantum memory and offering more parameter tradeoffs. While recent works have analyzed the concrete cost of the original algorithms (and variants) against CSIDH, nothing of this nature was previously available for the c-sieve.

This work fills that gap. Specifically, we generalize Kuperberg's collimation sieve to work for arbitrary finite cyclic groups, provide some practical efficiency improvements, give a classical (i.e., non-quantum) simulator, run experiments for a wide range of parameters up to the actual CSIDH-512 group order, and concretely quantify the complexity of the c-sieve against CSIDH.

Our main conclusion is that the proposed CSIDH parameters provide relatively little quantum security beyond what is given by the cost of quantumly evaluating the CSIDH group action itself (on a uniform superposition). For example, the cost of CSIDH-512 key recovery is only about 2^{16} quantum evaluations using 2^{40} bits of quantumly accessible *classical* memory (plus relatively small other resources). This improves upon a prior estimate of $2^{32.5}$ evaluations and 2^{31} qubits of *quantum* memory, for a variant of Kuperberg's original sieve.

Under the plausible assumption that quantum evaluation does not cost much more than what is given by a recent "best case" analysis, CSIDH-512 can therefore be broken using significantly less than 2^{64} quantum T-gates. This strongly invalidates its claimed NIST level 1 quantum security, especially when accounting for the MAXDEPTH restriction. Moreover, under analogous assumptions for CSIDH-1024 and -1792, which target higher NIST security levels, except near the high end of the MAXDEPTH range even these instantiations fall short of level 1.

This material is based upon work supported by the Patrick C. Fischer Development Chair and the National Science Foundation under Award CNS-1606362. The views expressed are those of the author and do not necessarily reflect the official policy or position of the National Science Foundation.

© International Association for Cryptologic Research 2020
A. Canteaut and Y. Ishai (Eds.): EUROCRYPT 2020, LNCS 12106, pp. 463–492, 2020.
https://doi.org/10.1007/978-3-030-45724-2_16

1   Introduction

In 1994, Shor [Sho94] upended cryptography by giving polynomial-time *quantum* algorithms for the integer factorization and discrete logarithm problems, which can be used (on sufficiently large-scale quantum computers) to break all widely deployed public-key cryptography. With the steady progress in engineering quantum computers, there is an increasing need for viable *post-quantum* cryptosystems, i.e., ones which can be run on today's classical computers but resist attacks by future quantum ones. Indeed, the US National Institute of Standards and Technology (NIST) has begun a post-quantum standardization effort [NIS], and recently selected the second-round candidates.

1.1   Isogeny-Based Cryptography

One prominent class of candidate post-quantum cryptosystems uses *isogenies* between elliptic curves over a common finite field. Isogeny-based cryptography began with the proposal of Couveignes in 1997, though it was not widely distributed until 2006 [Cou06]. The approach was independently rediscovered by Stolbunov (in his 2004 Master's thesis [Sto04]) and by Rostovtsev and Stolbunov [RS06] in 2006. The central object in these proposals is a (free and transitive) *group action* $\star\colon G \times Z \to Z$ of a finite *commutative* group G on a set Z. Group actions naturally generalize exponentiation in (finite) cyclic multiplicative groups C: we take $G = \mathbb{Z}_q^*$ to be the multiplicative group of integers modulo the order $q = |C|$ and Z to be the set of generators of C, and define $a \star z = z^a$.

The Couveignes–Rostovtsev–Stolbunov (hereafter CRS) proposal very naturally generalizes Diffie–Hellman [DH76] noninteractive key exchange to use a commutative group action: some $z \in Z$ is fixed for use by all parties; Alice chooses a secret $a \in G$ and publishes $p_A = a \star z$; Bob likewise chooses a secret $b \in G$ and publishes $p_B = b \star z$; then each of them can compute their shared key $(ab) \star z = a \star p_B = b \star p_A$. (Note the essential use of commutativity in the second equation, where $b \star (a \star z) = (ba) \star z = (ab) \star z$.)

Security. Of course, for the CRS system to have any hope of being secure, the analogue of the discrete logarithm problem for the group action must be hard, i.e., it must be infeasible to recover a (or some functional equivalent) from $p_A = a \star z$. In 2010, Childs, Jao, and Soukharev [CJS10] observed that, assuming a suitable algorithm for the group action, this problem reduces to the (injective) abelian hidden-shift problem on the group G. It happens that Kuperberg [Kup03] in 2003 and then Regev [Reg04] in 2004 had already given asymptotically subexponential quantum "sieve" algorithms for this problem. More specifically, Kuperberg's algorithm uses $\exp(O(\sqrt{n}))$ quantum time and space, whereas Regev's uses slightly larger $\exp(O(\sqrt{n \log n}))$ quantum time but only $\mathrm{poly}(n)$ quantum space, where $n = \log N$ is the bit length of the group order $N = |G|$. While these attacks do not necessarily render CRS-type systems insecure asymptotically, one must consider their concrete complexity when setting parameters to obtain a desired level of security.

We mention that these subexponential attacks against CRS motivated Jao and De Feo [JD11] to give a different approach to isogeny-based cryptography using *supersingular* curves, whose full endomorphism rings are non-commutative, which thwarts the Kuperberg-type attacks. The Jao–De Feo scheme, now known as Supersingular Isogeny Diffie–Helmman (SIDH), is also not based on a group action, and is inherently interactive. Most research on isogeny-based cryptography has focused on SIDH and closely related ideas.

CSIDH. The noninteractive nature and simplicity of the CRS approach are particularly attractive features, which motivated Castryck, Lange, Martindale, Panny, and Renes [CLM+18] to revisit the method recently. They proposed "Commutative SIDH," abbreviated CSIDH and pronounced "sea-side." Like SIDH, it relies on supersingular curves, but it uses a *commutative subring* of the full endomorphism ring, which naturally leads to a commutative group action. This design choice and other clever optimizations yield an impressive efficiency profile: for the CSIDH-512 parameters that were claimed in [CLM+18] to meet NIST security level 1, a full key exchange takes only about 80 milliseconds (improving upon several minutes for prior CRS prototypes), with key sizes of only 64 bytes (compared to hundreds of bytes for SIDH and derivatives).

In summary, the designers of CSIDH describe it as a primitive "that can serve as a drop-in replacement for the (EC)DH key-exchange protocol while maintaining security against quantum computers." As such, it has attracted a good deal of attention and interest. (For example, it received the 2019 Dutch Cybersecurity Research Paper Award.) In addition, a series of works [Sto11, DG19, BKV19, KKP20] used CSIDH to develop digital signature schemes having relatively small sizes and reasonable running times. E.g., for the same claimed security levels as above, the CSI-FiSh signature scheme [BKV19] can have a combined public key and signature size of 1468 bytes, which is better than all proposals to the NIST post-quantum cryptography effort.

1.2   Attacking the CSIDH

As mentioned above, when setting parameters for CSIDH and arriving at security claims, one must take into account known attacks. The main quantum approach is given by Kuperberg's abelian hidden-shift algorithm [Kup03] and descendants, where the hidden "shift" corresponds to the secret "discrete log" $a \in G$ for a given public key $p_A = a \star z \in Z$. Algorithms of this type have two main components:

1. a quantum *oracle* that, whenever queried, outputs a certain kind of random "labeled" quantum state, in part by evaluating the group action on a uniform superposition over the group;
2. a *sieving* procedure that combines labeled states in some way to generate "more favorable" ones.

By processing many fresh labeled states from the oracle, the sieve eventually creates some "highly favorable" states, which are then measured to reveal useful information about the hidden shift (i.e., the secret key).

The overall complexity of the attack is therefore mainly determined by the complexities of the quantum oracle and the sieve, where the latter includes the number of oracle queries. These can be analyzed independently, and for each there is a line of work with a focus on CRS/CSIDH.

The Oracle. To produce a labeled state, the oracle mainly needs to prepare a uniform superposition over the group G, and apply the group action to a superposition of the "base" $z \in Z$ and the public key $a \star z$. (It then does a certain measurement, takes a Fourier transform, and measures again to get a label.) In the context of isogenies, evaluating the group action on the superposition is presently the bottleneck, by a large amount.

The original work of Childs, Jao, and Soukharev [CJS10] implemented the oracle in $\exp(\tilde{O}(n^{1/2}))$ quantum time (assuming GRH) and space. Biasse, Iezzi, and Jacobson [BIJJ18] improved this to an oracle that (under different heuristics) runs in $\exp(\tilde{O}(n^{1/3}))$ quantum time and polynomial space, though they did not analyze the factors hidden by the $\tilde{O}$ notation.

More recently, Bernstein, Lange, Martindale, and Panny [BLMP19] analyzed the *concrete* cost of quantumly evaluating the CSIDH group action. For the CSIDH-512 parameters, they arrived at an estimate of less than 2^{40} nonlinear bit operations (which translates to between 2^{40} and 2^{44} quantum T-gates), with a failure probability below 2^{-32}, to evaluate the group action on a non-uniform "best conceivable" (for the attacker) distribution of group elements, namely, the one used in CSIDH key generation. Recent work by Beullens, Kleinjung, and Vercauteren [BKV19] suggests that the cost for a *uniform* superposition may be quite close to that of the "best conceivable" case; see Sect. 1.4 for further discussion.

The Sieve. Kuperberg's original algorithm [Kup03] has $\exp(O(\sqrt{n}))$ complexity in time, queries, *and* quantum space. More specifically, he rigorously proved a query bound of $O(2^{3\sqrt{n}})$, and a better time and query bound of $\tilde{O}(3^{\sqrt{2\log_3 N}})$ when $N = r^n$ for some small radix r (though this is very unlikely to be the case for CSIDH). As already mentioned, Regev reduced the quantum space to only polynomial in n, but at the cost of increasing the time and query complexity to $\exp(O(\sqrt{n \log n}))$; to our knowledge, precise hidden factors have not been worked out for this approach.

Bonnetain and Schrottenloher [BS18] provided a variant of Kuperberg's sieve for arbitrary cyclic groups, and gave more precise estimates of its query and quantum-space complexity. Specifically, using simulations up to $n = 100$ they estimate that $2^{1.8\sqrt{n}+2.3}$ queries and nearly the same number of qubits of memory are needed. For the CSIDH-512 parameters, this translates to $2^{32.5}$ queries and 2^{31} qubits.

Notably, in late 2011 Kuperberg gave a follow-up algorithm [Kup11], called the *collimation sieve* (or "c-sieve" for short), which subsumes his original one and Regev's variant.[1] Asymptotically, it still uses $\exp(O(\sqrt{n}))$ quantum time and classical space, but only *linear* $O(n)$ quantum space (in addition to the oracle's). Moreover, it provides other options and tradeoffs, most notably among classical time, quantum time, and *quantumly accessible classical* memory (QRACM, also known as QROM), i.e., classical memory that is readable (but not writeable) in superposition. As argued in [BHT98, Kup11], QRACM is plausibly much cheaper than fully quantum memory, because it does not need to be preserved in superposition. In particular, Kuperberg describes [Kup11, Proposition 2.2] how QRACM can be simulated using ordinary classical memory, at the cost of logarithmic quantum memory and quasilinear quantum time in the number of data cells; see [BGB+18, Section III.C] for a realization of this idea which has modest concrete cost.

Although Kuperberg's collimation sieve dates to about six years before the CSIDH proposal, and has been briefly cited in some of the prior literature on CSIDH, an analysis for concrete parameters was not previously available.[2] That is the topic we address in this work.

1.3 Our Contributions

We analyze the concrete complexity of Kuperberg's collimation sieve [Kup11], with a focus on CSIDH and its proposed parameterizations, although our results apply generally to *any* CRS-style commutative group action, including recent CSIDH variants [CD19, FTLX19].[3] Our study mainly treats the quantum oracle as a "black box," and focuses on the precise number of queries and amount of quantumly accessible classical memory (QRACM) the sieve uses. Following a suggestion by Schanck [Sch19], we also give a rough analysis of how these quantities translate to the quantum complexity of full attacks on proposed CSIDH parameters.

More specifically, we generalize the c-sieve to work for cyclic groups of arbitrary finite order (from power-of-two or other smooth orders, which CSIDH groups typically do not have), provide some practical improvements that extract more secret-key bits per run of the sieve and maintain better control of the memory and time complexities, give a classical simulator and run experiments on a wide range of parameters—including the actual CSIDH-512 group order of $N \approx 2^{257.1}$—and concretely quantify the complexity of the c-sieve against proposed CSIDH parameters. As far as we know, ours is the first work to simulate *any* kind of quantum sieve algorithm for groups as large as the actual CSIDH-512 group; previously, the largest simulations were for group orders $N \approx 2^{100}$.

---

[1] More recently, Kuperberg has given talks highlighting the virtues of the algorithm and its relevance to isogenies.

[2] Shortly after the announcement of this work, Bonnetain and Schrottenloher posted an updated version of [BS18], which had been under private review and which does contain such an analysis. See below for a comparison.

[3] Our work has no implications for SIDH [JD11] or the NIST submission SIKE, which do not use commutative group actions.

Conclusions. Our main conclusion is that the proposed CSIDH parameters provide relatively little quantum security beyond what is given by the cost of the quantum oracle. For example, for CSIDH-512 the secret key can be recovered from the public key with only about 2^{16} oracle queries and 2^{40} bits of QRACM, or about $2^{19.3}$ queries and 2^{32} bits of QRACM, plus insignificant other resources. This improves upon a prior estimate [BS18] of $2^{32.5}$ queries and 2^{31} qubits of *quantum* memory, for a variant of Kuperberg's first sieve algorithm. The key insight underlying our improvements is that when the oracle is expensive, trading oracle queries for QRACM can dramatically reduce the overall quantum time, while keeping the classical costs reasonable. (No such tradeoff is available for the earlier sieve algorithms.) In addition, we find that for the group orders of interest, the cost of implementing even substantial amounts of QRACM using [BGB+18] is dwarfed by that of the oracle queries (under current estimates for the latter). See Sect. 4 for the full details.

Under the plausible assumption that implementing the oracle does not cost much more than the "best conceivable case" estimate of [BLMP19], CSIDH-512 can therefore be broken using not much more than 2^{60} quantum T-gates, plus relatively small other resources. This strongly invalidates its claimed NIST level 1 quantum security, especially when accounting for the MAXDEPTH restriction, and even under much weaker assumptions about the cost of the oracle.[4]

Similarly, CSIDH-1024 and -1792, which respectively targeted NIST quantum security levels 2 and 3, can be broken with, e.g., about 2^{26} and 2^{39} oracle queries and 2^{40} bits of QRACM (plus insignificant other resources).[5] Under analogous assumptions about the cost of their oracles relative to the "best conceivable case," CSIDH-1024 therefore falls short of level 1 (and by a large margin for the low end and middle region of the MAXDEPTH range). Moreover, with the

---

[4] The main security claim in [CLM+18] for CSIDH-512 (which appears in the abstract, introduction, and security evaluation) is NIST level 1. However, in one location the paper also mentions, in a passing reference to CSIDH-512, a "conjectured post-quantum security level of 64 bits." This would constitute a different, significantly weaker security claim than NIST level 1, in part because the latter accounts for the cost of quantumly evaluating AES, and has a MAXDEPTH restriction. No definition for 'bits of post-quantum security' is given in [CLM+18], but the security analysis in Section 7.3 and Table 1 quantifies "costs for the complete attack" in terms of number of logical qubit operations, and targets 2^{64} or more for CSIDH-512. Under this implied interpretation of '64 bits of post-quantum security,' and our assumption on the cost of the oracle, our work even falsifies this security claim as well. We point out that other metrics like "depth times width" can be used to quantify security (see, e.g., [JS19]), and at present the complexity of our attack in this metric is unclear, in part because the precise depth and width of the oracle are unknown. However, under any reasonable metric the oracle calls are presently the bottleneck for sieve parameters of interest.

[5] We again emphasize that the c-sieve offers a flexible tradeoff among queries, QRACM, and classical time, so all these example query counts can be reduced somewhat by increasing these other resources.

possible exception of the high region of the MAXDEPTH range, even CSIDH-1792 also fails to reach level 1.

Comparison with [BS18]. Shortly after the initial announcement of this work, Bonnetain and Schrottenloher posted an update [BS18] to their earlier analysis of Kuperberg's first sieve algorithm, which now also analyzes variants of the collimation sieve. They arrive at similar conclusions, but their analysis is largely complementary to ours, in the following ways. They give a theoretical analysis that ignores some polynomial terms, whereas ours is fully concrete and supported by experiments (which reveal some unexpected phenomena that significantly affect the polynomial factors). They only consider large collimation arity r (see below) with correspondingly small fully quantum memory and large classical work and memory, whereas we mainly limit our attention to the binary case $r = 2$ with correspondingly larger QRACM and small classical work. Finally, we include optimizations that are not considered in [BS18], like the extraction of many secret-key bits from each run of the sieve. It seems likely that a combination of ideas from these works would yield additional points on the attack spectrum and somewhat improved bounds.

1.4   Further Research

A main question that remains to be addressed is the actual concrete cost of the requisite quantum oracle, i.e., evaluation of the CSIDH group action for a uniform superposition over the group. The results of [BS18] and even moreso [BKV19] suggest that for CSIDH-512, the cost may be close to the roughly 2^{40} nonlinear bit operations estimate [BLMP19] for the "best conceivable case"—perhaps even within a factor of two or less. This is because [BKV19] gives a fast method for mapping a uniformly random group element to a short exponent vector, whose norm statistics are very similar to those of the distribution analyzed in [BLMP19]. (In particular, the norm's expectation is only about 10% larger, and its variance is actually somewhat smaller.) Also, because the sieve requires so few oracle queries (e.g., 2^{16} or less for CSIDH-512), some improvement should be obtainable simply by increasing the oracle's error probability, from the 2^{-32} considered in [BLMP19]. Related questions are whether it is possible to accelerate the oracle computations by amortization, or by directly designing a quantum circuit rather than converting a Boolean one.

Our study is primarily focused on collimation arity $r = 2$, which corresponds to a sieve that produces a binary recursion tree. Using an arity $r > 2$ can reduce the number of queries and/or the needed amount of QRACM, at the cost of more classical time. In a bit more detail, the main collimation subroutine that for $r = 2$ takes quasilinear $\tilde{O}(L)$ classical time (in the amount L of QRACM) takes $\tilde{O}(L^{r-1})$ classical time in general (or even less time with more memory, using Schroeppel–Shamir [SS79]), but reduces the depth of the recursion tree by about an $r-1$ factor, which can significantly reduce the number of oracle queries. Our experiments demonstrate that the classical work for $r = 2$ is cryptanalytically small (on the order of several core-days), and our model suggests modest improvements in query complexity for slightly larger arities, so this direction may be worth investigating further, especially if the quantum oracle remains the main bottleneck.

A final interesting question is how many bits of a CSIDH secret are required to break the scheme. Our complexity estimates are for running the c-sieve several times to recover almost all of the secret bits (the remainder can be obtained by brute force). However, if partial information about the secret suffices to break the scheme through other means, then the number of sieve invocations and corresponding query complexity would be reduced.

1.5 Paper Organization

In Sect. 3 we describe and analyze our generalization of Kuperberg's collimation sieve to arbitrary cyclic groups. In Sect. 4 we draw conclusions about the quantum security of various CSIDH parameters. In Sect. 5 we describe our classical simulator for the collimation sieve, and report on our experiments with it.

2   Preliminaries

We let $\mathbb{N} = \{0, 1, 2, \ldots\}$ denote the set of nonnegative integers, and for a positive integer L we define $[L] := \{0, 1, \ldots, L - 1\}$. All logarithms have base 2 unless otherwise specified. Define $\chi(x) = \exp(2\pi i \cdot x)$ and observe that $\chi(x)\chi(y) = \chi(x + y)$.

2.1   CSIDH Group Action

Here we recall sufficient background on CSIDH for our purposes; for full details, see [CLM+18]. At its heart is a free and transitive group action $\star \colon G \times Z \to Z$, where the group G is the ideal class group $\mathrm{Cl}(\mathcal{O})$ of the order $\mathcal{O} = \mathbb{Z}[\sqrt{-p}]$ of the imaginary quadratic number field $\mathbb{Q}(\sqrt{-p})$, for a given prime p of a certain form. (The acted-upon set Z is a certain collection of elliptic curves over $\mathbb{F}_p$, each of which can be uniquely represented by a single element of $\mathbb{F}_p$, but this will not be important for our purposes.) Because $\mathcal{O}$ is commutative, its class group $G = \mathrm{Cl}(\mathcal{O})$ is abelian. Heuristically, G is cyclic or "almost cyclic" (i.e., it has a cyclic component of order nearly as large as $|G|$), and its order $N = |G|$ is approximately $\sqrt{p}$.

CSIDH uses d special ideals $\mathfrak{l}_i$ of the order $\mathcal{O}$. Heuristically, these ideals generate the class group or a very large subgroup thereof; for simplicity, assume the former. The ideals $\mathfrak{l}_i$ define an integer lattice of relations

$$\Lambda = \{\mathbf{z} = (z_1, \ldots, z_d) \in \mathbb{Z}^d : \mathfrak{l}_1^{z_1} \cdots \mathfrak{l}_d^{z_d} \text{ is principal}\},$$

so G is isomorphic to $\mathbb{Z}^d / \Lambda$, via (the inverse of) the map $\mathbf{e} \in \mathbb{Z}^d \mapsto \left[\prod_i \mathfrak{l}_i^{e_i} \right]$, of which Λ is the kernel.

A CSIDH secret key is a vector $\mathbf{e} \in \mathbb{Z}^d$ of "small" integer exponents representing a group element; more specifically, the e_i are drawn uniformly from some small interval $[-B, B]$. One evaluates the group action for the associated ideal class $[\mathfrak{l}_1^{e_1} \cdots \mathfrak{l}_d^{e_d}]$ by successively applying the action of each $[\mathfrak{l}_i]$ or its inverse, $|e_i|$ times. Therefore, the ℓ_1 norm of $\mathbf{e}$ largely determines the evaluation time. Note that a group element is not uniquely specified by an exponent vector; any vector in the same coset of Λ defines the same group element, but very "long" vectors are not immediately useful for computing the group action. However, if we have a basis of Λ made up of very short vectors, then given any exponent representation of a group element, we can efficiently reduce it to a rather short representation of the same element using standard lattice algorithms like Babai's nearest-plane algorithm [Bab85].

In the CSIDH-512 parameterization, for which $p \approx 2^{512}$, the class group $G = \mathrm{Cl}(\mathcal{O})$ has recently been computed [BKV19]: it is isomorphic to the additive cyclic group $\mathbb{Z}_N = \mathbb{Z}/N\mathbb{Z}$ of integers modulo

$$N = 3 \cdot 37 \cdot 1407181 \cdot 51593604295295867744293584889$$
$$\cdot 31599414504681995853008278745587832204909 \approx 2^{257.1},$$

and is in fact generated by the class of the ideal $\mathfrak{l}_1$. In addition, the lattice $\Lambda \subset \mathbb{Z}^{74}$ of relations among the ideals $\mathfrak{l}_i$ is known, along with a very high-quality (HKZ-reduced) basis. Indeed, the authors of [BKV19] showed that a uniformly random element of $\mathbb{Z}_N$ can be quickly reduced to a short exponent vector having a norm distribution very similar to the CSIDH-512 one. So, in summary, for CSIDH-512 we can efficiently represent the class group as $\mathbb{Z}_N$, and secret keys using the distinguished representatives $\{0, 1, \ldots, N-1\}$.

2.2   Abelian Hidden-Shift Problem

The hidden-shift problem on an additive abelian group G is as follows: given injective functions $f_0, f_1 \colon G \to X$ (for some arbitrary set X) such that $f_1(x) = f_0(x + s)$ for some secret "shift" $s \in G$ and all $x \in G$, the goal is to find s. For cyclic groups $G \cong \mathbb{Z}_N$, this hidden-shift problem is equivalent to the hidden-subgroup problem on the Nth dihedral group (which has order $2N$). Kuperberg [Kup03] gave the first nontrivial quantum algorithm for this problem, which uses subexponential $\exp(O(\sqrt{\log N}))$ quantum time and space.

As observed by Childs, Jao, and Soukharev [CJS10], there is a simple connection between the abelian hidden-shift problem and the key-recovery problem for Couveignes–Rostovtsev–Stolbunov-type systems: given the "base value" $z_0 \in Z$ and a public key $z_1 = s \star z_0$ for some secret key $s \in G$, where $\star \colon G \times Z \to Z$ is a free and transitive group action, define $f_b \colon G \to Z$ as $f_b(g) = g \star z_b$ for $b = 0, 1$. These f_b are injective because $\star$ is free and transitive, and $f_1(x) = x \star z_1 = x \star (s \star z_0) = (x + s) \star z_0 = f_0(x + s)$, as required. So, solving the hidden-shift problem for these f_b immediately yields the secret key.

3   Collimation Sieve for Cyclic Groups

In this section we generalize Kuperberg's collimation sieve [Kup11] to arbitrary cyclic groups $\mathbb{Z}_N$ of known order N. (The algorithm can also be made to work even if we only have a bound on the group order.) The algorithm works very much like Kuperberg's for power-of-two group orders $N = 2^n$, but with some implementation differences and optimizations inspired by improvements to Kuperberg's first sieve algorithm [Kup03].

The collimation sieve works with quantum states called *phase vectors*, each of which has some associated integer *(phase) multipliers* (see Sect. 3.1). The ultimate goal of the sieve (see Sect. 3.2) is to construct a length-L phase vector that is 'very nice,' meaning its multipliers come from a desired set of *small* size $S \lesssim L$, e.g., the interval $[S]$. (Additionally, the phase multipliers should be roughly uniformly distributed, which happens automatically.) From such a nice phase vector one can extract bits of the secret via the quantum Fourier transform and measurement (see Sect. 3.4). Initially, the sieve will only be able to construct very 'non-nice' phase vectors whose multipliers come from the huge set $\{0, 1, \ldots, N - 1\}$. It then repeatedly produces progressively 'nicer' phase vectors whose multipliers lie in successively smaller sets, by combining less-nice vectors via a process called *collimation* (see Sect. 3.3).

The differences between our version of the collimation sieve and Kuperberg's are summarized as follows:

1. The sieve creates phase vectors with multipliers in progressively smaller *intervals* of the integers, by collimating on the "most-significant bits" of the multipliers. (By contrast, Kuperberg makes the multipliers divisible by progressively larger powers of two, by collimating on the least-significant bits.)
2. After sieving down to an interval of size S, where S can be roughly as large as the amount of quantumly accessible classical memory (QRACM), the algorithm applies a quantum Fourier transform of dimension S and measures, to reveal about $\log S$ of the "most-significant bits" of the secret with good probability. (Kuperberg instead applies a two-dimensional Fourier transform and measures to recover the single least-significant bit of the secret, with certainty.)
3. Alternatively, instead of recovering just $\log(S)$ bits of the secret, the algorithm can perform additional independent sieves down to various "scaled" intervals. By combining the resulting phase vectors, the algorithm can recover about $\log(S)$ different secret bits per sieve, and in particular, it can recover the entire secret using about $\log(N)/\log(S) = \log_S(N)$ sieves. (Kuperberg's algorithm, after recovering the least-significant bit of the secret, effectively halves the secret and repeats to recover the remaining bits, using $\log(N)$ total sieves.)

The technique from Item 2 is reminiscent of one used by Levieil and Fouque [LF06] to recover several secret bits at once in the Learning Parity with Noise problem. The technique from Item 3 is analogous to one attributed to Høyer in [Kup03] for recovering the entire secret from about $\log(N)$ qubits obtained via Kuperberg's original sieving algorithm.

3.1   Phase Vectors

We first recall from [Kup11] the notion of a phase vector and some of its essential properties. Fix some positive integer N and $s \in \mathbb{Z}_N$. For a positive integer L, a *phase vector* of *length* L is a (pure) quantum state of the form

$$|\psi\rangle = L^{-1/2} \sum_{j\in[L]} \chi(b(j) \cdot s/N)|j\rangle$$

for some function $b\colon [L] \to \mathbb{Z}$, where the $b(j)$ are called the *(phase) multipliers*. In all the algorithms considered in this work, the multiplier functions b will be written down explicitly in a table, in sorted order by $b(j)$ for efficiency of collimation (see Sect. 3.3). Note that while this requires classical memory proportional to L, only $\log L$ qubits of quantum memory are needed for $|\psi\rangle$. Also observe that the multipliers are implicitly modulo N (because of the division by N inside χ), so we will use and store their distinguished integer representatives in $\{0, 1, \ldots, N - 1\}$. We say that $|\psi\rangle$ is *ranged on* (or just *on*) a particular set $S \subseteq \mathbb{Z}$ if every $b(j) \in S$.

Looking ahead a bit, the collimation sieve uses collimation to combine and produce phase vectors of roughly equal length L that are ranged on a sequence of geometrically smaller sets, starting from unrestricted ones on $\{0, 1, \ldots, N - 1\}$ and ultimately yielding one on a set of size $S \lesssim L$ (e.g., the interval $[S]$). Measuring the quantum Fourier transform of such a vector then yields part of the secret.

Creating and Combining Phase Vectors. Prior (finite) hidden-subgroup and hidden-shift algorithms use a simple quantum procedure (an "oracle") U_f that generates a special kind of one-qubit state, i.e., a length-2 phase vector. Given quantum procedures for computing injective functions $f_0, f_1\colon \mathbb{Z}_N \to X$ (for an arbitrary set X) such that $f_1(x) = f_0(x + s)$ for some secret s and all x, the procedure U_f outputs a uniformly random $b \in \mathbb{Z}_N$ along with a qubit

$$|\psi\rangle = \frac{1}{\sqrt{2}}(|0\rangle + \chi(b \cdot s/N)|1\rangle),$$

i.e., a length-2 phase vector with $b(0) = 0, b(1) = b$. The details of U_f are not material here; see [Kup03,Reg04] for accessible descriptions. However, we note that U_f evaluates the functions f_i in superposition, which in our context corresponds to evaluating the CSIDH group action.

Phase vectors can naturally be combined by tensoring: given r phase vectors $|\psi_i\rangle$ respectively having lengths L_i and multiplier functions b_i, we can form the following quantum state $|\psi'\rangle$ with index set $L = [L_1] \times \cdots \times [L_r]$:

$$|\psi'\rangle = |\psi_1, \ldots, \psi_r\rangle = |L|^{-1/2} \sum_{j_1\in[L_1]} \cdots \sum_{j_r\in[L_r]} \chi(b_1(j_1) \cdot s/N) \cdots \chi(b_r(j_r) \cdot s/N)|j_1, \ldots, j_r\rangle$$

$$\tag{1}$$

$$= |L|^{-1/2} \sum_{\jmath\in L} \chi(b'(\jmath) \cdot s/N)|\jmath\rangle,$$

where $b'(\jmath) = \sum_{i=1}^{r} b_i(j_i)$. Therefore, $|\psi'\rangle$ can be thought of as a kind of phase vector of length $|L| = \prod_{i=1}^{r} L_i$, except that its index set is not exactly $[|L|]$ (although there is a natural bijection between L and $[|L|]$). We note that in the context of collimation (Sect. 3.3), we do not explicitly write down the full multiplier function b', but instead first partially measure $|\psi'\rangle$ to lessen its length before storing its multiplier function.

3.2   Collimation Sieve

We now formally define the collimation sieve, in Algorithm 1. It constructs a phase vector on a desired interval by recursively constructing and collimating phase vectors on suitably larger intervals. The algorithm is essentially the same as Kuperberg's from [Kup11] (which incorporates a key insight of Regev's [Reg04]), except that it uses collimation on "high bits," along with a few tweaks to make it more practically efficient in simulations (see Sect. 3.2 below).

Algorithm 1. Collimation sieve for group $\mathbb{Z}_N$ and collimation arity r.

Input: Interval sizes $S_0 < S_1 < \cdots < S_d = N$, a desired phase-vector length L, and oracle access to U_f.
Output: A phase vector on $[S_0]$ of length $\approx L$.

Base case. If $S_0 = N$, generate $\ell \approx \log L$ length-2 phase vectors $|\psi_1\rangle, |\psi_2\rangle, \ldots, |\psi_\ell\rangle$ using U_f (see Section 3.1). Output the length-2^ℓ phase vector $|\psi\rangle = |\psi_1, \ldots, \psi_\ell\rangle$.
Recursive case. Otherwise:

1. Using r recursive calls for sizes $S_1 < \cdots < S_d = N$ and appropriate desired lengths, obtain r phase vectors $|\psi_1\rangle, \ldots, |\psi_r\rangle$ on $[S_1]$, the product of whose lengths is $\approx rL \cdot S_1/S_0$.
2. Collimate these phase vectors using Algorithm 2 to produce a phase vector $|\psi\rangle$ on $[S_0]$, and output it. (Or, if its length is much less than L, discard it and recompute from Step 1.)

In the base case, when a phase vector of length roughly L on $[N]$ is desired, the algorithm simply invokes the oracle U_f some $\ell \approx \log L$ times to get length-2 phase vectors $|\psi_i\rangle \propto |0\rangle + \chi(b_i \cdot s/N)|1\rangle$ for known uniformly random multipliers $b_i \in [N]$, then tensors them all together to get a length-2^ℓ phase vector whose multipliers are the mod-N subset-sums of the b_i values. (See Sect. 3.1.) In the recursive case, when a phase vector on $[S_i]$ for some $S_i < N$ is desired, the algorithm recursively obtains r phase vectors on $[S_{i+1}]$ of appropriate lengths, collimates them to interval $[S_i]$, and returns the result. (See Sect. 3.3 below for the definition and analysis of the collimation procedure.)

The sieve can traverse the recursion tree in any manner, e.g., depth first, breadth first, or some hybrid of the two. The choice offers a tradeoff between the quantum memory cost and parallelism of the sieve. Because each phase vector uses about $\log L$ qubits, a depth-first traversal would require only about

$(r-1)d \log L$ qubits of memory, but the collimation steps would need to be done sequentially. On the other extreme, a breadth-first traversal would allow all the oracle calls and collimation steps at each level of the tree to be done in parallel, but at the cost of about $r^d \log L$ qubits of memory.

Finally, we can also use the sieve to construct phase vectors on other desired output ranges, like scaled intervals $A \cdot [S]$, simply by tweaking the collimation procedure as described in Sect. 3.3. Combining phase vectors on different scaled intervals enables recovery of more (or even all) bits of the secret with a single measurement.

Parameters. Following the analysis of the collimation procedure (see Sect. 3.3 and Eq. (4) below), a top-level call to Algorithm 1 for arity $r \geq 2$ would typically be made on a sequence of interval sizes S_i where:

- $S_0 \approx L$, the desired length of the ultimate phase vector (which can be almost as large as the available amount of QRACM), and
- $S_{i+1} = \min\{\approx S_i \cdot L^{r-1}/r, N\}$, where the final $S_d = N$.

The depth d of the recursion tree is therefore given by

$$S_0(L^{r-1}/r)^d \geq N \Longrightarrow d = \left\lceil \frac{\log(N/S_0)}{\log(L^{r-1}/r)} \right\rceil \approx \frac{\log_L(N/S_0)}{r-1}. \qquad (2)$$

Practical Improvements. As detailed below in Sect. 3.3, the length of a phase vector output by collimation is unpredictable, and may be rather longer or shorter than expected. Because the lengths directly affect the required amount of QRACM and other resources required by the rest of the sieve, we would like to keep them under control as much as possible. We do so with two techniques:

1. *being adaptive* about the requested vector lengths in the recursive calls, and
2. *discarding* phase vectors that are unusually short, and recomputing from scratch.

Adaptivity means the following. Recall that to create a phase vector on $[S]$ of length $\approx L$, the algorithm recursively creates r phase vectors on $[S']$ for some given $S' \gg S$, the product of whose lengths we want to be $\approx L' = L \cdot (S'/S)$. So, on the first recursive call we request a vector of length $(L')^{1/r}$, and obtain a vector of some length $\tilde{L}$. Following that we want the product of the remaining $r-1$ vector lengths to be $\approx L'/\tilde{L}$, so we request a vector of length $(L'/\tilde{L})^{1/(r-1)}$, and so on. This immediately compensates for shorter-than-expected vectors, which helps to avoid cascading short vectors higher in the recursion tree and a useless final output. And in the fortunate event that we get a longer-than-expected vector, requesting correspondingly shorter vectors speeds up the remaining computation. In case there is a hard cap on the available amount of QRACM, it is also trivial to shorten a longer-than-expected vector via a partial measurement, which also beneficially shrinks the interval in which the phase multipliers lie.

Vectors that are *much* shorter than expected present a more significant problem, however. Compensating for them requires corresponding longer and/or more phase vectors for collimation, which require correspondingly more QRACM and computation. Moreover, getting another short vector in that part of the computation subtree further increases the required resources. Therefore, whenever a call to Algorithm 1 produces a candidate output vector that is shorter than the requested length by some fixed threshold factor, it simply discards it and computes a fresh one from scratch.[6]

Empirically, for arity $r = 2$ threshold factors of 0.25 or 0.4 seem to work well, causing a discard in only about 2% or 4.5% of calls (respectively), and keeping the maximum vector length across the entire sieve to within a factor of about 2^4–2^5 or $2^{2.5}$ (respectively) of the desired length L; moreover, that factor tends to decrease somewhat as L grows. (See Fig. 2 for details.) This modification was very important for the feasibility of our simulations: without the discard rule, the maximum vector length tended to be several hundreds or even thousands of times larger than L, yet the ultimate phase vector was often still much shorter than desired.

Oracle Query Complexity. Here we give a model for the number of queries to the oracle U_f made by the sieve. For the interval sizes S_i given above in Sect. 3.2, the recursion depth is given in Eq. (2) as

$$d = \left\lceil \frac{\log(N/S_0)}{\log(L^{r-1}/r)} \right\rceil.$$

At the base case (leaf level) of the recursion tree, where $S_d = N$, we typically need to make a phase vector of length about

$$L' = (rLS_d/S_{d-1})^{1/r} = (rLN/S_{d-1})^{1/r}.$$

We construct such a vector by making $\lfloor \log L' \rfloor$ oracle queries and tensoring the results.

Supposing that a random δ fraction of recursive calls to Algorithm 1 result in a discard (due to insufficient length), the arity of the recursion tree is effectively $r/(1 - \delta)$. Therefore, our model for the total number of oracle queries is

$$Q = (r/(1 - \delta))^d \cdot \log L'. \tag{3}$$

For arity $r = 2$ our experiments turn out to conform very closely to this model, especially for moderate and larger values of L. (For $r = 2$ it is slightly more accurate to replace r with $2r/3$ in the above expressions, but this has a negligible effect on the predictions.) See Sect. 5 for details.

---

[6] This is roughly analogous to what is done in Kuperberg's original sieve [Kup03], where combining two qubits has a 50% chance of producing a "useless" output that is then discarded.

3.3 Collimating Phase Vectors

The heart of the collimation sieve is the collimation procedure, which combines phase vectors to create a new one on a desired smaller interval. Algorithm 2 is our variant of Kuperberg's collimation procedure; the only significant difference is that it collimates according to "high bits" (or "middle bits"; see Sect. 3.3) rather than "low bits," which allows us to deal with arbitrary group orders N. More precisely, it collimates phase vectors according to the quotients (ignoring remainder) of their multipliers with the desired interval size S, yielding a new phase vector on $[S]$.

Algorithm 2. Collimation procedure for arity r.

Input: Phase vectors $|\psi_1\rangle, |\psi_2\rangle, \ldots, |\psi_r\rangle$ of respective lengths $L_1, \ldots, L_r$, and a desired interval size S.

Output: A phase vector $|\psi\rangle$ on $[S]$.

1. Form the phase vector $|\psi'\rangle = |\psi_1, \ldots, \psi_r\rangle$ having index set $[L_1] \times \cdots \times [L_r]$ and phase multiplier function $b'(\jmath) = \sum_{i=1}^{r} b_i(j_i)$.
2. Measure $|\psi'\rangle$ according to the value of $q = \lfloor b'(\jmath)/S \rfloor$ to obtain $P_q|\psi'\rangle$ for a certain subunitary P_q.
3. Find the set J of tuples $\jmath$ that satisfy the above. Let $L = |J|$ and choose a bijection $\pi \colon J \to [L]$.
4. Output phase vector $|\psi\rangle = U_\pi P_q |\psi'\rangle$ with index set $[L]$ and multiplier function $b(j) = b'(\pi^{-1}(j))$.

In more detail, given phase vectors $|\psi_i\rangle$ having lengths L_i and multiplier functions $b_i \colon [L_i] \to \mathbb{Z}$, the algorithm constructs a combined phase vector $|\psi'\rangle$ having multiplier function $b'(\jmath) = \sum_{i=1}^{r} b_i(j_i)$, as shown in Eq. (1) above. It then measures the quotient $q = \lfloor b'(\jmath)/S \rfloor$, so that the "surviving" indices $\jmath$ are exactly those for which $b'(\jmath) \in qS + [S]$. The common additive qS term corresponds to a global phase that has no effect, so the surviving phase multipliers can be seen to lie in $[S]$. Let J be the set of surviving indices $\jmath$ and suppose that $|J| = L$. Just as described in [Kup11], the algorithm (classically) constructs a bijection $\pi \colon J \to [L]$ and its inverse, then applies a corresponding unitary permutation operator U_π to the post-measurement state, finally yielding a true length-L phase vector on $[S]$.

We briefly summarize the main computational costs; see Sect. 3.3 for a detailed analysis in the case $r = 2$. Step 2 does a QRACM lookup for each $i = 1, \ldots, r$ to obtain $b_i(j_i)$, then quantumly adds the results and divides by S. Step 3 classically performs an r-way merge on the sorted lists of phase multipliers, and prepares associated lists for the next step. Finally, Step 4 computes $\pi(\jmath)$ by performing QRACM lookups on the entries of $\jmath$, and uncomputes $\jmath$ and all the scratch work via one or more additional lookups.

Length Analysis. Collimation is guaranteed to output a phase vector on $[S]$, but the length of the output is a random variable affected by the phase multipliers of the input vectors and the quantum measurement.

Let r be small, with $r = 2$ being the main case of interest. Suppose that the input vectors $|\psi_i\rangle$ have roughly uniformly distributed multipliers on $[S']$ for some $S' \gg S$, and let $L' = \prod_i L_i$ be the product of their lengths. Then the L' phase multipliers $b'(\jmath)$ are also very well distributed on $[rS']$, so we expect $L \approx L' \cdot S/(rS')$ indices to "survive" collimation.[7] Moreover, the surviving multipliers are well distributed on $[S]$, because it is a very narrow subinterval of $[rS']$.

Because we will want all the input and output vectors to have roughly the same lengths L, we can therefore take $rS'L \approx SL'$ where $L' = L^r$, i.e.,

$$S' \approx S \cdot L^{r-1}/r. \tag{4}$$

In other words, with one level of collimation we can narrow the size of the interval in which the multipliers lie by roughly an L^{r-1}/r factor, while expecting to roughly preserve the vector lengths.

Scaled Intervals. Collimation naturally generalizes to produce phase vectors on other sets, such as scaled intervals $A \cdot [S] = \{0, A, 2A, \ldots, (S-1)A\}$ for positive integers A. (We use such sets in Sect. 3.4 below.) Specifically, if we are given r phase vectors on $A \cdot [S']$, we can get a phase vector on certain scalings of $[S]$ as follows:

1. We can collimate according to $q = \lfloor b'(\jmath)/(AS) \rfloor$, thereby creating a phase vector on $A \cdot [S]$ (ignoring the global-phase term qAS), because all the $b'(\jmath)$ are divisible by A.
2. Alternatively, we can collimate according to $c = b'(\jmath) \bmod (AB)$ for $B = \lceil rS'/S \rceil$, thereby creating a phase vector on $AB \cdot [S]$ (ignoring the global-phase term c), because all the $b'(\jmath)$ are in $A \cdot [rS']$.
3. Finally, we can interpolate between the above two techniques, collimating according to both $q = \lfloor b'(\jmath)/(ABS) \rfloor$ and $c = b'(\jmath) \bmod (AB)$ for an arbitrary positive integer $B \leq \lceil rS'/S \rceil$, thereby creating a phase vector on $AB \cdot [S]$.

By appropriately composing these kinds of collimations, we can obtain any needed scaling factor. For all these options, adapting the above analyses yields the same ultimate conclusions, that collimation can decrease the range size by roughly an L^{r-1}/r factor while keeping the input and output vector lengths roughly equal.

---

[7] Note that the multipliers $b'(\jmath) \in [rS']$ are not quite uniformly distributed, because they are biased toward their expectation $rS'/2$, and extreme values are less likely. For $r = 2$, an easy calculation shows that due to this bias, $\mathbb{E}[L]$ is very close to $\frac{2}{3}L' \cdot S/S'$. This means that the output of the collimation step is slightly better than the above analysis indicates.

Complexity of Binary Collimation. We conclude our treatment of collimation by analyzing its complexity for the main arity $r = 2$ of interest, focusing especially on precise QRACM bounds. We adapt and refine Kuperberg's analysis [Kup11, Proposition 4.2] of his "low bits" collimation procedure. Letting $L_{\max}$ denote the maximum of the lengths of the input and output phase vectors, Kuperberg proved that low-bits collimation can be done with:

- $\tilde{O}(L_{\max})$ classical time, where $\tilde{O}$ hides logarithmic factors in both $L_{\max}$ and N,
- $O(L_{\max} \log N)$ classical space,
- $O(1)$ lookups into $O(L_{\max} \cdot \log \max\{S'/S, L_{\max}\})$ bits of QRACM, and
- $\mathrm{poly}(\log L_{\max})$ quantum time and $O(\log L_{\max})$ quantum space.

The same holds for our high-bits collimation, with one subtlety concerning the amount of QRACM. Naïvely, measuring $q = \lfloor b(\jmath)/S \rfloor$ requires storing the entire b_i vectors in QRACM, which requires up to $O(L_{\max} \log S') = O(L_{\max} \log N)$ bits. This is in contrast to Kuperberg's method, which requires only $O(L_{\max} \log(S'/S))$ bits, namely, the least-significant bits of the multipliers. We can obtain the latter bound by storing in QRACM only sufficiently many of the "most significant bits" of the $b_i(j_i)$, namely, $\hat{b}_i(j_i) = \lfloor b_i(j_i)/K \rfloor$ for some K moderately smaller than S. We then measure $q = \lfloor K \cdot \hat{b}(\jmath)/S \rfloor$, from which it follows that

$$\hat{b}(\jmath) \in qS/K + [0, S/K] \implies b(\jmath) \in qS + [0, S + rK].$$

By taking $K = (S/S')^\alpha \cdot S$ for some small positive α like $\alpha = 1$ or $\alpha = 1/2$, each entry of $\hat{b}_i(j_i)$ takes at most (the ceiling of) $\log(S'/K) \le (1+\alpha)\log(S'/S)$ bits. By Eq. (4), the range size for the collimated output vector is $S + rK \approx S(1 + r^{1+\alpha}/L^\alpha)$, which is insignificantly larger than S for the $L \ge 2^{16}$ of interest.

Concrete Constants for QRACM. A close inspection of [Kup11, Section 4.3] shows that the constant factor in the QRACM bound, and the associated $O(1)$ number of QRACM lookups, are small. The entire algorithm can be run with 9 lookups and as little as

$$R = L_{\max} \cdot \lceil \max\{(1+\alpha)\log(S'/S), \log L_{\max}\} \rceil \tag{5}$$

bits of reusable QRACM, or with as few as 4 lookups and $L_{\max} \cdot (2(1+\alpha)\log(S'/S) + 3\log L_{\max})$ bits, or with various intermediate combinations. (For our purposes, minimizing QRACM seems preferable because lookups are much cheaper than CSIDH evaluation.) This can be done as follows:

1. First, in new registers we look up each $\hat{b}_i(j_i)$ for $i = 1, 2$. As described above, arrays representing the functions $\hat{b}_i$ can be stored in QRACM with $\lceil (1+\alpha)\log(S'/S) \rceil$ bits per entry. (In all steps, the QRACM can be reused from one lookup to another.)

2. Following the measurement, in new registers we compute $j = \pi(j_1, j_2) \in [L]$ and a scratch value j_2'. An array representing the permutation $\pi: J \to [L]$ can be stored as a table mapping each j_1 to the smallest value j_2' such that $(j_1, j_2') \in J$, and the corresponding value of $\pi(j_1, j_2')$; each value takes $\lceil \log L_{\max} \rceil$ bits per entry. We look up, either sequentially or both at once, the appropriate values of $j_2', \pi(j_1, j_2')$ and then (reversibly) add $j_2 - j_2'$ to the latter quantity to get $j = \pi(j_1, j_2)$.

3. Lastly, we uncompute the five values j_2' and $j_i, \hat{b}_i(j_i)$ for $i = 1, 2$, leaving behind just j. One or more arrays (each requiring a lookup) mapping each j (or alternatively, j_1 or j_2) to one or more of these values can be stored in the natural way. We do the appropriate lookup(s) to uncompute all the values.

Finally, we remark that for the $L_{\max}$ of interest in this work, the $\mathrm{poly}(\log L_{\max})$ quantum time (which consists of just a few additions and subtractions, and one division) and $O(\log L_{\max})$ quantum space needed for collimation are insignificant compared to the estimated complexity of the quantum oracle U_f for CSIDH parameters of interest [BLMP19].

3.4   Post-processing

We now describe how phase vectors output by the collimation sieve can be used to recover information about the secret.

Regularization. A top-level call to Algorithm 1 outputs a phase vector $|\psi\rangle$ on $[S] = [S_0]$ of length $\tilde{L} \approx L$, which we want to be somewhat larger than S. Heuristically, for each $t \in [S]$ we expect about $\tilde{L}/S$ phase multipliers $b(j)$ to equal t; however, there is some variation in the number of each multiplier. Ideally, we would like a *regular* state, i.e., one which has exactly the same number of multipliers for each $t \in [S]$.

We can obtain one by generalizing [Kup11]: select a maximal subset $X \subseteq [\tilde{L}]$ for which $b(X)$ has an equal number of every $t \in [S]$. Then measure whether $|\psi\rangle$ is in $\mathbb{C}[X]$ (i.e., the Hilbert space with basis $|j\rangle$ for $j \in X$), which holds with probability $|X|/\tilde{L}$. If not, discard it and run the sieve again. If so, the measured form of $|\psi\rangle$ is regular, so it has a factor of the form

$$S^{-1/2} \sum_{j \in [S]} \chi(j \cdot s/N) |j\rangle,$$

which we can extract by reindexing. (This requires almost no work, because the multipliers are sorted.) Observe that the above state essentially corresponds to the dimension-S inverse quantum Fourier transform of a point function at sS/N; see Sect. 3.4 for details.

The probability of obtaining a regular phase vector is $|X|/\tilde{L} = mS/\tilde{L}$, where m is the frequency of the least-frequent phase multiplier $t \in [S]$. In our experiments, a length $\tilde{L} \approx 64S$ typically led to success probabilities in the 40–80% range, and a length $\tilde{L} \approx 128S$ usually led to an 80% or larger success probability.

Punctured Regularization. The above procedure is somewhat wasteful, because it loses a factor of $\tilde{L}/S \approx 2^7$ in the number of basis states $|j\rangle$ in the fortunate case (and loses all of them in the unfortunate case). Alternatively, we can use the following method for generating a "punctured" (regular) phase vector, which works for S as large as $\tilde{L}$ (or even a bit more), and which produces a state that is almost as good as a regular one on $[S]$. Empirically, this lets us extract almost $\log S$ bits of the secret.

Again suppose that the sieve produces a phase vector $|\psi\rangle$ on $[S]$ of length $\tilde{L}$. We make a pass over $j \in [\tilde{L}]$, forming a set X of one index j for each distinct value of $b(j)$, and ignoring duplicates. (This is trivial to do, because the multipliers are sorted.) We then measure whether $|\psi\rangle$ is in $\mathbb{C}[X]$, which holds with probability $|X|/\tilde{L}$. If not, we try again with a new choice of X on the leftover phase vector, as long as it remains long enough. If so, the restriction $b\colon X \to [S]$ is injective, so by a change of variable and reindexing the basis from $j \in X$ to $b(j) \in [S]$, we now have a state of the form

$$|X|^{-1/2} \sum_{j \in X} \chi(b(j) \cdot s/N)|j\rangle \equiv |X|^{-1/2} \sum_{j \in b(X)} \chi(j \cdot s/N)|j\rangle. \tag{6}$$

This state is a length-$|X|$ phase vector, except for the "punctured" index set $b(X) \subseteq [S]$. It is also almost as good as a regular phase vector on $[S]$, in the following sense. Heuristically, each of the multipliers $b(j)$ for $j \in [\tilde{L}]$ is uniformly random, so the multipliers $b(X) \subseteq [S]$ form a random subset of density

$$1 - (1 - 1/S)^{\tilde{L}} \approx 1 - \exp(-\tilde{L}/S).$$

(For example, this density is approximately 0.632, 0.864, and 0.981 for $\tilde{L} = S$, $2S$, and $4S$, respectively.) Therefore, the state in Eq. (6) corresponds to a kind of *densely subsampled* Fourier transform of a point function encoding the secret. Empirically, such states have enough information to let us extract about $\log S - 2$ bits of the secret in expectation; see Sect. 3.4 for details.

Combining (Punctured) Regular Phase Vectors. By combining k separately generated regular phase vectors for *scalings* of $[S]$, we can create a regular phase vector on $[T]$ for $T = S^k$, as shown below. In particular, for $k > \log_S N$ we can create a regular phase vector for $T > N$, which is large enough to recover s exactly (with good probability). Note that it might not be necessary to recover *all* of s in this manner; given partial information on s (say, half of its bits) it might be more efficient to use other methods to recover the rest.

We separately create k regular phase vectors

$$|\psi_i\rangle = S^{-1/2} \sum_{j \in [S]} \chi(S^i j \cdot s/N)|j\rangle$$

on the scaled intervals $S^i \cdot [S] = \{0, S^i, 2S^i, \dots, (S-1)S^i\}$, for $i = 0, 1, \dots, k-1$. Then their tensor product $|\psi\rangle = |\psi_0, \dots, \psi_{k-1}\rangle$ is

$$|\psi\rangle = T^{-1/2} \sum_{j_0 \in [S]} \cdots \sum_{j_{k-1} \in [S]} \chi\Big(\sum_{i=0}^{k-1} j_i S^i \cdot s/N\Big)|j_0, \dots, j_{k-1}\rangle = T^{-1/2} \sum_{j \in [T]} \chi(j \cdot s/N)|j\rangle,$$

where we have re-indexed using $j = \sum_{i=0}^{k-1} j_i S^i$. Therefore, $|\psi\rangle$ is a regular phase vector for $[T]$, as desired.

The same technique works for punctured regular states, where the tensored state's index set is the Cartesian product of the original states' index sets. To prevent the density from decreasing, we can use a scaling factor slightly smaller than S, e.g., δS where δ is the density of the input states. Then the density of the resulting state is about $(\delta S)^k/(\delta^{k-1} S^k) = \delta$.

Measurement. Now suppose we have a regular phase vector $|\psi\rangle = T^{-1/2} \sum_{j\in[T]} \chi(j \cdot s/N)|j\rangle$ on $[T]$. Then its T-dimensional quantum Fourier transform is

$$\mathrm{QFT}_T|\psi\rangle = T^{-1} \sum_{w\in[T]} \sum_{j\in[T]} \chi\Big(\frac{js}{N} - \frac{jw}{T}\Big)|w\rangle = T^{-1} \sum_w \Big(\sum_j \chi\Big(j\Big(\frac{s}{N} - \frac{w}{T}\Big)\Big)\Big)|w\rangle. \quad (7)$$

We compute this state and measure, obtaining some w that reveals information about s, as analyzed next.

If $N|(sT)$, then the amplitude associated with $w = sT/N \in [T]$ is nonzero and the amplitudes associated with all the other $w \in [T]$ are zero, so measuring the state yields w with certainty, from which we recover $s = wN/T$. Otherwise, fix some arbitrary $w \in [T]$ and let $\theta = s/N - w/T \notin \mathbb{Z}$. By summing the finite geometric series (over j), we see that the amplitude associated with $|w\rangle$ is

$$T^{-1}\Big|\frac{1 - \chi(T\theta)}{1 - \chi(\theta)}\Big| = T^{-1}\Big|\frac{\chi(T\theta/2)\cdot(\chi(-T\theta/2) - \chi(T\theta/2))}{\chi(\theta/2)\cdot(\chi(-\theta/2) - \chi(\theta/2))}\Big| = T^{-1}\Big|\frac{\sin(\pi T\theta)}{\sin(\pi\theta)}\Big|.$$

For $|\theta| \leq 1/(2T)$ this value is at least $(T\sin(\pi/(2T)))^{-1} \geq 2/\pi$. So when measuring the state, we obtain a w such that $|s/N - w/T| \leq 1/(2T)$ with probability at least $4/\pi^2 \geq 0.4$. In such a case, we have

$$s \in w \cdot \frac{N}{T} + \Big[-\frac{N}{2T}, \frac{N}{2T}\Big],$$

i.e., we know the $\log T$ "most-significant bits" of s. In particular, if $T > N$ then this defines s uniquely.

Measuring Punctured Phase Vectors. Now suppose instead that we have a *punctured* regular phase vector $|\psi\rangle = |Y|^{-1/2}\sum_{j\in Y} \chi(j\cdot s/N)|j\rangle$ on $[T]$, for a heuristically random index set $Y \subseteq [T]$ of significant density. Its QFT is exactly as in Eq. (7), but with normalizing factor $(YT)^{-1/2}$ instead of T, and with the index j running over Y instead of $[T]$. As above, when w/T is very close to s/N, the amplitudes $\chi(j(s/N - w/T)) \in \mathbb{C}$ all point in roughly the same direction, and accumulate. Otherwise, the amplitudes heuristically point in random directions and mostly cancel out. Therefore, the final measurement is likely to output a w close to sT/N.

As pointed out by an anonymous reviewer, the above argument can be made rigorous using the *fidelity* $|\langle \rho|\psi\rangle|$ between our punctured vector $|\psi\rangle$ with index set

$|Y| = \delta|T|$ and a regular phase vector $|\rho\rangle$ on $[T]$, which by an easy calculation is seen to be $\sqrt{\delta}$. Because the QFT preserves fidelity, with probability δ the outcome of the measurement is the same as measuring a regular vector.

For the values of S we used in our experiments, it is possible to efficiently compute the probability of obtaining any particular value of w when measuring (the QFT of) a particular punctured phase vector. Empirically, we usually observe a total probability (over the first several punctured vectors coming from the final sieve output) of about 40% or more in recovering the value of w closest to sT/N. This corresponds to extracting at least $\log T - 2$ bits of the secret in expectation. See Fig. 3.

4   Quantum (In)security of CSIDH

In this section come to some conclusions about the quantum security levels for various CSIDH parameters proposed in [CLM+18], based on our model from Sect. 3.2 and our experiments' close adherence to it (Sect. 5). See Fig. 1 for several representative estimates.

4.1   Oracle Query Complexity for Key Recovery

Our main conclusion is that key recovery for CSIDH-512 can be accomplished with a binary collimation sieve using, for example, about 2^{19} oracle queries and about 2^{32} bits of QRACM, or about 2^{16} oracle queries and about 2^{40} bits of QRACM (plus relatively small other resources); see Fig. 1. This significantly improves upon the prior estimate [BS18] of about $2^{32.5}$ queries plus 2^{31} *quantum* bits of memory, for a version of Kuperberg's original sieve algorithm [Kup03].

Similarly, Fig. 1 shows that key recovery for CSIDH-1024 and -1792 (using the same or somewhat more QRACM as above) requires only 2^b oracle queries, for values of b in the mid-20s and high-30s, respectively. For example, CSIDH-1024 can be broken using less than 2^{24} queries and about 2^{44} bits of QRACM.

According to our model, for arities $r = 3$ and $r = 4$ (and the same amounts of QRACM) the query complexities decrease modestly, by factors of about 2^2–$2^{3.5}$. Note that these arities require much more classical computation, but still may be cryptanalytically feasible. We stress that all these query complexities are for recovering *almost all* the bits of the secret. At present it is unclear whether the number of queries can be reduced even further by breaking the scheme using only partial information about the secret.

The estimates in Fig. 1 are based on the following:

$\log p$	$\log N$	$\log L$	$\log$ QRACM	depth	$\log \tilde{Q}_{\text{total}}$	$\log T \leq$
512	257.1	23.6	32	11	18.7	63
		27.4	36	9	17.0	61
		31.3	40	8	15.7	60
		35.1	44	7	14.9	59
		39.0	48	6	14.1	58
1024	512	27.4	36	19	27.9	76
		31.3	40	16	25.5	74
		35.1	44	14	23.5	72
		39.0	48	13	22.1	70
		42.9	52	12	20.8	69
1792	896	31.3	40	29	39.2	90
		35.1	44	25	35.8	87
		39.0	48	23	33.2	84
		42.9	52	21	30.9	82
		46.7	56	19	29.2	80

Fig. 1. Example complexity estimates for secret-key recovery against CSIDH-$\log p$ using the collimation sieve with arity $r = 2$, for various bit lengths (rounded to the nearest integer) of the CSIDH parameter p. Each missing entry is equal to the one above it. Here N is the estimated (or known, in the case of CSIDH-512) group order; $L = S$ are respectively the desired length and range size of the sieve's final phase vector; "QRACM" is the number of bits of quantumly accessible classical memory, which is given by Eq. (5) with $\alpha = 1/2$ for $\tilde{L}_{\max} = 8L$ indexable cells; "depth" is the depth of the sieve's recursion tree; $\tilde{Q}_{\text{total}}$ is the total number of queries to the quantum oracle to recover all but 56 bits of the secret; T is the total T-gate complexity of the attack, assuming the complexity of implementing the oracle is not much more than for evaluating on the "best conceivable" distribution.

- We take $S = L$ and use punctured regularity to obtain several bits of the secret (see Sect. 3.4). We assume that each run of the sieve reveals an expected $\log S - 2$ bits of the secret, which is consistent with our experiments.
- We quantify the total number $\tilde{Q}_{\text{total}}$ of oracle queries needed to recover all but 56 bits of the secret; the remainder can be obtained by classical brute force. We assume that the actual number of queries $\tilde{Q}$ made by a run of the sieve is within a $2^{0.3}$ factor of the estimated number Q from Eq. (3), which is consistent with our experiments.
- We impose a maximum phase-vector length of $\tilde{L}_{\max} = 8L$. This reflects the fact that the generated phase vectors are sometimes longer than the desired length L, but are almost always within a factor of 8, and we can enforce this as a hard bound by doing a partial measurement whenever a phase vector happens to be longer. We use Eq. (5) for the number of bits of QRACM as a function of $\tilde{L}_{\max}$.

4.2   T-Gate Complexity and NIST Security Levels

As shown below in Sect. 4.3, for all the sieve parameters appearing in Fig. 1, the quantum work of the collimation sieve itself—mainly, the QRACM lookups done during each collimation step—can be implemented more cheaply than the oracle calls, under optimistic estimates for the latter. (Moreover, the classical work of the sieve scales with the number of collimations, so as long as the quasilinear classical work of collimation is cheaper than the linear quantum work used to implement the QRACM, the total classical work is not significant.) So, if we assume that the actual cost of the oracle is not much more than what is given by the analysis of [BLMP19] for the "best conceivable" distribution (see Sect. 1.4 for discussion), we can give T-gate estimates for the full attacks, and compare them to what is needed to achieve the targeted NIST post-quantum security levels.

CSIDH-512 and Level 1. A CSIDH-512 oracle for the "best conceivable" distribution can be implemented in about 2^{40} nonlinear bit operations [BLMP19], which translates to between 2^{40} and 2^{44} T-gates. Under our assumption, CSIDH-512 key recovery therefore costs between roughly 2^{56} and 2^{60} T-gates with 2^{40} bits of QRACM, plus relatively small other resources. (See Fig. 1 for other options.) It would be prudent to expect that something toward the lower end of this range is attainable.

It follows that CSIDH-512 falls *far short* of its claimed NIST quantum security level 1, especially when accounting for the MAXDEPTH restriction, and even under a substantially weaker assumption about the oracle cost. Specifically, level 1 corresponds to the difficulty of key search for AES-128, and NIST's estimate for this is $2^{170}/\text{MAXDEPTH}$ quantum gates, where suggested plausible values of MAXDEPTH range between 2^{40} and 2^{96}. As seen in Sect. 3.2, the sieve can almost perfectly parallelize the oracle calls and collimation steps, so the depth of the full attack can be made quite close to the depth of the oracle, which certainly cannot exceed its gate count. So, the depth of the full attack can be brought close to the low end of the MAXDEPTH range or only somewhat larger, if the sieve works sequentially (which requires fewer qubits). In any case, the attack's quantum gate complexity of about 2^{56}–2^{60} is far below the required 2^{130} for the low end of the MAXDEPTH range, and even significantly below the required 2^{74} for the high end.

Other CSIDH Parameters. For a 1030-bit prime CSIDH parameter (namely, four times the product of the first 130 odd primes and 911, minus 1), using the software from [BLMP19] we determined that an oracle for the "best conceivable" distribution can be implemented in less than 2^{44} nonlinear bit operations, which translates to between 2^{44} and 2^{48} T-gates. Under our assumption, breaking this parameterization of CSIDH therefore takes no more than about 2^{74} T-gates using about 2^{40} bits of QRACM, 2^{72} T-gates using about 2^{44} bits, and so on (see Fig. 1). This is also below NIST quantum security level 1, and well below it for small and medium choices of MAXDEPTH.

Similarly, for a 1798-bit prime CSIDH parameter (namely, four times the product of the first 207 odd primes and 2273, minus 1), an oracle for the "best conceivable" distribution can be implemented in about 2^{47} nonlinear qubit operations, which translates to between 2^{47} and 2^{51} T-gates. Under our assumption, the attack therefore takes no more than about 2^{87} T-gates using 2^{44} bits of QRACM, 2^{84} T-gates using 2^{48} bits of QRACM, and so on. While [CLM+18] proposed a 1792-bit parameterization for NIST quantum security level 3—corresponding to security against $2^{233}/\text{MAXDEPTH}$ quantum gates—it falls far short of this target (even allowing for a much weaker assumption about the oracle). Indeed, with the possible exception of the high end of the MAXDEPTH range, it does not even reach level 1.

4.3   Quantum Complexity of the Sieve

Here we estimate the T-gate complexity of the quantum work of the collimation sieve using the QRACM implementation of [BGB+18], as suggested by Schanck [Sch19]. The main conclusion is that for parameters of interest, the quantum complexity of the sieve and the QRACM is dwarfed by that of the oracle calls (under current estimates for the latter).

Fix the collimation arity $r = 2$. The analysis below shows that the total T-gate complexity of the collimation sieve (apart from the oracle calls) is essentially

$$36\tilde{L} \cdot (2/(1-\delta))^d, \tag{8}$$

where $\tilde{L}$ is (an upper bound on) the typical phase-vector length, δ is the discard probability, and d is the depth of the sieve tree. For $\delta \approx 0.02$ and all the sieve parameters $(\log \tilde{L}, d)$ given in Fig. 1, this T-gate estimate is comfortably below even the most optimistic T-gate estimates for all the oracle calls, based on [BLMP19]. For example, for the sieve parameters given in Fig. 1 for CSIDH-512, the T-gate complexity of the sieve itself is between 2^{38} and 2^{47}, which in all cases is well below the lower bound of about 2^{53} for making at least 2^{14} calls to an oracle with T-gate complexity at least 2^{39}.

The estimate from Eq. (8) is obtained as follows. The full sieve is a traversal of a binary tree (modulo discards), with one collimation at each non-leaf node, and one or more oracle calls at each leaf node. Therefore, the T-gate complexity of the sieve itself (apart from the oracle calls) is essentially the number of non-leaf nodes times the T-gate complexity of collimation. For sieve tree depth d, the number of internal nodes is about $(2/(1-\delta))^d$ when accounting for discards.

The T-gate complexity of a single collimation step can be bounded as follows. As shown in Sect. 3.3, for input and output phase vectors having lengths bounded by D, the quantum work is dominated by nine lookups into a QRACM of D indexable cells. Because [BGB+18] implements such a QRACM (for cells of any uniform size) using classical memory plus just $4D$ T-gates (and only $\lceil \log D \rceil$ ancillary qubits), the claim follows.

5   Experiments

At present, there are no (publicly available) quantum computers capable of running the full quantum algorithm for nontrivial parameters. But fortunately, as pointed out in [Kup11], the collimation sieve itself (apart from the quantum oracle U_f and the final QFT) is *pseudoclassical*: it consists entirely of permutations of the computational basis and measurements in that basis, which are trivial to simulate classically. In addition, the needed part of the quantum oracle U_f is easy to simulate, just by generating a uniformly random phase multiplier $b \leftarrow \mathbb{Z}_N$ (for the qubit $|\psi\rangle \propto |0\rangle + \chi(b \cdot s/N)|1\rangle$, which we do not need to generate).

5.1   Sieve Simulator

Using the above observations, we implemented a classical simulator for our generalized collimation sieve.[8] The simulator is currently hard-coded for collimation arity $r = 2$, but would be easy to generalize to larger arities. It allows the user to specify:

- a group order N (including an option for the exact CSIDH-512 group order, as computed in [BKV19]);
- a desired typical phase vector length L;
- an interval size S for the ultimate phase vector.

The simulator logs its progress in a human-readable form, and finally outputs various statistics for the full sieve, including:

- the total number $\tilde{Q}$ of queries to the quantum oracle U_f;
- the number Q of queries predicted by the model of Eq. (3) from Sect. 3.2;
- the length $\tilde{L}_{\max}$ of the longest created phase vector;
- the probability of obtaining a *regular* phase vector from the final one, and the expected number of bits of the secret that can be recovered from the final phase vector via regularity;
- the probabilities of obtaining *punctured* regular phase vectors of sufficient length from the final phase vector, and the total probability of measuring a value that yields $\log S$ secret bits.

---

[8] The code for the simulator and instructions for running it are at https://github.com/cpeikert/CollimationSieve. The code is written in the author's favorite functional language Haskell, and has not been especially optimized for performance, but it suffices for the present purposes.

5.2   Experimental Results

We ran our simulator for a wide range of group orders N (focusing mainly on the exact CSIDH-512 group order), desired phase-vector lengths L, and range sizes S. Our results for the CSIDH-512 group order are given in Figs. 2 and 3; the former concerns full regularization of the final phase vector (Sect. 3.4), while the latter concerns punctured regularization (Sect. 3.4). In summary, the experiments strongly support the following conclusions:

- For all tested group orders and desired vector lengths $L \in [2^{16}, 2^{26}]$, the required *classical* resources are cryptanalytically insignificant: at most a few core-days on a commodity server with 128 GB or 512 GB of RAM, using only four CPU cores and less than 100 GB RAM per experiment.
- The actual number $\tilde{Q}$ of oracle queries conforms very closely to the model of Eq. (3) from Sect. 3.2, especially for relatively larger $L \geq 2^{22}$, where $\tilde{Q}$ was almost always within a factor of $2^{0.4} \approx 1.32$ of the predicted Q, and was usually even closer.
- Taking $L = 64S$ suffices to obtain a *regular* phase vector on $[S]$ with good probability, usually in the 45–80% range (see Sect. 3.4). Halving S, and hence making $L \approx 128S$, typically results in a regularity probability of 70% or more, often yielding slightly more expected number of bits of the secret.
- Taking $L = S$ typically suffices to obtain at least $\log S - 2$ bits of the secret in expectation, via punctured regularization (see Sect. 3.4). More specifically, we can create one or more punctured regular phase vectors that collectively represent a roughly 40% probability of yielding $\log S$ bits of the secret.

log $\tilde{Q}$	log Q	log $\tilde{L}_{\max}$	log L	log S	Pr[regular] (%)	bits	threshold	discard (%)	depth
19.4	19.1	23.9	18	10	78	7.8	0.25	2.8	15
19.4	19.2	23.8		11	95	10.5		3.6	
19.2	19.3	23.3		12	72	8.6		4.2	
18.3	18.2	24.3	19	11	95	10.5		2.3	14
18.4	18.1	23.5		12	82	9.8		2.3	
18.6	18.1	24.5		13	61	7.9		2.4	
17.6	17.4	24.3	20	12	84	10.1		2.0	13
17.7	17.4	25.2		13	56	7.3		2.0	
17.6	17.4	24.2		14	66	9.2		2.2	
17.2	16.7	25.2	21	13	64	8.3		2.1	12
17.2	16.7	25.7		14	71	10.0		2.0	
16.8	16.6	25.4		15	73	10.9		1.9	
16.6	16.3	26.8	22	14	72	10.0		2.0	12
16.3	16.2	26.6		15	55	8.2		1.9	
16.6	16.2	26.6		16	60	9.6		2.3	
16.3	15.7	26.4	23	15	79	11.9		2.0	11
15.6	15.6	26.9		16	66	10.5		1.8	
15.6	15.6	26.7		17	62	10.6		2.0	
15.4	15.4	28.0	24	16	71	11.3		2.4	11
15.5	15.3	28.6		17	85	14.4		2.1	
15.3	15.2	29.1		18	64	11.5		2.1	
14.9	14.8	28.7	25	17	62	10.5		1.8	10
14.8	14.8	29.6		17	93	15.7		1.9	
15.4	14.8	28.9		18	85	15.3		1.9	
14.9	14.8	29.2		19	60	11.4		2.1	
15.1	14.8	29.1		19	81	15.4		2.0	
15.0	14.7	29.6	26	18	92	16.5	0.40	3.5	10
15.3	14.8	29.3		18	88	15.8		4.1	
14.9	14.8	29.4		19	77	14.7		4.6	

Fig. 2. Statistics from representative runs of our collimation sieve simulator on the actual CSIDH-512 group, as computed by [BKV19]. Here $\tilde{Q}$ and Q are respectively the actual and predicted (by the model of Sect. 3.2) number of queries to the quantum oracle; $\tilde{L}_{\max}$ is the maximum length of all created phase vectors, and L is the requested (and typical) vector length; S is the range size for the final phase vector; "Pr[regular]" is the probability of obtaining a regular vector from the final phase vector (see Sect. 3.4); "bits" is the expected number of bits of the secret that can be recovered from the final phase vector; "threshold" is the threshold factor used for determining whether a phase vector is too short (see Sect. 3.2); "discard" is the fraction of recursive calls that were discarded for being below the threshold; "depth" is the recursion depth of the sieve. Each missing entry is equal to the one above it. Every experiment ran on at most four CPU cores on a commodity server, and completed in no more than a few core-days.

$\log \tilde{Q}$	$\log Q$	$\log \tilde{L}_{\max}$	$\log L$	$\log S$	bits	threshold	discard (%)	depth
17.2	17.0	25.3	20	20	19.1	0.25	2.2	13
18.1	17.1	24.3			18.1		2.2	
16.7	16.4	25.1	21	21	20.1		2.0	12
16.8	16.4	24.9			19.4		1.9	
16.6	16.4	24.8			17.7		2.0	
15.9	15.7	26.6	22	22	21.2		1.9	11
16.2	15.8	25.7			20.3		2.0	
16.4	15.8	25.8			20.4		2.0	
15.6	15.3	26.6	23	23	21.2		1.7	11
16.0	15.4	26.3			21.9		2.0	
15.9	15.4	26.7			21.3		1.9	
16.1	15.4	26.1			21.4		1.9	
14.9	14.8	26.8	24	24	22.5		1.8	10
15.6	14.8	27.3			23.2		1.9	
15.0	14.8	27.3			23.1		1.9	
15.0	14.6	28.3	25	25	22.4		2.3	10
14.5	14.5	27.9			23.5		1.6	
15.0	14.6	28.2			23.7		2.4	
14.5	14.3	29.1	26	26	25.2		3.0	10
14.7	14.2	29.0			24.1		2.4	
14.7	14.6	28.4			25.0	0.40	4.9	
14.2	14.1	29.6	27	27	25.7		4.1	9
14.5	14.1	29.6			25.3		4.6	
14.4	14.1	30.0			24.6		4.2	
14.0	13.8	30.4	28	28	25.6		3.9	9
14.3	13.8	30.4			26.3		3.7	
13.9	13.8	30.1			26.4		4.3	
14.0	13.9	30.4			25.5		4.5	

Fig. 3. Statistics from representative runs of our collimation sieve simulator on the actual CSIDH-512 group, as computed by [BKV19]. The column headers are the same as in Fig. 2, except that "bits" b is the expected number of secret bits obtainable by using punctured phase vectors obtained from the vector output by the sieve; see Sect. 3.4. Each missing entry is equal to the one above it. Every experiment ran on at most four CPU cores on a commodity server, and completed within several core-days.

Acknowledgments. We thank the organizers of the Oxford Post-Quantum Cryptography Workshop, at which we received our first detailed exposure to CSIDH; Michael Cafarella and J. Alex Halderman for the use of their servers to conduct experiments; Oded Regev and Greg Kuperberg for clarifying comments; Dan Bernstein for pointing out Kuperberg's recent talks and for comments on [BLMP19]; Léo Ducas for additional references; John Schanck and Sam Jaques for additional references and discussions about the full quantum complexity analysis; and the anonymous EUROCRYPT reviewers for many helpful comments and suggestions.

References

[Bab85]   Babai, L.: On Lovász' lattice reduction and the nearest lattice point prob-
           lem. Combinatorica **6**(1), 1–13 (1986). Preliminary version in STACS 1985
[BGB+18]   Babbush, R., et al.: Encoding electronic spectra in quantum cir-
           cuits with linear T complexity. Phys. Rev. X **8**, 041015 (2018).
           https://arxiv.org/pdf/1805.03662.pdf
[BHT98]   Brassard, G., Høyer, P., Tapp, A.: Quantum cryptanalysis of hash and
           claw-free functions. In: Lucchesi, C.L., Moura, A.V. (eds.) LATIN 1998.
           LNCS, vol. 1380, pp. 163–169. Springer, Heidelberg (1998). https://doi.
           org/10.1007/BFb0054319
[BIJJ18]   Biasse, J.-F., Iezzi, A., Jacobson, M.J.: A note on the security of CSIDH.
           In: Chakraborty, D., Iwata, T. (eds.) INDOCRYPT 2018. LNCS, vol.
           11356, pp. 153–168. Springer, Cham (2018). https://doi.org/10.1007/978-
           3-030-05378-9_9
[BKV19]   Beullens, W., Kleinjung, T., Vercauteren, F.: CSI-FiSh: efficient isogeny
           based signatures through class group computations. In: Galbraith, S.D.,
           Moriai, S. (eds.) ASIACRYPT 2019. LNCS, vol. 11921, pp. 227–247.
           Springer, Cham (2019). https://doi.org/10.1007/978-3-030-34578-5_9
[BLMP19]   Bernstein, D.J., Lange, T., Martindale, C., Panny, L.: Quantum circuits
           for the CSIDH: optimizing quantum evaluation of isogenies. In: Ishai, Y.,
           Rijmen, V. (eds.) EUROCRYPT 2019. LNCS, vol. 11477, pp. 409–441.
           Springer, Cham (2019). https://doi.org/10.1007/978-3-030-17656-3_15
[BS18]   Bonnetain, X., Schrottenloher, A.: Quantum security analysis of CSIDH
           and ordinary isogeny-based schemes. Cryptology ePrint Archive, Report
           2018/537 (2018). https://eprint.iacr.org/2018/537
[CD19]   Castryck, W., Decru, T.: CSIDH on the surface. Cryptology ePrint
           Archive, Report 2019/1404 (2019). https://eprint.iacr.org/2019/1404
[CJS10]   Childs, A.M., Jao, D., Soukharev, V.: Constructing elliptic curve isogenies
           in quantum subexponential time. J. Math. Cryptol. **8**(1), 1–29 (2014).
           https://arxiv.org/abs/1012.4019
[CLM+18]   Castryck, W., Lange, T., Martindale, C., Panny, L., Renes, J.: CSIDH: an
           efficient post-quantum commutative group action. In: Peyrin, T., Gal-
           braith, S. (eds.) ASIACRYPT 2018. LNCS, vol. 11274, pp. 395–427.
           Springer, Cham (2018). https://doi.org/10.1007/978-3-030-03332-3_15
[Cou06]   Couveignes, J.-M.: Hard homogeneous spaces. Cryptology ePrint Archive,
           Report 2006/291 (2006). https://eprint.iacr.org/2006/291
[DG19]   De Feo, L., Galbraith, S.D.: SeaSign: compact isogeny signatures from
           class group actions. In: Ishai, Y., Rijmen, V. (eds.) EUROCRYPT 2019.
           LNCS, vol. 11478, pp. 759–789. Springer, Cham (2019). https://doi.org/
           10.1007/978-3-030-17659-4_26
[DH76]   Diffie, W., Hellman, M.E.: New directions in cryptography. IEEE Trans.
           Inf. Theory **IT−22**(6), 644–654 (1976)
[FTLX19]   Fan, X., Tian, S., Li, B., Xu, X.: CSIDH on other form of elliptic curves.
           Cryptology ePrint Archive, Report 2019/1417 (2019). https://eprint.iacr.
           org/2019/1417
[JD11]   Jao, D., De Feo, L.: Towards quantum-resistant cryptosystems from super-
           singular elliptic curve isogenies. In: Yang, B.-Y. (ed.) PQCrypto 2011.
           LNCS, vol. 7071, pp. 19–34. Springer, Heidelberg (2011). https://doi.org/
           10.1007/978-3-642-25405-5_2

[JS19] Jaques, S., Schanck, J.M.: Quantum cryptanalysis in the RAM model: claw-finding attacks on SIKE. In: Boldyreva, A., Micciancio, D. (eds.) CRYPTO 2019. LNCS, vol. 11692, pp. 32–61. Springer, Cham (2019). https://doi.org/10.1007/978-3-030-26948-7_2

[KKP20] Kaafarani, A.E., Katsumata, S., Pintore, F.: Lossy CSI-FiSh: efficient signature scheme with tight reduction to decisional CSIDH-512. In: PKC (2020)

[Kup03] Kuperberg, G.: A subexponential-time quantum algorithm for the dihedral hidden subgroup problem. SIAM J. Comput. **35**(1), 170–188 (2005). Preliminary version in https://arxiv.org/abs/quant-ph/0302112

[Kup11] Kuperberg, G.: Another subexponential-time quantum algorithm for the dihedral hidden subgroup problem. In: 8th Conference on the Theory of Quantum Computation, Communication and Cryptography, TQC, pp. 20–34 (2013). Preliminary version in https://arxiv.org/abs/1112.3333

[LF06] Levieil, É., Fouque, P.-A.: An improved LPN algorithm. In: De Prisco, R., Yung, M. (eds.) SCN 2006. LNCS, vol. 4116, pp. 348–359. Springer, Heidelberg (2006). https://doi.org/10.1007/11832072_24

[NIS] NIST post-quantum cryptography project. https://csrc.nist.gov/Projects/Post-Quantum-Cryptography

[Reg04] Regev, O.: A subexponential time algorithm for the dihedral hidden subgroup problem with polynomial space. CoRR, quant-ph/0406151 (2004)

[RS06] Rostovtsev, A., Stolbunov, A.: Public-key cryptosystem based on isogenies. Cryptology ePrint Archive, Report 2006/145 (2006). https://eprint.iacr.org/2006/145

[Sch19] Schanck, J.: Personal communication, June 2019

[Sho94] Shor, P.W.: Polynomial-time algorithms for prime factorization and discrete logarithms on a quantum computer. SIAM J. Comput. **26**(5), 1484–1509 (1997). Preliminary version in FOCS 2004

[SS79] Schroeppel, R., Shamir, A.: A $t=o(2^{n/2})$, $s=o(2^{n/4})$ algorithm for certain NP-complete problems. SIAM J. Comput. **10**(3), 456–464 (1981). Preliminary version in FOCS 1979

[Sto04] Stolbunov, A.: Public-key encryption based on cycles of isogenous elliptic curves. Master's thesis, Saint-Petersburg State Polytechnical University (2004). (in Russian)

[Sto11] Stolbunov, A.: Cryptographic schemes based on isogenies. Ph.D. thesis, Norwegian University of Science and Technology (2011)

Quantum Security Analysis of CSIDH

Xavier Bonnetain[1,2](✉) and André Schrottenloher[2](✉)

[1] Sorbonne Université, Collège Doctoral, 75005 Paris, France
[2] Inria, Paris, France
{xavier.bonnetain,andre.schrottenloher}@inria.fr

Abstract. CSIDH is a recent proposal for post-quantum non-interactive key-exchange, based on supersingular elliptic curve isogenies. It is similar in design to a previous scheme by Couveignes, Rostovtsev and Stolbunov, but aims at an improved balance between efficiency and security. In the proposal, the authors suggest concrete parameters in order to meet some desired levels of quantum security. These parameters are based on the hardness of recovering a hidden isogeny between two elliptic curves, using a quantum subexponential algorithm of Childs, Jao and Soukharev. This algorithm combines two building blocks: first, a quantum algorithm for recovering a hidden shift in a commutative group. Second, a computation in superposition of all isogenies originating from a given curve, which the algorithm calls as a black box.

In this paper, we give a comprehensive security analysis of CSIDH. Our first step is to revisit three quantum algorithms for the abelian hidden shift problem from the perspective of non-asymptotic cost, with trade-offs between their quantum and classical complexities. Second, we complete the non-asymptotic study of the black box in the hidden shift algorithm. We give a quantum procedure that evaluates CSIDH-512 using less than 40 000 logical qubits.

This allows us to show that the parameters proposed by the authors of CSIDH do not meet their expected quantum security.

Keywords: Post-quantum cryptography · Isogeny-based cryptography · Quantum cryptanalysis · Quantum circuits · Hidden shift problem

1 Introduction

Problems such as factoring and solving discrete logarithms, believed to be classically intractable, underlie the security of most asymmetric cryptographic primitives in use today. After Shor found a quantum polynomial-time algorithm for both [44], the cryptographic community has been actively working on replacements, culminating with the ongoing NIST call for post-quantum primitives [37].

One of the families of problems studied concerns elliptic curve isogenies. In this setting, we consider a graph, whose vertices are elliptic curves, and whose edges are non constant morphisms (isogenies). The problem of finding a path

A. Canteaut and Y. Ishai (Eds.): EUROCRYPT 2020, LNCS 12106, pp. 493–522, 2020.
https://doi.org/10.1007/978-3-030-45724-2_17

between two given curves was first used in the design of the CGL hash functions [13] with supersingular isogeny graphs. Afterwards, a key-exchange based on ordinary curves (CRS) was proposed independently by Rostovtsev and Stolbunov [45] and Couveignes [18]. Later, a quantum algorithm was given in [16], that could find an isogeny between two such curves in subexponential time, a problem for which classical algorithms still require exponential time. Although it is not broken in quantum polynomial time, the scheme became considered as too inefficient with respect to its post-quantum security.

Meanwhile, a key-exchange based on *supersingular* elliptic curves isogenies was proposed [21], and the candidate SIKE was selected for the second round of the NIST standardization process. The quantum algorithm for finding ordinary isogenies cannot be applied for the supersingular graphs, and the best known quantum algorithm for breaking SIKE has an exponential time complexity.

CSIDH. CSIDH is a new primitive presented at ASIACRYPT 2018 [12]. Its name stands for "commutative supersingular isogeny Diffie-Hellman", and its goal is to make isogeny-based key exchange efficient in the *commutative* case, analogous to a regular non-interactive Diffie-Hellman key exchange. CSIDH uses supersingular elliptic curves defined over $\mathbb{F}_p$. In this case, the $\mathbb{F}_p$-isogeny graph has a structure analogous to the ordinary isogeny graph, and the subexponential quantum attack of [16] also applies. CSIDH aims at an improved balance between efficiency and security with respect to the original CRS scheme. However, it stands in a peculiar situation. To the best of our knowledge, it is the only post-quantum scheme actively studied[1] against which a quantum adversary enjoys more than a polynomial speedup. Schemes based on lattices, codes, or SIKE, rely on problems with a quantum speedup quadratic *at best*.

In only two years, CSIDH has been the subject of many publications, showing a renewed interest for protocols based on commutative elliptic curve isogenies. It has been used in [20] to devise the signature scheme SeaSign. CSIDH and SeaSign were further studied and their efficiency was improved in [22,26,35,36], the last two works published at PQCRYPTO 2019.

Meanwhile, there has been a few works dealing with the security of CSIDH. The asymptotic cost of attacking the scheme, with classical precomputations and a quantum polynomial-space algorithm, was studied in [7]. Asymptotically also, it was shown in [27] that CSIDH (and CRS) could be attacked in polynomial space. Next, a quantum-classical trade-off using Regev's variant [39] of Kuperberg's sieve was proposed in [8]. Only two works studied the concrete parameters proposed in [12]: independently from us, Peikert [38] attacked CSIDH-512 using Kuperberg's collimation sieve [32]. Contrary to us, he uses classical memory with quantum random access. Finally, the number of Toffoli gates required to implement a CSIDH-512 key-exchange in constant time has been studied in full detail in [4], published at EUROCRYPT 2019. However, the authors designed an irreversible classical circuit, and the memory usage of an immediate translation to a quantum circuit seems massive (see the appendix of [4]).

---

[1] Unfortunately, CSIDH was published after the beginning of the NIST call, and it could not be submitted to the standardization process.

Contributions. In this paper, we make a decisive move towards understanding the quantum security of CSIDH. First, we revisit three quantum abelian hidden shift algorithms from the available literature, that can be used to recover the secret key in a CSIDH key-exchange, from the point of view of non-asymptotic cost. We give a wide range of trade-offs between their quantum and classical time and memory complexities. Second, we give quantum circuits for computing the isogenies in CSIDH. Building on [4], with the addition of quantum time-space tradeoffs for reversible computations and refined quantum search, we give a quantum procedure that computes the action of the class group in CSIDH-512 using $2^{49.8}$ Toffoli gates and less than 40 000 qubits. Putting together our improved query complexities and this new quantum circuit, we are able to attack CSIDH-512, -1024 and -1792 in 2^{10} to 2^{48} less quantum time than expected, using only tens of thousands of logical qubits.

Paper Outline. Section 2 below presents the context of the CSIDH group action and outlines the attack. We next go into the details of the two building blocks: a quantum black-box hidden shift algorithm, and a quantum procedure to evaluate the *class group action*. In Sect. 3, we present the three main quantum algorithms for finding abelian hidden shifts. Our contribution here is to give non-asymptotic estimates of them, and to write a simple algorithm for cyclic hidden shift (Algorithm 2), which can be easily simulated. In Sect. 4, we show how to replace the *class group action oracle* by the *CSIDH group action oracle* using lattice reduction. We study the latter in Sect. 5. We summarize our complexity analysis in Sect. 6.

2 Preliminaries

In this section, we present the rationale of CSIDH and the main ideas of its quantum attack. Throughout this paper, we use extensively standard notions of quantum computing such as qubits, ancilla qubits, quantum gates, entanglement, uncomputing, quantum Fourier Transform (QFT), CNOT and Toffoli gates. We use the Dirac notation of quantum states $|\rangle$. We analyze quantum algorithms in the *quantum circuit model*, where the number of qubits represents the quantum space used, including *ancilla* qubits which are restored to their initial state after the computation. Time is the number of quantum gates in the circuit (we do not consider the metric of circuit depth). We use the standard "Clifford+T" universal gate set for all our benchmarks [25] and focus notably on the T-gate count, as T-gates are usually considered an order of magnitude harder to realize than Clifford gates. It is possible to realize the Toffoli gate with 7 T-gates.

2.1 Context of CSIDH

Let $p > 3$ be a prime number. In general, supersingular elliptic curves over $\overline{\mathbb{F}_p}$ are defined over a quadratic extension $\mathbb{F}_{p^2}$. However, the case of supersingular curves *defined over* $\mathbb{F}_p$ is special. When $\mathcal{O}$ is an order in an imaginary quadratic field, each supersingular elliptic curve defined over $\mathbb{F}_p$ having $\mathcal{O}$ as its $\mathbb{F}_p$-rational endomorphism ring corresponds to an element of $\mathcal{Cl}(\mathcal{O})$, the ideal class group of $\mathcal{O}$. Moreover, a rational ℓ-isogeny from such a curve corresponds to an ideal of norm ℓ in $\mathcal{Cl}(\mathcal{O})$. The (commutative) class group $\mathcal{Cl}(\mathcal{O})$ acts on the set of supersingular elliptic curves with $\mathbb{F}_p$-rational endomorphism ring $\mathcal{O}$.

One-way Group Action. All use cases of the CSIDH scheme can be pinned down to the definition of a *one-way group action* (this is also the definition of a *hard homogeneous space* by Couveignes [18]). A group G acts on a set X. Operations in G, and the action $g * x$ for $g \in G, x \in X$, are easy to compute. Recovering g given x and $x' = g * x$ is hard. In the case of CSIDH, X is a set of Montgomery curves of the form $E_A : y^2 = x^3 + Ax^2 + x$ for $A \in \mathbb{F}_p$, and the group G is $\mathcal{Cl}(\mathcal{O})$ for $\mathcal{O} = \mathbb{Z}[\sqrt{-p}]$. Taking $g * x$ for an element in $\mathcal{Cl}(\mathcal{O})$ (*i.e.* an isogeny) and a curve corresponds to computing the image curve of x by this isogeny.

CSIDH and CRS both benefit from this action of the class group, which also exists in the ordinary case. Quantum algorithms for recovering abelian hidden shifts solve exactly this problem of finding g when G is commutative. There exists a family of such algorithms, initiated by Kuperberg. The variant of [16] targets precisely the context of ordinary curves, and it can be applied to CSIDH.

Representation of $\mathcal{Cl}(\mathcal{O})$. The designers choose a prime p of the form: $p = 4 \cdot \ell_1 \cdots \ell_u - 1$ where $\ell_1, \ldots, \ell_u$ are small primes. This enables to represent the elements of $\mathcal{Cl}(\mathcal{O})$ (hence, the isogenies) in a way that is now specific to CSIDH, and the main reason of its efficiency. Indeed, since each of the ℓ_i divides $-p-1 = \pi^2 - 1$, the ideal $\ell_i \mathcal{O}$ splits and $\mathfrak{l}_i = (\ell_i, \pi - 1)$ is an ideal in $\mathcal{O}$. The image curves by these ideals can be computed efficiently [12, Section 8].

The designers consider the set $\{\prod_{i=1}^u [\mathfrak{l}_i]^{e_i}, -m \leq e_i \leq m\} \subseteq \mathcal{Cl}(\mathcal{O})$, where $[\mathfrak{l}_i]$ is the class of $\mathfrak{l}_i$. If we suppose that these products fall randomly in $\mathcal{Cl}(\mathcal{O})$, which has $O(\sqrt{p})$ elements, it suffices to take $2m + 1 \simeq p^{1/(2u)}$ in order to span the group $\mathcal{Cl}(\mathcal{O})$ or almost all of it. Since a greater m yields more isogeny computations, u should be the greatest possible. With this constraint in mind, we estimate $u = 132$ and $u = 209$ for CSIDH-1024 and CSIDH-1792 respectively (for CSIDH-512, we know that $u = 74$ and the list of primes is given in [12]).

Given an element of $\mathcal{Cl}(\mathcal{O})$ of the form $[\mathfrak{b}] = \prod_{i=1}^u [\mathfrak{l}_i]^{e_i}$, we compute $E' = [\mathfrak{b}] \cdot E$ by applying a sequence of $\sum_i e_i$ isogenies. The CSIDH public keys are curves. The secret keys are isogenies of this form.

CSIDH Original Security Analysis. The problem underlying the security of CSIDH is: given two Montgomery curves E_A and E_B, recover the isogeny $[\mathfrak{b}] \in \mathcal{Cl}(\mathcal{O})$ such that $E_B = [\mathfrak{b}] \cdot E_A$. Moreover, the ideal $\mathfrak{b}$ that represents it should be sufficiently "small", so that the action of $[\mathfrak{b}]$ on a curve can be evaluated. The authors study different ways of recovering $[\mathfrak{b}]$. The complexity of these methods depends on the size of the class group $N = \#\mathcal{Cl}(\mathcal{O}) = O(\sqrt{p})$. Classically, the best method seems the exhaustive key search of $[\mathfrak{b}]$ using a meet-in-the-middle approach: it costs $O(p^{1/4})$. Quantumly, they use the cost given in [16] for ordinary curves: $\exp\left((\sqrt{2} + o(1))\sqrt{\log N \log \log N}\right)$.

Levels of Security. In [12], the CSIDH parameters 512, 1024 and 1792 bits are conjectured secure up to the respective levels 1, 3 and 5 of the NIST call [37]. These levels correspond respectively to a key-recovery on AES-128, on AES-192 and AES-256. A cryptographic scheme, instantiated with some parameter size, matches level 1 if there is no quantum key-recovery running faster than quantum exhaustive search of the key for AES-128, and classical key-recovery running faster than classical exhaustive search. The NIST call considered the quantum gate counts given in [25]. These were improved later in [33], and we choose to adopt these improvements in this paper. For example, AES-128 key-recovery can be done with Grover search using $1.47 \cdot 2^{81}$ T-gates and 865 qubits. Hence any algorithm using less than $1.47 \cdot 2^{81}$ T-gates and 2^{128} classical computations breaks the NIST level 1 security, as it runs below the security level of AES-128.

2.2 Attack Outline

Algorithm 1 outlines a quantum key-recovery on CSIDH. Given E_A, E_B, we find a vector $\bar{e}$ such that $E_B = \prod_i [\mathfrak{l}_i]_i^e \cdot E_A$. We will not retrieve the exact secret key which was selected at the beginning, but the output $\bar{e}$ will have an L_1 norm small enough that it can be used instead, and impersonate effectively the secret key.

Algorithm 1. Key Recovery

    Input: The elements $([\mathfrak{l}_1], \ldots, [\mathfrak{l}_u])$, two curves E_B and E_A defined over $\mathbb{F}_p$, a generating set of $Cl(\mathcal{O})$: $([\mathfrak{g}_1], \ldots, [\mathfrak{g}_k])$
    Output: A vector $(e_1, \ldots, e_u)$ such that $\prod_{i=1}^u [\mathfrak{l}_i]^{e_i} \cdot E_A = E_B$
1: Define $f : [x] \in Cl(\mathcal{O}) \mapsto [x] \cdot E_A$ and $g : [x] \in Cl(\mathcal{O}) \mapsto [x] \cdot E_B$.
2: There exists $[\mathfrak{s}]$ such that $E_B = [\mathfrak{s}] \cdot E_A$, hence $f([\mathfrak{s}][x]) = g([x])$ for all $[x]$.
3: Apply a quantum abelian hidden shift algorithm, which recovers the "shift" between f and g. Obtain $[\mathfrak{s}]$.
4: Decompose $[\mathfrak{s}]$ as $\prod_{i=1}^u [\mathfrak{l}_i]^{e_i}$ with small e_i.
5: **return** $(e_1, \ldots, e_u)$

In order to evaluate the cost of Algorithm 1, we need to study the *quantum query complexity* of the black-box hidden shift algorithm applied, but also its classical complexity, as it will often contain some quantum-classical trade-off. Afterwards, we need to analyze the quantum gate complexity of an oracle for the action of the ideal class group on Montgomery curves. There will also be classical precomputations.

In [16], in the context of ordinary curves, the authors show how to evaluate $[x] \cdot E$ *for any ideal class* $[x]$ in superposition, in subexponential time. For CSIDH, in a non-asymptotic setting, it is best to use the structure provided by the scheme (contrary to [7]). We have supposed that the class group is spanned by products of the form $[\mathfrak{l}_1]^{e_1} \ldots [\mathfrak{l}_u]^{e_u}$ with small e_i. If we are able to rewrite any $[x]$ as such a product, then the evaluation of the *class group action* $[x] \cdot E$ costs no more than the evaluation of the *CSIDH group action* $\prod_i [\mathfrak{l}_i]^{e_i} \cdot E$. Here, a technique based on lattice reduction intervenes, following [6,7,18].

In general, although the class group is spanned by the products used in the CSIDH key-exchange: $\{[\mathfrak{l}_1]^{e_1} \dots [\mathfrak{l}_u]^{e_u}, -m \leq e_i \leq m\}$, we cannot retrieve the shortest representation of a given $[x]$. There is some approximation overhead, related to the quality of the lattice precomputations. In Sect. 4, we will show that this overhead is minor for the CSIDH original parameters.

3   Quantum Abelian Hidden Shift Algorithms

In this section, we present in detail three quantum algorithms for solving the hidden shift problem in commutative (abelian) groups. For each of them, we give tradeoff formulas and non-asymptotic estimates. The first one (Sect. 3.2) is a new variant of [31] for cyclic groups, whose behavior is easy to simulate. The second is by Regev [39] and Childs, Jao and Soukharev [16]. The third is Kuperberg's second algorithm [32].

3.1   Context

The hidden shift problem is defined as follows:

Problem 1 (Hidden shift problem). Let $(\mathbb{G}, +)$ be a group, $f, g : \mathbb{G} \to \mathbb{G}$ two permutations such that there exists $s \in \mathbb{G}$ such that, for all x, $f(x) = g(x + s)$. Find s.

Classically, this problem essentially reduces to a collision search, but in the case of commutative groups, there exists quantum subexponential algorithms. The first result on this topic was an algorithm with low query complexity, by Ettinger and Høyer [24], which needs $O(\log(N))$ queries and $O(N)$ classical computations to solve the hidden shift in $\mathbb{Z}/N\mathbb{Z}$. The first time-efficient algorithms were proposed by Kuperberg in [31]. His Algorithm 3 is shown to have a complexity in quantum queries and memory of $\widetilde{O}\left(2^{\sqrt{2\log_2(3)\log_2(N)}}\right)$ for the group $\mathbb{Z}/N\mathbb{Z}$ for smooth N, and his Algorithm 2 is in $O\left(2^{3\sqrt{\log_2(N)}}\right)$, for any N. This has been followed by a memory-efficient variant by Regev, with a query complexity in $L_N(1/2, \sqrt{2})$ and a polynomial memory complexity, in [39], which has been generalized by Kuperberg in [32], with an algorithm in $\widetilde{O}\left(2^{\sqrt{2\log_2(N)}}\right)$ quantum queries and classical memory, and a polynomial quantum memory. Regev's variant has been generalized to arbitrary commutative groups in the appendix of [16], with the same complexity. A complexity analysis of this algorithm with tighter exponents can be found in [9].

A broad presentation of subexponential-time quantum hidden shift algorithms can be found in [39]. Their common design is to start with a pool of *labeled qubits*, produced using quantum oracle queries for f and g. Each qubit contains information in the form of a phase shift between the states $|0\rangle$ and $|1\rangle$.

This phase shift depends on the (known) label ℓ and on the (unknown) hidden shift s. Then, they use a *combination procedure* that consumes labeled qubits and creates new ones. The goal is to make the label ℓ reach some wanted value (*e.g.* 2^{n-1}), at which point meaningful information on s (*e.g.* one bit) can be extracted.

Cyclic Groups and Concrete Estimates. In [10], the authors showed that the polynomial factor in the $\tilde{O}$, for a variant of Kuperberg's original algorithm, is a constant around 1 if N is a power of 2. In the context of CSIDH, the cardinality of the class group $\mathcal{C}\ell(\mathcal{O})$ is not a power of 2, but in most cases, its odd part is cyclic, as shown by the Cohen–Lenstra heuristics [17]. So we choose to approximate the class group as a cyclic group. This is why we propose in what follows a generalization of [10, Algorithm 2] that works for any N, at essentially the same cost. We suppose that an arbitrary representation of the class group is available; one could be obtained with the quantum polynomial-time algorithm of [14], as done in [16].

3.2 A First Hidden Shift Algorithm

In this section, we present a generic hidden shift algorithm for $\mathbb{Z}/N\mathbb{Z}$, which allows us to have the concrete estimates we need. We suppose an access to the quantum oracle that maps $|x\rangle|0\rangle|0\rangle$ to $|x\rangle|0\rangle|f(x)\rangle$, and $|x\rangle|1\rangle|0\rangle$ to $|x\rangle|1\rangle|g(x)\rangle$.

Producing the Labeled Qubits. We begin by constructing the uniform superposition on $N \times \{0,1\}$: $\frac{1}{\sqrt{2N}} \sum_{x=0}^{N-1} |x\rangle (|0\rangle + |1\rangle) |0\rangle$. Then, we apply the quantum oracle, and get

$$\frac{1}{\sqrt{2N}} \sum_{x=0}^{N-1} |x\rangle (|0\rangle|f(x)\rangle + |1\rangle|g(x)\rangle) .$$

We then measure the final register. We obtain a value $y = f(x_0) = g(x_0 + s)$ for some random x_0. The two first registers *collapse* on the superposition that corresponds to this measured value: $\frac{1}{\sqrt{2}} (|x_0\rangle|0\rangle + |x_0 + s\rangle|1\rangle)$.

Finally, we apply a Quantum Fourier Transform (QFT) on the first register and measure it, we obtain a label ℓ and the state

$$|\psi_\ell\rangle = \frac{1}{\sqrt{2}} \left(|0\rangle + \chi \left(s\frac{\ell}{N} \right) |1\rangle \right), \chi(x) = \exp(2i\pi x) .$$

The phase $\chi\left(s\frac{\ell}{N}\right)$, which depends on s and $\frac{\ell}{N}$, contains information on s. We now apply a *combination routine* on pairs of labeled qubits $(|\psi_\ell\rangle, \ell)$ as follows.

Combination Step. If we have obtained two qubits $|\psi_{\ell_1}\rangle$ and $|\psi_{\ell_2}\rangle$ with their corresponding labels ℓ_1 and ℓ_2, we can write the (disentangled) joint state of $|\psi_{\ell_1}\rangle$ and $|\psi_{\ell_2}\rangle$ as:

$$|\psi_{\ell_1}\rangle \otimes |\psi_{\ell_2}\rangle = \frac{1}{2} \left(|00\rangle + \chi \left(s\frac{\ell_1}{N} \right) |10\rangle + \chi \left(s\frac{\ell_2}{N} \right) |01\rangle + \chi \left(s\frac{\ell_1 + \ell_2}{N} \right) |11\rangle \right) .$$

We apply a CNOT gate, which maps $|00\rangle$ to $|00\rangle$, $|01\rangle$ to $|01\rangle$, $|10\rangle$ to $|11\rangle$ and $|11\rangle$ to $|10\rangle$. We obtain the state:

$$\frac{1}{2}\left(|00\rangle + \chi\left(s\frac{\ell_2}{N}\right)|01\rangle + \chi\left(s\frac{\ell_1+\ell_2}{N}\right)|10\rangle + \chi\left(s\frac{\ell_1}{N}\right)|11\rangle\right).$$

We measure the second qubit. If we measure 0, the first qubit collapses to:

$$\frac{1}{\sqrt{2}}\left(|0\rangle + \chi\left(s\frac{\ell_1+\ell_2}{N}\right)|1\rangle\right) = |\psi_{\ell_1+\ell_2}\rangle$$

and if we measure 1, it collapses to:

$$\frac{1}{\sqrt{2}}\left(\chi\left(s\frac{\ell_2}{N}\right)|0\rangle + \chi\left(s\frac{\ell_1}{N}\right)|1\rangle\right) = \chi\left(s\frac{\ell_2}{N}\right)|\psi_{\ell_1-\ell_2}\rangle.$$

A common phase factor has no incidence, so we can see that the combination either produces $|\psi_{\ell_1+\ell_2}\rangle$ or $|\psi_{\ell_1-\ell_2}\rangle$, with probability $\frac{1}{2}$. Furthermore, the measurement of the first qubit gives us which of the labels we have obtained. Although we cannot choose between the two cases, we can perform favorable combinations: we choose ℓ_1 and ℓ_2 such that $\ell_1 \pm \ell_2$ is a multiple of 2 with greater valuation than ℓ_1 and ℓ_2 themselves.

Goal of the Combinations. In order to retrieve s, we want to produce the qubits with label 2^i and apply a Quantum Fourier Transform. Indeed, we have

$$QFT \bigotimes_{i=0}^{n-1}|\psi_{2^i}\rangle = \frac{1}{2^{n/2}}QFT\sum_{k=0}^{2^n-1}\chi\left(\frac{ks}{N}\right)|k\rangle$$

$$= \frac{1}{2^n}\sum_{t=0}^{2^n-1}\left(\sum_{k=0}^{2^n-1}\chi\left(k\left(\frac{s}{N}+\frac{t}{2^n}\right)\right)\right)|t\rangle.$$

The amplitude associated with t is $\frac{1}{2^n}\left|\frac{1-\chi(2^n(\frac{s}{N}+\frac{t}{2^n}))}{1-\chi(\frac{s}{N}+\frac{t}{2^n})}\right|$. If we note $\theta = \frac{s}{N} + \frac{t}{2^n}$, this amplitude is $\frac{1}{2^n}\left|\frac{\sin(2^n\pi\theta)}{\sin(\pi\theta)}\right|$. For $\theta \in \left[0; \frac{1}{2^{n+1}}\right]$, this value is decreasing, from 1 to $\frac{1}{2^n\sin\frac{\pi}{2^{n+1}}} \simeq \frac{2}{\pi}$. Hence, when measuring, we obtain a t such that $\left|\frac{s}{N}+\frac{t}{2^n}\right| \le \frac{1}{2^{n+1}}$ with probability greater than $\frac{4}{\pi^2}$. Such a t always exists, and uniquely defines s if $n > \log_2(N)$.

From 2^n to any N. We want to apply this simple algorithm to any cyclic group, with any N. A solution is to *not* take into account the modulus N in the combination of labels. We only want combinations such that $\sum_k \pm\ell_k = 2^i$. At each combination step, we expect the 2-valuation of the output label to increase (we collide on the lowest significant bits), but its maximum size can also increase: $\ell_1 + \ell_2$ is bigger than ℓ_1 and ℓ_2. However, the size can increase of at most one bit per combination, while the lowest significant 1 position increases on average in $\sqrt{n}$. Hence, the algorithm will eventually produce the correct value.

We note $\mathrm{val}_2(x) = \max_i 2^i | x$ the 2-valuation of x. The procedure is Algorithm 2. Each label is associated to its corresponding qubit, and the operation $\pm$ corresponds to the combination.

Algorithm 2. Hidden shift algorithm for $\mathbb{Z}/N\mathbb{Z}$

Input: N, a number of queries Q, a quantum oracle access to f and g such that $f(x) = g(x + s), x \in \mathbb{Z}/N\mathbb{Z}$
Output: s
1: Generate Q random labels in $[0; N)$ using the quantum oracles
2: Separate them in pools P_i of elements e such that $\mathrm{val}_2(x) = i$
3: $i \leftarrow 0$, $R = \emptyset$, $n \leftarrow \lfloor \log_2(N) \rfloor$.
4: **while** some elements remain **do**
5:     **if** $i \leq n$ **then**
6:         Pop a few elements e from P_i, put (e, i) in R.
7:     **end if**
8:     **for** $(e, j) \in R$ **do**
9:         **if** $\mathrm{val}_2(e - 2^j) = i$ **then**
10:             Pop a of P_i which maximizes $\mathrm{val}_2(a + e - 2^j)$ or $\mathrm{val}_2(e - 2^j - a)$
11:             $e = e \pm a$
12:         **end if**
13:     **end for**
14:     **if** $\{(2^i, i) | 0 \leq i \leq n\} \subset R$ **then**
15:         Apply a QFT on the qubits, measure a t
16:         $s \leftarrow \lceil \frac{-Nt}{2^{n+1}} \rfloor \mod N$
17:         **return** s
18:     **end if**
19:     **while** $|P_i| \geq 2$ **do**
20:         Pop two elements (a, b) of P_i which maximizes $\mathrm{val}_2(a + b)$ or $\mathrm{val}_2(a - b)$
21:         $c = a \pm b$
22:         Insert c in the corresponding P_j
23:     **end while**
24:     $i \leftarrow i + 1$
25: **end while**
26: **return** Failure

Intuitively, the behavior of this algorithm will be close to the one of [10], as we only have a slightly higher amplitude in the values, and a few more elements to produce. The number of oracle queries Q is exactly the number of labeled qubits used during the combination step. Empirically, we only need to put 3 elements at each step in R in order to have a good success probability. This algorithm is easily simulated, because we only need to reproduce the combination step, by generating at random the new labels obtained at each combination. We estimate the total number of queries to be around $12 \times 2^{1.8\sqrt{n}}$ (Table 1).

Table 1. Simulation results for Algorithm 2, for 90% success

$\log_2(N)$	$\log_2(Q)$	$1.8\sqrt{\log_2(N)} + 2.3$	$\log_2(N)$	$\log_2(Q)$	$1.8\sqrt{\log_2(N)} + 2.3$
20	10.1	10.3	64	16.7	16.7
32	12.4	12.5	80	18.4	18.4
50	15.1	15.0	100	20.3	20.3

For the CSIDH parameters of [4], we have three group sizes (in bits): $n = 256$, 512 and 896 respectively. We obtain 2^{33}, 2^{45} and 2^{58} oracle queries to build the labeled qubits, with 2^{31}, 2^{43} and 2^{56} qubits to store in memory. A slight overhead in time stems from the probability of success of $\frac{4}{\pi^2}$; the procedure needs to be repeated at most 4 times. In CSIDH, the oracle has a high gate complexity. The number of CNOT quantum gates applied during the combination step (roughly equal to the number of labeled qubits at the beginning) is negligible. Notice also that the production of the labeled qubits can be perfectly parallelized.

3.3   An Approach Based on Subset-sums

Algorithm 2 is only a variant of the first subexponential algorithm by Kuperberg in [31]. We develop here on a later approach used by Regev [39] and Childs, Jao and Soukharev [16] for odd N.

Subset-sum Combination Routine. This algorithm uses the same labeled qubits as the previous one. The main idea is to combine not 2, but k qubits:

$$\bigotimes_{i \leq k} |\psi_{\ell_i}\rangle = \sum_{j \in \{0,1\}^k} \chi\left(\frac{j \cdot (\ell_1, \ldots, \ell_k)}{N}s\right) |j\rangle$$

and apply $|x\rangle|0\rangle \mapsto |x\rangle|\lfloor x \cdot (\ell_1, \ldots, \ell_k)/B\rfloor\rangle$ for a given B that controls the cost of the combination routine and depends on the tradeoffs of the complete algorithm. Measuring the second register yields a value $V = \lfloor x \cdot (\ell_1, \ldots, \ell_k)/B\rfloor$, the state becoming

$$\sum_{\lfloor j \cdot (\ell_1, \ldots, \ell_k)/B\rfloor = V} \chi\left(\frac{j \cdot (\ell_1, \ldots, \ell_k)}{N}s\right) |j\rangle.$$

In order to get a new labeled qubit, one can simply project on any pair (j_1, j_2) with j_1 and j_2 among this superposition of j. This is easy to do as long as the j are classically known. They can be computed by solving the equation $\lfloor j \cdot (\ell_1, \ldots, \ell_k)/B\rfloor = V$, which is an instance of the subset-sum problem.

This labeled qubit obtained is of the form:

$$\chi\left(\frac{j_1 \cdot (\ell_1, \ldots, \ell_k)}{N}s\right) |j_1\rangle + \chi\left(\frac{j_2 \cdot (\ell_1, \ldots, \ell_k)}{N}s\right) |j_2\rangle$$

which, up to a common phase factor, is:

$$|j_1\rangle + \chi\left(\frac{(j_2 - j_1) \cdot (\ell_1, \ldots, \ell_k)}{N}s\right) |j_2\rangle.$$

We observe that the new label in the phase, given by $(j_2 - j_1) \cdot (\ell_1, \ldots, \ell_k)$, is less than B. If we map j_1 and j_2 respectively to 0 and 1, we obtain a labeled qubit $|\psi_\ell\rangle$ with $\ell < B$. Now we can iterate this routine in order to get smaller and smaller labels, until the label 1 is produced. If N is odd, one reaches the other powers of 2 by multiplying all the initial labels by 2^{-a} and then applying normally the algorithm.

Algorithm 3. Combination routine

Input: $(|\psi_{\ell_1}\rangle, \ldots, |\psi_{\ell_k}\rangle)$, r
Output: $|\psi_{\ell'}\rangle$, $\ell' < B$

1: Tensor $\bigotimes_i |\psi_{\ell_i}\rangle = \sum_{j \in \{0,1\}^k} \chi\left(\frac{j \cdot (\ell_1, \ldots, \ell_k)}{N} s\right) |j\rangle$
2: Add an ancilla register, apply $|x\rangle|0\rangle \mapsto |x\rangle|\lfloor x \cdot (\ell_1, \ldots, \ell_k)/B \rfloor\rangle$
3: Measure the ancilla register, leaving with

$$V \text{ and } \sum_{\lfloor j \cdot (\ell_1, \ldots, \ell_k)/B \rfloor = V} \chi\left(\frac{j \cdot (\ell_1, \ldots, \ell_k)}{N} s\right) |j\rangle$$

4: Compute the corresponding j
5: Project to a pair (j_1, j_2).
   The register is now $\chi\left(\frac{j_1 \cdot (\ell_1, \ldots, \ell_k)}{N} s\right) |j_1\rangle + \chi\left(\frac{j_2 \cdot (\ell_1, \ldots, \ell_k)}{N} s\right) |j_2\rangle$
6: Map $|j_1\rangle$ to $|0\rangle$, $|j_2\rangle$ to $|1\rangle$
7: Return $|0\rangle + \chi\left(\frac{(j_2 - j_1) \cdot (\ell_1, \ldots, \ell_k)}{N} s\right) |1\rangle$

There are 2^k sums, and N/B possible values, hence we can expect to have $2^k B/N$ solutions. If we take $k \simeq \log_2(N/B)$, we can expect 2 solutions on average. In order to obtain a labeled qubit in the end, we need at least two solutions, and we need to successfully project to a pair (j_1, j_2) if there are more than two solutions.

The case where a single solution exists cannot happen more than half of the time, as there are twice many inputs as outputs. We consider the case where we have strictly more than one index j in the sum. If we have an even number of such indices, we simply divide the indices j into a set of pairs, project onto a pair, and map one of the remaining indexes to 0 and the other to 1. If we have an odd number of such indices, since it is greater or equal than 3, we single out a solitary element, and do the projections as in the even case. The probability to fall on this element is less than $\frac{1}{t} \leq \frac{1}{3}$ if there are t solutions, hence the probability of success in this case is more than $\frac{2}{3}$.

This combination routine can be used recursively to obtain the label we want.

Linear Number of Queries. Algorithm 3 can directly produce the label 1 if we choose $k = \lceil \log_2(N) \rceil$ and $B = 2$. In that case, we will either produce 1 or 0 with a uniform probability, as the input labels are uniformly distributed.

If the group has a component which is a small power of two, the previous routine can be used with $B = 1$ in order to force the odd cyclic component at zero. Then the algorithms of [10] can be used, with a negligible overhead.

Overall, the routine can generate the label 1 using $\log_2(N)$ queries with probability one half. This also requires to solve a subset-sum instance, which can be done in only $\widetilde{O}\left(2^{0.291\log_2(N)}\right)$ classical time and memory [2].

We need to obtain $\log_2(N)$ labels, and then we can apply the Quantum Fourier Transform as before, to recover s, with a success probability $\frac{4}{\pi^2}$. So we expect to reproduce this final step 3 times. The total number of queries will be $8\log_2(N)^2$, with a classical time and memory cost in $\widetilde{O}\left(2^{0.291\log_2(N)}\right)$.

We note that this variant is the most efficient in quantum resources, as we limit the quantum queries to a polynomial amount. The classical complexity remains exponential, but we replace the complexity of a collision search (with an exponent of 0.5) by that of the subset-sum problem (an exponent of 0.291). In the case $N \simeq 2^{256}$ (CSIDH-512), by taking into account the success probability of the final Quantum Fourier Transform, we obtain 2^{19} quantum queries and 2^{86} classical time and memory.

Time/Query Tradeoffs. There are many possible tradeoffs, as we can adjust the number of steps and their sizes. For example, we can proceed in two steps: the first step will produce labels smaller than $\sqrt{N}$, and the second will use them to produce the label 1. The subset-sum part of each step, done classically, will cost $\widetilde{O}\left(2^{0.291\log_2(N)/2}\right)$ time and memory, and it has to be repeated $\log(N)^2/4$ times per label. Hence, the total cost in queries is in $O(\log(N)^3)$, with a classical time and memory cost in $\widetilde{O}\left(2^{0.291\log_2(N)/2}\right)$.

For $N \simeq 2^{256}$, we can use Algorithm 3 to obtain roughly 130 labels that are smaller than 2^{128}, and then apply Algorithm 3 on them to obtain the label 1. We can estimate the cost to be roughly 2^{24} quantum queries, 2^{60} classical time and 2^{45} memory.

This method generalizes to any number of steps. If we want a subexponential classical time, then the number of steps has to depend on N. Many tradeoffs are possible, depending on the resources of the quantum attacker (see [9]).

3.4 Kuperberg's Second Algorithm

This section revisits the algorithm from [32] and builds upon tradeoffs developed in [9]. We remark that the previous labeled qubits $|\psi_\ell\rangle$ were a particular case of qubit registers of the form

$$|\psi_{(\ell_0,\dots,\ell_{k-1})}\rangle = \frac{1}{\sqrt{k}}\sum_{0\le i\le k-1}\chi\left(s\frac{\ell_i}{N}\right)|i\rangle.$$

These multi-labeled qubit registers become the new building blocks. They are not indexed by a label ℓ, but by a vector $(\ell_0,\dots,\ell_{k-1})$. We can remark that if we consider the joint state (tensor) of j single-label qubits $|\psi_{\ell_i}\rangle$, we directly obtain a multi-labeled qubit register of this form:

Algorithm 4. A general combination routine

> **Input:** $(|\psi_{(\ell_0,\ldots,\ell_{M-1})}\rangle, |\psi_{(\ell'_0,\ldots,\ell'_{M-1})}\rangle) : \forall i, \ell_i < 2^a, \ell'_i < 2^a, r$
>
> **Output:** $|\psi_{(v_0,\ldots,v_{M'-1})}\rangle : \forall i, v_i < 2^{a-r}$
>
> 1: Tensor $|\psi_{(\ell_0,\ldots,\ell_{M-1})}\rangle |\psi_{(\ell'_0,\ldots,\ell'_{M-1})}\rangle = \sum_{i,j=0}^{M-1} \chi\left(\frac{s(\ell_i+\ell'_j)}{N}\right) |i\rangle|j\rangle$
> 2: Add an ancilla register, apply $|i\rangle|j\rangle|0\rangle \mapsto |i\rangle|j\rangle|\lfloor(\ell_i+\ell'_j)/2^{a-r}\rfloor\rangle$
> 3: Measure the ancilla register, leaving with
>
> $$V \text{ and } \sum_{i,j:\lfloor(\ell_i+\ell'_j)/2^{a-r}\rfloor=V} \chi\left(\frac{s(\ell_i+\ell'_j)}{N}\right) |i\rangle|j\rangle$$
>
> 4: Compute the M' corresponding pairs (i,j)
> 5: Apply to the state a transformation f from (i,j) to $[0; M'-1]$.
> 6: Return the state and the vector v with $v_{f(i,j)} = \ell_i + \ell'_j$.

$$\bigotimes_{0 \leq i \leq j-1} |\psi_{\ell_i}\rangle = \left|\psi_{\left(\ell'_0,\ldots,\ell'_{2^j-1}\right)}\right\rangle, \quad \text{with } \ell'_k = k \cdot (\ell_0,\ldots,\ell_{j-1}).$$

These registers can again be combined by computing and measuring a partial sum, as in Algorithm 4. While Algorithm 3 was essentially a subset-sum routine, Algorithm 4 is a 2-list merging routine. Step 4 simply consists in iterating trough the sorted lists of $(\ell_0,\ldots,\ell_{M-1})$ and $(\ell'_0,\ldots,\ell'_{M-1})$ to find the matching values (and this is exactly a classical 2-list problem). Hence, it costs $\widetilde{O}(M)$ classical time, with the lists stored in classical memory. The memory cost is $\max(M, M')$. The quantum cost comes from the computation of the partial sum and from the relabeling. Both can be done sequentially, in $O(\max(M, M'))$ quantum time.

This routine can also be generalized to merge more than two lists. The only difference will be that at Step 4, we will need to apply another list-merging algorithm to find all the matching values. In particular, if we merge $4k$ lists, we can use the Schroeppel-Shamir algorithm [43], to obtain the solutions in $O(M^{2k})$ classical time and $O(M^k)$ classical memory.

Once we are finished, we project the vector to a pair of values with difference 1, as in Algorithm 3, with the same success probability, better than $1/3$.

Complete Algorithm. The complete algorithm uses Algorithm 4 recursively. As before, the final cost depends on the size of the lists, the number of steps and the number of lists we merge at each step. Then, we can see the algorithm as a merging tree.

The most time-efficient algorithms use 2-list merging. The merging tree is binary, the number of lists at each level is halved. We can save some time if we allow the lists to double in size after a merging step. In that case, the merging of two lists of size 2^m to one list of size 2^{m+1} allows to constrain $m-1$ bits[2],

---

[2] As in the end, we only need a list of size two, the bit we lose here is regained in the last step.

at a cost of $O(2^m)$ in classical and quantum time and classical memory. If we have e levels in the tree and begin with lists of size 2^{ℓ_0}, then the quantum query cost is $\ell_0 2^e$. The time cost will be in $\widetilde{O}\left(2^{\ell_0+e}\right)$, as the first step is performed 2^e times, the second 2^{e-1} times, and so on.

Allowing the lists to grow saves some time, but costs more memory. To save memory, we can also combine lists and force the output lists to be of roughly the same size. Hence, the optimal algorithm will double the list sizes in the first levels until the maximal memory is reached, when the list size has to stay fixed.

Overall, let us omit polynomial factors and denote the classical and quantum time as 2^t. We use at most 2^m memory and make 2^q quantum queries, begin with lists of size 2^{ℓ_0} and double the list sizes until we reach 2^m. Hence, the list size levels are distributed as in Fig. 1. We have q equal to the number of levels, and t equals the number of levels plus ℓ_0. As each level constrains as many bits as the log of its list size, the total amount of bits constrained by the algorithm corresponds to the hatched area.

Fig. 1. Size of the lists in function of the tree level, in $\log_2$ scale, annotated with the different parameters.

Hence, with $\max(m, q) \leq t \leq m + q$, we can solve the hidden shift problem for $N < 2^n$ with

$$-\frac{1}{2}(t - m - q)^2 + mq = n$$

We directly obtain the cost of $\widetilde{O}\left(2^{\sqrt{2n}}\right)$ from [32] if we consider $t = m = q$.

Classical/Quantum Tradeoffs. The previous approach had the inconvenience of using equal classical and quantum times, up to polynomial factors. In practice, we can expect to be allowed more classical operations than quantum gates. We can obtain different tradeoffs by reusing the previous 2-list merging tree, and seeing it as a 2^k-list merging tree. That is, we see k levels as one, and merge the 2^k lists at once. This allows to use the Schroeppel-Shamir algorithm for merging, with a classical time in $2^{2^k/2}$ and a classical memory in $2^{2^k/4}$. This operation is purely classical, as we are computing lists of labels, and it does not impact the quantum cost. Moreover, while we used to have a constraint on $\log(k)m$ bits, we now have a constraint on $(k-1)m$ bits.

For $k = 2$, omitting polynomial factors, with a classical time of 2^{2t} and quantum time of 2^t, a memory of 2^m, a number of quantum queries of 2^q and $\max(m, q) \leq t \leq m + q$, we can solve the hidden shift problem for $N < 2^n$ with

$$-\frac{1}{2}(t - m - q)^2 + mq = 2n/3.$$

In particular, if we consider that $t = m = q$, we obtain an algorithm with a quantum time and query and classical memory complexity of $\widetilde{O}(2^2\sqrt{\frac{n}{3}})$ and a classical time complexity of $\widetilde{O}(2^4\sqrt{\frac{n}{3}})$, and if we consider that $t = 2m = 2q$, we obtain a quantum query and classical memory cost in $\widetilde{O}(2\sqrt{\frac{2n}{3}})$, a classical time in $\widetilde{O}(2^4\sqrt{\frac{2n}{3}})$ and a quantum time in $\widetilde{O}(2^2\sqrt{\frac{2n}{3}})$.

Concrete Estimates. If we consider $N \simeq 2^{256}$, with the 2-list merging method we can succeed with 2^{23} initial lists of size 2. We double the size of the list at each level until we obtain a list of size 2^{24}. In that case, we obtain classical and quantum time cost in 2^{39}, a classical memory in 2^{29} and 2^{34} quantum queries.

Using the 4-list merging, we can achieve the same in 10 steps with roughly 2^{55} classical time, 2^{23} classical memory, 2^{35} quantum time, 2^{31} quantum queries.

Other tradeoffs are also possible. We can reduce the number of queries by beginning with larger lists. We can also combine the k-list approach with the subset-sum approach to reduce the quantum time (or the classical memory, if we use a low-memory subset-sum algorithm).

For example, if we consider a 4-level tree, with a 4-list merging, an initial list size of 2^{24} and lists that quadruple in size, the first combination step can constrain $24 \times 3 - 2 = 70$ bits, the second $26 \times 3 - 2 = 76$ and the last $28 \times 4 - 1 = 111$ bits (for the last step, we do not need to end with a large list, but only with an interesting element, hence we can constrain more). We bound the success probability by the success probability of one complete merging (greater than $1/3$) times the success probability of the Quantum Fourier Transform (greater than $\pi^2/4$), for a total probability greater than $1/8$.

The cost in memory is of 2^{30}, as we store at most 4 lists of size 2^{28}. For the number of quantum queries: there are $4^3 = 64$ initial lists in the tree, each costs 24 queries (to obtain a list of 2^{24} labels by combining). We have to redo this 256 times to obtain all the labels we want, and to repeat this 8 times due to the probability of success. Hence, the query cost is $24 \times 64 \times 256 \times 8 \simeq 2^{22}$. The classical time cost is in $256 \times 8 \times 3 \times 2^{28 \times 2} \simeq 2^{69}$. The quantum time cost is in $256 \times 8 \times 3 \times 2^{28} \simeq 2^{41}$.

We summarize the results of this section in Table 2.

Table 2. Hidden shift costs tradeoffs that will be used in the following sections. Quantum memory is only the inherent cost needed by the algorithm and excludes the oracle cost. $n = \log_2(N)$.

Classical time	Classical memory	Quantum memory	Quantum queries	Approach
$1.8\sqrt{n} + 4.3$	$1.8\sqrt{n} + 2.3$	$1.8\sqrt{n} + 2.3$	$1.8\sqrt{n} + 4.3$	Section 3.2
$0.291n + \log_2(n) + 3$	$0.291n$	$\log_2(n)$	$2\log_2(n) + 3$	Section 3.3
$4\sqrt{\frac{2n}{3}} + \log_2(n) + 3$	$\sqrt{2n/3}$	$\log_2(n)$	$\sqrt{\frac{2n}{3}} + \log_2(n) + 3$	Section 3.4

4 Reduction in the Lattice of Relations

This section reviews the lattice reduction technique that allows to go from an arbitrary representation of an ideal class $[x]$ to a representation on a basis of arbitrary ideals: $[x] = [\mathfrak{l}_i]^{x_i}$, with short exponents x_i. This allows to turn an oracle for the CSIDH group action, computing $\prod_i [\mathfrak{l}_i]^{e_i} \cdot E$, into an oracle for the action of $\mathcal{Cl}(\mathcal{O})$.

4.1 The Relation Lattice

Given p and the ideal classes $[\mathfrak{l}_1], \ldots, [\mathfrak{l}_u]$, the integer vectors $\bar{e} = (e_1, \ldots e_u)$ such that $[\mathfrak{l}_1]^{e_1} \ldots [\mathfrak{l}_u]^{e_u} = 1$ form an integer lattice in $\mathbb{R}^u$, that we denote $\mathcal{L}$, the *relation lattice*. This lattice is ubiquitous in the literature on CRS and CSIDH (see [6] or [27] for a CSIDH context).

The lattice $\mathcal{L}$ depends only on the prime parameter p, hence all computations involving $\mathcal{L}$ are precomputations. First, we notice that $\mathcal{L}$ is the kernel of the map: $(e_1, \ldots e_u) \mapsto [\mathfrak{l}_1]^{e_1} \ldots [\mathfrak{l}_u]^{e_u}$. Finding a basis of $\mathcal{L}$ is an instance of the *Abelian Stabilizer Problem*, that Kitaev introduces and solves in [28] in quantum polynomial time.

Lattice Reduction. Next, we compute an approximate short basis B and its Gram-Schmidt orthogonalization B^*. All this information about $\mathcal{L}$ will be stored classically. We compute B using the best known algorithm to date, the Block Korkine Zolotarev algorithm (BKZ) [42]. Its complexity depends on the dimension u and the *block size*, an additional parameter which determines the quality of the basis. For any dimension u, BKZ gives an *approximation factor* c^u for some constant c depending on the block size: $\|b_1\|_2 \leq c^u \lambda_1(\mathcal{L})$ where $\lambda_1(\mathcal{L})$ is the euclidean norm of the smallest vector in $\mathcal{L}$. In our case, assuming that the products $[\mathfrak{l}_i]^{e_i}$ with $-m \leq e_i \leq m$ span the whole class group, one of these falls on 1 and we have: $\lambda_1(\mathcal{L}) \leq 2m\sqrt{u}$.

4.2 Solving the Approximate CVP with a Reduced Basis

In this section, we suppose that a product $\prod_i [\mathfrak{l}_i]^{t_i}$ for some large t_i is given (possibly as large as the cardinality of the class group, hence $O(\sqrt{p})$). In order to evaluate the action of $\prod_i [\mathfrak{l}_i]^{t_i}$, we would like to reduce $\bar{t} = t_1, \ldots t_u$ to a vector $\bar{e} = e_1, \ldots e_u$ with small norm, such that $\prod_i [\mathfrak{l}_i]^{e_i} = \prod_i [\mathfrak{l}_i]^{t_i}$. In other words, we want to solve the approximate closest vector problem (CVP) in $\mathcal{L}$: given the target $\bar{t}$, we search for the closest vector $\bar{v}$ in $\mathcal{L}$ and set $\bar{e} = \bar{v} - \bar{t}$.

Babai's Algorithm. The computation of a short basis B of $\mathcal{L}$ has to be done only once, but the approximate CVP needs to be solved on the fly and for a target $\bar{t}$ in superposition. As in [7], we use a simple polynomial-time algorithm, relying on the quality of the basis B: Babai's nearest-plane algorithm [1]. We detail it in the full version of the paper [11]. Given the target vector $\bar{t}$, B and its Gram-Schmidt orthogonalization B^*, this algorithm outputs in polynomial time a vector $\bar{v}$ in the lattice $\mathcal{L}$ such that $||\bar{v} - \bar{t}||_2 \leq \frac{1}{2}\sqrt{\sum_{i=1}^{u} ||b_i^\star||_2^2}$. This bound holds simultaneously for every target vector $\bar{t}$ and corresponding output $\bar{v}$ (as $\bar{t}$ will actually be a superposition over all targets, this is important for us).

Effect on the L_1 Norm. Our primary concern is the number of isogenies that we compute, so we will measure the quality of our approximation with the L_1 norm of the obtained $\bar{e} = \bar{v} - \bar{t}$. The bound on the L_1 norm is: $||\bar{v} - \bar{t}||_1 \leq \sqrt{u}||\bar{v} - \bar{t}||_2 = \frac{\sqrt{u}}{2}\sqrt{\sum_{i=1}^{u}||b_i^\star||_2^2}$. Naturally, if we manage to solve the exact CVP, and obtain always the closest vector to $\bar{t}$, any evaluation of $[x] \cdot E_A$ will cost exactly the same as an evaluation of $\prod_i [\mathfrak{l}_i]^{e_i} \cdot E_A$ with the bounds on the exponents e_i specified by the CSIDH parameters; hence the class group action collapses to the CSIDH group action.

Our Simulations. We performed simulations by modeling $\mathcal{C}\ell(\mathcal{O})$ as a cyclic group of random cardinality $q \simeq \sqrt{p}$. Then we take u elements at random in this group, of the form g^{a_i} for some generator g and compute two-by-two relations between them, as: $(g^{a_i})^{a_{i+1}} \cdot (g^{a_{i+1}})^{-a_i} = 1$. With such a basis, the computational system Sage [46] performs BKZ reduction with block size 50 in a handful of minutes, even in dimension 200. We compute the L_1 bound $\frac{\sqrt{u}}{2}\sqrt{\sum_{i=1}^{u}||b_i^\star||_2^2}$ for many lattices generated as above, reduced with BKZ-50. We obtain on average, for CSIDH -512, -1024 and -1792 (of dimensions 74, 132 and 209 respectively), 1300, 4000 and 10000. The standard deviation of the values found does not exceed 10%. Notice that the bound is a property of the lattice, so we can take the average here, even though we will apply Babai's algorithm to a superposition of inputs.

Faster Evaluations of the Class Group Action. In the context of speeding up the classical group action, the authors of [5] computed the structure of the class group for CSIDH-512, the relation lattice and a small basis of it. They showed that the class group was cyclic. Given an ideal class $[x]$, they use Babai's algorithm with another refinement [23]. It consists in keeping a list of short vectors and adding them to the output of Babai's algorithm, trying to reduce further the L_1 norm of the result.

In particular for CSIDH-512, they are able to compute vectors of L_1 norm even shorter on average than the original bound of $5 \times 74 = 370$, reaching an average 240 with BKZ-40 reduction. This suggests that, with lattice reduction, there may be actually *less* isogenies to compute than in the original CSIDH group action. However, we need a bound guaranteed for all target vectors, since we are computing in superposition, which is why we keep the bounds of above.

5   A Quantum Circuit for the Class Group Action

In this section, we first analyze the cost of a quantum circuit that evaluates the *CSIDH group action* on a given Montgomery curve E_A represented by $A \in \mathbb{F}_p$:

$$|e_1, \ldots e_u\rangle |A\rangle |0\rangle \mapsto |e_1, \ldots e_u\rangle |A\rangle |L_{\ell_1}^{e_1} \circ \ldots \circ L_{\ell_u}^{e_u}(A)\rangle$$

where L_{ℓ_i} corresponds to applying $[l_i]$ to a given curve, and the e_i are possibly greater than the CSIDH original exponents. We will then move to the *class group action*, which computes $[x] \cdot E_A$ in superposition for any $[x]$.

Following previous literature on the topic [4,41], we count the number of Toffoli gates and logical qubits used, as both are considered the most determinant factors for implementations. Our goal is to give an upper bound of resources for CSIDH-512 and an estimate for any CSIDH parameters, given a prime p of n bits and the sequence of small primes ℓ_i such that $p = 4 \cdot \prod_i \ell_i - 1$.

It was shown in [27] that the group action could be computed in polynomial quantum space. A non-asymptotic study of the gate cost has been done in [4]. However, the authors of [4] were concerned with optimizing a *classical circuit* for CSIDH, without reversibility in mind. This is why the appendix of [4], mentions a bewildering amount of "537503414" logical qubits [4, Appendix C.6] (approx. 2^{29}). In this section, we will show that the CSIDH-512 group action can be squeezed into 40 000 logical qubits.

We adopt a bottom-up approach. We first introduce some significant tools and components, then show how to find, on an input curve E_A, a point that generates a subgroup of order ℓ. We give a circuit for computing an isogeny, a sequence of isogenies, and combine this with lattice reduction to compute the class group action.

5.1 Main Tools

Bennett's Conversion. One of the most versatile tools for converting an irreversible computation into a reversible one is Bennett's time-space tradeoff [3]. Precise evaluations were done in [30,34].

Assume that we want to compute, on an input x of n bits, a sequence $f_{t-1} \circ \dots \circ f_0(x)$, where each f_i can be computed *out of place* with a quantum circuit using T_f Toffoli gates and a ancilla qubits: $|x\rangle|0\rangle \mapsto |x\rangle|f_i(x)\rangle$. We could naturally compute the whole sequence using tn ancilla qubits, but this rapidly becomes enormous. Bennett remarks that we can separate the sequence $f_{t-1} \circ \dots \circ f_0 = G \circ F$, with F and G functions using m_F and m_G ancillas respectively, and compute:

$$
\begin{aligned}
&1.\ |x\rangle\ |F(x)\rangle\ |0\rangle \\
&2.\ |x\rangle\ |F(x)\rangle\ |G \circ F(x)\rangle \\
&3.\ |x\rangle\ |0\rangle\qquad |G \circ F(x)\rangle
\end{aligned}
$$

If T_F and T_G are the respective Toffoli counts of the circuits for F and G, the total is $2T_F + T_G$ and the number of ancillas used is $\max(m_F, m_G) + n$. Afterwards, we cut F and G recursively. Bennett obtains that for any $\epsilon > 0$, an irreversible circuit using S space and running in time T can be converted to a reversible circuit running in time $T^{1+\epsilon}$ and using $O(S \log T)$ space.

Adding One More Step. It often happens for us that the final result of the f_i-sequence is actually not needed, we need only to modify the value of another one-bit register depending on $f_{t-1} \circ \ldots \circ f_0(x)$ (for example, flipping the phase). This means that at the highest level of the conversion, *all* functions are actually uncomputed. This can also mean that we do not compute $f_{t-1} \circ \ldots \circ f_0(x)$, but $f \circ f_{t-1} \circ \ldots \circ f_0(x)$ for some new f. Hence the cost is the same as if we added one more step before the conversion, and often negligible.

Number of Steps Given a Memory Bound. We want to be as precise as possible, so we follow [30]. In general, we are free to cut the t operations in any way, and finding the best recursive way, given a certain ancilla budget, is an optimization problem. Let $B(t, s)$ be the least number of computation steps, for a total Toffoli cost $B(t, s)T_f$, given $sn + m$ available ancilla qubits, to obtain reversibly $f_{t-1} \circ \ldots \circ f_0(x)$ from input x. We have:

Theorem 1 (Adaptation of [30], Theorem 2.1). *$B(t, s)$ satisfies the recursion:*

$$B(t, s) = \begin{cases} 1 \text{ for } t = 1 \text{ and } s \geq 0 \\ \infty \text{ for } t \geq 2 \text{ and } s = 0 \\ \min_{1 \leq k < t} B(k, s) + B(k, s - 1) + B(t - k, s - 1) \text{ for } t \geq 2 \text{ and } s \geq 1 \end{cases}$$

In all the costs formulas that we write below, we add a trade-off parameter s in the memory used and $B(t, s)$ in the time.

Basic Arithmetic Modulo p. The Toffoli cost of the group action oracle is almost totally consumed by arithmetic operations modulo p (a prime of n bits), and in the following, we count the time in multiples of these basic operations. We do not make a difference between multiplication and squaring, as we use a single circuit for both, and denote T_M the Toffoli gate count of a multiplication in $\mathbb{F}_p$, using Q_M ancilla qubits. We also denote T_I the Toffoli count of an inversion and Q_I its ancilla count. As n will remain the same parameter throughout this section, we deliberately omit it in these notations, although T_M, T_I, Q_I, Q_M are functions of n. Note that [4] considers that the inversion modulo p costs an n-bit exponentiation, far more than with the circuit of [41].

Lemma 1 ([41], Table 1). *There is a quantum circuit for (out of place) inversion modulo a prime p of n bits: $|x\rangle|0\rangle \mapsto |x\rangle|x^{-1} \bmod p\rangle$ that uses $T_I = 32n^2 \log_2 n$ Toffoli gates and $Q_I = 5n + 2\lceil \log_2 n \rceil + 7$ qubits.*

This circuit is *out of place*: the input registers are left unchanged, and the result is written on an n-bit output register. Circuits for *in-place* modular addition and doubling are also given in [41] and their Toffoli counts remain in $O(n \log_2 n)$, hence negligible with respect to the multiplications.

We use the best modular multipliers given in [40] with $3n$ qubits and $4n^2$ Toffoli gates (dismissing terms of lower order). Note that, although the paper is focused on in-place multiplication by a classically known Y (*i.e.* computing $|x\rangle \mapsto |xY\rangle$), the same resource estimations apply to the out-of-place multiplication of two quantum registers: $|x\rangle|y\rangle|0\rangle \mapsto |x\rangle|y\rangle|xy\rangle$ (see [40, Section 2.5]). Implementing a controlled multiplication (an additional register chooses to apply it or not) is not much more difficult than a multiplication.

In-place Multiplication. The in-place multiplication: $|x\rangle|y\rangle \mapsto |x\rangle|x \cdot y\rangle$ is not reversible if x is not invertible, and in this case, we can simply rewrite $|y\rangle$ in the output register. We reuse the modular inversion circuit of [41] to compute $|x^{-1}\rangle$. Then we compute $|x \cdot y\rangle$ and erase the $|y\rangle$ register by computing $|x \cdot y \cdot x^{-1}\rangle$.

Lemma 2 (In-place multiplication). *There is a circuit that on input $|x\rangle|y\rangle$ returns $|x\rangle|x \cdot y\rangle$ if x is invertible and $|x\rangle|y\rangle$ otherwise. It uses $T'_M = 2T_M + 2T_I$ Toffoli gates and $Q'_M = Q_I + n$ ancillas.*

Modular Exponentiation. Given a t-bit exponent m, we write $m = \sum_{i=0}^{t-1} m_i 2^i$. We give a circuit that maps $|m\rangle|x\rangle|0\rangle$ to $|m\rangle|x\rangle|x^m\rangle$. Contrary to the modular exponentiation in Shor's algorithm, in our case, both x and m are quantum, which means that we cannot classically precompute powers of x (see *e.g.* [41]).

We use a simple square-and-multiply approach with Bennett's time-space tradeoff. We perform t steps requiring each a squaring and a controlled multiplication by x: on input $|y\rangle|0\rangle|0\rangle$, we compute $|y\rangle|x \cdot y\rangle|0\rangle$ then $|y\rangle|x \cdot y\rangle|0\rangle$, then $|y\rangle|x \cdot y\rangle|(x \cdot y)^2\rangle$ and erase the second register with another multiplication. Hence a single step uses $3T_M$ Toffolis and $Q_M + n$ ancillas.

Lemma 3. *There is a quantum circuit for t-bit modular exponentiation (with quantum input x and m) using $3B(t, s)T_M$ Toffolis and $(s + 1)n + Q_M$ ancillas, where s is a trade-off parameter.*

Legendre Symbol. The Legendre symbol of x modulo p is 1 if x is a square modulo p, -1 if not, 0 if x is a multiple of p. It can be computed as $x^{(p-1)/2}$ mod p. We deduce from Lemma 3, for an n-bit p, a cost of $3B(n, s)T_M$ Toffolis and $(s + 1)n + Q_M$ ancillas for any trade-off parameter s.

Reversible Montgomery Ladder. Most of the work in the group action oracle is spent computing the (x-coordinate of the) m-th multiple of a point P on a Montgomery elliptic curve given by its coefficient A, for a quantum input m. Following the presentation in [4, Section 3.3], made reversible and combined with Bennett's time-space tradeoff, we prove Lemma 4 in the full version of the paper [11]. Notice that mP can be transformed back to affine coordinates with little overhead, since the inversion in $\mathbb{F}_p$ costs $T_I = O\left(n^2 \log n\right)$ Toffolis.

Lemma 4. *There exists a circuit to compute, given A, on input P (a point in affine coordinates) and m (an integer of t bits), the x-coordinate of mP (in projective coordinates), using $15B(t, s)T_M$ Toffolis and $Q_M + 2n + 4sn$ ancilla qubits, where s is a trade-off parameter.*

5.2   Finding a Point of Order ℓ

Given A in input, we want to compute $B = L_\ell(A)$, the coefficient of the curve ℓ-isogenous to A. This requires to find a subgroup of order ℓ of the curve E_A. In CSIDH, this is done by first finding a point P on E_A, then computing $Q = ((p + 1)/\ell)P$. if Q is not the point at infinity, it generates a subgroup of order ℓ.

Quantum Search for a Good Point. Let test(x) be a function that, on input $x \in \mathbb{F}_p^*$, returns 1 if x is the x-coordinate x of such a good point P, and 0 otherwise. We will first build a quantum circuit that on input A and $x \in \mathbb{F}_p^*$, flips the phase: $|A\rangle|x\rangle \mapsto (-1)^{\text{test}(x)}|A\rangle|x\rangle$. We will use this circuit as a test in a modified Grover search.

Testing if P is on the Curve. We compute $x^3 + Ax^2 + x$ using some multiplications and squarings (a negligible amount), then the Legendre symbol of $x^3 + Ax^2 + x$. For exactly half of $\mathbb{F}_p^*$, we obtain 1, which means that x is the x-coordinate of a point on the curve. For the other half, we obtain -1, and x is actually the x-coordinate of a point on its twist.

Multiplication by the Cofactor. Assume that the x-coordinate obtained above is that of a point P on the curve. We compute $Q = ((p+1)/\ell)P$ using our reversible Montgomery ladder. Then, another failure occurs if $Q = \infty$. This happens with probability $1/\ell$. Hence, the probability of success of the sampling-and-multiplication operation is $\frac{1}{2}\left(1 - \frac{1}{\ell}\right)$. In the circuit that we are building right now, we don't need the value of Q, only the information whether $Q = \infty$ or not. Bennett's conversions of both the Legendre symbol computation and the Montgomery ladder can take into account the fact that we merely need to flip the phase of the input vector.

Lemma 5. *There exists a quantum circuit that, on input $|A\rangle|x\rangle$, flips the phase by $(-1)^{\text{test}(x)}$, using $15B(n, s)T_M + 3B(n, s')T_M$ Toffolis and $\max(Q_M + 2n + 4sn, (s'+1)n + Q_M)$ ancillas, where s and s' are trade-off parameters.*

With this phase-flip oracle, we can obtain a point of order ℓ with a quantum search. Instead of using Elligator as proposed in [4], we follow the "conventional" approach outlined in [4, Section 4.1], not only because it is simpler, but also because its probability of success is exactly known, which makes the search operator cheaper. More details are given in the full version of the paper [11].

Quantum Search with High Success Probability. We start by generating the *uniform superposition* $\sum_{x \in \mathbb{F}_p^*}|x\rangle$ using a Quantum Fourier Transform (this is very efficient with respect to arithmetic operations). We use a variant of amplitude amplification for the case where the probability of success is high [15]. This variant is exact, but requires to use a phase shift whose angle depends on the success probability.

We know that the proportion of good x is exactly $g = \frac{1}{2}\left(1 - \frac{1}{\ell}\right)$. Normally, a Grover search iteration contains a phase flip and a diffusion transform which, altogether, realize an "inversion about average" of the amplitudes of the vectors in the basis. In [15], this iteration is modified into a controlled-phase operator which multiplies the phase of "good vectors" by $e^{i\gamma}$ instead of -1 and a "β-phase diffusion transform". Then by [15, Theorem 1], if $\frac{1}{4} \leq g \leq 1$ and we set $\beta = \gamma = \arccos(1 - 1/(2g))$, the amplitude of the "bad" subspace is reduced to zero. Such a phase shift can be efficiently approximated with the Solovay-Kitaev algorithm [19]. For a phase shift gate synthesized from Clifford+T gates, we estimate from [29] that it can be approximated up to an error of 2^{-50} using around 2^{14} T-gates, which is negligible compared to the cost of the exponentiation in the test function.

Detecting the Errors. If the error probability is low enough, we can assume that the end state is perfect. However, we can avoid these errors if, after computing the superposition of good points, we reapply the test function, add the result in an ancilla qubit and *measure* this qubit. In general, such a measurement could disrupt the computation. This is not the case here: measuring whether x is a good point for A, while A is in superposition, does not affect the register A, as the set of good points is always of the same size. With probability $\geq 1 - 2^{-50}$ we measure 1 and the state collapses to the exact superposition of good points for the given A. Otherwise we stop the procedure here. When we need to uncompute this procedure, we revert the same single-iteration quantum search and perform the same measurement, with the same success probability.

Lemma 6. *There exists a quantum procedure that, on input (affine) A, finds the x-coordinate x of a "good" point on E_A: $|A\rangle|0\rangle \mapsto |A\rangle(\sum_x |x\rangle)$. It uses $30B(n, s)T_M + 6B(n, 4s)T_M$ Toffolis and $Q_M + 2n + 4sn$ ancillas, and its probability of failure is less than 2^{-50}.*

Proof. This procedure runs as follows (we say "procedure" instead of "circuit", since it contains a measurement):

- Compute the superposition of points $S = \sum_{x \in \mathbb{F}_p^*} |x\rangle$;
- Apply the modified Grover operator: it contains the computation of S (negligible) and the computation of $|x\rangle \mapsto \left(e^{i\gamma}\right)^{\text{test}(x)} |x\rangle$
- We actually do not obtain a single x, but a superposition close to the superposition of suitable x
- Recompute the test in a single-bit ancilla register: $|x\rangle|0\rangle \mapsto |x\rangle|\text{test}(x)\rangle$
- Measure the ancilla register, forcing a collapse on the exact superposition of suitable x.

We set $s' = 4s$ in Lemma 5. All in all, we use two Legendre symbol computations and two n-bit reversible Montgomery ladders. □

5.3 Computing an Isogeny

From the x-coordinate of a point Q on E_A of order ℓ, we can compute the coefficient B of the ℓ-isogenous curve E_B. The details are in the full version of the paper [11].

Lemma 7 (Isogeny from point). *There is a circuit that on input $|A\rangle|Q\rangle|0\rangle$, computes $|A\rangle|Q\rangle|B\rangle$ using $Q_I + (4s + 9)n$ ancilla qubits and*

$$7B\left(\frac{\ell - 1}{2} + 1, s\right)T_M + 6B(\lceil \log_2 \ell \rceil, 4s)T_M + (4\ell - 1)T_I + (4\ell + 3)T_M$$

Toffolis, where s is a tradeoff parameter.

We now put together the last subsections in order to perform an ℓ-isogeny mapping: $|A\rangle|0\rangle \mapsto |A\rangle|L_\ell(A)\rangle$ with overwhelming probability of success *and detectable failure*. We suppose that the *cofactor* $(p + 1)/\ell$ has been classically precomputed. The isogeny computation is performed as follows:

1. On input $|A\rangle$, produce the superposition of good points P, that are on E_A and have order $p + 1$ (detectable failures happen here)
2. On input $|A\rangle|P\rangle$, compute a reversible Montgomery ladder to obtain $Q = ((p + 1)/\ell)P$
3. On input $|A\rangle|Q\rangle$, obtain the coefficient $B = L_\ell(A)$ of the image curve
4. Uncompute the Montgomery ladder for Q
5. Uncompute the superposition of good points (detectable failures happen here)

The ancilla cost of an out of place isogeny computation is the maximum between $n + Q_M + 2n + 4sn$ (computing the good points and the ladder for $Q = ((p+1)/\ell)P$) and $n + Q_I + (4s' + 9)n$ (computing the image curve). We set $s = s'$ in order to use $Q_I + (4s + 11)n$ ancillas at most. Next, we denote $T_\ell(s)$ the Toffoli count of this operation. It sums $60B(n, s) + 12B(n, 4s)T_M$ (computing the good points), the cost of Lemma 7 and $30B(n, s)T_M$ (computing the ladder).

Computing the inverse of an isogeny is not difficult, as noticed in [4], as we have $L_\ell^{-1}(A) = -L_\ell(-A)$. Hence, by doubling the cost, we are able to compute isogenies *in place*. On input $|A\rangle$, we compute $|A\rangle|L_\ell(A)\rangle$, then we compute L_ℓ^{-1} to erase $|A\rangle$. We will see that most of the computation is spent computing the 12 reversible Montgomery ladders $P \mapsto ((p + 1)/\ell)P$.

Lemma 8. *There exists a quantum procedure that performs an ℓ-isogeny mapping in place:* $|A\rangle \mapsto |L_\ell(A)\rangle$ *with an overwhelming probability of success* $(\leq 2^{-50})$ *and detectable failure using* $2T_\ell(s)$ *Toffolis and* $Q_I + (4s+11)n$ *ancillas.*

5.4 Computing a Sequence of Isogenies

Using the computation in place of L_{ℓ_i}, we now compute the image of an input A by a sequence of isogenies, described by $\bar{e} = e_1, \ldots e_u$:

$$|e_1, \ldots e_u\rangle|A\rangle \mapsto |e_1, \ldots e_u\rangle|L_{\ell_1}^{e_1} \circ \ldots \circ L_{\ell_u}^{e_u}(A)\rangle.$$

If we need to apply the backwards and not the forwards isogeny (e_i is negative), we apply $L_{\ell_i}^{-1}(A) = -L_{\ell_i}(-A)$, so we just need to change the signs of the registers, in place, with negligible overheads (in computations and qubits). In general, contrary to the standard CSIDH key-exchange, we do not have a guarantee on $\max_i e_i$. Instead, we only know that $\|\bar{e}\|_1 = \sum_i |e_i| \leq M$ for some bound M. We follow the idea of [4] of having a single quantum circuit for *any* ℓ_i-isogeny computation, controlled by which isogeny we want to apply. Given an input vector $e_1, \ldots e_u$, we apply isogenies one by one by decrementing always the top nonzero exponent (or incrementing it, if it is negative).

Since the procedure for the isogeny sequence considers all cases in superposition, it will always apply exactly M controlled isogenies, depending only on the promised bound M. Contrary to modular exponentiation, we don't need a time-space tradeoff for this sequence of computations, as isogenies can be computed in place (Lemma 8). Finally, if single isogenies fail with probability f, the total failure probability is lower than Mf.

A Constant Success Probability is Enough. The success probability 2^{-50} given Lemma 8 is actually more than enough. Indeed, *failures are detected* and *failed oracle queries can be discarded*. One should note that the quantum hidden shift algorithms that apply to the cryptanalysis of CSIDH precisely allow this, since they start by applying the oracle many independent times before combining the results. Before the combination step, we can discard all the failed queries and the complexity is only multiplied by $1/(1 - (Mf))$. Hence, compared to [4], we do not only obtain a better success probability in a simpler way using quantum search, but we also reduce considerably the required success rate. In our case, we expect $M \lll 2^{50}$, a negligible failure probability, hence a negligible overhead.

Finally, we can transform the CSIDH group action into the class group action, using the lattice reduction technique of Sect. 4. We show in the full version of the paper [11] that, using [27] and Babai's algorithm together, we can achieve a negligible computational and memory overhead.

Lemma 9 (Group action). *Let M be the L_1 bound obtained by reducing the lattice of relations. Assume that $M \lll 2^{50}$ and ℓ is the maximal small prime used. Then there exists a quantum circuit for the class group action using $2MT_\ell(s)$ Toffolis and $Q_I + (4s + 11)n$ ancillas, where s is an integer trade-off parameter, with negligible probability of failure.*

6   Estimating the Security of CSIDH Parameters

In this section, we assess the quantum security of the original parameters proposed in [12]. We count the number of T-gates necessary to attack CSIDH and compare to the targeted security levels.

6.1   Cost of the Group Action Oracle

In CSIDH-512, the base prime p has $n = 511$ bits, and there are $u = 74$ small primes whose maximum is $\ell = 587$. We will first count the number of Toffoli gates required in terms of T_M and T_I, before plugging the cost of a reversible multiplication modulo p.

In Sect. 4, we have estimated that Babai's algorithm would return a vector of L_1 norm smaller than 1300. Hence, the oracle of Lemma 9 needs to apply $M = 1300$ in-place isogenies, more than the $74 \cdot 5 = 370$ required by the "legitimate" group action. We choose $s = 15$ in Lemma 9. Using Lemma 1, we compute $B(512, 15) = 3553$ and $B(512, 60) = 1925$. We further have $\lceil \log_2 \ell \rceil = 10$ and $B(10, 60) = 17$, $(\ell + 1)/2 = 294$ and $B(294, 15) = 1809$. For a single in-place isogeny, the number of multiplications is: $639540 = 2^{19.3}$ for the Montgomery ladders, 46200 for the Legendre symbols, 30232 for computing the isogeny from a point, and there are 4694 inversions. For 1300 isogenies, we need $2^{29.8}$ multiplications, among which $2^{29.6}$ for the Montgomery ladders. There are approximately 38912 ancillas. A 512-bit multiplication costs 2^{20} Toffoli [40], hence the 512-bit class group action can be performed with $2^{49.8}$ Toffoli gates, *i.e.* $2^{52.6}$ T-gates.

Time Complexity for CSIDH-1024 and CSIDH-1792. Since the time is dominated by the Montgomery ladders, and $Q_I \simeq 5n$, we simplify the Toffoli cost of an isogeny into $180B(n,s)T_M$ and the ancilla cost into $(4s + 16)n$. We compute $B(n,s)$ for various values of s and propose the trade-offs of Table 3.

Table 3. Quantum time and qubits for the *class group action* for the original CSIDH parameters (computed with the simplified formula). We put in bold the trade-offs selected for the next section.

Bit-size n of p	Number M of isogenies	T_M	s	$B(n,s)$	Toffoli gates	T-gates	Ancilla qubits
512	1300	2^{20}	15	3553	$2^{49.6}$	$2^{52.4}$	**< 40 000**
1024	4000	2^{22}	10	27231	$2^{56.2}$	$2^{59.0}$	< 60 000
1024	4000	2^{22}	15	10465	$2^{54.8}$	$2^{57.6}$	**< 80 000**
1792	10 000	$2^{23.6}$	11	51953	$2^{60.1}$	$2^{62.9}$	**< 110 000**
1792	10 000	$2^{23.6}$	15	22753	$2^{58.9}$	$2^{61.7}$	< 140 000

6.2 Attacking CSIDH

The parameters in [12] are aimed at three security levels defined by the NIST call [37]: NIST 1 should be as computationally hard as recovering the secret key of AES-128 (with quantum or classical resources), NIST 3 should be as hard as key-recovery of AES-192 and NIST 5 key-recovery of AES-256. The NIST call referred to quantum estimates of [25], but they have been improved in [33]. We plug our class group action oracle into the three quantum hidden shift algorithms of Sects. 3.2, 3.3 and 3.4, and compute the resulting complexities (note that, in terms of quantum time, we compare only the T-gate counts). The results are summarized in Table 4.

The first generic hidden-shift algorithm that we presented (Sect. 3.2) uses a large amount of quantum memory (resp. 2^{31}, 2^{43} and 2^{56} qubits), as it needs to store all of its labeled qubits. Besides, as the quantum queries are very costly in the case of CSIDH, it is advantageous to reduce their count, even by increasing the classical complexity.

With the variant of Sect. 3.3, we see that the quantum query complexity decreases dramatically. If N is the cardinality of the class group (roughly $\sqrt{p}$), we solve $8(\log_2 N)$ classical subset-sum instances on $\log_2 N$ bits (one for each label produced before the final QFT, and a success probability of $\frac{1}{8}$ in total), each of which costs $2^{0.291 \log_2 N}$.[3] We make a total $8(\log_2 N)^2$ quantum oracle queries. The quantum memory used depends only on the quantum oracle implementation.

---

[3] In classical time complexities, contrary to quantum time complexities, we dismiss the subset-sum polynomial factor, as we dismiss the cost of a single AES query, which is a standard approach.

Table 4. Attack trade-offs, in $\log_2$ scale, rounded to the first decimal. "$<$" in the quantum memory complexity means that the memory comes mainly from the oracle. We put in bold the most significant trade-offs that we obtained for each variant.

Conjectured level of security in [12] and corresp. resources			Attacks of this paper					
	C. time	T-gates [33]	Hidden shift variant	Quant. queries	T-gates		C. time	Q. mem
NIST 1 CSIDH- 512	128	81.6	Section 3.2	33	$33 + 52.6 = 85.6$		33	31
			Section 3.3	**19**	$\mathbf{19 + 52.6 = 71.6}$		86	< 15.3
			Section 3.4	24	$24 + 52.6 = 76.6$		63	< 15.3
NIST 3 CSIDH- 1024	192	114.7	Section 3.2	45	$45 + 57.6 = 102.6$		45	43
			Section 3.3	21	$21 + 57.6 = 78.6$		161	< 16.3
			Section 3.4	**30.5**	$\mathbf{30.5 + 57.6 = 88.1}$		86	< 16.3
NIST 5 CSIDH- 1792	256	147.0	Section 3.2	58	$58 + 62.9 = 120.9$		58	56
			Section 3.3	22	$22 + 62.9 = 84.9$		274	< 16.7
			Section 3.4	**37**	$\mathbf{37 + 62.9 = 99.9}$		111	< 16.7

Going further, we can trade between classical and quantum cost with the algorithm of Sect. 3.4. We use 4-list merging, equal quantum query and classical memory costs (excluding polynomial factors). Hence we consider lists of size $2^{\sqrt{2\log_2(N)/3}}$ everywhere and $\sqrt{\log_2(N)/6}$ steps, obtaining the costs of Table 4 with respectively 2^{18}, 2^{25} and 2^{31} classical memory.

6.3 Going Further

All the parameter sizes proposed in [12] fall below their targeted security levels. In Table 4, we see that the best strategy to apply varies with the size of the parameter p. With the small instance CSIDH-512, it is better to reduce at most the number of quantum queries, even if it means increasing the classical time complexity. With CSIDH-1792, the variant of Sect. 3.3 with a polynomial number of quantum queries cannot be applied anymore, due to a too high classical complexity. However, the trade-off that we propose with Kuperberg's second algorithm (Sect. 3.4) allows to attack CSIDH-1024 and CSIDH-1792 with a significant quantum advantage. In order to meet the NIST security levels, the bit-size of the parameter p needs to be increased.

For CSIDH-512, it seems unlikely to us that the query count of 2^{19} may be significantly decreased; however, there is room for improvement in the quantum oracle. Currently, our oracle performs 1300 in-place isogeny computations, each of which requires 12 Montgomery ladders with 512 steps. With more precise estimations, and improving our current use of Babai's algorithm, one might reduce the number of isogenies down to ~240 [5]. But this would require to implement the algorithm of [23] as a quantum circuit and requires further investigation. We use currently 40 000 logical qubits; this could be reduced with more aggressive optimizations (for example, using *dirty* ancillas that don't need to start in the state $|0\rangle$). We also notice that in general, quantum multiplication circuits are optimized in order to use few ancilla qubits, with Shor's algorithm in mind. In the case of CSIDH, the prime p is smaller than an RSA modulus, but the number of ancillas can be higher, and different trade-offs might be used.

7   Conclusion

We performed the first non-asymptotic quantum security assessment of CSIDH, a recent and promising key-exchange primitive based on supersingular elliptic curve isogenies. We presented the main variants of quantum commutative hidden shift algorithms, which are used as a building block in attacking CSIDH. There are many tradeoffs in quantum hidden shift algorithms. This makes the security analysis of CSIDH all the more challenging, and we tried to be as exhaustive as possible regarding the current literature.

We gave tradeoffs, estimates and experimental simulations of their complexities. Next, we gave a quantum procedure for the *class group action oracle* in CSIDH, completing and extending the previous literature. Consequently, we were able to propose the first non-asymptotic cost estimates of attacking CSIDH.

Comparing these to the targeted security levels, as defined in the ongoing NIST call, we showed that the parameters proposed [12] did not meet these levels. We used different trade-offs between classical and quantum computations depending on the parameters targeted. In particular, the CSIDH-512 proposal is *at least* 1 000 times easier to break quantumly than AES-128, using a variant *polynomial* in quantum queries and *exponential* in classical computations.

Safe Instances. The minimal size for which the attacks presented here are out of reach is highly dependent both on the way we estimate the costs (as they are subexponential) and the interpretation of the NIST metrics. In particular, does NIST 1 allows for a classical part with $\text{Time} = \text{Memory} = 2^{128}$, or only $\text{Time} \times \text{Memory} = 2^{128}$? Moreover, the oracle cost vastly depends on the amount of qubits used inside.

We can propose two sets of parameters for security level NIST 1: one aggressive, and one conservative. If we consider that NIST 1 allows for a classical time-memory product of 2^{128}, 2^{20} quantum queries and we neglect the polynomial factors, then the minimal size would be $p \sim 2260$ bits, which corresponds to a multiplication by 4 of the parameter size. Our best attack would use Kuperberg's second algorithm and 2-list merging, at a cost of 2^{69} classical time, 2^{59} classical memory, 2^{20} quantum queries and 2^{18} qubits.

For a more conservative estimation, we can consider that classical time can reach 2^{128} and classical memory 2^{64}, that the quantum oracle for CISDH can be reduced down to 2^{40} T-gates, that a quantum key recovery on AES-128 costs 2^{80} T-gates (which allows for 2^{40} queries and 2^{80} quantum time), and neglect polynomial factors. Then this would require $p \sim 5280$ bits, that is, multiplying by 10 the parameter size. Our best attack uses 4-list merging in Kuperberg's second algorithm, for a cost in classical time of 2^{128}, 2^{64} classical memory, 2^{40} quantum queries, and as many qubits as required by the hypothetical improved CSIDH oracle.

Acknowledgements. The authors want to thank María Naya-Plasencia for her helpful comments, Alain Couvreur and Jean-Pierre Tillich for helpful discussions on isogeny-based cryptography, Lorenz Panny and Joost Renes for their valuable comments on a draft of this paper. Thanks to Jean-François Biasse for pointing out the reference [6], Luca De Feo, Ben Smith and Steven Galbraith for helpful comments on Kuperberg's algorithm and discussions on the NIST benchmark. Thanks to the anonymous Eurocrypt referees for helpful remarks.

This project has received funding from the European Research Council (ERC) under the European Union's Horizon 2020 research and innovation programme (grant agreement n° 714294 - acronym QUASYModo).

References

1. Babai, L.: On Lovász' lattice reduction and the nearest lattice point problem. Combinatorica **6**(1), 1–13 (1986). https://doi.org/10.1007/BF02579403
2. Becker, A., Coron, J.-S., Joux, A.: Improved generic algorithms for hard knapsacks. In: Paterson, K.G. (ed.) EUROCRYPT 2011. LNCS, vol. 6632, pp. 364–385. Springer, Heidelberg (2011). https://doi.org/10.1007/978-3-642-20465-4_21
3. Bennett, C.H.: Time/space trade-offs for reversible computation. SIAM J. Comput. **18**(4), 766–776 (1989)
4. Bernstein, D.J., Lange, T., Martindale, C., Panny, L.: Quantum circuits for the CSIDH: optimizing quantum evaluation of isogenies. In: Ishai, Y., Rijmen, V. (eds.) EUROCRYPT 2019. LNCS, vol. 11477, pp. 409–441. Springer, Cham (2019). https://doi.org/10.1007/978-3-030-17656-3_15
5. Beullens, W., Kleinjung, T., Vercauteren, F.: CSI-FISh: efficient isogeny based signatures through class group computations. IACR Cryptology ePrint Archive 2019, 498 (2019). https://eprint.iacr.org/2019/498
6. Biasse, J.F., Fieker, C., Jacobson, M.J.: Fast heuristic algorithms for computing relations in the class group of a quadratic order, with applications to isogeny evaluation. LMS J. Comput. Math. **19**(A), 371–390 (2016)
7. Biasse, J.F., Iezzi, A., Jacobson, M.J.: A note on the security of CSIDH. In: Chakraborty, D., Iwata, T. (eds.) INDOCRYPT 2018. LNCS, vol. 11356, pp. 153–168. Springer, Cham (2018). https://doi.org/10.1007/978-3-030-05378-9_9
8. Biasse, J.F., Bonnetain, X., Pring, B., Schrottenloher, A., Youmans, W.: A trade-off between classical and quantum circuit size for an attack against CSIDH. J. Math. Cryptol. (2020, to appear)
9. Bonnetain, X.: Improved low-qubit hidden shift algorithms. CoRR abs/1901.11428 (2019). http://arxiv.org/abs/1901.11428
10. Bonnetain, X., Naya-Plasencia, M.: Hidden shift quantum cryptanalysis and implications. In: Peyrin, T., Galbraith, S. (eds.) ASIACRYPT 2018. LNCS, vol. 11272, pp. 560–592. Springer, Cham (2018). https://doi.org/10.1007/978-3-030-03326-2_19

11. Bonnetain, X., Schrottenloher, A.: Quantum security analysis of CSIDH. IACR Cryptology ePrint Archive 2018, 537 (2018). https://eprint.iacr.org/2018/537
12. Castryck, W., Lange, T., Martindale, C., Panny, L., Renes, J.: CSIDH: an efficient post-quantum commutative group action. In: Peyrin, T., Galbraith, S. (eds.) ASIACRYPT 2018. LNCS, vol. 11274, pp. 395–427. Springer, Cham (2018). https://doi.org/10.1007/978-3-030-03332-3_15
13. Charles, D.X., Lauter, K.E., Goren, E.Z.: Cryptographic hash functions from expander graphs. J. Cryptol. **22**(1), 93–113 (2009). https://doi.org/10.1007/s00145-007-9002-x
14. Cheung, K.K.H., Mosca, M.: Decomposing finite Abelian groups. Quantum Inf. Comput. **1**(3), 26–32 (2001). http://portal.acm.org/citation.cfm?id=2011341
15. Chi, D.P., Kim, J.: Quantum database search by a single query. In: Williams, C.P. (ed.) QCQC 1998. LNCS, vol. 1509, pp. 148–151. Springer, Heidelberg (1999). https://doi.org/10.1007/3-540-49208-9_11
16. Childs, A.M., Jao, D., Soukharev, V.: Constructing elliptic curve isogenies in quantum subexponential time. J. Math. Cryptol. **8**(1), 1–29 (2014)
17. Cohen, H., Lenstra, H.W.: Heuristics on class groups of number fields. In: Jager, H. (ed.) Number Theory Noordwijkerhout 1983. LNM, vol. 1068, pp. 33–62. Springer, Heidelberg (1984). https://doi.org/10.1007/BFb0099440
18. Couveignes, J.M.: Hard homogeneous spaces. Cryptology ePrint Archive, Report 2006/291 (2006). https://eprint.iacr.org/2006/291
19. Dawson, C.M., Nielsen, M.A.: The Solovay-Kitaev algorithm. Quantum Inf. Comput. **6**(1), 81–95 (2006)
20. De Feo, L., Galbraith, S.D.: SeaSign: compact isogeny signatures from class group actions. In: Ishai, Y., Rijmen, V. (eds.) EUROCRYPT 2019. LNCS, vol. 11478, pp. 759–789. Springer, Cham (2019). https://doi.org/10.1007/978-3-030-17659-4_26
21. De Feo, L., Jao, D., Plût, J.: Towards quantum-resistant cryptosystems from supersingular elliptic curve isogenies. J. Math. Cryptol. **8**(3), 209–247 (2014)
22. Decru, T., Panny, L., Vercauteren, F.: Faster SeaSign signatures through improved rejection sampling. IACR Cryptology ePrint Archive 2018, 1109 (2018)
23. Doulgerakis, E., Laarhoven, T., de Weger, B.: Finding closest lattice vectors using approximate Voronoi cells. In: Ding, J., Steinwandt, R. (eds.) PQCrypto 2019. LNCS, vol. 11505, pp. 3–22. Springer, Cham (2019). https://doi.org/10.1007/978-3-030-25510-7_1
24. Ettinger, M., Høyer, P.: On quantum algorithms for noncommutative hidden subgroups. In: Meinel, C., Tison, S. (eds.) STACS 1999. LNCS, vol. 1563, pp. 478–487. Springer, Heidelberg (1999). https://doi.org/10.1007/3-540-49116-3_45
25. Grassl, M., Langenberg, B., Roetteler, M., Steinwandt, R.: Applying Grover's algorithm to AES: quantum resource estimates. In: Takagi, T. (ed.) PQCrypto 2016. LNCS, vol. 9606, pp. 29–43. Springer, Cham (2016). https://doi.org/10.1007/978-3-319-29360-8_3
26. Jalali, A., Azarderakhsh, R., Kermani, M.M., Jao, D.: Towards optimized and constant-time CSIDH on embedded devices. In: Polian, I., Stöttinger, M. (eds.) COSADE 2019. LNCS, vol. 11421, pp. 215–231. Springer, Cham (2019). https://doi.org/10.1007/978-3-030-16350-1_12
27. Jao, D., LeGrow, J., Leonardi, C., Ruiz-Lopez, L.: A subexponential-time, polynomial quantum space algorithm for inverting the CM group action. J. Math. Cryptol. (2018)
28. Kitaev, A.Y.: Quantum measurements and the Abelian stabilizer problem. Electronic Colloquium on Computational Complexity (ECCC) 3(3) (1996)

29. Kliuchnikov, V., Maslov, D., Mosca, M.: Fast and efficient exact synthesis of single-qubit unitaries generated by Clifford and T gates. Quantum Inf. Comput. **13**(7–8), 607–630 (2013)

30. Knill, E.: An analysis of Bennett's pebble game. CoRR abs/math/9508218 (1995)

31. Kuperberg, G.: A subexponential-time quantum algorithm for the dihedral hidden subgroup problem. SIAM J. Comput. **35**(1), 170–188 (2005)

32. Kuperberg, G.: Another subexponential-time quantum algorithm for the dihedral hidden subgroup problem. In: 8th Conference on the Theory of Quantum Computation, Communication and Cryptography, TQC 2013, Guelph, Canada, 21–23 May 2013, pp. 20–34 (2013). https://doi.org/10.4230/LIPIcs.TQC.2013.20

33. Langenberg, B., Pham, H., Steinwandt, R.: Reducing the cost of implementing AES as a quantum circuit. IACR Cryptology ePrint Archive 2019, 854 (2019)

34. Levin, R.Y., Sherman, A.T.: A note on Bennett's time-space tradeoff for reversible computation. SIAM J. Comput. **19**(4), 673–677 (1990)

35. Meyer, M., Campos, F., Reith, S.: On Lions and Elligators: an efficient constant-time implementation of CSIDH. Cryptology ePrint Archive, Report 2018/1198 (2018). https://eprint.iacr.org/2018/1198

36. Meyer, M., Reith, S.: A faster way to the CSIDH. In: Chakraborty, D., Iwata, T. (eds.) INDOCRYPT 2018. LNCS, vol. 11356, pp. 137–152. Springer, Cham (2018). https://doi.org/10.1007/978-3-030-05378-9_8

37. NIST: Submission requirements and evaluation criteria for the post-quantum cryptography standardization process (2016). https://csrc.nist.gov/CSRC/media/Projects/Post-Quantum-Cryptography/documents/call-for-proposals-final-dec-2016.pdf

38. Peikert, C.: He gives C-Sieves on the CSIDH. IACR Cryptology ePrint Archive 2019, 725 (2019)

39. Regev, O.: A subexponential time algorithm for the dihedral hidden subgroup problem with polynomial space. CoRR (2004). http://arxiv.org/abs/quant-ph/0406151

40. Rines, R., Chuang, I.: High performance quantum modular multipliers. CoRR abs/1801.01081 (2018). http://arxiv.org/abs/1801.01081

41. Roetteler, M., Naehrig, M., Svore, K.M., Lauter, K.: Quantum resource estimates for computing elliptic curve discrete logarithms. In: Takagi, T., Peyrin, T. (eds.) ASIACRYPT 2017. LNCS, vol. 10625, pp. 241–270. Springer, Cham (2017). https://doi.org/10.1007/978-3-319-70697-9_9

42. Schnorr, C., Euchner, M.: Lattice basis reduction: improved practical algorithms and solving subset sum problems. Math. Program. **66**, 181–199 (1994)

43. Schroeppel, R., Shamir, A.: A $T = O(2^{n/2})$, $S = O(2^{n/4})$ algorithm for certain NP-complete problems. SIAM J. Comput. **10**(3), 456–464 (1981)

44. Shor, P.W.: Algorithms for quantum computation: discrete logarithms and factoring. In: 35th Annual Symposium on Foundations of Computer Science, Santa Fe, New Mexico, USA, 20–22 November 1994, pp. 124–134. IEEE Computer Society (1994). https://doi.org/10.1109/SFCS.1994.365700

45. Stolbunov, A.: Constructing public-key cryptographic schemes based on class group action on a set of isogenous elliptic curves. Adv. Math. Commun. **4**(2), 215–235 (2010). https://doi.org/10.3934/amc.2010.4.215

46. The Sage Developers: SageMath, the Sage Mathematics Software System. http://www.sagemath.org

Rational Isogenies
from Irrational Endomorphisms

Wouter Castryck[1]($\boxtimes$), Lorenz Panny[2]($\boxtimes$), and Frederik Vercauteren[1]($\boxtimes$)

[1] imec-COSIC, KU Leuven, Leuven, Belgium
{wouter.castryck,frederik.vercauteren}@esat.kuleuven.be
[2] Department of Mathematics and Computer Science,
Technische Universiteit Eindhoven, Eindhoven, The Netherlands
lorenz@yx7.cc

Abstract. In this paper, we introduce a polynomial-time algorithm to compute a connecting $\mathcal{O}$-ideal between two supersingular elliptic curves over $\mathbb{F}_p$ with common $\mathbb{F}_p$-endomorphism ring $\mathcal{O}$, given a description of their full endomorphism rings. This algorithm provides a reduction of the security of the CSIDH cryptosystem to the problem of computing endomorphism rings of supersingular elliptic curves. A similar reduction for SIDH appeared at Asiacrypt 2016, but relies on totally different techniques. Furthermore, we also show that any supersingular elliptic curve constructed using the complex-multiplication method can be located precisely in the supersingular isogeny graph by explicitly deriving a path to a known base curve. This result prohibits the use of such curves as a building block for a hash function into the supersingular isogeny graph.

Keywords: Isogeny-based cryptography · Endomorphism rings · CSIDH

1 Introduction

Isogeny-based cryptography is founded on the hardness of computing an isogeny between two isogenous elliptic curves over a finite field $\mathbb{F}_q$. Since this problem appears to remain hard even for quantum computers, it is one of the main candidates for building post-quantum cryptography [26]. Although the origins of isogeny-based cryptography go back to work by Couveignes from 1997 using ordinary elliptic curves [10], the currently most efficient instantiations rely on

Author list in alphabetical order; see https://www.ams.org/profession/leaders/culture/CultureStatement04.pdf. This work was supported in part by the Commission of the European Communities through the Horizon 2020 program under project number 643161 (ECRYPT-NET) and by the Research Council KU Leuven grants C14/18/067 and STG/17/019, and by CyberSecurity Research Flanders with reference number VR20192203. The first listed author was affiliated with the Department of Mathematics at KU Leuven during part of the preparation of this paper.
Date of this document: 2020-02-20.

© International Association for Cryptologic Research 2020
A. Canteaut and Y. Ishai (Eds.): EUROCRYPT 2020, LNCS 12106, pp. 523–548, 2020.
https://doi.org/10.1007/978-3-030-45724-2_18

supersingular curves. These instantiations can be broadly classified into two families, known as SIDH [19] and CSIDH [7], depending on which supersingular elliptic curves and connecting isogenies are being used.

The acronym SIDH is shorthand for "Supersingular-Isogeny Diffie–Hellman", a key-exchange protocol introduced by Jao and De Feo in 2011 [19]. SIDH works in the full supersingular ℓ-isogeny graph, i.e., one considers the graph consisting of all (isomorphism classes of) supersingular elliptic curves defined over $\overline{\mathbb{F}}_p$ for a specifically chosen prime p and connecting isogenies of small prime degree ℓ. The vertices of this graph are the j-invariants of the isomorphism classes and are all contained in $\mathbb{F}_{p^2}$. Finding a path between two given vertices $j(E_1)$ and $j(E_2)$ is equivalent to constructing an isogeny between E_1 and E_2 whose degree is a power of ℓ.

The full endomorphism ring of a supersingular elliptic curve is a maximal order in a quaternion algebra. Kohel, Lauter, Petit and Tignol [22] showed that the above path-finding problem can be solved in (heuristically) expected polynomial time when given the endomorphism rings of E_1 and E_2; we will refer to this algorithm as "KLPT". Galbraith, Petit, Shani and Ti [16] later extended the KLPT algorithm specifically for the SIDH setting and showed that knowledge of the endomorphism rings of E_1 and E_2 suffices to break SIDH. Results by Eisenträger, Hallgren, Lauter, Morrison and Petit [13] show that finding a path in the isogeny graph is essentially equivalent to computing endomorphism rings.

CSIDH stands for "Commutative SIDH" and was introduced by Castryck, Lange, Martindale, Panny, and Renes [7] in 2018. CSIDH restricts the isogeny graph under consideration to supersingular elliptic curves and isogenies *defined over* $\mathbb{F}_p$ and mimics Couveignes' construction of a "hard homogeneous space". In particular, if E is a supersingular elliptic curve over $\mathbb{F}_p$, then its ring of $\mathbb{F}_p$-rational endomorphisms is an imaginary quadratic order $\mathcal{O} \subseteq \mathbb{Q}(\sqrt{-p})$. The C in "CSIDH" refers to the commutativity of $\mathcal{O}$, which (much like the situation on ordinary curves used by Couveignes) gives rise to an action of the (commutative) ideal-class group $\mathrm{cl}(\mathcal{O})$ on the set of supersingular elliptic curves over $\mathbb{F}_p$ with $\mathcal{O}$ as their $\mathbb{F}_p$-rational endomorphisms. This class-group action immediately leads to several cryptographic primitives such as identification, non-interactive key agreement, and even signature schemes.

1.1 Contributions

Our first contribution reduces the key recovery problem in CSIDH to computing the full endomorphism ring of the target curve, where in many cases even one non-$\mathbb{F}_p$-rational endomorphism suffices. More precisely, given two supersingular elliptic curves E, E' over $\mathbb{F}_p$ with $\mathbb{F}_p$-rational endomorphism ring $\mathcal{O}$, assuming sufficient knowledge of their full endomorphism rings $\mathrm{End}(E)$ and $\mathrm{End}(E')$, we show how to compute in polynomial time an ideal $\mathfrak{a} \subseteq \mathcal{O}$ such that $E' = [\mathfrak{a}]E$. This result can be seen as an analogon of [16] for SIDH, but uses different techniques, and in particular it does not rely on the KLPT algorithm [22].

Several remarks on this result are in order:

- In CSIDH all curves have *the same known* $\mathbb{F}_p$-rational endomorphism ring $\mathcal{O}$, which therefore does not contain any information specific to E, nor to $[\mathfrak{a}]$. This explains why we require knowledge of at least one endomorphism of E that is not $\mathbb{F}_p$-rational.
- Since both $\mathrm{End}(E_0)$ and $\mathrm{End}(E)$ are assumed to be known, one can run the KLPT algorithm to obtain an isogeny $\alpha \colon E_0 \to E$. However, this isogeny is most likely not $\mathbb{F}_p$-rational and as such does not correspond to the CSIDH private key. It is easy to verify that the isogeny $\beta = \alpha \circ \pi_{E_0} + \pi_E \circ \alpha$, with π the p-power Frobenius endomorphism on the respective curves, is an $\mathbb{F}_p$-rational isogeny[1] from E_0 to E. Note that β can be evaluated efficiently on points of E_0, but it is unclear how to efficiently derive an invertible ideal $\mathfrak{b} \subseteq \mathcal{O}$ whose action on E_0 corresponds to β. Such an ideal $\mathfrak{b}$ is required to break the CSIDH Diffie–Hellman key agreement and other derived protocols, since it is essentially a curve-independent way of specifying an $\mathbb{F}_p$-rational isogeny.
- Our polynomial-time algorithm returns an ideal $\mathfrak{a}$ whose norm is not necessarily smooth. To efficiently compute the action of $[\mathfrak{a}]$ therefore requires an extra smoothing step, which obtains an ideal of smooth norm in the ideal class $[\mathfrak{a}]$. This smoothing step is standard and consists of a combination of a class-group computation and lattice reduction to solve an instance of the approximate closest-vector problem (CVP). The class-group computation requires subexponential time using classical computers [18], but runs in polynomial time on a quantum computer [21]. Using the BKZ algorithm [28], one can solve the CVP problem up to a subexponential approximation factor in subexponential time. This last step therefore implies that asymptotically, the smoothing step requires subexponential time. However, we note that for any *practical* instantiation of CSIDH, solving the approximate CVP problem can be done fairly efficiently [4].

Our second contribution is motivated by an important open problem in isogeny-based cryptography, namely how to hash into a supersingular isogeny graph without revealing a path to a known base curve. This problem remains open both in the SIDH (full isogeny graph) and the CSIDH ($\mathbb{F}_p$-rational isogeny graph) setting. The hash function introduced by Charles, Goren and Lauter [8] can be used to hash any string into the supersingular isogeny graph, but by construction, the hash function itself leaks an isogeny path from a base curve. To illustrate the issue, we can compare with the standard elliptic-curve discrete-logarithm setting: The equivalent of the CGL construction would start from the public base point $P \in E(\mathbb{F}_q)$ and construct a point Q by multiplying P with a scalar computed deterministically from the message. As such, anyone would know the discrete logarithm of Q with respect to P, which voids cryptographic applications relying on the assumption that the relationship between Q and P cannot be discovered. To remedy this, elliptic-curve cryptosystems instead hash to curve points using maps like Elligator [3], which computes a point directly without passing through a scalar first, but an equivalent of these constructions in isogeny-based cryptography is not known.

---

[1] Unless $\beta = 0$.

Besides the random-walk approach à la CGL, it is also possible to generate supersingular elliptic curves using the complex-multiplication (CM) method [6]. It is therefore natural to wonder whether CM can be useful to hash into the supersingular isogeny graph, and in particular, whether finding paths between the resulting curves could be computationally hard. Our second result squashes this hope by locating these curves (and therefore also a path to a base curve) in the supersingular isogeny graph, in a surprisingly explicit manner (see Theorem 26(iii) for the exact statement).

The remainder of the paper is organized as follows. In Sect. 2 we recall the necessary mathematical background. In Sect. 3 we introduce the notion of twisting endomorphisms and explain their relation to $\mathbb{F}_p$-rational isogenies. Section 4 describes our new algorithm to compute a connecting ideal between two supersingular elliptic curves over $\mathbb{F}_p$ given their endomorphism rings and argues that (at least classically) our approach appears to be optimal. Finally, Sect. 5 shows how to locate supersingular elliptic curves constructed via CM in the isogeny graph, by explicitly deriving a path to a known starting curve.

2   Preliminaries

In this section we recall the required mathematical background and fix notation. Our focus lies on supersingular elliptic curves over finite prime fields $\mathbb{F}_p$, although much of what follows readily generalizes to arbitrary elliptic curves over arbitrary finite fields. Some of the observations below seem new.

For ease of exposition, we shall assume $p > 3$ throughout, noting that this is not necessarily a requirement for all of the statements.

2.1   Quadratic Twisting

For each odd prime number p we fix a non-square element $\xi \in \mathbb{F}_p$ along with a square root $\sqrt{\xi} \in \mathbb{F}_{p^2} \setminus \mathbb{F}_p$; if $p \equiv 3 \pmod{4}$ then our default choice is $\xi = -1$ and we write $\mathbf{i} = \sqrt{-1}$. For an elliptic curve $E: y^2 = f(x)$ over $\mathbb{F}_p$ defined by some squarefree cubic polynomial $f(x) \in \mathbb{F}_p[x]$, we call the curve $E^t: \xi^{-1}y^2 = f(x)$ the *quadratic twist* of E over $\mathbb{F}_p$. The map $\tau_E: E \to E^t$, $(x, y) \mapsto (x, \sqrt{\xi} \cdot y)$ is a non-$\mathbb{F}_p$-rational isomorphism. From $\sqrt{\xi}^p = -\sqrt{\xi}$ one easily sees that

$$\tau_E \circ \pi_E = -\pi_{E^t} \circ \tau_E, \tag{1}$$

with π_E and π_{E^t} the respective Frobenius endomorphisms of E and E^t.

It can exceptionally happen that our definition of the quadratic twist is a trivial twist in the sense of [30, § X.2]:

Lemma 1. *An elliptic curve* $E/\mathbb{F}_p$ *is* $\mathbb{F}_p$-*isomorphic to its quadratic twist* E^t *if and only if* $p \equiv 3 \pmod{4}$ *and* $j(E) = 1728$.

Proof. After an $\mathbb{F}_p$-isomorphism, we can assume $E: y^2 = x^3 + Ax + B$ with $A, B \in \mathbb{F}_p$ satisfying $4A^3 + 27B^2 \neq 0$. Then its quadratic twist is $\mathbb{F}_p$-isomorphic to $y^2 = x^3 + A\xi^2 x + B\xi^3$ for some non-square ξ. According to [30, Prop. III.3.1] this curve is $\mathbb{F}_p$-isomorphic to E if and only if $A\xi^2 = Au^4$ and $B\xi^3 = Bu^6$ for some $u \in \mathbb{F}_p \setminus \{0\}$. This holds if and only if $B = 0$ and ξ^2 is a fourth power, from which the lemma follows. $\qquad\square$

2.2 Hard Homogeneous Spaces from Supersingular Curves

Fix a prime number $p > 3$ and consider the imaginary quadratic number field $K = \mathbb{Q}(\sqrt{-p})$ along with its maximal order $\mathcal{O}_K$. If E is a supersingular elliptic curve defined over $\mathbb{F}_p$, then its ring $\mathrm{End}_p(E)$ of $\mathbb{F}_p$-rational endomorphisms admits an isomorphism to an order $\mathcal{O} \subseteq K$, under which π_E is mapped to $\sqrt{-p}$. In particular, $\mathcal{O}$ always contains the subring $\mathbb{Z}[\sqrt{-p}]$, hence if $p \equiv 1 \pmod 4$ then $\mathcal{O} = \mathcal{O}_K = \mathbb{Z}[\sqrt{-p}]$, while if $p \equiv 3 \pmod 4$ then either $\mathcal{O} = \mathbb{Z}[\sqrt{-p}]$ or $\mathcal{O} = \mathcal{O}_K = \mathbb{Z}[(1+\sqrt{-p})/2]$. We write $\mathcal{Ell}_p(\mathcal{O})$ to denote the set of $\mathbb{F}_p$-isomorphism classes of supersingular elliptic curves having endomorphism $\mathcal{O}$.

Remark 2. If $p \equiv 3 \pmod 4$, then the $\mathbb{F}_p$-endomorphism ring of a supersingular elliptic curve $E/\mathbb{F}_p$ is determined by its 2-torsion; see [12]: either we have $\#E(\mathbb{F}_p)[2] = 2$, in which case $E \in \mathcal{Ell}_p(\mathbb{Z}[\sqrt{-p}])$, or $\#E(\mathbb{F}_p)[2] = 4$, in which case $E \in \mathcal{Ell}_p(\mathbb{Z}[(1+\sqrt{-p})/2])$.

Every such order $\mathcal{O}$ comes equipped with its (ideal-)class group $\mathrm{cl}(\mathcal{O})$, which consists of invertible ideals modulo non-zero principal ideals; the class of an invertible ideal $\mathfrak{a} \subseteq \mathcal{O}$ is denoted by $[\mathfrak{a}]$. The number of elements of $\mathrm{cl}(\mathcal{O})$ is called the class number and denoted by $h(\mathcal{O})$.

Lemma 3. *If $p \equiv 3 \pmod 4$ then $h(\mathcal{O})$ is odd, while if $p \equiv 1 \pmod 4$ then $\mathrm{cl}(\mathcal{O})$ has a unique element of order 2, in particular $h(\mathcal{O})$ is even.*

Proof. This follows from genus theory [11]. $\qquad\square$

Through
$$\mathrm{cl}(\mathcal{O}) \times \mathcal{Ell}_p(\mathcal{O}) \longrightarrow \mathcal{Ell}_p(\mathcal{O}): \quad ([\mathfrak{a}], E) \longmapsto [\mathfrak{a}]E := E/E[\mathfrak{a}]$$
the class group acts in a free and transitive manner on the set $\mathcal{Ell}_p(\mathcal{O})$ of ($\mathbb{F}_p$-isomorphism classes of) supersingular elliptic curves defined over $\mathbb{F}_p$ whose ring of $\mathbb{F}_p$-endomorphisms $\mathrm{End}_p(E)$ is isomorphic to $\mathcal{O}$ [31]. Here $E[\mathfrak{a}]$ denotes the intersection of the kernels of all elements of $\mathfrak{a}$ interpreted as endomorphisms of E; to compute this intersection it suffices to consider a set of generators of $\mathfrak{a}$.

Ignoring constructive issues, this group action (for large enough p) is conjectured to turn $\mathcal{Ell}_p(\mathcal{O})$ into a "hard homogeneous space", in which the following problems are assumed to be computationally infeasible:

Definition 4. (Vectorization problem.) *Given $E, E' \in \mathcal{Ell}_p(\mathcal{O})$, find the ideal class $[\mathfrak{a}] \in \mathrm{cl}(\mathcal{O})$ for which $E' = [\mathfrak{a}]E$.*
(Parallelization problem.) *Given $E, E', E'' \in \mathcal{Ell}_p(\mathcal{O})$, find the elliptic curve $[\mathfrak{a}][\mathfrak{b}]E$ where $[\mathfrak{a}], [\mathfrak{b}] \in \mathrm{cl}(\mathcal{O})$ are such that $E' = [\mathfrak{a}]E$ and $E'' = [\mathfrak{b}]E$.*

The hardness of the parallelization problem naturally relates to the security of the Diffie–Hellman-style key exchange protocol built from the above group action: starting from a publicly known base curve $E \in \mathscr{E}\ell\ell_p(\mathcal{O})$, the two parties Alice and Bob secretly sample $[\mathfrak{a}]$ resp. $[\mathfrak{b}]$ from $\mathrm{cl}(\mathcal{O})$, compute $[\mathfrak{a}]E$ resp. $[\mathfrak{b}]E$, and publish the result. The shared secret is then $[\mathfrak{a}][\mathfrak{b}]E$, which Alice computes as $[\mathfrak{a}]([\mathfrak{b}]E)$ and which Bob computes as $[\mathfrak{b}]([\mathfrak{a}]E)$. Clearly, in order to solve the parallelization problem, it suffices to solve the vectorization problem. On a quantum computer, the converse holds as well [14].

For later use we recall the following rule, which was pointed out in [7, Rem. 5], albeit very briefly and without proof (see also [1, Prop. 3.31]).

Lemma 5. *For all $[\mathfrak{a}] \in \mathrm{cl}(\mathcal{O})$ and all $E \in \mathscr{E}\ell\ell_p(\mathcal{O})$ we have $[\mathfrak{a}]^{-1}E = ([\mathfrak{a}]E^t)^t$.*

Proof. It is convenient to assume that $\mathfrak{a}$ is generated by elements of $\mathbb{Z}[\sqrt{-p}]$, which can be done without loss of generality by scaling with an appropriate principal ideal if needed. We claim that the composition

$$E \xrightarrow{\ \tau_E\ } E^t \longrightarrow E^t/E^t[\mathfrak{a}] = [\mathfrak{a}]E^t \xrightarrow{\ \tau_{[\mathfrak{a}]E^t}\ } ([\mathfrak{a}]E^t)^t$$

is an $\mathbb{F}_p$-rational isogeny whose kernel equals the ideal $\bar{\mathfrak{a}}$ obtained from $\mathfrak{a}$ by complex conjugation. This claim implies the lemma because $\mathfrak{a}\bar{\mathfrak{a}}$ is the principal ideal generated by $\mathrm{N}(\mathfrak{a})$.

Let φ be the middle isogeny $E^t \twoheadrightarrow E^t/E^t[\mathfrak{a}]$. Two applications of (1) yield

$$\pi_{([\mathfrak{a}]E^t)^t} \circ (\tau_{[\mathfrak{a}]E^t} \circ \varphi \circ \tau_E) = (\tau_{[\mathfrak{a}]E^t} \circ \varphi \circ \tau_E) \circ \pi_E,$$

implying the $\mathbb{F}_p$-rationality. One verifies that $a+b\sqrt{-p} \in \mathfrak{a}$ if and only if $a+b\pi_{E^t}$ vanishes on $\ker \varphi$, which holds if and only if $a - b\pi_E$ vanishes on $\ker(\varphi \circ \tau_E)$, from which it follows that $\ker(\tau_{[\mathfrak{a}]E^t} \circ \varphi \circ \tau_E) = \ker(\varphi \circ \tau_E) = E[\bar{\mathfrak{a}}]$. $\qquad\square$

2.3   CSIDH

CSIDH (pronounced "seaside") is an efficient instantiation of the more general supersingular hard-homogeneous-spaces construction described in the previous section. We let $r \in \mathbb{Z}_{\geq 1}$ and consider a prime p of the form $p = 4\ell_1\ell_2\cdots\ell_r - 1$, where the ℓ_i's are distinct odd prime numbers. This implies $p \equiv 3 \pmod 8$, so a priori there are two options for $\mathcal{O}$, namely $\mathbb{Z}[\sqrt{-p}]$ and the maximal order $\mathcal{O}_K = \mathbb{Z}[(1+\sqrt{-p})/2]$. CSIDH chooses the former option. Recall from Remark 2 that this corresponds to supersingular elliptic curves over $\mathbb{F}_p$ having a unique $\mathbb{F}_p$-rational point of order 2.

Remark 6. The set $\mathscr{E}\ell\ell_p(\mathbb{Z}[\sqrt{-p}])$ is sometimes referred to as the "floor", as opposed to $\mathscr{E}\ell\ell_p(\mathbb{Z}[(1+\sqrt{-p})/2])$ which is called the "surface". This terminology comes from the volcano structure of the 2-isogeny graph of supersingular elliptic curves over $\mathbb{F}_p$; see [12]. We stress that CSIDH can be set up equally well on the surface, although a convenient feature of the floor is that each $E \in \mathscr{E}\ell\ell_p(\mathbb{Z}[\sqrt{-p}])$ is $\mathbb{F}_p$-isomorphic to a Montgomery curve $E_A: y^2 = x^3 + Ax^2 + x$ for a unique coefficient $A \in \mathbb{F}_p$; furthermore, the coefficient defining E^t is then given by $-A$.

The prime p was chosen such that the primes $\ell_1, \ell_2, \ldots, \ell_r$ exhibit particularly easy splitting behaviour in $\mathbb{Z}[\sqrt{-p}]$, namely

$$(\ell_i) = (\ell_i, \sqrt{-p} - 1)(\ell_i, \sqrt{-p} + 1). \tag{2}$$

We refer to the respective factors, which are complex conjugates of each other, by $\mathfrak{l}_i$ and $\overline{\mathfrak{l}_i}$. If we define $\ell_0 := 4$ then (2) also applies to $i = 0$, so we can similarly define $\mathfrak{l}_0$ and $\overline{\mathfrak{l}_0}$. All these ideals are clearly invertible, so we can consider their classes $[\mathfrak{l}_i]$ and $[\overline{\mathfrak{l}_i}] = [\mathfrak{l}_i]^{-1}$ inside $\mathrm{cl}(\mathcal{O})$. Although this is not known in general, it seems likely that the $[\mathfrak{l}_i]$'s together generate the entire class group.

Example 7. The concrete instantiation CSIDH-512 from [7] has $r = 74$, where $\ell_1, \ell_2, \ldots, \ell_{73}$ are the odd primes up to 373 and where $\ell_{74} = 587$. This results in a 511-bit prime p. The structure of $\mathrm{cl}(\mathbb{Z}[\sqrt{-p}])$ was computed by Beullens, Kleinjung and Vercauteren [4], who verified that $[\mathfrak{l}_1] = [(3, \sqrt{-p} - 1)]$ is in fact a generator.

The basic idea is then to let Alice and Bob choose their secrets as

$$[\mathfrak{a}] = [\mathfrak{l}_1]^{a_1} [\mathfrak{l}_2]^{a_2} \cdots [\mathfrak{l}_r]^{a_r} \qquad \text{resp.} \qquad [\mathfrak{b}] = [\mathfrak{l}_1]^{b_1} [\mathfrak{l}_2]^{b_2} \cdots [\mathfrak{l}_r]^{b_r},$$

for exponent vectors $(a_1, a_2, \ldots, a_r)$ and $(b_1, b_2, \ldots, b_r)$ sampled at random from some bounded subset of $\mathbb{Z}^r$, for instance uniformly from a hypercube $[-B; B]^r$ of size $(2B+1)^r \approx h(\mathbb{Z}[\sqrt{-p}]) \approx \sqrt{p}$. The resulting public keys and shared secret are then computed using $|a_1| + \ldots + |a_r|$ resp. $|b_1| + \ldots + |b_r|$ repeated actions of $[\mathfrak{l}_i]$ or $[\mathfrak{l}_i]^{-1} = [\overline{\mathfrak{l}_i}]$. If $E \in \mathcal{Ell}_p(\mathbb{Z}[\sqrt{-p}])$ then the subgroups

$$E[\mathfrak{l}_i] = \{ P \in E[\ell_i] \mid \pi_E(P) = P \} = E(\mathbb{F}_p)[\ell_i]$$
$$E[\overline{\mathfrak{l}_i}] = \{ P \in E[\ell_i] \mid \pi_E(P) = -P \}$$

consist of points having $\mathbb{F}_p$-rational x-coordinates; therefore, these actions are easy to evaluate using low-degree Vélu-type formulas and involving only arithmetic in $\mathbb{F}_p$.

As far as we know, the following class group relations have not appeared in the literature before:[2]

Lemma 8. *In* $\mathrm{cl}(\mathbb{Z}[\sqrt{-p}])$*, we have*

$$[\mathfrak{l}_1][\mathfrak{l}_2] \cdots [\mathfrak{l}_r] = [\overline{\mathfrak{l}_0}] \neq [1] \qquad \text{and} \qquad [\mathfrak{l}_1]^3 [\mathfrak{l}_2]^3 \cdots [\mathfrak{l}_r]^3 = [1].$$

Proof. One easily verifies that

$$\mathfrak{l}_1 \mathfrak{l}_2 \cdots \mathfrak{l}_r = \left(\frac{p+1}{4}, \sqrt{-p} - 1 \right) \qquad \text{and} \qquad \mathfrak{l}_0 \mathfrak{l}_1 \mathfrak{l}_2 \cdots \mathfrak{l}_r = \left(\sqrt{-p} - 1 \right).$$

The latter identity implies $[\mathfrak{l}_1][\mathfrak{l}_2] \cdots [\mathfrak{l}_r] = [\mathfrak{l}_0]^{-1} = [\overline{\mathfrak{l}_0}]$, while the former shows that $[\mathfrak{l}_1][\mathfrak{l}_2] \cdots [\mathfrak{l}_r]$ is an element of order 3. Indeed, it represents a non-trivial

---

[2] After we posted a version of this paper online, we learned that this was observed independently and quasi-simultaneously in [27], with a more elaborate discussion.

ideal class because $\mathbb{Z}[\sqrt{-p}]$ contains no elements of norm $(p+1)/4$, while its order divides 3 since

$$\left(\frac{p+1}{4}, \sqrt{-p}-1\right)\mathcal{O}_K = \frac{1+\sqrt{-p}}{2}\mathcal{O}_K,$$

i.e., it belongs to the kernel of the group homomorphism

$$\mathrm{cl}(\mathcal{O}) \longrightarrow \mathrm{cl}(\mathcal{O}_K), \ \mathfrak{a} \longmapsto \mathfrak{a}\mathcal{O}_K$$

which is 3-to-1 by [9, Thm. 5.2].   □

Note that this allows for reduction of the secret exponent vectors of Alice and Bob modulo $(3, 3, \ldots, 3)$. It also shows that the action of $[\mathfrak{l}_1][\mathfrak{l}_2]\cdots[\mathfrak{l}_r]$ can be evaluated using a single application of $[\overline{\mathfrak{l}_0}] = [(4, \sqrt{-p}+1)]$. The latter step can be taken using an isogeny of degree 4, or using a composition of two isogenies of degree 2, which necessarily makes us pass through the surface.

2.4   The Full Endomorphism Ring

The "full" endomorphism ring of a supersingular elliptic curve, as opposed to merely the $\mathbb{F}_p$-rational endomorphisms, plays a fundamental role in the theory of supersingular isogeny graphs.

An elliptic curve E is supersingular if and only if $\mathrm{End}(E)$ is non-commutative. In that case, $\mathrm{End}(E)$ embeds as a maximal order into a certain quaternion algebra $B_{p,\infty}$ ramified at p and infinity, which is unique up to isomorphism. Concretely, $B_{p,\infty}$ can be constructed as a four-dimensional $\mathbb{Q}$-algebra of the form $\mathbb{Q} \oplus \mathbb{Q}\mathbf{i} \oplus \mathbb{Q}\mathbf{j} \oplus \mathbb{Q}\mathbf{ij}$, subject to the multiplication rules $\mathbf{i}^2 = -q$, $\mathbf{j}^2 = -p$, and $\mathbf{ji} = -\mathbf{ij}$, for some positive integer q that depends on p. In the common case that $p \equiv 3 \pmod 4$, we can and will use $q = 1$. (Thus $B_{p,\infty}$ may be viewed as two imaginary quadratic fields "glued together" non-commutatively.) We certainly cannot stress enough that the embedding $\mathrm{End}(E) \hookrightarrow B_{p,\infty}$ is *extremely non-unique*; in fact, there are always infinitely many choices, and usually none of them sticks out as being particularly natural.

The notions of dual, degree, and trace of endomorphisms carry over to $B_{p,\infty}$: Taking the dual corresponds to conjugation, which maps $\alpha = a + b\mathbf{i} + c\mathbf{j} + d\mathbf{ij}$ to $\overline{\alpha} = a - b\mathbf{i} - c\mathbf{j} - d\mathbf{ij}$. The degree turns into $\mathrm{N}(\alpha) = \alpha\overline{\alpha} = a^2 + b^2 q + c^2 p + d^2 qp$, and the trace is simply $\mathrm{tr}(\alpha) = \alpha + \overline{\alpha} = 2a$. Moreover, the trace yields a symmetric bilinear map $\langle \alpha, \beta \rangle = \mathrm{tr}(\overline{\alpha}\beta)$ on $B_{p,\infty}$, with respect to which the basis $1, \mathbf{i}, \mathbf{j}, \mathbf{ij}$ is orthogonal. With this, finding *an* embedding $\mathrm{End}(E) \hookrightarrow B_{p,\infty}$ when being given rational maps that span $\mathrm{End}(E)$ in some computationally effective way is easy: A variant of Schoof's point counting algorithm [29] can be used to compute traces of endomorphisms, and thereby the map $\langle \cdot, \cdot \rangle$, which can then be used in the Gram–Schmidt process to compute an orthogonal basis of the given endomorphism ring. Once the basis is orthogonal, some norm computations are necessary to align the given maps with the algebraic properties of the abstract quaternion representation. See [13, § 5.4] for details. We will commonly use the

$\mathbb{Q}$-basis $(1, \mathbf{i}, \mathbf{j}, \mathbf{ij})$ in the forthcoming algorithms to compute with $\mathrm{End}(E)$; the isomorphism to the corresponding rational maps of curves will be made explicit whenever it is realized computationally.

One reason why the endomorphism rings are interesting for cryptographic applications is because they contain all the information necessary to construct an isogeny between two curves: Given $\mathrm{End}(E)$ and $\mathrm{End}(E')$, it is easy to find a *connecting ideal* $\mathcal{I}$ between them; that is, a lattice in $B_{p,\infty}$ that is a left ideal of $\mathrm{End}(E)$ and a right ideal of $\mathrm{End}(E')$. For example, the following choice works:

Lemma 9. *Between any two maximal orders $\mathcal{Q}$ and $\mathcal{Q}'$ in $B_{p,\infty}$, the lattice $\mathcal{I} = \mathcal{Q}\mathcal{Q}' = \mathrm{span}\,\{ab \mid a \in \mathcal{Q}, b \in \mathcal{Q}'\}$ is a connecting ideal.*

Proof. This is an easy special case of [20, Algorithm 3.5]: Clearly $\mathcal{Q}\mathcal{I} \subseteq \mathcal{I}$, hence $\mathcal{O}_\mathsf{L}(\mathcal{I}) \supseteq \mathcal{Q}$, and equality follows since $\mathcal{Q}$ is maximal. Similarly, $\mathcal{O}_\mathsf{R}(\mathcal{I}) = \mathcal{Q}'$. $\square$

The intersection of all kernels of endomorphisms contained in this ideal is a finite subgroup determining a separable isogeny $E \longrightarrow E'$. One can prove that the codomain curve of the isogeny given by such a left ideal of $\mathrm{End}(E)$ only depends on the left-ideal *class* of $\mathcal{I}$: This is what the Kohel–Lauter–Petit–Tignol algorithm [22] exploits to find a *smooth-degree*, hence efficiently computable, isogeny between E and E' given their endomorphism rings.

Since we are concerned with supersingular elliptic curves defined over $\mathbb{F}_p$, our endomorphism rings—maximal orders in $B_{p,\infty}$—will always contain a copy of the Frobenius order $\mathbb{Z}[\sqrt{-p}] \cong \mathbb{Z}[\pi_E] \subseteq \mathrm{End}_p(E)$. It thus makes sense to fix the image of the Frobenius endomorphism π_E when embedding $\mathrm{End}(E)$ into $B_{p,\infty}$ once and for all: We will always assume that π_E is mapped to $\mathbf{j}$.

3   Twisting Endomorphisms

As before, we focus on the case of finite fields $\mathbb{F}_p$ with $p > 3$ prime.

Definition 10. *Let E be an elliptic curve defined over $\mathbb{F}_p$. An endomorphism $\alpha \in \mathrm{End}(E)$ is called a* twisting endomorphism *of E if*

$$\alpha \circ \pi_E = -\pi_E \circ \alpha.$$

(Note that E must necessarily be supersingular for this to be possible.)

Lemma 11. *Let E be an elliptic curve defined over $\mathbb{F}_p$. The non-zero twisting endomorphisms of E are precisely the elements of $\mathrm{End}(E)$ that are purely imaginary over $\mathrm{End}_p(E)$.*

Proof. Write $\alpha = a + b\mathbf{i} + c\mathbf{j} + d\mathbf{ij}$ with $a, b, c, d \in \mathbb{Q}$; then using the fact that π_E is mapped to $\mathbf{j}$, the equality $\alpha \circ \pi_E = -\pi_E \circ \alpha$ implies $a = c = 0$. $\square$

Lemma 12. *Twisting endomorphisms have kernels defined over $\mathbb{F}_p$. (Thus they always equal either the zero map or an $\mathbb{F}_p$-isogeny followed by an isomorphism.)*

Proof. Since $\pi_E^{-1}(\ker \alpha) = \ker(\alpha \circ \pi_E) = \ker(-\pi_E \circ \alpha) = \ker \alpha$, the subgroup $\ker \alpha$ is stable under the action of $\mathrm{Gal}(\overline{\mathbb{F}}_p/\mathbb{F}_p)$, hence $\mathbb{F}_p$-rational.   □

Lemma 13. *Let E be an elliptic curve as above and let α be a non-zero twisting endomorphism of E. Then $\tau_E \circ \alpha \colon E \to E^t$ is an $\mathbb{F}_p$-rational isogeny of degree $N(\alpha)$.*

Proof. Since τ_E is an isomorphism we have $\deg(\tau_E \circ \alpha) = \deg \alpha = N(\alpha)$, so it remains to prove the $\mathbb{F}_p$-rationality, which follows from

$$\tau_E \circ \alpha \circ \pi_E = -\tau_E \circ \pi_E \circ \alpha = \pi_{E^t} \circ \tau_E \circ \alpha$$

where the last equality uses that $\sqrt{\xi} \in \mathbb{F}_{p^2} \setminus \mathbb{F}_p$ and therefore $\sqrt{\xi}^p = -\sqrt{\xi}$.

4   Isogenies from Known Endomorphisms

In this section, we describe how to find a connecting ideal between two supersingular elliptic curves over $\mathbb{F}_p$ given their full endomorphism rings.

The basic idea behind our approach is to exploit the symmetry of the isogeny graph over $\mathbb{F}_p$ with respect to quadratic twisting; cf. Lemma 5: Intuitively, the distance between a curve and its quadratic twist tells us where in the graph it is located, and combining this information for two curves allows finding the distance between them. See Fig. 1 below for an illustration.

In more mathematical terms, the "distance" between E and its quadratic twist corresponds to an invertible ideal $\mathfrak{a} \subseteq \mathcal{O}$ that connects E to E^t, i.e., satisfies $[\mathfrak{a}]E = E^t$. We will show in Algorithm 1 how to find such an ideal, given the full endomorphism ring of E. Subsequently, given two arbitrary supersingular elliptic curves E, E' with the same $\mathbb{F}_p$-endomorphism ring $\mathcal{O}$ together with such a "twisting ideal" for each of them, Algorithm 2 can be used to find a connecting ideal from E to E', i.e., an invertible ideal $\mathfrak{c} \subseteq \mathcal{O}$ such that $[\mathfrak{c}]E = E'$.

The following lemma shows the relationship between ideals in $\mathrm{End}_p(E)$ and $\mathrm{End}(E)$ that determine the same subgroup; it is of crucial significance for the forthcoming algorithms.

Lemma 14. *Let E be a supersingular elliptic curve defined over $\mathbb{F}_p$. Consider a non-zero ideal $\mathfrak{c} \subseteq \mathrm{End}_p(E)$ and a non-zero left ideal $\mathcal{I} \subseteq \mathrm{End}(E)$ such that the corresponding subgroups $E[\mathcal{I}]$ and $E[\mathfrak{c}]$ are equal. Then $\mathcal{I} \cap \mathrm{End}_p(E) = \pi_E^k \mathfrak{c}$ for some $k \in \mathbb{Z}$.[3]*

Proof. Following [31, Thm. 4.5], we know that for every order $\mathcal{O}$ which can arise as an endomorphism ring, every ideal of $\mathcal{O}$ is a kernel ideal, and thus

$$\mathcal{I} = \{\gamma \in \mathrm{End}(E) \mid \ker \gamma \supseteq E[\mathcal{I}]\} \cdot \pi_E^r$$
$$\mathfrak{c} = \{\gamma \in \mathrm{End}_p(E) \mid \ker \gamma \supseteq E[\mathfrak{c}]\} \cdot \pi_E^s$$

with non-negative integers $r, s \in \mathbb{Z}$. Now $E[\mathcal{I}] = E[\mathfrak{c}]$ by assumption, hence it follows that $\mathcal{I} \cap \mathrm{End}_p(E) = \pi_E^{r-s} \mathfrak{c}$, which shows the claim.   □

---

[3] One could handle the purely inseparable part—powers of π_E—in a unified way by working with scheme-theoretic kernels. Since this issue is only tangential to our work, we will for simplicity avoid this technical complication and deal with π_E explicitly.

4.1   The Algorithm

Throughout this section, we write $\mathcal{O}_E := \mathrm{End}_p(E)$ for brevity.

Recall from Sect. 2.4 that we assume $\mathrm{End}(E)$ is represented as a maximal order in $B_{p,\infty}$ with respect to the $1, \mathbf{i}, \mathbf{j}, \mathbf{ij}$ basis, and such that the Frobenius endomorphism π_E is mapped to $\mathbf{j} \in B_{p,\infty}$ under the embedding.

We start off with an algorithm to find an ideal that connects a curve to its quadratic twist, which will be used as a building block for the main algorithm to connect two arbitrary curves with the same $\mathbb{F}_p$-endomorphism ring in the $\mathbb{F}_p$-isogeny graph.

Algorithm 1: Connecting ideal of a curve and its twist.

Input: a supersingular $E/\mathbb{F}_p$ and the full endomorphism ring $\mathrm{End}(E)$.

Output: an invertible ideal $\mathfrak{a} \subseteq \mathcal{O}_E$ such that $[\mathfrak{a}]E = E^t$.

Find a non-zero element $\alpha \in \mathrm{End}(E)$ of the form $x\mathbf{i} + y\mathbf{ij}$.

Compute the ideal $\mathfrak{a} := \big(\mathrm{End}(E) \cdot \alpha\big) \cap \mathcal{O}_E$.

Return $\mathfrak{a}$.

Lemma 15. *Algorithm 1 is correct and runs in polynomial time.*

Proof. Note that $\alpha \in \mathbf{i}\mathcal{O}_E$ is a twisting endomorphism of E due to Lemma 11. Hence, $E[\mathrm{End}(E) \cdot \alpha] = \ker \alpha$ is an $\mathbb{F}_p$-rational subgroup of E giving rise to an $\mathbb{F}_p$-rational isogeny $E \longrightarrow E^t$, which is necessarily horizontal since $\mathcal{O}_E = \mathcal{O}_{E^t}$. Therefore, there exists an invertible ideal $\mathfrak{c}$ of $\mathcal{O}_E$ such that $E[\mathfrak{c}] = \ker \alpha$, and we may apply Lemma 14 to conclude that $\mathfrak{a} = \big(\mathrm{End}(E) \cdot \alpha\big) \cap \mathcal{O}_E$ in fact equals the desired ideal $\mathfrak{c}$—up to powers of π_E, which is an endomorphism.

Regarding the runtime, everything consists of basic arithmetic in $B_{p,\infty}$ and some linear algebra over $\mathbb{Q}$ and $\mathbb{Z}$. $\square$

As mentioned before, the inherent symmetry of the $\mathbb{F}_p$-isogeny graph with respect to quadratic twisting implies that the "location" of a curve E in the graph is somehow related to the properties of ideals that connect E to its quadratic twist E^t. The following lemma makes this intuition precise, in the sense that it determines a connecting ideal between two curves almost uniquely when given a twisting ideal for each of them. This correspondence is then used in an explicit manner to compute a connecting ideal in Algorithm 2.

Lemma 16. *Let E_0 and E_1 be supersingular elliptic curves defined over $\mathbb{F}_p$ with $\mathrm{End}_p(E_0) \cong \mathrm{End}_p(E_1)$, such that we may simply write $\mathcal{O}$ for both. If $\mathfrak{b}, \mathfrak{c} \subseteq \mathcal{O}$ are invertible ideals such that $[\mathfrak{b}]E_0 = E_0^t$ and $[\mathfrak{c}]E_1 = E_1^t$, then the unique ideal class $[\mathfrak{a}]$ such that $[\mathfrak{a}]E_0 = E_1$ satisfies the equation $[\mathfrak{a}]^2 = [\mathfrak{b}][\mathfrak{c}]^{-1}$.*

Proof. By Lemma 5, applying the action of an ideal class $[\mathfrak{u}]$ to E^t gives the same result as first applying $[\overline{\mathfrak{u}}] = [\mathfrak{u}]^{-1}$ and then twisting. Hence, if $[\mathfrak{a}]E_0 = E_1$, then $[\mathfrak{a}]^{-1}E_0^t = E_1^t$. However, by the assumptions, we have $[\mathfrak{a}]^{-1}E_0^t = [\mathfrak{a}]^{-1}[\mathfrak{b}]E_0$ on the left-hand side and $E_1^t = [\mathfrak{c}]E_1 = [\mathfrak{c}][\mathfrak{a}]E_0$ on the right-hand side, which implies the claimed equality of ideal classes as the class-group action is free. See Fig. 1 for a visualization of the situation on an isogeny cycle. $\square$

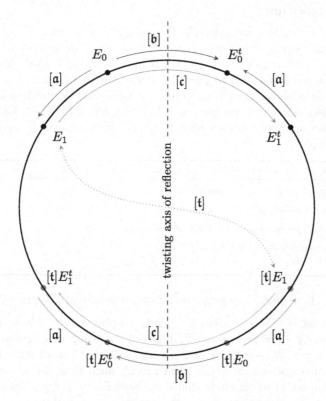

Fig. 1. Illustration of Lemma 16 and the square-root issue in Lemma 17. If the ideal $\mathfrak{t} = (2, \sqrt{-p})$ is non-principal and invertible in $\mathcal{O}$, it corresponds to a point symmetry with respect to the "center" of the isogeny cycle, and the entire relationship between $E_{0,1}$ and their twists is replicated on the "opposite" side with the "dual" curves $[\mathfrak{t}]E_{0,1}$ and their twists. This explains why the output of Algorithm 2 is a priori only correct up to multiplication by $\mathfrak{t}$; the quadratic equation determining $[\mathfrak{a}]$ simply cannot distinguish whether $[\mathfrak{a}]$ jumps between the two worlds or not.

Algorithm 2: Connecting ideal of two curves.

Input: supersingular elliptic curves $E_0, E_1/\mathbb{F}_p$ with $\mathcal{O}_{E_0} = \mathcal{O}_{E_1} = \mathcal{O}$,
            together with their full endomorphism rings $\mathrm{End}(E_0)$ and $\mathrm{End}(E_1)$.

Output: an invertible ideal $\mathfrak{a} \subseteq \mathcal{O}$ such that $[\mathfrak{a}]E_0 = E_1$.

Using Algorithm 1, find an invertible ideal $\mathfrak{b} \subseteq \mathcal{O}$ with $[\mathfrak{b}]E_0 = E_0^t$.

Likewise, find an invertible ideal $\mathfrak{c} \subseteq \mathcal{O}$ such that $[\mathfrak{c}]E_1 = E_1^t$.

Compute an ideal $\mathfrak{a} \subseteq \mathcal{O}$ such that $[\mathfrak{a}]^2 = [\mathfrak{b}][\mathfrak{c}]^{-1}$ in $\mathrm{cl}(\mathcal{O})$ using [5, § 6].

If $p \equiv 1 \pmod 4$ and the right order of $\mathrm{End}(E_0) \cdot \mathfrak{a}$ in $B_{p,\infty}$ is not isomorphic to $\mathrm{End}(E_1)$, then replace $\mathfrak{a}$ by $\mathfrak{a} \cdot (2, 1+\sqrt{-p})$.

Return $\mathfrak{a}$.

Lemma 17. *Algorithm 2 is correct and runs in polynomial time.*

Proof. Most of this follows from Lemmas 16 and 15. The square root in $cl(\mathcal{O})$ to determine the ideal $\mathfrak{a}$ can be computed in polynomial time using the algorithm in [5, §6].

Regarding the correctness of the output, recall from Lemma 3 that the class number of $\mathcal{O}$ is odd if $p \equiv 3 \pmod 4$, hence the square root $[\mathfrak{a}]$ is unique. On the other hand, if $p \equiv 1 \pmod 4$, then Lemma 3 implies that there are exactly two square roots. Now the order $\mathcal{O}$ has discriminant $-4p$, hence $(p) = (\sqrt{-p})^2$ and $(2) = (2, 1+\sqrt{-p})^2$ are the only ramified primes. The principal ideal $(\sqrt{-p})$ becomes trivial in $cl(\mathcal{O})$. However, $\mathfrak{t} := (2, 1+\sqrt{-p})$ is non-principal as there is no element of norm 2 in $\mathcal{O}$, hence $[\mathfrak{t}]$ is an element of order 2 in $cl(\mathcal{O})$. Thus the two square roots of $[\mathfrak{b}][\mathfrak{c}]^{-1}$ are $[\mathfrak{a}]$ and $[\mathfrak{at}]$. The final check in the algorithm identifies the correct choice by lifting $\mathfrak{a}$ to a left $End(E_0)$-ideal and comparing its right order to the endomorphism ring of E_1; they must be isomorphic if $\mathfrak{a}$ determines an isogeny $E_0 \to E_1$ as intended. $\square$

An Example. To illustrate the algorithms in this section, we will show their workings on a concrete, rather special example.

Lemma 18. *Assume $p \equiv 3 \pmod 4$ and let E_1 be a supersingular elliptic curve over $\mathbb{F}_p$ with $\mathbb{F}_p$-endomorphism ring $\mathcal{O}$. Let E_0 be the elliptic curve in $\mathcal{Ell}_p(\mathcal{O})$ having j-invariant 1728. If $\mathfrak{b} \subseteq \mathcal{O}$ is an invertible ideal such that $[\mathfrak{b}]E_1 = E_1^t$, then the unique ideal class $[\mathfrak{a}]$ such that $[\mathfrak{a}]E_0 = E_1$ is given by $[\mathfrak{b}]^{(h(\mathcal{O})-1)/2}$.*

Proof. This follows from Lemmas 1 and 16, together with the fact that the class number of $\mathcal{O}$ is odd. $\square$

Example 19. Assume that $p \equiv 11 \pmod{12}$. We illustrate Algorithm 2 by computing a connecting ideal $\mathfrak{a}$ between $E_0 \colon y^2 = x^3 + x$ and $E_1 \colon y^2 = x^3 + 1$. Note that both curves are contained in $\mathcal{Ell}_p(\mathbb{Z}[\sqrt{-p}])$, as can be seen by considering $E(\mathbb{F}_p)[2]$. If $\omega \in \mathbb{F}_{p^2} \setminus \mathbb{F}_p$ denotes a primitive 3rd root of unity, then E_1 admits the automorphism $(x, y) \mapsto (\omega x, y)$, which will, by abuse of notation, be denoted by ω as well. According to [25, Prop. 3.2],[4] the endomorphism ring of E_1 is isomorphic to the $B_{p,\infty}$-order

$$\mathcal{Q} = \mathbb{Z} + \mathbb{Z}\frac{-1 + \mathbf{i}}{2} + \mathbb{Z}\mathbf{j} + \mathbb{Z}\frac{3 + \mathbf{i} + 3\mathbf{j} + \mathbf{ij}}{6},$$

where $\mathbf{i}$ corresponds to $2\omega + 1$ and satisfies[5] $\mathbf{i}^2 = -3$, and as usual $\mathbf{j}$ corresponds to the Frobenius endomorphism π_{E_1}. If we choose the twisting endomorphism $\alpha = \mathbf{i}$ in Algorithm 1, then we find $\mathcal{Q}\mathbf{i} \cap \mathbb{Z}[\mathbf{j}] = (3, \mathbf{j} - 1)$. (Of course, this also

---

[4] Unfortunately, the statement of [25, Prop. 3.2] wrongly attributes this description to the quadratic twist of E_1.

[5] Here we deviate from our convention that $\mathbf{i}^2 = -1$ as soon as $p \equiv 3 \pmod 4$.

follows from the fact that $2\omega + 1$ is a degree-3 isogeny whose kernel $\{(0, \pm 1), \infty\}$ is $\mathbb{F}_p$-rational.) So $E_1^t = [(3, \sqrt{-p} - 1)]E_1$, and we can take

$$\mathfrak{a} = (3, \sqrt{-p} - 1)^{(h(\mathbb{Z}[\sqrt{-p}])-1)/2} \tag{3}$$

by Lemma 18. Thus, in the 3-isogeny graph associated with $\mathcal{E}\ell\ell_p(\mathbb{Z}[\sqrt{-p}])$, which is a union of cycles, the curve E_1 and its twist $E_1^t\colon y^2 = x^3 - 1$ can be found "opposite" of our starting curve E_0, on the same cycle. We will generalize this example in Sect. 5.

Example 20. In particular, the findings of Example 19 hold for a CSIDH prime $p = 4\ell_1\ell_2\cdots\ell_r - 1$ with $\ell_1 = 3$, so that $(3, \sqrt{-p} - 1) = \mathfrak{l}_1$. Note that $E\colon y^2 = x^3 + 1$ is isomorphic to the Montgomery curve $E_{-\sqrt{3}}\colon y^2 = x^3 - \sqrt{3}\cdot x^2 + x$ through

$$E_{-\sqrt{3}} \longrightarrow E, \quad (x, y) \longmapsto (\delta^2 x - 1, \delta^3 y),$$

where $\sqrt{3} \in \mathbb{F}_p$ denotes the square root of 3 which is a square itself, and $\delta^2 = \sqrt{3}$. In view of the class-group computation carried out in [4] for the CSIDH-512 parameter set, the previous example shows that the ideal

$$\mathfrak{l}_1^{1273262211147421375885150930053196010808102571527432117962854304877988805863095}$$

takes the starting Montgomery coefficient 0 to the coefficient $-\sqrt{3}$, and one further application of $\mathfrak{l}_1$ takes it to $\sqrt{3}$. Smoothing this ideal using the class-group relations of $\mathrm{cl}(\mathbb{Z}[\sqrt{-p}])$ from [4] yields (for instance) the CSIDH-512 exponent vector

$$\begin{aligned}
(&5, -7, -1, \ 1, -4, -5, -8, \ 4, -1, \ 5, \ 1, \ 0, -2, -4, -2, \ 2, -9, \ 4, \ 2, \\
&5, \ 1, \ 1, \ 1, \ 5, -4, \ 2, \ 6, \ 5, -1, \ 0, \ 0, -4, -1, -3, -1, -4, \ 1, \ 7, \\
&1, \ 4, \ 1, \ 4, -7, \ 0, -3, -1, \ 0, \ 1, \ 2, \ 3, \ 1, \ 2, -4, -5, \ 9, -1, \ 4, \\
&0, \ 5, \ 1, \ 0, \ 1, \ 1, \ 3, \ 0, \ 2, \ 2, \ 2, -1, \ 2, \ 1, -1, \ 11, \ 3),
\end{aligned}$$

which can indeed be readily verified to connect E_0 to $E_{-\sqrt{3}}$ by plugging it into a CSIDH-512 implementation, such as that of [7], as a private key.

Example 21. If in Example 19, we instead choose the twisting endomorphism

$$\alpha = \frac{\mathbf{i} + \mathbf{ij}}{3} = -1 - \mathbf{j} + 2\frac{3 + \mathbf{i} + 3\mathbf{j} + \mathbf{ij}}{6} \in \mathcal{Q},$$

then we obtain a twisting ideal of norm $(p + 1)/3$. In the CSIDH setting of Example 20 above, one can deduce that this ideal is nothing but $\bar{\mathfrak{l}}_0\bar{\mathfrak{l}}_2\bar{\mathfrak{l}}_3\cdots\bar{\mathfrak{l}}_r$, so this confirms the first class-group relation stated in Lemma 8.

4.2 Incomplete Knowledge of Endomorphism Rings

At first sight, there appears to be no strong reason why one requires the full endomorphism rings to be known exactly in Algorithm 1, rather than for instance a full-rank proper subring $\mathcal{Q} \subsetneq \mathrm{End}(E)$ containing $\mathcal{O}$: Twisting endomorphisms

α can clearly be found in every full-rank subring, and one can still compute the left ideal $\mathcal{Q} \cdot \alpha$, which can then be intersected with $\mathcal{O}$. The result is indeed an ideal $\mathfrak{a}$ of $\mathcal{O}$, as desired, but unfortunately it turns out that $\mathfrak{a}$ usually falls short of connecting E to its quadratic twist unless in fact $\mathcal{Q} = \mathrm{End}(E)$. This is not surprising: If $\mathcal{Q}$ is contained in multiple non-isomorphic maximal orders, then the algorithm would need to work for all those maximal orders—and therefore elliptic curves—simultaneously, which is absurd. However, luckily, one can prove that $\mathfrak{a}$ is only *locally* "wrong" at the conductor, i.e., the index $f := [\mathrm{End}(E) : \mathcal{Q}]$.

Lemma 22. *Let $\mathcal{Q} \subseteq \mathrm{End}(E)$ a full-rank subring containing $\mathcal{O}$ and $\alpha \in \mathcal{Q}\backslash\{0\}$ a twisting endomorphism. Defining $\mathfrak{a} := (\mathcal{Q}\cdot\alpha)\cap\mathcal{O}$ and $\mathfrak{b}_c := (\mathrm{End}(E)\cdot c\alpha)\cap\mathcal{O}$, we have inclusions of $\mathcal{O}$-ideals*

$$\mathfrak{b}_f \subseteq \mathfrak{a} \subseteq \mathfrak{b}_1,$$

where the norm of the quotient $(\mathfrak{b}_1 : \mathfrak{b}_f)$ divides the squared conductor f^2.

Proof. The inclusions are obvious from $\mathrm{End}(E) \cdot f \subseteq \mathcal{Q} \subseteq \mathrm{End}(E)$. Moreover,

$$f\mathfrak{b}_1 = (f \cdot \mathrm{End}(E) \cdot \alpha) \cap (f \cdot \mathcal{O}) \subseteq (\mathrm{End}(E) \cdot f\alpha) \cap \mathcal{O} = \mathfrak{b}_f,$$

and the inclusions we have just established imply a chain of surjections

$$\mathfrak{b}_1/f\mathfrak{b}_1 \longrightarrow\!\!\!\!\!\rightarrow \mathfrak{b}_1/\mathfrak{b}_f \longrightarrow\!\!\!\!\!\rightarrow \mathfrak{b}_1/\mathfrak{a}$$

on the quotients of $\mathfrak{b}_1$. The first module in this sequence is clearly isomorphic to $\mathbb{Z}^2/f\mathbb{Z}^2$, therefore the index $[\mathfrak{b}_1 : \mathfrak{b}_f]$ must be a divisor of $|\mathbb{Z}^2/f\mathbb{Z}^2| = f^2$. $\square$

Note that both ideals $\mathfrak{b}_1$ and $\mathfrak{b}_f$ from Lemma 22 would be correct outputs for a generalization of Algorithm 1 to proper subrings of $\mathrm{End}(E)$, but $\mathfrak{a}$ typically is not. However, the lemma still suggests an easy strategy for guessing $\mathfrak{b}_1$ after having obtained $\mathfrak{a}$ from the subring variant of Algorithm 1, at least when factoring f is feasible and there are not too many prime factors: In that case, one may simply brute-force through all ideals $\mathfrak{c} \subseteq \mathcal{O}$ of norm dividing f^2 and output $\mathfrak{ac}$ for each of them. The lemma guarantees that a correct such $\mathfrak{c}$ exists, since the ideal $(\mathfrak{b}_1 : \mathfrak{a})$ is a good choice. This procedure is summarized in Algorithm 3.

Algorithm 3: Twisting a curve using an endomorphism *subring*.

Input: a supersingular $E/\mathbb{F}_p$ and a rank-4 subring $\mathcal{Q} \subseteq \mathrm{End}(E)$ with $\mathcal{Q} \supseteq \mathcal{O}_E$.
Output: a set A of invertible ideals $\mathfrak{a} \subseteq \mathcal{O}_E$ such that $\exists\mathfrak{a}\in A$ with $[\mathfrak{a}]E = E^t$.

Find a non-zero element $\alpha \in \mathcal{Q}$ of the form $x\mathbf{i} + y\mathbf{ij}$.
Compute the ideal $\mathfrak{a} := (\mathcal{Q} \cdot \alpha) \cap \mathcal{O}_E$.
Determine $f = [\mathrm{End}(E) : \mathcal{Q}]$ as the (reduced) discriminant of $\mathcal{Q}$ divided by p.
Factor f and iterate through all ideals $\mathfrak{c} \subseteq \mathcal{O}$ of norm dividing f^2 to compute the set $A := \{\mathfrak{ac} \mid \mathfrak{c} \subseteq \mathcal{O}$ ideal, $\mathrm{N}(\mathfrak{c}) \mid f^2\}$.
Return A.

We can bound the size of the set A returned by the algorithm as follows: If the conductor f factors into primes as $f = \prod_{i=1}^{r} p_i^{e_i}$, then there are at most

$$\prod_{i=1}^{r} \binom{2e_i + 2}{2} \in O\left((\log f)^{2r}\right)$$

distinct $\mathcal{O}$-ideals of norm dividing f^2. Hence, if f is factorable in polynomial time and the number of distinct prime factors r is bounded by a constant, then Algorithm 3 takes polynomial time to output polynomially many ideals, and at least one of them is guaranteed to be correct.

4.3   Can We Do Better?

It is a natural question to ask whether one can tweak the KLPT quaternion-ideal algorithm [22] to simply output an ideal corresponding to an isogeny defined over $\mathbb{F}_p$, while preserving the main characteristics of the algorithm, namely the smoothness of the ideal that is returned and the (heuristic) polynomial runtime.

In this section, we argue that the answer is likely "no", at least for classical algorithms: More concretely, we show that such an algorithm can be used as a black-box oracle to construct, under a few mild assumptions, a polynomial-time algorithm for the discrete-logarithm problem in those imaginary-quadratic class groups where the prospective KLPT variant would apply. In contrast, the currently best known algorithm is only subexponential-time [18]. Thus, the basic conclusion appears to be that either our result is essentially optimal, or there exists an improved classical algorithm to compute class-group discrete logarithms in (at least) some cases.

In a sense, this is not surprising: The requirement that the output be generated by an ideal of the two-dimensional subring $\mathrm{End}_p(E)$ removes about the same amount of freedom as was "adjoined" when moving from $\mathbb{Q}(\sqrt{-p})$ to $B_{p,\infty}$ in the first place. In fact, the KLPT algorithm makes explicit constructive use of a quadratic subring of $B_{p,\infty}$ to achieve its functionality; an advantage that can be expected to cease when imposing strong restrictions on the output.

We formalize the situation as follows. Suppose we are given an algorithm $\mathcal{A}$ with the same interface as Algorithm 2, i.e., it takes as input two supersingular elliptic curves $E, E'/\mathbb{F}_p$ with the same $\mathbb{F}_p$-endomorphism ring $\mathcal{O}$, together with their full endomorphism rings, and outputs an ideal $\mathfrak{a} \subseteq \mathcal{O}$ such that $[\mathfrak{a}]E = E'$. In addition, our hypothetical algorithm $\mathcal{A}$ now guarantees that all prime factors of the returned ideal $\mathfrak{a}$ are elements of some polynomially-sized set $S_{\mathcal{O}}$, which may depend on the prime p or the ring $\mathcal{O}$ but not on the concrete input curves E and E'. For example, $S_{\mathcal{O}}$ might consist of the prime ideals of $\mathcal{O}$ with norm bounded by a polynomial in $\log p$.[6]

---

[6] Under GRH, Bach [2] proved that $\mathrm{cl}(\mathcal{O})$ is generated by prime ideals of norm less than $C(\log p)^2$ for an explicitly computable small constant C. It is not known unconditionally whether a polynomial bound on the norms suffices.

Then, Algorithm 5 can use such an oracle $\mathcal{A}$ to compute discrete logarithms in the subgroup of $\mathrm{cl}(\mathcal{O})$ generated by the subset $S_{\mathcal{O}}$ in expected polynomial time, assuming that querying $\mathcal{A}$ takes polynomial time. Note that the core of the reduction is Algorithm 4, which employs $\mathcal{A}$ to decompose class-group elements as a relation over the factor base $S_{\mathcal{O}}$, and those relations are subsequently used by Algorithm 5 in a generic and fairly standard index-calculus procedure.

A remark on notation: we make use of vectors and matrices indexed by finite sets I such as $S_{\mathcal{O}}$—in real implementations this would correspond to fixing an ordering of I and simply storing normal vectors or matrices of length $|I|$. We use the notation $|_{I'}$ to restrict a vector or matrix to the columns indexed by a subset $I' \subseteq I$.

Algorithm 4: Finding a class-group relation using $\mathcal{A}$.

Input: an oracle $\mathcal{A}$ as above, and an ideal $\mathfrak{a} \subseteq \mathcal{O}$ such that $[\mathfrak{a}] \in \langle [\mathfrak{s}] \mid \mathfrak{s} \in S_{\mathcal{O}} \rangle$.

Output: a vector $(e_{\mathfrak{s}} \mid \mathfrak{s} \in S_{\mathcal{O}}) \in \mathbb{Z}^{S_{\mathcal{O}}}$ such that $[\mathfrak{a}] = \left[\prod_{\mathfrak{s} \in S_{\mathcal{O}}} \mathfrak{s}^{e_{\mathfrak{s}}} \right]$.

Find a supersingular $E/\mathbb{F}_p$ with $\mathrm{End}_p(E) = \mathcal{O}$ and known $\mathrm{End}(E)$.

Apply KLPT to $\mathrm{End}(E) \cdot \mathfrak{a}$ to get an equivalent powersmooth left ideal $\mathcal{I}$.

Find the codomain $E' = [\mathfrak{a}]E$ by computing the isogeny defined by $\mathcal{I}$.

Compute $\mathrm{End}(E')$ as the right order of $\mathcal{I}$ in $B_{p,\infty}$.

Now query $\mathcal{A}$ to find an ideal $\mathfrak{c} \in \langle S_{\mathcal{O}} \rangle$ such that $[\mathfrak{c}]E = E' = [\mathfrak{a}]E$.

By assumption, $\mathfrak{c}$ is of the form $\prod_{\mathfrak{s} \in S_{\mathcal{O}}} \mathfrak{s}^{e_{\mathfrak{s}}}$.

Return that exponent vector $\underline{e} = (e_{\mathfrak{s}} \mid \mathfrak{s} \in S_{\mathcal{O}})$.

Lemma 23. *Algorithm 4 is correct. It takes polynomial time under the heuristic that the KLPT algorithm runs in polynomial time.*

Proof. Note that finding a curve E as desired is easy: first construct an arbitrary supersingular elliptic curve over $\mathbb{F}_p$ using [6], then potentially walk to the surface or floor of a 2-volcano. Next, note that the curve E' in fact equals $[\mathfrak{a}]E$, since $\mathrm{End}(E) \cdot \mathfrak{a}$ and $\mathfrak{a}$ define the same subgroup of E and $\mathcal{I}$ is equivalent as a left ideal to $\mathrm{End}(E) \cdot \mathfrak{a}$. Computing $\mathrm{End}(E')$ given $\mathcal{I}$ is easy linear algebra. Now, $\mathfrak{c}$ is a product of ideals in $S_{\mathcal{O}}$ by assumption on $\mathcal{A}$, and it must be equivalent to $\mathfrak{a}$ in $\mathrm{cl}(\mathcal{O})$ since the latter acts freely on $\mathcal{Ell}_p(\mathcal{O})$. In conclusion, Algorithm 4 indeed returns a correct relation vector for $\mathfrak{a}$ and takes polynomial time to do so. $\square$

Using Algorithm 4, we can then follow the generic index-calculus procedure shown in Algorithm 5 to compute discrete logarithms in $\mathrm{cl}(\mathcal{O})$:

Lemma 24. *Algorithm 5 is correct and runs in expected polynomial time.*[7]

Proof sketch. It is not hard to check that the output of the algorithm is correct if it terminates; we thus only have to bound the expected runtime.

---

[7] Note that this does not require *any* assumptions on the output distribution of $\Delta(\mathfrak{a})$, other than that the returned vectors are correct. (The algorithm still takes polynomial time if the oracle Δ only succeeds on an inverse polynomial fraction of inputs.).

Algorithm 5: Solving DLP using index calculus (generic).

Input: • a generating set S of a finite abelian group G.
  • an upper bound B on the cardinality $|G|$.
  • elements $\mathsf{g}, \mathsf{h} \in G$ such that $\mathsf{h} \in \langle \mathsf{g} \rangle$.
  • a probabilistic algorithm $\Delta \colon G \to \mathbb{Z}^S$, such that for all inputs $\mathsf{a} \in G$,
    we have $\|\Delta(\mathsf{a})\|_\infty < B$ and $\mathsf{a} = \prod_{\mathsf{b} \in S} \mathsf{b}^{\Delta(\mathsf{a})_{\mathsf{b}}}$.

Output: an integer x such that $\mathsf{g}^x = \mathsf{h}$.

Fix a large integer $H \gg B^{2|S|+1}$. (In practice, use much smaller H.)
Initialize empty matrices $M \in \mathbb{Z}^{0 \times 2}$ and $L \in \mathbb{Z}^{0 \times S}$.

For $n = 1, 2, \ldots$ **do**

  Pick integers u, v uniformly random in $\{-H, \ldots, H\}$.

  Invoke Δ to obtain a vector $\underline{e} \in \mathbb{Z}^S$ such that $\mathsf{g}^u \mathsf{h}^v = \prod_{\mathsf{b} \in S} \mathsf{b}^{e_{\mathsf{b}}}$.

  Append (u, v) to M as a new row. Append $\underline{e}$ to L as a new row.

  Compute a basis matrix $K \in \mathbb{Z}^{r \times n}$ of the left kernel of L, which is a lattice in $\mathbb{Z}^n$ of rank r.

  If the row span of $K \cdot M$ contains a vector of the form $(x, -1)$ **then**

   Return x.

Since the proof is rather technical, we will merely show the overall strategy. Note that it suffices to lower bound the success probability of the algorithm when $r = 2$ by a constant: Since $r \geq n - |S|$ throughout, it is evident that running $|S| + \alpha$ iterations of Algorithm 5 has success probability at least as big as $\lfloor \alpha/2 \rfloor$ independent executions of the modified algorithm. We thus want to lower bound the probability that two entries λ_1, λ_2 in the second column of $K \cdot M$ are coprime.

First, since Δ cannot distinguish from which scalars (u, v) the element $\mathsf{g}^u \mathsf{h}^v$ was obtained, the conditional distribution of each coefficient of M after fixing a certain oracle output $\underline{e}$ is close to uniform on $\{-H, \ldots, H\}$. As the lattice spanned by the rows of $K \cdot M$ is clearly independent of a basis choice, we may without loss of generality assume that the rows of K form a shortest basis of $\mathbb{Z}^r K$; using lattice techniques, one can then show that the norms of vectors in a shortest basis of $\mathbb{Z}^r K$ are upper bounded by $B^{2|S|}$. (This uses the bound on the size of integers returned by Δ.) Hence λ_i is a "small" coprime linear combination of random variables essentially uniform on $\{-H, \ldots, H\}$, which in turn implies that λ_i is close to uniform modulo all potential prime divisors. Thus the probability that $\gcd(\lambda_1, \lambda_2) = 1$ is lower bounded by a constant, similar to the well-known fact that the density of coprime pairs in $\mathbb{Z}^2$ is $\zeta(2)^{-1} = 6/\pi^2$. $\qquad \square$

For concreteness, we briefly spell out how to instantiate Algorithm 5 for our particular application to $\mathrm{cl}(\mathcal{O})$. Clearly, Algorithm 4 will serve as the oracle Δ, so the factor base S equals the set $S_\mathcal{O}$ from Algorithm 4. In order to keep the representation sizes limited and to obtain unique representatives of ideal classes, the required products $\mathsf{g}^u \mathsf{h}^v$ should be computed using the square-and-multiply algorithm combined with reduction of binary quadratic forms; see [11] for more context on the correspondence between quadratic forms and ideals (§ 7.B) and the notion of reduction (§ 2.A). To select the estimate B on the group order, recall the upper bound $h(\mathcal{O}) \in O(\sqrt{p} \log p)$ from the class number formula.

5   Vectorizing CM Curves

To the best of our knowledge, there exist two practical methods for constructing supersingular elliptic curves over a large finite field $\mathbb{F}_p$: either one reduces curves having CM by some order $\mathcal{R}$ in an imaginary quadratic field F modulo (appropriately chosen) primes that do not split in F, or one performs isogeny walks starting from known supersingular curves. As pointed out earlier, outside of trusted setup, the latter method is not suitable for most cryptographic applications. In this section we focus on the former method; additional details can be found in Bröker's paper [6] and the references therein. As we will see, from a security point of view, the situation is even more problematic in this case: we show that the vectorization problem associated with a CM-constructed supersingular elliptic curve over $\mathbb{F}_p$ admits a surprisingly easy and explicit solution.

In practice, when constructing supersingular elliptic curves over $\mathbb{F}_p$ one does not explicitly write down CM curves. Rather, one computes the Hilbert class polynomial $H_\mathcal{R}(T) \in \mathbb{Z}[T]$ for $\mathcal{R}$, which is a monic irreducible polynomial whose roots are the j-invariants of the curves having CM by $\mathcal{R}$. This polynomial can be computed effectively, although the existing methods are practical for orders having small discriminants only, one reason being that the degree of $H_\mathcal{R}(T)$ equals $h(\mathcal{R})$. The roots of $H_\mathcal{R}(T) \bmod p \in \mathbb{F}_p[T]$ are precisely those $j \in \overline{\mathbb{F}}_p$ which arise as the j-invariant of a supersingular elliptic curve obtained by reducing an elliptic curve having CM by $\mathcal{R}$. It is well-known that all these j-invariants are in fact elements of $\mathbb{F}_{p^2}$, i.e., the irreducible factors of $H_\mathcal{R}(T) \bmod p$ are at most quadratic. The linear factors then correspond to elliptic curves over $\mathbb{F}_p$.

Example 25. The Hilbert class polynomial for $\mathbb{Z}[\sqrt{-17}]$ is given by

$$H_{\mathbb{Z}[\sqrt{-17}]}(T) = T^4 - 178211040000T^3 - 758436921600000000T^2$$
$$-318507038720000000000T - 2089297506304000000000000,$$

whose reduction modulo 83 factors as $(T - 28)(T - 50)(T^2 + 7T + 73)$. This gives rise to two pairs of quadratic twists of elliptic curves over $\mathbb{F}_{83}$ that appear as the reduction modulo 83 of a curve with CM by $\mathbb{Z}[\sqrt{-17}]$.

The main result of this section is the following theorem; for conciseness, our focus lies on the setting where $p \equiv 3 \pmod 4$ and where

$$\mathbb{Z}[\sqrt{-\ell}] \subseteq \mathcal{R} \subseteq \mathbb{Q}(\sqrt{-\ell})$$

for some odd prime number ℓ, i.e., we want our CM curves to come equipped with an endomorphism Ψ satisfying $\Psi \circ \Psi = [-\ell]$. This leaves us with two options for $\mathcal{R}$, namely $\mathbb{Z}[\sqrt{-\ell}]$ and $\mathbb{Z}[(1+\sqrt{-\ell})/2]$. In Remark 32 we will briefly comment on how to locate curves having CM by more general imaginary quadratic orders.

Theorem 26. *Let $p \equiv 3 \pmod 4$ and $\ell < (p+1)/4$ be primes with $\left(\frac{-p}{\ell}\right) = 1$.*

(i) If $\ell \equiv 1 \pmod 4$ then

$$H_{\mathbb{Z}[\sqrt{-\ell}]}(T) \bmod p$$

has precisely two $\mathbb{F}_p$-rational roots, both corresponding to a pair of quadratic twists of supersingular elliptic curves. One pair is contained in $\mathscr{E}\ell\ell_p(\mathbb{Z}[\sqrt{-p}])$ while the other pair is contained in $\mathscr{E}\ell\ell_p(\mathbb{Z}[(1+\sqrt{-p})/2])$.

(ii) If $\ell \equiv 3 \pmod 4$ then both

$$H_{\mathbb{Z}[(1+\sqrt{-\ell})/2]}(T) \bmod p \qquad and \qquad H_{\mathbb{Z}[\sqrt{-\ell}]}(T) \bmod p$$

have exactly one $\mathbb{F}_p$-rational root each, in both cases corresponding to a pair of quadratic twists of elliptic curves. The first such pair is contained in $\mathscr{E}\ell\ell_p(\mathbb{Z}[\sqrt{-p}])$, while the other pair is contained in $\mathscr{E}\ell\ell_p(\mathbb{Z}[(1+\sqrt{-p})/2])$.

(iii) Let $\mathcal{O} \in \{\mathbb{Z}[\sqrt{-p}], \mathbb{Z}[(1+\sqrt{-p})/2]\}$ and let $E, E^t \in \mathscr{E}\ell\ell_p(\mathcal{O})$ be a pair of supersingular elliptic curves over $\mathbb{F}_p$ arising as above. Up to order, this pair is given by the curves

$$[\mathfrak{l}]^{(h(\mathcal{O})-1)/2} E_0 \qquad and \qquad [\mathfrak{l}]^{(h(\mathcal{O})+1)/2} E_0 \tag{4}$$

for any prime ideal $\mathfrak{l} \subseteq \mathcal{O}$ lying above ℓ. Here $E_0 \colon y^2 = x^3 \pm x$ is the unique curve with j-invariant 1728 in $\mathscr{E}\ell\ell_p(\mathcal{O})$.

This theorem can be seen as a vast generalization of (3) from Example 19, where we dealt with the reduction modulo p of the curve $E \colon y^2 = x^3 + 1$ over $\mathbb{Q}$ having CM by the ring of Eisenstein integers $\mathbb{Z}[e^{2\pi i/3}] = \mathbb{Z}[(1+\sqrt{-3})/2]$. Up to twisting it is the only such curve: the Hilbert class polynomial for $\mathbb{Z}[(1+\sqrt{-3})/2]$ is just T. An endomorphism Ψ satisfying $\Psi^2 = -3$ can be constructed as $2\omega + 1$, where ω is the automorphism $E \to E$, $(x,y) \mapsto (e^{2\pi i/3}x, y)$.

One particularly interesting range of parameters satisfying the stated assumptions is where

- $p = 4\ell_1\ell_2 \cdots \ell_r - 1$ is a CSIDH prime with $r \geq 2$, and
- $\ell = \ell_i$ for some $i \in \{1, 2, \ldots, r\}$.

If $r = 1$ then $\ell_1 = (p+1)/4$, so Theorem 26 can no longer be applied. However, the reasons for excluding the boundary case $\ell = (p+1)/4$ are rather superficial and the statement remains largely valid in this case (the exclusion is related to the possible occurrence of $j = 1728$ as a root of $H_{\mathcal{R}}(T) \bmod p$, which comes with some subtleties in terms of quadratic twisting; see the proof).

5.1   Twisting Endomorphisms from Deuring Reduction

Before proceeding to the proof of Theorem 26, we discuss Deuring lifting and reduction, with a focus on how the endomorphism Ψ behaves under reduction.

Theorem 27 (Deuring's reduction theorem). *Let p be a prime number and let E be an elliptic curve over a number field K which has CM by some order $\mathcal{R}$ in an imaginary quadratic number field F. Let $\mathfrak{p}$ be a prime of K above p at which E has good reduction. Then E mod $\mathfrak{p}$ is supersingular if and only if p ramifies or is inert in F.*

Proof. This is part of [23, Thm. 12 of Ch. 13]. □

When applying this to an elliptic curve E/K having CM by our order $\mathcal{R} \subseteq \mathbb{Q}(\sqrt{-\ell})$ from above, the endomorphism Ψ satisfying $\Psi \circ \Psi = [-\ell]$ reduces modulo $\mathfrak{p}$ to an endomorphism ψ which also satisfies $\psi \circ \psi = [-\ell]$. This is because reduction modulo $\mathfrak{p}$ induces an (injective) homomorphism of endomorphism rings; see for instance [23, § 2 of Ch. 9]. The following proposition gives sufficient conditions for ψ to be a twisting endomorphism.

Proposition 28. *Assume $K = \mathbb{Q}(j(E))$, $p > 2$ and $\ell \leq (p+1)/4$. If E mod $\mathfrak{p}$ is supersingular and $j(E$ mod $\mathfrak{p}) \in \mathbb{F}_p$ then $\deg \mathfrak{p} = 1$ and*

$$\pi_{E \text{ mod } \mathfrak{p}} \circ \psi = -\psi \circ \pi_{E \text{ mod } \mathfrak{p}}, \tag{5}$$

i.e., ψ anticommutes with the p-power Frobenius endomorphism of E mod $\mathfrak{p}$.

The proof of this proposition relies on the following observation:

Lemma 29. *Let α be an algebraic integer and $K = \mathbb{Q}(\alpha)$. Consider a prime number p and a prime ideal $\mathfrak{p} \subseteq \mathcal{O}_K$ above p. If $\mathbb{F}_p(\alpha$ mod $\mathfrak{p}) \subsetneq \mathcal{O}_K/\mathfrak{p}$, then p divides the discriminant of the minimal polynomial $f(x) \in \mathbb{Z}[x]$ of α over $\mathbb{Q}$.*

Proof. If p does not divide the discriminant of $f(x)$, then

$$\mathfrak{p} = (p, g(\alpha)),$$

where $g(x) \in \mathbb{Z}[x]$ is a monic polynomial of degree $\deg \mathfrak{p}$ whose reduction modulo p is an irreducible factor in $\mathbb{F}_p[x]$ of $f(x)$ mod p; this is a well-known fact, see e.g. [24, Thm. 27]. But this implies that α mod $\mathfrak{p}$ is a generator of $\mathcal{O}_K/\mathfrak{p}$ over $\mathbb{F}_p$, so the lemma follows by contradiction. □

Proof (of Proposition 28). The minimal polynomial of $j(E)$ over $\mathbb{Q}$ is precisely the Hilbert class polynomial $H_{\mathcal{R}}(T)$ for $\mathcal{R}$. The field $H = \mathbb{Q}(\sqrt{-\ell}, j(E))$ is a quadratic extension of K known as the ring class field for $\mathcal{R}$, see [11, proof of Prop. 1.32]. If $\mathcal{R}$ is a maximal order, then this is better known as the Hilbert class field.

Using that $\ell \leq (p+1)/4$, we see that p does not ramify in $\mathbb{Q}(\sqrt{-\ell})$, hence it must be inert by our assumption that E mod $\mathfrak{p}$ is supersingular. This implies that $p\mathcal{O}_H$ splits as a product of prime ideals $\mathfrak{P}$ of degree 2, see [11, Cor. 5.25] for a proof in case $\mathcal{R}$ is a maximal order and [11, proof of Prop. 9.4] for the general case (this is where we use the assumption $p > 2$). Our prime ideal $\mathfrak{p}$ is necessarily dominated by such a $\mathfrak{P}$, so it follows that

– either $\deg \mathfrak{p} = 1$, in which case $\mathfrak{p}$ must be inert in H, i.e., $\mathfrak{p}\mathcal{O}_H = \mathfrak{P}$,
– or $\deg \mathfrak{p} = 2$, in which case $\mathfrak{p}$ must split in H.

But the latter option would imply that

$$\mathbb{F}_p(j(E) \bmod \mathfrak{p}) = \mathbb{F}_p(j(E \bmod \mathfrak{p})) = \mathbb{F}_p \subsetneq \mathcal{O}_K/\mathfrak{p}$$

and therefore, in view of Lemma 29, it would follow that p divides the discriminant of $H_\mathcal{R}(T)$. This is impossible: by Gross–Zagier [17, p. 195] the primes p dividing the discriminant of $H_\mathcal{R}(T)$ cannot be larger than the absolute value of the discriminant of $\mathcal{R}$, which is at most 4ℓ.

We have thus established that $\deg \mathfrak{p} = 1$. Now let Σ be the non-trivial automorphism of H over K. From [23, §4 of Ch. 10] we see that Ψ is not defined over K and therefore $\Psi^\Sigma = -\Psi$. But Σ necessarily descends to the Frobenius automorphism σ of $\mathcal{O}_H/\mathfrak{P} \cong \mathbb{F}_{p^2}$ over $\mathcal{O}_K/\mathfrak{p} \cong \mathbb{F}_p$, from which it follows that $\psi^\sigma = -\psi$. This implies (5) and thereby concludes the proof. □

We remark that the last part of the preceding proof mimics the proof of [15, Prop. 6.1]. However, the statement of [15, Prop. 6.1] is lacking an assumption on $\deg \mathfrak{p}$. For instance, in our case, if $\deg \mathfrak{p} = 2$ and therefore $\mathfrak{p}$ splits in H, the reasoning fails because the extension $\mathcal{O}_H/\mathfrak{P}$ over $\mathcal{O}_K/\mathfrak{p}$ becomes trivial. And indeed, in these cases it may happen that the reduction of Ψ mod $\mathfrak{p}$ does *not* anticommute with Frobenius:

Example 30. The discriminant of the Hilbert class polynomial for $\mathbb{Z}[\sqrt{-29}]$ is divisible by 83. More precisely, its reduction modulo 83 factors as $T(T-50)(T-67)^2(T^2+7T+73)$. One can verify that inside $K = \mathbb{Q}[T]/(H_{\mathbb{Z}[\sqrt{-29}]}(T))$, we have

$$83\mathcal{O}_K = (83, T)(83, T-50)(83, T^2-7)(83, T^2+7T+73),$$

where the third factor is a degree-2 prime ideal $\mathfrak{p}$ modulo which T reduces to 67; note that $67^2 \equiv 7 \pmod{83}$. So in this case we have $\mathbb{F}_p(T \bmod \mathfrak{p}) \subsetneq \mathcal{O}_K/\mathfrak{p}$.

Let E be any of the two elliptic curves over $\mathbb{F}_{83}$ having j-invariant 67. By exhaustive search through the possible kernels of order 29, one can check that E admits four distinct automorphisms squaring to $[-29]$. These appear in the form $\pm\psi, \pm\psi^\sigma$, where as in the proof of Proposition 28 we use σ to denote the action of the p-power Frobenius. In particular ψ does not anticommute with π_E. Nevertheless, by Deuring's lifting theorem (recalled below), the pair (E, ψ) must arise as the reduction of some CM curve along with an endomorphism Ψ satisfying $\Psi \circ \Psi = [-29]$. (Note: this also applies to the pair (E, ψ^σ), which is reflected in the fact that 67 appears as a double root of $H_{\mathbb{Z}[\sqrt{-\ell}]}(T)$ mod 83.)

Theorem 31 (Deuring's lifting theorem). *Let $E/\overline{\mathbb{F}}_p$ be an elliptic curve and let $\alpha \in \mathrm{End}(E)$. There exists an elliptic curve E' over a number field K along with an endomorphism $\alpha' \in \mathrm{End}(E')$ and a prime $\mathfrak{p}$ of K above p at which E' has good reduction, such that E' mod $\mathfrak{p}$ is isomorphic to E and such that α' reduces to α modulo $\mathfrak{p}$.*

Proof. See [23, Thm. 14 of Ch. 13]. □

5.2 Proof of Theorem 26

Proof (of Theorem 26). Using quadratic reciprocity one checks that

$$\left(\frac{-p}{\ell}\right) = 1 \iff \left(\frac{-\ell}{p}\right) = -1,$$

from which we see that p is inert in $\mathbb{Q}(\sqrt{-\ell})$. Hence a curve with CM by $\mathbb{Z}[\sqrt{-\ell}]$ has supersingular reduction modulo p and therefore the $\mathbb{F}_p$-rational roots of the Hilbert class polynomial

$$H_{\mathbb{Z}[\sqrt{-\ell}]}(T) \bmod p$$

should correspond to pairs of quadratic twists in either the floor $\mathcal{E}\ell\ell_p(\mathbb{Z}[\sqrt{-p}])$ or the surface $\mathcal{E}\ell\ell_p(\mathbb{Z}[(1+\sqrt{-p})/2])$. If $\ell \equiv 3 \pmod 4$, then the same conclusions apply to $\mathbb{Z}[(1+\sqrt{-\ell})/2]$.

As a side note, we remark that $\ell < (p+1)/4$ implies that $y^2 = x^3 \pm x$ does not admit any twisting endomorphisms of norm ℓ, which is easy to elaborate from [25, Prop. 3.1]. In view of Proposition 28, we therefore see that the $\mathbb{F}_p$-rational roots of the Hilbert class polynomial never include 1728. Hence by Lemma 1 there is no ambiguity in what is meant by "pairs of quadratic twists". (Apart from this ambiguity, the theorem remains true under the weaker assumption $\ell \leq (p+1)/4$.)

We first claim that $\mathcal{E}\ell\ell_p(\mathbb{Z}[\sqrt{-p}])$ and $\mathcal{E}\ell\ell_p(\mathbb{Z}[(1+\sqrt{-p})/2])$ both contain *at most* one such pair E, E^t. Indeed, using Proposition 28 we see that E comes equipped with a twisting endomorphism ψ of degree ℓ, which by Lemma 13 corresponds to an $\mathbb{F}_p$-rational degree-ℓ isogeny $E \to E^t$. Its kernel is necessarily of the form $E[\mathfrak{l}]$ for some prime ideal $\mathfrak{l}$ above ℓ, i.e., we must have $E^t = [\mathfrak{l}]E$. But then we can solve the vectorization problem $E = [\mathfrak{a}]E_0$: from Lemma 18 we get that $[\mathfrak{a}] = [\mathfrak{l}]^{(h(\mathcal{O})-1)/2}$. Since the pair

$$\left\{ [\mathfrak{l}]^{(h(\mathcal{O})-1)/2}, \quad [\mathfrak{l}]^{(h(\mathcal{O})+1)/2} = [\bar{\mathfrak{l}}]^{(h(\mathcal{O})-1)/2} \right\}$$

does not depend on the choice of $\mathfrak{l}$, this shows that the pair $\{E, E^t\}$ is fully characterized by ℓ, implying the claim. At the same time this proves (iii).

Next, let us explain why $\mathcal{E}\ell\ell_p(\mathbb{Z}[\sqrt{-p}])$ and $\mathcal{E}\ell\ell_p(\mathbb{Z}[(1+\sqrt{-p})/2])$ contain *at least* one such pair E, E^t. We remark that this comes for free if $\ell \equiv 3 \pmod 4$, since in this case the Hilbert class polynomials for $\mathbb{Z}[\sqrt{-\ell}]$ and $\mathbb{Z}[(1+\sqrt{-\ell})/2]$ have odd degree and split over $\mathbb{F}_{p^2}$, their roots being supersingular j-invariants: hence they must admit at least one $\mathbb{F}_p$-rational root. In general, we can reverse the reasoning from the previous paragraph and *define* E, E^t using (4), for some choice of prime ideal $\mathfrak{l}$ above ℓ. In particular $E^t = [\mathfrak{l}]E$, which provides us with an $\mathbb{F}_p$-rational degree-ℓ isogeny $\varphi \colon E \to E^t$, which we use to construct an endomorphism $\psi = \tau_{E^t} \circ \varphi$ of E that is not $\mathbb{F}_p$-rational. In contrast, it is easily verified that $\psi \circ \psi$ is $\mathbb{F}_p$-rational. Therefore the minimal polynomial of ψ cannot admit a non-zero linear term, i.e., $\psi \circ \psi$ must be a scalar-multiplication map, necessarily of the form $[\pm \ell]$. By Deuring's lifting theorem E can be lifted to an elliptic curve over a number field carrying an endomorphism Ψ whose reduction modulo a suitable prime above p yields ψ. Since Ψ must belong to an imaginary quadratic ring we see that $\Psi \circ \Psi = [-\ell]$ as wanted.

Altogether this proves (i), while for (ii) it leaves us with the task of showing that if $\ell \equiv 3 \pmod 4$, then the unique $\mathbb{F}_p$-rational root of

$$H_{\mathbb{Z}[(1+\sqrt{-\ell})/2]}(T) \bmod p$$

corresponds to a pair of elliptic curves $\{E, E^t\}$ with endomorphism ring $\mathbb{Z}[\sqrt{-p}]$. Equivalently, we need to show that such curves admit a unique $\mathbb{F}_p$-rational point of order 2, rather than three such points. To this end, let $P \in E$ be an $\mathbb{F}_p$-rational point of order 2 and let φ be the endomorphism of E corresponding to $(1+\sqrt{-\ell})/2$. Proposition 28 implies that $\pi_E \circ \varphi = \overline{\varphi} \circ \pi_E$, where $\overline{\varphi}$ corresponds to $(1-\sqrt{-\ell})/2$. But then clearly $(\varphi + \overline{\varphi})(P) = P \neq \infty$, which implies that $\overline{\varphi}(P) \neq \varphi(P)$ and therefore that $\pi_E(\varphi(P)) \neq \varphi(P)$, i.e., $\varphi(P)$ is a non-rational point of order 2. This concludes the proof.   □

Remark 32. The above ideas can be generalized to locate reductions mod p of CM curves carrying an endomorphism Ψ such that $\Psi \circ \Psi = [-\ell_1\ell_2 \cdots \ell_s]$, where the $\ell_i \leq (p+1)/4$ are distinct odd primes for which

$$\left(\frac{-\ell_1\ell_2\cdots\ell_s}{p}\right) = -1. \tag{6}$$

We did not elaborate this in detail, but assume for instance that each ℓ_i splits in $\mathbb{Q}(\sqrt{-p})$; note that this implies (6). Letting $\mathcal{O} \in \{\mathbb{Z}[\sqrt{-p}], \mathbb{Z}[(1+\sqrt{-p})/2]\}$, one expects that 2^{s-1} pairs E, E^t in $\mathcal{Ell}_p(\mathcal{O})$ can be obtained as the reduction mod p of an elliptic curve carrying such an endomorphism Ψ. Fixing for each $i = 1, 2, \ldots, s$ a prime ideal $\mathfrak{l}_i \subseteq \mathcal{O}$ of norm ℓ_i, these pairs are characterized by

$$E^t = [\mathfrak{l}_1][\mathfrak{l}_2]^{e_2}[\mathfrak{l}_2]^{e_3} \cdots [\mathfrak{l}_s]^{e_s} E$$

with $(e_2, e_3, \ldots, e_s) \in \{\pm 1\}^{s-1}$. As before, an application of Lemma 18 then solves the corresponding vectorization problems.

Acknowledgements. The authors would like to thank Benjamin Wesolowski, Robert Granger, Christophe Petit, and Ben Smith for interesting discussions regarding this work, and Lixia Luo for pointing out an error in an earlier version of Lemma 22, as well as a few smaller mistakes. Thanks to Daniel J. Bernstein for providing key insights regarding the proof of Lemma 24.

References

1. Arpin, S., et al.: Adventures in Supersingularland. Cryptology ePrint Archive 2019/1056 (2018). https://ia.cr/2019/1056
2. Bach, E.: Explicit bounds for primality testing and related problems. Math. Comput. **55**(191), 355–380 (1990)
3. Bernstein, D.J., Hamburg, M., Krasnova, A., Lange, T.: Elligator: elliptic-curve points indistinguishable from uniform random strings. In: ACM Conference on Computer and Communications Security, pp. 967–980. ACM (2013). https://ia.cr/2013/325

4. Beullens, W., Kleinjung, T., Vercauteren, F.: CSI-FiSh: efficient isogeny based signatures through class group computations. In: Galbraith, S.D., Moriai, S. (eds.) ASIACRYPT 2019. LNCS, vol. 11921, pp. 227–247. Springer, Cham (2019). https://doi.org/10.1007/978-3-030-34578-5_9

5. Bosma, W., Stevenhagen, P.: On the computation of quadratic 2-class groups. J. de Théorie des Nombres de Bordeaux **8**(2), 283–313 (1996)

6. Bröker, R.: Constructing supersingular elliptic curves. J. Comb. Number Theory **1**(3), 273–469 (2009)

7. Castryck, W., Lange, T., Martindale, C., Panny, L., Renes, J.: CSIDH: an efficient post-quantum commutative group action. In: Peyrin, T., Galbraith, S. (eds.) ASIA-CRYPT 2018. LNCS, vol. 11274, pp. 395–427. Springer, Cham (2018). https://doi.org/10.1007/978-3-030-03332-3_15

8. Charles, D.X., Lauter, K.E., Goren, E.Z.: Cryptographic hash functions from expander graphs. J. Cryptol. **22**(1), 93–113 (2009). https://ia.cr/2006/021

9. Conrad, K.: The conductor ideal. Expository paper. https://kconrad.math.uconn.edu/blurbs/gradnumthy/conductor.pdf

10. Couveignes, J.-M.: Hard homogeneous spaces. IACR Cryptology ePrint Archive 2006/291 (1997). https://ia.cr/2006/291

11. Cox, D.A.: Primes of the Form $x^2 + ny^2$: Fermat, Class Field Theory, and Complex Multiplication. Pure Applied Mathematics, 2nd edn. Wiley, Hoboken (2013)

12. Delfs, C., Galbraith, S.D.: Computing isogenies between supersingular elliptic curves over $\mathbb{F}_p$. Des. Codes Cryptogr. **78**(2), 425–440 (2016). https://arxiv.org/abs/1310.7789

13. Eisenträger, K., Hallgren, S., Lauter, K., Morrison, T., Petit, C.: Supersingular isogeny graphs and endomorphism rings: reductions and solutions. In: Nielsen, J.B., Rijmen, V. (eds.) EUROCRYPT 2018. LNCS, vol. 10822, pp. 329–368. Springer, Cham (2018). https://doi.org/10.1007/978-3-319-78372-7_11

14. Galbraith, S., Panny, L., Smith, B., Vercauteren, F.: Quantum equivalence of the DLP and CDHP for group actions. Cryptology ePrint Archive 2018/1199 (2018). https://ia.cr/2018/1199

15. Galbraith, S., Rotger, V.: Easy decision Diffie-Hellman groups. LMS J. Comput. Math. **7**, 201–218 (2004). https://ia.cr/2004/070

16. Galbraith, S.D., Petit, C., Shani, B., Ti, Y.B.: On the security of supersingular isogeny cryptosystems. In: Cheon, J.H., Takagi, T. (eds.) ASIACRYPT 2016. LNCS, vol. 10031, pp. 63–91. Springer, Heidelberg (2016). https://doi.org/10.1007/978-3-662-53887-6_3

17. Gross, B.H., Zagier, D.B.: On singular moduli. J. für die Reine und Angewandte Mathematik **355**, 191–220 (1985)

18. Hafner, J.L., McCurley, K.S.: A rigorous subexponential algorithm for computation of class groups. J. Am. Math. Soc. **2**, 837–850 (1989)

19. Jao, D., De Feo, L.: Towards quantum-resistant cryptosystems from supersingular elliptic curve isogenies. In: Yang, B.-Y. (ed.) PQCrypto 2011. LNCS, vol. 7071, pp. 19–34. Springer, Heidelberg (2011). https://doi.org/10.1007/978-3-642-25405-5_2

20. Kirschmer, M., Voight, J.: Algorithmic enumeration of ideal classes for quaternion orders. SIAM J. Comput. **39**(5), 1714–1747 (2010). https://arxiv.org/abs/0808.3833

21. Kitaev, A.Y.: Quantum measurements and the Abelian stabilizer problem. Electron. Colloquium Comput. Complex. (ECCC) **3**(3) (1996). https://eccc.hpi-web.de/eccc-reports/1996/TR96-003

22. Kohel, D., Lauter, K., Petit, C., Tignol, J.-P.: On the quaternion ℓ-isogeny path problem. LMS J. Comput. Math. **17**(Suppl. A), 418–432 (2014). https://ia.cr/2014/505

23. Lang, S.: Elliptic Functions. Graduate Texts in Mathematics, vol. 112. Springer, Heidelberg (1987). https://doi.org/10.1007/978-1-4612-4752-4. With an appendix by John Tate

24. Marcus, D.A.: Number Fields. Universitext, 2nd edn. Springer, Heidelberg (2018). https://doi.org/10.1007/978-1-4684-9356-6. With a foreword by Barry Mazur

25. McMurdy, K.: Explicit representation of the endomorphism rings of supersingular elliptic curves (2014). Preprint. https://phobos.ramapo.edu/~kmcmurdy/research/McMurdy-ssEndoRings.pdf

26. National Institute of Standards and Technology: Post-Quantum Cryptography Standardization, December 2016. https://csrc.nist.gov/Projects/Post-Quantum-Cryptography/Post-Quantum-Cryptography-Standardization

27. Onuki, H., Takagi, T.: On collisions related to an ideal class of order 3 in CSIDH. Cryptology ePrint Archive 2019/1202 (2019). https://ia.cr/2019/1202

28. Schnorr, C.-P., Euchner, M.: Lattice basis reduction: improved practical algorithms and solving subset sum problems. Math. Program. **66**, 181–199 (1994)

29. Schoof, R.: Elliptic curves over finite fields and the computation of square roots mod p. Math. Comput. **44**(170), 483–494 (1985)

30. Silverman, J.H.: The Arithmetic of Elliptic Curves. Graduate Texts in Mathematics, vol. 106, 2nd edn. Springer, Heidelberg (2009). https://doi.org/10.1007/978-0-387-09494-6

31. Waterhouse, W.C.: Abelian varieties over finite fields. Annales scientifiques de l'École Normale Supérieure **2**, 521–560 (1969)

Lattice-Based Cryptography

Hardness of LWE on General Entropic Distributions

Zvika Brakerski[1(✉)] and Nico Döttling[2(✉)]

[1] Weizmann Institute of Science, Rehovot, Israel
zvika.brakerski@weizmann.ac.il
[2] CISPA Helmholtz Center for Information Security, Saarbrücken, Germany
doettling@cispa-helmholtz.de

Abstract. The hardness of the Learning with Errors (LWE) problem is by now a cornerstone of the cryptographic landscape. In many of its applications the so called "LWE secret" is not sampled uniformly, but comes from a distribution with some min-entropy. This variant, known as "Entropic LWE", has been studied in a number of works, starting with Goldwasser et al. (ICS 2010). However, so far it was only known how to prove the hardness of Entropic LWE for secret distributions supported inside a ball of small radius.

In this work we resolve the hardness of Entropic LWE with arbitrary long secrets, in the following sense. We show an entropy bound that guarantees the security of arbitrary Entropic LWE. This bound is higher than what is required in the ball-bounded setting, but we show that this is essentially tight. Tightness is shown unconditionally for highly-composite moduli, and using black-box impossibility for arbitrary moduli.

Technically, we show that the entropic hardness of LWE relies on a simple to describe lossiness property of the distribution of secrets itself. This is simply the probability of recovering a random sample from this distribution s, given $s + e$, where e is Gaussian noise (i.e. the quality of the distribution of secrets as an error correcting code for Gaussian noise). We hope that this characterization will make it easier to derive entropic LWE results more easily in the future. We also use our techniques to show new results for the ball-bounded setting, essentially showing that under a strong enough assumption even polylogarithmic entropy suffices.

1 Introduction

Lattice-based cryptography has emerged in the last few decades as one of the most important developments in cryptography. Lattice-based cryptographic schemes have been shown to achieve functionalities that are unknown under any

We encourage readers to refer to the full version of this work, available at https://eprint.iacr.org/2020/119.

Z. Brakerski—Supported by the Binational Science Foundation (Grant No. 2016726), and by the European Union Horizon 2020 Research and Innovation Program via ERC Project REACT (Grant 756482) and via Project PROMETHEUS (Grant 780701).

A. Canteaut and Y. Ishai (Eds.): EUROCRYPT 2020, LNCS 12106, pp. 551–575, 2020.
https://doi.org/10.1007/978-3-030-45724-2_19

other cryptographic structure (such as fully homomorphic encryption [Gen09, BV11], attribute-based encryption for circuits [GVW13] and many others). At the same time, it is possible in many cases to show strong security properties such as worst-case to average-case hardness results [Ajt96, AD97, MR04, Reg05] that relate the hardness of breaking the cryptographic scheme to that of solving approximate short-vector problems in worst-case lattices, a problem that resists algorithmic progress even when use of quantum computers is considered.

Much of the progress in advancing lattice-based cryptography can be attributed to the hardness of the Learning with Errors (LWE) problem, introduced by Regev [Reg05]. This problem can be stated in a very clean linear-algebraic syntax, which allows to utilize it for applications very easily, and at the same time was shown to enjoy worst-case hardness as explained above. An instance of the LWE problem has the following form. It is parameterized by a dimension n and modulus $q \gg n$. Consider the following distribution. Sample a (public) random matrix $\mathbf{A} \in \mathbb{Z}_q^{n \times m}$, for arbitrary $m = \mathsf{poly}(n)$, and a (secret) random vector $\mathbf{s} \in \mathbb{Z}_q^n$, and output $(\mathbf{A}, \mathbf{y})$, where $\mathbf{y} = \mathbf{s}\mathbf{A} + \mathbf{e} \pmod{q}$, and $\mathbf{e}$ is a noise vector selected from some distribution (often a Gaussian with parameter $\sigma \ll q$). The goal of the LWE solver is to find $\mathbf{s}$ given $(\mathbf{A}, \mathbf{y})$, where m can be as large as the adversary desires. In the most straightforward use of this assumption for cryptography (suggested in Regev's original paper), $(\mathbf{A}, \mathbf{y})$ are used as public key for an encryption scheme, and $\mathbf{s}$ is the secret key. Similar roles are assumed in other cryptographic constructions.

Goldwasser et al. [GKPV10] initiated a study on the hardness of LWE when $\mathbf{s}$ is not chosen uniformly at random. This study was motivated by the desire to achieve an *entropic* notion of security that will allow to guarantee that the problem remains hard even if some information about $\mathbf{s}$ is leaked. They showed that if $\mathbf{s}$ is sampled from a binary distribution (i.e. supported over $\{0, 1\}^n$), then LWE remains hard so long as $\mathbf{s}$ has sufficient entropy. In fact, sampling $\mathbf{s}$ from a (possibly sparse) binary distribution is attractive in other contexts such as constructing efficient post-quantum cryptographic objects [NIS], minimizing noise blowup in homomorphic encryption [BGV12], classical worst-case to average-case reduction [BLP+13] and proving hardness for the so-called Learning with Rounding (LWR) problem [BPR12, BGM+16]. Progress on understanding entropic LWE in the binary setting was made in subsequent works [BLP+13, Mic18].

However, the question of hardness of LWE on imperfect secret distributions carries significance beyond the binary setting. If we consider the key-leakage problem, then changing the honest key distribution to be binary just for the sake of improving robustness against key-leakage carries a heavy cost in the performance and security features in case no leakage occurs. An entropic hardness result for the general uniform setting is thus a natural question. Furthermore, for a problem as important as LWE, the mere scientific understanding of the robustness of the problem to small changes in the prescribed distributions and parameters stands as a self-supporting goal.

Alas, it appears that current approaches provide no insight for the general setting. Existing results can be extended beyond the binary setting so long as the norm of the vectors **s** is bounded, i.e. so long as the secret distribution is contained within some small enough ball, as was made explicit by Alwen et al. [AKPW13]. However this appeared to be an artifact of the proof technique and it was speculated by some that a general entropic LWE result should exist. Exploring the hardness of general entropic LWE is the goal of this work.

1.1 Our Results

We relate the hardness of Entropic LWE for arbitrary distributions to a basic property of the distribution, specifically to how *bad* the distribution performs as an error correcting code against Gaussian noise. Specifically, let $\mathcal{S}$ be some distribution over secrets in $\mathbb{Z}_q^n$. Recall the notion of conditional smooth min-entropy $\tilde{H}_\infty$ and define the *noise lossiness* of $\mathcal{S}$ as

$$\nu_\sigma(\mathcal{S}) = \tilde{H}_\infty(\mathbf{s}|\mathbf{s}+\mathbf{e}) = -\log\left(\Pr_{\mathbf{s},\mathbf{e}}[\mathcal{A}^*(\mathbf{s}+\mathbf{e}) = \mathbf{s}]\right), \tag{1}$$

where **s** is sampled from $\mathcal{S}$ and **e** is (continuous, say) Gaussian noise with parameter σ, and $\mathcal{A}^*$ is the optimal maximal likelihood decoder for **s**, namely $\mathcal{A}^*(\mathbf{y}) = \arg\max_{\mathbf{s}} \Pr_{\mathbf{s},\mathbf{e}}[\mathbf{s}|\mathbf{y} = \mathbf{s} + \mathbf{e}]$. This notion is a min-entropy analogue to the notion of *equivocation* for Shannon-entropy, and can be seen as a *guaranteed information loss* of a gaussian channel (rather than average information loss).

We advocate for noise lossiness as a new and natural measure for a distribution and show that it allows to get a good handle on the entropic LWE question. We do this by showing that distributions with sufficiently high noise lossiness lead to hard instances of Entropic LWE (under assumptions, see details below). We then show that high min-entropy implies (some limited level of) noise lossiness, which allows us to derive hardness results for general Entropic LWE. We furthermore show that results for distributions supported inside a ball can also be derived using our technique and show that noise lossiness of such distributions is larger than that of general distributions.[1] Finally, we show that our bounds for the general entropic setting are essentially tight. See below for details.

Noise Lossiness Implies Entropic LWE Hardness (Sect. 4). We show that high noise lossiness implies entropic hardness. Our result relies on the hardness of the decision version of LWE (with "standard" secret distribution). Whereas the variant we discussed so far is the search variant, which asserts that finding **s** given $(\mathbf{A}, \mathbf{y})$ should be hard, the decision variant dLWE asserts that it is computationally hard to even distinguish $(\mathbf{A}, \mathbf{y})$ from $(\mathbf{A}, \mathbf{u})$ where $\mathbf{u} \in \mathbb{Z}_q^m$ is uniform. The hardness of decision LWE immediately implies hardness for search LWE, and the converse is also true but not for every noise distribution and via

---

[1] In fact, noise lossiness provides a simple intuitive explanation on why ball-bounded distributions with given min-entropy yield harder Entropic LWE instances than general ones. This is due to the fact that packing the same number of elements in a small ball necessarily makes it harder to go back to the point of origin once noise is added.

a reduction that incurs some cost. This is also the case in the entropic setting. By default when we refer to (Entropic) LWE in this work, we refer to the search version. We will mention explicitly when referring to the decision version.

Our results in this setting are as follows.

Theorem 1.1 (Main Theorem, Informal). *Assume that decision LWE with dimension k, modulus q and Gaussian noise parameter γ is hard. Let $\mathcal{S}$ be a distribution over $\mathbb{Z}_q^n$ with $\nu_{\sigma_1}(\mathcal{S}) \geq k\log(q) + \omega(\log \lambda)$ for some parameter σ_1, then Entropic LWE with secret distribution $\mathcal{S}$ and Gaussian noise parameter $\sigma \approx \sigma_1 \gamma \sqrt{m}$ is hard.*

Our actual theorem is even more expressive on two aspects. First, while the above result applies for search Entropic LWE for all values of q, but in some cases, e.g. when q is prime, it also applies to decision Entropic LWE. Second, in the case where $\mathcal{S}$ is supported inside a ball, the term $k\log(q)$ can be relaxed to roughly $k\log(\gamma r)$ where r is the radius of the ball (this only applies to the search version).

We note that we incur a loss in noise that depends on $\sqrt{m}$, i.e. depends on the number of LWE samples. This is inherent in our proof technique, but using known statistical or computational rerandomization results, this dependence can be replaced by dependence on n, γ.

As explained above, most of our results imply hardness for search Entropic LWE and do not directly imply hardness for the decision version (albeit search-to-decision reductions can be applied, as we explained below). We note that this is an artifact of the applicability of our proof technique even in cases where the decision problem is not hard at all. We view this as a potentially useful property which may find future applications. To illustrate, consider the setting where the distributions of $\mathbf{s}$ and $\mathbf{e}$, as well as the modulus q, are all even. (Indeed, usually we consider the coordinates of $\mathbf{e}$ to be continuous Gaussians or a discrete Gaussians over $\mathbb{Z}$, but one may be interested in a setting where they are, say, discrete Gaussian over $2\mathbb{Z}$.) In this setting, decision LWE is trivially easy, but search LWE remains hard. Our techniques (as detailed in the technical overview below) naturally extend to this setting and can be used to prove entropic hardness in this case as well.

In the standard regime of parameters, where $\mathbf{e}$ is a continuous Gaussian, we can derive the hardness of the decision problem using known search-to-decision reductions. The most generic version, as in e.g. [Reg05], runs in time $q \cdot \text{poly}(n)$ but in many cases the dependence on q can be eliminated [Pei09,MM11]. In particular we note that in the ball-bounded setting, search-to-decision does not incur dependence on q.

Noise-Lossiness and Entropy (Sect. 5). We analyze the relation between noise-lossiness and min-entropy of a distribution both in the general setting and in the ball-bounded setting. We derive the following bounds.

Lemma 1.2 (Noise-Lossiness of General Distributions). *Let $\mathcal{S}$ be a general distribution over $\mathbb{Z}_q^n$, then $\nu_\sigma(\mathcal{S}) \geq \tilde{H}_\infty(\mathbf{s}) - n\log(q/\sigma) - 1$.*

Lemma 1.3 (Noise-Lossiness of Small Distributions). *Let S be a distribution over $\mathbb{Z}_q^n$ which is supported only inside a ball of radius r, then $\nu_\sigma(S) \geq \tilde{H}_\infty(\mathbf{s}) - 2r\sqrt{n}/\sigma$.*

Putting these results together with our main theorem, we get general Entropic LWE hardness whenever $\tilde{H}_\infty(\mathbf{s}) \gtrsim k \log(q) + n \log(q\gamma\sqrt{m}/\sigma)$. In the r-ball-bounded setting we require entropy $\tilde{H}_\infty(\mathbf{s}) \gtrsim k \log(\gamma r) + 2r\sqrt{nm}\gamma/\sigma$.[2] Note that if we make the very strong (yet not implausible) assumption that LWE is sub-exponentially secure, then we can use complexity leveraging and choose k to be polylogarithmic, we can choose σ to be large enough that the second term vanishes, and we get entropic hardness even with $\tilde{H}_\infty(\mathbf{s})$ which is polylogarithmic in the security parameter, in particular independent of $\log(q)$.

Tightness (Sects. 6 and 7). We provide two tightness results. The first one is essentially a restatement of a bound that was shown in the Ring-LWE setting by Bolboceanu et al. [BBPS19]. It is unconditional, but requires q to have a factor of a proper size.

Theorem 1.4 (Counterexample for Entropic LWE, Informal [BBPS19]). *Let n, q, σ be LWE parameters. Then if there exists p s.t. $p|q$ and $p \approx \sigma\sqrt{n}$, then there exists a distribution S with min-entropy roughly $n\log(q/\sigma)$, such that Entropic LWE is insecure with respect to S.*

However, the above requires that q has a factor of appropriate size. One could wonder whether one can do better for a prime q. While we do not have an explicit counterexample here, we can show that proving such a statement (i.e. security for Entropic LWE with entropy below roughly $n\log(q/\sigma)$) cannot be done by a black-box reduction to a standard "game based" assumption. In particular if the reduction can only access the adversary and to the distribution of secrets as black-box, then the entropy bound $n\log(q/\sigma)$ applies even for prime q.

Theorem 1.5 (Barrier for Entropic LWE, Informal). *Let n, q, σ be LWE parameters. Then there is no black-box reduction from Entropic LWE with entropy $\ll n\log(q/\sigma)$ to any game-based cryptographic assumption.*

1.2   Technical Overview

We provide a technical overview of our main contributions.

The Lossiness Approach to Entropic LWE. The starting point of our proof is the lossiness approach. This approach (in some small variants) was used in

---

[2] In the ball-bounded setting, our main improvement over [AKPW13, Appendix B] is that our entropy bound is independent of q. This is due to our use of Hermite normal form. Beyond this important difference, our flooding method and that of [AKPW13] are asymptotically similar *in the ball-bounded setting*. Our method of flooding at the source, however, is a general method that performs at least as well as the state of the art in the ball-bounded setting, and also implies tight results in the unbounded setting.

all existing hardness results for Entropic LWE [GKPV10]. However, prior works were only able to use it for norm-bounded secrets. We show a minor yet crucial modification that allows to relate the hardness of Entropic LWE to the noise-lossiness of the noise distribution.

Fix parameters n, q, σ and recall that the adversary is given $(\mathbf{A}, \mathbf{y})$, where $\mathbf{A}$ is uniform, $\mathbf{y} = \mathbf{sA} + \mathbf{e} \pmod{q}$, $\mathbf{s}$ sampled from $\mathcal{S}$ and $\mathbf{e}$ is a (continuous) Gaussian with parameter σ. The lossiness approach replaces the uniform matrix $\mathbf{A}$ with an "LWE matrix" of the form: $\mathbf{BC} + \mathbf{F}$, where $\mathbf{B} \in \mathbb{Z}_q^{n \times k}$, $\mathbf{C} \in \mathbb{Z}_q^{k \times m}$ are uniform, and $k \ll n, m$, and where $\mathbf{F}$ is a matrix whose every element is a (discrete) Gaussian with parameter γ. The *decisional* LWE assumption with dimension k, modulus q and noise parameter γ asserts that $\mathbf{BC} + \mathbf{F}$ is computationally indistinguishable from a uniform matrix, and therefore the adversary should also be able to recover $\mathbf{s}$ when $(\mathbf{A}, \mathbf{y})$ is generated using $\mathbf{A} = \mathbf{BC} + \mathbf{F}$. At this point, the vector $\mathbf{y}$ is distributed as

$$\mathbf{y} = \mathbf{sA} + \mathbf{e} = \mathbf{sBC} + \mathbf{sF} + \mathbf{e}.$$

The strategies on how to continue from here diverge. The [GKPV10] approach is to say that when $\mathbf{s}$ is confined inside a ball, and when $\mathbf{e}$ is a wide enough Gaussian, then the value $\mathbf{sF} + \mathbf{e}$ is "essentially independent" of $\mathbf{s}$. This is sometimes referred to as "noise flooding" since the noise $\mathbf{e}$ "floods" the value $\mathbf{sF}$ and minimizes its effect. This allows to apply the leftover hash lemma to argue that $\mathbf{sB}$ is statistically close to a uniform $\mathbf{s}'$ and obtain a new "standard" LWE instance. The [BLP+13,Mic18] approaches can be viewed as variants of this method, where the argument on $\mathbf{sF} + \mathbf{e}$ is refined in non-trivial ways to achieve better parameters.

This type of argument cannot work for the general setting (i.e. when $\mathbf{s}$ is not short) since in this case $\mathbf{sF} + \mathbf{e}$ can reveal noticeable information about $\mathbf{s}$. For example, if $\mathbf{s}$ is a multiple of some large enough factor then the noise $\mathbf{e}$ can just be rounded away (indeed this will be the starting point for our tightness result, as we explain further below).

Our approach therefore is to resort to a weaker claim. We do not try to change $\mathbf{y}$ into a form of standard LWE, but instead all we show is that $\mathbf{y}$ *loses information* about $\mathbf{s}$. Namely, we will show that even information-theoretically it is not possible to recover $\mathbf{s}$ from $(\mathbf{A}, \mathbf{y})$. This approach was taken, for example, by Alwen et al. [AKPW13], but they were unable to show lossiness for the general setting. The reason, essentially, is that they also use a refined version of noise flooding, one that did not require that $\mathbf{e}$ completely floods $\mathbf{sF}$, only slightly perturb it. We can call it "gentle flooding" for the purpose of this work. A similar argument was used in [DM13] to establish hardness of LWE with uniform errors from a short interval.

We note that in all flooding methods, it is beneficial if $\mathbf{F}$ contains small values as much as possible. Therefore in order to show hardness for $\mathbf{s}$ with as low entropy as possible, the parameter γ is to be taken as small as possible, while still supporting the hardness of distinguishing $\mathbf{BC} + \mathbf{F}$ from uniform.

Our Approach: Gentle Flooding at the Source. Our approach can be viewed in hindsight as a very simple modification of the lossiness/flooding approach, that results in a very clean statement, and the characterization of the noise lossiness as the "right" parameter for the hardness of Entropic LWE.

We take another look at the term $\mathbf{sF} + \mathbf{e}$ and recall that our goal is to use $\mathbf{e}$ to lose information about $\mathbf{s}$. Clearly, if $\mathbf{e}$ was of the form $\mathbf{e}_1\mathbf{F}$, then things would be more approachable since then we would simply have $(\mathbf{s} + \mathbf{e}_1)\mathbf{F}$, and we will simply need to argue about the lossiness of $\mathbf{s}$ under additive Gaussian noise (which is exactly our notion of noise lossiness for the distribution $\mathcal{S}$). Our observation is that even though $\mathbf{e}$ does not have this form, the properties of the Gaussian distribution allow to present $\mathbf{e}$ as $\mathbf{e} = \mathbf{e}_1\mathbf{F} + \mathbf{e}_2$, where $\mathbf{e}_1, \mathbf{e}_2$ are independent random variables (but the *distribution* of $\mathbf{e}_2$ depends on $\mathbf{F}$). This is easiest to analyze when $\mathbf{e}$ is a continuous Gaussian, which is the approach we take in this work.[3]

It can be shown essentially by definition that the sum of two independent Gaussian vectors with covariance matrices Σ_1, Σ_2 is a Gaussian with covariance matrix $\Sigma_1 + \Sigma_2$. It follows that if we choose $\mathbf{e}_1$ to be a spherical Gaussian with parameter σ_1 then $\mathbf{e}_1\mathbf{F}$ will have covariance matrix $\sigma_1\mathbf{F}^T\mathbf{F}$. Therefore if we choose $\mathbf{e}_2$ to be an aspherical Gaussian with covariance $\sigma\mathbf{I} - \sigma_1\mathbf{F}^T\mathbf{F}$, we get that $\mathbf{e} = \mathbf{e}_1\mathbf{F} + \mathbf{e}_2$ is indeed a spherical σ Gaussian. There is an important emphasis here, the matrix $\sigma\mathbf{I} - \sigma_1\mathbf{F}^T\mathbf{F}$ must be a valid covariance matrix, i.e. positive semidefinite. To guarantee this, we must set the ratio σ/σ_1 to be at least the largest singular value of the matrix $\mathbf{F}$. Standard results on singular values of Gaussian matrices imply that the largest singular value is roughly $\sqrt{m}\gamma$, which governs the ratio between σ_1 and σ. We stress again that $\mathbf{e}_1$ and $\mathbf{e}_2$ are independent random variables.

Once we established the decomposition of the Gaussian, we can write $\mathbf{y}$ as

$$\mathbf{y} = \mathbf{sA} + \mathbf{e} = \mathbf{sBC} + (\mathbf{s} + \mathbf{e}_1)\mathbf{F} + \mathbf{e}_2.$$

Now, our noise lossiness term $\nu_{\sigma_1}(\mathcal{S}) = \tilde{H}_\infty(\mathbf{s}|\mathbf{s} + \mathbf{e}_1)$ naturally emerges. Note that $\mathbf{y}$ cannot provide more information about $\mathbf{s}$ than the two variables $(\mathbf{sB}, \mathbf{s} + \mathbf{e}_1)$. Since the former contains only $k \log q$ bits, it follows that if the noise lossiness is sufficiently larger than $k \log q$, then naturally $\tilde{H}_\infty(\mathbf{s}|\mathbf{s} + \mathbf{e}_1, \mathbf{sB})$ is non-trivial (we need $\omega(\log \lambda)$ where λ is the security parameter), which implies that finding $\mathbf{s}$ is information theoretically hard. Thus the hardness of Entropic (search) LWE is established.

If in addition $\mathbf{B}$ can serve as an extractor (this is the case when the modulus q is prime, or when the $\mathcal{S}$ is binary), then we can make a stronger claim, that $\mathbf{sB}$ is statistically close to uniform, and then apply (standard) LWE again in order to obtain hardness for Entropic dLWE directly.

Finally, we notice that for norm-bounded distributions we can improve the parameters further by using LWE in *Hermite Normal Form* (HNF) which has

---

[3] It can be shown and is by now standard that the hardness of LWE is essentially equivalent whether $\mathbf{e}$ is a continuous Gaussian, discrete Gaussian, or "rounded" Gaussian [Pei10].

been shown to be equivalent to standard LWE in [ACPS09]. HNF LWE allows to argue that $\mathbf{BC} + \mathbf{F}$ is indistinguishable from uniform even when the elements of $\mathbf{B}$ are also sampled from a Gaussian with parameter γ (same as $\mathbf{F}$). Using HNF, we can further bound the entropy loss caused by the term $\mathbf{sB}$ and achieve a bound that is independent of q, and only depends on γ, r, σ. We can only apply this technique for Entropic search LWE.

For the complete analysis and formal statement of the result, see Sect. 4.

Computing The Noise Lossiness. We briefly explain the intuition behind the noise lossiness computation. The exact details require calculation and are detailed in Sect. 5.

For the sake of this overview, let us consider only "flat" distributions, i.e. ones that are uniform over a set of K strings (and thus have min-entropy $\log K$). We will provide an upper bound on the probability $\Pr_{\mathbf{s,e}}[\mathcal{A}^*(\mathbf{s+e}) = \mathbf{s}]$ from Eq. (1), which will immediately translate to a bound on the noise-lossiness.

For general distributions, we note that we can write

$$\Pr_{\mathbf{s,e}}[\mathcal{A}^*(\mathbf{s}+\mathbf{e}) = \mathbf{s}] = \int_{\mathbf{y}} \Pr_{\mathbf{s,e}}[\mathbf{s}+\mathbf{e} = \mathbf{y} \wedge \mathcal{A}^*(\mathbf{y}) = \mathbf{s}]dy,$$

where the integral is over the entire q-cube (we use integral since we use a continuous distribution for $\mathbf{e}$, but a calculation with discrete Gaussian will be very similar). Note that the expression $\Pr_{\mathbf{s,e}}[\mathbf{s} + \mathbf{e} = \mathbf{y} \wedge \mathcal{A}^*(\mathbf{y}) = \mathbf{s}]$ can be written as $\Pr_{\mathbf{s,e}}[\mathcal{A}^*(\mathbf{y}) + \mathbf{e} = \mathbf{y} \wedge \mathcal{A}^*(\mathbf{y}) = \mathbf{s}]$, which can then be decomposed since the event $\mathcal{A}^*(\mathbf{y}) + \mathbf{e} = \mathbf{y}$ depends only on $\mathbf{e}$ and the event $\mathcal{A}^*(\mathbf{y}) = \mathbf{s}$ depends only on $\mathbf{s}$ (recall that $\mathbf{y}$ is fixed at this point). We can therefore write

$$\Pr_{\mathbf{s,e}}[\mathcal{A}^*(\mathbf{s} + \mathbf{e}) = \mathbf{s}] = \int_{\mathbf{y}} \Pr_{\mathbf{e}}[\mathbf{e} = \mathbf{y} - \mathcal{A}^*(\mathbf{y})] \cdot \Pr_{\mathbf{s}}[\mathcal{A}^*(\mathbf{y}) = \mathbf{s}]dy.$$

Now, for all $\mathbf{y}$ it holds that $\Pr_{\mathbf{s}}[\mathcal{A}^*(\mathbf{y}) = \mathbf{s}] \leq 1/K$, simply since $\mathcal{A}^*(\mathbf{y})$ is a fixed value. It also holds that $\Pr_{\mathbf{e}}[\mathbf{e} = \mathbf{y} - \mathcal{A}^*(\mathbf{y})]$ is bounded by the maximum value of the Gaussian mass function, which is $1/\sigma^n$. We get that

$$\Pr_{\mathbf{s,e}}[\mathcal{A}^*(\mathbf{s} + \mathbf{e}) = \mathbf{s}] \leq \frac{1}{K\sigma^n} \int_{\mathbf{y}} dy = \frac{q^n}{K\sigma^n},$$

and Lemma 1.2 follows.

For the setting of Lemma 1.3, recall that $\mathcal{S}$ is supported only over r-norm-bounded vectors. Note that the analysis above is correct up to and including the conclusion that $\Pr_{\mathbf{s}}[\mathcal{A}^*(\mathbf{y}) = \mathbf{s}] \leq 1/K$. Furthermore, $\mathcal{A}^*(\mathbf{y})$ must return a value in the support of $\mathcal{S}$, that is small. We therefore remain with the challenge of bounding $\int_{\mathbf{y}} \Pr_{\mathbf{e}}[\mathbf{e} = \mathbf{y} - \mathcal{A}^*(\mathbf{y})]dy$, when we are guaranteed that $\|\mathcal{A}^*(\mathbf{y})\| \leq r$. We can deduce that this can only induce a minor perturbation to the $\mathbf{e}$ Gaussian. Using Gaussian tail bounds the result follows.

Tightness. The result of [BBPS19] (Theorem 1.4 above) is quite straightforward in our setting (they showed a ring variant which is somewhat more involved).

The idea to choose $\mathcal{S}$ to be uniform over the set of all vectors that are multiples of p (or in the [BBPS19] terminology, uniform over an ideal dividing the ideal q). This distribution has min-entropy $n \log(q/p) \approx n \log(q/\sigma)$ (since $p \approx \sigma$), and it clearly leads to an insecure LWE instance since the instance can be taken modulo p in order to recover the noise, and then once the noise is removed the secret can easily be recovered.

The above argument seems to "unfairly" rely on the structure of the modulus q, and one could hope that for prime q, which has no factors, a better result can be achieved. We extend a methodology due to Wichs [Wic13] to show that if such a result exists then it will require non-black-box use of the adversary and/or the sampler for the distribution $\mathcal{S}$. Consider a black-box reduction that given access to an entropic LWE adversary $\mathcal{A}$ and a sampler for $\mathcal{S}$ (we overload the notation and denote the sampler by $\mathcal{S}$ as well), manages to solve some hard problem, e.g. solve a standard LWE instance.

We show that it is possible to efficiently (jointly) simulate $\mathcal{A}, \mathcal{S}$, such that in the eyes of a reduction they are indistinguishable from a real high-entropy distribution $\mathcal{S}$ and an adversary $\mathcal{A}$ that solves Entropic LWE on it, thus leading to an efficient unconditional algorithm for said hard problem. The basic idea relies on the natural intuition that it is hard to generate a "valid" LWE instance without knowing the value of $\mathbf{s}$ that is being used. While this intuition is false in many situations, we show that in the entropic setting with black-box reductions it can be made formal.

Specifically, consider $\mathcal{S}$ that is just a uniform distribution over a set of K randomly chosen strings (note that this distribution does not have an efficient sampler, but a black-box reduction is required to work in such a setting as well, and we will show how to simulate $\mathcal{S}$ efficiently). The adversary $\mathcal{A}$, upon receiving an instance $(\mathbf{A}, \mathbf{y})$ first checks that $\mathbf{A}$ is full rank (otherwise return $\bot$), and if so it brute-forces $\mathbf{s}$ out of $\mathbf{y}$ by trying all possible $\mathbf{s}^*$ in the support of $\mathcal{S}$, and if there is one for which $\mathbf{y} - \mathbf{s}^* \mathbf{A} \pmod{q}$ is short (i.e. of the length that we expect from noise with Gaussian parameter σ), then return a random such $\mathbf{s}^*$ as answer (otherwise return $\bot$). This is a valid adversary for Entropic LWE and therefore it should allow the reduction to solve the hard problem.

Now, let us show how to simulate $\mathcal{S}, \mathcal{A}$ efficiently. The idea is to rely on the intuition that the reduction cannot generate valid LWE instances with values of $\mathcal{S}$ that it does not know, and since the distribution is sparse, the reduction cannot generate strings in the support of $\mathcal{S}$ in any way except calling the $\mathcal{S}$ sampler. Furthermore, since the reduction can only make polynomially many queries to the sampler, there are only polynomially many options for $\mathbf{s}$ for which it can generate valid LWE instances, and our efficient implementation of $\mathcal{A}$ can just check these polynomially many options. (Note that throughout this intuitive outline we keep referring to *valid* Entropic LWE instances, the above argument actually fails without a proper notion of validity as will be explained below.)

Concretely, we will simulate the adversary using a *stateful* procedure, i.e. one that keeps state. However, in the eyes of the reduction this will simulate the original stateless adversary and therefore will suffice for our argument. We will simulate $\mathcal{S}$ using "lazy sampling". Whenever the reduction makes a call to $\mathcal{S}$, we will just sample a new random string $\mathbf{s}$, and save the new sample to its internal state. When a query $(\mathbf{A}, \mathbf{y})$ to $\mathcal{A}$ is made, then we first check that $\mathbf{A}$ is indeed full rank (otherwise return $\perp$), and if it is the case, go over all vectors $\mathbf{s}^*$ that we generated so far (and are stored in the state), and check whether $\mathbf{y} - \mathbf{s}^*\mathbf{A}$ (mod q) is short (in the same sense as above, i.e. of the length that we expect from noise with Gaussian parameter σ). If it is the case then a random such $\mathbf{s}^*$ is returned as the Entropic LWE answer. If the scan did not reveal any adequate candidate, then return $\perp$.

We want to argue that the above simulates the stateless process. The first step is to show that if there is no $\mathbf{s}^*$ in the state and thus our simulated adversary returns $\perp$, then the inefficient adversary would also have returned $\perp$ with all but negligible probability. Secondly, noticing that when our simulated adversary does return a value $\mathbf{s}^*$, this $\mathbf{s}^*$ is a value that the reduction already received as a response to a $\mathcal{S}$ query, and only one such $\mathbf{s}^*$ exists. In fact, both of these concerns boil down to properly defining a notion of validity of the Entropic LWE instance that will prevent both of these concerns.

To this end, we notice that the original inefficient adversary return a non-$\perp$ value only on instances where $\mathbf{A}$ is full rank, and there exists a short $\mathbf{e}^*$ and value $\mathbf{s}^*$ in the support of $\mathcal{S}$ such that $\mathbf{y} = \mathbf{s}^*\mathbf{A} + \mathbf{e}^*$. We will prove that it is not possible to find an instance which is valid for $\mathbf{s}$ in the support of $\mathcal{S}$ which has not been seen by the reduction. This will address both concerns and can be proven since the unseen elements of $\mathcal{S}$ are just randomly sampled strings, so we can think of the vectors as sampled after the matrix $\mathbf{A}$ is determined. The probability of a random vector $\mathbf{s}$ to be s.t. $\mathbf{y} - \mathbf{s}\mathbf{A}$ is σ-short, where $\mathbf{y}$ is arbitrary and $\mathbf{A}$ is full rank, is roughly $(\sigma/q)^n$. This translates to the cardinality K of $\mathcal{S}$ being as large as (roughly) $n\log(q/\sigma)$ and still allowing to apply the union bound. The result thus follows.

Maybe somewhat interestingly, while our security proofs for entropic LWE are technically similar to *converse coding theorems* [Sha48, W+59], our barrier result resembles the random coding arguments used to prove the *coding theorem* [Sha48, Sha49].

2   Preliminaries

We will denote the security parameter by λ. We say a function $\nu(\lambda)$ is negligible if $\nu(\lambda) \in \lambda^{-\omega(1)}$. We will generally denote row vectors by $\mathbf{x}$ and column vectors by $\mathbf{x}^\top$. We will denote the L_2 norm of a vector $\mathbf{x}$ by $\|\mathbf{x}\| = \sqrt{\sum_i x_i^2}$ and the L_∞ norm by $\|\mathbf{x}\|_\infty = \max_i |x_i|$.

We denote by $\mathbb{T}_q = \mathbb{R}/q\mathbb{Z}$ be the real torus of scale q. We can embed $\mathbb{Z}_q = \mathbb{Z}/q\mathbb{Z}$ into $\mathbb{T}_q$ in the natural way. $\mathbb{T}_q$ is an abelian group and therefore a $\mathbb{Z}$-algebra. Thus multiplication of vectors from $\mathbb{T}_q^n$ with $\mathbb{Z}$-matrices is well-defined. $\mathbb{T}_q$ is however not a $\mathbb{Z}_q$-algebra. We will represent $\mathbb{T}_q$ elements by their central residue class representation in $[-q/2, q/2)$.

For a continuous random variable $\mathbf{x}$, we will denote the probability-density function of $\mathbf{x}$ by $p_{\mathbf{x}}(\cdot)$. We will denote the probability density of $\mathbf{x}$ conditioned on an event E by $p_{\mathbf{x}|E}(\cdot)$. Let X, Y be two discrete random variables defined on a common support $\mathcal{X}$. We define the statistical distance between X and Y as $\Delta(X, Y) = \sum_{x \in \mathcal{X}} |\Pr[X = x] - \Pr[Y = x]|$. Likewise, if X and Y are two continuous random variables defined on a measurable set $\mathcal{X}$, we define the statistical distance between X and Y as $\Delta(X, Y) = \int_{x \in \mathcal{X}} |p_X(x) - p_Y(x)|$.

Random Matrices. Let p be a prime modulus. Let $\mathbf{A} \leftarrow_{\$} \mathbb{Z}_p^{n \times m}$ be chosen uniformly at random. Then the probability that $\mathbf{A}$ is not invertible (i.e. does not have an invertible column-submatrix)

$$\Pr[\mathbf{A} \text{ not invertible}] = 1 - \prod_{i=0}^{n-1}(1 - p^{i-m}) \leq p^{n-m}.$$

For an arbitrary modulus q, a matrix $\mathbf{A}$ is invertible if and only if it is invertible modulo all prime factors p_i of q. As we can bound the number of prime factors of q by $\log(q)$, we get for an $\mathbf{A} \leftarrow_{\$} \mathbb{Z}_p^{n \times m}$ that

$$\Pr[\mathbf{A} \text{ not invertible}] \leq \log(q) \cdot 2^{n-m}.$$

2.1 Min-entropy

Let $\mathbf{x}$ be a discrete random variable supported on a set X and $\mathbf{z}$ be a possibly (continuous) random variable supported on a (measurable) set Z. The conditional min-entropy $\tilde{H}_\infty(\mathbf{x}|\mathbf{z})$ of $\mathbf{x}$ given $\mathbf{z}$ is defined by

$$\tilde{H}_\infty(\mathbf{x}|\mathbf{z}) = -\log\left(\mathsf{E}_{\mathbf{z}'}\left[\max_{\mathbf{x}' \in X} \Pr[\mathbf{x} = \mathbf{x}'|\mathbf{z} = \mathbf{z}']\right]\right).$$

In the case that $\mathbf{z}$ is continuous, this becomes

$$\tilde{H}_\infty(\mathbf{x}|\mathbf{z}) = -\log\left(\int_{\mathbf{z}'} p_{\mathbf{z}}(\mathbf{z}') \max_{\mathbf{x}' \in X} \Pr[\mathbf{x} = \mathbf{x}'|\mathbf{z} = \mathbf{z}']\right),$$

where $p_{\mathbf{z}}(\cdot)$ is the probability density of $\mathbf{z}$.

2.2 Leftover Hashing

We recall the generalized leftover hash lemma [DORS08, Reg05]

Lemma 2.1. *Let q be a modulus and let n, k be integers. Let $\mathbf{s}$ be a random variable defined on $\mathbb{Z}_q^n$ and let $\mathbf{B} \leftarrow_{\$} \mathbb{Z}_q^{n \times k}$ be chosen uniformly random. Furthermore let Y be a random-variable (possibly) correlated with $\mathbf{s}$. Then it holds that*

$$\Delta((\mathbf{B}, \mathbf{sB}, Y), (\mathbf{B}, \mathbf{u}, Y)) \leq \sqrt{q^k \cdot 2^{-\tilde{H}_\infty(\mathbf{s}|Y)}}.$$

2.3 Gaussians

Continuous Gaussians. A matrix $\boldsymbol{\Sigma} \in \mathbb{R}^{n \times n}$ is called positive definite, if it holds for every $\mathbf{x} \in \mathbb{R}^n \backslash \{\mathbf{0}\}$ that $\mathbf{x} \boldsymbol{\Sigma} \mathbf{x}^\top > 0$. For every positive definite matrix $\boldsymbol{\Sigma}$ there exists a unique positive definite matrix $\sqrt{\boldsymbol{\Sigma}}$ such that $(\sqrt{\boldsymbol{\Sigma}})^2 = \boldsymbol{\Sigma}$.

For a parameter $\sigma > 0$ define the n-dimensional gaussian function $\rho_\sigma : \mathbb{R}^n \to (0, 1]$ by

$$\rho_\sigma(\mathbf{x}) = e^{-\pi \|\mathbf{x}\|^2 / \sigma^2}.$$

For a positive definite matrix $\boldsymbol{\Sigma} \in \mathbb{R}^{n \times n}$, define the function $\rho_{\sqrt{\boldsymbol{\Sigma}}} : \mathbb{R}^n \to (0, 1]$ by

$$\rho_{\sqrt{\boldsymbol{\Sigma}}}(\mathbf{x}) := e^{-\pi \mathbf{x} \boldsymbol{\Sigma}^{-1} \mathbf{x}^\top}.$$

For a scalar $\sigma > 0$, we will define

$$\rho_\sigma(\mathbf{x}) := \rho_{\sigma \cdot \mathbf{I}}(\mathbf{x}) = e^{-\pi \|\mathbf{x}\|^2 / \sigma^2}.$$

The total measure of $\rho_{\sqrt{\boldsymbol{\Sigma}}}$ over $\mathbb{R}^n$ is

$$\rho_{\sqrt{\boldsymbol{\Sigma}}}(\mathbb{R}^n) = \int_{\mathbb{R}^n} \rho_{\sqrt{\boldsymbol{\Sigma}}}(\mathbf{x}) d\mathbf{x} = \sqrt{\det(\boldsymbol{\Sigma})}.$$

In the scalar case this becomes

$$\rho_\sigma(\mathbb{R}^n) = \int_{\mathbb{R}^n} \rho_\sigma(\mathbf{x}) d\mathbf{x} = \sigma^n.$$

Normalizing $\rho_{\sqrt{\boldsymbol{\Sigma}}}$ by $\rho_{\sqrt{\boldsymbol{\Sigma}}}(\mathbb{R}^n)$ yields the probability density for the continuous gaussian distribution $D_{\sqrt{\boldsymbol{\Sigma}}}$ over $\mathbb{R}^n$.

For a discrete set $S \subseteq \mathbb{R}^n$ we define $\rho_{\sqrt{\boldsymbol{\Sigma}}}(S)$ by

$$\rho_{\sqrt{\boldsymbol{\Sigma}}}(S) := \sum_{\mathbf{s} \in S} \rho_{\sqrt{\boldsymbol{\Sigma}}}(\mathbf{s}).$$

In particular, for a integer q we have

$$\rho_{\sqrt{\boldsymbol{\Sigma}}}(q\mathbb{Z}^n) = \sum_{\mathbf{z} \in q\mathbb{Z}^n} \rho_{\sqrt{\boldsymbol{\Sigma}}}(\mathbf{z}).$$

For a gaussian $x \sim D_\sigma$ we get the tail-bound

$$\Pr[|x| \geq t] \leq 2 \cdot e^{-\frac{t^2}{2\sigma^2}}.$$

As a simple consequence we get $\Pr[|x| \geq (\log(\lambda)) \cdot \sigma] \leq \mathsf{negl}(\lambda)$.

Discrete Gaussians. We say a random variable x defined on $\mathbb{Z}$ follows the discrete gaussian distribution $D_{\mathbb{Z}, \sigma}$ for a parameter $\sigma > 0$, if the probability mass function of x is given by

$$\Pr[x = x'] = \frac{\rho_\sigma(x')}{\rho_\sigma(\mathbb{Z})}$$

for every $x' \in \mathbb{Z}$.

Modular Gaussians. For a modulus q, we also define the q-periodic gaussian function $\tilde{\rho}_{q,\sqrt{\Sigma}}$: by

$$\tilde{\rho}_{q,\sqrt{\Sigma}}(\mathbf{x}) := \sum_{\mathbf{z} \in q\mathbb{Z}^n} \rho_{q,\sqrt{\Sigma}}(\mathbf{x} - \mathbf{z}).$$

We define $\tilde{\rho}_{q,\sqrt{\Sigma}}(\mathbb{T}_q^n)$ by

$$\tilde{\rho}_{q,\sqrt{\Sigma}}(\mathbb{T}_q^n) := \tilde{\rho}_{q,\sqrt{\Sigma}}([-q/2,q/2)^n) = \int_{[-q/2,q/2)^n} \tilde{\rho}_{q,\sqrt{\Sigma}}(\mathbf{x})d\mathbf{x} = \rho_{\sqrt{\Sigma}}(\mathbb{R}^n).$$

Consequently, normalizing $\tilde{\rho}_{q,\sqrt{\Sigma}}$ by $\tilde{\rho}_{q,\sqrt{\Sigma}}(\mathbb{T}_q^n)$ yields a probability density on $\mathbb{T}_q^n$. We call the corresponding distribution $D_{\sqrt{\Sigma}}$ mod q a modular gaussian. A $\mathbf{x} \sim D_{\sqrt{\Sigma}}$ mod q can be sampled by sampling and $\mathbf{x}' \leftarrow_{\$} D_{\sqrt{\Sigma}}$ and computing $\mathbf{x} \leftarrow \mathbf{x}'$ mod q.

In order to prove our strong converse coding theorems, we need various upper bounds for the periodic gaussian function. We will use the following variant of the smoothing lemma of Micciancio and Regev [MR04][4].

Lemma 2.2 (Smoothing Lemma [MR04]). *Let $\epsilon > 0$. Given that $\frac{1}{\sigma} \geq \sqrt{\frac{\ln(2n(1+1/\epsilon))}{\pi}} \cdot \frac{1}{q}$, then it holds that*

$$\rho_\sigma(q\mathbb{Z}^n \setminus \{\mathbf{0}\}) \leq \epsilon.$$

Lemma 2.3. *The periodic gaussian function $\tilde{\rho}_{q,\sigma}$ assumes its maximum at $q \cdot \mathbb{Z}^n$. In particular, it holds for all $\mathbf{x} \in \mathbb{R}^n$ that $\tilde{\rho}_{q,\sigma}(\mathbf{x}) \leq \tilde{\rho}_{q,\sigma}(\mathbf{0})$.*

See the full version [BD20] for proof.

Lemma 2.4. *If $\frac{q}{\sigma} \geq \sqrt{\frac{\ln(4n)}{\pi}}$, then it holds for all $\mathbf{x} \in \mathbb{R}^n$ that*

$$\tilde{\rho}_{q,\sigma}(\mathbf{x}) \leq 2.$$

See the full version [BD20] for proof.

We will use the following estimate for shifted gaussians.

Lemma 2.5. *Let $\sigma_2 > \sigma_1 > 0$. Then it holds for all $\mathbf{x} \in \mathbb{R}^n$ and $\mathbf{t} \in \mathbb{R}^n$ that*

$$\rho_{\sigma_1}(\mathbf{x} - \mathbf{t}) \leq e^{\pi \frac{\|\mathbf{t}\|^2}{\sigma_2^2 - \sigma_1^2}} \cdot \rho_{\sigma_2}(\mathbf{x}).$$

Moreover, the same holds for the q-periodic gaussian function $\hat{\rho}_{q\mathbb{Z}^n,\sigma_1}$, i.e.

$$\hat{\rho}_{q\mathbb{Z}^n,\sigma_1}(\mathbf{x} - \mathbf{t}) \leq e^{\pi \frac{\|\mathbf{t}\|^2}{\sigma_2^2 - \sigma_1^2}} \cdot \hat{\rho}_{q\mathbb{Z}^n,\sigma_2}(\mathbf{x}).$$

See the full version [BD20] for proof.

---

[4] We use the smoothing lemma with the parameter $s - 1/\sigma$ and the lattice $\Lambda = \frac{1}{q}\mathbb{Z}^n$. Note that for this lattice it holds that $\lambda_n = 1/q$.

2.4 Learning with Errors

The learning with errors (LWE) problem was defined by Regev [Reg05]. The search problem $\mathsf{LWE}(n, m, q, \chi)$, for $n, m, q \in \mathbb{N}$ and for a distribution χ supported over the torus $\mathbb{T}_q$ is to find $\mathbf{s}$ given $(\mathbf{A}, \mathbf{sA} + \mathbf{e})$, where $\mathbf{A} \leftarrow_\$ \mathbb{Z}_q^{n \times m}$ is chosen uniformly random and $\mathbf{e} \leftarrow_\$ \chi^m$ is chosen according to χ^m. The decisional version $\mathsf{dLWE}(n, m, q, \chi)$ asks to distinguish between the distributions $(\mathbf{A}, \mathbf{sA} + \mathbf{e})$ and $(\mathbf{A}, \mathbf{u} + \mathbf{e})$, where $\mathbf{A}$, $\mathbf{s}$ and $\mathbf{e}$ are as in the search version and $\mathbf{u} \leftarrow_\$ \mathbb{Z}_q^m$ is chosen uniformly random. We also consider the hardness of solving dLWE for *any* $m = \mathsf{poly}(n \log q)$. This problem is denoted $\mathsf{dLWE}(n, q, \chi)$. The matrix version of this problem asks to distinguish $(\mathbf{A}, \mathbf{S} \cdot \mathbf{A} + \mathbf{E})$ from $(\mathbf{A}, \mathbf{U})$, where $\mathbf{S} \leftarrow_\$ \mathbb{Z}_q^{k \times n}$, $\mathbf{E} \leftarrow_\$ \chi^{k \times m}$ and $\mathbf{U} \leftarrow \mathbb{Z}_q^{k \times m}$. The hardness of the matrix version for any $k = \mathsf{poly}(n)$ can be established from $\mathsf{dLWE}_{n,m,q,\chi}$ via a routine hybrid-argument. Moreover, Applebaum et al. [ACPS09] showed that if the error-distribution χ is supported on $\mathbb{Z}_q$, then the matrix $\mathbf{S}$ can also be chosen from $\chi^{k \times m}$ without affecting the hardness of the problem.

As shown in [Reg05], the $\mathsf{LWE}(n, q, \chi)$ problem with χ being a continuous Gaussian distribution with parameter $\sigma = \alpha q \geq 2\sqrt{n}$ is at least as hard as approximating the shortest independent vector problem (SIVP) to within a factor of $\gamma = \tilde{O}(n/\alpha)$ in *worst case* dimension n lattices. This is proven using a quantum reduction. Classical reductions (to a slightly different problem) exist as well [Pei09, BLP+13] but with somewhat worse parameters. The best known (classical or quantum) algorithms for these problems run in time $2^{\tilde{O}(n/\log \gamma)}$, and in particular they are conjectured to be intractable for $\gamma = \mathsf{poly}(n)$.

Regev also provided a search-to-decision reduction which bases the hardness of the decisional problem $\mathsf{dLWE}(n, q, \chi)$ on the search version $\mathsf{LWE}(n, q, \chi)$ whenever q is prime of polynomial size. This reduction has been generalized to more general classes of moduli [Pei09, BLP+13]. Moreover, there exists a *sample preserving* reduction which [MM11] which bases the hardness of $\mathsf{dLWE}(n, m, q, \chi)$ on $\mathsf{LWE}(n, m, q, \chi)$ for certain moduli q without affecting the number of samples m.

Finally, Peikert [Pei10] provided a randomized rounding algorithm which allows to base the hardness of $\mathsf{LWE}(n, m, q, D_{\mathbb{Z},\sigma'})$ (i.e. LWE with a discrete gaussian error $D_{\mathbb{Z},\sigma'}$) on $\mathsf{LWE}(n, m, q, D_\sigma)$ (continuous gaussian error), where σ' is only slightly larger than σ.

2.5 Entropic LWE

We will now consider LWE with entropic secrets, entropic LWE for short. In this variant, we allow the distribution of secrets $\mathcal{S}$ to be chosen from a family of distributions $\bar{\mathcal{S}} = \{\mathcal{S}_i\}_i$. This captures the idea the distribution of secrets can be worst-case from a certain family.

Definition 2.6 (Entropic LWE). *Let* $q = q(\lambda)$ *be a modulus and* $n, m = \mathsf{poly}(\lambda)$. *Let* χ *be an error-distribution on* $\mathbb{T}_q$. *Let* $\bar{\mathcal{S}} = \mathcal{S}(\lambda, q, n, m)$ *be a family* *of distributions on* $\mathbb{Z}_q^n$. *We say that the search problem* ent-LWE$(q, n, m, \bar{\mathcal{S}}, \chi)$ *is hard, if it holds for every PPT adversary $\mathcal{A}$ and every $\mathcal{S} \in \bar{\mathcal{S}}$ that*

$$\Pr[\mathcal{A}(1^\lambda, \mathbf{A}, \mathbf{s} \cdot \mathbf{A} + \mathbf{e}) = \mathbf{s}] \leq \mathsf{negl}(\lambda),$$

where $\mathbf{A} \leftarrow_\$ \mathbb{Z}_q^{m \times n}$, $\mathbf{s} \leftarrow_\$ \mathcal{S}$ *and* $\mathbf{e} \leftarrow_\$ \chi^m$. *Likewise, we say that the decisional problem* ent-dLWE$(q, n, m, \bar{\mathcal{S}}, \chi)$ *is hard, if it holds for every PPT distinguisher $\mathcal{D}$ and every $\mathcal{S} \in \bar{\mathcal{S}}$ that*

$$|\Pr[\mathcal{D}(1^\lambda, \mathbf{A}, \mathbf{s}\mathbf{A} + \mathbf{e}) = 1] - \Pr[\mathcal{D}(1^\lambda, \mathbf{u} + \mathbf{e}) = 1]| \leq \mathsf{negl}(\lambda),$$

where $\mathbf{A} \leftarrow_\$ \mathbb{Z}_q^{m \times n}$, $\mathbf{s} \leftarrow_\$ \mathcal{S}$, $\mathbf{e} \leftarrow_\$ \chi^m$ *and* $\mathbf{u} \leftarrow_\$ \mathbb{Z}_q^m$.

3   Probability-Theoretic Tools

3.1   Singular Values of Discrete Gaussian Matrices

Consider a real valued matrix $\mathbf{A} \in \mathbb{R}^{n \times m}$, assume for convenience that $m \geq n$. The singular values of $\mathbf{A}$ are the square roots of the eigenvalues of the positive semidefinite (PSD) matrix $\mathbf{A}\mathbf{A}^\top$. They are denoted $\sigma_1(\mathbf{A}) \geq \cdots \geq \sigma_n(\mathbf{A}) \geq 0$. The *spectral norm* of $\mathbf{A}$ is $\sigma_1(\mathbf{A})$, and we will also denote it by σ_A. It holds that

$$\sigma_\mathbf{A} = \sigma_1(\mathbf{A}) = \max_{\mathbf{x} \in \mathbb{R}^m \setminus \{\mathbf{0}\}} \frac{\|\mathbf{A}\mathbf{x}\|}{\|x\|}.$$

We will be interested in the of discrete Gaussian matrices.

Proposition 3.1 ([MP12, Lemma 2.8, 2.9]). *Let* $\mathbf{F} \sim D_{\mathbb{Z}, \gamma}^{n \times m}$, *assume for convenience that $m \geq n$. Then with all but 2^{-m} probability it holds that $\sigma_\mathbf{F} \leq \gamma \cdot C \cdot \sqrt{m}$, where C is a global constant.*

3.2   Decomposition Theorem for Continuous Gaussians

The following proposition is an immediate corollary of the properties of (continuous) Gaussian vectors. We provide a proof for the sake of completeness.

Proposition 3.2. *Let* $\mathbf{F} \in \mathbb{Z}^{n \times m}$ *be an arbitrary matrix with spectral norm* σ_F. *Let* $\sigma, \sigma_1 > 0$ *be s.t.* $\sigma > \sigma_1 \cdot \sigma_F$. *Let* $\mathbf{e}_1 \sim D_{\sigma_1}^n$ *and let* $\mathbf{e}_2 \sim D_{\sqrt{\Sigma}}$ *for* $\Sigma = \sigma^2 \mathbf{I} - \sigma_1^2 \mathbf{F}^\top \mathbf{F}$. *Then the random variable* $\mathbf{e} = \mathbf{e}_1 \mathbf{F} + \mathbf{e}_2$ *is distributed according to* D_σ^m.

Proof. First note that Σ is positive definite: It holds for any $\mathbf{x} \in \mathbb{R}^m \setminus \{\mathbf{0}\}$ that

$$\mathbf{x}\Sigma\mathbf{x}^\top = \sigma^2\|\mathbf{x}\|^2 - \sigma_1^2\|\mathbf{x}\mathbf{F}\|^2 \geq \sigma^2\|\mathbf{x}\| - \sigma^2\sigma_\mathbf{F}^2\|\mathbf{x}\|^2 \geq (\sigma^2 - \sigma_1^2\sigma_\mathbf{F}^2) \cdot \|\mathbf{x}\|^2 > 0,$$

as $\sigma > \sigma_1 \cdot \sigma_\mathbf{F}$. Since $\mathbf{e}_1, \mathbf{e}_2$ are independent Gaussian vectors, they are also jointly Gaussian, and therefore $\mathbf{e}$ is also a Gaussian vector. Since $\mathbf{e}_1, \mathbf{e}_2$ have expectation 0, then so does $\mathbf{e}$. The covariance matrix of $\mathbf{e}$ is given by a direct calculation, recalling that $\mathbf{e}_1, \mathbf{e}_2$ are independent:

$$\begin{aligned}
\mathbb{E}[\mathbf{e}^\top \mathbf{e}] &= \mathbb{E}[\mathbf{F}^\top \mathbf{e}^\top \mathbf{e} \mathbf{F}] + \mathbb{E}[\mathbf{e}_2^\top \mathbf{e}_2] \\
&= \mathbf{F}^\top \sigma_1^2 \mathbf{I} \mathbf{F} + \mathbf{\Sigma} \\
&= \sigma_1^2 \mathbf{F}^\top \mathbf{F} + \sigma^2 \mathbf{I} - \sigma_1^2 \mathbf{F}^\top \mathbf{F} \\
&= \sigma^2 \mathbf{I},
\end{aligned}$$

and the statement follows.   □

4   Hardness of Entropic LWE with Gaussian Noise

In this Section we will establish our main result, the hardness of entropic search LWE with continuous gaussian noise. Using standard techniques, we can conclude that entropic search LWE with discrete gaussian noise is also hard. Finally for suitable moduli a search-to-decision reduction can be used to establish the hardness of entropic decisional LWE.

Theorem 4.1. *Let C be the global constant from Proposition 3.1. Let $q = q(\lambda)$ be a modulus and $n, m = \mathrm{poly}(\lambda)$ where $m \geq n$, and let $r, \gamma, \sigma_1 > 0$. Let $\mathbf{s}$ be a random variable on $\mathbb{Z}_q^n$ distributed according to some distribution $\mathcal{S}$. Let $\mathbf{e}_1 \sim D_{\sigma_1} \mod q$ be an error term. Assume that $\mathbf{s}$ is r-bounded, where we assume that $r = q$ if no bound for $\mathbf{s}$ is known. Further assume that*

$$\tilde{H}_\infty(\mathbf{s}|\mathbf{s} + \mathbf{e}_1) \geq k \cdot \log(\min\{2C \cdot \gamma \cdot \sqrt{n}r, q\}) + \omega(\log(\lambda))$$

Let $\sigma > C \cdot \sqrt{m} \cdot \gamma \cdot \sigma_1$. Then the search problem $\mathsf{ent\text{-}LWE}(q, n, m, \mathcal{S}, D_\sigma)$ is hard, provided that $\mathsf{dLWE}(q, k, D_{\mathbb{Z}, \gamma})$ is hard.

Furthermore, if $\tilde{H}_\infty(\mathbf{s}|\mathbf{s} + \mathbf{e}_1) \geq k \cdot \log(q) + \omega(\log(\lambda))$ and we have that either q is prime or $\mathbf{s} \in \{0, 1\}^n$, then the decisional problem $\mathsf{ent\text{-}dLWE}(q, n, m, \mathcal{S}, D_\sigma)$ is hard, provided that $\mathsf{dLWE}(q, k, D_{\mathbb{Z}, \gamma})$ and $\mathsf{dLWE}(q, k, m, D_\sigma)$ are hard.

See the full version [BD20] for proof.

5   Noise-Lossiness for Modular Gaussians

In this Section, we will compute the noise lossiness for general high-minentropy distributions. We further show that considerable improvements can be achieved when considering short distributions. Our Lemmas in this Section can be seen as *strong converse coding theorems* for gaussian channels. I.e. if a distribution codes above a certain information rate, then information must be lost and noise lossiness quantifies how much information is lost. The following lemma will allow us to bound $\tilde{H}_\infty(\mathbf{s}|\mathbf{s} + \mathbf{e})$ by suitably bounding $\max_{\mathbf{s}^*} p_{\mathbf{e}}(\mathbf{y} - \mathbf{s}^*)$.

Lemma 5.1. *Let $q \in \mathbb{N}$ be a modulus and fix $n, m \in \mathbb{N}$ with $m > n$. Let $\mathbf{s}$ be a random variable on $\mathbb{Z}_q^k$ with min-entropy $\tilde{H}_\infty(\mathbf{s})$. Let χ be a noise distribution over $\mathbb{R}^n$ and let $\mathbf{e} \sim \chi$. Then it holds that*

$$\tilde{H}_\infty(\mathbf{s}|\mathbf{s} + \mathbf{e}) \geq \tilde{H}_\infty(\mathbf{s}) - \log\left(\int_\mathbf{y} \max_{\mathbf{s}^*} p_\mathbf{e}(\mathbf{y} - \mathbf{s}^*) d\mathbf{y}\right)$$

in the case that χ is continuous and

$$\tilde{H}_\infty(\mathbf{s}|\mathbf{s} + \mathbf{e}) \geq \tilde{H}_\infty(\mathbf{s}) - \log\left(\sum_\mathbf{y} \max_{\mathbf{s}^*} \Pr_\mathbf{e}[\mathbf{e} = \mathbf{y} - \mathbf{s}^*]\right)$$

in the case that χ is discrete. Moreover, if $\mathbf{s}$ is a flat distribution then equality holds.

Proof. The lemma follows from the following derivation in the continuous case. The discrete case follows analogously.

$$\tilde{H}_\infty(\mathbf{s}|\mathbf{s} + \mathbf{e}) = -\log\left(\mathbb{E}_\mathbf{y}[\max_{\mathbf{s}^* \in S} \Pr_{\mathbf{s},\mathbf{e}}[\mathbf{s} = \mathbf{s}^*|\mathbf{s} + \mathbf{e} = \mathbf{y}]]\right)$$

$$= -\log\left(\int_\mathbf{y} p_{\mathbf{s}+\mathbf{e}}(\mathbf{y}) \cdot \max_{\mathbf{s}^*} \Pr_{\mathbf{s},\mathbf{e}}[\mathbf{s} = \mathbf{s}^*|\mathbf{s} + \mathbf{e} = \mathbf{y}] d\mathbf{y}\right)$$

$$= -\log\left(\int_\mathbf{y} \max_{\mathbf{s}^*} p_{\mathbf{s},\mathbf{s}+\mathbf{e}}(\mathbf{s}^*, \mathbf{y}) d\mathbf{y}\right)$$

$$= -\log\left(\int_\mathbf{y} \max_{\mathbf{s}^*} p_{\mathbf{s}+\mathbf{e}|\mathbf{s}=\mathbf{s}^*}(\mathbf{y}) \cdot \underbrace{\Pr[\mathbf{s} = \mathbf{s}^*]}_{\leq 2^{-\tilde{H}_\infty(\mathbf{s})}} d\mathbf{y}\right)$$

$$\geq \tilde{H}_\infty(\mathbf{s}) - \log\left(\int_\mathbf{y} \max_{\mathbf{s}^*} p_\mathbf{e}(\mathbf{y} - \mathbf{s}^*) d\mathbf{y}\right).$$

To see that equality holds for flat distributions, note that in this case we have $\Pr[\mathbf{s} = \mathbf{s}^*] = 2^{-\tilde{H}_\infty(\mathbf{s})}$.

5.1   General High Entropy Secrets

We first turn to the case of general high-entropy secrets and prove the following lemma.

Lemma 5.2. *Let n be an integer, let q be a modulus and σ_1 be a parameter for a gaussian. Assume that*

$$\frac{q}{\sigma_1} \geq \sqrt{\frac{\ln(4n)}{\pi}}.$$

Let $\mathbf{s}$ be a random variable on $\mathbb{Z}_q^n$ and $\mathbf{e}_1 \sim D_{\sigma_1} \mod q$. Then it holds that

$$\tilde{H}_\infty(\mathbf{s}|\mathbf{s} + \mathbf{e}_1) \geq \tilde{H}_\infty(\mathbf{s}) - n \cdot \log(q/\sigma_1) - 1$$

We remark that the requirement $\frac{q}{\sigma_1} \geq \sqrt{\frac{\ln(4n)}{\pi}}$ is made for technical reasons, but we restrict ourselves to keep the proof simple. We also remark that this condition is essentially trivially fulfilled by interesting parameter choices.

We can instantiate Theorem 4.1 with Lemma 5.2 obtaining the following corollary.

Corollary 5.3. *Let C be a global constant. Let $q = q(\lambda)$ be a modulus and let $n, m, k = \mathsf{poly}(\lambda)$. Let $\gamma, \sigma_1 > 0$. Assume that $\mathcal{S}$ is a distribution on $\mathbb{Z}_q^n$ with $\tilde{H}_\infty(\mathbf{s}) > k \cdot \log(q) + n \cdot \log(q/\sigma_1) + \omega(\log(\lambda))$. Now let $\sigma > C \cdot \sqrt{m} \cdot \gamma \sigma_1$. Then $\mathsf{ent\text{-}LWE}(q, n, m, \mathcal{S}, D_\sigma)$ is hard, provided that $\mathsf{dLWE}(q, k, D_{\mathbb{Z},\gamma})$ is hard.*

Proof (of Lemma 5.2). It holds that

$$\int_{\mathbf{y}} \max_{\mathbf{s}^*} p_{\mathbf{e}}(\mathbf{y} - \mathbf{s}^*) d\mathbf{y} = \frac{1}{\rho_{\sigma_1}(\mathbb{R}^n)} \int_{\mathbf{y}} \max_{\mathbf{s}^*} \hat{\rho}_{q\mathbb{Z}^n, \sigma_1}(\mathbf{y} - \mathbf{s}^*) d\mathbf{y}$$

$$\leq \frac{1}{\rho_{\sigma_1}(\mathbb{R}^n)} \cdot \int_{\mathbf{y}} 2 d\mathbf{y}$$

$$= 2 \cdot \frac{q^n}{\rho_{\sigma_1}(\mathbb{R}^n)}$$

$$= 2 \cdot \frac{q^n}{\sigma_1^n},$$

where the $\hat{\rho}_{q\mathbb{Z}^n, \sigma_1}(\mathbf{y} - \mathbf{s}^*) \leq 2$ follows by Lemma 2.4 as $\frac{q}{\sigma_1} \geq \sqrt{\frac{\ln(4n)}{\pi}}$. We can conclude by Lemma 5.1 that

$$\tilde{H}_\infty(\mathbf{s}|\mathbf{s} + \mathbf{e}) \geq \tilde{H}_\infty(\mathbf{s}) - \log \left(\int_{\mathbf{y}} \max_{\mathbf{s}^*} p_{\mathbf{e}}(\mathbf{y} - \mathbf{s}^*) d\mathbf{y} \right)$$

$$\geq \tilde{H}_\infty(\mathbf{s}) - n \cdot \log(q/\sigma_1) - 1.$$

5.2   Short Secrets

We will now turn to the case where the secret has bounded norm.

Lemma 5.4. *Let n be an integer, let q be a modulus and σ_1 be a parameter for a gaussian. Assume that $\mathbf{s}$ is a random-variable on $\mathbb{Z}_q^n$ such that $\|\mathbf{s}\| \leq r$ for a parameter $r = r(\lambda)$. Let $\mathbf{e}_1 \sim D_{\sigma_1} \mod q$ Then it holds that*

$$\tilde{H}_\infty(\mathbf{s}|\mathbf{s} + \mathbf{e}_1) \geq \tilde{H}_\infty(\mathbf{s}) - \sqrt{2\pi n} \cdot \frac{r}{\sigma_1} \log(e).$$

In particular, if $\sigma_1 > \sqrt{n} \cdot r$, then $\tilde{H}_\infty(\mathbf{s}|\mathbf{s} + \mathbf{e}_1) \geq \tilde{H}_\infty(\mathbf{s}) - \pi \log(e)$. We can instantiate Theorem 4.1 with Lemma 5.4 obtaining the following corollary.

Corollary 5.5. *Let C be a global constant. Let $q = q(\lambda)$ be a modulus and let $n, m, k = \mathsf{poly}(\lambda)$. Let $\gamma = \gamma(\lambda) > 0$ and $\sigma_1 = \sigma_1(\lambda) > 0$. Assume that $\mathcal{S}$ is a r-bounded distribution with $\tilde{H}_\infty(\mathbf{s}) > k \cdot \log(2C \cdot \gamma \cdot \sigma_1) + \sqrt{2\pi n} \cdot \frac{r}{\sigma_1} \log(e) + \omega(\log(\lambda))$. Now let $\sigma > C \cdot \sqrt{m} \sigma_1 \cdot \gamma$. Then $\mathsf{ent\text{-}LWE}(q, n, m, \mathcal{S}, D_\sigma)$ is hard, provided that $\mathsf{dLWE}(q, k, D_{\mathbb{Z},\gamma})$ is hard.*

Proof (of Lemma 5.4). Fix some $\sigma_2 > \sigma_1$. Since it holds that $\|\mathbf{s}\| \leq r$, it holds that

$$
\begin{aligned}
\int_{\mathbf{y}} \max_{\mathbf{s}^*} p_{\mathbf{e}}(\mathbf{y} - \mathbf{s}^*) d\mathbf{y} &= \frac{1}{\rho_{\sigma_1}(\mathbb{R}^n)} \int_{\mathbf{y}} \max_{\mathbf{s}^*} \hat{\rho}_{q\mathbb{Z}^n, \sigma_1}(\mathbf{y} - \mathbf{s}^*) d\mathbf{y} \\
&\leq \frac{1}{\rho_{\sigma_1}(\mathbb{R}^n)} \int_{\mathbf{y}} \max_{\mathbf{s}^*} e^{\pi \frac{\|\mathbf{s}^*\|^2}{\sigma_2^2 - \sigma_1^2}} \cdot \hat{\rho}_{q\mathbb{Z}^n, \sigma_2}(\mathbf{y}) d\mathbf{y} \\
&\leq \frac{1}{\rho_{\sigma_1}(\mathbb{R}^n)} \cdot e^{\pi \frac{r^2}{\sigma_2^2 - \sigma_1^2}} \cdot \int_{\mathbf{y}} \hat{\rho}_{q\mathbb{Z}^n, \sigma_2}(\mathbf{y}) d\mathbf{y} \\
&= e^{\pi \frac{r^2}{\sigma_2^2 - \sigma_1^2}} \cdot \frac{\rho_{\sigma_2}(\mathbb{R}^n)}{\rho_{\sigma_1}(\mathbb{R}^n)} \\
&= e^{\pi \frac{r^2}{\sigma_2^2 - \sigma_1^2}} \cdot \left(\frac{\sigma_2}{\sigma_1}\right)^n
\end{aligned}
$$

Now, setting $\sigma_2 = \sigma_1 \cdot \sqrt{1 + \eta}$ we get that

$$
\int_{\mathbf{y}} \max_{\mathbf{s}^*} p_{\mathbf{e}}(\mathbf{y} - \mathbf{s}^*) d\mathbf{y} \leq e^{\pi \frac{r^2}{\sigma_2^2 - \sigma_1^2}} \cdot \left(\frac{\sigma_2}{\sigma_1}\right)^n = e^{\pi \frac{r^2}{\eta \sigma_1^2}} \cdot (1 + \eta)^{n/2} \leq e^{\pi \frac{r^2}{\eta \sigma_1^2} + \frac{n\eta}{2}}
$$

By Lemma 5.1, we can conclude that

$$
\tilde{H}_\infty(\mathbf{s}|\mathbf{s} + \mathbf{e}_1) \geq \tilde{H}_\infty(\mathbf{s}) - \left(\pi \frac{r^2}{\eta \sigma_1^2} + \frac{n\eta}{2}\right) \log(e).
$$

Recall that η is still a free parameter. This expression is minimized by choosing $\eta = \sqrt{\frac{2\pi}{n} \frac{r}{\sigma_1}}$, which yields

$$
\tilde{H}_\infty(\mathbf{s}|\mathbf{s} + \mathbf{e}_1) \geq \tilde{H}_\infty(\mathbf{s}) - \sqrt{2\pi n} \cdot \frac{r}{\sigma_1} \log(e).
$$

6 Tightness of the Result

In this Section, we will show that for general moduli and general min-entropy distributions our result is tight up to polynomial factors.

For a modulus q and a noise parameter σ, we will provide an example of a distribution $\mathbf{s}$ with min-entropy $\approx n \cdot \log(q/\sigma)$, such that ent-LWE$(q, n, m, \mathcal{X}, \chi)$ is easy. For this counter-example, the choice of the modulus q is critical.

Lemma 6.1. *Let $q = q(\lambda)$ be a modulus such that q has a divisor p of size $|p| > 2B + 1$, let $n, m = \mathrm{poly}(\lambda)$ and let χ be a B-bounded error-distribution. Define the distribution $\mathcal{S}$ to be the uniform distribution on $p \cdot \mathbb{Z}_q^n$. Then there exists an efficient algorithm $\mathcal{A}$ that solves ent-LWE$(q, n, m, \mathcal{S}, \chi)$.*

Corollary 6.2. *There exist moduli q and distributions $\mathcal{S}$ with min-entropy $\geq n \cdot (\log(q/\sigma) - \log(\log(\lambda)))$ such that ent-LWE$(q, n, m, \mathcal{S}, D_\sigma)$ is easy.*

The corollary follows from Lemma 6.1 by choosing p such that $p = 2\log(\lambda) \cdot \sigma + 1$ and noting that a gaussian of parameter σ is $\log(\lambda) \cdot \sigma$ bounded, except with negligible probability. Moreover, for this choice of p the distribution $\mathcal{S}$ in Lemma 6.1 has min-entropy $n \cdot \log(q/p) \geq n \cdot \log(q/\sigma) - 2\log(\log(\lambda))$.

Proof (of Lemma 6.1). Assume that reduction modulor p computes a *central residue class representation* in $[-p/2, p/2]$. The algorithm $\mathcal{A}$ proceeds as follows.

$\mathcal{A}(\mathbf{A}, \mathbf{y})$:
  - Compute $\mathbf{e} \leftarrow \mathbf{y} \mod p$.
  - Solve the equation system $\mathbf{s} \cdot \mathbf{A} = \mathbf{y} - \mathbf{e}$ for $\mathbf{s}$, e.g. via Gaussian elimination.
  - Output $\mathbf{s}$.
To see that the algorithm $\mathcal{A}$ is correct, note that

$$\mathbf{y} \mod p = (\mathbf{s} \cdot \mathbf{A} + \mathbf{e}) \mod p = (p \cdot \mathbf{r} \cdot \mathbf{A} + \mathbf{e}) \mod p = \mathbf{e}$$

as $p \geq 2B$ and $\|\mathbf{e}\| \leq B$.

7   Barriers for Entropic LWE

In the last Section we provided an attack on entropic LWE when the min-entropy of the secret is below $n \cdot \log(q/\sigma)$ for a worst-case choice of the modulus q. On might still hope that for more benign choices of the modulus q this problem might be hard in this entropy regime. In this section we will provide a barrier for the hardness of entropic LWE in this regime for any modulus. In particular, we will show that for entropies below $n \cdot \log(q/\sigma)$, the hardness of entropic LWE does not follow from any standard assumption in a black-box way. This leaves open the possibility that in this regime the hardness of entropic LWE may be established from more exotic *knowledge assumptions*. To establish our result, we will use a framework developed by Wichs [Wic13].

7.1   Simulatable Attacks

We first recall the notion of cryptographic games as a way to characterize cryptographic standard assumptions due to Haitner and Holenstein [HH09]. This characterization captures essentially all falsifiable assumptions [Nao03] used in cryptography, such as LWE.

Definition 7.1 (Cryptographic Games [HH09]). *A cryptographic game* $\mathcal{C} = (\Gamma, c)$ *is defined by a (possibly inefficient) randomized machine* Γ, *called the challenger, and a constant* $c \in [0, 1)$. *On input a security parameter* 1^λ, *the challenger interacts with an attack* $\mathcal{A}(1^\lambda)$ *and outputs a bit* b. *Denote this by* $\Gamma(1^\lambda) \leftrightarrows \mathcal{A}(1^\lambda)$. *The advantage of an attacker* $\mathcal{A}$ *against* $\mathcal{C}$ *is defined by*

$$\mathsf{Adv}_{\mathcal{C}}^{\mathcal{A}}(1^\lambda) = \Pr[(\Gamma(1^\lambda) \leftrightarrows \mathcal{A}(1^\lambda)) = 1] - c.$$

We say that a cryptographic game $\mathcal{C}$ *is secure if for all PPT attackers* $\mathcal{A}$ *the advantage* $\mathsf{Adv}_{\mathcal{C}}^{\mathcal{A}}(\lambda)$ *is negligible.*

Definition 7.2 (Black-Box Reduction). *Let C_1 and C_2 be cryptographic games. A black-box reduction deriving the security of C_2 from the security of C_1 is an oracle PPT-machine $\mathcal{B}^{(\cdot)}$ for which there are constants c, λ_0 such that for all $\lambda \geq \lambda_0$ and all (possibly inefficient, non-uniform) attackers $\mathcal{A}_\lambda$ with advantage $\mathsf{Adv}_{C_1}^{\mathcal{A}_\lambda}(\lambda) \geq 1/2$, we have $\mathsf{Adv}_{C_2}^{\mathcal{B}^{\mathcal{A}_\lambda}}(\lambda) \geq \lambda^{-c}$.*

We remark that the choice of the constant $1/2$ for the advantage of $\mathcal{A}_\lambda$ is arbitrary and can be replaced by a non-negligible function (depending $\mathcal{A}_\lambda$). We now recall the notion of *simulatable attacks* [Wic13].

Definition 7.3 (Simulatable Attacks [Wic13]). *An ϵ-simulatable attack on an assumption C is a tuple $(\mathcal{A}, \mathsf{Sim})$ such that $\mathcal{A}$ is a stateless, non-uniform possibly inefficient attacker against C, and Sim is a stateful PPT simulator. We require the following two properties to hold.*

- *The (inefficient) attacker $\mathcal{A}$ successfully breaks C with advantage $1 - \mathsf{negl}(\lambda)$.*
- *For every (possibly inefficient) oracle machine $\mathcal{M}^{(\cdot)}$ making at most q queries to its oracle it holds that*

$$|\Pr[\mathcal{M}^{\mathcal{A}(1^\lambda, 1)}(1^\lambda) = 1] - \Pr[\mathcal{M}^{\mathsf{Sim}(1^\lambda)} = 1]| \leq \mathsf{poly}(q) \cdot \epsilon.$$

where the probabilities are taken over all the random choices involved.

We use the shorthand simulatable attack for ϵ-simulatable attack with some negligible ϵ.

We remark that for reasons of conceptual simplicity Wichs [Wic13] required the advantage of the simulatable adversary $\mathcal{A}$ to be 1. But it can easily be verified that Theorem 7.4 below also works with our slightly relaxed notion which allows the unbounded adversary to have advantage $1 - \mathsf{negl}(\lambda)$. The following theorem by Wichs [Wic13] shows that the existence of a simulatable attack for some assumption C_1 implies that there cannot by a reduction $\mathcal{B}$ which reduces the hardness of C_1 to any standard assumption C_2, where C_1 and C_2 are cryptographic games in the sense of Definition 7.1.

Theorem 7.4 ([Wic13] Theorem 4.2). *If there exists a simulatable attack against some assumption C_1 and there is a black-box reduction $\mathcal{B}$ reducing the security of C_1 to some assumption C_2, then C_2 is not secure.*

The idea for the proof of this theorem is simple: If an attack $\mathcal{A}$ against C_1 is simulatable, then the behavior of $\mathcal{B}^{\mathsf{Sim}}$ will be indistinguishable from $\mathcal{B}^{\mathcal{A}}$. But since $\mathcal{A}$ breaks C_1, it holds that $\mathcal{B}^{\mathcal{A}}$ breaks C_2. Therefore, the efficient algorithm $\mathcal{B}^{\mathsf{Sim}}$ must also break C_2, implying that C_2 is insecure.

7.2   A Simulatable Attack for Entropic LWE

We will now provide a simulatable attack against entropic (search-)LWE. The attack consists of a pair of a min-entropy distribution $\mathcal{S}$ and an attacker $\mathcal{A}$.

Since we want to prove a result for general min-entropy distributions, we assume that both the adversary and the min-entropy distribution $\mathcal{S}$ are adversarially chosen. Thus, we can consider the distribution $\mathcal{S}$ as running a coordinated attack with the attacker $\mathcal{A}$. More importantly, any black-box reduction $\mathcal{B}$ reducing the entropic LWE to a standard assumption will only have black-box access to the distribution $\mathcal{S}$. We remark that, to the best of our knowledge, currently all reductions in the realm of leakage resilient cryptography only make black-box use of the distribution. Making effective non-black box use of an adversarially chosen sampling circuit seems out of reach for current techniques. Assume in the following that $m \geq 2n$ and let χ be a B-bounded error distribution. Furthermore let k be a positive integer. Consider the following attacker, consisting of the adversary $\mathcal{A}$ and the distribution $\mathcal{S}$.

- The distribution $\mathcal{S}$ is a flat distribution on a set S of size 2^k, where the set S is chosen uniformly random.
- $\mathcal{A}_S(\mathbf{A}, \mathbf{y})$: Given a pair $(\mathbf{A}, \mathbf{y})$, the attacker $\mathcal{A}$ proceeds as follows:
    - Check if the matrix $\mathbf{A}$ has an invertible column-submatrix, if not abort and output $\perp$ (this check can be performed efficiently using linear algebra).
    - Compute a set $I \subseteq [m]$ of size n such that the column-submatrix $\mathbf{A}_I$ is invertible (where $\mathbf{A}_I$ is obtained by dropping all columns of $\mathbf{A}$ that do not have indices in I).
    - Set $\mathbf{A}' = \mathbf{A}_I$ and $\mathbf{y}' = \mathbf{y}_I$ (i.e. $\mathbf{y}'$ is $\mathbf{y}$ projected to the coordinates in I).
    - Initialize a set $S' = \emptyset$.
    - For every $\mathbf{s} \in S$, check if $\|\mathbf{y} - \mathbf{s}\mathbf{A}\|_\infty \leq B$, if so include $\mathbf{s}$ in the set S'.
    - Choose an $\mathbf{s} \leftarrow_{\$} S'$ uniformly random and output $\mathbf{s}$.

First observe that whenever the matrix $\mathbf{A}$ has an invertible submatrix, then $\mathcal{A}$ does have advantage 1. The probability that $\mathbf{A}$ does not have an invertible submatrix is at most $\log(q) \cdot 2^{n-m} = \log(q) \cdot 2^{-n}$, which is negligible (see Sect. 2). Consequently, $\mathcal{A}$ breaks ent-LWE$(q, n, m, \mathcal{S}, \chi)$ with probability $1 - \mathsf{negl}(\lambda)$.

We will now provide our simulator for the adversary $\mathcal{A}$ and the distribution $\mathcal{S}$. The simulator jointly simulates the distribution $\mathcal{S}$ and the attacker $\mathcal{A}$, i.e. from the interface of an oracle machine $\mathcal{B}$ it holds that $\mathsf{Sim}(1^\lambda, \cdot, \cdot)$ simulates $(\mathcal{S}(\cdot), \mathcal{A}(\cdot))$. The advantage of the simulator stems from having a joint view of the samples provided so far and the inputs of the adversary $\mathcal{A}$. The main idea of our simulator is that is samples the set S lazily and keeps track of all the samples S^* it gave out so far. When provided with an instance $(\mathbf{A}, \mathbf{y})$, it will perform the same check as $\mathcal{A}$ but restricted to the set X' and therefore run in time $O(q)$. Recall that the simulator is stateful.

- Simulator $\mathsf{Sim}(1^\lambda, \cdot, \cdot)$:
    - Initialize a set $S^* = \emptyset$.
    - Whenever a sample is queried from $\mathcal{S}$, choose $\mathbf{s} \leftarrow_{\$} Z_q^n$ uniformly random, include $\mathbf{s}$ in the set S^* and output $\mathbf{s}$.
    - Whenever an instance is provided to $\mathcal{A}$, do the following:

* Initialize a set $S' = \emptyset$.
* Check for every $\mathbf{s} \in S^*$, check if $\|\mathbf{y} - \mathbf{sA}\|_\infty \leq B$, if so include $\mathbf{s}$ in the set S'.
* Choose an $\mathbf{s} \leftarrow_\$ S'$ uniformly random and output $\mathbf{s}$.

We will now show that the simulator Sim simulates the attack $(\mathcal{A}, \mathcal{X})$ with negligible error. We need the following lemma.

Lemma 7.5. *Let $\mathbf{z} \leftarrow_\$ \mathbb{Z}_q^n$ be distributed uniformly random. Then it holds that*

$$\Pr[\|\mathbf{z}\|_\infty \leq B] \leq ((2B+1)/q)^n.$$

Proof. Since all the components z_i of $\mathbf{z}$ are distributed uniformly and independently, it holds that

$$\Pr[\|\mathbf{z}\|_\infty \leq B] = \prod_{i=1}^{n} \Pr[|z_i| \leq B] \leq ((2B+1)/q)^n.$$

Theorem 7.6. *Let $\chi = \chi(\lambda)$ be a B-bounded error-distribution. Further, let $k < n \cdot \log(q/(2B+1)) - \omega(\log(\lambda))$ be an integer. Let $\bar{\mathcal{S}}$ be the family of all distributions on $\mathbb{Z}_q^n$ with min-entropy at most k. Then, if there is a reduction $\mathcal{B}$ from* ent-LWE$(q, n, m, \bar{\mathcal{S}}, \chi)$ *to any cryptographic game $\mathcal{C}$, then $\mathcal{C}$ is not secure.*

See the full version [BD20] for proof.

References

[ACPS09] Applebaum, B., Cash, D., Peikert, C., Sahai, A.: Fast cryptographic primitives and circular-secure encryption based on hard learning problems. In: Halevi, S. (ed.) CRYPTO 2009. LNCS, vol. 5677, pp. 595–618. Springer, Heidelberg (2009). https://doi.org/10.1007/978-3-642-03356-8_35

[AD97] Ajtai, M., Dwork, C.: A public-key cryptosystem with worst-case/average-case equivalence. In: 29th Annual ACM Symposium on Theory of Computing, El Paso, TX, USA, 4–6 May 1997, pp. 284–293. ACM Press (2017)

[Ajt96] Ajtai, M.: Generating hard instances of lattice problems (extended abstract). In: 28th Annual ACM Symposium on Theory of Computing, Philadephia, PA, USA, 22–24 May 1996, pp. 99–108. ACM Press (1996)

[AKPW13] Alwen, J., Krenn, S., Pietrzak, K., Wichs, D.: Learning with rounding, revisited. In: Canetti, R., Garay, J.A. (eds.) CRYPTO 2013. LNCS, vol. 8042, pp. 57–74. Springer, Heidelberg (2013). https://doi.org/10.1007/978-3-642-40041-4_4

[BBPS19] Bolboceanu, M., Brakerski, Z., Perlman, R., Sharma, D.: Order-LWE and the hardness of ring-LWE with entropic secrets. In: Galbraith, S.D., Moriai, S. (eds.) ASIACRYPT 2019. LNCS, vol. 11922, pp. 91–120. Springer, Cham (2019). https://doi.org/10.1007/978-3-030-34621-8_4. https://eprint.iacr.org/2018/494

[BD20] Brakerski, Z., Döttling, N.: Hardness of LWE on general entropic distributions. Cryptology ePrint Archive, Report 2020/119 (2020). https://eprint.iacr.org/2020/119 (Full version of this work)

[BGM+16] Bogdanov, A., Guo, S., Masny, D., Richelson, S., Rosen, A.: On the hardness of learning with rounding over small modulus. In: Kushilevitz, E., Malkin, T. (eds.) TCC 2016. LNCS, vol. 9562, pp. 209–224. Springer, Heidelberg (2016). https://doi.org/10.1007/978-3-662-49096-9_9

[BGV12] Brakerski, Z., Gentry, C., Vaikuntanathan, V.: (Leveled) fully homomorphic encryption without bootstrapping. In: Goldwasser, S. (ed.) ITCS 2012: 3rd Innovations in Theoretical Computer Science, Cambridge, MA, USA, 8–10 January 2012, pp. 309–325. Association for Computing Machinery (2012)

[BLP+13] Brakerski, Z., Langlois, A., Peikert, C., Regev, O., Stehlé, D.: Classical hardness of learning with errors. In: Boneh, D., Roughgarden, T., Feigenbaum, J. (eds.) 45th Annual ACM Symposium on Theory of Computing, Palo Alto, CA, USA, 1–4 June 2013, pp. 575–584. ACM Press (2013)

[BPR12] Banerjee, A., Peikert, C., Rosen, A.: Pseudorandom functions and lattices. In: Pointcheval, D., Johansson, T. (eds.) EUROCRYPT 2012. LNCS, vol. 7237, pp. 719–737. Springer, Heidelberg (2012). https://doi.org/10.1007/978-3-642-29011-4_42

[BV11] Brakerski, Z., Vaikuntanathan, V.: Efficient fully homomorphic encryption from (standard) LWE. In: Ostrovsky, R. (ed.) 52nd Annual Symposium on Foundations of Computer Science, Palm Springs, CA, USA, 22–25 October 2011, pp. 97–106. IEEE Computer Society Press (2011)

[DM13] Döttling, N., Müller-Quade, J.: Lossy codes and a new variant of the learning-with-errors problem. In: Johansson, T., Nguyen, P.Q. (eds.) EUROCRYPT 2013. LNCS, vol. 7881, pp. 18–34. Springer, Heidelberg (2013). https://doi.org/10.1007/978-3-642-38348-9_2

[DORS08] Dodis, Y., Ostrovsky, R., Reyzin, L., Smith, A.D.: Fuzzy extractors: how to generate strong keys from biometrics and other noisy data. SIAM J. Comput. **38**(1), 97–139 (2008)

[Gen09] Gentry, C.: Fully homomorphic encryption using ideal lattices. In: Mitzenmacher, M. (ed.) 41st Annual ACM Symposium on Theory of Computing, Bethesda, MD, USA, 31 May–2 June 2009, pp. 169–178. ACM Press (2009)

[GKPV10] Goldwasser, S., Kalai, Y.T., Peikert, C., Vaikuntanathan, V.: Robustness of the learning with errors assumption. In: Yao, A.C.-C (ed.) ICS 2010: 1st Innovations in Computer Science, Tsinghua University, Beijing, China, 5–7 January 2010, pp. 230–240. Tsinghua University Press (2010)

[GVW13] Gorbunov, S., Vaikuntanathan, V., Wee, H.: Attribute-based encryption for circuits. In: Boneh, D., Roughgarden, T., Feigenbaum, J. (eds.) 45th Annual ACM Symposium on Theory of Computing, Palo Alto, CA, USA, 1–4 June 2013, pp. 545–554. ACM Press (2013)

[HH09] Haitner, I., Holenstein, T.: On the (im)possibility of key dependent encryption. In: Reingold, O. (ed.) TCC 2009. LNCS, vol. 5444, pp. 202–219. Springer, Heidelberg (2009). https://doi.org/10.1007/978-3-642-00457-5_13

[Mic18] Micciancio, D.: On the hardness of learning with errors with binary secrets. Theory Comput. **14**(1), 1–17 (2018)

[MM11] Micciancio, D., Mol, P.: Pseudorandom knapsacks and the sample complexity of LWE search-to-decision reductions. In: Rogaway, P. (ed.) CRYPTO 2011. LNCS, vol. 6841, pp. 465–484. Springer, Heidelberg (2011). https://doi.org/10.1007/978-3-642-22792-9_26

[MP12] Micciancio, D., Peikert, C.: Trapdoors for lattices: simpler, tighter, faster, smaller. In: Pointcheval, D., Johansson, T. (eds.) EUROCRYPT 2012. LNCS, vol. 7237, pp. 700–718. Springer, Heidelberg (2012). https://doi.org/10.1007/978-3-642-29011-4_41

[MR04] Micciancio, D., Regev, O.: Worst-case to average-case reductions based on Gaussian measures. In: 45th Annual Symposium on Foundations of Computer Science, Rome, Italy, 17–19 October 2004, pp. 372–381. IEEE Computer Society Press (2004)

[Nao03] Naor, M.: On cryptographic assumptions and challenges. In: Boneh, D. (ed.) CRYPTO 2003. LNCS, vol. 2729, pp. 96–109. Springer, Heidelberg (2003). https://doi.org/10.1007/978-3-540-45146-4_6

[NIS] NIST: Post-quantum cryptography standardization. https://csrc.nist.gov/Projects/Post-Quantum-Cryptography

[Pei09] Peikert, C.: Public-key cryptosystems from the worst-case shortest vector problem: extended abstract. In: Mitzenmacher, M. (ed.) 41st Annual ACM Symposium on Theory of Computing, Bethesda, MD, USA, 31 May–2 June 2009, pp. 333–342. ACM Press (2009)

[Pei10] Peikert, C.: An efficient and parallel Gaussian sampler for lattices. In: Rabin, T. (ed.) CRYPTO 2010. LNCS, vol. 6223, pp. 80–97. Springer, Heidelberg (2010). https://doi.org/10.1007/978-3-642-14623-7_5

[Reg05] Regev, O.: On lattices, learning with errors, random linear codes, and cryptography. In: Gabow, H.N., Fagin, R. (eds.) 37th Annual ACM Symposium on Theory of Computing, Baltimore, MA, USA, 22–24 May 2005, pp. 84–93. ACM Press (2005)

[Sha48] Shannon, C.E.: A mathematical theory of communication. Bell Syst. Tech. J. **27**(3), 379–423 (1948)

[Sha49] Shannon, C.E.: Communication in the presence of noise. Proc. IRE **37**(1), 10–21 (1949)

[W+59] Wolfowitz, J., et al.: Strong converse of the coding theorem for semicontinuous channels. Ill. J. Math. **3**(4), 477–489 (1959)

[Wic13] Wichs, D.: Barriers in cryptography with weak, correlated and leaky sources. In: Kleinberg, R.D. (ed.) ITCS 2013: 4th Innovations in Theoretical Computer Science, Berkeley, CA, USA, 9–12 January 2013, pp. 111–126. Association for Computing Machinery (2013)

Key-Homomorphic Pseudorandom Functions from LWE with Small Modulus

Sam Kim[✉]

Stanford University, Stanford, USA
skim13@cs.stanford.edu

Abstract. Pseudorandom functions (PRFs) are fundamental objects in cryptography that play a central role in symmetric-key cryptography. Although PRFs can be constructed from one-way functions generically, these black-box constructions are usually inefficient and require deep circuits to evaluate compared to direct PRF constructions that rely on specific algebraic assumptions. From lattices, one can directly construct PRFs from the Learning with Errors (LWE) assumption (or its ring variant) using the result of Banerjee, Peikert, and Rosen (Eurocrypt 2012) and its subsequent works. However, all existing PRFs in this line of work rely on the hardness of the LWE problem where the associated modulus is super-polynomial in the security parameter.

In this work, we provide two new PRF constructions from the LWE problem. In each of these constructions, each focuses on either minimizing the depth of its evaluation circuit or providing key-homomorphism while relying on the hardness of the LWE problem with either a polynomial modulus or nearly polynomial modulus. Along the way, we introduce a new variant of the LWE problem called the Learning with Rounding and Errors (LWRE) problem. We show that for certain settings of parameters, the LWRE problem is as hard as the LWE problem. We then show that the hardness of the LWRE problem naturally induces a pseudorandom synthesizer that can be used to construct a low-depth PRF. The techniques that we introduce to study the LWRE problem can then be used to derive variants of existing key-homomorphic PRFs whose security can be reduced from the hardness of the LWE problem with a much smaller modulus.

1 Introduction

A pseudorandom function (PRF) [32] is a deterministic function $F : \mathcal{K} \times \mathcal{X} \to \mathcal{Y}$ that satisfies a specific security property: for a randomly sampled key $k \xleftarrow{\text{R}} \mathcal{K}$, the output of the function $F(k, \cdot)$ is computationally indistinguishable from those of a truly random function. PRFs are fundamental objects in cryptography that serve as a basis for symmetric cryptography. Even beyond symmetric cryptography, PRFs serve as one of the core building blocks for many advanced cryptographic constructions and protocols.

In theory, PRFs can be constructed from any one-way function via the transformation of [32,34]. However, the PRFs that are constructed from one-way

A. Canteaut and Y. Ishai (Eds.): EUROCRYPT 2020, LNCS 12106, pp. 576–607, 2020.
https://doi.org/10.1007/978-3-030-45724-2_20

functions in a blackbox way are generally inefficient. Furthermore, the transformation of [32,34] is inherently *sequential* and therefore, the resulting PRFs require deep circuits to evaluate. For practical deployment, this is problematic as symmetric objects like PRFs are often deployed inside designated hardware devices similar to how modern blockciphers, such as AES, are incorporated into many modern processors. For these settings, it is important for PRFs to exhibit *low depth* evaluation circuits that require few computing cycles to evaluate using multiple cores or processing units.

For these reasons, constructing low-depth pseudorandom functions from standard cryptographic assumptions have been a highly active area of research. Starting from the seminal work of Naor and Reingold [45], there have been great progress in constructing low-depth pseudorandom functions from *group-based* assumptions like the Decisional Diffie-Hellman (DDH) assumption [1,2,45]. However, constructing low-depth PRFs from standard lattice assumptions such as the Learning with Errors (LWE) assumption [48] has been surprisingly more difficult. Indeed, a low-depth PRF from LWE was constructed by a breakthrough result of Banerjee, Peikert, and Rosen [11], but only after the realization of seemingly more powerful primitives such as (lattice-based) identity-based encryption [3,4,27,31] and fully homomorphic encryption [22,23,30].

Key-Homomorphic PRFs. Since the work of [11], the study of lattice-based PRFs has become a highly productive area of research. There have been a sequence of results that further improve the constructions of [11] with various trade-offs in the parameters [10,17,28,35,43]. A long sequence of results also show how to construct PRFs with useful algebraic properties such as key-homomorphic PRFs [10,17,25], constrained PRFs [16,21,25,26], and even watermarkable PRFs [26,36,37,47] from LWE.

A special family of PRFs that are particularly useful for practical applications are key-homomorphic PRFs. The concept was first introduced by Naor, Pinkas, and Reingold [44] and it was first formalized as a cryptographic primitive by Boneh et al. [17]. We say that a pseudorandom function $F : \mathcal{K} \times \mathcal{X} \to \mathcal{Y}$ is *key-homomorphic* if the key-space $(\mathcal{K}, \oplus)$ and the range of the PRF $(\mathcal{Y}, \otimes)$ exhibit group structures such that for any two keys k_1, k_2 and input $x \in \mathcal{X}$, we have $F(k_1 \oplus k_2, x) = F(k_1, x) \otimes F(k_2, x)$. Key-homomorphic PRFs have many useful applications in symmetric cryptography and give rise to distributed PRFs, symmetric-key proxy re-encryption, and updatable encryption. The study of updatable encryption, in particular, have recently gained a considerable amount of traction [17,19,29,38,40]. Most of these existing proposals for updatable encryption rely on key-homomorphic PRFs or use direct updatable encryption constructions that take advantage of similar algebraic structures.

LWE Modulus. Despite significant progress in our understanding of lattice-based PRFs as described above, all existing direct PRF constructions suffer from one caveat: the modulus q, which defines the underlying ring for the PRF, must be set to be super-polynomial in the security parameter. The need for a large modulus q has several disadvantages. The first and immediate disadvantage is *efficiency*. A lattice-based PRF is generally defined with respect to a set of public matrices in $\mathbb{Z}_q^{n \times m}$ and a secret vector in $\mathbb{Z}_q^n$ for some suitable choice of parameters n and m. A bigger modulus q means that more space is required to store these values and more time is needed to evaluate the PRF.

Another disadvantage of a large modulus q is related to the *quality* of the LWE assumption that is needed to prove security. Generally, PRFs that are defined with a super-polynomial modulus q relies on the hardness of the LWE problem with a super-polynomial noise-to-modulus ratio. This means that the security of the PRF can only be based on the hardness of solving worst-case lattice problems with a super-polynomial approximation factor, which is a significantly stronger assumption than what is required by many other lattice-based cryptographic constructions. In fact, today, we can base seemingly stronger primitives like fully-homomorphic encryption [7,24] and attribute-based encryption [33] (when restricted to NC^1 computations) on the hardness of approximating worst-case lattice problems with only polynomial approximation factors. This clearly demonstrates that our current understanding of lattice-based PRFs is still quite limited.

Many existing lattice-based PRFs including the original constructions of [11] are, in fact, conjectured to be secure even when they are instantiated with much smaller values of the modulus q. However, their formal proof of security has been elusive for many years. An important question in the study of lattice-based PRFs is whether there exist direct lattice-based PRF constructions that rely on a polynomial modulus q that still exhibit some of the useful features not satisfied by the generic constructions [32,34] such as low-depth evaluation circuits or key-homomorphism.

1.1   Our Contributions

In this work, we present two PRF constructions from the hardness of the LWE problem with a small modulus q. For our first construction, we focus on minimizing the depth of the evaluation circuit while in our second construction, we focus on constructing a key-homomorphic PRF. In both settings, our goal is to construct lattice-based PRFs that work over small moduli q.

1.1.1   Low-Depth PRF

In our first PRF construction, our main focus is on minimizing the size of the modulus q while also minimizing the depth of the PRF evaluation circuit. We provide an overview of the construction in Sect. 2 and briefly discuss our approach below. The resulting PRF can be instantiated with a range of parameter settings that are determined by a trade-off between the depth of the evaluation circuit and the associated modulus q. We consider two types of parameter settings that provide different levels of security.

- *Theoretical security:* In this setting, we guarantee that any adversary has at most a negligible advantage in breaking the PRF. For this level of security, we can set the parameters of our PRF such that the modulus is polynomial in the security parameter $q = \tilde{O}(\lambda^{2.5})$ and the depth of the evaluation circuit is in NC^2.

- 2^λ-*security:* In this setting, we guarantee that an adversary's advantage in breaking the PRF degrades exponentially in the security parameter. For this level of security, we can set the parameters of our PRF such that the depth of the evaluation circuit is $\tilde{O}(\lambda/\log q)$. In particular, setting $q = 2^{\tilde{O}(\sqrt{\lambda})}$, the PRF evaluation can be done in depth $\tilde{O}(\sqrt{\lambda})$. Previously, all lattice-based PRFs either required that the depth of the evaluation circuit is at least $\tilde{O}(\lambda)$ or the modulus q to be at least $2^{\tilde{O}(\lambda)}$.

We provide a comparison of the size of the modulus q and the depth of the evaluation circuit that is needed for our PRF with those of existing LWE-based PRFs in Table 1. We further discuss how to interpret our parameter settings in Sect. 1.2 and how to concretely instantiate them in Sect. 4.3.

Synthesizers and LWRE. The main intermediate object that we use to construct our PRF is a pseudorandom synthesizer (Definition 4.5), which was first introduced by Naor and Reingold [45]. They showed that a pseudorandom synthesizer that can be computed by a low-depth circuit can be used to construct a PRF that can also be computed by a low-depth circuit. The work of Banerjee, Peikert, and Rosen [11] first showed that such pseudorandom synthesizers can be constructed from a natural variant of the LWE problem called the Learning with Rounding (LWR) problem. They showed that the hardness of the LWR problem can be reduced from the hardness of the LWE problem when the modulus q is set to be very large.

To construct a pseudorandom synthesizer from a small-modulus LWE problem, we introduce yet another variant of the LWE problem called the Learning with Rounding *and* Errors (LWRE) problem whose hardness naturally induces a pseudorandom synthesizer. The challenger for an LWRE problem chains multiple samples of the LWR and LWE problems together such that the error terms that are involved in each of the LWE samples are derived from the "noiseless" LWR samples. This specific way of chaining LWR and LWE samples together allows us to reduce the hardness of LWRE from the hardness of the LWE problem with a much smaller modulus q. We provide an overview of the LWRE problem and the reduction from LWE in Sect. 2. We precisely formulate the LWRE problem in Definition 4.1 and provide the formal reduction in the full version of this work.

The LWRE problem and our synthesizer construction naturally extend to the ring setting as well. In the full version of this work, we formulate the Ring-LWRE problem similarly to how the Ring-LWE and Ring-LWR problems are defined. Then, we show how to construct a pseudorandom synthesizer from the Ring-LWRE problem.

1.1.2 Key-Homomorphic PRF

For our second construction, we focus on constructing a key-homomorphic PRF with a small modulus q. Specifically, we provide a key-homomorphic PRF whose security (either theoretical or 2^λ-security) can be based on the hardness of LWE with a polynomial size q without relying on random oracles. All previous key-homomorphic PRFs from lattices either relied on LWE with a super-polynomial

Table 1. Comparison of the PRF constructions in this work and the existing PRF constructions based on LWE. For each of the PRF constructions, the table denotes the size of the modulus q that is needed to prove 2^λ-security from LWE and the depth of the evaluation circuit that is needed to evaluate the PRFs.

Construction	Size of modulus	Evaluation depth
[11, GGM]	$\lambda^{\Omega(1)}$	$\Omega(\lambda \log \lambda)$
[11, Synthesizer]	$2^{\Omega(\lambda)}$	$\Omega(\log^2 \lambda)$
[11, Direct]	$2^{\Omega(\lambda \log \lambda)}$	$\Omega(\log^2 \lambda)$
[17]	$2^{\Omega(\lambda \log \lambda)}$	$\Omega(\log^2 \lambda)$
[10]	$2^{\Omega(\lambda)}$	$\Omega(\log^2 \lambda)$
[28]	$2^{\Omega(\lambda)}$	$\Omega(\log^{1+o(1)} \lambda)$
[43]	$2^{\Omega(\lambda)}$	$\Omega(\log^2 \lambda)$
[35]	$2^{\Omega(\lambda)}$	$\Omega(\log^{1+o(1)} \lambda)$
This work: Synthesizer-based	$2^{\Omega(\sqrt{\lambda})}$	$\Omega(\sqrt{\lambda} \log \lambda)$
This work: BP-based	$\lambda^{\Omega(1)}$	$\Omega(\lambda^2 \log \lambda)$

modulus q [10,17,25] or random oracles [17,44]. As in previous LWE-based key-homomorphic PRFs, our construction is "almost" key-homomorphic in that the homomorphism on the PRF keys hold subject to some small rounding error, which does not significantly impact its usefulness to applications.

Our construction relies on the same chaining technique that is used to construct our first PRF. This time, instead of chaining multiple LWE and LWR samples together as was done in our first construction, we chain multiple instances of the existing lattice-based PRFs themselves. For most existing PRF constructions that are based on LWE, their proof of security proceeds in two steps:

1. Define a "noisy" variant of the deterministic PRF function whose security can be based on the hardness of the LWE problem.
2. Show that the deterministic PRF function and its "noisy" variant have the same input-output behavior with overwhelming probability over the randomness used to sample the noise.

Generally, in order to show that the deterministic PRF and its "noisy" variant are statistically indistinguishable in step 2 above, the modulus q has to be set to be super-polynomial in the security parameter.

To reduce the need for a large modulus q in step 2, we chain multiple instances of the deterministic PRF and its noisy variant. Namely, our PRF construction consists of many noisy variants of these PRFs that are chained together such that the noise that is needed to evaluate the noisy PRF in a chain is derived from a PRF in the previous level of the chain. By setting the initial PRF at the start of the chain to be the original deterministic PRF, the entire evaluation of the chained PRF can be made to be deterministic.

This simple way of chaining multiple instances of deterministic and noisy variants of PRFs allows us to prove the security of the final PRF from the hardness of LWE with a much smaller modulus q. In fact, when we chain multiple instances of a key-homomorphic PRF, the resulting PRF is also key-homomorphic. Instantiating the chain with the Banerjee-Peikert key-homomorphic PRF [10] results in a key-homomorphic PRF that works over a polynomial modulus q. We provide a detailed overview of our technique in Sect. 2 and provide the formal construction and its security proof in Sect. 5.

1.2 Discussions

Regarding Theoretical and 2^λ-Security. The reason why we present our results with respect to both theoretical and 2^λ-security is due to the fact that the generic PRF constructions [32] can already be used to construct a low-depth PRF that provides asymptotically equivalent level of security. Note that using a length-doubling pseudorandom generator, the Goldwasser, Goldreich and Micali [32] construction can be used to provide a PRF that can be evaluated in depth linear in the input size of the PRF. One way to achieve a poly-logarithmic depth PRF using the GGM construction is to first hash the input using a universal hash function into a domain of size $2^{\omega(\log \lambda)}$ and then apply the PRF on the hash of the message. As the hashed outputs are poly-logarithmic in length, the PRF can be evaluated in poly-logarithmic depth. At the same time, as long as the adversary is bounded to making a polynomial number of evaluation queries on the PRF, a collision on the hash function occurs with negligible probability and therefore, any efficient adversary can have at most negligible advantage in breaking the PRF. As a length-doubling PRG can be constructed from LWE with a polynomial modulus q, this gives an LWE-based PRF with both small evaluation depth and small modulus q. Of course, the actual security of this final PRF is quite poor since the probability that an adversary forces a collision on the hash function is barely negligible.

Therefore, the way to view our low-depth PRF is to consider its parameters when they are set to provide 2^λ-security. In this setting, our PRF provides security under the condition that $d \log q = \tilde{\Omega}(\lambda)$ where d is the depth of the evaluation circuit. When setting $\tilde{\Omega}(\log q) = \sqrt{\lambda}$, the evaluation circuit has depth that scales with $\sqrt{\lambda}$. This means that setting $\lambda = 128$ and ignoring arithmetic and vector operations, our PRF can be evaluated by a circuit with depth ≈ 11 that works over a ≈ 11-bit modulus. The GGM PRF, on the other hand, requires a circuit with depth at least $\lambda = 128$, which is prohibitive for practical use, while the existing lattice-based PRFs require $7 \approx \log \lambda$ circuit depth, but must operate over at least a 128-bit modulus. We discuss concrete instantiation of our scheme in Sect. 4.3.

We note that for key-homomorphic PRFs, no construction that works over a polynomial modulus was previously known. Therefore, our second PRF construction can be viewed as the first key-homomorphic PRF that works over a polynomial modulus independent of whether it provides theoretical or 2^λ-security.

On the Chaining Method and Blockciphers. The pseudorandom synthesizers or PRFs in this work consist of many repeated rounds of computation that are chained together in such a way that the output of each round of computation is affected by the output of the previous round. This way of chaining multiple rounds of computation is reminiscent of the structure of many existing blockciphers such as DES or AES, which also consist of many rounds of bit transformations that are chained together. Interestingly, chaining in blockciphers and chaining in our work seem to serve completely opposite roles. In blockcipher design, chaining is generally used to achieve the effect of *diffusion*, which guarantees that a small change to the input to the blockcipher significantly alters its final output. This assures that no correlation can be efficiently detected between the input and the output of the blockcipher. In this work, chaining is used to actually *prevent* diffusion. Namely, chaining guarantees that some small error that is induced by the PRF evaluation does not affect the final output of the PRF. This allows us to switch from the real PRF evaluation to the "noisy" PRF evaluation in our hybrid security argument such that we can embed an LWE challenge to the output of the PRF.

1.3   Other Related Work

PRF Cascades. The techniques that are used in this work are conceptually similar to PRF cascading, which is the process of chaining multiple small-domain PRFs to construct large-domain PRFs. The technique was first introduced by Bellare et al. [14] and was further studied by Boneh et al. [18]. PRF cascades serve as a basis for NMAC and HMAC PRFs [12,13].

LWR for Bounded Number of Samples. There have been a sequence of results that study the hardness of the Learning with Rounding problem when the number of samples are a priori bounded. Alwen et al. [8] first showed that such variant of LWR is as hard as LWE even when the modulus q is set to be polynomial in the security parameter. Bogdanov et al. [15] improved the statistical analysis of this reduction using Rényi divergence. Alperin-Sherif and Apon [6] further improved these previous results such that the reduction from LWE to LWR is sample-preserving.

2   Overview

In this section, we provide a high level overview of the main techniques that we use in this work. For the full details of our main results and proofs, we refer the readers to Sects. 4 and 5.

We divide the overview into three parts. In Sect. 2.1, we provide additional background on existing results on constructing lattice-based PRFs. In Sect. 2.2, we provide an overview of our synthesizer construction from a new computational problem called the Learning with Rounding and Errors (LWRE) problem. Then, in Sect. 2.3, we show how the technique that we use to prove the security of our synthesizer-based PRF can be applied to the parameters for existing lattice-based key-homomorphic PRFs.

2.1 Background on Lattice PRFs via Synthesizers

The main intermediate primitive that we use to construct our first lattice-based PRF is a special family of pseudorandom generators called *pseudorandom synthesizers* [45]. A pseudorandom synthesizer over a domain $\mathcal{D}$ is a two-to-one function $S : \mathcal{D} \times \mathcal{D} \to \mathcal{D}$ such that for any (a priori *unbounded*) polynomial number of inputs $a_1, \ldots, a_\ell \xleftarrow{R} \mathcal{D}$, and $b_1, \ldots, b_\ell \xleftarrow{R} \mathcal{D}$, the set of ℓ^2 elements $\{S(a_i, b_j)\}_{i,j \in [\ell]}$ are computationally indistinguishable from uniformly random elements $\{u_{i,j}\}_{i,j \in [\ell]} \xleftarrow{R} \mathcal{D}^{\ell^2}$.

A pseudorandom synthesizer $S : \mathcal{D} \times \mathcal{D} \to \mathcal{D}$ induces a PRF F with key space $\mathcal{D}^{2\ell}$, domain $\{0,1\}^\ell$, and range $\mathcal{D}$ for any positive power-of-two integer ℓ as follows:

- Define a PRF key to consist of 2ℓ uniformly random elements in $\mathcal{D}$:

$$\begin{pmatrix} s_{1,0} & s_{2,0} & \cdots & s_{\ell,0} \\ s_{1,1} & s_{2,1} & & s_{\ell,1} \end{pmatrix}.$$

- To evaluate the PRF on an input $x \in \{0,1\}^\ell$, compress the subset of the elements $s_{1,x_1}, \ldots, s_{\ell,x_\ell}$ into a single element of $\mathcal{D}$ by iteratively applying the synthesizer:

$$S\Big(\cdots S\big(S(s_{1,x_1}, s_{2,x_2}), S(s_{3,x_3}, s_{4,x_4}) \big), \cdots S(s_{\ell-1,x_{\ell-1}}, s_{\ell,x_\ell}) \cdots \Big).$$

The pseudorandomness of the output of the PRF can roughly be argued as follows. Since each of the ℓ elements $s_{1,x_1}, \ldots, s_{\ell,x_\ell} \in \mathcal{D}$ that are part of the PRF key are sampled uniformly at random, the compressed $\ell/2$ elements $S(s_{1,x_1}, s_{2,x_2}), \ldots, S(x_{\ell-1,x_{\ell-1}}, x_{\ell,x_\ell})$ are computationally indistinguishable from random elements in $\mathcal{D}$. This, in turn, implies that the compression of these $\ell/2$ elements into $\ell/4$ elements are pseudorandom. This argument can be applied iteratively to show that the final output of the PRF is computationally indistinguishable from uniform in $\mathcal{D}$.

LWE and Synthesizers. As pseudorandom synthesizers imply pseudorandom functions, one can naturally hope to construct a pseudorandom synthesizer from the LWE problem [48]. Recall that the $\mathsf{LWE}_{n,q,\chi}$ assumption, parameterized by positive integers n, q and a B-bounded error distribution χ, states that for any (a priori unbounded) $m = \mathsf{poly}(\lambda)$, if we sample a uniformly random secret vector $\mathbf{s} \xleftarrow{R} \mathbb{Z}_q^n$, uniformly random public vectors $\mathbf{a}_1, \ldots, \mathbf{a}_m \xleftarrow{R} \mathbb{Z}_q^n$, "small" error terms $e_1, \ldots, e_\ell \leftarrow \chi^m$, and uniformly random values $u_1, \ldots, u_m \xleftarrow{R} \mathbb{Z}_q$, the following distributions are computationally indistinguishable:

$$\begin{array}{ccc} (\mathbf{a}_1, \langle \mathbf{a}_1, \mathbf{s} \rangle + e_1) & \approx_c & (\mathbf{a}_1, u_1) \\ (\mathbf{a}_2, \langle \mathbf{a}_2, \mathbf{s} \rangle + e_2) & \approx_c & (\mathbf{a}_2, u_2) \\ \vdots & & \vdots \\ (\mathbf{a}_m, \langle \mathbf{a}_m, \mathbf{s} \rangle + e_m) & \approx_c & (\mathbf{a}_m, u_m). \end{array}$$

Given the $\mathsf{LWE}_{n,q,\chi}$ assumption, it is natural to define a (randomized) pseudorandom synthesizer $S : \mathbb{Z}_q^{n \times n} \times \mathbb{Z}_q^{n \times n} \to \mathbb{Z}_q^{n \times n}$ as follows

$$S(\mathbf{S}, \mathbf{A}) = \mathbf{S} \cdot \mathbf{A} + \mathbf{E},$$

where the error matrix $\mathbf{E} \leftarrow \chi^{n \times n}$ is sampled randomly by the synthesizer S. It is easy to show via a standard hybrid argument that for any set of matrices $\mathbf{S}_1, \ldots, \mathbf{S}_\ell \xleftarrow{\text{R}} \mathbb{Z}_q^{n \times n}$, $\mathbf{A}_1, \ldots, \mathbf{A}_\ell \xleftarrow{\text{R}} \mathbb{Z}_q^{n \times n}$, and $\mathbf{E}_{1,1}, \ldots, \mathbf{E}_{\ell,\ell} \leftarrow \chi^{n \times n}$, the pairwise applications of the synthesizer $\tilde{S}(\mathbf{S}_i, \mathbf{A}_j) = \mathbf{S}_i \cdot \mathbf{A}_j + \mathbf{E}_{i,j}$ for all $i, j \in [n]$ result in pseudorandom matrices.

Learning with Rounding. The problem with the synthesizer construction above is that the synthesizer must be randomized. Namely, in order to argue that the synthesizer's outputs are pseudorandom, the evaluation algorithm must flip random coins and sample independent error matrices $\mathbf{E}_{i,j} \leftarrow \chi^{n \times n}$ for each execution $S(\mathbf{S}_i, \mathbf{A}_j)$ for $i, j \in [\ell]$. Otherwise, if the error matrices are derived from an additional input to the synthesizer, then the error matrices for each evaluation of the synthesizer $S(\mathbf{S}_i, \mathbf{A}_j)$ for $i, j \in [\ell]$ must inevitably be correlated and hence, the security of the synthesizer cannot be shown from the hardness of $\mathsf{LWE}_{n,q,\chi}$.

Banerjee, Peikert and Rosen [11] provided a way to overcome this obstacle by introducing a way of derandomizing errors in LWE samples. The idea is quite simple and elegant: instead of adding small random error terms $e \leftarrow \chi$ to each inner product $\langle \mathbf{a}, \mathbf{s} \rangle \in \mathbb{Z}_q$, one can deterministically round it to one of $p < q$ partitions or "buckets" in $\mathbb{Z}_q$. Concretely, the idea can be implemented by applying the *modular rounding* operation $\lfloor \cdot \rceil_p : \mathbb{Z}_q \to \mathbb{Z}_p$ to the inner product $\langle \mathbf{a}, \mathbf{s} \rangle$, which maps $\langle \mathbf{a}, \mathbf{s} \rangle \mapsto \lfloor \langle \mathbf{a}, \mathbf{s} \rangle \cdot p/q \rceil$. Intuitively, adding a small noise term $e \leftarrow \chi$ to the inner product of $\langle \mathbf{a}, \mathbf{s} \rangle$ in the $\mathsf{LWE}_{n,q,\chi}$ problem *blinds* its low-ordered bits from a distinguisher. Therefore, applying the modular rounding operation to $\langle \mathbf{a}, \mathbf{s} \rangle$, which *removes* the low-ordered bits (albeit deterministically), should make the task of distinguishing it from random just as hard.

With this intuition, [11] introduced a new computational problem called the Learning with Rounding (LWR) problem. For parameters $n, q, p \in \mathbb{N}$ where $p < q$, the $\mathsf{LWR}_{n,q,p}$ problem asks an adversary to distinguish the distributions:

$$
\begin{array}{lcl}
(\mathbf{a}_1, \lfloor \langle \mathbf{a}_1, \mathbf{s} \rangle \rceil_p) & \approx_c & (\mathbf{a}_1, u_1) \\
(\mathbf{a}_2, \lfloor \langle \mathbf{a}_2, \mathbf{s} \rangle \rceil_p) & \approx_c & (\mathbf{a}_2, u_2) \\
\vdots & & \vdots \\
(\mathbf{a}_m, \lfloor \langle \mathbf{a}_m, \mathbf{s} \rangle \rceil_p) & \approx_c & (\mathbf{a}_m, u_m),
\end{array}
$$

where $\mathbf{s} \xleftarrow{\text{R}} \mathbb{Z}_q^n$, $\mathbf{a}_1, \ldots, \mathbf{a}_m \xleftarrow{\text{R}} \mathbb{Z}_q^n$, and $u_1, \ldots, u_m \xleftarrow{\text{R}} \mathbb{Z}_p$. The hardness of the LWR problem then induces a deterministic pseudorandom synthesizer $S : \mathbb{Z}_q^{n \times n} \times \mathbb{Z}_q^{n \times n} \to \mathbb{Z}_p^{n \times n}$ that is defined as follows:

$$S(\mathbf{S}, \mathbf{A}) = \lfloor \mathbf{S} \cdot \mathbf{A} \rceil_p,$$

where the modular rounding is done component-wise to each entry of the matrix $\mathbf{S} \cdot \mathbf{A} \in \mathbb{Z}_q^{n \times n}$.[1]

Reducing LWE to LWR. Now, the remaining question is whether the LWR problem can formally be shown to be as hard as the LWE problem. The work of [11] gave a positive answer to this question. They showed that for any B-bounded distribution χ and moduli q and p for which $q = 2Bp\lambda^{\omega(1)}$, the $\mathsf{LWR}_{n,q,p}$ problem is as hard as the $\mathsf{LWE}_{n,q,\chi}$ problem.[2] Given an adversary for the $\mathsf{LWR}_{n,q,p}$ problem $\mathcal{A}$, one can construct a simple algorithm $\mathcal{B}$ that uses $\mathcal{A}$ to solve $\mathsf{LWE}_{n,q,\chi}$. Specifically, on input an $\mathsf{LWE}_{n,q,\chi}$ challenge $(\mathbf{a}_1, b_1), \ldots, (\mathbf{a}_m, b_m) \in \mathbb{Z}_q^n \times \mathbb{Z}_q$, algorithm $\mathcal{B}$ simply provides $(\mathbf{a}_1, \lfloor b_1 \rceil_p), \ldots, (\mathbf{a}_m, \lfloor b_m \rceil_p)$ to $\mathcal{A}$.

- If the values $b_1, \ldots, b_m \in \mathbb{Z}_q$ are noisy inner products $b_1, = \langle \mathbf{a}_1, \mathbf{s} \rangle + e_1, \ldots, b_m = \langle \mathbf{a}_m, \mathbf{s} \rangle + e_m$, then we have

$$\lfloor b_i \rceil_p = \lfloor \langle \mathbf{a}_i, \mathbf{s} \rangle + e_i \rceil_p = \lfloor \langle \mathbf{a}_i, \mathbf{s} \rangle \rceil_p$$

  for all $i \in [m]$ except with negligible probability over $\mathbf{a}_1, \ldots, \mathbf{a}_m \xleftarrow{\mathsf{R}} \mathbb{Z}_q^n$.
- If the values $b_1, \ldots, b_m$ are uniformly random in $\mathbb{Z}_q$, then the values $\lfloor b_1 \rceil_p, \ldots, \lfloor b_m \rceil_p$ are also uniform in $\mathbb{Z}_p$.

Hence, the algorithm $\mathcal{B}$ statistically simulates the correct distribution of an $\mathsf{LWR}_{n,q,p}$ challenge for $\mathcal{A}$ and therefore, can solve the $\mathsf{LWE}_{n,q,\chi}$ problem with essentially the same advantage as $\mathcal{A}$.

The apparent limitation of this reduction is the need for the modulus q to be super-polynomial in the security parameter. If q is only polynomial, then with noticeable probability, the inner product $\langle \mathbf{a}_i, \mathbf{s} \rangle \in \mathbb{Z}_q$ for any $i \in [m]$ lands on a rounding "borderline" set

$$\mathsf{Borderline}_B = [-B, B] + q/p \cdot (\mathbb{Z} + 1/2)$$
$$FV = \{ v \in \mathbb{Z}_q \mid \exists\, e \in [-B, B] \text{ such that } \lfloor v \rceil_p \neq \lfloor v + e \rceil_p \},$$

and hence $\lfloor \langle \mathbf{a}_i, \mathbf{s} \rangle + e_i \rceil_p \neq \lfloor \langle \mathbf{a}_i, \mathbf{s} \rangle \rceil_p$. In this case, one cannot guarantee that an adversary $\mathcal{A}$ for the $\mathsf{LWR}_{n,q,p}$ problem correctly distinguishes the samples $(\mathbf{a}_1, \lfloor \langle \mathbf{a}_1, \mathbf{s} \rangle + e_1 \rceil_p), \ldots, (\mathbf{a}_m, \lfloor \langle \mathbf{a}_m, \mathbf{s} \rangle + e_m \rceil_p)$ from purely random samples.

---

[1] Note that the synthesizer maps matrices in $\mathbb{Z}_q^{n \times n}$ to matrices in $\mathbb{Z}_p^{n \times n}$ for $p < q$ and hence violates the original syntax of a synthesizer. This is a minor technicality, which can be addressed in multiple ways. One option is to have a sequence of rounding moduli $p_1, \ldots, p_{\log \ell}$ such that the synthesizer can be applied iteratively. Another option is to take a pseudorandom generator $G : \mathbb{Z}_p^{n \times n} \to \mathbb{Z}_q^{n \times n}$ and define $S(\mathbf{S}, \mathbf{A}) = G(\lfloor \mathbf{S} \cdot \mathbf{A} \rceil_p)$. Finally, one can define the synthesizer $S(\mathbf{S}, \mathbf{A}) = \lfloor \mathbf{S} \cdot \mathbf{A} \rceil_p$ with respect to non-square matrices $S : \mathbb{Z}_q^{m \times n} \times \mathbb{Z}_q^{n \times m} \to \mathbb{Z}_p^{m \times m}$ such that the sets $\mathbb{Z}_q^{m \times n}, \mathbb{Z}_q^{n \times m}$, and $\mathbb{Z}_p^{m \times m}$ have the same cardinality $|\mathbb{Z}_q^{m \times n}| = |\mathbb{Z}_q^{n \times m}| = |\mathbb{Z}_p^{m \times m}|$.

[2] For the reduction to succeed with probability $1 - 2^{-\lambda}$, we must set $q \geq 2Bp \cdot 2^{\lambda}$. For simplicity throughout the overview, we restrict to the "negligible vs. non-negligible" type security as opposed to 2^{λ}-security. See Sect. 1.2 for further discussions.

2.2   Learning with Rounding and Errors

Chaining LWE Samples. We get around the limitation of the reduction above by using what we call the *chaining method*. To demonstrate the idea, let us consider a challenge oracle $\mathcal{O}_{\tau,\mathbf{S}}$ that chains multiple $\mathsf{LWE}_{n,q,\chi}$ samples together. The oracle $\mathcal{O}_{\tau,\mathbf{S}}$ is parameterized by a chaining parameter $\tau \in \mathbb{N}$, a set of secret vectors $\mathbf{S} = (\mathbf{s}_1, \ldots, \mathbf{s}_\tau) \in \mathbb{Z}_q^{n \times \tau}$, and is defined with respect to a sampling algorithm $D_\chi : \{0,1\}^{\lfloor \log p \rfloor} \to \mathbb{Z}$, which takes in as input $\lfloor \log p \rfloor$ random coins and samples an error value $e \in \mathbb{Z}$ according to the B-bounded error distribution χ.

- $\mathcal{O}_{\tau,\mathbf{S}}$: On its invocation, the oracle samples a public vector $\mathbf{a} \xleftarrow{\text{R}} \mathbb{Z}_q^n$ and an error term $e_1 \leftarrow \chi$. Then, for $1 \leq i < \tau$, it iteratively computes:
  - $r_i \leftarrow \lfloor \langle \mathbf{a}, \mathbf{s}_i \rangle + e_i \rceil_p$.
  - $e_{i+1} \leftarrow D_\chi(r_i)$.
  It then returns $(\mathbf{a}, \lfloor \langle \mathbf{a}, \mathbf{s}_\tau \rangle + e_\tau \rceil_p)$.

In words, the oracle $\mathcal{O}_{\tau,\mathbf{S}}$ generates (the rounding of) an $\mathsf{LWE}_{n,q,\chi}$ sample $(\mathbf{a}, \lfloor \langle \mathbf{a}, \mathbf{s}_1 \rangle + e_1 \rceil_p)$ and uses $r_1 \leftarrow \lfloor \langle \mathbf{a}, \mathbf{s}_1 \rangle + e_1 \rceil_p$ as the random coins to sample $e_2 \leftarrow D_\chi(r_1)$. It then computes $r_2 \leftarrow \lfloor \langle \mathbf{a}, \mathbf{s}_2 \rangle + e_2 \rceil_p$ and uses r_2 to sample the next error term $e_3 \leftarrow D_\chi(r_2)$ for the next iteration. The oracle iterates this procedure for τ steps and finally returns $(\mathbf{a}, \lfloor \langle \mathbf{a}, \mathbf{s}_\tau \rangle + e_\tau \rceil_p)$.

Now, suppose that p divides q. Then a hybrid argument shows that assuming the hardness of $\mathsf{LWE}_{n,q,\chi}$, a sample $(\mathbf{a}, b) \leftarrow \mathcal{O}_{\tau,\mathbf{S}}$ is computationally indistinguishable from uniform in $\mathbb{Z}_q^n \times \mathbb{Z}_p$. Specifically, we can argue that the first term (random coins) $r_1 \leftarrow \lfloor \langle \mathbf{a}, \mathbf{s}_1 \rangle + e_1 \rceil_p$ is computationally indistinguishable from uniform in $\{0,1\}^{\lfloor \log p \rfloor}$ by the hardness of $\mathsf{LWE}_{n,q,\chi}$. Then, since r_1 is uniform, the error term $e_2 \leftarrow D_\chi(r_1)$ is correctly distributed according to χ, which implies that $r_2 \leftarrow \lfloor \langle \mathbf{a}, \mathbf{s}_2 \rangle + e_2 \rceil_p$ is also computationally indistinguishable from uniform. Continuing this argument for τ iterations, we can prove that the final output $(\mathbf{a}, \lfloor \langle \mathbf{a}, \mathbf{s}_\tau \rangle + e_\tau \rceil_p)$ is computationally indistinguishable from uniform in $\mathbb{Z}_q^n \times \mathbb{Z}_p$.

Chaining LWR and LWE Samples. So far, it seems as if we have not made much progress. Although the oracle $\mathcal{O}_{\tau,\mathbf{S}}$ returns an "LWR looking" sample $(\mathbf{a}, b) \in \mathbb{Z}_q \times \mathbb{Z}_p$, it must still randomly sample the initial noise term $e_1 \leftarrow \chi$, which makes it useless for constructing a deterministic pseudorandom synthesizer. Our key observation, however, is that when the chaining parameter τ is big enough, then the initial error term e_1 does not affect the final output $(\mathbf{a}, \lfloor \langle \mathbf{a}, \mathbf{s}_\tau \rangle + e_\tau \rceil_p)$ with overwhelming probability. In other words, e_1 can always be set to be 0 without negatively impacting the pseudorandomness of $\mathcal{O}_{\tau,\mathbf{S}}$.

To see this, consider the following modification of the oracle $\mathcal{O}_{\tau,\mathbf{S}}$:

- $\mathcal{O}_{\tau,\mathbf{S}}^{(\mathsf{lwre})}$: On its invocation, the oracle samples a public vector $\mathbf{a} \xleftarrow{\text{R}} \mathbb{Z}_q^n$ and initializes $e_1 = 0$. Then, for $1 \leq i < \tau$, it iteratively computes:
  - $r_i \leftarrow \lfloor \langle \mathbf{a}, \mathbf{s}_i \rangle + e_i \rceil_p$.
  - $e_{i+1} \leftarrow D_\chi(r_i)$.
  It returns $(\mathbf{a}, \lfloor \langle \mathbf{a}, \mathbf{s}_\tau \rangle + e_\tau \rceil_p)$.

In contrast to $\mathcal{O}_{\tau,\mathbf{S}}$, the oracle $\mathcal{O}_{\tau,\mathbf{S}}^{(\mathsf{lwre})}$ derives the first set of random coins r_1 from an errorless $\mathsf{LWR}_{n,q,p}$ sample $r_1 \leftarrow \lfloor \langle \mathbf{a}, \mathbf{s}_1 \rangle \rceil_p$. It then uses r_1 to sample the error term $e_2 \leftarrow D_\chi(r_1)$ for the next $\mathsf{LWE}_{n,q,\chi}$ sample to derive $r_2 \leftarrow \lfloor \langle \mathbf{a}, \mathbf{s}_2 \rangle + e_2 \rceil_p$, and it continues this procedure for τ iterations. As the oracle $\mathcal{O}_{\tau,\mathbf{S}}^{(\mathsf{lwre})}$ is, in effect, chaining $\mathsf{LWR}_{n,q,p}$ and $\mathsf{LWE}_{n,q,\chi}$ samples together, we refer to $\mathcal{O}_{\tau,\mathbf{S}}^{(\mathsf{lwre})}$ as the *Learning with (both) Rounding and Errors* (LWRE) oracle.

We claim that even when q is small, as long as the chaining parameter τ is big enough, the samples that are output by the oracles $\mathcal{O}_{\tau,\mathbf{S}}$ and $\mathcal{O}_{\tau,\mathbf{S}}^{(\mathsf{lwre})}$ are identical except with negligible probability. For simplicity, let us fix the modulus to be $q = 4Bp$ such that for $u \overset{\mathsf{R}}{\leftarrow} \mathbb{Z}_q$, $e_1, e_2 \leftarrow \chi$, we have

$$\Pr[\lfloor u + e_1 \rceil_p \neq \lfloor u + e_2 \rceil_p] \leq \frac{1}{2}. \tag{2.1}$$

Now, consider a transcript of an execution of the oracles $\mathcal{O}_{\tau,\mathbf{S}}$ and $\mathcal{O}_{\tau,\mathbf{S}}^{(\mathsf{lwre})}$ for $\mathbf{S} \overset{\mathsf{R}}{\leftarrow} \mathbb{Z}_q^{n \times \tau}$, $\mathbf{a} \overset{\mathsf{R}}{\leftarrow} \mathbb{Z}_q^n$, and any fixed error value $e_1 \in [-B, B]$:

$$
\begin{array}{ll}
\mathcal{O}_{\tau,\mathbf{S}}: & \mathcal{O}_{\tau,\mathbf{S}}^{(\mathsf{lwre})}: \\[4pt]
r_1 \leftarrow \lfloor \langle \mathbf{a}, \mathbf{s}_1 \rangle + e_1 \rceil_p & \tilde{r}_1 \leftarrow \lfloor \langle \mathbf{a}, \mathbf{s}_1 \rangle + 0 \rceil_p \\[4pt]
r_2 \leftarrow \lfloor \langle \mathbf{a}, \mathbf{s}_2 \rangle + e_2 \rceil_p & \tilde{r}_2 \leftarrow \lfloor \langle \mathbf{a}, \mathbf{s}_2 \rangle + \tilde{e}_2 \rceil_p \\[4pt]
\quad\vdots & \quad\vdots \\[4pt]
r_\tau \leftarrow \lfloor \langle \mathbf{a}, \mathbf{s}_\tau \rangle + e_\tau \rceil_p & \tilde{r}_\tau \leftarrow \lfloor \langle \mathbf{a}, \mathbf{s}_\tau \rangle + \tilde{e}_\tau \rceil_p
\end{array}
$$

We make the following observations:

1. Since the sampler D_χ is deterministic, if there exists an index $1 \leq i^* \leq \tau$ for which $r_{i^*} = \tilde{r}_{i^*}$, then this implies that $r_i = \tilde{r}_i$ for all $i^* \leq i \leq \tau$.
2. Since the vectors $\mathbf{s}_1, \ldots, \mathbf{s}_\tau$ are sampled uniformly at random from $\mathbb{Z}_q^n$, the inner products $\langle \mathbf{a}, \mathbf{s}_i \rangle$ for any $1 \leq i \leq \tau$ are distributed statistically close to uniform in $\mathbb{Z}_q$.[3] Therefore, using (2.1), we have

$$\Pr\left[\lfloor \langle \mathbf{a}, \mathbf{s}_i \rangle + e_i \rceil_p \neq \lfloor \langle \mathbf{a}, \mathbf{s}_i \rangle + \tilde{e}_i \rceil_p\right] \leq \frac{1}{2} + \mathsf{negl},$$

for any $1 \leq i \leq \tau$.

These observations imply that unless all of the inner products $\langle \mathbf{a}, \mathbf{s}_1 \rangle, \ldots, \langle \mathbf{a}, \mathbf{s}_\tau \rangle$ land on the "borderline" set of $\mathbb{Z}_q$, the samples of $\mathcal{O}_{\tau,\mathbf{S}}$ and $\mathcal{O}_{\tau,\mathbf{S}}^{(\mathsf{lwre})}$ coincide for $\mathbf{a} \overset{\mathsf{R}}{\leftarrow} \mathbb{Z}_q^n$. Furthermore, such bad event occurs with probability at most $\approx 1/2^\tau$. Hence, even for very small values of the chaining parameter $\tau = \omega(\log \lambda)$, with overwhelming probability over the matrix $\mathbf{S} \overset{\mathsf{R}}{\leftarrow} \mathbb{Z}_q^{n \times \tau}$, no information about the

---

[3] When the modulus q is prime, then the inner product $\langle \mathbf{a}, \mathbf{s}_i \rangle$ is certainly uniform in $\mathbb{Z}_q$. Even when q is composite (i.e. q is divisible by p), under mild requirements on q, the inner product $\langle \mathbf{a}, \mathbf{s}_i \rangle$ is statistically close to uniform in $\mathbb{Z}_q$.

initial error term e_1 is revealed from a single sample of $\mathcal{O}_{\tau,\mathbf{S}}$ or $\mathcal{O}_{\tau,\mathbf{S}}^{(\text{lwre})}$. This can be extended to argue that no information about e_1 is leaked from any polynomial number of samples via the union bound. Hence, for $\tau = \omega(\log \lambda)$, any polynomial number of samples from $\mathcal{O}_{\tau,\mathbf{S}}$ or $\mathcal{O}_{\tau,\mathbf{S}}^{(\text{lwre})}$ are statistically indistinguishable.

In the discussion above, we set the modulus $q = 4Bp$ purely for simplicity. If we set q to be slightly greater than $2Bp$ (by a polynomial factor), the chaining parameter τ can be set to be any super-constant function $\tau = \omega(1)$ to guarantee that the output of the oracles $\mathcal{O}_{\tau,\mathbf{S}}$ and $\mathcal{O}_{\tau,\mathbf{S}}^{(\text{lwre})}$ are statistically indistinguishable.

Synthesizer from LWRE. The oracle $\mathcal{O}_{\tau,\mathbf{S}}^{(\text{lwre})}$ naturally induces a computational problem. Namely, for a set of parameters n, q, p, χ, and τ, we define the $\text{LWRE}_{n,q,p,\chi,\tau}$ problem that asks an adversary to distinguish the samples $(\mathbf{a}_1, b_1), \ldots, (\mathbf{a}_m, b_m) \leftarrow \mathcal{O}_{\tau,\mathbf{S}}^{(\text{lwre})}$ from uniformly random samples $(\mathbf{a}_1, \hat{b}_1), \ldots, (\mathbf{a}_m, \hat{b}_m) \xleftarrow{\text{R}} \mathbb{Z}_q^n \times \mathbb{Z}_p$. Using the ideas highlighted above, we can show that for small values of q and τ, the $\text{LWRE}_{n,q,p,\chi,\tau}$ is at least as hard as the $\text{LWE}_{n,m,q,\chi}$ problem. Specifically, we can first show that the oracle $\mathcal{O}_{\tau,\mathbf{S}}^{(\text{lwre})}$ is statistically indistinguishable from $\mathcal{O}_{\tau,\mathbf{S}}$. Then, via a hybrid argument, we can show that the oracle $\mathcal{O}_{\tau,\mathbf{S}}$ is computationally indistinguishable from a uniform sampler over $\mathbb{Z}_q^n \times \mathbb{Z}_p$ by the hardness of $\text{LWE}_{n,q,\chi}$.

The $\text{LWRE}_{n,q,p,\chi,\tau}$ problem naturally induces a pseudorandom synthesizer. One can first define an "almost" pseudorandom synthesizer $\mathcal{G} : \mathbb{Z}_q^n \times \mathbb{Z}_q^{n \times \tau} \to \mathbb{Z}_p$ that emulates the $\text{LWRE}_{n,q,p,\chi,\tau}$ oracle as follows:

– $\mathcal{G}(\mathbf{a}, \mathbf{S})$: On input $\mathbf{a} \in \mathbb{Z}_q^n$ and $\mathbf{S} = (\mathbf{s}_1, \ldots, \mathbf{s}_\tau) \in \mathbb{Z}_q^{n \times \tau}$, the LWRE function sets $e_1 = 0$ and computes for $i = 1, \ldots, \tau - 1$:
  1. $r_i \leftarrow \lfloor \langle \mathbf{a}, \mathbf{s}_i \rangle + e_i \rceil_p$,
  2. $e_{i+1} \leftarrow D_\chi(r_i)$.
It then sets $b = \lfloor \langle \mathbf{a}, \mathbf{s}_\tau \rangle + e_\tau \rceil_p$ and returns $b \in \mathbb{Z}_p$.

It is easy to see that as long as the $\text{LWRE}_{n,q,p,\chi,\tau}$ problem is hard, then for any $\ell = \text{poly}(\lambda)$, $\mathbf{a}_1, \ldots, \mathbf{a}_\ell \xleftarrow{\text{R}} \mathbb{Z}_q^n$, $\mathbf{S}_1, \ldots, \mathbf{S}_\ell \leftarrow \mathbb{Z}_q^{n \times \tau}$, and $u_{1,1}, \ldots, u_{\ell,\ell} \xleftarrow{\text{R}} \mathbb{Z}_p$, we have

$$\left\{ \mathcal{G}(\mathbf{a}_i, \mathbf{S}_j) \right\}_{i,j \in [\ell]} \approx_c \left\{ u_{i,j} \right\}_{i,j \in [\ell]} \in \mathbb{Z}_p^{\ell^2}.$$

Furthermore, this indistinguishability holds even for small values of the chaining parameter $\tau = \omega(1)$ and hence, the function $\mathcal{G}$ can be computed by shallow circuits.

The only reason why $\mathcal{G} : \mathbb{Z}_q^n \times \mathbb{Z}_q^{n \times \tau} \to \mathbb{Z}_p$ is not a pseudorandom synthesizer is that the cardinality of the sets $\mathbb{Z}_q^n$, $\mathbb{Z}_q^{n \times \tau}$, and $\mathbb{Z}_p$ are different. However, this can easily be fixed by defining a synthesizer $S : (\mathbb{Z}_q^n)^{\ell_1} \times (\mathbb{Z}_q^{n \times \tau})^{\ell_2} \to (\mathbb{Z}_p)^{\ell_1 \times \ell_2}$ that takes in a set of ℓ_1 vectors $(\mathbf{a}_1, \ldots, \mathbf{a}_\ell) \in (\mathbb{Z}_q^n)^{\ell_1}$, and ℓ_2 matrices $(\mathbf{S}_1, \ldots, \mathbf{S}_\tau) \in (\mathbb{Z}_q^{n \times \tau})^{\ell_2}$, and then returns $\{\mathcal{G}(\mathbf{a}_i, \mathbf{S}_j)\}_{i,j \in [\ell]}$. The parameters ℓ_1 and ℓ_2 can be set to be any positive integers such that

$$\left| (\mathbb{Z}_q^n)^{\ell_1} \right| = \left| (\mathbb{Z}_q^{n \times \tau})^{\ell_2} \right| = \left| \mathbb{Z}_p^{\ell_1 \times \ell_2} \right|,$$

which makes S to be a two-to-one function over a fixed domain. The PRF that is induced by the synthesizer $S : (\mathbb{Z}_q^n)^{\ell_1} \times (\mathbb{Z}_q^{n\times\tau})^{\ell_2} \to (\mathbb{Z}_p)^{\ell_1\times\ell_2}$ corresponds to our first PRF construction.

We note that for practical implementation of the synthesizer, the large PRF key can be derived from a λ-bit PRG seed. Furthermore, the discrete Gaussian sampler D_χ can always be replaced by a suitable look-up table with pre-computed Gaussian noise as the modulus p is small. Therefore, the synthesizer can be implemented quite efficiently as it simply consists of τ inner products of two vectors modulo a small integer and their rounding. We refer to Sect. 4.3 for a discussion on the parameters and implementations.

2.3 Chaining Key-Homomorphic PRFs

The method of chaining multiple LWR/LWE samples can also be applied directly to existing lattice-based PRF constructions to improve their parameters. Furthermore, when applied to existing key-homomorphic PRFs, the resulting PRF is also key-homomorphic. Here, we demonstrate the idea with the PRF construction of [17] as it can be described quite compactly. In the technical section (Sect. 5), we show how to chain the PRF construction of [10] as it is a generalization of the previous PRF constructions of [11,17] and it also allows us to set the parameters such that the underlying modulus q is only polynomial in the security parameter.

Background on BLMR [17]. Recall that the BLMR PRF is defined with respect to two public binary matrices $\mathbf{A}_0, \mathbf{A}_1 \in \{0,1\}^{n\times n}$ for a suitable choice of $n = \mathsf{poly}(\lambda)$. A PRF key is set to be a vector $\mathbf{s} \in \mathbb{Z}_q^n$, and the PRF evaluation for an input $x \in \{0,1\}^\ell$ is defined to be the rounded matrix product

$$F^{(\mathsf{BLMR})}(\mathbf{s}, x) = \left\lfloor \mathbf{s}^\intercal \prod_{i=1}^{\ell} \mathbf{A}_{x_i} \right\rceil_p.$$

We can reason about the security of the BLMR PRF by considering its "noisy" variant that is defined as follows:

$F^{(\mathsf{noise})}(\mathbf{s}, x)$:
1. Sample error vectors $\mathbf{e}_1, \dots, \mathbf{e}_\ell \leftarrow \chi^n$,
2. Return the vector

$$\left\lfloor \left(\left((\mathbf{s}^\intercal \mathbf{A}_{x_1} + \mathbf{e}_1^\intercal) \cdot \mathbf{A}_{x_2} + \mathbf{e}_2^\intercal\right) \cdots \right) \cdot \mathbf{A}_{x_\ell} + \mathbf{e}_\ell^\intercal \right\rceil_p$$

$$= \left\lfloor \mathbf{s}^\intercal \prod_{i=1}^{\ell} \mathbf{A}_{x_i} + \underbrace{\sum_{i=1}^{\ell-1} \mathbf{e}_i^\intercal \prod_{j=i+1}^{\ell-1} \mathbf{A}_{x_j} + \mathbf{e}_\ell^\intercal}_{\mathbf{e}^*} \right\rceil_p.$$

Since the error vectors $\mathbf{e}_1, \ldots, \mathbf{e}_\ell \leftarrow \chi^n$ has small norm and the matrices $\mathbf{A}_0, \mathbf{A}_1 \in \{0,1\}^{n \times n}$ are binary, the error term $\mathbf{e}^*$ is also small. Therefore, if the modulus q is sufficiently big, then with overwhelming probability, the error vector $\mathbf{e}^*$ is "rounded away" and does not contribute to the final output of the PRF. This shows that when the modulus q is big, the evaluations of the functions $F(\mathbf{s}, \cdot)$ and $F^{(\text{noise})}(\mathbf{s}, \cdot)$ are statistically indistinguishable.

Now, it is easy to show that $F^{(\text{noise})}(\mathbf{s}, \cdot)$ is computationally indistinguishable from a truly random function using the hardness of the $\text{LWE}_{n,q,\chi}$ problem.[4] We can first argue that the vector $\mathbf{s}_1^\mathsf{T} \mathbf{A}_{1,x_1} + \mathbf{e}_1^\mathsf{T}$ is computationally indistinguishable from a uniformly random vector $\mathbf{s}_2 \xleftarrow{\text{R}} \mathbb{Z}_q^n$. This implies that the vector $\mathbf{s}_2^\mathsf{T} \mathbf{A}_{2,x_2} + \mathbf{e}_2^\mathsf{T}$ is computationally indistinguishable from a random vector $\mathbf{s}_3 \xleftarrow{\text{R}} \mathbb{Z}_q^n$. We can repeat the argument for ℓ steps to prove that the final output of the PRF is computationally indistinguishable from a uniformly random output.

Chaining BLMR. For the security argument of the BLMR PRF to be valid, it is crucial that the modulus q is large enough such that the error term $\mathbf{e}^*$ rounds away with the modular rounding operation. Specifically, the modulus q must be set to be greater than the maximum possible norm of the error term $\|\mathbf{e}^*\|$ by a super-polynomial factor in the security parameter.

To prevent this blow-up in the size of q, we can chain multiple instances of the functions $F^{(\text{BLMR})}$ and $F^{(\text{noise})}$ together. Consider the following chained PRF $F^{(\text{chain})} : \mathbb{Z}_q^{n \times \tau} \times \{0,1\}^\ell \to \mathbb{Z}_p^n$:

$F^{(\text{chain})}(\mathbf{S} = (\mathbf{s}_1, \ldots, \mathbf{s}_\tau), x)$:
  1. Evaluate $r_2 \leftarrow F^{(\text{BLMR})}(\mathbf{s}_1, x)$.
  2. For $i = 2, \ldots, \tau - 1$, compute:
     - $r_{i+1} \leftarrow F^{(\text{noise})}(\mathbf{s}_i, x; r_i)$.
  3. Return $F^{(\text{noise})}(\mathbf{s}_\tau, x; r_\tau)$.

In words, the chained PRF $F^{(\text{chain})}(\mathbf{s}, x)$ evaluates the "random coins" that are needed to evaluate the randomized PRF $F^{(\text{noise})}(\mathbf{s}_i, x)$ from the previous execution of $F^{(\text{noise})}(\mathbf{s}_{i-1}, x)$. The initial random coins are derived from the errorless BLMR PRF $F^{(\text{BLMR})}(\mathbf{s}_1, x)$.

We can prove that the chained PRF $F^{(\text{chain})}$ is secure using the same argument that was used to show the hardness of the LWRE problem. Namely, we first argue that even if the modulus q is greater than the maximum possible norm of the error term $\|\mathbf{e}^*\|$ only by a polynomial factor, for any two random coins r_i, r_i', we have $F^{(\text{noise})}(\mathbf{s}_i, x; r_i) = F^{(\text{noise})}(\mathbf{s}_i, x; r_i')$ with noticeable probability. Therefore, if we set τ to be sufficiently big, then we can replace $F^{(\text{BLMR})}(\mathbf{s}_1, \cdot)$ with the randomized function $F^{(\text{noise})}(\mathbf{s}_1, \cdot)$ without changing the output of the PRF. Now, we can use the fact that $F^{(\text{noise})}(\mathbf{s}_1, \cdot)$ is computationally indistinguishable from a

---

[4] Technically, the reduction uses the hardness of the *non-uniform* variant of the LWE problem [17] where the challenger samples the public vectors $\mathbf{a}_1, \ldots, \mathbf{a}_m$ uniformly at random from $\{0,1\}^n$ as opposed to sampling them from $\mathbb{Z}_q^n$. The work of [17] shows that this variant of the LWE problem is as hard as the traditional version of LWE for suitable choices of parameters.

truly random function to argue that the function $F^{(\text{chain})}(\mathbf{S}, \cdot)$ is computationally indistinguishable from a truly random function.

The parameters for the chained PRF $F^{(\text{chain})}$ provide a trade-off between the depth of the evaluation circuit and the size of the modulus q (and therefore, the quality of the LWE assumption). If we set $\tau = 1$, then we recover the original BLMR PRF, which requires very large values of the modulus q. As we increase τ, the modulus q can be set to be arbitrarily close to the maximum possible value of the error vector $\|\mathbf{e}^*\|$ for $F^{(\text{noise})}(\mathbf{s}, x)$. For the Banerjee-Peikert PRF [10], the maximum possible value of the error vector $\|\mathbf{e}^*\|$ can be made to be only polynomial in the security parameter, thereby allowing us to set q to be a polynomial function of the security parameter.

Key-Homomorphism. The BLMR PRF is key-homomorphic because the modular rounding operation is an almost linear operation. Namely, for any input $x \in \{0,1\}^{\ell}$ and any two keys $\mathbf{s}, \tilde{\mathbf{s}} \in \mathbb{Z}_q^n$, we have

$$F^{(\text{BLMR})}(\mathbf{s}, x) + F^{(\text{BLMR})}(\tilde{\mathbf{s}}, x) = \left\lfloor \mathbf{s}^{\mathsf{T}} \prod_{i=1}^{\ell} \mathbf{A}_{x_i} \right\rceil_p + \left\lfloor \tilde{\mathbf{s}}^{\mathsf{T}} \prod_{i=1}^{\ell} \mathbf{A}_{x_i} \right\rceil_p$$

$$\approx \left\lfloor (\mathbf{s} + \tilde{\mathbf{s}})^{\mathsf{T}} \prod_{i=1}^{\ell} \mathbf{A}_{x_i} \right\rceil_p$$

$$= F^{(\text{BLMR})}(\mathbf{s} + \tilde{\mathbf{s}}, x).$$

Due to this algebraic structure, the "noisy" variant of the BLMR PRF is also key-homomorphic. Namely, for any input $x \in \{0,1\}^{\ell}$, any two keys $\mathbf{s}, \tilde{\mathbf{s}} \in \mathbb{Z}_q^n$, and any *random coins* $r, \tilde{r}, r'$ that is used to sample the noise, we have

$$F^{(\text{noise})}(\mathbf{s}, x; r) + F^{(\text{noise})}(\tilde{\mathbf{s}}, x; \tilde{r}) = \left\lfloor (\mathbf{s} + \tilde{\mathbf{s}})^{\mathsf{T}} \prod_{i=1}^{\ell} \mathbf{A}_{x_i} + (\mathbf{e}^* + \tilde{\mathbf{e}}^*) \right\rceil_p$$

$$\approx F^{(\text{noise})}(\mathbf{s} + \tilde{\mathbf{s}}, x; r'),$$

Now, note that the final output of the chained PRF $F^{(\text{chain})}$ on an input $x \in \{0,1\}^{\ell}$ and a key $(\mathbf{s}_1, \ldots, \mathbf{s}_{\tau}) \in \mathbb{Z}_q^{n \times \tau}$ with chaining parameter τ is simply the output of the noisy PRF $F^{(\text{noise})}(\mathbf{s}_{\tau}, x; r_{\tau})$ where r_{τ} is the randomness that is derived from the previous execution of $r_{\tau} \leftarrow F^{(\text{noise})}(\mathbf{s}_{\tau-1}, x; r_{\tau-1})$. Therefore, for any input $x \in \{0,1\}^{\ell}$, and two keys $\mathbf{S}, \tilde{\mathbf{S}} \in \mathbb{Z}_q^{n \times \tau}$, we can show that

$$F^{(\text{chain})}(\mathbf{S}, x) + F^{(\text{chain})}(\tilde{\mathbf{S}}, x) = F^{(\text{noise})}(\mathbf{s}_{\tau}, x; r_{\tau}) + F^{(\text{noise})}(\tilde{\mathbf{s}}_{\tau}, x; \tilde{r}_{\tau})$$

$$\approx F^{(\text{noise})}(\mathbf{s}_{\tau} + \tilde{\mathbf{s}}_{\tau}, x)$$

$$\approx F^{(\text{chain})}(\mathbf{S} + \tilde{\mathbf{S}}, x)$$

Specifically, we can show that for a suitable choice of the modulus q, the resulting PRF is *2-almost* key-homomorphic in that for any input $x \in \{0,1\}^{\ell}$ and two keys $\mathbf{S}, \tilde{\mathbf{S}} \in \mathbb{Z}_q^{n \times \tau}$, there exists an error vector $\boldsymbol{\eta} \in [0,2]^n$ such that

$$F^{(\text{chain})}(\mathbf{S}, x) + F^{(\text{chain})}(\tilde{\mathbf{S}}, x) = F^{(\text{chain})}(\mathbf{S} + \tilde{\mathbf{S}}, x) + \boldsymbol{\eta}.$$

The exact argument to show that the chained BLMR PRF is 2-almost key-homomorphic can be used to show that the chained BP PRF [10] is also 2-almost key-homomorphic. We provide the formal details in Sect. 5.

3   Preliminaries

Basic Notations. Unless specified otherwise, we use λ to denote the security parameter. We say a function $f(\lambda)$ is negligible in λ, denoted by $\mathsf{negl}(\lambda)$, if $f(\lambda) = o(1/\lambda^c)$ for all $c \in \mathbb{N}$. We say that a function $f(\lambda)$ is noticeable in λ if $f(\lambda) = \Omega(1/\lambda^c)$ for some $c \in \mathbb{N}$. We say that an event happens with overwhelming probability if its complement happens with negligible probability. We say that an algorithm is efficient if it runs in probabilistic polynomial time in the length of its input. We use $\mathsf{poly}(\lambda)$ to denote a quantity whose value is bounded by a fixed polynomial in λ.

For an integer $n \geq 1$, we write $[n]$ to denote the set of integers $\{1, \ldots, n\}$. For a distribution $\mathcal{D}$, we write $x \leftarrow \mathcal{D}$ to denote that x is sampled from $\mathcal{D}$; for a finite set S, we write $x \xleftarrow{\text{R}} S$ to denote that x is sampled uniformly from S. For a positive integer B, we say that a distribution $\mathcal{D}$ over $\mathbb{Z}$ is B-bounded if $\Pr[x \leftarrow \mathcal{D} \wedge |x| > B]$ is negligible. Finally, we write $\mathsf{Funs}[\mathcal{X}, \mathcal{Y}]$ to denote the set of all functions mapping from a domain $\mathcal{X}$ to a range $\mathcal{Y}$.

Vectors and Matrices. We use bold lowercase letters (*e.g.*, $\mathbf{v}, \mathbf{w}$) to denote vectors and bold uppercase letters (*e.g.*, $\mathbf{A}, \mathbf{B}$) to denote matrices. Throughout this work, we always use the infinity norm for vectors and matrices. Therefore, for a vector $\mathbf{x}$, we write $\|\mathbf{x}\|$ to denote $\max_i |x_i|$. Similarly, for a matrix $\mathbf{A}$, we write $\|\mathbf{A}\|$ to denote $\max_{i,j} |A_{i,j}|$. If $\mathbf{x} \in \mathbb{Z}^n$ and $\mathbf{A} \in \mathbb{Z}^{n \times m}$, then $\|\mathbf{x}\mathbf{A}\| \leq n \cdot \|\mathbf{x}\| \cdot \|\mathbf{A}\|$.

Modular Rounding. For an integer $p \leq q$, we define the modular "rounding" function

$$\lfloor \cdot \rceil_p \colon \mathbb{Z}_q \to \mathbb{Z}_p \text{ that maps } x \to \lfloor (p/q) \cdot x \rceil$$

and extend it coordinate-wise to matrices and vectors over $\mathbb{Z}_q$. Here, the operation $\lfloor \cdot \rceil$ is the integer rounding operation over the real numbers. It can be readily checked that for any two values $x, y \in \mathbb{Z}_q$, there exists some $\eta \in \{0, 1\}$ such that $\lfloor x \rceil_p + \lfloor y \rceil_p = \lfloor x + y \rceil_p + \eta$.

Bit-Decomposition. Let n and q be positive integers. Then we define the "gadget matrix" $\mathbf{G} = \mathbf{g} \otimes \mathbf{I}_n \in \mathbb{Z}_q^{n \times n \cdot \lceil \log q \rceil}$ where $\mathbf{g} = (1, 2, 4, \ldots, 2^{\lceil \log q \rceil - 1})$. We define the inverse bit-decomposition function $\mathbf{G}^{-1} : \mathbb{Z}_q^{n \times m} \to \mathbb{Z}_q^{n \lceil \log q \rceil \times m}$ which expands each entry $x \in \mathbb{Z}_q$ in the input matrix into a column of size $\lceil \log q \rceil$ that consists of the bits of the binary representation of x.

3.1   Learning with Errors

In this section, we define the Learning with Errors (LWE) problem [48].

Learning with Errors. We define the LWE problem with respect to the real and ideal oracles.

Definition 3.1 (Learning with Errors). *Let $\lambda \in \mathbb{N}$ be the security parameter. Then the learning with errors (LWE) problem is parameterized by a dimension $n = n(\lambda)$, modulus $q = q(\lambda)$, and error distribution $\chi = \chi(\lambda)$. It is defined with respect to the real and ideal oracles $\mathcal{O}_s^{(\text{lwe})}$ and $\mathcal{O}^{(\text{ideal})}$ that are defined as follows:*

- $\mathcal{O}_s^{(\text{lwe})}$: *The real oracle is parameterized by a vector $\mathbf{s} \in \mathbb{Z}_q^n$. On its invocation, the oracle samples a random vector $\mathbf{a} \stackrel{R}{\leftarrow} \mathbb{Z}_q^n$, and an error term $e \leftarrow \chi$. It sets $b = \langle \mathbf{a}, \mathbf{s} \rangle + e$, and returns $(\mathbf{a}, b) \in \mathbb{Z}_q^n \times \mathbb{Z}_q$.*
- $\mathcal{O}^{(\text{ideal})}$: *On its invocation, the ideal oracle samples a random vector $\mathbf{a} \stackrel{R}{\leftarrow} \mathbb{Z}_q^n$, random element $u \stackrel{R}{\leftarrow} \mathbb{Z}_q$, and returns $(\mathbf{a}, u) \in \mathbb{Z}_q^n \times \mathbb{Z}_q$.*

The $\mathsf{LWE}_{n,q,\chi}$ problem is to distinguish the oracles $\mathcal{O}_s^{(\text{lwe})}$ and $\mathcal{O}^{(\text{ideal})}$. More precisely, we define an adversary $\mathcal{A}$'s distinguishing advantage $\mathsf{Adv}_{\mathsf{LWE}}(n, q, \chi, \mathcal{A})$ as the probability

$$\mathsf{Adv}_{\mathsf{LWE}}(n, q, \chi, \mathcal{A}) = \left| \Pr\left[\mathcal{A}^{\mathcal{O}_s^{(\text{lwe})}}(1^\lambda) = 1 \right] - \Pr\left[\mathcal{A}^{\mathcal{O}^{(\text{ideal})}}(1^\lambda) = 1 \right] \right|,$$

where $\mathbf{s} \stackrel{R}{\leftarrow} \mathbb{Z}_q^n$. The $\mathsf{LWE}_{n,q,\chi}$ assumption state that for any efficient adversary $\mathcal{A}$, its distinguishing advantage is negligible $\mathsf{Adv}_{\mathsf{LWE}}(n, q, \chi, \mathcal{A}) = \mathsf{negl}(\lambda)$.

Compactly, the $\mathsf{LWE}_{n,q,\chi}$ assumption states that for any $m = \mathsf{poly}(\lambda)$, $\mathbf{s} \stackrel{R}{\leftarrow} \mathbb{Z}_q^n$, $\mathbf{A} \leftarrow \mathbb{Z}_q^{n \times m}$, $\mathbf{e} \leftarrow \chi^m$, and $\mathbf{u} \leftarrow \mathbb{Z}_q^m$, the noisy vector-matrix product $(\mathbf{A}, \mathbf{s}^\mathsf{T}\mathbf{A} + \mathbf{e}^\mathsf{T})$ is computationally indistinguishable from $(\mathbf{A}, \mathbf{u}^\mathsf{T})$. It follows from a standard hybrid argument that for any $m, \ell = \mathsf{poly}(\lambda)$, $\mathbf{S} \stackrel{R}{\leftarrow} \mathbb{Z}_q^{\ell \times n}$, $\mathbf{A} \stackrel{R}{\leftarrow} \mathbb{Z}_q^{n \times m}$, $\mathbf{E} \leftarrow \chi^{\ell \times m}$, and $\mathbf{U} \stackrel{R}{\leftarrow} \mathbb{Z}_q^{\ell \times m}$, the noisy matrix product $(\mathbf{A}, \mathbf{S} \cdot \mathbf{A} + \mathbf{E})$ is computationally indistinguishable from $(\mathbf{A}, \mathbf{U})$ by the $\mathsf{LWE}_{n,q,\chi}$ assumption.

Let $n = \mathsf{poly}(\lambda)$ and χ be a B-bounded discrete Gaussian distribution. Then the $\mathsf{LWE}_{n,q,\chi}$ assumption is true assuming that various worst-case lattice problems such as GapSVP and SIVP on n-dimensional lattices are hard to approximate to within a factor of $\tilde{O}(n \cdot q / B)$ by a quantum algorithm [48]. Similar reductions of $\mathsf{LWE}_{n,q,\chi}$ to the *classical* hardness of approximating worst-case lattice problems are also known [9,20,41,42,46].

3.2 Elementary Number Theory

In this section, we state and prove an elementary fact in number theory that we use for our technical sections. Specifically, we analyze the distribution of the inner product of two uniformly random vectors $\langle \mathbf{a}, \mathbf{s} \rangle$ where $\mathbf{a}, \mathbf{s} \stackrel{R}{\leftarrow} \mathbb{Z}_q^n$ for some positive integers n and q. When n is sufficiently big, then with overwhelming probability, one of the components of $\mathbf{a}$ (or $\mathbf{s}$) will be a multiplicative unit in $\mathbb{Z}_q$ and therefore, the inner product $\langle \mathbf{a}, \mathbf{s} \rangle$ will be uniform in $\mathbb{Z}_q$. We formally state and prove this elementary fact in the lemma below. We first recall a general fact of the Euler totient function.

Fact 3.2 ([39]). Let $\varphi : \mathbb{Z} \to \mathbb{Z}$ be the Euler totient function. Then, there exists a constant c such that for any $q > 264$, we have $q/\varphi(q) = c \cdot \log\log q$.

The following lemma follows immediately from Fact 3.2.

Lemma 3.3. *Let $n = n(\lambda)$ and $q = q(\lambda)$ be positive integers such that $n = \Omega(\lambda \log\log q)$. Then, for any element $d \in \mathbb{Z}_q$, we have*

$$\Pr[\ \langle \mathbf{a}, \mathbf{s} \rangle = d\ ] \leq 1/q + 2^{-\lambda},$$

for $\mathbf{a}, \mathbf{s} \xleftarrow{\text{R}} \mathbb{Z}_q^n$.

Proof. If the vector $\mathbf{a} \in \mathbb{Z}_q^n$ has at least one component that is a multiplicative unit in $\mathbb{Z}_q$, then since $\mathbf{s}$ is sampled uniformly at random from $\mathbb{Z}_q^n$, we have $\langle \mathbf{a}, \mathbf{s} \rangle = d$ with probability $1/q$. By Fact 3.2, the probability that all components of $\mathbf{a}$ is *not* a unit in $\mathbb{Z}_q$ is bounded by the probability

$$\left(1 - \frac{1}{c \cdot \log\log q} \right)^n$$

for some constant c. Setting $\lambda = \Omega(n/\log\log q)$, this probability is bounded by $e^{-\lambda} < 2^{-\lambda}$. The lemma follows.

3.3   Pseudorandom Functions and Key-Homomorphic PRFs

In this section, we formally define pseudorandom functions [32] and key-homomorphic PRFs [17].

Definition 3.4 (Pseudorandom Functions [32]). *A pseudorandom function for a key space $\mathcal{K}$, domain $\mathcal{X}$, and range $\mathcal{Y}$ is an efficiently computable deterministic function $F : \mathcal{K} \times \mathcal{X} \to \mathcal{Y}$ such that for any efficient adversary $\mathcal{A}$, we have*

$$\left| \Pr\left[k \xleftarrow{\text{R}} \mathcal{K} : \mathcal{A}^{F(k,\cdot)}(1^\lambda) = 1 \right] - \Pr\left[f \xleftarrow{\text{R}} \mathsf{Funs}[\mathcal{X}, \mathcal{Y}] : \mathcal{A}^{f(\cdot)}(1^\lambda) = 1 \right] \right| = \mathsf{negl}(\lambda),$$

We generally refer to the experiment where the adversary $\mathcal{A}$ is given oracle access to the real PRF $F(k, \cdot)$ as the *real* PRF experiment. Analogously, we refer to the experiment where the adversary $\mathcal{A}$ is given oracle access to a truly random function $f(\cdot)$ as the *ideal* PRF experiment.

Key-homomorphic PRFs are special family of pseudorandom function that satisfy an additional algebraic property. Specifically, for a key-homomorphic PRF, the key space $\mathcal{K}$ and the range $\mathcal{Y}$ of the PRF exhibit certain group structures such that its evaluation on any fixed input $x \in \mathcal{X}$ is homomorphic with respect to these group structures. Formally, we define a key-homomorphic PRF as follows.

Definition 3.5 (Key-Homomorphic PRFs [17,44]). *Let $(\mathcal{K}, \oplus)$, $(\mathcal{Y}, \otimes)$ be groups. Then, an efficiently computable deterministic function $F : \mathcal{K} \times \mathcal{X} \to \mathcal{Y}$ is a key-homomorphic PRF if*

- F is a secure PRF (Definition 3.4).
- For every key $k_1, k_2 \in \mathcal{K}$ and every $x \in \mathcal{X}$, we have $F(k_1, x) \otimes F(k_2, x) = F(k_1 \oplus k_2, x)$.

In this work, we will work with a slight relaxation of the notion of key-homomorphic PRFs. Namely, instead of requiring that the PRF outputs are perfectly homomorphic with respect to the PRF keys, we require that they are "almost" homomorphic in that $F(k_1, x) \otimes F(k_2, x) \approx F(k_1 \oplus k_2, x)$. Precisely, we define an almost key-homomorphic PRF as follows.

Definition 3.6 (Almost Key-Homomorphic PRFs [17]). *Let* $(\mathcal{K}, \oplus)$, $(\mathcal{Y}, \otimes)$ *be groups and let* m *and* p *be positive integers. Then, an efficiently computable deterministic function* $F : \mathcal{K} \times \mathcal{X} \to \mathbb{Z}_p^m$ *is a* γ-*almost key-homomorphic PRF if*

- *F is a secure PRF (Definition 3.4).*
- *For every key* $k_1, k_2 \in \mathcal{K}$ *and every* $x \in \mathcal{X}$, *there exists a vector* $\mathbf{e} \in [0, \gamma]^m$ *such that*

$$F(k_1, x) + F(k_2, x) = F(k_1 \oplus k_2, x) + \mathbf{e} \quad (mod \ p).$$

Naor et al. [44] and Boneh et al. [17] gave a number of applications of (almost) key-homomorphic PRFs including distributed PRFs, symmetric-key proxy re-encryption, updatable encryption, and PRFs secure against related-key attacks.

4   Learning with Rounding and Errors

In this section, we present our new lattice-based synthesizer construction. We first define the Learning with Rounding and Errors (LWRE) problem in Sect. 4.1. We then show how to use the LWRE problem to construct a synthesizer in Sect. 4.2 and discuss its parameters in Sect. 4.3. We show that the LWRE problem is as hard as the standard LWE problem for suitable choices of parameters in the full version of this work.

4.1   Learning with Rounding and Errors

Definition 4.1 (Learning with Rounding and Errors). *Let* $\lambda \in \mathbb{N}$ *be the security parameter. The* learning with rounding and errors *(LWRE) problem is defined with respect to the parameters*

- *LWE parameters* (n, q, χ),
- *Rounding modulus* $p \in \mathbb{N}$ *such that* $p < q$,
- *Chaining parameter* $\tau \in \mathbb{N}$,

that are defined as functions of λ. *Additionally, let* $D_\chi : \{0,1\}^{\lfloor \log p \rfloor} \to \mathbb{Z}$ *be a sampling algorithm for the error distribution* χ. *Then, we define the* $\mathsf{LWRE}_{n,q,p,\chi,\tau}$ *real and ideal oracles* $\mathcal{O}_{\tau,\mathbf{S}}^{(\mathsf{lwre})}$ *and* $\mathcal{O}^{(\mathsf{ideal})}$ *as follows:*

- $\mathcal{O}_{\tau,\mathbf{S}}^{(\text{lwre})}$: *The real oracle is defined with respect to a chaining parameter* $\tau \in \mathbb{N}$, *and a secret matrix* $\mathbf{S} = (\mathbf{s}_1, \ldots, \mathbf{s}_\tau) \in \mathbb{Z}_q^{n \times \tau}$. *On its invocation, the real oracle samples a vector* $\mathbf{a} \xleftarrow{\text{R}} \mathbb{Z}_q^n$ *and initializes* $e_1 = 0$. *Then, for* $1 \leq i < \tau$, *it iteratively computes:*
  1. $r_i \leftarrow \lfloor \langle \mathbf{a}, \mathbf{s}_i \rangle + e_i \rceil_p$.
  2. $e_{i+1} \leftarrow D_\chi(r_i)$.
  It then sets $b = \lfloor \langle \mathbf{a}, \mathbf{s}_\tau \rangle + e_\tau \rceil_p$, *and returns* $(\mathbf{a}, b) \in \mathbb{Z}_q^n \times \mathbb{Z}_p$.
- $\mathcal{O}^{(\text{ideal})}$: *On its invocation, the ideal oracle samples a random vector* $\mathbf{a} \xleftarrow{\text{R}} \mathbb{Z}_q^n$, *a random element* $u \xleftarrow{\text{R}} \mathbb{Z}_p$, *and returns* $(\mathbf{a}, u) \in \mathbb{Z}_q^n \times \mathbb{Z}_p$.

The $\text{LWRE}_{n,q,p,\chi,\tau}$ *problem is to distinguish the oracles* $\mathcal{O}_{\mathbf{S}}^{(\text{lwre})}$ *and* $\mathcal{O}^{(\text{ideal})}$ *for* $\mathbf{S} \xleftarrow{\text{R}} \mathbb{Z}_q^{n \times \tau}$. *More precisely, we define an adversary* $\mathcal{A}$*'s distinguishing advantage* $\text{Adv}_{\text{LWRE}}(n, q, p, \chi, \tau, \mathcal{A})$ *as the probability*

$$\text{Adv}_{\text{LWRE}}(n, q, p, \chi, \tau, \mathcal{A}) = \left| \Pr\left[\mathcal{A}^{\mathcal{O}_{\tau,\mathbf{S}}^{(\text{lwre})}}(1^\lambda) = 1 \right] - \Pr\left[\mathcal{A}^{\mathcal{O}^{(\text{ideal})}}(1^\lambda) = 1 \right] \right|,$$

for $\mathbf{S} \xleftarrow{\text{R}} \mathbb{Z}_q^{n \times \tau}$.

It is easy to see that when $\tau = 1$, the $\text{LWRE}_{n,q,p,\chi,\tau}$ problem is identical to the standard Learning with Rounding problem [11]. Hence, the reduction in [11] immediately shows that for $\tau = 1$, if the modulus q is sufficiently large such that $q = 2Bpn^{\omega(1)}$, then the $\text{LWRE}_{n,q,p,\chi,\tau}$ problem is as hard as the $\text{LWE}_{n,q,\chi}$ problem. We show that when τ is set to be larger, then the modulus q can be set to be significantly smaller.

Theorem 4.2. *Let* λ *be the security parameter and* n, q, p, χ, τ *be a set of parameters for the* $\text{LWRE}_{n,q,p,\chi,\tau}$ *problem such that* p *divides* q. *Then, for any efficient adversary* $\mathcal{A}$ *making at most* Q *number of oracle calls, we have*

$$\text{Adv}_{\text{LWRE}}(n, q, p, \chi, \tau, \mathcal{A}) \leq Q\left(2Bp/q + 1/2^\lambda \right)^\tau + \tau \cdot \text{Adv}_{\text{LWE}}(n, q, \chi, \mathcal{A}).$$

In particular, if $Q(2Bp/q + 1/2^\lambda)^\tau = \text{negl}(\lambda)$, *then the* $\text{LWRE}_{n,q,p,\chi,\tau}$ *problem is as hard as the* $\text{LWE}_{n,q,\chi}$ *problem.*

We provide the proof of the theorem in the full version of this work. We provide the high-level ideas of the proof in Sect. 2.

Remark 4.3. The $\text{LWRE}_{n,q,p,\chi,\tau}$ problem is well-defined only when there exists a concrete sampler $D_\chi : \{0,1\}^{\lfloor \log p \rfloor} \to \mathbb{Z}$, which uses at most $\lfloor \log p \rfloor$ random bits to sample from χ. For the discrete Gaussian distribution (over $\mathbb{Z}$) with Gaussian parameter $\sigma > \sqrt{n}$, there exist Gaussian samplers (i.e., [31]) that require $O(\log \lambda)$ random bits. Therefore, one can always set $p = \text{poly}(\lambda)$ to be big enough such that $\text{LWRE}_{n,q,p,\chi,\tau}$ is well defined for the discrete Gaussian distribution.

To set p to be even smaller, one can alternatively use a pseudorandom generator (PRG) to stretch the random coins that are needed by the sampler. A single element in $\mathbb{Z}_p$ for $p = \text{poly}(\lambda)$ is not large enough to serve as a seed for a

PRG. However, one can modify the oracle $\mathcal{O}_{\tau,\mathbf{S}}^{(\mathsf{lwre})}$ such that it samples multiples vectors $\mathbf{a}_1, \ldots, \mathbf{a}_\ell \xleftarrow{\text{R}} \mathbb{Z}_q^n$ for some $\ell = \mathsf{poly}(\lambda)$ and then derives a vector of elements $\mathbf{r}_i = (r_{i,1}, \ldots, r_{i,\ell}) \in \mathbb{Z}_p^\ell$ that can serve as a seed for any (lattice-based) pseudorandom generator.

Remark 4.4. We note that in Theorem 4.2, we impose the requirement that p perfectly divides q. This requirement is needed purely to guarantee that the rounding $\lfloor r \rceil_p$ of a uniformly random element $r \xleftarrow{\text{R}} \mathbb{Z}_q$ results in a uniformly random element in $\mathbb{Z}_p$. However, even when q is not perfectly divisible by p (i.e. q is prime), the rounding $\lfloor r \rceil_p$ of $r \xleftarrow{\text{R}} \mathbb{Z}_q$ still results in a highly unpredictable element in $\mathbb{Z}_p$. Therefore, by modifying the oracle $\mathcal{O}_{\tau,\mathbf{S}}^{(\mathsf{lwre})}$ such that it applies a randomness extractor after each of the modular rounding operation, one can remove the requirement on the structure of q with respect to p.

4.2 Pseudorandom Synthesizers from LWRE

In this section, we construct our new pseudorandom synthesizer from the hardness of the $\mathsf{LWRE}_{n,q,p,\chi,\tau}$ problem. A pseudorandom synthesizer over a domain $\mathcal{D}$ is a function $S : \mathcal{D} \times \mathcal{D} \to \mathcal{D}$ satisfying a specific pseudorandomness property as formulated below. We first recall the formal definition as presented in [45]. As observed in [11], one can also relax the traditional definition of a pseudorandom synthesizer by allowing the synthesizer function $S : \mathcal{D}_1 \times \mathcal{D}_1 \to \mathcal{D}_2$ to have differing domain $\mathcal{D}_1$ and range $\mathcal{D}_2$. A synthesizer satisfying this relaxed definition still induces a PRF as long as the function can be applied iteratively. For this work, we restrict to the original definition for a simpler presentation.

Definition 4.5 (Pseudorandom Synthesizer [45]). *Let $\mathcal{D}$ be a finite set. An efficiently computable function $S : \mathcal{D} \times \mathcal{D} \to \mathcal{D}$ is a secure pseudorandom synthesizer if for any polynomial $\ell = \ell(\lambda)$, the following distributions are computational indistinguishable*

$$\{S(a_i, b_j)\}_{i,j \in [\ell]} \approx_c \{u_{i,j}\}_{i,j \in [\ell]},$$

where $(a_1, \ldots, a_\ell) \xleftarrow{\text{R}} \mathcal{D}^\ell$, $(b_1, \ldots, b_\ell) \xleftarrow{\text{R}} \mathcal{D}^\ell$, and $(u_{i,j})_{i,j \in [\ell]} \leftarrow \mathcal{D}^{\ell \times \ell}$.

Naor and Reingold [45] showed that a secure pseudorandom synthesizer induces a secure pseudorandom function. Furthermore, if the synthesizer can be computed by a low-depth circuit, then the final PRF can also be evaluated by a low-depth circuit. We formally state their result in the following theorem.

Theorem 4.6 ([11,45]). *Suppose that there exists a pseudorandom synthesizer $S : \mathcal{D} \times \mathcal{D} \to \mathcal{D}$ over a finite set $\mathcal{D}$ that is computable by a circuit of size s and depth d. Then, for any $\ell = \mathsf{poly}(\lambda)$, there exists a pseudorandom function $F : \mathcal{D}^{2\ell} \times \{0,1\}^\ell \to \mathcal{D}$ with key space $\mathcal{D}^{2\ell}$, domain $\{0,1\}^\ell$, and range $\mathcal{D}$ that is computable by a circuit of size $O(s\ell)$ and depth $O(d \log \ell)$.*

As was shown in [11], the hardness of the Learning with Rounding (LWR) problem (Definition 4.1 for $\tau = 1$) naturally induces a secure pseudorandom synthesizer $S : \mathbb{Z}_q^{n \times n} \to \mathbb{Z}_q^{n \times n} \to \mathbb{Z}_p^{n \times n}$ that can be compactly defined as $S(\mathbf{S}, \mathbf{A}) = \lfloor \mathbf{S} \cdot \mathbf{A} \rceil_p$.[5] One can naturally extend this construction to $\mathsf{LWRE}_{n,q,p,\chi,\tau}$ for $\tau > 1$. Unfortunately, as the $\mathsf{LWRE}_{n,q,p,\chi,\tau}$ requires the chaining of many samples, the synthesizer does not exhibit a compact description like the LWR synthesizer. We describe the LWRE synthesizer in two steps. We first define an *LWRE function*, which satisfies the security requirement of a pseudorandom synthesizer, but does not satisfy the strict restriction on the domain and range of a synthesizer. Then, we show how to modify the LWRE function to achieve a synthesizer that satisfies Definition 4.5.

Definition 4.7 (LWRE Function). *Let λ be the security parameter and let n, q, p, χ, τ be a set of* LWRE *parameters. Then, we define the* $\mathsf{LWRE}_{n,q,p,\chi,\tau}$ *function $\mathcal{G}_{n,q,p,\chi,\tau} : \mathbb{Z}_q^n \times \mathbb{Z}_q^{n \times \tau} \to \mathbb{Z}_p$ as follows:*

– $\mathcal{G}_{n,q,p,\chi,\tau}(\mathbf{a}, \mathbf{S})$: *On input $\mathbf{a} \in \mathbb{Z}_q^n$ and $\mathbf{S} = (\mathbf{s}_1, \ldots, \mathbf{s}_\tau) \in \mathbb{Z}_q^{n \times \tau}$, the LWRE function sets $e_1 = 0$ and computes for $1 \leq i < \tau$:*
  1. $r_i \leftarrow \lfloor \langle \mathbf{a}, \mathbf{s}_i \rangle + e_i \rceil_p$,
  2. $e_{i+1} \leftarrow D(r_i)$.
  It then sets $b = \lfloor \langle \mathbf{a}, \mathbf{s}_\tau \rangle + e_\tau \rceil_p$ and returns $b \in \mathbb{Z}_p$.

For any $\ell = \mathsf{poly}(\lambda)$, we can use a standard hybrid argument to show that for $\mathbf{a}_1, \ldots, \mathbf{a}_\ell \xleftarrow{\text{R}} \mathbb{Z}_q^n$ and $\mathbf{S}_1, \ldots, \mathbf{S}_\ell \xleftarrow{\text{R}} \mathbb{Z}_q^{n \times \tau}$, the set of elements $\{\mathcal{G}_{n,q,p,\chi,\tau}(\mathbf{a}_i, \mathbf{S}_j)\}_{i,j \in [\ell]}$ are computationally indistinguishable from ℓ^2 uniformly random elements in $\mathbb{Z}_p$. It readily follows that for any $\ell_1, \ell_2 = \mathsf{poly}(\lambda)$, the function $S : \mathbb{Z}_q^{n \times \ell_1} \times (\mathbb{Z}_q^{n \times \tau})^{\ell_2} \to \mathbb{Z}_p^{\ell_1 \times \ell_2}$ that takes in as input $\mathbf{A} = (\mathbf{a}_1, \ldots, \mathbf{a}_{\ell_1}) \xleftarrow{\text{R}} \mathbb{Z}_q^{n \times \ell_1}$, $(\mathbf{S}_1, \ldots, \mathbf{S}_{\ell_2}) \xleftarrow{\text{R}} (\mathbb{Z}_q^{n \times \tau})^{\ell_2}$, and returns the pairwise application of the LWRE function

$$\left\{ \mathcal{G}_{n,q,p,\chi,\tau}(\mathbf{a}_i, \mathbf{S}_j) \right\}_{i \in [\ell_1], j \in [\ell_2]}$$

satisfies the security requirements for a synthesizer. Therefore, as long as ℓ_1 and ℓ_2 are set such that the cardinality of the sets $\mathbb{Z}_q^{n \times \ell_1}$, $(\mathbb{Z}_q^{n \times \tau})^{\ell_2}$, and $\mathbb{Z}_p^{\ell_1 \times \ell_2}$ have the same cardinality, the function $S : \mathbb{Z}_q^{n \times \ell_1} \times (\mathbb{Z}_q^{n \times \tau})^{\ell_2} \to \mathbb{Z}_p^{\ell_1 \times \ell_2}$ satisfies Definition 4.5. We can naturally set the parameters ℓ_1 and ℓ_2 as

$$\ell_1 = n\tau \left\lceil \frac{\log q}{\log p} \right\rceil, \quad \ell_2 = n \left\lceil \frac{\log q}{\log p} \right\rceil.$$

Formally, we define our LWRE synthesizer as follows.

Construction 4.8 (LWRE Synthesizer). Let λ be the security parameter, let n, q, p, χ, τ be a set of LWRE parameters, and let $\ell = n\tau \lceil \log q / \log p \rceil$. We define the LWRE synthesizer $S : \mathbb{Z}_q^{n \times \ell} \times \mathbb{Z}_q^{n \times \ell} \to \mathbb{Z}_q^{n \times \ell}$ as follows:

---

[5] The LWR synthesizer satisfies the more general definition of a pseudorandom synthesizer where the domain and range of the synthesizer can differ.

– $S(\mathbf{A}, \mathbf{S})$: On input $\mathbf{A}, \mathbf{S} \in \mathbb{Z}_q^{n \times \ell}$, the synthesizer parses the matrices
- $\mathbf{A} = (\mathbf{a}_1, \ldots, \mathbf{a}_{\ell_1})$ where $\mathbf{a}_i \in \mathbb{Z}_q^n$ and $\ell_1 = n\tau\lceil \log q / \log p \rceil$,
- $\mathbf{S} = (\mathbf{S}_1, \ldots, \mathbf{S}_{\ell_2})$ where $\mathbf{S}_j \in \mathbb{Z}_q^{n \times \tau}$ and $\ell_2 = n\lceil \log q / \log p \rceil$.

Then, the synthesizer computes the $\mathsf{LWRE}_{n,q,p,\chi,\tau}$ function $b_{i,j} \leftarrow \mathcal{G}_{n,q,p,\chi,\tau}(\mathbf{a}_i, \mathbf{S}_j)$ for all $i \in [\ell_1]$ and $j \in [\ell_2]$. It translates the bits of $\{b_{i,j}\}_{j \in [\ell_1], i \in [\ell_2]} \in \mathbb{Z}_p^{\ell_1 \times \ell_2}$ as the representation of a matrix $\mathbf{B} \in \mathbb{Z}_q^{n \times \ell}$. It returns $\mathbf{B}$.

We now state the formal security statement for the LWRE synthesizer in Construction 4.8. The proof follows immediately from Definitions 4.1, 4.7 and Theorem 4.2.

Theorem 4.9 (Security). *Let λ be the security parameter and let n, q, p, χ, τ be a set of LWRE parameters. Then, assuming that the $\mathsf{LWRE}_{n,q,p,\chi,\tau}$ problem is hard, the LWRE synthesizer in Construction 4.8 is a secure pseudorandom synthesizer (Definition 4.5).*

By combining Theorems 4.2, 4.6 and 4.9, we get the following corollary.

Corollary 4.10. *Let λ be a security parameter and $n = \mathsf{poly}(\lambda)$ be a positive integer. Then, there exists a pseudorandom function $F : \mathcal{K} \times \{0,1\}^{\mathsf{poly}(\lambda)} \to \mathcal{Y}$ that can be computed by a circuit in NC^3, and whose security can be reduced from the worst-case hardness of approximating GapSVP and SIVP to a polynomial approximation factor on n-dimensional lattices.*

We additionally discuss the parameter choices for our PRF in Sect. 4.3.

4.3 Parameter Instantiations

In this section, we discuss the various ways of instantiating the parameters for the LWRE synthesizer from Construction 4.8. As discussed in Sect. 1.2, we consider two parameter settings that provide different level of security against an adversary. For *theoretical* security, we require that an efficient adversary's distinguishing advantage of the LWRE synthesizer to degrade super-polynomially in λ. For 2^λ-security, we require that an efficient adversary's advantage degrades exponentially in λ. By Theorem 4.2, the main factor that we consider in determining the security of the synthesizer is the term $(2Bp/q + 1/2^\lambda)^\tau$.

Theoretical Security. For theoretical security, we must let $(2Bp/q + 1/2^\lambda)^\tau = \mathsf{negl}(\lambda)$. In one extreme, we can set $\tau = 1$ and q to be greater than $2Bp$ by a super-polynomial factor in λ, which reproduces the result of [11].[6] As both vector-matrix multiplication and the rounding operation can be implemented in NC^1, the resulting PRF can be implemented in NC^2 for input space $\{0,1\}^\ell$ where $\ell = \mathsf{poly}(\lambda)$.

If we set $\tau = \omega(1)$, then we can set q to be any function that is greater than $2Bp$ by a polynomial factor in λ. In this case, when considering the depth

---

[6] We note that the term $1/2^\lambda$ is needed for Lemma 3.3. If q is set to be prime, then this factor can be ignored.

of the evaluation circuit, we must take into account the depth of the sampling algorithm D_χ for the error distribution χ. To base security on approximating worst-case lattice problems such as GapSVP or SIVP, we must set χ to be the discrete Gaussian distribution over $\mathbb{Z}$ with Gaussian parameter $\sigma > \sqrt{n}$. In this case, we can either use the rejection sampling algorithm of [31] or pre-compute the samples for each possible seed for the sampler and use a look-up table. In both cases, we can guarantee that a random element in $\mathbb{Z}_p$ provides enough entropy to the Gaussian sampler by setting $p = \omega(\lambda^2)$.

Since the Gaussian function can be computed by an arithmetic circuit with depth $O(\log p)$, the rejection sampling algorithm can be implemented by a circuit of depth $\omega(\log \lambda \cdot \log \log \lambda)$. Therefore, the synthesizer can be evaluated by a circuit in $\mathsf{NC}^{2+\varepsilon}$ for any constant $\varepsilon > 0$ and the final PRF can be evaluated by a circuit in $\mathsf{NC}^{3+\varepsilon}$ for input space $\{0,1\}^\ell$ where $\ell = \mathrm{poly}(\lambda)$. When using a look-up table, the synthesizer can be evaluated by a circuit in $\mathsf{NC}^{1+\varepsilon}$ for any constant $\varepsilon > 0$, and the final PRF can be evaluated in $\mathsf{NC}^{2+\varepsilon}$.

2^λ-**Security.** For 2^λ-security, we must let $(2Bp/q)^\tau = 1/2^{\Omega(\lambda)}$ or equivalently, $\tau \cdot \log q = \tilde{\Omega}(\lambda)$ for q prime. This provides a trade-off between the size of q and the chaining parameter τ, which dictates the depth needed to evaluate the PRF. In one extreme, we can set $\tau = 1$ and require the modulus to be greater than $2Bp$ by an exponential factor in λ. In the other extreme, we can let τ be linear in λ and decrease the modulus to be only a constant factor greater than $2Bp$. For practical implementations, a natural choice of parameters would be to set both τ and $\log q$ to be $\Omega(\sqrt{\lambda})$. For practical implementations, one can derive the secret keys from a single λ-bit seed using a pseudorandom generator.

Concrete Instantiations. The concrete parameters for our PRF can be instantiated quite flexibly depending on the applications. The modulus p can first be set to determine the output of the PRF. For instance, as the range of the PRF is $\mathbb{Z}_p$, the modulus p can be set to be 2^8 or 2^{16} such that the output of the PRF is byte-aligned. Then the PRF can be run multiple times (in parallel) to produce a 128-bit output.

Once p is set, the modulus q and τ can be set such that $\tau \cdot \log q \approx \lambda \cdot \log p$. For instance, to provide 2^λ-bit security, one can reasonable set q to be a 20-bit prime number and $\tau = 12$. Finally, after q is set, the LWE parameter n and noise distribution χ can be set such that the resulting LWE problem provides λ-bit level of security. Following the analysis in [5], we can set n to be around 600 (classical security) or 800 (quantum security), and χ to be either a uniform distribution over $[-24, 24]$ or an analogous Gaussian distribution with similar bits of entropy.

5   Key-Homomorphic PRFs

In this section, we show how to use the chaining method to construct key-homomorphic PRFs directly from the Learning with Errors assumption with a polynomial modulus q. Our construction is the modification of the Banerjee-Peikert (BP) PRF of [10], which generalizes the algebraic structure of previous LWE-based PRFs [11,17].

To be precise, the BP PRF is not a single PRF family, but rather multiple PRF families that are each defined with respect to a full binary tree. The LWE parameters that govern the security of a BP PRF are determined by the structure of the corresponding binary tree. In order to construct a key-homomorphic PRF that relies on the hardness of LWE with a polynomial modulus q, we must use the BP PRF that is defined with respect to the "right-spine" tree. However, as our modification works over any BP PRF family, we present our construction with respect to any general BP PRF. For general BP PRFs, our modification is not enough to bring the size of the modulus q to be polynomial in λ, but it still reduces its size by superpolynomial factors.

We provide our main construction in Sect. 5.1 and discuss its parameters in Sect. 5.2. We provide the proof of security and key-homomorphism in the full version.

5.1   Construction

The BP PRF construction is defined with respect to full (but not necessarily complete) binary trees. Formally, a full binary tree T is a binary tree for which every non-leaf node has two children. The shape of the full binary tree T that is used to define the PRF determines various trade-offs in the parameters and evaluation depth. As we only consider full binary trees in this work, we will implicitly refer to any tree T as a full binary tree.

Throughout the construction description and analysis, we let $|T|$ denote the number of its leaves. For any tree with $|T| \geq 1$, we let $T.\ell$ and $T.r$ denote the left and the right subtrees of T respectively (which may be empty trees). Finally, for a full binary tree T, we define its expansion factor $e(T)$ recursively as follows:

$$e(T) = \begin{cases} 0 & \text{if } |T| = 1 \\ \max\{e(T.\ell) + 1, e(T.r)\} & \text{otherwise.} \end{cases}$$

This is simply the "left-depth" of the tree, i.e., the maximum length of a root-to-leaf path, counting edges from parents to their left children.

With these notations, we define our PRF construction in a sequence of steps. We first define an input-to-matrix mapping $\mathbf{A}_T : \{0,1\}^{|T|} \to \mathbb{Z}_q^{n \times m}$ as follows.

Definition 5.1. *Let n, q, χ be a set of LWE parameters, let $p < q$ be a rounding modulus, and let $m = n\lceil \log q \rceil$. Then, for a full binary tree T, and matrices $\mathbf{A}_0, \mathbf{A}_1 \in \mathbb{Z}_q^{n \times m}$, define the function $\mathbf{A}_T : \{0,1\}^{|T|} \to \mathbb{Z}_q^{n \times m}$ recursively:*

$$\mathbf{A}_T(x) = \begin{cases} \mathbf{A}_x & \text{if } |T| = 1 \\ \mathbf{A}_{T.\ell}(x_\ell) \cdot \mathbf{G}^{-1}(\mathbf{A}_{T.r}(x_r)) & \text{otherwise,} \end{cases}$$

where $x = x_\ell \| x_r$ for $|x_\ell| = |T.\ell|$, $|x_r| = |T.r|$.

Then, for a binary tree T, and a PRF key $\mathbf{s} \in \mathbb{Z}_q^n$, the BP PRF $F^{(\mathrm{BP})}$: $\{0,1\}^{|T|} \to \mathbb{Z}_p^m$ is defined as $F_{\mathbf{s}}^{(\mathrm{BP})}(x) = \lfloor \mathbf{s}^T \mathbf{A}_T(x) \rceil_p$. To define our new PRF, we must first define its "noisy" variant $\mathcal{G}_{\mathbf{s},\mathbf{E},T} : \{0,1\}^{|T|} \to \mathbb{Z}_p^m$ as follows.

Definition 5.2. *Let n, q, χ be a set of LWE parameters, let $p < q$ be a rounding modulus, and let $m = n\lceil \log q \rceil$. Then, for a full binary tree T, public matrices $\mathbf{A}_0, \mathbf{A}_1 \in \mathbb{Z}_q^{n \times m}$, error matrix $\mathbf{E} = (\mathbf{e}_1, \ldots, \mathbf{e}_{e(T)}) \in \mathbb{Z}^{m \times e(T)}$, and a secret vector $\mathbf{s} \in \mathbb{Z}_q^n$, we define the function $\mathcal{G}_{\mathbf{s},\mathbf{E},T} : \{0,1\}^{|T|} \to \mathbb{Z}_p^m$:*

$$
\mathcal{G}_{\mathbf{s},\mathbf{E},T}(x) = \begin{cases} \mathbf{s}^T \mathbf{A}_T(x) + \mathbf{e}_1^T & \text{if } |T| = 1 \\ \mathcal{G}_{\mathbf{s},\mathbf{E},T.\ell}(x_\ell) \cdot \mathbf{G}^{-1}\big(\mathbf{A}_{T.r}(x_r)\big) + \mathbf{e}_{e(T)} & \text{otherwise,} \end{cases}
$$

where $x = x_\ell \| x_r$ for $|x_\ell| = |T.\ell|$, $|x_r| = |T.r|$.

We note that when the error matrix $\mathbf{E}$ is set to be an all-zero matrix $\mathbf{E} = \mathbf{0} \in \mathbb{Z}^{m \times e(T)}$, then the function $\lfloor \mathcal{G}_{\mathbf{s},\mathbf{0},T}(\cdot) \rceil_p$ is precisely the BP PRF.

We define our new PRF to be the iterative chaining of the function $\mathcal{G}_{\mathbf{s},\mathbf{E},T}$. Specifically, our PRF is defined with respect to τ secret vectors $\mathbf{s}_1, \ldots, \mathbf{s}_\tau \in \mathbb{Z}_q^n$ where $\tau \in \mathbb{N}$ is the chaining parameter. On input $x \in \{0,1\}^{|T|}$, the PRF evaluation function computes $\mathbf{r}_1 \leftarrow \lfloor \mathcal{G}_{\mathbf{s}_1,\mathbf{0},T}(x) \rceil_p$ and uses $\mathbf{r}_1 \in \mathbb{Z}_p^m$ as a seed to derive the noise term $\mathbf{E}_2$ for the next iteration $\mathbf{r}_2 \leftarrow \lfloor \mathcal{G}_{\mathbf{s}_2,\mathbf{E}_2,T}(x) \rceil_p$. The evaluation function repeats this procedure for $\tau - 1$ iterations and returns $\mathbf{r}_\tau \leftarrow \lfloor \mathcal{G}_{\mathbf{s}_{\tau-1},\mathbf{E}_{\tau-1},T}(x) \rceil_p$ as the final PRF evaluation.

Construction 5.3. Let n, m, q, and χ be LWE parameters and $p < q$ be an additional rounding modulus. Then, our PRF construction is defined with respect to a full binary tree T, two public matrices $\mathbf{A}_0, \mathbf{A}_1 \in \mathbb{Z}_q^{n \times m}$, a secret matrix $\mathbf{S} \in \mathbb{Z}_q^{m \times \tau}$, and a sampler $D_\chi : \{0,1\}^{m \lfloor \log p \rfloor} \to \mathbb{Z}^{m \times e(T)}$ for the noise distribution χ. We define our PRF $F_{\mathbf{S}} : \{0,1\}^{|T|} \to \mathbb{Z}_q^m$ as follows:

- $F_{\mathbf{S}}(x)$: On input $x \in \{0,1\}^{|T|}$, the evaluation algorithm sets $\mathbf{E}_1 = \mathbf{0} \in \mathbb{Z}_q^{m \times e(T)}$. Then, for $i = 1, \ldots, \tau - 1$, it iteratively computes
  1. $\mathbf{r}_i \leftarrow \lfloor \mathcal{G}_{\mathbf{s}_i,\mathbf{E}_i,T}(x) \rceil_p$.
  2. $\mathbf{E}_{i+1} \leftarrow D_\chi(\mathbf{r}_i)$.
  It sets $\mathbf{y} \leftarrow \lfloor \mathcal{G}_{\mathbf{s}_\tau,\mathbf{E}_\tau,T}(x) \rceil_p$, and returns $\mathbf{y} \in \mathbb{Z}_p^m$.

For the PRF to be well-defined, we must make sure that a seed $\mathbf{r}_i \leftarrow \lfloor \mathcal{G}_{\mathbf{s}_i,\mathbf{E}_i,T}(x) \rceil_p \in \mathbb{Z}_p^m$ for $i \in [\tau - 1]$ provides enough entropy to derive the noise terms $\mathbf{E}_{i+1} \leftarrow \chi^{m \times e(T)}$. As in the case of LWRE (Remark 4.3), there are two main ways of ensuring this condition. One method is to set the rounding modulus p to be big enough such that there exists a sampler $D_\chi : \{0,1\}^{m \lfloor \log p \rfloor} \to \mathbb{Z}^{m \times e(T)}$ for the noise distribution $\chi^{m \times e(T)}$. Alternatively, one can expand the seed $\mathbf{r}_i \in \mathbb{Z}_p^m$ using a pseudorandom generator to derive sufficiently many bits to sample from $\chi^{m \times e(T)}$. Since the issue of deriving the noise terms $\mathbf{E}_{i+1}$ from the seeds $\mathbf{r}_i$ is mostly orthogonal to the central ideas of our PRF construction, we assume that the rounding modulus p is set to be big enough such that the noise terms $\mathbf{E}_{i+1}$ can be derived from the bits of $\mathbf{r}_i$.

We now state the main security theorem for the PRF in Construction 5.3.

Theorem 5.4. *Let T be any full binary tree, λ the security parameter, n, m, q, p, τ positive integers and χ a B-bounded distribution such that $m = n\lceil \log q \rceil > 2$, $(2Rmp/q)^{\tau-1} = \mathsf{negl}(\lambda)$ for $R = |T|Bm^{e(T)}$ and p divides q. Then, assuming that the $\mathsf{LWE}_{n,q,\chi}$ problem is hard, the PRF in Construction 5.3 is a 2-almost key-homomorphic PRF (Definition 3.5).*

We provide the proof of Theorem 5.4 in the full version. Except for the components on chaining, the proof inherits many of the arguments that are already used in [10]. For the main intuition behind the proof, we refer the readers to Sect. 2.3.

5.2   Instantiating the Parameters

As in the original Banerjee-Peikert PRF [10], the size of the modulus q and the depth of the evaluation circuit is determined by the structure of the full binary tree T. The size of the modulus q is determined by the expansion factor $e(T)$ or equivalently, the length of the maximum root-to-leaf path to the left children of T. Namely, to satisfy Theorem 5.4, we require q to be large enough such that $(2Rmp/q)^{\tau-1} = \mathsf{negl}(\lambda)$ for $R = |T|Bm^{e(T)}$.

The depth of the evaluation circuit is determined by the *sequentiality* factor $s(T)$ of the tree, which is formally defined by the recurrence

$$s(T) = \begin{cases} 0 & \text{if } |T| = 1 \\ \max\{s(T.\ell), s(T.r) + 1\} & \text{otherwise.} \end{cases}$$

Combinatorially, $s(T)$ denotes the length of the maximum root-to-leaf path to the right children of T. For a tree T, our PRF can be evaluated by depth $\tau \cdot s(T) \log |T|$.

When we restrict the chaining parameter to be $\tau = 1$, then we recover the parameters of the Banerjee-Peikert PRF where the modulus q is required to be $q = Rmp\lambda^{\omega(1)}$. However, setting τ to be a super-constant function $\omega(1)$, we can set $q = 2Rmp \cdot \lambda^c$ for any constant $c > 0$, which reduces the size of the modulus q by a super-polynomial factor. To guarantee that an adversary's advantage in breaking the PRF degrades exponentially in λ, we can set τ to be linear in λ.

To set q to be polynomial in the security parameter, we can instantiate the construction with respect to the "right-spine" binary tree where the left child of any node in the tree is a leaf node. In this tree T, the sequentiality factor becomes linear in the size of the tree $s(T) = |T|$, but the expansion factor becomes a constant $e(T) = 1$. Therefore, when $\tau = \omega(1)$ (or linear in λ for 2^λ-security), the modulus q can be set to be $q = 2mp\lambda^c$ for any constant $c > 0$. The concrete parameters for our PRF can be set similarly to our synthesizer construction (see Sect. 4.3).

Acknowledgments. We thank the Eurocrypt reviewers for their helpful comments. This work was funded by NSF, DARPA, a grant from ONR, and the Simons Foundation. Opinions, findings and conclusions or recommendations expressed in this material are those of the authors and do not necessarily reflect the views of DARPA.

References

1. Abdalla, M., Benhamouda, F., Passelègue, A.: An algebraic framework for pseudorandom functions and applications to related-key security. In: Gennaro, R., Robshaw, M. (eds.) CRYPTO 2015. LNCS, vol. 9215, pp. 388–409. Springer, Heidelberg (2015). https://doi.org/10.1007/978-3-662-47989-6_19

2. Abdalla, M., Benhamouda, F., Passelègue, A.: Multilinear and aggregate pseudorandom functions: new constructions and improved security. In: Iwata, T., Cheon, J.H. (eds.) ASIACRYPT 2015. LNCS, vol. 9452, pp. 103–120. Springer, Heidelberg (2015). https://doi.org/10.1007/978-3-662-48797-6_5

3. Agrawal, S., Boneh, D., Boyen, X.: Efficient lattice (H)IBE in the standard model. In: Gilbert, H. (ed.) EUROCRYPT 2010. LNCS, vol. 6110, pp. 553–572. Springer, Heidelberg (2010). https://doi.org/10.1007/978-3-642-13190-5_28

4. Agrawal, S., Boneh, D., Boyen, X.: Lattice basis delegation in fixed dimension and shorter-ciphertext hierarchical IBE. In: Rabin, T. (ed.) CRYPTO 2010. LNCS, vol. 6223, pp. 98–115. Springer, Heidelberg (2010). https://doi.org/10.1007/978-3-642-14623-7_6

5. Albrecht, M.R., Player, R., Scott, S.: On the concrete hardness of learning with errors. J. Math. Cryptol. 9(3), 169–203 (2015)

6. Alperin-Sheriff, J., Apon, D.: Dimension-preserving reductions from LWE to LWR. IACR Cryptology ePrint Archive, 2016(589) (2016)

7. Alperin-Sheriff, J., Peikert, C.: Faster bootstrapping with polynomial error. In: Garay, J.A., Gennaro, R. (eds.) CRYPTO 2014. LNCS, vol. 8616, pp. 297–314. Springer, Heidelberg (2014). https://doi.org/10.1007/978-3-662-44371-2_17

8. Alwen, J., Krenn, S., Pietrzak, K., Wichs, D.: Learning with rounding, revisited. In: Canetti, R., Garay, J.A. (eds.) CRYPTO 2013. LNCS, vol. 8042, pp. 57–74. Springer, Heidelberg (2013). https://doi.org/10.1007/978-3-642-40041-4_4

9. Applebaum, B., Cash, D., Peikert, C., Sahai, A.: Fast cryptographic primitives and circular-secure encryption based on hard learning problems. In: Halevi, S. (ed.) CRYPTO 2009. LNCS, vol. 5677, pp. 595–618. Springer, Heidelberg (2009). https://doi.org/10.1007/978-3-642-03356-8_35

10. Banerjee, A., Peikert, C.: New and improved key-homomorphic pseudorandom functions. In: Garay, J.A., Gennaro, R. (eds.) CRYPTO 2014. LNCS, vol. 8616, pp. 353–370. Springer, Heidelberg (2014). https://doi.org/10.1007/978-3-662-44371-2_20

11. Banerjee, A., Peikert, C., Rosen, A.: Pseudorandom functions and lattices. In: Pointcheval, D., Johansson, T. (eds.) EUROCRYPT 2012. LNCS, vol. 7237, pp. 719–737. Springer, Heidelberg (2012). https://doi.org/10.1007/978-3-642-29011-4_42

12. Bellare, M.: New proofs for NMAC and HMAC: security without collision-resistance. In: Dwork, C. (ed.) CRYPTO 2006. LNCS, vol. 4117, pp. 602–619. Springer, Heidelberg (2006). https://doi.org/10.1007/11818175_36

13. Bellare, M., Canetti, R., Krawczyk, H.: Keying hash functions for message authentication. In: Koblitz, N. (ed.) CRYPTO 1996. LNCS, vol. 1109, pp. 1–15. Springer, Heidelberg (1996). https://doi.org/10.1007/3-540-68697-5_1

14. Bellare, M., Canetti, R., Krawczyk, H.: Pseudorandom functions revisited: the cascade construction and its concrete security. In: FOCS (1996)

15. Bogdanov, A., Guo, S., Masny, D., Richelson, S., Rosen, A.: On the hardness of learning with rounding over small modulus. In: Kushilevitz, E., Malkin, T. (eds.) TCC 2016. LNCS, vol. 9562, pp. 209–224. Springer, Heidelberg (2016). https://doi.org/10.1007/978-3-662-49096-9_9

16. Boneh, D., Kim, S., Montgomery, H.: Private puncturable PRFs from standard lattice assumptions. In: Coron, J.-S., Nielsen, J.B. (eds.) EUROCRYPT 2017. LNCS, vol. 10210, pp. 415–445. Springer, Cham (2017). https://doi.org/10.1007/978-3-319-56620-7_15

17. Boneh, D., Lewi, K., Montgomery, H., Raghunathan, A.: Key homomorphic PRFs and their applications. In: Canetti, R., Garay, J.A. (eds.) CRYPTO 2013. LNCS, vol. 8042, pp. 410–428. Springer, Heidelberg (2013). https://doi.org/10.1007/978-3-642-40041-4_23

18. Boneh, D., Montgomery, H.W., Raghunathan, A.: Algebraic pseudorandom functions with improved efficiency from the augmented cascade. In: CCS (2010)

19. Boyd, C., Davies, G.T., Gjøsteen, K., Jiang, Y.: Rise and shine: fast and secure updatable encryption. Cryptology ePrint Archive, Report 2019/1457 (2019). https://eprint.iacr.org/2019/1457

20. Brakerski, Z., Langlois, A., Peikert, C., Regev, O., Stehlé, D.: Classical hardness of learning with errors. In: STOC (2013)

21. Brakerski, Z., Tsabary, R., Vaikuntanathan, V., Wee, H.: Private constrained PRFs (and more) from LWE. In: Kalai, Y., Reyzin, L. (eds.) TCC 2017. LNCS, vol. 10677, pp. 264–302. Springer, Cham (2017). https://doi.org/10.1007/978-3-319-70500-2_10

22. Brakerski, Z., Vaikuntanathan, V.: Efficient fully homomorphic encryption from (standard) LWE. In: FOCS (2011)

23. Brakerski, Z., Vaikuntanathan, V.: Fully homomorphic encryption from Ring-LWE and security for key dependent messages. In: Rogaway, P. (ed.) CRYPTO 2011. LNCS, vol. 6841, pp. 505–524. Springer, Heidelberg (2011). https://doi.org/10.1007/978-3-642-22792-9_29

24. Brakerski, Z., Vaikuntanathan, V.: Lattice-based FHE as secure as PKE. In: ITCS (2014)

25. Brakerski, Z., Vaikuntanathan, V.: Constrained key-homomorphic PRFs from standard lattice assumptions. In: Dodis, Y., Nielsen, J.B. (eds.) TCC 2015. LNCS, vol. 9015, pp. 1–30. Springer, Heidelberg (2015). https://doi.org/10.1007/978-3-662-46497-7_1

26. Canetti, R., Chen, Y.: Constraint-hiding constrained PRFs for NC^1 from LWE. In: Coron, J.-S., Nielsen, J.B. (eds.) EUROCRYPT 2017. LNCS, vol. 10210, pp. 446–476. Springer, Cham (2017). https://doi.org/10.1007/978-3-319-56620-7_16

27. Cash, D., Hofheinz, D., Kiltz, E., Peikert, C.: Bonsai trees, or how to delegate a lattice basis. In: Gilbert, H. (ed.) EUROCRYPT 2010. LNCS, vol. 6110, pp. 523–552. Springer, Heidelberg (2010). https://doi.org/10.1007/978-3-642-13190-5_27

28. Döttling, N., Schröder, D.: Efficient pseudorandom functions via on-the-fly adaptation. In: Gennaro, R., Robshaw, M. (eds.) CRYPTO 2015. LNCS, vol. 9215, pp. 329–350. Springer, Heidelberg (2015). https://doi.org/10.1007/978-3-662-47989-6_16

29. Everspaugh, A., Paterson, K., Ristenpart, T., Scott, S.: Key rotation for authenticated encryption. In: Katz, J., Shacham, H. (eds.) CRYPTO 2017. LNCS, vol. 10403, pp. 98–129. Springer, Cham (2017). https://doi.org/10.1007/978-3-319-63697-9_4

30. Gentry, C.: Fully homomorphic encryption using ideal lattices. In: STOC (2009)

31. Gentry, C., Peikert, C., Vaikuntanathan, V.: Trapdoors for hard lattices and new cryptographic constructions. In: STOC (2008)

32. Goldreich, O., Goldwasser, S., Micali, S.: How to construct random functions. J. ACM (JACM) 33(4), 792–807 (1986)

33. Gorbunov, S., Vinayagamurthy, D.: Riding on asymmetry: efficient ABE for branching programs. In: Iwata, T., Cheon, J.H. (eds.) ASIACRYPT 2015. LNCS, vol. 9452, pp. 550–574. Springer, Heidelberg (2015). https://doi.org/10.1007/978-3-662-48797-6_23

34. Håstad, J., Impagliazzo, R., Levin, L.A., Luby, M.: A pseudorandom generator from any one-way function. SIAM J. Comput. **28**(4), 1364–1396 (1999)

35. Jager, T., Kurek, R., Pan, J.: Simple and more efficient PRFs with tight security from LWE and matrix-DDH. In: Peyrin, T., Galbraith, S. (eds.) ASIACRYPT 2018. LNCS, vol. 11274, pp. 490–518. Springer, Cham (2018). https://doi.org/10.1007/978-3-030-03332-3_18

36. Kim, S., Wu, D.J.: Watermarking cryptographic functionalities from standard lattice assumptions. In: Katz, J., Shacham, H. (eds.) CRYPTO 2017. LNCS, vol. 10401, pp. 503–536. Springer, Cham (2017). https://doi.org/10.1007/978-3-319-63688-7_17

37. Kim, S., Wu, D.J.: Watermarking PRFs from lattices: stronger security via extractable PRFs. In: Boldyreva, A., Micciancio, D. (eds.) CRYPTO 2019. LNCS, vol. 11694, pp. 335–366. Springer, Cham (2019). https://doi.org/10.1007/978-3-030-26954-8_11

38. Klooß, M., Lehmann, A., Rupp, A.: (R)CCA secure updatable encryption with integrity protection. In: Ishai, Y., Rijmen, V. (eds.) EUROCRYPT 2019. LNCS, vol. 11476, pp. 68–99. Springer, Cham (2019). https://doi.org/10.1007/978-3-030-17653-2_3

39. Landau, E.: Handbuch der Lehre von der Verteilung der Primzahlen, vol. 1. Ripol Classic Publishing House, Moscow (2000)

40. Lehmann, A., Tackmann, B.: Updatable encryption with post-compromise security. In: Nielsen, J.B., Rijmen, V. (eds.) EUROCRYPT 2018. LNCS, vol. 10822, pp. 685–716. Springer, Cham (2018). https://doi.org/10.1007/978-3-319-78372-7_22

41. Micciancio, D., Mol, P.: Pseudorandom knapsacks and the sample complexity of LWE search-to-decision reductions. In: Rogaway, P. (ed.) CRYPTO 2011. LNCS, vol. 6841, pp. 465–484. Springer, Heidelberg (2011). https://doi.org/10.1007/978-3-642-22792-9_26

42. Micciancio, D., Peikert, C.: Trapdoors for lattices: simpler, tighter, faster, smaller. In: Pointcheval, D., Johansson, T. (eds.) EUROCRYPT 2012. LNCS, vol. 7237, pp. 700–718. Springer, Heidelberg (2012). https://doi.org/10.1007/978-3-642-29011-4_41

43. Montgomery, H.: More efficient lattice PRFs from keyed pseudorandom synthesizers. In: Chakraborty, D., Iwata, T. (eds.) INDOCRYPT 2018. LNCS, vol. 11356, pp. 190–211. Springer, Cham (2018). https://doi.org/10.1007/978-3-030-05378-9_11

44. Naor, M., Pinkas, B., Reingold, O.: Distributed pseudo-random functions and KDCs. In: Stern, J. (ed.) EUROCRYPT 1999. LNCS, vol. 1592, pp. 327–346. Springer, Heidelberg (1999). https://doi.org/10.1007/3-540-48910-X_23

45. Naor, M., Reingold, O.: Synthesizers and their application to the parallel construction of pseudo-random functions. J. Comput. Syst. Sci. **58**(2), 336–375 (1999)

46. Peikert, C.: Public-key cryptosystems from the worst-case shortest vector problem. In: STOC (2009)

47. Quach, W., Wichs, D., Zirdelis, G.: Watermarking PRFs under standard assumptions: public marking and security with extraction queries. In: Beimel, A., Dziembowski, S. (eds.) TCC 2018. LNCS, vol. 11240, pp. 669–698. Springer, Cham (2018). https://doi.org/10.1007/978-3-030-03810-6_24
48. Regev, O.: On lattices, learning with errors, random linear codes, and cryptography. J. ACM (JACM) **56**(6), 34 (2009)

Integral Matrix Gram Root and Lattice Gaussian Sampling Without Floats

Léo Ducas[1], Steven Galbraith[2], Thomas Prest[3], and Yang Yu[4(✉)]

[1] Centrum Wiskunde en Informatica, Amsterdam, The Netherlands
ducas@cwi.nl
[2] Mathematics Department, University of Auckland, Auckland, New Zealand
s.galbraith@auckland.ac.nz
[3] PQShield Ltd, Oxford, UK
thomas.prest@pqshield.com
[4] Univ Rennes, CNRS, IRISA, Rennes, France
yang.yu0986@gmail.com

Abstract. Many advanced lattice based cryptosystems require to sample lattice points from Gaussian distributions. One challenge for this task is that all current algorithms resort to floating-point arithmetic (FPA) at some point, which has numerous drawbacks in practice: it requires numerical stability analysis, extra storage for high-precision, lazy/backtracking techniques for efficiency, and may suffer from weak determinism which can completely break certain schemes.

In this paper, we give techniques to implement Gaussian sampling over general lattices without using FPA. To this end, we revisit the approach of Peikert, using perturbation sampling. Peikert's approach uses continuous Gaussian sampling and some decomposition $\Sigma = \mathbf{A}\mathbf{A}^t$ of the target covariance matrix Σ. The suggested decomposition, e.g. the Cholesky decomposition, gives rise to a square matrix $\mathbf{A}$ with real (not integer) entries. Our idea, in a nutshell, is to replace this decomposition by an integral one. While there is in general no integer solution if we restrict $\mathbf{A}$ to being a square matrix, we show that such a decomposition can be efficiently found by allowing $\mathbf{A}$ to be wider (say $n \times 9n$). This can be viewed as an extension of Lagrange's four-square theorem to matrices. In addition, we adapt our integral decomposition algorithm to the ring setting: for power-of-2 cyclotomics, we can exploit the tower of rings structure for improved complexity and compactness.

1 Introduction

Lattice based cryptography is a promising post-quantum alternative to cryptography based on integer factorization and discrete logarithms. One of its attractive features is that lattices can be used to build various powerful cryptographic primitives including identity based encryption (IBE) [1,8,11,19], attribute based encryption (ABE) [5,20], functional encryption [2], group signatures [22,23,31]

© International Association for Cryptologic Research 2020
A. Canteaut and Y. Ishai (Eds.): EUROCRYPT 2020, LNCS 12106, pp. 608–637, 2020.
https://doi.org/10.1007/978-3-030-45724-2_21

and so on [7,18]. A core component of many advanced lattice based cryptosystems is sampling lattice points from discrete Gaussians, given a short basis (i.e. a trapdoor) [19,25,32].

Gaussian sampling is important to prevent leaking secret information. Indeed early lattice trapdoors have suffered from statistical attacks [14,30,37]. In 2008, Gentry, Peikert and Vaikuntanathan first showed that Gaussian distributions [19] can prevent such leaks, and that Klein's algorithm [21] could sample efficiently from a negligibly close distribution. This algorithm uses the Gram-Schmidt orthogonalization, which requires either arithmetic over the rationals with very large denominators, or floating-point approximations. An alternative algorithm was proposed by Peikert in [32], where most of the expensive computation, including floating-point arithmetic, can be done in an offline phase at the cost of somewhat increasing the width of the sampled Gaussian. This technique turned out to be particularly convenient in the lattice-trapdoor framework of Micciancio and Peikert [25].

We now explain Peikert's algorithm in more details. Let $\mathbf{B}$ be the input basis and the target distribution be a spherical discrete Gaussian of width s, center $\mathbf{c}$ and over the lattice $\mathcal{L}$ spanned by $\mathbf{B}$. Note that spherical Gaussian sampling over $\mathbb{Z}^n$ is easy, by applying $\mathbf{B}$ as a transformation, it is also easy to sample a Gaussian over $\mathcal{L}$ but of covariance $\mathbf{\Sigma} = \mathbf{BB}^t$. To produce target samples, Peikert proposed to use convolution, that is adding some perturbation vector of covariance $\mathbf{\Sigma}_p = s^2\mathbf{I} - \mathbf{\Sigma}$ on the center $\mathbf{c}$. Indeed for continuous Gaussians, the resulting distribution is of covariance $s^2\mathbf{I}$. In [32], Peikert showed that this fact also holds for discrete Gaussians under some conditions. In summary, Peikert's approach consists of two phases:

- offline phase: one samples a perturbation vector of covariance $\mathbf{\Sigma}_p = s^2\mathbf{I} - \mathbf{\Sigma}$;
- online phase: one first samples a spherical Gaussian over $\mathbb{Z}^n$ and then applies the transformation of $\mathbf{B}$.

The online sampling can be rather efficient and fully performed over the integers [17,25,32]. By contrast, the offline sampling uses continuous Gaussian sampling and requires some matrix $\mathbf{A}$ such that $\mathbf{\Sigma}_p = \mathbf{AA}^t$. The only suggested way to find such $\mathbf{A}$ is the Cholesky decomposition. Therefore high-precision floating-point arithmetic is still heavily used in the offline phase.

We now list some of the numerous drawbacks of high-precision FPA when it comes to practical efficiency and security in the wild.

- First, one needs to perform a *tedious numerical stability analysis* to determine what level of precision is admissible, and how much security is lost. Indeed, while such analysis may be reasonable when done asymptotically, doing a concrete and tight analysis requires significant effort [3,13,33,34], and may be considered too error-prone for deployed cryptography. Moreover, efficient numerical stability analysis for cryptosystems based on generic decision problems remain open.

- Second, for a security level of λ-bits, it incurs *significant storage overheads* as one requires at least a precision of $\lambda/2$ bits[1] for each matrix entry, while the trapdoor basis itself only needs $\log(s)$ bits per entry, where $s = \mathrm{poly}(\lambda)$ in simple cryptosystems.
- Thirdly, the requirement for high-precision arithmetic would *significantly slow down* those sampling algorithms (may it be fix-point or floating-point arithmetic). While it has been shown in [13] that one can do most of the operations at lower precision, the proposed technique requires *complicated backtracking*, and high-precision arithmetic from time to time. While asymptotically interesting, it is unclear whether this technique is practical; in particular it has, to our knowledge never been implemented. It also seems particularly hard to protect against timing attacks.
- Finally we mention the intrinsic *weak determinism* of floating-point arithmetic. It is essential to de-randomize trapdoor sampling, as revealing two different vectors close to a single target instantly reveals a (secret) short vector of the lattice. Even with the same random stream, we need to assume that the rest of the algorithm is deterministic. In the case of high-precision arithmetic, one would for example have to assume that the mpfr library behaves exactly the same across different architectures and versions. But even at low precision, the use of native floats can be tricky despite deterministic IEEE standards. For example, while both ADD and MULTIPLY instructions are deterministically defined by the IEEE standard, the standard also allows the combined 'MULTIPLY-AND-ACCUMULATE' instruction to behave differently from applying both instructions sequentially, as long as the result is at least as precise [36]. As FPA addition is *not associative*, it is crucial to specify the order of operations for matrix-vector products as part of the scheme, and to not leave it as an implementation detail. Furthermore, compilers such as gcc do not guarantee determinism when considering code optimization over floating-point computation [29].

Our contribution. We present a new perturbation sampling algorithm in which no floating-point arithmetic is used. Compared with Peikert's algorithm [32], our new algorithm has the following features. A more detailed comparison is available in Sect. 5, with Tables 2 and 3.

- *Similar quality.* The final Gaussian width s achieved by our technique is only larger than its minimum by a factor of $1 + o(1)$: the parameters of the whole cryptosystems will be unaffected.
- *No need for FPA and less precision.* All operations are performed over integers of length about $\log s$, while previous algorithms required floating points with a mantissa of length at least $\lambda/2 + \log s$.
- *Less memory.* While the intermediate matrix, i.e. the Gram root of the covariance, is rectangular, it is integral and of a regular structure, requiring only $\approx n^2 \log s$, instead of $n^2(\lambda + \log s)/2$ bits for Cholesky decomposition [25,32].

---

[1] Unless one assumes strong bounds on the number of attackers' queries, as done in [34].

– *Simpler base sampling.* Only two kinds of base samplers are required: $D_{\mathbb{Z},Lr}$ and $D_{\mathbb{Z},r,c}$ with $c \in \frac{1}{L} \cdot \mathbb{Z}$, where L can be any integer larger than a polynomial bound; choosing L as a power of two is known to be particularly convenient [28].

In summary, not only do we get rid of FPA and its weak determinism, we also improve time and memory consumption; when $s = \text{poly}(\lambda)$ this improvement factor is quasilinear. In practice, it may allow to implement an HIBE or ABE with a few levels before having to resort to multi-precision arithmetic (note that the parameter s grows exponentially with the depth of such schemes). Compared to traditional samplers, we expect that the absence of floating-point arithmetic in our sampler will make it more amenable to side-channel countermeasures such as masking. We leave this for future work.

Techniques. Our main idea stems from the observation that, at least in the continuous case, sampling a Gaussian of covariance Σ can be done with using a matrix $\mathbf{A}$ such that $\mathbf{A}\mathbf{A}^t = \Sigma$, may $\mathbf{A}$ not be a square matrix. This idea was already implicit in [28,32], and we push it further.

The first step is to prove that the above statement also holds in the discrete case. We show that when $\mathbf{A} \cdot \mathbb{Z}^m = \mathbb{Z}^n$, the distribution of $\mathbf{A}\mathbf{x}$ where $\mathbf{x}$ is drawn from $D_{\mathbb{Z}^m,r}$ is statistically close to $D_{\mathbb{Z}^n,r\sqrt{\mathbf{A}\mathbf{A}^t}}$ under some smoothness condition with respect to the orthogonal lattice $\Lambda^\perp(\mathbf{A})$.

Now the difficult step under study boils down to finding a Gram root of a given matrix (in the context of Peikert's algorithm, $\mathbf{A}\mathbf{A}^t = d\mathbf{I} - \Sigma$). To avoid the FPA issues, we want this Gram root integral. Driven by this, we proceed to study the Integral Gram Decomposition Problem denoted by $\mathsf{IGDP}_{n,B,d,m}$ as follows: given an integral symmetric matrix $\Sigma \in \mathbb{Z}^{n \times n}$ with $\|\Sigma\|_2 \leq B$, find an integral matrix $\mathbf{A} \in \mathbb{Z}^{n \times m}$ such that $\mathbf{A}\mathbf{A}^t = d\mathbf{I}_n - \Sigma$. For $n = 1$, Lagrange's 4-square theorem has provided a solution to IGDP. Our goal is finding an algorithmic generalization of such a decomposition to larger matrices, which will be bootstrapped from the case of $n = 1$. Aiming at $\mathsf{IGDP}_{n,B,d,m}$, our initial method is recursive, and can be summarized as the following reduction

$$\mathsf{IGDP}_{n,B,d,m} \rightarrow \mathsf{IGDP}_{n-1,B',d,m'}$$

where $B' \approx B$, $m = m' + \lceil \log_b B \rceil + 4$ and b is the base of the used gadget decomposition. The reduction is constructive: by gadget decomposition (also called b-ary decomposition), one first finds a matrix $\mathbf{T}$ such that $\mathbf{T}\mathbf{T}^t$ has the same first row and column as $d\mathbf{I}_n - \Sigma$ except the diagonal element, and then clears out the remaining diagonal element by the 4-square decomposition given by Lagrange's theorem. However, this decomposition requires $d \gg B$, which significantly enlarges the width of corresponding Gaussian. To overcome this issue, we develop another tool called eigenvalue reduction, which can be viewed as the following reduction:

$$\mathsf{IGDP}_{n,B,d,m} \rightarrow \mathsf{IGDP}_{n,B',d-B,m-n}$$

with $B' \ll B$. By eigenvalue reduction, the final overhead on the Gaussian width is introduced during the decomposition on a small matrix, which becomes negligible compared with the original parameter. Combining the integral decomposition for $d \gg B$ and the eigenvalue reduction, we arrive at a solution to $\mathsf{IGDP}_{n,B,d,m}$ of a somewhat large B, say $B = \omega(n^4)$. This is the case of some advanced lattice based schemes, such as hierarchical IBE [1,8] and ABE [20]. Furthermore, if a few, say $O(\log n)$, bits of rational precision are permitted, we can find an almost integral Gram root for general positive definite matrices.

Techniques in the ring setting. The aforementioned algorithms apply to the ring setting, but the decompositions break the ring structure and thus lose the efficiency improvement provided by rings. To improve efficiency, we devised ring-based algorithms. The $\mathsf{IGDP}_{n,B,d,m}$ problem is naturally generalized to the ring setting by adding the underlying ring $\mathcal{R}$ as a parameter. To tackle the $\mathsf{IGDP}_{\mathcal{R},n,B,d,m}$ problem, we first study the special case $\mathsf{IGDP}_{\mathcal{R},1,B,d,m}$. We propose an analogue of 4-square decomposition in the power-of-2 cyclotomic ring, i.e. $\mathcal{R}_{2w} = \mathbb{Z}[x]/(x^w + 1)$ where $w = 2^l$. At a high level, our solution performs the reduction

$$\mathsf{IGDP}_{\mathcal{R}_{2w},1,B,d,m} \to \mathsf{IGDP}_{\mathcal{R}_w,1,B',d',m'},$$

where $B' \approx B$, $d = d' + \frac{b^{2k}-1}{b^2-1}$, $m = m' + k$ and b is the gadget base, $k = \lceil \log_b B \rceil$, which projects the problem onto a subring. To build this reduction, we make use of ring gadgets: given $f \in \mathcal{R}_{2w}$, the ring gadget computes a set of $a_i = b^{i-1} + x c_i(x^2) \in \mathcal{R}_{2w}$ such that $f + \sum_{i=1}^{k} a_i a_i^*$ can be viewed as an element in the subring $\mathcal{R}_w$ and all c_i's are small. The resulting integral decomposition inherits the tower of rings structure and hence can be stored efficiently despite the output being wider by a factor of $O(\log w)$. Finally, this decomposition in the ring setting can be combined with the previous integer setting algorithm to yield an algorithm for solving $\mathsf{IGDP}_{\mathcal{R}_{2w},n,B,d,m}$.

Related work. While we are not aware of works on the Integral Gram Decomposition Problem, the rational version of this question arises as a natural mathematical and algorithmic question for the representation of quadratic forms. For example, Cassel [9] showed that a rational solution exists for $m = n + 3$; we are unaware of an efficient algorithm to find such a solution. Lenstra [24] proposed a polynomial time rational solution for $m = 4n$.

However, such rational solutions are not very satisfactory in our context, as the denominators can get as large as the determinant of the input lattice. In fact, if rational arithmetic with such large coefficient is deemed acceptable, then one could directly use an implementation of Klein-GPV [19,21] algorithm over the rationals.

In a concurrent work [10], Chen, Genise and Mukherjee proposed a notion of approximate trapdoor and adapted the Micciancio-Peikert trapdoor [25] to the approximate trapdoor setting. In the analysis of the preimage distribution, they used a similar linear transformation theorem for discrete Gaussians. Their preimage sampling calls perturbation sampling as a "black-box" so that our technique is well compatible with [10].

Furthermore in [15], Ducas and Prest applied FFT techniques to improve the Klein-GPV algorithm in the ring setting. Similarly, Genise and Micciancio exploited the Schur complement and developed a discrete perturbation algorithm in [17]. Yet in practice these methods still resort to floating-point arithmetic.

Roadmap. We start in Sect. 2 with some preliminary material. Section 3 shows that rectangular Gram roots allow to sample according to the desired distribution. In Sect. 4, we introduce the Integral Gram Decomposition Problem and detail the algorithms to solve it. We provide a detailed comparison with Peikert's perturbation sampler in Sect. 5. Finally we propose a variant of our integral matrix decomposition geared to the ring setting in Sect. 6.

2 Preliminaries

2.1 Notations

We use log and ln to denote respectively the base 2 logarithm and the natural logarithm. Let $\epsilon > 0$ denote some very small number; we use the notational shortcut $\hat{\epsilon} = \epsilon + O(\epsilon^2)$. One can check that $\frac{1+\epsilon}{1-\epsilon} = 1 + 2\hat{\epsilon}$ and $\ln\left(\frac{1+\epsilon}{1-\epsilon}\right) = 2\hat{\epsilon}$.

For a distribution D over a countable set, we write $z \hookleftarrow D$ when the random variable z is sampled from D, and denote by $D(x)$ the probability of $z = x$. For a real-valued function f and a countable set S, we write $f(S) = \sum_{x \in S} f(x)$ assuming that this sum is absolutely convergent (which is always the case in this paper). Given two distributions D_1 and D_2 of common support E, the *max-log distance* between D_1 and D_2 is

$$\Delta_{\mathrm{ML}}(D_1, D_2) = \max_{x \in E} |\ln(D_1(x)) - \ln(D_2(x))|.$$

As shown in [28], it holds that $\Delta_{\mathrm{ML}}(D_1, D_2) \leq \Delta_{\mathrm{ML}}(D_1, D_3) + \Delta_{\mathrm{ML}}(D_2, D_3)$.

2.2 Linear Algebra

We use bold lower case letters to denote vectors, and bold upper case letters to denote matrices. By convention, vectors are in column form. For a matrix $\mathbf{A}$, we denote by $\mathbf{A}_{i,j}$ the element in the i-th row and j-th column, and by $\mathbf{A}_{i:j,k:l}$ the sub-block $(\mathbf{A}_{a,b})_{a \in \{i, \cdots, j\}, b \in \{k, \cdots, l\}}$. Let $\lfloor \mathbf{A} \rceil$ be the matrix obtained by rounding each entry of $\mathbf{A}$ to the nearest integer. Let $\mathbf{I}_n$ be the n-dimensional identity matrix.

Let $\boldsymbol{\Sigma} \in \mathbb{R}^{n \times n}$ be a symmetric matrix. We write $\boldsymbol{\Sigma} > 0$ when $\boldsymbol{\Sigma}$ is *positive definite*, i.e. $\mathbf{x}^t \boldsymbol{\Sigma} \mathbf{x} > 0$ for all non-zero $\mathbf{x} \in \mathbb{R}^n$. It is known that $\boldsymbol{\Sigma} > 0$ if and only if $\boldsymbol{\Sigma}^{-1} > 0$. We also write $\boldsymbol{\Sigma}_1 > \boldsymbol{\Sigma}_2$ when $\boldsymbol{\Sigma}_1 - \boldsymbol{\Sigma}_2 > 0$. It holds that $\boldsymbol{\Sigma}_1 > \boldsymbol{\Sigma}_2 > 0$ if and only if $\boldsymbol{\Sigma}_2^{-1} > \boldsymbol{\Sigma}_1^{-1} > 0$. Similarly, we write $\boldsymbol{\Sigma}_1 \geq \boldsymbol{\Sigma}_2$ or $\boldsymbol{\Sigma}_1 - \boldsymbol{\Sigma}_2 \geq 0$ to state that $\boldsymbol{\Sigma}_1 - \boldsymbol{\Sigma}_2$ is positive semi-definite. If $\boldsymbol{\Sigma} = \mathbf{A}\mathbf{A}^t$, we call

A a *Gram root* of $\boldsymbol{\Sigma}$. In particular, if a Gram root **A** is a square and invertible matrix, we call **A** a *square Gram root*[2]. When the context permits it, we denote $\sqrt{\boldsymbol{\Sigma}}$ for any square Gram root of $\boldsymbol{\Sigma}$.

For a positive definite matrix $\boldsymbol{\Sigma}$, let $e_1(\boldsymbol{\Sigma})$ be the largest eigenvalue of $\boldsymbol{\Sigma}$, then $e_1(\boldsymbol{\Sigma}) > 0$. Let $\boldsymbol{\Sigma}_1, \boldsymbol{\Sigma}_2$ be positive definite matrices and $\boldsymbol{\Sigma} = \boldsymbol{\Sigma}_1 + \boldsymbol{\Sigma}_2$, then $\boldsymbol{\Sigma} > 0$ and $e_1(\boldsymbol{\Sigma}) \leq e_1(\boldsymbol{\Sigma}_1) + e_1(\boldsymbol{\Sigma}_2)$. We recall the spectral norm $\|\mathbf{A}\|_2 = \max_{\mathbf{x} \neq 0} \frac{\|\mathbf{Ax}\|}{\|\mathbf{x}\|} = \sqrt{e_1(\mathbf{A}^t \mathbf{A})}$ and the Frobenius norm $\|\mathbf{A}\|_F = \sqrt{\sum_{i,j} \mathbf{A}_{i,j}^2}$. It is known that $\|\mathbf{A}^t\|_2 = \|\mathbf{A}\|_2$, $\|\mathbf{AB}\|_2 \leq \|\mathbf{A}\|_2 \|\mathbf{B}\|_2$ and $\|\mathbf{A}\|_2 \leq \|\mathbf{A}\|_F$. We also write $\|\mathbf{A}\|_{\max} = \max_{i,j} |\mathbf{A}_{i,j}|$ and $\|\mathbf{A}\|_{\mathrm{col}} = \max_j \sqrt{\sum_i \mathbf{A}_{i,j}^2}$.

2.3 Lattices

A lattice is a discrete additive subgroup of $\mathbb{R}^m$, and is the set of all integer linear combinations of linearly independent vectors $\mathbf{b}_1, \cdots, \mathbf{b}_n \in \mathbb{R}^m$. We call $\mathbf{B} = \begin{pmatrix} \mathbf{b}_1 \cdots \mathbf{b}_n \end{pmatrix}$ a basis and n the dimension of the lattice. If $n = m$, we call the lattice *full-rank*. We denote by $\mathcal{L}(\mathbf{B})$ the lattice generated by the basis **B**. Let $\widehat{\mathcal{L}} = \{\mathbf{u} \in \mathrm{span}(\mathcal{L}) \mid \forall \mathbf{v} \in \mathcal{L}, \langle \mathbf{u}, \mathbf{v} \rangle \in \mathbb{Z}\}$ be the dual lattice of $\mathcal{L}$. For $k \leq n$, the k-th minimum $\lambda_k(\mathcal{L})$ is the smallest value $r \in \mathbb{R}$ such that there are at least k linearly independent vectors in $\mathcal{L}$ whose lengths are not greater than r.

Given $\mathbf{A} \in \mathbb{Z}^{n \times m}$ with $m \geq n$, we denote the *orthogonal lattice*[3] defined by **A** by $\Lambda^\perp(\mathbf{A}) = \{\mathbf{v} \in \mathbb{Z}^m \mid \mathbf{Av} = \mathbf{0}\}$. When the rank of **A** is n, the dimension of $\Lambda^\perp(\mathbf{A})$ is $(m - n)$.

2.4 Gaussians

Let $\rho_{\mathbf{R},\mathbf{c}}(\mathbf{x}) = \exp\left(-\pi(\mathbf{x} - \mathbf{c})^t \mathbf{R}^{-t} \mathbf{R}^{-1}(\mathbf{x} - \mathbf{c})\right)$ be the n-dimensional Gaussian weight with center $\mathbf{c} \in \mathbb{R}^n$ and (scaled)[4] covariance matrix $\boldsymbol{\Sigma} = \mathbf{RR}^t$. Because $\rho_{\mathbf{R},\mathbf{c}}(\mathbf{x}) = \exp\left(-\pi(\mathbf{x} - \mathbf{c})^t \boldsymbol{\Sigma}^{-1}(\mathbf{x} - \mathbf{c})\right)$ is exactly determined by $\boldsymbol{\Sigma}$, we also write $\rho_{\mathbf{R},\mathbf{c}}$ as $\rho_{\sqrt{\boldsymbol{\Sigma}},\mathbf{c}}$. When $\mathbf{c} = \mathbf{0}$, the Gaussian function is written as $\rho_{\mathbf{R}}$ or $\rho_{\sqrt{\boldsymbol{\Sigma}}}$ and is called *centered*. When $\boldsymbol{\Sigma} = s^2 \mathbf{I}_n$, we write the subscript $\sqrt{\boldsymbol{\Sigma}}$ as s directly, and call s the *width*.

The *discrete Gaussian distribution* over a lattice $\mathcal{L}$ with center $\mathbf{c}$ and covariance matrix $\boldsymbol{\Sigma}$ is defined by the probability function $D_{\mathcal{L},\sqrt{\boldsymbol{\Sigma}},\mathbf{c}}(\mathbf{x}) = \frac{\rho_{\sqrt{\boldsymbol{\Sigma}},\mathbf{c}}(\mathbf{x})}{\rho_{\sqrt{\boldsymbol{\Sigma}},\mathbf{c}}(\mathcal{L})}$ for any $\mathbf{x} \in \mathcal{L}$. We recall some notions related to the *smoothing parameter*.

Definition 1 ([27], Definition 3.1). *Given a lattice $\mathcal{L}$ and $\epsilon > 0$, the ϵ-smoothing parameter of $\mathcal{L}$ is* $\eta_\epsilon(\mathcal{L}) = \min\left\{s \mid \rho_{1/s}\left(\widehat{\mathcal{L}}\right) \leq 1 + \epsilon\right\}$.

---

[2] When $n \geq 2$, any $\boldsymbol{\Sigma} > 0$ has infinitely many square Gram roots.

[3] Take note that we are here not considering the "q-ary orthogonal lattice" $\Lambda_q^\perp(\mathbf{A}) = \{\mathbf{v} \in \mathbb{Z}^m \mid \mathbf{Av} = \mathbf{0} \bmod q\}$.

[4] The scaling factor is 2π and we omit it in this paper for convenience.

Definition 2 ([32], Definition 2.3). *Given a full-rank lattice $\mathcal{L}$, $\epsilon > 0$ and a positive definite matrix Σ, we write $\sqrt{\Sigma} \geq \eta_\epsilon(\mathcal{L})$ if $\eta_\epsilon\left(\sqrt{\Sigma}^{-1} \cdot \mathcal{L}\right) \leq 1$ i.e. $\rho_{\sqrt{\Sigma^{-1}}}\left(\widehat{\mathcal{L}}\right) \leq 1 + \epsilon$.*

We define $\eta_\epsilon^{\leq}(\mathbb{Z}^n) = \sqrt{\frac{\ln(2n(1+1/\epsilon))}{\pi}}$. We will use the following results later.

Proposition 1. *Given a lattice $\mathcal{L}$ and $\epsilon > 0$, then $\eta_\epsilon(r\mathcal{L}) = r \cdot \eta_\epsilon(\mathcal{L})$ for arbitrary $r > 0$.*

Proposition 2. *Let $\Sigma_1 \geq \Sigma_2 > 0$ be two positive definite matrices. Let $\mathcal{L}$ be a full-rank lattice and $\epsilon \in (0,1)$. If $\sqrt{\Sigma_2} \geq \eta_\epsilon(\mathcal{L})$, then $\sqrt{\Sigma_1} \geq \eta_\epsilon(\mathcal{L})$.*

Proof. Notice that $\rho_{\sqrt{\Sigma_1^{-1}}}(\mathbf{x}) = \exp(-\pi \mathbf{x}^t \Sigma_1 \mathbf{x}) \leq \exp(-\pi \mathbf{x}^t \Sigma_2 \mathbf{x}) = \rho_{\sqrt{\Sigma_2^{-1}}}(\mathbf{x})$, hence $\rho_{\sqrt{\Sigma_1^{-1}}}\left(\widehat{\mathcal{L}}\right) \leq \rho_{\sqrt{\Sigma_2^{-1}}}\left(\widehat{\mathcal{L}}\right)$. By Definition 2, we complete the proof. ☐

Lemma 1 ([27], Lemma 3.3). *Let $\mathcal{L}$ be an n-dimensional lattice and $\epsilon \in (0,1)$. Then $\eta_\epsilon(\mathcal{L}) \leq \eta_\epsilon^{\leq}(\mathbb{Z}^n) \cdot \lambda_n(\mathcal{L})$. In particular, for any $\omega(\sqrt{\log n})$ function, there is a negligible ϵ such that $\eta_\epsilon(\mathbb{Z}^n) \leq \omega(\sqrt{\log n})$.*

Lemma 2 ([27], implicit in Lemma 4.4). *Let $\mathcal{L}$ be a lattice and $\epsilon \in (0,1)$. If $r \geq \eta_\epsilon(\mathcal{L})$, then $\rho_r(\mathbf{c} + \mathcal{L}) \in [\frac{1-\epsilon}{1+\epsilon}, 1]\rho_r(\mathcal{L})$ for any $\mathbf{c} \in \mathrm{span}(\mathcal{L})$.*

We recall the convolution theorem with respect to discrete Gaussians that was introduced in [32].

Theorem 1 (Adapted from Theorem 3.1 [32]). *Let $\Sigma_1, \Sigma_2 \in \mathbb{R}^{n \times n}$ be positive definite matrices. Let $\Sigma = \Sigma_1 + \Sigma_2$ and let $\Sigma_3 \in \mathbb{R}^{n \times n}$ be such that $\Sigma_3^{-1} = \Sigma_1^{-1} + \Sigma_2^{-1}$. Let $\mathcal{L}_1, \mathcal{L}_2$ be two full-rank lattices in $\mathbb{R}^n$ such that $\sqrt{\Sigma_1} \geq \eta_\epsilon(\mathcal{L}_1)$ and $\sqrt{\Sigma_3} \geq \eta_\epsilon(\mathcal{L}_2)$ for $\epsilon \in (0, 1/2)$. Let $\mathbf{c}_1, \mathbf{c}_2 \in \mathbb{R}^n$. Then the distribution of $\mathbf{x}_1 \hookleftarrow D_{\mathcal{L}_1, \sqrt{\Sigma_1}, \mathbf{x}_2 - \mathbf{c}_2 + \mathbf{c}_1}$ where $\mathbf{x}_2 \hookleftarrow D_{\mathcal{L}_2, \sqrt{\Sigma_2}, \mathbf{c}_2}$ is within max-log distance $4\hat{\epsilon}$ of $D_{\mathcal{L}_1, \sqrt{\Sigma}, \mathbf{c}_1}$.*

2.5 Integral Decompositions

Lagrange's four-square theorem states that every natural number can be represented as the sum of four integer squares. An efficient algorithm to find such a decomposition was given by Rabin and Shallit [35].

Theorem 2 (Rabin-Shallit algorithm [35]). *There is a randomized algorithm for expressing $N \in \mathbb{N}$ as a sum of four squares which requires an expected number of $O(\log^2 N \log \log N)$ operations with integers smaller than N.*

Another important integral decomposition for our work is the b-ary decomposition, more conveniently formalized with the *gadget vector* $\mathbf{g} = (1, b, \cdots, b^{k-1})^t$ in [25], hence called *gadget decomposition*. It says that for any $n \in (-b^k, b^k) \cap \mathbb{Z}$, there exists a vector $\mathbf{c} \in \mathbb{Z}^k$ such that $\langle \mathbf{c}, \mathbf{g} \rangle = n$ and $\|\mathbf{c}\|_\infty < b$. The cost of such a decomposition is dominated by $O(k)$ Euclidean divisions by b that are particularly efficient in practice when b is a power of 2. Note that $\|\mathbf{g}\|^2 = (b^{2k} - 1)/(b^2 - 1)$.

3 Gaussian Sampling with an Integral Gram Root

In Peikert's sampler [32], one samples perturbation vectors from a Gaussian with certain covariance, say $D_{\mathbb{Z}^n, r\sqrt{\Sigma}}$ during the offline phase. Among existing perturbation samplers [17,25,32] this requires floating-point arithmetic in the linear algebraic steps.

To avoid FPA, our starting point is the following observation: given an integral Gram root of $\Sigma - I_n$, one can sample from $D_{\mathbb{Z}^n, r\sqrt{\Sigma}}$ without resorting to FPA and in a quite simple manner. The main result of this section is the following theorem.

Theorem 3 (Sampling theorem). *Let* $\Sigma \in \mathbb{Z}^{n\times n}$ *such that* $\Sigma - I_n \geq I_n$. *Given* $A \in \mathbb{Z}^{n\times(n+m)}$ *such that* $AA^t = \Sigma - I_n$, $A \cdot \mathbb{Z}^{n+m} = \mathbb{Z}^n$ *and* $\lambda_m(\Lambda^\perp(A)) \leq L$, *let* $\widetilde{D}_A(L', r)$ *denote the distribution of* $D_{\mathbb{Z}^n, r, \frac{1}{L'}\cdot c}$ *where* $c = Ax$ *with* $x \hookleftarrow D_{\mathbb{Z}^{n+m}, L'r}$. *For* $\epsilon \in (0, 1/2)$, $r \geq \eta_\epsilon(\mathbb{Z}^n)$ *and* $L' \geq \max\{\sqrt{2}, (L/r) \cdot \eta_\epsilon^{\leq}(\mathbb{Z}^m)\}$, *then*

$$\Delta_{\mathrm{ML}}\left(\widetilde{D}_A(L', r), D_{\mathbb{Z}^n, r\sqrt{\Sigma}}\right) \leq 8\hat{\epsilon}.$$

We give an algorithmic description in Algorithm 1.

Algorithm 1. New perturbation sampling algorithm $\mathsf{NewPert}(r, \Sigma)$

Input: a covariance matrix $\Sigma \in \mathbb{Z}^{n\times n}$ and some $r \geq \eta_\epsilon(\mathbb{Z}^n)$.
Output: a sample x from a distribution within max-log distance $8\hat{\epsilon}$ of $D_{\mathbb{Z}^n, r\sqrt{\Sigma}}$.
Precomputation:
1: compute $A \in \mathbb{Z}^{n\times(n+m)}$ such that $AA^t = \Sigma - I_n$, $A \cdot \mathbb{Z}^{n+m} = \mathbb{Z}^n$ and $\lambda_m(\Lambda^\perp(A)) \leq L$ (see Sect. 4 for details)
   Sampling:
2: sample $x \hookleftarrow D_{\mathbb{Z}^{n+m}, Lr}$ by base sampler $D_{\mathbb{Z}, Lr}$
3: $c \leftarrow Ax$
4: sample $y \hookleftarrow D_{\mathbb{Z}^n, r, \frac{1}{L}\cdot c}$ by base samplers $D_{\mathbb{Z}, r, \frac{c}{L}}$ with $c \in \{0, 1, \cdots, L-1\}$
5: return y

To prove Theorem 3, we need the following linear transformation lemma for discrete Gaussians.

Lemma 3 (Linear Transformation Lemma). *Let* $A \in \mathbb{Z}^{n\times m}$ *such that* $A \cdot \mathbb{Z}^m = \mathbb{Z}^n$. *Let* $\Sigma = AA^t$. *For* $\epsilon \in (0, 1/2)$, *if* $r \geq \eta_\epsilon(\Lambda^\perp(A))$, *then the max-log distance between the distribution of* $y = Ax$ *where* $x \hookleftarrow D_{\mathbb{Z}^m, r}$ *and* $D_{\mathbb{Z}^n, r\sqrt{\Sigma}}$ *is at most* $4\hat{\epsilon}$.

Remark 1. Lemma 3 was used implicitly in [6,26]. Its proof is given in the full version [16]. Again, a general linear transformation theorem is stated in [10].

Remark 2. Lemma 3 implies similar bounds for other metrics, such as the Kullback-Leibler divergence [33] and the Rényi divergence [3,34].

Proof of Theorem 3. By Lemmata 3 and 1, the max-log distance between the distribution of $\mathbf{c} = \mathbf{A}\mathbf{x}$ and $D_{\mathbb{Z}^n, L'r\sqrt{\mathbf{\Sigma} - \mathbf{I}_n}}$ is at most $4\hat{\epsilon}$. By scaling, we have that the max-log distance between the distribution of $\frac{1}{L'} \cdot \mathbf{c}$ and $D_{\frac{1}{L'} \cdot \mathbb{Z}^n, r\sqrt{\mathbf{\Sigma} - \mathbf{I}_n}}$ is still at most $4\hat{\epsilon}$. It can be verified that

$$r\sqrt{\left((\mathbf{\Sigma} - \mathbf{I}_n)^{-1} + \mathbf{I}_n^{-1}\right)^{-1}} \geq \eta_\epsilon \left(\frac{1}{L'} \cdot \mathbb{Z}^n\right).$$

Combining Theorem 1, the proof follows. □

3.1 Reducing $\lambda_m(\Lambda^\perp(\mathbf{A}))$

As shown in Theorem 3, with an integral Gram root, the sampling of $D_{\mathbb{Z}^n, r\sqrt{\mathbf{\Sigma}}}$ is converted into two kinds of base samplings: $D_{\mathbb{Z}, L'r}$ and $D_{\mathbb{Z}, r, c}$ with $c \in \frac{1}{L'} \cdot \mathbb{Z}$. One sometimes may prefer to work with small L' whose size is mainly determined by $\lambda_m(\Lambda^\perp(\mathbf{A}))$. The following lemma suggests that given a matrix $\mathbf{A}$, one can construct an orthogonal lattice of relatively small successive minima by padding $\mathbf{A}$ with some gadget matrices $\left(\mathbf{I}_n \ b\mathbf{I}_n \ \cdots \ b^{k-1}\mathbf{I}_n\right)$.

Lemma 4. *Let* $\mathbf{A} \in \mathbb{Z}^{n \times m}$ *with* $\|\mathbf{A}\|_2 \leq B$. *For* $b, k \in \mathbb{N}$ *such that* $b^k > B$, *let* $\mathbf{A}' = \left(\mathbf{I}_n \ b\mathbf{I}_n \ \cdots \ b^{k-1}\mathbf{I}_n \ \mathbf{A}\right)$, *then* $\lambda_{m+(k-1)n}(\Lambda^\perp(\mathbf{A}')) \leq \sqrt{nk(b-1)^2 + 1}$.

The proof of Lemma 4 is given in the full version [16].

Remark 3. Lemma 4 provides a solution to reduce L' at the cost of more base samplings and some overhead on the final Gaussian width. In practice, it is optional to pad gadget matrices considering the tradeoff. In later discussions, we shall omit this trick and just focus on $\lambda_m(\Lambda^\perp(\mathbf{A}))$.

4 Integral Gram Decompositions

In Sect. 3, we have explicated how to sample perturbation vectors using no FPA with an integral Gram root. The computation of such an integral Gram root is developed in this section. Let us first formally define the *Integral Gram Decomposition Problem*.

Definition 3 ($\mathsf{IGDP}_{n,B,d,m}$). *Let* $n, B, d, m \in \mathbb{N}$. *The Integral Gram Decomposition Problem, denoted by* $\mathsf{IGDP}_{n,B,d,m}$, *is defined as follows: given an integral symmetric matrix* $\mathbf{\Sigma} \in \mathbb{Z}^{n \times n}$ *with* $\|\mathbf{\Sigma}\|_2 \leq B$, *find an integral matrix* $\mathbf{A} \in \mathbb{Z}^{n \times m}$ *such that* $\mathbf{A}\mathbf{A}^t = d\mathbf{I}_n - \mathbf{\Sigma}$.

Our final goal is to solve $\mathsf{IGDP}_{n,B,d,m}$ with fixed (n, B) while keeping $d = (1 + o(1))B$ and m relatively small.

Our first approach (Sect. 4.1) only allows a decomposition of sufficiently diagonally dominant matrices, i.e. $d \gg B$, which implies a large overhead on the final width of the Gaussian. Fortunately, when the parameter B is somewhat large, say $\omega(n^4)$, this can be fixed by first resorting to some integral approximations of Cholesky Gram roots and then working on the left-over matrix of small norm. We call this procedure eigenvalue reduction and describe it in Sect. 4.2. Finally, we combine these two algorithms and give several example instances in Sect. 4.3.

4.1   Decomposition for Diagonally Dominant Matrices

We present an algorithm to compute an integral Gram root of $\mathbf{\Sigma}' = d\mathbf{I}_n - \mathbf{\Sigma}$ for a relatively large d. It is formally described in Algorithm 2.

The algorithm proceeds by induction, reducing $\mathsf{IGDP}_{n,B,d,m}$ to $\mathsf{IGDP}_{n-1,B',d,m'}$ where B' and m are slightly larger than B and m' respectively. To do so, one first constructs $\mathbf{T} \in \mathbb{Z}^{n \times k}$ such that $\mathbf{TT}^t$ and $\mathbf{\Sigma}'$ have the same first row and column, and then proceeds iteratively over $(\mathbf{\Sigma}' - \mathbf{TT}^t)_{2:n,2:n}$. In the construction of $\mathbf{T}$, to clear out the off-diagonal elements, we make use of a gadget decomposition $\langle \mathbf{c}_i, \mathbf{g} \rangle = \mathbf{\Sigma}'_{1,i}$ $(i > 1)$. The remaining diagonal element, namely $\mathbf{\Sigma}'_{1,1} - \|\mathbf{g}\|^2$, is then handled by the 4-square theorem.

To ensure the inductive construction goes through, Algorithm 2 requires a certain strongly positive definiteness condition. We need that $d - \mathbf{\Sigma}_{i,i} \geq \|\mathbf{g}\|^2$, but we also need to account for the perturbation $\mathbf{TT}^t$ subtracted from $\mathbf{\Sigma}'$ during the induction. The correctness and efficiency of this algorithm is given in Lemma 5.

Remark 4. For tighter parameters, we consider $\|\mathbf{\Sigma}\|_{\max}$ instead of direct $\|\mathbf{\Sigma}\|_2$ in Algorithm 2, which does not affect the main result, i.e. Corollary 1.

Lemma 5. *Algorithm 2 is correct. More precisely, let $\mathbf{\Sigma} \in \mathbb{Z}^{n \times n}$ be symmetric and $d, b, k \in \mathbb{Z}$ such that $b^k \geq \|\mathbf{\Sigma}\|_{\max} + k(n-1)b^2$ and $d \geq \frac{b^{2k}-1}{b^2-1} + b^k$. Then $\mathsf{DiagDomIGD}(\mathbf{\Sigma}, d, b, k)$ outputs $\mathbf{A} \in \mathbb{Z}^{n \times n(k+4)}$ such that $\mathbf{AA}^t = d\mathbf{I}_n - \mathbf{\Sigma}$.*

Moreover, $\mathsf{DiagDomIGD}(\mathbf{\Sigma}, d, b, k)$ performs $O(kn^3 + n\log^2 d \log\log d)$ arithmetic operations on integers of bitsize $O(\log d)$.

Proof. There are n calls to the Rabin-Shallit algorithm in Algorithm 2, and all input integers are at most $2d$. Thus the total cost of the Rabin-Shallit algorithm is $O(n\log^2 d \log\log d)$ operations on integers of bitsize $O(\log d)$. There are also $\frac{n(n-1)}{2}$ gadget decompositions, and the total cost is $O(n^2 k)$ operations on integers of bitsize at most $k \log b \leq \log d$. For matrix multiplication, we follow the textbook algorithm, thus the total cost is $O(n^3 k)$ operations on integers of bitsize at most $O(\log d)$. This yields the overall running time complexity.

We now prove the correctness. Since $d - \mathbf{\Sigma}_{1,1} \geq d - \|\mathbf{\Sigma}\|_{\max} \geq \|\mathbf{g}\|^2$, the existence of a 4-square decomposition $\mathbf{x}$ is ensured. For $\mathbf{\Sigma}_{1,j}$ with $j > 1$, we have $|\mathbf{\Sigma}_{1,j}| \leq \|\mathbf{\Sigma}\|_{\max} < b^k$, which implies the existence of $\mathbf{c}_j$ and $\|\mathbf{c}_j\|_\infty < b$. Then it can be verified that

$$d\mathbf{I}_n - \mathbf{\Sigma} - \mathbf{TT}^t = \begin{pmatrix} 0 & \mathbf{0}^t \\ \mathbf{0} & \mathbf{\Pi}' \end{pmatrix}$$

where $\mathbf{\Pi}' = d\mathbf{I}_{n-1} - \mathbf{\Pi} \in \mathbb{Z}^{(n-1)\times(n-1)}$ and $\mathbf{\Pi} = \mathbf{\Sigma}_{2:n,2:n} + \mathbf{\Xi}$ with $\mathbf{\Xi} = \mathbf{CC}^t$. Notice that $\|\mathbf{c}_j\| \leq b\sqrt{k}$, hence $\|\mathbf{\Pi}\|_{\max} \leq \|\mathbf{\Sigma}\|_{\max} + kb^2$. Further we have that

$$b^k \geq \|\mathbf{\Pi}\|_{\max} + k(n-2)b^2 \quad \text{and} \quad d \geq \frac{b^{2k}-1}{b^2-1} + b^k.$$

So far, all parameter conditions indeed hold for d and $\mathbf{\Pi}$ correspondingly. Therefore, the induction goes through and Algorithm 2 is correct. □

Algorithm 2. Integral matrix decomposition for a strongly diagonally dominant matrix $\mathsf{DiagDomIGD}(\boldsymbol{\Sigma}, d, b, k)$

Input: a symmetric matrix $\boldsymbol{\Sigma} \in \mathbb{Z}^{n \times n}$,

    two integers $b, k \geq 2$ such that $b^k \geq \|\boldsymbol{\Sigma}\|_{\max} + k(n-1)b^2$,

    an integer d such that $d \geq \frac{b^{2k}-1}{b^2-1} + b^k$.

Output: $\mathbf{A} = \begin{pmatrix} \mathbf{L}_1 \cdots \mathbf{L}_k \ \mathbf{D}_1 \cdots \mathbf{D}_4 \end{pmatrix} \in \mathbb{Z}^{n \times n(k+4)}$ such that $\mathbf{A}\mathbf{A}^t = d\mathbf{I}_n - \boldsymbol{\Sigma}$

    where $\mathbf{L}_i \in \mathbb{Z}^{n \times n}$ is a lower-triangular matrix whose diagonal elements are b^{i-1}

    and $\mathbf{D}_i \in \mathbb{Z}^{n \times n}$ is a diagonal matrix.

1: $\mathbf{g} \leftarrow (1, b, \cdots, b^{k-1})^t$
2: calculate $\mathbf{x} = (x_1, x_2, x_3, x_4)^t \in \mathbb{Z}^4$ such that $\|\mathbf{x}\|^2 = d - \boldsymbol{\Sigma}_{1,1} - \|\mathbf{g}\|^2$ using Rabin-Shallit algorithm (Theorem 2)
3: **if** $n = 1$ **then**
4:     return $(\mathbf{g}^t, \mathbf{x}^t)$
5: **end if**
6: **for** $j = 2, \cdots, n$ **do**
7:     calculate $\mathbf{c}_j \in \mathbb{Z}^k$ such that $\langle \mathbf{c}_j, \mathbf{g} \rangle = -\boldsymbol{\Sigma}_{1,j}$ by gadget decomposition
8: **end for**
9: $\mathbf{C} \leftarrow \begin{pmatrix} \mathbf{c}_2 \cdots \mathbf{c}_n \end{pmatrix}^t \in \mathbb{Z}^{(n-1) \times k}$, $\mathbf{T} \leftarrow \begin{pmatrix} \mathbf{g}^t \ \mathbf{x}^t \\ \mathbf{C} \end{pmatrix} \in \mathbb{Z}^{n \times (4+k)}$
10: $\boldsymbol{\Pi} \leftarrow (\boldsymbol{\Sigma} + \mathbf{T}\mathbf{T}^t)_{2:n, 2:n}$
11: $\begin{pmatrix} \mathbf{L}'_1 \cdots \mathbf{L}'_k \ \mathbf{D}'_1 \cdots \mathbf{D}'_4 \end{pmatrix} \leftarrow \mathsf{DiagDomIGD}(\boldsymbol{\Pi}, d, b, k)$ {Recursive call}
12: $\begin{pmatrix} \mathbf{v}'_1 \cdots \mathbf{v}'_k \end{pmatrix} \leftarrow \mathbf{C}$
13: $\mathbf{L}_i \leftarrow \begin{pmatrix} b^{i-1} \\ \mathbf{v}'_i \ \mathbf{L}'_i \end{pmatrix} \in \mathbb{Z}^{n \times n}$ for $i = 1, \cdots, k$
14: $\mathbf{D}_i \leftarrow \begin{pmatrix} x_i \\ & \mathbf{D}'_i \end{pmatrix} \in \mathbb{Z}^{n \times n}$ for $i = 1, \cdots, 4$
15: return $\mathbf{A} = \begin{pmatrix} \mathbf{L}_1 \cdots \mathbf{L}_k \ \mathbf{D}_1 \cdots \mathbf{D}_4 \end{pmatrix}$

Notice that $\|\boldsymbol{\Sigma}\|_{\max} \leq \|\boldsymbol{\Sigma}\|_2$, we immediately get the following result.

Corollary 1. Let $n, B, d, b, k \in \mathbb{N}$ such that $b^k \geq B + k(n-1)b^2$ and $d \geq \frac{b^{2k}-1}{b^2-1} + b^k$. Then there exists a solution to $\mathsf{IGDP}_{n,B,d,n(k+4)}$ and it can be calculated by Algorithm 2.

To use such a decomposition for perturbation sampling, we also need to control $\lambda_{m-n}(\Lambda^\perp(\mathbf{A}))$. Lemma 6 shows that this can easily be done by padding the output $\mathbf{A}$ with an identity matrix $\mathbf{I}_n$.

Lemma 6. Let $\mathbf{A} = \mathsf{DiagDomIGD}(\boldsymbol{\Sigma}, d-1, b, k) \in \mathbb{Z}^{n \times m}$ where $m = n(k+4)$. Let $\mathbf{A}' = \begin{pmatrix} \mathbf{I}_n \ \mathbf{A} \end{pmatrix}$, then $\mathbf{A}' \cdot \mathbb{Z}^{n+m} = \mathbb{Z}^n$, the dimension of $\Lambda^\perp(\mathbf{A}')$ is m, and

$$\lambda_m(\Lambda^\perp(\mathbf{A}')) \leq \max\left\{ b^2\sqrt{n}, \sqrt{d - \frac{b^{2k}-1}{b^2-1} + \|\boldsymbol{\Sigma}\|_{\max}} \right\}.$$

Proof. Let $\mathbf{S} = \begin{pmatrix} 1 & -b \\ & 1 & -b \\ & & \ddots & -b \\ & & & 1 \end{pmatrix} \in \mathbb{Z}^{(k-1) \times (k-1)}$. We define $\mathbf{D} = \begin{pmatrix} \mathbf{D}_1 \cdots \mathbf{D}_4 \end{pmatrix}$ $\in \mathbb{Z}^{n \times 4n}$, $\mathbf{L} = \begin{pmatrix} \mathbf{L}_1 \cdots \mathbf{L}_k \end{pmatrix} \in \mathbb{Z}^{n \times kn}$ such that $\mathbf{A} = \begin{pmatrix} \mathbf{L} \ \mathbf{D} \end{pmatrix}$. We also define

$\overline{\mathbf{L}} = \mathbf{L} \cdot (\mathbf{S} \otimes \mathbf{I}_n) = \begin{pmatrix} \mathbf{L}_1 & \mathbf{L}_2 - b\mathbf{L}_1 & \cdots & \mathbf{L}_k - b\mathbf{L}_{k-1} \end{pmatrix}$, then $\|\overline{\mathbf{L}}\|_{\max} < b^2$ and the diagonal elements of $\mathbf{L}_i - b\mathbf{L}_{i-1}$ are 0. Let

$$\mathbf{P} = \begin{pmatrix} \mathbf{A} \\ -\mathbf{I}_m \end{pmatrix} \cdot \begin{pmatrix} \mathbf{S} \otimes \mathbf{I}_n \\ & \mathbf{I}_{4n} \end{pmatrix} = \begin{pmatrix} \overline{\mathbf{L}} & \mathbf{D} \\ -\mathbf{S} \otimes \mathbf{I}_n \\ & -\mathbf{I}_{4n} \end{pmatrix},$$

then $\mathbf{P}$ contains m linearly independent vectors of $\Lambda^{\perp}(\mathbf{A}')$. A straightforward computation yields that

$$\|\mathbf{P}\|_{\mathrm{col}} \leq \max \left\{ b^2 \sqrt{n}, \sqrt{d - \frac{b^{2k} - 1}{b^2 - 1} + \|\mathbf{\Sigma}\|_{\max}} \right\},$$

which implies the conclusion immediately.   □

4.2   Eigenvalue Reduction

The parameter requirements of Corollary 1 are rather demanding. Indeed, the minimal d is at least $B + b^{2k-2} + k(n-1)b^2 > 2B\sqrt{k(n-1)}$, which results in costly overhead on the final Gaussian width, and therefore on all the parameters of the cryptosystem. Yet we claim that for some large B, say $\omega(n^4)$, one can overcome this issue with the help of some integral approximations of Cholesky decompositions. The case of large B is of interest in advanced lattice based schemes [1,8,20]. Note that by scaling, this constraint on B can even be removed if one accepts to include a few $(O(\log n))$ rational bits in the Gram decomposition.

This technique essentially can be summarized as a reduction from $\mathsf{IGDP}_{n,B,d,m}$ to $\mathsf{IGDP}_{n,B',d-B,m-n}$ in which $B' \ll B$. One first splits $d\mathbf{I}_n - \mathbf{\Sigma}$ into two parts: $\mathbf{\Sigma}' = B \cdot \mathbf{I}_n - \mathbf{\Sigma}$ and $(d - B) \cdot \mathbf{I}_n$. Exploiting an integral approximation of Cholesky decomposition, one decomposes $\mathbf{\Sigma}'$ as a Gram matrix $\mathbf{L}\mathbf{L}^t$ and a small matrix $\mathbf{\Sigma}''$. Then it suffices to decompose $(d - B)\mathbf{I}_n + \mathbf{\Sigma}''$, which implies the reduction. As $B' \ll B$, the overhead introduced by $\mathsf{IGDP}_{n,B',d-B,m-n}$ can be negligible compared with the original B. The formal description is illustrated in Algorithm 3, and an upper bound of B' is shown in Lemma 7.

Algorithm 3. Eigenvalue reduction $\mathsf{EigenRed}(\mathbf{\Sigma}, B)$

Input: a symmetric matrix $\mathbf{\Sigma} \in \mathbb{Z}^{n \times n}$ with $\|\mathbf{\Sigma}\|_2 \leq B$.
Output: $(\mathbf{L}, \mathbf{\Pi})$ where $\mathbf{L} \in \mathbb{Z}^{n \times n}$, $\mathbf{\Pi} \in \mathbb{Z}^{n \times n}$ is symmetric and
    $B \cdot \mathbf{I}_n - \mathbf{\Sigma} = \mathbf{L}\mathbf{L}^t - \mathbf{\Pi}$.
1: $\mathbf{L} \leftarrow \left\lfloor \widetilde{\mathbf{L}} \right\rceil$ where $\widetilde{\mathbf{L}}$ is the Cholesky Gram root of $B \cdot \mathbf{I}_n - \mathbf{\Sigma}$
2: $\mathbf{\Pi} \leftarrow \mathbf{L}\mathbf{L}^t - (B \cdot \mathbf{I}_n - \mathbf{\Sigma})$
3: return $(\mathbf{L}, \mathbf{\Pi})$

For better description, we define a function $F_n : \mathbb{N} \to \mathbb{N}$ specified by n as

$$F_n(x) = \left\lceil \sqrt{n(n+1)x} + \frac{n(n+1)}{8} \right\rceil.$$

Lemma 7. *Let $\boldsymbol{\Sigma} \in \mathbb{Z}^{n \times n}$ be a symmetric matrix and $B \geq \|\boldsymbol{\Sigma}\|_2$. Let $(\mathbf{L}, \boldsymbol{\Pi}) = \mathsf{EigenRed}(\boldsymbol{\Sigma}, B)$, then $\|\boldsymbol{\Pi}\|_2 \leq F_n(B)$.*

Proof. Let $\boldsymbol{\Delta} = \mathbf{L} - \widetilde{\mathbf{L}}$, then $\|\boldsymbol{\Delta}\|_{\max} \leq \frac{1}{2}$ and $\boldsymbol{\Delta}$ is lower triangular. We have $\|\boldsymbol{\Delta}\|_2 \leq \|\boldsymbol{\Delta}\|_F \leq \frac{1}{2} \cdot \sqrt{\frac{n(n+1)}{2}}$ and $\|\widetilde{\mathbf{L}}\|_2 \leq \sqrt{2B}$, then

$$\|\boldsymbol{\Pi}\|_2 = \|\boldsymbol{\Delta}\widetilde{\mathbf{L}}^t + \widetilde{\mathbf{L}}\boldsymbol{\Delta}^t + \boldsymbol{\Delta}\boldsymbol{\Delta}^t\|_2 \leq 2\|\widetilde{\mathbf{L}}\|_2\|\boldsymbol{\Delta}\|_2 + \|\boldsymbol{\Delta}\|_2^2 \leq F_n(B).$$

We complete the proof. □

Corollary 2. *Let $n, B, d, m \in \mathbb{N}$. There is a deterministic reduction from $\mathsf{IGDP}_{n,B,d,m}$ to $\mathsf{IGDP}_{n,F_n(B),d-B,m-n}$ whose cost is dominated by one call to Cholesky decomposition on some positive semi-definite matrix $\boldsymbol{\Sigma} \in \mathbb{Z}^{n \times n}$ with $\|\boldsymbol{\Sigma}\|_2 \leq 2B$.*

Remark 5. One may fear the re-introduction of Cholesky within our algorithm, however we argue that it is in this context much less of an issue:

- costly FPA computation may still be needed, but they are now confined to a one-time pre-computation, rather than a many-time off-line phase,
- the weak determinism of this FPA computation can be mitigated by running pre-computation as part of the trapdoor generation algorithm, and providing the pre-computed integral Gram decomposition as part of the secret key,
- the eigenvalue reduction algorithm can tolerate a rather crude approximation of Cholesky without leading to a hard to detect statistical leak. At worse, insufficient precision will simply fail to solve the IGDP instance at hand. That is, only completeness is at stake, not security, and one may tolerate rare failures.
- one may also completely avoid FPA by resorting to potentially less efficient though more convenient square root approximation algorithm. In particular, we note that the Taylor series of $\sqrt{1-x}$ involves only power-of-2 denominators: one can design a "strongly deterministic" algorithm.

4.3 Putting Them Together

So far, we have introduced two algorithmic tools for $\mathsf{IGDP}_{n,B,d,m}$: the integral decomposition for diagonally dominant matrices $\mathsf{DiagDomIGD}(\boldsymbol{\Sigma}, d, b, k)$ and the eigenvalue reduction $\mathsf{EigenRed}(\boldsymbol{\Sigma}, B)$. They can be combined as follows: one first applies the eigenvalue reduction iteratively and then decomposes the final left-over matrix. We summarize this as $\mathsf{IGD}(\boldsymbol{\Sigma}, d, B, t, b, k)$ in Algorithm 4, and prove its correctness in Lemma 8.

We follow the notation F_n given in Sect. 4.2, and also define its iterated function $F_n^{(i)} : \mathbb{N} \to \mathbb{N}$ for $i \in \mathbb{N}$ by: $F_n^{(0)}(x) = x$ and $F_n^{(i+1)}(x) = F_n\left(F_n^{(i)}(x)\right)$.

Algorithm 4. Integral matrix decomposition $\mathsf{IGD}(\boldsymbol{\Sigma}, d, B, t, b, k)$

Input: a symmetric matrix $\boldsymbol{\Sigma} \in \mathbb{Z}^{n \times n}$ with $\|\boldsymbol{\Sigma}\|_2 \leq B$,
     non-negative integers b, k, t such that $b^k \geq F_n^{(t)}(B) + k(n-1)b^2$,
     an integer d such that $d \geq \frac{b^{2k}-1}{b^2-1} + b^k + \sum_{i=0}^{t-1} F_n^{(i)}(B)$.

Output: $\mathbf{A} = \begin{pmatrix} \mathbf{A}_1 & \mathbf{A}_2 \end{pmatrix} \in \mathbb{Z}^{n \times (m_1 + m_2)}$ such that $\mathbf{A}\mathbf{A}^t = d\mathbf{I}_n - \boldsymbol{\Sigma}$ where
     $m_1 = nt$ and $m_2 = n(k+4)$,
     $\mathbf{A}_1 \in \mathbb{Z}^{n \times m_1}$ consists of t lower-triangular matrices,
     $\mathbf{A}_2 = \mathsf{DiagDomIGD}(\boldsymbol{\Pi}, d - \sum_{i=0}^{t-1} F_n^{(i)}(B), b, k) \in \mathbb{Z}^{n \times m_2}$ where $\|\boldsymbol{\Pi}\|_2 \leq F_n^{(t)}(B)$.
1: $\mathbf{A}_1 \leftarrow ()$ (an empty matrix $\in \mathbb{Z}^{n \times 0 \cdot n}$), $\boldsymbol{\Pi} \leftarrow \boldsymbol{\Sigma}$
2: **for** $i = 1, \cdots, t$ **do**
3:      $(\mathbf{L}, \boldsymbol{\Pi}) \leftarrow \mathsf{EigenRed}(\boldsymbol{\Pi}, F_n^{(i-1)}(B))$
4:      $\mathbf{A}_1 \leftarrow \begin{pmatrix} \mathbf{A}_1 & \mathbf{L} \end{pmatrix}$
5: **end for**
6: $\mathbf{A}_2 \leftarrow \mathsf{DiagDomIGD}(\boldsymbol{\Pi}, d - \sum_{i=0}^{t-1} F_n^{(i)}(B), b, k) \in \mathbb{Z}^{n \times m_2}$
7: **return** $\begin{pmatrix} \mathbf{A}_1 & \mathbf{A}_2 \end{pmatrix}$

Lemma 8. *Algorithm 4 is correct. More precisely, let $\boldsymbol{\Sigma} \in \mathbb{Z}^{n \times n}$ be symmetric and $d, B, t, b, k \in \mathbb{N}$ such that $\|\boldsymbol{\Sigma}\|_2 \leq B$, $b^k \geq F_n^{(t)}(B) + k(n-1)b^2$ and $d \geq \frac{b^{2k}-1}{b^2-1} + b^k + \sum_{i=0}^{t-1} F_n^{(i)}(B)$. Then $\mathsf{IGD}(\boldsymbol{\Sigma}, d, B, t, b, k)$ outputs $\mathbf{A} \in \mathbb{Z}^{n \times m}$ such that $\mathbf{A}\mathbf{A}^t = d\mathbf{I}_n - \boldsymbol{\Sigma}$ and $m = n(t + k + 4)$.*

Remark 6. In practice, the calculation of the Gram root $\mathbf{A}$ can be accomplished during the key generation and needs to run only once. Therefore, we do not take into account the complexity of $\mathsf{IGD}(\boldsymbol{\Sigma}, d, B, t, b, k)$.

Proof. It can be verified that

$$\mathbf{A}_1 \mathbf{A}_1^t = \left(\sum_{i=0}^{t-1} F_n^{(i)}(B) \right) \cdot \mathbf{I}_n - \boldsymbol{\Sigma} + \boldsymbol{\Pi}$$

and

$$\mathbf{A}_2 \mathbf{A}_2^t = \left(d - \sum_{i=0}^{t-1} F_n^{(i)}(B) \right) \cdot \mathbf{I}_n - \boldsymbol{\Pi},$$

hence $\mathbf{A}\mathbf{A}^t = d\mathbf{I}_n - \boldsymbol{\Sigma}$. According to Lemmata 5 and 7, all conditions required by the calls of $\mathsf{EigenRed}(\boldsymbol{\Pi}, F_n^{(i-1)}(B))$ and $\mathsf{DiagDomIGD}(\boldsymbol{\Pi}, d - \sum_{i=0}^{t-1} F_n^{(i)}(B), b, k)$ are satisfied. Therefore, Algorithm 4 is correct. $\qquad\square$

Now we give an upper bound of $\lambda_{m-n}(\Lambda^\perp(\mathbf{A}))$ in Lemma 9. Similar to Lemma 6, we also pad the Gram root $\mathbf{A}$ with $\mathbf{I}_n$.

Lemma 9. *Let* $\mathbf{A} = \mathsf{IGD}(\Sigma, d-1, B, t, b, k) \in \mathbb{Z}^{n \times m}$ *where* $m = n(t+k+4)$. *Let* $\mathbf{A}' = \begin{pmatrix} \mathbf{I}_n & \mathbf{A} \end{pmatrix}$, *then* $\mathbf{A}' \cdot \mathbb{Z}^{n+m} = \mathbb{Z}^n$, *the dimension of* $\Lambda^\perp(\mathbf{A}')$ *is* m, *and*

$$\lambda_m(\Lambda^\perp(\mathbf{A}')) \leq \max\left\{ b^2\sqrt{n}, \sqrt{d + F_n^{(t)}(B) - \frac{b^{2k}-1}{b^2-1} - \sum_{i=0}^{t-1} F_n^{(i)}(B)}, \max_{0 \leq i < t} \sqrt{2F_n^{(i)}(B)} + n \right\}.$$

Proof. Let $\mathbf{A} = \begin{pmatrix} \mathbf{A}_1 & \mathbf{A}_2 \end{pmatrix}$ where $\mathbf{A}_1 \in \mathbb{Z}^{n \times m_1}$ with $m_1 = nt$ and $\mathbf{A}_2 \in \mathbb{Z}^{n \times m_2}$ with $m_2 = n(k+4)$. Let $\mathbf{A}_1' = \begin{pmatrix} \mathbf{I}_n & \mathbf{A}_1 \end{pmatrix}$ and $\mathbf{A}_2' = \begin{pmatrix} \mathbf{I}_n & \mathbf{A}_2 \end{pmatrix}$, then

$$\lambda_m(\Lambda^\perp(\mathbf{A}')) \leq \max\{\lambda_{m_1}(\Lambda^\perp(\mathbf{A}_1')), \lambda_{m_2}(\Lambda^\perp(\mathbf{A}_2'))\}.$$

The matrix $\mathbf{A}_1$ consists of t lower-triangular matrices, denoted by $\mathbf{L}_1, \cdots, \mathbf{L}_t$, such that $\mathbf{L}_i = \left\lfloor \widetilde{\mathbf{L}_i} \right\rceil$ and $\|\widetilde{\mathbf{L}_i}\|_{\mathrm{col}} \leq \|\widetilde{\mathbf{L}_i}\|_2 \leq \sqrt{2F_n^{(i-1)}(B)}$ by Lemma 7. It follows that $\|\mathbf{L}_i\|_{\mathrm{col}} \leq \|\widetilde{\mathbf{L}_i}\|_{\mathrm{col}} + \frac{\sqrt{n}}{2} \leq \sqrt{2F_n^{(i-1)}(B)} + \frac{\sqrt{n}}{2}$, and then we have

$$\lambda_{m_1}(\Lambda^\perp(\mathbf{A}_1')) \leq \max_{1 \leq i \leq t} \sqrt{\|\mathbf{L}_i\|_{\mathrm{col}}^2 + 1} \leq \max_{0 \leq i < t} \sqrt{2F_n^{(i)}(B)} + n.$$

As for $\lambda_{m_2}(\Lambda^\perp(\mathbf{A}_2'))$, combining Lemmata 6 and 7 leads to that

$$\lambda_{m_2}(\Lambda^\perp(\mathbf{A}_2')) \leq \max\left\{ b^2\sqrt{n}, \sqrt{d + F_n^{(t)}(B) - \frac{b^{2k}-1}{b^2-1} - \sum_{i=0}^{t-1} F_n^{(i)}(B)} \right\}.$$

The proof is completed. □

As the parameters n and B have been determined before the key generation, one can first choose suitable (t, b, k) and then proceed to minimize d satisfying the requirements of Algorithm 4. We next discuss concrete parameter selections according to the size of B.

Case 1: $B = \omega(n^6)$. In this case, we insist on a common gadget setting: $b = 2$. One can first fix $(t, b) = (2, 2)$ and then choose $k = 1 + \lceil \frac{3}{2}\log(n+1) + \frac{1}{4}\log B \rceil$. The minimal d is bounded by $B + 2(n+1)^3\sqrt{B} = (1 + o(1))B$.

Under this setting, the final integral Gram root $\mathbf{A}' = \begin{pmatrix} \mathbf{I}_n & \mathbf{A} \end{pmatrix}$ is of size $n \times (n+m)$ with $m = n(k+6)$, and $\lambda_m(\Lambda^\perp(\mathbf{A}')) \leq \sqrt{2B} + n$ for $d \leq 3B$.

Case 2: $B = \omega(n^4)$. We now insist on minimizing the total size of the output $\mathbf{A}$. To this end, one first sets $(t, k) = (1, 3)$ and then selects $b = \left\lceil 3n + \sqrt{2}n^{\frac{1}{3}}B^{\frac{1}{6}} \right\rceil$. The minimal d is bounded by $B + 2b^4 = (1 + o(1))B$.

Under this setting, the final integral Gram root $\mathbf{A}' = \begin{pmatrix} \mathbf{I}_n & \mathbf{A} \end{pmatrix}$ is of size $n \times (n+m)$ with $m = 8n$, and $\lambda_m(\Lambda^\perp(\mathbf{A}')) \leq \max\{\sqrt{2B} + n, b^2\sqrt{n} = O(n^{\frac{7}{6}}B^{\frac{1}{3}})\}$ for $d \leq 3B$.

Case 3: $B = O(n^4)$. In some scenarios, B can be relatively small, say $\widetilde{O}(n)$ [4,25], so that the current algorithm does not work directly. But we can still compute an *almost integral* Gram root of $d\mathbf{I}_n - \mathbf{\Sigma}$. By *almost integral*, we mean that we resort to rationals of the form $i/2^\nu$, with only a few rational bits $\nu = O(\log n)$.

The trick is rather simple: by scaling both d and B by a factor of $2^{2\nu}$, one can reduce the case of small B to the case of a large one. This technique indeed applies for any B and $d > B + 1$, when the scaling factor is sufficiently large.

As an example, we choose arbitrary $\nu \in \mathbb{Z}$ such that $2^{2\nu}B = \omega(n^4)$. As shown in Case 2, selecting $(t, k, b) = \left(1, 3, \left\lceil 3n + \sqrt{2}n^{\frac{1}{3}}(2^{2\nu}B)^{\frac{1}{6}} \right\rceil\right)$ allows an almost integral decomposition, and the minimal d is bounded by $B + 2b^4 \cdot 2^{-2\nu} = (1 + o(1))B$.

Under this setting, the final integral Gram root $\mathbf{A}' = 2^{-\nu} \cdot \left(\mathbf{I}_n\ \mathbf{A}\right)$ is of size $n \times (n + m)$ with $m = 8n$. A minor modification to apply Theorem 3 is that one should consider $\lambda_m(\Lambda^\perp(2^\nu \cdot \mathbf{A}'))$ to fulfil Lemma 3. This can be done similarly: $\lambda_m(\Lambda^\perp(2^\nu \cdot \mathbf{A}')) \leq \max\{2^\nu\sqrt{2B} + n, b^2\sqrt{n} = O(2^{\frac{2}{3}\nu}n^{\frac{7}{6}}B^{\frac{1}{3}})\}$ for $d \leq 3B$.

We compare above parameter selections according to some values including: (1) $\overline{m} = m + n$, determining the size of the Gram root; (2) L, an upper bound of $\lambda_m(\Lambda^\perp(\mathbf{A}'))$ dominating L' in Theorem 3; and (3) d_{min}, the minimum of d proportional to the minimal final width. We summarize three cases in Table 1.

Table 1. Parameter selections of the integral Gram decomposition. In the first two cases, the final Gram root $\mathbf{A}'$ is integral of size $n \times \overline{m}$. In the third one, the final Gram root is $2^{-\nu}\mathbf{A}'$ where $\mathbf{A}' \in \mathbb{Z}^{n \times \overline{m}}$ and $\nu = 2\log n - \frac{1}{2}\log B + \omega(1)$ is an integer.

	$\overline{m} = m + n$	L	d_{min}
Gadget base $b = 2$: $B = \omega(n^6)$	$O(n \log B)$	$O\left(\sqrt{B}\right)$	$(1 + o(1))B$
Large gadget base: $B = \omega(n^4)$	$9n$	$O\left(\sqrt{B} + n^{\frac{7}{6}}B^{\frac{1}{3}}\right)$	$(1 + o(1))B$
Almost integral: $B = O(n^4)$	$9n$	$O\left(2^\nu\sqrt{B} + 2^{\frac{2}{3}\nu}n^{\frac{7}{6}}B^{\frac{1}{3}}\right)$	$(1 + o(1))B$

5   Comparisons with Peikert's Perturbation Sampler

Throughout this section, $\mathbf{\Sigma} \in \mathbb{Z}^{n \times n}$ is a positive semi-definite matrix, and $s = rs'$ is the final Gaussian width where r is the base sampling parameter and $s'^2 \in \mathbb{Z}$ such that $s'^2 \geq e_1(\mathbf{\Sigma}) + 1$. The covariance of perturbation vectors is $r^2(s'^2\mathbf{I}_n - \mathbf{\Sigma})$. The later discussions specialize to $e_1(\mathbf{\Sigma}) = \omega(n^6)$, which can occur in advanced cryptosystems, e.g. hierarchical IBE [1,8] and ABE [20].[5]

---

[5] When $e_1(\mathbf{\Sigma})$ is small, one can resort to the almost integral Gram root in Sect. 4.3.

Applying the integral matrix decomposition from Sect. 4 along with Theorem 3, we devise a variant of Peikert's perturbation sampling algorithm. This variant requires no floating-point arithmetic, and the intermediate matrix is integral. The centers of the base Gaussian samplings are integers scaled by a common factor L', which is easier to deal with. Moreover, our approach only enlarges the final width by a factor of $1 + o(1)$.

We next compare our sampler with Peikert's one [32] from the following aspects: the storage of the Gram root (Sect. 5.1), required base samplings (Sect. 5.2) and the quality of final Gaussians (Sect. 5.3). Additionally, we discuss the applications within the Micciancio-Peikert trapdoor framework [25] in Sect. 5.4, and show that exploiting the trapdoor, one can significantly reduce the size of the matrix to be decomposed.

5.1   Required Storage

For Peikert's sampler, we follow the suggested setting where the precomputation is a standard (real) Cholesky Gram root of $\sqrt{(s'^2 - 1)\mathbf{I}_n - \mathbf{\Sigma}}$. It requires $\frac{n(n+1)}{2}(\log s' + \lambda)$ bits of storage, where λ is a security parameter that is usually set to $O(n)$.

In our sampler, the intermediate matrix is $\mathbf{A} = \begin{pmatrix} \mathbf{I}_n \ \mathbf{A}_1 \ \mathbf{A}_2 \end{pmatrix} \in \mathbb{Z}^{n+m}$ where $\begin{pmatrix} \mathbf{A}_1 \ \mathbf{A}_2 \end{pmatrix} = \mathsf{IGD}(\mathbf{\Sigma}, s'^2 - 2, B, t, b, k) \in \mathbb{Z}^{n \times m}$ and $m = n(t + k + 4)$. The sub-matrix $\mathbf{A}_1$ consists of t lower-triangular matrices, and its storage is about $\frac{n(n+1)}{2}\left(\sum_{i=0}^{t-1} \log \sqrt{F_n^{(i)}(B)}\right)$ bits. The parameter t can be very small, say $t = 1, 2$ (see Sect. 4.3), and $\{F_n^{(i)}(B)\}_i$ decreases very fast at the beginning for large B. Therefore, the actual storage of $\mathbf{A}_1$ is well bounded. As for $\mathbf{A}_2$, while it is even wider, namely $n \times n(k + 4)$, its regular structure allows an efficient storage. More precisely, treating (b, k) as global variables, it suffices to store off-diagonal entries that are in $(-b, b)$ in the first k blocks and diagonal ones in the rest blocks (see Algorithm 2). Thus the storage of $\mathbf{A}_2$ is bounded by $\frac{n(n-1)}{2}k \log b + 2n \log(s')$, which is about $\frac{n(n-1)}{2} \log(F_n^{(t)}(B)) + 2n \log(s')$ when $b^k = O(F_n^{(t)}(B))$.

We summarize in Table 2 the storage comparison. Despite the integral Gram root $\mathbf{A}$ being wider, it can achieve asymptotically better storage efficiency than the FPA solution. In fact, the storage is still an advantage even we apply the almost integral decomposition in Sect. 4.3 to deal with small $e_1(\mathbf{\Sigma})$.

5.2   Base Samplings

To generate an integral perturbation, one first samples from a Gaussian of covariance $r^2((s'^2 - 1)\mathbf{I}_n - \mathbf{\Sigma})$. In Peikert's sampler, this is accomplished by continuous Gaussian sampling with high precision, which is expensive. In our sampler, this is accomplished by sampling from $D_{\mathbb{Z}^{n+m}, L'r}$ and then multiplying a scaled integral Gram root, i.e. $\frac{1}{L'}\mathbf{A}$.

Table 2. The storage comparison. The concrete parameter selections of $t = 1, 2$ are discussed in Sect. 4.3.

	Storage of Gram root
Peikert's sampler	$\approx \frac{n^2}{2}(\log s' + \lambda)$ where λ is the security parameter
Ours	$\approx \frac{n^2}{4}\left(\sum_{i=0}^{t} \log(F_n^{(i)}(s'^2)) + \log(F_n^{(t)}(s'^2))\right)$
Ours with $t = 1$	$\approx n^2(\log s' + \frac{1}{2}\log n)$
Ours with $t = 2$	$\approx n^2(\log s' + \log n)$

There are also some non-centered samplings. Peikert's algorithm requires to sample from $D_{\mathbb{Z},r,c}$ with a floating-point center. In our sampler, all Gaussian centers are in $\frac{1}{L'} \cdot \mathbb{Z}$ with some $L' \geq \lambda_m(\Lambda^\perp(\mathbf{A}))$.

We exhibit the comparison on the base samplings in Table 3. As shown in Sect. 4.3, we may choose some $L' = O(s' + n^{\frac{7}{6}}s'^{\frac{2}{3}})$. When the padding trick is used (see Sect. 3.1), L' can be even smaller, namely $O\left(\sqrt{n \log s'}\right)$. In concrete implementations, we would suggest to set L' to be a power-of-2 so that with a minor modification, all samplings can be done by only two base samplers $D_{\mathbb{Z},r}$ and $D_{\mathbb{Z},r,1/2}$ as in [28]. Therefore, the base samplings required by us are easier to implement than that by Peikert. While our sampler requires more centered samples, $(n + m)$ is $O(n \log s')$ even $O(n)$, which does not increase the base sample number too much.

Table 3. The base sampling comparison. Here $D_{\mathbb{R},r}$ denotes the continuous Gaussian over $\mathbb{R}$ of width r. In our sampler, the Gram root $\mathbf{A} \in \mathbb{Z}^{n \times (n+m)}$. If no padding, $m = O(n)$ (say $8n$) and $L' = O(s' + n^{\frac{7}{6}}s'^{\frac{2}{3}}) \geq \lambda_m(\Lambda^\perp(\mathbf{A}))$. If padding is used, $m = O(n \log s')$ and $L' = O(\sqrt{n \log s'})$.

	Centered samplings	Non-centered samplings
Peikert's sampler	$D_{\mathbb{R},r}$	$D_{\mathbb{Z},r,c}$ with $c \in \mathbb{R}$
	n times	n times
Ours	$D_{\mathbb{Z},L'r}$	$D_{\mathbb{Z},r,c}$ with $c \in \frac{1}{L'} \cdot \mathbb{Z}$
	$O(n)$ times	n times
Ours with padding	$D_{\mathbb{Z},L'r}$	$D_{\mathbb{Z},r,c}$ with $c \in \frac{1}{L'} \cdot \mathbb{Z}$
(Sect. 3.1)	$O(n \log s')$ times	n times

5.3   The Quality of Final Gaussians

In Peikert's sampler, $r \geq \eta_\epsilon(\mathbb{Z}^n)$ and $s'^2 \geq e_1(\Sigma) + 1$ so that the minimal s is $\eta_\epsilon(\mathbb{Z}^n)\sqrt{e_1(\Sigma) + 1}$. Our sampler also applies to any $r \geq \eta_\epsilon(\mathbb{Z}^n)$ according to Theorem 3. As for s', its minimum is $(1 + o(1))\sqrt{e_1(\Sigma)}$ (see Sect. 4.3). Thus the minimal s achieved by us is $(1 + o(1)) \cdot \eta_\epsilon(\mathbb{Z}^n)\sqrt{e_1(\Sigma)}$. As a conclusion, our sampler only leads to a very small loss in the quality of final Gaussians.

5.4 The Case of the Micciancio-Peikert Trapdoor

In [25], Micciancio and Peikert propose a celebrated trapdoor framework which has been the basis of various primitives [4,12,20]. In this framework, the matrix $\Sigma = \begin{pmatrix} \mathbf{T} \\ \mathbf{I} \end{pmatrix} (\mathbf{T}^t \ \mathbf{I})$ where $\mathbf{T} \in \mathbb{Z}^{n_1 \times n_2}$ is the trapdoor with $n_1 \ll n_1 + n_2$. The Gaussian sampling is performed by an entity that knows the trapdoor $\mathbf{T}$.

We now explain how to use the trapdoor to reduce the input size at the beginning of the matrix decomposition of $\Sigma' = d\mathbf{I}_n - \Sigma$ (a similar idea is used in [17]). More precisely, notice that

$$\Sigma' = d\mathbf{I}_n - \Sigma = \begin{pmatrix} d\mathbf{I}_{n_1} - 2\mathbf{T}\mathbf{T}^t \\ & (d-2)\mathbf{I}_{n_2} \end{pmatrix} + \begin{pmatrix} \mathbf{T} \\ -\mathbf{I} \end{pmatrix} (\mathbf{T}^t \ -\mathbf{I}).$$

Hence, it suffices to decompose $\Sigma'_{new} = d\mathbf{I}_{n_1} - 2\mathbf{T}\mathbf{T}^t$ whose dimension is n_1, which is much less than $n = n_1 + n_2$.[6] This trick needs neither extra computation nor storage, and only enlarges the maximal elements in $\Sigma_{new} (= 2\mathbf{T}\mathbf{T}^t)$ by a factor of 2. Therefore we suggest to use this trick as the preprocessing of the integral decomposition in the Micciancio-Peikert trapdoor framework.[7]

6 The Ring Setting

Many lattice cryptosystems use polynomial rings. In this setting, vectors and matrices consist of ring elements, which improves storage and running time. Some previous works [15,17,25,32] provide ring-efficient Gaussian sampling in which intermediate matrices preserve the ring structure, but require high-precision FPA. One the other hand, the generic techniques in Sect. 4 avoid high-precision FPA but require to take $\mathbb{Z}$ as a base ring, therefore not benefiting from efficiency gains that are typically expected in the ring setting.

The goal of this section is to get *the best of both worlds*: being ring-efficient and avoiding high-precision FPA. We realize that by proposing an integral decomposition algorithm for the ring setting. By Theorem 3, this will imply a Gaussian sampler that is both ring-efficient and FPA-free. To this end, we first formally define the *Integral Gram Decomposition Problem over the ring $\mathcal{R}$*.

Definition 4 (IGDP$_{\mathcal{R},n,B,d,m}$). *Let $\mathcal{R} = \mathbb{Z}[x]/\Phi(x)$ where $\Phi(x) \in \mathbb{Z}[x]$ and $n, B, d, m \in \mathbb{N}$. The Integral Gram Decomposition Problem over $\mathcal{R}$, denoted by IGDP$_{\mathcal{R},n,B,d,m}$, is defined as follows: given an integral symmetric matrix $\Sigma \in \mathcal{R}^{n \times n}$ with $\|\Sigma\|_2 \leq B$, find an integral matrix $\mathbf{A} \in \mathcal{R}^{n \times m}$ such that $\mathbf{A}\mathbf{A}^t = d\mathbf{I}_n - \Sigma$.*

Clearly, IGDP$_{\mathcal{R},n,B,d,m}$ is a natural generalization of the IGDP problem which introduces a new parameter: the ring $\mathcal{R}$. The initial definition of IGDP$_{n,B,d,m}$ (Definition 3) corresponds to the case $\mathcal{R} = \mathbb{Z}$. For simplicity we only discuss

---

[6] The other block can be addressed by 4-square decomposition directly.

[7] Note that this requires some new analysis of smoothness conditions.

power-of-2 cyclotomic rings, i.e. $\mathcal{R}_{2w} = \mathbb{Z}[x]/(x^w + 1)$ with $w = 2^\ell$. Similarly to [15], the results can be extended to more general cyclotomic rings and convolution rings with smooth conductors. Why do we care about solving $\mathsf{IGDP}_{\mathcal{R},n,B,d,m}$ for trapdoor sampling? Indeed, a naive and functional approach is to embed Σ in $\mathbb{Z}^{wn \times wn}$ via the coefficient embedding, then solve $\mathsf{IGDP}_{\mathbb{Z},wn,B,d',m'}$ as in Sect. 4. However, that would break the ring structure and cancel the main advantage of rings: efficiency. Therefore our goal is to directly solve $\mathsf{IGDP}_{\mathcal{R},n,B,d,m}$; if $m' = m \cdot \tilde{\omega}(w)$, this improves the storage and running time (via the number theoretic transform) of lattice Gaussian sampling by a factor $\tilde{O}(w)$ compared to the naive approach.

Technical roadmap. We first recall some preliminaries on cyclotomic rings (Sect. 6.1). Next, we propose a solution for the special case $\mathsf{IGDP}_{\mathcal{R}_{2w},1,B,d,m}$; this particular case is also a generalization of the 4-square decomposition, for self-adjoint ring elements instead of natural numbers. Our solution relies on a technique called *ring gadgets* to reduce $\mathsf{IGDP}_{\mathcal{R}_{2w},1,B,d,m}$ to $\mathsf{IGDP}_{\mathcal{R}_w,1,B',d',m'}$. Naturally, a repeated application of ring gadgets allows to project the initial problem onto $\mathbb{Z}$ eventually, which is then solved by 4-square decomposition.

Once we know how to decompose a single polynomial, a general solution to $\mathsf{IGDP}_{\mathcal{R}_{2w},n,B,d,m}$ is easily derived by adapting Algorithm 2 to the ring setting (Sect. 6.3). Compared with the generic solution (Sect. 4), the ring-based integral decomposition reduces storage by a factor $O(w)$ and running time by a factor $\tilde{O}(w)$, at the cost of increasing the number of columns of the integral Gram root by $O(\log w)$. This leads to a simple ring-based sampler achieving the same efficiency as the state of the art [17] (Sect. 6.4).

Comparison with the generic technique. Algorithms in Sect. 4 and in this section operate on the same central idea: to recursively project the initial problem into smaller dimensions. The only conceptual difference is how this projection is done; as we now impose an additional constraint, i.e. preserving the ring structure, projection requires to use ring gadgets in addition to matrix decomposition. In addition, these algorithms treat the eigenvalue reduction and the bottom case differently. We summarize used techniques as Table 4.

Table 4. Different techniques in integral decompositions.

	Section 4 $\mathsf{IGDP}_{n,B,d,m}$	Section 6.2 $\mathsf{IGDP}_{\mathcal{R}_{2w},1,B,d,m}$	Section 6.3 $\mathsf{IGDP}_{\mathcal{R}_{2w},n,B,d,m}$
Eigenvalue reduction	Cholesky	–	Structured Cholesky
Projection	Integer gadget	Ring gadget	Integer gadget
Bottom case	4-square	4-square	$\mathsf{IGDP}_{\mathcal{R}_{2w},1,B,d,m}$

6.1 Preliminaries on Cyclotomic Rings

Let $w \in \mathbb{N}$ and $\Phi_w(x) \in \mathbb{Z}[x]$ be the w-th cyclotomic polynomial. The w-th *cyclotomic ring* is $\mathcal{R}_w = \mathbb{Z}[x]/(\Phi_w(x))$ and the w-th *cyclotomic field* is $\mathbb{K}_w = \mathbb{Q}[x]/(\Phi_w(x))$. In this paper, we only discuss the case of power-of-2 cyclotomic rings where $w = 2^\ell$ and $\Phi_{2w}(x) = x^w + 1$. For such kind of rings, we have the following *tower of rings*:

$$\mathcal{R}_{2w} \supseteq \mathcal{R}_w \supseteq \cdots \supseteq \mathcal{R}_2 = \mathbb{Z}. \tag{1}$$

Adjoints. Let $\Phi \in \mathbb{R}[x]$ be monic with distinct roots over $\mathbb{C}$, and $f, g \in \mathbb{R}[x]/(\Phi(x))$. We denote by $f^\star$ the (Hermitian) adjoint of f, that is, the unique element of $\mathbb{R}[x]/(\Phi(x))$ such that $f^\star(\xi) = \overline{f(\xi)}$ for any root ξ of Φ. This generalizes the complex conjugation of real numbers. We say that f is *self-adjoint* if $f = f^\star$. It is easy to verify that $ff^\star$ is self-adjoint and all self-adjoint elements form a ring. When Φ is a cyclotomic polynomial, it holds that $f^\star(x) = f(x^{-1})$.

Norms and gadgets. For $f = \sum_{i=0}^{w-1} f_i x^i \in \mathbb{K}_{2w}$, let $\|f\| = \sqrt{\sum_{i=0}^{w-1} |f_i|^2}$ be its ℓ_2-*norm*, and $\|f\|_\infty = \max_i |f_i|$ be its ℓ_∞-*norm*. For $\mathbf{f} = (f_0, \cdots, f_{n-1})^t$ and $\mathbf{g} = (g_0, \cdots, g_{n-1})^t$ in $\mathbb{K}_{2w}^n$, let $\|\mathbf{f}\| = \sqrt{\sum_{i=0}^{n-1} \|f_i\|^2}$, $\|\mathbf{f}\|_\infty = \max_i \|f_i\|_\infty$ and $\langle \mathbf{f}, \mathbf{g} \rangle = \sum_i f_i g_i^\star \in \mathbb{K}_{2w}$. For $\mathbf{\Sigma} \in \mathbb{K}_{2w}^{n \times n}$, let $\|\mathbf{\Sigma}\|_2 = \max_{\mathbf{x} \neq \mathbf{0}} \frac{\|\mathbf{\Sigma}\mathbf{x}\|}{\|\mathbf{x}\|}$ and $\|\mathbf{\Sigma}\|_{\max} = \max_{i,j} \|\mathbf{\Sigma}_{i,j}\|_\infty$. Moreover, the gadget decomposition generalizes naturally: given the gadget vector $\mathbf{g} = (1, b, \cdots, b^{k-1})^t \in \mathcal{R}_{2w}^k$, for any $f \in \mathcal{R}_{2w}$ with $\|f\|_\infty < b^k$, there exists $\mathbf{c} \in \mathcal{R}_{2w}^k$ such that $\langle \mathbf{c}, \mathbf{g} \rangle = f$ and $\|\mathbf{c}\|_\infty < b$, and it can be efficiently computed.

Even and odd polynomials. Each $f \in \mathcal{R}_{2w}$ can be uniquely written as:

$$f(x) = f_e(x^2) + x f_o(x^2),$$

where f_e, f_o are elements of the subring $\mathcal{R}_w \subset \mathcal{R}_{2w}$. We say that f_e (resp. f_o) is the even (resp. odd) part of f, and indeed it consists of the even-index (resp. odd-index) coefficients of f, respectively. We also say that a polynomial is even (resp. odd) if its odd (resp. even) part is zero. Any even polynomial of $\mathbb{Z}[x]/(x^w + 1)$ can be seen as an element of $\mathbb{Z}[y]/(y^{w/2} + 1)$ by the ring morphism $y \to x^2$.

Ring gadgets. A key technical component of our algorithms in the ring setting consists of projecting a self-adjoint polynomial $f \in \mathcal{R}_{2w}$ onto the subring $\mathcal{R}_w$. More precisely, we exhibit a polynomial $a \in \mathcal{R}_{2w}$ such that $aa^\star + f$ is even (hence is in the subring $\mathcal{R}_w$) and self-adjoint. Let us write $f = f_e(x^2) + x f_o(x^2)$; since f is self-adjoint, it holds that $f_i = -f_{w-i}$ for each coefficient f_i of f, and we can therefore write $xf_o(x^2) = x\bar{f}_o(x^2) + (x\bar{f}_o(x^2))^*$ for some polynomial $\bar{f}_o \in \mathcal{R}_w$ with only its lower-half coefficients nonzero. Taking $a = 1 - x\bar{f}_o(x^2)$, we have:

$$f + aa^* = f_e(x^2) + x\bar{f}_o(x^2) + (x\bar{f}_o(x^2))^* + (1 - x\bar{f}_o(x^2))(1 - x\bar{f}_o(x^2))^*$$
$$= f_e(x^2) + \bar{f}_o(x^2)(\bar{f}_o(x^2))^* + 1$$

All the odd terms have been eliminated, and $f + aa^*$ is isomorphic to an element of $\mathcal{R}_w$. As an example, let us consider the following self-adjoint element of $\mathcal{R}_{16}$:

$$f = 32 - 8x + 2x^2 - 9x^3 + 9x^5 - 2x^6 + 8x^7,$$
$$f = (32 + 2x^2 - 2x^6) + x(-8 - 9x^2) + (x(-8 - 9x^2))^*.$$

Then we will take: $a = 1 - x\bar{f}_o(x^2) = 1 + 8x + 9x^3$. One can check that:

$$f + aa^* = -74x^6 + 74x^2 + 178,$$

which is indeed in the subring $\mathcal{R}_8$. This projection is compatible with the use of gadget matrices; more precisely, we can first decompose a polynomial using gadget decomposition, and then apply the projection to each element of the decomposition. Finally we have $f + \sum_{i=1}^{k} a_i a_i^*$ is even, where $a_i = b^{i-1} + xc_i(x^2)$ and $\sum_{i=1}^{k} b^{i-1}c_i = -\bar{f}_o$. We will refer to these combined decomposition and projection as *ring gadgets*.

6.2   Decomposition for Ring Elements

We proceed to generalize 4-square decomposition to the ring setting. Precisely, our goal is to represent one integral self-adjoint ring element $f \in \mathcal{R}_{2w}$ as $\langle \mathbf{a}, \mathbf{a} \rangle$ where $\mathbf{a} \in \mathcal{R}_{2w}^m$ is an integral polynomial vector. Equivalently, we seek to solve the special case $\mathsf{IGDP}_{\mathcal{R}_{2w},1,B,d,m}$.

Our solution is build upon the use of *ring gadgets*, defined at the end of Sect. 6.1. As previously illustrated, a single application of a ring gadget can be viewed as the reduction $\mathsf{IGDP}_{\mathcal{R}_{2w},1,B,d,m} \to \mathsf{IGDP}_{\mathcal{R}_w,1,B',d',m'}$. Hence, we have projected our problem onto a subring.

We can go further. As recalled in (1), the $\mathcal{R}_i$'s are arranged in a tower of rings structure, thus we can repeatedly apply ring gadgets to project $\mathsf{IGDP}_{\mathcal{R},1,B,d,m}$ onto a subring, until it is projected in $\mathcal{R}_4$. We note that the set of all self-adjoint elements of $\mathcal{R}_4$ is exactly $\mathbb{Z}$ and thus $\mathsf{IGDP}_{\mathcal{R}_4,1,B,B,4}$ is easily solved via the Rabin-Shallit algorithm. We have this chain of reductions:

$$\mathsf{IGDP}_{\mathcal{R}_{2w},1,B,d,m} \to \mathsf{IGDP}_{\mathcal{R}_w,1,B',d',m'} \to \cdots \to \mathsf{IGDP}_{\mathcal{R}_4,1,B'',d'',m''}$$

We formally describe the procedure in Algorithm 5.

Lemma 10 shows the correctness and the complexity analysis of Algorithm 5.

Algorithm 5. Decomposition of a single ring element $\mathsf{REIGD}(d, f, b, k)$

Input: a self-adjoint $f \in \mathcal{R}_{2w}$ with $w = 2^\ell \geq 2$,
  two integers $b, k \geq 2$ such that $b^k \geq \|f\|_\infty + kwb^2$,
  an integer d such that $d \geq \frac{b^{2k}-1}{b^2-1}(\ell - 1) + b^k$.

Output: $\mathbf{a} = \begin{pmatrix} a_1 \cdots a_{k(\ell-1)} & x_1 \ x_2 \ x_3 \ x_4 \end{pmatrix} \in \mathcal{R}_{2w}^{k(\ell-1)+4}$ such that $\langle \mathbf{a}, \mathbf{a} \rangle = d - f$,
  where $x_1, x_2, x_3, x_4 \in \mathbb{Z}$ and $a_{1+jk+i} = b^i + a'_{i,j}\left(x^{2^{\ell-2-j}}\right)$ with $a'_{i,j} \in \mathcal{R}_{2^{j+2}}$
  for any $0 \leq i < k$ and $0 \leq j < \ell - 1$.

1: $\mathbf{g} \leftarrow (1, b, \cdots, b^{k-1})^t$
2: **if** $w = 2$ **then**
3:     calculate $\mathbf{x} = (x_1, x_2, x_3, x_4)^t \in \mathbb{Z}^4$ such that $\|\mathbf{x}\|^2 = d - f$ using the
    Rabin-Shallit algorithm (Theorem 2)
4:     **return** $\mathbf{x}$
5: **end if**
6: calculate $\begin{pmatrix} a_1 \cdots a_k \end{pmatrix} \in \mathcal{R}_{2w}^k$ by using ring gadgets such that $f + \sum_i a_i a_i^\star$ is even
7: let $f' \in \mathcal{R}_w$ such that $f'(x^2) = f - \frac{b^{2k}-1}{b^2-1} + \sum_i a_i a_i^\star$
8: $\mathbf{a}' = \begin{pmatrix} a'_1 \cdots a'_{k(\ell-2)} & x_1 \ x_2 \ x_3 \ x_4 \end{pmatrix} \leftarrow \mathsf{REIGD}\left(d - \frac{b^{2k}-1}{b^2-1}, f', b, k\right)$
9: **return** $\mathbf{a} = \begin{pmatrix} a'_1(x^2) \cdots a'_{k(\ell-2)}(x^2) \parallel a_1 \cdots a_k \parallel x_1 \ x_2 \ x_3 \ x_4 \end{pmatrix} \in \mathcal{R}_{2w}^{k(\ell-1)+4}$

Lemma 10. *Algorithm 5 is correct. More precisely, let $w = 2^\ell \geq 2$ and $f \in \mathcal{R}_{2w}$ be a self-adjoint polynomial, let $d, b, k \in \mathbb{Z}$ such that $b^k \geq \|f\|_\infty + kwb^2$ and $d \geq \frac{b^{2k}-1}{b^2-1}(\ell - 1) + b^k$. Then $\mathsf{REIGD}(d, f, b, k)$ outputs $\mathbf{a} \in \mathcal{R}_{2w}^{k(\ell-1)+4}$ such that $\langle \mathbf{a}, \mathbf{a} \rangle = d - f$.*

Moreover, $\mathsf{REIGD}(d, f, b, k)$ performs $O(kw \log w + \log^2 d' \log \log d')$ arithmetic operations on integers of bitsize $O(\log d')$ where $d' = d - \frac{b^{2k}-1}{b^2-1}(\ell - 1)$.

Proof. Let $f_e \in \mathcal{R}_w$ be the even part of f. Let $a_i = b^{i-1} + x c_i(x^2)$ where $c_i \in \mathcal{R}_w$ with $\|c_i\|_\infty < b$ and only its lower-half coefficients nonzero. Since $f(x) + \sum_i a_i a_i^\star = f'(x^2) + \frac{b^{2k}-1}{b^2-1}$, we inductively conclude that $\langle \mathbf{a}, \mathbf{a} \rangle = d - f$. A routine computation shows that $f' = f_e + \sum_i c_i c_i^\star$ and that $\|c_i c_i^\star\|_\infty \leq \frac{w}{2} b^2$. By the same argument as in the proof of Lemma 5, the correctness follows.

Algorithm 5 proceeds recursively. At the highest level, there is one gadget decomposition of $(-\bar{f}_o)$, k polynomial multiplications over $\mathcal{R}_w$ and one recursive call. At the bottom level, there is one 4-square decomposition. Thus the total complexity is $O(kw \log w + \log^2 d' \log \log d')$ if one uses NTT techniques during multiplication, and all involved integers are of bitsize at most $O(\log d')$. $\square$

Lemma 10 implies a solution to $\mathsf{IGDP}_{\mathcal{R}_{2w}, 1, B, d, m}$ as the following corollary.

Corollary 3. *Let $\ell, B, d, b, k \in \mathbb{N}$ and $w = 2^\ell \geq 2$ such that $m = k(\ell-1)+4$ and $d - \frac{b^{2k}-1}{b^2-1}(\ell-1) \geq b^k \geq B + kwb^2$. Then there exists a solution to $\mathsf{IGDP}_{\mathcal{R}_{2w}, 1, B, d, m}$ and it can be calculated by Algorithm 5.*

The output of Algorithm 5 consists of a series of vectors built upon the tower of rings followed by 4 integers, hence the storage can be essentially the same as that of f due to the polynomials in the tower of rings being gradually sparser. Detailed argument on the storage is given in Lemma 11.

Lemma 11. *Let* $\mathbf{a}$ *be the output of Algorithm 5, then* $\mathbf{a}$ *can be stored using* $\left(\frac{kw}{2}\log b + 2\log(2d')\right)$ *bits where* $d' = d - \frac{b^{2k}-1}{b^2-1}(\ell - 1)$. *In particular, when* $d' = O\left(\|f\|_\infty\right)$, *the required storage is* $\left(\frac{w}{2} + 2\right)\left(\log\|f\|_\infty + O(1)\right)$ *bits.*

Proof. The storage of $(x_1, x_2, x_3, x_4) \in \mathbb{Z}^4$ is bounded by $2\log(2d')$. We notice that $a_{1+jk+i} = b^i + a'_{i,j}\left(x^{2^{\ell-2-j}}\right)$ for some $a'_{i,j} \in \mathcal{R}_{2^{j+2}}$ with even coefficients being 0, odd coefficients in $(-b, b)$, hence the storage of a_{1+jk+i} is $2^j\log b$ and then the storage of $\mathbf{a}$ is $\frac{kw}{2}\log b + 2\log(2d')$. □

6.3 Decomposition for Positive Definite $\mathbf{\Sigma}' \in \mathcal{R}_{2w}^{n \times n}$

We now show how to solve the generalized problem $\mathsf{IGDP}_{\mathcal{R}_{2w},n,B,d,m}$. Our ring-setting matrix decomposition is illustrated in Algorithm 6. The high level idea is the same in spirit to Algorithm 4, except that we replace the Rabin-Shallit algorithm with a decomposition based on ring gadgets (Algorithm 5). For $\mathbf{\Sigma}' = d\mathbf{I}_n - \mathbf{\Sigma} \in \mathcal{R}_{2w}^{n \times n}$, one first calculates some $\mathbf{T} \in \mathcal{R}_{2w}^{n \times k}$ such that $\mathbf{T}\mathbf{T}^t$ has the same first row and column as $\mathbf{\Sigma}'$, except the diagonal element, and then proceeds iteratively over $(\mathbf{\Sigma}' - \mathbf{T}\mathbf{T}^t)_{2:n,2:n} \in \mathcal{R}_{2w}^{(n-1)\times(n-1)}$. During construction of $\mathbf{T}$ we deal with off-diagonal elements by gadget decomposition, and decompose the remaining diagonal element with Algorithm 5. Detailed analysis is shown in Lemma 12.

Lemma 12. *Algorithm 6 is correct. More precisely, let* $w = 2^\ell \geq 2$ *and* $\mathbf{\Sigma} \in \mathcal{R}_{2w}^{n \times n}$ *be a symmetric matrix, let* $d, b, k \in \mathbb{Z}$ *such that* $b^k \geq \|\mathbf{\Sigma}\|_{\max} + knwb^2$ *and* $d \geq \frac{b^{2k}-1}{b^2-1}\ell + b^k$. *Then* $\mathsf{RMIGD}(d, \mathbf{\Sigma}, b, k)$ *outputs* $\mathbf{A} \in \mathcal{R}_{2w}^{n \times n(k\ell+4)}$ *such that* $\mathbf{A}\mathbf{A}^t = d\mathbf{I}_n - \mathbf{\Sigma}$.

Moreover, $\mathsf{RMIGD}(d, \mathbf{\Sigma}, b, k)$ *performs* $O(n^3 kw \log w + n \log^2 d' \log\log d')$ *arithmetic operations on integers of bitsize at most* $O(\log d')$, *and* $\mathbf{A}$ *can be stored using* $\left(\frac{n^2}{2}kw \log b + 2n\log(2d')\right)$ *bits where* $d' = d - \frac{b^{2k}-1}{b^2-1}\ell$.

Proof (sketch). A routine computation shows that $\|\mathbf{C}\mathbf{C}^t\|_{\max} \leq kwb^2$. Following the same argument as the proof of Lemma 5, we confirm the correctness.

According to Lemma 10, all involved integers are of bitsize at most $O(\log d')$, and the complexity is mainly contributed by (1) the gadget decompositions, (2) calls to Algorithm 5 and (3) matrix multiplications. More specifically, there are $O(n^2)$ times gadget decompositions, hence the total complexity of this part is $O(kwn^2)$. There are n calls to Algorithm 5 that entirely costs $O(nkw \log w + n \log^2 d' \log\log d')$ according to Lemma 10. Furthermore, the cost of all matrix multiplications is bounded by $O(kn^3 w \log w)$. To sum up, the running time of $\mathsf{RMIGD}(d, \mathbf{\Sigma}, b, k)$ is dominated by $O(n^3 kw \log w + n \log^2 d' \log\log d')$.

From Lemma 11, the storage of $\mathbf{D}$ is $n\left(\frac{kw}{2}\log b + 2\log(2d')\right)$ and that of each $\mathbf{L}_i$ is $\frac{n(n-1)}{2}w\log b$. The overall storage thus is $\left(\frac{n^2}{2}kw\log b + 2n\log(2d')\right)$. □

Algorithm 6. Integral matrix decomposition in ring setting
$\mathsf{RMIGD}(d, \mathbf{\Sigma}, b, k)$

Input: a symmetric matrix $\mathbf{\Sigma} \in \mathcal{R}_{2w}^{n \times n}$ with $w = 2^{\ell} \geq 2$,
    integers $d, b, k \geq 2$ such that $b^k \geq \|\mathbf{\Sigma}\|_{\max} + knwb^2$ and $d \geq \frac{b^{2k}-1}{b^2-1}\ell + b^k$.

Output: $\mathbf{A} = \left(\mathbf{L}_1 \cdots \mathbf{L}_k \ \mathbf{D}\right) \in \mathcal{R}_{2w}^{n \times n(k\ell+4)}$ such that $\mathbf{A}\mathbf{A}^t = d\mathbf{I}_n - \mathbf{\Sigma}$
    where $\mathbf{L}_i \in \mathcal{R}_{2w}^{n \times n}$ is a lower-triangular matrix with diagonal elements being
    b^{i-1} and off-diagonal elements of ℓ_{∞}-norm less than b,
    $\mathbf{D} \in \mathcal{R}_w^{n \times n(k(\ell-1)+4)}$ is a block diagonal matrix with each block being the
    output of $\mathsf{REIGD}(d, f, b, k)$ for some $f \in \mathcal{R}_{2w}$.

1: $\mathbf{g} \leftarrow (1, b, \cdots, b^{k-1})^t \in \mathcal{R}_{2w}^k$

2: $\mathbf{x} \leftarrow \mathsf{REIGD}(d - \|\mathbf{g}\|^2, \mathbf{\Sigma}_{1,1}, b, k) \in \mathcal{R}_{2w}^{k(\ell-1)+4}$ {Call to Algorithm 5}

3: **if** $n = 1$ **then**

4:     return $(\mathbf{g}^t, \mathbf{x}^t)$

5: **end if**

6: **for** $j = 2, \cdots, n$ **do**

7:     calculate $\mathbf{c}_j \in \mathcal{R}_{2w}^k$ such that $\langle \mathbf{c}_j, \mathbf{g} \rangle = -\mathbf{\Sigma}_{1,j}$ by gadget decomposition

8: **end for**

9: $\mathbf{C} \leftarrow \left(\mathbf{c}_2 \cdots \mathbf{c}_n\right)^t \in \mathcal{R}_{2w}^{(n-1) \times k}$, $\mathbf{T} \leftarrow \begin{pmatrix} \mathbf{g}^t \ \mathbf{x}^t \\ \mathbf{C} \end{pmatrix} \in \mathcal{R}_{2w}^{n \times (k\ell+4)}$

10: $\mathbf{\Pi} \leftarrow \left(\mathbf{\Sigma} + \mathbf{T}\mathbf{T}^t\right)_{2:n, 2:n}$

11: $\left(\mathbf{L}_1' \cdots \mathbf{L}_k' \ \mathbf{D}'\right) \leftarrow \mathsf{RMIGD}(d, \mathbf{\Pi}, b, k)$ {Recursive call}

12: $\left(\mathbf{v}_1' \cdots \mathbf{v}_k'\right) \leftarrow \mathbf{C}$

13: $\mathbf{L}_i \leftarrow \begin{pmatrix} b^{i-1} & \\ \mathbf{v}_i' & \mathbf{L}_i' \end{pmatrix} \in \mathcal{R}_{2w}^{n \times n}$ for $i = 1, \cdots, k$

14: $\mathbf{D} \leftarrow \begin{pmatrix} \mathbf{x}^t & \\ & \mathbf{D}' \end{pmatrix} \in \mathcal{R}_{2w}^{n \times n(k(\ell-1)+4)}$

15: return $\mathbf{A} = \left(\mathbf{L}_1 \cdots \mathbf{L}_k \ \mathbf{D}\right)$

Corollary 4. *Let $\ell, B, d, b, k \in \mathbb{N}$ and $w = 2^{\ell} \geq 2$ such that $m = n(k\ell + 4)$ and $d - \frac{b^{2k}-1}{b^2-1}\ell \geq b^k \geq B + knwb^2$. Then there exists a solution to $\mathsf{IGDP}_{\mathcal{R}_{2w}, n, B, d, m}$ and it can be calculated by Algorithm 6.*

Lemma 13 shows a result related to the smoothness condition. Arguments in the proof of Lemma 9 still apply to the ring setting due to the similar structure of the output Gram root. The minor difference is that we should use the ℓ_2-norm to measure the "size" of each entry that is a ring element instead of an integer. Therefore we omit the proof.

Lemma 13. *Let $\mathbf{A}' = \mathsf{RMIGD}(d, \mathbf{\Sigma}, b, k) \in \mathcal{R}_{2w}^{n \times m}$ with $w = 2^{\ell} \geq 2$ and $m = n(k\ell + 4)$ and $\mathbf{A} = \left(\mathbf{I}_{nw} \ \mathcal{M}_w(\mathbf{A}')\right) \in \mathbb{Z}^{nw \times (n+m)w}$ where $\mathcal{M}_w$ maps each entry of $\mathbf{A}'$ to its coefficient matrix of size $w \times w$. Then*

$$\lambda_{mw}(\Lambda^{\perp}(\mathbf{A})) \leq \max\left\{b^2\sqrt{nw}, \sqrt{d - \frac{b^{2k}-1}{b^2-1}\ell + b^k + 1}\right\}.$$

The idea of eigenvalue reduction (Sect. 4.2) is compatible with the ring setting as well, if one uses structure-preserving Cholesky decomposition as in [15].

Additionally, for Algorithm 5, one may also subtract some $gg^\star$ approximation from f at the beginning, and then work on a small polynomial.

6.4 Comparative Results of the Ring-Based Sampler

Combining the eigenvalue reduction and Algorithm 6, a ring-based integral decomposition is available. Based on it, one can devise a perturbation sampler for the ring case. Here we skip detailed arguments and just present some comparisons. Let us first recall the following notations:

- $\ell \in \mathbb{N}$, $w = 2^\ell$, $n \in \mathbb{N}$ and $N = nw$.
- $\boldsymbol{\Sigma} \in \mathcal{R}_{2w}^{n \times n}$ is a symmetric matrix over $\mathcal{R}_{2w}$ that is identified with a symmetric matrix over $\mathbb{Z}^{N \times N}$. We focus on the case of $e_1(\boldsymbol{\Sigma}) = \omega(N^7)$.
- $s'^2 \in \mathbb{N}$ and $s'^2 > e_1(\boldsymbol{\Sigma}) + 1$.
- $M \in \mathbb{N}$ such that the integral Gram root $\mathbf{A} = \left(\mathbf{I}_N \ \mathbf{A}' \right) \in \mathbb{Z}^{N \times (N+M)}$.
- $L \in \mathbb{N}$ is an upper bound of $\lambda_M(\Lambda^\perp(\mathbf{A}))$. The base samplings include $D_{\mathbb{Z},L'r}$ and $D_{\mathbb{Z},r,c}$ with $c \in \frac{1}{L'} \cdot \mathbb{Z}$, where $L' \approx L$.

Comparison with the generic sampler. Table 5 shows the comparison between the ring-based sampler and the generic one. Note that in both the generic and ring cases, the parameter $L = O(s')$ and the minimal Gaussian width $s_{min} = (1 + o(1))\sqrt{e_1(\boldsymbol{\Sigma})}$. Thus we do not include them in Table 5.

Table 5. Comparisons between the ring-based sampler and the generic ones.

	Storage	M
Ring, large gadget base	$\approx N(\frac{2n+1}{2}\log s' + \frac{n}{2}\log N)$	$O(Nl)$
Generic, large gadget base	$\approx N^2(\log s' + \frac{1}{2}\log N)$	$O(N)$
Ring, gadget base $b = 2$	$\approx N(\frac{4n+3}{4}\log s' + n\log N)$	$O(Nl\log s')$
Generic, gadget base $b = 2$	$\approx N^2(\log s' + \log N)$	$O(N\log s')$

As a conclusion, our ring-based integral decomposition reduces the required memory by a factor of $O(w)$ but increases the number of centered base samplings (i.e. M) by $O(\log w)$. The smoothness condition and the quality of the output Gaussian are asymptotically the same in two kinds of samplers.

Comparison with the sampler of [17]. Genise and Micciancio proposed a ring-based perturbation sampler in [17]. To generate a perturbation vector in $\mathbb{Z}^{w(2+\log q)}$, they first sample $w \log q$ integer Gaussians and then sample a Gaussian of covariance $d\mathbf{I}_2 - \boldsymbol{\Sigma} \in \mathcal{R}_{2w}^{2 \times 2}$. To minimize the storage, the sampler only stores the matrix $\boldsymbol{\Sigma}$ and performs all algebraic computation on the fly.[8]

As shown in Sect. 5.4, our ring-based sampler can also reduce the procedure to the sampling of $D_{\mathbb{Z}^{2w}, \sqrt{d\mathbf{I}_2 - \boldsymbol{\Sigma}}}$ in which $n = 2$. The storage comes from the integral Gram root of $\sqrt{d\mathbf{I}_2 - \boldsymbol{\Sigma}}$. We summarize the comparison in Table 6.

---

[8] It suffices to store 3 polynomials due to the symmetry.

Table 6. Comparisons between the Genise-Micciancio sampler and ours. We use large gadget base in our sampler. We do not take into account the storage of the trapdoor itself that is $O(w \log q \log s')$.

	Storage	Time
Genise-Micciancio sampler	$\approx 6w \log s'$	$\Theta(w \log w \log q)$
Our ring-based sampler	$\approx w(5 \log s' + 2 \log w)$	$\Theta(w \log w \log q)$

The Genise-Micciancio sampler and ours require asymptotically the same memory. Particularly, if one regards the integral Gram root as a part of the trapdoor, the increase is *negligible* compared with the storage of trapdoor itself. As for running time, the costs of two samplers are dominated by the matrix multiplication of the trapdoor $\mathbf{T} \in \mathcal{R}_{2w}^{2 \times \log q}$. Applying FFT or NTT techniques yields the same complexity of $\Theta(w \log w \log q)$. Nevertheless, our sampler (Theorem 3) just requires base samplings and integral polynomial multiplications. This not only gets rid of FPA, but also makes the whole algorithm much simpler and highly parallelizable.

As a conclusion, our ring-based sampler achieves the same storage and time efficiency asymptotically as the state of the art [17] but in a simpler manner.

Acknowledgements. Léo Ducas is supported by a Veni Innovational Research Grant from NWO under project number 639.021.645 and by the European Union Horizon 2020 Research and Innovation Program Grant 780701 (PROMETHEUS). Steven Galbraith is funded by the Royal Society of New Zealand, Marsden Fund project 16-UOA-144. Thomas Prest is supported by the Innovate UK Research Grant 104423 (PQ Cybersecurity). Yang Yu is funded by a French government support managed by the National Research Agency in the "Investing for the Future" program, under the national project RISQ P141580-2660001/DOS0044216, and under the project TYREX granted by the CominLabs excellence laboratory with reference ANR-10-LABX-07-01.

References

1. Agrawal, S., Boneh, D., Boyen, X.: Efficient lattice (H)IBE in the standard model. In: Gilbert, H. (ed.) EUROCRYPT 2010. LNCS, vol. 6110, pp. 553–572. Springer, Heidelberg (2010). https://doi.org/10.1007/978-3-642-13190-5_28
2. Agrawal, S., Freeman, D.M., Vaikuntanathan, V.: Functional encryption for inner product predicates from learning with errors. In: Lee, D.H., Wang, X. (eds.) ASIACRYPT 2011. LNCS, vol. 7073, pp. 21–40. Springer, Heidelberg (2011). https://doi.org/10.1007/978-3-642-25385-0_2
3. Bai, S., Langlois, A., Lepoint, T., Stehlé, D., Steinfeld, R.: Improved security proofs in lattice-based cryptography: using the Rényi divergence rather than the statistical distance. In: Iwata, T., Cheon, J.H. (eds.) ASIACRYPT 2015. LNCS, vol. 9452, pp. 3–24. Springer, Heidelberg (2015). https://doi.org/10.1007/978-3-662-48797-6_1
4. Bert, P., Fouque, P.-A., Roux-Langlois, A., Sabt, M.: Practical implementation of ring-SIS/LWE based signature and IBE. In: Lange, T., Steinwandt, R. (eds.)

PQCrypto 2018. LNCS, vol. 10786, pp. 271–291. Springer, Cham (2018). https://doi.org/10.1007/978-3-319-79063-3_13

5. Boneh, D., et al.: Fully key-homomorphic encryption, arithmetic circuit ABE and compact garbled circuits. In: Nguyen, P.Q., Oswald, E. (eds.) EUROCRYPT 2014. LNCS, vol. 8441, pp. 533–556. Springer, Heidelberg (2014). https://doi.org/10.1007/978-3-642-55220-5_30

6. Bourse, F., Del Pino, R., Minelli, M., Wee, H.: FHE circuit privacy almost for free. In: Robshaw, M., Katz, J. (eds.) CRYPTO 2016. LNCS, vol. 9815, pp. 62–89. Springer, Heidelberg (2016). https://doi.org/10.1007/978-3-662-53008-5_3

7. Brakerski, Z., Vaikuntanathan, V.: Efficient fully homomorphic encryption from (standard) LWE. In: FOCS 2011, pp. 97–106 (2011)

8. Cash, D., Hofheinz, D., Kiltz, E., Peikert, C.: Bonsai trees, or how to delegate a lattice basis. In: Gilbert, H. (ed.) EUROCRYPT 2010. LNCS, vol. 6110, pp. 523–552. Springer, Heidelberg (2010). https://doi.org/10.1007/978-3-642-13190-5_27

9. Cassels, J.W.S.: Rational quadratic forms. In: North-Holland Mathematics Studies, vol. 74 (1982)

10. Chen, Y., Genise, N., Mukherjee, P.: Approximate trapdoors for lattices and smaller hash-and-sign signatures. In: Galbraith, S.D., Moriai, S. (eds.) ASIACRYPT 2019. LNCS, vol. 11923, pp. 3–32. Springer, Cham (2019). https://doi.org/10.1007/978-3-030-34618-8_1

11. Ducas, L., Lyubashevsky, V., Prest, T.: Efficient identity-based encryption over NTRU lattices. In: Sarkar, P., Iwata, T. (eds.) ASIACRYPT 2014. LNCS, vol. 8874, pp. 22–41. Springer, Heidelberg (2014). https://doi.org/10.1007/978-3-662-45608-8_2

12. Ducas, L., Micciancio, D.: Improved short lattice signatures in the standard model. In: Garay, J.A., Gennaro, R. (eds.) CRYPTO 2014. LNCS, vol. 8616, pp. 335–352. Springer, Heidelberg (2014). https://doi.org/10.1007/978-3-662-44371-2_19

13. Ducas, L., Nguyen, P.Q.: Faster Gaussian lattice sampling using lazy floating-point arithmetic. In: Wang, X., Sako, K. (eds.) ASIACRYPT 2012. LNCS, vol. 7658, pp. 415–432. Springer, Heidelberg (2012). https://doi.org/10.1007/978-3-642-34961-4_26

14. Ducas, L., Nguyen, P.Q.: Learning a zonotope and more: cryptanalysis of NTRUSign countermeasures. In: Wang, X., Sako, K. (eds.) ASIACRYPT 2012. LNCS, vol. 7658, pp. 433–450. Springer, Heidelberg (2012). https://doi.org/10.1007/978-3-642-34961-4_27

15. Ducas, L., Prest, T.: Fast fourier orthogonalization. In: ISSAC 2016, pp. 191–198 (2016)

16. Ducas, L., Galbraith, S., Prest, T., Yu, Y.: Integral matrix gram root and lattice Gaussian sampling without floats. IACR Cryptology ePrint Archive, report 2019/320 (2019)

17. Genise, N., Micciancio, D.: Faster Gaussian sampling for trapdoor lattices with arbitrary modulus. In: Nielsen, J.B., Rijmen, V. (eds.) EUROCRYPT 2018. LNCS, vol. 10820, pp. 174–203. Springer, Cham (2018). https://doi.org/10.1007/978-3-319-78381-9_7

18. Gentry, C.: Fully homomorphic encryption using ideal lattices. In: STOC 2009, pp. 169–178 (2009)

19. Gentry, C., Peikert, C., Vaikuntanathan, V.: Trapdoors for hard lattices and new cryptographic constructions. In: STOC 2008, pp. 197–206 (2008)

20. Gorbunov, S., Vaikuntanathan, V., Wee, H.: Attribute-based encryption for circuits. In: STOC 2013, pp. 545–554 (2013)

21. Klein, P.N.: Finding the closest lattice vector when it's unusually close. In: SODA 2000, pp. 937–941 (2000). http://dl.acm.org/citation.cfm?id=338219.338661
22. Laguillaumie, F., Langlois, A., Libert, B., Stehlé, D.: Lattice-based group signatures with logarithmic signature size. In: Sako, K., Sarkar, P. (eds.) ASIACRYPT 2013. LNCS, vol. 8270, pp. 41–61. Springer, Heidelberg (2013). https://doi.org/10.1007/978-3-642-42045-0_3
23. Langlois, A., Ling, S., Nguyen, K., Wang, H.: Lattice-based group signature scheme with verifier-local revocation. In: Krawczyk, H. (ed.) PKC 2014. LNCS, vol. 8383, pp. 345–361. Springer, Heidelberg (2014). https://doi.org/10.1007/978-3-642-54631-0_20
24. Lenstra, H.W.: Lattices (2008). http://www.math.leidenuniv.nl/~psh/ANTproc/06hwl.pdf
25. Micciancio, D., Peikert, C.: Trapdoors for lattices: simpler, tighter, faster, smaller. In: Pointcheval, D., Johansson, T. (eds.) EUROCRYPT 2012. LNCS, vol. 7237, pp. 700–718. Springer, Heidelberg (2012). https://doi.org/10.1007/978-3-642-29011-4_41
26. Micciancio, D., Peikert, C.: Hardness of SIS and LWE with small parameters. In: Canetti, R., Garay, J.A. (eds.) CRYPTO 2013. LNCS, vol. 8042, pp. 21–39. Springer, Heidelberg (2013). https://doi.org/10.1007/978-3-642-40041-4_2
27. Micciancio, D., Regev, O.: Worst-case to average-case reductions based on Gaussian measures. SIAM J. Comput. **37**(1), 267–302 (2007)
28. Micciancio, D., Walter, M.: Gaussian sampling over the integers: efficient, generic, constant-time. In: Katz, J., Shacham, H. (eds.) CRYPTO 2017. LNCS, vol. 10402, pp. 455–485. Springer, Cham (2017). https://doi.org/10.1007/978-3-319-63715-0_16
29. mirtich: Bug 323 - optimized code gives strange floating point results. GCC Bugzilla. https://gcc.gnu.org/bugzilla/show_bug.cgi?id=323
30. Nguyen, P.Q., Regev, O.: Learning a parallelepiped: cryptanalysis of GGH and NTRU signatures. In: Vaudenay, S. (ed.) EUROCRYPT 2006. LNCS, vol. 4004, pp. 271–288. Springer, Heidelberg (2006). https://doi.org/10.1007/11761679_17
31. Nguyen, P.Q., Zhang, J., Zhang, Z.: Simpler efficient group signatures from lattices. In: Katz, J. (ed.) PKC 2015. LNCS, vol. 9020, pp. 401–426. Springer, Heidelberg (2015). https://doi.org/10.1007/978-3-662-46447-2_18
32. Peikert, C.: An efficient and parallel Gaussian sampler for lattices. In: Rabin, T. (ed.) CRYPTO 2010. LNCS, vol. 6223, pp. 80–97. Springer, Heidelberg (2010). https://doi.org/10.1007/978-3-642-14623-7_5
33. Pöppelmann, T., Ducas, L., Güneysu, T.: Enhanced lattice-based signatures on reconfigurable hardware. In: Batina, L., Robshaw, M. (eds.) CHES 2014. LNCS, vol. 8731, pp. 353–370. Springer, Heidelberg (2014). https://doi.org/10.1007/978-3-662-44709-3_20
34. Prest, T.: Sharper bounds in lattice-based cryptography using the Rényi divergence. In: Takagi, T., Peyrin, T. (eds.) ASIACRYPT 2017. LNCS, vol. 10624, pp. 347–374. Springer, Cham (2017). https://doi.org/10.1007/978-3-319-70694-8_13
35. Rabin, M.O., Shallit, J.O.: Randomized algorithms in number theory. Commun. Pure Appl. Math. **39**(S1), S239–S256 (1986)
36. Wilson, J.: Floating point trouble with x86's extended precision. The gcc@gcc.gnu.org mailing list for the GCC project. https://gcc.gnu.org/ml/gcc/2003-08/msg01195.html
37. Yu, Y., Ducas, L.: Learning strikes again: the case of the DRS signature scheme. In: Peyrin, T., Galbraith, S. (eds.) ASIACRYPT 2018. LNCS, vol. 11273, pp. 525–543. Springer, Cham (2018). https://doi.org/10.1007/978-3-030-03329-3_18

Symmetric Cryptography II

TNT: How to Tweak a Block Cipher

Zhenzhen Bao[1], Chun Guo[2,3(✉)], Jian Guo[1], and Ling Song[4,5]

[1] Division of Mathematical Sciences, School of Physical and Mathematical Sciences,
Nanyang Technological University, Singapore, Singapore
{zzbao,guojian}@ntu.edu.sg
[2] Key Laboratory of Cryptologic Technology and Information Security
of Ministry of Education, Shandong University, Qingdao, China
[3] School of Cyber Science and Technology, Shandong University, Qingdao, China
chun.guo@sdu.edu.cn
[4] State Key Laboratory of Information Security, Institute of Information
Engineering, Chinese Academy of Sciences, Beijing, China
[5] Jinan University, Guangzhou, China
songling.qs@gmail.com

Abstract. In this paper, we propose Tweak-aNd-Tweak (TNT for short) mode, which builds a tweakable block cipher from three independent block ciphers. TNT handles the tweak input by simply XOR-ing the unmodified tweak into the internal state of block ciphers twice. Due to its simplicity, TNT can also be viewed as a way of turning a block cipher into a tweakable block cipher by dividing the block cipher into three chunks, and adding the tweak at the two cutting points only. TNT is proven to be of beyond-birthday-bound $2^{2n/3}$ security, under the assumption that the three chunks are independent secure n-bit SPRPs. It clearly brings minimum possible overhead to both software and hardware implementations. To demonstrate this, an instantiation named TNT-AES with 6, 6, 6 rounds of AES as the underlying block ciphers is proposed. Besides the inherent proven security bound and tweak-independent rekeying feature of the TNT mode, the performance of TNT-AES is comparable with all existing TBCs designed through modular methods.

Keywords: AES · Tweakable block cipher · χ^2 method · Proof

1 Introduction

1.1 Background - The Need of BBB TBC

Together with the development of authenticated encryption (AE) in CAESAR competition [1] and the on-going lightweight cryptography competition [64], tweakable block ciphers (TBC) are playing a more and more important role. Besides the plaintext, TBCs take a *tweak* as an additional input, which can be viewed as an index to the underlying block cipher, so it becomes a family of (independent) block ciphers v.s. a single instance of block cipher. Its formalization is motivated by the needs of (more than one) independent block ciphers in

© International Association for Cryptologic Research 2020
A. Canteaut and Y. Ishai (Eds.): EUROCRYPT 2020, LNCS 12106, pp. 641–673, 2020.
https://doi.org/10.1007/978-3-030-45724-2_22

some modes, e.g., OCB [67], while using multiple independent ciphers or keys could cause efficiency issues. In contrast, using a TBC that typically lends itself to very efficient (both software and hardware) implementations, a new instance of block cipher could be obtained by simply choosing a new value of the tweak.

Beyond-Birthday-Bound Security. Most of the current (tweakable) block cipher standards have a block length of 128 bits or less, providing a security level at most 64 bits when instantiated in designs offering only birthday-bound security. Such a security level has become largely inadequate [35]. Even worse, in order to save hardware implementation costs, many lightweight block cipher designs tend to have a smaller block length like 64 bits, providing a birthday security of 32 bits only. Hence, the needs of modes providing BBB security are emerging, and the same has been observed by Gueron and Lindell [35] and in this whitepaper [2].

There are two different ways to construct TBCs. Following the modular approach, they can be built from classical block ciphers via various modular constructions, and security is ensured by a reduction to that of the underlying block ciphers. Alternatively, one could appeal to (probably more efficient) dedicated algorithms, the security guarantees of which come from comprehensive cryptanalysis. Below we'll review both methods.

1.2   Modular Approach: TBCs from Block Ciphers

A classical popular approach is to construct TBCs from existing (traditional) block ciphers in a black-box fashion. Such proposals are further divided into two classes. The "old school" approach, initiated by Liskov et al. [54], works in the so-called standard model, models the underlying block cipher as a *pseudorandom permutation*. The "new school" approach recently popularized by Mennink [56] models the block cipher as an *ideal cipher*. The two approaches deviate not only in their security assumptions, but also in their design philosophies. Concretely, standard assumption-based constructions typically tried to avoid tweak-dependent rekeying, which were deemed as (arguably) costly. Another shortage of rekeying is the unavoidable "hybrid security loss" in their security bounds [58,69] (some withstand this loss using carefully-chosen parameters [17,61]). Such a loss doesn't appear in the ideal cipher model, and this is leveraged by many constructions for good bounds and efficiency at the same time. Indeed, ideal cipher-based TBCs have achieved $\geq n$-bit security within 1 or 2 cipher-calls [43,53,77].

In this paper we follow the standard model. In this respect, the original Liskov et al.'s paper [54] proposed two constructions that were subsequently named LRW1 and LRW2 by Landecker et al. [51]. The former is based on a block cipher E with key space $\mathcal{K}_E$ and message space $\{0,1\}^n$, and is defined as

$$\mathsf{LRW1}((K, K'), T, X) = E_{K'}(T \oplus E_K(X)). \tag{1}$$

where $(K, K') \in \mathcal{K}_E \times \mathcal{K}_E$ is the key, $T \in \mathcal{T}$ is the tweak, and $X \in \{0,1\}^n$ is the message. Unfortunately it is only CPA secure up to a tight birthday bound, *i.e.*, $2^{n/2}$ adversarial queries. Actually, achieving CCA security was an important motivation for their second proposal LRW2, which is based on a block cipher E and message space $\{0,1\}^n$ and an almost XOR-universal (AXU) family of hash functions $\mathcal{H} = (H_K)_{K \in \mathcal{K}_H}$ from some set $\mathcal{T}$ to $\{0,1\}^n$, and defined as

$$\text{LRW2}((K, K'), T, X) = H_{K'}(T) \oplus E_K(H_{K'}(T) \oplus X), \tag{2}$$

where $(K, K') \in \mathcal{K}_E \times \mathcal{K}_H$ is the key. This construction was proved CCA secure in [54] up to a tight birthday bound. To seek for beyond-birthday-bound (BBB) secure TBCs, pioneered by Landecker et al. [51], subsequent works studied cascade of LRW2 (with independent underlying keys): its 2-cascade was first proved secure up to about $2^{2n/3}$ queries [51] and latter improved to a tight bound of $2^{3n/4}$ queries [44,59], while its r-cascade for general r was proved secure up to roughly $2^{\frac{rn}{r+2}}$ adversarial queries.

A somewhat independent series of works considered tweakable Even-Mansour (TEM) ciphers that are built upon public random permutations [18,20,57], which could also be instantiated with fixed-key block ciphers. It is important to note their security is only provable in the ideal (permutation) model.

1.3 Development of Dedicated TBCs

The Tweakey framework was introduced in 2014 by Jean et al. [41], which provides a general guideline for TBC designs. The core idea is to treat the key and tweak in the same way during the primitive design process so that the cryptanalysis can be unified, and becomes simpler than before. So the word "tweakey" is invented to reflect the combined input of tweak and key. Following tweakey framework, various dedicated algorithms such as the Deoxys-BC in the Deoxys AE design [42], SKINNY [7], and Kiasu [40] have been proposed. In detail, SKINNY takes lightweightness into account, and hence makes use of lightweight linear layer—0/1 matrices—almost MDS rather than MDS, although it still follows AES-like design strategy. Up to date, Deoxys is one of the finalists of the CAESAR competition and SKINNY is one of the lightest TBCs in terms of area in the optimized hardware implementations.

When the tweak length is long, TBC-based designs [3,38] can take advantage of its efficiency to process additional input such as associated data. There is also a recent direction of designing TBCs of short tweaks to offer a small family of yet independent block ciphers [12], where tweaks are mainly used as domain separators in the design of authenticated encryption schemes.

It is well-known that, to hide the key of a block cipher, it requires several iterations of the simple round functions. Since Tweakey framework does not distinguish key and tweak, the tweak input has been iterated the same amount of rounds as well. We notice that, rather than hiding, the functionality of a tweak is no more than an index to the block cipher in most of use-cases, and are even assumed to be under attacker's full control in some cryptanalytic settings. Hence, the required level of "protection" for a tweak is essentially lower than that for the key. Inspired by this observation, a natural question to be asked is: what is the minimum number of iterations (or tweak addition) required to produce a secure TBC (especially those with BBB security), with provable security.

1.4 Our Approach (Hybrid of Two Approaches), Provable Security of TBC Modes, and Instantiation with Long-Standing Modules (Similar with AES-PRF)

We seek for an approach slotting between the above two and (hopefully) enjoying the advantages of both, *i.e.*, achieving (some level of) provable guarantees and high efficiency at the same time. Our result is a proposal of a new design of dedicated TBCs based on AES. Our approach is "prove-then-prune", *i.e.*, proving security and then instantiating with a scaled-down primitive (a reduced-round block cipher), that has been used in symmetric designs for a long time, see e.g., [60] (while the terminology was due to Hoang *et al.* [37]). Below we elaborate in detail.

TNT: A New TBC Construction with BBB Security. Our starting point is a new block cipher-based TBC construction with provable BBB security. Concretely, the idealized version of our mode is built upon three secret independent random permutations π_1, π_2, and π_3, and is defined as

$$\mathsf{TNT}^{\pi_1,\pi_2,\pi_3}(T,X) = \pi_3\big(T \oplus \pi_2\big(T \oplus \pi_1(X)\big)\big),$$

as pictured in Fig. 1. We term our mode as TNT, meaning Tweak-aNd-Tweak. It can also be viewed as a cascaded LRW1 TBC construction (if we "split" π_2 into two permutations, then the scheme turns into a cascade of two LRW1 constructions).

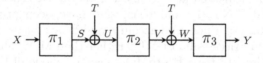

Fig. 1. The $\mathsf{TNT}^{\pi_1,\pi_2,\pi_3}$ mode with the notations (for the intermediate values) used in this paper.

While the original (two-permutation-based) LRW1 construction was proved CPA secure up to birthday $2^{n/2}$ queries and it turns out to be tight, the security of TNT (or cascaded LRW1) remains as a long-standing open problem. In this paper, using the χ^2 technique recently proposed by Dai *et al.* [24], we prove the idealized TNT construction is CCA secure up to BBB $2^{2n/3}$ queries. To our knowledge, this constitutes the first "non-trivial" application of the χ^2 technique to domain expanding constructions, and our proof thus demonstrates relevant issues and their solutions.

We refer to Table 1 for a summary of comparison to existing TBC constructions (we omit the TEM ciphers as they either appear a bit theoretical or are specific for sponges [57]). It is rather difficult to make a comparison with the ideal cipher-based designs [43,53,56,77]. In general, they achieve $\geq n$ bits security (as mentioned) at the expense of a smaller safety margin (similar concern

Table 1. Comparison with previous TBCs. The column ⊗/AXU states if the design relies on AXU hash or field multiplications ⊗. The column tdk states if the design relies on tweak-dependent rekeying. For all the ideal cipher-based designs, we assume using an ideal cipher with n-bit keys and n-bit blocks.

	#tweak	#cost	⊗/AXU?	tdk	security ($\log_2$)
LRW1	n	2 SPRPs	no	no	$n/2$ [54]
XEX	n	1 SPRP	yes	no	$n/2$ [67]
LRW2	arbitrary	1 SPRP	yes	no	$n/2$ [54]
CLRW2$_2$	arbitrary	2 SPRPs	yes	no	$3n/4$ [44,59]
CLRW2$_r$	arbitrary	r SPRPs	yes	no	$rn/(r+2)$ [50]
Min	t	2 SPRPs	no	yes	$\max\{n/2, n-t\}$ [61]
$\widetilde{F}[1]$	n	1 ideal cipher	no	yes	$2n/3$ [56]
$\widetilde{F}[2]$	n	2 ideal ciphers	no	yes	n [56]
$\widetilde{E1}, \ldots, \widetilde{E32}$	n	2 ideal ciphers	no	yes	n [77]
XHX	arbitrary	1 ideal cipher	yes	yes	n [43]
XHX2	arbitrary	2 ideal ciphers	yes	yes	$4n/3$ [53]
TNT	n	3 SPRPs	no	no	$2n/3$

has been raised in other settings [36]). Also, their provable bounds should be interpreted with a bit of caution [58]. In terms of efficiency, it is widely believed that tweak-dependent rekeying used in the above designs as well as [61] is a bit costly, particularly when AES-NI is available.

It appears that LRW2 and its cascades are the closest designs. In short, while LRW2 and CLRW2 accept long tweaks, their uses of AXU hash are expected to result in a lower efficiency when n-bit tweaks already suffice. The additional requirement of AXU hash usually results in lower software efficiency and/or higher gate counts as additional registers and operations are needed.

Instantiation from AES. To take the advantage of the AES-NI for better software performance, it is natural for us to instantiate TNT with AES. To further improve the software performance, we reduce the number of rounds of each of the permutations π_1, π_2, and π_3 to 6, 6, and 6 rounds respectively (rather than the full AES itself), which are named TNT-AES. Although, it is not possible to assume the round-reduced AES to be ideal any more, we show, through comprehensive cryptanalysis, the security of TNT-AES are sound. Similar design strategy was introduced by Hoang *et al.* [37] and used in the design of AES-PRF [60] by Mennink and Neves. The estimated performance shows, with help from AES-NI, TNT-AES is among the fastest TBCs in software, and in some cases it can be implemented as light as AES itself in area constrained hardware environment thanks to the simplicity of TNT, smaller than most of the existing TBCs.

Organization. The rest of the paper is organized as follows. Section 2 gives the preliminary necessary for the introduction of the new mode in Sect. 3. The security TNT is proven in Sect. 4. Section 5 proposes a concrete design following TNT based on AES, and finally Sect. 6 concludes the paper.

2 Preliminary

2.1 Notation

For a finite set $\mathcal{X}$, $X \xleftarrow{\$} \mathcal{X}$ denotes selecting an element from $\mathcal{X}$ uniformly at random and $|\mathcal{X}|$ denotes its cardinality.

2.2 TBC and Its Security

A tweakable permutation with tweak space $\mathcal{T}$ and message space $\mathcal{M}$ is a mapping $\widetilde{\Pi} : \mathcal{T} \times \mathcal{M} \to \mathcal{M}$ such that for any tweak $T \in \mathcal{T}$, $X \mapsto \widetilde{\Pi}(T, X)$ is a permutation of $\mathcal{M}$. We denote $\mathsf{TP}(\mathcal{T}, n)$ the set of all tweakable permutations with tweak space $\mathcal{T}$ and message space $\{0,1\}^n$. A tweakable block cipher with key space $\mathcal{K}$, tweak space $\mathcal{T}$, and message space $\mathcal{M}$ is a mapping $\mathsf{TBC} : \mathcal{K} \times \mathcal{T} \times \mathcal{M} \to \mathcal{M}$ such that for any key $K \in \mathcal{K}$, $(T, X) \mapsto \mathsf{TBC}(K, T, X)$ is a tweakable permutation in $\mathsf{TP}(\mathcal{T}, n)$.

A secure TBC should be indistinguishable from a tweakable random permutation. As our mode TNT is specified in an idealized manner, our security definition is also given for such cases. For this, we denote $\mathsf{P}(n)$ the set of all n-bit permutations. By default, we always allow $\mathcal{D}$ to make forward and inverse queries to its tweakable permutation oracle (though we do not write this explicitly). With these, for the TBC construction $C^{\pi_1,\dots,\pi_r}$ built upon r independent secret n-bit permutations, we define the advantage of any distinguisher $\mathcal{D}$ breaking its *strong tweakable pseudorandomness (STPRP)* as

$$\mathbf{Adv}_C^{\mathrm{stprp}}(\mathcal{D}) = \left| \Pr[\pi_1, \dots, \pi_r \xleftarrow{\$} \mathsf{P}(n) : \mathcal{D}^{C^{\pi_1,\dots,\pi_r}} = 1] - \Pr[\widetilde{\Pi} \xleftarrow{\$} \mathsf{TP}(\mathcal{T}, n) : \mathcal{D}^{\widetilde{\Pi}} = 1] \right|.$$

And for any non-negative integer q, we define the insecurity of $C^{\pi_1,\dots,\pi_r}$ as

$$\mathbf{Adv}_C^{\mathrm{stprp}}(q) = \max_{\mathcal{D}} \mathbf{Adv}_C^{\mathrm{stprp}}(\mathcal{D}),$$

where the maximum is taken over all distinguishers $\mathcal{D}$ making exactly q queries to the oracle.

The above definition focuses on the information-theoretic setting. Later in Sect. 5 we will instantiate the multiple secret permutations $\pi_1, \dots, \pi_r$ with multiple "independent" block ciphers $E_1, \dots, E_r$ using the *same* secret key K (thus the key space does not increase with the number of permutations). Proving the indistinguishability of such two systems $(\pi_1, \dots, \pi_r)$ and $((E_1)_K, \dots, (E_r)_K)$ seems out of reach of current techniques (note that existing works typically instantiated $\pi_1, \dots, \pi_r$ with the *same* block cipher using r *independent keys* $K_1, \dots, K_r$, which deviates from us). As such, our mode TNT will be specified only in the idealized manner.

2.3 χ^2 Method

For the proof, we will employ the χ^2 method of Dai *et al.* [24]. We recall this technique here. Below we mainly follow Dai *et al.*'s notations (with some necessary supplementaries borrowed from Chen *et al.* [13]). Concretely, consider two stateless systems $\mathbf{S}_0$ and $\mathbf{S}_1$ (e.g., $\mathbf{S}_0$ and $\mathbf{S}_1$ may be the tweakable random permutation $\widetilde{\Pi}$ and the TNT construction $\mathsf{TNT}^{\pi_1,\pi_2,\pi_3}$ respectively) and any computationally unbounded deterministic distinguisher $\mathcal{D}$ that has query access to either of these systems. The distinguisher's goal is to distinguish the two systems. It is well-known that, the distinguishing advantage $\mathbf{Adv}_{\mathbf{S}_0,\mathbf{S}_1}(\mathcal{D})$ is bounded by the statistical distance $\|\mathsf{p}_{\mathbf{S}_0,\mathcal{D}}(\cdot) - \mathsf{p}_{\mathbf{S}_1,\mathcal{D}}(\cdot)\|$, where $\mathsf{p}_{\mathbf{S}_0,\mathcal{D}}(\cdot)$ and $\mathsf{p}_{\mathbf{S}_1,\mathcal{D}}(\cdot)$ are the respective probability distributions of the answers obtained by $\mathcal{D}$. The χ^2 method concerns with bounding $\|\mathsf{p}_{\mathbf{S}_0,\mathcal{D}}(\cdot) - \mathsf{p}_{\mathbf{S}_1,\mathcal{D}}(\cdot)\|$. To this end, if we denote the maximum amount of queries by q, we can define a transcript $\mathcal{Q} = (\tau_1,\ldots,\tau_q)$ with $\tau_i = (T_i, X_i, Y_i)$, and let $\mathcal{Q}_\ell = (\tau_1,\ldots,\tau_\ell)$ for every $\ell \leq q$. The distinguisher $\mathcal{D}$ can make its queries adaptively, but as it makes them in a deterministic manner, the ℓ-th query input is determined by the first $\ell - 1$ query-responses $\mathcal{Q}_{\ell-1}$.

For system $\mathbf{S}_b$ with $b \in \{0,1\}$ and fixed tuple $\mathcal{Q}_{\ell-1}$, we denote by $\mathsf{p}_{\mathbf{S}_b,\mathcal{D}}(\mathcal{Q}_{\ell-1})$ the probability that $\mathcal{D}$ interacting with $\mathbf{S}_b$ yields transcript $\mathcal{Q}_{\ell-1}$ for its first $\ell-1$ queries. If $\mathsf{p}_{\mathbf{S}_b,\mathcal{D}}(\mathcal{Q}_{\ell-1}) > 0$, then we denote by $\mathsf{p}_{\mathbf{S}_b,\mathcal{D}}(R_\ell \mid \mathcal{Q}_{\ell-1})$ the conditional probability that $\mathcal{D}$ receives response R_ℓ upon its ℓ-th query, given transcript $\mathcal{Q}_{\ell-1}$ of the first $\ell - 1$ queries (that deterministically fixes the ℓ-th query). Define for any $\ell \in \{1,\ldots,q\}$ and any query-response tuple $\mathcal{Q}_{\ell-1}$:

$$\chi^2(\mathcal{Q}_{\ell-1}) = \sum_{R_\ell} \frac{\left(\mathsf{p}_{\mathbf{S}_1,\mathcal{D}}(R_\ell \mid \mathcal{Q}_{\ell-1}) - \mathsf{p}_{\mathbf{S}_0,\mathcal{D}}(R_\ell \mid \mathcal{Q}_{\ell-1})\right)^2}{\mathsf{p}_{\mathbf{S}_0,\mathcal{D}}(R_\ell \mid \mathcal{Q}_{\ell-1})}, \tag{3}$$

where the sum is taken over all R_ℓ in the support of the distribution $\mathsf{p}_{\mathbf{S}_0,\mathcal{D}}(\cdot \mid \mathcal{Q}_{\ell-1})$. The χ^2 method states the following:

Lemma 1 *(χ^2 method [24, Lemma 3]). Consider a fixed deterministic distinguisher $\mathcal{D}$ and two systems $\mathbf{S}_0, \mathbf{S}_1$. Suppose that for any $\ell \in \{1,\ldots,q\}$ and any query-response tuple $\mathcal{Q}_\ell$, $\mathsf{p}_{\mathbf{S}_0,\mathcal{D}}(\mathcal{Q}_\ell) > 0$ whenever $\mathsf{p}_{\mathbf{S}_1,\mathcal{D}}(\mathcal{Q}_\ell) > 0$. Then:*

$$\|\mathsf{p}_{\mathbf{S}_0,\mathcal{D}}(\cdot) - \mathsf{p}_{\mathbf{S}_1,\mathcal{D}}(\cdot)\| \leq \left(\frac{1}{2}\sum_{\ell=1}^q \mathbf{E}\left[\chi^2(\mathcal{Q}_{\ell-1})\right]\right)^{1/2}, \tag{4}$$

where the expectation is taken over $\mathcal{Q}_{\ell-1}$ of the $\ell - 1$ first answers sampled according to interaction with $\mathbf{S}_1$.

3 The Idealized TNT Mode

In this section, we describe our mode TNT. As discussed in Sect. 2, we only give its idealized description, which is built upon *secret random permutations* rather than efficient block ciphers.

Concretely, TNT is built upon three independent secret random permutations $\pi_1, \pi_2,$ and $\pi_3,$ and is formally defined as

$$\mathsf{TNT}^{\pi_1, \pi_2, \pi_3}(T, X) = \pi_3\big(T \oplus \pi_2\big(T \oplus \pi_1(X)\big)\big). \tag{5}$$

4   Security Proof for TNT Mode

Theorem 1. *When $q \leq 2^n/2$, it holds*

$$\mathbf{Adv}_{\mathsf{TNT}}^{\mathrm{stprp}}(q) \leq \frac{8q^{1.5}}{2^n}. \tag{6}$$

Proof. In our proof, $\mathbf{S_0}$ denotes the tweakable random permutation $\widetilde{\Pi}$, while $\mathbf{S_1}$ denotes the $\mathsf{TNT}^{\pi_1, \pi_2, \pi_3}$ TBC. The condition stated in Lemma 1, *i.e.*, $\forall \mathcal{Q}_\ell$, $\mathsf{p}_{\mathbf{S_0}, \mathcal{D}}(\mathcal{Q}_\ell) > 0$ whenever $\mathsf{p}_{\mathbf{S_1}, \mathcal{D}}(\mathcal{Q}_\ell) > 0$, is clearly satisfied.

Given $\mathcal{Q}_{\ell-1}$, let T_ℓ be the tweak of the ℓ-th query (note that it is determined by $\mathcal{Q}_{\ell-1}$). It is easy to see that, regardless of the direction of this query, it holds

$$\mathsf{p}_{\widetilde{\Pi}, \mathcal{D}}(R_\ell \mid \mathcal{Q}_{\ell-1}) = \frac{1}{2^n - \mu_\ell},$$

where $\mu_\ell \leq \ell - 1$ is the frequency of the tweak value T_ℓ in $\mathcal{Q}_{\ell-1}$, *i.e.*,

$$\mu_\ell = \Big|\big\{(X, Y) : (T_\ell, X, Y) \in \mathcal{Q}_{\ell-1}\big\}\Big|.$$

The real world probability $\mathsf{p}_{\mathsf{TNT}, \mathcal{D}}(R_\ell \mid \mathcal{Q}_{\ell-1})$ however depends on the concrete state of the ℓ-th query and $\mathcal{Q}_{\ell-1}$, for which we distinguish eight cases as follows.

Case 1: the ℓ-th query is forward $\mathsf{TNT}(T_\ell, X_\ell) \to Y_\ell$, and $X_\ell, Y_\ell \in \mathcal{Q}_{\ell-1}$, *i.e.*, $\exists T', X', T^*, Y^* : (T', X', Y_\ell), (T^*, X_\ell, Y^*) \in \mathcal{Q}_{\ell-1}$. We write

$$\mathsf{p}_{\mathsf{TNT}, \mathcal{D}}(Y_\ell \mid \mathcal{Q}_{\ell-1}) = \Pr[\mathsf{TNT}(T_\ell, X_\ell) \to Y_\ell \mid \mathcal{Q}_{\ell-1}]$$

$$= \sum_{\mathbf{Inter}} \Pr[\mathsf{TNT}(T_\ell, X_\ell) \to Y_\ell \mid \mathbf{Inter}] \cdot \Pr[\mathbf{Inter} \mid \mathcal{Q}_{\ell-1}],$$

where the sum is taken over all the vectors of intermediate values

$$\mathbf{Inter} = \Big((S_1, \ldots, S_{\ell-1}), (U_1, \ldots, U_{\ell-1}), (V_1, \ldots, V_{\ell-1}), (W_1, \ldots, W_{\ell-1})\Big)$$

that are possible to appear given $\mathcal{Q}_{\ell-1}$.

Now, for a certain intermediate vector **Inter**, it can be seen that there are three possibilities, according to which we divide all intermediate vectors into three disjoint classes $\mathcal{A}$, $\mathcal{B}$, and $\mathcal{C}$:

- Class $\mathcal{A}$: $\Pr[\mathsf{TNT}(T_\ell, X_\ell) \to Y_\ell \mid \mathbf{Inter}] = 1$;
  - *i.e.*, the vector **Inter** specifies S_ℓ and W_ℓ as the values corresponding to X_ℓ and Y_ℓ, as well as a input-output relation on π_2 (subsequently abbreviated as π_2-relation) (U_i, V_i) such that $T_\ell \oplus S_\ell = U_i$ and $T_\ell \oplus W_\ell = V_i$.

– Class $\mathcal{B}$: $\Pr[\mathsf{TNT}(T_\ell, X_\ell) \to Y_\ell \mid \mathbf{Inter}] = \frac{1}{N - \beta(\mathbf{Inter})}$, where $\beta(\mathbf{Inter})$ is the number of distinct U values in $(U_1, \ldots, U_{\ell-1})$;

- *i.e.*, the two corresponding values $U_\ell = T_\ell \oplus S_\ell$ and $V_\ell = T_\ell \oplus W_\ell$ (as before) are "free", so that $\Pr[\pi_2(U_\ell) = V_\ell \mid \mathbf{Inter}] = \frac{1}{N - \beta(\mathbf{Inter})}$.

– Class $\mathcal{C}$: $\Pr[\mathsf{TNT}(T_\ell, X_\ell) \to Y_\ell \mid \mathbf{Inter}] = 0$.

- *i.e.*, the two corresponding values $U_\ell = T_\ell \oplus S_\ell$ and $V_\ell = T_\ell \oplus W_\ell$ (as before) are "contradictory" to $\mathbf{Inter}$: there exists a π_2-relation (U_i, V_i) in $\mathbf{Inter}$ such that
  * $T_\ell \oplus S_\ell = U_i$ yet $T_\ell \oplus W_\ell \neq V_i$; or
  * $T_\ell \oplus S_\ell \neq U_i$ yet $T_\ell \oplus W_\ell = V_i$.

By these, we have

$$\Pr[\mathsf{TNT}(T_\ell, X_\ell) \to Y_\ell \mid \mathcal{Q}_{\ell-1}]$$

$$= \sum_{\mathbf{Inter} \in \mathcal{A}} \Pr[\mathbf{Inter} \mid \mathcal{Q}_{\ell-1}] + \sum_{\mathbf{Inter} \in \mathcal{B}} \Pr[\mathbf{Inter} \mid \mathcal{Q}_{\ell-1}] \cdot \frac{1}{N - \beta(\mathbf{Inter})}. \quad (7)$$

With this, we derive upper and lower bounds as follows.

The Upper Bound: It's easy to see $\beta(\mathbf{Inter}) \leq \ell - 1$. By this and Eq. (7), it holds

$$\Pr[\mathsf{TNT}(T_\ell, X_\ell) \to Y_\ell \mid \mathcal{Q}_{\ell-1}]$$

$$\leq \Pr[\mathbf{Inter} \in \mathcal{A} \mid \mathcal{Q}_{\ell-1}] + \underbrace{\Pr[\mathbf{Inter} \in \mathcal{B} \mid \mathcal{Q}_{\ell-1}]}_{\leq 1} \cdot \frac{1}{2^n - \ell}. \quad (8)$$

It remains to bound $\Pr[\mathbf{Inter} \in \mathcal{A} \mid \mathcal{Q}_{\ell-1}]$. For this, note that once the values in $\mathbf{Inter}$ except for (S_ℓ, W_ℓ) have been fixed, the number of choices for (S_ℓ, W_ℓ) is at least $(2^n - \alpha(\mathcal{Q}_{\ell-1}))(2^n - \gamma(\mathcal{Q}_{\ell-1})) \geq 2^{2n}/4$, where $\alpha(\mathcal{Q}_{\ell-1}) \leq q \leq 2^n/2$ and $\gamma(\mathcal{Q}_{\ell-1}) \leq q \leq 2^n/2$ are the number of distinct values in $(S_1, \ldots, S_{\ell-1})$ and $(W_1, \ldots, W_{\ell-1})$. Out of these $\geq 2^{2n}/4$ choices, the number of choices that ensure the desired property $\mathsf{TNT}(T_\ell, X_\ell) = Y_\ell$ is at most $\ell - 1$, which results from the following selection process: we first pick a pair of input-output (U_i, V_i) with $i \leq \ell - 1$, and then set $S_\ell = T_\ell \oplus U_i$ and $W_\ell = T_\ell \oplus V_i$. Therefore, $\Pr[\mathbf{Inter} \in \mathcal{A} \mid \mathcal{Q}_{\ell-1}] \leq \frac{4\ell}{2^{2n}}$, and thus the upper bound in this case is

$$\Pr[\mathsf{TNT}(T_\ell, X_\ell) \to Y_\ell \mid \mathcal{Q}_{\ell-1}] \leq \frac{4\ell}{2^{2n}} + \frac{1}{2^n - \ell}. \quad (9)$$

The Lower Bound: It can be seen $\beta(\mathbf{Inter}) \geq \mu_\ell$, since every previous query under the tweak T_ℓ gives rise to a unique pair (U, V) in $((U_1, V_1), \ldots, (U_{\ell-1}, V_{\ell-1}))$. Therefore, still from Eq. (7), we have

$$\Pr[\mathsf{TNT}(T_\ell, X_\ell) \to Y_\ell \mid \mathcal{Q}_{\ell-1}] \geq \sum_{\mathbf{Inter} \in \mathcal{B}} \Pr[\mathbf{Inter} \mid \mathcal{Q}_{\ell-1}] \cdot \frac{1}{2^n - \mu_\ell}$$

$$= \Pr[\mathbf{Inter} \in \mathcal{B} \mid \mathcal{Q}_{\ell-1}] \cdot \frac{1}{2^n - \mu_\ell}.$$

As before, out of the $(2^n - \alpha(\mathcal{Q}_{\ell-1}))(2^n - \gamma(\mathcal{Q}_{\ell-1}))$ choices of (S_ℓ, W_ℓ), the number of choices that ensure the desired property $T_\ell \oplus S_\ell \notin \{U_1, \ldots, U_{\ell-1}\}$ and $T_\ell \oplus W_\ell \notin \{V_1, \ldots, V_{\ell-1}\}$ is at least $(2^n - \ell)^2$. This means $\Pr[\mathbf{Inter} \in \mathcal{B} \mid \mathcal{Q}_{\ell-1}] \geq \frac{2^n - \ell}{2^n - \alpha(\mathcal{Q}_{\ell-1})} \cdot \frac{2^n - \ell}{2^n - \gamma(\mathcal{Q}_{\ell-1})} \geq (1 - \frac{\ell}{2^n})^2 \geq 1 - \frac{2\ell}{2^n}$, and thus

$$\Pr[\mathsf{TNT}(T_\ell, X_\ell) \to Y_\ell \mid \mathcal{Q}_{\ell-1}] \geq \left(1 - \frac{2\ell}{2^n}\right) \cdot \frac{1}{2^n - \mu_\ell}. \tag{10}$$

Summary. In all, in the first case, we have

$$\left| \Pr[\mathsf{TNT}(T_\ell, X_\ell) \to Y_\ell \mid \mathcal{Q}_{\ell-1}] - \frac{1}{2^n - \mu_\ell} \right|$$

$$\leq \max\left\{ \frac{4\ell}{2^{2n}} + \frac{\ell - \mu_\ell}{(2^n - \mu_\ell)(2^n - \ell)}, \frac{2\ell}{2^n} \cdot \frac{1}{2^n - \mu_\ell} \right\} \leq \frac{8\ell}{2^{2n}}. \tag{11}$$

Case 2: the ℓ-th query is forward $\mathsf{TNT}(T_\ell, X_\ell) \to Y_\ell$, and $X_\ell \in \mathcal{Q}_{\ell-1}$, $Y_\ell \notin \mathcal{Q}_{\ell-1}$, i.e., $\exists T', Y' : (T', X_\ell, Y') \in \mathcal{Q}_{\ell-1}$, yet $\forall T, X : (T, X, Y_\ell) \notin \mathcal{Q}_{\ell-1}$. Now, for a certain intermediate vector $\mathbf{Inter}$, there are three possibilities, according to which we divide all intermediate vectors into three disjoint classes $\mathcal{A}$, $\mathcal{B}$, and $\mathcal{C}$:

- Class $\mathcal{A}$: there does not exist (U_i, V_i) such that $U_i = T_\ell \oplus S_\ell$, where S_ℓ is specified by $\mathbf{Inter}$ and corresponds to X_ℓ.
- Class $\mathcal{B}$: there exists (U_i, V_i) such that $U_i = T_\ell \oplus S_\ell$, and $\Pr[\pi_3(T_\ell \oplus V_i) = Y_\ell] = \frac{1}{2^n - \gamma(\mathcal{Q}_{\ell-1})}$, where $\gamma(\mathcal{Q}_{\ell-1})$ is the number of distinct values in $(Y_1, \ldots, Y_{\ell-1})$.
- Class $\mathcal{C}$: there exists (U_i, V_i) such that $U_i = T_\ell \oplus S_\ell$, and $\Pr[\pi_3(T_\ell \oplus V_i) = Y_\ell] = 0$.

By these, we have

$$\Pr[\mathsf{TNT}(T_\ell, X_\ell) \to Y_\ell \mid \mathcal{Q}_{\ell-1}]$$

$$= \sum_{\mathbf{Inter} \in \mathcal{A}} \Pr[\mathbf{Inter} \mid \mathcal{Q}_{\ell-1}] \cdot \Pr[\mathsf{TNT}(T_\ell, X_\ell) \to Y_\ell \mid \mathbf{Inter}]$$

$$+ \sum_{\mathbf{Inter} \in \mathcal{B}} \Pr[\mathbf{Inter} \mid \mathcal{Q}_{\ell-1}] \cdot \frac{1}{2^n - \gamma(\mathcal{Q}_{\ell-1})}. \tag{12}$$

The Upper Bound: For this we need to consider $\Pr[\mathsf{TNT}(T_\ell, X_\ell) \to Y_\ell \mid \mathbf{Inter}]$ for any $\mathbf{Inter} \in \mathcal{A}$. Let $U_\ell = T_\ell \oplus S_\ell$. Then it can be seen

$$\Pr[\mathsf{TNT}(T_\ell, X_\ell) \to Y_\ell \mid \mathbf{Inter}]$$

$$= \sum_{V_\ell \in \{0,1\}^n} \Pr[\pi_2(U_\ell) = V_\ell \mid \mathbf{Inter}] \cdot \Pr[\pi_3(T_\ell \oplus V_\ell) = Y_\ell \mid \mathbf{Inter}] \tag{13}$$

$$\leq \underbrace{\sum_{V_\ell \in \{0,1\}^n} \Pr[\pi_2(U_\ell) = V_\ell \mid \mathbf{Inter}]}_{\leq 1} \cdot \frac{1}{2^n - \gamma(\mathcal{Q}_{\ell-1})}.$$

By this, the upper bound in this case is

$$\Pr[\mathsf{TNT}(T_\ell, X_\ell) \to Y_\ell \mid \mathcal{Q}_{\ell-1}] \leq \sum_{\mathbf{Inter} \in \mathcal{A} \cup \mathcal{B}} \Pr[\mathbf{Inter} \mid \mathcal{Q}_{\ell-1}] \cdot \frac{1}{2^n - \gamma(\mathcal{Q}_{\ell-1})}$$

$$\leq \frac{1}{2^n - \gamma(\mathcal{Q}_{\ell-1})} \leq \frac{1}{2^n - \ell}.$$

The Lower Bound: Still by Eq. (13), for any $\mathbf{Inter} \in \mathcal{A}$ we have

$$\Pr[\mathsf{TNT}(T_\ell, X_\ell) \to Y_\ell \mid \mathbf{Inter}]$$

$$\geq \sum_{W_\ell \in \mathcal{GW}} \Pr[\pi_2(U_\ell) = T_\ell \oplus W_\ell \mid \mathbf{Inter}] \cdot \Pr[\pi_3(W_\ell) = Y_\ell \mid \mathbf{Inter}],$$

where $\mathcal{GW}$ ("good W set") is the set of W_ℓ such that:
- $W_\ell \notin \{W_1, \ldots, W_{\ell-1}\}$, and
- $T_\ell \oplus W_\ell \notin \{V_1, \ldots, V_{\ell-1}\}$.

It can seen that $|\mathcal{GW}| \geq 2^n - \ell - \ell + \mu_\ell = 2^n - 2\ell + \mu_\ell$: the reason is, for any $(T_i, X_i, Y_i) \in \mathcal{Q}_{\ell-1}$ with $T_i = T_\ell$, $W_\ell \neq W_i \Leftrightarrow T_\ell \oplus W_\ell \neq V_i$. On the other hand, $\Pr[\pi_3(W_\ell) = Y_\ell \mid \mathbf{Inter}] = \frac{1}{2^n - \gamma(\mathcal{Q}_{\ell-1})} \geq \frac{1}{2^n - \mu_\ell}$, and $\Pr[\pi_2(U_\ell) = T_\ell \oplus W_\ell \mid \mathbf{Inter}] = \frac{1}{2^n - \beta(\mathbf{Inter})} \geq \frac{1}{2^n - \mu_\ell}$. Therefore, for any $\mathbf{Inter} \in \mathcal{A}$ we have

$$\Pr[\mathsf{TNT}(T_\ell, X_\ell) \to Y_\ell \mid \mathbf{Inter}] \geq \frac{2^n - 2\ell + \mu_\ell}{(2^n - \mu_\ell)^2}.$$

By these and Eq. (12), we have

$$\Pr[\mathsf{TNT}(T_\ell, X_\ell) \to Y_\ell \mid \mathcal{Q}_{\ell-1}]$$

$$\geq \sum_{\mathbf{Inter} \in \mathcal{A} \cup \mathcal{B}} \Pr[\mathbf{Inter} \mid \mathcal{Q}_{\ell-1}] \cdot \frac{2^n - 2\ell + \mu_\ell}{(2^n - \mu_\ell)^2}$$

$$= \left(1 - \Pr[\mathbf{Inter} \in \mathcal{C} \mid \mathcal{Q}_{\ell-1}]\right) \cdot \frac{2^n - 2\ell + \mu_\ell}{(2^n - \mu_\ell)^2}.$$

To bound $\Pr[\mathbf{Inter} \in \mathcal{C} \mid \mathcal{Q}_{\ell-1}]$, note that if $\mathbf{Inter} \in \mathcal{C}$, then there exists $Y_i \in \{Y_1, \ldots, Y_{\ell-1}\}$ such that $\Pr[\mathsf{TNT}(T_\ell, X_\ell) = Y_i \mid \mathcal{Q}_{\ell-1}] = 1$. For each such Y_i the probability is at most $\frac{4\ell}{2^{2n}}$ as analyzed in Case 1. Since there are at most $\ell - 1 \leq \ell$ choices for this Y_i, we obtain

$$\Pr[\mathsf{TNT}(T_\ell, X_\ell) \to Y_\ell \mid \mathcal{Q}_{\ell-1}] \geq \left(1 - \frac{4\ell^2}{2^{2n}}\right) \cdot \frac{2^n - 2\ell + \mu_\ell}{(2^n - \mu_\ell)^2}$$

as the lower bound. Further note that

$$\frac{1}{2^n - \mu_\ell} - \left(1 - \frac{4\ell^2}{2^{2n}}\right) \cdot \frac{2^n - 2\ell + \mu_\ell}{(2^n - \mu_\ell)^2}$$

$$\leq \frac{1}{2^n - \mu_\ell} - \frac{2^n - 2\ell + \mu_\ell}{(2^n - \mu_\ell)^2} + \frac{4\ell^2}{2^{2n}} \cdot \frac{2^n - 2\ell + \mu_\ell}{(2^n - \mu_\ell)^2}$$

$$\leq \frac{2(\ell - \mu_\ell)}{(2^n - \mu_\ell)^2} + \frac{8\ell^2}{2^{3n}} \leq \frac{8\ell}{2^{2n}} + \frac{8\ell}{2^{2n}} = \frac{16\ell}{2^{2n}}.$$

Summary. In all, in the second case, we have

$$\left| \Pr[\mathsf{TNT}(T_\ell, X_\ell) \to Y_\ell \mid \mathcal{Q}_{\ell-1}] - \frac{1}{2^n - \mu_\ell} \right|$$

$$\leq \max \left\{ \frac{1}{2^n - \ell} - \frac{1}{2^n - \mu_\ell}, \frac{16\ell}{2^{2n}} \right\} \leq \frac{16\ell}{2^{2n}}. \tag{14}$$

Case 3: the ℓ-th query is forward $\mathsf{TNT}(T_\ell, X_\ell) \to Y_\ell$, and $X_\ell \notin \mathcal{Q}_{\ell-1}$, $Y_\ell \in \mathcal{Q}_{\ell-1}$. The analysis is similar to Case 2 by symmetry, resulting in the same bound

$$\left| \Pr[\mathsf{TNT}(T_\ell, X_\ell) \to Y_\ell \mid \mathcal{Q}_{\ell-1}] - \frac{1}{2^n - \mu_\ell} \right| \leq \frac{16\ell}{2^{2n}}. \tag{15}$$

Case 4: the ℓ-th query is forward $\mathsf{TNT}(T_\ell, X_\ell) \to Y_\ell$, and $X_\ell, Y_\ell \notin \mathcal{Q}_{\ell-1}$. The analyses for this case heavily resemble Case 2. First, the same upper bound

$$\Pr[\mathsf{TNT}(T_\ell, X_\ell) \to Y_\ell \mid \mathcal{Q}_{\ell-1}] \leq \frac{1}{2^n - \gamma(\mathcal{Q}_{\ell-1})} \leq \frac{1}{2^n - \ell}$$

can be established. Second, for any **Inter** such that $\Pr[\mathbf{Inter} \mid \mathcal{Q}_{\ell-1}] > 0$, we have

$$\Pr[\mathsf{TNT}(T_\ell, X_\ell) \to Y_\ell \mid \mathbf{Inter}]$$

$$\geq \sum_{S_\ell \in \mathcal{GS}, W_\ell \in \mathcal{GW}} \Pr[\pi_1(X_\ell) = S_\ell \mid \mathbf{Inter}] \cdot \Pr[\pi_2(T_\ell \oplus S_\ell) = T_\ell \oplus W_\ell \mid \mathbf{Inter}]$$

$$\cdot \Pr[\pi_3(W_\ell) = Y_\ell \mid \mathbf{Inter}],$$

where $\mathcal{GS}$ is the set of S_ℓ such that:

- $S_\ell \notin \{S_1, \ldots, S_{\ell-1}\}$, and
- $T_\ell \oplus S_\ell \notin \{U_1, \ldots, U_{\ell-1}\}$,

and $\mathcal{GW}$ is the set of W_ℓ such that:

- $W_\ell \notin \{W_1, \ldots, W_{\ell-1}\}$, and
- $T_\ell \oplus W_\ell \notin \{V_1, \ldots, V_{\ell-1}\}$.

It is easy to see $|\mathcal{GS}|, |\mathcal{GW}| \geq 2^n - 2\ell + \mu_\ell$, $\Pr[\pi_1(X_\ell) = S_\ell \mid \mathbf{Inter}] = \frac{1}{2^n - \alpha(\mathcal{Q}_{\ell-1})} \geq \frac{1}{2^n - \mu_\ell}$, $\Pr[\pi_3(W_\ell) = Y_\ell \mid \mathbf{Inter}] = \frac{1}{2^n - \gamma(\mathcal{Q}_{\ell-1})} \geq \frac{1}{2^n - \mu_\ell}$, and $\Pr[\pi_2(U_\ell) = T_\ell \oplus W_\ell \mid \mathbf{Inter}] = \frac{1}{2^n - \beta(\mathbf{Inter})} \geq \frac{1}{2^n - \mu_\ell}$. Therefore, we have

$$\Pr[\mathsf{TNT}(T_\ell, X_\ell) \to Y_\ell \mid \mathbf{Inter}] \geq \frac{(2^n - 2\ell + \mu_\ell)^2}{(2^n - \mu_\ell)^3},$$

for which

$$\frac{1}{2^n - \mu_\ell} - \frac{(2^n - 2\ell + \mu_\ell)^2}{(2^n - \mu_\ell)^3} \leq \frac{4(\ell - \mu_\ell)(2^n - \ell)}{(2^n - \mu_\ell)^3} \leq \frac{16\ell}{2^{2n}}.$$

Therefore,

$$\left| \Pr[\mathsf{TNT}(T_\ell, X_\ell) \to Y_\ell \mid \mathcal{Q}_{\ell-1}] - \frac{1}{2^n - \mu_\ell} \right|$$

$$\leq \max\left\{ \frac{1}{2^n - \ell} - \frac{1}{2^n - \mu_\ell}, \frac{16\ell}{2^{2n}} \right\} \leq \frac{16\ell}{2^{2n}}. \qquad (16)$$

To conclude, when the ℓ-th query is forward, from Eqs. (11), (14), (15), and (16) we have

$$\left(\mathsf{p}_{\mathsf{TNT},\mathcal{D}}(Y_\ell \mid \mathcal{Q}_{\ell-1}) - \frac{1}{2^n - \mu_\ell} \right)^2 \leq \left(\frac{16\ell}{2^{2n}} \right)^2 \leq \frac{256\ell^2}{2^{4n}}.$$

The remaining Cases 5, 6, 7, and 8 concern with the case where the ℓ-th query is backward, and the analyses are similar to Cases 1, 2, 3, and 4 by symmetry, resulting in the same bound

$$\left(\mathsf{p}_{\mathsf{TNT},\mathcal{D}}(X_\ell \mid \mathcal{Q}_{\ell-1}) - \frac{1}{2^n - \mu_\ell} \right)^2 \leq \left(\frac{16\ell}{2^{2n}} \right)^2 \leq \frac{256\ell^2}{2^{4n}}.$$

Consequently,

$$\chi^2(\mathcal{Q}_{\ell-1}) \leq \sum_{R_\ell} \frac{256\ell^2/2^{4n}}{1/(2^n - \mu_\ell)} \leq 2^n \cdot 2^n \cdot \frac{256\ell^2}{2^{4n}} \leq \frac{256\ell^2}{2^{2n}},$$

and

$$\frac{1}{2} \sum_{\ell=1}^{q} \mathbf{E}[\chi^2(\mathcal{Q}_{\ell-1})] \leq \frac{1}{2} \sum_{\ell=1}^{q} \frac{256\ell^2}{2^{2n}} \leq \frac{1}{2} \cdot \frac{128q^3}{2^{2n}} = \frac{64q^3}{2^{2n}},$$

which implies Eq. (6) by Lemma 1. $\square$

5   Concrete Proposals

In this section, we propose our instantiation of the TNT construction based on AES, which allows fast software implementations when AES-NI are available. We call the instantiation TNT-AES. To also enjoy the long-standing security of AES, we try to make minimum possible modifications over AES. Following these considerations, we only extend the number of rounds without any modification to its round function or key schedule, and pick the respective numbers of rounds for the three permutations π_1, π_2, and π_3 so that the design is secure against all relevant attacks. More explicitly, when the tweak $T = 0$, TNT-AES simply becomes AES with more rounds, which clearly leaves higher security margins over AES. Besides, we let the last round be complete instead of missing the MixColumns operation. In the remainder of the section, we give the description of TNT-AES, followed by a comprehensive cryptanalysis, and a comparison of software and hardware performances against other existing TBCs with similar security levels.

5.1 Instantiation Based on AES

The Advanced Encryption Standard (AES) [23] is an iterated block cipher with block size 128 bits and secret key sizes 128, 192, and 256 bits. The internal state of AES, as well as the round keys, can be represented as a 4×4 matrix whose elements are byte value (8 bits). The round function consists of four basic transformations in the following order (see Fig. 2):

- SubBytes (SB) is a nonlinear substitution that applies the same S-box to each byte of the internal state.
- ShiftRows (SR) is a cyclic rotation of the i-th row by i bytes to the left, for $i = 0, 1, 2, 3$.
- MixColumns (MC) is a multiplication of each column with a Maximum Distance Separable (MDS) matrix over $GF(2^8)$.
- AddRoundKey (AK) is an exclusive-or with the round key.

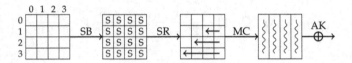

Fig. 2. AES round function

At the very beginning of the encryption, an additional pre-whitening key addition is performed, and the last round is different from the normal rounds by omitting the MixColumns operation. AES-128, AES-192, and AES-256 share the same round function with different numbers of rounds: 10, 12, and 14, respectively.

The key schedule of AES transforms the master key into subkeys that are used in each of the rounds. Here, we describe the key schedule of AES-128. The 128-bit master key is divided into four 32-bit words $(W[0], W[1], W[2], W[3])$, then $W[i]$ for $i \geqslant 4$ is computed as

$$W[i] = \begin{cases} W[i-4] \oplus \mathsf{SB}(\mathtt{RotByte}(W[i-1])) \oplus Rcon[i/4] & i \equiv 0 \bmod 4, \\ W[i-4] \oplus W[i-1] & \text{otherwise.} \end{cases}$$

The i-th round key is the concatenation of 4 words $W[4i] \parallel W[4i+1] \parallel W[4i+2] \parallel W[4i+3]$. $\mathtt{RotByte}$ is a cyclic shift by one byte to the left, and $Rcon$ are the round constants defined as

$$Rcon[i] = \begin{cases} 1 & i = 0, \\ 2 \cdot Rcon[i-1] & \text{otherwise,} \end{cases}$$

where '$\cdot$' denotes multiplication in $GF(2^8)$ with irreducible polynomial $x^8 + x^4 + x^3 + x + 1$.

Although AES-128 consists of 10 rounds, it can be naturally extended to more rounds, each composed of all 4 transformations (AddRoundKey ∘ MixColumns ∘ ShiftRows ∘ SubBytes), and the pre-whitening key addition to the first round is kept as it is. Then, TNT-AES[n_1, n_2, n_3] is defined to be the extension of AES to ($n_1 + n_2 + n_3$) rounds, i.e., π_1, π_2, π_3 are of n_1, n_2, n_3 full AES rounds respectively, and the 128-bit tweak is XOR-ed into the internal state at the output of π_1 and π_2. It is natural to set $n_1 = n_3$ due to the symmetry of the design. Concretely, we define TNT-AES[6, 6, 6], and will use TNT-AES to denote this choice for the sake of simplicity. We will justify the round numbers in the security analysis below.

5.2   Preliminary Cryptanalysis

In this subsection, we give our preliminary cryptanalysis against TNT-AES. As TNT-AES consists of 18 rounds in total, which is 8 more rounds than AES-128, we expect higher security margins of TNT-AES when the tweak is treated as a given constant. Hence, we focus on only the cases where the tweaks help the attack from cryptanalysts' point of view, i.e., it is assumed the tweak is under the attacker's full control (*open* tweak), and possibly extends the existing attacks against round-reduced AES. Under such a setting, we verify the most efficient attacks in terms of number of attacked rounds, against TNT-AES and claim the absence of key-recovery attack against the full TNT-AES in the single-key setting. While we do not claim security under the related-key setting for TNT-AES due to lack of security proof for TNT in such setting, our preliminary cryptanalysis below shows that there is no key-recovery attack either.

Following the proven security bound of TNT, TNT-AES offers $2n/3$-bit security, i.e., there exists no key-recovery attack, given that the data (the combination of tweak and plaintext with no restriction on individual input) and time complexities are bounded by $2^{2 \cdot 128/3} \simeq 2^{85}$. Due to the fact that there is no attack against TNT matching the $2^{2n/3}$ bound, all our security analysis against TNT-AES are following the $2^n = 2^{128}$ bound for both data and time. This allows TNT-AES offering higher security strength should a better than $2n/3$-bit bound be proven for TNT. In summary, we claim that there is no shortcut attack on TNT-AES better than the generic attacks against the corresponding TNT mode.

In what follows, explicit security margins are given under each attack method whenever possible. Before moving to the individual attack methods, an overview of the impact of the tweak to the security at model level is given as follows. As mentioned above, the security margin will be higher for TNT-AES when tweak is a given constant, and we call such a tweak *inactive*. When the tweak is *active*, it may be used to cancel differences in differential attack, or to be used as the source of input structure in integral attacks. Under the single-key setting, the activeness of the round functions will be consistent within each of the three permutations $\pi_1, \pi_2,$ and π_3. This allows us using 0/1 to denote the activeness of the permutations with 1 for active (0 for inactive), and a simple exhaustive search shows there are activity patterns $\{(0, 1, 0), (0, 1, 1), (1, 1, 0), (1, 0, 1), (1, 1, 1)\}$ for differential attacks, and $\{(1, 1, 1), (1, 1, 0), (0, 1, 1)\}$ for integral attacks and alike.

Differential and Linear Attacks. In the single-key setting, we will employ the known results of 4-round AES to justify the security of TNT-AES. It is well-known that there are at least 25 active S-boxes in 4 rounds of AES, which makes sure that there exists no 4-round differential characteristic (resp. linear approximation) with differential probability (resp. linear correlation) higher than $2^{-6 \times 25}$ (resp. $2^{-3 \times 25}$) [22]. For the maximum expected differential and linear probability (MEDP and MELP), known results can be obtained following the work of Keliher and Sui [47], which suggests that the upper bound on the MEDP (and MELP) of 4-round AES is about $(53/2^{34})^4 \approx 2^{-110}$. For TNT-AES in the single-key setting where the difference can be injected on the plaintext or the tweak, there is at least one active permutation among π_1, π_2, π_3 since their activity patterns fall in $\{(0,1,0), (0,1,1), (1,1,0), (1,0,1), (1,1,1)\}$. As long as π_2 is active, there must be more than 25 active S-boxes. In the case of $(1,0,1)$, it happens only when the first addition of the tweak cancels out the differences introduced from plaintext through π_1, and the same difference is then re-introduced through the second addition of tweak through π_3. Due to the fact that the same tweak is added and the difference in tweak is the same as well, π_1 and π_3 can be concatenated together with respective to differences. Note that $\pi_1 + \pi_3$ is of 12 rounds in total, out of which any 4 consecutive rounds will ensure 25 active S-boxes. We also note the security analysis of TNT under such a setting is very similar to that of AES-PRF [60] except one has the control over the extra input tweak in TNT added to the unknown internal state.

In the related-key setting, we only considered differential cryptanalysis, as there is no cancellation of active S-boxes between subkeys and the state in linear approximations. In [73], it is shown that in the related-key setting, there are at least 21 active S-boxes in consecutive 6 rounds of AES-128, and the optimal 6-round differential has probability 2^{-131}. Therefore, no useful related-key differential characteristic covering more than π_2 can be found no matter whether there is a difference in the tweak or not.

Impossible-Differential Attacks. In [71], it is proven that there does not exist any truncated impossible-differential of AES which covers more than 5 rounds. Furthermore, the best impossible-differential attack, in terms of number of attacked rounds, is 7 rounds against AES-128 [55]. Following a similar discussion for differential attacks, when π_2 is active, impossible-differential attack does not apply naturally since π_2 is of 6 rounds, more than what impossible-differential distinguisher can cover. For the case of activity pattern $(1,0,1)$, there are 12 rounds in total for $\pi_1 + \pi_3$, more than the best attack against AES-128 can cover.

The Demirci-Selçuk Meet-in-the-Middle Attack. The Demirci-Selçuk meet-in-the-middle attack led to the best cryptanalytic result on 7 rounds of AES-128 in the single-key setting, where data/time/memory complexities are below 2^{100} [25]. The distinguisher covers 4 rounds, following a differential characteristic. Note, the distinguisher here tries to limit the number of possibilities for the actual values related to the differential characteristic, and it is not clear how the addition of the tweak helps reduce that. Actually, it is not even clear the addition of round key can help reduce the counts either. Hence, round keys are treated as independent fixed constants in such attacks. Thus, we can treat the tweak in the same way. Therefore, the Demirci-Selçuk meet-in-the-middle attack would work in the same way on TNT-AES as on AES, and 7 rounds of TNT-AES can be attacked.

Yoyo Tricks. In [68], Rønjom *et al.* presented several key-independent yoyo-distinguishers on 3- to 5-round AES, which require up to $2^{25.8}$ data and $2^{24.8}$ XOR computations. A key-independent impossible-differential yoyo-distinguisher on 6-round AES requiring an amount of $2^{122.83}$ data was also proposed. Besides, a key-recovery attack on 5-round AES requiring practical complexities was devised based on the 4-round yoyo-distinguisher. In these attacks, the attacker queries pair of plaintexts to the encryption and uses swap operation on the obtained pair of ciphertexts to generate new queries to the decryption, and observes difference in the obtained pair of plaintexts, then she may continually construct new pairs of plaintexts by swapping words in the obtained pairs and iterate the same procedure enough times. It can be seen that, instead of collecting all chosen plaintexts/ciphertexts (CPs/CCs) at once, these attacks use adaptively-chosen-plaintexts/-ciphertexts (ACPs/ACCs). In TNT-AES, tweaks are always inserted as input to the encryption/decryption, and will never be output. So, for activity pattern $(0, 1, 1)$ (resp. $(1, 1, 0)$ for decryption), the attacker cannot play the yoyo game by adaptively choosing and observing the differences of tweak pairs and ciphertext (resp. plaintext) pairs. Accordingly, we claim that these yoyo-distinguishers and yoyo-distinguisher-based key-recovery attacks cannot be directly applied in their current form to TNT-AES.

Subspace Trail Attacks. Subspace trail cryptanalysis [32] can be seen as a generalization of invariant subspace cryptanalysis [52], whereas it can be launched independently on specific choices of round constants or subkeys. By analyzing subspace trails, Grassi *et al.* re-interpreted the 3-round truncated differential and integral, the 4-round impossible-differential and integral distinguishers on AES [33]. Besides, new distinguishers on round-reduced AES are found using subspace trail cryptanalysis, including the 5-round impossible-differential distinguisher [33], the 5-round multiple-of-8 distinguisher [34], the 4-round mixture-differential [31], and the 5-round (probabilistic, threshold, and impossible) mixture-differential distinguishers [30]. Exploiting the 4-round mixture-differential distinguisher, a record for key-recovery attack on 5-round AES-128 in single-key model is set [4]. In [6], Bardeh and Rønjom proposed the exchange attacks. Like in yoyo and mixture-differential attacks, exchange attacks also involve swap (exchange) operations on the pairs of chosen data. On 6-round AES, the exchange distinguishers requires $2^{88.2}$ CPs and $2^{88.2}$ encryptions. In the attacks, new plaintext pairs are obtained by exchanging certain active diagonal of other pairs that are different in diagonals, and an invariant property on the number of active columns of the differences of ciphertext pairs under such exchange operation are considered.

Using subspace trail cryptanalysis and comparing with distinguishers on round-reduced AES, we analyze distinguishers and corresponding attacks on round-reduced TNT-AES. The activity patterns of the three permutations that we considered are $(0, 1, 0)$, $(1, 0, 1)$, $(0, 1, 1)$, $(1, 1, 0)$, and $(1, 1, 1)$. The activity pattern $(0, 1, 0)$ requires that all differences are comes from tweaks and canceled by the same tweaks through n_2 (*i.e.*, 6) AES-rounds, which has no shortcut method up to now. Considering that all subspace-trail-based distinguishers on round-reduced AES are no more than n_2 (*i.e.*, 6) AES-rounds, it seems hard to construct an exploitable subspace trail under activity patterns $(0, 1, 1)$, $(1, 1, 0)$, $(1, 1, 1)$, which indicate more than a chunk of active 6-round AES. The activity pattern $(1, 0, 1)$ implies that the coset of subspace related to the internal states at the end of π_1 (resulted from a set of plaintexts) equals a coset of the same subspace formed by the chosen tweaks (and the differences between tweak pairs should cancel the differences caused by the plaintext pairs), and thus the coset of subspace formed by the chosen tweaks will cause the internal states at the beginning of π_3 forming a coset of the same subspace. A subspace trail on internal states can be seen as bypassing π_2 via choosing a coset of subspace of the tweak. Thus, devising an attack using a subspace trail under activity pattern $(1, 0, 1)$ requires that one can devise a subspace trail attack on the concatenated permutation $\pi_3 \circ \pi_1$ that is of $(n_1 + n_3)$ AES-rounds, which is unknown when $(n_1 + n_3) > 6$. In Appendix A, we discuss in detail the subspace-trail-based distinguishers and key-recovery attacks on round-reduced TNT-AES.

Cube Attack, Dynamic Cube Attack. AES is immune to cube attacks [27] or dynamic cube attacks [28] due to the high algebraic degree of the AES S-box. Specifically, the algebraic degree is 7 for one round of AES and increases to 32 ($<7^2$) and 128 ($<32 \times 7$) for two and three rounds. Therefore, AES, which has 10 rounds, is believed to be resistant to such types of attacks. So is TNT-AES since it has more rounds than AES.

Integral Attacks and Division Property. The integral attacks utilize an integral distinguisher for 3 rounds (or 4 rounds without MixColumns for the last round), with a starting point of *ALL* values for a diagonal and a *BALANCED* output, *i.e.*, the sum of each individual byte is 0. The best attack setting will be to utilize the degrees of freedom from the tweak to achieve the distinguisher starting from the input of π_2 in forward direction with activity pattern $(0, 1, 1)$ (or output of π_2 in backward direction with activity pattern $(1, 1, 0)$). The attack will start with a fixed plaintext, and take ALL values of a diagonal from tweak. Thus, the target is $\pi_2 + \pi_3$ only with a secret input to π_2. In the key-recovery phase, the attacker is able to append one round only, so this attack will work for at most $n_1 + 5$ out of $(n_1 + n_2 + n_3)$ rounds, *i.e.*, $6 + 5$ out of 18 for TNT-AES.

The division property due to Todo *et al.* [74,75] can be viewed as an extension of integral distinguisher, which has been successfully applied to many block ciphers. However, there is no reported results on AES better than integral attack so far.

Slide Attacks. The slide attack was first described by Biryukov and Wagner [10,11] in 1999 to attack round-reduced DES. The core idea is to make use of the similarity of the round functions and that of key schedule. Thus, the difference of encryption process in its original form and one (or few) rounds shifted is within control, *e.g.*, with high probability. The addition of tweak will allow canceling the difference in at most one round, while TNT-AES has 8 more rounds than AES-128. Hence, we expect higher security margin here. Furthermore, there is no reported slide attack against full AES-128 so far.

(Related-Subkey) Boomerang Attacks. Boomerang attacks [76] construct long distinguishers by connecting two short differential characteristics. Recently, a new tool named Boomerang Connectivity Table [16] was proposed to formulate the dependency that the two differential characteristics contain and offer guidance towards better boomerang distinguishers. We utilize the framework of the boomerang connectivity table when mounting boomerang attacks on TNT-AES. First, we consider the single-key setting where the difference can be introduced on the plaintext or the tweak. When the difference is introduced only on the tweak, as shown in Fig. 3 in Appendix B, high-probability boomerang distinguishers can be constructed on $n_1 + n_2 + n_3$ rounds, where n_1, n_3 can be any number and $n_2 < 6$. When $n_2 \geq 6$, such high-probability distinguishers do not exist. Note that these distinguishers with zero plaintext and ciphertext difference are not useful in key-recovery attacks. When the difference is also introduced to the plaintext or ciphertext, by making π_2 inactive through the tweak difference, the cipher can be seen as $\pi_1 \circ \pi_3$ with respective to differences and boomerang attacks of $n_2 + r$ rounds can be mounted, where r is the number of rounds that boomerang attacks of AES-128 can cover and is 5. That is, only 11 rounds can be attacked. Next, we consider the related-subkey setting where the key difference can be injected on a round key. The related-subkey setting is more powerful and usually allows longer boomerang distinguishers than the related-key setting where the difference is injected on the master key. In the related-subkey setting, there exists a 6-round boomerang distinguisher of AES-128 with probability $2^{-109.42}$ [70]. This distinguisher can be naturally extended to the 7 middle rounds of TNT-AES with the same probability under the condition that the tweak difference cancels the input difference or the output difference of the 6-round boomerang distinguisher. When we add one more round to the bottom or to the top of the 7-round distinguisher, the numbers of active S-boxes will increase at least by one, leading to a negligible probability. Therefore, there seem no boomerang distinguishers of TNT-AES in the related-subkey setting that cover more than 8 rounds.

5.3   Performance

Software Performance. We estimate the software performance of TNT-AES on the basis of the best results of AES software provided by Park *et al.* [65]. In what follows, we consider both "Plaintext" and "Tweak" as data since when used in some authenticated encryption schemes, both of them are used to process data such as associated data. Hence, the software performance is then calculated as the total number of CPU cycles divided by the total byte length of plaintext and tweak of the TBCs. To obtain a fair comparison, we estimate the same for other existing TBCs as well (omitting their additional cost for updating tweaks), using the following formula:

$$\text{original speed} \times \frac{\text{block size}}{\text{block size} + \text{tweak size}}. \tag{17}$$

For TNT-AES, the number of rounds are different from AES. To evaluate the performance, we multiply a factor to the speed of AES. Accordingly, the formula we used to calculate the software speed of TNT-AES is (where, AES means AES-128):

$$\text{speed of AES} \times \frac{\text{block size}}{\text{block size} + \text{tweak size}} \times \frac{\text{TNT-AES round number}}{\text{AES round number}}. \tag{18}$$

We note that the optimization technique proposed in [65] is for the CTR mode of AES, which extends the counter-mode caching [9,78]. It caches and reuses intermediate results up to AES round 1 (R1) or up to AES round 2 (R2). For TNT-AES, tweaks are added until round $(n_1 + 1)$. Thus, this optimization technique is applicable. Whereas, for other TBCs in which tweaks are added before the first round, this technique may not be applicable.

Table 2 presents the estimated results on software performance of TNT-AES, together with the results of other TBCs under the similar setting (considering both "Plaintext" and "Tweak" as data).

Rekeying and Retweaking. To see the scenario that profits considerably by using a tweakable block cipher processing tweak efficiently, we performed a performance comparison between retweaking in TNT-AES and rekeying in AES-128. Table 3 reports the timing results. Because in the AES-NI set, the reciprocal throughput of the AESKEYGENASSIST instruction that assists the key-schedule is higher than that of the instruction AESENC that executes one round of encryption, in Table 3, it can be seen that the process of rekeying in AES becomes slower. Whereas, the process of retweaking in TNT-AES benefits a lot from the fast AES-NI instruction for encryption.[1]

---

[1] Please refer to https://github.com/TNT-AES/Rekeying_vs_Retweaking for a very simple implementation of the TNT-AES encryption and this performance comparison.

Table 2. A table of comparison with other TBCs on software (all TBCs are with 128-bit block, 128-bit master key). The platform is Intel Haswell CPU i7-4770, which is the commonly used CPU in references [8, 40, 42, 65].

Cipher	Data type	Tech.	Speed in cycles per byte, given messages in bytes										Ref.
			128	256	512	1024	2048	4096	8192	20480	40960	65536	
AES	Plaintext	Table-based				8.38		8.34		8.37	8.37		[65]
	Plaintext	Bitsliced				4.70		4.43		4.40	4.40		[65]
	Plaintext	AES-NI 1 × 1 R1				1.03		1.02		1.07	1.07		[65]
	Plaintext	AES-NI 1 × 1 R2				0.93		0.92		1.04	1.04		[65]
	Plaintext	AES-NI 1 x 4 R1				0.63		0.62		0.62	0.62		[65]
	Plaintext	AES-NI 1 x 4 R2				0.59		0.58		0.58	0.58		[65]
TNT- AES	Plaintext + Tweak	Table-based				7.54		7.51		7.53	7.53		★ [65]
	Plaintext + Tweak	Bitsliced				4.23		3.99		3.96	3.96		★ [65]
	Plaintext + Tweak	AES-NI 1 × 1 R1				0.92		0.92		0.97	0.96		★ [65]
	Plaintext + Tweak	AES-NI 1 × 1 R2				0.83		0.83		0.94	0.94		★ [65]
	Plaintext + Tweak	AES-NI 1 × 4 R1				0.57		0.56		0.56	0.56		★ [65]
	Plaintext + Tweak	AES-NI 1 × 4 R2				0.53		0.52		0.52	0.52		★ [65]
SKINNY -128-128	Plaintext	Bitsliced-64-block				† 3.78							[8]
SKINNY -128-256	Plaintext + Tweak	Bitsliced-64-block				‡ 2.27							[8]
Deoxys -BC-256	Plaintext	AES-NI	4.74	2.85	1.90	1.43	1.18	1.07	1.01		0.96		[42]
	Plaintext + Tweak	AES-NI	2.37	1.43	0.95	0.72	0.59	0.54	0.51		0.48		[42]
Kiasu≠ -BC-64	Plaintext	AES-NI	0.97	0.84	0.78	0.76	0.75	0.74					[40]
	Plaintext + Tweak	AES-NI	0.65	0.56	0.52	0.51	0.50	0.49					[40]

- The reference for TNT-AES indicated by ★ means that basing on the results of AES in [65] and using Eq. (18), we calculated the presented results for TNT-AES.
- The value for SKINNY-128-256 indicated by ‡ is calculated using the value for SKINNY-128-128 indicated by † basing on a formula similar to Eq. (18).

Hardware Performance. We estimate the hardware performance of TNT-AES with area minimization as optimizations target. The current record of minimized area of AES is kept by the bit-serial implementations provided by Jean *et al.* [39]. Apart from AES, Jean *et al.* also provided bit-serial implementations of another tweakable block cipher SKINNY. Using those state-of-the-art results provided by Jean *et al.* [39], we estimate the area and latency of TNT-AES and make comparisons with other TBCs. The results are summarized in Table 5.

In the table, results for AES, SKINNY-128-256, and Deoxys-BC-256 are all from existing studies. The results for TNT-AES are calculated using the following method based on the results for AES. Let δ be the number of bits in the data path in all implementations. Let C_{1DFF} be the cost of a 1-bit D flip-flop (D FF), let C_{XOR} be the cost of a 2-input XOR gate, and let C_{MUX} be the cost of a 2-to-1 Multiplexer in a library. We use Table 4 to estimate C_{1DFF}, C_{XOR}, and C_{MUX} in various libraries.

Table 3. Software performance of AES-128 when rekeying for every block and that of TNT-AES when fixing a key but retweaking for every block, both with plaintexts as data (unlike in Table 2 where we consider both "Plaintext" and "Tweak" as data), and both with help of AES-NI (on an Intel(R) Core(TM) i7-8565U CPU 1.80 GHz, which belongs to products formerly Whiskey Lake).

$|M|$ (bytes)	Rekeying in AES-128 (cycles/byte)	Retweaking in TNT-AES (cycles/byte)
128	4.60	1.50
256	4.60	1.00
512	4.60	0.80
1024	4.60	0.70
2048	4.60	0.60
4096	4.60	0.60
8192	4.60	0.60

Compared with implementations of AES, the additional area cost for implementations of TNT-AES comes from the cost for storing a 128-bit tweak and the cost for implementing the XOR with tweak (we ignore the additional cost for the signals controlling the tweak/key inputs). We note that there are cases where as input, the tweak can be sent twice by the external provider. In such cases, extra storage for the tweak can be saved. We note that this is possible for a design without a "tweak-schedule". For other designs, such as that permute the bytes of the tweak, this becomes difficult as it requires this permutation to be followed by external provider if not stored locally. In TNT-AES, there is no tweak-schedule, hence no storage for tweak is required. When storage is required, the 128-bit tweak can be stored using 128 1-bit D FF. To implement the XOR with tweak, besides δ 2-input XOR gates, δ 2-to-1 multiplexers are also required for selecting the bits of tweak after the n_1-th round and the (n_1+n_2)-th round and selecting constant 0 after other rounds. The additional area cost for XOR gates and multiplexers is $\delta \times (C_{XOR} + C_{MUX})$. Thus, additional area cost is $128 \times C_{1DFF} + \delta \times (C_{XOR} + C_{MUX})$ when the tweak needs to be stored locally, and $\delta \times (C_{XOR} + C_{MUX})$ otherwise. To get a better view of the performances, we provide the gate sizes for both scenarios.

Table 4. The (estimated) cost (in Gate Equivalent, GE) of regular flip-flops, scan flip-flops, 2-input XOR gates, and 2-to-1 Multiplexers in different libraries.

	UMC 180	UMC 130	UMC 90	Ngate 45	IBM 130
1-bit D FF	4.67	5.00	4.25	5.67	4.25
1-bit Scan FF	6.00	6.25	5.75	7.67	5.50
1-bit XOR	2.67	2.75	2.50	2.00	2.00
2-to-1 MUX	2.33	2.25	2.25	2.33	2.25

Table 5. A table of comparison with other TBCs on hardware area (in GEs) and latency (all TBCs are with 128-bit block, 128-bit master key, and 128-bit tweak)

Cipher	data path Bits	UMC 180 GEs	UMC 130 GEs	UMC 90 GEs	Ngate 45 GEs	IBM 130 GEs	Latency Cycles	Ref.
AES	1	1727	1902	1596	1982	1560	* 1776/168	[39]
	2	1796	1992	1667	2054	1625	* 888/84	[39]
	4	1920	2168	1784	2146	1731	* 520/50	[39]
	8	2112	2360	1968	2337	1912	* 282/27	[39]
	8	2400	3574	2292	2768	2182	* 226/21	[63]
TNT- AES	1	† 2330/1732	† 2547/1907	† 2145/1601	† 2712/1986	† 2108/1564	3152 ⋆	[39]
	2	† 2404/1806	† 2642/2002	† 2221/1677	† 2788/2063	† 2178/1634	1576 ⋆	[39]
	4	† 2538/1940	† 2828/2188	† 2347/1803	† 2889/2163	† 2292/1748	932 ⋆	[39]
	8	† 2750/2152	† 3040/2400	† 2550/2006	† 3097/2372	† 2490/1946	502 ⋆	[39]
	8	† 3038/2440	† 4254/3614	† 2874/2330	† 3528/2803	† 2760/2216	394 ⋆	[63]
SKINNY- 128-256	1	2082	2278	1937	2501	1905	8448	[39]
	2	2130	2318	1988	2554	1941	4224	[39]
	4	2248	2433	2108	2694	2044	2112	[39]
	8	2456	2662	2325	2949	2223	1056	[39]
Deoxys- BC-256	8	2860					338	[42]

* In column 8 for **AES**, in the form x/y, x is the number of cycles taken by the entire encryption, y is the number of cycles taken by one full round which is used to estimate the latency of **TNT-AES**.
† In column 3–7 for **TNT-AES**, in the form x/y, x is the area when the tweak is stored locally, y is the area when the tweak is not stored locally.
⋆ The references for **TNT-AES** indicated by ⋆ means that basing on the results of **AES** in these works, we calculated the presented results for **TNT-AES**.

For latency, selecting and XOR-ing bits of tweak can be implemented in the same clock cycles for AddRoundKey and SubBytes, thus cost no additional cycles. The additional cycle-cost comes from the fact that TNT-AES has more rounds and the last round is complete instead of missing the MixColumns. Thus, to estimate the latency of TNT-AES, we use the clock cycles taken by one full round of AES (denoted by $Cycles_{round}$), times the total number of rounds ($n_1+n_2+n_3$), plus the cycles taken by the last AddRoundKey ($128/\delta$ cycles), *i.e.*, $Cycles_{round} \times (n_1 + n_2 + n_3) + 128/\delta$, where $Cycles_{round}$ is listed in Table 5 (column 8 for AES).

From Table 5, when the tweak has to be stored locally, the hardware performance of TNT-AES is slightly inferior to those of SKINNY-128-256 and Deoxys-BC-256, otherwise, the hardware performance of TNT-AES can be superior.

Comparison to TAES. Here, we briefly discuss the comparison between the performance of TNT-AES and that of TAES, where TAES is an AES-based TBC used to instantiate ZOCB and ZOTR that are two tweakable blockcipher modes for authenticated encryption with full absorption [3]. TAES tweaks AES-256 by simply replacing the second half part of the secrete key with 128-bit tweak and keeping all other operations and parameters unchanged. Thus, it has 14 rounds, 128-bit blocks, 128-bit keys, and 128-bit tweaks.

Because TNT-AES consists of 18 AES-rounds, *i.e.*, 4 more rounds than TAES, under the use-cases where both the key and the tweak are fixed and all sub-tweaks/sub-keys can be precomputed, TAES outperforms TNT-AES. Whereas, for other use-cases where retweaking is necessary, TNT-AES is expected to perform better. The reasons are as follows. TNT-AES has no tweak-schedule, while that for TAES is related to the key-schedule for AES-256. For software implementation using AES-NI, the instruction for one-round encryption outperforms that for the key-schedule as mentioned above. Thus, in retweaking use-cases, TNT-AES will be much faster than TAES. For hardware implementation, when the 128-bit tweak can be stored in external storage, TNT-AES does not need additional storage to process the tweak. The area requirement is hence much less than that of TAES, which requires local storage to hold and process the tweak.

6   Conclusion and Open Questions

In this paper, we proposed a new mode named TNT for constructing tweakable block ciphers with proven BBB security based on three block ciphers. To demonstrate the effectiveness of the mode, an instantiation based on AES named TNT-AES was proposed, which enjoys the long-standing security of AES, fast software performance due to AES new instructions, and hardware efficiency due to the simplicity of TNT mode. Following the prove-then-prune design strategy, we reduced the number of rounds of the three underlying AES-based block ciphers from 10 for the original AES, to 6, 6, and 6, respectively. Our comprehensive cryptanalysis shows no security issues against TNT-AES, while the reduced number of rounds allow achieving competitive software and hardware performances with existing TBCs designed through modular methods. We expect TNT to be a generic way to turn a block cipher into a tweakable block cipher securely, especially for those lightweight block ciphers with smaller block lengths.

Potential Applications. While TNT-AES only supports n-bit tweaks which seems a limitation compared to CLRW2$_2$, such a parameter has already been sufficient for many important applications. For example, many TBC-based MACs, including the chaining-via-tweak mode proposed by Liskov *et al.* [54] (its security was later proved optimal by Landecker *et al.* [51]) and the AXU-hash-based MACs proposed by Cogliati *et al.* [19], are exactly built from TBCs with n-bit tweaks, and thus instantiating the TBCs with CLRW2$_2$ (as done in [51]) clearly wastes power and causes unnecessary efficiency loss. Consequently, TNT-AES would probably be a better building block. Moreover, TNT-AES could also be used to build BBB secure variable length domain extenders via the construction of Chen *et al.* [13] or double-length block cipher via the construction of Coron *et al.* [21]. As discussed in [13], such construction may further motivate highly secure format-preserving encryption schemes might be a very valuable alternative to the recently broken standards.

Besides, TNT-AES could be used to replace the TBC module in the standard OCB3 mode and the OTR mode [62] (the 2nd round candidate during CAESAR competition). Both modes are optimally secure when the underlying TBC-module is optimal [49,62] but fall down to the birthday bound due to instantiating the TBC with XEX-like constructions [67]. Therefore, once instantiating with TNT-AES, we obtain corresponding variants secure against BBB $2^{2n/3}$ queries in both cases. Consider the application to OCB3 for concreteness. The resulting AE TNT-AES-ΘCB is a ΘCB instance [49] with TNT-AES being its underlying TBC, and the security is boosted from $n/2$ bits of OCB3 to $2n/3$ bits. Perhaps surprisingly, the hardware efficiency might be improved as well: the original OCB3 mode requires to store an AXU hash key $E_K(0)$ during the lifetime of the master key K, which is avoided in TNT-AES-TAE.

We anticipate more such applications, especially when AES-based TBCs are used and constructed from other modes than TNT.

The Security Gap. Although the security of TNT is proven to be $2^{2n/3}$, there is no matching attack – note that Dinur *et al.*'s attack strategy [26] against the 3-round Even-Mansour ciphers does not help here since the permutations in TNT cannot be queried by the adversary, and Mennink's distinguisher [59] does not work directly either due to the $2^{3n/2}$ offline computational complexity besides the $2^{3n/4}$ online query complexity. Then, the same applies to the instantiation TNT-AES. It will be interesting to see the closure of this gap, by either improving the proven security bound or finding a better attack. We leave this as an open problem to the community.

Acknowledgements. We thank the anonymous reviewers for their helpful comments and thank Tetsu Iwata, Eik List and Kazuhiko Minematsu for fruitful discussions. This research is supported by the National Research Foundation, Prime Minister's Office, Singapore, under its Strategic Capability Research Centres Funding Initiative, Nanyang Technological University under grant M4082123, Singapore's Ministry of Education under grants RG 18/19 and MOE2019-T2-1-060, and National Natural Science Foundation of China (No. 61961146004). The second author is partially supported by the Program of Qilu Young Scholars (Grant No. 61580089963177) of Shandong University. The fourth author is partially supported by the National Natural Science Foundation of China (Grants No. 61802399, 61802400, 61732021 and 61772519), the Youth Innovation Promotion Association CAS, the National Key Research and Development Project (Grant No. 2018YFA0704704) and Chinese Major Program of National Cryptography Development Foundation (Grant No. MMJJ20180102).

A   Subspace Trail Cryptanalysis of TNT-AES

In this section, we discuss subspace-trail-based distinguishers and key-recovery attacks on TNT-AES under the activity pattern $(0, 1, 1)$. Attacking encryption under the pattern $(1, 1, 0)$ can be seen as attacking decryption with the pattern $(0, 1, 1)$. Thus, similar attacks under the pattern $(1, 1, 0)$ can be devised once attacks under the pattern $(0, 1, 1)$ are established. Subspace trail cryptanalysis of TNT-AES under the activity pattern $(0, 1, 1)$ can be compared with subspace trail cryptanalysis of $(n_2 + n_3)$-round AES. The difference lies in that the initial coset of concerned subspace is formed by chosen tweaks instead of by chosen plaintext and elements in the coset will be XOR-ed with the internal state (an unknown constant) c^* which can not be observed during the attack. Besides, the same chosen tweaks are XOR-ed after π_2.

As introduced in Sect. 5.2, a series of attacks on round-reduced (no more than 6 rounds) AES based on subspace trail cryptanalysis and the extended mixture-differential, exchange attacks were proposed in [4–6, 31–34]. Among these r-round distinguishers, those which do not require the knowledge of part of the secret key can be directly turned into $(n_1 + r)$-round distinguishers with the same complexity on round-reduced TNT-AES. This can be done by using a unique plaintext p and a structure of tweaks to construct required cosets of concerned subspace at the beginning of π_2. Although the exact cosets are unknown, required relations among input states at the beginning of the active permutation can be constructed using chosen tweaks. For example, when turn the 4-round mixture-differential distinguisher on AES [4, 30] into an $(n_1 + 4)$-round distinguisher on TNT-AES, if some chosen tweaks can form mixture quadruples, then after being XOR-ed with a common unknown internal state, the resulting states still keep the relation of being mixture quadruples. There are r-round distinguishers on round-reduced AES that require considering part of the key, which can also be turned into $(n_1 + r)$-round distinguisher on TNT-AES. Take the 5-round impossible-differential distinguishers based on the impossible subspace trail on 4-round AES [33] for example. When we turn it into $(n_1 + 5)$-round distinguisher on TNT-AES, we use a unique plaintext p and structures of chosen tweaks (chosen in the way of choosing plaintexts in the original distinguisher). Then, unlike in the original distinguisher on AES, where we guess the single-byte key difference $k_{0,0} \oplus k_{1,1}$, we guess the single-byte difference $c_{0,0}^* \oplus c_{1,1}^*$, where c^* is the unknown internal state before XOR-ing the tweak. Again, the complexities of these $(n_1 + r)$-round distinguishers on TNT-AES will be almost the same with those r-round distinguishers on AES.

As for key-recovery attacks exploiting those r-round distinguishers on round-reduced AES (*e.g.*, the 5-round key-recovery attack exploiting the 4-round mixture-differential distinguisher [4] and the 6-round key-recovery attack exploiting the 5-round probabilistic mixture-differential distinguisher [30]), they add one round in front of the distinguisher, and guess parts of the whitening key (*e.g.*, key bits in $SR^{-1}(Col(i))$, or say in diagonal space $\mathcal{D}_i$, $i \in \{0, 1, 2, 3\}$) to filter out useful plaintexts from a chosen structure or to classify chosen plaintexts into properly defined sets. Such attacks may not be directly used to construct corresponding attacks on $(n_1 + 1 + r)$-round TNT-AES by guessing part of the subkey, because the internal state is also unknown. However, by guessing the internal state before XOR-ing the tweak, we can recover this unknown state part by part (instead of recovering key bits). Using this recovered internal state, one may further analyze π_1 to recover the key. However, because the dependent unknown values are in the diagonal $SR^{-1}(Col(i))$ that depend on the full state one round before, extending such attacks to cover one more round seems to be difficult. Thus, exploiting current techniques in such attacks on r-round AES-128, an attack on TNT-AES is limited to be no more than $(n_1 + 1 + r)$ rounds. Key-recovery attacks using those $(n_1 + r)$-round ($r \geq 5$) distinguishers to recovery the subkey in an appended (complete) round seems also very hard. That is because, the considered cosets at the end of the exploited distinguishers are commonly cosets of mixed space $\mathcal{M}_I$ ($I \subseteq \{0, 1, 2, 3\}$), which are mapped into the full state. Thus, in an $(n_1 + r + 1)$-round ($r \geq 5$) key-recovery attack, checking the distinguishable properties one round before the last round requires guessing the entire key.

Based on these analyses and together with previous analyses of other activity patterns, we believe TNT-AES is strong enough to resist subspace trail attacks.

B   Examples of the Related-Tweak Boomerang Distinguishers of TNT-AES

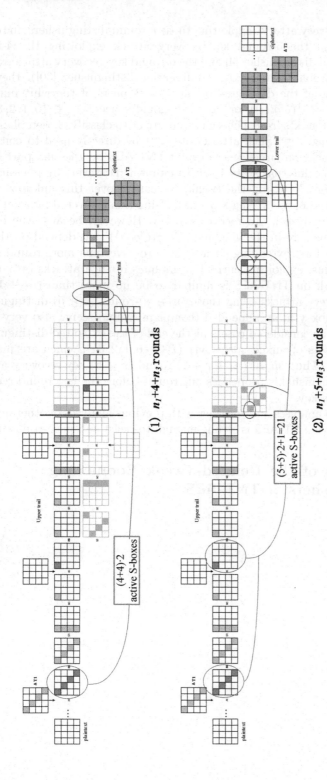

Fig. 3. Examples of the related-tweak boomerang distinguishers of TNT-AES, where the $(n_1 + 4 + n_3)$-round distinguisher has probability 2^{-96} and the $(n_1 + 5 + n_3)$-round distinguisher has probability slightly higher than 2^{-128}.

References

1. CAESAR: Competition for Authenticated Encryption: Security, Applicability, and Robustness (2014–2019). https://competitions.cr.yp.to/caesar.html
2. Aumasson, J.P., et al.: Challenges in authenticated encryption, March 2017. https://chae.cr.yp.to/chae-20170301.pdf
3. Bao, Z., Guo, J., Iwata, T., Minematsu, K.: ZOCB and ZOTR: tweakable blockcipher modes for authenticated encryption with full absorption. IACR Trans. Symmetr. Cryptol. **2019**(2), 1–54 (2019)
4. Bar-On, A., Dunkelman, O., Keller, N., Ronen, E., Shamir, A.: Improved key recovery attacks on reduced-round AES with practical data and memory complexities. In: Shacham, H., Boldyreva, A. (eds.) CRYPTO 2018, Part II. LNCS, vol. 10992, pp. 185–212. Springer, Cham (2018). https://doi.org/10.1007/978-3-319-96881-0_7
5. Bardeh, N.G.: A key-independent distinguisher for 6-round AES in an adaptive setting. Cryptology ePrint Archive, Report 2019/945 (2019). https://eprint.iacr.org/2019/945
6. Bardeh, N.G., Rønjom, S.: The exchange attack: how to distinguish six rounds of AES with $2^{88.2}$ chosen plaintexts. In: Galbraith, S.D., Moriai, S. (eds.) ASIACRYPT 2019. LNCS, vol. 11923, pp. 347–370. Springer, Cham (2019). https://doi.org/10.1007/978-3-030-34618-8_12
7. Beierle, C., et al.: The SKINNY family of block ciphers and its low-latency variant MANTIS. In: Robshaw, M., Katz, J. (eds.) CRYPTO 2016, Part II. LNCS, vol. 9815, pp. 123–153. Springer, Heidelberg (2016). https://doi.org/10.1007/978-3-662-53008-5_5
8. Beierle, C., et al.: The SKINNY family of block ciphers and its low-latency variant MANTIS. Cryptology ePrint Archive, Report 2016/660 (2016). http://eprint.iacr.org/2016/660
9. Bernstein, D.J., Schwabe, P.: New AES software speed records. In: Chowdhury et al. [15], pp. 322–336 (2008)
10. Biryukov, A., Wagner, D.: Slide attacks. In: Knudsen [48], pp. 245–259 (1999)
11. Biryukov, A., Wagner, D.: Advanced slide attacks. In: Preneel, B. (ed.) EUROCRYPT 2000. LNCS, vol. 1807, pp. 589–606. Springer, Heidelberg (2000). https://doi.org/10.1007/3-540-45539-6_41
12. Chakraborti, A., Datta, N., Jha, A., Lopez, C.M., Nandi, M., Sasaki, Y.: Elastictweak: a framework for short tweak tweakable block cipher. Cryptology ePrint Archive, Report 2019/440 (2019). https://eprint.iacr.org/2019/440
13. Chen, Y.L., Mennink, B., Nandi, M.: Short variable length domain extenders with beyond birthday bound security. In: Peyrin and Galbraith [66], pp. 244–274 (2018)
14. Cheon, J.H., Takagi, T. (eds.): Advances in Cryptology - ASIACRYPT 2016, Part I, Hanoi, Vietnam, 4–8 December 2016. LNCS, vol. 10031. Springer, Heidelberg (2016). https://doi.org/10.1007/978-3-662-53887-6
15. Chowdhury, D.R., Rijmen, V., Das, A. (eds.): Progress in Cryptology - INDOCRYPT 2008: 9th International Conference in Cryptology in India, Kharagpur, India 14–17 December 2008. LNCS, vol. 5365. Springer, Heidelberg (2008). https://doi.org/10.1007/978-3-540-89754-5
16. Cid, C., Huang, T., Peyrin, T., Sasaki, Y., Song, L.: Boomerang connectivity table: a new cryptanalysis tool. In: Nielsen, J.B., Rijmen, V. (eds.) EUROCRYPT 2018, Part II. LNCS, vol. 10821, pp. 683–714. Springer, Cham (2018). https://doi.org/10.1007/978-3-319-78375-8_22

17. Cogliati, B.: Tweaking a block cipher: multi-user beyond-birthday-bound security in the standard model. Des. Codes Cryptogr. **86**(12), 2747–2763 (2018). https://doi.org/10.1007/s10623-018-0471-8
18. Cogliati, B., Lampe, R., Seurin, Y.: Tweaking even-mansour ciphers. In: Gennaro and Robshaw [29], pp. 189–208 (2015)
19. Cogliati, B., Lee, J., Seurin, Y.: New constructions of MACs from (tweakable) block ciphers. IACR Trans. Symmetr. Cryptol. **2017**(2), 27–58 (2017)
20. Cogliati, B., Seurin, Y.: Beyond-birthday-bound security for tweakable even-mansour ciphers with linear tweak and key mixing. In: Iwata, T., Cheon, J.H. (eds.) ASIACRYPT 2015, Part II. LNCS, vol. 9453, pp. 134–158. Springer, Heidelberg (2015). https://doi.org/10.1007/978-3-662-48800-3_6
21. Coron, J.-S., Dodis, Y., Mandal, A., Seurin, Y.: A domain extender for the ideal cipher. In: Micciancio, D. (ed.) TCC 2010. LNCS, vol. 5978, pp. 273–289. Springer, Heidelberg (2010). https://doi.org/10.1007/978-3-642-11799-2_17
22. Daemen, J., Rijmen, V.: AES Proposal: Rijndael (1999)
23. Daemen, J., Rijmen, V.: The Design of Rijndael: AES - The Advanced Encryption Standard. Information Security and Cryptography. Springer, Heidelberg (2002). https://doi.org/10.1007/978-3-662-04722-4
24. Dai, W., Hoang, V.T., Tessaro, S.: Information-theoretic indistinguishability via the Chi-Squared method. In: Katz and Shacham [46], pp. 497–523 (2017)
25. Derbez, P., Fouque, P.-A., Jean, J.: Improved key recovery attacks on reduced-round, in the single-key setting. In: Johansson, T., Nguyen, P.Q. (eds.) EUROCRYPT 2013. LNCS, vol. 7881, pp. 371–387. Springer, Heidelberg (2013). https://doi.org/10.1007/978-3-642-38348-9_23
26. Dinur, I., Dunkelman, O., Keller, N., Shamir, A.: Key recovery attacks on 3-round even-mansour, 8-step LED-128, and Full AES^2. In: Sako, K., Sarkar, P. (eds.) ASIACRYPT 2013, Part I. LNCS, vol. 8269, pp. 337–356. Springer, Heidelberg (2013). https://doi.org/10.1007/978-3-642-42033-7_18
27. Dinur, I., Shamir, A.: Cube attacks on tweakable black box polynomials. In: Joux, A. (ed.) EUROCRYPT 2009. LNCS, vol. 5479, pp. 278–299. Springer, Heidelberg (2009). https://doi.org/10.1007/978-3-642-01001-9_16
28. Dinur, I., Shamir, A.: Breaking grain-128 with dynamic cube attacks. In: Joux [45], pp. 167–187 (2011)
29. Gennaro, R., Robshaw, M.J.B. (eds.): Advances in Cryptology - CRYPTO 2015, Part I, Santa Barbara, CA, USA, 16–20 August 2015. LNCS, vol. 9215. Springer, Heidelberg (2015). https://doi.org/10.1007/978-3-662-48000-7
30. Grassi, L.: Structural truncated differential attacks on round-reduced AES. Cryptology ePrint Archive, Report 2017/832 (2017). http://eprint.iacr.org/2017/832
31. Grassi, L.: Mixture differential cryptanalysis: a new approach to distinguishers and attacks on round-reduced AES. IACR Trans. Symmetr. Cryptol. **2018**(2), 133–160 (2018)
32. Grassi, L., Rechberger, C., Rønjom, S.: Subspace trail cryptanalysis and its applications to AES. IACR Trans. Symmetr. Cryptol. **2016**(2), 192–225 (2016). http://tosc.iacr.org/index.php/ToSC/article/view/571
33. Grassi, L., Rechberger, C., Rønjom, S.: Subspace trail cryptanalysis and its applications to AES. Cryptology ePrint Archive, Report 2016/592 (2016). http://eprint.iacr.org/2016/592
34. Grassi, L., Rechberger, C., Rønjom, S.: A new structural-differential property of 5-Round AES. In: Coron, J.-S., Nielsen, J.B. (eds.) EUROCRYPT 2017, Part II. LNCS, vol. 10211, pp. 289–317. Springer, Cham (2017). https://doi.org/10.1007/978-3-319-56614-6_10

35. Gueron, S., Lindell, Y.: Better bounds for block cipher modes of operation via nonce-based key derivation. In: Thuraisingham, B.M., Evans, D., Malkin, T., Xu, D. (eds.) ACM CCS 2017: 24th Conference on Computer and Communications Security, 31 October–2 November 2017, pp. 1019–1036. ACM Press, Dallas (2017)

36. Gueron, S., Lindell, Y., Nof, A., Pinkas, B.: Fast garbling of circuits under standard assumptions. J. Cryptol. **31**(3), 798–844 (2018)

37. Hoang, V.T., Krovetz, T., Rogaway, P.: Robust authenticated-encryption AEZ and the problem that it solves. In: Oswald, E., Fischlin, M. (eds.) EUROCRYPT 2015, Part I. LNCS, vol. 9056, pp. 15–44. Springer, Heidelberg (2015). https://doi.org/10.1007/978-3-662-46800-5_2

38. Iwata, T., Minematsu, K., Peyrin, T., Seurin, Y.: ZMAC: a fast tweakable block cipher mode for highly secure message authentication. In: Katz and Shacham [46], pp. 34–65

39. Jean, J., Moradi, A., Peyrin, T., Sasdrich, P.: Bit-sliding: a generic technique for bit-serial implementations of SPN-based primitives. In: Fischer, W., Homma, N. (eds.) CHES 2017. LNCS, vol. 10529, pp. 687–707. Springer, Cham (2017). https://doi.org/10.1007/978-3-319-66787-4_33

40. Jean, J., Nikolić, I., Peyrin, T.: KIASU v1. Additional first-round candidates of CAESAR compeition (2014). https://competitions.cr.yp.to/caesar-submissions.html

41. Jean, J., Nikolić, I., Peyrin, T.: Tweaks and keys for block ciphers: the TWEAKEY framework. In: Sarkar, P., Iwata, T. (eds.) ASIACRYPT 2014, Part II. LNCS, vol. 8874, pp. 274–288. Springer, Heidelberg (2014). https://doi.org/10.1007/978-3-662-45608-8_15

42. Jean, J., Nikolić, I., Peyrin, T., Seurin, Y.: Deoxys-II. Finalist of CAESAR compeition (2014). https://competitions.cr.yp.to/caesar-submissions.html

43. Jha, A., List, E., Minematsu, K., Mishra, S., Nandi, M.: XHX - a framework for optimally secure tweakable block ciphers from classical block ciphers and universal hashing. Cryptology ePrint Archive, Report 2017/1075 (2017). https://eprint.iacr.org/2017/1075

44. Jha, A., Nandi, M.: Tight security of cascaded LRW2. Cryptology ePrint Archive, Report 2019/1495 (2019). https://eprint.iacr.org/2019/1495

45. Joux, A. (ed.): Fast Software Encryption - FSE 2011, Lyngby, Denmark, 13–16 February 2011. LNCS, vol. 6733. Springer, Heidelberg (2011). https://doi.org/10.1007/978-3-642-21702-9

46. Katz, J., Shacham, H. (eds.): Advances in Cryptology - CRYPTO 2017, Part III, Santa Barbara, CA, USA, 20–24 August 2017. LNCS, vol. 10403. Springer, Heidelberg (2017). https://doi.org/10.1007/978-3-319-63688-7

47. Keliher, L., Sui, J.: Exact maximum expected differential and linear probability for 2-round advanced encryption standard (AES). Cryptology ePrint Archive, Report 2005/321 (2005). http://eprint.iacr.org/2005/321

48. Knudsen, L.R. (ed.): Fast Software Encryption - FSE 1999, Germany, Rome, Italy 24–26 March 1999. LNCS, vol. 1636. Springer, Heidelberg (1999)

49. Krovetz, T., Rogaway, P.: The software performance of authenticated-encryption modes. In: Joux [45], pp. 306–327 (2011)

50. Lampe, R., Seurin, Y.: Tweakable blockciphers with asymptotically optimal security. In: Moriai, S. (ed.) FSE 2013. LNCS, vol. 8424, pp. 133–151. Springer, Heidelberg (2014). https://doi.org/10.1007/978-3-662-43933-3_8

51. Landecker, W., Shrimpton, T., Terashima, R.S.: Tweakable blockciphers with beyond birthday-bound security. In: Safavi-Naini, R., Canetti, R. (eds.) CRYPTO 2012. LNCS, vol. 7417, pp. 14–30. Springer, Heidelberg (2012). https://doi.org/10. 1007/978-3-642-32009-5_2

52. Leander, G., Abdelraheem, M.A., AlKhzaimi, H., Zenner, E.: A cryptanalysis of PRINTcipher: the invariant subspace attack. In: Rogaway, P. (ed.) CRYPTO 2011. LNCS, vol. 6841, pp. 206–221. Springer, Heidelberg (2011). https://doi.org/10. 1007/978-3-642-22792-9_12

53. Lee, B., Lee, J.: Tweakable block ciphers secure beyond the birthday bound in the ideal cipher model. In: Peyrin and Galbraith [66], pp. 305–335

54. Liskov, M., Rivest, R.L., Wagner, D.: Tweakable block ciphers. In: Yung, M. (ed.) CRYPTO 2002. LNCS, vol. 2442, pp. 31–46. Springer, Heidelberg (2002). https:// doi.org/10.1007/3-540-45708-9_3

55. Lu, J., Dunkelman, O., Keller, N., Kim, J.: New impossible differential attacks on AES. In: Chowdhury et al. [15], pp. 279–293 (2011)

56. Mennink, B.: Optimally secure tweakable blockciphers. Cryptology ePrint Archive, Report 2015/363 (2015). http://eprint.iacr.org/2015/363

57. Mennink, B.: XPX: generalized tweakable Even-Mansour with improved security guarantees. In: Robshaw, M., Katz, J. (eds.) CRYPTO 2016, Part I. LNCS, vol. 9814, pp. 64–94. Springer, Heidelberg (2016). https://doi.org/10.1007/978-3-662-53018-4_3

58. Mennink, B.: Insuperability of the standard versus ideal model gap for tweakable blockcipher security. In: Katz, J., Shacham, H. (eds.) CRYPTO 2017, Part II. LNCS, vol. 10402, pp. 708–732. Springer, Cham (2017). https://doi.org/10.1007/978-3-319-63715-0_24

59. Mennink, B.: Towards tight security of cascaded LRW2. In: Beimel, A., Dziembowski, S. (eds.) TCC 2018, Part II. LNCS, vol. 11240, pp. 192–222. Springer, Cham (2018). https://doi.org/10.1007/978-3-030-03810-6_8

60. Mennink, B., Neves, S.: Optimal PRFs from blockcipher designs. IACR Trans. Symmetr. Cryptol. 2017(3), 228–252 (2017)

61. Minematsu, K.: Beyond-birthday-bound security based on tweakable block cipher. In: Dunkelman, O. (ed.) FSE 2009. LNCS, vol. 5665, pp. 308–326. Springer, Heidelberg (2009). https://doi.org/10.1007/978-3-642-03317-9_19

62. Minematsu, K.: Parallelizable rate-1 authenticated encryption from pseudorandom functions. In: Nguyen, P.Q., Oswald, E. (eds.) EUROCRYPT 2014. LNCS, vol. 8441, pp. 275–292. Springer, Heidelberg (2014). https://doi.org/10.1007/978-3-642-55220-5_16

63. Moradi, A., Poschmann, A., Ling, S., Paar, C., Wang, H.: Pushing the limits: a very compact and a threshold implementation of AES. In: Paterson, K.G. (ed.) EUROCRYPT 2011. LNCS, vol. 6632, pp. 69–88. Springer, Heidelberg (2011). https://doi.org/10.1007/978-3-642-20465-4_6

64. NIST: Lightweight Cryptography Competition (2019). https://csrc.nist.gov/projects/lightweight-cryptography

65. Park, J.H., Lee, D.H.: FACE: Fast AES CTR mode encryption techniques based on the reuse of repetitive data. IACR Trans. Cryptogr. Hardw. Embedd. Syst. 2018(3), 469–499 (2018). https://tches.iacr.org/index.php/TCHES/article/view/7283

66. Peyrin, T., Galbraith, S. (eds.): Advances in Cryptology - ASIACRYPT 2018, Part I, Brisbane, Queensland, Australia, 2–6 December 2018. LNCS, vol. 11272. Springer, Heidelberg (2018). https://doi.org/10.1007/978-3-030-03326-2

67. Rogaway, P.: Efficient instantiations of tweakable blockciphers and refinements to modes OCB and PMAC. In: Lee, P.J. (ed.) ASIACRYPT 2004. LNCS, vol. 3329, pp. 16–31. Springer, Heidelberg (2004). https://doi.org/10.1007/978-3-540-30539-2_2

68. Rønjom, S., Bardeh, N.G., Helleseth, T.: Yoyo tricks with AES. In: Takagi, T., Peyrin, T. (eds.) ASIACRYPT 2017, Part I. LNCS, vol. 10624, pp. 217–243. Springer, Cham (2017). https://doi.org/10.1007/978-3-319-70694-8_8

69. Shrimpton, T., Terashima, R.S.: Salvaging weak security bounds for blockcipher-based constructions. In: Cheon and Takagi [14], pp. 429–454 (2016)

70. Song, L., Qin, X., Hu, L.: Boomerang connectivity table revisited. IACR Trans. Symmetr. Cryptol. **2019**(1), 118–141 (2019)

71. Sun, B., Liu, M., Guo, J., Rijmen, V., Li, R.: Provable security evaluation of structures against impossible differential and zero correlation linear cryptanalysis. In: Fischlin, M., Coron, J.-S. (eds.) EUROCRYPT 2016, Part I. LNCS, vol. 9665, pp. 196–213. Springer, Heidelberg (2016). https://doi.org/10.1007/978-3-662-49890-3_8

72. Sun, B., et al.: Links among impossible differential, integral and zero correlation linear cryptanalysis. In: Gennaro and Robshaw [29], pp. 95–115 (2015)

73. Sun, S., et al.: Analysis of AES, SKINNY, and others with constraint programming. IACR Trans. Symmetr. Cryptol. **2017**(1), 281–306 (2017)

74. Todo, Y.: Integral cryptanalysis on full MISTY1. In: Gennaro and Robshaw [29], pp. 413–432 (2015)

75. Todo, Y., Morii, M.: Bit-based division property and application to Simon family. In: Peyrin, T. (ed.) FSE 2016. LNCS, vol. 9783, pp. 357–377. Springer, Heidelberg (2016). https://doi.org/10.1007/978-3-662-52993-5_18

76. Wagner, D.: The boomerang attack. In: Knudsen [48], pp. 156–170 (1999)

77. Wang, L., Guo, J., Zhang, G., Zhao, J., Gu, D.: How to build fully secure tweakable blockciphers from classical blockciphers. In: Cheon and Takagi [14], pp. 455–483 (2016)

78. Wu, H.: Hongjun's optimized C-code for AES-128 and AES-256. eSTREAM project (2007). http://www.ecrypt.eu.org/stream/svn/viewcvs.cgi/ecrypt/trunk/benchmarks/aes-ctr/aes-128/hongjun/v1/?rev=203#dirlist

On a Generalization of Substitution-Permutation Networks: The HADES Design Strategy

Lorenzo Grassi[1,3]($\boxtimes$), Reinhard Lüftenegger[1]($\boxtimes$), Christian Rechberger[1], Dragos Rotaru[2,4], and Markus Schofnegger[1]

[1] IAIK, Graz University of Technology, Graz, Austria
L.Grassi@science.ru.nl, {reinhard.luftenegger,
christian.rechberger,markus.schofnegger}@iaik.tugraz.at
[2] University of Bristol, Bristol, UK
[3] Know-Center, TU Graz, Graz, Austria
[4] imec-Cosic, Department of Electrical Engineering, KU Leuven, Leuven, Belgium
dragos.rotaru@esat.kuleuven.be

Abstract. Keyed and unkeyed cryptographic permutations often iterate simple round functions. Substitution-permutation networks (SPNs) are an approach that is popular since the mid 1990s. One of the new directions in the design of these round functions is to reduce the substitution (S-Box) layer from a full one to a partial one, uniformly distributed over all the rounds. LowMC and Zorro are examples of this approach.

A relevant freedom in the design space is to allow for a highly non-uniform distribution of S-Boxes. However, choosing rounds that are so different from each other is very rarely done, as it makes security analysis and implementation much harder.

We develop the design strategy HADES and an analysis framework for it, which despite this increased complexity allows for security arguments against many classes of attacks, similar to earlier simpler SPNs. The framework builds upon the wide trail design strategy, and it additionally allows for security arguments against algebraic attacks, which are much more of a concern when algebraically simple S-Boxes are used.

Subsequently, this is put into practice by concrete instances and benchmarks for a use case that generally benefits from a smaller number of S-Boxes and showcases the diversity of design options we support: A candidate cipher natively working with objects in $GF(p)$, for securing data transfers with distributed databases using secure multiparty computation (MPC). Compared to the currently fastest design MiMC, we observe significant improvements in online bandwidth requirements and throughput with a simultaneous reduction of preprocessing effort, while having a comparable online latency.

Keywords: HADES strategy · Cryptographic permutations · Secure Multiparty Computation (MPC)

© International Association for Cryptologic Research 2020
A. Canteaut and Y. Ishai (Eds.): EUROCRYPT 2020, LNCS 12106, pp. 674–704, 2020.
https://doi.org/10.1007/978-3-030-45724-2_23

1   Introduction

Starting out with a layer of local substitution boxes (S-Boxes), combining it with a global permutation box (sometimes merely wires, sometimes affine transformations), and iterating such a round a number of times is a major design approach in symmetric cryptography. The resulting constructions are often referred to as substitution-permutation networks (SPNs) and are used to instantiate block ciphers, permutations, pseudo-random functions (PRFs), one-way functions, hash functions, and various other constructions. The approach can be traced back to Shannon's confusion-diffusion paradigm. There is a huge amount of efficient designs that exploit this design strategy, including Rijndael/AES [20] which is perhaps the most important one. Theoretical aspects have been analyzed too, which include the asymptotic analysis by Miles and Viola [41], and more recent results in the provable security framework [16, 26].

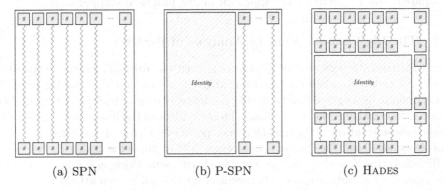

(a) SPN   (b) P-SPN   (c) HADES

Fig. 1. SP-Networks and Generalizations (P-SPNs and HADES).

Driven by various new application areas and settings, a variation of the SPN approach – the so-called partial substitution-permutation network (P-SPN) – has been proposed and investigated on the practical side [5, 27]. The idea is to replace parts of the substitution layer with an identity mapping, leading to substantial practical advantages. A big caveat of this approach is that existing elegant approaches to rule out large classes of attacks via the so-called *wide trail strategy* [19] are no longer applicable and have to be replaced by more ad-hoc approaches, as discussed in more details in Sect. 1.1. We note that the well studied Feistel approach and its generalizations, when the round function is using S-Boxes, also have the property that only a part of the internal state is affected by S-Boxes in a given round.

Our Contribution in a Nutshell: We propose a new generalization of SPNs, which we call the "HADES" approach[1]. This is illustrated in Fig. 1. It *(1st)* restores the ability to apply the elegant wide trail strategy to rule out important classes of attacks, *(2nd)* is accompanied with a broad framework to rule out various other attack vectors for many relevant instantiation possibilities, and *(3rd)* is demonstrated to result in even better implementation characteristics in the same application domains P-SPNs have been introduced for.

We use the rest of the introduction to explain this further. In Sect. 1.1 we explain the difficulty of the security analysis of P-SPNs, in Sect. 1.2 we outline our alternative generalization of SPNs called HADES. A big part of the paper will then be spent on detailing the approach and its framework for the security analysis. On the practical side, in Sect. 1.4 we will discuss how applications which rely on properties like a small number of S-Boxes can benefit from this framework. A very recent and independent work [3] explores various generalized Feistel networks as a method benefiting similar settings. This nicely complements our paper, and we include this approach in our practical comparisons.

1.1   The Big Caveat: Security Analysis of P-SPNs

The wide trail strategy cannot guarantee security against all attacks in the literature. As a concrete example, algebraic attacks that exploit the low degree of the encryption or decryption function – like the interpolation attack [33] or the higher-order differential one [36] – are (almost) independent of the linear layer used in the round transformation[2], which is the crucial point of such a design strategy. In other words, especially in the case of a low-degree S-Box, the wide trail strategy is not sufficient by itself, and it must be combined with something else (e.g., increasing the number of rounds) to guarantee security against all known attacks.

Moreover, the "hidden" assumption of such a strategy is that each round contains a full S-Box layer. Even if this is a well accepted practice, there are various applications/contexts in which non-linear operations are much less expensive than linear ones. For example, this includes masking and practical applications of secure multi-party computation (MPC), fully homomorphic encryption (FHE), and zero-knowledge proofs (ZK) that use symmetric primitives.

A possible way to achieve a lower implementation cost is by designing a primitive minimizing the number of non-linear operations. To achieve this goal, possible strategies are looking for low-degree S-Boxes and/or exploiting SPN structures where not all the state goes through the S-Boxes in each round. This second approach has been proposed for the first time by Gérard *et al.* [27] at CHES 2013. Such partial non-linear SP networks – in which the non-linear operation is applied to only part of the state in every round – contain a wide range of possible concrete schemes that were not considered so far, some of which have

---

[1] Referring to Fig. 1 and 2, if one highlights the S-Boxes per round, the obtained picture resembles a "*bident*". In classical mythology, the bident is a weapon associated with Hades, the ruler of the underworld.

[2] We remark that a linear/affine function does in general not increase/change the degree.

performance advantages on certain platforms. A concrete instantiation of their methodology is Zorro [27], a 128-bit lightweight AES-like cipher which reduces the number of S-Boxes per round from 16 to only 4 (to compensate, the number of rounds has been increased to 24).

A similar approach has then been considered by Albrecht *et al.* [5] in the recent design of a family of block ciphers called LowMC proposed at Eurocrypt 2015. LowMC is a flexible block cipher based on an SPN structure and designed for MPC/FHE/ZK applications. It combines an incomplete S-Box layer with a strong linear layer to reduce the total number of AND gates.

How Risky Are Partial SP Networks? The wide trail strategy and tools that were developed in order to formally prove the security of block ciphers against standard differential and linear cryptanalysis do not apply to partial SP networks such as Zorro, and authors use heuristic arguments instead.

For the case of Zorro, the simple bounds on the number of active S-Boxes in linear and differential characteristics cannot be used due to the modified Sub-Bytes operation. Even though the authors came up with a dedicated approach to show the security of their design, this turned out to be insufficient, as Wang *et al.* [46] found iterative differential and linear characteristics that were missed by the heuristic and used them to break full Zorro. An automated characteristic search tool and dedicated key-recovery algorithms for SP networks with partial non-linear layers have been presented in [8]. In there, the authors propose generic techniques for differential and linear cryptanalysis of SP networks with partial non-linear layers. Besides obtaining practical attacks on P-SPN ciphers, the authors concluded that even if *"the methodology of building PSP networks based on AES in a straightforward way is flawed, [...] the basic PSP network design methodology can potentially be reused in future secure designs"*.

Similarly, the authors of LowMC chose the number of rounds in order to guarantee that no differential/linear characteristic can cover the whole cipher with *non-negligible probability*. However, they do not provide such strong security arguments against other attack vectors including algebraic attacks. As a result, the security of earlier versions of LowMC against algebraic attacks was found to be lower than expected [23,25], and full key-recovery attacks on LowMC have been set up. More recently, generalizations of impossible differential attacks have been found for some LowMC instances [43].

1.2   The Idea in a Nutshell – The HADES Strategy

Summarizing the current situation: The wide trail strategy is appealing due to its simplicity, but limited to differential and linear attacks, and does not work with partial S-Box layers. Additionally, when S-Boxes are chosen to have a low degree, other attacks vectors are more relevant anyhow. Designs of this type, like Zorro and LowMC, require a lot of ad-hoc analysis.

To address this issue we propose to start with a classical wide trail design, i.e., with a full S-Box layer (outer layer), and then add a part with full and/or partial S-Box layers in the middle. Even without the middle part, the outer layer in itself is supposed to give arguments against differential and linear attacks in exactly the same way the wide trail strategy does. At the same time, arguments against low-degree attacks can be obtained working on the middle layer. Since algebraic attacks exploit the small degree of the encryption/decryption function, the main role of this middle part is to achieve a high degree, with perhaps only few (e.g., one) S-Boxes per round. Depending on the cost metric of the target application one has in mind (e.g., minimizing the total number of non-linear operations), we show that the best solution is to choose the optimal ratio between the number of rounds with full S-Box layers and with partial S-Box layers in order to achieve both security and performance. We refer to this high-level approach as the "HADES" strategy and will be more concrete in the following.

1.3   Related Work – Designs with Different Round Functions

Almost all designs for block ciphers and permutations, not only those following the wide trail design strategy, use round functions that are very similar, differing often only in so-called round constants which break symmetries in order to prevent attacks like slide attacks. Notable exceptions to this are the AES finalist MARS, the lightweight cipher PRINCE [14] and the cipher *Rescue* [6], recently proposed for ZK-STARK proof system and MPC applications. MARS has whitening rounds with a different structure than the inner rounds with the idea to frustrate cryptanalytic attacks. A downside was perhaps that it also complicated cryptanalysis. PRINCE rounds differ in that the later half of the rounds is essentially the inverse of the first half of the rounds, and a special middle round is introduced. This allows to achieve a special property, namely that a circuit describing PRINCE computes its own inverse (when keyed in a particular way). Similar to PRINCE, each round of *Rescue* is composed of two steps, which are respectively a non-linear S-Box layer and its inverse (that is, $R(\cdot) = M' \circ S^{-1} \circ M \circ S(\cdot)$ for particular affine layers M, M'). Finally, we mention the cases of LowMC [5] and Rasta [24], for which different (independent and random) linear layers are used in each round. Due to their particular design strategies, this allows to maximize the amount of diffusion achieved by the linear layer. In none of these cases, however, the *amount* of non-linearity, and hence their cryptographic strength, differs over the rounds.

1.4   HADESMiMC: Concrete Instantiations for MPC Applications

We briefly outline the use cases in the following and discuss how our new design compares against the best-in-class.

MPC. There is a large application area around secure multi-party computation. The setting is a secret-sharing-based MPC system where data is often shared as elements of a finite field $\mathbb{F}_p$ for large p. In order to get data securely in and out of such a system, an efficient solution can be to directly evaluate a symmetric primitive within such an MPC system. Note that "traditional" PRFs such as AES are not efficient in this setting, since they are built for computational engines which work over data types that do not easily match the operations possible in the MPC engine. For example, AES is a byte-oriented cipher, which is hard to represent using arithmetic in $\mathbb{F}_p$. More details can be found in [32], where for the first time this setting was explicitly analyzed and where the authors concluded that among various other options MiMC [4] was competitive. After these initial works, several new primitives have been proposed for MPC applications, including GMiMC [3] (a generalization of MiMC based on Feistel networks), JARVIS and FRIDAY [7], and *Rescue* and *Vision* [6]. GMiMC was recently broken [13] by exploiting its weak key schedule, and Gröbner basis attacks were found against JARVIS and FRIDAY [2].

Concrete Instances. For our concrete instantiations of HADESMiMC, we borrow ideas from the pre-predecessor of AES, namely SHARK [44], an SPN design with a single large MDS layer covering the whole internal state. Concretely specified instances, both full and toy versions, together with their reference implementation, test vectors, and helper scripts are available online[3].

When benchmarking our new design HADESMiMC for MPC applications, we observe significant improvements in online bandwidth requirements and throughput with a simultaneous reduction of preprocessing effort with respect to MiMC and *Rescue*, while having a comparable online latency. The same holds also for the comparison between HADESMiMC and GMiMC, with the exception for the online throughput when the number of blocks is bigger than or equal to 16.

New Instances for Future Use Cases. HADESMiMC is a very parameterizable design approach: Given any block size and a cost metric that one aims to minimize, a concrete secure instantiation – hence, the best S-Box size and the best ratio between rounds with full S-Box and partial S-Box layers – can be created easily using our scripts. In fact we can already report on such usage: Variants of HADESMiMC have been proposed [29] for use cases of efficient proof systems like STARKs, SNARKs and Bulletproofs, for which they outperform competing designs, often by a large margin.

2   Description of the HADES Strategy

Block ciphers and cryptographic permutations are typically designed by iterating an efficiently implementable round function many times in the hope that the resulting composition behaves like a randomly drawn permutation. In general, the same round function is iterated enough times to make sure that any symmetries and structural properties that might exist in the round function vanish. In our case, instead of considering the same non-linear layer for all rounds, we propose to consider *a variable number of S-Boxes per round*, that is, to use different S-Box layers in the round functions.

Each round of a cipher based on HADES is composed of three steps:

1. *Add Round Key* – denoted by $ARK(\cdot)$;
2. *SubWords* – denoted by S-Box$(\cdot)$;
3. *MixLayer* – denoted by $M(\cdot)$.

---

[3] https://extgit.iaik.tugraz.at/krypto/hadesmimc.

A final round key addition is then performed, and the final MixLayer operation can be omitted (we sometimes include it in this description for simplicity):

$$\underbrace{ARK \rightarrow \text{S-Box} \rightarrow M}_{1st \text{ round}} \rightarrow \dots \rightarrow \underbrace{ARK \rightarrow \text{S-Box} \rightarrow M}_{(R-1)\text{-}th \text{ round}} \rightarrow \underbrace{ARK \rightarrow \text{S-Box}}_{R\text{-}th \text{ round}} \rightarrow ARK$$

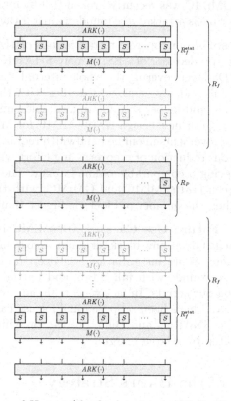

Fig. 2. Construction of HADES (the final matrix multiplication can be omitted).

The crucial property of HADES is that the number of S-Boxes per round is not the same for every round:

- a certain number of rounds – denoted by R_F – has a *full* S-Box layer, i.e., t S-Box functions;
- a certain number of rounds – denoted by R_P – has a *partial* S-Box layer, i.e., $1 \le s < t$ S-Boxes and $(t - s)$ identity functions.

In the following, we only consider the case $s = 1$, that is, R_P rounds have a single S-Box per round and $t - 1$ identity functions. However, we remark that this construction can be easily generalized (e.g., like LowMC) allowing more than a single S-Box per round in the middle R_P rounds.

In more details, assume $R_F = 2 \cdot R_f$ is an even number. Then

– the first R_f rounds have a full S-Box layer,
– the middle R_P rounds have a partial S-Box layer (i.e., 1 S-Box per round),
– the last R_f rounds have a full S-Box layer.

Note that the rounds with a partial S-Box layer are "masked" by the rounds with a full S-Box layer, which means that an attacker should not (directly) take advantage of the rounds with a partial S-Box layer.

Crucial Points of the HADES Strategy. In the HADES design, R_f^{stat} rounds with full S-Box layers situated at the beginning and the end guarantee security against statistical attacks, yielding a total of $R_F^{\text{stat}} = 2 \cdot R_f^{\text{stat}}$ rounds with full S-Box layers. As we are going to show, they are sufficient in order to apply the wide trail strategy, even without the middle rounds with partial S-Box layers. Moreover, the choice to have the same number of rounds with full non-linear layers at the beginning and at the end aims to provide the same security with respect to chosen-plaintext and chosen-ciphertext attacks.

Security against all algebraic attacks is achieved working both with rounds $R_F = R_F^{\text{stat}} + R_F' \geq R_F^{\text{stat}}$ with full S-Box layers and rounds $R_P \geq 0$ with partial S-Box layers. The degree of the encryption/decryption function has a major impact on the cost of an algebraic attack. Even if one S-Box per round is potentially sufficient to increase this degree, other factors can have a crucial impact on the cost of such attacks too (e.g., a Gröbner basis attack also depends on the number of non-linear equations and variables).

Finally, another crucial point of our HADES strategy regards the possibility to choose among several possible combinations of rounds ($R_F \geq R_F^{\text{stat}}, R_P \geq 0$) that provide the *same* security level. Namely, one can potentially decrease (resp. increase) the number of rounds with partial S-Box layers and add (resp. remove) $R_F' = 2 \cdot R_f' \geq 0$ rounds with full S-Box layers instead *without affecting the security level*. This freedom allows to choose the best combination of rounds (R_F, R_P) that minimizes a given cost metric. Roughly speaking, the idea is to find a balance between the approach in an SPN and a P-SPN cipher.

Choosing the Field and the Linear/Non-linear Layer. Our strategy does not pose any restriction/constriction on the choice of the field, on the linear layer, or on the choice of the S-Box. The idea is to consider a "traditional" SPN cipher – defined over $(\mathbb{F}_{q^n})^t$ for $q = 2$ or $q = p$ prime – based on the wide trail strategy, and then to replace a certain number of rounds with full S-Box layers with the same number of rounds with partial S-Box layers in order to reduce the number of non-linear operations, but without affecting the security. The HADES strategy has a considerable impact especially in the case of ciphers with low-degree S-Boxes, since in this case a large number of rounds is required to guarantee security against algebraic attacks.

3   The Keyed Permutation HADESMiMC

HADESMiMC is a construction for cryptographic permutations based on the strategy just proposed. It is obtained by applying the HADES strategy to the cipher SHARK [44] proposed by Rijmen *et al.* in 1996 and based on the wide trail strategy. Our design works with texts of $t \geq 2$ words[4] in $(\mathbb{F}_p, +, \times) \equiv (\mathrm{GF}(p), +, \times)$, where p is a prime of size $p \approx 2^n \geq 11$ (namely, the smallest prime bigger than $2^3 = 8$) and where $+$ and $\times$ are resp. the addition and the multiplication in $\mathbb{F}_p$. In the following, N denotes $N := \lceil \log_2 p \rceil \cdot t$.

3.1 Specification of HADESMiMC

Each round $R_k(\cdot) : (\mathbb{F}_p)^t \to (\mathbb{F}_p)^t$ of HADESMiMC is defined as

$$R_k(\cdot) = k + M \times \mathcal{S}(\cdot),$$

where $k \in (\mathbb{F}_p)^t$ is the secret subkey, $M \in (\mathbb{F}_p)^{t \times t}$ is an invertible matrix that defines the linear layer, $\mathcal{S}(\cdot) : (\mathbb{F}_p)^t \to (\mathbb{F}_p)^t$ is the S-Box layer, defined as $\mathcal{S} = [S(\cdot), ..., S(\cdot)]$ for the rounds with full S-Box layers and as $\mathcal{S} = [S(\cdot), I(\cdot), ..., I(\cdot)]$ for the rounds with partial S-Box layers, where $S(\cdot) : \mathbb{F}_p \to \mathbb{F}_p$ is a non-linear S-Box and $I(\cdot)$ is the identity function.

The number of rounds $R = 2 \cdot R_f + R_P$ depends on the choice of the S-Box and of the parameters p and t. For the MPC applications we have in mind, we usually consider a large prime number (namely, $p \geq 2^{64}$, e.g. $p \approx 2^{128}$), and each round is composed of the following operations:

- the non-linear S-Box is defined as the *cube* one, namely S-Box$(x) = x^3$; we recall that x^3 is a permutation[5] in $\mathrm{GF}(p)$ if and only if $p \neq 1 \bmod 3$;
- as in SHARK, the MixLayer of HADESMiMC is defined by a multiplication with a fixed $t \times t$ MDS matrix.

Details about the MDS matrix, the key schedule, and the number of rounds are given in the following. Test vectors are provided in [30, App. A].

About the MDS Matrix. A $t \times t$ MDS matrix[6] M with elements in $\mathrm{GF}(p)$ exists if the condition $2t + 1 \leq p$ is satisfied (see [39] for details). Since there are several ways to construct an MDS matrix, we recall in [30, App. B] some concrete strategies proposed in the literature. We also provide a script that, given an input p and t, returns an MDS matrix.

Security Level κ and Key Schedule. For our goals, we define two security levels, respectively $\kappa = \log_2(p) \cdot t \approx n \cdot t = N$ and $\kappa = \log_2(p) \approx n$ (note that $n = \lceil \log_2(p) \rceil$ is the field size in bits).

Case: $\kappa = \log_2(p) \cdot t \approx N$. Let $k \in (\mathbb{F}_p)^t$ be the secret key of size $N \approx t \cdot \log_2(p)$ bits, and let $k = [k_0, k_1, ..., k_{t-1}]$ be its representation over $\mathbb{F}_p$ (namely,

---

[4] The case $t = 1$ corresponds to MiMC [4].

[5] More generally, a power map $x \mapsto x^\alpha$ is a permutation over $\mathbb{F}_p$ if and only if $\gcd(\alpha, p-1) \neq 1$ – see e.g. Hermite's criterion for more details.

[6] A matrix $M \in \mathbb{F}^{t \times t}$ is called a *Maximum Distance Separable* (MDS) matrix iff it has a branch number $\mathcal{B}(M)$ equal to $\mathcal{B}(M) = t + 1$. The branch number is defined as $\mathcal{B}(M) = \min_{x \in \mathbb{F}^t \setminus \{0\}} \{wt(x) + wt(M(x))\}$, where wt is the bundle weight in wide trail terminology. Equally, a matrix M is MDS iff every submatrix of M is non-singular.

$k_j \in \mathbb{F}_p$ for each $0 \leq j < t$). We define the i-th round key $k^{(i)}$ for $0 \leq i \leq R$ (where R is the number of rounds) as follows. For the first round $i = 0$, the subkey is simply given by the whitening key, that is, $k^{(0)} := k$. For the next rounds, the subkeys are defined by a linear key schedule as

$$\forall i = 1, ..., R: \quad k^{(i)} := \hat{M} \cdot k^{(i-1)} + RC^{(i)},$$

where $RC^{(i)} \neq 0$ are random round constants and $\hat{M}$ is an MDS matrix[7]. For the matrix $\hat{M}$ we require that $\hat{M}^i = \prod_{i=1}^{R} \hat{M}$ has no zero coefficient[8], where $1 \leq i \leq R$ and R is the total number of rounds. This condition implies that each word of each subkey $k^{(i)}$ (linearly) depends on all words of k. As a result, even if an attacker guesses a certain number of words of a subkey $k^{(i)}$, she does not have information about other subkeys (more precisely, she cannot deduce any words of other subkeys).

Case: $\kappa = \log_2(p) \approx n$ *(for MPC Applications).* Let $k' \in \mathbb{F}_p$ be the secret key of size $n \approx \log_2(p)$ bits. We define the subkeys as

$$\forall i = 0, ..., R: \quad k^{(i)} = [\underbrace{k', k', \cdots, k'}_{t \text{ times}}] \oplus RC^{(i)},$$

for random round constants $RC^{(i)}$.

Efficient Implementation and Decryption. Like for LowMC, the amount of operations required in each round with a partial non-linear layer can be reduced. Referring to the idea proposed in [22], in [30, App. C] we recall an equivalent representation of an SPN with partial non-linear layers that can be exploited for an efficient implementation of HADESMiMC.

Finally, we mention that – as for MiMC [4] – decryption is much more expensive than encryption (e.g., $x^{1/3} \equiv x^{(2p-1)/3}$ over $\mathbb{F}_p$). However, we emphasize that HADESMiMC has been proposed for applications where the decryption process (hence, computing the inverse) is not required. We therefore provide benchmark results only for the encryption function. If used for confidentiality, we suggest to use modes where the inverse is not needed (e.g., the counter (CTR) mode).

3.2   Design Considerations: Reviving "Old" Design Ideas

Why SHARK Among Many Others? Since in our practical applications (e.g., the MPC use case which we will mainly consider) the cost of linear operations is much lower than the cost of non-linear ones, we decided to focus on the most efficient linear layer (from the security point of view) to construct HADESMiMC, namely the one that provides the fastest diffusion at word level. This corresponds to a linear layer defined as a multiplication with an MDS matrix that involves the entire state, which is exactly the case for SHARK.

Since our design strategy can be applied to any SPN design, a possible interesting future problem would be to apply HADES to e.g. AES, in order to see if a certain number of rounds of AES can be replaced with rounds that contain partial non-linear layers without decreasing its security.

---

[7] To be as general as possible, $\hat{M}$ can be equal or different from M.
[8] If this is not possible, one must minimize the number of zero coefficients.

Choosing the S-Box. Before going on, we mention that we also considered possible variants of HADESMiMC instantiated by S-Boxes defined by e.g. a different power exponent. In order to motivate our choice, we remember that, since our final goal is to use HADESMiMC for MPC applications over a LAN, the performance in such application is mainly influenced by the total number of non-linear operations (the AND depth/multiplication depth has a small impact on the cost of an MPC application over a LAN, while it could play a crucial role in the case of a WAN). Since linear operations are basically free, the choice to consider a cube S-Box among many other non-linear permutations is motivated by the following considerations:

- First of all, since there are no quadratic permutation polynomials (namely, $x \mapsto x^2 + a \cdot x + b$ for $a, b \in \mathbb{F}_p$) over the finite field $\mathbb{F}_p$ (see e.g. [38, Theorem 6–7] and [21, Sect. 2] for details), the cube S-Box requires the smallest number of non-linear operations (namely, two) and at the same time it offers high security against statistical attacks (e.g. its maximum differential probability satisfies $DP_{max} \leq 2/|\mathbb{F}|$ where $|\mathbb{F}|$ is the size of the field $\mathbb{F}$);
- Secondly, let us focus on algebraic attacks when using an S-Box of the form $\text{S-Box}(x) = x^d$. An S-Box with a higher degree than the cube one allows to reach the maximum degree faster, hence a smaller number of rounds is potentially sufficient to provide security. However, an S-Box with a higher degree requires more operations to be computed. As a result, even if the number of rounds can *potentially* be decreased[9], in general the total number of non-linear operations does not change significantly (see e.g. [4, Sect. 5] for a detailed analysis[10]). Thus, from this point of view, *the choice of the S-Box is in continuity with the choice of the cube S-Box made e.g. for MiMC and for Rescue* [6] *for similar applications.*

4   Security Analysis

It is paramount for a new design to present a concrete security analysis. In the following, we provide an in-depth analysis of the security of the HADESMiMC family of block ciphers. Since we cannot ensure that a cipher is secure against all possible attacks, the best option of determining its security is to ensure that it is secure against all known attacks. We follow this strategy for our proposals and the number of rounds of HADESMiMC is then chosen accordingly.

The crucial points of our security analysis are the following:

---

[9] *We emphasize that this is not always the case.* For a concrete example, we analyze the security of HADESMiMC instantiated by the inverse S-Box $\text{S-Box}(x) = 1/x$ in [30, App. F]. In there, we show that, even though this S-Box has the highest possible degree, the number of rounds needed for security is of the same order as the number of rounds required for the cubic case (see also [33, Sect. 3.4] for more details).

[10] In there, authors showed e.g. that the total number of non-linear operations over $\mathbb{F}_p$ (hence, including the square operations) is constant for each permutation function of the form $x \mapsto x^d$ for $d = 2^{d'} - 1$.

- Security against statistical attacks is obtained exploiting the wide trail strategy by using $R_F^{\mathrm{stat}} = 2 \cdot R_f^{\mathrm{stat}}$ rounds with full S-Box layers.
- The combination of both rounds $R_F = R_F^{\mathrm{stat}} + R'$ with full S-Box layers *and/or* rounds $R_P \geq 0$ with partial S-Box layers provide security against all other possible attacks. Indeed, even if rounds with partial S-Box layers are sufficient to increase the degree of the encryption/decryption function, other factors can also have a crucial impact on the cost of an algebraic attack.

In the following, we present our security analysis for the case $\kappa = N$ (and full data case). Then, we adapt it for the case $\kappa = n$ (together with the restriction $p^{t/2} \approx 2^{N/2}$) used for the MPC applications we have in mind.

4.1   Main Points of Our Cryptanalysis Results

Here we limit ourselves to highlight the main points of our cryptanalysis results – a detailed description of the attacks can be found in the following.

Number of Rounds. In the following, given the number of rounds of a distinguisher which is independent of the key, we add at least 2 rounds *with full S-Box layers* to prevent key-guessing attacks. This choice is motivated by the fact that it is not possible to skip more than a single round with a full S-Box layer without guessing the entire key. Indeed, one round of HADESMiMC already provides full diffusion at word level, while the S-Box provides full diffusion at bit level.

Statistical Attacks. As we are going to show, at least 6 rounds with full S-Box layers are needed to protect HADESMiMC against all statistical attacks in the literature (that is, differential, linear, truncated/impossible differential, boomerang, ...). Depending on p and t, in some cases 10 rounds are necessary in order to guarantee security against these attacks.

Algebraic Attacks. Algebraic attacks exploit mainly the low degree of the encryption/decryption function in order to break the cipher. However, as already mentioned, other factors can influence the cost of such attacks.

Interpolation Attack. The goal of an interpolation attack is to construct the polynomial that describes the function: If the number of monomials is too large, then such a polynomial cannot be constructed faster than via a brute force attack. A (lower/upper) bound of the number of different monomials can be estimated given the degree of the function. We show that – when the polynomial is dense – the attack complexity is approximately $\mathcal{O}(d^t)$, where d is the degree of the polynomial after r rounds. Since $d = 3^r$ for the cubic case, $\log_3(p) + \log_3(t)$ rounds with partial S-Box layers are necessary to guarantee security, where $\log_3(t)$ more rounds guarantee that the polynomial is dense. The cost of the attack does not change when working with rounds with full S-Box layers.

We finally remark that the degree of a function can also depend on its "representation". To give a concrete example, the function x^{-1} can be written as a function of degree $p - 2$ (namely, $x^{-1} \equiv x^{p-2}$ for $x \neq 0$) or using the "fraction representation" $1/x$ as introduced in [33], where both the numerator and the denominator are functions of degree at most 1 (see [30, App. F] for more details on the influence of such representation on the interpolation attack).

Gröbner Basis Attack. In a Gröbner basis attack, one tries to solve a system of non-linear equations that describe the cipher. The cost of such an attack depends on the degree of the equations, but also on the number of equations and on the number of variables. We show that – when working with rounds with full S-Box layers – the attack complexity is approximately $\mathcal{O}((d/t)^t)$. If a partial S-Box layer is used in order to guarantee security against this attack, it could become more efficient to consider degree-3 equations for single S-Boxes. In this case, a higher number of rounds may be necessary to provide security.

To summarize, a round with a partial S-Box layer can be described by just 1 non-linear equation of degree d and $t - 1$ linear equations, while a round with a full S-Box layer can be described by t non-linear equations of degree d. If the cost of the attack depends on other properties than just the degree (as in the case of a Gröbner basis attack), this fact can influence its final cost.

Higher-Order Differential Attack. The higher-order differential attack exploits the property that given a function $f(\cdot)$ of algebraic degree δ, then $\bigoplus_{x \in V \oplus \phi} f(x) = 0$ if the dimension of the subspace V satisfies $\dim(V) \geq \delta + 1$ (where the algebraic degree δ of a function $f(x) = x^d$ is given by the hamming weight of d, which we denote by $hw(d)$). If the algebraic degree is sufficiently high, then the attack does not work. In the case in which HADESMiMC is instantiated over $\mathbb{F}_p$, we conjecture that security against the interpolation attack implies security against this attack.

Other Attacks. *Related-Key Attacks.* The related-key attack model is a class of cryptanalytic attacks in which the attacker knows or chooses a relation between several keys and is given access to encryption/decryption functions with all these keys. We explicitly state that we do *not* make claims in the related-key model as we do not consider it to be relevant for the intended use case.

HADES*MiMc Permutation: Security.* Since we do not require the indistinguishability of the permutation obtained by HADESMiMC with a fixed key from a "randomly drawn" permutation[11] in the practical applications considered in the following, we explicitly state that we do *not* make claims about the indistinguishability of the HADESMiMC Permutation.

---

[11] This basically corresponds to the known-key or chosen-key models, where the attacker can have access or even choose the key(s) used, and where the goal is to find some (plaintext, ciphertext) pairs having a certain property with a complexity lower than what is expected for randomly chosen permutations.

4.2   Statistical Attacks – Security Level: $\kappa = N$

Differential Cryptanalysis. Differential cryptanalysis [11] and its variations are the most widely used techniques to analyze symmetric-key primitives. The differential probability of any function over the finite field $(\mathbb{F}, +, \times)$ is defined as

$$\text{Prob}[\alpha \to \beta] := |\{x : f(x + \alpha) - f(x) = \beta\}|/|\mathbb{F}|$$

where $|\mathbb{F}|$ is the size of the field and where "$-$" denotes the subtraction operation ($x - y = z$ iff $x = z + y$). The probability for the cube function $f(x) = x^3$ is bounded above by $2/|\mathbb{F}_p| = 2/p$, i.e., it has an optimal differential probability over a prime field [42].

As largely done in the literature, we first compute the number of rounds necessary to guarantee that each characteristic has probability at most $p^{-t} \approx 2^{-N}$. Since more characteristics can be used simultaneously in order to set up a differential attack, the previous number of rounds is in general not sufficient to guarantee security. For this reason, we claim that HADESMiMC is secure against differential cryptanalysis if each characteristic has probability smaller than $p^{-2 \cdot t} \approx 2^{-2 \cdot N}$. We emphasize that *(1st)* this basically corresponds to double the number of rounds necessary to guarantee that each characteristic has probability at most 2^{-N} and *(2nd)* that a similar strategy is largely used in the literature (including e.g. AES).

As we are going to show, the idea is to compute the *minimum number of rounds with full S-Box layers* that guarantee this. In other words, we consider a "weaker" version of the cipher defined as

$$R^{R_f} \circ L \circ R^{R_f}(\cdot), \text{ where} \tag{1}$$

- L is an *invertible linear layer* (which is the "weakest" possible assumption),
- $R(\cdot) = M \circ \text{S-Box} \circ ARK(\cdot)$ where S-Box$(\cdot)$ is a full S-Box layer (remember that M is an MDS matrix).

We show that this "weaker" cipher is secure against differential cryptanalysis for

$$R_F^{\text{stat}} = \begin{cases} 6 & \text{if } p \geq 2^{t+1}, \\ 10 & \text{otherwise.} \end{cases} \tag{2}$$

As a result, it follows that also HADESMiMC (instantiated with R_F rounds with full S-Box layers) is secure against such an attack. Indeed, if the linear layer L (which we only assume to be invertible) is replaced by R_P rounds of HADESMiMC, its security cannot decrease. *The same strategy is exploited in the following in order to prove security against all attacks in this subsection.*

In order to prove the result just given, we need a lower bound on the (minimum) number of active S-Boxes. Observe that the minimum number of active S-Boxes of a cipher of the form

$$R^s \circ L \circ R^r(\cdot) \equiv SB \circ \underbrace{M \circ SB}_{s-1 \text{ times}} \circ \underbrace{L'}_{\equiv L \circ M(\cdot)} \circ SB \circ \underbrace{M \circ SB}_{r-1 \text{ times}}(\cdot),$$

where $s, r \geq 1$, $R(\cdot)$ is a round with a full S-Box layer and where L' is an invertible linear layer, is at least[12]

$$\text{number } active \text{ S-Boxes} \geq (\lfloor s/2 \rfloor + \lfloor r/2 \rfloor) \times (t+1) + (s \bmod 2) + (r \bmod 2).$$

We emphasize that the middle linear layer $L'(\cdot) \equiv L \circ M(\cdot)$ plays *no* role in the computation of the previous number (it has branch number equal to 2). By choosing $s = r = 2$, it follows that – since at least $2 \cdot (t+1)$ S-Boxes are active in the weaker cipher $R^2 \circ L \circ R^2(\cdot)$ and since the maximum differential probability of the cube S-Box is $DP_{max} = 2/p$ – each characteristic has probability at most

$$\left(\frac{2}{p}\right)^{2 \cdot (t+1)} = \begin{cases} p^{-2t} \cdot \frac{4^{t+1}}{p^2} \leq p^{-2 \cdot t} \approx 2^{-2 \cdot N} & if \, p \geq 2^{t+1} \\ p^{-1.25 \cdot t} \cdot \frac{4^{t+1}}{p^{0.75 \cdot t+2}} < p^{-1.25 \cdot t} \approx 2^{-1.25 \cdot N} & since \, p^{0.75} > 6 \end{cases}$$

where remember that $p \geq 11$. By doubling this number of rounds (i.e., by choosing $s = r = 4$), we get that each characteristic has probability at most $p^{-2.5 \cdot t} \approx 2^{-2.5 \cdot N}$. Finally, 2 more rounds with full S-Box layers guarantee that no differential attack can be set up by key guessing. Indeed, note that *(1st)* given a partial round key, one has no information about the other round keys (due to the key schedule), and *(2nd)* 1 round with a full S-Box layer is sufficient to provide full diffusion. Hence, no more than a single round can be skipped by exploiting a partial guessed key.

Other Attacks. In [30, App. D], we present a (detailed) security analysis against other statistical attacks, including the linear one [40], truncated [36] and impossible differential attacks [10], Meet-in-the-Middle statistical attacks, the integral attack [18], the boomerang attack [45], the multiple-of-8 distinguisher [31], the mixture differential attack [28], and the invariant subspace attack [37]. *In there, we argue that (the "basic" variants of) all these attacks do not outperform the differential attack discussed here.* Finally, a discussion about biclique cryptanalysis [12] is provided.

4.3   Algebraic Attacks – Security Level: $\kappa = N$

Interpolation Attack. One of the most powerful attacks against HADESMiMC is the interpolation attack, introduced by Jakobsen and Knudsen [33] in 1997.

The strategy of the attack is to construct a polynomial corresponding to the encryption function without knowledge of the secret key. Let $E_k : \mathbb{F} \to \mathbb{F}$ be an encryption function. For a randomly fixed key k, the interpolation polynomial $P(\cdot)$ representing $E_k(\cdot)$ can be constructed using e.g. the Vandermonde matrix (cost of $\approx \mathcal{O}(t^2)$) or Lagrange's theorem (cost of $\approx \mathcal{O}(t \cdot \log t)$). If an adversary can construct such an interpolation polynomial without using the full codebook, then she can potentially use it to set up a forgery attack or a key-recovery attack.

---

[12] If $s = 2 \cdot s'$ is even, then the minimum number of active S-Boxes over $R^s(\cdot)$ rounds with full S-Box layers is $\lfloor s/2 \rfloor \cdot (t+1)$. Instead, if $s = 2 \cdot s' + 1$ is odd, then the minimum number of active S-Boxes over $R^s(\cdot)$ rounds with full S-Box layers is $\lfloor s/2 \rfloor \cdot (t+1) + 1$.

The attack proceeds by simply guessing the key of the final round, decrypting the ciphertexts and constructing the polynomial for $r - 1$ rounds[13]. With one extra (plaintext, ciphertext) pair, the attacker checks whether the polynomial is correct. The data cost of the attack is well approximated by the number of texts necessary to construct the interpolation polynomial.

Considering HADESMiMC, since the S-Box is the cube function, the degree of each word after r rounds is roughly approximated by 3^r. In particular, since in each round at least one S-Box is applied and since the affine layer does not change the degree, the degree of one round is three as well. It follows that, if the degree of each word after $r \geq 1$ rounds is 3^r, then the degree of each word after $r + 1$ rounds is well approximated by 3^{r+1} even if only one S-Box per round (together with a linear layer that provides "sufficiently good" diffusion at word level, in our case the multiplication with an MDS matrix) is applied. For this reason, in the following we consider a *weaker cipher* in which each round contains only a single S-Box. If such a cipher is secure against the interpolation attack, then our design is also secure (more S-Boxes per round do not decrease the security). Finally, we recall that since at least 3 rounds with a full S-Box layer are applied at the beginning and at the end, our design prevents the possibility to skip a certain number of rounds by a proper choice of the input texts (e.g., by having no active S-Box), as happens for the case of partial SPN ciphers. For this reason, we do not take care of this last event.

Note that not all terms of (total) degree 3^r appear *before* the $(r + 1)$-th round[14]. Thus, assuming the interpolation polynomial of degree 3^{r-1} is *not sparse* in the r-th round, a (rough) estimation for the number of monomials of the interpolation polynomial (and so of the attack complexity) is given by

$$(3^{r-1} + 1)^t \geq 3^{(r-1)\cdot t},$$

since after r rounds there are t words each of degree *at least* 3^{r-1}. By requiring that the number of monomials is equal to the full codebook ($3^{(r-1)\cdot t} \simeq p^t$, that is, $3^{r-1} \simeq p$), the number of rounds must be at least $r \simeq 1 + \log_3(p)$. However, this estimation for the number of rounds does not guarantee that the interpolation polynomial is dense. For this reason, since the cipher works over a finite field with characteristic p and due to the specific algebraic structure of the cube function, we add $\lceil \log_3(t) \rceil$ more rounds in order to guarantee that the interpolation polynomial is not sparse – see [30, App. E] for details.

A MitM variant of the interpolation attack can also be performed. To thwart this variant and due to the high degree of S-Box$^{-1}(x) = x^{1/3} = x^{(2p-1)/3}$, it is sufficient to add 2 rounds. Finally, 2 more rounds are added to prevent key-

---

13 The "hidden" assumption is that the cost to construct such a polynomial is smaller than the cost of an encryption. If this assumption does not hold, then the cost of the attack is bigger than the cost of a brute-force attack.

14 E.g., after the first round not all words of degree 3 appear. Indeed, the input of each S-Box in the first round is composed of a single word, which means that after the first round there is no *non-linear* mixing of different words. Similarly, not all terms of (total) degree 3^r appear *before* the $(r + 1)$-th round.

guessing attacks. As a result, the total number of rounds R must satisfy[15]

$$R = R_P + R_F \geq R^{\text{inter}}(N, t) \equiv 5 + \lceil \log_3(p) \rceil + \lceil \log_3(t) \rceil \tag{3}$$

to thwart the interpolation attack.

Gröbner Basis and GCD Attacks. In the Greatest Common Divisors (GCD) attack [4], given more than one known (plaintext, ciphertext) pair or working on the output of each S-Box of a single (known) pair, one constructs their polynomial representations and computes their polynomial GCD to recover a multiple of the key. We refer to [30, App. E] for all details about the GCD attack.

The natural generalization of GCDs is the notion of Gröbner bases [17]. The attack proceeds like the GCD attack with the final GCD computation replaced by a Gröbner basis computation. As our design exhibits a strong algebraic structure, it is paramount to carefully analyze its resistance against Gröbner basis attacks. For example, it has been shown recently that this attack vector has been able to break two proposed primitives which do not seem to be vulnerable to other types of classical algebraic attacks [2].

A Gröbner basis attack consists of the following steps:

1. computing the Gröbner basis in *degrevlex* order;
2. converting the Gröbner basis into *lex* order;
3. factorizing the univariate polynomial, and back-substituting its roots.

As largely done in the literature, we assume that *the security of ciphers against Gröbner basis attacks follows from the infeasible complexity of computing the Gröbner basis in degrevlex order.* For generic systems, the complexity of this step (hence, a lower bound for the complexity of computing a Gröbner basis) for a system of n_e polynomials f_i in n_v variables is $\mathcal{O}\left(\binom{n_v + D_{\text{reg}}}{D_{\text{reg}}}^{\omega} \right)$ operations over the base field $\mathbb{F}$ [17], where D_{reg} is the *degree of regularity* and $2 \leq \omega < 3$ is the linear algebra constant (the memory requirement of these algorithms is of the same order as the running time). The degree of regularity depends on the degrees of the polynomials d and the number of polynomials n_e.

In the following, we provide three different strategies to attack our design using Gröbner bases. We give a brief overview here, while we provide more details in [30, App. E].

First Strategy. The first strategy consists in using t variables $k_0, ..., k_{t-1}$ and t equations for each (plaintext, ciphertext) pair. When being provided at most $p^t - 1$ (plaintext, ciphertext) pairs, the system of equations that describes the cipher is composed of at most $n_e = t \cdot (p^t - 1)$ equations of the form $\hat{c}_i = f_i(\hat{p}_0, ..., \hat{p}_{t-1}, k_0, ..., k_{t-1})$ in $n_v = t$ variables $k_0, ..., k_{t-1}$ (remember that the key schedule is linear). In this over-determined case $(n_e > n_v)$, there is no closed-form expression to compute D_{reg}, which is defined as the index of the first non-positive coefficient in

$$H(z) = \frac{\prod_{i=1}^{n_e}(1 - z^{d_i})}{(1 - z)^{n_v}} = \frac{(1 - z^{3^r})^{n_e}}{(1 - z)^{n_v}} = (1 - z^{3^r})^{n_e - n_v} \cdot (1 + z + z^2)^{n_v},$$

---

[15] We emphasize that *in this analysis we do not take into account the cost to construct the interpolation polynomial, which is (in general) non-negligible.*

where $d_i = 3^r$ is the degree of the i-th equation. By simple observation, the index of the first non-positive coefficient cannot be smaller than $d = 3^r$, since $(1 + z + z^2)^{n_v}$ contains only positive terms.

Depending on parameter choices, the hybrid approach [9], which combines exhaustive search with Gröbner basis computations, may lead to a reduced cost. Following [9], guessing $\kappa < t$ parts of the key leads to a complexity of

$$\mathcal{O}\left(p^{\kappa} \cdot \binom{t - \kappa + D'_{\text{reg}}}{D'_{\text{reg}}}^{\omega} \right), \tag{4}$$

where $D'_{\text{reg}} \leq D_{\text{reg}}$ is the degree of regularity for the system of equations after substituting κ variables with their guesses. It follows that to prevent Gröbner basis attacks, the minimum number of rounds r must satisfy $p^{\kappa} \cdot \binom{t-\kappa+D'_{\text{reg}}}{D'_{\text{reg}}}^{\omega} \geq p^t$ for all $0 \leq \kappa \leq t - 1$, and where the degree of regularity $D'_{\text{reg}} = \mathcal{O}(d) \approx 3^r$. In our cases, the expression (4) is minimized by $\kappa = 0$, which implies that

$$\binom{t + d}{d} = \frac{1}{t!} \cdot \prod_{i=1}^{t} (d + i) \geq \frac{d^t}{t!} \geq \left(\frac{d}{t}\right)^t = 2^{t \log_2(d/t)},$$

where $x! \leq x^x$ for $x \geq 1$. Setting $\omega = 2$, we obtain $2t \log_2(d/t) \approx \log_2(p) \cdot t$ and

$$r \geq 2 + \log_3(p)/2 + \log_3(t), \tag{5}$$

where 2 rounds are added to thwart the MitM version of the attack (note that the degree of the S-Box in the decryption direction is $(2p - 1)/3$). As a result, $R \geq \lceil \log_3(p)/2 + \log_3(t) \rceil + 2$ rounds are sufficient to protect the cipher from this attack. Note that the analysis just proposed is independent of the fact whether the rounds contain a full or a partial S-Box layer.

Second Strategy. While we use only t variables in the first strategy, the second strategy is to add intermediate variables in each round. Specifically for the rounds with a partial S-Box layer, it is sufficient to add only one intermediate variable. In total, we get a system with more variables and equations compared to the first strategy, but with much lower degrees. We describe this strategy in detail in [30, App. E], where we conclude that R_F and R_P have to fulfill

$$R_F \cdot t + R_P \geq \left\lceil \frac{N}{2 \cdot (\log_2(27) - 2)} \right\rceil + \left\lceil \frac{N}{2 \cdot (\log_2(2p - 1) - \log_2(3))} \right\rceil$$

in order for our design to be secure against this type of attack.

Third Strategy. The third strategy is merely a combination of the previous two strategies. We use $2t$ variables for the R_F rounds with full S-box layers (i.e., we do not add intermediate variables in these rounds), but we apply the idea from the second strategy during the R_P rounds with partial S-box layers (i.e., we add intermediate variables in these rounds). This approach gives us a system of $2t$ equations of degree 3^{R_f} and R_P equations of degree 3 in $2t + R_P$ variables (t variables for the key and $t + R_P$ intermediate variables). Since the number of variables is the same as the number of equations, we can estimate D_{reg} and conclude that our design is secure if[16]

$$R_F \geq 2 + \log_3(2) \cdot \left(\frac{N}{2t + R_P} + 2 \cdot \log_2(t + R_P) - 2 \cdot \log_2(t) \right),$$

is fulfilled (see [30, App. E] for more details).

Conclusion. We claim that if R_F and R_P satisfy

$$
\begin{cases}
R_P + R_F \geq R^{\text{1st-Grob}}(N, t) \equiv 2 + \lceil \log_3(p)/2 + \log_3(t) \rceil \\
R_F \cdot t + R_P \geq R^{\text{2nd-Grob}}(N, t) \equiv \lceil N/[2 \cdot \log_2(27/4)] \rceil + \lceil N/[2 \cdot \log_2((2p-1)/3)] \rceil \\
R_F \geq R^{\text{3rd-Grob}}(N, t, R_P) \equiv 2 + \log_3(2) \cdot \left(\frac{N}{2t + R_P} + 2 \cdot \log_2(t + R_P) - 2 \cdot \log_2(t) \right)
\end{cases}
$$
$$(6)$$

for $N \approx t \cdot \log_2(p)$, then HADESMiMC can be considered secure against the Gröbner basis attacks proposed here. We mention that if R_F satisfies $R_F \geq R^{\text{1st-Grob}}(N, t) \equiv 2 + \lceil \log_3(p)/2 + \log_3(t) \rceil$ (namely, rounds with full S-Box layers are sufficient to provide security w.r.t. the first strategy), then the second and the third condition are also satisfied.

Higher-Order Differential Attack. A well-known result from the theory of Boolean functions is that if the algebraic degree of a vectorial Boolean function $f(\cdot)$ (like a permutation) is d, then the sum over the outputs of the function applied to all elements of an affine vector space $\mathcal{V} \oplus c$ of dimension $\geq d + 1$ for an arbitrary constant c is zero, that is, $\sum_{v \in \mathcal{V} \oplus c} v = \sum_{v \in \mathcal{V} \oplus c} f(v) = 0$.

This property is exploited by higher-order differential attacks [36]. However, it only holds if $\mathcal{V}$ is a subspace, and not just a generic set of elements. While $\mathbb{F}_{2^m}$ is always a subspace of $\mathbb{F}_{2^n}$ for each $m \leq n$, the only subspaces of $\mathbb{F}_p$ are $\{0\}$ and $\mathbb{F}_p$. It follows that the biggest subspace of $(\mathbb{F}_p)^t$ has dimension t, in contrast to the biggest subspace of $(\mathbb{F}_{2^n})^t$, which has dimension $n \cdot t = N$. As a result, in the case in which a cipher is instantiated over $\mathbb{F}_p$, a lower degree (and hence a smaller number of rounds) is sufficient to protect it against the higher-order differential attack w.r.t. the number of rounds needed for the $\mathbb{F}_{2^n}$ case.

Security Analysis: HADESMiMc Instantiated Over $\mathbb{F}_p$. Due to the discussion just given (namely, the fact that the biggest (non-trivial) subspace of $(\mathbb{F}_p)^t$ has dimension at most $t - 1$), we conjecture that the number of rounds necessary to achieve maximum degree guarantees security against higher-order differential attacks over $\mathbb{F}_p$. In other words, we conjecture that if HADESMiMC over $\mathbb{F}_p$ is secure against the interpolation attack, then it is also secure against the higher-order differential attack[17].

---

[16] A "more precise" condition can be found in [30, App. E].

[17] We emphasize that this does not hold in general. In particular, working over $\mathbb{F}_2^N$, note that a scheme is secure against the interpolation attack if the corresponding polynomial is full/dense. However, for security against higher-order differential attacks, we want a maximum algebraic degree. These two things are in general not strictly related.

5   Security Analysis for MPC: $\kappa = n$ and Data $\leq p^{1/2}$

In this section, we will adjust our security arguments in order to provide a security level of only $\log_2(p) \approx n$ bits (instead of the previous $\log_2(p^t) \approx N$ bits). At the same time, we only allow an attacker to use $p^{1/2}$ data.

5.1   Statistical Attacks

Differential Attack. As before, we assume that the cipher is secure if every characteristic has probability smaller than p^{-2} (namely, smaller than the square of the data complexity equal to $\sqrt{p}$). Working with the weaker cipher $R^{R_f} \circ L \circ R^{R_f}(\cdot)$ defined as in (1), it follows that $R_f = 2$ rounds with full S-Box layers are sufficient, since each characteristic has a probability of at most

$$\left(\frac{2}{p}\right)^{2(t+1)} = \frac{1}{p^{1.25 \cdot t}} \cdot \frac{4^{t+1}}{(p^{0.75})^{t+1.25}} < p^{-2.5},$$

since $p^{1/2} \geq 11^{1/2} \approx 3.3$. However, since a total number of $R_F = 2$ full rounds would not lead to 2 consecutive full rounds in our design (recall that we use partial rounds in the middle), we add two other rounds to have at least 2 consecutive rounds both at the beginning and at the end. Finally, we add two more rounds to prevent differential attacks with key guessing and conclude that $R_F \geq R_F^{\text{stat}} = 6$ rounds are needed in this setting.

Other Attacks. The situation in this setting does not differ from the situation analyzed in Sect. 4.2 (namely, other statistical attacks do not outperform the differential attack just discussed). Therefore, we argue that $R_F = 6$ rounds also prevent (the "basic" variant of) all other statistical attacks in the literature.

5.2   Algebraic Attacks

Interpolation Attack. The approach in this setting follows the analysis given in Sect. 4.3. By choosing plaintexts with *just one active word*, the interpolation polynomial depends on a single variable (namely, the active word). Hence, the number of monomials after r rounds is approximated by $3^r + 1$. Since the data complexity is limited to $\sqrt{p}$, here we require that $3^r + 1 \geq \sqrt{p} \implies r \geq 0.5 \cdot \log_3(p)$. We finally add $\log_3(t) + 4$ rounds due to the reasons given in Sect. 4.3 and conclude that

$$R_F + R_P \geq R^{\text{inter}}(p, t) \equiv 4 + \left\lceil \frac{\log_3(p)}{2} \right\rceil + \lceil \log_3(t) \rceil \tag{7}$$

rounds are needed to prevent the interpolation attack.

GCD and Gröbner Basis Attack. As further explained in [30, App. E], the GCD attack for a key from $(\mathbb{F}_p)^t$ works by first guessing $t-1$ components of the key in order to have a univariate polynomial in the last component. Since we are using only one key component in this setting, we do not need to guess these components. With other words, the encryption path alone already yields a univariate polynomial. Since the cost of the GCD computation is approximated by $\mathcal{O}\left(d\log_2^2 d\right)$, we target a complexity of $d\log_2^2 d \approx p$, where d is well approximated by 3^{r-1} when using a cubic S-Box, and thus require that

$$R_F + R_P \geq R^{\mathrm{GCD}}(p,t) \equiv 4 + \lceil \log_3(p) \rceil - \lfloor 2\log_3(\log_2(p)) \rfloor. \tag{8}$$

Finally, since computing the Gröbner Basis of a univariate system of equations is equivalent to computing the greatest common divisor (GCD) [15], we expect that this attack does not outperform the GCD one just discussed (we refer to [30, App. E] for more details).

6   Number of Rounds: Security and Efficiency

The design goal of HADESMiMC is to offer a cipher optimized for schemes whose performance critically depends on the MULTdepth/ANDdepth, the number of MULTs/ANDs, or the number of MULTs/ANDs per bit. We thus try to be as close to the number of rounds needed for security as possible.

Security. HADESMiMC with a security level equal to $\kappa = N$ is secure iff

$$\begin{cases} R_F \geq \max\{R_F^{\mathrm{stat}}; R^{\mathrm{3rd\text{-}Grob}}(p,t,R_P)\}, \\ R_P + R_F \geq \Psi^{(1)}(p,t) \equiv \max\{R^{\mathrm{inter}}(p,t); R^{\mathrm{1st\text{-}Grob}}(p,t); R^{\mathrm{GCD}}(p,t)\} = R^{\mathrm{inter}}(p,t), \\ R_P + t \cdot R_F \geq \Psi^{(t)}(p,t) \equiv R^{\mathrm{2nd\text{-}Grob}}(p,t), \end{cases}$$

where $R^{\mathrm{inter}}(p,t)$ and $R^{\mathrm{1st\text{-}Grob}}(p,t)$, $R^{\mathrm{2nd\text{-}Grob}}(p,t)$, $R^{\mathrm{3rd\text{-}Grob}}(p,t,R_P)$ are resp. defined in (3) and (6) for the case $\kappa = N$. The analogous case $\kappa = n$ (used for the MPC applications that we have in mind) is discussed in the following.

Several Combinations of (R_F, R_P) for the *Same* Security Level. Besides the possibility to choose the size of the S-Box, we emphasize that *one of the strengths of our design is the freedom to choose the ratio between the number of rounds R_F with full S-Box layers and the number of rounds R_P with partial S-Box layers without affecting the security level.* In other words, the crucial point here is that for each given p and t, the designer has in general the freedom to choose among several combinations of rounds (R_F, R_P) – that guarantee the same security – in order to minimize the analyzed cost metric.

In the following, we show how to choose the best combination of (R_F, R_P) in order to minimize a given cost metric (for the same security level). We provide *a script*[18] *that, given an input p, returns the best t and the best ratio between R_P and R_F for several cost metrics* – as the total number of non-linear operations, the depth, etc., *for both $\kappa = N$ and $\kappa = n$.*

---

[18] We mention that we propose also a variant of such script that takes p and t as input, and that returns the best choice of R_F and R_P that minimizes the given cost metric.

6.1   Efficiency in the Case of MPC Applications

Consider a generic scenario in which the main goal is to minimize the total number of non-linear operations (namely, the number of S-Boxes in our case) and/or the depth and/or the total number of linear operations proportional respectively to some parameters $0 \leq \varphi, \psi, \rho \leq 1$ s.t. $\varphi + \psi + \rho = 1$. Among all possible combinations of rounds (R_F, R_P) that provides the same security level, the goal is to find the one that minimizes the metric given by

$$\frac{\varphi}{\varphi + \psi + \rho} \times \# \text{ S-Boxes} + \frac{\psi}{\varphi + \psi + \rho} \times \text{ depth} + \frac{\rho}{\varphi + \psi + \rho} \times \# \text{ Linear Op.} =$$

$$= \frac{\varphi \times (t \cdot R_F + R_P) + \psi \times (R_F + R_P) + \rho \times (t^2 \cdot R_F + (3t - 2) \cdot R_P)}{\varphi + \psi + \rho}$$

where the equality holds *only* for the HADESMiMC design (a precise estimation of the number of linear operations in the case of an efficient implementation of HADESMiMC is provided in [30, App. C]).

Cost Metric for MPC: "Number of S-Boxes" and Depth. Due to the MPC applications we have in mind, we limit ourselves to optimize HADESMiMC w.r.t. the metric that takes into account both the number of multiplications/S-Boxes and the depth. Motivated by real-life applications, the goal that we face is to reduce the total runtime (described in details in the following). Since the main bottleneck of a protocol run on top of the SPDZ framework is the triple generation mechanism, which is given by the number of non-linear operations, in such a case the goal would be to minimize the total number of S-Boxes, while the depth plays a minor role (and where the cost of a single linear operation is negligible compared to the cost of a single non-linear operation). Due to this consideration, here we focus only on the case $0 \leq \rho \ll \varphi$. For the simplified case $\rho = 0$, the previous metric can be simplified as follows:

$$\alpha \times \text{ number of S-Boxes } + (1 - \alpha) \times \text{ depth } =$$

$$= \alpha \times (t \cdot R_F + R_P) + (1 - \alpha) \times (R_F + R_P) = R_F \times [1 + \alpha \cdot (t - 1)] + R_P \tag{9}$$

for different values of a parameter α, where $0 \leq \alpha \leq 1$. Note that $\alpha = 1$ and $\alpha = 0$ correspond to the cases in which one aims to minimize the total number of S-Boxes and the depth, respectively.

6.2   Best Ratio Between R_F and R_P – MPC Application

We focus on HADESMiMC with a security level of $\kappa = n$ (and the data complexity allowed for the attack is less than $p^{1/2}$), namely the case suitable for the MPC applications we have in mind.

Security. Due to the analysis provided in the previous section, HADESMiMC is secure if the following inequalities are satisfied:

$$\begin{cases} R_F \geq R_F^{\text{stat}} & \text{and} \quad R_P \geq 0; \\ R_P + R_F \geq \Psi(p, t) \equiv \max\{R^{\text{GCD}}(p, t); R^{\text{inter}}(p, t)\} \end{cases}$$

where $R^{\mathrm{GCD}}(p,t)$ and $R^{\mathrm{inter}}(p,t)$ are defined resp. in (8) and in (7).

Efficiency – Best Combination ($\mathbf{R_F}, \mathbf{R_P}$). The goal is to find the best combination of rounds $R_F = R_F^{\mathrm{stat}} + R_F' \geq R_F^{\mathrm{stat}}$ and R_P that minimizes the cost for different values of α, assuming $\Psi(p,t)$ is fixed (equivalently, both p and t are fixed). As we are going to show, in the case in which a single inequality of the form $R_P + R_F \geq \Psi(p,t)$ must be satisfied, for each α the cost metric (9) is always *minimized by choosing the smallest possible R_F* (namely, $R_F = R_F^{\mathrm{stat}}$).

By combining the equation $R_P + R_F \geq \Psi(p,t)$ with the cost metric for generic α, we get that the cost is upper bounded by

$$R_F \times [1 + \alpha \cdot (t-1)] + R_P \Big|_{R_P + R_F \geq \Psi} \geq R_F \times \alpha \times (t-1) + \Psi,$$

which is minimized by the following choice:

- if $\alpha \neq 0$, then the cost is minimized by taking the *minimum* value of R_F (where note that Ψ is fixed for t and N fixed), that is $R_F = R_F^{\mathrm{stat}}$;
- if $\alpha = 0$, then the cost is equal for each choice of (R_F, R_P) s.t. $R_P + R_F = \Psi$.

Let us analyze the case in which $\alpha = 0$ in more details. Even if every choice of R_F and R_P lead to the same cost w.r.t. the metric $R_F + R_P$ (namely, the depth), one possibility would be to choose the combination that minimizes other metrics. By taking into account the number of non-linear and linear operations, it turns out that the best choice is to take the *minimum* value of R_F, since

$$\# \text{ S-Boxes: } \quad t \times R_F + R_P \Big|_{R_P + R_F \geq \Psi} \geq R_F \times (t-1) + \Psi$$

$$\# \text{ Linear Op.: } \quad t^2 \times R_F + (3t-2) \times R_P \Big|_{R_P + R_F \geq \Psi} \geq R_F \times (\underbrace{t^2 - 3t + 2}_{\geq 0 \text{ for each } t \geq 2}) + \Psi$$

are both minimized by taking the minimum $R_F \geq R_F^{\mathrm{stat}}$.

6.3 Concrete Instantiations of HADESMiMC

Based on the security analysis just proposed, in Table 1 we present concrete instantiations of HADESMiMC for different security levels and/or applications. The corresponding test vectors of HADESMiMC are given in [30, App. A].

Reduced and Toy Versions. Many classes of cryptanalytic attacks become more difficult with an increased number of rounds. In order to facilitate third-party cryptanalysis and estimate the security margin, reduced-round variants need to be considered. Hence we encourage to study reduced-round variants of HADESMiMC where the symmetry around the middle is kept. For this reason, we highlight that it is also possible to specify toy versions of our cipher which aim at achieving, e.g., only 32 bits of security.

Table 1. *A range of different parameter sets for* HADESMiMC *offering different trade-offs. The first set is for AES-like security ($\approx$128 bits). The second set is for MPC applications (where the ratio between R_F and R_P is chosen in order to minimize the metric cost for given values of α). The last set includes an example of a toy version useful to facilitate third-party cryptanalysis.*

Text size $\log_2 p \times t$	Security κ	S-Box size $(\log_2 p)$	# S-Box (t)	α	Rounds R_F (Full S-Box)	Rounds R_P (Partial S-Box)
128	128	8	16	–	10	4
128	128	16	8	–	8	10
256	128	128	2	$0, 0.25, 0.5, 0.75, 1$	6	71
256	256	128	2	$0, 0.25, 0.5, 0.75, 1$	12	76
512	128	128	4	$0, 0.25, 0.5, 0.75, 1$	6	71
512	512	128	4	$0, 0.25, 0.5, 0.75, 1$	12	76
1 024	128	128	8	$0, 0.25, 0.5, 0.75, 1$	6	71
1 024	1 024	128	8	$0, 0.25$	16	72
1 024	1 024	128	8	$0.5, 0.75, 1$	14	79
2 048	128	128	16	$0, 0.25, 0.5, 0.75, 1$	6	71
2 048	2 048	128	16	$0, 0.25, 0.5$	20	69
2 048	2 048	128	16	$0.75, 1$	18	93
4 096	128	128	32	$0, 0.25, 0.5, 0.75, 1$	6	71
4 096	4 096	128	32	0	24	66
4 096	4 096	128	32	$0.25, 0.5$	22	83
4 096	4 096	128	32	$0.75, 1$	20	121
8 192	128	128	64	$0, 0.25, 0.5, 0.75, 1$	6	71
8 192	8 192	128	64	0	32	58
8 192	8 192	128	64	$0.25, 0.5$	22	151
8 192	8 192	128	64	$0.75, 1$	20	240
32	32	8	4	–	6	7

About the case in which the security level κ is equal to the size of the S-Box (namely, $\kappa = \log_2 p$): the given number of rounds provided security only if the data used for the attack is smaller than $p^{1/2}$ – no restriction for the case $\kappa = \log_2 p \cdot t \approx N$.

Comparison with Ciphers in "Traditional Use Cases". We remark that our strategy is *not* primarily intended to be used for pure encryption/decryption purposes, and that it is specifically tailored towards new applications like the MPC use case explained previously.

However, if only encryption/decryption is needed, we still expect HADESMiMC to not be significantly worse than more suitable constructions when considering the number of S-Boxes. E.g, when choosing the first instance given in Table 1 (namely, $p \approx 2^8$ and $t = 16$) and comparing it to AES-128, we can observe that the total number of S-Boxes is $10 \cdot (16 + 4) = 200$ in AES-128 (including the key schedule), and only $10 \cdot 16 + 4 = 164$ in our design. At the same time, we point out that the linear layer of HADESMiMC compared to the one of AES is likely to be a bottleneck when trying to reduce the number of operations.

7 MPC Applications

For MPC applications, we evaluated the HADESMiMC cipher using the SPDZ framework [35] within a prime field $\mathbb{F}_p$ following the reasoning of [32].

Preliminaries. In the following, we denote by $[x]$ a sharing of x, where each party P_i holds a random $x_i \in \mathbb{F}_p$. The process of parties reconstructing x is called an opening, i.e., going from a shared value $[x]$ to a public value x known to all parties. As with modern MPC frameworks, a protocol is split into two steps: an input-independent preprocessing phase where parties generate random Beaver triples $[a] = [b] \cdot [c]$, and an input-dependent online phase where parties share their inputs and use the triples generated in the preprocessing phase. The cost of a multiplication between two secret values $[z] \leftarrow [x] \cdot [y]$ is twofold: one Beaver triple generated in the preprocessing phase as well as two openings and one round of communications in the online phase. Since secretly shared multiplications can be done in parallel, the number of communication rounds in the online phase is given by the multiplicative depth of the circuit (AND depth) to be evaluated. Linear operations such as additions and multiplications by public scalars are non-interactive and require only a small computational overhead.

To evaluate a blockcipher in our setting, both the key $[k]$ and the message $[m]$ are secretly shared between the parties. Since most of the computation is linear and is computed locally by the parties the last thing to show is how to compute the S-Box. The trivial way is to perform $[x^2] \leftarrow [x] \cdot [x]$ and then $[x^3] \leftarrow [x^2] \cdot [x]$ using two triples. This can be done with two communication rounds and it has an online cost of 3 openings and uses two triples. However, we use the Grassi *et al.* version [32] to reduce the online cost to one communication round with the same amount of openings and triples. Note that every multiplication translates into two field elements broadcasted by each party (256 bits for $p \approx 2^{128}$).

Standard Benchmarks. We implemented and benchmarked HADESMiMC with a security level of $\kappa = 128 \approx \log_2 p$ bits using the SPDZ protocol in the MP-SPDZ library[19] between two computers equipped with i7-7700K CPUs, 32GB RAM, and connected via a 10Gb/s LAN connection with an average round-trip time of 0.47 ms. The choice of MP-SPDZ was due to having the fastest triple generation mechanism for a dishonest majority [34] and because it integrates the preprocessing with the online phase to check the end-to-end runtime of a protocol.

In Table 2, we present a comparison between HADESMiMC and other existing PRFs/block-ciphers proposed in the literature for MPC applications – namely, MiMC and GMiMC$_{\text{eff}}$ (both with a security level of $\kappa = 128$ bits) and *Rescue* (with a security level of $\kappa = t \cdot 128$ bits) – in terms of four metrics:

1. *latency* represents the best running time of a single cipher evaluation by running sequential single-threaded executions of it;

---

[19] https://github.com/data61/MP-SPDZ.

2. *throughput* represents the encryption rate given in the number of field elements that can be encrypted in parallel per second by running multiple executions using different threads;
3. *communication* done by each party per encrypted field element;
4. *round complexity* which is the multiplicative depth of the circuit when computed in MPC.

Moreover, we show the difference in throughput and communication between the online phase (columns denoted by 'Online') and when running the entire end-to-end protocols (Runtime).

Experiment Results: Table 2. Our design is better in all metrics for $t = 2$ compared to all other blockciphers (except round complexity when looking at MiMC in CTR mode), and also enjoys the smallest online latency for all t's.

In terms of online throughput it is surpassed by GMiMC$_{erf}$ from $t \geq 16$ due to the local computation involving MDS matrices. In more details, from $t \geq 16$ GMiMC$_{erf}$ has the best online throughput due to a low number of openings in the online phase and a low computational overhead as it is just swapping and adding states.

When looking at the Runtime column, we see that HADESMiMC outperforms all the existing work from $t = 2$ and the gap increases by a factor of four for $t = 64$ when comparing with GMiMC$_{erf}$. Note that for the runtime column one has to choose carefully the number of encryptions done in parallel. This is because for different t's MP-SPDZ produces triples in a batch of size 524288 and some of them might be unused. We tried to diminish this gap by tweaking the number of encryptions to be produced when benchmarking such that it utilizes a maximum number of triples from the last batch.

Remarks About GMiMC$_{erf}$ *and Rescue.* In order to understand the previous results, we emphasize two facts. First, all versions of GMiMC$_{erf}$ with $n \approx \log_2 p$ bits of security are vulnerable to an attack presented in [13]. Specifically, in [3] the authors propose a number of rounds for $n \approx \log_2 p$ bits of security, assuming the attacker has access to the full codebook (up to $p^t \approx 2^N$ different texts). Secondly, in order to have a more precise comparison, in [30, App. G] we adapt their analysis in the case in which the attacker has access to at most $p^{1/2}$ different chosen texts. This attack – which is reminiscent of a slide attack – makes *only* use of the weak key schedule and does not exploit any particular properties of the cipher. Hence, while the versions of GMiMC$_{erf}$ used here are broken in theory, we conjecture that a stronger key schedule can help to avoid this attack. Therefore, since in MPC applications round keys are precomputed (the cost of MPC applications is not influenced by the key schedule), we decided to keep the corresponding numbers in the table, noting that a secure variant of GMiMC$_{erf}$ using an appropriate key schedule would yield the same results.

We highlight that *Rescue* is specified with a security level of $p^t \approx 2^N$ bits only, besides a conservative security margin of 100%. Due to the particular design of *Rescue* (each round contains a non-linear layer and its inverse), this choice has been made due to the fact that *"[...] the field of algebraic attacks seems rather*

Table 2. Two-party costs for *Rescue*, MiMC$_t$ (namely, t parallel MiMC-128/128 in CTR mode), GMiMC$_{erf}$ and HMiMC≡HADESMiMC over a 10Gb/s LAN. Communication is given in KiloBytes. Runtime column represents the entire protocol execution, including preprocessing.

Cipher	Text size	Online				Runtime (multi-thread)	
	$\log_2 p \times t$	(MPC) Rounds	Lat. (ms) (s-thr)	$\mathbb{F}_p$/s (m-thr)	Comm. per $\mathbb{F}_p$	$\mathbb{F}_p$/s	Comm. per $\mathbb{F}_p$
Rescue	256	98	5.54	23 464	6.10	70	971
MiMC$_2$	256	73	3.53	79 728	3.50	192	366
GMiMC$_{erf}$	256	146	7.50	71 661	3.50	137	487
HMiMC	256	78	3.85	117 358	1.90	261	266
Rescue	512	50	1.25	46 890	3.08	136	485
MiMC$_4$	512	73	1.69	83 876	3.50	192	366
GMiMC$_{erf}$	512	150	3.42	137 058	1.80	274	243
HMiMC	512	78	1.90	185 160	1.14	526	133.2
Rescue	1024	32	0.59	72 689	1.93	137	484
MiMC$_8$	1024	73	1.08	85 795	3.50	192	366
GMiMC$_{erf}$	1024	158	1.98	252 102	0.94	271	241
HMiMC	1024	78	0.98	253 475	0.71	1045	66.8
Rescue	2048	32	0.45	66 830	1.93	273	243
MiMC$_{16}$	2048	73	0.63	87 318	3.50	192	366
GMiMC$_{erf}$	2048	174	1.09	425 717	0.52	137	483
HMiMC	2048	78	0.5	283 678	0.50	1088	60.9
Rescue	4096	32	0.42	57 695	1.93	274	243
MiMC$_{32}$	4096	73	0.34	87 831	3.5	192	366
GMiMC$_{erf}$	4096	206	0.68	637 747	0.3	276	241
HMiMC	4096	78	0.32	258 610	0.39	1098	60.8
Rescue	8192	32	0.31	44 697	1.93	283	243
MiMC$_{64}$	8192	73	0.20	87 773	3.50	192	366
GMiMC$_{erf}$	8192	323	0.50	664 091	0.24	550	120
HMiMC	8192	78	0.11	189 772	0.32	2189	30.6

underexplored. As a result, it is difficult to make a compelling security argument valid for the entire family of attacks" (see [6, Sect. 3.5]). Hence, we mention that it is potentially possible that the gap (in term of performance) between *Rescue* and HADESMiMC can be actually reduced in the case in which the "*design choices [of Rescue are] indeed too conservative, and that the complexity and security margins can safely be reduced*" (see [6, Sect. 4.6]).

Related Work. At CCS'18, Agrawal *et al.* [1] applied a threshold PRF to compute an encryption between several parties where one party P_{ext} holds a plaintext m, does a 2-round protocol with multiple servers, and P_{ext} receives an encryption $E_k(m)$ where the key k is shared among the servers. This use case is covered by us as well by having the servers computing the blockcipher in MPC with P_{ext} as an external party providing the input m and getting the output $E_k(m)$. In the two-server case where one external party gets the ciphertext, Agrawal *et al.* obtain a latency of 0.05 ms and a throughput of around 2 million encrypted blocks. HADESMiMC with $t = 2$ blocks can achieve an online latency of 3.85 ms and an online throughput of more than 117 000 blocks per second.

Although this design performs orders of magnitude slower than Agrawal et al.'s, we provide more flexibility: *(1st)* P_{ext} does not have to be online with the other servers as in Agrawal *et al.* to compute the encryption; *(2nd)* it is more friendly towards working with encrypted databases: servers upload the ciphertext to a DB and anyone holding k can decrypt, whereas for Agrawal *et al.* each party (P_{ext} or else) needs to be online with the servers to decrypt.

Acknowledgements. The authors thank the anonymous reviewers for their valuable comments and suggestions. L. Grassi has been supported by IOV42. D. Rotaru has been supported in part by the Defense Advanced Research Projects Agency (DARPA) and Space and Naval Warfare Systems Center, Pacific (SSC Pacific) under contract No. N66001-15-C-4070, by the Office of the Director of National Intelligence (ODNI), Intelligence Advanced Research Projects Activity (IARPA) via Contract No. 2019-1902070006 and by the CyberSecurity Research Flanders with reference number VR20192203. Any opinions, findings and conclusions or recommendations expressed in this material are those of the author(s) and do not necessarily reflect the views of the ODNI, United States Air Force, IARPA, DARPA, the US Government or FWO. The U.S. Government is authorized to reproduce and distribute reprints for governmental purposes notwithstanding any copyright annotation therein.

References

1. Agrawal, S., Mohassel, P., Mukherjee, P., Rindal, P.: DiSE: distributed symmetric-key encryption. In: CCS, pp. 1993–2010. ACM (2018)
2. Albrecht, M.R., et al.: Algebraic cryptanalysis of STARK-friendly designs: application to MARVELLOUS and MiMC. In: Galbraith, S.D., Moriai, S. (eds.) ASIACRYPT 2019. LNCS, vol. 11923, pp. 371–397. Springer, Cham (2019). https://doi.org/10.1007/978-3-030-34618-8_13
3. Albrecht, M.R., et al.: Feistel structures for MPC, and more. In: Sako, K., Schneider, S., Ryan, P.Y.A. (eds.) ESORICS 2019. LNCS, vol. 11736, pp. 151–171. Springer, Cham (2019). https://doi.org/10.1007/978-3-030-29962-0_8
4. Albrecht, M.R., Grassi, L., Rechberger, C., Roy, A., Tiessen, T.: MiMC: efficient encryption and cryptographic hashing with minimal multiplicative complexity. In: Cheon, J.H., Takagi, T. (eds.) ASIACRYPT 2016. LNCS, vol. 10031, pp. 191–219. Springer, Heidelberg (2016). https://doi.org/10.1007/978-3-662-53887-6_7
5. Albrecht, M.R., Rechberger, C., Schneider, T., Tiessen, T., Zohner, M.: Ciphers for MPC and FHE. In: Oswald, E., Fischlin, M. (eds.) EUROCRYPT 2015. LNCS, vol. 9056, pp. 430–454. Springer, Heidelberg (2015). https://doi.org/10.1007/978-3-662-46800-5_17
6. Aly, A., Ashur, T., Ben-Sasson, E., Dhooghe, S., Szepieniec, A.: Design of Symmetric-Key Primitives for Advanced Cryptographic Protocols. Cryptology ePrint Archive, Report 2019/426 (2019). https://eprint.iacr.org/2019/426

7. Ashur, T., Dhooghe, S.: MARVELlous: a STARK-Friendly Family of Cryptographic Primitives. Cryptology ePrint Archive, Report 2018/1098 (2018)

8. Bar-On, A., Dinur, I., Dunkelman, O., Lallemand, V., Keller, N., Tsaban, B.: Cryptanalysis of SP networks with partial non-linear layers. In: Oswald, E., Fischlin, M. (eds.) EUROCRYPT 2015. LNCS, vol. 9056, pp. 315–342. Springer, Heidelberg (2015). https://doi.org/10.1007/978-3-662-46800-5_13

9. Bettale, L., Faugère, J.C., Perret, L.: Hybrid approach for solving multivariate systems over finite fields. J. Math. Cryptol. **3**(3), 177–197 (2009)

10. Biham, E., Biryukov, A., Shamir, A.: Cryptanalysis of skipjack reduced to 31 rounds using impossible differentials. In: Stern, J. (ed.) EUROCRYPT 1999. LNCS, vol. 1592, pp. 12–23. Springer, Heidelberg (1999). https://doi.org/10.1007/3-540-48910-X_2

11. Biham, E., Shamir, A.: Differential cryptanalysis of DES-like cryptosystems. J. Cryptol. **4**(1), 3–72 (1991)

12. Bogdanov, A., Khovratovich, D., Rechberger, C.: Biclique cryptanalysis of the full AES. In: Lee, D.H., Wang, X. (eds.) ASIACRYPT 2011. LNCS, vol. 7073, pp. 344–371. Springer, Heidelberg (2011). https://doi.org/10.1007/978-3-642-25385-0_19

13. Bonnetain, X.: Collisions on Feistel-MiMC and univariate GMiMC. Cryptology ePrint Archive, Report 2019/951 (2019). https://eprint.iacr.org/2019/951

14. Borghoff, J., et al.: PRINCE – a low-latency block cipher for pervasive computing applications. In: Wang, X., Sako, K. (eds.) ASIACRYPT 2012. LNCS, vol. 7658, pp. 208–225. Springer, Heidelberg (2012). https://doi.org/10.1007/978-3-642-34961-4_14

15. Buchberger, B.: Bruno Buchberger's PhD thesis 1965: an algorithm for finding the basis elements of the residue class ring of a zero dimensional polynomial ideal. J. Symb. Comput. **41**, 475–511 (2006)

16. Cogliati, B., et al.: Provable security of (tweakable) block ciphers based on substitution-permutation networks. In: Shacham, H., Boldyreva, A. (eds.) CRYPTO 2018. LNCS, vol. 10991, pp. 722–753. Springer, Cham (2018). https://doi.org/10.1007/978-3-319-96884-1_24

17. Cox, D.A., Little, J., O'Shea, D.: Ideals, Varieties, and Algorithms - An Introduction to Computational Algebraic Geometry and Commutative Algebra. UTM. Springer, Cham (2015). https://doi.org/10.1007/978-3-319-16721-3

18. Daemen, J., Knudsen, L.R., Rijmen, V.: The block cipher Square. In: Biham, E. (ed.) FSE 1997. LNCS, vol. 1267, pp. 149–165. Springer, Heidelberg (1997). https://doi.org/10.1007/BFb0052343

19. Daemen, J., Rijmen, V.: The wide trail design strategy. In: Honary, B. (ed.) Cryptography and Coding 2001. LNCS, vol. 2260, pp. 222–238. Springer, Heidelberg (2001). https://doi.org/10.1007/3-540-45325-3_20

20. Daemen, J., Rijmen, V.: The Design of Rijndael: AES - The Advanced Encryption Standard. Information Security and Cryptography. Springer, Heidelberg (2002). https://doi.org/10.1007/978-3-662-04722-4

21. Diaz-Vargas, J., Rubio-Barrios, C.J., Sozaya-Chan, J.A., Tapia-Recillas, H.: Self-invertible permutation polynomials over $\mathbb{Z}_m$. Int. J. Algebra **5**(23), 1135–1153 (2011)

22. Dinur, I., Kales, D., Promitzer, A., Ramacher, S., Rechberger, C.: Linear equivalence of block ciphers with partial non-linear layers: application to LowMC. In: Ishai, Y., Rijmen, V. (eds.) EUROCRYPT 2019. LNCS, vol. 11476, pp. 343–372. Springer, Cham (2019). https://doi.org/10.1007/978-3-030-17653-2_12

23. Dinur, I., Liu, Y., Meier, W., Wang, Q.: Optimized interpolation attacks on LowMC. In: Iwata, T., Cheon, J.H. (eds.) ASIACRYPT 2015. LNCS, vol. 9453, pp. 535–560. Springer, Heidelberg (2015). https://doi.org/10.1007/978-3-662-48800-3_22

24. Dobraunig, C., et al.: Rasta: a cipher with low ANDdepth and Few ANDs per bit. In: Shacham, H., Boldyreva, A. (eds.) CRYPTO 2018. LNCS, vol. 10991, pp. 662–692. Springer, Cham (2018). https://doi.org/10.1007/978-3-319-96884-1_22

25. Dobraunig, C., Eichlseder, M., Mendel, F.: Higher-order cryptanalysis of LowMC. In: Kwon, S., Yun, A. (eds.) ICISC 2015. LNCS, vol. 9558, pp. 87–101. Springer, Cham (2016). https://doi.org/10.1007/978-3-319-30840-1_6

26. Dodis, Y., Stam, M., Steinberger, J.P., Liu, T.: Indifferentiability of confusion-diffusion networks. In: Fischlin, M., Coron, J.-S. (eds.) EUROCRYPT 2016. LNCS, vol. 9666, pp. 679–704. Springer, Heidelberg (2016). https://doi.org/10.1007/978-3-662-49896-5_24

27. Gérard, B., Grosso, V., Naya-Plasencia, M., Standaert, F.-X.: Block ciphers that are easier to mask: how far can we go? In: Bertoni, G., Coron, J.-S. (eds.) CHES 2013. LNCS, vol. 8086, pp. 383–399. Springer, Heidelberg (2013). https://doi.org/10.1007/978-3-642-40349-1_22

28. Grassi, L.: Mixture differential cryptanalysis: a new approach to distinguishers and attacks on round-reduced AES. IACR Trans. Symmetric Cryptol. 2018(2), 133–160 (2018)

29. Grassi, L., Kales, D., Khovratovich, D., Roy, A., Rechberger, C., Schofnegger, M.: Starkad and Poseidon: New Hash Functions for Zero Knowledge Proof Systems. Cryptology ePrint Archive, Report 2019/458 (2019)

30. Grassi, L., Lüfteneggr, R., Rechberger, C., Rotaru, D., Schofnegger, M.: On a Generalization of Substitution-Permutation Networks: The HADES Design Strategy. Cryptology ePrint Archive, Report 2019/1107 (2019)

31. Grassi, L., Rechberger, C., Rønjom, S.: A new structural-differential property of 5-round AES. In: Coron, J.-S., Nielsen, J.B. (eds.) EUROCRYPT 2017. LNCS, vol. 10211, pp. 289–317. Springer, Cham (2017). https://doi.org/10.1007/978-3-319-56614-6_10

32. Grassi, L., Rechberger, C., Rotaru, D., Scholl, P., Smart, N.P.: MPC-friendly symmetric key primitives. In: CCS, pp. 430–443. ACM (2016)

33. Jakobsen, T., Knudsen, L.R.: The interpolation attack on block ciphers. In: Biham, E. (ed.) FSE 1997. LNCS, vol. 1267, pp. 28–40. Springer, Heidelberg (1997). https://doi.org/10.1007/BFb0052332

34. Keller, M., Pastro, V., Rotaru, D.: Overdrive: making SPDZ great again. In: Nielsen, J.B., Rijmen, V. (eds.) EUROCRYPT 2018. LNCS, vol. 10822, pp. 158–189. Springer, Cham (2018). https://doi.org/10.1007/978-3-319-78372-7_6

35. Keller, M., Scholl, P., Smart, N.P.: An architecture for practical actively secure MPC with dishonest majority. In: CCS, pp. 549–560. ACM (2013)

36. Knudsen, L.R.: Truncated and higher order differentials. In: Preneel, B. (ed.) FSE 1994. LNCS, vol. 1008, pp. 196–211. Springer, Heidelberg (1995). https://doi.org/10.1007/3-540-60590-8_16

37. Leander, G., Abdelraheem, M.A., AlKhzaimi, H., Zenner, E.: A cryptanalysis of PRINTCIPHER: the invariant subspace attack. In: Rogaway, P. (ed.) CRYPTO 2011. LNCS, vol. 6841, pp. 206–221. Springer, Heidelberg (2011). https://doi.org/10.1007/978-3-642-22792-9_12

38. Li, S.: Permutation Polynomials modulo m. arXiv Mathematics e-prints (2005)

39. MacWilliams, F.J., Sloane, N.J.A.: The Theory of Error-Correcting Codes. North-Holland Publishing Company, Amsterdam (1978)

40. Matsui, M.: Linear cryptanalysis method for DES cipher. In: Helleseth, T. (ed.) EUROCRYPT 1993. LNCS, vol. 765, pp. 386–397. Springer, Heidelberg (1994). https://doi.org/10.1007/3-540-48285-7_33
41. Miles, E., Viola, E.: Substitution-permutation networks, pseudorandom functions, and natural proofs. J. ACM **62**(6), 46:1–46:29 (2015)
42. Nyberg, K., Knudsen, L.R.: Provable security against differential cryptanalysis. In: Brickell, E.F. (ed.) CRYPTO 1992. LNCS, vol. 740, pp. 566–574. Springer, Heidelberg (1993). https://doi.org/10.1007/3-540-48071-4_41
43. Rechberger, C., Soleimany, H., Tiessen, T.: Cryptanalysis of low-data instances of full LowMCv2. IACR Trans. Symmetric Cryptol. **2018**(3), 163–181 (2018)
44. Rijmen, V., Daemen, J., Preneel, B., Bosselaers, A., De Win, E.D.: The cipher SHARK. In: Gollmann, D. (ed.) FSE 1996. LNCS, vol. 1039, pp. 99–111. Springer, Heidelberg (1996). https://doi.org/10.1007/3-540-60865-6_47
45. Wagner, D.: The Boomerang attack. In: Knudsen, L. (ed.) FSE 1999. LNCS, vol. 1636, pp. 156–170. Springer, Heidelberg (1999). https://doi.org/10.1007/3-540-48519-8_12
46. Wang, Y., Wu, W., Guo, Z., Yu, X.: Differential cryptanalysis and linear distinguisher of full-round zorro. In: Boureanu, I., Owesarski, P., Vaudenay, S. (eds.) ACNS 2014. LNCS, vol. 8479, pp. 308–323. Springer, Cham (2014). https://doi.org/10.1007/978-3-319-07536-5_19

Lightweight Authenticated Encryption Mode Suitable for Threshold Implementation

Yusuke Naito[1]([⊠]), Yu Sasaki[2]([⊠]), and Takeshi Sugawara[3]([⊠])

[1] Mitsubishi Electric Corporation, Kamakura, Kanagawa, Japan
Naito.Yusuke@ce.MitsubishiElectric.co.jp
[2] NTT Secure Platform Laboratories, Tokyo, Japan
yu.sasaki.sk@hco.ntt.co.jp
[3] The University of Electro-Communications, Tokyo, Japan
sugawara@uec.ac.jp

Abstract. This paper proposes tweakable block cipher (TBC) based modes PFB_Plus and PFBω that are efficient in threshold implementations (TI). Let t be an algebraic degree of a target function, e.g. $t = 1$ (resp. $t > 1$) for linear (resp. non-linear) function. The d-th order TI encodes the internal state into $dt+1$ shares. Hence, the area size increases proportionally to the number of shares. This implies that TBC based modes can be smaller than block cipher (BC) based modes in TI because TBC requires s-bit block to ensure s-bit security, e.g. PFB and Romulus, while BC requires $2s$-bit block. However, even with those TBC based modes, the minimum we can reach is 3 shares of s-bit state with $t = 2$ and the first-order TI ($d = 1$).

Our first design PFB_Plus aims to break the barrier of the $3s$-bit state in TI. The block size of an underlying TBC is $s/2$ bits and the output of TBC is linearly expanded to s bits. This expanded state requires only 2 shares in the first-order TI, which makes the total state size $2.5s$ bits. We also provide rigorous security proof of PFB_Plus. Our second design PFBω further increases a parameter ω: a ratio of the security level s to the block size of an underlying TBC. We prove security of PFBω for any ω under some assumptions for an underlying TBC and for parameters used to update a state. Next, we show a concrete instantiation of PFB_Plus for 128-bit security. It requires a TBC with 64-bit block, 128-bit key and 128-bit tweak, while no existing TBC can support it. We design a new TBC by extending SKINNY and provide basic security evaluation. Finally, we give hardware benchmarks of PFB_Plus in the first-order TI to show that TI of PFB_Plus is smaller than that of PFB by more than one thousand gates and is the smallest within the schemes having 128-bit security.

Keywords: Authenticated encryption · Threshold implementation · Beyond-birthday-bound security · Tweakable block cipher · Lightweight

© International Association for Cryptologic Research 2020
A. Canteaut and Y. Ishai (Eds.): EUROCRYPT 2020, LNCS 12106, pp. 705–735, 2020.
https://doi.org/10.1007/978-3-030-45724-2_24

1   Introduction

Data communication through IoT devices is getting more and more popular. This requires lightweight authenticated encryption (AE) schemes that can be used comfortably in a resource-restricted environment. Since March 2019, NIST has organized a competition for determining the lightweight AE standard [38]. 56 designs were chosen as Round 1 candidates and 32 designs have been chosen as Round 2 candidates in August 2019. The design of lightweight AE schemes is one of the most actively discussed topics in the symmetric-key research filed.

Many of AE designs with provable security adopt a block cipher (BC), a cryptographic permutation, or a tweakable block cipher (TBC) as an underlying primitive. The conventional security model regards those modules as a black box and discusses the security under the black box setting. In contract, NIST's competition optionally takes into account the security in the grey box setting, where the cryptographic modules leak side-channel information. It is now important to design lightweight AE schemes such that countermeasures against side-channel attacks (SCA) can be implemented efficiently.

Masking is by far the most common countermeasure against SCA [25,37], and thus implementing an AE scheme using a BC/TBC primitive protected by masking is the natural way to realize an SCA-resistant AE. Threshold implementation (TI) introduced by Nikova et al. [37] is a masking particularly popular for hardware implementation. Masking, however, easily multiply the computational cost. Although hardware designers have been tackling the problem by designing serialized implementations in order to achieve an extreme of the area-speed trade-off, implementation-level optimization is reaching its limit. To push the limit further, researchers have been studying a BC optimized for TI by design, mostly focusing on TI-friendly Sboxes [13,21]. In this paper, we follow this line of research and go one step further by introducing the TI-friendly AE mode.

TI encodes the internal state (mostly consists of the internal state to compute the underlying primitive) into multiple shares, and apply the round transformation to each of them. Hence, the area size in TI increases proportionally to the number of shares. The number of shares is $dt+1$ for the order of masking d and the algebraic degree of a target function t, and thus it is $t+1$ for the first-order TI with $d=1$.

In lightweight AE schemes, register occupies the major circuit area. To be more precise, let b and s be the bit sizes of the underlying primitive and the aiming security, respectively. Then the key size needs to be at least s, and thus we need a b-bit register for the data block and an s-bit key for the key. We need different number of shares for the data and key because the data needs three shares for the nonlinear round function ($t > 1$), but the key needs only two shares because the key schedule function is often linear for recent algorithms. Naito and Sugawara recently proposed a TBC-based scheme which is particularly efficient with TI by exploiting this asymmetry [34].

The problem we address in this paper is to further exploit this asymmetry. More specifically, we let $\omega = s/b$ be an indicator of the asymmetry, and consider designing a scheme with higher ω. Following Naito and Sugawara, we pursue TBC-based schemes because of disadvantages of other approaches as follows. The comparison is also given in Table 1.

Drawbacks of BC based schemes: To minimize a register size, i.e., the register size is (almost) equal to the BC size, the security level is compromised to the birthday-bound security regarding the block size, because birthday attacks are principally unavoidable. Hence, $2s$-bit block and s-bit key are necessary to ensure s-bit security even without TI. SAEB [33] is an example of this case. To apply the first-order TI by assuming a linear key schedule, we need 3 shares for the data block and 2 shares for the key. Hence, we need a register of size $8s(= 3 \times 2s + 2 \times s)$ bits. Note that the key register may not be protected in the same level as the data block register because computation of the key schedule is not dependent on the value of the data block. In this strategy, the register size is $7s(= 3 \times 2s + s)$ bits. Note that there are several beyond-the-birthday-bound (BBB) modes, but those require very unsuitable structures for TI i.e., in TI the register sizes of BBB modes are grater than those of birthday-bound ones.

Drawbacks of permutation based schemes: Let r and c be the number of bits for the rate and the capacity, respectively. When attackers are allowed to make decryption queries, the security of the simple duplex construction can be proven only up to the birthday bound of the capacity [12,28]. Hence to ensure s-bit security, the permutation size must be at least $2s + r$ bits. For the first-order TI, we need $3 \times (2s + r)$ bits of the register size. Beetle [14], a recently proposed design, is provably security up to $\min(c - \log r, b/2, r)$. To ensure s-bit security, we basically balance r and c to s bits for the second term, but slightly increases c to compensate '$- \log r$' in the first term. Hence, the register size is $2s + \log s$ bits without TI and $3 \times (2s + \log s)$ for TI.

Advantages of TBC based schemes: To ensure s-bit security, the block size can be s bits. Along with an s-bit key and an s-bit tweak, the register size without TI is $3s$ bits, e.g. PFB [34] and Romulus [26]. To apply the first-order TI by assuming a linear key schedule, we need 3 shares for the data block and 2 shares for the key. s-bit tweak is a public value, and it does not need any protection. Hence, we need a register of size $6s(= 3s + 2s + s)$ bits for TI. By the same analogy for BC, the protection of the key register may not be needed. In this case, the register size for TI becomes $5s$ bits.

Form the above comparison, we investigate a TBC-based scheme to design a mode that is efficient for TI. In particular, we focus our attention on the property that the area size of TI mainly depends on how big $\omega(= s/b)$ is, and we aim a TBC-based mode with a large ω.

Before stepping into the TI-friendly design, we first briefly introduce some knowledge that is general to the designs of AE schemes.

- To be lightweight, the use of "nonce", a value that is never repeated under the same key, offers significant advantages.
- As shown by ΘCB [29], privacy can be ensured by injecting the nonce and the block counter into the tweak for an underlying TBC.
- Authenticity can be ensured by preparing the double internal state size (the block size of an underlying TBC is a part of the internal state size) of the security level.

Table 1. Comparison of State Sizes with and without (w/o) TI. The (twea)key functions are assumed to be linear. Without TI, permutation based schemes achieve the smallest state size by using a small rate, while with TI, TBC based schemes in particular PFB_Plus outperform the others.

		base	BC	Permutation		TBC		
	example mode	SAEB	Duplex	Beetle	PFB,Romulus	PFB_Plus	PFBω
	reference	[33]	[12, 28]	[14]	[26, 34]	Ours	Ours
w/o TI	data block	$2s$	$2s + r$	$2s + \log s$	s	$0.5s$	s/ω
	key	s	s	s	s	s	s
	tweak	–	–	–	s	s	s
	extra state	–	–	–	–	$0.5s$	$s - s/\omega$
	total	$3s$	$2s + r$	$2s + \log s$	$3s$	$3s$	$3s$
TI	protect key	$8s$	$6s + 3r$	$6s + 3\log s$	$6s$	$5.5s$	$5s + s/\omega$
	not protect key	$7s$	$6s + 3r$	$6s + 3\log s$	$5s$	$4.5s$	$4s + s/\omega$

- The key size must be greater than or equal to the security level.
- The maximum number of processed input blocks by all queries should be equal to the security level.

Our goal is to design a TBC-based AE mode that has a large $\omega(= s/b)$. The biggest ω among the exiting TBC modes is 1, hence we first aim a TBC-based AE mode with $\omega = 2$. To achieve the goal, we have the following obstacles.

- b is a block size of TBC. For $\omega = 2$, we need to ensure the security up to the double of the block size. Hence, we need to design a mode that expands an b-bit TBC output to a $2b$-bit internal state. The expanded state needs to be updated only linearly, otherwise we need 3 shares for the expanded state in TI and thus does not yield any advantage compared to the case with $\omega = 1$.
- To avoid using 3 shares for the key, the key schedule must be linear. To leave the tweak state unprotected (only with 1 share), the tweak and key states must be kept independent. We observe that the tweakey framework [27] is suitable for this design.
- The key size must be $2b$ bits. To process up to $2b$-bit block inputs, the size of the combination of the nonce and the block counter must be $2b$ bits. Namely, we need to process $4b$ bits for the key plus tweak, which is not easy with existing TBCs. The tweakey framework conceptually defines a way to process $4b$-bit tweakey (tweak plus key), while exiting concrete designs only support up to $3b$-bit tweakey. Note that Lilliput-AE [1], one of the first-round candidates at the NIST competition, specifies TBCs with $5b$-, $6b$-, and $7b$-bit tweakeys. However, those ignored the rationale of the original tweakey framework to ensure the security, and were actually attacked practically [20].

Our Contributions. This paper proposes new TBC based modes that are efficient for TI. We first propose our new mode PFB_Plus (Fig. 1) that is a TI-friendly TBC-based mode for $\omega = 2$ with rigorous security proof. The block size

b of the underlying TBC is $0.5s$ bits for s-bit security. As its construction, we combine the structure of PFB with f9 [43] in order to generate $2b$-bit internal state from b-bit TBC outputs and only use linear operations to update the expanded state. We then provide rigorous security proofs of PFB_Plus. The proof is advantageous in a sense that the security only depends on the number of decryption queries and independent of the length of the each query. PFB_Plus is optimized for the first-order TI, namely, 3 shares for the TBC of $0.5s$-bit block, 2 shares for the $0.5s$-bit extended state, 2 shares for the s-bit key and no protection (1 share) for the s-bit tweak. The total state size is $5.5s$ in TI or even $4.5s$ when the key is not protected. Those are shown in Table 1[1]. We also provide a tradeoff between the area size and the target security by truncating the extended $2b$-bit internal state, which offers arbitrary security level between b to $2b$ bits. Note that such a feature cannot be achieved by PFB and Romulus: one of the second-round candidates in the NIST competition.

While PFB_Plus is optimized for the first-order TI, one may be interested in finding the theoretical limitation of our approach, i.e. how large ω can be. To answer this question, we propose an extended version called PFBω (Fig. 2) that can handle an arbitrary ω with security proof under some assumptions for the existence of the underlying primitives (a TBC with $2\omega b$-bit tweakey and suitable coefficients for multiplications over a finite field). When ω becomes larger, to satisfy the assumption becomes more difficult and the number of operations increases, while the area size in TI becomes smaller. The state size of PFBω is shown in Table 1.

Next, we design a concrete TBC for PFB_Plus. The underlying TBC must be small in area and needs to support $4b$-bit tweakey. In addition, to increase the efficiency in TI, the tweakey schedule should not contain any non-linear operation. We choose SKINNY with 64-bit block as a base of our TBC because SKINNY is lightweight and indeed used in several designs submitted to the NIST competition. We extend the design of SKINNY to support TK4 so that the existing third-party security analysis remains available up to TK3. With this approach, our SKINNY-64-256 up to TK3 is secure as long as the original SKINNY is secure. We then provide the lower bounds of the number of active S-boxes in TK4 as the designers of SKINNY did the same. Moreover, we update the security analysis of SKINNY in the single key: the designers of SKINNY sometimes provided upper bounds of the number of active S-boxes both in differential and linear cryptanalysis. Alfarano *et al.* updated the bounds for differential cryptanalysis [4], while we update the bounds for linear cryptanalysis with the tight ones. Finally, we benchmark TI of PFB_Plus instantiated with SKINNY-64-256 in hardware by using the most practical parameters for TI.[2]

---

[1] In the table, the (twea)key functions are assumed to be linear. If the functions are non-linear, 3 shares of the functions are required, and the state sizes of the TBC-based modes are grater than those of the permutation-based ones.

[2] With respect to the reliability, it can be disadvantageous that our modes cannot be instantiated with existing well-known TBCs. However, from a different viewpoint, PFB_Plus is the first use case where $2n$-bit tweak and $2n$-bit key sizes are useful. This can give new insight to TBC designers considering that there is no consensus about the adequate tweak size to support.

Finally, we give hardware performance evaluation of PFB_Plus combined with SKINNY-64-256, and compare it with the conventional PFB. As a masking scheme, we choose the first-order TI in which the TBC state and key are protected with three and two shares, respectively. Thanks to the larger ω, the TI of PFB_Plus is smaller than that of PFB by more than one thousand gates (7,439 and 8,448 [GE], respectively), and is the smallest within the schemes having 128-bit security.

Recommendation. PFBω is designed as a proof-of-concept of using a smaller block size, and our recommendation is PFB_Plus.

Limitations. The proposed method becomes efficient with TI, and the benefit extends to other masking schemes with $dt + 1$ shares (for $t > 1$) [25]; meanwhile, it is no longer efficient with $(d + 1)$-share masking schemes [16]. We believe that $(dt + 1)$-shares schemes are still important. First, the 1st-order TI is a very practical option because of its reasonable circuit area and no need for fresh randomness. Second, $(dt + 1)$-share schemes can be an only option under some security requirements, e.g., when we need non-completeness to eliminate leakage by glitches without relying on registers in between gates.

PFB_Plus and PFBω are secure if no unverified plaintext is released and no nonce is repeated, and we do not ensure the misuse security.

Previous Works. In this paper, we focus on designing TI-friendly AE schemes with respect to implementation size. Another approach to design an AE scheme with SCA resistance is leakage-resilient cryptography. The schemes [9–11,23,24] based on the Pereira et al.'s approach [39] assume a leak-free component, and are optimized for minimizing the number of calls to it[3]. However, the way how to realize the leak-free component, that determines the implementation size, is usually out of scope. Moreover, they need additional components such as hash function and pseudo-random function. Barwell et al. [7] studied another approach using pairing-based cryptography, but it is also costly.

The Sponge-based leakage resilient AE scheme ISAP [18] has a potential for lightweight implementation because it does not rely on a leak-free component. However, its implementation cost (14 [kGE]) is still larger than PFB_Plus (7.439 [kGE]). There are recent works following ISAP. The works [17,19] gave security proofs for the Sponge-based schemes which was missing in the original paper. Degabriele et al. [17] proposed a variant using a random function. Dobraunig and Mennink [19] gave the security proof of the duplex [12] with respect to leakage resiliency.

Another line of research is to design cryptographic primitives using minimum number of non-linear operations thereby reducing the cost for TI [2,3]. In contrast to those studies, we approach the problem from the mode of operation by exploiting the asymmetry between non-linear round function and linear key scheduling, rather than improving the non-linear function itself. We designed SKINNY-64-256 for providing a small block length and a larger tweakey state,

---

[3] Note that some works even have misuse resistance that our research does not.

and not for minimizing the number of non-linear operations. We also note that the conventional works focus on minimizing non-linear operations and thus their target primitive is BC rather than TBC (TBCs typically require a higher amount of operations than BCs in order to process a tweak), while the use of TBC is the central part of our study.

2   Preliminaries

Notation. Let ε be an empty string and $\{0,1\}^*$ be the set of all bit strings. For an integer $i \geq 0$, let $\{0,1\}^i$ be the set of all i-bit strings, $\{0,1\}^0 := \{\varepsilon\}$, and $\{0,1\}^{\leq i} := \{0,1\}^1 \cup \{0,1\}^2 \cup \cdots \cup \{0,1\}^i$ be the set of all bit strings of length at most i, except for ε. Let 0^i resp. 1^i be the bit string of i-bit zeros resp. ones. For an integer $i \geq 1$, let $[i] := \{1, 2, \ldots, i\}$ be the set of positive integers less than or equal to i, and $(i] := \{0\} \cup [i]$. For a non-empty set $\mathcal{T}$, $T \xleftarrow{\$} \mathcal{T}$ means that an element is chosen uniformly at random from $\mathcal{T}$ and is assigned to T. The concatenation of two bit strings X and Y is written as $X \| Y$ or XY when no confusion is possible. For integers $0 \leq i \leq j$ and $X \in \{0,1\}^j$, let $\mathsf{msb}_i(X)$ resp. $\mathsf{lsb}_i(X)$ be the most resp. least significant i bits of X, and $|X|$ be the number of bits of X, i.e., $|X| = j$. For integers i and j with $0 \leq i < 2^j$, let $\mathsf{str}_j(i)$ be the j-bit binary representation of i. For an integer $b \geq 0$ and a bit string X, we denote the parsing into fixed-length b-bit strings as $(X_1, X_2, \ldots, X_\ell) \xleftarrow{b} X$, where if $X \neq \varepsilon$ then $X = X_1 \| X_2 \| \cdots \| X_\ell$, $|X_i| = b$ for $i \in [\ell - 1]$, and $0 < |X_\ell| \leq b$; if $X = \varepsilon$ then $\ell = 1$ and $X_1 = \varepsilon$. For an integer $b > 0$, let $\mathsf{ozp} : \{0,1\}^{\leq b} \to \{0,1\}^b$ be a one-zero padding function: for a bit string $X \in \{0,1\}^{\leq b}$, $\mathsf{ozp}(X) = X$ if $|X| = b$; $\mathsf{ozp}(X) = X \| 10^{b-1-|X|}$ if $|X| < b$.

Tweakable Block Cipher. A tweakable blockcipher (TBC) is a set of permutations indexed by a key and a public input called tweak. Let $\mathcal{K}$ be the key space, $\mathcal{TW}$ be the tweak space, and b be the input/output-block size. An encryption is denoted by $\widetilde{E} : \mathcal{K} \times \mathcal{TW} \times \{0,1\}^b \to \{0,1\}^b$, $\widetilde{E}$ having a key $K \in \mathcal{K}$ is denoted by $\widetilde{E}_K$, and $\widetilde{E}_K$ having a tweak $TW \in \mathcal{TW}$ is denoted by $\widetilde{E}_K^{TW}$.

In this paper, a keyed TBC is assumed to be a secure tweakable-pseudorandom permutation (TPRP), i.e., indistinguishable from a tweakable random permutation (TRP). A tweakable permutation (TP) $\widetilde{P} : \mathcal{TW} \times \{0,1\}^b \to \{0,1\}^b$ is a set of b-bit permutations indexed by a tweak in $\mathcal{TW}$. A TP $\widetilde{P}$ having a tweak $TW \in \mathcal{TW}$ is denoted by $\widetilde{P}^{TW}$. Let $\widetilde{\mathsf{Perm}}(\mathcal{TW}, \{0,1\}^b)$ be the set of all TPs. For a set of all TPs: $\mathcal{TW} \times \{0,1\}^b \to \{0,1\}^b$ denoted by $\widetilde{\mathsf{Perm}}(\mathcal{TW}, \{0,1\}^b)$, a TRP is defined as $\widetilde{P} \xleftarrow{\$} \widetilde{\mathsf{Perm}}(\mathcal{TW}, \{0,1\}^b)$. In the TPRP-security game, an adversary $\mathbf{A}$ has access to either the keyed TBC $\widetilde{E}_K$ or a TRP $\widetilde{P}$, where $K \xleftarrow{\$} \mathcal{K}$ and $\widetilde{P} \xleftarrow{\$} \widetilde{\mathsf{Perm}}(\mathcal{TW}, \{0,1\}^b)$, and after the interaction, $\mathbf{A}$ returns a decision bit $y \in \{0,1\}$. The output of $\mathbf{A}$ with access to $\mathcal{O}$ is denoted by $\mathbf{A}^{\mathcal{O}}$. The TPRP-security advantage function of $\mathbf{A}$ is defined as

$$\mathbf{Adv}_{\widetilde{E}_K}^{\mathsf{tprp}}(\mathbf{A}) := \Pr\left[K \xleftarrow{\$} \mathcal{K}; \mathbf{A}^{\widetilde{E}_K} = 1\right] - \Pr\left[\widetilde{P} \xleftarrow{\$} \widetilde{\mathsf{Perm}}(\mathcal{TW}, \{0,1\}^b); \mathbf{A}^{\widetilde{P}} = 1\right],$$

where the probabilities are taken over $K, \widetilde{P}$ and $\mathbf{A}$.

Nonce-Based Authenticated Encryption with Associated Data. A nonce-based authenticated encryption with associated data (nAEAD) scheme based on a keyed TBC $\widetilde{E}_K$, denoted by $\Pi[\widetilde{E}_K]$, is a pair of encryption and decryption algorithms $(\Pi.\mathsf{Enc}[\widetilde{E}_K], \Pi.\mathsf{Dec}[\widetilde{E}_K])$. $\mathcal{K}, \mathcal{N}, \mathcal{M}, \mathcal{C}, \mathcal{A}$ and $\mathcal{T}$ are the sets of keys, nonces, plaintexts, ciphertexts, associated data (AD) and tags of $\Pi[\widetilde{E}_K]$, respectively. In this paper, the key space of $\Pi[\widetilde{E}_K]$ is equal to that of the underlying TBC. The encryption algorithm takes a nonce $N \in \mathcal{N}$, AD $A \in \mathcal{A}$, and a plaintext $M \in \mathcal{M}$, and returns, deterministically, a pair of a ciphertext $C \in \mathcal{C}$ and a tag $T \in \mathcal{T}$. The decryption algorithm takes a tuple $(N, A, C, T) \in \mathcal{N} \times \mathcal{A} \times \mathcal{C} \times \mathcal{T}$, and returns, deterministically, either the distinguished invalid (reject) symbol **reject** $\notin \mathcal{M}$ or a plaintext $M \in \mathcal{M}$. We require $|\Pi.\mathsf{Enc}[\widetilde{E}_K](N, A, M)| = |\Pi.\mathsf{Enc}[\widetilde{E}_K](N, A, M')|$ when these outputs are strings and $|M| = |M'|$. We consider two security notions of nAEAD, privacy and authenticity. Hereafter, we call queries to the encryption resp. decryption oracle "encryption queries" resp. "decryption queries."

The privacy notion considers the indistinguishability between the encryption $\Pi.\mathsf{Enc}[\widetilde{E}_K]$ and a random-bits oracle \$, in the nonce-respecting setting. \$ has the same interface as $\Pi.\mathsf{Enc}[\widetilde{E}_K]$ and for a query (N, A, M) returns a random bit string of length $|\Pi.\mathsf{Enc}[\widetilde{E}_K](N, A, M)|$. In the privacy game, an adversary **A** interacts with either $\Pi.\mathsf{Enc}[\widetilde{E}_K]$ or \$, and then returns a decision bit $y \in \{0, 1\}$. The privacy advantage function of an adversary **A** is defined as

$$\mathbf{Adv}^{\mathsf{priv}}_{\Pi[\widetilde{E}_K]}(\mathbf{A}) := \Pr[K \xleftarrow{\$} \mathcal{K}; \mathbf{A}^{\Pi.\mathsf{Enc}[\widetilde{E}_K]} = 1] - \Pr[\mathbf{A}^{\$} = 1],$$

where the probabilities are taken over $K, \$$ and **A**. We demand that **A** is nonce-respecting (all nonces in encryption queries are distinct).

The maximum over all adversaries, running in time at most t and making encryption queries of $\sigma_\mathcal{E}$ the total number of TBC calls invoked by all encryption queries, is denoted by $\mathbf{Adv}^{\mathsf{priv}}_{\Pi[\widetilde{E}_K]}(\sigma_\mathcal{E}, t) := \max_{\mathbf{A}} \mathbf{Adv}^{\mathsf{priv}}_{\Pi[\widetilde{E}_K]}(\mathbf{A})$. When an adversary is a computationally unbounded algorithm, the time t is disregarded.

The authenticity notion considers the unforgeability in the nonce-respecting setting. In the authenticity game, an adversary **A** interacts with $\Pi[\widetilde{E}_K] = (\Pi.\mathsf{Enc}[\widetilde{E}_K], \Pi.\mathsf{Dec}[\widetilde{E}_K])$, and the goal of the adversary is to make a non-trivial decryption query whose response is not **reject**. The authenticity advantage of an adversary **A** is defined as

$$\mathbf{Adv}^{\mathsf{auth}}_{\Pi[\widetilde{E}_K]}(\mathbf{A}) := \Pr[K \xleftarrow{\$} \mathcal{K}; \mathbf{A}^{\Pi.\mathsf{Enc}[\widetilde{E}_K], \Pi.\mathsf{Dec}[\widetilde{E}_K]} \text{ forges}],$$

where the probabilities are taken over K and **A**. We demand that **A** is nonce-respecting (all nonces in encryption queries are distinct), that **A** never asks a trivial decryption query (N, A, C, T), i.e., there is a prior encryption query (N, A, M) with $(C, T) = \Pi.\mathsf{Enc}[\widetilde{E}_K](N, A, M)$, and that **A** never repeats a query. $\mathbf{A}^{\Pi.\mathsf{Enc}[\widetilde{E}_K], \Pi.\mathsf{Dec}[\widetilde{E}_K]}$ forges means that **A** makes a decryption query whose response is not **reject**.

The maximum over all adversaries, running in time at most t and making at most $q_{\mathcal{E}}$ encryption queries and $q_{\mathcal{D}}$ decryption queries of σ the total number of TBC calls invoked by all queries, is denoted by $\mathbf{Adv}^{\mathrm{auth}}_{\Pi[\widetilde{E}_K]}((q_{\mathcal{E}}, q_{\mathcal{D}}, \sigma), t) :=$ $\max_{\mathbf{A}} \mathbf{Adv}^{\mathrm{auth}}_{\Pi[\widetilde{E}_K]}(\mathbf{A})$. When an adversary is a computationally unbounded algorithm, the time t is disregarded.

3   PFB_Plus: Specification and Security Bounds

We design PFB_Plus, a TBC-based nAEAD mode with $b + \tau$-bit security where $0 \leq \tau \leq b$, by extending the existing TBC-based lightweight mode PFB [34]. Regarding the relation between security and internal state size, in order to achieve s-bit security, the internal state size must be at least s bits. Thus PFB_Plus is designed so that the internal state size is minimum, i.e., $b + \tau$ bits. To do so, we extend PFB, which is a b-bit secure nAEAD mode and whose security level equals to the internal state size. For the extension, we need to define an additional τ-bit internal state in order to have $b + \tau$-bit security. The additional internal state is designed using the idea of f9 [43], which is a BC-based message authentication code.

- The first b-bit internal state is updated by iterating a TBC and absorbing a data block (AD/plaintext/ciphertext block), and the output of the last TBC call becomes the first b-bit tag. The idea comes from PFB.
- The remaining τ-bit internal state is defined by XORing outputs of TBC calls. The idea comes from f9, but our structure is slightly different from f9. In PFB_Plus, a TBC is not performed after XORing all outputs of TBC calls (with $b - \tau$-bit truncation), which keeps the internal state size $b + \tau$ bits. On the other hand, in f9, a block cipher is performed after XORing all outputs of block cipher calls.

Regarding tweak elements, as shown by ΘCB [29], for the sake of perfect privacy, the nonce and the block counter are injected.

3.1   Specification

The specification of PFB_Plus is given in Algorithm 1 and is illustrated in Fig. 1.

Let ℓ_{max} be a maximum number of AD/plaintext/ciphertext blocks, i.e., $a \leq \ell_{\mathsf{max}}$ and $m \leq \ell_{\mathsf{max}}$. The tweak space $\mathcal{TW}$ consists of a nonce space $\mathcal{N} := \{0, 1\}^n$, a block counter space $(\ell_{\mathsf{max}}]$ and a space for tweak separations $(15]$. The space for tweak separations $(15]$ is used to offer distinct permutations for handing AD, encrypting plaintexts (or decrypting ciphertexts) and generating a tag. Hence, the tweak space is defined as $\mathcal{TW} := \{0, 1\}^n \times (\ell_{\mathsf{max}}] \times (15]$.

The procedure of handing AD is given in PFB_Plus.Hash. The procedure of encrypting a plaintext is given in the steps 2–5 of PFB_Plus.Enc, and the procedure of generating a tag is given in the steps 6–9. The procedure of decrypting a ciphertext is given in the steps 2–5 of PFB_Plus.Dec, and the procedure of verifying a tag is given in the steps 6–9. Note that the tweaks x and y are defined according to the lengths of AD A and of a plaintext M (more precisely, whether

Algorithm 1. PFB_Plus

Encryption PFB_Plus.Enc$[\widetilde{E}_K](N, A, M)$

1: $(M_0, T_2) \leftarrow$ PFB_Plus.Hash$[\widetilde{E}_K](A)$
2: **if** $A = \varepsilon$ **then** $x \leftarrow 1$; **else if** $A \neq \varepsilon \wedge |A| \mod b = 0$ **then** $x \leftarrow 6$; **else** $x \leftarrow 11$
3: $M_1, \ldots, M_m \xleftarrow{b} M$; **if** $M = \varepsilon$ **then** $\{m \leftarrow 0; S_1 \leftarrow M_0;$ **goto** Step 7$\}$
4: **for** $i = 1, \ldots, m-1$ **do** $\{W_i \leftarrow \widetilde{E}_K^{N,i,x}(M_{i-1}); C_i \leftarrow W_i \oplus M_i; T_2 \leftarrow T_2 \oplus \mathsf{lsb}_\tau(W_i)\}$
5: $W_m \leftarrow \widetilde{E}_K^{N,m,x}(M_{m-1}); C_m \leftarrow \mathsf{msb}_{|M_m|}(W_m) \oplus M_m$
6: $T_2 \leftarrow T_2 \oplus \mathsf{lsb}_\tau(W_m); S_1 \leftarrow \mathsf{ozp}(M_m) \oplus (0^{|M_m|} \| \mathsf{lsb}_{b-|M_m|}(W_m))$
7: **if** $|M| \mod b = 0$ **then** $y \leftarrow x+1$; **else** $y \leftarrow x+3$
8: $S_2 \leftarrow \widetilde{E}_K^{N,m,y}(S_1); T_2 \leftarrow \mathsf{lsb}_\tau(S_2) \oplus T_2; T_1 \leftarrow \widetilde{E}_K^{N,m,y+1}(S_2)$
9: $C \leftarrow C_1 \| \cdots \| C_m; T \leftarrow T_1 \| T_2;$ **return** (C, T)

Decryption PFB_Plus.Dec$[\widetilde{E}_K](N, A, C, \hat{T})$

1: $(M_0, T_2) \leftarrow$ PFB_Plus.Hash$[\widetilde{E}_K](A)$
2: **if** $A = \varepsilon$ **then** $x \leftarrow 1$; **else if** $A \neq \varepsilon \wedge |A| \mod b = 0$ **then** $x \leftarrow 6$; **else** $x \leftarrow 11$
3: $C_1, \ldots, C_m \xleftarrow{b} C$; **if** $C = \varepsilon$ **then** $\{m \leftarrow 0; S_1 \leftarrow M_0;$ **goto** Step 7$\}$
4: **for** $i = 1, \ldots, m-1$ **do** $\{W_i \leftarrow \widetilde{E}_K^{N,i,x}(M_{i-1}); M_i \leftarrow W_i \oplus C_i; T_2 \leftarrow T_2 \oplus \mathsf{lsb}_\tau(W_i)\}$
5: $W_m \leftarrow \widetilde{E}_K^{N,m,x}(M_m); M_m \leftarrow \mathsf{msb}_{|C_m|}(W_m) \oplus C_m$
6: $T_2 \leftarrow T_2 \oplus \mathsf{lsb}_\tau(W_m); S_1 \leftarrow \mathsf{ozp}(M_m) \oplus (0^{|C_m|} \| \mathsf{lsb}_{b-|C_m|}(W_m))$
7: **if** $|C| \mod b = 0$ **then** $y \leftarrow x+1$; **else** $y \leftarrow x+3$
8: $S_2 \leftarrow \widetilde{E}_K^{N,m,y}(S_1); T_2 \leftarrow \mathsf{lsb}_\tau(S_2) \oplus T_2; T_1 \leftarrow \widetilde{E}_K^{N,m,y+1}(S_2); T \leftarrow T_1 \| T_2$
9: **if** $T = \hat{T}$ **then return** $M \leftarrow M_1 \| \cdots \| M_m;$ **else return reject**

Hash PFB_Plus.Hash$[\widetilde{E}_K](A)$

1: **if** $A = \varepsilon$ **then return** $(0^b, 0^\tau)$
2: $V_0 \leftarrow 0^b; H_2 \leftarrow 0^\tau; A_1, \ldots, A_a \xleftarrow{b} A$
3: **for** $i = 1, \ldots, a-1$ **do** $\{V_i \leftarrow \widetilde{E}_K^{0^n,i,0}(A_i \oplus V_{i-1}); H_2 \leftarrow \mathsf{lsb}_\tau(V_i) \oplus H_2\}$
4: $V_a \leftarrow \widetilde{E}_K^{0^n,a,0}(\mathsf{ozp}(A_a) \oplus V_{a-1}); H_1 \leftarrow V_a; H_2 \leftarrow \mathsf{lsb}_\tau(V_a) \oplus H_2;$ **return** (H_1, H_2)

AD is empty or not, whether the one-zero padding is applied to A or not, and whether it is applied to M or not). The concrete values are given below:

- if $A = \varepsilon \wedge |M| \mod b = 0$ then $(x, y) = (1, 2)$,
- if $A = \varepsilon \wedge |M| \mod b \neq 0$ then $(x, y) = (1, 4)$,
- if $A \neq \varepsilon \wedge |A| \mod b = 0 \wedge |M| \mod b = 0$ then $(x, y) = (6, 7)$,
- if $A \neq \varepsilon \wedge |A| \mod b = 0 \wedge |M| \mod b \neq 0$ then $(x, y) = (6, 9)$,
- if $A \neq \varepsilon \wedge |A| \mod b \neq 0 \wedge |M| \mod b = 0$ then $(x, y) = (11, 12)$, and
- if $A \neq \varepsilon \wedge |A| \mod b \neq 0 \wedge |M| \mod b \neq 0$ then $(x, y) = (11, 14)$.

3.2   Privacy and Authenticity Bounds of PFB_Plus

Theorem 1.

$$\mathbf{Adv}^{\mathsf{priv}}_{\mathsf{PFB\_Plus}[\widetilde{E}_K]}(\sigma_\mathcal{E}, t) \leq \mathbf{Adv}^{\mathsf{tprp}}_{\widetilde{E}_K}(\sigma_\mathcal{E}, t + O(\sigma_\mathcal{E})),$$

$$\mathbf{Adv}^{\mathsf{auth}}_{\mathsf{PFB\_Plus}[\widetilde{E}_K]}((q_\mathcal{E}, q_\mathcal{D}, \sigma), t) \leq \frac{q_\mathcal{D} \cdot 2^{b-\tau+1}}{(2^b - 1)^2} + \mathbf{Adv}^{\mathsf{tprp}}_{\widetilde{E}_K}(\sigma, t + O(\sigma)).$$

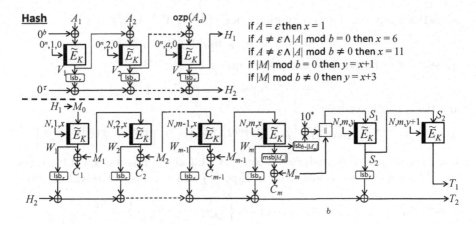

Fig. 1. PFB_Plus.Hash and PFB_Plus.Enc. $A_1, \ldots, A_a \xleftarrow{b} A$ (in the hash procedure); $M_1, \ldots, M_m \xleftarrow{b} M$ (in the encryption procedure).

4 Proof of Theorem 1

Firstly, the keyed TBC $\widetilde{E}_K$ for $K \xleftarrow{\$} \mathcal{K}$ is replaced with a TRP $\widetilde{P} \xleftarrow{\$} \widetilde{\mathrm{Perm}}\,(\mathcal{TW}, \{0,1\}^b)$. The replacement offers the TPRP-terms $\mathbf{Adv}^{\mathrm{tprp}}_{\widetilde{E}_K}(\sigma_{\mathcal{E}}, t + O(\sigma_{\mathcal{E}}))$ and $\mathbf{Adv}^{\mathrm{tprp}}_{\widetilde{E}_K}(\sigma, t + O(\sigma))$, and then the remaining works are to upper-bound the advantages $\mathbf{Adv}^{\mathrm{priv}}_{\mathrm{PFB\_Plus}[\widetilde{P}]}(\sigma_{\mathcal{E}})$ and $\mathbf{Adv}^{\mathrm{auth}}_{\mathrm{PFB\_Plus}[\widetilde{P}]}(q_{\mathcal{E}}, q_{\mathcal{D}}, \sigma)$, where adversaries are computationally unbounded algorithms and the complexities are solely measured by the numbers of queries. Without loss of generality, adversaries are deterministic.

Regarding $\mathbf{Adv}^{\mathrm{priv}}_{\mathrm{PFB\_Plus}[\widetilde{P}]}(\sigma_{\mathcal{E}})$, as tweaks of $\widetilde{P}$ are all distinct, all output blocks of $\widetilde{P}$ defined by encryption queries are chosen independently and uniformly at random from $\{0,1\}^b$. We thus have $\mathbf{Adv}^{\mathrm{priv}}_{\mathrm{PFB\_Plus}[\widetilde{P}]}(\sigma_{\mathcal{E}}) = 0$.

In the following, we focus on upper-bounding $\mathbf{Adv}^{\mathrm{auth}}_{\mathrm{PFB\_Plus}[\widetilde{P}]}(q_{\mathcal{E}}, q_{\mathcal{D}}, \sigma)$.

4.1 Upper-Bounding $\mathbf{Adv}^{\mathrm{auth}}_{\mathrm{PFB\_Plus}[\widetilde{P}]}(q_{\mathcal{E}}, q_{\mathcal{D}}, \sigma)$

Firstly, we fix a decryption query $(N^{(d)}, A^{(d)}, C^{(d)}, \hat{T}^{(d)})$, and upper-bound the probability that an adversary forges at the decryption query.

In the analysis, we use the following notations. Values/variables corresponding with the decryption query are denoted by using the superscript of (d) such as $N^{(d)}, M^{(d)}$, etc. Hence, this analysis upper-bounds $\Pr[T^{(d)} = \hat{T}^{(d)}]$. The lengths a and m are denoted by a_d and m_d, respectively. Similarly, for an encryption query $(N^{(e)}, A^{(e)}, M^{(e)})$, values/variables corresponding with the encryption query are denoted by using the superscript of (e), and the lengths a and m are denoted by a_e and m_e, respectively.

We next define two cases that are used to upper-bound $\Pr[T^{(d)} = \hat{T}^{(d)}]$.

- Case1: for any previous encryption query $(N^{(e)}, A^{(e)}, M^{(e)})$,

$$N^{(e)} \neq N^{(d)} \vee m_e \neq m_d \vee y^{(e)} \neq y^{(d)}.$$

- Case2: for some previous encryption query $(N^{(e)}, A^{(e)}, M^{(e)})$,

$$N^{(e)} = N^{(d)} \wedge m_e = m_d \wedge y^{(e)} = y^{(d)}.$$

Using these cases, we have

$$\Pr[T^{(d)} = \hat{T}^{(d)}] \leq \max \left\{ \Pr\left[T^{(d)} = \hat{T}^{(d)} \middle| \mathsf{Case1}\right], \Pr\left[T^{(d)} = \hat{T}^{(d)} \middle| \mathsf{Case2}\right] \right\}.$$

These probabilities are analyzed in Subsect. 4.2 and Subsects. 4.3–4.9, respectively. The upper-bounds are given in Eqs. (1) and (4), respectively, and give

$$\mathbf{Adv}^{\mathrm{auth}}_{\mathrm{PFB\_Plus}[\widetilde{P}]}(q_{\mathcal{E}}, q_{\mathcal{D}}, \sigma) \leq q_{\mathcal{D}} \cdot \max \left\{ \frac{1}{2^{b+\tau}}, \frac{2^{b-\tau+1}}{(2^b-1)^2} \right\} = \frac{q_{\mathcal{D}} \cdot 2^{b-\tau+1}}{(2^b-1)^2}.$$

4.2   Upper-Bounding $\Pr\left[T^{(d)} = \hat{T}^{(d)} \middle| \mathsf{Case1}\right]$

In Case1, the tweak tuples $(y^{(d)}, N^{(d)}, z^{(d)})$ and $(y^{(d)}+1, N^{(d)}, z^{(d)})$ with which the outputs of $\widetilde{P}$ define $S_2^{(d)}$ and $T_1^{(d)}$ are distinct from the tweak triples defined by the previous encryption queries. Hence, $T_1^{(d)}$ and $T_2^{(d)}$ are chosen uniformly at random from $\{0,1\}^b$ and independently of the previous outputs of $\widetilde{P}$. We thus have

$$\Pr\left[T^{(d)} = \hat{T}^{(d)} \middle| \mathsf{Case1}\right] \leq \frac{1}{2^{b+\tau}}. \tag{1}$$

4.3   Upper-Bounding $\Pr\left[T^{(d)} = \hat{T}^{(d)} \middle| \mathsf{Case2}\right]$

In Case2, $S_2^{(d)} = S_2^{(e)} \Leftrightarrow S_1^{(d)} = S_1^{(e)}$ is satisfied (as $\widetilde{P}^{N^{(d)}, y^{(d)}, m_d}$ and $\widetilde{P}^{N^{(e)}, y^{(e)}, m_e}$ are the same permutation). Hence, we can focus on the cases: $S_1^{(d)} \neq S_1^{(e)} \wedge S_2^{(d)} \neq S_2^{(e)}$; $S_1^{(d)} = S_1^{(e)} \wedge S_2^{(d)} = S_2^{(e)}$. Using these cases, we have

$$\Pr\left[T^{(d)} = \hat{T}^{(d)} \middle| \mathsf{Case2}\right] = \Pr\left[T^{(d)} = \hat{T}^{(d)} \wedge S_1^{(d)} \neq S_1^{(e)} \wedge S_2^{(d)} \neq S_2^{(e)} \middle| \mathsf{Case2}\right]$$

$$+ \Pr\left[T^{(d)} = \hat{T}^{(d)} \wedge S_1^{(d)} = S_1^{(e)} \wedge S_2^{(d)} = S_2^{(e)} \middle| \mathsf{Case2}\right]$$

$$\leq \underbrace{\Pr\left[T^{(d)} = \hat{T}^{(d)} \middle| \mathsf{Case2} \wedge S_1^{(d)} \neq S_1^{(e)} \wedge S_2^{(d)} \neq S_2^{(e)}\right]}_{=:p_1} \tag{2}$$

$$+ \underbrace{\Pr\left[S_1^{(d)} = S_1^{(e)} \wedge T_2^{(d)} = \hat{T}_2^{(d)} \middle| \mathsf{Case2}\right]}_{=:p_2}. \tag{3}$$

The probabilities p_1 and p_2 are analyzed in Subsect. 4.4 and Subsects. 4.4–4.9, respectively. The upper-bounds are given in Eqs. (5) and (6), respectively, and give

$$\Pr\left[T^{(d)} = \hat{T}^{(d)} \middle| \mathsf{Case2}\right] \leq \frac{2^{b-\tau}}{(2^b-1)^2} + \frac{2^{b-\tau}}{(2^b-1)^2} = \frac{2^{b-\tau+1}}{(2^b-1)^2}. \tag{4}$$

4.4 Upper-Bounding p_1 in (2)

By $S_1^{(d)} \neq S_1^{(e)} \wedge S_2^{(d)} \neq S_2^{(e)}$, $T_1^{(d)}$ is chosen uniformly at random from $\{0,1\}^b \backslash \{T_1^{(e)}\}$, and $S_2^{(d)}$ is chosen uniformly at random from $\{0,1\}^b \backslash \{S_2^{(e)}\}$, i.e., $T_2^{(d)}$ is chosen uniformly at random from at least $(2^b - 1)/2^{b-\tau}$ values. Hence, we have

$$p_1 = \Pr\left[\hat{T}^{(d)} = T^{(d)} \middle| S_1^{(d)} \neq S_1^{(e)} \wedge S_2^{(d)} \neq S_2^{(e)} \wedge \mathsf{Case2}\right] \leq \frac{2^{b-\tau}}{(2^b - 1)^2}. \tag{5}$$

4.5 Upper-Bounding p_2 in (3)

Let

$$\mathcal{I}_V^{\neq} = \left\{i \in [\max\{a_e, a_d\}] \middle| V_i^{(d)} \neq V_i^{(e)}\right\}, \quad \mathcal{I}_W^{\neq} = \left\{i \in [m_d] \middle| W_i^{(d)} \neq W_i^{(e)}\right\}$$

be sets of indexes with distinct blocks for V and W, respectively, where $V_i^{(d)} := \varepsilon$ for $i > a_d$, and $V_i^{(e)} := \varepsilon$ for $i > a_e$.

This analysis uses the following four sub-cases of Case2.

- Case2-1 : $\mathsf{Case2} \wedge a_d = a_e \wedge |\mathcal{I}_V^{\neq}| + |\mathcal{I}_W^{\neq}| = 1$.
- Case2-2 : $\mathsf{Case2} \wedge a_d = a_e \wedge |\mathcal{I}_V^{\neq}| + |\mathcal{I}_W^{\neq}| \geq 2$.
- Case2-3 : $\mathsf{Case2} \wedge a_d \neq a_e \wedge |\mathcal{I}_W^{\neq}| = 0 \wedge A^{(d)} \neq \varepsilon \wedge A^{(e)} \neq \varepsilon$.
- Case2-4 : $\mathsf{Case2} \wedge a_d \neq a_e \wedge |\mathcal{I}_W^{\neq}| \geq 1 \wedge A^{(d)} \neq \varepsilon \wedge A^{(e)} \neq \varepsilon$.

Note that $\mathsf{Case2} \Rightarrow \mathsf{Case2\text{-}1} \vee \mathsf{Case2\text{-}2} \vee \mathsf{Case2\text{-}3} \vee \mathsf{Case2\text{-}4}$ is satisfied by the following reasons. Regarding the sets $\mathcal{I}_V^{\neq}$ and $\mathcal{I}_W^{\neq}$, the non-equation $(A^{(d)}, C^{(d)}) \neq (A^{(e)}, C^{(e)})$ and the condition $y^{(e)} = y^{(d)}$ (from Case2) ensure the following:

$$|\mathcal{I}_V^{\neq}| + |\mathcal{I}_W^{\neq}| \geq 1.$$

Regarding the AD $A^{(d)}$ and $A^{(e)}$, the condition $y^{(e)} = y^{(d)}$ ensures the following:

$$\left(A^{(d)} = A^{(e)} = \varepsilon\right) \vee \left(A^{(d)} \neq \varepsilon, A^{(e)} \neq \varepsilon\right).$$

Let $\mathsf{Coll}_{S,T} := S_1^{(d)} = S_1^{(e)} \wedge \hat{T}_2^{(d)} = T_2^{(e)}$. Then, using the four cases, we have

$$p_2 = \Pr\left[\mathsf{Coll}_{S,T} | \mathsf{Case2}\right] \leq \max\left\{\Pr\left[\mathsf{Coll}_{S,T} | \mathsf{Case2\text{-}1}\right], \Pr\left[\mathsf{Coll}_{S,T} | \mathsf{Case2\text{-}2}\right],\right.$$

$$\left.\Pr\left[\mathsf{Coll}_{S,T} | \mathsf{Case2\text{-}3}\right], \Pr\left[\mathsf{Coll}_{S,T} | \mathsf{Case2\text{-}4}\right]\right\}.$$

These probabilities are analyzed in Subsects. 4.6, 4.7, 4.8, and 4.9, respectively. These upper-bounds are given in Eqs. (7), (8), (9), and (10), respectively, and give

$$p_2 \leq \frac{2^{b-\tau}}{(2^b - 1)^2}. \tag{6}$$

4.6 Upper-Bounding $\Pr\left[S_1^{(d)} = S_1^{(e)} \wedge T_2^{(d)} = \hat{T}_2^{(d)} \middle| \text{Case2-1}\right]$

In Case2-1, the number of positions with distinct output blocks is 1, and thus the output difference is propagated to S_1, i.e., $S_1^{(d)} \neq S_1^{(e)}$ is satisfied. Hence, we have

$$\Pr\left[S_1^{(d)} = S_1^{(e)} \wedge T_2^{(d)} = \hat{T}_2^{(d)} \middle| \text{Case2-1}\right] = 0. \qquad (7)$$

4.7 Upper-Bounding $\Pr\left[S_1^{(d)} = S_1^{(e)} \wedge T_2^{(d)} = \hat{T}_2^{(d)} \middle| \text{Case2-2}\right]$

First, notations used in the analysis are introduced. Let $\mathcal{I}^{\neq} = \mathcal{I}_V^{\neq} \cup \left\{i + a_d \middle| i \in \mathcal{I}_W^{\neq}\right\}$ be the set of indexes with distinct output blocks (counting from the hash function). Let $\mathcal{I}^{\neq} = \{i_1, i_2, \ldots, i_\gamma\}$ where $i_1 < i_2 < \cdots < i_\gamma$ and $\gamma \geq 2$. For $i \in \mathcal{I}^{\neq}$, the i-th output block is denoted as Z_i, where $Z_i := V_i$ if $i \leq a_d$; $Z_i := W_{i-a_d}$ if $i > a_d$, and the data block (AD or ciphertext block) XORed with Z_i is denoted as D_i: $D_i = A_{i+1}$ (if $i \leq a_d - 2$); $D_{a_d-1} = \text{ozp}(A_{a_d})$; $D_{a_d} = 0^b$; $D_i = C_{i-a_d}$ (if $a_d < i < a_d + m_d$); $D_{a_d+m_d} = \text{ozp}(C_{m_d})$.

Then, the collision $S_1^{(d)} = S_1^{(e)}$ is considered. The collision occurs if and only if $Z_{i_\gamma}^{(d)} \oplus D_{i_\gamma}^{(d)} = Z_{i_\gamma}^{(e)} \oplus D_{i_\gamma}^{(e)}$ is satisfied. In order to satisfy the equation, $D_{i_\gamma}^{(d)} \neq D_{i_\gamma}^{(e)}$ and $Z_{i_\gamma}^{(d)} \neq Z_{i_\gamma}^{(e)}$ must be satisfied. As $Z_{i_\gamma}^{(d)}$ is chosen uniformly at random from $\{0,1\}^b \backslash \{Z_{i_\gamma}^{(e)}\}$, we have $\Pr[S_1^{(d)} = S_1^{(e)}] = \Pr[Z_{i_\gamma}^{(d)} \oplus D_{i_\gamma}^{(d)} = Z_{i_\gamma}^{(e)} \oplus D_{i_\gamma}^{(e)}] \leq 1/(2^b - 1)$.

Next, the collision $T_2^{(d)} = \hat{T}_2^{(d)}$ is considered. The collision is of the form: $\text{lsb}_\tau\left(Z_{i_1}^{(d)}\right) = \hat{T}_2^{(d)} \oplus \text{lsb}_\tau\left(\bigoplus_{i \in [a_d+m_d] \backslash \{i_1\}} Z_i^{(d)} \oplus S_2^{(d)}\right)$. As $Z_{i_1}^{(d)}$ is chosen uniformly at random from $\{0,1\}^b \backslash \{Z_{i_1}^{(e)}\}$, we have $\Pr[T_2^{(d)} = \hat{T}_2^{(d)}] \leq 2^{b-\tau}/(2^b - 1)$.

These upper-bounds give

$$\Pr\left[S_1^{(d)} = S_1^{(e)} \wedge T_2^{(d)} = \hat{T}_2^{(d)} \middle| \text{Case2-2}\right] \leq \frac{2^{b-\tau}}{(2^b - 1)^2}. \qquad (8)$$

4.8 Upper-Bounding $\Pr\left[S_1^{(d)} = S_1^{(e)} \wedge T_2^{(d)} = \hat{T}_2^{(d)} \middle| \text{Case2-3}\right]$

First, the collision $T_2^{(d)} = \hat{T}_2^{(d)}$ is considered. The collision is of the form $\text{lsb}_\tau(V_1^{(d)}) = \hat{T}_2^{(d)} \oplus \text{lsb}_\tau\left(\bigoplus_{i=2}^{a_d} V_i^{(d)} \oplus \bigoplus_{i=1}^{m_d} W_i^{(d)} \oplus S_2^{(d)}\right)$. As $V_1^{(d)}$ is chosen uniformly at random from $\{0,1\}^b \backslash \{V_1^{(e)}\}$ (if the input blocks of $V_1^{(d)}$ and $V_1^{(e)}$ are the same, "$\backslash \{V_1^{(e)}\}$" is removed), we have $\Pr[T_2^{(d)} = \hat{T}_2^{(d)}] \leq 2^{b-\tau}/(2^b - 1)$.

Next, the collision $S_1^{(d)} = S_1^{(e)}$ is considered. In Case2-3, $S_1^{(d)} = S_1^{(e)} \Leftrightarrow H_1^{(d)} = H_1^{(e)} \Leftrightarrow V_{a_d}^{(d)} = V_{a_e}^{(e)}$ is satisfied. When $a_d > a_e \geq 1$, $V_{a_d}^{(d)}$ is chosen independently of $V_1^{(d)}$, and chosen uniformly at random from $\{0,1\}^b$. When $1 \leq a_d < a_e$, $V_{a_e}^{(e)}$ is chosen independently of $V_1^{(d)}$, and chosen uniformly at random from $\{0,1\}^b$. Hence, we have $\Pr[S_1^{(d)} = S_1^{(e)}] \leq 1/2^b$.

These upper-bounds give

$$\Pr\left[S_1^{(d)} = S_1^{(e)} \wedge T_2^{(d)} = \hat{T}_2^{(e)}\Big|\mathsf{Case2\text{-}3}\right] \le \frac{1}{2^\tau(2^b-1)}. \tag{9}$$

4.9 Upper-Bounding $\Pr\left[S_1^{(d)} = S_1^{(e)} \wedge T_2^{(d)} = \hat{T}_2^{(d)}\Big|\mathsf{Case2\text{-}4}\right]$

First, the collision $S_1^{(d)} = S_1^{(e)}$ is considered. Let $i = \max \mathcal{I}_W^{\neq}$. The collision implies $W_i^{(d)} \oplus C_i^{(d)} = W_i^{(e)} \oplus C_i^{(e)}$. As $W_i^{(d)}$ are chosen uniformly at random from $\{0,1\}^b \backslash \{W_i^{(e)}\}$, we have $\Pr[S_1^{(d)} = S_1^{(e)}] \le 1/(2^b-1)$.

Next, the collision $T_2^{(d)} = \hat{T}_2^{(d)}$ is considered. The collision is of the form $\mathsf{lsb}_\tau\left(V_1^{(d)}\right) = \hat{T}_2^{(d)} \oplus \mathsf{lsb}_\tau\left(\bigoplus_{i=2}^{a_d} V_i^{(d)} \oplus \bigoplus_{i=1}^{m_d} W_i^{(d)} \oplus S_2^{(d)}\right)$. As $V_1^{(d)}$ is chosen uniformly at random from $\{0,1\}^b \backslash \{V_1^{(d)}\}$ (if the input blocks of $V_1^{(d)}$ and $V_1^{(e)}$ are the same, "$\backslash \{V_1^{(e)}\}$" is removed), we have $\Pr[T_2^{(d)} = \hat{T}_2^{(d)}] \le 2^{b-\tau}/(2^b-1)$.

These upper-bounds give

$$\Pr\left[S_1^{(d)} = S_1^{(e)} \wedge T_2^{(d)} = \hat{T}_2^{(d)}\Big|\mathsf{Case2\text{-}4}\right] \le \frac{2^{b-\tau}}{(2^b-1)^2}. \tag{10}$$

5 PFBω: Specification and Security Bounds

We design PFBω, a TBC-based nAEAD mode with ωb-bit security (under some condition), where $1 \le \omega$. PFBω is an extension of PFB_Plus, and the internal state size is ωb bits for achieving ωb-bit security. The procedure of updating the first b-bit internal state of PFBω is designed by using the PFB's idea [34]. The procedure of updating the remaining $(\omega - 1)b$-bit internal sate is designed by extending the PMAC_Plus's idea [45][4]. Using these ideas, the procedure of updating the internal state of PFBω is designed as follows.

- The first b-bit internal state is updated by iterating a TBC and absorbing a data block (AD/plaintext/ciphertext block), and the output of the last TBC call becomes the first b-bit tag. The idea comes from PFB.
- The i-th b-bit internal state ($2 \le i \le \omega$) is updated by multiplying an output of a TBC with a constant over $GF(2^b)^*$ and then XORing the result with the current internal state. This is an extension of the PMAC_Plus's idea. In order to have ωb-bit security, a condition on the constants is required, which is given in the next subsection.

Regarding tweak elements, as PFB_Plus, the nonce and the block counter are injected in order to ensure perfect privacy.

---

[4] PMAC_Plus is a block-cipher-based message authentication code and has $2b$-bit internal state, which is updated by using outputs of BC calls, XOR operations and constant field multiplications.

Algorithm 2. PFBω

Encryption PFBω.Enc$[\widetilde{E}_K](N, A, M)$

1: $M_1, \ldots, M_m \xleftarrow{b} M$; $(M_0, S_2, \ldots, S_\omega, a, \ell) \leftarrow$ PFBω.Hash$[\widetilde{E}_K](A, m)$
2: **if** $M = \varepsilon$ **then** $\{m \leftarrow 0;$ **goto** Step 7$\}$
3: **for** $j = 1, \ldots, m$ **do**
4:   $Z_{a+j-1} \leftarrow \widetilde{E}_K^{N,a,j,0}(M_{j-1})$; $C_j \leftarrow Z_{a+j-1} \oplus M_j$
5:     **for** $i = 2, \ldots, \omega$ **do** $\{S_i \leftarrow \alpha_{i,a+j-1}^{(\ell)} \cdot Z_{a+j-1} \oplus S_i\}$
6: **end for**
7: $S_1 \leftarrow M_m$; $Z_{a+m} \leftarrow \widetilde{E}_K^{N,a,m,1}(S_1)$; $T_1 \leftarrow Z_{a+m}$
8: **for** $i = 2, \ldots, \omega$ **do** $\{S_i \leftarrow \alpha_{i,a+m}^{(\ell)} \cdot Z_{a+m} \oplus S_i;$ $T_i \leftarrow \widetilde{E}_K^{N,a,m,i}(S_i)\}$
9: $C \leftarrow C_1 \| \cdots \| C_m$; $T \leftarrow T_1 \| \cdots \| T_\omega$; **return** (C, T)

Decryption PFBω.Dec$[\widetilde{E}_K](N, A, C, \hat{T})$

1: $(M_0, S_2, \ldots, S_\omega, a, \ell) \leftarrow$ PFBω.Hash$[\widetilde{E}_K](A, m)$; $C_1, \ldots, C_m \xleftarrow{b} C$
2: **if** $C = \varepsilon$ **then** $\{m \leftarrow 0;$ **goto** Step 7$\}$
3: **for** $j = 1, \ldots, m$ **do**
4:   $Z_{a+j-1} \leftarrow \widetilde{E}_K^{N,a,j,0}(M_{j-1})$; $M_j \leftarrow Z_{a+j-1} \oplus C_j$;
5:     **for** $i = 2, \ldots, \omega$ **do** $\{S_i \leftarrow \alpha_{i,a+j-1}^{(\ell)} \cdot W_{a+j-1} \oplus S_i\}$
6: **end for**
7: $S_1 \leftarrow M_m$; $Z_{a+m} \leftarrow \widetilde{E}_K^{N,a,m,1}(S_1)$; $T_1 \leftarrow Z_{a+m}$
8: **for** $i = 2, \ldots, \omega$ **do** $\{S_i \leftarrow \alpha_{i,a+m}^{(\ell)} \cdot Z_{a+m} \oplus S_i;$ $T_i \leftarrow \widetilde{E}_K^{N,a,m,i}(S_i)\}$
9: $T \leftarrow T_1 \| \cdots \| T_\omega$; **if** $T = \hat{T}$ **then return** $M \leftarrow M_1 \| \cdots \| M_m$; **else return reject**

Hash PFBω.Hash$[\widetilde{E}_K](A, m)$

1: **if** $A = \varepsilon$ **then return** $(0^b, \ldots, 0^b, 0, m)$
2: $Z_0 \leftarrow 0^b$; $A_1, \ldots, A_a \xleftarrow{b} A$; $\ell \leftarrow a + m$; **for** $i = 2, \ldots, \omega$ **do** $H_i \leftarrow 0^b$
3: **for** $j = 1, \ldots, a - 1$ **do**
4:   $Z_j \leftarrow \widetilde{E}_K^{0^n,j,0,0}(Z_{j-1} \oplus A_j)$; **for** $i = 2, \ldots, \omega$ **do** $H_i \leftarrow \alpha_{i,j}^{(\ell)} \cdot Z_j \oplus H_i$
5: **end for**
6: $H_1 \leftarrow Z_{a-1} \oplus A_a$ **return** $(H_1, \ldots, H_\omega, a, \ell)$

5.1 Specification

For the sake of simplifying the specification and the security proof, we consider only the case where the bit lengths of AD and plaintext/ciphertext are multiple of b, i.e., $|A| \mod b = 0$, $|M| \mod b = 0$ and $|C| \mod b = 0$. Note that arbitrary length data can be handled by introducing the one-zero padding ozp as PFB_Plus, and an extra TBC call by the padding can be avoided by adding 2 bits to the tweak space for distinguishing whether the padding is applied or not for each of AD and plaintext/ciphertext.

The specification of PFBω is given in Algorithm 2 and is illustrated in Fig. 2.

Let a_{max} be a maximum number of AD blocks, i.e., $a \leq a_{\mathsf{max}}$, and m_{max} be a maximum number of plaintext/ciphertext blocks, i.e., $m \leq m_{\mathsf{max}}$. The tweak space $\mathcal{TW}$ consists of a nonce space $\mathcal{N} := \{0, 1\}^n$, a counter space for AD blocks $(a_{\mathsf{max}}]$,

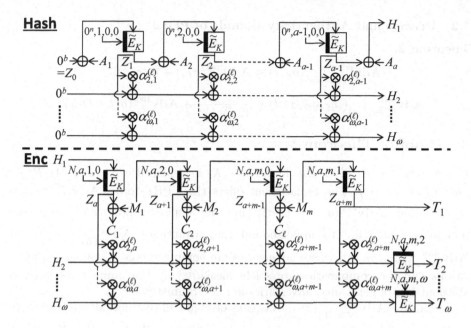

Fig. 2. PFBω.Enc and PFBω.Hash.

a counter space for plaintext/ciphertext blocks $(m_{max}]$, and a space for tweak separations $(\omega]$. Hence, the tweak space is defined as $\mathcal{TW} := \mathcal{N} \times (a_{max}] \times (m_{max}] \times (\omega]$. Let $\alpha_{i,j}^{(\ell)}$ be a b-bit constant in $GF(2^b)^*$ with the following condition.

- Cond: for any $1 \leq \ell \leq a_{max} + m_{max}$, a $\omega - 1 \times \ell$ matrix with an i-th row and j-th column element $\alpha_{i,j}^{(\ell)}$ is MDS, i.e., for any $1 \leq \mu \leq \min\{\ell, \omega - 1\}$, $2 \leq i_1 < i_2 < \cdots < i_\mu \leq \omega$, and $1 \leq j_1 < j_2 < \cdots < j_\mu \leq \ell$, the rank of the $\mu \times \mu$ sub-matrix where for each $u, v \in [\mu]$, the u-th row and v-th column element is $\alpha_{i_u,j_v}^{(\ell)}$ is μ.

Examples of constants for $\omega = 2, 3$ are given below.

- $\omega = 2$: $\alpha_{2,j}^{(\ell)} := 1$ for all ℓ, j. The second b-bit internal state is updated by XORing all outputs of TBC calls. This is the same as the PFB_Plus's internal state updating (without truncations).
- $\omega = 3$: $\alpha_{2,j}^{(\ell)} := 1$ and $\alpha_{3,j}^{(\ell)} := 2^{\ell-j}$ for all ℓ, j. This is the same as the PMAC_Plus's internal state updating.

5.2   Privacy and Authenticity Bounds of PFBω

Theorem 2.

$$\mathbf{Adv}^{\mathrm{priv}}_{\mathsf{PFB}\omega[\widetilde{E}_K]}(\sigma_{\mathcal{E}}, t) \leq \mathbf{Adv}^{\mathrm{tprp}}_{\widetilde{E}_K}(\sigma_{\mathcal{E}}, t + O(\sigma_{\mathcal{E}})),$$

$$\mathbf{Adv}^{\mathrm{auth}}_{\mathsf{PFB}\omega[\widetilde{E}_K]}((q_{\mathcal{E}}, q_{\mathcal{D}}, \sigma), t) \leq \frac{2^{\omega} \cdot q_{\mathcal{D}}}{(2^b - 1)^{\omega}} + \mathbf{Adv}^{\mathrm{tprp}}_{\widetilde{E}_K}(\sigma, t + O(\sigma)).$$

6   Proof of Theorem 2

Firstly, the keyed TBC $\widetilde{E}_K$ for $K \xleftarrow{\$} \mathcal{K}$ is replaced with a TRP $\widetilde{P} \xleftarrow{\$}$ $\widetilde{\mathsf{Perm}}\,(\mathcal{TW}, \{0,1\}^b)$. The replacement offers the TPRP-terms $\mathbf{Adv}^{\mathrm{tprp}}_{\widetilde{E}_K}(\sigma_{\mathcal{E}}, t + O(\sigma_{\mathcal{E}}))$ and $\mathbf{Adv}^{\mathrm{tprp}}_{\widetilde{E}_K}(\sigma, t + O(\sigma))$ in the upper-bounds, and then the remaining works are to upper-bound the advantages $\mathbf{Adv}^{\mathrm{priv}}_{\mathsf{PFB}\omega[\widetilde{P}]}(\sigma_{\mathcal{E}})$ and $\mathbf{Adv}^{\mathrm{auth}}_{\mathsf{PFB}\omega[\widetilde{P}]}(q_{\mathcal{E}}, q_{\mathcal{D}}, \sigma)$, where adversaries are computationally unbounded algorithms and the complexities are solely measured by the numbers of queries. Without loss of generality, adversaries are deterministic.

Regarding $\mathbf{Adv}^{\mathrm{priv}}_{\mathsf{PFB}\omega[\widetilde{P}]}(\sigma_{\mathcal{E}})$, as tweaks of $\widetilde{P}$ are all distinct, all output blocks of $\widetilde{P}$ defined by encryption queries are chosen independently and uniformly at random from $\{0,1\}^b$. We thus have $\mathbf{Adv}^{\mathrm{priv}}_{\mathsf{PFB}\omega[\widetilde{P}]}(\sigma_{\mathcal{E}}) = 0$.

Hereafter, we focus on upper-bounding $\mathbf{Adv}^{\mathrm{auth}}_{\mathsf{PFB}\omega[\widetilde{P}]}(q_{\mathcal{E}}, q_{\mathcal{D}}, \sigma)$.

6.1   Upper-Bonding $\mathbf{Adv}^{\mathrm{auth}}_{\mathsf{PFB}\omega[\widetilde{P}]}(q_{\mathcal{E}}, q_{\mathcal{D}}, \sigma)$

We first fix a decryption query $(N^{(d)}, A^{(d)}, C^{(d)}, \hat{T}^{(d)})$ and upper-bound the probability that $\mathbf{A}$ forges at the decryption query. Values/variables corresponding with the decryption query are denoted by using the superscript of (d) such as $N^{(d)}$, $M^{(d)}$, etc. The lengths a, m and ℓ are denoted by a_d, m_d and ℓ_d, respectively. Thus $\Pr[T^{(d)} = \hat{T}^{(d)}]$ is upper-bounded in the analysis. Similarly, for an encryption query $(N^{(e)}, A^{(e)}, M^{(e)})$, values/variables corresponding with the decryption query are denoted by using the superscript of (e), and the lengths a, m and ℓ are denoted by a_e, m_e and ℓ_e, respectively.

Then, $\Pr[T^{(d)} = \hat{T}^{(d)}]$ is upper-bounded using the following two cases.

– Case1: $\forall$enc. query $(N^{(e)}, A^{(e)}, M^{(e)})$: $N^{(e)} \neq N^{(d)} \vee a_e \neq a_d \vee m_e \neq m_d$.
– Case2: $\exists$enc. query $(N^{(e)}, A^{(e)}, M^{(e)})$ s.t. $N^{(e)} = N^{(d)} \wedge a_e = a_d \wedge m_e = m_d$.

Using these cases, we have

$$\Pr[T^{(d)} = \hat{T}^{(d)}] \leq \max \left\{ \Pr\left[T^{(d)} = \hat{T}^{(d)} \Big| \mathsf{Case1}\right], \Pr\left[T^{(d)} = \hat{T}^{(d)} \Big| \mathsf{Case2}\right] \right\}.$$

These probabilities are analyzed in Subsects. 6.2 and 6.3, respectively. The upper-bounds are given in Eqs. (12) and (13), respectively, and give

$$\mathbf{Adv}^{\mathrm{auth}}_{\mathsf{PFB}\omega[\widetilde{P}]}(q_{\mathcal{E}}, q_{\mathcal{D}}, \sigma) \leq \frac{2^{\omega} \cdot q_{\mathcal{D}}}{(2^b - 1)^{\omega}}. \tag{11}$$

6.2   Upper-Bounding $\Pr\left[T^{(d)} = \hat{T}^{(d)} \middle| \mathsf{Case1}\right]$

In Case1, tag blocks $T_1^{(d)}, T_2^{(d)}, \ldots, T_\omega^{(d)}$ are chosen independently and uniformly at random from $\{0,1\}^b$. Hence, we have

$$\Pr\left[T^{(d)} = \hat{T}^{(d)} \middle| \mathsf{Case1}\right] \leq \frac{1}{2^{\omega b}}. \tag{12}$$

6.3   Upper-Bounding $\Pr\left[\hat{T}^{(d)} = T^{(d)} \middle| \mathsf{Case2}\right]$

Let $(N^{(e)}, A^{(e)}, M^{(e)})$ be an encryption query with $N^{(e)} = N^{(d)} \wedge a_e = a_d \wedge m_e = m_d$. The analysis considers the following sub-cases where $0 \leq \mu \leq \omega$.

$\mathsf{Case2}\text{-}\mu : \exists \mu$ indexes $i_1 < \cdots < i_\mu$ s.t. $\left(\forall i \in [i_1, \ldots, i_\mu] : S_i^{(d)} = S_i^{(e)}\right) \wedge$

$$\left(\forall i \in [\omega]\backslash\{i_1, \ldots, i_\mu\} : S_i^{(d)} \neq S_i^{(e)}\right).$$

Using the sub-cases, we have

$$\Pr\left[T^{(d)} = \hat{T}^{(d)} \middle| \mathsf{Case2}\right] \leq \sum_{\mu=0}^{\omega} \Pr\left[T^{(d)} = \hat{T}^{(d)} \wedge \mathsf{Case2}\text{-}\mu \middle| \mathsf{Case2}\right]$$

$$\leq \frac{1}{(2^b - 1)^\omega} + \sum_{\mu=1}^{\omega} 2 \cdot \binom{\omega - 1}{\mu - 1} \cdot \frac{1}{(2^b - 1)^\omega} \leq \frac{2^\omega}{(2^b - 1)^\omega}. \tag{13}$$

The probabilities $\Pr\left[T^{(d)} = \hat{T}^{(d)} \wedge \mathsf{Case2}\text{-}\mu \middle| \mathsf{Case2}\right]$ for $0 \leq \mu \leq \omega$ are upper-bounded below. In the analyses, the following set is used: $\mathcal{I}^{\neq} = \left\{j \middle| Z_j^{(e)} \neq Z_j^{(d)}\right\}$.

- $\mu = 0$. In this case, for all i, $S_i^{(d)} \neq S_i^{(e)}$ is satisfied, and thus $T_i^{(d)}$ is chosen uniformly at random from $\{0,1\}^b\backslash\{T_i^{(e)}\}$ (as both $T_i^{(e)}$ and $T_i^{(d)}$ are defined by the same permutation $\widetilde{P}^{N^{(d)},a_d,m_d,i}$). Hence, we have

$$\Pr\left[T^{(d)} = \hat{T}^{(d)} \wedge \mathsf{Case2}\text{-}0 \middle| \mathsf{Case2}\right] \leq \frac{1}{(2^b - 1)^\omega}.$$

- $1 \leq \mu \leq \omega - 1 \wedge S_1^{(d)} = S_1^{(e)}$. Note that one has $i_1 = 1$. First, $\mu - 1$ indexes $1 < i_2 < \cdots < i_\mu$ are fixed, and the following case is considered:

  – $\forall i \in \{1, i_2, \ldots, i_\mu\} : S_i^{(d)} = S_i^{(e)}$ is satisfied, and
  – $\forall i \in [\omega]\backslash\{1, i_2, \ldots, i_\mu\} : S_i^{(d)} \neq S_i^{(e)}$ is satisfied.

  For each $i \in [\omega]\backslash\{1, i_2, \ldots, i_\mu\}$, $T_i^{(d)}$ is chosen uniformly at random from $\{0,1\}^b\backslash\{T_i^{(e)}\}$, we have $\Pr[\forall i \in [\omega]\backslash\{1, i_2, \ldots, i_\mu\} : T_i^{(d)} = \hat{T}_i^{(d)}] \leq 1/(2^b - 1)^{\omega - \mu}$.

Next, the collisions $S_i^{(d)} = S_i^{(e)}$ where $i \in \{1, i_2, \ldots, i_\mu\}$ are considered. Let $\mathcal{I}^{\neq} = \{J_1, \ldots, j_\gamma\}$ such that $j_1 < \cdots < j_\gamma$ (note that $\forall j \in \mathcal{I}^{\neq} : Z_j^{(d)} \neq Z_j^{(e)}$). The collisions are of the following forms:

$$S_1^{(d)} = S_1^{(e)} \Leftrightarrow \underbrace{Z_{j_\gamma}^{(d)} \oplus Z_{j_\gamma}^{(e)}}_{=:Z_{j_\gamma}} = D_{j_\gamma+1}^{(d)} \oplus D_{j_\gamma+1}^{(e)},$$

where $D_{j_\gamma+1} \in \{A_{j_\gamma+1}, C_{j_\gamma-a+1}\}$, and for $i \in \{i_2, \ldots, i_\mu\}$,

$$S_i^{(d)} = S_i^{(e)} \Leftrightarrow \alpha_{i,j_1}^{(\ell_d)} \cdot \underbrace{(Z_{j_1}^{(e)} \oplus Z_{j_1}^{(d)})}_{=:Z_{j_1}} \oplus \cdots \oplus \alpha_{i,j_\gamma}^{(\ell_d)} \cdot \underbrace{(Z_{j_\gamma}^{(e)} \oplus Z_{j_\gamma}^{(d)})}_{=:Z_{j_\gamma}} = 0^b.$$

If $\gamma \leq \mu - 1$, by Cond, the collisions $S_i^{(d)} = S_i^{(e)}$ where $i \in \{i_2, \ldots, i_\mu\}$ offer a unique solution $(Z_{j_1}, \ldots, Z_{j_\gamma}) = (0^b, \cdots, 0^b)$. Hence, the collisions do not occur. If $\gamma \geq \mu$, then the collision $S_1^{(d)} = S_1^{(e)}$ offers a solution $Z_{j_\gamma} = D_{j_\gamma+1}^{(d)} \oplus D_{j_\gamma+1}^{(e)}$. The collisions $S_{i_2}^{(d)} = S_{i_2}^{(e)}, \ldots, S_{i_\mu}^{(d)} = S_{i_\mu}^{(e)}$, fixing $Z_{j_\omega}, \ldots, Z_{j_{\gamma-1}}$, offer a unique solution for $(Z_{j_1}, \ldots, Z_{j_\omega-1})$ by Cond. Since for each $j \in \{j_1, \ldots, j_{\omega-1}, j_\gamma\}$, $Z_j^{(d)}$ is chosen uniformly at random from $\{0,1\}^b \backslash \{Z_j^{(e)}\}$, we have $\Pr[\forall i \in \{1, i_2, \ldots, i_\mu\} : S_i^{(d)} = S_i^{(e)}] \leq 1/(2^b - 1)^\mu$.

These upper-bounds give

$$\Pr\left[T^{(d)} = \hat{T}^{(d)} \wedge \mathsf{Case2\text{-}}\mu \middle| \mathsf{Case2}\right] \leq \binom{\omega-1}{\mu-1} \cdot \frac{1}{(2^b-1)^\omega}.$$

- $1 \leq \mu \leq \omega - 1 \wedge S_1^{(d)} \neq S_1^{(e)}$: This analysis is the same as that of the case: $1 \leq \mu \leq \omega - 1 \wedge S_1^{(d)} = S_1^{(e)}$. μ indexes $1 < i_1 < i_2 < \cdots < i_\mu$ are fixed, and the following case is considered:

  - $\forall i \in \{i_1, i_2, \ldots, i_\mu\} : S_i^{(d)} = S_i^{(e)}$ is satisfied, and
  - $\forall i \in [\omega] \backslash \{i_1, i_2, \ldots, i_\mu\} : S_i^{(d)} \neq S_i^{(e)}$ is satisfied.

Using the same analysis, we have $\Pr[\forall i \in \{i_1, i_2, \ldots, i_\mu\} : S_i^{(d)} = S_i^{(e)}] \leq 1/(2^b - 1)^\mu$, and $\Pr[\forall i \in [\omega] \backslash \{i_1, i_2, \ldots, i_\mu\} : T_i^{(d)} = \hat{T}_i^{(d)}] \leq 1/(2^b - 1)^{\omega-\mu}$. These upper-bounds give

$$\Pr\left[T^{(d)} = \hat{T}^{(d)} \wedge \mathsf{Case2\text{-}}\mu \middle| \mathsf{Case2}\right] \leq \binom{\omega-1}{\mu-1} \cdot \frac{1}{(2^b-1)^\omega}.$$

7 SKINNY-64-256

SKINNY [8] is a tweakable block cipher adopting the tweakey framework [27] that treats the key input and the tweak input in the same way. The combined state is called tweakey which does not make a particular distinction about which part is used as a key and the tweak. For the 64-bit block, SKINNY supports the tweakey sizes up to 192 bits, (i.e. SKINNY-64-192) while what we need is SKINNY-64-256. In Sect. 7.1, we show how to extend the design of SKINNY to support a 256-bit tweakey. The rationale of our design choices are explained in Sect. 7.2. Security evaluation of SKINNY-64-256 is given in Sect. 7.3.

7.1 Specification

Round Transformation. We only briefly recall the round transformation of SKINNY-64-256 because SKINNY-64-256 does not modify the round transformation. Refer to the original SKINNY document [8] for the details of each operation.

The 64-bit internal state is viewed as a 4×4 square array of nibbles. SKINNY-64-256 consists of 44 rounds, in which one round transformation is defined as an application of the following 5 operations: SubCells, AddRoundConstant, AddRoundTweakey, ShiftRows and MixColumns.

SubCells. A 4-bit S-box is applied for each nibble.

AddRoundConstant. A 6-bit constant generated by an LFSR and a single fixed bit are XORed to the top three rows of the first column.

AddRoundTweakey. The top two rows of all tweakey arrays are extracted and XORed to the top two rows of the state.

ShiftRows. Each nibble in row i is rotated by i positions to the right.

MixColumns. Each column is multiplied by a 4×4 binary matrix.

New Tweakey Schedule. The 256-bit tweakey state consists of four 4×4 square arrays of nibbles. Each of them are called $TK1$, $TK2$, $TK3$ and $TK4$.

The tweakey states are updated as follows. First, a permutation P_T is applied on the nibble positions of all tweakey arrays $TK1$, $TK2$, $TK3$, and $TK4$, where P_T is defined as $(0, \ldots, 15) \xmapsto{P_T} (9, 15, 8, 13, 10, 14, 12, 11, 0, 1, 2, 3, 4, 5, 6, 7)$.

Finally, every nibble of the first and second rows of $TK2$, $TK3$, and $TK4$ are individually updated with the following LFSRs.

$$TK2 : (x_3\|x_2\|x_1\|x_0) \rightarrow (x_2\|x_1\|x_0\|x_3 \oplus x_2)$$
$$TK3 : (x_3\|x_2\|x_1\|x_0) \rightarrow (x_0 \oplus x_3\|x_3\|x_2\|x_1)$$
$$TK4 : (x_3\|x_2\|x_1\|x_0) \rightarrow (x_2\|x_1\|x_2 \oplus x_0\|x_3 \oplus x_2 \oplus x_1)$$

7.2 Rationale for Newly Designed Parts

Design from Scratch vs Extension of the Original. The designers of SKINNY first searched for good parameters of ShiftRows and MixColumns to maximize the security in the single-key setting, and then later searched for the tweakey schedule to maximize the security in the TK2 and TK3 settings. Later Nikolić searched for better parameters to achieve higher number of active S-boxes [36]. The first choice we made is whether we should search for good parameters for TK4 from scratch as Nikolić did or we should extend the original SKINNY that was optimized for TK1, TK2, and TK3. In the end, we determined to design

SKINNY-64-256 as a natural extension of the original SKINNY-64, i.e. not modify any components to realize $TK1$, $TK2$, and $TK3$, though we do not have any application to use smaller tweakey sizes. This is all for higher reliability. The original SKINNY has received a lot of cryptanalytic effort by third-party and seems to generate a consensus that the design choice of SKINNY is conservative, and thus secure. We would like to design SKINNY-64-256 so that those existing results contribute to the reliability of the security of SKINNY-64-256.

Number of Rounds. Once the above strategy was established, the only components we need to design are an LFSR to update the $TK4$ state and the number of rounds. In SKINNY, the number of rounds for $TK1$, $TK2$ and $TK3$ are defined to be 32, 36, and 40, respectively. As mentioned above, those choices look quite conservative. Indeed, the maximum number of attacked rounds so far is 19 for $TK1$ by related-tweakey impossible differential attacks [30,41], 23 for $TK2$ by related-tweakey impossible differential attacks [5,30,41], and 27 for $TK3$ by a related-tweakey rectangle attack [30]. This made us think about not increasing the number of rounds from $TK3$. In the end, to be consistent with the first decision, i.e. to make it a natural extension of the original SKINNY, we determined to keep the same rate for increasing the number of rounds, namely 44 for $TK4$.

LFSR for $TK4$. To be a secure instantiation of the tweakey framework [27], the LFSR must have a cycle of 15. The original LFSRs in SKINNY for $TK2$ and $TK3$ are quite efficient: they only require a single XOR to the LFSR. By the exhaustive search, We found that there is no more LFSR achieving cycle 15 only with a single XOR. Moreover, we found that

- there is no LFSR having cycle 15 even with two XORs.
- it is impossible to achieve cycle 15 only by updating one output bit

In the end, we picked up the LFSR that updates 2 output bits with 3 XORs.

7.3   Bounds of the Number of Active S-boxes

Bounds for SKINNY-64-256 (TK4). The designers of SKINNY evaluated the tight bounds of the number of active S-boxes by using Mixed Integer Linear Programming (MILP) by describing how to model the problem in details. We extended their MILP model to derive the number of active S-boxes of SKINNY-64-256 (in TK4). The lower bounds of the number of active S-boxes for SK, TK1, TK2, TK3 and TK4 are compared in Table 2. Note that according to the designers, MILP sometimes took too long, and the designers only could give upper bounds of the number of active S-boxes in such cases. The upper bounds are denoted with the upper bar in Table 2.

Table 2 shows that TK4 is a natural extension of TK3 also for the increase of the bounds. In particular, the comparison is clear in the following part.

- The bounds for 21 to 24 rounds for TK2 are 59, 64, 67, and 72, respectively.
- The bounds for 24 to 27 rounds for TK3 are 58, 60, 65, and 72, respectively.
- The bounds for 27 to 30 rounds for TK4 are 58, 62, 66, and 72, respectively.

Table 2. Lower bounds on the number of active Sboxes. The numbers for **SK**, **TK1**, **TK2**, **TK3** and **Lin** are from the evaluation by the designers [8], where numbers with upper line are the upper bounds. **SK**[4] shows the updated tight bounds by Alfarano *et al.* [4]. Numbers for **Lin'** and **TK4** were derived by us.

	1	2	3	4	5	6	7	8	9	10	11	12	13	14	15
SK	1	2	5	8	12	16	26	36	41	46	51	55	58	61	66
TK1	0	0	1	2	3	6	10	13	16	23	32	38	41	45	49
TK2	0	0	0	0	1	2	3	6	9	12	16	21	25	31	35
TK3	0	0	0	0	0	0	1	2	3	6	10	13	16	19	24
TK4	0	0	0	0	0	0	0	0	1	2	3	6	9	12	16
Lin	1	2	5	8	13	19	25	32	38	43	48	52	55	58	64

	16	17	18	19	20	21	22	23	24	25	26	27	28	29	30
SK	75	82	88	92	96	102	108	$\overline{114}$	$\overline{116}$	$\overline{124}$	$\overline{132}$	$\overline{138}$	$\overline{136}$	$\overline{148}$	$\overline{158}$
SK[4]	75	82	88	92	96	102	108	112	116	124	128	132	136	142	148
TK1	54	59	62	66	70	75	79	83	85	88	95	102	$\overline{108}$	$\overline{112}$	$\overline{120}$
TK2	40	43	47	52	57	59	64	67	72	75	82	85	88	92	96
TK3	27	31	35	43	45	48	51	55	58	60	65	72	77	81	85
TK4	19	21	24	30	35	39	41	43	46	50	54	58	62	66	72
Lin	70	76	80	85	90	96	102	107	$\overline{110}$	$\overline{118}$	$\overline{122}$	$\overline{128}$	$\overline{136}$	$\overline{141}$	$\overline{143}$
Lin'	70	76	80	85	90	96	102	107	110	115	121	127	130	135	141

The bounds for r rounds in TK2, $r+3$ rounds in TK3, and $r+6$ rounds in TK4 are almost the same. This also implies that our choice of the total number of rounds (44 rounds for TK4, while 40 rounds for TK3 and 36 rounds for TK2) is quite reasonable.

To be more precise, the designers of SKINNY need to ensure at least 64 active S-boxes because their 8-bit S-box for 128-bit block versions also allows differential propagation with probability 2^{-2}. For SKINNY-64, to ensure at least 32 active S-boxes is sufficient to resist a single differential characteristic, which is ensured only by 20 rounds even in TK4. Hence, our choice of 44 rounds is more conservative than the original SKINNY supporting the 128-bit block.

Deriving Tight Bounds for Linear Cryptanalysis. As mentioned above, the designers sometimes could not derive the tight bounds. Alfarano *et al.* [4] later identified the tight bound for differential cryptanalysis in **SK**, but did not show the bound for linear cryptanalysis. To present a better picture, we tried to derive the tight bounds.

Our approach is to apply the combination of Matsui's search strategy [31] with MILP proposed by Zhang et al. [46]. In short, this considers the bound derived for $r-1$ rounds to efficiently search for the bounds for r rounds. In more precise, it restricts the sum of the number of active S-boxes from round 1 to round $r-1$ and from round 2 to round r. This small changes actually allowed us to derive the tight bounds for **Lin** up to 30 rounds.

8   Hardware Performance Evaluation

We evaluate the hardware performance of PFB_Plus combined with SKINNY-64-256 and compare it with a conventional BBB scheme, namely PFB.

Choice of Competitor. We choose PFB as a competitor in hardware performance evaluation because (i) it is the scheme PFB_Plus based on, and (ii) it shows the best performance in TI at the time of writing [34]. To achieve the same security level, we use a 128-bit variant of the SKINNY family, namely SKINNY-128-256 as an underlying cipher.

Design Policy. We follow the design policy for the previous PFB implementation [34]. The design defines a set of commands for processing block-aligned data, and an external microcontroller is supposed to dispatches the commands in an appropriate order to realize AD processing, encryption, and decryption of AEAD. The design aims to accelerate the main processing part, while the microcontroller is responsible for preparing the block-aligned data by padding and choosing an appropriate ID. The designs store a key, nonce, and tweak in its internal registers, and can process multiple data blocks without feeding the data redundantly. For the purpose, the tweak is updated in place by integrated nonce-updating circuitry.

Side-Channel Attack Countermeasure. We implement unprotected and protected designs for each of the algorithms. For protected implementation, we implement 3-share TI secure up to the first-order attacks. For protected implementations, we also protect the on-the-fly tweakey schedule considering a profiling attack[5].

Register Cost. We first compare the register costs of PFB_Plus[SKINNY-64-256] and PFB[SKINNY-128-256] with and without TI in Table 3. The table also shows PFB[SKINNY-64-192] and SAEB[GIFT-128-128] in the previous work [34] for comparison. Without TI, the security level determines the register cost: the ones with 128- and 64-bit security need 386 and 256 bits of registers, respectively. With TI, on the other hand, PFB_Plus[SKINNY-64-256] uses a smaller number of registers than PFB[SKINNY-128-256]. The difference comes from the different number of shares for each component: the state needs three shares, while the key and tag need only two shares because the operation is linear. There are 2-share masking schemes that can protect the state with two shares [15], but we do not consider them because they need fresh randomness during the execution and the cost for random number generation is overwhelming [42].

8.1   PFB_Plus with SKINNY-64-256

Tweakey Configuration. We use the tweakey **TK1** and **TK2** for storing a 128-bit secret key, and **TK3** and **TK4** for a tweak. The tweak comprises the

---

[5] The designs in this paper has a room for more aggressive optimization by skipping protection of (twea)key-scheduling [8,40,44].

Table 3. Comparison of the number of registers with and without TI. We implement and evaluate the ones with 128-bit security (PFB_Plus[SKINNY-64-256] and PFB[SKINNY-128-256]) in this section. The table also shows the conventional ones with 64-bit security (PFB[SKINNY-64-192] and SAEB[GIFT-128-128]) [34] for comparison.

Name	TI	Sec.	Total	State	Key	Tweak	Tag	Ref.
PFB_Plus[SKINNY-64-256]	—	128	386	64	128	128	64	Ours
PFB[SKINNY-128-256]	—	128	386	128	128	128	0	Ours
PFB_Plus[SKINNY-64-256]	✓	128	704	192	256	128	128	Ours
PFB[SKINNY-128-256]	✓	128	768	384	256	128	0	Ours
PFB[SKINNY-64-192]	—	64	256	64	128	64	0	[34]
SAEB[GIFT-128-128]	—	64	256	128	128	0	0	[34]
PFB[SKINNY-64-192]	✓	64	512	192	256	64	0	[34]
SAEB[GIFT128-128]	✓	64	640	384	256	0	0	[34]

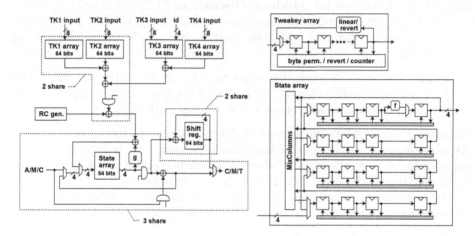

Fig. 3. Hardware architecture of PFB_Plus[SKINNY-64-256]. f and g functions are the decomposed 4-bit S-box [8].

4-bit ID x, 96-bit nonce N, and a 28-bit counter ctr. **TK3** and **TK4** combined store these values as:

$$\mathbf{TK3}\|\mathbf{TK4} = \mathsf{str}_4(x)\|\mathsf{str}_{96}(N)\|\mathsf{str}_{28}(ctr). \tag{14}$$

Circuit Architecture for SKINNY-64-256. Following the conventional SKINNY implementations, we use the nibble-serial architecture based on 2-dimensional arrays of scan flip-flops [8,32,34] with the decomposed 4-bit S-box (f and g functions) integrated. The design uses in-place on-the-fly tweakey schedule capable of reverting it to the original state after the final round [34]. Moreover, the **TK4** array has an integrated 28-bit adder for incrementing ctr in place.

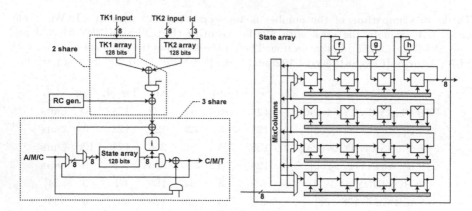

Fig. 4. Hardware architecture of PFB[SKINNY-128-256]. f, g, h, and i functions are the decomposed 8-bit S-box [8].

Circuit Architecture for Mode of Operation. PFB_Plus is a thin wrapper on top of the SKINNY-64-256 circuit similar to the conventional PFB implementation. The shift register (4×16 bits) with a feedback XOR realizes the tag accumulator.

Latency. The design finishes the round function in 16 cycles, and the entire SKINNY-64-256 in 704 ($=16 \times 44$) cycles. With one more cycle for updating the tweak, the circuit consumes a single-block message with 705 cycles.

Sharing. Figure 3 shows the number of shares in the protected implementation. As mentioned in the previous section, the implementation is heterogeneous in terms of the number of shares: (I) there is no sharing on **TK3** and **TK4** storing the public tweak, (II) **TK1**, **TK2**, and the tag accumulator use 2-share representation as they use linear operations only, and (III) the state array that goes through the non-linear S-box operation has three shares.

8.2   PFB with SKINNY-128-256

Tweakey Configuration. The first tweakey array **TK1** stores a 128-bit secret key, and another tweakey **TK2** stores a tweak comprising the 3-bit ID x, 96-bit nonce N, and a 29-bit counter ctr:

$$\mathbf{TK2} = \mathsf{str}_3(x)\|\mathsf{str}_{96}(N)\|\mathsf{str}_{29}(ctr). \tag{15}$$

Circuit Architecture for SKINNY-128-256. Figure 4 shows the circuit architecture of PFB_Plus with SKINNY-128-256. The circuit architecture of SKINNY-128-256 follows the previous implementation [8]: the byte-serial architecture with the decomposed 8-bit S-box (f, g, h, and i functions) integrated into the state array. The **TK1** and **TK2** arrays have the same structure as the SKINNY-64-256 circuit (see Fig. 3), and support in-pace tweak updating and reverting after on-the-fly tweakey schedule.

Circuit Architecture for Mode of Operation. The circuit architecture for PFB is similar to the previous PFB_Plus and also the conventional implementation [34].

Latency. The design finishes the SKINNY-64-256 encryption in 768 (= 16 × 44 + 1) cycles.

Sharing. This circuit also has a heterogeneous sharing, as shown in Fig. 4: (I) there is no sharing on **TK2** storing the public tweak, (II) the secret key in **TK1** represented by two shares, and (III) the state array in three shares.

8.3   Performance Evaluation and Comparison

Implementation and Evaluation Procedure. We implemented the designs in the register-transfer level with a single exception: explicit instantiation of

Table 4. Circuit area breakdown of PFB_Plus[SKINNY-64-256] and PFB[SKINNY-128-256]

Target	Component	Circuit area [GE]	
		Normal	TI
PFB_Plus with	Total	**4,351**	**7,439**
SKINNY-64-256	Total/Shift register	444	888
	Total/TBC	3,713	6,292
	Total/TBC/State	532	1,646
	Total/TBC/Key	1,268	2,620
	Total/TBC/Tweak	1,551	1,551
PFB with	Total	**4,400**	**8,448**
SKINNY-128-256	Total/TBC	4,218	8,159
	Total/TBC/State	1,098	3,517
	Total/TBC/Key	1,224	2,546
	Total/TBC/Tweak	1,421	1,470

Table 5. Comparison with previous AEAD implementations with TI: the latency shows that of a single primitive call.

Target	Sec. [bits]	Area [GE]	Latency [cycles]	Standard-cell library	Ref.
PFB_Plus[SKINNY-64-256]	128	7,439	705	NanGate 45-nm	**Ours**
PFB[SKINNY-128-256]	128	8,448	768	NanGate 45-nm	**Ours**
PFB[SKINNY-64-192]	64	5,858	641	NanGate 45-nm	[34]
SAEB[GIFT128-128]	64	6,229	1,320	NanGate 45-nm	[34]
Ascon w/o IF	128	7,970	3,072	UMC 90-nm	[22]
Ascon w/ IF	128	9,190	3,072	UMC 90-nm	[22]
Ketje-JR	96	18,335	16	NanGate 45-nm	[6]

scan flip-flops following the previous works [32]. We synthesized the design using Synopsys Design Compiler with the NanGate 45-nm standard cell library [35] while preserving the structure of major components, as shown in Table 4.

Performance without TI. PFB_Plus[SKINNY-64-256] and PFB[SKINNY-128-256] have similar circuit areas without TI: 4,351 and 4,400 [GE], respectively. As consistent with the register counts in Table 3, PFB_Plus[SKINNY-64-256] has the smaller state array (532 compared to 1,098 [GE], but needs the additional shift register.

Performance with TI. With TI, on the other hand, PFB_Plus[SKINNY-64-256] is smaller than PFB[SKINNY-128-256] by 1,009 [GE] (7,439 and 8,448 [GE]). That is also consistent with Table 3 as PFB_Plus[SKINNY-64-256] has 64-bit fewer registers. A smaller S-box circuit of PFB_Plus[SKINNY-64-256] (nibblewise and two stages) compared to that of PFB[SKINNY-128-256] (byte-wise and four stages) also contributes to this advantage of over one thousand gates.

Comparison with other AEAD. Table 5 compares the proposed method with conventional implementations of AEADs protected with TI. PFB[SKINNY-64-192] is a predecessor with a lower security level and is smaller than PFB_Plus[SKINNY-64-256] by 1,581 [GE] because it has fewer registers as summarized in Table 3. In comparison with Ascon having the same 128-bit security level, PFB_Plus[SKINNY-64-256] has a smaller circuit area even compared with the one having no interface[6]. The advantage of PFB_Plus[SKINNY-64-256] comes from heterogeneous sharing: PFB_Plus[SKINNY-64-256] can use fewer shares for the tweak, key, and tag meanwhile Ascon needs three shares for the entire 320-bit state. We also note that the Ascon implementation has longer latency and needs fresh random bits during the execution. Based on the comparison, we can conclude that PFB_Plus[SKINNY-64-256] has the smallest circuit area in TI among the schemes having 128-bit security.

References

1. Adomnicai, A., et al.: Lilliput-AE: a new lightweight tweakable block cipher for authenticated encryption with associated data. Submitted to NIST Lightweight Project (2019)
2. Albrecht, M., Grassi, L., Rechberger, C., Roy, A., Tiessen, T.: MiMC: efficient encryption and cryptographic hashing with minimal multiplicative complexity. In: Cheon, J.H., Takagi, T. (eds.) ASIACRYPT 2016. LNCS, vol. 10031, pp. 191–219. Springer, Heidelberg (2016). https://doi.org/10.1007/978-3-662-53887-6_7
3. Albrecht, M.R., Rechberger, C., Schneider, T., Tiessen, T., Zohner, M.: Ciphers for MPC and FHE. In: Oswald, E., Fischlin, M. (eds.) EUROCRYPT 2015. LNCS, vol. 9056, pp. 430–454. Springer, Heidelberg (2015). https://doi.org/10.1007/978-3-662-46800-5_17

---

[6] The Ascon implementation excludes a 128-bit key register (640 [GE] for 5 [GE/bit]) needed to run another encryption/decryption with the same key.

4. Alfarano, G.N., Beierle, C., Isobe, T., Kölbl, S., Leander, G.: ShiftRows alternatives for AES-like ciphers and optimal cell permutations for Midori and Skinny. IACR Trans. Symmetric Cryptol. **2018**(2), 20–47 (2018)
5. Ankele, R., et al.: Related-key impossible-differential attack on reduced-round SKINNY. In: Gollmann, D., Miyaji, A., Kikuchi, H. (eds.) ACNS 2017. LNCS, vol. 10355, pp. 208–228. Springer, Cham (2017). https://doi.org/10.1007/978-3-319-61204-1_11
6. Arribas, V., Nikova, S., Rijmen, V.: Guards in action: first-order SCA secure implementations of Ketje without additional randomness. In: DSD 2018, pp. 492–499. IEEE Computer Society (2018)
7. Barwell, G., Martin, D.P., Oswald, E., Stam, M.: Authenticated encryption in the face of protocol and side channel leakage. In: Takagi, T., Peyrin, T. (eds.) ASIACRYPT 2017. LNCS, vol. 10624, pp. 693–723. Springer, Cham (2017). https://doi.org/10.1007/978-3-319-70694-8_24
8. Beierle, C., et al.: The SKINNY family of block ciphers and its low-latency variant MANTIS. In: Robshaw, M., Katz, J. (eds.) CRYPTO 2016. LNCS, vol. 9815, pp. 123–153. Springer, Heidelberg (2016). https://doi.org/10.1007/978-3-662-53008-5_5
9. Berti, F., Koeune, F., Pereira, O., Peters, T., Standaert, F.: Ciphertext integrity with misuse and leakage: definition and efficient constructions with symmetric primitives. In: AsiaCCS 2018, pp. 37–50. ACM (2018)
10. Berti, F., Pereira, O., Peters, T., Standaert, F.: On leakage-resilient authenticated encryption with decryption leakages. IACR Trans. Symmetric Cryptol. **2017**(3), 271–293 (2017)
11. Berti, F., Pereira, O., Standaert, F.-X.: Reducing the cost of authenticity with leakages: a CIML2-secure AE scheme with one call to a strongly protected tweakable block cipher. In: Buchmann, J., Nitaj, A., Rachidi, T. (eds.) AFRICACRYPT 2019. LNCS, vol. 11627, pp. 229–249. Springer, Cham (2019). https://doi.org/10.1007/978-3-030-23696-0_12
12. Bertoni, G., Daemen, J., Peeters, M., Van Assche, G.: Duplexing the sponge: single-pass authenticated encryption and other applications. In: Miri, A., Vaudenay, S. (eds.) SAC 2011. LNCS, vol. 7118, pp. 320–337. Springer, Heidelberg (2012). https://doi.org/10.1007/978-3-642-28496-0_19
13. Beyne, T., Bilgin, B.: Uniform first-order threshold implementations. In: Avanzi, R., Heys, H. (eds.) SAC 2016. LNCS, vol. 10532, pp. 79–98. Springer, Cham (2017). https://doi.org/10.1007/978-3-319-69453-5_5
14. Chakraborti, A., Datta, N., Nandi, M., Yasuda, K.: Beetle family of lightweight and secure authenticated encryption ciphers. IACR Trans. Cryptogr. Hardw. Embed. Syst. **2018**(2), 218–241 (2018)
15. Chen, C., Farmani, M., Eisenbarth, T.: A tale of two shares: why two-share threshold implementation seems worthwhile—and why it is not. In: Cheon, J.H., Takagi, T. (eds.) ASIACRYPT 2016. LNCS, vol. 10031, pp. 819–843. Springer, Heidelberg (2016). https://doi.org/10.1007/978-3-662-53887-6_30
16. De Cnudde, T., Reparaz, O., Bilgin, B., Nikova, S., Nikov, V., Rijmen, V.: Masking AES with $d+1$ shares in hardware. In: Gierlichs, B., Poschmann, A.Y. (eds.) CHES 2016. LNCS, vol. 9813, pp. 194–212. Springer, Heidelberg (2016). https://doi.org/10.1007/978-3-662-53140-2_10
17. Degabriele, J.P., Janson, C., Struck, P.: Sponges resist leakage: the case of authenticated encryption. In: Galbraith, S.D., Moriai, S. (eds.) ASIACRYPT 2019. LNCS, Part II, vol. 11922, pp. 209–240. Springer, Cham (2019). https://doi.org/10.1007/978-3-030-34621-8_8

734   Y. Naito et al.

18. Dobraunig, C., Eichlseder, M., Mangard, S., Mendel, F., Unterluggauer, T.: ISAP - towards side-channel secure authenticated encryption. IACR Trans. Symmetric Cryptol. **2017**(1), 80–105 (2017)

19. Dobraunig, C., Mennink, B.: Leakage resilience of the duplex construction. In: Galbraith, S.D., Moriai, S. (eds.) ASIACRYPT 2019. LNCS, Part III, vol. 11923, pp. 225–255. Springer, Cham (2019). https://doi.org/10.1007/978-3-030-34618-8_8

20. Dunkelman, O., Keller, N., Lambooij, E., Sasaki, Y.: A practical forgery attack on Lilliput-AE. IACR Cryptology ePrint Archive 2019/867 (2019)

21. Gao, S., Roy, A., Oswald, E.: Constructing TI-friendly substitution boxes using shift-invariant permutations. In: Matsui, M. (ed.) CT-RSA 2019. LNCS, vol. 11405, pp. 433–452. Springer, Cham (2019). https://doi.org/10.1007/978-3-030-12612-4_22

22. Groß, H., Wenger, E., Dobraunig, C., Ehrenhöfer, C.: Suit up! - made-to-measure hardware implementations of ASCON. In: DSD 2015, pp. 645–652. IEEE Computer Society (2015)

23. Guo, C., Pereira, O., Peters, T., Standaert, F.-X.: Authenticated encryption with nonce misuse and physical leakage: definitions, separation results and first construction. In: Schwabe, P., Thériault, N. (eds.) LATINCRYPT 2019. LNCS, vol. 11774, pp. 150–172. Springer, Cham (2019). https://doi.org/10.1007/978-3-030-30530-7_8

24. Guo, C., Pereira, O., Peters, T., Standaert, F.: Towards lightweight side-channel security and the leakage-resilience of the duplex sponge. IACR Cryptology ePrint Archive 2019/193 (2019)

25. Ishai, Y., Sahai, A., Wagner, D.: Private circuits: securing hardware against probing attacks. In: Boneh, D. (ed.) CRYPTO 2003. LNCS, vol. 2729, pp. 463–481. Springer, Heidelberg (2003). https://doi.org/10.1007/978-3-540-45146-4_27

26. Iwata, T., Khairallah, M., Minematsu, K., Peyrin, T.: Romulus v1.0. Submitted to NIST Lightweight Project (2019)

27. Jean, J., Nikolić, I., Peyrin, T.: Tweaks and keys for block ciphers: the TWEAKEY framework. In: Sarkar, P., Iwata, T. (eds.) ASIACRYPT 2014. LNCS, vol. 8874, pp. 274–288. Springer, Heidelberg (2014). https://doi.org/10.1007/978-3-662-45608-8_15

28. Jovanovic, P., Luykx, A., Mennink, B., Sasaki, Y., Yasuda, K.: Beyond conventional security in sponge-based authenticated encryption modes. J. Cryptol. **32**(3), 895–940 (2018). https://doi.org/10.1007/s00145-018-9299-7

29. Krovetz, T., Rogaway, P.: The software performance of authenticated-encryption modes. In: Joux, A. (ed.) FSE 2011. LNCS, vol. 6733, pp. 306–327. Springer, Heidelberg (2011). https://doi.org/10.1007/978-3-642-21702-9_18

30. Liu, G., Ghosh, M., Song, L.: Security analysis of SKINNY under related-tweakey settings (long paper). IACR Trans. Symmetric Cryptol. **2017**(3), 37–72 (2017)

31. Matsui, M.: On correlation between the order of S-boxes and the strength of DES. In: De Santis, A. (ed.) EUROCRYPT 1994. LNCS, vol. 950, pp. 366–375. Springer, Heidelberg (1995). https://doi.org/10.1007/BFb0053451

32. Moradi, A., Poschmann, A., Ling, S., Paar, C., Wang, H.: Pushing the limits: a very compact and a threshold implementation of AES. In: Paterson, K.G. (ed.) EUROCRYPT 2011. LNCS, vol. 6632, pp. 69–88. Springer, Heidelberg (2011). https://doi.org/10.1007/978-3-642-20465-4_6

33. Naito, Y., Matsui, M., Sugawara, T., Suzuki, D.: SAEB: a lightweight blockcipher-based AEAD mode of operation. IACR Trans. Cryptogr. Hardw. Embed. Syst. **2018**(2), 192–217 (2018)

34. Naito, Y., Sugawara, T.: Lightweight authenticated encryption mode of operation for tweakable block ciphers. IACR Trans. Cryptogr. Hardw. Embed. Syst. **2020**(1), 66–94 (2020)
35. NanGate: NanGate FreePDK45 open cell library. http://www.nangate.com
36. Nikolić, I.: How to use metaheuristics for design of symmetric-key primitives. In: Takagi, T., Peyrin, T. (eds.) ASIACRYPT 2017. LNCS, vol. 10626, pp. 369–391. Springer, Cham (2017). https://doi.org/10.1007/978-3-319-70700-6_13
37. Nikova, S., Rechberger, C., Rijmen, V.: Threshold implementations against side-channel attacks and glitches. In: Ning, P., Qing, S., Li, N. (eds.) ICICS 2006. LNCS, vol. 4307, pp. 529–545. Springer, Heidelberg (2006). https://doi.org/10.1007/11935308_38
38. NIST: Submission requirements and evaluation criteria for the lightweight cryptography standardization process (2018). https://csrc.nist.gov/Projects/lightweight-cryptography
39. Pereira, O., Standaert, F., Vivek, S.: Leakage-resilient authentication and encryption from symmetric cryptographic primitives. In: CCS 2015, pp. 96–108. ACM (2015)
40. Poschmann, A., Moradi, A., Khoo, K., Lim, C., Wang, H., Ling, S.: Side-channel resistant crypto for less than 2,300 GE. J. Cryptol. **24**(2), 322–345 (2011). https://doi.org/10.1007/s00145-010-9086-6
41. Sadeghi, S., Mohammadi, T., Bagheri, N.: Cryptanalysis of reduced round SKINNY block cipher. IACR Trans. Symmetric Cryptol. **2018**(3), 124–162 (2018)
42. Sugawara, T.: 3-share threshold implementation of AES S-box without fresh randomness. IACR Trans. Cryptogr. Hardw. Embed. Syst. **2019**(1), 123–145 (2019)
43. TS35.201: 3G Security; Specification of the 3GPP confidentiality and integrity algorithms; Document 1: f8 and f9 specification (1999)
44. Ueno, R., Homma, N., Aoki, T.: Toward more efficient DPA-resistant AES hardware architecture based on threshold implementation. In: Guilley, S. (ed.) COSADE 2017. LNCS, vol. 10348, pp. 50–64. Springer, Cham (2017). https://doi.org/10.1007/978-3-319-64647-3_4
45. Yasuda, K.: A new variant of PMAC: beyond the birthday bound. In: Rogaway, P. (ed.) CRYPTO 2011. LNCS, vol. 6841, pp. 596–609. Springer, Heidelberg (2011). https://doi.org/10.1007/978-3-642-22792-9_34
46. Zhang, Y., Sun, S., Cai, J., Hu, L.: Speeding up MILP aided differential characteristic search with Matsui's strategy. In: Chen, L., Manulis, M., Schneider, S. (eds.) ISC 2018. LNCS, vol. 11060, pp. 101–115. Springer, Cham (2018). https://doi.org/10.1007/978-3-319-99136-8_6

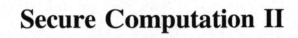

Secure Computation II

PSI from PaXoS: Fast, Malicious Private Set Intersection

Benny Pinkas[1]([⊠]), Mike Rosulek[2]([⊠]), Ni Trieu[2], and Avishay Yanai[3]

[1] Bar-Ilan University, Ramat Gan, Israel
benny.pinkas@biu.ac.il
[2] Oregon State University, Corvallis, USA
{rosulekm,trieun}@oregonstate.edu
[3] VMware Research, Herzliya, Israel
yanaia@vmware.com

Abstract. We present a 2-party private set intersection (PSI) protocol which provides security against malicious participants, yet is almost as fast as the fastest known *semi-honest* PSI protocol of Kolesnikov et al. (CCS 2016).

Our protocol is based on a new approach for two-party PSI, which can be instantiated to provide security against either malicious or semi-honest adversaries. The protocol is unique in that the only difference between the semi-honest and malicious versions is an instantiation with different parameters for a linear error-correction code. It is also the first PSI protocol which is concretely efficient while having linear communication and security against malicious adversaries, while running in the OT-hybrid model (assuming a non-programmable random oracle).

State of the art semi-honest PSI protocols take advantage of cuckoo hashing, but it has proven a challenge to use cuckoo hashing for malicious security. Our protocol is the first to use cuckoo hashing for malicious-secure PSI. We do so via a new data structure, called a probe-and-XOR of strings (PaXoS), which may be of independent interest. This abstraction captures important properties of previous data structures, most notably garbled Bloom filters. While an encoding by a garbled Bloom filter is larger by a factor of $\Omega(\lambda)$ than the original data, we describe a significantly improved PaXoS based on cuckoo hashing that achieves constant rate while being no worse in other relevant efficiency measures.

The first and fourth authors are supported by the BIU Center for Research in Applied Cryptography and Cyber Security in conjunction with the Israel National Cyber Bureau in the Prime Minister's Office and by a grant from the Israel Science Foundation. The second and third authors are supported by NSF award 1617197, a Google faculty award, and a Visa faculty award. Part of the work was done while the fourth author is at Bar-Ilan University. This research is based upon work supported in part by the Office of the Director of National Intelligence (ODNI), Intelligence Advanced Research Projects Activity (IARPA), via 2019-19-020700006. The views and conclusions contained herein are those of the authors and should not be interpreted as necessarily representing the official policies, either expressed or implied, of ODNI, IARPA, or the U.S. Government. The U.S. Government is authorized to reproduce and distribute reprints for governmental purposes notwithstanding any copyright annotation therein.

© International Association for Cryptologic Research 2020
A. Canteaut and Y. Ishai (Eds.): EUROCRYPT 2020, LNCS 12106, pp. 739–767, 2020.
https://doi.org/10.1007/978-3-030-45724-2_25

1   Introduction

Private set intersection (PSI) allows two parties with respective input sets X and Y to compute the intersection of the two sets without revealing anything else about their inputs. PSI and its variants have numerous applications, such as for contact discovery, threat detection, advertising, etc. (see e.g., [14,31] and references within). Privately computing the size of the intersection (known as 'PSI cardinality') is also important for computing conditional probabilities, which are useful for computing different analytics of private distributed data.

While there are generic methods for secure multi-party computation of any function (MPC), finding a specific protocol for PSI is interesting in its own sake since generic MPC protocols are relatively inefficient for computing PSI: generic MPC operates on a circuit representation of the computed functionality, while the intersection functionality can be represented only by relatively large circuits (the naive circuit for computing the intersection of two sets of size n is of size $O(n^2)$; a circuit based on sorting networks is of size $O(n \log n)$ [12]; and new results reduce the circuit to size $O(n)$ by utilizing different hashing schemes, but seem to be hard to be adapted to the malicious setting [28,29].)

There has been tremendous progress in computing PSI in the semi-honest model, where the parties are assured to follow the protocol (see [19,26,28]). However, protocols for the malicious setting, where parties can behave arbitrarily, are much slower, with the protocol of Rosulek and Rindal [34] being the best in terms of concrete efficiency. Protocols in both settings reduce the computation of PSI to computing many oblivious transfers (OT), which can be implemented extremely efficiently using oblivious transfer extension [1,15]. The protocols also benefit from hashing the items of the input sets to many bins, and computing the intersection separately on each bin. In the semi-honest setting it was possible to use Cuckoo hashing, which is a very efficient hashing method that maps each item to one of *two* possible locations [17,25]. However, it was unknown how to use Cuckoo hashing in the malicious setting: the problem was that a malicious party Alice can learn the location to which an input element of Bob is mapped. The choice of this location by Bob leaks information about the other inputs of Bob, including items which are not in the intersection.

1.1   Our Contributions

Our protocol is the first to use Cuckoo hashing for PSI in the malicious setting. This is done by introducing a new data structure, called a probe-and-XOR of strings (PaXoS). This is a randomized function, mapping n binary strings to m binary strings, where each of the n original strings can be retrieved by XOR'ing a specific subset of the m strings. PaXoS can be trivially implemented using a random $m \times n$ matrix, but then the encoding and decoding times are prohibitively high when n is large. We show how to implement PaXoS using a Cuckoo graph (a graph representing the mapping in Cuckoo hashing), with efficient encoding and decoding algorithms. This is essentially equivalent to Cuckoo hashing where instead of storing an item in one of two locations, we set the values of these two locations such that their XOR is equal to the stored value. As a side-effect, this does away with the drawback of using Cuckoo hashing in malicious PSI. Namely, parties do not need to *choose one of two locations* in which an input item is stored, and thus there is no potential information leakage by Cuckoo hashing.

Our protocol uses a PaXoS data structure D as a key-value store, mapping the inputs values (aka keys) of one of the parties to values which are encoded as linear combinations of the string in D. It then uses the OT extension protocol of Orrù et al. [23] (OOS), to build a PSI protocol from this data structure. The OOS protocol is secure against malicious adversaries, and is parameterized by a linear error-correcting code. Our PSI construction is unique in that the only difference between the semi-honest and malicious instantiations is only in the parameters of this code.

The semi-honest instantiation improves over the state of the art KKRT protocol [19] by 25% in concrete communication cost, while having a comparable running time. More importantly, the malicious instantiation has only slightly higher overhead than the best *semi-honest* protocol, and significantly better performance than the state of the art for malicious security [34] (about 8× less communication, and 3× faster computation). Source code is available at github.com/cryptobiu/PaXoS_PSI.

From a theory perspective, we introduce the first concretely efficient protocol in the OT-hybrid model (assuming a non-programmable random oracle), which is secure in the malicious setting and has *linear* communication. The previous state-of-the-art [34] has $O(n \log n)$ communication complexity.

1.2 Related Work

We focus on the discussion of the state-of-the-art of semi-honest PSI protocols. We note that the earliest PSI protocols, based on Diffie-Hellman assumptions, can be traced back to the 1980s [13,20,35], and refer the reader to [30] for an overview of the different PSI paradigms for PSI. Protocols [26] based on oblivious transfer extension have proven to be the fastest in practice.

A more popular public-key based approach to low-communication PSI is based on Diffie-Hellman key agreement, and presented in the 1980s [13,21] in the random oracle model. The high-level idea is for the parties to compute the intersection of $\{(H(x_i)^k)^r \mid x \in X\}$ and $\{(H(y_i)^r)^k \mid y \in Y\}$ in the clear, where r and k are secrets known by receiver and sender, respectively. However, This protocol requires $O(n)$ exponentiations.

Current state-of-the-art semi-honest PSI protocols in the two-party setting are [19,26,31]. They all rely on oblivious transfer. Most work on concretely efficient PSI is in the random oracle model, and with security against semi-honest, rather than malicious, adversaries. Some notable exceptions are [7,11,16] in the standard model, and [4,7,33,34] with security against malicious adversaries.

We refer the reader to the full paper [27] for a detailed and technical comparison of the many different protocol paradigms for PSI.

1.3   Organization

In Sect. 2 we present the preliminaries required in order to understand our techniques (linear codes, correlation-robustness, oblivious transfer and PSI). We then introduce the notion of Probe and Xor of Strings (PaXoS) in Sect. 3 and show an efficient construction of a PaXoS in Sect. 5. In Sect. 4 we present and prove our PSI protocol, which is obtained from any PaXoS. We show our main construction of an efficient PaXoS in Sect. 3.2 (and an alternative, more compact one, in the full paper [27]). We present a detailed, qualitative as well as experimental, comparison to previous work in Sects. 6 and 7.

2   Preliminaries

We denote the computational and statistical security parameters by κ and λ respectively. We say that a function $\mu : \mathbb{N} \to \mathbb{N}$ is *negligible* if for every positive polynomial $p(\cdot)$ and all sufficiently large κ it holds that $\mu(\kappa) < \frac{1}{p(\kappa)}$. For a bit string x (or a vector) of length m, we refer to the j-th coordinate of x by x_j. A matrix is denoted by a capital letter. For a matrix X, we refer to the j-th row of X by x_j and the j-th column of X by x^j. For two bit strings a, b with $|a| = |b|$, $a \wedge b$ (resp. $a \oplus b$) denotes the bitwise-AND (resp. bitwise-XOR) of a and b.

Error-correcting codes.   A binary linear code $\mathcal{C}$ with length $n_\mathcal{C}$, dimension $k_\mathcal{C}$ and minimum distance $d_\mathcal{C}$ is denoted $[n_\mathcal{C}, k_\mathcal{C}, d_\mathcal{C}]$. So $\mathcal{C} : \mathbb{F}_2^{k_\mathcal{C}} \to \mathbb{F}_2^{n_\mathcal{C}}$ is a linear map such that for every nonzero $m \in \mathbb{F}_2^{k_\mathcal{C}}$, the Hamming weight of $\mathcal{C}(m)$ is at least $d_\mathcal{C}$.

Code-correlation-robustness of random oracles.   Our construction uses the fact that when H is a random oracle, C is a linear code with minimum distance κ, and s is secret, terms of the form $H(a \oplus C(b) \wedge s)$ look random. This property was introduced in [18] as a generalization of correlation-robust hashing (from [15]), and a variant is also used in the context of PSI in [19]. It is described in the following lemma.

Lemma 1 ([18]).   *Let C be a linear error correcting code $[n, k, d]$ with $d \geq \kappa$. Let H be a random oracle and let $s \leftarrow \{0, 1\}^n$ be chosen uniformly at random. Then for all $a_1, \ldots, a_m \in \{0, 1\}^n$ and nonzero $b_1, \ldots, b_m \in \{0, 1\}^k$, the following values are indistinguishable from random:*

$$H(a_1 \oplus C(b_1) \wedge s), \ldots, H(a_m \oplus C(b_m) \wedge s),$$

Proof (Proof Sketch). If C has minimum distance κ, then any nonzero codeword $C(b_i)$ has hamming weight at least κ, so the term $C(b_i) \wedge s$ involves at least κ unknown bits of the secret s. Hence, each argument of the form $H(a_i \oplus C(b_i) \wedge s)$ has at least κ bits of entropy, from the point of view of the distinguisher, so it is negligibly likely that the distinguisher will ever query H at such a point.

Oblivious transfer. Oblivious Transfer (OT) is a central cryptographic primitive in the area of secure computation. It was introduced by Rabin [6,32]. 1-out-of-2 OT is a two-party protocol between a sender, who inputs two messages v_0, v_1, and a receiver who inputs a choice bit b and learns as output v_b and nothing about v_{1-b}. The sender remains oblivious as what message was received by the receiver. The general case of 1-out-of-N OT on τ-bit strings is defined as the functionality:

$$\mathcal{F}_{N\text{-OT}}^{\tau}\left[(v_0, \ldots, v_{N-1}), c\right] \to [\perp, v_c]$$

where $v_0, \ldots, v_{N-1} \in \{0,1\}^{\tau}$ are the sender's inputs and $c \in \{0, \ldots, N-1\}$ is the receiver's input. We denote by $\mathcal{F}_{N\text{-OT}}^{\tau,m}$ the functionality that runs $\mathcal{F}_{N\text{-OT}}$ for m times on messages in $\{0,1\}^{\tau}$. An important variant is the *random* OT functionality, denoted $\mathcal{F}_{N\text{-ROT}}^{\tau,m}$ in which the sender provides no input, but receives from the functionality as output random messages $(v_0, \ldots, v_{N-1})$ (or a key which enables to compute these messages).

The OOS oblivious transfer functionality. We will use a specific construction, by Orrù, Orsini and Scholl [23] (hereafter referred to as OOS) that realizes $\mathcal{F}_{N\text{-ROT}}^{\tau,m}$, and supports an exponentially large N, e.g. $N = 2^{\tau}$. OOS is parameterized with a binary linear code $[n_C, k_C, d_C]$ where $k_C = \tau$ and $d_C \geq \kappa$. OOS features a useful homomorphism property that we use in our PSI construction (see Sect. 4).

Specifically, we describe OOS as the functionality:

$$\mathcal{F}_{\text{OOS}}\left[s, (d_1, \ldots, d_m)\right] \to \left[(q_1, \ldots, q_m), (r_1, \ldots, r_m)\right]$$

where $r_i = q_i \oplus s \wedge C(d_i)$, $s, q_i \in \mathbb{F}_2^{n_c}$ and $d_i \in \mathbb{F}_2^{k_c}$ for every $i \in [m]$.

These outputs can be used for m instances of 1-out-of-N OT as follows. The random OT values for the ith OT instance are $H(q_i \oplus s \wedge C(x))$, where H is a random oracle and x ranges over all N possible τ-bit strings. The sender can compute any of these values as desired, whereas the receiver can compute only $H(r_i) = H(q_i \oplus s \wedge C(d_i))$, which is the OT value corresponding to choice index d_i. The fact that other OT values $H(q_i \oplus s \wedge C(d'))$, for $d' \neq d_i$, are pseudorandom is due to Lemma 1. Specifically, we can write

$$q_i \oplus s \wedge C(d') = q_i \oplus s \wedge \left[C(d_i) \oplus C(d_i \oplus d')\right] = r_i \oplus s \wedge C(d_i \oplus d')$$

and observe that $C(d_i \oplus d')$ has Hamming weight at least $d_C \geq \kappa$. Hence Lemma 1 applies. Note that the "raw outputs" of the OOS functionality are XOR-homomorphic in the following sense: for every $i, j \in [m]$,

$$r_i \oplus r_j = \left(q_i \oplus s \wedge C(d_i)\right) \oplus \left(q_j \oplus s \wedge C(d_j)\right) = q_i \oplus q_j \oplus s \wedge C(d_i \oplus d_j)$$

In this expression we use the fact that C is a linear code.

Secure computation and 2-party PSI. Informally, security is defined in the real/ideal paradigm [9, Chapter 7]. A protocol is secure if, for any attack against the protocol, there is an equivalent attack in an "ideal" world where the function is computed by a trusted third party. More formally, a functionality is a trusted third party who cannot be corrupted and who carries out a specific task in response to invocations (with arguments) from parties. This is considered as the ideal world. Parties interact with each other according to some prescribed protocol; in other words, the parties execute a protocol in the real world. Parties, who execute some protocol, may interact/invoke functionalities as well, in which case we consider this to be a hybrid world. A semi-honest adversary may corrupt parties and obtain their entire state and all subsequent received messages; a malicious adversary may additionally cause them deviate, arbitrarily, from their interaction with each other and with a functionality (i.e. modify/omit messages, etc.). In this work there are only two parties, sender and receiver, and the adversary may *statically* corrupt one of them (at the onset of the execution).

We denote by $\text{IDEAL}_{f,\mathcal{A}}(x,y)$ the joint execution of some task f by an ideal world functionality, under inputs x and y of the receiver and sender, resp., in the presence of an adversary $\mathcal{A}$. In addition, we denote by $\text{REAL}_{\pi,\mathcal{A}}(x,y)$ the joint execution of some task f by a protocol π in the real world, under inputs x and y of the receiver and sender, resp., in the presence of an adversary $\mathcal{A}$.

Definition 2. *A protocol π is said to securely compute f (in the malicious model) if for every probabilistic polynomial time adversary $\mathcal{A}$ there exists a probabilistic polynomial time simulator $\mathcal{S}$ such that*

$$\{\text{IDEAL}_{f,\mathcal{S}}(x,y)\}_{x,y} \overset{c}{\equiv} \{\text{REAL}_{\pi,\mathcal{A}}(x,y)\}_{x,y}$$

We consider a 2-party PSI functionality, described in Fig. 1, that **does not strictly enforce the size of a corrupt party's input set.** In other words, while ostensibly running the protocol on sets of size n, an adversary may learn as much as if he used a set of bounded size $n' > n$ in the ideal world (typically, $n' = c \cdot n$ for some constant c, This is the case in this work as well). This property is shared by several other 2-party malicious PSI protocols [33,34].

3   Probe-and-XOR of Strings (PaXoS)

3.1   Definitions

Our main tool is a mapping which has good linearity properties.

Definition 3. *A $(n,m,2^{-\lambda})$-**probe and XOR of strings** (PaXoS) is an oracle function $\boldsymbol{v}^H : \{0,1\}^* \to \{0,1\}^m$ such that for any distinct $x_1,\ldots,x_n \in \{0,1\}^*$,*

$$\Pr[\boldsymbol{v}^H(x_1),\ldots,\boldsymbol{v}^H(x_n) \text{ are linearly independent}] \geq 1 - 1/2^\lambda$$

Parameters:
- Two parties: a sender and receiver.
- Set size n for honest parties and n' for corrupt parties.

Functionality:
1. Wait for input $Y = \{y_1, y_2, \ldots\}$ from the receiver. Abort if the receiver is corrupt and $|Y| > n'$.
2. Wait for input $X = \{x_1, x_2, \ldots\}$ from the sender. Abort if the sender is corrupt and $|X| > n'$.
3. Give output $X \cap Y$ to the receiver.

Fig. 1. Ideal functionality for 2-party PSI.

where the probability is over choice of random function H, and linear independence is over the vector space $(\mathbb{Z}_2)^m$, i.e. for $x \in \{0,1\}^*$ we look at $\boldsymbol{v}^H(x)$ as a vector from $(\mathbb{Z}_2)^m$. We often let H be implicit and eliminate it from the notation.

In other words, this is a randomized function mapping n binary strings to binary vectors of length m, satisfying the property that the output strings are independent except with probability $2^{-\lambda}$.

We would like the output/input rate, m/n, to be as close as possible to 1. A random mapping would satisfy the PaXoS definition and will have a good rate, but will be bad in terms of encoding/decoding efficiency properties that will be defined in Sect. 3.4.

A PaXoS has the implicit property that the mapping is independent of the inputs. Namely, the goal is not to find a function that works well for a specific set of inputs, but rather to find a function that works well with high probability for any input set. This is crucial in terms of privacy, since the function must not depend on any input, as this would leak information about the input.

3.2 PaXoS as Key-Value Mapping

A key-value store, or mapping, is a database which maps a set of keys to corresponding values.[1] A PaXoS leads to a method for **encoding a key-value mapping into a concise data structure**, as follows:

$\underline{\mathsf{Encode}((x_1, y_1), \ldots, (x_n, y_n))}$: Given n items (x_i, y_i) with $x_i \in \{0,1\}^*$ and $y_i \in \{0,1\}^\ell$, denote by M the $n \times m$ matrix where the ith row is $\boldsymbol{v}(x_i)$. One can solve for a data structure (matrix) $D = (d_1, \ldots, d_m)^\top \in (\{0,1\}^\ell)^m$ such that $M \times D = (y_1, \ldots, y_n)^\top$. Namely, the following linear system of equations

---

[1] A hash table is a simple key-value mapping, but it encounters issues such as collisions. More importantly for our application, a hash table explicitly reveals whether an item is encoded in it and therefore has a privacy leakage.

(over the field of order 2^ℓ) is satisfied:

$$
\begin{bmatrix}
- \ v(x_1) \ - \\
- \ v(x_2) \ - \\
\vdots \\
- \ v(x_n) \ -
\end{bmatrix}
\times
\begin{bmatrix}
d_1 \\
d_2 \\
\vdots \\
d_m
\end{bmatrix}
=
\begin{bmatrix}
y_1 \\
y_2 \\
\vdots \\
y_n
\end{bmatrix}
$$

When the $v(x_i)$'s are linearly independent, a solution to this system of equations must exist. Therefore, when $v(\cdot)$ is a PaXoS, the system has a solution except with probability $1/2^\lambda$.

Decode(D, x): Given a data structure $D \in (\{0,1\}^\ell)^m$ and a "key" $x \in \{0,1\}^*$, we can retrieve its corresponding "value" via

$$
y = \langle v(x), D \rangle \overset{\text{def}}{=} \bigoplus_{j:v(x)_j=1} d_j
$$

In other words, probing D for a key x amounts to computing the XOR of specific positions in D, where the choice of positions is defined by $v(x)$ and depends only on x (not D). It is easy to see that when x is among the x_i values that was used to create D as above, then y obtained this way is equal to the corresponding y_i. However, the PaXoS can be probed on any key x.

It is often more convenient to discuss PaXoS in terms of the corresponding Encode/Decode algorithms than the v mapping.

3.3 Homomorphic Properties

The Decode algorithm enjoys the following **homomorphic properties**. Let $D = (d_1, \ldots, d_m) \in (\{0,1\}^\ell)^m$. Then:

- For any **linear** map $L : \{0,1\}^\ell \to \{0,1\}^{\ell'}$, extend the notation $L(D)$ to mean $(L(d_1), \ldots, L(d_m))$. Then we have

$$
\text{Decode}(L(D), x) = L(\text{Decode}(D, x)).
$$

- If D and D' have the same dimension, then define $D \oplus D' = (d_1 \oplus d'_1, \ldots, d_m \oplus d'_m)$. Then we have

$$
\text{Decode}(D, x) \oplus \text{Decode}(D', x) = \text{Decode}(D \oplus D', x).
$$

- With $s \in \{0,1\}^\ell$, define $D \wedge s = (d_1 \wedge s, d_2 \wedge s, \ldots, d_m \wedge s)$, where "$\wedge$" refers to bitwise-AND. Then we have

$$
\text{Decode}(D \wedge s, x) = \text{Decode}(D, x) \wedge s.
$$

3.4   Efficiency Measures

The following measures of efficiency are relevant in our work, and are crucial for the efficiency of the resulting PSI protocols:

- **Rate:** The Encode algorithm must encode n values $(y_1, \ldots, y_n)$, which have total length $n\ell$ bits, into a data structure D of total length $m\ell$ bits. The ratio n/m defines the **rate** of the PaXoS scheme, with rate 1 being optimal and constant rate being desirable.
- **Encoding complexity:** What is the computational cost of the Encode algorithm, as a function of the number n of key-value pairs? In general, solving a system of n linear equations requires $O(n^3)$ computation using Gaussian elimination. However, the structure of the $v(x)$ constraints may lead to a more efficient method for solving the system. We strive for an encoding procedure that is linear in n, for example $O(n\lambda)$ where λ is the statistical security parameter.
- **Decoding complexity:** What is the computational cost of the Decode algorithm? The cost is proportional to the Hamming weight of the $v(k)$ vectors—i.e., the number of positions of D that are XOR'ed to give the final result. We strive for decoding which is sublinear in n, for example $O(\lambda)$ or $O(\log n)$.[2]

3.5   Examples and Simple Constructions

Below are some existing concepts that fall within the abstraction of a PaXoS:

Random Boolean Matrix. A natural approach is to let $v(x)$ simply be a random vector for each distinct x.[3] It is elementary to show that a random boolean matrix of dimension $n \times (n + \lambda)$ has full rank with probability at least $1 - 1/2^\lambda$. This leads to a $(n, m, 2^{-\lambda})$-PaXoS scheme with $m = n + \lambda$.

This scheme has excellent rate $n/(n + \lambda)$ (which is likely optimal), but poor efficiency of encoding/decoding. Encoding corresponds to solving a random linear system of equations, requiring $O(n^3)$ if done via Gaussian elimination. Decoding one item requires computing the XOR of $\sim n/2$ positions from the data structure.

Garbled Bloom Filter. A garbled Bloom filter works in the following way: Let $h_1, \ldots, h_\lambda$ be random functions with range $\{1, \ldots, m\}$. To query the data structure at a key x, compute the XOR of positions $h_1(x), \ldots, h_\lambda(x)$ in the data structure. In our terminology, $v(x)$ is the vector that is 1 at position i if and only if $\exists j : h_j(x) = i$.

---

[2] When defining the cost of encoding and decoding we ignore the length (m) of the y-values.

[3] I.e., $v^H(x) = H(x)$ where H is a random oracle with m output bits.

Garbled Bloom Filters were introduced by Dong, Chen, Wen in [5]. They showed that if the Bloom filter has size $m = \Theta(\lambda n)$ then the Encode algorithm succeeds with probability $1 - 1/2^\lambda$. The concrete error probability is identical to the false-positive probability of a standard Bloom filter.

Garbled Bloom filters are an instance of $(n, m, 2^{-\lambda})$-PaXoS with $m = \Theta(\lambda n)$ and therefore rate $\Theta(1/\lambda)$. Items can be inserted into the garbled Bloom filter in an online manner, leading to a total cost of $O(n\lambda)$ to encode n items. Decoding requires taking the XOR of at most λ positions per item.

Garbled Cuckoo table. We introduce in Sect. 5 a new PaXoS construction, garbled Cuckoo table, with a size which is almost optimal, and optimal encoding and decoding times.

It is also worth mentioning a variant of Bloomier filters that was introduced in [3], is similar to our garbled Cuckoo table construction, and yet is *insecure* for our purposes. The construction of [3] works for a specific input set S. It chooses random hash functions and generates a graph by mapping the items of S to edges. The construction works well if the graph is acyclic. If the graph contains cycles then a new set of hash functions is chosen, until finding hash functions which map S to an acyclic graph. This construction is not a PaXoS since the choice of hash functions depends on the input and therefore leaks information about it. (Our garbled Cuckoo table construction, on the other hand, chooses the hash functions independently of the inputs, and works properly, except with negligible probability, even if the graph has cycles (Fig. 2).)

scheme	size m	encoding (n items)	decoding (single item)
random matrix	$n + \lambda$	$O(n^3)$	$\Theta(n)$
garbled Bloom filter	$O(\lambda n)$	$O(\lambda n)$	λ
garbled Cuckoo	$(2 + \epsilon)n + d + \lambda$	$O((\lambda + d)n)$	$(\lambda + d + 2)/2$ in avg.

Fig. 2. A comparison between the different PaXoS schemes, where n is the number of items, λ is a statistical security parameter (e.g., $\lambda = 40$), ϵ is the a Cuckoo hash parameter (typically $\epsilon = 0.4$), and d is an upper bound the number of cycles of a Cuckoo hash graph ($d = \log n$ except with negligible probability, and therefore for all reasonable input sizes $d < \lambda$).

4   PSI from PaXoS

In this section we describe a generic construction of PSI from PaXoS.

4.1   Overview

The fastest existing 2-party PSI protocols [19,34] are all based on efficient OT extension and its variants. The leading OT extension protocol for malicious security is due to Orrù *et al.* [23] (hereby called OOS), and it serves as the basis of our PSI protocol.

The OOS OT extension protocol implements the OOS functionality defined in Sect. 2, and provides many instances of 1-out-of-N OT of random strings, where N can even be exponentially large. Our PSI protocol involves the internals of the OOS protocol to some extent, so let us start by reviewing the relevant details. Suppose we are interested in 1-out-of-N OT for $N = 2^t$. In OOS, the sender chooses a string s and receives a string q_i for each OT instance. In this OT instance, the sender can derive N random values as follows:

$$H\big(q_i \oplus C(00\cdots0) \wedge s\big); \quad H\big(q_i \oplus C(00\cdots01) \wedge s\big); \quad \cdots \quad H\big(q_i \oplus C(11\cdots1) \wedge s\big);$$

where C is a linear error-correcting code with t input/data bits, H is a correlation-robust hash function, and "$\wedge$" denotes bitwise-AND (whenever we write $a \oplus b \wedge s$ we mean $a \oplus (b \wedge s)$).

The receiver has a "choice string" $d_i \in \{0,1\}^t$ for each instance, and as a result of the OOS protocol he receives

$$r_i = q_i \oplus C(d_i) \wedge s \qquad (1)$$

Clearly $H(r_i)$ is one of the N random values that the sender can compute for this OT instance. The security of the OOS protocol is that the $N-1$ other values look pseudorandom to the receiver, given r_i, despite the fact that the same s is used in all OT instances.

One important property of the OOS values is that they enjoy an XOR-homomorphic property:

$$r_i \oplus r_j = (q_i \oplus C(d_i) \wedge s) \oplus (q_j \oplus C(d_j) \wedge s) = q_i \oplus q_j \oplus C(d_i \oplus d_j) \wedge s$$

Note that we use the fact that C is a linear code. The fact that these values have such a homomorphic property was already pointed out and used in the OOS protocol as a way to check consistency for a corrupt receiver. Our main contribution is to point out how to leverage this homomorphic property for PSI as well.

Suppose the receiver uses the strings of a PaXoS $D = (d_1, \ldots, d_m)$ as its OOS inputs, and the parties further interpret their OOS outputs $Q = (q_1, \ldots, q_m)$ (for the sender) and $R = (r_1, \ldots, r_m)$ (for the receiver) as PaXoS data structures as well. Then we find that the identity $r_i = q_i \oplus C(d_i) \wedge s$ facilitates the homomorphic properties of PaXoS:

$$\begin{aligned}
\mathsf{Decode}(R, x) &= \mathsf{Decode}(Q \oplus C(D) \wedge s, x) \\
&= \mathsf{Decode}(Q, x) \oplus C(\mathsf{Decode}(D, x)) \wedge s
\end{aligned}$$

Suppose the receiver encodes the PaXoS D so that $\mathsf{Decode}(D, x)$ is something "recognizable" (say, x itself) for every item x in his PSI input set. Then the expression above is something that both parties can compute: the receiver computes it as $\mathsf{Decode}(R, x)$, and the sender computes it as $\mathsf{Decode}(Q, x) \oplus C(x) \wedge s$.

Hence, we can obtain a PSI protocol by having the sender send $H(\mathsf{Decode}(Q, x) \oplus C(x) \wedge s)$ for each of her items x. The receiver compares these values to $H(\mathsf{Decode}(R, y))$ for each of his items y, to determine the intersection.

4.2 Protocol Details

Our full protocol follows the general outline described above, but with some minor technical changes to facilitate the security proof.

One change is that instead of generating a PaXoS D where $\mathsf{Decode}(D, x) = x$, the receiver arranges for $\mathsf{Decode}(D, x) = H_1(x)$ (for x in his input set) where H_1 is a random oracle. This modification allows the simulator to extract a malicious receiver's effective input set by observing D (used as input to OOS) and the receiver's queries to H_1.

Also, instead of sending values of the form $H(\mathsf{Decode}(Q, x) \oplus C(H_1(x)) \wedge s)$, we have the sender send values of the form $H(x, \mathsf{Decode}(Q, x) \cdots)$. That is, the item x is included in the clear as an additional argument to H (named H_2 in our construction to avoid confusion with H_1). Additionally, H (H_2) is a (non-programmable) random oracle. As above, this allows the simulator to extract a malicious sender's effective input by observing its random-oracle queries.

The protocol is described formally in Fig. 3.

4.3 Security Analysis

Recall that we are using as our definition an ideal PSI functionality (Fig. 1) that does not strictly enforce the size of a corrupt party's set. In other words, a corrupt party may provide more items (n') than they claim (n). We prove security of our construction without making explicit reference to the relationship between n' and n. That is, in the proofs below we show that a simulator is able to extract *some* set (of size polynomial in the security parameter) in the ideal interaction, but the proofs do not explicitly bound the size of these sets.

The protocol contains several parameters ℓ_1 and ℓ_2 which affect the value of n' that can be proven. We discuss how to choose these parameters, and the resulting n' that one obtains, in Sect. 4.4.

Theorem 4. *The protocol of Fig. 3 is a secure 2-party PSI protocol against malicious adversaries in the random oracle model.*

We prove the theorem in the following two lemmas:

Lemma 5. *The protocol of Fig. 3 is secure against a malicious receiver in the random oracle model.*

Parameters:

- Computational and statistical security parameters κ and λ
- Sender with set $X \subseteq \{0,1\}^*$ of size n
- Receiver with set $Y \subseteq \{0,1\}^*$ of size n
- $(n, m, 2^{-\lambda})$-PaXoS scheme (Encode, Decode)
- Random oracles $H_1 : \{0,1\}^* \to \{0,1\}^{\ell_1}$ and $H_2 : \{0,1\}^* \to \{0,1\}^{\ell_2}$, where $\ell_2, \ell_1 \geq \lambda + 2 \log n$
- Linear error correcting code $C : [t, \ell_1, \kappa]$

Protocol:

1. The receiver generates a PaXoS $D = \mathsf{Encode}(\{(y, H_1(y)) \mid y \in Y\})$.
2. The parties run the OOS functionality (as defined in Section 2) where the receiver uses as input $D = (d_1, \ldots, d_m)$ and the sender uses a random string s as input. As a result, the sender obtains output strings $Q = (q_1, \ldots, q_m)$ and the receiver obtains output strings $R = (r_1, \ldots, r_m)$ that follow Eq, (1). We interpret both D, Q and R as PaXoS data structures.
3. The sender computes and sends the set

$$M = \left\{ H_2\Big(x, \mathsf{Decode}(Q, x) \oplus C(H_1(x)) \wedge s \Big) \;\Big|\; x \in X \right\}$$

   randomly permuted.
4. The receiver coutputs $\{y \in Y \mid H_2(y, \mathsf{Decode}(R, y)) \in M\}$.

Fig. 3. Our PaXoS-PSI protocol

Proof. The simulator for a corrupt receiver behaves as follows:

- It observes the receiver's input D to OOS, and also observes all of the receiver's queries to random oracle H_1.
- The simulator computes $\tilde{Y} = \{y \mid y$ was queried to H_1 and $\mathsf{Decode}(D, y) = H_1(y)\}$ and sends this to the ideal functionality as the receiver's effective input.
- Upon receiving from the ideal functionality the intersection $Z = X \cap \tilde{Y}$, the simulator simulates the sender's message M as $\{H_2(z, \mathsf{Decode}(R, z)) \mid z \in Z\}$ along with $|X \setminus Z|$ additional random values.

We prove the indistinguishability of this simulation in the following sequence of hybrids:

- Hybrid 1: Same as the real protocol interaction, but the simulator maintains a list L of all queries that the adversary makes to random oracle H_1. When the adversary selects its OOS input D, the simulator checks all $y \in L$ and defines the set $\tilde{Y} = \{y \in L \mid \mathsf{Decode}(D, y) = H_1(y)\}$. This hybrid is indistinguishable from the real protocol interaction, since the only difference is in internal bookkeeping information that is not used.

– Hybrid 2: Same as Hybrid 1, except that immediately after defining $\tilde{Y}$, the simulator aborts if the honest sender holds an $x \in X$ where $\mathsf{Decode}(D, x) = H_1(x)$ but $x \notin \tilde{Y}$. It suffices to show that the probability of this artificial abort is negligible.

  • Case $x \in L$: then $H_1(x)$ was known at the time $\tilde{Y}$ was defined. Therefore it is by construction that $x \in \tilde{Y} \Leftrightarrow \mathsf{Decode}(D, x) = H_1(x)$. In other words, the abort does not happen in this case

  • Case $x \notin L$: then $H_1(x)$ is independent of D, and thus $\mathsf{Decode}(D, x) = H_1(x)$ with probability $1/2^{\ell_1}$ where ℓ_1 is the output length of H_1.

  If $\ell_1 = \lambda + \log_2 n$ then by a union bound over at most n possible sender's values $x \in X$, the abort probability is indeed bounded by $1/2^{\lambda}$.

– Hybrid 3: Same as Hybrid 2, except we can rewrite the computation that defines the sender's message M. Observe that

$$
\begin{aligned}
\mathsf{Decode}(Q, x) &\oplus C(H_1(x)) \wedge s \\
&= \mathsf{Decode}(R \oplus C(D) \wedge s, x) \oplus C(H_1(x)) \wedge s \\
&= \Big[\mathsf{Decode}(R, x) \oplus \mathsf{Decode}(C(D), x) \wedge s \Big] \oplus C(H_1(x)) \wedge s \\
&= \mathsf{Decode}(R, x) \oplus \Big[C(\mathsf{Decode}(D, x)) \oplus C(H_1(x)) \Big] \wedge s \\
&= \mathsf{Decode}(R, x) \oplus C\Big(\mathsf{Decode}(D, x) \oplus H_1(x) \Big) \wedge s
\end{aligned}
$$

In particular, the term inside C is zero if and only if $\mathsf{Decode}(D, x) = H_1(x)$. Furthermore, because of the artificial abort introduced in the previous hybrid, this happens for $x \in X$ if and only if $x \in X \cap \tilde{Y}$. Hence, we can rewrite the sender's message M as:

$$
\begin{aligned}
M &= \{ H_2(x, \mathsf{Decode}(Q, x) \oplus C(H_1(x)) \wedge s) \mid x \in X \} \\
&= \{ H_2(x, \mathsf{Decode}(R, x)) \mid x \in X \cap \tilde{Y} \} \\
&\quad \cup \{ H_2(x, \mathsf{Decode}(R, x) \oplus C(\delta_x) \wedge s) \mid x \in X \setminus \tilde{Y} \}
\end{aligned}
$$

where the $\delta_x := \mathsf{Decode}(D, x) \oplus H_1(x)$ values are guaranteed to be nonzero. This hybrid is identical to the previous one, as we have only rewritten the same computation in an equivalent way.

– Hybrid 4: Same as Hybrid 3, except we replace every term of the form $H_2(x, \mathsf{Decode}(R, x) \oplus C(\delta_x) \wedge s)$ with random. The two hybrids are indistinguishable by Lemma 1 since $C(\delta_x)$ are nonzero codewords and hence have Hamming weight at least κ. Now note that the sender's message M is generated as:

$$
M = \{ H_2(x, \mathsf{Decode}(R, x)) \mid x \in X \cap \tilde{Y} \} \cup \{ m_1, \ldots, m_{|X \setminus \tilde{Y}|} \}
$$

where each m_i is uniformly chosen in $\{0, 1\}^{\ell_2}$.

– Hybrid 5: Same as Hybrid 4, except the simulator no longer artificially aborts in the manner introduced in Hybrid 2. The hybrids are indistinguishable for the same reasoning as before. Now the simulator does not use the items of $X \setminus \tilde{Y}$ at all. We conclude the proof by observing that this hybrid exactly describes the final ideal-world simulation: the simulator extracts $\tilde{Y}$, sends it to the ideal PSI functionality, receives $Z = X \cap \tilde{Y}$, and uses it to simulate the sender's message M.

Lemma 6. *The protocol of Fig. 3 is secure against a malicious sender in the random oracle model.*

Proof. The simulator for a corrupt sender behaves as follows:

- It observes the sender's input s and output Q from OOS, and also observes all of the sender's queries to random oracle H_2.
- When the sender produces protocol message M, the simulator computes

$$\tilde{X} = \{x \mid x \text{ was queried to } H_2 \text{ and } H_2(x, \mathsf{Decode}(Q, x) \oplus C(H_1(x)) \wedge s) \in M\}$$

and sends this to the ideal functionality as the sender's effective input.

We prove the indistinguishability of this simulation in the following sequence of hybrids:

- Hybrid 1: Same as the real protocol interaction, except that the simulator observes the sender's input s and output Q for OOS, and additionally observes all queries made to random oracle H_2. The simulator defines a set L of all the values x such that the adversary queried H_2 on the "correct" value $(x, \mathsf{Decode}(Q, x) \oplus C(H_1(x)) \wedge s)$. When the sender gives protocol message M, the simulator defines the set $\tilde{X} := \{x \in L \mid H_2(x, \mathsf{Decode}(Q, x) \oplus C(H_1(x)) \wedge s) \in M\}$. This hybrid is identical to the real protocol interaction, since the only change is to record bookkeeping information that is not used.
- Hybrid 2: Same as Hybrid 1, except the simulator aborts if the honest receiver holds $y \in Y \setminus \tilde{X}$ where $H_2(y, \mathsf{Decode}(Q, y) \oplus C(H_1(y)) \wedge s) \in M$. There are two cases for why such a y may not be in $\tilde{X}$:
  - Case $y \in L$: then the value $H_2(y, \mathsf{Decode}(Q, y) \oplus C(H_1(y)) \wedge s)$ was defined at the time $\tilde{X}$ was computed, and y was excluded because the correct value was not in M. The simulator will never abort in this case.
  - Case $y \notin L$: the adversary never queried H_2 at $H_2(y, \mathsf{Decode}(Q, y) \oplus C(H_1(y)) \wedge s)$ before sending M, so this output of H_2 is random and independent of M. The probability that this H_2-output appears in M is thus $|M|/2^{\ell_2}$ where ℓ_2 is the output length of H_2.

  Overall, the probability of such an artificial abort is bounded by $n|M|/2^{\ell_2} \leq n^2/2^{\ell_1} \leq 1/2^\lambda$ (since $\ell_1 < \ell_2$ and $\ell_1 \geq \lambda + 2\log n$). Hence the two hybrids are indistinguishable.
- Hybrid 3: Same as Hybrid 2, except we change the way the honest receiver's output is computed. In Hybrid 2, the honest receiver computes output as in the protocol specification:

$$\{y \in Y \mid H_2(y, \mathsf{Decode}(R, y)) \in M\}$$

In this hybrid we make the honest receiver compute its output as, simply, $\tilde{X} \cap Y$. These two expressions are in fact equivalent, from the definition of $\tilde{X}$, the artificial abort introduced in the previous expression, and the equivalence of $\mathsf{Decode}(R, y)$ and $\mathsf{Decode}(Q, y) \oplus C(H_1(y)) \wedge s$ discussed in the previous proof.

- Hybrid 4: Same as Hybrid 3, except we remove the artificial abort condition that was introduced in Hybrid 2. The hybrids are indistinguishable for the same reason as before. Note that in this hybrid, the simulator does not use the honest receiver's input Y except to compute the receiver's final output. We conclude the proof by observing that this hybrid exactly describes the ideal world simulation: The simulator observes s, Q and the sender's oracle queries to determine a set $\tilde{X}$. It sends $\tilde{X}$ to the ideal functionality and $\tilde{X} \cap Y$ is delivered to the receiver.

4.4 Choosing Parameters

The protocol contains several parameters:

- A linear binary code $C : \{0, 1\}^{\ell_1} \to \{0, 1\}^t$.
- Random oracle output lengths ℓ_1, ℓ_2.

As shown in the security proof, the following facts must be true in order for security to hold:

- C must have minimum distance at least κ (the computational security parameter).
- $\ell_1, \ell_2 \geq \lambda + 2 \log n$, where λ is the statistical security parameter.

However, the parameters ℓ_1, ℓ_2 also have an effect on the size of the corrupt party's set, as extracted by the simulator. In particular, increasing these values causes the protocol to more tightly enforce the size (n') of the corrupt party's input set.

We note that the communication cost of the protocol is roughly ℓ_2 bits per item from the sender and roughly t bits per item from the receiver (sent as part of the OOS protocol, where t is the length of the code used in the OOS protocol).

Semi-honest security. To instantiate our protocol for semi-honest security, it is enough to set $\ell_1 = \ell_2 = \lambda + 2 \log n$, the minimum possible value for security. The issue of extracting a corrupt party's input, which involves further increasing ℓ_1, ℓ_2, is not relevant in the semi-honest case.

It therefore suffices to identify linear (binary) codes with suitable minimum distance, for the different values of ℓ_1 that result. We identify good choices in Fig. 4, all of which are the result of concatenating a Reed-Solomon code with a small (optimal) binary code.

n	$\ell_1 = \ell_2 = \lambda + 2\log n$	codeword length t	choice of code
2^{12}	64	448	$RS[28, 13, 16]_{32}$ composed with $(16, 5, 8)_2$
2^{16}	72	473	$RS[42, 12, 32]_{64}$ composed with $(11, 6, 4)_2$
2^{20}	80	495	$RS[45, 14, 32]_{64}$ composed with $(11, 6, 4)_2$
2^{24}	88	506	$RS[46, 15, 32]_{64}$ composed with $(11, 6, 4)_2$

Fig. 4. Parameters for semi-honest instantiation of PaXoS-PSI, with $\kappa = 128$ and $\lambda = 40$.

Malicious sender's set size. Consider a malicious sender and recall how the simulator extracts an effective input for that sender. The sender gives protocol message M and the simulator extracts via

$$\tilde{X} := \{x \in L \mid H_2(x, \mathsf{Decode}(Q, x) \oplus C(H_1(x)) \wedge s) \in M\}$$

where L is the set of x values such that the adversary has queried $H_2(x, \cdot)$. The protocol limits the protocol message M to have n items, but still $\tilde{X}$ may have many more than n items if the adversary manages to find collisions in H_2. If we set ℓ_2 (the output length of H_2) to be 2κ, then collisions are negligibly likely and indeed $|\tilde{X}| \leq n$ except with negligible probability.

While it is possible to set $\ell_2 < 2\kappa$, doing so has less impact on the protocol than the other parameters (ℓ_1 and hence t). One can reduce ℓ_2 only very slightly before the adversary can find a very large amount (e.g., superlinear in n) of collisions. For these reasons, **we recommend setting $\ell_2 = 2\kappa$** in our malicious instantiation.

Malicious receiver's set size. Consider a malicious receiver and recall how the simulator extracts an effective input for that receiver. The simulator observes the receiver's input D (a PaXoS) to OOS and also observes all queries made to the random oracle H_1. Then the simulator extracts via:

$$\tilde{Y} := \{y \in L \mid \mathsf{Decode}(D, y) = H_1(y)\}$$

where L is the set of queries made to H_1. The question becomes: as a function of $|D|$ and ℓ_1 (the output length of H_1), what is an upper bound on the number of items in $\tilde{Y}$?

In the full version [27] we prove the following, using an information-theoretic compression argument:

Claim. Suppose an adversary makes q queries to random oracle H_1 with output length ℓ_1 and then generates a PaXoS D of size m (hence $m\ell_1$ bits) total. Fix a value n' and let $\mathcal{E}$ denote the event that $\mathsf{Decode}(D, y) = H_1(y)$ for at least n' values y that were queried to H_1. Then

$$\Pr[\mathcal{E}] \leq \binom{q}{n'} / 2^{(n'-m)\ell_1}.$$

The idea behind the proof is that if a PaXoS D happens to encode many $H_1(y)$ values, then D could be used to compress H_1. However, this is unlikely due to H_1 being a random object and therefore incompressible.

For reference, we have computed some concrete parameter settings so that $\Pr[\mathcal{E}] < 2^{-40}$ (the probability that the simulator extracts more than n' items). The values are given in Fig. 5. We consider an adversary making $q = 2^{128}$ queries to H_1, which is rather conservative (in terms of security). In practice significantly smaller parameters may be possible.[4] Note that if the PaXoS has size m, then a compression argument such as the one we use only starts to apply when $n' > m$. Hence all of our bounds are expressed as $n' = cm$ where $c > 1$ is a small constant.

Recall that ℓ_1 is the input length to the linear code C, so increasing it has the effect of increasing t (the codeword length) as well. We include good choices of codes (achieving minimum distance $\kappa = 128$) in the figure as well.

m	n'	ℓ_1	codeword len t	choice of code
2^{12}	$2m$	233	776	$RS[97, 34, 64]_{128}$ composed with $(8, 7, 2)_2$
2^{12}	$3m$	174	660	$RS[60, 29, 32]_{64}$ composed with $(11, 6, 4)_2$
2^{12}	$4m$	154	627	$RS[57, 26, 32]_{64}$ composed with $(11, 6, 4)_2$
2^{12}	$5m$	144	605	$RS[55, 24, 32]_{64}$ composed with $(11, 6, 4)_2$
2^{16}	$2m$	225	768	$RS[64, 33, 32]_{128}$ composed with $(12, 7, 4)_2$
2^{16}	$3m$	168	649	$RS[59, 28, 32]_{64}$ composed with $(11, 6, 4)_2$
2^{16}	$4m$	149	616	$RS[56, 25, 32]_{64}$ composed with $(11, 6, 4)_2$
2^{16}	$5m$	139	605	$RS[55, 24, 32]_{64}$ composed with $(11, 6, 4)_2$
2^{20}	$2m$	217	744	$RS[62, 31, 32]_{128}$ composed with $(12, 7, 4)_2$
2^{20}	$3m$	162	638	$RS[58, 27, 32]_{64}$ composed with $(11, 6, 4)_2$
2^{20}	$4m$	144	605	$RS[55, 24, 32]_{64}$ composed with $(11, 6, 4)_2$
2^{20}	$5m$	134	594	$RS[54, 23, 32]_{64}$ composed with $(11, 6, 4)_2$
2^{24}	$2m$	209	732	$RS[61, 30, 32]_{128}$ composed with $(12, 7, 4)_2$
2^{24}	$3m$	156	627	$RS[57, 26, 32]_{64}$ composed with $(11, 6, 4)_2$
2^{24}	$4m$	138	594	$RS[54, 23, 32]_{64}$ composed with $(11, 6, 4)_2$
2^{24}	$5m$	129	583	$RS[53, 22, 32]_{64}$ composed with $(11, 6, 4)_2$

Fig. 5. Parameters for malicious PaXoS-PSI with $\kappa = 128$ and $\Pr[\text{simulator extracts} >$ n' items from malicious receiver$] < 1/2^{40}$, where adversary makes 2^{128} queries to H_1.

5   Garbled Cuckoo Table

We introduce a new approach for PaXoS that enjoys the best of all worlds: it has the same asymptotic encoding and decoding costs as a garbled Bloom filter, but with constant rate (e.g., $\sim 1/(2 + \epsilon)$) rather than a $O(1/\lambda)$ rate.

---

[4] For example, considering an adversary who makes $q = 2^{80}$ queries to H_1 leads to ℓ_1 in the range of 70 to 90, and codeword length t in the range of 460 to 510.

Furthermore, it has a linear time construction, just like the modified Bloomier filter of [3], but with the advantage of having the hash function(s) independent of the keys/values.

5.1   Overview

Our construction uses ideas from both garbled Bloom filters as well as Cuckoo hashing. Recall that in Cuckoo hashing, it is typical to have only 2 hash functions h_1, h_2, where an item x is associated with positions $h_1(x)$ and $h_2(x)$ in the data structure.

So as a starting point, consider a garbled Bloom filter with just 2 hash functions rather than λ. Such a data structure corresponds to the decoding function $\mathsf{Decode}(D, x) = d_{h_1(x)} \oplus d_{h_2(x)}$.[5] (Using the PaXoS key-value mapping terminology of Sect. 3.2, the vector $v(x)$ has only two non-zero entries, in locations $h_1(x)$ and $h_2(x)$.) Given n key-value pairs (x_i, y_i), how can we generate a data structure $D = (d_1, \ldots, d_m)$ that encodes them in this way?

An important object in analyzing our construction is the **cuckoo graph**. The vertices in the cuckoo graph are numbered 1 through m, and correspond to the positions in the data structure D. The (undirected) edges of the graph correspond to items that are meant to be inserted. An item x corresponds to the edge $\{h_1(x), h_2(x)\}$. (The graph may contain self-loops and repeated edges.) We refer to such graphs with m vertices and n edges as (n, m)-**cuckoo graphs** and note that the distribution over such graphs is independent of X. We write $G_{h_1, h_2, X}$ to refer to the specific (n, m)-cuckoo graph corresponding to a particular set of hash functions and keys X. All properties of our PaXoS can be understood in terms of properties of random (n, m)-cuckoo graphs.

In the simplest case, suppose that $G_{h_1, h_2, X}$ happens to be a **tree**. Our goal is to encode the items X into the data structure D. Each node g in the graph corresponds to a row d_g of D. Then we can do this encoding in linear time as follows: We choose an arbitrary root vertex r of the tree and set d_r of the data structure arbitrarily. We then traverse the tree, say, in DFS or BFS order. Each time we visit a vertex j for the first time, we set its corresponding value d_j in the data structure, to agree with the edge we just traversed. This is done as follows.

Recall that each edge ij corresponds to a key-value pair (x, y) in the sense that $\{i, j\} = \{h_1(x), h_2(x)\}$ and our goal is to arrange that $d_i \oplus d_j = y$. As we cross an edge from i to j in the traversal, we have the invariant that position d_i in the data structure has been already fixed but d_j is still undefined. Hence, we can always set $d_j := d_i \oplus y$.

Handling Cycles. When $m = O(n)$, corresponding to a PaXoS of constant rate, the corresponding Cuckoo graph is unlikely to be acyclic [10]. In this case the encoding procedure that we just outlined does not work, since when the graph traversal closes a circuit it encounters a vertex whose value has already been defined and cannot be set to satisfy the constraint imposed by the current edge.

---

[5] For now, we ignore the case where $h_1(x) = h_2(x)$.

We can handle acyclic Cuckoo graphs by adding $d+\lambda$ additional entries to the data structure D. We first describe an analysis where d is an upper bound on the size χ of the 2-core of the graph, and then an analysis where d is an upper bound on the cyclomatic number σ of the graph. (These bounds are $O((\log n)^{1+\omega(1)})$ and $\log n$, respectively.) We recall below the definitions of both these values, and note that $\sigma < \chi$ always.

The **2-core** of a graph is the maximum subgraph where each node has degree at least 2 (namely, the subgraph containing all cycles, as well as all paths connecting cycles). We use χ to denote the number of edges in the 2-core. The **cyclomatic number** of a graph is the minimum number of edges to remove to leave an acyclic graph. Equivalently, it is the number of non-tree edges (back edges) in a DFS traversal of the graph. We use σ to denote the cyclomatic number. The cyclomatic number is equal to the minimal number of independent cycles in the graph, and is therefore smaller than or equal to the number of cycles. It is also always strictly less than the size of the 2-core.

The construction. D will be structured as $D = L \| R$, where $|L| = m$ (the number of vertices in the Cuckoo graph) and $|R| = d+\lambda$. Each decoding/constraint vector $\boldsymbol{v}(x)$ then has the form $\boldsymbol{v}(x) = \boldsymbol{l}(x) \| \boldsymbol{r}(x)$, where $\boldsymbol{l}(x)$ determines the positions of L to be XOR'ed and $\boldsymbol{r}(x)$ determines the positions of R to be XOR'ed. We will let L correspond to the simple Cuckoo hashing idea above, so each $\boldsymbol{l}(x)$ vector is zeroes everywhere except for two 1s. We will let $\boldsymbol{r}(x)$ be determined uniformly at random for each x (similar to the random matrix construction of a PaXoS).

To encode n key-value pairs into the data structure in this way, first consider the system of linear equations induced by the constraints $\langle \boldsymbol{v}(x_i), D \rangle = y_i$, **restricted to only the χ items (edges) in the 2-core.** (Once we set values that encode the items in the 2-core, we will be able to encode the other items using graph traversal as in an acyclic graph.) These constraints refer to a vertex u of G only if that vertex is in the 2-core. We get χ equations over $m + d + \lambda$ variables, where the coefficients of the last $d + \lambda$ variables (the $\boldsymbol{r}(x)$ part) are random. If we set d to be an upper bound on χ then we get that the system has a solution with probability $1 - 2^{-\lambda}$.

So, using a general-purpose linear solver we can find values for R and for the subset of L corresponding to the vertices in the 2-core, that satisfies these constraints. This can be done in $O((d + \lambda)^3)$ time. For vertices u outside of the 2-core, the value of d_u in the data structure remains undefined. But after removing the 2-core, the rest of the graph is such that these values in the data structure can be fixed according to a tree traversal process:

Every edge *not* in the 2-core can be oriented away from all cycles (if an edge leads to a cycle in both directions, then that edge would have been part of the 2-core). We traverse those edges following the direction of their orientation. Let edge $i \rightarrow j$ correspond to a key-value pair (x, y). Let d_j denote the position in D (in its "L region") corresponding to vertex j. By our invariant, d_j is not yet fixed when we traverse $i \rightarrow j$. Yet it is the only undefined value relevant to the constraint $\langle v(x), D \rangle = y$, so we can satisfy the constraint by solving for d_j. Hence with a linear pass over all remaining items, we finish constructing the data structure D.

The total cost of encoding is therefore $O((d + \lambda)^3 + n\lambda)$. We explained above that we can set d to be an upper bound on the size of the 2-core.[6] As we shall see (in Sect. 5.2), it is possible to set d to be the cyclomatic number of the Cuckoo graph, which is logarithmic in n. Therefore the dominating part of the expression is $n\lambda$.

5.2   Details

The garbled-cuckoo construction is presented formally in Fig. 6.

Analysis & Costs. In the full version of the paper [27] we show that the number σ of cycles is smaller than $\log n + O(1)$ except with negligible probability. Therefore we can set $d = (1 + \varepsilon) \log n$.[7] This bound also applies to the cyclomatic number (which is always smaller than or equal to the number of cycles). Theorem 7 shows that it is sufficient to set d to be equal to this upper bound on the cyclomatic number.

Recall that each item is mapped to a row $l(x_i) \| r(x_i)$ which contains an $l(x_i)$ part with two 1 entries, and a random binary vector $r(x_i)$ of length $\lambda + d$. We set $\lambda = 40$, and therefore for all practical input sizes we get that $d < \lambda$. We conclude that the number of 1 entries in the row vector is $O(\lambda)$.

The encoding processes each of n edges once during the traversal. The computation involves XORing the locations pointed to by 1 entries in the row. The overhead of encoding all rows is $O(n\lambda)$. The decoding of a single item involves XORing the rows pointed by the two rows to which it is mapped, and is $O(\lambda)$.

Theorem 7. *When setting $d = (1 + \varepsilon) \log n$, the garbled cuckoo* PaXoS *of Fig. 6 with parameter λ is a $(n, m, \epsilon + 2^{-\lambda})$-*PaXoS *where*

$$\epsilon = \Pr[\text{the cyclomatic number of a random } (n, m)\text{-cuckoo graph} > \log n + O(1)]$$

Proof. As discussed above, we use here an upper bound d for the cyclomatic number of the graph. Setting the bound to $d = (1 + \varepsilon) \log n$ works excepts with a negligible failure probability.

---

[6] Such an upper bound for the case of Cuckoo hashing can be derived from [24, Lemma 3.4], but that analysis assumes that the graph has $8n$ edges, and shows that an upper bound of size d fails with probability $n/2^{-\Omega(d)}$. Therefore we must set $d = (\log n)^{1+\epsilon}$ to get a negligible failure probability.

[7] The parameter ε used here is independent of the parameter ϵ used in Cuckoo hashing.

Parameters:

- upper bound d on the cyclomatic number of the Cuckoo graph
- error parameter λ
- random functions $h_1, h_2 : \{0,1\}^* \to \{1, \ldots, m\}$
- random function $r : \{0,1\}^* \to \{0,1\}^{d+\lambda}$

Decode(D, x):

1. Parse D as $D = L \| R$ where $|L| = m$ and $|R| = d + \lambda$
2. Set $l(x) \in \{0,1\}^m$ to be all zeroes except 1s at positions $h_1(x)$ and $h_2(x)$
3. Return $\langle l(x), L \rangle \oplus \langle r(x), R \rangle$

Encode$((x_1, y_1), \ldots, (x_n, y_n))$:

1. Construct the Cuckoo graph $G_{h_1,h_2,X}$ for $X = \{x_1, \ldots, x_n\}$ and let $\tilde{V}, \tilde{E}$ be the vertices and edges of its 2-core. If the number of cycles is greater than d then abort.
2. Initialize variables $L = (l_1, \ldots, l_m)$ and $R = (r_1, \ldots, r_{d+\lambda})$.
3. Solve (e.g., with Gaussian elimination) for variables $\{l_u \mid u \in \tilde{V}\} \cup R$ that satisfy:
$$\langle l(x_i) \| r(x_i), L \| R \rangle = y_i, \quad \forall x_i \in \tilde{E}$$
where $l(\cdot), r(\cdot)$ are as above.
4. For each connected component which is a tree, pick an arbitrary vertex v as the root of the tree. Set the variable l_v to a random value.
5. For each item/edge $x_i \notin \tilde{E}$, in order of a DFS traversal directed away from the 2-core (in connected components which include a cycle), or directed away from the root (in connected components which do not include a cycle)
   (a) Let $\{u, v\} = \{h_1(x_i), h_2(x_i)\}$ so that l_u is already defined and l_v is not.
   (b) Set $l_v := l_u \oplus \langle r(x_i), R \rangle \oplus y_i$
6. Output $D = L \| R$

Fig. 6. Garbled Cuckoo PaXoS

The proof bounds the probability that the Encode algorithm fails to satisfy the linear constraints $\langle v(x_i), D \rangle = y_i$ for every i. For items x_i that do not correspond to edges in the 2-core, Step 4 of Encode satisfies the appropriate linear constraint, by construction. For items in the 2-core, their linear constraints are fixed all at once in Step 3 of Encode. Hence, the construction only fails if Step 3 fails. Step 3 solves for the following system of equations:

$$\langle l(x_i) \| r(x_i), L \| R \rangle = y_i, \quad \forall x_i \in \tilde{E}$$

We interpret $\{l(x_i)\|r(x_i)\}_{x_i \in \tilde{E}}$ as a matrix $M_L|M_R$ where the first m columns (i.e., M_L) are $\{l(x_i)\}_{x_i \in \tilde{E}}$ and the remaining $d + \lambda$ columns (i.e., M_R) are $\{r(x_i)\}_{x_i \in \tilde{E}}$. We therefore ask whether the rows of the matrix $M_L|M_R$ are linearly independent.

There are up to d cycles in the graph, denoted as $C_1, \ldots, C_d$. Let us focus on the matrix M_L, and more specifically on the rows corresponding an arbitrary cycle C_i (each of these rows has two 1 entries, at the locations of the vertices touching the corresponding edge). It is easy to see that there is a single linear combination D_i of these rows which is 0 (the XOR of all these rows). Any linear combination of $D_1, \ldots, D_d$ is 0, and these are the only linear combinations of rows which are equal to 0. Therefore there are at most 2^d such combinations and the kernel of M_L is of dimension at most d.

Our goal is to find the probability of the existence of a zero linear combination of the rows of $M_L|M_R$, rather than the rows of M_L alone. Since in M_R each row contains $d + \lambda$ random bits, this probability is at most $2^{-\lambda}$.   □

5.3 Comparison

Our construction shares many features with garbled Bloom filters (GBF), and indeed is somewhat inspired by them. Both our construction and GBF involve probing about the same number of positions per item ($\frac{\lambda + \chi + 2}{2}$ in average vs. $O(\lambda)$), however we are able to obtain constant rate while GBFs have rate $O(1/\lambda)$. We point out that GBFs inherit from standard Bloom filters their support for fully online insertion; that is, their analysis proves that items can be added to a GBF in any order. Our approach builds the data structure in a very particular order (according to a global tree or tree-like structure of a graph). This qualitative difference seems important for achieving constant rate.

We also use much of the analysis techniques and terminology from cuckoo hashing (especially cuckoo hashing with a stash). However, one important difference with typical cuckoo hashing is that our construction can handle multiple cycles in a connected component of the cuckoo graph. Indeed, usual cuckoo hashing (without a stash) succeeds if each connected component of the graph has at most one cycle. The items in a cycle can be handled by arbitrarily assigning an orientation to the cycle, and assigning each edge (item) to its forward endpoint (position in the table). In our case, if some items form a cycle, their corresponding constraint vectors become linearly dependent and we cannot solve the system of linear equations. In general, our approach has a larger class of subgraphs which present a "barrier" to the process (where graphs with only 1 cycle are a barrier for us but not for standard cuckoo hashing), making the analyses slightly different.

5.4 An Alternative Construction

In full version of the paper [27] we describe a modified construction which is based on a DFS traversal of the graph, and has a similar overhead to the construction described in this section.

6 A Theoretical Comparison

In Table 1 we show the *theoretical* communication complexity of our protocol compared with the Diffie-Hellman based PSI, the KKRT protocol [19] and the SpoT protocol [26] in the semi-honest setting, and the Rindal-Rosulek [34] and Ghosh-Nilges [8] protocols in the malicious setting. This comparison measures how much communication the protocols require on an idealized network where we do not care about protocol metadata, realistic encodings, byte alignment, etc. In practice, data is split up into multiples of bytes (or CPU words), and different data is encoded with headers, etc.—empirical measurements of such real-world costs are given later in Sect. 7.

Table 1. Theoretical communication costs of PSI protocols (in bits), calculated using computational security $\kappa = 128$ and statistical security $\lambda = 40$. Ignores cost of base OTs (in our protocol, KKRT, Sp) which are independent of input size. n_1 and n_2 are the input sizes of the sender and receiver respectively. ϕ is the size of elliptic curve group elements (256 is used here). ℓ is width of OT extension matrix (depends on n_1 and protocol. χ is the upper bound on the number of cycles in a cuckoo graph. σ is the length of items ($\sigma = 64$ in the concrete numbers). "SH" and "M" denotes semi-honest and malicious setting. In RR protocols, EC-ROM and SM respectively denote their encode-commit model and the standard model dual execution variant.

Protocol	Communication	$n = n_1 = n_2$		
		2^{16}	2^{20}	2^{24}
Semi Honest				
DH-PSI	$\phi n_1 z + (\phi + \lambda + \log(n_1 n_2))n_2$	$584n$	$592n$	$600n$
KKRT [19]	$(3 + s)(\lambda + \log(n_1 n_2))n_1 + 1.2\ell n_2$	$1042n$	$1018n$	$978n$
SpoT-low-comm [26]	$1.02(\lambda + \log_2(n_2) + 2)n_1 + \ell n_2$	$488n$	$500n$	$512n$
SpoT-fast [26]	$2(\lambda + \log(n_1 n_2))n_1 + \ell(1 + 1/\lambda)n_2$	$583n$	$609n$	$634n$
ours	$(\lambda + \log_2(n_1 n_2))n_1 + \ell(2.4n_2 + \lambda + \chi)$	$\sim 1207n$	$\sim 1268n$	$\sim 1302n$
Malicious				
RR (EC-ROM) [34]	$3\kappa n + n(2\kappa + \kappa \log n + \log^2 n)$	$10112n$	$10576n$	$11024n$
RR (SM) [34]	$3\kappa n + n(2\kappa + \sigma\kappa \log n + \log^2 n)$	$(200k)n$	$(220k)n$	$> (240k)n$
GN [8]	at least $8(n + 1)(\kappa + 2\sigma)$	$> 3072n$	$> 3072n$	$> 3072n$
ours	$(\lambda + \log_2(n_1 n_2))n_1 + \ell(2.4n_2 + 2\lambda + \chi) + \lambda(2.4n_2 + 2\ell)$	$\sim 1623n$	$\sim 1621n$	$\sim 1602n$

PaXoS PSI has linear communication complexity. Let us clarify our claim of "linear communication." Consider the *insecure* intersection protocol where Alice sends $H(x)$ for every x in her set. H could have output length equal to security parameter, giving $O(n \cdot \kappa)$ communication. But with semi-honest parties H can also have output length as small as $\lambda + 2\log(n)$ to ensure correctness with probability $1 - 1/2^\lambda$. When viewed this way, it looks like the protocol has complexity $O(n \log n)$! However, if $1/2^\lambda$ is supposed to be negligible then certainly $\log n \ll \lambda$, so one could still write $O(n \cdot \lambda)$.

If we let L be a length that depends on the security parameters and $\log n$ (which is inherent to all intersection protocols, secure or not), then insecure PSI and PaXoS-PSI have complexity $O(L \cdot n)$, while previous OT-based malicious

PSI [34] has complexity $O(L \cdot n \log n)$ or even $O(L \cdot n\kappa)$ [33]. For comparison, semi-honest KKRT [19] protocol has complexity $\omega(L \cdot n)$ (from the stash growing as $\omega(1)$) and semi-honest PRTY [26] has complexity $O(L \cdot n)$.

In [26] and in this work, L can depend on the security parameter alone, leading to a $O(n \cdot \kappa)$ communication, which we would characterize as linear in n. But when choosing concrete parameters (just like in the insecure protocol) L can be made smaller by involving a $O(\log n)$ term. Again, this is endemic to all intersection protocols.

7 Implementation and Evaluation

7.1 Implementation Details

We now present a comparison based on implementations of all protocols. We used the implementation of KKRT [19], RR [34], HD-PSI, spot-low, spot-fast [26] from the open source-code[8] provided by the authors.

We evaluate the DH-PSI protocol, instantiated with two different elliptic curves: Curve25519 [2] and Koblitz-283. Curve25519 elements are 256 bits while K-283 elements are 283 bits. Using the Miracl library, K-283 operations are faster than Curve25519, giving us a tradeoff of running time vs. communication for DH-PSI.

All OT-based PSI protocols [19,26,34] (including our protocols) require the same underlying primitives: a Hamming correlation-robust function H, a pseudorandom function F, and base OTs for OT extension. We instantiated these primitives exactly as in previous protocols (e.g, KKRT, RR): both H and F instantiated using AES, and base OTs instantiated using Naor-Pinkas [22]. We use the implementation of base OTs from the libOTe library[9]. All protocols use a computational security parameter of $\kappa = 128$ and a statistical security parameter $\lambda = 40$.

For our own protocols, we implemented two variants of our PaXoS. We implemented the DFS traversal of the cuckoo graph (see the full version [27]) using the boost library. We used additional libraries linbox, gmp, ntl, givaro iml, blas for solving systems for linear equations and generating the required concatenated linear codes needed for the 2-core based variant of Sect. 5. We use $2n$ bins in our DFS based PaXoS, and $2.4n$ bin in our 2-core based variant.

7.2 Experimental Setup

We performed a series of benchmarks on the Amazon web services (AWS) EC2 cloud computing service. We used the M5.large machine class with 2.5 GHz Intel Xeon and 8 GB RAM.6

---

[8] https://github.com/osu-crypto.
[9] https://github.com/osu-crypto/libOTe.

We tested the protocols over three different network settings: LAN – two machines in the same region (N.Virginia) with bandwidth 4.97 GiB/s; WAN1 – one machine in N.Virginia and the other in Oregon with bandwidth 155 MiB/s; and WAN2 – one machine in N.Virginia and the other in Sydney with bandwidth 55 MiB/s. All experiments are performed with a single thread (with an additional thread used for communication). Find the result of the WAN2 setting in the full version of the paper [27].

7.3   Experimental Results

A detailed benchmark for set sizes $n = \{2^{12}, 2^{16}, 2^{20}\}$ is given in Table 2.

Semi-honest PSI Comparison. Our best protocol in terms of communication is PaXoS-DFS. The communication of this protocol is less than 10% larger than that of KKRT [19], and slightly more than twice the communication of SpOT-low.

Our best protocol in terms of run time is PaXoS 2-core. In the LAN setting for 2^{20} inputs, it runs only 18% slower than KKRT. In the two WAN settings it is about 80% slower.

Table 2. Communication in MB and run time in milliseconds for related works over $n = \{2^{12}, 2^{16}, 2^{20}\}$ items and over three network settings as described in the text. DH-PSI has two versions, with two different curves: K-283 and 25519. EC-ROM is the encode-commit version in [34] and σ is the input length of the parties. All protocols run with $\sigma = 128$ except RR (SM) that can run with 64 at most bit items. The upper part of the table refers to semi-honest (SH) protocols whereas the lower part refers to malicious (M) protocols. Missing entries refer to experiment that failed due to lack of memory or they took too much time.

Protocol	comm (MB)			LAN			WAN		
	2^{12}	2^{16}	2^{20}	2^{12}	2^{16}	2^{20}	2^{12}	2^{16}	2^{20}
Semi Honest									
DH-PSI (K-283)	0.32	5.2	84.0	4597	73511		6529	75839	
DH-PSI (25519)	0.29	4.7	76.1	8797	140507		12558	142922	
KKRT [19]	0.53	8.06	127	177	339	4551	586	1361	9809
SpOT-low [26]	**0.25**	**3.9**	**63.1**	898	10173		3693	18068	
SpOT-fast [26]	0.3	4.71	76.4	460	1964	24442	6464	11602	31944
PaXoS 2-core (Sect. 5)	0.65	10.19	163.63	16	235	5378	641	1664	17628
Malicious									
RR (EC-ROM) [34]	4.8	79	1322	144	828	13996	1723	5061	69003
RR (SM, $\sigma = 64$) [34]	92	1317	22183	596	7330		6190	67310	
PaXoS 2-core (Sect. 5)	0.81	12.59	202.04	**120**	**257**	**5598**	**644**	**1800**	**18621**

Malicious PSI Comparison. The communication of both implementations of our protocol is better than that of RR. For 2^{20} items, PaXoS-DFS uses almost 8 times less communication, and PaXoS 2-core uses 6.5 less communication.

In terms of run time, PaXoS 2-core is faster than RR by a factor of about 2.5 on a LAN, and factors of 3.7–4 in the two WAN settings. The larger improvement in the WAN settings is probably due to the larger effect that the improvement in the communication has over a WAN.

Semi-honest vs. Malicious. In both our implementations of PaXoS the malicious implementation uses only about 25% more communication than the semi-honest implementation. In the LAN setting, our malicious protocols run about 4% slower than our corresponding semi-honest protocols.

References

1. Asharov, G., Lindell, Y., Schneider, T., Zohner, M.: More efficient oblivious transfer and extensions for faster secure computation. In: ACM CCS, pp. 535–548 (2013)
2. Bernstein, D.J.: Curve25519: new Diffie-Hellman speed records. In: Yung, M., Dodis, Y., Kiayias, A., Malkin, T. (eds.) PKC 2006. LNCS, vol. 3958, pp. 207–228. Springer, Heidelberg (2006). https://doi.org/10.1007/11745853_14
3. Charles, D., Chellapilla, K.: Bloomier filters: a second look. In: Halperin, D., Mehlhorn, K. (eds.) ESA 2008. LNCS, vol. 5193, pp. 259–270. Springer, Heidelberg (2008). https://doi.org/10.1007/978-3-540-87744-8_22
4. Chen, H., Huang, Z., Laine, K., Rindal, P.: Labeled PSI from fully homomorphic encryption with malicious security. In: Proceedings of the 2018 ACM SIGSAC Conference on Computer and Communications Security, CCS 2018, Toronto, ON, Canada, 15–19 October 2018, pp. 1223–1237 (2018)
5. Dong, C., Chen, L., Wen, Z.: When private set intersection meets big data: an efficient and scalable protocol. In: ACM CCS 2013, pp. 789–800 (2013)
6. Even, S., Goldreich, O., Lempel, A.: A randomized protocol for signing contracts. Commun. ACM **28**, 637–647 (1985)
7. Freedman, M.J., Nissim, K., Pinkas, B.: Efficient private matching and set intersection. In: Cachin, C., Camenisch, J.L. (eds.) EUROCRYPT 2004. LNCS, vol. 3027, pp. 1–19. Springer, Heidelberg (2004). https://doi.org/10.1007/978-3-540-24676-3_1
8. Ghosh, S., Nilges, T.: An algebraic approach to maliciously secure private set intersection. In: Ishai, Y., Rijmen, V. (eds.) EUROCRYPT 2019. LNCS, vol. 11478, pp. 154–185. Springer, Cham (2019). https://doi.org/10.1007/978-3-030-17659-4_6
9. Goldreich, O.: Foundations of Cryptography, Volume 2: Basic Applications. Cambridge University Press, Cambridge (2004)
10. Havas, G., Majewski, B.S., Wormald, N.C., Czech, Z.J.: Graphs, hypergraphs and hashing. In: van Leeuwen, J. (ed.) WG 1993. LNCS, vol. 790, pp. 153–165. Springer, Heidelberg (1994). https://doi.org/10.1007/3-540-57899-4_49
11. Hazay, C., Lindell, Y.: Efficient protocols for set intersection and pattern matching with security against malicious and covert adversaries. J. Cryptology **23**(3), 422–456 (2010). https://doi.org/10.1007/s00145-008-9034-x
12. Huang, Y., Evans, D., Katz, J.: Private set intersection: are garbled circuits better than custom protocols? In: NDSS (2012)

13. Huberman, B.A., Franklin, M.K., Hogg, T.: Enhancing privacy and trust in electronic communities. In: EC, pp. 78–86 (1999)
14. Ion, M., et al.: Private intersection-sum protocol with applications to attributing aggregate ad conversions. ePrint Archive 2017/738 (2017)
15. Ishai, Y., Kilian, J., Nissim, K., Petrank, E.: Extending oblivious transfers efficiently. In: Boneh, D. (ed.) CRYPTO 2003. LNCS, vol. 2729, pp. 145–161. Springer, Heidelberg (2003). https://doi.org/10.1007/978-3-540-45146-4_9
16. Jarecki, S., Liu, X.: Efficient oblivious pseudorandom function with applications to adaptive OT and secure computation of set intersection. In: Reingold, O. (ed.) TCC 2009. LNCS, vol. 5444, pp. 577–594. Springer, Heidelberg (2009). https://doi.org/10.1007/978-3-642-00457-5_34
17. Kirsch, A., Mitzenmacher, M., Wieder, U.: More robust hashing: cuckoo hashing with a stash. SIAM J. Comput. 39(4), 1543–1561 (2009)
18. Kolesnikov, V., Kumaresan, R.: Improved OT extension for transferring short secrets. In: Canetti, R., Garay, J.A. (eds.) CRYPTO 2013. LNCS, vol. 8043, pp. 54–70. Springer, Heidelberg (2013). https://doi.org/10.1007/978-3-642-40084-1_4
19. Kolesnikov, V., Kumaresan, R., Rosulek, M., Trieu, N.: Efficient batched OPRF with applications to PSI. In: ACM CCS (2016)
20. Meadows, C.: A more efficient cryptographic matchmaking protocol for use in the absence of a continuously available third party. In: IEEE S&P (1986)
21. Meadows, C.A.: A more efficient cryptographic matchmaking protocol for use in the absence of a continuously available third party. In: Proceedings of the 1986 IEEE Symposium on Security and Privacy, Oakland, California, USA, 7–9 April 1986, pp. 134–137 (1986)
22. Naor, M., Pinkas, B.: Efficient oblivious transfer protocols. In: Kosaraju, S.R. (ed.) 12th SODA, pp. 448–457. ACM-SIAM, January 2001
23. Orrú, M., Orsini, E., Scholl, P.: Actively secure 1-out-of-N OT extension with application to private set intersection. In: Handschuh, H. (ed.) CT-RSA 2017. LNCS, vol. 10159, pp. 381–396. Springer, Cham (2017). https://doi.org/10.1007/978-3-319-52153-4_22
24. Pagh, A., Pagh, R.: Uniform hashing in constant time and optimal space. SIAM J. Comput. 38(1), 85–96 (2008)
25. Pagh, R., Rodler, F.F.: Cuckoo hashing. J. Algorithms 51(2), 122–144 (2004)
26. Pinkas, B., Rosulek, M., Trieu, N., Yanai, A.: SpOT-light: lightweight private set intersection from sparse OT extension. In: Boldyreva, A., Micciancio, D. (eds.) CRYPTO 2019. LNCS, vol. 11694, pp. 401–431. Springer, Cham (2019). https://doi.org/10.1007/978-3-030-26954-8_13
27. Pinkas, B., Rosulek, M., Trieu, N., Yanai, A.: PSI from PaXoS: fast, malicious private set intersection. ePrint archive 2020/193 (2020)
28. Pinkas, B., Schneider, T., Tkachenko, O., Yanai, A.: Efficient circuit-based PSI with linear communication. In: Ishai, Y., Rijmen, V. (eds.) EUROCRYPT 2019. LNCS, vol. 11478, pp. 122–153. Springer, Cham (2019). https://doi.org/10.1007/978-3-030-17659-4_5
29. Pinkas, B., Schneider, T., Weinert, C., Wieder, U.: Efficient circuit-based PSI via cuckoo hashing. In: Nielsen, J.B., Rijmen, V. (eds.) EUROCRYPT 2018. LNCS, vol. 10822, pp. 125–157. Springer, Cham (2018). https://doi.org/10.1007/978-3-319-78372-7_5
30. Pinkas, B., Schneider, T., Zohner, M.: Faster private set intersection based on OT extension. In: USENIX 2014, pp. 797–812 (2014)
31. Pinkas, B., Schneider, T., Zohner, M.: Scalable private set intersection based on OT extension. ACM Trans. Priv. Secur. 21(2), 7:1–7:35 (2018)

32. Rabin, M.O.: How to exchange secrets with oblivious transfer. ePrint Archive 2005/187 (2005)
33. Rindal, P., Rosulek, M.: Improved private set intersection against malicious adversaries. In: Coron, J.-S., Nielsen, J.B. (eds.) EUROCRYPT 2017. LNCS, vol. 10210, pp. 235–259. Springer, Cham (2017). https://doi.org/10.1007/978-3-319-56620-7_9
34. Rindal, P., Rosulek, M.: Malicious-secure private set intersection via dual execution. In: Thuraisingham, B.M., Evans, D., Malkin, T., Xu, D. (eds.) ACM CCS 2017, pp. 1229–1242. ACM Press, October 2017
35. Shamir, A.: On the power of commutativity in cryptography. In: de Bakker, J., van Leeuwen, J. (eds.) ICALP 1980. LNCS, vol. 85, pp. 582–595. Springer, Heidelberg (1980). https://doi.org/10.1007/3-540-10003-2_100

Two-Round Oblivious Transfer
from CDH or LPN

Nico Döttling[1(✉)], Sanjam Garg[2(✉)], Mohammad Hajiabadi[2], Daniel Masny[3], and Daniel Wichs[4]

[1] CISPA Helmholtz Center for Information Security, Saarbrücken, Germany
doettling@cispa-helmholtz.de
[2] UC Berkeley, Berkeley, USA
sanjamg@berkeley.edu
[3] VISA Research, Palo Alto, USA
[4] Northeastern University, Boston, USA

Abstract. We show a new general approach for constructing maliciously-secure two-round oblivious transfer (OT). Specifically, we provide a generic sequence of transformations to upgrade a very basic notion of two-round OT, which we call *elementary OT*, to UC-secure OT. We then give simple constructions of elementary OT under the Computational Diffie-Hellman (CDH) assumption or the Learning Parity with Noise (LPN) assumption, yielding the first constructions of malicious (UC-secure) two-round OT under these assumptions. Since two-round OT is complete for two-round 2-party and multi-party computation in the malicious setting, we also achieve the first constructions of the latter under these assumptions.

1 Introduction

Oblivious transfer (OT) [Rab05, EGL85], is a fundamental primitive in cryptography. An OT protocol consists of two parties: a *sender* and a *receiver*. The sender's input is composed of two strings (m_0, m_1) and the receiver's input is a bit c. At the end of the execution of the OT protocol, the receiver should only learn the value m_c, but should not learn anything about the other value m_{1-c}. The sender should gain no information about the choice bit c. This very simple primitive is often used as the foundational building block for realizing secure computation protocols [Yao82, GMW87]. Thus, the efficiency characteristics of the OT protocol directly affect the efficiency of the resulting secure computation

S. Garg—Supported in part from AFOSR Award FA9550-19-1-0200, AFOSR YIP Award, NSF CNS Award 1936826, DARPA and SPAWAR under contract N66001-15-C-4065, a Hellman Award and research grants by the Okawa Foundation, Visa Inc., and Center for Long-Term Cybersecurity (CLTC, UC Berkeley). The views expressed are those of the authors and do not reflect the official policy or position of the funding agencies.
D. Masny—Part of the research was done at UC Berkeley supported by the Center for Long-Term Cybersecurity (CLTC, UC Berkeley).
D. Wichs—Research supported by NSF grants CNS-1314722, CNS-1413964, CNS-1750795 and the Alfred P. Sloan Research Fellowship.

A. Canteaut and Y. Ishai (Eds.): EUROCRYPT 2020, LNCS 12106, pp. 768–797, 2020.
https://doi.org/10.1007/978-3-030-45724-2_26

protocol. As such, several notions of OT, achieving varying security and efficiency properties, have been devised (see e.g., [Lin16]). Ideally, we want to achieve a *simulation-based* definition of OT, where we require that malicious behavior in the real world can be simulated in an ideal world with an ideal OT functionality, and even more desirably, we want to do so in the *universal composability* (UC) framework [Can01].

OT in Two-Rounds. As the name suggests, a two-round OT protocols allows the OT functionality to be implemented in just the minimal two-rounds of communication. Namely, the receiver sends the first-round message based on her input bit c. Next, using his input (m_0, m_1) and the first message of the protocol, the sender generates and sends the second-round message of the protocol. Finally, the receiver uses the second-round protocol message to recover m_c.

OT protocols that require *only* two rounds of communication are often desirable. Most importantly, two-round OT protocols are complete (necessary and sufficient) for general two-round (i.e., round optima) two-party [Yao82] and multiparty secure computation (2PC, MPC) [GS18,BL18] in both the semi-honest and malicious settings. Unfortunately, constructing two-round OT is typically much harder than constructing OT protocols with a larger round complexity. In particular, by relying on ZK proofs, we can construct constant-round malicious OT assuming only constant-round semi-honest OT and the latter follows from essentially all known assumptions that imply public-cryptography. On the other hand, no such equivalence is known for 2-round protocols since zero-knowledge proofs add more round. Furthermore, we know that two-round simulation-secure malicious OT is impossible in the plain model, and therefore we consider security in the common reference string (CRS) model.

Assumptions. Over the years, tremendous progress has been made in constructing both *semi-honest* and *maliciously* secure two-round OT protocols [CCM98, NP01, AIR01, DHRS04, PVW08, HK12, BD18] from a wide variety of assumptions. However, there are still gaps in our understanding—namely, constructing two-round OT typically requires stronger assumptions than what known to be sufficient for just OT. This is especially true for the case of maliciously secure OT. In this work, we attempt to bridge this gap. More specifically, we ask:

> *Can maliciously secure two-round OT and be based on the Computational Diffie-Hellman (CDH) assumption or the Learning Parity with Noise (LPN) assumption?*

Since two-round malicious (UC) OT is complete for two-round malicious (UC) 2PC and MPC, the above is equivalent to asking whether the latter can be instantiated under the CDH and LPN assumptions. While constructions of UC-secure two-round OT under the Decisional Diffie-Hellman (DDH) assumption and the Learning with Errors (LWE) assumption are known [PVW08], the question of constructing the same under CDH and LPN has so far remained open. Moreover, we do not even have two-round constructions under CDH or LPN that satisfy any alternate weaker notions of malicious OT security that have been previously proposed in the literature.

1.1   Why Is Two-Round Maliciously Secure OT Difficult?

One reason that (two-round) OT is difficult to construct is that this notion is even difficult to define. Simulation-based definitions of security are complex and impose requirements that often seem stronger than necessary and hard to achieve. Unlike (say) public-key encryption, where we have simple game-based definitions that imply simulation-based (semantic) security, we do not have any simpler definitions of malicious OT security that suffice for simulation. All prior attempts from the literature to weaken the definition of OT security are still complex and require some form of extraction/simulation. In particular, to meaningfully define that the malicious receiver only learns one of the two sender values m_0, m_1, all known definitions require that we can somehow *extract* the receiver's choice bit c from the first OT message and then argue that the second message hides the value m_{1-c}.

To meet any such extraction-based definition, we need to start with an OT where the receiver's choice bit is statistically committed in the first OT message. This seems like a significant restriction. For example there is a natural construction of OT from CDH due to Bellare and Micali [BM90], which achieves semi-honest security in the standard model or a weak form of malicious security in the random-oracle model. However, in this construction, the first message only commits the receiver computationally to the choice bit and hence there is no hope of extracting it. Therefore, it appears difficult to prove any meaningful notion of malicious security without resorting to the random oracle model.

Overall, we are aware of only two approaches towards achieving maliciously-secure OT. The first starts with semi-honest OT and then compiles it to malicious OT using zero-knowledge proofs. Unfortunately, if we want two-round OT we would need to use non-interactive zero-knowledge (NIZK) proofs and we do not have instantiations of such NIZKs under many natural assumptions such as CDH or LPN (or LWE). The other approach, used by Peikert, Vaikuntanathan and Waters [PVW08] (and to some extent also e.g., [NP01, AIR01, BD18]) takes advantage of a statistically "lossy" mode of DDH/LWE based encryption. Unfortunately, we do not have any such analogous "lossy" mode for CDH/LPN based encryption and therefore this approach too appears to be fundamentally stuck.

1.2   Our Results

In this work, we give a new general approach for constructing UC-secure two-round OT.[1] Specifically, we introduce an extremely weak and simple notion of two-round OT, which we call *elementary* OT. This notion is defined via a game-based definition and, in contrast to all prior notions of OT, does not rely on an extractor. We then provide a series of generic transformations that upgrade the security of elementary OT, eventually culminating in a UC-secure two-round OT. These transformations are the main technically challenging contributions of the

---

[1] Although we achieve UC security, it does not appear that achieving stand-alone security would make our solutions significantly simpler.

paper. Lastly, we show simple constructions of two-round *elementary* OT under the Computational Diffie-Hellman (CDH) assumption or the Learning Parity with Noise (LPN) assumption, yielding the first constructions of UC-secure two-round OT under these assumptions. We rely on a variant of LPN with noise-rate $1/n^\varepsilon$ for some arbitrary constant $\varepsilon > \frac{1}{2}$.[2]

Applications to Two-Round MPC. As mentioned earlier, two-round OT is known to be complete for constructing two-round MPC [GS18, BL18]. Thus, our results also yield the first constructions of two-round malicious (UC-secure) MPC under the Computational Diffie-Hellman (CDH) assumption or the Learning Parity with Noise (LPN) assumption.

Open Problems. Interestingly, our generic transformations use garbled circuits that make a non-black-box use of the underlying cryptographic primitives. We leave it as an open problem to obtain a black-box construction or show the impossibility thereof.

Follow-Up Work. Subsequently to our work, techniques and results of our paper were used in some follow-up works. Lombardi et al. [LQR+19] used our main result to obtain the first construction of maliciously-secure designated-verifier NIZK (MDV-NIZK) from CDH. MDV-NIZK may be though of as a two-round ZK protocol in the CRS model with a reusable first-round message. Technically, [LQR+19] gives constructionist of MDV-NIZK from a combination of key-dependent-message (KDM) secure private-key encryption for projection functions and a receiver-extractable two-round OT protocol. (See Definition 15.) They used the main result of our paper in order to realize their OT component. (The KDM component is already known from CDH [BLSV18].) In another work, Döttling, Garg and Malavolta [DGM19] use and extend techniques form our work (especially those from Sect. 6) in order to build protocols for Malicious Laconic Function Evaluation (among others).

2   Technical Overview

Our results are obtained via a sequence of transformations between various notions of OT. We give an overview of this sequence in Fig. 1 and explain each of the steps below. All of the notions of OT that we consider are two-round and can rely on a *common reference string* (CRS), which is generated by a trusted third party and given to both the sender and the receiver. For simplicity, we often ignore the CRS in the discussion below.

Elementary OT. We begin by defining an extremely weak and simple notion of OT, called elementary OT. The receiver uses her choice bit c to generate a first round message otr. The sender then uses otr to generate a second-round message ots together with two values y_0, y_1. The receiver gets ots and uses it to recover the value y_c. Note that, unlike in standard OT, the sender does not choose the

---

[2] This is marginally stronger than the variant used in constructing public-key encryption due to Alekhnovich [Ale03], which relies on a noise-rate $1/\Theta(n^{1/2})$.

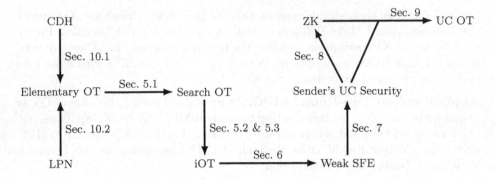

Fig. 1. Sequence of transformations leading to our results.

two values y_0, y_1 himself, but instead generates them together with ots. (One may think of this as analogous to the distinction between key-encapsulation and encryption.) The security of elementary OT is defined via the following two game-based requirements:

1. Receiver Security: The receiver's choice bit c is computationally hidden by the first-round OT message otr.
2. Sender Security: A malicious receiver who creates the first-round message otr maliciously and is then given an honestly generated second-round message ots cannot simultaneously output both of the values y_0, y_1 except with negligible probability.

Note that elementary OT provides a very weak notion of sender security. Firstly, it only provides unpredictability, rather than indistinguishability, based security – the malicious receiver cannot output both values y_0, y_1, but may learn some partial information about each of the two values. Second of all, it does not require that the there is a consistent bit w such that the value y_w is hidden from the malicious receiver – it may be that, even after the receiver maliciously chooses otr, for some choices of ots she learns y_0 and for other choices she learns y_1. We fix the second issue first.

From Elementary OT to Search OT. We define a strengthening of elementary OT, which we call *search OT*. The syntax and the receiver security remain the same. For sender security, we still keep an unpredictability (search) based security definition. But now we want to ensure that, for any choice of the malicious receiver's message otr, there is a consistent bit w such that y_w is hidden. We want to capture this property without requiring the existence of an (even inefficient) extractor that can find such w. We do so as follows. For any choice of the malicious receiver's first message otr (along with all her random coins and the CRS), we define two probabilities $\varepsilon_0, \varepsilon_1$ which denote the probability of the receiver outputting y_0 and y_1 respectively, taken only over the choice of ots. We require that for any polynomial p, with overwhelming probability over the receiver's choices, at least one of ε_0 or ε_1 is smaller than $1/p$. In particular, this means that with overwhelming probability over the malicious receiver's choice of otr, there is a fixed and consistent bit w such that the receiver will be unable to recover y_w from the sender's message ots. Note that the value w may not be extractable (even inefficiently) from otr alone since the way that w is defined is "adversary-dependent".

To go from elementary OT to search OT, we rely on techniques from "hardness amplification". The difficulty of using a search-OT adversary to break elementary-OT security is that a search-OT adversary can, for example, have $\varepsilon_0 = \varepsilon_1 = \frac{1}{2}$, but for half the value of ots it outputs the correct y_0 and for half it outputs the correct y_1, yet it never output both correct values simultaneously. However, if we could ensure that $\varepsilon_0, \varepsilon_1$ are both much larger than $\frac{1}{2}$, then this could not happen. We use hardness amplification to achieve this. In particular, we construct search OT scheme from elementary OT by having the sender generate λ (security parameter) different second-round messages of the elementary OT and set the search OT values to be the concatenations $\mathsf{OTS} = (\mathsf{ots}^1, \dots, \mathsf{ots}^\lambda)$ and $Y_0 = (y_0^1, \dots, y_0^\lambda), Y_1 = (y_1^1, \dots, y_1^\lambda)$. By hardness amplification, if for some choice of otr the malicious receiver can separately predict each of Y_0, Y_1 with probability better than some inverse polynomial $1/p$, then that means it can separately predict each of the components y_0, y_1 with extremely high probability $> \frac{3}{4}$, and by the union bound, can therefore predict both components y_0, y_1 simultaneously with probability $> \frac{1}{4}$.

From Search OT to Indistinguishability OT. Next, we define a notion that we call *indistinguishability OT*. Here, just like in standard OT, the sender gets to choose his two values m_0, m_1 himself, rather than having the scheme generate values y_0, y_1 for him, as was the case in elementary and search OT. The receiver security remains the same as in elementary and search OT: the receiver's choice bit c is hidden by her first-round message otr. The sender security is defined in a similar manner to search OT, except that we now require indistinguishability rather than unpredictability. In particular, the malicious receiver chooses two values m_0, m_1 and a maliciously generated otr. For any such choice, we define two probabilities $\varepsilon_0, \varepsilon_1$, where ε_b denotes the receiver's advantage, calculated only over the random coins of the sender, in distinguishing between ots generated with the messages (m_0, m_1) versus (m'_0, m'_1) where m'_b is uniformly random and $m'_{1-b} = m_{1-b}$. We require that for any polynomial p, with overwhelming probability over the receiver's choices, at least one of ε_0 or ε_1 is smaller than $1/p$. In particular, this means that, with overwhelming probability, the malicious receiver's choice of otr fixes a consistent bit w such that the receiver does not learn anything about m_w.

To go from search OT to indistinguishability OT with 1-bit values m_0, m_1, we rely on the Goldreich-Levin hardcore bit [GL89]. In particular, we use search OT to generate ots along with values y_0, y_1 and then use the Goldreich-Levin hardcore bits of y_0, y_1 to mask m_0, m_1 respectively. To then allow for multi-bit values m_0, m_1, we simply have the sender send each bit separately, by reusing the same receiver message otr for all bits.

From Indistinguishability OT to Weak SFE. Next, we generalize from OT and define a weak form of (two-round) *secure function evaluation (weak-SFE)*. Here, there is a receiver with an input x and a sender with a circuit f. The receiver learns the output $f(x)$ in the second round. We define a very simple (but weak) game-based notion of malicious security, without relying on a simulator or extractor:

- Receiver Security: The receiver's first-round message hides the input x from the sender.
- Sender Security: A malicious receiver cannot distinguish between any two functionally equivalent circuits f_0, f_1 used by the sender.

We show how to compile indistinguishability OT to weak SFE. Indeed, the construction is the same as the standard construction of (standard) SFE from (standard) OT: the receiver sends first-round OT messages corresponding to the bits of the input x and the sender creates a garbled circuit for f and uses the two input labels as the values for the second-round OT messages.

The proof of sender security, however, is very different than that for the standard construction of SFE from OT, which relies on extracting the receiver's OT choice bits. Instead, we rely on technical ideas that are similar to and inspired by those recently used in the context of *distinguisher-dependent simulation* [JKKR17] and have a sequence of hybrids that depends on the adversary. More concretely, indistinguishability OT guarantees that for each input wire, there is some bit w such that the adversary cannot tell if we replace the label for w by uniform. However, this bit w is defined in an adversary-dependent manner. This effectively allows us to extract the adversary's OT choice bits. Therefore, we have a sequence of adversary-dependent hybrids where we switch the OT values used by the sender and replace the labels for the bits w by random values. We then rely on garbled circuit security to argue that garblings of f_0 and f_1 are indistinguishable, and conclude that the adversary's advantage is negligible.

Formalizing the above high-level approach is the most technically involved component of the paper.

From Weak SFE to OT with UC Sender Security. We show how to go from weak SFE to an OT scheme that has UC-security for the sender. In particular, this means we can extract the choice bit c from the receiver's first-round message otr and simulate the sender's second-round message ots given only m_c, without knowing the "other" value m_{1-c}. For the receiver's security, we maintain the same indistinguishability-based requirement as in elementary/search/indistinguishability OT, which guarantees that the choice bit c is hidden by the first-round OT message otr. We refer to this as a "half-UC OT" for short. This is the first step where we introduce a simulation/extraction based notion of security.

Our compiler places a public-key pk of a public-key encryption (PKE) scheme to the CRS. The receiver encrypts her choice bit c under pk using randomness r and sends the resulting ciphertext $ct = E_{pk}(c; r)$ as part of her first-round OT message. At the same time, the receiver and sender run an instance of weak SFE, where the receiver's input is $x = (c, r)$ and the sender's circuit is $f_{\mathsf{pk},\mathsf{ct},m_0,m_1}(c, r)$, which output m_c if $\mathsf{ct} = \mathsf{E}_{\mathsf{pk}}(c; r)$ and $\perp$ otherwise. The indistinguishability-based security of the receiver directly follows from that of the SFE and the PKE, which together guarantees that c is hidden by the first-round message. To argue UC security of the sender, we now extract the receiver's bit c by decrypting the ciphertext ct. If ct is an encryption of c then $f_{\mathsf{pk},\mathsf{ct},m_0,m_1}$ is functionally equivalent to $f_{\mathsf{pk},\mathsf{ct},m_0',m_1'}$ where $m_c' = m_c$ and m_{1-c}' is replaced by an arbitrary value, say all 0s. Therefore, we can simulate the sender's second-round OT message by using the circuit $f_{\mathsf{pk},\mathsf{ct},m_0',m_1'}$, which only relies on knowledge of m_c without knowing m_{1-c}, and weak SFE security guarantees that this is indistinguishable from the real world.

From UC Sender Security to Full UC OT. Finally, we show how to use an OT scheme with UC-security of the sender and indistinguishability-based security for the receiver ("half-UC OT") to get a full UC-secure OT. In particular, this means that we need to simulate the receiver's first-round message without knowing c and extract two values m_0, m_1 from a malicious sender such that, if the receiver's bit was c, he would get m_c.

Before we give our actual construction, it is useful to examine a naive proposal and why it fails. In the naive proposal, the sender commits to both values m_0, m_1 using an extractable commitment (e.g., PKE where the public key is in the CRS); the parties use a half-UC OT where the sender puts the two decommitments as his OT values and also sends the commitments as part of the second-round OT message. We can extract two values m_0, m_1 from the commitment and are guaranteed that the receiver either outputs the value m_c or $\perp$ (if the decommitment he receives via the underlying OT is incorrect). But we are unable to say which of the two cases will occur. This is insufficient for full security.

We solve the above problem via two steps:

- We first give a solution using a two-round zero-knowledge (ZK) argument and an extractable commitment (both in the CRS model). The sender and receiver run the half-UC OT protocol where the receiver uses her choice bit c and the sender uses his two values m_0, m_1. In the first round, the receiver also sends the first-round verifier message of the ZK argument. In the second round, the sender also commits to his two messages m_0, m_1 using an extractable commitment and uses the ZK argument system to prove that he computed the second-round OT message correctly using the same values m_0, m_1 as in the commitment. This provides UC security for the receiver since, if the ZK argument verifies, we can extract the values m_0, m_1 from the commitment and know that the receiver would recover the correct value m_c. The transformation also preserves UC security for the sender since the ZK argument can be simulated.
- We then show how to construct a two-round ZK argument using half-UC OT. We rely on a Σ-protocol for NP where the prover sends a value a, receives a 1-bit challenge $b \in \{0, 1\}$, and sends a response z; the verifier checks that the transcript (a, b, z) is valid for the statement being proved and accepts or

rejects accordingly. We can compile a Σ-protocol to a two-round ZK argument using OT. The verifier sends a first-round OT message for a random bit b. The prover chooses a and computes both responses z_0, z_1 corresponding to both possible values of the challenge b; he then sends a and uses z_0, z_1 as the values for the second-round OT message. The verifier recovers z_b from the OT and checks that (a, b, z_b) is a valid transcript of the Σ-protocol. We repeat this in parallel λ (security parameter) times to get negligible soundness error. It turns out that we can prove ZK security by relying on the UC-security for the sender; we can extract the OT choice bits b in each execution and then simulate the Σ-protocol transcript after knowing the challenge bit b. It would also be easy to prove soundness using UC-security for the receiver, but we want to only rely on a "half-UC" OT where we only have indistinguishability security of the receiver. To solve this, we rely on a special type of "extractable" Σ-protocol [HL18] in the CRS model, where, for every choice of a there is a unique "bad challenge" b such that, if the statement is false, there exists a valid response z that results in a valid transcript (a, b, z). Furthermore, this unique bad challenge b should be efficiently extractable from a using a trapdoor to the CRS. Such "extractable" Σ-protocols can be constructed from only public-key encryption. If the Σ-protocol is extractable and the OT scheme has indistinguishability-based receiver security then the resulting two-round ZK is computationally sound. This is because, the only way that the prover can succeed is if in each of the λ invocations he chooses a first message a such that the receiver's OT choice bit b is the unique bad challenge for a, but this means that the prover can predict the receiver's OT choice bits (the reduction uses the trapdoor for the Σ-protocol to extract the unique bad challenge from a).

Combined together, the above two steps give a general compiler from half-UC OT to fully secure UC OT.

Instantiation from CDH. We now give our simple instantiation of elementary OT under the CDH assumption. The construction is based on a scheme of Bellare and Micali [BM90], which achieves a weak form of malicious security in the random-oracle model. Our protocol is somewhat simplified and does not require a random oracle. Recall that the CDH assumption states that, given a generator g of some cyclic group $\mathbb{G}$ of order p, along with values g^a, g^b for random $a, b \in \mathbb{Z}_p$, it is hard to compute g^{ab}.

The CRS of the OT scheme consists of $A = g^a$ for random $a \in \mathbb{Z}_p$. The receiver with a choice bit c computes two value $h_c = g^r$ and $h_{1-c} = A/h_c$ for a random $r \in \mathbb{Z}_p$ and sends $\mathsf{otr} := h_0$ as the first-round OT message. The sender computes $h_1 = A/h_0$. It chooses a random $b \in \mathbb{Z}_p$, sets $\mathsf{ots} := B = g^b$ as the second-round message, and generates the two values $y_0 = h_0^b, y_1 = h_1^b$. The receiver outputs $\hat{y}_c = B^r$.

This ensures correctness since $\hat{y}_c = B^r = g^{br} = h_c^b = y_c$. Also, h_0 is uniformly random over $\mathbb{G}$ no matter what the receiver bit c is, and therefore this provides (statistic) indistinguishability-based receiver security. Lastly, we argue that we get elementary OT security for the sender, meaning that a malicious receiver cannot simultaneously compute both y_0, y_1. Note that the only values seen by the malicious receiver during the game are $A = g^a, B = g^b$. If the receiver outputs $y_0 = h_0^b, y_1 = h_1^b = (A/h_0)^b$ then we can use these values to compute $y_0 \cdot y_1 = A^b = g^{ab}$, which breaks CDH.

Instantiation from LPN. We also give a simple instantiation of elementary OT under the LPN assumption. This construction closely mirrors the CDH one. We use a variant of the LPN problem with noise-rate $1/n^\varepsilon$ for an arbitrary constant $\varepsilon > \frac{1}{2}$. We also rely on a variant of the LPN problem where the secret is chosen from the error distribution, which is known to be equivalent to standard LPN where the secret is uniformly random [ACPS09]. In particular this variant of the LPN problem states that, for a Bernoulli distribution $\mathcal{B}_\rho$ which outputs 1 with probability $\rho = 1/n^\varepsilon$, and for $A \leftarrow \mathbb{Z}_2^{n \times n}$, $s, e \leftarrow \mathcal{B}_\rho^n$, the values $(A, sA + e)$ are indistinguishable from uniformly random values.

The CRS of the OT scheme consists of a tuple (A, v) where $A \leftarrow \mathbb{Z}_2^{n \times n}$ and $v \leftarrow \mathbb{Z}_2^n$. The receiver chooses $x, e \leftarrow \mathcal{B}_\rho^n$ and sets $h_c = Ax + e$ and $h_{1-c} = v - h_c$ and sends $\mathsf{otr} = h_0$ as the first-round OT message. The sender computes $h_1 = h_0 + v$, chooses $S, E \leftarrow \mathcal{B}_\rho^{\lambda \times n}$ where λ is the security parameter and sends $\mathsf{ots} := B = SA + E$ as the second-round OT message. The sender computes the values $y_0 = Sh_0, y_1 = Sh_1$. The receiver outputs $\hat{y}_c = Bx$.

This ensures correctness with a small inverse-polynomial error probability. In particular, $y_c = Sh_c = S(Ax + e) = Bx + Se - Ex = \hat{y}_c + (Se - Ex)$ where $Ex + Se = 0$ except with a small error probability, which we can make an arbitrarily small inverse polynomial in λ by setting n to be a sufficiently large polynomial in λ. The receiver's (computational) indistinguishability-based security holds under LPN since h_0 is indistinguishable from uniform no matter what c is. We also get elementary OT security for the sender under the LPN assumption. A malicious receiver only sees the values A, v and $B = SA + E$ during the game. If the receiver outputs $y_0 = Sh_0, y_1 = Sh_1$, then we can use it to compute $y_0 + y_1 = S(h_0 + h_1) = Sv$. But, since S is hard to compute given A, B, we can argue that Sv is indistinguishable form uniform under the LPN assumption, by thinking of the i'th of Sv as a Goldreich-Levin hardcore bit for the i'th row of S. Therefore, is should be hard to output Sv except with negligible probability.

The fact that we get a small (inverse polynomial) error probability does not affect the security of the generic transformations going from elementary OT to indistinguishability OT for 1-bit messages. Then, when we go from 1-bit messages to multi-bit messages we can also use an error-correcting code to amplify correctness and get a negligible correctness error.

3   Preliminaries

Notation. We use λ for the security parameter. We use $\overset{c}{\equiv}$ to denote computational indistinguishability between two distributions and use $\equiv$ to denote two distributions are identical. For a distribution D we use $x \overset{\$}{\leftarrow} D$ to mean x is sampled according to D and use $y \in D$ to mean y is in the support of D. For a set S we overload the notation to use $x \overset{\$}{\leftarrow} S$ to indicate that x is chosen uniformly at random from S.

3.1   Basic Inequalities

Lemma 1 (Markov Inequality for Advantages). *Let $A(Z)$ and $B(Z)$ be two random variables depending on a random variable Z and potentially additional random choices. Assume that $|\Pr_Z[A(Z) = 1] - \Pr_Z[B(Z) = 1]| \geq \epsilon \geq 0$. Then*

$$\Pr_Z[|\Pr[A(Z) = 1] - \Pr[B(Z) = 1]| \geq \epsilon/2] \geq \epsilon/2.$$

Proof. Let $a := \Pr_Z[|\Pr[A(Z) = 1] - \Pr[B(Z) = 1]| \geq \epsilon/2]$. We have $\epsilon \leq a \times 1 + (1 - a) \times \epsilon/2$. Since $0 \leq 1 - a \leq 1$, we obtain $\epsilon \leq a + \epsilon/2$. The inequality now follows. $\square$

Theorem 2 (Hoeffding Inequality). *Let $X_1, \ldots, X_N \in [0,1]$ be i.i.d. random variables with expectation $E[X_1]$. Then it holds that*

$$\Pr\left[\left|\frac{1}{N}\sum_i X_i - E[X_1]\right| > \delta\right] \leq 2e^{-2N\delta^2}.$$

3.2   Standard Primitives

Definition 3 (PKE). *The notion of CPA security for a PKE scheme $\mathsf{PKE} = (\mathsf{KeyGen}, \mathsf{E}, \mathsf{Dec})$ is standard. We say that PKE is perfectly correct if $\Pr[\exists(\mathsf{m}, \mathsf{r})$ s.t. $\mathsf{Dec}(\mathsf{sk}, \mathsf{E}(\mathsf{pk}, \mathsf{m}; \mathsf{r})) \neq \mathsf{m}] = \mathsf{negl}(\lambda)$, where $(\mathsf{pk}, \mathsf{sk}) \overset{\$}{\leftarrow} \mathsf{KeyGen}(1^\lambda)$.*

Definition 4 (Garbled Circuits). *A garbling scheme for a class of circuits $\mathcal{C}$ with n-bit inputs consists of $(\mathsf{Garble}, \mathsf{Eval}, \mathsf{Sim})$ with the following correctness and security properties.*

- *Correctness: for all $\mathsf{C} \in \mathcal{C}$, $\mathsf{x} \in \{0,1\}^n$, we have $\Pr[\mathsf{Eval}(\widehat{\mathsf{C}}, \mathsf{GarbleInput}(\vec{\mathsf{lb}}^0, \vec{\mathsf{lb}}^1, \mathsf{x})) = \mathsf{C}(\mathsf{x})] = 1$, where $(\widehat{\mathsf{C}}, \vec{\mathsf{lb}}^0, \vec{\mathsf{lb}}^1) \overset{\$}{\leftarrow} \mathsf{Garble}(1^\lambda, \mathsf{C})$, $\vec{\mathsf{lb}}^0 := (\mathsf{lb}_1^0, \ldots, \mathsf{lb}_n^0)$, $\vec{\mathsf{lb}}^1 := (\mathsf{lb}_1^1, \ldots, \mathsf{lb}_n^1)$ and we define $\mathsf{GarbleInput}(\vec{\mathsf{lb}}^0, \vec{\mathsf{lb}}^1, \mathsf{x}) := (\mathsf{lb}_1^{\mathsf{x}_1}, \ldots, \mathsf{lb}_n^{\mathsf{x}_n})$.*
- *Security: For any $\mathsf{C} \in \mathcal{C}$ and $\mathsf{x} \in \{0,1\}^n$: $(\widehat{\mathsf{C}}, \mathsf{GarbleInput}(\vec{\mathsf{lb}}^0, \vec{\mathsf{lb}}^1, \mathsf{x})) \overset{c}{\equiv} \mathsf{Sim}(1^\lambda, \mathsf{C}(\mathsf{x}))$, where $(\widehat{\mathsf{C}}, \vec{\mathsf{lb}}^0, \vec{\mathsf{lb}}^1) \overset{\$}{\leftarrow} \mathsf{Garble}(1^\lambda, \mathsf{C})$.*

4   Definitions of Two-Round Oblivious Transfer

A two-round oblivious transfer (OT) protocol (we use the definition from [BGI+17]) is given by algorithms (Setup, OT_1, OT_2, OT_3), where the setup algorithm Setup generates a CRS value crs $\xleftarrow{\$}$ Setup(1^λ).[3] The receiver runs the algorithm OT_1 which takes crs and a choice bit $c \in \{0,1\}$ as input and outputs (otr, st). The receiver then sends otr to the sender, who obtains ots by evaluating $OT_2(1^\lambda, \text{otr}, m_0, m_1)$, where m_0 and m_1 (such that $m_0, m_1 \in \{0,1\}^\lambda$) are its inputs. The sender then sends ots to the receiver who obtains m_c by evaluating $OT_3(1^\lambda, \text{st}, \text{ots})$.

4.1   Correctness

We say that a two-round OT scheme is *perfectly correct*, if with probability $1 - \text{negl}(\lambda)$ over the choice of crs $\xleftarrow{\$}$ Setup(1^λ) the following holds: for every choice bit $c \in \{0,1\}$ of the receiver and input messages m_0 and m_1 of the sender, and for any (otr, st) $\in OT_1(\text{crs}, c)$ and ots $\in OT_2(\text{crs}, \text{otr}, m_0, m_1)$, we have $OT_3(\text{st}, \text{ots}) = m_c$. (Recall that $x \in \mathcal{D}$ for a distributions $\mathcal{D}$ means that x is in the support of $\mathcal{D}$.)

4.2   Receiver's Security Notions

We consider two notions of receiver's security—namely, notions that require security against a malicious sender. We describe them next.

Receiver's indistinguishability security. For every non-uniform polynomial-time adversary $\mathcal{A}$: $|\Pr[\mathcal{A}(\text{crs}, OT_1(\text{crs}, 0)) = 1] - \Pr[\mathcal{A}(\text{crs}, OT_1(\text{crs}, 1)) = 1]| = \text{negl}(\lambda)$, where crs $\xleftarrow{\$}$ Setup(1^λ).

Receiver's UC-Security. We work in Canetti's UC framework with static corruptions [Can01]. We assume familiarity with this model. We use $\mathcal{Z}$ for denoting the underlying environment. For a real protocol Π and an adversary $\mathcal{A}$, we use EXEC$_{\Pi,\mathcal{A},\mathcal{Z}}$ to denote the real-world ensemble. Also, for an ideal functionality $\mathcal{F}$ and an adversary $\mathcal{S}$ we denote IDEAL$_{\mathcal{F},\mathcal{S},\mathcal{Z}}$ to denote the ideal-world ensemble.

We say that an OT protocol OT is receiver-UC secure if for any adversary $\mathcal{A}$ corrupting the sender, there exists a simulator $\mathcal{S}$ such that for all environments $\mathcal{Z}$:

$$\text{IDEAL}_{\mathcal{F}_{\text{OT}},\mathcal{S},\mathcal{Z}} \overset{c}{\equiv} \text{EXEC}_{\text{OT},\mathcal{A},\mathcal{Z}},$$

where the ideal functionality $\mathcal{F}_{\text{OT}}$ is defined in Fig. 2. (We will follow the same style as in [CLOS02, PVW08].)

---

[3] Some variants of two-round OT do not need a CRS. In this case, we will assume Setup as the identity function.

$\mathcal{F}_{\text{OT}}$ interacts with an ideal sender **S** and an ideal receiver **R**.

1. On input $(\text{sid}, \text{sender}, m_0, m_1)$ from the sender, store (m_0, m_1).
2. On input $(\text{sid}, \text{receiver}, b)$, check if a pair of inputs (m_0, m_1) has been already recorded for session sid; if so, send m_b to **R** and send sid to the adversary and halt; else, send nothing.

Fig. 2. Ideal functionality $\mathcal{F}_{\text{OT}}$

Since our OT protocols are in the CRS model, we also give the $\mathcal{F}_{\text{CRS}}$ idea functionality below (Fig. 3).

$\mathcal{F}_{\text{CRS}}^{\mathcal{D}}$: parameterized over a distribution $\mathcal{D}$, run by parties $P_1, \ldots, P_n$, and an adversary $\mathcal{S}$:

- Whenever receiving message a message (sid, P_i, P_j) from party P_i, sample $\text{crs} \xleftarrow{\$} \mathcal{D}$ and send (sid, crs) to P_i and send $(\text{sid}, \text{crs}, P_i, P_j)$ to $\mathcal{S}$. Whenever receiving the message (sid, P_i, P_j) from P_j, send (sid, crs) to P_j and $\mathcal{S}$.

Fig. 3. Ideal functionality $\mathcal{F}_{\text{CRS}}^{\mathcal{D}}$ [CR03]

4.3 Sender's Security Notions

We consider several different notions of sender's security that we define below. In the first two notions of security, namely elementary and search notions, we change the syntax of OT_2 a bit. More specifically, instead of taking m_0 and m_1 as input, OT_2 outputs two masks y_0 and y_1 where the receiver only gets y_c, where c is the receiver's choice bit.

Sender's Elementary Security. The elementary sender security corresponds to the weakest security notion against a malicious receiver that is considered in this work. This notion requires that the receiver actually compute both the strings y_0 and y_1 used by the sender. Let $\mathcal{A} = (\mathcal{A}_1, \mathcal{A}_2)$ be an adversary. Consider the following experiment $\text{Exp}_{\text{eOT}}^{\lambda}(\mathcal{A})$:

1. Run $\text{crs} \xleftarrow{\$} \text{Setup}(1^\lambda)$.
2. Run $(\text{otr}, \text{st}) \xleftarrow{\$} \mathcal{A}_1(1^\lambda, \text{crs})$
3. Compute $(\text{ots}, y_0, y_1) \xleftarrow{\$} \text{OT}_2(\text{crs}, \text{otr})$
4. Compute $(y_0^*, y_1^*) \xleftarrow{\$} \mathcal{A}_2(\text{st}, \text{ots})$ and output 1 iff $(y_0^*, y_1^*) = (y_0, y_1)$

We say that a scheme satisfies eOT security if $\Pr[\mathsf{Exp}^\lambda_{\mathsf{eOT}}(\mathcal{A}) = 1] = \mathsf{negl}(\lambda)$.

Sender's Search Security. Next, we consider the search security notion. In this stronger security notion, the adversary is expected to still compute both y_0 and y_1 but perhaps not necessarily at the same time. More formally, let $\mathcal{A} = (\mathcal{A}_1, \mathcal{A}_2)$ be an adversary where $\mathcal{A}_2$ outputs a message y^*. Consider the following experiment $\mathsf{Exp}^{\mathsf{crs},r,w}_{\mathsf{sOT}}(\mathcal{A})$, indexed by a crs, random coins $r \in \{0,1\}^\lambda$ and a bit $w \in \{0,1\}$.

1. Run $(\mathsf{otr}, \mathsf{st}) \xleftarrow{\$} \mathcal{A}_1(1^\lambda, \mathsf{crs}; r)$
2. Compute $(\mathsf{ots}, y_0, y_1) \xleftarrow{\$} \mathsf{OT}_2(\mathsf{crs}, \mathsf{otr})$
3. Compute $y^* \xleftarrow{\$} \mathcal{A}_2(\mathsf{st}, \mathsf{ots}, w)$ and output 1 iff $y^* = y_w$

We say a PPT adversary $\mathcal{A}$ breaks the sender search privacy if there exist a non-negligible function ϵ such that

$$\Pr_{\mathsf{crs},r}[\Pr[\mathsf{Exp}^{\mathsf{crs},r,0}_{\mathsf{sOT}}(\mathcal{A}) = 1] > \epsilon \text{ and } \Pr[\mathsf{Exp}^{\mathsf{crs},r,1}_{\mathsf{sOT}}(\mathcal{A}) = 1] > \epsilon] > \epsilon,$$

where $\mathsf{crs} \xleftarrow{\$} \mathsf{Setup}(1^\lambda)$ and $r \xleftarrow{\$} \{0,1\}^\lambda$.

Sender's Indistinguishability Security (iOT). Moving on, we consider the sender's indistinguishability security notion (or the iOT notion for short). In this notion, we require that the receiver does not learn any information about either m_0 or m_1. More formally, let $\mathcal{A} = (\mathcal{A}_1, \mathcal{A}_2)$ be an adversary where $\mathcal{A}_2$ outputs a bit s. Consider the following experiment $\mathsf{Exp}^{\mathsf{crs},r,w,b}_{\mathsf{iOT}}(\mathcal{A})$, indexed by a crs, random coins $r \in \{0,1\}^\lambda$, a bit $w \in \{0,1\}$ and a bit $b \in \{0,1\}$.

1. Run $(m_0, m_1, \mathsf{otr}, \mathsf{st}) \xleftarrow{\$} \mathcal{A}_1(1^\lambda, \mathsf{crs}; r)$
2. If $b = 0$ compute $\mathsf{ots} \xleftarrow{\$} \mathsf{OT}_2(\mathsf{crs}, \mathsf{otr}, m_0, m_1)$
3. Otherwise, if $b = 1$ compute $\mathsf{ots} \xleftarrow{\$} \mathsf{OT}_2(\mathsf{crs}, \mathsf{otr}, m'_0, m'_1)$ where $m'_w \xleftarrow{\$} \{0,1\}^n$ and $m'_{1-w} = m_{1-w}$.
4. Compute and output $s \xleftarrow{\$} \mathcal{A}_2(\mathsf{st}, \mathsf{ots})$

Define the advantage of $\mathcal{A}$ as $\mathsf{Adv}^{\mathsf{crs},r,w}_{\mathsf{iOT}}(\mathcal{A}) = |\Pr[\mathsf{Exp}^{\mathsf{crs},r,w,0}_{\mathsf{iOT}}(\mathcal{A}) = 1] - \Pr[\mathsf{Exp}^{\mathsf{crs},r,w,1}_{\mathsf{iOT}}(\mathcal{A}) = 1]|$. We say a PPT adversary $\mathcal{A}$ breaks the sender's indistinguishability security if there exist a non-negligible function ϵ such that

$$\Pr_{\mathsf{crs},r}[\mathsf{Adv}^{\mathsf{crs},r,0}_{\mathsf{iOT}}(\mathcal{A}) > \epsilon \text{ and } \mathsf{Adv}^{\mathsf{crs},r,1}_{\mathsf{iOT}}(\mathcal{A}) > \epsilon] > \epsilon,$$

where $\mathsf{crs} \xleftarrow{\$} \mathsf{Setup}(1^\lambda)$ and $r \xleftarrow{\$} \{0,1\}^\lambda$.

In the experiment above, if the two messages m_0 and m_1 are single-bits, then call the notion bit iOT. Otherwise, we call the notion string iOT.

Sender's UC-Security. We say that an OT protocol OT is sender-UC secure if for any adversary $\mathcal{A}$ corrupting the receiver, there exists a simulator $\mathcal{S}$ such that for all environments $\mathcal{Z}$:

$$\text{IDEAL}_{\mathcal{F}_{\text{OT}}, \mathcal{S}, \mathcal{Z}} \stackrel{c}{\equiv} \text{EXEC}_{\text{OT}, \mathcal{A}, \mathcal{Z}},$$

where the ideal functionality $\mathcal{F}_{\text{OT}}$ is defined in Fig. 2.

Definition 5. *For* $\mathcal{X} \in \{$*elementary, search, indistinguishability*$\}$, *we call a two-round OT scheme* $\mathcal{X}$*-secure if it has sender's* $\mathcal{X}$ *security and receiver's indistinguishability security. Moreover, we call a two-round OT scheme UC-secure if it has sender's UC-security and receiver's UC-security.*

5   Transformations for Achieving Sender's Indistinguishability

In this section, we give a sequence of transformations which leads us to sender's indistinguishability security, starting with sender's elementary security.

5.1   From Elementary OT to Search OT

We rely on a result of [CHS05] on hardness amplification of weakly verifiable puzzles. In such puzzles, a puzzle generator can efficiently verify solutions but others need not be able to; we rely on a restricted case where the solution is unique and the puzzle generator generates the puzzle with the solution. The result essentially says that solving many puzzles is much harder than solving a single puzzle. For simplicity, we state a simplified version of their result (restatement of Lemma 1 in [CHS05]) with a restricted range of parameters. It shows that, if there is a "weak solver" that has some inverse polynomial advantage in solving λ puzzles simultaneously, then there is an "amplified solver" that has extremely high advantage (arbitrarily close to 1) in solving an individual puzzle.

Lemma 6 (Hardness Amplification [CHS05]). *For every polynomial p and every constant $\delta > 0$ there exists a PPT algorithm* Amp *such that the following holds for all sufficiently large $\lambda \in \mathbb{N}$. Let G be some distribution over pairs* (puzzle, solution) $\leftarrow G$. *Let* WS *be a "weak solver" such that*

$$\Pr[\text{WS}(\text{puzzle}_1, \dots, \text{puzzle}_\lambda) = (\text{solution}_1, \dots, \text{solution}_\lambda)] \geq 1/p(\lambda)$$

where (puzzle$_i$, solution$_i$) $\stackrel{\$}{\leftarrow} G$ *for $i \in \{1, \dots, \lambda\}$. Then*

$$\Pr[\text{Amp}^{\text{WS}, G}(1^\lambda, \text{puzzle}^*) = \text{solution}^*] \geq \delta$$

where (puzzle*, solution*) $\stackrel{\$}{\leftarrow} G$.

Construction of Search OT. Let $\Pi = (\text{Setup}, \text{OT}_1, \text{OT}_2, \text{OT}_3)$ be an elementary OT. We construct a search OT scheme $\Pi' = (\text{Setup}, \text{OT}_1, \text{OT}_2', \text{OT}_3')$ as follows:

- $(\mathsf{ots}', Y_0, Y_1) \xleftarrow{\$} \mathsf{OT}'_2(\mathsf{otr}')$: Sample $(\mathsf{ots}^i, \mathsf{y}^i_0, \mathsf{y}^i_1) \xleftarrow{\$} \mathsf{OT}_2(\mathsf{crs}, \mathsf{otr})$ for $i = 1, \ldots, \lambda$. Output $\mathsf{ots}' = (\mathsf{ots}^1, \ldots, \mathsf{ots}^\lambda)$ and $Y_0 = (\mathsf{y}^1_0, \ldots, \mathsf{y}^\lambda_0)$, $Y_1 = (\mathsf{y}^1_1, \ldots, \mathsf{y}^\lambda_1)$.
- $Y \xleftarrow{\$} \mathsf{OT}'_3(\mathsf{ots}', \mathsf{st})$: Parse $\mathsf{ots}' = (\mathsf{ots}^1, \ldots, \mathsf{ots}^\lambda)$. Let $\mathsf{y}_i \xleftarrow{\$} \mathsf{OT}_3(\mathsf{ots}^i, \mathsf{st})$ for $i = 1, \ldots, \lambda$. Output $Y = (\mathsf{y}_1, \ldots, \mathsf{y}_\lambda)$.

Theorem 7. *If Π is an elementary OT then Π' described above is a search OT.*

The proof can be found in the full version of the paper.

5.2 From Search OT to Bit iOT

Let $\Pi = (\mathsf{Setup}, \mathsf{OT}_1, \mathsf{OT}_2, \mathsf{OT}_3)$ be a *search OT* with message length $n = n(\lambda)$. We construct an iOT scheme $\Pi' = (\mathsf{Setup}, \mathsf{OT}'_1, \mathsf{OT}'_2, \mathsf{OT}'_3)$ with 1-bit message as follows:

- $(\mathsf{otr}', \mathsf{st}') \xleftarrow{\$} \mathsf{OT}'_1(\mathsf{crs}, b)$: Let $(\mathsf{otr}, \mathsf{st}) \xleftarrow{\$} \mathsf{OT}_1(\mathsf{crs}, b)$. Output $\mathsf{otr}' = \mathsf{otr}, \mathsf{st}' = (\mathsf{st}, b)$.
- $\mathsf{ots}' \xleftarrow{\$} \mathsf{OT}'_2(\mathsf{otr}', \mathsf{m}_0, \mathsf{m}_1)$: Sample $(\mathsf{ots}, \mathsf{y}_0, \mathsf{y}_1) \xleftarrow{\$} \mathsf{OT}_2(\mathsf{crs}, \mathsf{otr})$. Choose $s_0, s_1 \xleftarrow{\$} \{0,1\}^n$. For $b \in \{0,1\}$, let $c_b = \langle \mathsf{y}_b, s_b \rangle \oplus \mathsf{m}_b$. Output $\mathsf{ots}' = (\mathsf{ots}, s_0, s_1, c_0, c_1)$.
- $M \xleftarrow{\$} \mathsf{OT}'_3(\mathsf{st}', \mathsf{ots}')$: Parse $\mathsf{ots}' = (\mathsf{ots}, s_0, s_1, c_0, c_1)$, $\mathsf{st}' = (\mathsf{st}, b)$. Let $\mathsf{y} \xleftarrow{\$} \mathsf{OT}_3(\mathsf{ots}, \mathsf{st})$. Output $M = c_b \oplus \langle \mathsf{y}, s_b \rangle$.

Theorem 8. *If Π is a search OT then Π' is an iOT with 1-bit messages.*

The proof can be found in the full version of the paper.

5.3 From Bit iOT to String iOT

Let $\Pi = (\mathsf{Setup}, \mathsf{OT}_1, \mathsf{OT}_2, \mathsf{OT}_3)$ be an iOT scheme with 1 bit messages. Then, we construct an iOT scheme $\Pi' = (\mathsf{Setup}, \mathsf{OT}'_1, \mathsf{OT}'_2, \mathsf{OT}'_3)$ with message length $n = n(\lambda)$ as follows:

- $(\mathsf{otr}', \mathsf{st}') \xleftarrow{\$} \mathsf{OT}'_1(\mathsf{crs}, b)$: Let $(\mathsf{otr}, \mathsf{st}) \xleftarrow{\$} \mathsf{OT}_1(\mathsf{crs}, b)$. Output $\mathsf{otr}' = \mathsf{otr}, \mathsf{st}' = \mathsf{st}$.
- $\mathsf{ots}' \xleftarrow{\$} \mathsf{OT}'_2(\mathsf{otr}', \mathsf{m}_0, \mathsf{m}_1)$: For each $i \in [n]$, sample $\mathsf{ots}^{(i)} \xleftarrow{\$} \mathsf{OT}_2(\mathsf{crs}, \mathsf{otr}, \mathsf{m}^{(i)}_0, \mathsf{m}^{(i)}_1)$, where $\mathsf{m}^{(i)}_0$ and $\mathsf{m}^{(i)}_1$ are the ith bits of m_0 and m_1, respectively. Output $\mathsf{ots}' = \{\mathsf{ots}^{(i)}\}_{i \in [n]}$.
- $M \xleftarrow{\$} \mathsf{OT}'_3(\mathsf{ots}', \mathsf{st}')$: Parse $\mathsf{ots}' = \{\mathsf{ots}^{(i)}\}$, $\mathsf{st}' = (\mathsf{st}, b)$. Let $M^{(i)} \xleftarrow{\$} \mathsf{OT}_3(\mathsf{ots}^{(i)}, \mathsf{st})$ and output M.

Theorem 9. *If Π is iOT with 1-bit messages then Π' is an iOT with messages of length n.*

The proof can be found in the full version of the paper.

6   Weak Secure Function Evaluation

In this section, we will define our notion of weak secure function evaluation and provide instantiations of the new notion.

6.1   Definitions

Definition 10. *A weak secure function evaluation scheme* wSFE *for a function class $\mathcal{F}$ consists of four PPT algorithms* (Setup, Receiver$_1$, Sender, Receiver$_2$) *with the following syntax.*

Setup(1^λ): *Takes as input a security parameter and outputs a common reference string* crs

Receiver$_1$(crs, x): *Takes as input a common reference string* crs *and an input* x *and outputs a message* z_1 *and a state* st

Sender(crs, f, z_1): *Takes as input a common reference string* crs, *a function* $f \in \mathcal{F}$ *and a receiver message* z_1 *and outputs a sender message* z_2

Receiver$_2$(st, z_2): *Takes as input a state* st *and a sender message* z_2 *and outputs a value* y.

We require the following properties.

- **Correctness:** *It holds for any* λ, *any* $f \in \mathcal{F}$ *and any* x *in the domain of* f *that*
$$\text{Receiver}_2(\text{st}, \text{Sender}(\text{crs}, f, z_1)) = f(x),$$
where crs $\overset{\$}{\leftarrow}$ Setup(1^λ) *and* (z_1, st) $\overset{\$}{\leftarrow}$ Receiver$_1$(crs, x)

- **Receiver Privacy:** *Let* $\mathcal{A} = (\mathcal{A}_1, \mathcal{A}_2)$ *be an adversary where* $\mathcal{A}_2$ *outputs a bit and let the experiment* $\text{Exp}_{RP}(\mathcal{A})$ *be defined as follows:*
  - *Compute* crs $\overset{\$}{\leftarrow}$ Setup(1^λ)
  - *Compute* $(x_0, x_1) \overset{\$}{\leftarrow} \mathcal{A}_1(\text{crs})$
  - *Choose* $b \overset{\$}{\leftarrow} \{0, 1\}$
  - *Compute* $z_1^* \overset{\$}{\leftarrow}$ Receiver$_1$(crs, x_b)
  - *Compute* $b' \overset{\$}{\leftarrow} \mathcal{A}_2(\text{crs}, z_1^*)$
  - *If* $b' = b$ *output 1, otherwise 0*

  Define $\text{Adv}_{RP}(\mathcal{A}) = |\Pr[\text{Exp}_{RP}(\mathcal{A}) = 1] - 1/2|$. *We say that* wSFE *has computational receiver privacy, if it holds for all PPT adversaries* $\mathcal{A}$ *that* $\text{Adv}_{RP}(\mathcal{A}) < \text{negl}(\lambda)$. *Likewise, we say that* wSFE *has statistical receiver privacy, if it holds for all unbounded (non-uniform) adversaries* $\mathcal{A}$ *that* $\text{Adv}_{RP}(\mathcal{A}) < \text{negl}(\lambda)$.

- **Sender Privacy:** *Let* $\mathcal{A} = (\mathcal{A}_1, \mathcal{A}_2)$ *be an adversary where* $\mathcal{A}_2$ *outputs a bit and let the experiment* $\text{Exp}_{SP}(\mathcal{A})$ *be defined as follows:*
  - *Compute* crs $\overset{\$}{\leftarrow}$ Setup(1^λ)
  - *Compute* $(f_0, f_1, z_1) \overset{\$}{\leftarrow} \mathcal{A}_1(\text{crs})$
  - *Choose* $b \overset{\$}{\leftarrow} \{0, 1\}$

- *Compute* $z_2^* \xleftarrow{\$} \mathsf{Sender}(\mathsf{crs}, f_b, z_1)$
- *Compute* $b' \xleftarrow{\$} \mathcal{A}_2(\mathsf{crs}, z_2^*)$
- *If* $b' = b$ *output 1, otherwise 0*

Define $\mathsf{Adv}_{SP}(\mathcal{A}) = |\Pr[\mathsf{Exp}_{SP}(\mathcal{A}) = 1] - 1/2|$. *We say that* wSFE *has computational sender privacy, if it holds for all PPT adversaries* $\mathcal{A} = (\mathcal{A}_1, \mathcal{A}_2)$ *which output equivalent functions* $f_0 \equiv f_1$ *in the first stage that* $\mathsf{Adv}_{SP}(\mathcal{A}) < \mathsf{negl}(\lambda)$. *Likewise, we say that* wSFE *has statistical sender privacy, if it holds for all unbounded (non-uniform) adversaries* $\mathcal{A}$ *which output equivalent functions* $f_0 \equiv f_1$ *in the first stage that* $\mathsf{Adv}_{SP}(\mathcal{A}) < \mathsf{negl}(\lambda)$.

6.2   wSFE for All Circuits from iOT and Garbled Circuits

Let $\mathsf{iOT} = (\mathsf{Setup}, \mathsf{OT}_1, \mathsf{OT}_2, \mathsf{OT}_3)$ be an iOT protocol and let $(\mathsf{Garble}, \mathsf{Eval})$ be a garbling scheme. Overloading notation, assume that if $\vec{x} = (x_1, \ldots, x_n) \in \{0,1\}^n$ is an input vector, then $\mathsf{OT}_1(\mathsf{crs}, \vec{x}) = (\mathsf{OT}_1(\mathsf{crs}, x_1), \ldots, \mathsf{OT}_1(\mathsf{crs}, x_n))$. Similarly, if $\vec{m}_0 = (m_{0,1}, \ldots, m_{0,n})$ and $\vec{m}_1 = (m_{1,1}, \ldots, m_{1,n})$ are two vectors of messages, then denote

$$\mathsf{OT}_2(\mathsf{crs}, \vec{\mathsf{otr}}, \vec{m}_0, \vec{m}_1) = (\mathsf{OT}_2(\mathsf{crs}, \mathsf{otr}^1, m_{0,1}, m_{1,1}), \ldots, \mathsf{OT}_2(\mathsf{crs}, \mathsf{otr}^n, m_{0,n}, m_{1,n}))$$

The scheme wSFE is given as follows.

$\mathsf{Setup}(1^\lambda)$: Compute and output $\mathsf{crs} \xleftarrow{\$} \mathsf{iOT.Setup}(1^\lambda)$

$\mathsf{Receiver}_1(\mathsf{crs}, \vec{x} \in \{0,1\}^n)$: Compute $(\vec{\mathsf{otr}}, \vec{\mathsf{st}}') \xleftarrow{\$} \mathsf{iOT.OT}_1(\mathsf{crs}, \vec{x})$. Output $z_1 \xleftarrow{\$} \vec{\mathsf{otr}}$ and $\mathsf{st} \xleftarrow{\$} \vec{\mathsf{st}}'$.

$\mathsf{Sender}(\mathsf{crs}, z_1 = \vec{\mathsf{otr}}, C)$:
  - Compute $(\widehat{C}, \vec{\mathsf{lb}}^0, \vec{\mathsf{lb}}^1) \xleftarrow{\$} \mathsf{Garble}(1^\lambda, C)$
  - Compute $\vec{\mathsf{ots}} \xleftarrow{\$} \mathsf{iOT.OT}_2(\mathsf{crs}, \vec{\mathsf{otr}}, \vec{\mathsf{lb}}^0, \vec{\mathsf{lb}}^1)$.
  - Output $z_2 \xleftarrow{\$} (\vec{\mathsf{ots}}, \widehat{C})$.

$\mathsf{Receiver}_2(\mathsf{st} = \vec{\mathsf{st}}', z_2)$:
  - Parse $z_2 = (\vec{\mathsf{ots}}, \widehat{C})$.
  - Compute $\vec{\mathsf{lb}} \xleftarrow{\$} \mathsf{iOT.OT}_3(\vec{\mathsf{st}}', \vec{\mathsf{ots}})$
  - Compute $m \xleftarrow{\$} \mathsf{Eval}(\widehat{C}, \vec{\mathsf{lb}})$.
  - Output m

Correctness. We will briefly argue that the scheme is correct. Thus, let $\mathsf{crs} \xleftarrow{\$} \mathsf{iOT.Setup}(1^\lambda)$ and $(\vec{\mathsf{otr}}, \vec{\mathsf{st}}) \xleftarrow{\$} \mathsf{iOT.OT}_1(\mathsf{crs}, \vec{x})$. Further let $(\widehat{C}, \vec{\mathsf{lb}}^0, \vec{\mathsf{lb}}^1) \xleftarrow{\$} \mathsf{Garble}(1^\lambda, C)$ and $\vec{\mathsf{ots}} \xleftarrow{\$} \mathsf{iOT.OT}_2(\mathsf{crs}, \vec{\mathsf{otr}}, \vec{\mathsf{lb}}^0, \vec{\mathsf{lb}}^1)$. By the correctness of iOT it holds that

$$\vec{\mathsf{lb}} = \mathsf{iOT.OT}_3(\vec{\mathsf{st}}, \vec{\mathsf{ots}}) = \mathsf{GarbleInput}(\vec{\mathsf{lb}}^0, \vec{\mathsf{lb}}^1, \vec{x}).$$

Furthermore, by the correctness of the garbling scheme $(\mathsf{Garble}, \mathsf{Eval})$ it holds that

$$m = \mathsf{Eval}(\widehat{C}, \vec{\mathsf{lb}}) = \mathsf{Eval}(\widehat{C}, \mathsf{GarbleInput}(\vec{\mathsf{lb}}^0, \vec{\mathsf{lb}}^1, \vec{x})) = C(\vec{x}),$$

and we get that wSFE is correct.

Receiver Privacy. We will first establish receiver privacy of wSFE.

Theorem 11. *Assume that iOT has receiver indistinguishability security. The* wSFE *has receiver privacy.*

The proof can be found in the full version of the paper.

Sender Privacy. We will now proceed to show sender privacy of wSFE against malicious receivers.

Theorem 12. *Assuming that iOT has indistinguishability sender privacy and that* (Garble, Eval) *is a simulation secure garbling scheme, it holds that* wSFE *has sender privacy.*

The proof can be found in the full version of the paper.

7   Sender-UC OT from wSFE

In this section we will provide a two-round OT protocol with sender's UC security and receiver's indistinguishability security from any CPA-secure PKE and a two-round wSFE for a specific class of functions.

Let $\mathsf{PKE} := (\mathsf{KeyGen}, \mathsf{E}, \mathsf{Dec})$ be a PKE scheme and let wSFE be a two-round wSFE, i.e. $\mathsf{wSFE} := (\mathsf{Setup}, \mathsf{Receiver}_1, \mathsf{Sender}, \mathsf{Receiver}_2)$, for a function class $\mathcal{F}$ defined as follows: any function in this class is of the form $C[\mathsf{pk}, \mathsf{ct}, \mathsf{m}_0, \mathsf{m}_1]$, parameterized over a public key pk, a ciphertext ct and two messages m_0 and m_1, and is defined as follows:

$C[\mathsf{pk}, \mathsf{ct}, \mathsf{m}_0, \mathsf{m}_1](b, r)$: If $\mathsf{PKE.E}(\mathsf{pk}, b; r) = \mathsf{ct}$, output m_b; otherwise $\bot$.

Construction 13 (Sender-UC OT). *The OT-protocol is based on the above two primitives* PKE *and* wSFE, *and is described as follows.*

$\mathsf{Setup}(1^\lambda)$: *Compute* $\mathsf{crs}' \xleftarrow{\$} \mathsf{wSFE.Setup}(1^\lambda)$ *and* $(\mathsf{pk}, \mathsf{sk}) \xleftarrow{\$} \mathsf{PKE.KeyGen}(1^\lambda)$. *Output* $\mathsf{crs} := (\mathsf{crs}', \mathsf{pk})$.

$\mathsf{OT}_1(\mathsf{crs} = (\mathsf{crs}', \mathsf{pk}), b)$: *Choose* $r \xleftarrow{\$} \{0, 1\}^\lambda$ *and compute* $\mathsf{ct} \xleftarrow{\$} \mathsf{PKE.E}(\mathsf{pk}, b; r)$. *Set* $\vec{x} := (b, r)$ *and compute* $(\mathsf{z}_1, \mathsf{st}) \xleftarrow{\$} \mathsf{wSFE.Receiver}_1(\mathsf{crs}', \vec{x})$. *Output* $\mathsf{otr} := (\mathsf{ct}, \mathsf{z}_1)$ *as the OT message and* st *as the private state.*

$\mathsf{OT}_2(\mathsf{crs}, \mathsf{otr}, \mathsf{m}_0, \mathsf{m}_1)$: *Parse* $\mathsf{crs} = (\mathsf{crs}', \mathsf{pk})$, $\mathsf{otr} = (\mathsf{ct}, \mathsf{z}_1)$ *and compute* $\mathsf{z}_2 \xleftarrow{\$} \mathsf{wSFE.Sender}(\mathsf{crs}', C[\mathsf{pk}, \mathsf{ct}, \mathsf{m}_0, \mathsf{m}_1], \mathsf{z}_1)$. *Output* $\mathsf{ots} := \mathsf{z}_2$.

$\mathsf{OT}_3(\mathsf{st}, \mathsf{ots})$: *Let* $\mathsf{z}_2 := \mathsf{ots}$. *Compute and output* $\mathsf{Receiver}_2(\mathsf{st}, \mathsf{z}_2)$.

Theorem 14. *Assuming* PKE *is CPA-secure and perfectly correct (Definition 3), and that* wSFE *satisfies correctness, receiver privacy and sender privacy (Definition 10), then the OT given in Construction 13 provides receiver's indistinguishability security and sender's UC security.*

The proof can be found in the full version of the paper.

Finally, we mention that the OT protocol constructed in Construction 13 satisfies a receiver-extractability property, which was (implicitly) used in the proof of sender's UC security. Since we will use this definition later, we formalize it below.

Definition 15. *We say that an OT protocol* (Setup, OT_1, OT_2, OT_3) *has receiver extractability if the setup algorithm* Setup(1^λ) *in addition to* crs *also outputs a trapdoor key* σ *and if there is a PPT algorithm* Extract, *for which the following holds: for any stateful PPT adversary* $\mathcal{A} := (\mathcal{A}_1, \mathcal{A}_2)$, *assuming* $(m_0, m_1, otr) \overset{\$}{\leftarrow} \mathcal{A}_1(crs)$ *and* $b = $ Extract(σ, otr), *then* $\mathcal{A}_2$ *cannot distinguish between the outputs of* $OT_2(crs, otr, (m_0, m_1))$ *and* $OT_2(crs, otr, (m_b, m_b))$.

8   2-Round ZK from Sender-UC OT and Σ-Protocols

In this section we give a two-round (statement-independent) ZK protocol against malicious verifiers in the CRS model based on a special type of Σ-protocols and an OT with sender's UC-security and receiver's indistinguishability security.

We first start by defining the properties we require of our Σ-protocol, and will then define the notion of statement-independent ZK protocols that we would like to achieve. Our notion of Σ-protocols is what Holmgren and Lombardi [HL18] called *extractable Σ-protocols*, defined as follows.

Definition 16 (Extractable Σ-protocols [HL18]). *A CRS-based Σ-protocol* (Setup, P, V, Extract, Sim) *for a language* L $\in$ NP *is a three-round argument system between a prover* P := (P_1, P_2) *and a verifier* V, *where the prover is the initiator of the protocol and where the verifier's only message is a random bit* $b \in \{0, 1\}$. *The setup algorithm* (crs, σ) $\overset{\$}{\leftarrow}$ Setup(1^λ) *returns a CRS value* crs *together with an associated trapdoor key* σ. *The trapdoor key* σ *will only play a role in the extractability requirement. We require the following properties:*

– *Completeness: For all λ, all* (x, w) $\in$ R *(where R is the underlying relation), we have* $\Pr[V(crs, x, a, b, z) = 1] = 1$, *where the probability is taken over* (crs, σ) $\overset{\$}{\leftarrow}$ Setup(1^λ), (a, st) $\overset{\$}{\leftarrow}$ P_1(crs, x, w), $b \overset{\$}{\leftarrow} \{0, 1\}$ *and* $z \overset{\$}{\leftarrow}$ P_2(st, b).

– *Special soundness and extractability: For any value* crs *generated as* (crs, σ) $\overset{\$}{\leftarrow}$ Setup(1^λ), *any* x $\notin$ L *and any (possibly malicious) first-round message* a, *there exists at most one* $b \in \{0, 1\}$ *for which there exists* z *such that* V(crs, x, a, b, z) = 1. *Moreover, for such parameters, this unique value of b (if any) can be computed efficiently as* Extract(σ, x, a).

– *Honest-verifier zero knowledge: For any value* crs *generated as* (crs, σ) $\overset{\$}{\leftarrow}$ Setup(1^λ), *any* $b \in \{0, 1\}$ *and any* (x, w) $\in$ R:

$$(crs, x, a, b, z) \overset{c}{\equiv} (crs, x, a', b, z'),   (1)$$

where (a, st) $\overset{\$}{\leftarrow}$ P_1(crs, x, w), $z \overset{\$}{\leftarrow}$ P_2(st, b) *and* (a', z') $\overset{\$}{\leftarrow}$ Sim(crs, x, b).

We will now define out notion of CRS-based two-round statement-independent ZK. Informally, a two-round ZK protocol is statement-independent if the verifier's message in the protocol is independent of the statement being proven.

Definition 17 (Two-round statement-independent zero knowledge). *A two-round zero-knowledge argument system for a language* $L \in NP$ *with a corresponding relation* R *in the CRS model consists of four PPT algorithms* $ZK = (Setup, P, V := (V_1, V_2), Sim := (Sim_1, Sim_2))$, *defined as follows. The setup algorithm* Setup *on input* 1^λ *outputs a value* crs. *The verifier algorithm* $V_1(crs)$ *on input* crs *returns a message* msgv *together with a private state* st. *We stress that the verifier does not take as input any statement* x, *hence the "statement-independent" name. The prover algorithm* $P(crs, x, w, msgv)$ *on input* crs, *a statement* x *with a corresponding witness* w *and a verifier's message* msgv, *outputs a message* msgp. *Finally, the algorithm* $V_2(st, x, msgp)$ *outputs a bit* b. *We require the following properties.*

- *Completeness: For all* $(x, w) \in L$ *we have* $\Pr[V_2(st, x, msgp) = 1] = 1$, *where* $crs \xleftarrow{\$} Setup(1^\lambda)$, $(msgv, st) \xleftarrow{\$} V_1(crs)$ *and* $msgp \xleftarrow{\$} P(crs, x, w, msgv)$.
- *Adaptive soundness: No PPT malicious prover can convince an honest verifier of a false statement, even if the statement is chosen adaptively after seeing* crs *and the verifier's (statement-independent) message. Formally, for any PPT adversary* P^* *the following holds:* $\Pr[V_2(st, x, msgp) = 1 \land x \notin L] = negl(\lambda)$, *where* $crs \xleftarrow{\$} Setup(1^\lambda)$, $(msgv, st) \xleftarrow{\$} V_1(crs)$, $(x, msgp) \xleftarrow{\$} P^*(crs, msgv)$.
- *Adaptive Malicious Zero-Knowledge (ZK): Let* $V^* = (V_1^*, V_2^*)$ *be a stateful two-phase adversary where* V_2^* *outputs a bit. Let the experiment* $Exp_{ZK}(V^*)$ *be defined as follows:*
  1. *Choose* $b \xleftarrow{\$} \{0, 1\}$
  2. *If* $b = 0$, *sample* $crs \xleftarrow{\$} Setup(1^\lambda)$. *Else, sample* $(crs, \sigma) \xleftarrow{\$} Sim_1(1^\lambda)$.
  3. *Let* $(x, w, msgv) \xleftarrow{\$} V_1^*(crs)$. *If* $R(x, w) = 0$, *then halt.*
  4. *If* $b = 0$, *let* $msgp \xleftarrow{\$} P(crs, x, w, msgv)$. *Else, let* $msgp \xleftarrow{\$} Sim_2(\sigma, x, msgv)$.
  5. *Compute* $b' \xleftarrow{\$} V_2^*(msgp)$.
  6. *If* $b' = b$ *output 1, otherwise 0.*

  Define $Adv_{ZK}(V^*) = |\Pr[Exp_{ZK}(V^*) = 1] - 1/2|$. *We say that the scheme is zero-knowledge if for all PPT adversaries* V^*, $Adv_{ZK}(V^*) = negl(\lambda)$.

Construction 18 (Two-round ZK). *Let* $OT := (Setup, OT_1, OT_2, OT_3)$ *be an* OT *protocol and let* $SIGM := (Setup, P, V, Extract, Sim)$ *be an extractable* Σ-*protocol for a language* $L \in NP$ *(Definition 16). We give a two-round ZK protocol* $ZK := (Setup, P, V := (V_1, V_2))$ *for* L *as follows. The construction is parameterized over a polynomial* $r := r(\lambda)$, *which we will instantiate in the soundness proof.*

- ZK.Setup(1^λ): *Run* $crs_{ot} \xleftarrow{\$} OT.Setup(1^\lambda)$ *and* $(crs_{sig}, \sigma) \xleftarrow{\$} SIGM.Setup(1^\lambda)$. *Return* $crs := (crs_{ot}, crs_{sig})$.

- ZK.V_1(crs := (crs_{ot}, crs_{sig})): *For each* $i \in [r]$, *sample* $b_i \overset{\$}{\leftarrow} \{0,1\}$. *Let* ($o\vec{t}r, \vec{st}_{ot}$) $\overset{\$}{\leftarrow}$ $OT_1(crs_{ot}, \vec{b})$, *where* $\vec{b}$:= ($b_1, \ldots, b_r$). *Return* (msgv, st), *where* msgv := $o\vec{t}r$ *is the message to the prover* P, *and* st := ($b_1, \ldots, b_r, \vec{st}_{ot}$) *is the private state.*

- ZK.P(crs := (crs_{ot}, crs_{sig}), x, w, msgv): *For each* $i \in [r]$ *sample* (a_i, sts_i) $\overset{\$}{\leftarrow}$ SIGM.P_1(crs_{sig}, x, w). *For each* $i \in [r]$ *and* $b \in \{0,1\}$, *form* $z_{i,b} \overset{\$}{\leftarrow}$ SIGM.P_2(sts_i, b), *which is the prover's last message in the Σ-protocol when his first message was* a_i *and when the verifier's challenge bit is* b. *Return* msgp := ($\vec{a}, OT_2(crs_{ot}, o\vec{t}r, \vec{z_0}, \vec{z_1})$), *where* $\vec{a}$:= ($a_1, \ldots, a_r$), $\vec{z_0}$:= ($z_{1,0}, \ldots, z_{r,0}$) *and* $\vec{z_1}$:= ($z_{1,1}, \ldots, z_{r,1}$).

- ZK.V_2(st, x, msgp): *Parse* st := ($b_1, \ldots, b_r, \vec{st}_{ot}$), msgp := ($\vec{a}, \vec{ots}$) *and* $\vec{a}$:= ($a_1, \ldots, a_r$). *Let* ($z_1, \ldots, z_r$) = $OT_3(\vec{st}_{ot}, \vec{ots})$. *Return* 1 *if for all* $i \in [r]$: SIGM.V(crs_{sig}, x, a_i, b_i, z_i) = 1. *Otherwise, return* 0.

Theorem 19. *Assuming that* SIGM := (Setup, P, V, Extract, Sim) *is an extractable Σ-protocol for a language* L *(Definition 16) and* OT := (Setup, OT_1, OT_2, OT_3) *provides sender's UC-security and receiver's indistinguishability security, then the protocol* ZK *given in Construction 18 satisfies completeness, adaptive soundness and adaptive malicious zero knowledge for* L.

The proof can be found in the full version of the paper.

9 UC-Secure OT from Sender-UC OT and Zero Knowledge

We will now show how to build a UC-secure OT scheme (with both receiver's and sender's UC security) from the combination of a CPA-secure PKE scheme, a CRS-based two-round statement-independent ZK protocol, and a two-round OT scheme with sender's UC-security and receiver's indistinguishability security.

Let PKE := (KeyGen, E, Dec) be the PKE scheme, (Setup, OT_1, OT_2, OT_3) be the base two-round OT scheme and ZK = (Setup, P, V := (V_1, V_2), Sim := (Sim_1, Sim_2)) be a two-round statement-independent ZK protocol for the language $L_{pk,crs_{ot},otr} \in NP$, parameterized over a public key pk of the PKE scheme, a CRS value crs_{ot} of the OT scheme and an OT-receiver's message otr, defined as follows:

$$L_{pk,crs_{ot},otr} = \{(ct_0, ct_1, ots) \mid \exists(m_0, m_1, r_0, r_1, r) \text{ s.t.}$$
$$ct_0 = E(pk, m_0; r_0), ct_1 = E(pk, m_1; r_1), ots = OT_2(crs_{ot}, otr, m_0, m_1; r)\}. \quad (2)$$

Construction 20 (UC-secure OT). *We build* OT' := (Setup', OT'_1, OT'_2, OT'_3) *from the above primitives as follows.*

Setup'(1^λ): *Sample* (pk, sk) $\overset{\$}{\leftarrow}$ PKE.Gen(1^λ), $crs_{ot} \overset{\$}{\leftarrow}$ OT.Setup(1^λ) *and* $crs_{zk} \overset{\$}{\leftarrow}$ ZK.Setup(1^λ). *Output* crs := (pk, crs_{ot}, crs_{zk}).

$\mathsf{OT}'_1(\mathsf{crs}, b)$: *Parse* $\mathsf{crs} := (\mathsf{pk}, \mathsf{crs}_{\mathsf{ot}}, \mathsf{crs}_{\mathsf{zk}})$. *Sample* $(\mathsf{otr}, \mathsf{st}_{\mathsf{ot}}) \xleftarrow{\$} \mathsf{OT}_1(\mathsf{crs}_{\mathsf{ot}}, b)$ *and*
$(\mathsf{msgv}, \mathsf{st}_{\mathsf{zk}}) \xleftarrow{\$} \mathsf{ZK.V}_1(\mathsf{crs}_{\mathsf{zk}})$. *Output* $\mathsf{otr}' := (\mathsf{otr}, \mathsf{msgv})$ *as the message to the*
sender and output $\mathsf{st} := (\mathsf{st}_{\mathsf{ot}}, \mathsf{st}_{\mathsf{zk}})$ *as the private state.*
$\mathsf{OT}'_2(\mathsf{crs}, \mathsf{otr}', m_0, m_1)$: *Parse* $\mathsf{crs} := (\mathsf{pk}, \mathsf{crs}_{\mathsf{ot}}, \mathsf{crs}_{\mathsf{zk}})$ *and* $\mathsf{otr}' := (\mathsf{otr}, \mathsf{msgv})$. *Sam-*
ple $r, r_0, r_1 \xleftarrow{\$} \{0,1\}^*$. *Let* $\mathsf{ct}_0 := \mathsf{E}(\mathsf{pk}, m_0; r_0)$, $\mathsf{ct}_1 = \mathsf{E}(\mathsf{pk}, m_1; r_1)$, *and* $\mathsf{ots} = $
$\mathsf{OT}_2(\mathsf{crs}_{\mathsf{ot}}, \mathsf{otr}, m_0, m_1; r)$. *Set* $\mathsf{x} := (\mathsf{ct}_0, \mathsf{ct}_1, \mathsf{ots})$ *and* $\mathsf{w} := (m_0, m_1, r_0, r_1, r)$.
Output $\mathsf{ots}' := (\mathsf{ct}_0, \mathsf{ct}_1, \mathsf{ots}, \mathsf{msgp})$, *where* $\mathsf{msgp} \xleftarrow{\$} \mathsf{ZK.P}(\mathsf{crs}_{\mathsf{zk}}, \mathsf{x}, \mathsf{w}, \mathsf{msgv})$.
$\mathsf{OT}'_3(\mathsf{st}, \mathsf{ots}')$: *Parse* $\mathsf{st} := (\mathsf{st}_{\mathsf{ot}}, \mathsf{st}_{\mathsf{zk}})$, $\mathsf{ots}' := (\mathsf{ct}_0, \mathsf{ct}_1, \mathsf{ots}, \mathsf{msgp})$ *and let* $\mathsf{x} :=$
$(\mathsf{ct}_0, \mathsf{ct}_1, \mathsf{ots})$. *If* $\mathsf{ZK.V}_2(\mathsf{st}_{\mathsf{zk}}, \mathsf{x}, \mathsf{msgp}) \neq 1$, *then return* $\bot$. *Otherwise, return*
$\mathsf{OT}_3(\mathsf{st}_{\mathsf{ot}}, \mathsf{ots})$.

Theorem 21. *Assuming that* $\mathsf{OT} := (\mathsf{Setup}, \mathsf{OT}_1, \mathsf{OT}_2, \mathsf{OT}_3)$ *provides sender's*
UC-security and receiver's indistinguishability security, that $\mathsf{PKE} := (\mathsf{KeyGen}, \mathsf{E},$
$\mathsf{Dec})$ *is a CPA-secure scheme, and that* ZK *is a two-round ZK protocol for the lan-*
guage L *described in Eq. 2, then the OT protocol* OT' *given in Construction 20 sat-*
isfies completeness and UC security.

The proof can be found in the full version of the paper.

10 Instantiations from CDH and LPN

10.1 Instantiation from CDH

We first give a construction of elementary OT from CDH. In fact, we show that
the construction also already directly satisfies the stronger notion of search OT
security. The protocol is given in Fig. 4.

Definition 22 (Computational Diffie-Hellman (CDH) assumption). *Let*
$\mathbb{G}$ *be a group-generator scheme, which on input* 1^λ *outputs* $(\mathbb{G}, p, g)$, *where* $\mathbb{G}$
is the description of a group, p *is the order of the group which is always a*
prime number and g *is a generator of the group. We say that* G *is CDH-hard*
if for any PPT adversary $\mathcal{A}$: $\Pr[\mathcal{A}(\mathbb{G}, p, g, g^{a_1}, g^{a_2}) = g^{a_1 a_2}] = \mathsf{negl}(\lambda)$, *where*
$(\mathbb{G}, p, g) \xleftarrow{\$} \mathsf{G}(1^\lambda)$ *and* $a_1, a_2 \xleftarrow{\$} \mathbb{Z}_p$.

Lemma 23. *The protocol in Fig. 4 satisfies statistical receiver's indistinguisha-*
bility security.

Proof. The distribution of the receiver's message $h_0 = g^r X^{-c}$ is uniformly random over the group $\mathbb{G}$ no matter that the receiver's bit c is. ☐

Lemma 24. *The protocol in Fig. 4 satisfies sender's elementary security based*
on the CDH assumption.

Sender(X):   CRS: $X := g^x$ Receiver(X, c):

$$r \leftarrow \mathbb{Z}_p$$

$$\xleftarrow{\quad \text{otr} := h_0 \quad} \qquad h_0 := g^r X^{-c}$$

$h_1 := h_0 X$

$s \leftarrow \mathbb{Z}_p$

$S := g^s$ $\xrightarrow{\quad \text{ots} := S \quad}$

output $y_0 := h_0^s, y_1 := h_1^s$ output $y_c := h_c^s = S^r$

Fig. 4. Elementary and search OT from CDH.

Proof. Let there be a PPT adversary $\mathcal{A}$ that breaks the elementary security of the sender. Then we are able to construct a PPT adversary $\mathcal{B}$ that breaks the CDH assumption. Recall that $\mathcal{A}$ receives a CRS $X = g^x$, sends a group element h_0, receives $S = g^s$ for a uniform s, and succeeds if he outputs $y_0 = h_0^s$, $y_1 = h_1^s = (h_0 X)^s$. Our adversary against the CDH assumption receives $\mathbb{G}$, p, g, $A_1 := g^{a_1}$, $A_2 := g^{a_2}$ from his challenger, gives CRS $X := A_1$ to $\mathcal{A}$, receives h_0, gives $S := A_2$ to $\mathcal{A}$, receives y_0, y_1 and outputs y_1/y_0. If $\mathcal{A}$ succeeds then $y_0 = h_0^s = h_0^{a_2}$, $y_1 = h_1^s = (h_0 X)^s = h_0^b A_1^{a_2} = h_0^{a_2} g^{a_1 a_2}$ and therefore $y_1/y_0 = g^{a_1 a_2}$, meaning that $\mathcal{B}$ succeeds in solving CDH. $\qquad\square$

The above two lemmas already show that the scheme in Fig. 4 is a elementary OT scheme and we can then rely on our black-box transformations from the previous sections to then get UC secure OT under CDH assumption. Therefore, the following Theorem follows as a corollary.

Theorem 25. *Under the CDH assumption there exists a 2-round UC OT.*

Although the above lemmas already suffice to show the above corollary, we note that we can actually show something stronger about the scheme in Fig. 4. Not only does it satisfy sender's elementary security, it already also satisfies the stronger notion of sender's search security. To show this, we implicitly rely on the random self-reducibility of the CDH problem.

Lemma 26. *The protocol in Fig. 4 satisfies sender's search security based on the CDH assumption.*

Proof. Let there be an adversary $\mathcal{A} = (\mathcal{A}_1, \mathcal{A}_2)$ with

$$\Pr_{\text{crs},r}[\Pr[\text{Exp}_{\text{sOTiOT}}^{\text{crs},r,0}(\mathcal{A}) = 1] > \epsilon \text{ and } \Pr[\text{Exp}_{\text{sOTiOT}}^{\text{crs},r,1}(\mathcal{A}) = 1] > \epsilon] > \epsilon,$$

the we can construct an adversary $\mathcal{A}'$ that solves CDH at least with probability ϵ^3. $\mathcal{A}'$ receives a CDH challenge $\mathbb{G}, p, g, A_1, A_2$. It sets crs $X := A_1$, chooses random coins r and invokes $\mathcal{A}_1$ which outputs a state st and OT message otr $= h_0$. $\mathcal{A}'$ samples $d_1, d_2 \leftarrow \mathbb{Z}_p$, defines $S_0 := A_2 \cdot g^{d_1}$, $S_1 := A_2 \cdot g^{d_2}$ and invokes for $i \in \{0, 1\}$ $\mathcal{A}_2(\text{st}, S_i, i)$ which outputs y_i. $\mathcal{A}'$ returns solution $(h_0^{d_1} \cdot y_1)/(h_0^{d_2} \cdot y_0 \cdot A_1^{d_2})$ to the CDH challenger.

With probability ϵ, crs X and random coins r are good, i.e. $\Pr[\mathsf{Exp}^{\mathsf{crs},r,0}_{\mathsf{sOTiOT}}(\mathcal{A}) = 1] > \epsilon$ and $\Pr[\mathsf{Exp}^{\mathsf{crs},r,1}_{\mathsf{sOTiOT}}(\mathcal{A}) = 1] > \epsilon$. We condition on that being the case. Since S_0 and S_1 are independent, it holds with probability ϵ^2 that $\mathcal{A}_2$ is successful for input $(\mathsf{st}, S_0, 0)$ and input $(\mathsf{st}, S_1, 1)$. Conditioned on that being the case, $y_0 = h_0^{s_0} = h_0^{a_2+d_1}$ and $y_1 = h_1^{s_1} = (h_0 \cdot A_1)^{d_2+a_2}$. Therefore it holds that the submitted CDH solution is

$$\frac{h_0^{d_1} \cdot y_1}{h_0^{d_2} \cdot y_0 \cdot A_1^{d_1}} = \frac{h_0^{d_1} \cdot (h_0 \cdot A_1)^{d_2+a_2}}{h_0^{d_2} \cdot h_0^{a_2+d_1} \cdot A_1^{d_2}} = A_1^{a_2}.$$

Hence, $\mathcal{A}'$ solves CDH with at least probability ϵ^3.   □

10.2   Instantiation from LPN

We now give an instantiation of an elementary OT under the *learning parity with noise* (LPN) assumption with noise rate $\rho = n^{-\varepsilon}$ for $\varepsilon > \frac{1}{2}$. This protocol only achieves imperfect correctness, with an inverse-polynomial failure probability, but we argue that this is sufficient to get UC OT with negligible error probability.

Definition 27 (Learning Parity with Noise). *For a uniform $s \in \mathbb{Z}_2^n$, oracle $\mathcal{O}_{\mathsf{LPN}}$ outputs samples of the form $a, z = as + e$, where $a \xleftarrow{\$} \mathbb{Z}_2^n$ and Bernoulli distributed noise term $e \xleftarrow{\$} \mathcal{B}_\rho$ for parameter ρ. Oracle $\mathcal{O}_{\mathsf{uniform}}$ outputs uniform samples $a, z \in \mathbb{Z}_2^n \times \mathbb{Z}_2$. We say Learning with Parity (LPN) for dimension n and noise distribution $\mathcal{B}_\rho$ is hard iff for any ppt adversary $\mathcal{A}$,*

$$|\Pr[\mathcal{A}^{\mathcal{O}_{\mathsf{LPN}}}(1^n) = 1] - \Pr[\mathcal{A}^{\mathcal{O}_{\mathsf{uniform}}}(1^n) = 1]| \leq \mathsf{negl}.$$

In the following, we will use a variant of LPN, where the secret is sampled from the noise distribution rather than the uniform distribution and the first sample is errorless. This variant is known to be as hard as standard LPN. The two following lemmata give a more precise relation between LPN and its above described variant.

Lemma 28 ([BLP+13], Lemma 4.3). *There is an efficient reduction from LPN with dimension n and noise distribution $\mathcal{B}_\rho$ to LPN where the first sample is errorless with dimension $n - 1$ and noise distribution $\mathcal{B}_\rho$ that reduces the advantage by at most probability 2^{-n}.*

Lemma 29 ([ACPS09] Adaptation of Lemma 2). *LPN samples of the from $a, as + e$ with uniform $a, s \in \mathbb{Z}_2^n$ and $e \xleftarrow{\$} \mathcal{B}_\rho$ can be efficiently transformed into samples $a', a's' + e$, where $s' \xleftarrow{\$} \mathcal{B}_\rho^n$ and uniform $a' \in \mathbb{Z}_2^n$. This also holds when $e = 0$, i.e. first is errorless LPN. The same transformation maintains the uniformity of samples in $\mathbb{Z}_2^n \times \mathbb{Z}_2$.*

Proof (Proof Sketch). The transformation queries LPN samples $A, z_A = As + e_s$ until $A \in \mathbb{Z}_2^{n \times n}$ is invertible. Then, $A^{-1}, A^{-1}z_A = s + A^{-1}e_s$ will allow mapping LPN samples $a, z = as + e$ to samples with secret $s' = e_s$ by computing the new sample $a' = aA^{-1}$, $z + aA^{-1}z_A = a's' + e$. In the case where $e = 0$, i.e. an errorless LPN sample, the resulting sample will also be errorless.   □

Sender(A, v):   CRS: $(A, v) \in \mathbb{Z}_2^{n \times (n+1)}$ Receiver(A, v, c):

$$x, e \leftarrow \mathcal{B}_\rho^n$$

$$\xleftarrow{\quad \mathsf{otr} := h_0 \quad}$$

$$h_0 := Ax + e + cv$$

$h_1 := h_0 + v$

$S, E \leftarrow \mathcal{B}_\rho^{\lambda \times n}$

$$\xrightarrow{\quad \mathsf{ots} := Z \quad}$$

$Z := SA + E$

output $y_0 := Sh_0, y_1 := Sh_1$ output $y_c := Zx$

Fig. 5. Elementary OT from LPN with imperfect correctness.

Lemma 30. *The protocol in Fig. 5 satisfies receiver's indistinguishability security based on the LPN assumption with dimension n and noise distribution $\mathcal{B}_\rho$.*

Proof. The receiver's bit c is masked by an LPN sample $Ax + e$. Therefore, distinguishing the case $c = 0$ versus $c = 1$ is equivalent to breaking LPN. ☐

Lemma 31. *The protocol in Fig. 5 satisfies sender's elementary OT security based on the LPN assumption with dimension $n - 1$ and noise distribution $\mathcal{B}_\rho$.*

Proof. We use a hybrid version of first is errorless LPN with a secret sampled from the noise distribution which is hard based on standard LPN with the same noise distribution and dimension $n - 1$, see Lemma 28 and Lemma 29. Hybrid LPN is as hard as standard LPN losing a factor $\frac{1}{\lambda}$ in the advantage.

Let there be a malicious receiver that outputs y_0, y_1 with probability $\epsilon >$ negl then there is a LPN distinguisher $\mathcal{A}$ that breaks hybrid first is errorless LPN with advantage ϵ. $\mathcal{A}$ operates as follows. It receives a LPN challenge v, A, z_v, Z and sets CRS to A, v. After receiving h_0, it sends Z to the malicious receiver and obtains y_0, y_1. If $y_0 + y_1 = z_v$ it outputs 1 otherwise 0.

Let $Z = SA + E$, $z_v = Sv$, then $\mathcal{A}$ faithfully simulates the actual protocol. With probability ϵ, the malicious receiver will output $(y_0, y_1) = (Sh_0, Sh_1)$. In this case $y_0 + y_1 = Sv$ equals z_v and $\mathcal{A}$ will output 1. In the uniform case, i.e. Z_A and z_v are uniform, hence the malicious receiver can output y_0, y_1 such that $y_0 + y_1 = z_v$ at most with probability $2^{-\lambda}$. Hence $\mathcal{A}$ breaks LPN with advantage $\frac{\epsilon}{\lambda} - 2^{-\lambda} >$ negl. ☐

Lemma 32 (Imperfect Correctness). *Let a sender and a receiver interact in the protocol in Fig. 5 with parameter $\rho \leq \frac{1}{n^\epsilon}$, for constant $1 > \epsilon > \frac{1}{2}$. Then with overwhelming probability $1 - \mathsf{negl}(\lambda)$ over the coins of the receiver (i.e., x, e) we have the following probability of correctness over the coins of the sender (i.e., S, E):*

$$\Pr_{S, E}[Sh_c = Zx] \geq 1 - 4\lambda n^{1 - 2\epsilon},$$

where $4\lambda n^{1 - 2\epsilon}$ can be an arbitrary $\frac{1}{\mathsf{poly}(\lambda)}$ for a suitable choice of $n = \mathsf{poly}(\lambda)$.

Proof. The protocol is correct iff the receivers output Zx matches the senders output Sh_c. By construction, $Zx = SAx + Ex$, whereas $Sh_c = SAx + Se$. Hence correctness holds when $Ex - Se = 0$.

By Chernoff,

$$\Pr[|x| > 2\rho n \vee |e| > 2\rho n] \leq 2e^{-\frac{\rho n}{3}},$$

which is negligible for $\epsilon < 1$. Given that $|x| \leq 2\rho n$, for all rows e_i of E, $e_i x$ is distributed as the sum of at most $2\rho n$ Bernoulli variables with parameter ρ. Hence, by a union bound over the $2\rho n$ variables $\Pr_{e_i}[e_i x = 1] \leq 2\rho^2 n$. Using another union bound over all λ rows yields $\Pr_E[Ex \neq 0 \in \mathbb{Z}_2^\lambda] \leq 2\lambda\rho^2 n$. Because of symmetry,

$$\Pr_{E,S}[Ex - Se = 0] \geq 1 - 4\lambda\rho^2 n.$$

□

Dealing with Imperfect Correctness. The above gives us an elementary OT scheme with imperfect correctness under LPN: with overwhelming probability over the coins of the receiver, we have a $1/p(\lambda)$ error-probability over the coins of the sender, where we can choose $p(\lambda)$ to be an arbitrary polynomial. For concreteness we set $p(\lambda) = \lambda^2$, so the error probability is $1/\lambda^2$. We outline how to leverage the series of generic transformations from the previous sections to get UC OT with a negligible correctness error. This requires only minor modifications throughout.

Elementary OT $\rightarrow$ Search OT (Theorem 7): This transformation performs a λ-wise parallel repetition on the sender message and therefore, by the union bound, increases the correctness error from $1/\lambda^2$ to $1/\lambda$. Security is unaffected.

Search OT $\rightarrow$ bit-iOT (Theorem 8): This transformation preserves the correctness error of $1/\lambda$. Security is unaffected.

bit-iOT $\rightarrow$ string iOT (Theorem 9): Here, we can modify the transformation slightly and first encode the strings using an error-correcting code and have the receiver apply error correction. Since each bit has an independent error probability of $1/\lambda$, we can set the parameters of the error-correcting code to get an exponentially small error probability, say $2^{-2\lambda}$. Security is unaffected by this modification.

Imperfect $\rightarrow$ Perfect Correctness: The above gives a scheme where, with overwhelming probability over the receiver's coins, we have a $2^{-2\lambda}$ error probability over the sender's coins. However, our definition of OT correctness in Sect. 4.1 requires a stronger notion of *perfect correctness*: with overwhelming over the receiver's coins and the CRS, *all* choices of the sender coins yield the correct output. This is needed in two places: (1) In the construction of 2-round ZK arguments (Theorem 19), we rely on extractable commitments, which in turn require a PKE with perfect correctness (Definition 3). Constructing PKE from OT requires the same perfect correctness for the OT. (2) In the construction of UC OT from Sender-UC OT and ZK (Theorem 21) we also need the underlying Sender-UC OT to have perfect correctness. This is because we rely on the fact that if a malicious sender computes the second-round OT message correctly with some choice of random coins (which he proves via the ZK argument), then the receiver gets the correct value. We can generically achieve such perfect correctness, using an idea similar to the one behind Naor's commitments [Nao90]. We add an additional random value r^* to the CRS. The sender computes his second-round OT message by relying on a pseudorandom generator G and setting the random coins to be $G(s) \oplus r^*$ where s is small seed of length (e.g.,) λ. By a counting argument, with overwhelming probability over r^* and the receiver's random coins, there is no choice of the sender's coins s that results in an error. Security is preserved by relying on the security of the PRG.

Combining the above, the following theorem follows as a corollary.

Theorem 33. *Under the LPN assumption with noise rate $\rho = n^{-\varepsilon}$ for $\varepsilon > \frac{1}{2}$ there exists a 2-round UC OT.*

References

[ACPS09] Applebaum, B., Cash, D., Peikert, C., Sahai, A.: Fast cryptographic primitives and circular-secure encryption based on hard learning problems. In: Halevi, S. (ed.) CRYPTO 2009. LNCS, vol. 5677, pp. 595–618. Springer, Heidelberg (2009). https://doi.org/10.1007/978-3-642-03356-8_35

[AIR01] Aiello, B., Ishai, Y., Reingold, O.: Priced oblivious transfer: how to sell digital goods. In: Pfitzmann, B. (ed.) EUROCRYPT 2001. LNCS, vol. 2045, pp. 119–135. Springer, Heidelberg (2001). https://doi.org/10.1007/3-540-44987-6_8

[Ale03] Alekhnovich, M.: More on average case vs approximation complexity. In: 44th FOCS, Cambridge, MA, USA, 11–14 October 2003, pp. 298–307. IEEE Computer Society Press (2003)

[BD18] Brakerski, Z., Döttling, N.: Two-message statistically sender-private OT from LWE. In: Beimel, A., Dziembowski, S. (eds.) TCC 2018, Part II. LNCS, vol. 11240, pp. 370–390. Springer, Cham (2018). https://doi.org/10.1007/978-3-030-03810-6_14

[BGI+17] Badrinarayanan, S., Garg, S., Ishai, Y., Sahai, A., Wadia, A.: Two-message witness indistinguishability and secure computation in the plain model from new assumptions. In: Takagi, T., Peyrin, T. (eds.) ASIACRYPT 2017, Part III. LNCS, vol. 10626, pp. 275–303. Springer, Cham (2017). https://doi.org/10.1007/978-3-319-70700-6_10

[BL18] Benhamouda, F., Lin, H.: k-round multiparty computation from k-round oblivious transfer via garbled interactive circuits. In: Nielsen, J.B., Rijmen, V. (eds.) EUROCRYPT 2018, Part II. LNCS, vol. 10821, pp. 500–532. Springer, Cham (2018). https://doi.org/10.1007/978-3-319-78375-8_17

[BLP+13] Brakerski, Z., Langlois, A., Peikert, C., Regev, O., Stehlé, D.: Classical hardness of learning with errors. In: Boneh, D., Roughgarden, T., Feigenbaum, J. (eds.) 45th ACM STOC, Palo Alto, CA, USA, 1–4 June 2013, pp. 575–584. ACM Press (2013)

[BLSV18] Brakerski, Z., Lombardi, A., Segev, G., Vaikuntanathan, V.: Anonymous IBE, leakage resilience and circular security from new assumptions. In: Nielsen, J.B., Rijmen, V. (eds.) EUROCRYPT 2018, Part I. LNCS, vol. 10820, pp. 535–564. Springer, Cham (2018). https://doi.org/10.1007/978-3-319-78381-9_20

[BM90] Bellare, M., Micali, S.: Non-interactive oblivious transfer and applications. In: Brassard, G. (ed.) CRYPTO 1989. LNCS, vol. 435, pp. 547–557. Springer, New York (1990). https://doi.org/10.1007/0-387-34805-0_48

[Can01] Canetti, R.: Universally composable security: a new paradigm for cryptographic protocols. In: 42nd FOCS, Las Vegas, NV, USA, 14–17 October 2001, pp. 136–145. IEEE Computer Society Press (2001)

[CCM98] Cachin, C., Crépeau, C., Marcil, J.: Oblivious transfer with a memory-bounded receiver. In: 39th FOCS, Palo Alto, CA, USA, 8–11 November 1998, pp. 493–502. IEEE Computer Society Press (1998)

[CHS05] Canetti, R., Halevi, S., Steiner, M.: Hardness amplification of weakly verifiable puzzles. In: Kilian, J. (ed.) TCC 2005. LNCS, vol. 3378, pp. 17–33. Springer, Heidelberg (2005). https://doi.org/10.1007/978-3-540-30576-7_2

[CLOS02] Canetti, R., Lindell, Y., Ostrovsky, R., Sahai, A.: Universally composable two-party and multi-party secure computation. In: 34th ACM STOC, Montréal, Québec, Canada, 19–21 May 2002, pp. 494–503. ACM Press (2002)

[CR03] Canetti, R., Rabin, T.: Universal composition with joint state. In: Boneh, D. (ed.) CRYPTO 2003. LNCS, vol. 2729, pp. 265–281. Springer, Heidelberg (2003). https://doi.org/10.1007/978-3-540-45146-4_16

[DGM19] Döttling, N., Garg, S., Malavolta, G.: Laconic conditional disclosure of secrets and applications. In: 2019 IEEE 58th Annual Symposium on Foundations of Computer Science (FOCS). IEEE (2019)

[DHRS04] Ding, Y.Z., Harnik, D., Rosen, A., Shaltiel, R.: Constant-round oblivious transfer in the bounded storage model. In: Naor, M. (ed.) TCC 2004. LNCS, vol. 2951, pp. 446–472. Springer, Heidelberg (2004). https://doi.org/10.1007/978-3-540-24638-1_25

[EGL85] Even, S., Goldreich, O., Lempel, A.: A randomized protocol for signing contracts. Commun. ACM 28(6), 637–647 (1985)

[GL89] Goldreich, O., Levin, L.A.: A hard-core predicate for all one-way functions. In: 21st ACM STOC, Seattle, WA, USA, 15–17 May 1989, pp. 25–32. ACM Press (1989)

[GMW87] Goldreich, O., Micali, S., Wigderson, A.: How to play any mental game or a completeness theorem for protocols with honest majority. In: Aho, A. (ed.) 19th ACM STOC, New York City, NY, USA, 25–27 May 1987, pp. 218–229. ACM Press (1987)

[GS18] Garg, S., Srinivasan, A.: Two-round multiparty secure computation from minimal assumptions. In: Nielsen, J.B., Rijmen, V. (eds.) EUROCRYPT 2018, Part II. LNCS, vol. 10821, pp. 468–499. Springer, Cham (2018). https://doi.org/10.1007/978-3-319-78375-8_16

[HK12] Halevi, S., Kalai, Y.T.: Smooth projective hashing and two-message oblivious transfer. J. Cryptol. 25(1), 158–193 (2012)

[HL18] Holmgren, J., Lombardi, A.: Cryptographic hashing from strong one-way functions (or: one-way product functions and their applications). In: 59th FOCS, pp. 850–858. IEEE Computer Society Press (2018)

[JKKR17] Jain, A., Kalai, Y.T., Khurana, D., Rothblum, R.: Distinguisher-dependent simulation in two rounds and its applications. In: Katz, J., Shacham, H. (eds.) CRYPTO 2017, Part II. LNCS, vol. 10402, pp. 158–189. Springer, Cham (2017). https://doi.org/10.1007/978-3-319-63715-0_6

[Lin16] Lindell, Y.: How to simulate it - a tutorial on the simulation proof technique. Cryptology ePrint Archive, Report 2016/046 (2016). http://eprint.iacr.org/2016/046

[LQR+19] Lombardi, A., Quach, W., Rothblum, R.D., Wichs, D., Wu, D.J.: New constructions of reusable designated-verifier NIZKs. In: Boldyreva, A., Micciancio, D. (eds.) CRYPTO 2019. LNCS, vol. 11694, pp. 670–700. Springer, Cham (2019). https://doi.org/10.1007/978-3-030-26954-8_22

[Nao90] Naor, M.: Bit commitment using pseudo-randomness. In: Brassard, G. (ed.) CRYPTO 1989. LNCS, vol. 435, pp. 128–136. Springer, New York (1990). https://doi.org/10.1007/0-387-34805-0_13

[NP01] Naor, M., Pinkas, B.: Efficient oblivious transfer protocols. In: Rao Kosaraju, S. (ed.) 12th SODA, Washington, DC, USA, 7–9 January 2001, pp. 448–457. ACM-SIAM (2001)

[PVW08] Peikert, C., Vaikuntanathan, V., Waters, B.: A framework for efficient and composable oblivious transfer. In: Wagner, D. (ed.) CRYPTO 2008. LNCS, vol. 5157, pp. 554–571. Springer, Heidelberg (2008). https://doi.org/10.1007/978-3-540-85174-5_31

[Rab05] Rabin, M.O.: How to exchange secrets with oblivious transfer. Cryptology ePrint Archive, Report 2005/187 (2005). http://eprint.iacr.org/2005/187

[Yao82] Yao, A.C.-C.: Protocols for secure computations (extended abstract). In: 23rd FOCS, Chicago, Illinois, 3–5 November 1982, pp. 160–164. IEEE Computer Society Press (1982)

Private Aggregation from Fewer Anonymous Messages

Badih Ghazi[1]($\boxtimes$), Pasin Manurangsi[1]($\boxtimes$), Rasmus Pagh[1,2], and Ameya Velingker[1]

[1] Google Research, Mountain View, CA 94043, USA
badihghazi@google.com, pasin@google.com, pagh@google.com,
ameyav@google.com
[2] IT University of Copenhagen, Copenhagen, Denmark

Abstract. Consider the setup where n parties are each given an element x_i in the finite field $\mathbb{F}_q$ and the goal is to compute the sum $\sum_i x_i$ in a secure fashion and with as little communication as possible. We study this problem in the *anonymized model* of Ishai et al. (FOCS 2006) where each party may broadcast anonymous messages on an insecure channel.

We present a new analysis of the one-round "split and mix" protocol of Ishai et al. In order to achieve the same security parameter, our analysis reduces the required number of messages by a $\Theta(\log n)$ multiplicative factor.

We also prove lower bounds showing that the dependence of the number of messages on the domain size, the number of parties, and the security parameter is essentially tight.

Using a reduction of Balle et al. (2019), our improved analysis of the protocol of Ishai et al. yields, in the same model, an (ε, δ)-differentially private protocol for aggregation that, for any constant $\varepsilon > 0$ and any $\delta = \frac{1}{\text{poly}(n)}$, incurs only a constant error and requires only a *constant number of messages* per party. Previously, such a protocol was known only for $\Omega(\log n)$ messages per party.

Keywords: Secure aggregation · Anonymous channel · Shuffled model · Differential privacy

1 Introduction

We study one-round multi-party protocols for the problem of secure aggregation: Each of n parties holds an element of the field $\mathbb{F}_q$ and we wish to compute the sum of these numbers, while satisfying the security property that for every two inputs with the same sum, their transcripts are "indistinguishable." The protocols we consider work in the *anonymized model*, where parties are able to send anonymous messages through an insecure channel and indistinguishability is in terms of the *statistical distance* between the two transcripts (i.e., this is information-theoretic security rather than computational security). This model was introduced by Ishai et al. [17] in their work on cryptography from

© International Association for Cryptologic Research 2020
A. Canteaut and Y. Ishai (Eds.): EUROCRYPT 2020, LNCS 12106, pp. 798–827, 2020.
https://doi.org/10.1007/978-3-030-45724-2_27

anonymity[1]. We refer to [8,17] for a discussion of cryptographic realizations of an anonymous channel.

The secure aggregation problem in the anonymized model was studied already by Ishai et al. [17], who gave a very elegant one-round "split and mix" protocol. Under their protocol, each party i holds a private input x_i and sends m anonymized messages consisting of random elements of $\mathbb{F}_q$ that are conditioned on summing to x_i. Upon receiving these mn anonymized messages from n parties, the server adds them up and outputs the result. Pseudocode of this protocol is shown as Algorithm 1. Ishai et al. [17] show that as long as m exceeds a threshold of $\Theta(\log n + \sigma + \log q)$, this protocol is σ-secure in the sense that the statistical distance between transcripts resulting from inputs with the same sum is at most $2^{-\sigma}$.

Differentially Private Aggregation in the Shuffled Model. An exciting recent development in differential privacy is the *shuffled model*, which is closely related to the aforementioned anonymized model. The shuffled model provides a middle ground between two widely-studied models of differential privacy. In the *central model*, the data structure released by the analyst is required to be differentially private, whereas the *local model* enforces the more stringent requirement that the messages sent by each party be private. While protocols in the central model generally allow better accuracy, they require a much greater level of trust to be placed in the analyzer, an assumption that may be unsuitable for certain applications. The *shuffled model* is based on the Encode-Shuffle-Analyze architecture of [6] and was first analytically studied by [8,12] and further studied in recent work [4,13]. It seeks to bridge the two aforementioned models and assumes the presence of a trusted shuffler that randomly permutes all incoming messages from the parties before passing them to the analyzer (see Sect. 2 for formal definitions.) The shuffled model is particularly compelling because it allows the possibility of obtaining more accurate communication-efficient protocols than in the local model while placing far less trust in the analyzer than in the central model. Indeed, the power of the shuffled model has been illustrated by a number of recent works that have designed algorithms in this model for a wide range of problems such as privacy amplification, histograms, heavy hitters, and range queries [4,8,11–13].

The appeal of the shuffled model provides the basis for our study of differentially private protocols for aggregation in this work. Most relevant to the present work are the recent differentially private protocols for aggregation of real numbers in the shuffled model provided by [3,4,8,15]. The strongest of these results [3] shows that an extension of the split and mix protocol yields an (ε, δ)-differentially private protocol for aggregation with error $O(1 + 1/\varepsilon)$ and $m = O(\log(n/\delta))$ messages, each consisting of $O(\log n)$ bits.

---

[1] Ishai et al. in fact considered a more general model in which the adversary is allowed to corrupt some of the parties; please refer to the discussion at the end of Sect. 1.1 for more details.

1.1   Our Results

Upper Bound. We prove that the split and mix protocol is in fact secure for a much smaller number of messages. In particular, for the same security parameter σ, the number of messages required in our analysis is $\Theta(\log n)$ times smaller than the bound in [17]:

Theorem 1 (Improved upper bound for split and mix). *Let n and q be positive integers and σ be a positive real number. The split and mix protocol (Algorithm 1 and [17]) with n parties and inputs in $\mathbb{F}_q$ is σ-secure for m messages, where $m = O\left(1 + \frac{\sigma + \log q}{\log n}\right)$.*

An interesting case to keep in mind is when the field size q and the inverse statistical distance 2^σ are bounded by a polynomial in n. In this case, Theorem 1 implies that the protocol works already with a *constant* number of messages, improving upon the known $O(\log n)$ bound.

Lower Bound. We show that, in terms of the number of messages m sent by each party, Theorem 1 is essentially tight not only for just the split and mix protocol but also for *every* one-round protocol.

Theorem 2 (Lower bound for every one-round protocol). *Let n and q be positive integers, and $\sigma \geq 1$ be a real number. In any σ-secure, one-round aggregation protocol over $\mathbb{F}_q$ in the anonymized model, each of the n parties must send $\Omega\left(1 + \frac{\sigma}{\log(\sigma n)} + \frac{\log q}{\log n}\right)$ messages.*

The lower bound holds regardless of the message size and asymptotically matches the upper bound under the very mild assumption that σ is bounded by a polynomial in n. Furthermore, when σ is larger, the bound is tight up to a factor $O\left(\frac{\log \sigma}{\log n}\right)$.

We point out that Theorem 2 provides a nearly-tight lower bound on the *number of messages*. In terms of the total communication per party, improvements are still possible when $\sigma + \log q = \omega(\log n)$. We discuss this further, along with other interesting open questions, in Sect. 5.

Corollary for Differentially Private Aggregation. As stated earlier, the differentially private aggregation protocols of [3,15] both use extensions of the split and mix protocol. Moreover, Balle et al. use the security guarantee of the split and mix protocol as a blackbox and derive a differential privacy guarantee from it [3, Lemma 4.1]. Specifically, when ε is a constant and $\delta \geq \frac{1}{\text{poly}(n)}$, their proof uses the split and mix protocol with field size $q = \text{poly}(n)$. Previous analyses required $m = \Omega(\log n)$; however, our analysis works with a *constant* number of messages. In general, Theorem 1 implies (ε, δ)-differential privacy with a factor $\Theta(\log n)$ fewer messages than known before:

Corollary 1 (Differentially private aggregation in the shuffled model). *Let n be a positive integer, and let ε, δ be positive real numbers. There is an (ε, δ)-differentially private aggregation protocol in the shuffled model for inputs in $[0, 1]$ having absolute error $O(1 + 1/\varepsilon)$ in expectation, using $O\left(1 + \frac{\log(1/\delta)}{\log n}\right)$ messages per party, each consisting of $O(\log n)$ bits.*

A more comprehensive comparison between our differentially private aggregation protocol in Corollary 1 and previous protocols is presented in Fig. 1.

We end this subsection by remarking that Ishai et al. [17] in fact considered a setting that is more general than what we have described so far. Specifically, they allow the adversary to corrupt a certain number of parties. In addition to the transcript of the protocol, the adversary knows the input and messages of these corrupted parties. (Alternatively, one can think of these corrupted parties as if they are colluding to learn the information about the remaining parties.) As already observed in [17], the security of the split and mix protocol still holds in this setting except that n is now the number of honest (i.e., uncorrupted) parties. In other words, Theorem 1 remains true in this more general setup but with n being the number of honest parties instead of the total number of parties.

Discussion and Comparison of Parallel and Subsequent Work. Concurrently and independently of our work, Balle et al. [2,5] obtained an upper bound that is asymptotically the same as the one in Theorem 1. They also give explicit constants, whereas we state our theorem in asymptotic notation and do not attempt to optimize the constants in our proof.

A key difference between our work and theirs is that in addition to the analysis of the split and mix protocol, we manage to prove a matching lower bound on the required number of messages for any protocol (see Theorem 2), which establishes the near-tightness of the algorithmic guarantees in our upper bound. Our lower bound approach could potentially be applied to other problems pertaining to the anonymous model and possibly differential privacy.

The upper bound proofs use different techniques. Balle et al. reduce the question to an analysis of the number of connected components of a certain random graph, while our proof analyzes the rank deficiency of a carefully-constructed random matrix. While the upper bound of Balle et al. is shown for summation over any abelian group, our proofs are presented for finite fields. We note, though, that our lower bound proof carries over verbatim to any abelian group.

A subsequent work [14] obtained an $(\varepsilon, 0)$-differentially private aggregation protocol with error $O_\varepsilon(1)$ and where each user sends $O_\varepsilon(\log^3 n)$ messages each consisting of $O(\log \log n)$ bits (see Fig. 1 for the explicit bounds).

1.2 Applications and Related Work

At first glance it may seem that aggregation is a rather limited primitive for combining data from many sources in order to analyze it. However, in important approaches to machine learning and distributed/parallel data processing, the mechanism for combining computations of different parties is *aggregation of vectors*. Since we can build vector aggregation in a straightforward way from scalar aggregation, our results can be applied in these settings.

Before discussing this in more detail, we mention that it is shown in [17] that summation protocols can be used as building blocks for realizing *general* secure computations in a specific setup where a server mediates computation of a function on data held by n other parties. However, the result assumes a somewhat weak security model (see in Appendix D of [17] for more details).

Machine Learning and Data Analytics. Secure aggregation has applications in so-called *federated* machine learning [21] (see, e.g., [18] for a recent survey). The idea is to train a machine learning model without collecting data from any party, and instead compute weight updates in a distributed manner by sending model parameters to all parties, locally running stochastic gradient descent on private data, and aggregating model updates over all parties. For learning algorithms based on gradient descent, a secure aggregation primitive can be used to compute global weight updates without compromising privacy [23,24]. It is known that gradient descent can work well even if data is accessible only in noised form, in order to achieve differential privacy (e.g., [1,25]).

Beyond gradient descent, as observed in [8], we can translate any *statistical query* over a distributed data set to an aggregation problem over numbers in $[0, 1]$. That is, every learning problem solvable using a small number of statistical queries [19] can be solved privately and efficiently based on secure aggregation.

Moreover, very recent work in eye-tracking research [22,29] study differential privacy for eye-tracking tasks, the most basic of which is the *aggregation* of users' gaze maps.

Sketching. Research in the area of data stream algorithms has uncovered many non-trivial algorithms that are compact *linear sketches*, see, e.g., [9,31]. As noted already in [17], linear sketches can be implemented using secure aggregation by computing linear sketches locally, and then using aggregation to compute their sum which yields the sketch of the whole dataset. Typically, linear sketches do not reveal much information about their input, and are robust to the noise needed to ensure differential privacy, though specific guarantees depend on the sketch in question. We refer to [20,26,27] for examples and further discussion.

Secure Aggregation Protocols. Secure aggregation protocols are well-studied, both under cryptographic assumptions and with respect to differential privacy. We refer to the survey of Goryczka et al. [16] for an overview, but note that our approach leads to protocols that use less communication than existing (multi-round) protocols. The trust assumptions needed for implementing a shuffler (e.g., using a mixnet) are, however, slightly different from the assumptions typically used for secure aggregation protocols. Practical secure aggregation typically relies on an honest-but-curious assumption, see e.g. [7]. In that setting, such protocols typically require five rounds of communication with $\Omega(n)$ bits of communication and $\Omega(n^2)$ computation per party. A more recent work [28] using

Reference	#messages / n	Message size	Expected error
Cheu et al. [8]	$\dfrac{\varepsilon\sqrt{n}}{\ell}$	1	$\dfrac{1}{\varepsilon}\log\frac{n}{\delta}$ $\sqrt{n}/\ell + \frac{1}{\varepsilon}\log\frac{1}{\delta}$
Balle et al. [4]	1	$\log n$	$\dfrac{n^{1/6}\log^{1/3}(1/\delta)}{\varepsilon^{2/3}}$
Ghazi et al. [15]	$\log(\frac{n}{\varepsilon\delta})$	$\log(\frac{n}{\delta})$	$\frac{1}{\varepsilon}\sqrt{\log\frac{1}{\delta}}$
Balle et al. [3]	$\log(\frac{n}{\delta})$	$\log n$	$\frac{1}{\varepsilon}$
This work (Corollary 1)	$1 + \dfrac{\log(1/\delta)}{\log n}$	$\log n$	$\frac{1}{\varepsilon}$
Ghazi et al. [14] ($\delta = 0$)	$\dfrac{\log^3 n}{\varepsilon}$	$\log\log n$	$\dfrac{\sqrt{\log(1/\varepsilon)}}{\varepsilon^{3/2}}$

Fig. 1. Comparison of differentially private aggregation protocols in the shuffled model with (ε, δ)-differential privacy. The number of parties is n, and ℓ is an integer parameter. Message sizes are in bits. For readability, we assume that $\varepsilon \leq O(1)$, and asymptotic notations are suppressed.

homomorphic threshold encryption gives a protocol with three messages and constant communication and computation per party in addition to a (reusable) two-message setup (consisting of $\Omega(n)$ communication per party). By contrast, our aggregation protocol has a single round of constant communication and computation per party, albeit in the presence of a trusted shuffler. We note that for an apples to apples comparison of these approaches, one would need to look at actual implementations of the shuffler which is beyond the scope of this work.

Other Related Models. A very recent work [30] has designed an extension of the shuffled model, called *Multi Uniform Random Shufflers* and analyzed its trust model and privacy-utility tradeoffs. Since they consider a more general model, our differentially private aggregation protocol would hold in their setup as well.

There has also been work on aggregation protocols in the multiple servers setting, e.g., the PRIO system [10]; here the protocol is secure as long as at least one server is honest. Thus trust assumptions of PRIO are somewhat different from those underlying shuffling and mixnets. While each party would be able to check the output of a shuffler, to see if its message is present, such a check is not possible in the PRIO protocol making server manipulation invisible even if the number of parties is known. On the other hand, PRIO handles malicious parties that try to manipulate the result of a summation by submitting illegal data—a challenge that has not been addressed yet for summation in the shuffled model but that would be interesting future work.

1.3   The Split and Mix Protocol

The protocol of [17] is shown in Algorithm 1. To describe the main guarantee proved in [17] regarding Algorithm 1, we need some notation. For any input sequence $\mathbf{x} \in \mathbb{F}_q^n$, we denote by $\mathcal{S}_{\mathbf{x}}$ the distribution on $\mathbb{F}_q^{mn}$ obtained by sampling

$y_{m(i-1)+1}, \ldots, y_{mi} \in \mathbb{F}_q$ uniformly at random conditioned on $y_{m(i-1)+1} + \cdots + y_{mi} = x_i$, sampling a random permutation $\pi : [mn] \rightarrow [mn]$, and outputting $(y_{\pi(1)}, \ldots, y_{\pi(mn)})$. Ishai et al. [17] proved that for some $m = O(\log n + \sigma + \log q)$ and for any two input sequences $\mathbf{x}, \mathbf{x}' \in \mathbb{F}_q^n$ having the same sum (in $\mathbb{F}_q$), the distributions $\mathcal{S}_{\mathbf{x}}$ and $\mathcal{S}_{\mathbf{x}'}$ are $2^{-\sigma}$-close in statistical distance.

Algorithm 1. Split and mix encoder from [17]

> **Input:** $x \in \mathbb{F}_q$, positive integer parameter m
> **Output:** Multiset $\{y_1, \ldots, y_m\} \subseteq \mathbb{F}_q$
>
> **for** $j = 1, \ldots, m-1$ **do**
> $\quad \lfloor \; y_j \leftarrow \text{Uniform}(\mathbb{F}_q)$
> $y_m \leftarrow x - \sum_{j=1}^{m-1} y_j$ (in $\mathbb{F}_q$)
> **return** $\{y_1, \ldots, y_m\}$

1.4 Overview of Proofs

We now give a short overview of the proofs of Theorems 1 and 2. For ease of notation, we define $\mathcal{B}_s$ to be the set of all input vectors $\mathbf{x} = (x_1, x_2, \ldots, x_n) \in \mathbb{F}_q^n$ with a fixed sum $x_1 + x_2 + \cdots + x_n = s$.

Upper Bound. To describe the main idea behind our upper bound, we start with the following notation. For every $x \in \mathbb{F}_q$, we denote by $\mathcal{S}_x$ the uniform distribution on $\mathbb{F}_q^{mn}$ conditioned on all coordinates summing to x.

To prove Theorem 1, we have to show that for any two input sequences $\mathbf{x}, \mathbf{x}' \in \mathbb{F}_q^n$ such that $\sum_{i \in [n]} x_i = \sum_{i \in [n]} x_i'$, the statistical distance between $\mathcal{S}_{\mathbf{x}}$ and $\mathcal{S}_{\mathbf{x}'}$ is at most $\gamma = 2^{-\sigma}$. By the triangle inequality, it suffices to show that the statistical distance between $\mathcal{S}_{\mathbf{x}}$ and $\mathcal{S}_{x_1 + \cdots + x_n}$ is at most $\gamma/2$. (Theorem 3). Note that $\mathcal{S}_{x_1 + \cdots + x_n}$ puts equal mass on all vectors in $\mathbb{F}_q^{mn}$ whose sum is equal to $x_1 + \cdots + x_n$. Thus, our task boils down to showing that the mass put by $\mathcal{S}_{\mathbf{x}}$ on a random sample from $\mathcal{S}_{x_1 + \cdots + x_n}$ is well-concentrated. We prove this via a second order method (specifically, Chebyshev's inequality). This amounts to computing the mean and bounding the variance. The former is a simple calculation whereas the latter is more technically involved and reduces to proving a probabilistic bound (Theorem 4) on the rank deficit of a certain random matrix (specified in Definitions 7 and 8). A main ingredient in the proof of this bound is a combinatorial characterization (Lemma 2) of the rank deficit of the relevant matrices in terms of *matching partitions* (given in Definition 9).

Lower Bound. For the lower bound (Theorem 2), our proof consists of two parts: a "security-dependent" lower bound $m \geq \Omega\left(\frac{\sigma}{\log(\sigma n)}\right)$ and a "field-dependent" lower bound $m \geq \Omega\left(\frac{\log q}{\log n}\right)$. Combining these two yields Theorem 2. We start by outlining the field-dependent bound as it is simpler before we outline the security-dependent lower bound which is technically more challenging.

Field-Dependent Lower Bound. To prove the field-dependent lower bound (formally stated in Theorem 5), the key idea is to show that for any $s \in \mathbb{F}_q$, there exist distinct inputs $\mathbf{x}, \mathbf{x}' \in \mathcal{B}_s$ such that the statistical distance between $\mathcal{S}_\mathbf{x}$ and $\mathcal{S}_{\mathbf{x}'}$ is at least $1 - n^{nm}/q^{n-1}$ (see Lemma 4). We do so by proving the same quantitative lower bound on the *average* statistical distance between $\mathcal{S}_\mathbf{x}$ and $\mathcal{S}_{\mathbf{x}'}$ over all pairs $\mathbf{x}, \mathbf{x}' \in \mathcal{B}_s$.

The average statistical distance described above can be written as the sum, over all $\mathbf{y}$, of the average difference in probability mass assigned to $\mathbf{y}$ by $\mathbf{x}$ and $\mathbf{x}'$. Thus, we consider how to lower bound this coordinate-wise probability mass difference for an arbitrary $\mathbf{y}$.

There are at most n^{nm} ways to associate each of the nm elements of $\mathbf{y}$ with a particular party. Since any individual party's encoding uniquely determines the corresponding input, it follows that any shuffled output $\mathbf{y}$ could have arisen from at most n^{nm} inputs $\mathbf{x}$. Moreover, since there are exactly q^{n-1} input vectors $\mathbf{x} \in \mathcal{B}_s$, it follows that there are at least $q^{n-1} - n^{nm}$ possible inputs $\mathbf{x} \in \mathcal{B}_s$ that cannot possibly result in $\mathbf{y}$ as an output. This implies that the average coordinate-wise probability mass difference, over all $\mathbf{x}, \mathbf{x}' \in \mathcal{B}_s$, is at least $\left(1 - \frac{q^{n-1}}{n^{nm}}\right)$ times the average probability mass assigned to $\mathbf{y}$ over all inputs in $\mathcal{B}_s$. Summing this up over all $\mathbf{y}$ yields the desired bound.

Security-Dependent Lower Bound. To prove the security-dependent lower bound, it suffices to prove the following statement (see Theorem 7): if Enc is the encoder of any aggregation protocol in the anonymized model for $n > 2$ parties with m messages sent per party, then there is a vector $\mathbf{x} \in \mathcal{B}_0$ such that the statistical distance between the distributions of the shuffled output $\mathbf{y}$ corresponding to inputs $\mathbf{0}$ and $\mathbf{x}$ is at least $\frac{1}{(10nm)^{5m}}$.

Let us first sketch a proof for the particular case of the split and mix protocol. In this case, we set $\mathbf{x} = (\underbrace{1, 1, \ldots, 1}_{n-1}, -(n-1))$, and we will bound from below the statistical distance by considering the "distinguisher" $\mathcal{A}$ which chooses a random permutation $\pi : [nm] \to [nm]$ and accepts iff $y_{\pi(1)} + \cdots + y_{\pi(m)} = 0$. We can argue (see Subsect. 4.2) that the probability that $\mathcal{A}$ accepts under the distribution $\mathcal{S}_\mathbf{0}$ is larger by an additive factor of $\frac{1}{(en)^m}$ than the probability that it accepts under the distribution $\mathcal{S}_\mathbf{x}$. To generalize this idea to arbitrary encoders (beyond Ishai et al.'s protocol), it is natural to consider a distinguisher which accepts iff $y_{\pi(1)}, \ldots, y_{\pi(m)}$ is a valid output of the encoder when the input is zero. Unlike the case of Ishai et al., in general when $\pi(1), \ldots, \pi(m)$ do not all come from the same party, it is not necessarily true that the acceptance probability would be the same for both distributions. To circumvent this, we pick the smallest integer t such that the t-message marginal of the encoding of 0 and that of input 1 are substantially different, and we let the distinguisher perform an analogous check on $y_{\pi(1)}, \ldots, y_{\pi(t)}$ (instead of $y_{\pi(1)}, \ldots, y_{\pi(m)}$ as before). Another complication that we have to deal with is that we can no longer consider the input vector $(1, \cdots, 1, -(n-1))$ as in the lower bound for Ishai et al.'s protocol sketched above. This is because the t-message marginal of the encoding of $-(n-1)$ could deviate from that for input 0 more substantially than from that for input 1, which could significantly affect the acceptance probability. Hence, to overcome this issue, we instead set x^* to the minimizer of this value t among all elements of $\mathbb{F}_q$, and use the input vector $\mathbf{x} = (x^*, \ldots, x^*, -(n-1)x^*)$ (for more details we refer the reader to the full proof in Subsect. 4.2).

Organization of the Rest of the Paper

We start with some preliminaries in Sect. 2. We prove our main upper bound (Theorem 1) in Sect. 3. We prove our lower bound (Theorem 2) in Sect. 4. The proof of Corollary 1 appears in Appendix B.

2   Preliminaries

2.1   Protocols

In this paper, we are concerned with answering the question of how many messages are needed for protocols to achieve certain security or cryptographic guarantees. We formally define the notion of protocols in the models of interest to us.

We first define the notion of a *secure protocol* in the *shuffled model*. An n-user *secure protocol* in the *shuffled model*, $\mathcal{P} = (\mathsf{Enc}, \mathcal{A})$, consists of a randomized *encoder* (also known as *local randomizer*) $\mathsf{Enc} : \mathcal{X} \to \mathcal{Y}^m$ and an *analyzer* $\mathcal{A} : \mathcal{Y}^{nm} \to \mathcal{Z}$. Here, $\mathcal{Y}$ is known as the *message alphabet*, $\mathcal{Y}^m$ is the *message space* for each user, and $\mathcal{Z}$ is the *output space* of the protocol. The protocol $\mathcal{P}$ implements the following mechanism: each party i holds an input $x_i \in \mathcal{X}$ and encodes x_i as Enc_{x_i}. (Note that Enc_{x_i} is possibly random based on the private randomness of party i.) The concatenation of the encodings, $\mathbf{y} = (\mathsf{Enc}_{x_1}, \mathsf{Enc}_{x_2}, \ldots, \mathsf{Enc}_{x_n}) \in \mathcal{Y}^{nm}$ is then passed to a trusted *shuffler*, who chooses a uniformly random permutation π on nm elements and applies π to $\mathbf{y}$. The output is submitted to the analyzer, which then outputs $\mathcal{P}(\mathbf{x}) = \mathcal{A}(\pi(\mathbf{y})) \in \mathcal{Z}$.

In this paper, we will be concerned with protocols for *aggregation*, in which $\mathcal{X} = \mathcal{Z} = \mathbb{F}_q$ (a finite field on q elements) and $\mathcal{Y} = [\ell] = \{1, 2, \ldots, \ell\}$, and

$$\mathcal{A}(\pi(\mathsf{Enc}_{x_1}, \mathsf{Enc}_{x_2}, \ldots, \mathsf{Enc}_{x_n})) = \sum_{i=1}^{n} x_i,$$

i.e., the protocol always outputs the sum of the parties' inputs, regardless of the randomness over the encoder and the shuffler.

A related notion that we consider in this work is a one-round protocol $\mathcal{P} = (\mathsf{Enc}, \mathcal{A})$ in the *anonymized model*. The notion is similar to that of a secure protocol in the shuffled model except that there is no shuffler. Rather, the analyzer $\mathcal{A}$ receives a *multiset* of nm messages obtained by enumerating all m messages of each of the n parties' encodings. It is straightforward to see that the two models are equivalent, in the sense that a protocol in one model works in the other and the distributions of the view of the analyzer are the same.

2.2   Distributions Related to a Protocol

To study a protocol and determine its security and privacy, it is convenient to define notations for several probability distributions related to the protocol. First, we use $\mathcal{E}_x^{\mathsf{Enc}}$ to denote the distribution of the (random) encoding of x:

Definition 1. *For a protocol $\mathcal{P}$ with encoding function Enc, we let $\mathcal{E}_x^{\mathsf{Enc}}$ denote the distribution of outputs over $\mathcal{Y}^m$ obtained by applying Enc to $x \in \mathcal{X}$.*

Furthermore, for a vector $\mathbf{x} \in \mathcal{X}^n$, we use $\mathcal{E}_{\mathbf{x}}^{\mathsf{Enc}}$ to denote the distribution of the concatenation of encodings of $x_1, \ldots, x_n$, as stated more formally below.

Definition 2. *For an n-party protocol $\mathcal{P}$ with encoding function Enc and $\mathbf{x} \in \mathcal{X}^n$, we let $\mathcal{E}_{\mathbf{x}}^{\mathsf{Enc}}$ denote the distribution over $\mathcal{Y}^{nm}$ obtained by applying Enc individually to each element of $\mathbf{x}$, i.e.,*

$$\mathcal{E}_{\mathbf{x}}^{\mathsf{Enc}} \sim \left(\mathcal{E}_{x_1}^{\mathsf{Enc}}, \mathcal{E}_{x_2}^{\mathsf{Enc}}, \ldots, \mathcal{E}_{x_n}^{\mathsf{Enc}} \right).$$

Finally, we define $\mathcal{S}_{\mathbf{x}}^{\mathsf{Enc}}$ to be $\mathcal{E}_{\mathbf{x}}^{\mathsf{Enc}}$ after random shuffling. Notice that $\mathcal{S}_{\mathbf{x}}^{\mathsf{Enc}}$ is the distribution of the transcript seen at the analyzer.

Definition 3. *For an n-party protocol $\mathcal{P}$ with encoding function Enc and $\mathbf{x} \in \mathcal{X}^n$, we let $\mathcal{S}_{\mathbf{x}}^{\mathsf{Enc}}$ denote the distribution over $\mathcal{Y}^{nm}$ obtained by applying Enc to the elements of $\mathbf{x}$ and then shuffling the resulting nm-tuple, i.e.,*

$$\mathcal{S}_{\mathbf{x}}^{\mathsf{Enc}} \sim \pi \circ \mathcal{E}_{\mathbf{x}}^{\mathsf{Enc}}$$

for π a uniformly random permutation over nm elements.

2.3   Security and Privacy

Given two distributions $\mathcal{D}_1$ and $\mathcal{D}_2$, we let $\mathrm{SD}(\mathcal{D}_1, \mathcal{D}_2)$ denote the *statistical distance* (aka the total variation distance) between $\mathcal{D}_1$ and $\mathcal{D}_2$.

We begin with a notion of σ-security for computation of a function f, which essentially says that distinct inputs with a common function value should be (almost) indistinguishable:

Definition 4 (σ-security). *An n-user one-round protocol $\mathcal{P} = (\mathsf{Enc}, \mathcal{A})$ in the anonymized model is said to be σ-secure for computing a function $f : \mathcal{X}^n \to \mathcal{Z}$ if for any $\mathbf{x}, \mathbf{x}' \in \mathcal{X}^n$ such that $f(\mathbf{x}) = f(\mathbf{x}')$, we have*

$$\mathrm{SD}\left(\mathcal{S}_{\mathbf{x}}^{\mathsf{Enc}}, \mathcal{S}_{\mathbf{x}'}^{\mathsf{Enc}} \right) \leq 2^{-\sigma}.$$

In this paper, we will primarily be concerned with the function that sums the inputs of each party, i.e., $f : \mathbb{F}_q^n \to \mathbb{F}_q$ given by $f(x_1, x_2, \ldots, x_n) = \sum_{i=1}^{n} x_i$.

We now define the notion of (ε, δ)-*differential privacy*. We say that two input vectors $\mathbf{x} = (x_1, x_2, \ldots, x_n) \in \mathcal{X}^n$ and $\mathbf{x}' = (x_1', x_2', \ldots, x_n') \in \mathcal{X}^n$ are *neighboring* if they differ on at most one party's data, i.e., $x_i = x_i'$ for all but one value of i.

Definition 5 ((ε, δ)-differential privacy). *An algorithm $M : \mathcal{X}^* \to \mathcal{Z}$ is (ε, δ)-differentially private if for every neighboring input vectors $\mathbf{x}, \mathbf{x}' \in \mathcal{X}^n$ and every $S \subseteq \mathcal{Z}$, we have*

$$\Pr[M(\mathbf{x}) \in S] \leq e^\varepsilon \cdot \Pr[M(\mathbf{x}') \in S] + \delta,$$

where probability is over the randomness of M.

We now define (ε, δ)-differential privacy specifically in the *shuffled model*.

Definition 6. *A protocol $\mathcal{P}$ with encoder $\mathsf{Enc} : \mathcal{X} \to \mathcal{Z}^m$ is (ε, δ)-differentially private in the shuffled model if the algorithm $M : \mathcal{X}^n \to \mathcal{Z}^{nm}$ given by*

$$M(x_1, x_2, \ldots, x_n) = \pi(\mathsf{Enc}_{x_1}, \mathsf{Enc}_{x_2}, \ldots, \mathsf{Enc}_{x_n})$$

is (ε, δ)-differentially private, where π is a uniformly random permutation on nm elements.

3   Proof of Theorem 1

In this section, we prove Theorem 1, i.e., that the split and mix protocol of Ishai et al. is σ-secure even for $m = \Theta\left(1 + \frac{\sigma + \log q}{\log n}\right)$ messages, improving upon the known bounds of $O(\log n + \sigma + \log q)$ [3,15,17].

Since we only consider Ishai et al.'s split and mix protocol in this section, we will drop the superscript from $\mathcal{S}_{\mathbf{x}}^{\mathsf{Enc}}$ and simply write $\mathcal{S}_{\mathbf{x}}$ to refer to the shuffled output distribution of the protocol. Recall that, by the definition of the protocol, $\mathcal{S}_{\mathbf{x}}$ is generated as follows: for every $i \in [n]$, sample $y_{m(i-1)+1}, \ldots, y_{mi} \in \mathbb{F}_q$ uniformly at random conditioned on $y_{m(i-1)+1} + \cdots + y_{mi} = x_i$. Then, pick a random permutation $\pi : [mn] \to [mn]$ and output $(y_{\pi(1)}, \ldots, y_{\pi(mn)})$.

Showing that the protocol is σ-secure is by definition equivalent to showing that $\mathrm{SD}(\mathcal{S}_{\mathbf{x}}, \mathcal{S}_{\mathbf{x}'}) \leq 2^{-\sigma}$ for all inputs $\mathbf{x}, \mathbf{x}' \in \mathbb{F}_q^n$ such that $\sum_{i \in [n]} x_i = \sum_{i \in [n]} x_i'$.

In fact, we prove a stronger statement, that each $\mathcal{S}_{\mathbf{x}}$ is γ-close (in statistical distance) to the distribution that is uniform over all vectors in $\mathbb{F}_q^{mn}$ whose sum of all coordinates is equal to $\sum_{i \in [n]} x_i$, as stated below.

Theorem 3. *For every $a \in \mathbb{F}_q$, let $\mathcal{S}_a$ denote the distribution on $\mathbb{F}_q^{mn}$ generated uniformly at random conditioned on all coordinates summing to a. For any parameter $\gamma > 0$ and any $m \geq \Theta(1 + \log_n(q/\gamma))$, the following holds: for every $\mathbf{x} \in \mathbb{F}_q^n$, the statistical distance between $\mathcal{S}_{\mathbf{x}}$ and $\mathcal{S}_{x_1 + \cdots + x_n}$ is at most γ.*

When plugging in $\gamma = 2^{-\sigma-1}$, Theorem 3 immediately implies Theorem 1 via the triangle inequality.

We now outline the overall proof approach. First, observe that $\mathcal{S}_{x_1+\cdots+x_n}$ puts probability mass equally across all vectors $\mathbf{t} \in \mathbb{F}_q^{mn}$ whose sum of all coordinates is $x_1+\cdots+x_n$, whereas $\mathcal{S}_{\mathbf{x}}$ puts mass proportional to the number of permutations $\pi : [mn] \to [mn]$ such that $\mathbf{y} := (t_{\pi^{-1}(1)}, \ldots, t_{\pi^{-1}(mn)})$ satisfies $y_{m(i-1)+1} + \cdots + y_{mi} = x_i$ for all $i \in [n]$. Thus, our task boils down to proving that this latter number is well-concentrated (for a random $\mathbf{t} \in \text{supp}(\mathcal{S}_{x_1+\cdots+x_n})$). We prove this via a second moment method (specifically Chebyshev's inequality). Carrying this out amounts to computing the first moment and upper-bounding the second moment of this number. The former is a simple calculation, whereas the latter involves proving an inequality regarding the rank of a certain random matrix (Theorem 4). We do so by providing a combinatorial characterization of the rank deficit of the relevant matrices (Lemma 2).

The rest of this section is organized as follows. In Subsect. 3.1, we define appropriate random variables, state the bound we want for the second moment (Lemma 4), and show how it implies our main theorem (Theorem 3). Then, in Subsect. 3.2, we relate the second moment to the rank of a random matrix (Proposition 1). Finally, we give a probabilistic bound on the rank of such a random matrix in Subsect. 3.3 (Theorem 4).

3.1 Bounding Statistical Distance via Second Moment Method

From now on, let us fix $\mathbf{x} \in \mathbb{F}_q^n$, and let $a = x_1 + \cdots + x_n$. The variables we define below will depend on $\mathbf{x}$ (or a), but, for notational convenience, we avoid indicating these dependencies in the variables' names.

For every $\mathbf{t} \in \mathbb{F}_q^{mn}$, let $Z_{\mathbf{t}}$ denote the number of permutations $\pi : [mn] \to [mn]$ such that $t_{\pi(m(i-1)+1)} + \cdots + t_{\pi(mi)} = x_i$ for all $i \in [n]$. From the definition[2] of $\mathcal{S}_{\mathbf{x}}$, its probability mass function is

$$f_{\mathcal{S}_{\mathbf{x}}}(\mathbf{t}) = \frac{Z_{\mathbf{t}}}{(mn)! \cdot q^{(m-1)n}}. \tag{1}$$

As stated earlier, Theorem 3 is essentially about the concentration of $Z_{\mathbf{t}}$, which we will prove via the second moment method. To facilitate the proof, for every $\pi : [mn] \to [mn]$, let us also denote by $Y_{\mathbf{t},\pi}$ the indicator variable of "$t_{\pi(r(i-1)+1)} + \cdots + t_{\pi(ri)} = x_i$ for all $i \in [n]$". Note that by definition we have

$$Z_{\mathbf{t}} = \sum_{\pi \in \Pi_{mn}} Y_{\mathbf{t},\pi} \tag{2}$$

where Π_{mn} denotes the set of all permutations of $[mn]$.

When we think of $\mathbf{t}$ as a random variable distributed according to $\mathcal{S}_a$, the mean of $Y_{\mathbf{t},\pi}$ (and hence of $Z_{\mathbf{t}}$) can be easily computed: the probability that $\mathbf{t}$

---

[2] Note that, if derived directly from the definition of $\mathcal{S}_{\mathbf{x}}$, π here should be replaced by π^{-1}. However, these two definitions are equivalent since $\pi \mapsto \pi^{-1}$ is a bijection.

satisfies "$t_{\pi(m(i-1)+1)} + \cdots + t_{\pi(mi)} = x_i$" is exactly $1/q$ for each $i \in [n-1]$, and these events are independent. Furthermore, when these events are true, it is automatically the case that the condition holds for $i = n$. Hence, we immediately have:

Observation 1. *For every* $\pi \in \Pi_{mn}$,

$$\underset{t \sim \mathcal{S}_a}{\mathbb{E}} [Y_{t,\pi}] = \frac{1}{q^{n-1}}. \tag{3}$$

The more challenging part is upper-bounding the second moment of Z_t (where we once again think of t as a random variable drawn from $\mathcal{S}_a$). This is equivalent to upper-bounding the expectation of $Y_{t,\pi} \cdot Y_{t,\pi'}$, where π, π' are independent uniformly random permutations of $[mn]$ and t is once again drawn from $\mathcal{S}_a$. On this front, we will show the following bound in the next subsections.

Lemma 1. *For every* $\pi \in \Pi_{mn}$, *we have*

$$\underset{\pi,\pi' \sim \Pi_{mn}, t \sim \mathcal{S}_a}{\mathbb{E}} [Y_{t,\pi} \cdot Y_{t,\pi'}] \leq \sum_{k \geq 1} \frac{q^k}{q^{2n-1}} \cdot \left(\frac{n^2}{(n/2)^{m-2}} \right)^{\frac{k-1}{2}}. \tag{4}$$

Since there are many parameters, the bound might look a bit confusing. However, the only property we need in order to show concentration of Z_t is that the right-hand side of (4) is dominated by the $k = 1$ term. This is the case when the term inside the parenthesis is $q^{-\Omega(1)}$, which indeed occurs when $m \geq 4 + \Omega(\log_n q)$.

The bound in Lemma 1 will be proved in the subsequent sections. For now, let us argue why such a bound implies our main theorem (Theorem 3).

Proof of Theorem 3. First, notice that (2) and Observation 1 together imply that

$$\underset{t \sim \mathcal{S}_a}{\mathbb{E}} [Z_t] = \frac{(mn)!}{q^{n-1}}. \tag{5}$$

For convenience, let us define μ as $\frac{(mn)!}{q^{n-1}}$.

We now bound the second moment of Z_t as follows:

$$\underset{t \sim \mathcal{S}_a}{\mathbb{E}} [Z_t^2] = \underset{t \sim \mathcal{S}_a}{\mathbb{E}} \left[\left(\sum_{\pi \in \Pi_{mn}} Y_{t,\pi} \right)^2 \right]$$

$$= ((mn)!)^2 \cdot \underset{\pi,\pi' \sim \Pi_{mn}, t \sim \mathcal{S}_a}{\mathbb{E}} [Y_{t,\pi} \cdot Y_{t,\pi'}]$$

$$\overset{(4)}{\leq} ((mn)!)^2 \cdot \left(\sum_{k \geq 1} \frac{q^k}{q^{2n-1}} \cdot \left(\frac{n^2}{(n/2)^{m-2}} \right)^{\frac{k-1}{2}} \right)$$

$$= ((mn)!)^2 \cdot \frac{1}{q^{2(n-1)}} \cdot \left(1 + \sum_{k \geq 2} q^{k-1} \cdot \left(\frac{n^2}{(n/2)^{m-2}} \right)^{\frac{k-1}{2}} \right)$$

$$= \mu^2 \cdot \left(1 + \sum_{k \geq 2} \left(\frac{(qn)^2}{(n/2)^{m-2}} \right)^{\frac{k-1}{2}} \right).$$

Now, let $p = \left(\frac{(qn)^2}{(n/2)^{m-2}} \right)^{\frac{1}{2}}$. If $m \geq 4 + 100 \log_{n/2}(q/\gamma)$, then we have $p \leq 0.01\gamma^4$. Plugging this back in the above inequality gives

$$\operatorname*{\mathbb{E}}_{t \sim \mathcal{S}_a} [Z_t^2] \leq \mu^2 \left(\frac{1}{1-p} \right) \leq \mu^2 \left(\frac{1}{1 - 0.01\gamma^4} \right) \leq \mu^2 (1 + 0.02\gamma^4).$$

In other words, we have $\operatorname{Var}_{t \sim \mathcal{S}_a}(Z_t) \leq (0.2\gamma^2 \cdot \mu)^2$. Hence, by Chebyshev's inequality, we have

$$\operatorname*{Pr}_{t \sim \mathcal{S}_a} [Z_t \leq (1 - 0.5\gamma)\mu] \leq 0.5\gamma. \tag{6}$$

Finally, notice that the statistical distance between $\mathcal{S}_x$ and $\mathcal{S}_a$ is

$$\sum_{t \in \mathbb{F}_q^{mn}} \max\{ f_{\mathcal{S}_a}(t) - f_{\mathcal{S}_x}(t), 0 \} = \sum_{\substack{t \in \mathbb{F}_q^{mn} \\ t_1 + \cdots + t_{mn} = a}} \max\left\{ \frac{1}{q^{mn-1}} - \frac{Z_t}{(mn)! \cdot q^{(m-1)n}}, 0 \right\}$$

$$= \sum_{\substack{t \in \mathbb{F}_q^{mn} \\ t_1 + \cdots + t_{mn} = a}} f_{\mathcal{S}_a}(t) \cdot \max\{ 1 - Z_t/\mu, 0 \}$$

$$= \operatorname*{\mathbb{E}}_{t \sim \mathcal{S}_a} [\max\{ 1 - Z_t/\mu, 0 \}]$$

$$\leq \operatorname*{Pr}_{t \sim \mathcal{S}_a} [Z_t \leq (1 - 0.5\gamma)\mu] \cdot 1 + \operatorname*{Pr}_{t \sim \mathcal{S}_a} [Z_t > (1 - 0.5\gamma)\mu] \cdot (0.5\gamma)$$

$$\overset{(6)}{\leq} (0.5\gamma) \cdot 1 + 1 \cdot (0.5\gamma)$$

$$= \gamma. \qquad \square$$

3.2   Relating Moments to Rank of Random Matrices

Having shown how Lemma 1 implies our main theorem (Theorem 3), we now move on to prove Lemma 1 itself. In this subsection, we deal with the first half of the proof by relating the quantity on the left-hand side of (4) to a quantity involving the rank of a certain random matrix.

Warm-Up: (Re-)Computing the First Moment. As a first step, let us define below a class of matrices that will be used throughout.

Definition 7. *For every permutation $\pi : [mn] \to [mn]$, let us denote by $\mathbf{A}_\pi \in \mathbb{F}_q^{n \times mn}$ the matrix whose i-th row is the indicator vector for $\pi(\{m(i - 1) + 1, \ldots, mi\})$. More formally,*

$$(\mathbf{A}_\pi)_{i,j} = \begin{cases} 1 & \textit{if } j \in \pi(\{m(i-1) + 1, \ldots, mi\}), \\ 0 & \textit{otherwise.} \end{cases}$$

Before we describe how these matrices relate to the second moment, let us illustrate their relation to the first moment, by sketching an alternative way to prove Observation 1. To do so, let us rearrange the left-hand side of (3) as $\mathbb{E}_{\mathbf{t}\sim\mathcal{S}_a}[Y_{\mathbf{t},\pi}] = \frac{1}{q^{mn-1}}\sum_{\mathbf{t}\in\mathbb{F}_q^{mn}} Y_{\mathbf{t},\pi}$. Now, observe that $Y_{\mathbf{t},\pi} = 1$ iff $\mathbf{A}_\pi \mathbf{t} = \mathbf{x}$. Since the rows of the matrix $\mathbf{A}_\pi$ have pairwise-disjoint supports, the matrix is always full rank (over $\mathbb{F}_q$), i.e., $\mathrm{rank}(\mathbf{A}_\pi) = n$. This means that the number of values of $\mathbf{t}$ satisfying the aforementioned equation is q^{mn-n}. Plugging this into the above expansion gives $\mathbb{E}_{\mathbf{t}\sim\mathcal{S}_a}[Y_{\mathbf{t},\pi}] = \frac{q^{mn-n}}{q^{mn-1}} = \frac{1}{q^{n-1}}$. Hence, we have rederived (3).

Relating Second Moment to Rank. In the previous subsection, we have seen the relation of matrix $\mathbf{A}_\pi$ to the first moment. We will now state such a relation for the second moment. Specifically, we will rephrase the left-hand side of (4) as a quantity involving matrices $\mathbf{A}_\pi$ and $\mathbf{A}_{\pi'}$. To do so, we will need the following additional notations:

Definition 8. *For a pair of permutations* $\pi, \pi' : [mn] \to [mn]$, *we let* $\mathbf{A}_{\pi,\pi'} \in \mathbb{F}_q^{2n\times mn}$ *denote the (column-wise) concatenation of* $\mathbf{A}_\pi$ *and* $\mathbf{A}_{\pi'}$, *i.e.,*

$$\mathbf{A}_{\pi,\pi'} = \begin{bmatrix} \mathbf{A}_\pi \\ \mathbf{A}_{\pi'} \end{bmatrix}.$$

Furthermore, let[3] the rank deficit *of* $\mathbf{A}_{\pi,\pi'}$ *be* $\mathrm{defc}(\mathbf{A}_{\pi,\pi'}) := 2n - \mathrm{rank}(\mathbf{A}_{\pi,\pi'})$.

Analogous to the relationship between the first moment and $\mathbf{A}_\pi$ seen in the previous subsection, the quantity $\mathbb{E}_{\mathbf{t}\sim\mathcal{S}_a}[Y_{\mathbf{t},\pi} \cdot Y_{\mathbf{t},\pi'}]$ is in fact proportional to the number of solutions to certain linear equations, which is represented by $\mathbf{A}_{\pi,\pi'}$. This allows us to give the bound to the former, as formalized below.

Proposition 1. *For every pair of permutations* $\pi, \pi' : [mn] \to [mn]$, *we have*

$$\mathbb{E}_{\mathbf{t}\sim\mathcal{S}_a}[Y_{\mathbf{t},\pi} \cdot Y_{\mathbf{t},\pi'}] \le \frac{q^{\mathrm{defc}(\mathbf{A}_{\pi,\pi'})}}{q^{2n-1}}.$$

Proof. First, let us rearrange the left-hand side term as

$$\mathbb{E}_{\mathbf{t}\sim\mathcal{S}_a}[Y_{\mathbf{t},\pi} \cdot Y_{\mathbf{t},\pi'}] = \frac{1}{q^{mn-1}} \sum_{\mathbf{t}\in\mathbb{F}_q^{mn}} Y_{\mathbf{t},\pi} \cdot Y_{\mathbf{t}\cdot\pi'}. \tag{7}$$

Now, notice that $Y_{\mathbf{t},\pi} = 1$ iff $\mathbf{A}_\pi \mathbf{t} = \mathbf{x}$. Similarly, $Y_{\mathbf{t},\pi'} = 1$ iff $\mathbf{A}_{\pi'}\mathbf{t} = \mathbf{x}$. In other words, $Y_{\mathbf{t},\pi} \cdot Y_{\mathbf{t}\cdot\pi'} = 1$ iff

$$\mathbf{A}_{\pi,\pi'}\mathbf{t} = \begin{bmatrix} \mathbf{x} \\ \mathbf{x} \end{bmatrix}.$$

---

[3] Note that $\mathrm{defc}(\mathbf{A}_{\pi,\pi'})$ is equal to the *corank* of $\mathbf{A}_{\pi,\pi'}^T$.

The number of solutions $\mathbf{t} \in \mathbb{F}_q^{mn}$ to the above equation is at most $q^{mn-\mathrm{rank}(\mathbf{A}_{\pi,\pi'})} = q^{(m-2)n+\mathrm{defc}(\mathbf{A}_{\pi,\pi'}^T)}$. Plugging this back into (7), we get

$$\mathop{\mathbb{E}}_{\mathbf{t} \sim \mathcal{S}_a} [Y_{\mathbf{t},\pi} \cdot Y_{\mathbf{t},\pi'}] \le \frac{1}{q^{mn-1}} \cdot q^{(m-2)n+\mathrm{defc}(\mathbf{A}_{\pi,\pi'})} = \frac{q^{\mathrm{defc}(\mathbf{A}_{\pi,\pi'})}}{q^{2n-1}},$$

as desired. □

3.3   Probabilistic Bound on Rank Deficit of Random Matrices

The final step of our proof is to bound the probability that the rank deficit of $\mathbf{A}_{\pi,\pi'}$ is large. Such a bound is encapsulated in Theorem 4 below. Notice that Proposition 1 and Theorem 4 immediately yield Lemma 1.

Theorem 4. *For all $m \ge 3$ and $k \in \mathbb{N}$, we have*

$$\mathop{\Pr}_{\pi,\pi' \sim \Pi_{mn}} [\mathrm{defc}(\mathbf{A}_{\pi,\pi'}) \ge k] \le \left(\frac{n^2}{(n/2)^{m-2}} \right)^{\frac{k-1}{2}}.$$

Characterization of Rank Deficit via Matching Partitions. To prove Theorem 4, we first give a "compact" and convenient characterization of the rank deficit of $\mathbf{A}_{\pi,\pi'}$. In order to do this, we need several additional notations: we say that a partition $S_1 \sqcup \cdots \sqcup S_k = U$ of a universe U is *non-empty* if $S_1, \ldots, S_k \ne \emptyset$. Moreover, for a set $S \subseteq [n]$, we use $S^{\to m} \subseteq [mn]$ to denote the set $\cup_{i \in S}\{m(i-1)+1, \ldots, mi\}$. Finally, we need the following definition of *matching partitions*.

Definition 9. *Let π, π' be any pair of permutations of $[mn]$. A pair of non-empty partitions $S_1 \sqcup \cdots \sqcup S_k = [n]$ and $S_1' \sqcup \cdots \sqcup S_k' = [n]$ is said to* match *with respect to π, π' iff*

$$\pi\left(S_j^{\to m}\right) = \pi'\left((S_j')^{\to m}\right) \tag{8}$$

for all $j \in [k]$. When π, π' are clear from the context, we may omit "with respect to π, π'" from the terminology.

Condition (8) might look a bit mysterious at first glance. However, there is a very simple equivalent condition in terms of the matrices $\mathbf{A}_\pi, \mathbf{A}_{\pi'}$: $S_1 \sqcup \cdots \sqcup S_k = [n]$ and $S_1' \sqcup \cdots \sqcup S_k' = [n]$ match iff the sum of rows $i \in S_j$ of $\mathbf{A}_\pi$ coincides with the sum of rows $i' \in S_j'$ of $\mathbf{A}_{\pi'}$, i.e., $\sum_{i \in S_j}(\mathbf{A}_\pi)_i = \sum_{i' \in S_j'}(\mathbf{A}_{\pi'})_{i'}$.

An easy-to-use equivalence of $\mathrm{defc}(\mathbf{A}_{\pi,\pi'}) = k$ is that a pair of matching partitions $S_1 \sqcup \cdots \sqcup S_k = [n]$ and $S_1' \sqcup \cdots \sqcup S_k' = [n]$ exists. We only use one direction of this relation, which we prove below.

Lemma 2. *For any permutations $\pi, \pi' : [mn] \to [mn]$, if $\mathrm{defc}(\mathbf{A}_{\pi,\pi'}) \ge k$, then there exists a pair of matching partitions $S_1 \sqcup \cdots \sqcup S_k = [n]$ and $S_1' \sqcup \cdots \sqcup S_k' = [n]$.*

Proof. We will prove the contrapositive. Let $\pi, \pi' : [mn] \rightarrow [mn]$ be any permutations, and suppose that there is no pair of matching partitions $S_1 \sqcup \cdots \sqcup S_k = [n]$ and $S'_1 \sqcup \cdots \sqcup S'_k = [n]$. We will show that $\mathrm{defc}(\mathbf{A}_{\pi,\pi'}) < k$, or equivalently $\mathrm{rank}(\mathbf{A}_{\pi,\pi'}) > 2n - k$.

Consider any pair of matching partitions[4] $S_1 \sqcup \cdots \sqcup S_t = [n]$ and $S'_1 \sqcup \cdots \sqcup S'_t = [n]$ that maximizes the number of parts t. From our assumption, we must have $t < k$.

For every part $j \in [t]$, let us pick an arbritrary element $i_j \in S_j$. Consider all rows of $\mathbf{A}_{\pi,\pi'}$, except the i_j-th rows for all $j \in [t]$ (i.e. $\{(\mathbf{A}_{\pi,\pi'})_i\}_{i \notin \{i_1,\ldots,i_t\}}$). We claim that these rows are linearly independent. Before we prove this, note that this imply that the rank of $\mathbf{A}_{\pi,\pi'}$ is at least $2n - t > 2n - k$, which would complete our proof.

We now move on to prove the linear independence of $\{(\mathbf{A}_{\pi,\pi'})_i\}_{i \notin \{i_1,\ldots,i_t\}}$. Suppose for the sake of contradiction that these rows are not linearly independent. Since the matrix $\mathbf{A}_{\pi,\pi'}$ is simply a concatenation of $\mathbf{A}_\pi$ and $\mathbf{A}_{\pi'}$, we have that $\{(\mathbf{A}_{\pi,\pi'})_i\}_{i \notin \{i_1,\ldots,i_t\}} = \{(\mathbf{A}_\pi)_i\}_{i \in [n] \setminus \{i_1,\ldots,i_t\}} \cup \{(\mathbf{A}_{\pi'})_{i'}\}_{i' \in [n]}$. The linear dependency of these rows mean that there exists a non-zero vector of coefficients $(c_1, \ldots, c_n, c'_1, \ldots, c'_n) \in \mathbb{F}_q^{2n}$ with $c_{i_1} = \cdots = c_{i_t} = 0$ such that

$$0 = \sum_{i \in [n]} c_i \cdot (\mathbf{A}_\pi)_i + \sum_{i' \in [n]} c'_{i'} \cdot (\mathbf{A}_{\pi'})_{i'}. \tag{9}$$

Since the rows of $\mathbf{A}_{\pi'}$ are linearly independent, there must exist $i^* \in [n]$ such that $c_{i^*} \neq 0$. Let $j \in [t]$ denote the index of the partition to which i^* belongs, i.e., $i^* \in S_j$. For notational convenience, we will assume, without loss of generality, that $j = t$.

Let $P_t : \mathbb{F}_q^{mn} \rightarrow \mathbb{F}_q^{(S_t^{\rightarrow m})}$ denote the projection operator that sends a vector $(v_\ell)_{\ell \in [mn]}$ to its restriction on coordinates in $S_t^{\rightarrow m}$, i.e., $(v_\ell)_{\ell \in S_t^{\rightarrow m}}$. Observe that $P_t((\mathbf{A}_\pi)_i)$ is non-zero iff $i \in S_t$ and $P_t((\mathbf{A}_{\pi'})_{i'})$ is non-zero iff $i' \in S'_t$. Thus, by taking P_t on both sides of (9), we have

$$0 = \sum_{i \in S_t} c_i \cdot P_t((\mathbf{A}_\pi)_i) + \sum_{i' \in S'_t} c_{i'} \cdot P_t((\mathbf{A}_\pi)_{i'}) \tag{10}$$

Now, let $T = \{i \in S_t \mid c_i \neq 0\}$ and $T' = \{i' \in S'_t \mid c_{i'} \neq 0\}$. Notice that $\mathrm{supp}\left(\sum_{i \in S_t} c_i \cdot P_t((\mathbf{A}_\pi)_i)\right) = \pi(T^{\rightarrow m})$ and $\mathrm{supp}\left(\sum_{i' \in S'_t} c_{i'} \cdot P_t((\mathbf{A}_\pi)_{i'})\right) = \pi'((T')^{\rightarrow m})$. Hence, from (10), we have

$$\pi(T^{\rightarrow m}) = \pi'((T')^{\rightarrow m}). \tag{11}$$

Consider the pair of partitions $S_1 \sqcup \cdots S_{t-1} \sqcup T \sqcup (S_t \setminus T) = [n]$ and $S'_1 \sqcup \cdots S'_{t-1} \sqcup T' \sqcup (S'_t \setminus T') = [n]$. From the definition of T, we must have $T \neq \emptyset$ because i^* belongs to T, and $(S_t \setminus T) \neq \emptyset$ because i_t does not belong to T. From this and (11), these partitions are non-empty and they match. However, these matching partitions have $t + 1$ parts, which contradicts the maximality of the number of parts of $S_1 \sqcup \cdots \sqcup S_t$ and $S'_1 \sqcup \cdots \sqcup S'_t$. This concludes our proof. $\square$

---

[4] Note that at least one matching partition always exists: $S_1 = [n] = S'_1$.

Proof of Theorem 4. With the characterization from the previous subsection ready, we can now easily prove our main theorem of this section (Theorem 4). We will also use two simple inequalities regarding the multinomial coefficients stated below. For completeness, we provide their proofs in the appendix.

Fact 1. *For every* $a_1, \ldots, a_k, a_1', \ldots, a_k' \in \mathbb{N}$, *we have*

$$\binom{a_1 + \cdots + a_k + a_1' + \cdots + a_k'}{a_1 + a_1', \ldots, a_k + a_k'} \geq \binom{a_1 + \cdots + a_k}{a_1, \ldots, a_k} \cdot \binom{a_1' + \cdots + a_k'}{a_1', \ldots, a_k'}$$

Fact 2. *For every* $k \in \mathbb{N}$ *and* $a_1, \ldots, a_k \in \mathbb{N}$, *we have*

$$\binom{a_1 + \cdots + a_k}{a_1, \ldots, a_k} \geq \left(\frac{a_1 + \cdots + a_k}{2} \right)^{\lfloor k/2 \rfloor}$$

Proof of Theorem 4. Let us fix a pair of non-empty partitions $S_1 \sqcup \cdots \sqcup S_k = [n]$ and $S_1' \sqcup \cdots \sqcup S_k' = [n]$ such that[5] $|S_i| = |S_i'|$ for all $i \in [k]$. Notice that, when we pick $\pi : [mn] \to [mn]$ uniformly at random, $(\pi(S_1^{\to m}), \cdots, \pi(S_k^{\to m}))$ is simply a random partition of $[mn]$ into subsets of size $m|S_1|, \ldots, m|S_k|$. Hence, the probability that these partitions match is equal to

$$\frac{1}{\binom{mn}{m|S_1|, \ldots, m|S_k|}}.$$

Hence, by evoking Lemma 2 and taking union bound over all pairs of partitions $S_1 \sqcup \cdots \sqcup S_k = [n]$ and $S_1' \sqcup \cdots \sqcup S_k' = [n]$, we have

$$\Pr_{\pi, \pi' \sim \Pi_{mn}} [\mathrm{defc}(\mathbf{A}_{\pi, \pi'}^T) \geq k] \leq \sum_{\substack{S_1 \sqcup \cdots \sqcup S_k = [n], S_1' \sqcup \cdots \sqcup S_k' = [n] \\ |S_1| = |S_1'| > 0, \ldots, |S_k| = |S_k'| > 0}} \frac{1}{\binom{mn}{m|S_1|, \ldots, m|S_k|}}$$

$$= \sum_{\substack{a_1, \ldots, a_k \in \mathbb{N} \\ a_1 + \cdots + a_k = n}} \sum_{\substack{S_1 \sqcup \cdots \sqcup S_k = [n], S_1' \sqcup \cdots \sqcup S_k' = [n] \\ |S_1| = |S_1'| = a_1, \ldots, |S_k| = |S_k'| = a_k}} \frac{1}{\binom{mn}{ma_1, \ldots, ma_k}}$$

$$= \sum_{\substack{a_1, \ldots, a_k \in \mathbb{N} \\ a_1 + \cdots + a_k = n}} \frac{\binom{n}{a_1, \ldots, a_k}^2}{\binom{mn}{ma_1, \ldots, ma_k}}$$

$$(\text{Fact 1}) \leq \sum_{\substack{a_1, \ldots, a_k \in \mathbb{N} \\ a_1 + \cdots + a_k = n}} \frac{1}{\binom{n}{a_1, \ldots, a_k}^{(m-2)}}$$

$$(\text{Fact 2}) \leq \sum_{\substack{a_1, \ldots, a_k \in \mathbb{N} \\ a_1 + \cdots + a_k = n}} \frac{1}{(n/2)^{(m-2) \cdot \lfloor k/2 \rfloor}}$$

$$\leq \frac{n^{k-1}}{(n/2)^{(m-2) \cdot \lfloor k/2 \rfloor}}$$

$$\leq \left(\frac{n^2}{(n/2)^{m-2}} \right)^{\frac{k-1}{2}} \qquad \qquad \square$$

---

[5] We may assume that $|S_i| = |S_i'|$; otherwise, $\pi(S_i^{\to m})$ and $\pi'((S_i')^{\to m})$ are obviously not equal and hence $S_1 \sqcup \cdots \sqcup S_k = [n]$ and $S_1' \sqcup \cdots \sqcup S_k' = [n]$ do not match.

4   Lower Bound Proofs

In this section, we prove our lower bound on the number of messages (Theorem 2), which is a direct consequence of the following two theorems:

Theorem 5. *Suppose $\sigma \geq 1$. Then, for any σ-secure n-party aggregation protocol over $\mathbb{F}_q$ in which each party sends m messages, we have $m = \Omega(\log_n q)$.*

Theorem 6. *For any σ-secure n-party aggregation protocol over $\mathbb{F}_q$ in which each party sends m messages, we have $m = \Omega\left(\frac{\sigma}{\log(\sigma n)}\right)$.*

We prove Theorem 5 in Sect. 4.1, while we prove Theorem 6 in Sect. 4.2. Before we proceed to the proofs, let us start by proving the following fact that will be used in both proofs: the output of the encoder on a party's input must uniquely determine the input held by the party.

Lemma 3. *For any n-party aggregation protocol $\mathcal{P}$ with encoder $\mathsf{Enc} : \mathbb{F}_q \to [\ell]^m$, we have that for any $x, x' \in \mathbb{F}_q$ with $x \neq x'$, the distributions $\mathcal{E}_x^{\mathsf{Enc}}$ and $\mathcal{E}_{x'}^{\mathsf{Enc}}$ have disjoint supports.*

As a consequence, for any output vector $\mathbf{y} \in [\ell]^{nm}$, there exists at most one $\mathbf{x} = (x_1, x_2, \ldots, x_n) \in \mathbb{F}_q^n$ such that $\mathbf{y}$ is a possible output $(\mathsf{Enc}_{x_1}, \mathsf{Enc}_{x_2}, \ldots, \mathsf{Enc}_{x_n})$.

Proof. For the sake of contradiction, suppose there exist $x, x' \in \mathbb{F}_q$ with $x \neq x'$ such that $\mathcal{E}_x^{\mathsf{Enc}}$ and $\mathcal{E}_{x'}^{\mathsf{Enc}}$ have a common element in the support, say $\mathbf{z}$. Then, let $\mathbf{z}' \in [\ell]^m$ be an element in the support of $\mathcal{E}_0^{\mathsf{Enc}}$. Note that it follows that $(\mathbf{z}, \underbrace{\mathbf{z}', \mathbf{z}', \ldots, \mathbf{z}'}_{n-1})$ is a possible output of inputs $(x, \mathbf{0}^{n-1})$ and $(x', \mathbf{0}^{n-1})$, which means that the analyzer cannot uniquely determine the parties' inputs from the output, thereby contradicting the correctness of the protocol. This completes the proof. $\square$

4.1   Field-Dependent Bound

We now present the proof of Theorem 5. Recall from Sect. 1.4 that $\mathcal{B}_s$ is defined as $\{\mathbf{x} \in \mathbb{F}_q^n \mid \sum_i x_i = s\}$. The key technical lemma is the following.

Lemma 4. *For each $s \in \mathbb{F}_q$ and every n-user one-round aggregation protocol $\mathcal{P}$ in the anonymized model with encoder $\mathsf{Enc} : \mathbb{F}_q \to [\ell]^m$, there exists a pair of inputs $\mathbf{x}, \mathbf{x}' \in \mathcal{B}_s$ such that $\mathrm{SD}\left(\mathcal{S}_{\mathbf{x}}^{\mathsf{Enc}}, \mathcal{S}_{\mathbf{x}'}^{\mathsf{Enc}}\right) \geq 1 - n^{nm}/q^{n-1}$.*

Throughout this subsection, let us fix $s \in \mathbb{F}_q$. Before proving Lemma 4, we first define some notation. For every possible shuffler output vector $\mathbf{y}$ and input $\mathbf{x} \in \mathcal{B}_s$, let $p_{\mathbf{x},\mathbf{y}}$ denote the probability that on input $\mathbf{x}$ the encoder outputs $\mathbf{y}$, i.e., $\Pr_{Y \sim \mathcal{S}_{\mathbf{x}}^{\mathsf{Enc}}}[Y = \mathbf{y}]$. Moreover, let $\mathrm{Inv}_{\mathbf{y}} = \{\mathbf{x} \in \mathcal{B}_s \mid p_{\mathbf{x},\mathbf{y}} > 0\}$ denote the set of sum-s inputs that are possible given that the output is $\mathbf{y}$.

Lemma 5. $|\mathrm{Inv_y}| \leq n^{nm}$.

Proof. Suppose $\mathbf{y}$ is an output vector consisting of nm messages with $|\mathrm{Inv_y}| > 0$. Consider a function $g : [nm] \rightarrow [n]$ that associates each of the mn messages to a single party. Note that $\mathbf{y}$ and g uniquely identify the set of messages Y_i sent by each party i. In turn, Y_i must correspond to a unique input x_i to party i by Lemma 3. Then, it follows that $\mathbf{y}$ and g can determine at most one input $\mathbf{x} \in \mathrm{Inv_y}$. Since there are at most n^{nm} valid functions g, the desired bound on $|\mathrm{Inv_y}|$ follows. $\qquad\square$

Let $p_{\mathbf{y}} = \sum_{\mathbf{x} \in \mathcal{B}_s} p_{\mathbf{x},\mathbf{y}}$, and define $d_{\mathbf{y}} = \frac{1}{q^{2n-2}} \sum_{\mathbf{x} \in \mathcal{B}_s} \sum_{\mathbf{x'} \in \mathcal{B}_s} |p_{\mathbf{x},\mathbf{y}} - p_{\mathbf{x'},\mathbf{y}}|$ as the average difference between probabilities $p_{\mathbf{x},\mathbf{y}}$ and $p_{\mathbf{x'},\mathbf{y}}$ over all pairs of inputs $\mathbf{x}, \mathbf{x'}$ with sum s. Then, we have the following lemma.

Lemma 6. $d_{\mathbf{y}} \geq 2 \left(1 - \frac{n^{nm}}{q^{n-1}} \right) p_{\mathbf{y}}/q^{n-1}$.

Proof. We have

$$q^{2n-2} d_{\mathbf{y}} \geq 2 \sum_{\mathbf{x} \in \mathrm{Inv_y}} \sum_{\mathbf{x'} \in \mathcal{B}_s \setminus \mathrm{Inv_y}} |p_{\mathbf{x},\mathbf{y}} - 0|$$

$$= 2 |\mathcal{B}_s \setminus \mathrm{Inv_y}| \sum_{\mathbf{x} \in \mathrm{Inv_y}} p_{\mathbf{x},\mathbf{y}}$$

$$= 2 \left(q^{n-1} - |\mathrm{Inv_y}| \right) p_{\mathbf{y}}$$

$$(\text{Lemma 5}) \geq 2 \left(q^{n-1} - n^{nm} \right) p_{\mathbf{y}}. \qquad\square$$

We now prove Lemma 4.

Proof of Lemma 4. We will in fact show the stronger statement that the (scaled) *average* statistical distance for pairs of inputs in $\mathcal{B}_s$ is lower bounded by $1 - n^{nm}/q^{n-1}$, i.e.,

$$d_{\mathrm{avg}} \geq 1 - \frac{n^{nm}}{q^{n-1}},$$

where

$$d_{\mathrm{avg}} = \frac{1}{q^{2n-2}} \sum_{\mathbf{x} \in \mathcal{B}_s} \sum_{\mathbf{x'} \in \mathcal{B}_s} \mathrm{SD} \left(\mathcal{S}_{\mathbf{x}}^{\mathsf{Enc}}, \mathcal{S}_{\mathbf{x'}}^{\mathsf{Enc}} \right). \tag{12}$$

Note that by Lemma 6, we have

$$d_{\mathrm{avg}} = \sum_{\mathbf{y}} \frac{d_{\mathbf{y}}}{2}$$

$$\geq \frac{1}{q^{n-1}} \left(1 - \frac{n^{nm}}{q^{n-1}} \right) \sum_{\mathbf{y}} p_{\mathbf{y}}$$

$$\geq \frac{1}{q^{n-1}} \left(1 - \frac{n^{nm}}{q^{n-1}} \right) \sum_{\mathbf{y}} \sum_{\mathbf{x} \in \mathcal{B}_s} p_{\mathbf{x},\mathbf{y}}$$

$$= 1 - \frac{n^{nm}}{q^{n-1}},$$

where the last line follows from the fact that $|\mathcal{B}_s| = q^{n-1}$. To conclude, note that it follows that at least one of the summands in (12) must be at least $1 - \frac{n^{nm}}{q^{n-1}}$, as desired. $\square$

Theorem 5 now follows easily from Lemma 4.

Proof of Theorem 5. Suppose $\mathcal{P}$ is such a σ-secure n-party aggregation protocol with encoder $\mathsf{Enc} : \mathbb{F}_q \to [\ell]^m$. Then, choose an arbitrary $s \in \mathbb{F}_q$. Note that by Lemma 4, there exist $\mathbf{x}, \mathbf{x}' \in \mathcal{B}_s$ such that $2^{-\sigma} \geq \mathrm{SD}\left(\mathcal{S}_{\mathbf{x}}^{\mathsf{Enc}}, \mathcal{S}_{\mathbf{x}'}^{\mathsf{Enc}}\right) \geq 1 - \frac{n^{nm}}{q^{n-1}}$. Thus, if $\sigma \geq 1$, it follows that $m = \Omega(\log_n q)$, as desired. $\square$

4.2 Security-Dependent Bound

We now turn to the proof of Theorem 6, which follows from the next theorem.

Theorem 7. *Let* Enc *be the encoder of any summation protocol for* $n > 2$ *parties with* m *messages sent per party. Then, there exists a vector* $\mathbf{x} \in \mathcal{B}_0$ *such that the statistical distance between* $\mathcal{S}_0^{\mathsf{Enc}}$ *and* $\mathcal{S}_{\mathbf{x}}^{\mathsf{Enc}}$ *is at least* $\frac{1}{(10nm)^{5m}}$.

It is not hard to see that Theorem 6 follows from Theorem 7:

Proof of Theorem 6. Simply note that by Theorem 7 and the definition of σ-security, we can find $\mathbf{x} \in \mathcal{B}_0$ such that $2^{-\sigma} \geq \mathrm{SD}\left(\mathcal{S}_0^{\mathsf{Enc}}, \mathcal{S}_{\mathbf{x}}^{\mathsf{Enc}}\right) \geq \frac{1}{(10nm)^{5m}}$, which immediately implies that $m = \Omega\left(\frac{\sigma}{\log(\sigma n)}\right)$, as desired. $\square$

Henceforth, we focus on proving Theorem 7.

Warm-up: Proof of Theorem 7 for Ishai et al.'s Protocol. Before we prove Theorem 7 for the general case, let us sketch a proof specific to Ishai et al.'s protocol. The input vector $\mathbf{x}$ we will use is simply $\mathbf{x} = (1, \cdots, 1, -(n-1))$.

To lower bound $\mathrm{SD}(\mathcal{S}_0, \mathcal{S}_{\mathbf{x}})$, we give a "distinguisher" $\mathcal{A}$ that takes in the output $(y_1, \ldots, y_{\pi(mn)})$ of the shuffler and outputs either 1 (i.e. "accept") or 0 (i.e. "reject"). Its key property will be that the probability that $\mathcal{A}$ accepts when $(y_{\pi(1)}, \ldots, y_{\pi(mn)}) \sim \mathcal{S}_0$ is more than that of when $(y_{\pi(1)}, \ldots, y_{\pi(mn)}) \sim \mathcal{S}_{\mathbf{x}}$ by an additive factor of $\frac{1}{(en)^m}$. This immediately implies that the distributions $\mathcal{S}_0$ and $\mathcal{S}_{\mathbf{x}}$ are at a statistical distance of at least $\frac{1}{(en)^m}$ as well. (Note that this bound is slightly better than the one in Theorem 7.)

The distinguisher $\mathcal{A}$ is incredibly simple here: $\mathcal{A}$ accepts iff $y_{\pi(1)} + \cdots + y_{\pi(m)} = 0$. To see that it satisfies the claim property, observe that, when $\pi(1), \ldots, \pi(m)$ not all come from the same party, $y_{\pi(1)} + \cdots + y_{\pi(m)}$ is simply a random number in $\mathbb{F}_q$, meaning that $\mathcal{A}$ accepts with probability $1/q$ (in both distributions). On the other hand, when $\pi(1), \ldots, \pi(m)$ come from the same party, $y_{\pi(1)} + \cdots + y_{\pi(m)}$ is always zero in the distribution $\mathcal{S}_0$ and hence $\mathcal{A}$ always accept. For the distribution $\mathcal{S}_{\mathbf{x}}$, if $\pi(1), \ldots, \pi(m)$ comes from the same party $i \neq n$, then the sum $y_{\pi(1)} + \cdots + y_{\pi(m)}$ is always one and hence $\mathcal{A}$ rejects. Thus, the probability that $\mathcal{A}$ accepts in the former distribution is more than that of the latter by an additive factor of $\frac{n-1}{\binom{nm}{m}} \geq \frac{1}{(en)^m}$. (The -1 factor corresponds to the case where $p(1), \cdots, p(m)$ comes from party $i = n$; here $\mathcal{A}$ might accept if $-(n-1) = 0$ in $\mathbb{F}_q$.) This concludes the proof sketch.

From Ishai et al.'s Protocol to General Protocols. Having sketched the argument for Ishai et al.'s protocol, one might wonder whether the same approach would work for general protocols. In particular, here instead of checking if $y_{\pi(1)} + \cdots + y_{\pi(m)} = 0$, we would check whether $y_{\pi(1)}, \ldots, y_{\pi(m)}$ is a valid output of the encoder when the input is zero. Now, the statement for when $\pi(1), \ldots, \pi(m)$ comes from the same party remains true. However, the issue is that, when $\pi(1), \ldots, \pi(m)$ do not all come from the same party, it is not necessarily true that the acceptance probability of $\mathcal{A}$ would be the same for both distributions.

To avoid having these "cross terms" affect the probability of acceptance of $\mathcal{A}$ too much, we pick the smallest integer t such that the "t-message marginals" (defined formally below) of $\mathcal{E}_0^{\mathsf{Enc}}$ and $\mathcal{E}_1^{\mathsf{Enc}}$ differ "substantially". Then, we modify $\mathcal{A}$ so that it performs an analogous check on $y_{\pi(1)}, \ldots, y_{\pi(t)}$ (instead of $y_{\pi(1)}, \ldots, y_{\pi(m)}$ as before). Once again, we will have that, if $\pi(1), \ldots, \pi(t)$ corresponds to the same party, then the probability that $\mathcal{A}$ accepts differs significantly between the two cases. On the other hand, due to the minimality of t, we can also argue that, when $\pi(1), \ldots, \pi(t)$ are not all from the same parties (i.e. "cross terms"), the difference is small. Hence, the former case would dominate and we can get a lower bound on the difference as desired. This is roughly the approach we take in the proof of Theorem 7 below. There are subtle points we have to change in the actual proof below. For instance, we cannot simply use the input $(1, \cdots, 1, -(n-1))$ as in the case of Ishai et al. protocol because, if the t-marginal of $\mathcal{E}_{-(n-1)}^{\mathsf{Enc}}$ deviates from $\mathcal{E}_0^{\mathsf{Enc}}$ more substantially than that of $\mathcal{E}_1^{\mathsf{Enc}}$, then this could affect the acceptance probability by a lot. Hence, in the actual proof, we instead pick x^* that minimizes the value of such t among all numbers in $\mathbb{F}_q$, and use the input vector $\mathbf{x} = (x^*, \ldots, x^*, -(n-1)x^*)$.

Additional Notation and Observation. To formally prove Theorem 7 in the general form, we need to formally define the notion of t-marginal. For a distribution $\mathcal{D}$ supported on $[\ell]^m$ and a positive integer $t \leq m$, its *t-marginal*, denoted by $\mathcal{D}|_t$, supported on $[\ell]^t$ is simply the marginal of $\mathcal{D}$ on the first t-coordinates; more formally, for all $\mathbf{y} \in [\ell]^t$, we have

$$\Pr_{Y \sim \mathcal{D}|_t}[Y = \mathbf{y}] = \sum_{y_{t+1}, \ldots, y_m \in [\ell]} \Pr_{Y \sim \mathcal{D}}[Y = \mathbf{y} \circ (y_{t+1}, \ldots, y_m)].$$

An observation that will simplify our proof is that we may assume w.l.o.g. that the distribution $\mathcal{E}_x^{\mathsf{Enc}}$ for every $x \in \mathbb{F}_q$ is permutation invariant, i.e., that for any $\pi : [m] \to [m]$ and any $\mathbf{y} \in [\ell]^m$, we have

$$\Pr_{Y \sim \mathcal{E}_x^{\mathsf{Enc}}}[Y = \mathbf{y}] = \Pr_{Y \sim \mathcal{E}_x^{\mathsf{Enc}}}[Y = \pi(\mathbf{y})].$$

This is because we may apply a random permutation to the encoding Enc_x before sending it to the shuffler, which does not change the distribution $\mathcal{S}_{\mathsf{Enc}}^x$. Notice that our observation implies that $\mathcal{E}_x^{\mathsf{Enc}}|_t$ is also permutation invariant.

Proof of Theorem 7. Let $t \leq m$ be the smallest positive integer such that $\max_{x \in \mathbb{F}_q} SD(\mathcal{E}_0^{\mathsf{Enc}}|_t, \mathcal{E}_x^{\mathsf{Enc}}|_t)$ is at least $\frac{1}{(10nm)^{4(m-t)}}$. Note that such t always exist because the requirement holds for $t = m$, at which $\mathcal{E}_0^{\mathsf{Enc}}|_t = \mathcal{E}_0^{\mathsf{Enc}}$ and $\mathcal{E}_1^{\mathsf{Enc}}|_t = \mathcal{E}_1^{\mathsf{Enc}}$ have statistical distance 1 (as their supports are disjoint due to Lemma 3).

For t as defined above, let $x^* = \operatorname{argmax}_{x \in \mathbb{F}_q} SD(\mathcal{E}_0^{\mathsf{Enc}}|_t, \mathcal{E}_x^{\mathsf{Enc}}|_t)$ and let us defined H as the set of elements of $[\ell]^t$ whose probability under $\mathcal{E}_0^{\mathsf{Enc}}|_t$ is higher than under $\mathcal{E}_{x^*}^{\mathsf{Enc}}|_t$. More formally, $H = \{\mathbf{y} \in [\ell]^t : \mathcal{E}_0^{\mathsf{Enc}}|_t(\mathbf{y}) > \mathcal{E}_{x^*}^{\mathsf{Enc}}|_t(\mathbf{y})\}$. By definition of statistical distance, we have

$$\Pr_{\mathbf{y} \in \mathcal{E}_0^{\mathsf{Enc}}|_t}[\mathbf{y} \in H] - \Pr_{\mathbf{y} \in \mathcal{E}_{x^*}^{\mathsf{Enc}}|_t}[\mathbf{y} \in H] = SD(\mathcal{E}_0^{\mathsf{Enc}}|_t, \mathcal{E}_{x^*}^{\mathsf{Enc}}|_t) \geq \frac{1}{(10nm)^{4(m-t)}}, \quad (13)$$

where the inequality follows from our choice of t.

Let $\mathbf{x} = (x^*, \ldots, x^*, -(n-1)x^*)$; clearly, $\mathbf{x} \in \mathcal{B}_0$ as desired. We next give a distinguisher for the distributions $\mathcal{S}_0^{\mathsf{Enc}}$ and $\mathcal{S}_{\mathbf{x}}^{\mathsf{Enc}}$. The distinguisher $\mathcal{A}$ takes in the permuted output $(y_{\pi(1)}, \ldots, y_{\pi(nm)})$. It returns one (i.e., "accept") if $(y_{\pi(1)}, \ldots, y_{\pi(t)})$ belongs to H and it returns zero (i.e., "reject") otherwise.

We will show that the probability that $\mathcal{A}$ accepts on $\mathcal{S}_0^{\mathsf{Enc}}$ is more than the probability that it accepts on $\mathcal{S}_{\mathbf{x}}^{\mathsf{Enc}}$ by at least $\frac{1}{(10nm)^{5m}}$, which implies that the statistical distance between $\mathcal{S}_0^{\mathsf{Enc}}$ and $\mathcal{S}_{\mathbf{x}}^{\mathsf{Enc}}$ is also at least $\frac{1}{(10nm)^{5m}}$ as desired.

To argue about the acceptance probability of $\mathcal{A}$, it is worth noting that there are two sources of randomness here: the output $\mathbf{y}$ (sampled from $\mathcal{E}_0^{\mathsf{Enc}}$ or $\mathcal{E}_{\mathbf{x}}^{\mathsf{Enc}}$) and the permutation π. More formally, we may write the probability that $\mathcal{A}$ accepts on $\mathcal{S}_0^{\mathsf{Enc}}$ and that on $\mathcal{S}_{\mathbf{x}}^{\mathsf{Enc}}$ as $\Pr_{\pi \sim \Pi_{mn}, \mathbf{y} \sim \mathcal{E}_0^{\mathsf{Enc}}}[\mathcal{A}(\pi(y)) = 1]$ and $\Pr_{\pi \sim \Pi_{mn}, \mathbf{y} \sim \mathcal{E}_{\mathbf{x}}^{\mathsf{Enc}}}[\mathcal{A}(\pi(y)) = 1]$ respectively. Hence, the difference between the probability that $\mathcal{A}$ accepts on $\mathcal{S}_0^{\mathsf{Enc}}$ and that on $\mathcal{S}_{\mathbf{x}}^{\mathsf{Enc}}$ is

$$\Pr_{\pi \sim \Pi_{mn}, \mathbf{y} \sim \mathcal{S}_0^{\mathsf{Enc}}}[\mathcal{A}(\pi(y)) = 1] - \Pr_{\pi \sim \Pi_{mn}, \mathbf{y} \sim \mathcal{S}_{\mathbf{x}}^{\mathsf{Enc}}}[\mathcal{A}(\pi(y)) = 1]$$

$$= \mathbb{E}_{\pi \sim \Pi_{mn}}\left[\Pr_{\mathbf{y} \sim \mathcal{S}_0^{\mathsf{Enc}}}[\mathcal{A}(\pi(y)) = 1] - \Pr_{\mathbf{y} \sim \mathcal{S}_{\mathbf{x}}^{\mathsf{Enc}}}[\mathcal{A}(\pi(y)) = 1]\right].$$

For brevity, let us define Δ_π as

$$\Delta_\pi := \Pr_{\mathbf{y} \sim \mathcal{S}_0^{\mathsf{Enc}}}[\mathcal{A}(\pi(y)) = 1] - \Pr_{\mathbf{y} \sim \mathcal{S}_{\mathbf{x}}^{\mathsf{Enc}}}[\mathcal{A}(\pi(y)) = 1].$$

Note that the quantity we would like to lower bound is now simply $\mathbb{E}_\pi[\Delta_\pi]$.

For each party $i \in \{1, \ldots, n\}$ and any permutation $\pi : [mn] \to [mn]$, we use U_π^i to denote $\{\pi(1), \ldots, \pi(t)\} \cap \{m(i-1)+1, \ldots, mi\}$. Furthermore, we define *the largest number of messages from a single party* for a permutation π as $C_\pi := \max_{i=1, \ldots, n} |U_\pi^i|$.

In the next part of the proof, we classify π into three categories, as listed below. For each category, we prove either a lower or an upper bound on Δ_π and the probability that a random permutation falls into that category.

I. $C_\pi = t$ and $|U_\pi^n| \neq t$. In other words, all of $\{\pi(1), \ldots, \pi(t)\}$ correspond to a single party and that party is not the last party.

II. $C_\pi = t$ and $|U_\pi^n| = t$. In other words, all of $\{\pi(1), \ldots, \pi(t)\}$ correspond to the last party n.

III. $C_\pi < t$. Not all of $\pi(1), \ldots, \pi(t)$ comes from the same party.

We will show that for category I permutations, Δ_π is large (Lemma 11) and the probability that a random permutation belongs to this category is not too small (Lemma 8). For both categories II and III, we show that $|\Delta_\pi|$ is small (Lemmas 9 and 11) and the probabilities that a random permutation belongs to each of these two categories are not too large (Lemmas 10 and 12).

These quantitative bounds are such that the first category dominates $\mathbb{E}_\pi[\Delta_\pi]$, meaning that we get a lower bound on this expectation as desired; this is done at the very end of the proof.

Category I: $C_\pi = t$ and $|U_\pi^n| \neq t$.

We now consider the first case: when $\{\pi(1), \ldots, \pi(t)\}$ corresponds to a single party $i \neq n$. In this case, Δ_π is exactly equal to the statistical distance between $\mathcal{E}_0^{\mathsf{Enc}}$ and $\mathcal{E}_{x^*}^{\mathsf{Enc}}$ (which we know from (13) to be large):

Lemma 7. *For any π such that $C_\pi = t$ and $|U_\pi^n| \neq t$, we have $\Delta_\pi = \mathrm{SD}(\mathcal{E}_0^{\mathsf{Enc}}|_t, \mathcal{E}_{x^*}^{\mathsf{Enc}}|_t)$.*

Proof. Let $i \in \{1, \ldots, n\}$ be the party such that $|U_\pi^i| = C_\pi = t$. When $\mathbf{y}$ is drawn from $\mathcal{E}_{\mathbf{x}}^{\mathsf{Enc}}$ (respectively $\mathcal{E}_0^{\mathsf{Enc}}$), $\{\pi(1), \cdots, \pi(t)\} \subseteq \{m(i-1)+1, \ldots, mi\}$, it is the case that $(y_{\pi(1)}, \ldots, y_{\pi(t)})$ is simply distributed as $\mathcal{E}_{x_i}^{\mathsf{Enc}}|_t$ (respectively $\mathcal{E}_0^{\mathsf{Enc}}|_t$). Recall that we assume that $U_\pi^n \neq t$, which means that $i \neq n$ or equivalently $x_i = x^*$. Hence, we have

$$\Pr_{\mathbf{y} \sim \mathcal{E}_{\mathbf{x}}^{\mathsf{Enc}}}[\mathcal{A}(\pi(\mathbf{y})) = 1] = \Pr_{\mathbf{y}' \sim \mathcal{E}_{x_i}^{\mathsf{Enc}}|_t}[\mathbf{y}' \in H] = \Pr_{\mathbf{y}' \sim \mathcal{E}_{x^*}^{\mathsf{Enc}}|_t}[\mathbf{y}' \in H].$$

and

$$\Pr_{\mathbf{y} \sim \mathcal{E}_0^{\mathsf{Enc}}}[\mathcal{A}(\pi(\mathbf{y})) = 1] = \Pr_{\mathbf{y}' \sim \mathcal{E}_0^{\mathsf{Enc}}|_t}[\mathbf{y}' \in H].$$

Combining the above two equalities with (13) implies that $\Delta_\pi = \mathrm{SD}(\mathcal{E}_0^{\mathsf{Enc}}|_t, \mathcal{E}_{x^*}^{\mathsf{Enc}}|_t)$ as desired. □

The probability that π falls into this category can be simply computed:

Lemma 8. $\Pr_\pi[C_\pi = t \wedge U_\pi^n \neq t] = \dfrac{(n-1) \cdot \binom{m}{t}}{\binom{nm}{t}}.$

Proof. $C_\pi = t$ and $|U_\pi^n| \neq t$ if and only if there exists a party $i \in \{1, \ldots, n-1\}$ such that $\pi(\{1, \ldots, t\}) \subseteq \{m(i-1) + 1, \ldots, mi\}$. For a fixed i, this happens with probability $\frac{\binom{m}{t}}{\binom{nm}{t}}$. Notice also that the event is disjoint for different i's. As a result, the total probability that this event occurs for at least one i is $(n-1) \cdot \frac{\binom{m}{t}}{\binom{nm}{t}}$. □

Category II: $C_\pi = t$ and $|U_\pi^n| = t$.

We now consider the second category: when $\{\pi(1), \ldots, \pi(t)\}$ corresponds to the last party n. In this case, our choice of x^* implies that $|\Delta_\pi|$ is upper bounded by the statistical distance between $\mathcal{E}_0^{\mathsf{Enc}}|_t$ and $\mathcal{E}_{x^*}^{\mathsf{Enc}}|_t$, as formalized below.

Lemma 9. *For any π such that $C_\pi = t$ and $|U_\pi^n| = t$, we have $|\Delta_\pi| \leq \mathrm{SD}(\mathcal{E}_0^{\mathsf{Enc}}|_t, \mathcal{E}_{x^*}^{\mathsf{Enc}}|_t)$.*

Proof. In this case, we have $\{\pi(1), \cdots, \pi(i)\} \subseteq \{m(n-1) + 1, \ldots, mn\}$. Thus, when $\mathbf{y}$ is drawn from $\mathcal{E}_{\mathbf{x}}^{\mathsf{Enc}}$ (respectively $\mathcal{E}_0^{\mathsf{Enc}}$), it is the case that $(y_{\pi(1)}, \ldots, y_{\pi(t)})$ is simply distributed as $\mathcal{E}_{x_n}^{\mathsf{Enc}}|_t$ (respectively $\mathcal{E}_0^{\mathsf{Enc}}|_t$). Hence, we have $\Pr_{\mathbf{y} \sim \mathcal{E}_{\mathbf{x}}^{\mathsf{Enc}}}[\mathcal{A}(\pi(\mathbf{y})) = 1] = \Pr_{\mathbf{y}' \sim \mathcal{E}_{x_n}^{\mathsf{Enc}}|_t}[\mathbf{y}' \in H]$ and $\Pr_{\mathbf{y} \sim \mathcal{E}_0^{\mathsf{Enc}}}[\mathcal{A}(\pi(\mathbf{y})) = 1] = \Pr_{\mathbf{y}' \sim \mathcal{E}_0^{\mathsf{Enc}}|_t}[\mathbf{y}' \in H]$. Combining the above two equalities implies that $|\Delta_\pi| \leq \mathrm{SD}(\mathcal{E}_0^{\mathsf{Enc}}|_t, \mathcal{E}_{x_n}^{\mathsf{Enc}}|_t)$. Recall that x^* is chosen to maximize $\mathrm{SD}(\mathcal{E}_0^{\mathsf{Enc}}|_t, \mathcal{E}_{x^*}^{\mathsf{Enc}}|_t)$, which means that $\mathrm{SD}(\mathcal{E}_0^{\mathsf{Enc}}|_t, \mathcal{E}_{x_n}^{\mathsf{Enc}}|_t) \leq \mathrm{SD}(\mathcal{E}_0^{\mathsf{Enc}}|_t, \mathcal{E}_{x^*}^{\mathsf{Enc}}|_t)$. Hence, we have $|\Delta_\pi| \leq \mathrm{SD}(\mathcal{E}_0^{\mathsf{Enc}}|_t, \mathcal{E}_{x^*}^{\mathsf{Enc}}|_t)$ as desired. □

The probability that π falls into this category can be simply computed in a similar manner as in the first case:

Lemma 10. $\Pr_\pi[C_\pi = t \land |U_\pi^n| = t] = \frac{\binom{m}{t}}{\binom{nm}{t}}$.

Proof. $C_\pi = t$ and $|U_\pi^n| = t$ if and only if $\pi(\{1, \ldots, t\}) \subseteq \{m(n-1)+1, \ldots, mn\}$. This happens with probability exactly $\frac{\binom{m}{t}}{\binom{nm}{t}}$. □

Category III: $C_\pi < t$.

Finally, we consider any permutation π such that not all of $\{\pi(1), \ldots, \pi(t)\}$ correspond to a single party. On this front, we may use our choice of t to give an upper bound on $|\Delta_\pi|$ as follows.

Lemma 11. *For any π such that $C_\pi < t$, we have $|\Delta_\pi| < m \cdot \frac{1}{(10nm)^{4(m-C_\pi)}}$.*

Proof. In fact, we will show something even stronger: that the statistical distance of $(y_{\pi(1)}, \ldots, y_{\pi(t)})$ when $\mathbf{y}$ is drawn from $\mathcal{E}_0^{\mathsf{Enc}}$ and that when $\mathbf{y}$ is drawn from $\mathcal{E}_{\mathbf{x}}^{\mathsf{Enc}}$ is at most $m \cdot \frac{1}{(10nm)^{4(m-C_\pi)}}$. The desired bound immediately follows.

Let I denote the set of all parties i such that $U_i \neq \emptyset$. Observe that, when $\mathbf{y}$ is drawn from $\mathcal{E}_{\mathbf{x}}^{\mathsf{Enc}}$ (respectively $\mathcal{E}_0^{\mathsf{Enc}}$), $(y_p)_{p \in U_i}$ is simply distributed as $\mathcal{E}_{x_i}^{\mathsf{Enc}}|_{|U_i|}$ (respectively $\mathcal{E}_0^{\mathsf{Enc}}|_{|U_i|}$) and that these are independent for different i. In other words, $(y_{\pi(1)}, \ldots, y_{\pi(t)})$ is (after appropriate rearrangement) just the product distribution $\prod_{i \in I} \mathcal{E}^{\mathsf{Enc}}_{x_i}|_{|U_i|}$ (respectively $\prod_{i \in I} \mathcal{E}^{\mathsf{Enc}}_0|_{|U_i|}$).

Recall from the definition of C_π that $|U_i|$ is at most C_π for all i. Since $C_\pi < t$ and from our choice of t, we must have $\mathrm{SD}(\mathcal{E}^{\mathsf{Enc}}_0|_{|U_i|}, \mathcal{E}^{\mathsf{Enc}}_{x_i}|_{|U_i|}) < \frac{1}{(10nm)^{4(m-C_\pi)}}$ for all $i \in I$. Hence, we also have

$$\mathrm{SD}\left(\prod_{i \in I} \mathcal{E}^{\mathsf{Enc}}_0|_{|U_i|}, \prod_{i \in I} \mathcal{E}^{\mathsf{Enc}}_{x_i}|_{|U_i|}\right) < |I| \cdot \frac{1}{(10nm)^{4(m-C_\pi)}} \leq m \cdot \frac{1}{(10nm)^{4(m-C_\pi)}},$$

which concludes the proof. $\qquad \square$

Next, we bound the probability that a random permutation π belongs to this category:

Lemma 12. *For all $j < t$, we have $\Pr_\pi[C_\pi = j] \leq \frac{n \cdot \binom{m}{t}}{\binom{nm}{t}} \cdot (nm)^{3(t-j)}$.*

Proof. If $C_\pi = j$, there must exist a subset $T \subseteq \{1, \ldots, t\}$ of size j and a party $i \in \{1, \ldots, n\}$ such that $\pi(T) \subseteq \{m(i-1)+1, \ldots, mi\}$. For a fixed T and i, this happens with probability exactly $\frac{\binom{m}{j}}{\binom{nm}{j}}$. Hence, by union bound over all T and i, we have

$$\Pr_\pi[C_\pi = j] \leq n \cdot \binom{t}{j} \cdot \frac{\binom{m}{j}}{\binom{nm}{j}} \leq \frac{n \cdot \binom{m}{t}}{\binom{nm}{t}} \cdot \frac{\binom{t}{j} \cdot m^{t-j}}{(nm)^{j-t}} \leq \frac{n \cdot \binom{m}{t}}{\binom{nm}{t}} \cdot (nm)^{3(t-j)}. \quad \square$$

Putting Things Together. With all the claims ready, it is now simple to finish the proof of Theorem 7. The difference between the probability that $\mathcal{A}$ accepts on $\mathcal{S}^{\mathsf{Enc}}_0$ and that on $\mathcal{S}^{\mathsf{Enc}}_x$ is

$$\mathbb{E}_\pi[\Delta_\pi] = \Pr_\pi[C_\pi = t \wedge |U^n_\pi| \neq t] \cdot \mathbb{E}_\pi[\Delta_\pi \mid C_\pi = t \wedge |U^n_\pi| \neq t]$$

$$+ \Pr_\pi[C_\pi = t \wedge |U^n_\pi| = t] \cdot \mathbb{E}_\pi[\Delta_\pi \mid C_\pi = t \wedge |U^n_\pi| = t]$$

$$+ \sum_{j=1}^{t-1} \Pr_\pi[C_\pi = j] \cdot \mathbb{E}_\pi[\Delta_\pi \mid C_\pi = j]$$

$$\text{(Lemmas 7, 8, 9, 10)} \geq \frac{(n-1) \cdot \binom{m}{t}}{\binom{nm}{t}} \cdot \mathrm{SD}(\mathcal{E}^{\mathsf{Enc}}_0|_t, \mathcal{E}^{\mathsf{Enc}}_{x^*}|_t) - \frac{\binom{m}{t}}{\binom{nm}{t}} \cdot \mathrm{SD}(\mathcal{E}^{\mathsf{Enc}}_0|_t, \mathcal{E}^{\mathsf{Enc}}_{x^*}|_t)$$

$$+ \sum_{j=1}^{t-1} \Pr_\pi[C_\pi = j] \cdot \mathbb{E}_\pi[\Delta_\pi \mid C_\pi = j]$$

$$\text{(From } n \geq 3) \geq \frac{n \cdot \binom{m}{t}}{3\binom{nm}{t}} \cdot \mathrm{SD}(\mathcal{E}^{\mathsf{Enc}}_0|_t, \mathcal{E}^{\mathsf{Enc}}_{x^*}|_t) + \sum_{j=1}^{t-1} \Pr_\pi[C_\pi = j] \cdot \mathbb{E}_\pi[\Delta_\pi \mid C_\pi = j]$$

$$\text{((13) and Lemma 11)} \geq \frac{n \cdot \binom{m}{t}}{3\binom{nm}{t}} \cdot \frac{1}{(10nm)^{4(m-t)}} - \sum_{j=1}^{t-1} \frac{\Pr_\pi[C_\pi = j] \cdot m}{(10nm)^{4(m-j)}}$$

$$
\text{(Lemma 12)} \geq \frac{n \cdot \binom{m}{t}}{\binom{nm}{t}} \cdot \left(\frac{1}{3} \cdot \frac{1}{(10nm)^{4(m-t)}} - \sum_{j=1}^{t-1} \frac{(nm)^{3(t-j)}m}{(10nm)^{4(m-j)}} \right)
$$

$$
\geq \frac{n \cdot \binom{m}{t}}{\binom{nm}{t}} \cdot \left(\frac{1}{3} - \sum_{j=1}^{t-1} \frac{1}{10^{t-j}} \right) \cdot \frac{1}{(10nm)^{4(m-t)}}
$$

$$
\geq \frac{n \cdot \binom{m}{t}}{\binom{nm}{t}} \cdot \frac{1}{10} \cdot \frac{1}{(10nm)^{4(m-t)}}
$$

$$
\geq \frac{1}{(nm)^t} \cdot \frac{1}{10} \cdot \frac{1}{(10nm)^{4(m-t)}}
$$

$$
\geq \frac{1}{(10nm)^{5m}}. \qquad \qquad \square
$$

5   Conclusion and Open Questions

In this work, we provide an improved analysis for the split and mix protocol of Ishai et al. [17] in the shuffled model. Our analysis reduces the number of messages required by the protocol by a logarithmic factor. Moreover, for a large range of parameters, we give an asymptotically tight lower bound in terms of the number of messages that each party needs to send for *any* protocol for secure summation.

Although our lower bound is tight in terms of the number of messages, it does not immediately imply any communication lower bound beyond the trivial $\log q$ bound. For instance, when $q = n^{\log n}$ and σ is a constant, then the number of messages needed by Ishai et al.'s protocol is $O\left(\frac{\log q}{\log n}\right) = O(\log n)$ but each message is also of length $O(\log q)$. However, our lower bound does not preclude a protocol with the same number of messages but of length only $O(\log n)$ bits. It remains an interesting open question to close this gap.

Another interesting open question is whether we can give a lower bound for (ε, δ)-differentially private summation protocols when ε is a constant. Currently, our lower bound does not give anything in this regime. In fact, to the best of our knowledge, it remains possible that an $(\varepsilon, 0)$-differentially private summation protocol exists with error $O(1/\varepsilon)$ and where each party sends only $O_\varepsilon(\log n)$ bits. Coming up with such a protocol, or proving that one does not exist, would be a significant step in understanding the power of differential private algorithms in the shuffled model. We point out that following up on this work, [14] studied this question obtaining a pure differentially protocol for summation along with a lower bound, though the tight answer remains unknown.

A   Proofs of Bounds for Multinomial Coefficients

Below we prove Facts 1 and 2 from Sect. 3.

Proof of Fact 1. Let $U = [a_1 + a'_1 + \cdots + a_k + a'_k]$, $A = [a_1 + \cdots + a_k]$ and $B = U \setminus A$.

Consider the following process of generating a partition $S_1 \sqcup \cdots \sqcup S_k = U$. First, take a partition $T_1 \sqcup \cdots \sqcup T_k = A$ and a partition $T'_1 \sqcup \cdots \sqcup T'_k = B$. Then, let $S_i = T_i \cup T'_i$ for all $i \in [k]$.

Notice that each pair of $T_1 \sqcup \cdots \sqcup T_k$ with $|T_i| = a_i$ and $T'_1 \sqcup \cdots \sqcup T'_k$ with $|P_i| = a'_i$ produces different $S_1 \sqcup \cdots \sqcup S_k = U$ with $|S_i| = a_i + a'_i$. Since the number of such pairs $T_1 \sqcup \cdots \sqcup T_k$ and $T'_1 \sqcup \cdots \sqcup T'_k$ is $\binom{a_1 + \cdots + a_k}{a_1, \ldots, a_k} \cdot \binom{a'_1 + \cdots + a'_k}{a'_1, \ldots, a'_k}$ and the number of $S_1 \sqcup \cdots \sqcup S_k = U$ with $|S_i| = a_i + a'_i$ is only $\binom{a_1 + \cdots + a_k + a'_1 + \cdots + a'_k}{a_1 + a'_1, \ldots, a_k + a'_k}$, we have

$$\binom{a_1 + \cdots + a_k + a'_1 + \cdots + a'_k}{a_1 + a'_1, \ldots, a_k + a'_k} \geq \binom{a_1 + \cdots + a_k}{a_1, \ldots, a_k} \cdot \binom{a'_1 + \cdots + a'_k}{a'_1, \ldots, a'_k}$$

as desired. □

Proof of Fact 2. Assume w.l.o.g. that $a_1 \leq a_2 \leq \cdots \leq a_k$. We have

$$\binom{a_1 + \cdots + a_k}{a_1, \ldots, a_k} = \prod_{i=1}^{k} \binom{a_i + \cdots + a_k}{a_i} \geq \prod_{i=1}^{\lfloor k/2 \rfloor} \binom{a_i + \cdots + a_k}{a_i}$$

$$\geq \prod_{i=1}^{\lfloor k/2 \rfloor} (a_i + \cdots + a_k)$$

$$\geq \left(\frac{a_1 + \cdots + a_k}{2} \right)^{\lfloor k/2 \rfloor},$$

where the last inequality uses the fact that $a_1 \leq \cdots \leq a_k$. □

B   Proof of Corollary 1

Corollary 1 follows from our main theorem (Theorem 1) and the connection between secure summation protocols and differentially private summation protocols due to Balle et al. [3]. We recall the latter below.

Lemma 13 (Lemma 4.1 of [3]). *Given a σ-secure protocol in the anonymized setting for n-party summation over the domain $\mathbb{F}_q$, where each party sends $f(q, n, \sigma)$ messages each of $g(q, n, \sigma)$ bits, there exists an $(\varepsilon, (1 + e^\varepsilon)2^{-\sigma-1})$-differentially private protocol in the shuffled model for real summation with absolute error $O(1 + 1/\varepsilon)$ where each party sends $f(O(n^{3/2}), n, \sigma)$ messages each of $g(O(n^{3/2}), n, \sigma)$ bits.*

Corollary 1 now follows immediately by applying Lemma 13 and Theorem 1 with $\sigma = 1 + \log\left(\frac{1 + e^\varepsilon}{\delta}\right) = O\left(1 + \varepsilon + \log(1/\delta)\right)$.

We remark here that Lemma 13 as stated above is slightly different from Lemma 4.1 of [3]. In particular, in [3], the statement requires the secure summation protocol to works for any $\mathbb{Z}_q$ even when q is not a prime power. On the other hand, our analysis in this paper (which uses rank of matrices) only applies to when q is a prime power (i.e., $\mathbb{F}_q$ is a field). However, it turns out that this does not affect the connection too much: instead of picking $q = 2\lceil n^{3/2}\rceil$ as in [3], we may pick q to be the smallest prime larger than $2n^{3/2}$. In this case, q remains $O(n^{3/2})$ and the remaining argument of [3] remains exactly the same.

References

1. Abadi, M., et al.: Deep learning with differential privacy. In: Proceedings of the 2016 ACM SIGSAC Conference on Computer and Communications Security, pp. 308–318. ACM (2016)
2. Balle, B., Bell, J., Gascón, A., Nissim, K.: Improved summation from shuffling (2019). http://arxiv.org/abs/1909.11225
3. Balle, B., Bell, J., Gascón, A., Nissim, K.: Differentially private summation with multi-message shuffling. CoRR abs/1906.09116 (2019). http://arxiv.org/abs/1906.09116
4. Balle, B., Bell, J., Gascón, A., Nissim, K.: The privacy blanket of the shuffle model. In: Boldyreva, A., Micciancio, D. (eds.) CRYPTO 2019, Part II. LNCS, vol. 11693, pp. 638–667. Springer, Cham (2019). https://doi.org/10.1007/978-3-030-26951-7_22
5. Balle, B., Bell, J., Gascón, A., Nissim, K.: Private summation in the multi-message shuffle model. arXiv: 2002.00817 (2020)
6. Bittau, A., et al.: PROCHLO: strong privacy for analytics in the crowd. In: Proceedings of the 26th Symposium on Operating Systems Principles, Shanghai, China, 28–31 October 2017, pp. 441–459 (2017)
7. Bonawitz, K., et al.: Practical secure aggregation for privacy-preserving machine learning. In: Thuraisingham, B.M., Evans, D., Malkin, T., Xu, D. (eds.) Proceedings of the 2017 ACM SIGSAC Conference on Computer and Communications Security, CCS 2017, Dallas, TX, USA, 30 October–03 November 2017, pp. 1175–1191. ACM (2017)
8. Cheu, A., Smith, A., Ullman, J., Zeber, D., Zhilyaev, M.: Distributed differential privacy via shuffling. In: Ishai, Y., Rijmen, V. (eds.) EUROCRYPT 2019, Part I. LNCS, vol. 11476, pp. 375–403. Springer, Cham (2019). https://doi.org/10.1007/978-3-030-17653-2_13
9. Cormode, G., Garofalakis, M., Haas, P.J., Jermaine, C., et al.: Synopses for massive data: samples, histograms, wavelets, sketches. Found. Trends Databases **4**(1–3), 1–294 (2011)
10. Corrigan-Gibbs, H., Boneh, D.: Prio: private, robust, and scalable computation of aggregate statistics. In: NSDI (2017)
11. Erlingsson, Ú., et al.: Encode, shuffle, analyze privacy revisited: formalizations and empirical evaluation. arXiv preprint arXiv:2001.03618 (2020)
12. Erlingsson, Ú., Feldman, V., Mironov, I., Raghunathan, A., Talwar, K., Thakurta, A.: Amplification by shuffling: from local to central differential privacy via anonymity. In: SODA, pp. 2468–2479 (2019)
13. Ghazi, B., Golowich, N., Kumar, R., Pagh, R., Velingker, A.: On the power of multiple anonymous messages. arXiv preprint arXiv:1908.11358 (2019)
14. Ghazi, B., Kumar, R., Manurangsi, P., Pagh, R., Velingker, A.: Pure differentially private summation from anonymous messages. arXiv: 2020.01919 (2020)

15. Ghazi, B., Pagh, R., Velingker, A.: Scalable and differentially private distributed aggregation in the shuffled model (2019). http://arxiv.org/abs/1906.08320
16. Goryczka, S., Xiong, L., Sunderam, V.: Secure multiparty aggregation with differential privacy: a comparative study. In: EDBT/ICDT 2013 Workshops (2013)
17. Ishai, Y., Kushilevitz, E., Ostrovsky, R., Sahai, A.: Cryptography from anonymity. In: IEEE Symposium on Foundations of Computer Science (FOCS) (2006)
18. Kairouz, P., et al.: Advances and open problems in federated learning. arXiv: 1912.04977 (2019)
19. Kearns, M.: Efficient noise-tolerant learning from statistical queries. JACM 45(6), 983–1006 (1998)
20. Kenthapadi, K., Korolova, A., Mironov, I., Mishra, N.: Privacy via the Johnson-Lindenstrauss transform. J. Privacy Confid. 5, 39–71 (2013)
21. Konečný, J., McMahan, H.B., Yu, F.X., Richtárik, P., Suresh, A.T., Bacon, D.: Federated learning: strategies for improving communication efficiency. arXiv preprint arXiv:1610.05492 (2016)
22. Liu, A., Xia, L., Duchowski, A., Bailey, R., Holmqvist, K., Jain, E.: Differential privacy for eye-tracking data. In: Proceedings of the 11th ACM Symposium on Eye Tracking Research & Applications, pp. 1–10 (2019)
23. McMahan, B., Moore, E., Ramage, D., Hampson, S., Arcas, B.A.: Communication-efficient learning of deep networks from decentralized data. In: Artificial Intelligence and Statistics, pp. 1273–1282 (2017)
24. McMahan, H.B., Ramage, D.: Federated learning: collaborative machine learning without centralized training data. Google AI Blog, April 2017. https://ai.googleblog.com/2017/04/federated-learning-collaborative.html
25. McMahan, H.B., Ramage, D., Talwar, K., Zhang, L.: Learning differentially private recurrent language models. arXiv preprint arXiv:1710.06963 (2017)
26. Melis, L., Danezis, G., Cristofaro, E.D.: Efficient private statistics with succinct sketches. In: NDSS (2016)
27. Mishra, N., Sandler, M.: Privacy via pseudorandom sketches. In: PODS (2006)
28. Reyzin, L., Smith, A.D., Yakoubov, S.: Turning hate into love: homomorphic ad hoc threshold encryption for scalable MPC. IACR Cryptology ePrint Archive (2018)
29. Steil, J., Hagestedt, I., Huang, M.X., Bulling, A.: Privacy-aware eye tracking using differential privacy. In: Proceedings of the 11th ACM Symposium on Eye Tracking Research & Applications, pp. 1–9 (2019)
30. Wang, T., Xu, M., Ding, B., Zhou, J., Li, N., Jha, S.: Practical and robust privacy amplification with multi-party differential privacy. arXiv:1908.11515 (2019)
31. Woodruff, D.P., et al.: Sketching as a tool for numerical linear algebra. Found. Trends Theor. Comput. Sci. 10(1–2), 1–157 (2014)

Broadcast-Optimal Two-Round MPC

Ran Cohen[1]([✉]), Juan Garay[2]([✉]), and Vassilis Zikas[3]

[1] Northeastern University, Boston, USA
rancohen@ccs.neu.edu
[2] Texas A&M University, College Station, USA
garay@cse.tamu.edu
[3] School of Informatics, University of Edinburgh & IOHK, Edinburgh, UK
vzikas@inf.ed.ac.uk

Abstract. An intensive effort by the cryptographic community to mini-mize the round complexity of secure multi-party computation (MPC) has recently led to optimal two-round protocols from minimal assumptions. Most of the proposed solutions, however, make use of a broadcast channel in every round, and it is unclear if the broadcast channel can be replaced by standard point-to-point communication in a round-preserving man-ner, and if so, at what cost on the resulting security.

In this work, we provide a complete characterization of the trade-off between number of broadcast rounds and achievable security level for two-round MPC tolerating arbitrarily many active corruptions. Specif-ically, we consider all possible combinations of broadcast and point-to-point rounds against the three standard levels of security for maliciously secure MPC protocols, namely, security with identifiable, unanimous, and selective abort. For each of these notions and each combination of broadcast and point-to-point rounds, we provide either a tight feasibility or an infeasibility result of two-round MPC. Our feasibility results hold assuming two-round OT in the CRS model, whereas our impossibility results hold given any correlated randomness.

1 Introduction

Round complexity is an important efficiency measure of secure multi-party com-putation protocols (MPC) [40,67], with a large body of research focusing on how it can be minimized. The "holy grail" in this thread has been two-round proto-cols, as single-round MPC for a large set of functions cannot be achieved [43]. The first solutions to this problem were based on strong cryptographic assump-tions (FHE [5,59], iO [34], witness encryption [42], and spooky encryption [26]), whereas more recent results showed how to build two-round MPC resilient to any number of active corruptions from standard assumptions, such as two-round oblivious transfer (OT) [9,10,33] or OT-correlation setup and one-way functions (OWF) [35] (we discuss the state of the art in Sect. 1.1).

The full version of this paper can be found at the *IACR Cryptology ePrint Archive*, report 2019/1183.

The advantage of such two-round MPC protocols, however, is often dulled by the fact that the protocols make use of a broadcast channel in the case of malicious adversaries. Indeed, in practice such a broadcast channel is typically not available to the parties, who instead need to use a broadcast protocol over point-to-point communication for this task. Classical impossibility results from distributed computing imply that any such deterministic protocol tolerating (up to) t corruptions requires $t + 1$ rounds of communication [27,28]; these bounds extend to *randomized* broadcast, showing that termination cannot be guaranteed in constant rounds [17,52]. Even when considering *expected* round complexity, randomized broadcast would require $\Omega(n/(n-t))$ rounds [30] when the adversary can corrupt a majority of parties (i.e., $t \geq n/2$), and *expected two rounds* are unlikely to suffice for reaching agreement, even with weak guarantees, as long as $t > n/4$ [24] (as opposed to expected *three* rounds [58]). Furthermore, while the above lower bounds consider broadcasting just a single message, known techniques for composing randomized broadcast protocols with non-simultaneous termination require a multiplicative blowup of $c > 2$ rounds [7,20,22,53,55].

The above state of affairs motivated a line of work investigating the effect in the round complexity of removing the assumption of broadcast from two-round MPC protocols [2,4,49,51,60]. In order to do so, however, one needs to settle for weaker security definitions. In other words, one needs to trade off security guarantees for lower round complexity.

In this work, we fully characterize the optimal trade-off between security and use of broadcast in two-round MPC protocols against a malicious adversary who corrupts any number of parties: In a nutshell, for each of the three standard security definitions that are achievable against such adversaries in the round-unrestricted setting—namely, security with *identifiable*, *unanimous*, or *selective* abort—we provide protocols that use the provably minimal number of broadcast rounds (a broadcast round is a round in which at least one party broadcasts a message using a broadcast channel). Our positive results assume, as in the state-of-the-art solutions, existence of a two-round oblivious transfer (OT) protocol in the CRS model (alternatively, OT-correlation setup and OWF), whereas our impossibility results hold for any correlated randomness setup.

1.1   Background

Starting with the seminal works on MPC [8,16,40,65,67], a major goal has been to strike a favorable balance between the resources required for the computation (e.g., the protocol's round complexity), the underlying assumptions (e.g., the existence of oblivious transfer), and the security guarantees that can be achieved.

Since in the (potentially) dishonest-majority setting, which is the focus in this work, *fairness* (either all parties learn the output or nobody does) cannot be achieved generically [18], the standard security requirement is weakened by allowing the adversary to prematurely abort the computation even after learning the output value. Three main flavors of this definition—distinguished by the guarantees that honest parties receive upon abort—have been considered in the literature:

1. Security with *identifiable abort* [19,50] allows the honest parties to identify cheating parties in case of an abort;
2. security with *unanimous abort* [29,40] allows the honest parties to detect that an attack took place, but not to catch the culprits; and, finally,
3. security with *selective (non-unanimous) abort* [41,49] guarantees that every honest party either obtains the correct output from the computation or locally detects an attack and aborts.

We note in passing that the above ordering reflects the strength of the security definition, i.e., if a protocol is secure with identifiable abort then it is also secure with unanimous abort; and if a protocol is secure with unanimous abort, then it is also secure with selective abort. The opposite is not true in general.

A common design principle for MPC protocols, used in the vast majority of works in the literature, is to consider a *broadcast channel* as an atomic resource of the communication model. The ability to broadcast messages greatly simplifies protocols secure against malicious parties (see, e.g., the discussion in Goldreich's book [39, Sec. 7]) and is known to be necessary for achieving security with identifiable abort [19]. Indeed, broadcast protocols that run over authenticated channels exist assuming a public-key infrastructure (PKI) for digital signatures [27], with information-theoretic variants in the private-channels setting [63]. Therefore, in terms of *feasibility results* for MPC, the broadcast resource is interchangeable with a PKI setup. In fact, if merely *unanimous abort* is required, even this setup assumption can be removed [29].[1]

However, as discussed above, in terms of *round efficiency*, removing the broadcast resource is not for free and one needs to either pay with more rounds to emulate broadcast [27,30], or lessen the obtained security guarantees. However, very few generic ways to trade-off broadcast for weaker security have been proposed. A notable case is that of Goldwasser and Lindell [41], who showed how to compile any r-round MPC protocol π that is designed in the broadcast model into a $2r$-round MPC protocol over point-to-point channels at the cost of settling for the weakest security guarantee of *selective abort*, even if the original protocol π was secure with unanimous or identifiable abort. Interestingly, since as mentioned earlier broadcast protocols are expensive in terms of rounds and communication, most (if not all) practical implementations of MPC protocols use this compiler and therefore can only achieve selective abort [44,45,54,56,57,66].

But even at this security cost, the compiler from Goldwasser and Lindell [41] does not achieve a round-preserving reduction as it induces a constant multiplicative blowup in the number of rounds. The reason is that, in a nutshell, this compiler has every broadcast round being emulated by a two-round echo multicast approach, where every party sends the message he intends to broadcast to all other parties, who then echo it to ensure that if two honest parties received inconsistent messages everyone can observe. Such a blowup is unacceptable when we are after protocols with the minimal round complexity of two rounds.

---

[1] In some cases, the PKI assumption can be removed even for the strong notion of *guaranteed output delivery*, see [19,21].

Two-round MPC protocols in the malicious setting were first explored in [37,38], while recent years have witnessed exciting developments in two-round MPC [1–5,9–11,15,25,26,31–36,42,49,51,59,60,64]. The current state of the art can be summarized as follows:

- Garg and Srinivasan [33] and Benhamouda and Lin [9] showed how to balance between the optimal round complexity and minimal cryptographic assumptions for MPC in the broadcast model, by showing that every function can be computed with unanimous abort using two broadcast rounds, assuming two-round oblivious transfer (OT) and tolerating $t < n$ corruptions.
- In the honest-majority setting, Ananth et al. [2] and Applebaum et al. [4] showed that security with selective abort can be achieved using two point-to-point rounds assuming OWF.
- Patra and Ravi [60] showed that in the plain model (without any setup assumptions, such as a PKI) security with unanimous abort cannot be achieved in two point-to-point rounds, and even if the first round can use a broadcast channel. As pointed out in [62], the lower-bounds proofs from [60] do not extend to a setting with private-coins setup.

While advancing our understanding of what kind of security can be achieved in two rounds, the picture derived from the results above is only partial and does not resolve the question of whether the feasibility results can be pushed further. For example, is it possible to obtain identifiable abort via two broadcast rounds for $t < n$? Is it possible to achieve selective abort via two point-to-point rounds for $t < n$? What security can be achieved when broadcast is used only in a single round in a two-round MPC protocol? This motivates the main question we study in this paper:

What is the tradeoff between the use of broadcast and achievable security in two-round MPC?

1.2   Our Contributions

We devise a complete characterization of the feasibility landscape of two-round MPC against arbitrarily many malicious corruptions, with respect to the above three levels of security (with abort) depending on availability of a broadcast channel. Specifically, we consider all possible combinations of broadcast and point-to-point rounds—where a point-to-point round consists of only point-to-point communication whereas in a broadcast round at least one party uses the broadcast channel—i.e., no broadcast round, one broadcast round, and two broadcast rounds.

Our results are summarized in Table 1. For simplicity we prove our positive results secure against a static t-adversary, for $t < n$. Although we do not see a specific reason why an adaptive adversary cannot be tolerated, treating this stronger case would need a careful modification of our arguments; we leave a formal treatment of an adaptive adversary as an open question. All our negative results hold for a static adversary, and hence also for an adaptive adversary, since

Table 1. Feasibility and infeasibility of two-round MPC facing a static, malicious $(n-1)$-adversary. Feasibility results hold assuming two-round OT in the CRS model. Impossibility results hold given any correlated randomness. A corollary with a citation of a paper should be interpreted as corollary of the results of the paper that was not explicitly stated in the paper.

Rounds		Security with abort		
First	Second	Selective	Unanimous	Identifiable
BC	BC	✓	✓ GS [33], BL [9]	✓ **Corollary** 1 [9,33]
P2P	BC	✓	✓ **Theorem** 11	✗ **Theorem** 7
BC	P2P	✓	✗ **Theorem** 1	✗
P2P	P2P	✓ **Theorem** 11	✗ **Theorem** 1	✗
BC	–	✗ HLP [43]	✗	✗

the latter is a stronger adversary. We note that due to the ordering in strength of the security definitions discussed above, any positive (feasibility) result implies feasibility for any column to its left in the same row, and an impossibility result implies impossibility for any column to its right in the same row.

Next, we give a more detailed description of the results and how they complement the current landscape.

Two Broadcast Rounds MPC. First, as a justification of our search for round-optimal protocols, we observe that as a straightforward corollary of Halevi et al. [43], we can exclude the existence of a single-round general MPC protocol—i.e., MPC for any function. This is true for any of the three security definitions, independently of whether or not the protocol uses a broadcast channel. We can thus focus our attention to protocols with two rounds.

Let us first consider the case where both rounds use a broadcast channel. A simple observation reveals that in this case the strongest notion of security with identifiable abort is feasible. Indeed, the recent results by Garg and Srinivasan [33] and Benhamouda and Lin [9] prove that assuming two-round OT, every function can be securely computed with unanimous abort, tolerating static, malicious corruptions of any subset of the parties.[2] A simple corollary shows that when starting with an inner protocol that is secure with identifiable abort (e.g., the GMW protocol [40]), the compiled protocol will also be secure with identifiable abort. The proof follows directly by inspecting either one of the proofs of [9,33]. For completeness, we state this as a corollary below.

Corollary 1 ([9,33]). *Assume the existence of a two-round OT protocol secure against a static malicious adversary in the CRS model and let $t < n$. Then, every efficiently computable n-party function can be securely computed with identifiable abort in the CRS model using two broadcast rounds tolerating a static malicious t-adversary.*

---

[2] In fact, [9] also requires NIZK, but this assumption can be removed (see [10]).

This leaves open the cases of both rounds being point-to-point rounds, and of one broadcast round and one point-to-point round, which constitute our main contributions. Interestingly, in the latter case the order of the rounds makes a difference on what security can be achieved.

Impossibility Results. We start our investigation with proving the lower bounds illustrated in Table 1. Towards this goal, we describe a simple three-party function which, due to its properties, can be used in all the associated lower bounds. At a very high level, the chosen function f enjoys two core properties that will be crucial in our impossibility proofs: First, the function takes two inputs from a dedicated party, say P_3, but in any evaluation, the output depends on only one of these values (which of the two inputs is actually used is mandated by the input of the other two parties). Second, f has input independence with respect to P_1's input, i.e., an adversary corrupting P_2 and P_3 cannot bias their inputs depending on P_1's input. (See Sect. 3 for the function's definition.)

We note in passing that all our impossibility results hold assuming an arbitrary private-coin setup and are therefore not implied by any existing work. As a result, wherever in our statements broadcast is assumed for some round, the impossibility holds even if point-to-point channels are also available in this round. The reason is that as our proofs hold assuming an arbitrary private-coins setup (e.g, a PKI), the setup can be leveraged to implement secure point-to-point communication over broadcast (using encryption). Thus, adding point-to-point communication in a broadcast round cannot circumvent our impossibilities. This is not necessarily the case when no setup is allowed by the proof, which is an additional justification for proving impossibilities which hold even assuming setup.

Here is how we proceed in gradually more involved steps to complete the impossibility landscape: As a first, easy step we show, using the line of argumentation of HLP [43], that our function f is one of the functions which cannot be computed in a single round even against any one party being semi-honest. This excludes existence of single-round maliciously secure generic MPC protocol against dishonest majorities, even if the single round is a broadcast round, and even if we are settling for security with selective abort and assume an arbitrary correlated-randomness setup (last row in Table 1).

Unanimous Abort Requires Second Round over Broadcast. Next, we turn to two-round protocols and prove impossibility for securely computing f with unanimous abort when only the first round might use broadcast, i.e., the second round is exclusively over point-to-point (rows 3 and 4 in Table 1). This implies that under this communication pattern, security with identifiable abort is also impossible. Looking ahead, this impossibility result is complemented by Theorem 11 (Item 2), which shows that security with selective abort can be achieved in this setting.

The proof is somewhat involved, although not uncommon in lower bounds, but can be summarized as follows: We assume, towards a contradiction, that a protocol π computing f with unanimous abort exists. We then look at an adversary corrupting P_1 and define a sequence of worlds in which P_1's second-round messages are gradually dropped—so that in the last world, (the adversarial) P_1 sends no messages to the other parties. By sequentially comparing neighboring worlds, we prove that in all of them, the parties cannot abort and they have to output the output of the function evaluated on the original inputs that were given to the parties. However, as in the last scenario P_1 sends no message in the second round, this means that P_2 and P_3 can compute the output (which incorporates P_1's input) already in the first round. This enables a rushing adversary corrupting P_2 and P_3 to evaluate $f(x_1, x_2, x_3)$ on his favorite inputs for x_2 and x_3 before even sending any protocol message, and depending on the output y decide whether he wants to continue playing with those inputs—and induce the output $y = f(x_1, x_2, x_3)$ on P_1—or change his choice of inputs to some x'_2 and x'_3 and induce the output $y' = f(x_1, x'_2, x'_3)$ on P_1. This contradicts the second property of f, i.e., input independence with respect to P_1's input against corrupted P_2 and P_3.

We note in passing that a corollary of [60, Thm. 5] (explicitly stated in the full version [61, Cor. 1]) excluded security with unanimous abort for the case of an honest majority, but only for protocols that are defined in the plain model, without any trusted setup assumptions. Indeed, as pointed out by the authors in [62], their proof technique does not extend to the setting with private-coin setup. In more detail, and to illustrate the difference, consider the setting where the first round is over broadcast (and possibly point-to-point channels) and the second is over point-to-point. The argument for ruling out unanimous abort in [61, Cor. 1] crucially relies on P_3 not be able to distinguish between the case where P_2 does not send messages to P_1 (over a private channel) and the case where P_1 claims not to receive any message. However, given a PKI and a CRS for NIZK, the private channel can be emulated over the broadcast message, and the sender can prove honest behaviour. In this case, P_3 can detect the event where P_2 is cheating towards P_1 in the first round; hence, P_1 and P_3 can jointly detect the attack.

Identifiable Abort Requires Two Broadcast Rounds. As a final step, we consider the case where only the second round might use broadcast—i.e., the first round is over a point-to-point channel. In this case we prove that security with identifiable abort is impossible (row 2 in Table 1). This result, which constitutes the core technical contribution of our work, is once again, complemented by a positive result which shows how to obtain unanimous abort with this communication pattern (Theorem 11). The idea of the impossibility proof is as follows: Once again we start with an assumed protocol π (towards contradiction) and compare two scenarios, where the adversary corrupts P_1 in the first and P_2 in the second. The adversary lets the corrupted party run π, but drops any message exchanged between P_1 and P_2 in the first (point-to-point) round. By comparing the views on the two scenarios we show that aborting is not an option. Intuitively, the reason is that identifiable abort requires the parties to agree on the identity of a corrupted party; but the transcripts of the two executions are identical despite the corrupted party's identity being different, which means that if the parties try to identify a cheater, they will get it wrong (with noticeable probability) in one of the two scenarios.

Subsequently, we compare the world where P_2 is corrupted with one where the adversary corrupts also P_1 but has him play honestly; the correctness of the protocol (and the fact that the protocol machines are not aware of who is corrupted) ensures that despite the fact that P_1 is corrupted, his initial input will be used for computing the output of the honest party (which recall cannot abort as its view is identical to the other two scenarios). In this world, P_2 sends nothing to P_3 in Round 1, but P_1 and P_3 exchange their first-round messages. Therefore, a rushing adversary can obtain P_3's second-round message before sending any message on behalf of P_2. Using this information, the adversary can run in its head two executions of the protocol using the same messages for P_3 (and same first-round messages for P_1) but on different inputs for P_2. This will allow extracting both inputs of P_3, thereby violating the first property of the function discussed above.

Note that this proof is more involved than the previous one excluding unanimous abort. For example, while the previous proof merely required the adversary to "bias" the output, the current proof requires the adversary to extract both inputs of the honest P_3; essentially, we use the indistinguishable hybrids to construct an extractor. Indeed, the above is only a sketch of the argument, and the formal proof needs to take care of a number of issues: First, since an honest P_3 can detect that P_2 is cheating, the security definition only guarantees that P_3's output will be consistent with *some* input value of P_2. In that case, it is not clear that the adversary can have strategies which yield both inputs of P_3, which would exclude the possibility of the above attack. We prove that this is not the case, and that using the honest strategy, the adversary can induce an execution in which the different input distributions required by the proofs are used in the evaluation of the function. Second, in order to extract the two inputs of P_3, the adversary needs to know the output as well as the effective corrupted inputs on which the function is evaluated under our above attack scenarios. We ensure this by a simple syntactic manipulation of the function, i.e., by requiring each party to locally (and privately) output its own input as used in the evaluation of the function's output.

Observe that although our results are proved for three parties, they can be easily extended to n parties by a standard player-simulation argument [46]—in fact, because our adversary corrupts 2 out of the 3 parties, our result exclude any adversary corrupting $t \geq 2n/3$ of the parties.

Feasibility Results. Next, we proceed to provide matching upper bounds, showing that security with *unanimous* abort is feasible when the second round is over broadcast (even if the first round is over point-to-point), and that security with *selective* abort can be achieved when both rounds are over point-to-point channels. Our results are based on the compiler of Ananth et al. [2], who focused on information-theoretic security of two-round MPC in the honest-majority setting.[3] Ananth et al. [2], initially adjusted the two-round protocol from [1] to provide information-theoretic security with unanimous abort in the broadcast model (for NC^1 circuits), and then compiled it to provide security with selective abort over point-to-point channels.[4]

Compiling Two-Broadcast-Round Protocols. We start by presenting an adaptation of the compiler from [2] to the dishonest-majority setting. Let π_{bc} be a two-round MPC protocol in the broadcast model that is secure with unanimous abort. We first discuss how to compile π_{bc} to a protocol in which the first round is over point-to-point and the second round is over broadcast.

- In the compiled protocol, every party P_i starts by computing its first-round message in π_{bc}, denoted m_i^1. In addition, P_i considers its next-message function for the second round $\mathsf{second\text{-}msg}_i(x_i, r_i, m_1^1, \ldots, m_n^1)$ (that computes P_i's second round message based on its input x_i, randomness r_i, and all first-round messages). Each party "hard-wires" its input and randomness to the circuit computing $\mathsf{second\text{-}msg}_i$ such that given all first-round messages as input, the circuit outputs P_i's second-round message. Next, P_i garbles this circuit and secret-shares each input label using an additive secret-sharing scheme. In the first round of the compiled protocol, each party sends to each other party over private channels his first-round message from π_{bc} and one share of each garbled label. (Note that for all the parties, the "adjusted" second-round circuits should receive the same input values, i.e., the first-broadcast-round messages.)
- In case P_i didn't receive messages from all other parties he aborts. Otherwise, P_i receives from every P_j the message $m_{j \to i}^1$ (i.e., first-round messages of π_{bc}) and for each input wire of the next-message function of P_j, two shares: one for value 0 and the other for value 1 (recall that each bit that is broadcasted in the first round of π_{bc} forms an input wire in each circuit). In the second round, every party sends to all other parties the garbled circuit as well as one share from each pair, according to the messages received in the first round $(m_{1 \to i}^1, \ldots, m_{n \to i}^1)$.
- Next, every party reconstructs all garbled labels and evaluates each garbled circuit to obtain the second-round messages of π_{bc}. Using these messages the output value from π_{bc} is obtained.

Proof Intuition. Intuitively, if all honest parties receive the same "common part" of the first-round message (corresponding to the first broadcast round of π_{bc}), they will be able to reconstruct the garbled labels and obtain the second-round message of each party by evaluating the garbled circuits. Note that since the second round is over broadcast, it is guaranteed that all honest parties will evaluate the same garbled circuits using the same garbled inputs, and will obtain

---

[3] A similar technique was used by Garg et al. [35] to compile two-round MPC to a client-server MPC, albeit in the semi-honest setting.

[4] We note that the approach of Applebaum et al. [4] does not extend to the dishonest-majority setting in a straightforward way.

the same output value. If there exists a pair of parties that received different first-round messages, then none of the parties will be able to reconstruct the correct labels.

Given an adversary $\mathcal{A}_{\text{out}}$ to the outer protocol (that uses a first point-to-point round) a simulator $\mathcal{S}_{\text{out}}$ is constructed using a simulator $\mathcal{S}_{\text{in}}$ for the inner protocol (in the broadcast model). At a high level, $\mathcal{S}_{\text{out}}$ will use $\mathcal{S}_{\text{in}}$ to simulate the first-round messages of the honest parties, send them (with the appropriate synthetic adjustments) to $\mathcal{A}_{\text{out}}$, and get the corrupted parties' first-round messages.

- In case they are not consistent, $\mathcal{S}_{\text{out}}$ will send abort to the trusted party and resume by simulating garbled circuits that output dummy values in the second round—this is secure since the labels for these garbled circuits will not be revealed.
- In case they are consistent, $\mathcal{S}_{\text{out}}$ will use the inner simulator $\mathcal{S}_{\text{in}}$ to extract the input values of the corrupted parties and send them to the trusted party. Once receiving the output, $\mathcal{S}_{\text{out}}$ can hand it to $\mathcal{S}_{\text{in}}$ who outputs the second-round messages for the honest parties. Next, $\mathcal{S}_{\text{out}}$ will use these messages to simulate the garbled circuits of the honest parties and hand them to $\mathcal{A}_{\text{out}}$. Based on the response from $\mathcal{A}_{\text{out}}$ (i.e., the second-round messages) $\mathcal{S}_{\text{out}}$ will send abort or continue to the trusted party and halt.

We remark that the proof in [2] also follows this intuition; however, that proof uses specific properties of the (simulator for the) broadcast-model protocol constructed in [2] (which in turn is based on the protocol from [1]). Our goal is to provide a generic compiler, which works for *any* two-round broadcast-model protocol, and so our use of the simulator for the broadcast-model protocol must be black-box. For that purpose, we devise non-trivial new simulation techniques, which we believe might be of independent interest. Our proof can be adapted to demonstrate that the original compilation technique of [2] is, in fact, generic, i.e., can securely compile any broadcast-hybrid protocol.

To explain the technical challenge and our solution, let us discuss the above issue in more detail: Recall that the security definition for the stand-alone model[5] from [39] guarantees that for every adversary there is a simulator for the ideal computation (in the current case, ideal computation with unanimous abort). The simulator is invoked with some auxiliary information, and starts by sending to the trusted party inputs for the corrupted parties (or abort). Upon receiving the output value, the simulator responds with abort/continue, and finally generates its output which is computationally indistinguishable from the view of the adversary in a protocol (where the honest parties' outputs are distributed according to the extracted corrupted-parties' inputs).

Given an adversary $\mathcal{A}_{\text{out}}$ for the compiled protocol π, we would like to use the security of π_{bc} to construct a simulator $\mathcal{S}_{\text{out}}$ and simulate the "common part"

---

[5] Our choice to describe the results in the stand-alone model is for simplicity and for providing stronger impossibility results. Our feasibility results extend to the UC framework [13] via standard technical adjustments, as our simulators are black-box and straight-line. We note that the same simulation techniques discussed in this section are also needed for adjusting the proof to the UC model.

of the honest parties' messages (i.e., the messages $m^1_{i \to j}$ from an honest P_i to a corrupted P_j). However, the adversary $\mathcal{A}_{\mathsf{out}}$ induces *multiple adversaries* for π_{bc}, one for every honest party and it is not clear which simulator (i.e., for which of these adversaries) should be used. In fact, before interacting with $\mathcal{A}_{\mathsf{out}}$ and sending him the first-round messages of honest parties, $\mathcal{S}_{\mathsf{out}}$ should first run one (or a few) of the aforementioned simulators to get the inputs for the corrupted parties, invoke the trusted party with the input values, and get back the output. (At this point the simulator is committed to the corrupted parties' inputs.)[6] Only then can $\mathcal{S}_{\mathsf{out}}$ send the output back to the inner simulator(s) and get the view of the inner adversary (adversaries) in the execution, and use it to interact with $\mathcal{A}_{\mathsf{out}}$.

Receiver-Specific Adversaries. To solve this conundrum, we construct our simulator as follows: For every honest party P_j we define a *receiver-specific adversary* $\mathcal{A}^j_{\mathsf{in}}$ for π_{bc}, by forwarding the first-broadcast-round messages to $\mathcal{A}_{\mathsf{out}}$ and responding with the messages $\mathcal{A}_{\mathsf{out}}$ sends to P_j (recall that $\mathcal{A}_{\mathsf{out}}$ can send different messages to different honest parties in π). By the security of π_{bc}, for every such $\mathcal{A}^j_{\mathsf{in}}$ there exists a simulator $\mathcal{S}^j_{\mathsf{in}}$.

To define the simulator $\mathcal{S}_{\mathsf{out}}$ (for the adversary $\mathcal{A}_{\mathsf{out}}$), we use one of the simulators $\mathcal{S}^j_{\mathsf{in}}$ corresponding to the honest parties. $\mathcal{S}_{\mathsf{out}}$ initially receives from $\mathcal{S}^j_{\mathsf{in}}$ either the corrupted parties' inputs or an abort message, and forwards the received message to the trusted party. If $\mathcal{S}^j_{\mathsf{in}}$ does not abort, $\mathcal{S}_{\mathsf{out}}$ receives back the output value y, forwards y to $\mathcal{S}^j_{\mathsf{in}}$ and receives the simulated second-round messages from $\mathcal{S}^j_{\mathsf{in}}$'s output. Next, $\mathcal{S}_{\mathsf{out}}$ invokes $\mathcal{A}_{\mathsf{out}}$ and simulates the first-round messages of π (using the simulated first-round messages for π_{bc} obtained from $\mathcal{S}^j_{\mathsf{in}}$), receives back the first-round messages from $\mathcal{A}_{\mathsf{out}}$, and checks whether these messages are consistent. If so, $\mathcal{S}_{\mathsf{out}}$ completes the simulation by constructing simulated garbled circuits that output the correct second-round messages (if $\mathcal{A}_{\mathsf{out}}$'s messages are consistent, the simulated messages by $\mathcal{S}^j_{\mathsf{in}}$ are valid for all honest parties). If $\mathcal{A}_{\mathsf{out}}$'s messages are inconsistent, $\mathcal{S}_{\mathsf{out}}$ simulates garbled circuits that output dummy values (e.g., zeros), which is acceptable since the $\mathcal{A}_{\mathsf{out}}$ will not learn the labels to open them. We refer the reader to Sect. 4.2 for a detailed discussion and a formal proof.

Selective Abort via Two point-to-point Rounds. After showing that the compiler from [2] can be adjusted to achieve unanimous abort when the first round is over point-to-point and the second is over broadcast, we proceed to achieve selective abort when both rounds are over point-to-point, facing any number of corruptions. The main difference from the previous case is that the adversary can send different garbled circuits to different honest parties in the second round, potentially causing them to obtain different output values, which would violate

---

[6] This is challenging because we use the broadcast-hybrid protocol in a black-box manner. Restricting to subclasses of protocols with specific properties—e.g., the view of the adversary in the first round is distributed independently of the function's output—may enable more straightforward simulation strategies.

correctness (recall that the definition of security with selective abort permits some honest parties to abort while other obtain the correct output, but it is forbidden for two honest parties to obtain two different output values). However, we reduce this attack to the security of π_{bc} and show that it can only succeed with negligible probability.

Organization of the Paper. Preliminaries are presented in Sect. 2. In Sect. 3 we present our impossibility results and in Sect. 4 our feasibility results. Due to space limitations, complementary material and some of the proofs can be found in the full version [23].

2   Preliminaries

In this section, we introduce some necessary notation and terminology. We denote by κ the security parameter. For $n \in \mathbb{N}$, let $[n] = \{1, \cdots, n\}$. Let poly denote the set of all positive polynomials and let PPT denote a probabilistic algorithm that runs in *strictly* polynomial time. A function $\nu \colon \mathbb{N} \to [0, 1]$ is *negligible* if $\nu(\kappa) < 1/p(\kappa)$ for every $p \in$ poly and large enough κ. Given a random variable X, we write $x \leftarrow X$ to indicate that x is selected according to X.

2.1   Security Model

We provide the basic definitions for secure multiparty computation according to the real/ideal paradigm (see [12,13,39] for further details), capturing in particular the various types of unsuccessful termination ("abort") that may occur. For simplicity, we state our results in the stand-alone setting, however, all of our results can be extended to the UC framework [13].

Real-World Execution. An n-party protocol $\pi = (P_1, \ldots, P_n)$ is an n-tuple of PPT interactive Turing machines. The term *party* P_i refers to the i'th interactive Turing machine. Each party P_i starts with input $x_i \in \{0, 1\}^*$ and random coins $r_i \in \{0, 1\}^*$. Without loss of generality, the input length of each party is assumed to be the security parameter κ. An *adversary* $\mathcal{A}$ is another interactive TM describing the behavior of the corrupted parties. It starts the execution with input that contains the identities of the corrupted parties and their private inputs, and an additional auxiliary input. The parties execute the protocol in a synchronous network. That is, the execution proceeds in rounds: Each round consists of a *send phase* (where parties send their messages from this round) followed by a *receive phase* (where they receive messages from other parties). The adversary is assumed to be *rushing*, which means that he can see the messages the honest parties send in a round before determining the messages that the corrupted parties send in that round.

The parties can communicate in every round over a broadcast channel or using a fully connected point-to-point network. The communication lines between the parties are assumed to be ideally authenticated and private (and thus the adversary cannot modify messages sent between two honest parties nor read them).[7]

Throughout the execution of the protocol, all the honest parties follow the instructions of the prescribed protocol, whereas the corrupted parties receive their instructions from the adversary. The adversary is considered to be actively malicious, meaning that he can instruct the corrupted parties to deviate from the protocol in any arbitrary way. At the conclusion of the execution, the honest parties output their prescribed output from the protocol, the corrupted parties do not output anything and the adversary outputs an (arbitrary) function of its view of the computation (containing the views of the corrupted parties). The view of a party in a given execution of the protocol consists of its input, its random coins, and the messages it sees throughout this execution.

Definition 1 (Real-world execution). *Let* $\pi = (P_1, \ldots, P_n)$ *be an n-party protocol and let* $\mathcal{I} \subseteq [n]$ *denote the set of indices of the parties corrupted by* $\mathcal{A}$. *The* joint execution *of* π *under* $(\mathcal{A}, \mathcal{I})$ *in the* real model, *on input vector* $\boldsymbol{x} = (x_1, \ldots, x_n)$, *auxiliary input* aux *and security parameter* κ, *denoted* $\mathrm{REAL}_{\pi, \mathcal{I}, \mathcal{A}(\mathsf{aux})}(\boldsymbol{x}, \kappa)$, *is defined as the output vector of* $P_1, \ldots, P_n$ *and* $\mathcal{A}(\mathsf{aux})$ *resulting from the protocol interaction.*

Ideal-World Execution (with abort). We now present standard definitions of ideal computations that are used to define security with identifiable abort, unanimous abort, and selective (non-unanimous) abort. For further details see [19,41,50].

An ideal computation with abort of an n-party functionality f on input $\boldsymbol{x} = (x_1, \ldots, x_n)$ for parties $(P_1, \ldots, P_n)$ in the presence of an adversary (a simulator) $\mathcal{S}$ controlling the parties indexed by $\mathcal{I} \subseteq [n]$, proceeds via the following steps.

Sending inputs to trusted party: An honest party P_i sends its input x_i to the trusted party. The adversary may send to the trusted party arbitrary inputs for the corrupted parties. Let x_i' be the value actually sent as the input of party P_i.

Trusted party answers adversary: The trusted party computes $y = f(x_1', \ldots, x_n')$. If there are corrupted parties, i.e., if $\mathcal{I} \neq \emptyset$, send y to $\mathcal{S}$. Otherwise, proceed to step *Trusted party answers remaining parties*.

Adversary responds to trusted party: The adversary $\mathcal{S}$ can either select a set of parties that will not get the output by sending an (abort, $\mathcal{J}$) message with $\mathcal{J} \subseteq [n] \setminus \mathcal{I}$, or allow all honest parties to obtain the output by sending a continue message.

Trusted party answers remaining parties: If $\mathcal{S}$ has sent an (abort, $\mathcal{J}$) message with $\mathcal{J} \subseteq [n] \setminus \mathcal{I}$ and $\mathcal{I} \neq \emptyset$, the trusted party sends $\perp$ to every party P_j with $j \in \mathcal{J}$ and y to every P_j with $j \notin \mathcal{J} \cup \mathcal{I}$. Otherwise, if the adversary sends a continue message or if $\mathcal{I} = \emptyset$, the trusted party sends y to P_i for every $i \notin \mathcal{I}$.

Outputs: Honest parties always output the message received from the trusted party while the corrupted parties output nothing. The adversary $\mathcal{S}$ outputs

---

[7] Private channels can be realized over authenticated channels without increasing the round complexity given a PKI for public-key encryption.

an arbitrary function of the initial inputs $\{x_i\}_{i \in \mathcal{I}}$, the messages received by the corrupted parties from the trusted party and its auxiliary input.

Definition 2 (Ideal computation with *selective* abort). *Let* $f \colon (\{0,1\}^*)^n$ $\to (\{0,1\}^*)^n$ *be an n-party functionality and let* $\mathcal{I} \subseteq [n]$ *be the set of indices of the corrupted parties. Then, the* joint execution *of* f *under* $(\mathcal{S}, \mathcal{I})$ *in the ideal computation, on input vector* $\boldsymbol{x} = (x_1, \ldots, x_n)$, *auxiliary input* aux *to* $\mathcal{S}$ *and security parameter* κ, *denoted* $\mathrm{IDEAL}^{\mathsf{sl\text{-}abort}}_{f,\mathcal{I},\mathcal{S}(\mathsf{aux})}(\boldsymbol{x}, \kappa)$, *is defined as the output vector of* $P_1, \ldots, P_n$ *and* $\mathcal{S}$ *resulting from the above described ideal process.*

We now define the following variants of this ideal computation:

- **Ideal computation with *unanimous* abort.** This ideal computation proceeds as in Definition 2, with the difference that in order to abort the computation, the adversary simply sends abort to the trusted party (without specifying a set $\mathcal{J}$). In this case, the trusted party responds with $\bot$ to all honest parties. This ideal computation is denoted as $\mathrm{IDEAL}^{\mathsf{un\text{-}abort}}_{f,\mathcal{I},\mathcal{S}(\mathsf{aux})}(\boldsymbol{x}, \kappa)$.
- **Ideal computation with *identifiable* abort.** This ideal computation proceeds as the ideal computation with unanimous abort, with the exception that in order to abort the computation, the adversary chooses an index of a corrupted party $i^* \in \mathcal{I}$ and sends (abort, i^*) to the trusted party. In this case, the trusted party responds with $(\bot, i^*)$ to all parties. This ideal computation is denoted as $\mathrm{IDEAL}^{\mathsf{id\text{-}abort}}_{f,\mathcal{I},\mathcal{S}(\mathsf{aux})}(\boldsymbol{x}, \kappa)$.

Security Definitions. Having defined the real and ideal computations, we can now define security of protocols.

Definition 3. *Let* type $\in \{\mathsf{sl\text{-}abort}, \mathsf{un\text{-}abort}, \mathsf{id\text{-}abort}\}$. *Let* $f \colon (\{0,1\}^*)^n \to (\{0,1\}^*)^n$ *be an n-party functionality. A protocol* π *t-securely computes* f *with "type" if for every PPT real-world adversary* $\mathcal{A}$, *there exists a PPT adversary* $\mathcal{S}$, *such that for every* $\mathcal{I} \subseteq [n]$ *of size at most* t, *it holds that*

$$\left\{\mathrm{REAL}_{\pi,\mathcal{I},\mathcal{A}(\mathsf{aux})}(\boldsymbol{x}, \kappa)\right\}_{(\boldsymbol{x},\mathsf{aux}) \in (\{0,1\}^*)^{n+1}, \kappa \in \mathbb{N}} \overset{c}{\equiv} \left\{\mathrm{IDEAL}^{\mathsf{type}}_{f,\mathcal{I},\mathcal{S}(\mathsf{aux})}(\boldsymbol{x}, \kappa)\right\}_{(\boldsymbol{x},\mathsf{aux}) \in (\{0,1\}^*)^{n+1}, \kappa \in \mathbb{N}}.$$

3 Impossibility Results

In this section, we prove our impossibility results. Concretely, in Sect. 3.1, we argue that there is no single-round maliciously secure generic MPC protocol against dishonest majorities, even if the single round is a broadcast round, and even if we are settling for security with selective abort and we assume an arbitrary correlated-randomness setup. Subsequently, in Sect. 3.2, we prove that no generic two-round MPC protocol can achieve security with identifiable abort, while making use of broadcast in only one of the two rounds. This holds irrespective of whether the broadcast round is the first or second one. Towards this goal, we start by proving that no two-round protocol in which the broadcast round is first—i.e., the second round is over point-to-point— can achieve *identifiable* abort. This is proved in Theorem 1; in fact, the theorem proves a stronger statement, namely, that there is a function f such that no protocol with the above structure can securely compute f with *unanimous* abort.[8]

Theorem 1 implies that the only option for a two-round protocol with only one broadcast round to securely compute f with identifiable abort, is if the broadcast round is the second round—i.e., the first round is over point-to-point. We prove (Theorem 7) that this is also impossible, i.e., f cannot be computed by such a protocol. This proves that the result from Theorem 11 (Item 1), which achieves security with unanimous abort in this case, is also tight and completes the (in)feasibility landscape for two-round protocols. Furthermore, we note that all the results proved in this section hold for both computational and information-theoretic security, even if we assume access to an arbitrary correlated-randomness setup.

A Simple Function. Before starting our sequence of impossibility results, we first introduce a simple function which we will use throughout this section. Consider the following three-party public-output function (i.e., all three parties receive the output): The parties, P_1, P_2, and P_3, hold inputs $x_1 \in \{0,1\} \times \{0,1\}$, $x_2 \in \{0,1\}$ and $x_3 \in \{0,1\}^\kappa \times \{0,1\}^\kappa$, respectively, where $x_1 = (x_{1,1}, x_{1,2})$ and $x_3 = (x_{3,1}, x_{3,2})$. For a bit b we denote by b^κ the string resulting from concatenating κ times the bit b (recall that κ denotes the security parameter). The function is defined as follows:

$$f(x_1, x_2, x_3) = \begin{cases} x_{1,1}^\kappa \oplus x_2^\kappa \oplus x_{3,1}, & \text{if } x_{1,2} = x_2 \\ x_{1,1}^\kappa \oplus x_2^\kappa \oplus x_{3,2}, & \text{if } x_{1,2} \neq x_2. \end{cases}$$

Note that in the above function, the first bit of P_1, i.e., $x_{1,1}$ contributes to the computed XOR, whereas the relation between the second bit of P_1, i.e., $x_{1,2}$, and the input-bit x_2 of P_2 is the one which defines which of the $x_{3,1}$ or $x_{3,2}$ will be used in the output. One can easily verify that the following is a more compact representation of f:

$$f(x_1, x_2, x_3) = x_{1,1}^\kappa \oplus x_2^\kappa \oplus x_{3,1+(x_{1,2} \oplus x_2)}.$$

The latter representation will be useful in the proof of Theorem 7.

As discussed in the introduction, the above function enjoys the following two useful properties: First, it is impossible in the ideal world (where parties and an adversary/simulator have access to a TTP for f) for the simulator to learn both inputs of P_3 even if he corrupts both P_1 and P_2. Second, assuming the input $x_{1,1}$ of P_1 is chosen uniformly at random, it is impossible for a simulator corrupting P_2 and P_3 to fix the output to 0. We prove these two properties in the corresponding theorems where they are used.

---

[8] Recall that there is a trivial reduction from security with unanimous abort to security with identifiable abort: Run the protocol and in case it aborts with the ID of some party P_i, output abort and ignore the identity of the corrupted party.

3.1 Impossibility of Single-Round MPC

As a simple corollary of HLP [43] (see also [60]), we can exclude the existence of a semi-honestly secure MPC protocol for the above function.

Corollary 2 ([43]). *The function f cannot be computed with selective abort by a single-round protocol tolerating one semi-honest corrupted party.*

Extending Corollary 2 to the multi-party case (involving more than three parties) follows using a player-simulation argument, and the following facts that are implied by our definition of security with selective abort: (1) If the adversary follows his protocol, the evaluation cannot abort even if parties are corrupted; this follows from the non-triviality condition and the fact that when the adversary follows the protocol with his corrupted parties, the protocol cannot deviate based on the fact that parties are corrupted; (2) for such an honest-looking adversary [14], the protocol achieves all the guarantees required for semi-honest security—i.e., there is a simulator which simulates the adversary's entire view from the inputs and outputs of corrupted parties.

Corollary 3. *For $n \geq 3$, there exist an n-party function f_n for which there is no single-round protocol π which securely computes f_n with selective abort against even a single corruption. The statement is true even if π uses a broadcast channel in its single round.*

3.2 Impossibility of Single-Broadcast Two-Round MPC

Having excluded the possibility of single-round MPC protocols, we next turn to two rounds. Throughout this section, we prove impossibility statements for three-party protocols (for the function f). As discussed in the introduction, all our statements can be directly extended to the multi-party setting using the straightforward extension of f to n parties (cf. function f_n in Corollary 3).

Impossibility of Unanimous Abort When Broadcast Is First Round.
We start by proving impossibility of security with unanimous abort for f against corrupted majorities. Analogous to [43] we will say that *an adversary learns the residual function $f(x_1, \cdot, \cdot)$* to denote the event that the adversary learns enough information to locally and efficiently compute $f(x_1, x_2^*, x_3^*)$ on any (and as many) inputs x_2^* and x_3^* as he wants.

Theorem 1. *There exists no two-round protocol π which securely computes f with unanimous abort against corrupted majorities while making use of the broadcast channel only in the first round (i.e., where the second round is over point-to-point channels). The statement is true even assuming an arbitrary correlated randomness setup.*

Proof. Towards a contradiction, assume that there is protocol $\pi = (\pi_1, \pi_2, \pi_3)$, where π_i is the code (e.g., interactive Turing machine) of P_i, for computing f

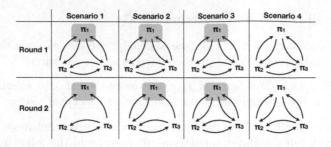

Fig. 1. The scenarios from the proof. All protocols are executed as specified; whenever an arrow is present it indicates that the message that the corresponding protocol would send is indeed sent; missing arrows indicate that respective messages are dropped. A shade on the background of a protocol indicates that the corresponding party is corrupted (but the adversary still executes the respective protocol on the honest input, but might drop some messages).

with unanimous abort which uses broadcast in its first round, but only point-to-point in the second round. Consider executions of π on uniformly random inputs x_1 and x_2 for P_1 and P_2 and on input $x_3 \in \{(0^\kappa, 1^\kappa), (1^\kappa, 0^\kappa)\}$ from P_3 in the following scenarios (see Fig. 1 for an illustration). In all four scenarios, the adversary uses the honest input for the corrupted party and allows him to execute his honest protocol on uniform random coins, but might drop some of the messages the corrupted party's protocol attempts to send in Round 2.

Scenario 1: The adversary corrupts P_1, plays the first round according to π but sends no messages in the second round.

Scenario 2: The adversary corrupts P_1, plays both rounds according to π, but does not send his second-round message towards P_3; party P_2 receives his second-round message according to the honest protocol.

Scenario 3: The adversary corrupts P_1 but plays the honest protocols in both rounds.

Scenario 4: No party is corrupted.

The proof of the theorem proceeds as follows: By a sequence of comparisons between the four scenarios we show that in Scenario 1, π_2 and π_3 cannot abort and will have to produce output equal to $f(x_1, x_2, x_3)$ with overwhelming probability despite the fact that P_1 sends no message in Round 2. This means that a (rushing)[9] adversary corrupting P_2 can learn the residual function $f(x_1, \cdot, \cdot)$

---

[9] Our impossibility results consider standard, worst-case and rushing adversaries. One might investigate how the landscape looks like against non-rushing adversaries, but this is typically considered too strong an assumption for protocols, as it implies feasibility of fair exchange (a task impossible in the standard rushing-adversary with dishonest majority realm) and even in a single round. We do not consider this theoretical question here.

already in Round 1 and before committing to any inputs for P_2 and P_3. This allows him to choose corrupted inputs depending on (the honest input) x_1 violating the security (in particular the input-independence property)[10] of π. The formal argument follows. For notational clarity, we will denote the message that P_i sends to P_j over a point to point channel in round ρ by $m_{\rho,i\to j}$; if in round ρ a party P_i broadcasts a messages, we will denote this message by $m_{\rho,i\to *}$. Due to space limitations, the proof for these claim are deferred to the full version [23].

Claim 2. In Scenario 3, parties P_2 and P_3 output $f(x_1, x_2, x_3)$ with overwhelming probability.

Claim 3. In Scenario 2, parties P_2 and P_3 output $f(x_1, x_2, x_3)$ with overwhelming probability.

Claim 4. In Scenario 1, parties P_2 and P_3 output $f(x_1, x_2, x_3)$ with overwhelming probability.

Claim 5. An adversary corrupting P_2 and P_3 can learn the residual function $f(x_1, \cdot, \cdot)$ before P_2 or P_3 send any message.

To complete the proof of the theorem, we show that existence of the above adversary $\mathcal{A}$ implies an adversary $\mathcal{A}'$ that can break the security (in particular, the input independence) of π. Intuitively, $\mathcal{A}'$ will corrupt P_2 and P_3 and use the strategy of the adversary $\mathcal{A}$ from the above claim to learn the residual function before committing to his own input to f; thus $\mathcal{A}'$ is free to choose this inputs for P_2 and P_3 depending on x_1. We next provide a formal proof of this fact by describing a strategy for biasing the output (depending on x_1) which cannot be simulated.

Concretely, consider the following $\mathcal{A}'$ that corrupts P_2 and P_3: $\mathcal{A}'$ receives $m_{1,1\to *}$ from P_1 and using $\mathcal{A}$, for $x_2^* = 0$ and $x_{3,1}* = 0^\kappa$ and $x_{3,2}* = 1^\kappa$, $\mathcal{A}'$ computes $y = f(x_1, 0, (0^\kappa, 1^\kappa))$. Then, dependent on whether y is 0^κ or 1^κ—observe that by definition of the function, these are the only two possible outcomes given the above inputs of P_3—$\mathcal{A}'$ distinguishes two cases:

Case 1: If $y = 0^\kappa$ then execute the honest protocol for P_2 and P_3 with these inputs, i.e., $x_2 = 0$ and $x_{3,1} = 0^\kappa$ and $x_{3,2} = 1^\kappa$.

Case 2: If $y = 1^\kappa$, then execute the honest protocol for P_2 and P_3 with the inputs of P_3 swapped, i.e., $x_2 = 0$ and $x_{3,1} = 1^\kappa$ and $x_{3,2} = 0^\kappa$.

Note that in both cases P_1 witnesses a view which is indistinguishable from the honest protocol with inputs: $x_2 = 0$ and $x_{3,1} = 0^\kappa$ and $x_{3,2} = 1^\kappa$ (Case 1) or $x_2 = 0$ and $x_{3,1} = 1^\kappa$ and $x_{3,2} = 0^\kappa$ (Case 2); hence, the correctness of π implies that with overwhelming probability if $y = f(x_1, 0, (0^\kappa, 1^\kappa)) = 0^\kappa$ then P_1 will output it, otherwise, i.e., if $y = f(x_1, 0, (0^\kappa, 1^\kappa)) = 1^\kappa$ he will output $y = f(x_1, 0, (1^\kappa, 0^\kappa))$; but in this latter case $y = 0^\kappa$ by the definition of f. Hence, this adversary always makes P_1 output 0^κ.

---

[10] Informally, input independence, a property implied by the standard simulation-based security definition (see Sect. 2.1), requires that the adversary cannot choose his inputs depending on the inputs of honest parties.

To complete the proof we prove that in an ideal evaluation of f with an honest P_1 and corrupted P_2 and P_3, if P_1 uses a uniformly random input and no abort occurs, then the output can be 0^κ with probability at most $1/2 \pm \mathsf{negl}(\kappa)$.

Claim 6. For any simulator $\mathcal{S}$ corrupting P_2 and P_3 and not causing the ideal execution to abort, if P_1's input is chosen uniformly at random, then for any choice of inputs for P_2 and P_3, there exist a string $z \in \{0,1\}^\kappa$ such that the output of P_1 will be z or $\bar{z}$ each with probability $1/2 \pm \mathsf{negl}(\kappa)$.

The above claim implies that for any simulator, with probability at least $1/2$ the output will be different than 0^κ. Hence the adversary $\mathcal{A}'$ (who, recall, always fixes the output to 0^κ) cannot be simulated which contradicts the assumed security of π.

Impossibility of Identifiable Abort. Next, we proceed to the proof of our second, and main, impossibility theorem about identifiable abort. For this proof we make the following modification to f: In addition to its output from f, every party P_i is required to locally output his own input x_i. We denote this function by $\hat{f}$. Specifically, the output of $\hat{f}$ consists of two parts: A public part that is identical to f, which is the same for all parties (without loss of generality, we will use $f(x_1, x_2, x_3)$ to denote this part), and a private part which for each P_i is its own input.

$$\hat{f}(x_1, x_2, x_3) = \big((y, x_1), (y, x_2), (y, x_3)\big) \quad \text{where} \quad y = f(x_1, x_2, x_3).$$

We remark that impossibility for such a public/private output function $\hat{f}$ implies impossibility of public output functions via the standard reduction of private to public input functions (see [39]).

Theorem 7. *The function $\hat{f}$ cannot be securely computed with identifiable abort by a three-party protocol that uses one point-to-point round and one broadcast round, tolerating (up to) two corrupted parties. This is true even assuming an arbitrary correlated-randomness setup.*

Proof. Assume, towards a contradiction, that a protocol π exists for the function $\hat{f}$. First, note that due to Theorem 1, the broadcast round cannot be the first round. (This holds because security with identifiable abort implies security with unanimous abort.) Hence, the first round of π must be the point-to-point round and the second can be a broadcast round. In the following, we will assume that the second round uses only the broadcast channel; this is without loss of generality as we allow π to be in the correlated-randomness model, which means that parties might share keys that they can use to emulate point-to-point communication over the broadcast network. (Proving impossibility in the correlated-randomness model implies impossibility in the plain model.)

Consider the parties P_1, P_2, and P_3 holding uniformly chosen inputs x_1, x_2, and x_3 for $\hat{f}$. Let π_i denote the code executed by P_i in π (i.e., P_i's protocol machine), and consider the following scenarios (also illustrated in Fig. 2):

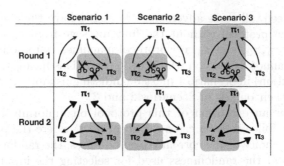

Fig. 2. The scenarios from the proof. All protocols are executed as specified. A shade on the background of a protocol indicates that the corresponding party is corrupted (the adversary still executes the respective protocol on the honest input, but may drop some messages). A solid arrow indicates that the message that the corresponding protocol would send is indeed sent; cut arrows indicate that respective messages are dropped, where we illustrate which adversarial behavior is the reason for dropping a message by scissors; bold arrows indicate that this second-round message depends on the protocol having seen some incomplete transcript (due to dropped messages) in the first round and might therefore adapt its behavior accordingly.

Scenario 1: The adversary corrupts only P_3 and has him play π_3, but drops the message $m_{1,3\to2}$ that π_3 sends to P_2 in the first round (i.e., the message is never delivered to π_2) and does not deliver to π_3 the message $m_{1,2\to3}$ received from P_2 in the first round. Other than this intervention, all machines execute their prescribed code and all other messages are sent and delivered as specified by the protocol π.

In particular, the instance of π_3 which the adversary emulates is not aware that the message $m_{1,3\to2}$ (which it generated and tried to send to π_2 in the first round) was never delivered, and is not aware that P_2 did send a message $m_{1,2\to3}$ in the first round, which was blocked. In other words, the internal state of π_2 (resp., π_3) reflects the fact that the message to π_3 (resp., π_2) is sent, but the message from π_3 (resp., π_2) did not arrive.

Scenario 2: The adversary corrupts only P_2 and has him play π_2 with the modification that he drops the first-round message $m_{1,3\to2}$ received from P_3 (again, the message is never delivered to π_2) and the message $m_{1,2\to3}$ that π_2 sends to P_3. Other than this specific intervention, all machines execute their prescribed code and all other messages are sent and delivered as specified by the protocol π.

In particular, the simulated instance of π_2 is not aware that its first round message $m_{1,2\to3}$ for P_3 was never delivered, and is not aware that P_3 did send the message $m_{1,3\to2}$ in the first round, which was blocked, as above.

Scenario 3: The adversary corrupts P_1 and P_2. Both parties play exactly the same protocol as in Scenario 2.

First we observe the following: In all three scenarios the three machines witness the same interaction—i.e., their (joint) internal states are identically distributed. Indeed, all three adversarial strategies have the effect of execution of the prescribed protocol without the first message from π_3 to π_2 and from π_2 to π_3. Since π_1, π_2, and π_3 are protocol-machines (interactive algorithms), their behavior cannot depend on who is corrupted. This means that their (joint) output (distribution) in Scenario 1 must be indistinguishable (in fact, identically distributed) to their output in Scenarios 2 and 3.

Now consider an execution of this protocol on uniformly random inputs. We consider the following two cases for Scenario 1, where the probabilities are defined over the choice of the correlated randomness, the random coins used by the protocols, and the randomness used for selecting the inputs, and analyze them in turn.

Case 1: The Honest Parties Abort (with noticeable probability). We prove that if an abort occurs with noticeable probability, then the security of the protocol is violated: Due to the identifiability requirement, if in Scenario 1 there is an abort, then both π_1 and π_2 need to output the identity of P_3 (as a cheater) as he is the only corrupted party. However, since as argued above the output distributions in the two scenarios are indistinguishable, the fact that in Scenario 1, π_1 aborts with the identity of P_3 with noticeable probability implies that also in Scenario 2, π_1 will also abort identifying P_3 with noticeable probability.

By the assumption that π is secure with identifiable abort—which implies that honest parties agree on the identity of a corrupted party in case of abort— the latter statement implies that in Scenario 2, with noticeable probability, π_3 will abort with the same cheater, i.e., the honest party P_3 (who is running π_3) will abort identifying itself as a cheater contradicting the fact that π is secure with identifiable abort. (Security with identifiable abort only allows an abort identifying a corrupted party.) This means that the protocol cannot abort with noticeable probability which leaves Case 2, below, as the only alternative.

Case 2: The Honest Parties Do Not Abort (with overwhelming probability). We prove that an adversary corrupting P_1 in addition to P_2 can learn both $x_{3,1}$ and $x_{3,2}$ with noticeable probability, which is impossible in an ideal evaluation of $\hat{f}$, as follows. Observe that since, in this case, the probability of aborting in Scenario 1 is negligible and the joint views of the parties are indistinguishable between the two scenarios, the probability that an abort occurs in Scenario 2 or Scenario 3 is also negligible. Furthermore, because Scenario 3 consist of the same protocols in exactly the same configuration and with the same messages dropped, the output of the protocols in Scenario 3 is distributed identically to the output of the protocol in Scenario 2, namely it is the output of the function on the actual inputs of P_1 and P_3 and *some* input from P_2.

Next, observe that the security of π for this case implies that for every adversary in Scenario 2 there exists a simulator corrupting P_2. Let $\mathcal{A}_2$ denote the adversary that chooses an input for π_2 uniformly at random and plays the strategy specified in Scenario 2, and let $\mathcal{S}_2$ denote the corresponding simulator. Denote by X_2^* the random variable corresponding to the input x_2^* that $\mathcal{S}_2$ hands to the functionality for $\hat{f}$ on behalf of P_2, and denote by $X_1 = (X_{1,1}, X_{1,2})$ and

$X_3 = (X_{3,1}, X_{3,2})$ the random variables corresponding to the inputs of the honest parties. The following claim states that X_2^* might take any of the values 0 or 1 with noticeable probability.

Claim 8. For each $b \in \{0, 1\}$, $\Pr[X_2^* = b]$ is noticeable.

Proof. First we note that due to input independence—i.e., because in the ideal experiment the simulator needs to hand inputs corresponding to the corrupted parties before seeing any information about the honest parties' inputs—it must hold that $\Pr[X_2^* = b] = \Pr[X_2^* = b \mid X_1, X_3]$. Hence, it suffices to prove that $\Pr[X_2^* = x_2^* \mid X_1, X_3]$ is noticeable for each of the two possible input choices $x_2^* \in \{0, 1\}$ for the simulator. Assume towards a contradiction that this is not true. This means that with overwhelming probability the simulator always inputs the same $x_2^* = b$. Without loss of generality, assume that $b = 0$ (the argument for $b = 1$ is symmetric). Since the protocol aborts only with negligible probability, security implies that the distribution of the public output for every P_i with this simulator S_2 is (computationally) indistinguishable from $f(X_1, 0, X_3) = X_{1,1}^{\kappa} \oplus X_{3,(1+X_{1,2})}$.

However, since S_2 is a simulator for π with adversary A_2 who uses a uniform input in his π_2 emulation, this implies that the interaction of the protocols π_1, π_2, and π_3 in Scenario 2 must also have as public output a value with distribution indistinguishable from $X_{1,1}^{\kappa} \oplus X_{3,(1+X_{1,2})}$. Now, using the fact that the views which the protocol machines in Scenario 2 and 1 are indistinguishable,[11] we can deduce that the public output in Scenario 1 needs to also be distributed indistinguishably from $X_{1,1}^{\kappa} \oplus X_{3,(1+X_{1,2})}$.

However, in Scenario 1, party P_2 is not corrupted which means that the public output distribution needs to be indistinguishable from $f(X_1, X_2, X_3^*)$, where $X_3^* = (X_{3,1}^*, X_{3,2}^*)$ is the input distribution of the simulator S_3 for the corrupted P_3, existence of which is implied by the security of π. But this means that S_3 will have to come up with X_3^* such that the public-output distribution $f(X_1, X_2, X_3^*) = X_{1,1}^{\kappa} \oplus X_2^{\kappa} \oplus X_{3,1+(X_{1,2} \oplus X_2)}^*$ is distributed indistinguishably from $X_{1,1}^{\kappa} \oplus X_{3,(1+X_{1,2})}^*$. Since X_3^* cannot depend on X_1 or X_2, this is impossible.

The following claim follows directly from Claim 8 and the security of π (recall that we are under the assumption that Scenario 2 terminates without abort except with negligible probability).

Claim 9. For any inputs x_1 and x_3 for protocol-machines π_1 and π_3 in Scenario 2, the probability (over the input-choice of x_2 and the local randomness r_2 given to π_2) that the public output is $x_{1,1}^{\kappa} \oplus x_2^{\kappa} \oplus x_{3,1}$ (i.e., $x_{1,2} = x_2$) is noticeable, and so is the probability that the public output $x_{1,1}^{\kappa} \oplus x_2^{\kappa} \oplus x_{3,2}$ (i.e., $x_{1,2} \neq x_2$).

---

[11] Note that although parties P_3 and P_2 are corrupted in these scenarios, the corresponding adversary still executes π_3 and π_2, respectively and has some transmitted message dropped. Hence, we can define the view of these protocols in this concrete attack scenario although they are controlled by the adversary.

The final claim that we prove provides the attack discussed at the beginning of the proof for Case 2. We refer to the full version [23] for a proof.

Claim 10. An adversary $\mathcal{A}$ corrupting both P_1 and P_2 can learn both $x_{3,1}$ and $x_{3,2}$ with noticeable probability.

Finally, we observe that, by the definition of the function, the probability that a simulator $\mathcal{S}$ for the adversary $\mathcal{A}$ from Claim 10 (who corrupts P_1 and P_2) outputs both inputs of π_3 is negligible. Hence, Claim 10 contradicts the assumed security of π.

4   Feasibility of Two-Round MPC with Limited Use of Broadcast

In this section, we present our feasibility results, showing how to compute any function with unanimous abort when only the second round of the MPC protocol is over broadcast, and with selective abort purely over pairwise channels. More formally:

Theorem 11. *Assume the existence of a two-round maliciously secure OT protocol, let f be an efficiently computable n-party function, and let $t < n$. Then,*

1. *f can be securely computed with unanimous abort, tolerating a PPT static, malicious t-adversary, by a two-round protocol in which the first round is over private channels and the second over broadcast.*
2. *f can be securely computed with selective abort, tolerating a PPT static, malicious t-adversary, by a two-round protocol over private channels.*

The proof of Theorem 11 follows from Lemmas 1 and 2 that show how to compile any two-broadcast-round protocol secure with unanimous (resp., selective) abort by a black-box straight-line simulation, to the desired result. Theorem 11 follows from that fact, and the two-broadcast-round MPC protocols presented in [9,33].

The only cryptographic assumption used in our compiler is a garbling scheme that is used to garble the second-round next-message function of the protocol. As observed in [2], for the protocol from [33] the second-round next-message function is in NC^1. Therefore, by using information-theoretic garbling schemes for NC^1 [47,48] and the information-theoretic two-broadcast-round protocol of [35] (in the OT-correlation model, where parties receive correlated randomness for precomputed OT [6]), we obtain the following corollary.

Corollary 4. *Let f be an efficiently computable n-party function and let $t < n$. Then,*

1. *f can be computed with information-theoretic security and unanimous abort in the OT-correlation model, tolerating a static, malicious t-adversary, by a two-round protocol in which the first round is over private channels and the second over broadcast.*

2. f can be computed with information-theoretic security and selective abort in the OT-correlation model, tolerating a static, malicious t-adversary, by a two-round protocol over private channels.

Structure of Two-Round Protocols. Before proving Theorem 11, we present the notations that will be used for the proof. We consider n-party protocols defined in the correlated-randomness hybrid model, where a trusted party samples $(r_1, \ldots, r_n) \leftarrow D_{\text{corr}}$ from some predefined efficiently sampleable distribution D_{corr}, and each party P_i receives r_i at the onset of the protocol. For simplicity, and without loss of generality, we assume that the random coins of each party are a part of the correlated randomness. The probabilities below are over the random coins for sampling the correlated randomness and the random coins of the adversary.

The two-round n-party protocol is then defined by the set of three functions per party $\{(\text{first-msg}_i, \text{second-msg}_i, \text{output}_i)\}_{i \in [n]}$. Every party P_i operates as follows:

- The first-round messages are computed by the function $(m^1_{i \to 1}, \ldots, m^1_{i \to n}) = \text{first-msg}_i(x_i, r_i)$, which is a deterministic function of his input x_i and randomness r_i. If the first round is over broadcast it holds that $m^1_{i \to 1} = \ldots = m^1_{i \to n}$, and we denote the unique message as m^1_i.
- The second-round messages are computed by the next-message function $(m^2_{i \to 1}, \ldots, m^2_{i \to n}) = \text{second-msg}_i(x_i, r_i, m^1_{1 \to i}, \ldots, m^1_{n \to i})$, which is a deterministic function of x_i, r_i and the first-round message $m^1_{j \to i}$ received from each P_j. As before, if the second round is over broadcast we denote the unique message as m^2_i.
- The output is computed by the function $y = \text{output}_i(x_i, r_i, m^1_{1 \to i}, \ldots, m^1_{n \to i}, m^2_{1 \to i}, \ldots, m^2_{n \to i})$, which is a deterministic function of x_i, r_i and the first-round and second-round messages.

4.1 Compiling Two-Broadcast-Round Protocols

In this section, we present a compiler which transforms a two-broadcast-round MPC protocol into a two-round protocol suitable for a point-to-point network. The compiler is based on the compiler presented in Ananth et al. [2], which considered information-theoretic honest-majority protocols that are executed over both private point-to-point channels and a broadcast channel. We adapt this compiler to the dishonest-majority setting, where the input protocol is defined purely over a broadcast channel. See the full version [23] for a formal specification of the compiler.

Let π_{bc} be a two-round MPC protocol in the broadcast model. Initially, every party "hard-wires" his input and randomness to the circuit computing the second-round next-message function $\text{second-msg}_{i,x,r}(m_1, \ldots, m_n)$ on the first-broadcast-round messages. Next, each party garbles this circuit and secret-shares each label using an additive secret-sharing scheme.

In the first round, each party sends to each other party over private channels[12] his first-round message from π_{bc} and one share of each garbled label. Note that all of these "adjusted" second-round circuits (one circuit generated by each party) should receive the same input values, i.e., the first-broadcast-round messages. For each input wire, corresponding to one broadcast bit, each party receives two shares (one for value 0 and the other for value 1). In the second round, every party sends to all other parties the garbled circuit as well as one share from each pair, according to the messages received in the first round. Since each party sends the same second-round message to all others, each party can either send the second-round message over a broadcast channel (in which case it is guaranteed that all parties receive the same messages) or multicast the message over (authenticated) point-to-point channels.

Next, every party reconstructs all garbled labels and evaluates each garbled circuit to obtain the second-round messages of π_{bc}. Using these messages each party can recover the output value from π_{bc}.

4.2 Unanimous Abort with a Single Broadcast Round

We start by proving that the compiled protocol $\pi = \mathsf{Comp}(\pi_{bc})$ is secure with unanimous abort when the second-round message is over a broadcast channel. Intuitively, if all honest parties receive the same "common part" of the first-round message (corresponding to the first broadcast round of π_{bc}), they will be able to reconstruct the garbled labels and obtain the second-round message of each party by evaluating the garbled circuits. Note that since the second round is over broadcast, it is guaranteed that all honest parties will evaluate the same garbled circuits using the same garbled inputs, and will obtain the same output value. If there exist a pair of parties that received different first-round messages, then none of the parties will be able to reconstruct the correct labels.

The security of the compiled protocol reduces to the security of the broadcast-model protocol; however, some subtleties arise in the simulation. The simulation of the garbled circuits requires the simulated second-round messages for π_{bc} (as this is the output from the garbled circuit). To simulate the second-round message of π_{bc}, the simulator must obtain the output value that corresponds to the input values that are extracted from the corrupted parties in the first round. However, since the adversary can send different first-round messages to different honest parties over the point-to-point channels, there may be multiple input values that can be extracted—in fact, the messages received by every honest party can define a different set of input values for the corrupted parties.

In more detail, given an adversary $\mathcal{A}$ for the compiled protocol π, we construct a simulator $\mathcal{S}$. We would like to use the security of π_{bc} to simulate the "common part" of the honest parties' messages. However, the adversary $\mathcal{A}$ induces *multiple adversaries* for π_{bc}, one for every honest party. For every honest party P_j we

---

[12] Private channels can be realized over authenticated channels without additional rounds assuming a public-key infrastructure (PKI) for public-key encryption.

define a *receiver-specific adversary* $\mathcal{A}_j$ for π_{bc}, by forwarding the first-broadcast-round messages to $\mathcal{A}$ and responding with the messages $\mathcal{A}$ sends to P_j (recall that $\mathcal{A}$ can send different messages to different honest parties in π). By the security of π_{bc}, for every such $\mathcal{A}_j$ there exists a simulator $\mathcal{S}_j$.

To define the simulator $\mathcal{S}$ (for the adversary $\mathcal{A}$), we use one of the simulators $\mathcal{S}_j$ corresponding to the honest parties (the choice of which simulator to use is arbitrary). $\mathcal{S}$ initially receives from $\mathcal{S}_j$ either the corrupted parties' inputs or an abort message, and forwards the received message to the trusted party. If $\mathcal{S}_j$ does not abort, $\mathcal{S}$ receives back the output value y, forwards y to $\mathcal{S}_j$ and receives the simulated second-round messages from $\mathcal{S}_j$'s output. Next, $\mathcal{S}$ invokes $\mathcal{A}$ and simulates the first-round messages of π (using the simulated first-round messages for π_{bc} obtained from $\mathcal{S}_j$), receives back the first-round messages from $\mathcal{A}$, and checks whether these messages are consistent. If so, $\mathcal{S}$ completes the simulation by constructing simulated garbled circuits that output the correct second-round messages (if $\mathcal{A}$'s messages are consistent, the simulated messages by $\mathcal{S}_j$ are valid for all honest parties). If $\mathcal{A}$'s messages are inconsistent, $\mathcal{S}$ simulates garbled circuit that output dummy values (e.g., zeros), which is ok since the $\mathcal{A}$ will not learn the labels to open them.

Lemma 1. *Let f be an efficiently computable n-party function and let $t < n$. Let π_{bc} be a two-broadcast-round protocol that securely computes f with unanimous abort by a black-box straight-line simulation and assume that garbling schemes exist. Consider the protocol $\pi = \mathsf{Comp}(\pi_{bc})$ where the first round is over secure point-to-point channels and the second round is over broadcast. Then, π securely computes f with unanimous abort.*

The proof of Lemma 1 can be found in the full version [23].

4.3   Selective Abort with Two point-to-point Rounds

We proceed by proving our second result, that the compiled protocol $\pi = \mathsf{Comp}(\pi_{bc})$ is secure with *selective* abort when the second-round message is over a point-to-point channel. The main difference from the previous case (Sect. 4.2) is that the adversary can send different garbled circuits to different honest parties in the second round, potentially causing them to obtain different output values, which would violate correctness (recall that the definition of security with selective abort permits some honest parties to abort while other obtain the correct output, but it is forbidden for two honest parties to obtain two different output values.)

Lemma 2. *Let f be an efficiently computable n-party function and let $t < n$. Let π_{bc} be a two-broadcast-round protocol that securely computes f with unanimous abort by a black-box straight-line simulation and assume that garbling schemes exist. Consider the protocol $\pi = \mathsf{Comp}(\pi_{bc})$ where both rounds are over secure point-to-point channels. Then, π securely computes f with selective abort.*

The proof of Lemma 2 can be found in the full version [23].

Acknowledgements. We would like to thank Prabhanjan Ananth, Arpita Patra, and Divya Ravi for useful discussions and comments. We also thank the anonymous reviewers of Eurocrypt 2020 for pointing us to the client-server protocol MPC of [35].

Ran Cohen's research was supported in part by the Office of the Director of National Intelligence (ODNI), Intelligence Advanced Research Project Activity (IARPA) under contract number 2019-19-020700009 (ACHILLES). Juan Garay and Vassilis Zikas were supported in part by the Office of the Director of National Intelligence (ODNI), Intelligence Advanced Research Projects Activity (IARPA), via 2019-1902070008.

The views and conclusions contained herein are those of the authors and should not be interpreted as necessarily representing the official policies or endorsements, either expressed or implied, of ODNI, IARPA, DoI/NBC, or the U.S. Government. The U.S. Government is authorized to reproduce and distribute reprints for Governmental purposes notwithstanding any copyright annotation thereon.

This work was done in part while Vassilis Zikas was visiting the Simons Institute for the Theory of Computing, UC Berkeley, and UCLA.

References

1. Ananth, P., Choudhuri, A.R., Goel, A., Jain, A.: Round-optimal secure multiparty computation with honest majority. In: Shacham, H., Boldyreva, A. (eds.) CRYPTO 2018, Part II. LNCS, vol. 10992, pp. 395–424. Springer, Cham (2018). https://doi.org/10.1007/978-3-319-96881-0_14

2. Ananth, P., Choudhuri, A.R., Goel, A., Jain, A.: Two round information-theoretic MPC with malicious security. In: Ishai, Y., Rijmen, V. (eds.) EUROCRYPT 2019, Part II. LNCS, vol. 11477, pp. 532–561. Springer, Cham (2019). https://doi.org/10.1007/978-3-030-17656-3_19

3. Applebaum, B., Brakerski, Z., Tsabary, R.: Perfect secure computation in two rounds. In: Beimel, A., Dziembowski, S. (eds.) TCC 2018, Part I. LNCS, vol. 11239, pp. 152–174. Springer, Cham (2018). https://doi.org/10.1007/978-3-030-03807-6_6

4. Applebaum, B., Brakerski, Z., Tsabary, R.: Degree 2 is complete for the round-complexity of malicious MPC. In: Ishai, Y., Rijmen, V. (eds.) EUROCRYPT 2019, Part II. LNCS, vol. 11477, pp. 504–531. Springer, Cham (2019). https://doi.org/10.1007/978-3-030-17656-3_18

5. Asharov, G., Jain, A., López-Alt, A., Tromer, E., Vaikuntanathan, V., Wichs, D.: Multiparty computation with low communication, computation and interaction via threshold FHE. In: Pointcheval, D., Johansson, T. (eds.) EUROCRYPT 2012. LNCS, vol. 7237, pp. 483–501. Springer, Heidelberg (2012). https://doi.org/10.1007/978-3-642-29011-4_29

6. Beaver, D.: Precomputing oblivious transfer. In: Coppersmith, D. (ed.) CRYPTO 1995. LNCS, vol. 963, pp. 97–109. Springer, Heidelberg (1995). https://doi.org/10.1007/3-540-44750-4_8

7. Ben-Or, M., El-Yaniv, R.: Resilient-optimal interactive consistency in constant time. Distrib. Comput. 16(4), 249–262 (2003)

8. Ben-Or, M., Goldwasser, S., Wigderson, A.: Completeness theorems for non-cryptographic fault-tolerant distributed computation (extended abstract). In: 20th ACM STOC, pp. 1–10. ACM Press (1988)

9. Benhamouda, F., Lin, H.: k-Round multiparty computation from k-round oblivious transfer via garbled interactive circuits. In: Nielsen, J.B., Rijmen, V. (eds.) EURO-CRYPT 2018, Part II. LNCS, vol. 10821, pp. 500–532. Springer, Cham (2018). https://doi.org/10.1007/978-3-319-78375-8_17

10. Benhamouda, F., Lin, H., Polychroniadou, A., Venkitasubramaniam, M.: Two-round adaptively secure multiparty computation from standard assumptions. In: Beimel, A., Dziembowski, S. (eds.) TCC 2018, Part I. LNCS, vol. 11239, pp. 175–205. Springer, Cham (2018). https://doi.org/10.1007/978-3-030-03807-6_7

11. Boyle, E., Gilboa, N., Ishai, Y.: Group-based secure computation: optimizing rounds, communication, and computation. In: Coron, J.-S., Nielsen, J.B. (eds.) EUROCRYPT 2017, Part II. LNCS, vol. 10211, pp. 163–193. Springer, Cham (2017). https://doi.org/10.1007/978-3-319-56614-6_6

12. Canetti, R.: Security and composition of multiparty cryptographic protocols. J. Cryptol. **13**(1), 143–202 (2000). https://doi.org/10.1007/s001459910006

13. Canetti, R.: Universally composable security: a new paradigm for cryptographic protocols. In: 42nd FOCS, pp. 136–145. IEEE Computer Society Press (2001)

14. Canetti, R., Ostrovsky, R.: Secure computation with honest-looking parties: what if nobody is truly honest? (extended abstract). In: 31st ACM STOC, pp. 255–264. ACM Press (1999)

15. Canetti, R., Poburinnaya, O., Venkitasubramaniam, M.: Better two-round adaptive multi-party computation. In: Fehr, S. (ed.) PKC 2017, Part II. LNCS, vol. 10175, pp. 396–427. Springer, Heidelberg (2017). https://doi.org/10.1007/978-3-662-54388-7_14

16. Chaum, D., Crépeau, C., Damgård, I.: Multiparty unconditionally secure protocols (extended abstract). In: 20th ACM STOC, pp. 11–19. ACM Press (1988)

17. Chor, B., Merritt, M., Shmoys, D.B.: Simple constant-time consensus protocols in realistic failure models. J. ACM **36**(3), 591–614 (1989)

18. Cleve, R.: Limits on the security of coin flips when half the processors are faulty (extended abstract). In: 18th ACM STOC, pp. 364–369. ACM Press (1986)

19. Cohen, R., Lindell, Y.: Fairness versus guaranteed output delivery in secure multiparty computation. J. Cryptol. **30**(4), 1157–1186 (2017). https://doi.org/10.1007/s00145-016-9245-5

20. Cohen, R., Coretti, S., Garay, J.A., Zikas, V.: Round-preserving parallel composition of probabilistic-termination cryptographic protocols. In: ICALP 2017. LIPIcs, vol. 80, pp. 37:1–37:15. Schloss Dagstuhl (2017)

21. Cohen, R., Haitner, I., Omri, E., Rotem, L.: Characterization of secure multiparty computation without broadcast. J. Cryptol. **31**(2), 587–609 (2018). https://doi.org/10.1007/s00145-017-9264-x

22. Cohen, R., Coretti, S., Garay, J., Zikas, V.: Probabilistic termination and composability of cryptographic protocols. J. Cryptol. **32**(3), 690–741 (2019). https://doi.org/10.1007/s00145-018-9279-y

23. Cohen, R., Garay, J.A., Zikas, V.: Broadcast-optimal two-round MPC. Cryptology ePrint Archive, Report 2019/1183 (2019)

24. Cohen, R., Haitner, I., Makriyannis, N., Orland, M., Samorodnitsky, A.: On the round complexity of randomized Byzantine agreement. In: DISC, pp. 12:1–12:17 (2019)

25. Cohen, R., Shelat, A., Wichs, D.: Adaptively secure MPC with sublinear communication complexity. In: Boldyreva, A., Micciancio, D. (eds.) CRYPTO 2019, Part II. LNCS, vol. 11693, pp. 30–60. Springer, Cham (2019). https://doi.org/10.1007/978-3-030-26951-7_2

26. Dodis, Y., Halevi, S., Rothblum, R.D., Wichs, D.: Spooky encryption and its applications. In: Robshaw, M., Katz, J. (eds.) CRYPTO 2016, Part III. LNCS, vol. 9816, pp. 93–122. Springer, Heidelberg (2016). https://doi.org/10.1007/978-3-662-53015-3_4

27. Dolev, D., Strong, H.R.: Authenticated algorithms for Byzantine agreement. SIAM J. Comput. **12**(4), 656–666 (1983)

28. Fischer, M.J., Lynch, N.A.: A lower bound for the time to assure interactive consistency. Inf. Process. Lett. **14**(4), 183–186 (1982)

29. Fitzi, M., Gottesman, D., Hirt, M., Holenstein, T., Smith, A.: Detectable Byzantine agreement secure against faulty majorities. In: 21st ACM PODC, pp. 118–126. ACM (2002)

30. Garay, J.A., Katz, J., Koo, C.-Y., Ostrovsky, R.: Round complexity of authenticated broadcast with a dishonest majority. In: 48th FOCS, pp. 658–668. IEEE Computer Society Press (2007)

31. Garg, S., Polychroniadou, A.: Two-round adaptively secure MPC from indistinguishability obfuscation. In: Dodis, Y., Nielsen, J.B. (eds.) TCC 2015, Part II. LNCS, vol. 9015, pp. 614–637. Springer, Heidelberg (2015). https://doi.org/10.1007/978-3-662-46497-7_24

32. Garg, S., Srinivasan, A.: Garbled protocols and two-round MPC from bilinear maps. In: 58th FOCS, pp. 588–599. IEEE Computer Society Press (2017)

33. Garg, S., Srinivasan, A.: Two-round multiparty secure computation from minimal assumptions. In: Nielsen, J.B., Rijmen, V. (eds.) EUROCRYPT 2018, Part II. LNCS, vol. 10821, pp. 468–499. Springer, Cham (2018). https://doi.org/10.1007/978-3-319-78375-8_16

34. Garg, S., Gentry, C., Halevi, S., Raykova, M.: Two-round secure MPC from indistinguishability obfuscation. In: Lindell, Y. (ed.) TCC 2014. LNCS, vol. 8349, pp. 74–94. Springer, Heidelberg (2014). https://doi.org/10.1007/978-3-642-54242-8_4

35. Garg, S., Ishai, Y., Srinivasan, A.: Two-round MPC: information-theoretic and black-box. In: Beimel, A., Dziembowski, S. (eds.) TCC 2018, Part I. LNCS, vol. 11239, pp. 123–151. Springer, Cham (2018). https://doi.org/10.1007/978-3-030-03807-6_5

36. Garg, S., Miao, P., Srinivasan, A.: Two-round multiparty secure computation minimizing public key operations. In: Shacham, H., Boldyreva, A. (eds.) CRYPTO 2018, Part III. LNCS, vol. 10993, pp. 273–301. Springer, Cham (2018). https://doi.org/10.1007/978-3-319-96878-0_10

37. Gennaro, R., Ishai, Y., Kushilevitz, E., Rabin, T.: The round complexity of verifiable secret sharing and secure multicast. In: 33rd ACM STOC, pp. 580–589. ACM Press (2001)

38. Gennaro, R., Ishai, Y., Kushilevitz, E., Rabin, T.: On 2-round secure multiparty computation. In: Yung, M. (ed.) CRYPTO 2002. LNCS, vol. 2442, pp. 178–193. Springer, Heidelberg (2002). https://doi.org/10.1007/3-540-45708-9_12

39. Goldreich, O.: Foundations of Cryptography: Basic Applications, vol. 2. Cambridge University Press, Cambridge (2004). ISBN 0-521-83084-2 (hardback)

40. Goldreich, O., Micali, S., Wigderson, A.: How to play any mental game or a completeness theorem for protocols with honest majority. In: 19th ACM STOC, pp. 218–229. ACM Press (1987)

41. Goldwasser, S., Lindell, Y.: Secure multi-party computation without agreement. J. Cryptol. **18**(3), 247–287 (2005)

42. Dov Gordon, S., Liu, F.-H., Shi, E.: Constant-round MPC with fairness and guarantee of output delivery. In: Gennaro, R., Robshaw, M. (eds.) CRYPTO 2015, Part II. LNCS, vol. 9216, pp. 63–82. Springer, Heidelberg (2015). https://doi.org/10.1007/978-3-662-48000-7_4

43. Halevi, S., Lindell, Y., Pinkas, B.: Secure computation on the web: computing without simultaneous interaction. In: Rogaway, P. (ed.) CRYPTO 2011. LNCS, vol. 6841, pp. 132–150. Springer, Heidelberg (2011). https://doi.org/10.1007/978-3-642-22792-9_8

44. Hazay, C., Scholl, P., Soria-Vazquez, E.: Low cost constant round MPC combining BMR and oblivious transfer. In: Takagi, T., Peyrin, T. (eds.) ASIACRYPT 2017, Part I. LNCS, vol. 10624, pp. 598–628. Springer, Cham (2017). https://doi.org/10.1007/978-3-319-70694-8_21

45. Hazay, C., Orsini, E., Scholl, P., Soria-Vazquez, E.: Concretely efficient large-scale MPC with active security (or, TinyKeys for TinyOT). In: Peyrin, T., Galbraith, S. (eds.) ASIACRYPT 2018, Part III. LNCS, vol. 11274, pp. 86–117. Springer, Cham (2018). https://doi.org/10.1007/978-3-030-03332-3_4

46. Hirt, M., Maurer, U.M.: Player simulation and general adversary structures in perfect multiparty computation. J. Cryptol. **13**(1), 31–60 (2000). https://doi.org/10.1007/s001459910003

47. Ishai, Y., Kushilevitz, E.: Randomizing polynomials: a new representation with applications to round-efficient secure computation. In: 41st FOCS, pp. 294–304. IEEE Computer Society Press (2000)

48. Ishai, Y., Kushilevitz, E.: Perfect constant-round secure computation via perfect randomizing polynomials. In: Widmayer, P., Eidenbenz, S., Triguero, F., Morales, R., Conejo, R., Hennessy, M. (eds.) ICALP 2002. LNCS, vol. 2380, pp. 244–256. Springer, Heidelberg (2002). https://doi.org/10.1007/3-540-45465-9_22

49. Ishai, Y., Kushilevitz, E., Paskin, A.: Secure multiparty computation with minimal interaction. In: Rabin, T. (ed.) CRYPTO 2010. LNCS, vol. 6223, pp. 577–594. Springer, Heidelberg (2010). https://doi.org/10.1007/978-3-642-14623-7_31

50. Ishai, Y., Ostrovsky, R., Zikas, V.: Secure multi-party computation with identifiable abort. In: Garay, J.A., Gennaro, R. (eds.) CRYPTO 2014, Part II. LNCS, vol. 8617, pp. 369–386. Springer, Heidelberg (2014). https://doi.org/10.1007/978-3-662-44381-1_21

51. Ishai, Y., Kumaresan, R., Kushilevitz, E., Paskin-Cherniavsky, A.: Secure computation with minimal interaction, revisited. In: Gennaro, R., Robshaw, M. (eds.) CRYPTO 2015, Part II. LNCS, vol. 9216, pp. 359–378. Springer, Heidelberg (2015). https://doi.org/10.1007/978-3-662-48000-7_18

52. Karlin, A.R., Yao, A.C.: Probabilistic lower bounds for Byzantine agreement and clock synchronization (1986). Unpublished manuscript

53. Katz, J., Koo, C.-Y.: On expected constant-round protocols for Byzantine agreement. In: Dwork, C. (ed.) CRYPTO 2006. LNCS, vol. 4117, pp. 445–462. Springer, Heidelberg (2006). https://doi.org/10.1007/11818175_27

54. Lindell, Y., Nof, A.: A framework for constructing fast MPC over arithmetic circuits with malicious adversaries and an honest-majority. In: ACM CCS 2017, pp. 259–276. ACM Press (2017)

55. Lindell, Y., Lysyanskaya, A., Rabin, T.: Sequential composition of protocols without simultaneous termination. In: 21st ACM PODC, pp. 203–212. ACM (2002)

56. Lindell, Y., Pinkas, B., Smart, N.P., Yanai, A.: Efficient constant round multiparty computation combining BMR and SPDZ. In: Gennaro, R., Robshaw, M. (eds.) CRYPTO 2015, Part II. LNCS, vol. 9216, pp. 319–338. Springer, Heidelberg (2015). https://doi.org/10.1007/978-3-662-48000-7_16

57. Lindell, Y., Smart, N.P., Soria-Vazquez, E.: More efficient constant-round multi-party computation from BMR and SHE. In: Hirt, M., Smith, A. (eds.) TCC 2016, Part I. LNCS, vol. 9985, pp. 554–581. Springer, Heidelberg (2016). https://doi.org/10.1007/978-3-662-53641-4_21

58. Micali, S.: Very simple and efficient Byzantine agreement. In: Papadimitriou, C.H. (ed.) ITCS 2017, LIPIcs, vol. 4266, pp. 6:1–6:1, 67, January 2017. https://doi.org/10.4230/LIPIcs.ITCS.2017.6

59. Mukherjee, P., Wichs, D.: Two round multiparty computation via multi-key FHE. In: Fischlin, M., Coron, J.-S. (eds.) EUROCRYPT 2016, Part II. LNCS, vol. 9666, pp. 735–763. Springer, Heidelberg (2016). https://doi.org/10.1007/978-3-662-49896-5_26

60. Patra, A., Ravi, D.: On the exact round complexity of secure three-party computation. In: Shacham, H., Boldyreva, A. (eds.) CRYPTO 2018, Part II. LNCS, vol. 10992, pp. 425–458. Springer, Cham (2018). https://doi.org/10.1007/978-3-319-96881-0_15

61. Patra, A., Ravi, D.: On the exact round complexity of secure three-party computation. Cryptology ePrint Archive, Report 2018/481 (2018)

62. Patra, A., Ravi, D.: Beyond honest majority: the round complexity of fair and robust multi-party computation. In: Galbraith, S.D., Moriai, S. (eds.) ASIACRYPT 2019, Part I. LNCS, vol. 11921, pp. 456–487. Springer, Cham (2019). https://doi.org/10.1007/978-3-030-34578-5_17

63. Pfitzmann, B., Waidner, M.: Unconditional Byzantine agreement for any number of faulty processors. In: Finkel, A., Jantzen, M. (eds.) STACS 1992. LNCS, vol. 577, pp. 337–350. Springer, Heidelberg (1992). https://doi.org/10.1007/3-540-55210-3_195

64. Quach, W., Wee, H., Wichs, D.: Laconic function evaluation and applications. In: 59th FOCS, pp. 859–870. IEEE Computer Society Press (2018)

65. Rabin, T., Ben-Or, M.: Verifiable secret sharing and multiparty protocols with honest majority (extended abstract). In: 21st ACM STOC, pp. 73–85. ACM Press (1989)

66. Wang, X., Ranellucci, S., Katz, J.: Global-scale secure multiparty computation. In: ACM CCS 2017, pp. 39–56. ACM Press (2017)

67. Yao, A.C.-C.: Protocols for secure computations (extended abstract). In: 23rd FOCS, pp. 160–164. IEEE Computer Society Press (1982)

Correction to: Optimal Merging in Quantum k-xor and k-sum Algorithms

María Naya-Plasencia and André Schrottenloher

Correction to:
Chapter "Optimal Merging in Quantum k-xor and k-sum Algorithms" in: A. Canteaut and Y. Ishai (Eds.): *Advances in Cryptology – EUROCRYPT 2020*, **LNCS 12106,**
https://doi.org/10.1007/978-3-030-45724-2_11

In the originally published version of the chapter 11, the title of the paper was incorrect. The title has been corrected as "Optimal Merging in Quantum k-xor and k-sum Algorithms".

The updated version of this chapter can be found at
https://doi.org/10.1007/978-3-030-45724-2_11

Author Index

Printed in the United States
By Bookmasters